D1552837

Empirical Direction in Design and Analysis

Empirical Direction
in Design and Analysis

Norman H. Anderson
University of California, San Diego

LAWRENCE ERLBAUM ASSOCIATES, PUBLISHERS
2001   Mahwah, New Jersey   London

President/CEO:	Lawrence Erlbaum
Executive Vice-President, Marketing:	Joseph Petrowski
Senior Vice-President, Book Production:	Art Lizza
Director, Editorial:	Lane Akers
Director, Sales and Marketing:	Robert Sidor
Director, Customer Relations:	Nancy Seitz
Senior Editor:	Debra Riegert
Textbook Marketing Manager:	Marisol Kozlovski
Editorial Assistant:	Jason Planer
Cover Design:	Kathryn Houghtaling Lacey
Textbook Production Manager:	Paul Smolenski
Text and Cover Printer:	Hamilton Printing Company

The final camera copy for this work was prepared by the author.

Lawrence Erlbaum Associates, Inc., Publishers
10 Industrial Avenue
Mahwah, New Jersey 07430

Library of Congress Cataloging-in-Publication Data

Anderson, Norman H.
Empirical direction in design and analysis / Norman H. Anderson
    p. cm.
    Includes bibliographical references and index.
ISBN 0-8058-3978-X (cloth : alk. paper)
1. Psychometrics. 2. Psychology—Methodology. I. Title.

BF39 .A49 2001
150'.1'5195—dc21   2001033377
                                                          CIP

Printed in the United States of America
10 9 8 7 6 5 4 3 2

DEDICATION

This book is dedicated to the many students who have been in my courses for the last 40 years. You have taught me a lot; I deeply appreciate this unique learning experience. I hope your lives have been rewarding. This book seeks to continue as coach and aide, passing on to new students what we together have learned.

This book has benefited from comments of numerous persons. I owe special thanks to Richard Bogartz, Edward Karpp, Pamela Moses, Charles Reichardt, Anne Schlottmann, Ewart Thomas, and James Zalinski. Many others have made helpful comments on various issues and sections. Among these are James Alexander, Gwendolyn Alexander, James Anderson, Mark Appelbaum, Margaret Armstrong, Ann Norman Atkinson, Rita Atkinson, Eileen Beier, Michael Birnbaum, Donnie Bocko, Lyle Bourne, Gordon Bower, Clifford Butzin, Robert Calfee, Edward Carr, Jenny Cantor, John Clavadetscher, Diane Cuneo, Claire Ernhart, Robert Farber, Arthur Farkas, Philip Gallo, William Gaver, Anthony Greenwald, Reid Hastie, Wilfried Hommers, Stephen Hubert, James Jaccard, Beth Jaworski, Martin Kaplan, Eileen Karsh, Lucille Kirsch, James Kulik, Andrius Kulikauskas, Anita Lampel, Irwin Levin, Stephen Link, Frank Logan, Lola Lopes, Jordan Louviere, Tracy Love-Geffen, Donald MacLeod, Irving Maltzman, George Mandler, Jean Mandler, Sergio Masin, Mark McDaniel, Jennifer McDowell, William McGill, William McGuire, Craig McKenzie, Colleen Surber Moore, Philip Moore, Etienne Mullet, Gregg Oden, Allen Osman, Allen Parducci, Mary Pendery, Joan Prentice, Mike Rinck, Maria Teresa Sastre, Shlomo Sawilowsky, Sandra Scarr, Laura Schreibman, John Shaughnessy, Juliet Shaffer, James Shanteau, Ling-Po Shiu, Ramadhar Singh, Cheryl Graesser Stecher, Jeff Steinberg, Saul Sternberg, Billy Vaughn, John Verdi, Mingshen Wang, David Weiss, Ben Williams, Wendy Williams, Friedrich Wilkening, John Wixted, Yuval Wolf, Chungfang Yang, Gregory Zarow, and Shu-Hong Zhu.

FOREWORD

Statistics should be an organic component of substantive investigation. This is how statistics should be learned—and how it should be taught.

A text should aim to give students what they will later need to know. What students will later need to know is how to utilize statistics in their empirical work. To get such transfer requires that statistics be embedded within a framework of substantive inquiry.

Substantive investigation rests on *extrastatistical inference*—substantive considerations concerning validity of task–procedure and generality of results. Practical understanding—transfer to empirical analysis—requires that statistics be integrated into a larger framework of extrastatistical inference.

This extrastatistical theme is embodied in the *Experimental Pyramid* of Figure 1.1. The six levels of the Pyramid portray a hierarchy of considerations involved in empirical investigation. Statistics, to be effective, needs to be integrated into the substantive considerations at each level of the Pyramid.

The main value of statistics is in planning the investigation, long before the data are collected. Contrary to the standard stereotype, the main function of statistics is to get more information *into* the data.

Current texts pursue two largely incompatible goals: To be a text for first-year graduate students and to serve as a reference handbook for advanced researchers. Both audiences suffer thereby, especially first-year students. Facing a plethora of formulas, uncertain which are basic, doing exercises largely devoted to numerical calculations, first-year students are hindered and side-tracked from developing understanding and research judgment.

Chapters 1–12 present a core intended for first-year graduate students. Far fewer formulas are presented than in other texts, which is intended to facilitate conceptual and empirical understanding. Two novelties are the heavy emphasis on confidence intervals and the separate chapters on confounding and single subject design.

Chapters 13–21 serve in part a reference handbook function, for they take up more specialized topics: within-versus-between design, Latin squares, multiple regression, analysis of covariance, quasi-experimental design, multiple comparisons, and the difficult problem of measuring effect size. Also included are chapters on the foundations of statistics, on mathematical models in psychology, and on psychological measurement theory. These chapters aim to give conceptual understanding that will facilitate empirical analysis.

The "Empirical Direction" in this book is not essentially new. It is a return to and unification of statistics with the extrastatistical nature of empirical science. Further discussion is given in Chapter 23, *Lifelong Learning*.

C O N T E N T S

PREFACE

Generality is a prime goal of scientific inference because science depends on evidence from **samples**. In psychology, experimental results are typically obtained from a small sample of subjects tested in one narrow experimental situation, with a very small sample of stimulus conditions and usually a single task and a single measure of behavior. These results have value only to the extent that they generalize. No one is interested, for example, in those particular infant monkeys in Harlow's experiments on mother love; their behavior is of interest only insofar as it generalizes to other infants, especially human infants, across a wider range of test situations than Harlow used. The four kinds of generality implicit in the previous sentence are discussed on pages 20-24.

Reliability, or replicability, is one aspect of generality. Different samples of subjects will yield different results. Perhaps the effect observed in your sample is merely a chance accident of which subjects chanced to get into your particular sample. Any claim for a real effect should be prefaced by evidence that it is reliable—not likely to be produced by chance alone. Statistics can help assess reliability. Not less important, statistics can help you plan your experiments to get more reliability for less cost (pages 16-20).

Validity, which is far more important than reliability, is primarily an extra-statistical issue—which must be answered in terms of substantive knowledge. The ubiquitous threat to validity is **confounding**. Confounding arises because the experimenter employs some concrete stimulus manipulation that is intended to elicit a specified process. But this manipulation may also elicit some other process that undercuts the interpretation. The classic example of confounding is the placebo effect, in which the suggestion produced by giving a medicine has beneficial effects even though the medicine itself is worthless. Validity is more complex, however, as discussed on pages 8-16.

Generality, reliability, and validity are mainly extrastatistical problems. Statistics can furnish valuable assistance with some aspects of these problems, but effective use of statistics depends on integration of statistics with extra-statistical, empirical knowledge.

Six levels of knowledge are distinguished in the **Experimental Pyramid** (page 3). Each lower level is more important. Statistics, although mainly applicable at the top level, can also help at each lower level. Your labors will be more productive the more you learn how to integrate statistical inference into an empirical framework of extrastatistical, scientific inference. This **empirical direction** is the main theme of this initial chapter and of the entire book.

Chapter 1

SCIENTIFIC INFERENCE

Statistics teaching should be integrated with empirical substance. Statistics is not varnish, to be applied after the experiment is done. Statistics is an integral component of the research plan—beginning with choice of problem for investigation. Statistics is important at every intermediate level, including apparatus and procedure, and concluding in the interpretation of the results.

Students almost inevitably come to view the significance test as the be-all and end-all. This test condenses the entire study into a single number of pivotal importance for making claims about what the study shows. A positive answer to the question, "Is it significant?" thus comes to be considered the ultimate goal. "*It is significant!*" seems all the more potent because "significant" carries undertones of everyday meaning.

The essential question, of course, is what the results mean. The significance test has the necessary—but minor—function of providing evidence of whether there is a result to interpret. What this result may mean depends on considerations at deeper levels.

The more important functions of statistics are in these deeper levels. These more important functions apply at the planning stage, before the data are collected. These more important functions condition the meaning and interpretation of any result that may be obtained. These more important functions of statistics need to be understood in organic relation to the substantive inquiry.

The significance test, in contrast, applies after the data have been collected. It is then too late to correct missed opportunities and shortcomings in the research plan. Finding a significant decrease in felt pain may not be worth much if the placebo control was overlooked. The placebo control may not be valid if the treatment was not "blind." And even the most careful procedure may founder if you or your research assistant stumbled with the random assignment. These three examples illustrate vital functions of statistics that operate in the planning stage, before the data are collected. This is where statistics is most needed—and most effective.

Some writers argue strenuously against using significance tests. There is something to be said for their argument; it would force people to look more closely at their data. Many statisticians voice similar complaints about the fixation on significance tests and seek to emphasize the more important functions of statistics by avoiding that term and speaking of experimental design, data analysis, and so forth. The significance test has an essential role, however, a role that it performs reasonably well.

The real difficulty is how to integrate statistics–design with empirical inquiry. A very modest number of statistical ideas and formulas will cover most situations that arise in experimental research, as this book will show. What is not so easy is to develop the research judgment to integrate statistical considerations into the planning stage of an experiment. A conceptual framework that puts statistics in its proper place—as an aide to scientific inference—is given by the Experimental Pyramid taken up next.

1.1 EXPERIMENTAL PYRAMID

Scientific inference is central to empirical research. Our empirical observations are clues to deeper reality. How we make inferences from these clues may be considered within the *Experimental Pyramid* of Figure 1.1. Each level of the Experimental Pyramid corresponds to different aspects of empirical investigation. These levels range from statistical inference and experimental design at the top to the conceptual framework at the bottom.

The lower levels are more fundamental. Validity at lower levels is prerequisite to validity at higher levels. The different levels are not separate and distinct, as the dashed lines might suggest; all levels interrelate as facets of an organic whole. Each following section comments briefly on one level of the Experimental Pyramid.

1.1.1 STATISTICAL INFERENCE

The significance test is a minor concern of scientific investigation. It is needed as evidence whether the result you observe is real, rather than chance. Unless you have reasonable evidence that your result is real, there is little point in trying to decide what it means. Before expounding your result, therefore, you owe it to your readers, and to yourself, to show that you have something to expound. This is why the significance test is ubiquitous.

Despite its ubiquity, the significance test is only a minor aspect of substantive inference. What your result means depends on substantive considerations: What experimental task you choose, what response measure you use, your control conditions, and so forth. Such substantive inference depends on considerations at more basic levels of the Pyramid.

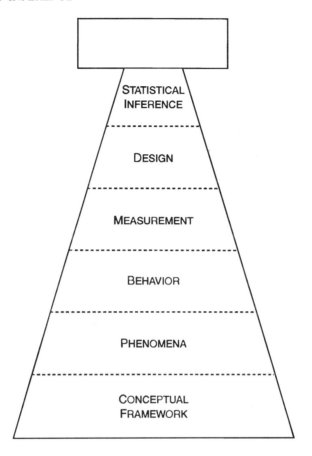

Figure 1.1. Experimental Pyramid.

Even within statistical inference, the significance test has a minor function. More important functions of statistical analysis concern other aspects of *reliability*, especially confidence intervals that describe a sample mean as an interval of likely error. Even more important is *validity*. When measuring each subject under multiple conditions, for example, statistical inference is essential for dealing with sticky problems of practice, adaptation, and transfer from initial conditions that confound the response to conditions that follow.

Validity, reliability, and other functions of statistical analysis share one common property. Unlike the test of significance, these other functions operate before or during the data collection. This is because these other functions are interwoven with substantive considerations at the lower levels. Some of these are taken up in the following discussions of the other levels of the Pyramid. Others will appear in the later sections on validity, reliability, and samples.

1.1.2 EXPERIMENTAL DESIGN

The experimental design mirrors and embodies questions being asked by the investigator. Almost the simplest design involves two treatments, experimental and control, the question being whether the experimental treatment has real effects on the behavior. The significance test aims to provide an objective answer. But the design is more basic—it determines what the data mean.

It is at this design stage—before any subject is run—that statistics has its greatest value. Most valuable is the function of controlling variables that might confound the interpretation. One notable example is the principle of random assignment discussed in Section 1.4.1, which has the vital function of controlling unknown variables.

Statistics can also help at the design stage by calculating the probability of success/failure, formally called the *power* of the experiment. If this power calculation indicates the experiment is too weak to detect the expected effect, design changes may be possible that will yield adequate power.

Still another design function of statistics arises in analysis of multiple determination. Multiple determination is fundamental in psychological science because most behavior depends on joint action of two or more variables. Among the questions of interest are whether two variables "interact," and if so, in what way. One major achievement of twentieth century statistics has been the development of tools to study multiple determination (Section 1.5).

Although the questions asked by the investigator are defined formally in the design, their substantive meaning depends on what is measured. Substantive meaning requires consideration of the next two levels of the Pyramid.

1.1.3 MEASUREMENT

Measurement has a unique role in the Experimental Pyramid. It is the link between the world of behavior and the world of science. Measurement is thus a transformation, or mapping, from the real world of objects and events to a conceptual world of ideas and symbols.

This measurement transformation is a vital feature of science. Our measurements are produced by our experimental task, apparatus, and procedure. Measurement is thus grounded in experimental specifics that define the transformation from the behavioral world to the conceptual world.

This empirical grounding of measurement will be emphasized in the later discussions of *validity* and *reliability*. These two concepts subsume virtually all of measurement. Reliability represents intrinsic informational content of our measurements; validity represents substantive or conceptual informational content. Both depend on the three lower levels of the Pyramid, beginning with the level of behavior.

1.1.4 BEHAVIOR

Behavior is the central level of the Experimental Pyramid. Behavior, however, is not autonomous. It is partly created by the investigator's choices in the experimental setup, which include organism, task, apparatus, procedure, response measure, and so forth. These choices determine what the measured data mean.

Progress in any science depends on development of "good" experimental setups. Among the criteria of a good setup are importance of the behavior, its simplicity and generalizability, statistical properties of the response measure, and cost, including time and trouble.

Pavlov's studies of conditioned salivary reflexes in dogs are famous because of the seeming simplicity of the behavior and its presumed generality, not merely as a base for psychological theory, but also as a model and tool for analysis of behavior. The white rat is more popular, partly because of cheapness and convenience, but also because the rat exhibits a broad spectrum of behaviors common with us humans.

The importance of choices in the experimental setup is visible in controversies in the literature. Many, perhaps most, are concerned with confoundings that may undercut the interpretation of the results. These controversies provide useful lore for newcomers in any field.

The choices in the experimental setup are in mutual interaction with the upper levels of the Pyramid. These choices are determiners of the quality and validity of the response measure, as well as its reliability. Mutually, requirements at upper levels guide choices at the behavioral level. The final setup requires compromises between aspiration and practicality, compromises that not infrequently must be made without adequate information. Early work on some problems can look strangely crude until it is recognized how subsequent work transformed our knowledge system.

Experimental setups should be treated as a matter of continuing development. A major impetus to such development stems from arguments over confounding and validity. Similar arguments over reliability would also be useful. In experimental psychology, however, they remain infrequent—in dark contrast to the attention lavished on the significance test.

1.1.5 PHENOMENA

We usually aim to study some phenomenon—information integration, memory, color vision, intuitive physics, language, social attitudes, and so forth. What we actually study is some observable behavior, which we hope is a good measure of the phenomenon. The difference is one of kind: between the fact of behavior and the name given the phenomenon, which usually carries a conceptual interpretation of the behavior.

We usually conflate the behavior and the phenomenon, presuming that the name we impose on the behavior is warranted. This presumption is more than a convenience; it is the most important determinant of our choices in the experimental setup. But this presumption may be unwarranted. The innumerable arguments over confounding in the literature demonstrate the difference between behavior and phenomenon. This central issue of confounding is discussed in Section 1.2.3 and Chapter 8 is devoted to it.

A related reason for distinguishing behavior from phenomenon is that performance in any setup involves other abilities besides the focal behavior. This is a recurrent difficulty in studying young children's development of concepts such as time and number. Younger children may be handicapped by lesser development of verbal ability, for example, that interferes with their performance on the focal concept. Such confounding is frequent in Piaget's work, to take one example from Chapter 8. This example has statistical relevance because statistical design techniques can remove some of these confoundings.

A further aspect of the behavior–phenomenon distinction concerns generality. Any given setup must be restricted to one or a few exemplars of the phenomenon. Generality for other exemplars is a primary desideratum. Studies of learning, for example, usually concentrate on a single task, hoping the results will hold for other tasks. Sometimes this happens, sometimes not. Pavlov's salivary reflex, surprisingly, yielded findings and principles of considerable generality. Ebbinghaus' rote memory tasks, on the other hand, were a disappointment in the search for general principles of memory.

The most important problems in experimental analysis are at the interface and interaction between the levels of behavior and phenomena. This is widely understood, but this understanding remains largely localized in the lore of particular substantive areas. Such lore represents general problems of method that deserve more focused and systematic discussion than they receive. How the investigator resolves these problems is a primary component of scientific inference.

1.1.6 CONCEPTUAL FRAMEWORK

The base of the Experimental Pyramid is the conceptual framework of the investigator. This framework is most apparent in the interpretation of results in the discussion section of an article. This framework is a major determinant of choices at all upper levels. The experimental design, as one example, is often constructed specifically to support one theoretical interpretation and eliminate alternatives. Studies that are primarily observational or exploratory generally stem from and embody preconceptions about what constitutes interesting aspects of behavior.

Conceptual frameworks are strong determiners of what phenomena are studied. Learning theory was the dominating framework during 1930–1960, but suffered eclipse in the later cognitive movement. Even in its dominant period, however, learning theory concentrated on a few narrow tasks. This led to neglect of the field of education, for one, which suffered further from trying to make do with theories developed for animal conditioning and rote learning.

Conceptual frameworks also strongly influence choice of behavioral task and measure. The memory domain, for example, has been almost totally dominated by a reproductive conception of memory, epitomized in rote learning. The stimulus material is given; the subject's task is to remember it correctly. The hallmark of reproductive memory is reliance on accuracy as the basic measure. Everyday life, however, operates largely through functional memory; reproductive memory has a relatively minor role. Different tasks and measures are needed to study functional memory.

These brief remarks indicate the pervasive role of conceptual frameworks at every level of investigation. A conceptual framework is a complex of knowledge systems, with interconnected levels of generality. Some of the broadest levels appears in the classic polarities of psychology, or dualities, as they might better be called: observational–experimental, association–gestalt, molecular–molar, central–peripheral, behavioral–cognitive, nature–nature, and individual–society, to name some of the more prominent. More specific conceptual frameworks underlie the choice and definition of phenomena, as with the example of memory in the previous paragraph.

The issue of conceptual frameworks has been discussed in various forms by many writers, who have emphasized their appearance and change in the various movements that take place in science. Present concern, however, is more limited and specific, namely, to emphasize the pervasive influence of conceptual frameworks in every aspect and level of experimental analysis.

Conceptual frameworks are personal knowledge systems. Each investigator has his or her own, undergoing continuous change and development. These personal differences are desirable, for they mean that different ones of us will study different phenomena and pursue different directions in prospecting Nature's boundless riches.

1.1.7 THE CAP ON THE PYRAMID

The cap on the Experimental Pyramid represents the theoretical interpretation put on the results of a given investigation. This is what appears in *Discussion* sections. These discussions integrate considerations from all levels of the Pyramid: statistical significance; possible confounds; the quality of the response measure and its relation to phenomena at issue; how far the results may be expected to generalize; alternative conceptual interpretations; and so forth. Discussion sections of published articles exhibit science at work.

Discussion sections are concerned with substantive inference. Much of this is extrastatistical in nature, but it is all concerned with the multiple aspects of validity of the results and their interpretation. The Discussion section thus involves integration of statistical and extrastatistical inference, considered further in Section 1.2.

1.1.8 THE EXPERIMENTAL PYRAMID

The Experimental Pyramid calls attention to important aspects of research endeavor. It makes explicit a multiplicity of considerations that arise in even the simplest experiment. This brief overview emphasizes the functional role of statistics as a way of thinking—a knowledge system—that integrates statistical and substantive considerations at every level of investigation.

Problems of reliability and validity, in particular, occur at all levels of the Experimental Pyramid; they need to be handled in relation to substantive considerations. A seeming exception is the significance test itself. It is applied after the data have been collected, as already observed, and it has been largely separated and divorced from substantive considerations. It is a significant commentary on current outlooks that the significance test came to be the apotheosis of statistics, not that more substantive and more important pair of concepts, **validity** and **reliability**. To these, we now turn.

1.2 VALIDITY

Validity is a primary concern at every level of the Experimental Pyramid. The most important aspect of validity is whether your measures are a veridical representation of the phenomenon or process you seek to study. No less important is the generality of your results. Validity questions are ubiquitous. Concerns about validity underlie most audience questions to colloquium speakers, questions to you by your Ph.D. committee, and criticisms by reviewers of the papers you submit for publication.

A useful research perspective on validity is given by the two distinctions of the validity diagram of Figure 1.2. The *outcome–process* distinction reflects two foci of concern: with observable results or with underlying process.

The *internal–external* distinction refers to generality: internally within the particular research setting, and externally to other settings, more or less different. This distinction will reappear later in the related distinction of *statistical–extrastatistical* inference.

Both distinctions are important for effective research, as indicated in the next two sections. Subsequent sections take up some intertwined aspects of validity that deserve specific discussion, especially confounding and measurement.

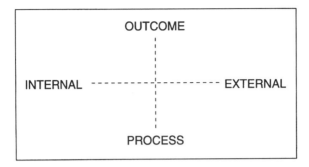

Figure 1.2. Validity diagram: Two continuous validity distinctions.

1.2.1 PROCESS VALIDITY AND OUTCOME VALIDITY

Process and outcome correspond to two quite different research goals. *Outcome validity* is mainly concerned with the observable level of behavior and is a prime goal in applied research. In an accident prevention program, for example, observable frequency of accidents has direct interest in itself. In a Head Start program, similarly, vocabulary size and social skills are outcomes desirable in themselves. The main validity issue concerns how far a given outcome can be generalized beyond the particular situation in which it was obtained.

Process validity is mainly concerned with conceptual interpretation. The observed behavioral outcome is taken to reflect some underlying process. In Pavlov's work on the salivary reflex, for example, there is little interest in salivation in dogs or in humans. Outcome generality is not at issue. Instead, the goal is to illuminate a general process, associative conditioning, dramatically portrayed in Aldous Huxley's novel, *Brave New World*. Process analysis is the focus of much psychological research: perceptual development in children, intuitive statistics, person cognition, and numerous others. Even phenomena of everyday life, such as self-esteem and family interaction, are often, perhaps too often, more focused on process than outcome.

Outcome validity and process validity both have two levels: internal and external. The *internal level* refers to the particular setting in which the study is performed; the *external level* refers to generality across other settings. Internal validity is, of course, prerequisite to external validity (see Section 18.4.1).

Assessment of internal validity begins by assessing whether the result is real, rather than chance, within the specific situation at hand. This is the function of the statistical significance test. A statistically significant result implies internal outcome validity. To assess internal process validity, in contrast, is far more difficult, an issue considered further in Section 1.2.3 on confounding.

The usefulness of the significance test for assessing internal outcome validity suggests that it should be equally useful for assessing external outcome validity. It would be, except that it assumes random samples, and random samples are uncommon. With rare exceptions, experimental analysis employs *handy samples* (see Section 1.4.1). Although statistical inference is central in assessing outcome validity within the handy sample, external outcome validity requires something more.

This something more is *extrastatistical inference*: Inference based on substantive considerations about whether or how much a result obtained in one particular situation will generalize to other situations. The necessity for extrastatistical inference is clear in generalizing from animal studies to humans.

Extrastatistical inference is essential for establishing process validity, both internal and external. This is because process validity is not factual in nature, but conceptual.

Extrastatistical inference is thus the backbone of science, both in the laboratory and in field applications. This fundamental fact of scientific life is glossed over in statistics instruction. Statistics texts and teachers, striving to motivate often ambivalent, statistics-averse students, shrink from emphasizing its limits and inadequacies. Statistical theory itself is elegant and self-contained, well-suited to autonomous instruction, and it comes to be taught this way. A hazy illusion thus develops that the internal outcome validity certified by the significance test somehow confers more or less internal process validity, and external validity to boot. Quite naturally, but unfortunately, the fact that the main validity questions require extrastatistical inference is avoided. Both kinds of inference, statistical and extrastatistical, will be more effective when they are employed as a team. Statistics should, in short, be appreciated and understood within the context of the Experimental Pyramid.

1.2.2 PROCESS–OUTCOME DISCORDANCE

Choices of research problem and research method are primary determinants of achievement, whether the goal be process validity or outcome validity. These two goals, regrettably, are typically discordant at the external level. Design and procedure that facilitate outcome validity are likely to undercut process validity, and vice versa. Attempts to achieve both goals are likely to achieve neither.

External outcome validity is best obtained when the situation studied is "realistic," that is, similar to or representative of a target situation to which generalization is desired. These target situations are typically complex; behavior is governed by numerous determinants, some not measurable, some not even known. Similarity between experimental and target situations helps ensure that similar determinants are operative and hence that similar outcomes will be obtained.

Outcome-oriented research is typically concerned with behavior change and social action. Educational psychology is a prime example. Comparative studies of teaching methods may not make sense outside of classroom situations. The one-hour experiments so common in process studies may sometimes be useful for pilot work, but classroom life contains numerous determinants of learning that are not simulated in the laboratory.

The goal of process validity requires an almost opposite strategy. A primary consideration is to simplify the situation in order to eliminate confounding from other processes. The usual aim is to study processes that are sufficiently basic that generality can reasonably be expected. Generality of specific outcomes is not usually of much concern in the process orientation. It is notable how so many of the famous tasks in psychology, the salivary reflex, the rat bar-press, and optical illusions, for example, are so far from everyday experience.

Process–outcome discordance deserves careful consideration. This discordance is regrettable, for it is desirable to derive social value from process research. However, the two orientations impose different constraints on design, measurement, and analysis. It is hard enough to attain even one kind of validity, as may be seen in the criticisms of articles in the literature. To seek both kinds of validity together will typically require compromises in research problem and research method that will compromise both goals.

Choice of research problem and research method are complicated by the fact that the process–outcome distinction is blurred in practice. Few outcome studies are without some process considerations, which may obscure an underlying outcome orientation. Even workers who emphasize social relevance often appeal to process explanations. Many process studies, on the other hand, are under pressure to justify themselves by dubious analogies of outcome generality. The difficulty, as already indicated, is that pursuing two discordant goals is a recipe for failure (see examples in Section 20.2.3; Anderson & Shanteau, 1977; Cook & Campbell, 1979, Chapter 8).

Outcome and process studies are both important. They can be mutually beneficial. They will work together better if the nature of their discordance is recognized. Outcome studies frequently raise new and important questions for process analysis. Such questions can ameliorate the dead-ending and trivialization that beset the process orientation. In return, process studies can be indispensable for testing and developing ideas suggested by outcome studies. The emphasis on process-outcome discordance is an argument against good-intentioned but ineffectual compromise in design and procedure.

1.2.3 CONFOUNDING

The main threat to process validity is *confounding*. We seek to manipulate some designated factor in an experiment, planning to attribute any observable effect to the operation of that factor. Some additional factor may intrude, however, that may also cause the observed effect, undercutting our planned interpretation. The two factors are thus confounded in operation and, using the term in a related sense, this confounds our interpretation.

Two important examples of confounding are noted here. The first appears in within subject design, in which each subject serves in two or more treatment conditions. Within subject design has notable advantages (Chapter 6), but it suffers potential confounding from order effects. Some condition must come second; thereby it is confounded with possible practice and other transfer from the first. The second treatment may seem good only because it benefits from practice on the first. Or it may seem bad only because it suffers from interference. Such confounding with order of presentation is a stumbling block in attempts to exploit the several advantages of within subject design. Statistical theory provides helpful ways of dealing with this form of confounding, discussed in later chapters.

The second example of confounding appears in the classical concept of *control group*. Suppose we give a treatment to an experimental group, measuring response before and after treatment. The natural measure of the treatment seems to be the change score, (after − before). We might be shot down, of course, if we did not include a control group, that is, a comparable group of subjects, measured similarly, who did not receive the treatment.

The control group is needed because the experimental group might change even if no treatment was given. Such autonomous change can occur for various reasons, including extraneous happenstance and natural growth and development. Such change is then confounded with our experimental treatment.

This confounding is resolved with the control group. By comparing the experimental group with the control, we assess the effect of the treatment itself, freed from whatever confounding was operative.

A more subtle aspect of confounding appears with the *placebo effect*. In medical psychology, the placebo effect refers to improvements reported by patients given a neutral treatment that has no medicinal properties in its own right. Patients' beliefs that they are getting a medicine is enough to make them feel better in surprisingly many cases.

The control problem is more difficult with the placebo effect. Unlike the autonomous changes just considered, the placebo effect is part of the treatment. A control group that received no treatment would not generally do. What is desired is a control treatment similar to the experimental treatment in all respects except the one under test. Sometimes this is as easy as giving the controls a sugar tablet or saline injection. Sometimes this is hardly feasible, as with surgical treatments.

Furthermore, "double blind" treatments may be necessary. The patients, obviously, should not know whether they receive the experimental or control treatment. Less obvious, but hardly less necessary, those who administer the treatments should also be blind to which treatment they are giving lest their expectations influence the treatment or bias their recording of the response.

A notable example of nonblind confounding appeared in the much-publicized claim that personality type is highly correlated with bodily build, or somatotype. This was an old idea, but it gained new respectability from a careful, rational method for measuring somatotype. These body–mind correlations were exceptionally impressive. For some time they were a staple of introductory texts. But the high correlations turned out to be merely personal bias of the investigators. They knew the somatotype of each subject when they evaluated his personality type; they worked their theory into their data (page 222). This wasteful commotion would have been avoided with rudimentary respect for experimental design. So important is the issue of confounding that a separate core chapter is devoted to it.

1.2.4 MEASUREMENT VALIDITY

Measurement is the link between two very different worlds: a real world of objects and events and a conceptual world of ideas and symbols. This function of measurement appeared in the Experimental Pyramid. The substantive virtue of our theories, accordingly, is bound up with the validity of our measurements. Measurement is thus an integral part of substantive theory.

Measurement has two aspects: *quantity* and *quality*. Quantity is concerned with "how much," which physics made into the essential currency of science and which is also important in psychology. Psychological science, however, faces difficult questions whether our observable response measure, score on a test, for example, or latency in reaction to an emotional stimulus, is a true quantitative measure of the phenomenon under investigation. This question of quantity underlies the concern with linear (equal interval) scales considered in Section 7.2 and in Chapter 21 on psychological measurement theory.

The more important aspect of measurement concerns the quality, or conceptual nature, of what is measured. Quality is the primary issue in measurement validity—whether the numbers are a veridical representation of the quality or process at issue.

Measurement has a twofold empirical base: in the task and procedure on one hand, and in the organism on the other hand. These interact to determine what is observed and what its quality may be. The main function of pilot work is to develop and shape both parts of this empirical base. These empirical operations determine the validity of the measurement transformation.

Measurement also has a conceptual base, manifest in the names we give to our measures: learning, memory, intelligence, expectancy, blame, and so forth. These are not simple object properties, like mass or length. Most refer to complex phenomena, whose definition involves successive approximation within an ever-developing conceptual framework.

This issue may be illustrated with the concept of intelligence. Scientific understanding of intelligence began with Binet's search for objective tests to improve on teacher's decisions about which children should be sent to special schools for mentally retarded. The conceptual framework of that era dictated the use of such tests as reaction time and sensory acuity. These proved useless. Not without trouble, Binet developed better tests, forerunners of the IQ tests of today. Even today, of course, the concept of intelligence is by no means agreed upon. It undergoes continued change and development, as do many other psychological concepts.

A basic validity consideration in psychological measurement is that many entities are complex, only partially representable in terms of a numerical scale. Verbal and quantitative abilities, for example, both operate in intelligent behavior. Some individuals may be high in one, yet low in the other. Hence a single "IQ" score cannot fully represent the concept of intelligence.

But multiple measures to represent multiple abilities are still only partial measures. Basic processes and even a quality itself are in good part not representable in quantitative terms. Analogous complexity appears with concepts in many areas, from visual perception to self-cognition.

A partial measure of a complex entity may be entirely adequate for the purpose at hand. A test of sentence understanding may be a fine indicator of usefulness of a Head Start program, even though it leaves much unassessed.

Partial measures are more common than is ordinarily realized. We are accustomed to considering number of drops of saliva in the conditioned dog as a measure of learning. The same applies to bar press rate by the rat and to error frequency in a human memory task. Obviously, these are not measures of the learning itself, only one particular product or output of that learning.

Although partial measures are invaluable in life science, two limits on their usefulness should be kept in mind. The name given the measure often becomes reified; the measure is identified with the concept. Part of the confusion over intelligence tests resulted from failure to realize that one-dimensional conceptions are inherently too narrow to represent the phenomena. Similar problems trouble the study of beliefs and values, standardly measured with one-dimensional scales, even though they are complex knowledge systems.

Partial measures can also be dangerous by delimiting the scope of inquiry. A single task and measure can thus become autonomous, surviving long after its usefulness has dwindled away. Memory research thus became trapped within a reproductive framework, defined by reliance on accuracy measures. Much work on social attitudes, to take another example, rests on superficial measures obtained in short experiments that have little relevance to social attitudes of everyday life.

Because of the unique role of measurement in the Experimental Pyramid, measurement validity is entwined with all other aspects of validity.

Confounding, in particular, is essentially a problem of measurement validity. The process–outcome distinction, similarly, implies rather different measurement criteria for outcome validity than for process validity. Much of progress consists of improvements in measurement, both in its empirical base and in its conceptual base.

1.2.5 CONCEPTUAL VALIDITY

Conceptual validity refers to the interpretation we place on particular results. More generally, it may refer to our overall conceptual framework, which generates such particular interpretations.

In the Experimental Pyramid, the conceptual framework constitutes the foundation. Your conceptual framework is the primary determinant of your judgments and decisions in any investigation: About which phenomena are important, which are tractable, which particular tasks will pay off, which aspects of behavior you measure, what confounds are likely, how you analyze the data, and how you interpret the outcome.

Many major advances in psychology consisted mainly of broadening our conceptual frameworks, as with the once-foreign idea that the study of animals could be part of our field. The modern cognitive movement, similarly, made its main contribution by liberalizing and broadening the scope of inquiry, as with consciousness and mother love. Equally instructive is the work of the ethologists, who showed the insufficiency of the prevailing experimental framework by demonstrating the effectiveness of field observation for revealing the nature of animal behavior.

A more specific example of this foundation role of conceptual framework in experimental analysis appears with *simplification strategy*. In developmental psychology, to take one instance of simplification strategy, knowledge of the external physical world is a basic component of cognition, and much effort sought to trace out the development of concepts of time, speed, and so forth. A popular question asked at what ages different concepts emerged, whether 5-year-olds, for example, have concepts of time or speed, and whether one concept is necessary as a precursor to the other.

A recurrent objection to such studies was that the tasks used for concept assessment depended on auxiliary abilities, verbal abilities, for example, which are confounded with the concept under study. Confounding from inadequate verbal ability is especially likely at early ages. This makes it uncertain which concepts are primitive, which are derived. The simplification strategy was intended to ameliorate this objection by finding tasks that required minimal auxiliary abilities.

Implicit in simplification strategy, however, is an assumption that the concepts are autonomous, well-defined, and can be studied in isolation. When made explicit, this assumption becomes questionable. Instead, the concept may begin as a tenuous component of other abilities, only gradually and partially becoming autonomous. Under this alternative conceptual framework, the basic assumption of simplification strategy, namely, well-defined autonomous concepts, becomes increasingly inappropriate at younger ages. Simplification strategy thus becomes increasingly difficult to apply the more it is needed.

One alternative to simplification strategy is to study the focal concept in tandem with auxiliary abilities. This strategy of multiple determination, as it may be called, has some effectiveness (see e.g., Figures 1.3 and 20.1). The main point here, however, is that these two strategies embody very different conceptual frameworks and lead to very different experimental approaches to cognitive development.

A second example appears in attempts to apply standard statistical tools of "interaction" to study joint action of multiple determinants. These begin from a conceptual framework that takes the additive model as basic and also assumes linearity ("equal intervals") of the measuring scale. Both assumptions are often false (Chapter 7). Here again, the validity of particular studies depends on the larger validity of the overall conceptual framework.

We tend to take our conceptual frameworks for granted. To some extent, we are unaware of them until they are challenged. It is at this level, however, that new ideas can have greatest impact.

1.3 VARIABILITY

That variability can serve as a yardstick to assess real effects is a basic statistical principle. Although this principle may seem paradoxical, it makes perfect sense. To claim a real effect of the experimental treatment, it must be shown that the mean difference *between* experimental and control treatments is greater than expected by chance from the variability *within* each treatment—this variability thus constitutes the yardstick. Almost miraculously, statistical theory transformed this qualitative principle to exact formulas (Sections 2.2.0 and 3.2).

This statistical principle has an important empirical implication:

Reduce Variability!

Variability obscures the signals Nature sends us. Such variability, accordingly, is called *error variability* or just *error*. If this variability can be reduced, Nature's signal will be clearer. Ways to reduce error variability are considered in the first three following sections.

More closely considered, variability is seen to be a substantive phenomenon. It arises from causal factors, especially individual differences, that deserve substantive consideration. The last section focuses on individual differences as a desirable phenomenon, not to be reduced, but to be studied in their own right and even to serve as a tool for theory construction.

1.3.1 INDIVIDUAL DIFFERENCES

The main source of variability in many investigations is individual differences. If their effect can be reduced, the results will be more precise. This is an important consideration in designing an investigation.

One way to reduce the effect of individual differences is through experimental hygiene. Subjects find it surprisingly easy to misunderstand instructions, for example, so instructions should be carefully developed in pilot work. The way in which they are presented should also be designed to minimize misunderstanding (see further Section 14.1.2, page 405).

More generally, experimental procedure should follow the principle of task–subject congruence. A good start with a child is to appreciate its name; a good start with a rat is to "gentle" it to reduce its fear in the hands of this huge monster. In addition to reducing error variability, experimental hygiene should yield a cleaner measure of response.

A second way to reduce the effect of individual differences is by stratification of the subject population. One form of stratification is seen in screening tests, in which certain classes of subjects are screened out of the investigation. Screening is common in studies of sensory function, usually to screen out persons with sensory defects such as color weakness or hearing loss. Sometimes, however, the normals may be screened out in order to study the sensory defect. Screening criteria may be similarly used with patient groups or children to ensure some acceptable degree of task functioning. Thus, a pretest may be given to assess whether the subject possesses the background skills or knowledge to perform acceptably in the assigned task.

Screening has more potential than is often realized, especially for situations in which occasional extreme subjects appear. Even one extreme score in a small sample can markedly increase the error variance and decrease power to detect treatment effects. For continuing work in such situations, development of a screening test could be very useful. This is one reason for always looking through your data for extreme scores. Such scores may also point to improvements in procedure and should be reported as a guide to other workers.

Subject stratification can also be incorporated into the experimental design. This can provide a double benefit. In one experimental study of two methods of language learning, for example, subjects were stratified on the basis of their grades in Spanish I (A and B students in one group, C and D students in the other). The two learning methods were then tested with both groups of subjects. One benefit was a substantial reduction in error variability. This came about because part of individual differences that correlated with grade in Spanish I was fractionated out of the error (detailed in Section 14.2.2, page 409).

More important, this stratified design yielded information on the generality of the result. The same teaching method was superior for both the better and the poorer students. Stratification thus yielded a substantive as well as a statistical benefit. Stratified design is discussed further under block design in Section 14.2 and analysis of covariance in Chapter 13.

A third way of dealing with individual differences is to give several treatments to each subject. Subjects thus serve as their own controls, so to speak. Statistically, the main effect of individual differences is fractionated out, typically decreasing manyfold the variability yardstick. This tremendous statistical advantage has made within subject designs widely popular (Chapter 6).

1.3.2 EXTRANEOUS VARIABLES

Aside from individual differences, extraneous variables also contribute to variability. One major class of extraneous variables consists of attentional factors. Human subjects should generally be run one at a time, not together in batches or classroom groups, for example, because their attention is then under poor control. This threatens the validity of the experiment more than its reliability. In particular, success in working with young children often requires experimenter skills to maintain a forward pace that keeps the child's interest and attention centered on the task.

One way to control extraneous variables is to reduce them through experimental hygiene, as with the attentional factors just noted. Also important is preliminary practice to adjust the subject to the task. Experimental procedure and apparatus, similarly, should be monitored for trouble-free functioning.

A different way to control extraneous variables is to incorporate them in the design. To illustrate, suppose subjects are to be run by two experimenters. It could be unfortunate if one of them was obtuse with subjects or careless with data recording. One function of the pilot work, accordingly, would be to train the experimenters so that both used reasonably similar procedure. In addition, experimenters would be included as a variable in the experimental design, each running half of the subjects in each treatment condition. This design has a double benefit, for it avoids confounding the experimenters with treatments, as would happen if each ran half of the treatments, for example, and it provides an assessment of their performance (see *Factorial Design*, Chapter 5).

This same technique may be used to control other minor variables. One common minor variable is position of a goal object, as in two-choice discrimination learning in children. Right and left are routinely balanced to avoid bias from the child's position preference. In within subject design, similarly, the treatments may be presented to different subjects in different orders. Order and serial position of treatments may then be included as variables in the experimental design. Even though these minor variables may often be expected to have minor effects, this design technique provides insurance for the investigator and assurance for reviewers and readers of the written report that the experimental procedure was indeed under control.

Not all extraneous variables are truly extraneous. Some represent aspects of the experimental situation that are also important for validity. Some stimulus variables, in particular, may represent substantive variability that should be incorporated into the design (Section 1.4.3).

1.3.3 RESPONSE MEASURE

Variability also depends on how the response is measured. The time it takes a rat to run a maze or a child to do a sum may be expressed instead as a speed score, that is, the reciprocal of the time score. Galvanic skin resistance, similarly, may be measured instead as the reciprocal conductance. In each case, the two measures are essentially equivalent, but one may yield lower variability.

Alternatively, the task itself may be changed to get a less variable response process. One major function of pilot work is to shape the task toward lower variability, much discussed under the concept of reliability in test theory. Analogous general methodology does not seem possible in experimental psychology because of the great diversity of experimental tasks. Much can be learned, however, from *Method* sections of published articles in your field.

In general, the investigator has some freedom of choice with the response measure and with the task. These choices are opportunities for decreasing variability and increasing power.

1.3.4 VARIABILITY AS SUBSTANTIVE PHENOMENON

In life sciences, unlike physical sciences, the main source of variability is real individual differences rather than error of measurement. This variability has basic substantive interest. In physical sciences, at least above the quantum level, variability typically resides in the measuring apparatus, not in the entity to be measured. The mean electric charge measured for different electrons represents a universal constant. In life sciences, however, a mean over a group of individuals has mainly a conventional significance, not corresponding to any natural entity. The statistical principle that a mean is meaningless without reference to variability thus has a second, deeper significance in life sciences.

Indeed, an experimental treatment may have opposite effects for different individuals; it may be beneficial to the group as a whole, yet harmful to a minority. Some medical drugs, for example, have noxious side effects to which a few individuals are susceptible. This problem of opposite effects is also a concern in educational psychology, as in the praise–blame study of Note 5.2.2a, and has general relevance in practical applications.

In most theory-oriented research, in contrast, individual differences are ignored. The general run of experimental process studies take for granted either that essentially all individuals in a given condition will exhibit the same directional effect or that any opposite effects by a minority of subjects would not trouble the face value of the means. This may usually be justified, but the massive unconcern with obtaining such justification is disturbing.

This ignoral of individual differences in experimental analysis has been criticized in other areas of psychology. Educational psychology is concerned with all learners; optimal methods of instruction may differ across abilities and aptitudes. Personality psychology emphasizes an idiographic approach that insists on the uniqueness of the individual, as may be seen in the popularity of case histories. In both these fields, the consignment of individual differences to the statistical error term so common in experimental psychology seems horrifying.

One way to get evidence on individual differences uses stratification technique. In educational psychology, for example, different instruction methods are commonly expected to be more effective with different levels of aptitude. Accordingly, subjects would be stratified on aptitude prior to testing the different methods, as in the foregoing example of language teaching. Stratification thus yields a win–win design, all outcomes being instructive.

A quite different approach employs individual response patterns. Each individual is tested under multiple conditions, and the analysis focuses on the pattern of response for each individual. This approach may be seen in fields as diverse as perception, operant behavior, judgment–decision, and person cognition (see *Single Subject Design*, Chapter 11). Individual differences in response pattern have potential as a tool for general theory, as demonstrated with algebraic models of psychological process (Chapters 20 and 21).

1.4 SAMPLES AND GENERALITY

All scientific inference rests on samples, but seldom are these samples random as statistical theory requires. Scientific inference is mainly extrastatistical. Statistical inference must be integrated into extrastatistical inference.

The primacy of extrastatistical inference is underscored by the fact that sampling occurs at many levels in our experiments. Subject sampling, the usual referent, is only one of these levels. Three other kinds of sampling, no less important, are also discussed here.

1.4.1 SUBJECT SAMPLES

Subject samples are historical accidents. They seldom have intrinsic interest. Their value lies in whatever generality they may have beyond the accidental. Scientific truth must thus be founded on evanescent behavior.

In fact, subject samples are nearly always samples of convenience—*handy samples*. The college students who serve in so many research studies are not random samples from their own colleges, much less from all colleges in the English speaking countries, and much much less from students yet unborn.

Handy samples are also standard in animal research. Monkeys are hard to get, and those who work with them are grateful for every one they can lay hands on. Those who work with rats take what the supply company dispenses.

Scientific inference must thus be founded on handy samples. Statistical inference must do the same, if it is to be helpful. In fact, statistical inference can cope with handy samples through a ingenious device.

This ingenious device is *randomization*: Subjects in the handy sample are randomly assigned to experimental conditions. A statistical significance test can then be used to assess whether the observed effect can reasonably be considered real for this handy sample. This test provides a solid base for extrastatistical inference to larger classes of subjects (see further Section 3.3.2).

Extrastatistical inference, although more or less uncertain, does command considerable consensus. Many experiments on visual perception, such as the line–box optical illusion of Figure 8.1 (page 226), use two or three subjects with confidence that similar results would be found in China and Poland. Experiments on language, on the other hand, or on social attitudes, may be expected to have much less generality.

The issue of generality is usually left implicit, however, except for the usual disclaimer that generality must be assessed in future work. This approach seems reasonable. Requiring arguments about generality would produce much bootless speculation in journal articles, a nuisance for writer and reader alike.

Some additional aspects of extrastatistical inference also require discussion. One appeared in the distinction between outcome validity and process validity of Section 1.2.1. Three others relate to three other kinds of sampling, noted briefly in the following sections.

1.4.2 ORGANISM SAMPLES

Much psychological research is done with animals in the expectation that the results may have some generality beyond the particular species being studied. Indeed, most prominent learning theories have been based primarily on animal data, especially from dogs, rats, and pigeons.

Organism sampling is also governed by considerations of convenience and generality. Fruit flies have long been a favorite in genetic research for practical reasons, including rapid breeding, with good hope of finding panspecies properties of genes. Indeed, Mendel's classic work foreshadowing gene theory was based on a shrewd choice of peas. The popularity of the white rat rests on an impressive list of experimental advantages, such as hardiness and small size, as well as similarities to humans in motivation and learning.

Generalization across species is necessarily extrastatistical. Some investigators demur at attempting cross-species generalization, advocating a philosophy of "rat for rat's sake." One virtue of this philosophy is that it removes the pressure of attempting to justify rat studies by forced, dubious analogies to humans.

Another virtue is that the rat does deserve to be studied for its own sake, as one of Nature's functional biological systems. Moreover, development of interlocking knowledge systems about each species separately is an important base for extrastatistical generalization. Even those who emphasize "rat for rat's sake" expect some degree of cross-species generality.

1.4.3 STIMULUS SAMPLES

The stimuli used in an experiment are often more or less arbitrary, a sample from some larger class of stimuli. In studies of face memory, for example, the stimulus faces may be a sample from some student yearbook. In person cognition, similarly, person descriptions may be constructed from a standardized set of personality trait adjectives. The outcome, however, may be peculiar to the arbitrary choice of stimuli. The examples given in Chapter 8 on confounding show that this problem of stimulus generality should not be taken lightly.

Stimulus generality can be assessed with stimulus replication: Include stimulus materials as an additional variable in the experimental design. Thus, two or more different sets of faces could be constructed by using yearbooks from different schools. Similarly, two or more person descriptions could be constructed, equivalent except for using different trait adjectives. If it turns out that different stimulus materials yield different results, generalization from a study that included only one would have been dangerous. On the other hand, generality is enhanced if different stimulus materials yield equivalent results. Stimulus replication is thus a win–win design. Statistically, stimulus replication may be handled with factorial design (Section 1.5.2).

In some areas, background knowledge will suggest that different stimulus samples will yield equivalent results. A single list of nonsense syllables might be considered enough in a learning study, partly on the basis of common sense, partly because the items of the list themselves constitute a sample. A single example of an optical illusion, similarly, would usually suffice to demonstrate the illusion, since background knowledge indicates size–independence, in particular. Even so, it may be advisable to use more than one set of stimulus materials, expecting to demonstrate that they do yield equivalent results. This can often be done with little cost to the investigator and helpful reassurance to the reader.

In other areas, such as psycholinguistics and personality–social, stimulus replication seems more generally necessary. A single metaphor would hardly suffice as a base for a general theory of metaphor; and an entire class of ambiguous expressions would only illuminate a small part of the general issue of ambiguity in communication. In personality–social, it would be risky to attempt any general conclusion with a single person description, for example, or a single communication in attitude research, or a single moral dilemma in moral judgment. Here again, the method of factorial design is useful.

The stimulus itself is complex in many experimental situations. In education, for example, the teacher is perhaps the most important aspect of the stimulus situation, a primary determinant of relative effectiveness of different teaching methods. It is certainly desirable, if not essential, therefore, to replicate by including more than one teacher for each teaching method. Similar replication is desirable with studies of counseling, therapy, and behavior change generally. Experimental studies with a single teacher, counselor, or therapist can be useful, but they are severely limited.

This too-brief discussion suggests that stimulus sampling may approach subject sampling in importance. This matter is often overlooked, as various writers have complained. Often, it is true, stimulus replication will merely verify an obvious expectation that different stimulus materials yield equivalent results. But such verification may help the reader's evaluation of the study; and failure to verify may be important for the investigator to learn about. In other cases, the behavior may depend as much on the stimulus sample as on the primary experimental variable. Although this can be distressing, it is the better part of workmanship to uncover this dependence.

1.4.4 TASK–BEHAVIOR SAMPLES

The behavior we observe in any study is always a sample, often several levels removed from our focal concern. Classic examples are Pavlov's salivary reflex and Ebbinghaus' rote learning of nonsense syllables. Neither of these behaviors had much interest in its own right. Both investigators considered their findings about learning of these peculiarly specific behaviors to hold far more generally. Most experimental studies throughout psychology are similarly based on very specific behaviors in very specific tasks.

Choice of experimental task is thus a basic determinant of the behavior sampling process. Choice of experimental task is also a basic determinant of the meaningfulness and generality of the results.

Among the criteria for choosing a task are interest and importance of the task behavior, convenience, simplicity, unitariness, and generalizability. Convenience, a practical virtue, includes cost and availability of subjects, apparatus, and so forth. Convenience especially includes a body of prior work that indicates what confounds are harmful, what controls are important, and what kinds of substantive inferences seem tenable.

Simplicity is a universal virtue. A simple task has less to go wrong and is easier to understand. The simplicity of many psychological tasks deserves reflection. The T-maze, for example, is a descendant of the complex, real-life Hampton Court maze. The rat bar-press seems even simpler, one reason for its great popularity.

The related virtue of unitariness refers to the fact that the focal behavior in any task always involves auxiliary abilities that may confound the interpretation. This problem of auxiliary abilities can be especially difficult in developmental psychology. Stage theories of moral judgment, for example, relied almost entirely on extensive interviews about moral dilemmas that have little relevance to everyday life, even for adults, and can hardly be used below 10–12 years of age. Simpler tasks, such as the blame task shown later in Figure 1.3, are applicable down to at least 4 years. That results with such tasks infirmed the stage theories is only a sign of their more important accomplishment of being applicable with far younger children.

The final criterion, generalizability, is not independent of the others, but it is often the most important. The observed data are only a sample of the behavior of the sample of organisms in the sample task, thus involving at least three levels of generalization. And this behavior itself is usually of interest only as an index of some phenomenon or process at each level of generalization.

Choice of task for eliciting behavior is a central determinant of achievement in research. Most workers begin with existing tasks. This is sensible because developing any new task is often arduous and sometimes unrewarding. This is one reason for attending to *Method* sections in published articles, which often contain useful hints about pitfalls to be avoided. Similarly, existing tasks offer opportunities to tie into current issues and problems.

At the same time, an existing task often develops intellectual inertia that continues its life long past its usefulness, as happened with Piaget's standard choice task in developmental psychology. Similarly, the monolithic conception of memory as reproductive, descended from Ebbinghaus' pioneering work, helped fix this field in an admittedly unproductive rut, and obstructed recognition of the very different functional conceptions, which study memory as it functions in school learning and in everyday life.

Much of the value of the recent cognitive movement consists of greater openness to phenomena and tasks to which the behavioral outlook was uncongenial or inimical. Much is made of the return of consciousness from exile, perhaps too much. No less important, perhaps more, are other "soft" phenomena, such as beliefs and attitudes, probability concepts, self-esteem, excuses and other forms of ego defense, health, play, and many, many other aspects of everyday life. Development of new issues and tasks is a continual source of fundamental contributions.

1.5 MULTIPLE DETERMINATION

Behavior characteristically depends on many determinants, not just one. This multiple determination appears everywhere in psychology, from contrast effects in psychophysics to motive conflicts in everyday life, and from food preferences to marital satisfaction. Prediction of behavior thus requires capabilities for dealing with multiple determinants. Understanding behavior similarly involves reference to its multiple determinants. The fact of multiple determination is thus a central problem for psychological theory and application.

There is a qualitative difference between experiments with one variable and experiments with two. The two-variable experiment is more than two one-variable experiments joined together. Two variables have a combined action that may not be determinable from their separate actions. No number of one-variable experiments can suffice to understand behavior or to predict it. The fact of multiple determination must be addressed in any attempt to develop psychological theory or to apply it.

Statistical theory provides two general methods for analysis of multiple determination: *regression analysis* and *analysis of variance*. These two methods, especially the latter, are the ground for most of the statistical material in this book. A preview is given here.

1.5.1 REGRESSION ANALYSIS

The psychology department at a major university realized that large amounts of time were spent every year evaluating the hundreds and hundreds of applications for graduate study. Despite earnest efforts by the admissions committee, a considerable fraction of those admitted did not do well. Perhaps, someone thought, a statistical prediction equation could do as well or better.

Two predictor variables were the applicant's grade point average (GPA) and score on the graduate record exam (GRE). The response measure Y was success in graduate school. The prediction equation was very simple, just a weighted sum of the two predictors:

$$Y = w_1 \, \text{GPA} + w_2 \, \text{GRE}.$$

The weights, w_1 and w_2, represent the predictive importance of the two variables. These weights are related to the correlations between these predictor variables and the specified response measure.

If these weights are known, they may be applied to each applicant's GPA and GRE scores to determine his/her predicted Y. To find these weights requires a set of calibration cases, for which GPA, GRE, and Y are known. In the present example, these calibration cases were graduate students from previous years, whose success in graduate school was known. A regression analysis was applied to these calibration data to obtain the weights. With these weights,

Y can be predicted for new applicants. Applicants for each new year can then be admitted in rank order of their predicted success.

How well does this statistical method compare with human judgment? In the given example, the statistical equation did somewhat better than the admissions committee. It was adopted, accordingly, freeing the committee members for other work. This illustrates a useful social resource, considering that even in 1970 there were more than seven million applications for graduate school, counting multiple applications by the same person to different schools. Furthermore, the predictive weights were later made public so potential applicants could calculate their own Y score. If this was unduly low, they might prefer not to apply, saving time, trouble, and the application fee.

Similar comparisons of statistical method with expert judgment have been made in numerous fields, including personnel selection, pilot trainee selection, diagnosis of disease from medical tests, parole decisions, and clinical diagnosis. A rough summary is that the statistical method ranges from perhaps a little inferior to the best experts in a few fields, such as radiography, to somewhat superior in most fields, such as personnel selection and clinical psychology.

Experts often vehemently disbelieve that an unthinking, statistical method can outpredict them. This outcome, however, is not surprising. One reason is that cognitive integration often follows an averaging process rather than the statistically optimal adding process. A second reason is that the statistical equation usually has, in effect, much more experience: It is constructed from an extensive set of calibration cases with known outcomes (see Section 16.1.3).

1.5.2 FACTORIAL DESIGN

The concept of factorial design is one of the fundamental ideas of experimental analysis. It opens a way to systematic study of causal inference when multiple determinants are operative. An example of factorial design is shown in Figure 1.3, based on a study of moral development. Children were told about a boy who interfered with some workmen painting a house. They judged how much blame or punishment the boy deserved, depending on two specified variables: his intent to harm and how much damage he caused.

The plan, or *design*, of the experiment is shown in the design table at the left of Figure 1.3. Intent of the harmdoer and amount of damage done are the variables, or *factors*, of this design. There were three levels of intent, listed as the rows of the table. Similarly, there were four graded levels of damage, listed as the columns of the table. As this design table indicates, each level of intent was paired with each level of damage to yield a total of $3 \times 4 = 12$ experimental conditions. Each cell of this factorial design thus corresponds to one of the 12 intent–damage combinations.

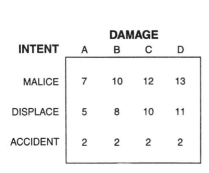
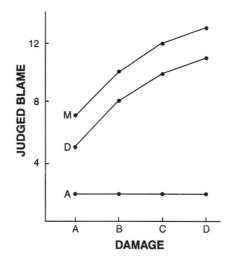

Figure 1.3. Integration schema for blame. Subject assigns blame for harmful actions, given the *intent* behind the action and the *damage* caused by the action. Left panel shows *factorial design*, with three levels of intent (purposive malice, displaced aggression, accident) combined with four levels of damage, graded from A to D. Entry in each cell is the blame assigned for the corresponding levels of intent and damage. Right panel shows *factorial graph* of data in left panel. After Leon (1980).

The number in each cell is the response to the intent–damage combination for that cell. Thus, the top row represents blame judgments for all four cases of malicious intent to harm; blame is least when no damage is done, and increases steadily as damage increases. A parallel pattern is visible with displaced aggression, listed in the second row of the table. For accidental damage in the last row, blame is constant, independent of damage. These data are slightly idealized from an actual experiment (see Figure 11.3, page 318).

The *factorial graph* at the right of Figure 1.3 presents the same data. Each row of data in the design table corresponds to one curve in the graph. Graph and table are thus isomorphic forms of the same data.

The trends in the data table are visible in the factorial graph. The upward trend of the top curve represents the relative effects of the four levels of damage. The elevations of the three curves represent the relative effects of the three levels of intent.

In this particular study, the *pattern* in the factorial graph has primary interest. The top two curves are parallel. Parallelism suggests an *addition rule*: Blame = Intent + Damage. Since the two curves are a constant distance apart, it is as though increasing the level of intent adds a constant amount of blame, regardless of level of damage.

In contrast, the bottom curve, for accidental damage, is flat, independent of damage. Taken together, the three curves thus exhibit a *configural effect*, in which the response depends on the configuration of the stimulus variables.

This factorial graph thus suggests the operation of two cognitive processes in moral judgment, the addition rule and the accident–configural rule. Neither process could have been revealed without joint manipulation of both variables.

In this example, the factorial graph stands up and tells us what the data mean. In practice, the factorial pattern will be more or less variable and the interpretation less definite. It is often desirable, accordingly, to augment the visual inspection with statistical assessment. Analysis of variance is useful for this purpose, as will be seen in Chapter 5 on factorial design.

1.5.3 MULTIPLE DETERMINATION

Two kinds of multiple determination were illustrated in the two foregoing examples. The first involves uncontrolled observational data, the second involves controlled experimental data. In each example, additional variables are also important. The prediction equation for graduate selection actually involved a third variable, namely, quality of the applicant's undergraduate institution. The study of blame needs to consider other determinants such as extenuating circumstances, apology, and atonement, as well as age and gender of the harmdoer.

These two kinds of multiple determination are ubiquitous in psychological science, a consequence of the basic fact that perception, thought, and action are generally determined by multiple factors. Statistical methods for studying these two forms of multiple determination are presented in the following chapters. Basic ideas and techniques are most easily presented for a single variable, as is done in Chapters 3, 4, and 9. Following chapters extend these ideas and techniques to multiple determinants.

1.5.4 TOWARD UNIFIED THEORY

Perception, thought, and action are always determined by multiple factors; multiple determination is a basic fact of psychology. Unified science depends on development of methods to analyze processes of multiple determination. Some assistance has been provided by the statistical tools of regression analysis and factorial design, as just illustrated.

But multiple determination is more subtle. These statistical tools, despite their usefulness, have strong limitations, as will be shown when discussing measurement and models in Chapter 7. In some situations, fortunately, these limitations can be transcended by incorporating these tools within a larger theory of functional cognition, a theory that has had some success in developing unified theory of psychological science (Chapter 21).

PREFACE

The sample mean should be considered an interval of uncertainty. Although the sample mean appears as a specific number, this appearance is misleading because it is only an uncertain clue to the population mean. To understand the sample mean, this uncertainty must be included.

Statistical theory shows how to make precise this idea of the sample mean as a range of uncertainty. This range of uncertainty can be quantified with two simple formulas; the information in the sample can be used to construct an interval within which the population mean is included with specified confidence. This *confidence interval* properly represents the sample mean.

As a confidence interval, the sample lifts itself by its bootstraps to the level of the population. Thereby, it provides a foundation for statistical inference.

The logic of the confidence interval is developed along a seven-step road in Section 2.2. Each step on the road involves some fundamental concept. Taken together, the seven steps constitute a chain of reasoning that deserves admiration for internal beauty as well as for practical value. The confidence interval reveals order in disorder; the variability and uncertainty of the sample data are transformed into a precision tool.

The confidence interval can be used as a test of statistical significance—whether experimental manipulations have real effect. Significance tests, however, involve additional concepts, of null hypothesis, false alarm, power, and so forth. Limitations and misuses of significance tests are also discussed.

BASIC CONCEPTS

sample and population	significance test
sampling distribution	null hypothesis
variance and standard deviation	2×2 decision table
confidence interval	false alarm and power
law of sample size	individual differences
central limit theorem	principle of replication

Chapter 2

STATISTICAL INFERENCE[*]

All science rests on evidence from samples. A sample, however, cannot provide an exact picture of the population from which it came. A sample mean, in particular, will always differ from the population mean.

It follows that a sample mean should be represented as an *interval of uncertainty*. It is only meaningful when accompanied by its *likely error* from the population mean.[a]

This view of the sample mean as an interval of likely error is vital in principle. In practice, this view may seem too vague, too indeterminate to be useful. Is it really possible to specify an exact value of likely error?

Remarkably, the answer is *yes*: Statistical theory has found a way to measure uncertainty. The sow's ear of variability in the sample can be transformed into the silk purse of a confidence interval. The confidence interval epitomizes statistical inference—and provides a tool for empirical analysis.

2.1 SAMPLE AND POPULATION

The prototypical problem of statistics is to use *sample* data to make inferences about *populations*. This requires an idealization in which we consider a *random sample* of elements drawn from some specified population. The elements are assumed to be *independent*: Knowledge of any one element tells nothing about any other element; each added element carries equal information.

---

[*] A review of basic concepts is given in the last chapter of this book.

2.1.1 RANDOM SAMPLE

Statistical theory rests squarely on *randomness.* A random sample, in its simplest form, includes each element of the population with equal probability. Randomness has two interrelated consequences.

First, randomness avoids *bias,* that is, systematic or long-run misrepresentation of the population. Nonrandom samples are susceptible to bias, and many notorious examples of such bias have been recorded. Some investigators have sought to avoid bias by selecting representative samples. However, when people try to construct a sample that is representative of some population, they invariably introduce bias. Random sampling, accordingly, has come to be considered vital.

Second, randomness allows the laws of probability to be applied. These laws enable us to determine the likely error of the sample mean.

The best-known case of random sampling is in election polls, which customarily include a warning about "margin of error." A notable statistical result for large populations is that the likely error of the sample depends only on the sample size—regardless of population size. A random poll of 1200 voters will be equally reliable with populations of 20 thousand and 20 million voters. This would yield a typical margin of error near 1.4%, which makes random polling an expensive but cost-effective tool for social issues (Section 0.1.4).

In experimental work, randomness is usually obtained by *randomization,* that is, by assigning subjects at random to the experimental conditions (see Section 3.3.2, page 69). Our subjects are usually handy samples, chosen for convenience. Randomization not only avoids bias in assigning subjects to conditions, but also allows statistical inference to be applied. Randomization confers empirical reality on the foregoing idealization of random sample.

2.1.2 SAMPLE MEAN AS INTERVAL OF UNCERTAINTY

The most common statistical inference uses sample data to estimate the population mean. This sample–population inference faces a basic difficulty: Different samples from the same population will yield different sample means; all will differ from the population mean; all will be more or less in error. We must live with this error, and statistical theory gives us a rational way to do so.

The rational way to live with sampling error is to specify its likely size. We take the sample mean as an estimate of the population mean, but we know it will be in error. How far wrong is it likely to be? Statistical theory formalizes this goal as follows: Specify a range about the sample mean such that the population mean will lie within this range for 95% (say) of all such sample means. For our one particular sample, we may then have 95% confidence that the population mean lies within the specified range of our sample mean. This range may be considered the *likely error* of our sample mean.

How is it possible to calculate the likely error of our sample mean? If we could draw many samples, the variability among their means would give us an indication of their likely error. But—we have only one sample. How can we use this one sample to determine the likely error of its own mean?

The answer comes from common sense: Look at the variability within our one sample. If our sample data show little variability among themselves, we expect their mean to be close to the population mean. If our sample data are highly variable, we fear their mean may be far away from the population mean. With statistical theory, this commonsense reasoning can be made precise.

This discussion of sample–population inference brings out an interesting subtlety. A sample is a historical accident; it has no meaning in itself. All its meaning is limited to what it can tell us about the population. But all it can tell us is an interval that is likely to contain the population mean.

From this perspective, the customary sample mean is misleading because it is a single number. Central tendency from the sample data should not be identified with the sample mean or any other single number. Instead, the sample mean should be seen as an interval of uncertainty. Of course, the same applies to any other measure of central tendency, such as the sample median. This interval conception of central tendency is taken up next.

2.2 CONFIDENCE INTERVAL

The *confidence interval* is an epitome of sample–population inference. It summarizes the information in the sample in such a way as to put likely bounds on the population mean. This remarkable result is summarized in the following seven sections.

This seven-step road to the confidence interval involves concepts that have general importance in statistical thinking. These concepts will appear repeatedly in later chapters. Each section thus has the collateral purpose of explaining one or more basic concepts.

This seven-step road to the confidence interval also illustrates the nature of statistical reasoning. All seven steps are essential; every bit of available information is needed; there is nothing to spare. The goal is just attainable, and the last step comes from an unexpected beneficence. Everything fits together in perfect harmony. This seven-step road is a godsend; besides its practical value, it deserves your understanding and appreciation for its simplicity and beauty.

2.2.0 TWO FORMULAS FOR CONFIDENCE INTERVALS

Before setting off on the seven-step road, a glance at the final destination may be helpful. Accordingly, two formulas for confidence intervals are given here. Both formulas assume normal distributions, which seems a severe limitation.

However, the last step on the seven-step road will show that they are practically correct for most nonnormal distributions.

The first formula specifies the 95% confidence interval for the mean of a sample of size n:

$$\overline{Y} \pm t^* s / \sqrt{n}, \qquad\qquad df = n - 1 \qquad\qquad (1)$$

where $\overline{Y}$ is the sample mean,
        s is the sample standard deviation,
        t^* is the .05 criterial value of Student's t on $n - 1$ df (see page 813).

We may have 95% confidence that the true mean, μ, lies within this interval, between $\overline{Y} - t^* s / \sqrt{n}$ and $\overline{Y} + t^* s / \sqrt{n}$.

Confidence intervals are narrower for larger samples. The main reason is $\sqrt{n}$ in the denominator of Expression 1. If n is increased by a factor of 4, $\sqrt{n}$ is increased by a factor of 2, and this halves the width of the confidence interval. A secondary reason is that the value of t^* decreases with larger n. For a single mean, t^* equals 2.26, 2.09 and 2.00, for $n = 10$, 20 and 60, respectively. The confidence interval shortens because s is less variable with larger n.

The second formula gives the confidence interval for the difference between two means, $\overline{Y}_1$ and $\overline{Y}_2$, each from a sample of size n. This is simple. In Expression 1, just replace the standard deviation for a single mean by the standard deviation for the difference between two means—replace s by $\sqrt{2}\, s$.

$$\overline{Y}_1 - \overline{Y}_2 \pm t^* \sqrt{2}\, s / \sqrt{n}. \qquad\qquad df = 2(n - 1) \qquad\qquad (2)$$

If 0 lies outside this interval, we can be 95% confident the difference between the two groups is real (Section 2.3). Student's t ratio is closely related to confidence intervals; its equations are given in Note 2.2.0a (page 53).[a]

We now start down the seven-step road to these confidence intervals.

2.2.1 MEAN, VARIANCE, AND STANDARD DEVIATION

We assume a random sample of n independent scores from some population with mean μ and variance σ^2. Let Y_i denote the score for the ith subject or case, with $\overline{Y}$ the mean of the Y_i:[a]

$$\overline{Y} = \frac{1}{n} \sum_{i=1}^{n} Y_i. \qquad\qquad (3)$$

We wish to use this sample mean $\overline{Y}$ as an estimate of the population mean μ. Since $\overline{Y}$ will differ from μ because of sampling variability, we desire some indication of the likely error.

To get the likely error of the sample mean, use the variability within the sample itself. The common sense of this approach has already been stated: If the individual Y_i are close together, we think $\overline{Y}$ will be close to μ; if the individual Y_i are far apart, we think $\overline{Y}$ may be far from μ. Our problem is to make this idea precise. To do this, we need a formula to quantify the variability among the Y_i.

A natural measure of sample variability begins with the deviation of each score from the sample mean, namely, $(Y_i - \overline{Y})$. If these deviations are small, variability is low; if large, high. However, averaging these deviations to get a single overall measure of variability goes nowhere because this average is equal to 0. Averaging the magnitude of these deviations, ignoring the minus signs, is attractive but runs into technical difficulties.

Surprisingly, but happily, averaging the squared deviations leads to simple, effective statistical theory. The *sample variance*, accordingly, is defined as

$$s^2 = \frac{1}{n-1} \sum_{i=1}^{n} (Y_i - \overline{Y})^2 = \frac{1}{n-1} \left[\sum_{i=1}^{n} Y_i^2 - n\overline{Y}^2 \right]. \tag{4}$$

Dividing by $n - 1$ instead of n makes s^2 an unbiased estimate of the population variance, σ^2. The second sum is easier for hand calculation.

The variance has the great virtue of *additivity*: The variance of a sum of independent scores is the sum of their variances. For any two independent variables, X and Y, the variance of their sum, and of their difference, is given by the addition formula

$$\sigma_{X+Y}^2 = \sigma_{X-Y}^2 = \sigma_X^2 + \sigma_Y^2. \tag{5}$$

This additive property leads to the law of sample size below. Also, it underlies the *analysis of variance*, taken up in the next chapter.

For assessing the likely error of a mean, it is preferable to use the *standard deviation*, which is the square root of the variance. Thus, $\sigma = \sqrt{\sigma^2}$, and $s = \sqrt{s^2}$ denote the standard deviations for population and sample.

The name, *standard* deviation, is apt because s lies on the same scale with the same unit as the measured data. If any constant is added to each sample score, the standard deviation remains unchanged. If each score is multiplied by any positive constant, the standard deviation will be multiplied by the same constant. Hence the standard deviation always has the same unit as the response scale. For example, if you measure in inches (centimeters), your standard deviation will also be in inches (centimeters). Because of these properties, the standard deviation is indeed a standard unit of variability.

By itself, however, the standard deviation is not enough to tell us the likely error of our sample mean. Ideally, we could state that 95% of the sample means lie within two standard deviations of the population mean. We would then have

95% confidence that the population mean lay within two standard deviations of our sample mean. But this 95% figure depends on the shape of the population. It applies specifically to the bell-shaped populations called *normal.*

Some empirical populations are approximately normal, but many are not. In fact, we are typically far more uncertain about the shape of a population than about the value of its mean. Unless we know the population shape, we cannot determine the likely error of a sample mean.

We thus face a seemingly insuperable obstacle. Statistical theory, however, has engineered a road through this obstacle. There are six more steps along this road, taken in the next six sections. The last step will bring us to our goal: likely bounds on the population mean.

2.2.2 SAMPLING DISTRIBUTION

The *sampling distribution* of any sample statistic gives the probability of each possible sample outcome. This distribution may be portrayed as a curve with the possible values of the sample statistic on the horizontal axis and their probability on the vertical axis. The sampling distribution thus summarizes the outcomes of all possible samples, giving the probability of each outcome.

All sample inferences rest on sampling distributions. All general properties of a sample statistic are contained in its sampling distribution:

> *Inference from our particular sample is only justified if the same inference would follow from most of the possible samples—as represented in the sampling distribution.*

This statement reemphasizes that the sample is important only as a clue, an uncertain clue, about the population. Sampling distribution is really a basic concept of common sense, therefore, as indicated under *Sample Principle* in Section 0.1.1 (page 783). This common sense concept of sampling distribution can be given a precision edge with statistical theory.

The concept of sampling distribution brings us face to face with a formidable problem. Inference is from the sampling distribution, as the italicized sentence indicates, not from the sample itself. But in practice, we have only one single sample. How can we possibly get beyond our one single sample to the sampling distribution of all possible samples? That this can be possible, even easy, is a stellar achievement of statistical theory.

2.2.3 SAMPLING DISTRIBUTION OF THE MEAN

Since the sample mean is such a useful statistic, its sampling distribution deserves special consideration. Conceptually, the *sampling distribution of the sample mean* is itself a population, namely, a population of means of samples (of size *n*) from the parent population. For brevity, it will be called the sample mean distribution. This *sample mean distribution* specifies the probability of obtaining each possible sample mean when we take a random sample of given size from the population. We must rely on this sample mean distribution to tell us about the likely error of our sample mean.

We now have two populations under consideration: The parent population from which we draw our samples—and the population of sample means. Each of these two populations has a population mean, denoted by μ and μ_{mean}, respectively. It is not hard to prove that these two are equal:

$$\mu_{mean} = \mu. \tag{6}$$

Although equal numerically, these two means are quite different conceptually. Hence we use the subscript to distinguish the mean of the sample mean distribution from the mean of the population.

The variability of our sample mean is represented by *its* sampling distribution. There is a natural tendency, even for statisticians, to take a sample mean at face value, without adequate appreciation of its variability (see Section 1.3, pages 16-20). Such appreciation may be gained empirically: Take repeated samples and observe the variability among successive sample means. Even a few samples will give some feeling for the likely error of a single mean.

With numerous samples, a histogram would approximate the shape of the sampling distribution of the sample mean. Such empirical experience can be illuminating and is highly recommended. In experimental work, of course, repeated sampling would require repeating the experiment, which is not often practicable. Even when practicable, it is generally inefficient.

Statistical theory can do as well—even better. Statistical analysis of a single sample can yield better information than empirical analysis of several samples. The next four sections show how we can use the variability within a single sample to determine its likely error.

2.2.4 LAW OF SAMPLE SIZE

What happens to the sampling distribution of the mean when we use larger samples? Intuitively, larger samples should give more reliable means, closer to the population mean. In other words, the spread, or variance, of the sample mean distribution should be smaller for larger samples.

This intuition, fortunately for us, leads to a simple formula. Let σ^2_{mean} be the variance of the sample mean distribution. This variance equals the population variance divided by the sample size:

$$\sigma^2_{mean} = \sigma^2 / n. \tag{7a}$$

This formula follows from the additivity rule for variance (Equation 5).

Equation 7a for σ^2_{mean} has great generality. It holds almost regardless of the shape of the population distribution. Equation 7a thus provides a simple, direct relation between the variance of the population, σ^2, and the variance of the sample mean distribution, σ^2_{mean}.

The standard deviation is in some ways more meaningful than the variance as an index of average deviations from the mean. From Equation 7a

$$\sigma_{mean} = \sigma/\sqrt{n}. \tag{7b}$$

Parallel to Equation 7b, a similar formula holds for s_{mean}, the standard deviation of a sample mean. First calculate the standard deviation s of the sample, taking the square root in Equation 4. Then

$$s_{mean} = s/\sqrt{n}. \tag{7c}$$

Equation 7c, the *square root law of sample size*, shows how the standard deviation of our one particular sample estimates the standard deviation of the sample mean distribution for all possible samples. This law of sample size is a critical step on our road to the confidence interval.

It is worth pausing to comment on one practical consequence of this square root law of sample size: Increasing sample size yields decreasing benefits. In the denominator of s_{mean}, the $\sqrt{n}$ corresponds to a law of diminishing returns for sample size. To halve the standard deviation of the sample mean requires not doubling but quadrupling the size of the sample. Thus, to get a sample standard deviation around half the size of the population standard deviation would require a sample size of 4. To halve that would require increasing sample size from 4 to 16; halving that would require a further increase from 16 to 64.

This square root law means that each additional subject you run adds less benefit. This is one reason why so much experimental analysis relies on small samples, mainly in the range from 6 to 24. Some lines of inquiry do require samples of size 50, 200, and above, but most experimental studies employ small samples, as you can verify by looking at Method sections of current articles. If you need samples of size 30 to get statsig results, you should think about changing your problem or your task–procedure. For the same reason, two related experiments with 16 subjects per condition might well be preferable to a single experiment with 32 subjects per condition.

The conceptual distinction between s and s_{mean} deserves heavy emphasis. The former refers to the parent population; the latter refers to the sample mean distribution. These two distributions are easily confused. This confusion appears in the not uncommon statement that variability can be reduced by increasing sample size. "The" variability refers to the parent population, which consists mainly of individual differences in typical experiments. It is obviously incorrect to think that sampling more individuals reduces the variability among them. This statement is quasi-correct—s_{mean} decreases as n increases—but this refers to a distribution different from the parent population.

There is, in fact, a different sample mean distribution for each sample size. The foregoing discussion slurred over this by considering the general case of sample size n. Each n, however, yields a different sampling distribution. These distributions are all alike in one respect, for all have a mean equal to μ, as shown in Equation 6. They all differ, however, in their standard deviations, as shown in Equation 7b.

To emphasize the distinction between s and s_{mean}, the latter standard deviation is often called the *standard error of the mean*. These standard errors are sometimes presented as *error bars* in published articles (Section 4.1.2, page 92).

2.2.5 CONFIDENCE INTERVALS: **NORMAL DISTRIBUTION**

Given a normal distribution, likely error of a sample mean can be specified exactly with its standard deviation, namely, $\sigma/\sqrt{n}$. The mathematical formula for the normal distribution shows that 95% of the probability in the sampling distribution of the mean lies less than 1.96 standard deviations from the mean of this sampling distribution. More succinctly, 95% of the sample means will lie within 1.96 standard deviations of μ.

Equivalently, μ will lie less than 1.96 standard deviations from $\bar{Y}$ for 95% of the samples. Accordingly, the expression

$$\bar{Y} \pm 1.96\sigma/\sqrt{n} \tag{8}$$

is called the 95% *normal confidence interval*. By this formula, the sample mean, together with its standard deviation, provide likely bounds on the true mean. The smaller the standard deviation, the tighter these bounds.

Two serious obstacles stand in the way of using the normal confidence interval of Expression 8. First, the population σ is unknown. The natural step is to substitute the sample estimate s. But s is subject to sampling error, with greater error for smaller samples. Because of this uncertainty about s, we can no longer have 95% confidence. The 1.96 figure is too small; it yields more confidence than the sample warrants.

This obstacle was resolved by Student with his t distribution. This distribution gives us a t^* value to use in place of 1.96, depending on the size of our sample (Table A4, page 813). If our parent population is normal, we can thus obtain the confidence interval for 95% or any other desired degree of confidence. Correct confidence intervals can thus be calculated from the sample data in the manner already specified in Expressions 1 and 2.

The second obstacle has a higher order of difficulty. The 1.96 figure in Expression 8 assumes samples from a normal distribution; so does Student's t. But many populations are nonnormal. Perhaps the 1.96 figure is far off for nonnormal populations. This obstacle, most fortunately, can be surmounted with the central limit theorem, which is taken up next.

2.2.6 CENTRAL LIMIT THEOREM

We now come to a powerful result—the *central limit theorem*. This theorem shows that the normal distribution has a central place in statistical theory: It is a limit toward which other distributions converge. Specifically, the central limit theorem shows that the shape of the sample mean distribution becomes more and more normal as sample size increases—almost regardless of the shape of population from which the samples are drawn (but see Section 4.1.5, page 94).

Furthermore, this convergence toward normality is usually rapid. Even with rather nonnormal populations, the sample mean distribution may be practically normal for n as small as 5 or 10. With a flat parent population, for example, the distribution of sample means will be nearly normal even for $n = 4$.

2.2.7 CONFIDENCE INTERVALS: **NONNORMAL DISTRIBUTIONS**

The central limit theorem resolves the second obstacle for constructing confidence intervals, namely, that many data distributions are nonnormal.

We obtain the confidence interval for the sample mean distribution, not for the parent data distribution from which our sample is drawn.

By the central limit theorem, this sample mean distribution will be approximately normal in most applications. Hence the normal confidence interval will be approximately correct. It will provide good likely bounds on the true mean of the sample mean distribution. But this true mean equals the mean of the parent population, by Equation 6. We have thus obtained the confidence interval that we sought. This seven-step road of reasoning justifies the formulas for confidence intervals listed in Expressions 1 and 2 at the beginning.

This confidence interval is a powerful tool. It means that the sample can lift itself by its bootstraps to make precise statements about the population—with specifiable limits of likely error. The variability among the sample elements is essential information; this variability allows the likely error to be estimated. With this simple, elegant chain of reasoning, statistical theory arrives at a fundamental goal. The crucial link in the chain is the central limit theorem, but each other link is also necessary.

It is worth pausing to appreciate how valuable the confidence interval is. Conceptually, the confidence interval emphasizes that the sample mean should be considered a range or interval of uncertainty. It is really an illusion that the sample mean has a specific numerical value. This specific value is meaningless without information about variability in the sample. Viewed in this way, the sample mean is indeed a range of likely values. Conceptually, therefore, the appropriate estimate of the population mean is not the sample mean as a single number, but the confidence interval about the sample mean.

For many experimental applications, moreover, the confidence interval can be employed as a significance test. To illustrate, suppose Y_i is a measure of how much subject i improves under some experimental treatment. Construct the 95% confidence interval for the sample mean $\bar{Y}$. If 0 lies outside this interval, we may have 95% confidence that the true mean is not 0. In this way, the confidence interval quantifies the sample uncertainty, thereby transforming variability into a precision tool.

One conceptual peculiarity of the confidence interval deserves notice. Different samples will give different confidence intervals, of which 95% will contain the true mean. Before we draw a sample, therefore, we can rightly say there is .95 probability that the confidence interval we will get after we have drawn the sample will contain the true mean. Now suppose we draw a sample and construct the confidence interval. This interval is now fixed; the true mean lies either inside or outside this one specific interval. We do not know whether it lies inside or out, of course, but the matter is no longer probabilistic. This is why we use the term *confidence* rather than probability (Section 4.1.6, page 94).

The seven-step road has thus solved the "formidable problem" noted on page 36. The confidence interval constitutes a tool for going beyond our one single sample to the sampling distribution of the means for all possible samples.

2.3 STATISTICAL SIGNIFICANCE TEST

The statistical significance test assesses whether some observed difference is reasonable evidence for a real difference. The classic example involves comparison of experimental and control treatments, E and C. Subjects are randomly assigned to two groups, the treatments are administered, and some response is measured. The question is whether E is better than C.

Implicit in—and essential to—this question is the sample–population distinction. The observed means are only sample results. It is not enough to show that the observed mean response is higher for E than for C. This can readily happen by chance in the sample, even when both treatments have identical effects in the population. The question becomes whether the higher performance of E is reliable.

This question of reliability is answered by the statistical significance test. By looking at the sample data, the significance test tells you whether the observed difference in the sample is reasonable evidence for a real difference.

The following sections are concerned with the conceptual basis and framework for the statistical significance test. Equations and formulas are deferred to the next chapter.

2.3.1 LOGIC OF SIGNIFICANCE TEST

The *significance test* assesses whether the sample data provide reasonable evidence to believe a real effect. The question is: Does the difference between *sample* means warrant the conclusion of a real difference between the corresponding *population* means?

The difficulty of this question about real effects becomes clear upon considering individual differences, prominent in every area of psychology. In any task, some subjects are better, some poorer. If we randomly assign different subjects to the two conditions, chance may put more of the better subjects in group E, more of the poorer subjects in group C. Chance alone could thus produce the difference between the sample means. Unless this operation of chance can reasonably be ruled out, it is not reasonable to decide that the experimental treatment had a real effect. The significance test assesses whether the sample information implies that chance is an unlikely explanation of the observed difference.

The idea of a significance test is straightforward and simple. Small differences between sample means are likely to occur by chance alone. Large differences, in contrast, are unlikely to occur by chance—but likely if there is a substantial real effect. If the observed sample difference is "large enough," therefore, we infer a real effect.

This "large enough" idea of a significance test can be expressed as the symbolic ratio:

$$\text{Test Ratio} = \frac{\text{Observed Difference}}{\text{Chance Difference}}. \tag{9a}$$

If there is no real difference between E and C, the Observed Difference in the numerator will be only chance. The Test Ratio is then expected to be around 1. But if there is a real difference between E and C, the Observed Difference is expected to be greater than chance. The Test Ratio will then be greater than 1, at least on average.

A large Test Ratio thus suggests a real difference between groups. If the Test Ratio is large enough, we infer a real difference. This same logic also holds with more than two groups.

How large is "large enough?" This question has a quantitative answer. To get this answer, replace the symbolic numerator and denominator of the Test Ratio by algebraic formulas for variability, namely, the variances.

The Chance Difference in the denominator of the Test Ratio is the variability *within* each condition. This variability is mainly individual differences; since all subjects within each condition are treated alike, the observed differences in their scores reflect individual differences. Because subjects were assigned randomly to conditions, these individual differences represent the prevailing chance variability, also called *Within Variability*.

The Observed Difference in the numerator of the Test Ratio is the variability between the sample means for the experimental conditions. This is accordingly called the *Between Variability*. With no real effect, the Between Variability will be merely chance, just like the Within Variability, and the Test Ratio will be around 1. Any real effect makes the sample means differ more than chance; the bigger the real effect, the bigger the Between Variability. A large Test Ratio thus argues for a real effect.

In short, a significance test compares variability *between groups* to variability *within groups*. This comparison may be done with Fisher's F ratio:

$$F = \frac{\text{Between variance}}{\text{Within variance}}. \qquad (9b)$$

If F is greater than some criterial value F^*, the difference between conditions is "large enough" to justify the conclusion of a real effect. Formulas for this F ratio are given in the next chapter. Here, however, these numerical details are not of concern; Equations 9a and 9b express the logic of the significance test.

Fisher's F ratio also applies with three or more experimental conditions, a notable "first" in statistical theory. Student's t test is limited to one or two groups, so F is used instead.[a]

2.3.2 LOGIC OF THE NULL HYPOTHESIS

The significance test involves a *null hypothesis*—that there is no real effect. The null hypothesis asserts that the observed differences between the sample means are merely chance variability. Our *experimental hypothesis*, in contrast, typically asserts that there is a real effect, over and above chance effects. To accept this experimental hypothesis, it is necessary (though not sufficient) to show that chance alone is not a likely cause of the observed difference.

The null hypothesis is denoted H_0. For the example of Experimental versus Control group, H_0 may be written

$$H_0: \mu_E = \mu_C \qquad \text{or} \qquad H_0: \mu_E - \mu_C = 0.$$

We reject H_0, as already noted, if the F ratio is large enough. The significance test, accordingly, is said to be a test of the null hypothesis.

This null hypothesis logic may seem odd, as though we are setting up a straw hypothesis to knock down in order to accept our experimental hypothesis. A little reflection, however, shows this logic is essential. Chance alone will produce some differences among the sample means. To claim a real effect, we should begin by showing that chance alone is not likely to cause a difference as large as that observed. This null hypothesis logic is just common sense.

2.3.3 TWO SAMPLING DISTRIBUTIONS

The null hypothesis logic may be elucidated with the two curves of Figure 2.1. The curve labeled "H_0 true" is the sampling distribution of F under the assumption of no real difference between groups. This sampling distribution gives the probability density (vertical axis) of obtaining various values of F (horizontal axis)—**given** H_0 true. The point labeled F_α^* is chosen so the area under the curve to the right of F_α^* equals the proportion α of the total area under this curve. This figure shows F^* for α of .05 and .01.

Even more important is the second curve in Figure 2.1, labeled "H_0 false." This curve is also a sampling distribution of the F ratio—calculated under the assumption that there is a real effect, that is, that H_0 is false. This curve is shifted to the right of the first curve, reflecting the fact that F tends to be larger when H_0 is false. The bigger the real effect, the bigger the rightward shift.

The logic of the null hypothesis may be summarized in terms of these two sampling distributions:

If our observed F is greater than F^*, we call it *statsig*,
     reject H_0, and decide there is a real effect.
This decision is justified on the ground that
     a. If H_0 is true, a statsig F is unlikely (α probability);
     b. If H_0 is false, a statsig F is more likely than α;
        the more false is H_0, the more likely is a statsig F.

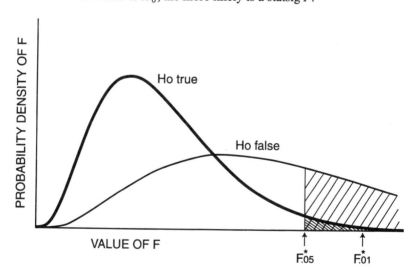

Figure 2.1. Two sampling distributions of F ratios: H_0 true (heavier curve); H_0 false (lighter curve). Vertical axis plots probability density of each value of F on horizontal axis. Points labeled F^* cut off .05 or .01 tail areas under the curve for H_0 true.

2.3.4 THE 2 × 2 DECISION TABLE

The point F_α^* divides each curve of Figure 2.1 into two regions, each with its own meaning. Each region corresponds to one of the four outcome cells in the 2 × 2 decision table of Figure 2.2.

In the right column of this decision table, H_0 is false. In this case, a statsig result is good, for then we reject H_0, correctly claiming a real effect. This is a *hit*, in other words, a correct claim for a real effect. A nonstatsig result is bad, for this is a *miss*, that is, a failure to detect a real effect.

In the left column of the decision table, H_0 is true. In this case, a statsig result is bad, for then we reject H_0, falsely claiming a real effect. This is called a *false rejection*, *false positive*, or *false alarm*, denoted F.A. The good outcome is a nonstatsig result, for then we do not reject H_0.

The probability of false alarm is α—**if H_0 is true.**

The probability of false alarm is 0—**if H_0 is false.**

The probability of a miss (given H_0 false) is denoted β. Correspondingly, the probability of a hit is $1 - \beta$, which is also called *power*. The power of your experiment has paramount importance. *If you have low power, don't do the experiment.* Even power as high as .70 means you have 30% chance of a miss.

Every experiment is predicated on an assumption that it has adequate power, that enough subjects are being run. Most investigators, however, still decide how many subjects to run by guess and by God. But a simple power formula is available to help with this important, difficult decision. This problem of estimating power before doing the experiment is taken up in Chapter 4.

		H_0 true	H_0 false
Decision:	statsig	F. A.	Hit
Decision:	nonstatisg	o. k.	Miss

Figure 2.2. 2 × 2 decision table for significance test. Each decision yields one good outcome, one bad outcome, depending on whether H_0 is true or false.

A false alarm is usually called a *Type I error* and a miss is called a *Type II error*. This statistical terminology requires learning two arbitrary terms when two meaningful terms are available, as in Figure 2.2.

The 2 × 2 decision table may seem overly constrictive in that it entails yes–no decisions about marginal results. This yes–no view can be made more flexible by including a band near the .05 level, from .03 to .06, for example, that may be called marginal. Such marginal results are often best handled by replication, as discussed in the last section of this chapter. Similar ideas have been suggested by a number of writers, and they seem sensible to me. Accordingly, this yes–marginal–no view will be implicitly adopted in this book.

Of course, any decision based on sample data is only provisional. "Reject H_0" merely indicates reasonable evidence for a tentative decision.

2.3.5 α–β TRADEOFF DILEMMA

You set the false alarm parameter α at whatever value you desire. Perhaps you feel that α = .05 is too weak, too risky, for it means you have 1 chance in 20 of falsely claiming a real effect when there is none. You can reduce this risk to 1 in 100 merely by changing α to .01. This certainly gives you more reassurance about false alarms.

But—you pay a big price in power. To see this price, look back at Figure 2.1. To change α from .05 to .01 is equivalent to changing from $F_{.05}^{*}$ to $F_{.01}^{*}$ in the figure. This increases the miss rate, β, which corresponds to the area under the H_0 false curve to the *left* of the new F^{*}. Power is thus decreased. Other things being equal, α and β stand in a see-saw, tradeoff relation.

The choice of α depends on the *costs and benefits* of the outcomes listed in the decision table of Figure 2.2. In screening numerous drugs for potential activity, false alarms might be inexpensive because they could be detected in follow-up tests. To avoid a miss of some useful drug, accordingly, a weak α of .10 or higher might be used. Costs and benefits are quite different in preparing to manufacture and market a drug. The cost of a false alarm could be enormous, and a single experiment even with α = .001 would seem inadequate.

Scientific studies use α = .05 for most purposes. I consider .05 somewhat weak, but it seems to work fairly well in practice. Further discussion of this issue is given in Section 19.2, but the conventional .05 will be used throughout this book for simplicity of exposition.

2.3.6 DO NOT ACCEPT H_0

Failure to establish a real effect does not mean the real effect is zero. The 2 × 2 decision table allows two conclusions: "Reject H_0" and "Do not reject H_0." Of course, "Do not reject H_0" does not mean "Accept H_0" any more than "Not guilty" means "Innocent." Trial evidence may incline jurors toward "Guilty," but not beyond reasonable doubt.

Do not accept H_0 needs emphasis. When the effect of A is not statsig, it seems natural to say "*A* had no effect." This is a loose way of speaking, convenient but often harmful (see, e.g., *"Inconsistencies" in the Literature* in Section 4.3.1, page 103). That the sample evidence is not strong enough to meet your criterion for a real effect does not imply zero effect. For scientific communication, such loose speaking seems better avoided.

A deeper, substantive reason for not accepting H_0 is that most experimental manipulations involve observable surface variables, intended to manipulate some underlying process. Failure to demonstrate an effect may merely reflect inappropriate choice of experimental task and procedure; some alternative task–procedure might have succeeded. Human infants, for example, have shown striking perceptual–cognitive abilities in the last two decades, previously unsuspected, through development of new kinds of experimental tasks.

2.3.7 REDUCE VARIABILITY!

Variability is an eternal companion and enemy of experimental analysis. The confidence interval and significance test seize variability by the horns and incorporate it into the data analysis. In doing so, they conceptualize the problem to make clear there is no alternative way.

At the same time, the confidence interval and significance test show that reducing variability has valuable benefits. These benefits were signaled in Equation 9b, in which the denominator is a measure of chance variability. The smaller this denominator, the larger is F and the stronger is the evidence for a real effect. Another sign of these benefits appeared in Expressions 1 and 2, in which lower variability, s, yields tighter confidence intervals.

Variability needs to be reduced before the first subject is run. One function of pilot work is to find ways to reduce variability. Good method is important. Make sure you are in tune with your subjects, that your subjects are in tune with the task, and that your procedure is in smooth working order. The experimental design, similarly, can sometimes confer substantial reductions in variability (see further Section 4.3.4, *Nine Ways to Increase Power*, pages 107*ff*).

2.4 BEFORE AND BEYOND SIGNIFICANCE TESTS

Statistics has its most important functions in designing an investigation, long before any significance test is made. Significance tests are a minor part of statistical analysis. This basic fact inevitably gets obscured because a significance test is generally essential as a minimal indication that the observed effect is real, not chance. *Is it statsig?* thus comes to seem all-important, whereas it is least important.

It is so easy to fall into viewing the significance test as the be-all and end-all of scientific investigation. Statistics texts have difficulty going beyond the significance test because doing so involves substantive considerations, different for different substantive areas. Indeed, statistical inference so easily lends itself to abstract, context-free presentation that it comes to be taught that way.

Such misconceptions about significance tests are aggravated by the common language meanings of "significant" and "highly significant." These surplus meanings divert attention from more basic problems of data analysis and substantive inference. This is why the term "statsig" is used in this book.

This point was foreshadowed in the discussion of confidence intervals, which go beyond the significance test in an important way by setting likely bounds on the size of the effect. Other limitations and inadequacies of the significance test are taken up in the next few sections. These are not criticisms of a useful tool, but guidance in its use.

2.4.1 SIZE AND IMPORTANCE OF EFFECTS

The significance test applies mainly to just one major class of questions, namely, hypothesis testing. The most glamorous hypotheses are critical predictions from some theory. Other sources of hypotheses are practical assessment of some remedial treatment and hunches that some variable will meaningfully affect some behavior. When the first goal is to show that the effect is not zero, the null hypothesis logic is appropriate (see also Sections 4.1.3 and 19.2).

A second class of investigations is more concerned with estimation. The main interest is to measure the size of some effect, not merely to show it is nonzero, as in hypothesis testing. Observational studies are often of this class, as in studying age trends in vocabulary, or in estimating size of wildlife populations, as with the census of bowhead whales in Section 19.1.3.

As a concrete example of estimation, consider the fact that male births outnumber female births by 106 to 100 in humans. This curious near-equality might be illuminated by investigating nonhuman species. The main concern, however, would be to estimate the size of the inequality in different species, not to show it was nonzero. In statistical terms, the main concern would be the center—and width—of the confidence interval, not whether it excluded zero.

Even for hypothesis testing, the significance test might almost be considered a necessary evil. It is an important first step, for it gives a reasonable modicum of evidence for a real effect. This is surely minimal, as a rule, for asking others to spend their time evaluating your method and procedure, scrutinizing your data analysis, pondering your theoretical interpretation, and relating all this to their own work. The evils of the significance test do not arise from its limitations, but from users who fail to appreciate these limitations.

One major limitation is that a statsig result says little about the size of the effect or about its importance. A small effect can be made "highly significant" by running a large number of subjects. Conversely, a marginally statsig result may represent a large effect. Of course, a statsig result says even less about the importance of the effect than about its size (see further Section 18.1).

2.4.2 INDIVIDUAL DIFFERENCES

In life sciences, the significance test has a limitation that deserves serious consideration. This concerns individual differences. A test of the mean may be misleading if the treatment induces opposite shifts in a minority of cases. A medicine that cures 90% of the patients is a fine discovery, but it would be bad medicine for you if you are one of the 10% who suffer harmful side-effects.

The significance test is not at fault for neglecting individual differences in this way—that is the substantive business of the investigator. The test performs its proper function on whatever data the investigator sees fit to give it. The investigator should be sensitive to the possibility that a significance test on means may be misleading—*because the means themselves may be misleading by masking individual differences*.

How individual differences should be handled depends on a complex of substantive and statistical considerations. This issue will appear repeatedly in this book. This issue is a never-ending concern in empirical analysis.

2.4.3 MISUNDERSTANDING p VALUES

The p value of an F test can be visualized in the "H_0 true" distribution shown in Figure 2.1. The p value is the area under this curve and to the right of the observed F. An F that large or larger occurs with probability p—**if H_0 is true**. This p value is printed out by the computer. If $p < \alpha$, the result is statsig. Other than this, the p value has little use.

It is tempting but fallacious to think that $1 - p$ is the probability that H_0 is false. This fallacy is undeniably attractive: A statsig result is unlikely if H_0 is true; hence a statsig result *seems* to imply some other cause is indeed likely. This seeming, however, implicitly relies on extrastatistical belief that some other cause is indeed likely.

The implicit operation of extrastatistical belief can be made explicit with an experiment to test whether praying over plants will increase their growth. Suppose we get devout persons to pray over 20 corn seedlings, with a proper control condition, and find a statsig result, with $p = .05$. By the given reasoning, the null hypothesis would have probability of .95 of being false. Even devout persons would hesitate to believe prayer–plus–statistics can yield such potent conclusions. And virtually any outcome would yield a value of $(1 - p)$ substantially greater than the presumably true value of $0.[a]$

In practice, of course, we do take a statsig result to imply that the null hypothesis is false, that is, that our result was caused by a real effect. But the main justification is empirical, not statistical. This justification lies in our prior, extrastatistical belief that there is a real effect, a belief that led us to do the experiment. Experiments are not done at random, but emerge from our knowledge systems, as indicated in the Experimental Pyramid of Chapter 1. The practical effectiveness of the significance test rests squarely on implicit appeal to our prior belief in a nonchance cause. The significance test works in practice because our prior beliefs generally have some measure of truth (see further Section 19.2.2, page 628).

You can easily avoid this logical fallacy. Don't say a word about the probability of the null hypothesis or the alternative hypothesis. Just say the test was statsig, and that you provisionally consider the effect to be real. Then proceed to the more important issue of what it means.

The exact value of p should ordinarily be ignored for the same reason. Some texts and some articles are enamored of such phrases as "highly significant" for $p < .01$, indexing it as **, and even using *** for $p < .001$. Such asterisking is specious glitter.

The significance test is a simple-minded technique, useful for making provisional reject–do not reject decisions. A statsig result represents a provisional claim that the results are not due to chance alone. Any conclusion about a real effect must integrate other, extrastatistical information.

A decision to publish ordinarily represents a reject H_0 decision, more precisely, a claim that the results constitute sufficient evidence to warrant expense of editorial time and reader time. Once the result appears in the literature, it has a claim on the time and attention of other investigators. Given this, primary concern should be with more important issues beyond the p value.

Among these more important issues are effect size and power, of which the p value is a poor measure (Note 18.1.3c, page 590). Even more important are validity considerations, especially confounding, to which the p value is irrelevant. Few arguments in the literature concern the value of p itself; most concern validity issues of experimental design, procedure, and confounding. Not only do p values have little bearing on these issues, they obscure them.

2.4.4 POWER

Power is a basic consideration in experimental design. For the H_0 false curve in Figure 2.1, power is markedly less than ½ for $\alpha = .05$. This seems far too low to make the experiment advisable. Even granted that there is a real effect, doing the experiment would seem a mistake for there is less than one chance in two of getting reasonable evidence for this real effect. If the result did chance to be statsig, moreover, it would seem a poor bet for follow-up work. Will-o'-the-wisp phenomena are generally unpromising for scientific inquiry.

Low power does not mean you must abandon your experiment. Rather, it suggests you seek to increase power. The power calculation is thus a guide to improving your experiment.

A formula for calculating power is given in Section 4.3, together with nine ways to increase power. It is prudent, of course, to apply the power formula before doing the experiment. This can provide a warning to avoid weak experiments. At the same time, it may suggest ways to increase power. A power calculation is the ounce of foresight that prevents the pound of regret.

2.4.5 EXPERIMENTAL DESIGN: VALIDITY

A statsig result says nothing whatever about substantive meaning or validity. Validity of any statsig result may be undercut by *confounding*. Confounding means that a manipulation of some specified variable is accompanied by variation in some other variable. Then the observed effect may be due to the other variable, not to the specified variable.

A standard example of confounding appears in before–after design. Some response is measured on each of a group of subjects, they are given an experimental treatment, and the response is measured again. The response might be reaction time, say, or degree of felt pain. The experimental hypothesis is that the treatment will yield a faster response or less pain. But a statsig change in response can hardly be interpreted as an effect of the experimental treatment; it might instead be an effect of practice with the reaction time or an effect of suggestion with the pain.

Another class of confounding arises from failure to randomize, which allows bias to enter. A classic example is the large-scale study to test whether supplementary nutrition would increase weight gain in British school children, retrospectively discussed by Student (1931). This was a large, well-planned investigation, impressive even today, with an initial random assignment of children to experimental conditions. Understandably, but most unfortunately, the investigators were nervous about leaving this assignment entirely to chance. Accordingly, they gave teachers in each school some flexibility to adjust the randomization for apparent mischance. But what evidently happened is that the teachers humanitarianly assigned more of the needier-looking children to the experimental group, which got the supplementary nutrition. These children would weigh less, and in fact the experimental group did weigh markedly less than the control before the experiment began. This bias was confounded with the experimental variable. This violation of the randomization largely destroyed the value of this expensive experiment (see page 81 of Chapter 3). This and other violations of the principle of randomization are discussed in Section 8.1.5 (pages 235ff).

Confounding can take many, many forms, as will appear in later chapters. So important is confounding that Chapter 8 is devoted to it. Here it may be re-emphasized that the significance test addresses only the issue of reliability. The significance test is oblivious to substantive confounding and other issues of validity. Validity depends on extrastatistical inference, based on substantive considerations at the lower levels of the Experimental Pyramid.

2.4.6 PRINCIPLE OF REPLICATION

The principle that results must be replicable is basic to experimental science. One reason is substantive. Any single experiment must be carried out under specific choices of task, stimulus materials, response measure, and subjects. The results may be peculiar to these specific choices, lacking generality (Section 1.4, pages 20-24). Moreover, the results may arise from some confounded variable within the specific situation that compromises the conceptual interpretation. Such considerations underlie the general consensus that knowledge develops gradually and solidifies as an interlocking network of results.

The term *replication* refers here to follow-up studies that pursue aims and findings of an initial study. Although follow-up studies may well include some literal replication of an initial study, completely literal replication is not usually desirable. Replication is most useful when it extends the scope of the initial work.

Replication might include some additional variable, for example, to extend the generality of the results. Or some aspect of procedure might be changed to reduce variability, especially to reduce extreme scores, or to rule out some objection about confounding.

Indeed, potential for such extended replication should be a major consideration already in planning the initial experiment, for it is through replication that an interlocking network of results is built up. A task–procedure that lacks potential for extended replication is usually inadvisable.

A second reason for replication is statistical. A result from any single experiment is only provisional. It cannot be well trusted unless it has been replicated, a point emphasized by Fisher long ago. A significance test provides provisional confidence, justification for further work, but such further work is necessary for solidity. An associated reason is that a result can be statsig without being especially replicable (see *Are Statsig Results Reliable?* on page 104).

Replication has a notable advantage over a test of significance. The latter is only a hopeful promise of replicability, the former is empirical reality.

Furthermore, replication obviates much of the concern and anxiety over significance testing. One concern is with statistical assumptions, such as normality, that are required in the formal statistical analysis, but may be poorly satisfied in the data (Section 3.3). Another concern is with false alarm escalation that occurs when making multiple tests (Section 4.2.2, pages 99*ff*). These and other statistical perplexities can be greatly eased through replication. A bird in the hand is worth a covey in the statistical bushes.

In general, single experiments are weak in solidity and in informativeness as well. This line of thought implies that the normal unit for publication is an integrated set of experiments. Even a single replication experiment can add valuable solidity. Replication has become increasingly required for publication in psychological journals.

There are, of course, various exceptions. Some studies provide valuable qualitative information, as with observational or case studies. In some studies, the behavior may be sufficiently important that the results deserve publication regardless of whether they are statsig, especially if the study is expensive. Some studies use a factorial design that provides, in effect, substantial replication as part of a single large experiment. Some studies present useful new methods or techniques. Allowing for such exceptions, however, the principle of replication says that a statsig result in a single experiment is not generally enough to warrant consideration by the scientific community.

NOTES

2a. The sample mean could equal the population mean in special cases of little practical importance, for example, when the population has only one element. In this case, as in others, a nonconsequential technical misstatement markedly simplifies the exposition.

2.2.0a. The formula for Student's t is closely related to Expressions 1 and 2 for confidence intervals. To test H_0: $\mu = 0$ for a single group:

$$t = \bar{Y} \div s / \sqrt{n}. \qquad df = n - 1.$$

To test H_0: $\mu_E - \mu_C = 0$ for two groups, make the denominator larger by $\sqrt{2}$:

$$t = (\bar{Y}_E - \bar{Y}_C) \div \sqrt{2}\, s / \sqrt{n}. \qquad df = 2(n - 1).$$

If 0 lies just at either end of the confidence interval, then t equals t^*.

2.2.1a. I use Y, not X, as the response measure to be consistent with near-universal usage in regression analysis, in which X denotes the stimulus variable or the predictor, and Y denotes the response.

2.3.1a. Student's t ratio also has the symbolic form of Between Variability divided by Within Variability, namely, $(\bar{Y}_E - \bar{Y}_C) \div \sqrt{2}\, s / \sqrt{n}$. But $t^2 = F$, so F always applies, even with two groups. Since F is more general, it is used throughout this book.

2.4.3a. For a more direct argument against the probability interpretation of p value, look at the H_0 true curve in Figure 2.1. For any F, $(1 - p)$ equals the area under this curve to the left of that F. But roughly half of these Fs have $(1 - p)$ at least ½. Virtually none have $(1 - p)$ equal to its true value of 0.

HOW TO DO EXERCISES

Exercises can help you develop research judgment. This is part of the "Empirical Direction" pursued in this book. Exercises in other texts on psychological statistics are mostly numerical calculations, fossils from the precomputer age. Exercises in this book aim instead at integration of statistical and extrastatistical knowledge (see *Exercises* in the concluding chapter, *Lifelong Learning*).

The more important exercises concern conceptual issues. They deserve thought and reflection. Answers to some exercises depend on your personal research judgment, and should be discussed with classmates. There need not be a single best answer, nor are those I give in the Instructor's Manual necessarily the best.

What is important is the understanding you gain from thinking and writing your answers, not your answers themselves. A wrong answer can be a good learning experience; a hasty correct answer can be a poor learning experience.

Development of good exercises should be a cooperative effort by all of us, *students above all*. I shall greatly appreciate hearing from you which exercises you do and do not consider useful. Suggestions for improvement and for new exercises will be most welcome. You can reach me at

> Norman H. Anderson
> Psychology—0109
> University of California, San Diego
> 9500 Gilman Drive
> La Jolla, CA 92093-0109
> nanderson@ucsd.edu

EXERCISES FOR CHAPTER 2

NOTE. Some exercises are intended to help develop skills of visual inspection and familiarity with certain formulas. To this end, exercises indicated "by hand" (which includes hand calculator), are intended to be done without a packaged program, even if available on the hand calculator. Mere drudgery of getting sums of squares, of course, is appropriate for a hand calculator.

1. By 1890, it was accepted that air was composed solely of oxygen and nitrogen; assiduous chemical investigations had revealed no other chemically active components. To measure density of nitrogen, Lord Rayleigh used hydrogen to burn out the oxygen from a sample containing both oxygen and nitrogen, eliminated the resultant water with a dessicant, and weighed the remainder gas (overcoming considerable difficulties). (With thanks to Tukey, 1977, pp. 49*ff*.)

    a. Graph Lord Rayleigh's data in some meaningful way.

    b. Find the "anomaly" by visual inspection.

c. How did you recognize this anomaly? What is the statistical principle?

d. Argue against application of a *t* test to verify the anomaly.

e. From the table, what seems to be the immediate cause of this anomaly?

f. What might underlie the immediate cause of (e)?

g. What other features of the data strike your eye?

Rayleigh's values of density of nitrogen

Date	Source	Density
29 Nov. 1893	Nitrous oxide	2.30143
2 Dec. 1893	Nitrous oxide	2.29890
5 Dec. 1893	Nitrous oxide	2.29816
6 Dec. 1893	Nitrous oxide	2.30182
12 Dec. 1893	Air	2.31017
14 Dec. 1893	Air	2.30986
19 Dec. 1893	Air	2.31010
22 Dec. 1893	Air	2.31001
26 Dec. 1893	Nitric oxide	2.29869
28 Dec. 1983	Nitric oxide	2.29940
9 Jan. 1894	Ammon. nitrite	2.29849
13 Jan. 1894	Ammon. nitrite	2.29889
27 Jan. 1984	Air	2.31024
30 Jan. 1894	Air	2.31010
1 Feb. 1894	Air	2.31028

NOTE: Data from "On an anomaly encountered in determinations of the density of nitrogen gas" by Lord Rayleigh (1894), *Proceedings of the Royal Society of London, 55*, 340-344.

2. An experiment with $n = 10$ subjects in each of two groups yields $\bar{Y}_E = 8$ and $\bar{Y}_C = 4$, with $s = 3$.

a. Show that the 95% confidence interval for the mean difference is 4 ± 2.82.

b. Show that the *t* ratio for the mean difference is 2.98 (see Note 2.2.0a).

c. Compare and contrast the implications of (a) and (b).

3. By visual inspection of Figure 2.1, estimate power for $\alpha = .05$ and also for $\alpha = .01$, assuming the given curve for H_0 false applies.

4. Consider the sample {1, 1, 1, 2, 2, 2, 3, 3, 3, 4, 4, 4, 5, 5, 5}.

   a. Show by visual inspection that the sample mean is 3.

   b. Calculate the sample variance by hand from Equation 4.

   c. Show that the 95% confidence interval for the sample mean is 3 ± .81.

   d. Construct the 99% confidence interval for the sample mean.

   e. Explain the difference in width of these two confidence intervals.

   f. In your opinion, is the 4% increase in confidence worth the increase in width of the interval?

5. Prove the assertion of Section 2.2.7 that if 95% of the sample means lie within 2 standard deviations of the population mean, then an interval of width ±2 standard deviations about the sample mean assures you 95% confidence that this interval contains the population mean.

6. What does the text mean by saying in Section 2.3.4 that "Every experiment is predicated on the assumption it has adequate power"?

7. You are TA in an undergraduate class on research methods.

   a. Write a paragraph for your students giving an intuitive rationale why larger samples have narrower confidence intervals for the sample mean.

   b. Show how this intuition is quantified with a formula in the text.

8. You are TA in undergraduate research methods. Write a paragraph giving your students an intuitive explanation about the common sense of "likely error" as discussed in the fourth paragraph of Section 2.1.2.

9. In what way does the standard deviation of the sample mean distribution differ from the standard deviation of the population distribution?

10. a. In what *qualitative* ways will the sample mean distribution for samples of size 3 differ from that for samples of size 2?

   b. In what way will they be the same?

11. What relation is there between the distribution of heights of a population of adult women and the corresponding sample mean distribution for:

   a. samples of 1 woman?

   b. samples of 2 women?

   c. samples of n women?

12. This exercise concerns similarities and differences between a jury trial and a significance test.

  a. What is the legal analogue of the false alarm parameter, α?

  b. What are the legal analogues of miss and false alarm?

  c. P says the analogue of the null hypothesis is "The defendant is guilty." Q argues for "The defendant is innocent." What do you say?

  d. What is the legal analogue of the stricture, "Do not accept H_0?

  e. What is the legal analogue of the α–β tradeoff?
How does the legal system handle this tradeoff?

  f. What is the legal analogue of power?

  g. How does power affect the behavior of prosecuting attorneys?

  h. How does power affect the behavior of defense attorneys?

  i. Do you see any logical difference between the decision of a jury and the decision of the journal editor on your thesis you submit for publication?

  j. Jurors may judge whether the defendant deserves to be punished by taking extenuating circumstances into account, not merely whether he or she is guilty of having performed a certain action. In your opinion, how much does this consideration change the foregoing decision analysis?

(As a case with historic interest, Daniel Sickles shot and killed his wife's lover, not under the compulsion of momentary emotion, but with deliberate premeditation. There was no doubt about his action; nor that such action was criminal. Yet he was acquitted by the jury. Perhaps the jury would not have bent the law so far had they foreseen that in his later career as a brash, political general in the Civil War, Sickles would put the Union army in dire peril at the Peach Orchard at Gettysburg on 2 July, 1863. Some truly wonderful letters by his wife are quoted in *Sickles, the Incredible*, Swanberg, 1956.)

13. You study efficacy of prayer by having devout persons pray over corn seedlings, using a t test to compare their growth amount with a control.

  a. Your data analysis yields $t(60) = 2.00$. How confident are you *personally* that *prayer* had the observed effect? How confident are you *statistically*?

  b. You do an exact replication of the experiment and get similar results. Now how confident are you personally that prayer had the observed effect?

14. An undergraduate in your class on research methods measures the stocking-foot height of all persons in a certain class and constructs a confidence interval. She finds mean height statsig greater for females than males. What different explanations would you consider possible?

15. What mental model do you think underlies the intuitive feeling that larger populations require larger samples to get same accuracy?

PREFACE

A useful way to look at data is in terms of *variance*: If the differences *between* our treatment means are large—compared to individual differences *within* each treatment condition—this is a sign of real treatment effects.

This intuitive decision process is made precise in this chapter through analysis of variance (Anova). Formulas are presented for the variance between treatment means ($MS_{between}$) and for the variance of the individual responses within a single treatment (MS_{within}). The ratio,

$$F = MS_{between} / MS_{within},$$

becomes our decision guide. A larger F is stronger evidence for real differences between our treatments. If F is "large enough," we have a statistically significant result, provisional evidence for real treatment effects.

Anova makes "large enough" precise. In terms of Chapter 1, your F ratio is an index of reliability, that is, the reliability of the observed differences between the treatment means.

In practice, a significance test is easy. Just give your data to the computer. It will calculate your F ratio and tell you whether it is "large enough."

The F test applies to two *or more* conditions; it includes the t test as a special case. Further, $MS_{within} = s^2$, which may be used to construct confidence intervals using the expressions in Chapter 2. Confidence intervals can be very helpful to your reader when you describe your data.

Anova depends on certain assumptions. Two of these, *normal distribution* and *equal variance*, are not usually problematic in experimental studies. *Independence* is critical, but can usually be ensured through careful procedure and random assignment. Practical aspects of *How to Randomize* are discussed in the appendix beginning on page 77.

It cannot be emphasized too much that the statistical significance test says nothing whatever about substantive significance of your results. The significance test merely tells whether your result has some minimum degree of reliability. This is a minimum first step; unless the result is reliable, there is little point in worrying what it might mean.

Questions of meaning, however, are primarily extrastatistical. Questions of meaning involve considerations at lower levels of the Experimental Pyramid of Chapter 1. Statistics can help with some of these questions, as will be seen in later chapters, but this help requires going beyond the significance test to issues of experimental design.

Chapter 3

ELEMENTS OF ANALYSIS OF VARIANCE   I

This chapter and the next give the elements of analysis of variance (Anova). Different subjects are assumed in each experimental condition, with a single score for each subject.

3.1 ALGEBRAIC MODEL FOR ANALYSIS OF VARIANCE

All Anova rests on some algebraic model. This model represents each response as a sum of empirical quantities: effects of the experimental manipulations, together with response variability.

3.1.1 POPULATION MODEL

The experimental variable is denoted A, with a specific *levels*, A_j, and with n different subjects assigned to each A_j. The A_j are experimental *treatments* or *conditions*, and the n subjects or scores for each treatment condition are sometimes called a *group*.

The score of individual i in condition j is denoted Y_{ij}. The population mean for condition j is denoted μ_j, the sample mean by $\overline{Y}_j$. The mean over all the conditions is denoted $\overline{\mu}$ for population and $\overline{Y}$ for sample.

For a single variable, the Anova model is so simple it hardly deserves the dignity of being called a model. Its simplicity, however, underlies its usefulness. For the population, the model represents each score as the sum of the treatment mean, μ_j, plus an individual subject deviation from that mean, ε_{ij}:

$$Y_{ij} = \mu_j + \varepsilon_{ij}. \tag{1a}$$

By rewriting the treatment mean as $\mu_j = \bar{\mu} + (\mu_j - \bar{\mu})$, we get

$$Y_{ij} = \bar{\mu} + (\mu_j - \bar{\mu}) + \varepsilon_{ij}$$

$$= \bar{\mu} + \alpha_j + \varepsilon_{ij}. \tag{1b}$$

The α_j in this Anova model represent the relative treatment effects: $\alpha_j = (\mu_j - \bar{\mu})$ is the *difference*, or *deviation*, of the condition mean μ_j from the overall mean $\bar{\mu}$. In this deviation form, α_j represents the *relative effect* of treatment A_j. If all treatments had equal effect, all μ_j would be equal—each μ_j would equal $\bar{\mu}$—and each α_j would be zero.

Differences in treatment effects are thus represented as nonzero α_j. The purpose of the experiment is to estimate these relative effects.

The ε_{ij} in the Anova model measure variability between individuals. From Equation 1a, $\varepsilon_{ij} = Y_{ij} - \mu_j$, that is, the *deviation* of individual i in condition A_j from the mean for that condition. These ε_{ij} thus represent variability between individuals who receive the same experimental treatment. The variance of ε_{ij} for group j is denoted $\sigma^2_{\varepsilon j}$. Equal variance is assumed, unless otherwise noted, so we drop the j subscript and simply write σ^2_{ε}.

This population model is true by definition. It is imposed on the data because it turns out to be useful. Each deviation score in Equation 1b represents a pertinent empirical quantity. This idea of deviation scores is basic, and will reappear continually in later chapters.

3.1.2 SAMPLE MODEL

Exactly parallel to the foregoing population model is the model for the observed sample of data,

$$Y_{ij} = \bar{Y}_j + e_{ij}. \tag{2a}$$

The error term is denoted e for the sample model rather than ε for the population model. In terms of deviation scores, the sample model has exactly the same form as the population model of Equation 1b:

$$Y_{ij} = \bar{Y} + (\bar{Y}_j - \bar{Y}) + e_{ij}$$

$$= \bar{Y} + \hat{\alpha}_j + e_{ij}. \tag{2b}$$

The "hat" on α_j denotes the sample estimate of the population parameter, α_j.

We rely—perforce—on these sample data to make inferences about the population. Specifically, we wish to test whether the $\hat{\alpha}_j$ from the sample are large enough to infer real differences among the α_j.

3.2 SIGNIFICANCE TESTS

Inferences about real differences between treatments employ the idea of Section 2.3.1. Real effects are measured by the variability *between* groups; chance effects are measured by the variability *within* groups. Comparison of these two yields the F ratio:

$$F = \frac{\text{Between variability}}{\text{Within variability}}.$$

Real effects tend to yield larger F ratios. Conversely, larger F ratios suggest the operation of real effects. We need to put this idea into quantitative form, which can be done with mean squares, or variances, of the sample data.

3.2.1 MEAN SQUARES AND F

The denominator of the F ratio is just the within group variance. It is computed separately for each group and averaged across groups. This is conveniently done in terms of *sum of squares* (SS) and *mean square* (MS). For group j, the within group SS is

$$SS_{within,j} = \sum_{i=1}^{n} (Y_{ij} - \bar{Y}_j)^2, \tag{3}$$

Each $(Y_{ij} - \bar{Y}_j)$ represents the deviation of individual i from the mean of all individuals who get the same treatment. The SS is the sum of these deviations squared. This is a general rule: Every SS is a sum of squared deviations.

Summing Equation 3 over groups yields

$$SS_{within} = \sum_{j=1}^{a} SS_{within,j} = \sum_{j=1}^{a}\sum_{i=1}^{n} (Y_{ij} - \bar{Y}_j)^2. \tag{4a}$$

Dividing SS_{within} by $(na - a) = a(n - 1)$ yields the *within group variance*,

$$MS_{within} = SS_{within}/a(n - 1). \tag{4b}$$

This within groups variance is the denominator of F.

The numerator of F is obtained using analogous formulas for the *between groups variance*. In this case, the deviations are between the group means, $\bar{Y}_j$, and the overall mean, $\bar{Y}$. Thus,

$$SS_{between} = \sum_{j=1}^{a}\sum_{i=1}^{n}(Y_j - \bar{Y})^2 = n\sum_{j=1}^{a}(\bar{Y}_j - \bar{Y})^2; \tag{5a}$$

$$MS_{between} = SS_{between}/(a - 1). \tag{5b}$$

These two between formulas are directly analogous to the two preceding within formulas of Equations 4.

Finally, F is obtained as the ratio of the MSs for between and within:

$$F = \frac{MS_{between}}{MS_{within}}. \qquad df = (a - 1)/(na - a) \qquad (6)$$

Here "df" is an abbreviation for *degrees of freedom*, or information units, discussed in Section 3.2.4. The df for the numerator of F are $(a - 1)$, the number of groups minus 1. The df for the denominator are $(na - a)$, the total number of scores minus the number of groups.

A larger F ratio is stronger evidence for real effects. If the real effects are zero, the F ratio tends to be near 1. If there are real effects, F tends to be larger than 1, by an amount related to their size. If the observed F is large enough, accordingly, we conclude that our treatments did have real effects.

How large is "large enough"—that is the question. We desire a *criterial value*, F^*, such that an observed F greater than F^* warrants a decision that our treatments really did have different effects. It is astonishing that this question has an answer that is both exact and general, regardless of the substantive nature of the experiment.[a]

3.2.2 FINDING F^*

How to find F^* is the concern of this section. In practice, you can simply look up F^* in Table A5 (page 815), corresponding to the df listed in Equation 6. Note that F^* is smaller for greater df. The df for MS_{within}, namely, $(na - a)$, equals the number of information units used to estimate this within variability. More df means a more reliable estimate. The same size effect is thus more reliable with more information units, a fact that is quantified through the concept of df. A related argument holds for the numerator df.

Statistically, the value of F^* is obtained as shown in Figure 3.1, repeated here from the previous chapter. As explained in Section 2.3.3 (pages 43f), F^* is chosen so that α of the area under the H_0 true distribution lies to the right of F^*.

To get the values of F^* in Table A5, Fisher had to derive a mathematical formula for the curve labeled "H_0 true" in Figure 3.1, which is the sampling distribution of F, given H_0 true. With this formula, we can choose F^* so that the proportion of the area under the curve that lies to the right of F^* is equal to α. This sets the false alarm parameter at α.

The formula for this sampling distribution can be derived with four assumptions: random sample, independence, and equinormality (normal distribution and equal variance), discussed in Section 3.3. Fisher's derivation of this formula involved a fundamentally new conceptual framework for statistical theory. In this book, however, we do not need to know this formula, only that it was the basis for constructing Table A5, which gives us F^* with no effort.[a]

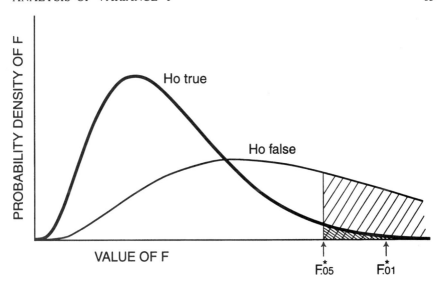

Figure 3.1. Two sampling distributions of F ratios: H_0 true (heavier curve); H_0 false (lighter curve). Vertical axis plots probability density of each value of F listed on horizontal axis. Points labeled F^* cut off .05 or .01 of the area under curve for H_0 true.

3.2.3 SIGNIFICANCE TEST

Testing the Null Hypothesis. The F ratio tests the overall null hypothesis that all treatments have the same effect. More precisely, this null hypothesis asserts that the true means of the a treatment groups are all equal:

$$\text{overall } H_0: \ \mu_1 = \mu_2 = \ldots = \mu_a. \tag{7}$$

If our observed F is larger than our criterial F^*, we reject the overall H_0. The logic of this significance test has been given in Section 2.3 (pages 41*ff*)

The formula for the sampling distribution of F in Figure 3.1, given H_0 true, depends only on the degrees of freedom (see Note 3.2.2a). Most fortunately, it does not depend on the error variance. For given df, a single formula holds—regardless of the particulars of the experiment. This formula is used to construct the curve for H_0 true in Figure 3.1 and thereby to determine the criterial F^* for the chosen α. In this way, the probability of getting a larger F—if chance alone is operative—is set at α.

Actually, you seldom have to bother looking up F^* in Table A5. Computer programs print out the "*p* value," which is the area in the upper tail to the right of the F obtained from the data. If $p < \alpha$, then the observed F is greater than F^* In this way, the p value provides a significance test. This is almost the only use of the p value. The fallacy that p equals the probability that H_0 is false is a treacherous cognitive illusion (Section 2.4.3, pages 49*f*).

Numerical Example. The Anova formulas may be illustrated with the following example of two groups, each with three subjects.

group 1: {1, 3, 5}   group 2: {7, 7, 10}

Our first step is to calculate the variance *within* groups, MS_{within}. Since $\bar{Y}_1 = 3$ and $\bar{Y}_2 = 8$, Equation 3 yields

$$SS_{within, 1} = (1 - 3)^2 + (3 - 3)^2 + (5 - 3)^2 = 8;$$

$$SS_{within, 2} = (7 - 8)^2 + (7 - 8)^2 + (10 - 8)^2 = 6.$$

By Equations 4a and 4b,

$$MS_{within} = (8 + 6)/2(3 - 1) = 3.5.$$

This is the variance within groups, or error variance.

Our second step is to calculate the variance *between* groups, $MS_{between}$. Since $\bar{Y} = 5.5$, Equations 5a and 5b yield

$$MS_{between} = 3[(3 - 5.5)^2 + (8 - 5.5)^2]/(2 - 1) = 37.5.$$

Our third and final step is to calculate F with Equation 6:

$$F = 37.5/3.5 = 10.71; \quad df = 1/4.$$

From Table A5, F^* on 1/4 df is 7.71 for $\alpha = .05$. Since $10.71 > 7.71$, the sample gives reasonable evidence for a real difference between the two groups.[a]

Why the .05 Level? The standard α of .05 is obviously a convenient round number and has been the target of various criticisms. One common concern is that false alarms tend to get published whereas failures to replicate generally do not. Hence, it is argued, the literature is filling up with false alarms. Student and Fisher could as easily have constructed their tables for $\alpha = .02$, and perhaps they should have done so.

In practice, however, the .05 level seems to work reasonably well. One reason lies in the principle of replication. When results agree across a series of experiments, the danger of false alarms is greatly reduced (Section 2.4.6).

A second reason lies in the role of extrastatistical background knowledge, which acts as a primary filter of false alarms. No experimental result stands alone. All are evaluated relative to a network of background knowledge, based in part on results from similar experiments, in part on general empirical sense. A prudent investigator will hesitate to publish a statsig result that appears to disagree with prevailing knowledge without replicating it. Reviewers and editors, similarly, may request replication in such cases.

Much the same point appears in the fact that experimental studies grow out of prevailing knowledge and expectation. Many results thus possess reasonable prior validity. With such prior belief against false alarms, α need not be so stringent (see also *One-Tailed Tests* on page 98). Although I personally consider the .05 level somewhat weak, this convention evidently works fairly well, not only in psychology, but also in other sciences.

3.2.4 MEAN SQUARES AS VARIANCES

The mean squares in the preceding section are actually variances, a statistical fact that is relevant to experimental design.

Error Variance. MS_{within} of Equation 4b is the error variance s^2 of the sample data—differences among subjects treated alike. By Equation 4 of Chapter 2, the sample variance for group j is the SS of Equation 3 above divided by $(n - 1)$:

$$MS_{within,j} = SS_{within,j}/(n - 1) = s_{e,j}^2. \tag{8a}$$

Since $MS_{within,j}$ measures variability between subjects treated alike, it serves as an error yardstick.

Pooling these MSs across groups yields MS_{within} of Equation 4b. Assuming equal true variance, we may drop the j subscript to get

$$MS_{within} = s_e^2. \tag{8b}$$

Hence $\sqrt{MS_{within}} = s_e$, which may be used as s in the two expressions for confidence intervals on page 34.

Although MS_{within} varies from sample to sample, its average value, also called its *expected value*, equals the population variance. The symbol E is used to denote expected values so

$$E(MS_{within}) = E(s_e^2) = \sigma_\varepsilon^2. \tag{8c}$$

Treatment Variance. The variance of the sample treatment means is given similarly by Equation 5b. It is just the average of the squared deviations of the sample means from their overall mean. It may seem odd to average across the a groups by dividing by $(a - 1)$. This is a little statistical device that makes the sample variance an unbiased estimate of the population variance. This device applies generally, as in Equation 8a for error variance.

The treatment variance, however, has two components. One is the error variability, which will cause the sample means to differ even if the true means are equal. The other is real differences, if any, among the true means. This latter component is the variance among the population means, written as[a]

$$\sigma_A^2 = \sum(\mu_j - \bar{\mu})^2/a = \sum \alpha_j^2/a.$$

The two components of the treatment variance are additive. In terms of expected values,

$$E(\text{MS}_{\text{between}}) = \sigma_\varepsilon^2 + n\sigma_A^2. \tag{8d}$$

F as Ratio of Variances. From the two foregoing subsections, it follows that the F ratio of Equation 6 is the ratio of two variances: the variance between treatment means divided by the error variance. The meaning of F may be appreciated by looking at its expected value (see also Note 5.1.4a):

$$E(F) = E\left[\frac{\text{MS}_{\text{between}}}{\text{MS}_{\text{within}}}\right]$$

$$= \frac{\text{df}_{\text{denom}}}{\text{df}_{\text{denom}} - 2} \times \left[1 + \frac{\text{df}_{\text{num}} + 1}{\text{df}_{\text{num}}} \times \frac{E(\text{MS}_{\text{between}}) - E(\text{MS}_{\text{within}})}{E(\text{MS}_{\text{within}})}\right]$$

$$= \frac{\text{df}_{\text{denom}}}{\text{df}_{\text{denom}} - 2} \times \left[1 + \frac{\text{df}_{\text{num}} + 1}{\text{df}_{\text{num}}} \times \frac{n\sigma_A^2}{\sigma_\varepsilon^2}\right]. \tag{9}$$

Equation 9 makes explicit three major determinants of the power of your experiment. All three appear in the last term, $n\sigma_A^2/\sigma_\varepsilon^2$. As this expression shows, two ways to increase power are to increase sample size, n, and to increase the real effect, σ_A^2. The third way to increase power is to decrease error variability, σ_ε^2. In fact, reducing error variability is often the most effective way (see *Nine Ways to Increase Power*, pages 107ff).

Note that $E(F)$ will ordinarily be near 1 when H_0 is true. For then $\sigma_A^2 = 0$ and $E(F) = \text{df}_{\text{denom}}/(\text{df}_{\text{denom}} - 2)$, which will be near 1 unless the error df are small. An observed F near 1 thus indicates nonstatsig results (Note 3.2.3a).

Degrees of Freedom. A degree of freedom may be considered a statistical unit of information—the amount of information in a single score. With N independent scores, there are N information units, or N df. These N df are divided among the Anova sources to index the amount of information in each source.

Each mean represents one unit of information. With a independent groups, there are a df for their means. But we are usually interested in differences among these means, namely, the relative effects, $\alpha_j = \mu_j - \bar{\mu}$, in the Anova model. Only $a - 1$ of these α_j are independent, since their sum is always zero. This is why the between groups source has $a - 1$ df in the Anova table.

A similar argument holds for a single group of n scores. Their mean has 1 df, leaving $n - 1$ df for deviations from their mean. These deviations yield the variance within group j, shown in Equation 8a, which thus has $n - 1$ df. Pooling across the a groups yields $a(n - 1)$ df for $\text{MS}_{\text{within}}$.

The df for numerator and denominator in Equation 6 are parameters in the theoretical formula for the F ratio (Note 3.2.2a). They govern the shape of the H_0 true distribution in Figure 3.1. Thereby they also determine F^*.

The error df reflect the reliability of the error mean square. Each error df represents one unit of information about reliability used to calculate MS_{error}. The more df, the more reliable is the estimate of MS_{error}, and the smaller is the criterial F^*.

Error as Yardstick. The use of error variability as a yardstick or reference standard for real effects is basic in data analysis. The smaller this yardstick, the better. Reducing error variability through experimental procedure and statistical design should thus be a primary concern. In this endeavor, it is helpful to recognize that the error term has multiple components: individual differences, variability within individuals, apparatus variability, procedural shortcomings, and ambient environmental influences.

Individual differences is usually the largest component of error by far, so reducing their effect is most desirable. Good procedure can help. The subject should be put at ease, whether rat, child, patient, or college sophomore. Task and instructions should be carefully piloted to remove the ambiguities that can trip up an occasional subject and produce an extreme score. Statistical designs to reduce effect of individual differences include screening subjects, stratification, repeated measures, and single subject design, discussed in later chapters.

Error variability is almost more important than the treatment means. Error variability determines the width of your confidence intervals, for example, which confer meaning on the mean. Moreover, your error variability mirrors the effectiveness of your task and procedure; it stands as a measure of the quality of your work.

3.2.5 HAND CALCULATION OF SS

Hand calculation of an SS is sometimes necessary, but Equations 3–5 should not generally be used for this purpose. The deviation scores in Equations 3 and 5a have conceptual meaning as expressions of within and between variability, respectively. Deviation scores exhibit the logic of Anova.

Deviation scores, however, typically involve decimal places, which makes them time-consuming, not to mention error-producing, for hand calculation. The following hand formulas are considerably easier.[a]

Hand Formulas for Equal n. The hand formula for $SS_{between}$ is

$$SS_{between} = n \sum_{j=1}^{a} \bar{Y}_j^2 - SS_{mean}. \tag{10a}$$

This equation exhibits a pattern that appears repeatedly in Anova. It is easiest to remember its schema:

> Square each treatment mean.
>
> Multiply each by the number of scores in that mean (in this case n).
>
> Add.
>
> Subtract SS_{mean} (given by Equation 10b just below).

Two other formulas complete the Anova:

$$SS_{mean} = an\,\overline{Y}_{.}^{2} \tag{10b}$$

$$SS_{within} = \sum_{j=1}^{a}\sum_{i=1}^{n} Y_{ij}^{2} - SS_{between} - SS_{mean}. \tag{10c}$$

These equations can be useful in reanalysis of published data. You may wish to test between a subset of treatment means for which only the overall F is reported. Using the means for this subset of treatments from the published graph or table, apply Equations 10ab to get $SS_{between}$ for this subset. If MS_{error} is not given in the article, you can reconstruct it from the reported means and F (Exercise 4).

Hand Formulas for Unequal n. The foregoing schema for hand formulas also applies when the groups have unequal size. Thus,

$$SS_{between} = \left(n_1\,\overline{Y}_1^2 + n_2\,\overline{Y}_2^2 + \ldots + n_a\,\overline{Y}_a^2\right) - SS_{mean}, \tag{11a}$$

where n_j is the number of scores that go into the mean for group j. This equation reduces to Equation 10a when all n_j are equal to n, as you can readily show. The df for $SS_{between}$ are $a - 1$ in either case.

Similarly, the total number of subjects is $N = n_1 + n_2 + \ldots + n_a$, so

$$SS_{mean} = N\overline{Y}^2, \qquad (\overline{Y} = \sum\sum Y_{ij}/N = \sum n_j\overline{Y}_j/N). \tag{11b}$$

The formula for SS_{within} is still given by Equation 10c. The error df are $N - a$.

3.3 VIOLATIONS OF ASSUMPTIONS

The four statistical assumptions of Anova listed in Section 3.2.2, page 62, will never be exactly true. It is necessary, accordingly, to inquire how sensitive the statistical analysis is to deviations from these assumptions. Independence is vital, so this assumption is considered first. Hardly less important is the assumption of random sampling.

Nonnormal distribution, on the other hand, often has little adverse effect. The same also holds for unequal variance (with equal n). Understanding the causes and consequences of violations of these two distributional assumptions can help you improve your experimental design and your data analysis.

3.3.1 INDEPENDENCE

Independence is violated when one score carries information about some other score. One common source of nonindependence is natural groupings among the subjects: classroom groups or discussion groups in educational psychology, work groups in industrial psychology, and families in social or counseling psychology. Subjects' responses may be expected to be more similar within groups than between groups, thereby violating independence.

Nonindependence can also arise when otherwise independent subjects are run in batches or ad hoc groups. Within each group, subjects may be influenced similarly by the same extraneous factor. In one group, for example, some subject may ask a question about the instructions that affects other subjects in that group. Such effects may usually be small and unimportant, but it seems generally preferable to avoid danger by using appropriate design.[a]

Independence can also be violated when treatments are applied in blocks rather than randomly. Apparatus settings, for example, may not be easy to change from one subject to the next, especially when each change requires recalibration. It then seems attractive to set the apparatus once and run several subjects before changing the setting. Unless done appropriately, however, this can introduce serious nonindependence.[b]

3.3.2 RANDOM SAMPLES AND HANDY SAMPLES

The foundation of statistical theory is the assumption that the observed data are a random sample from some well-defined population. But actual samples are nearly always handy, convenience samples from some ill-defined population. How is it possible to apply statistical theory to handy samples?

The answer lies in *randomization*—random assignment of subjects to experimental conditions. Randomization allows a statistical inference from the data to a well-defined population, namely, the population of all possible random assignments of subjects to conditions. A statsig result means our observed effect is not limited to our one random assignment, but would have been observed for most other random assignments. We may thus reasonably reject the null hypothesis and decide our result is real for our handy sample.

Statistical inference thus takes us no further than our handy sample. This limitation may seem disappointing, but doing this much is a notable achievement. Further, it makes explicit the deeper importance of extrastatistical judgment in the Experimental Pyramid and helps avoid the common confusion of statistical with extrastatistical inference. Establishing the reality of the difference for our handy sample provides a firm base for extrastatistical inference.

With nonrandom groups, statistics cannot control confounds from preexperimental differences. A significance test may merely reflect these differences. Without randomization, a statsig result for a handy sample does not imply a real treatment effect (Sections 13.2, 15.5, and 16.2).

3.3.3 NONNORMAL SHAPE

With most common nonnormal distributions, Anova keeps α under good control. This is a valuable result because it means that departures from the normal shape do not seriously bias the false alarm parameter.

Several studies have investigated this issue with rating scales, which often have five or even fewer steps. As an extreme case, consider a rating scale with just two response steps, 0 and 1. This two-point distribution is certainly far from the normal bell shape, yet Anova handles it quite well. As long as the frequencies of the two responses are not too extreme, say between 20% and 80%, even 20 df for error yields an effective α close to the assigned .05 or .01. The reason, of course, is that the sampling distribution of the *mean* is fairly normal by virtue of the central limit theorem.

Power, on the other hand, can be suboptimal with distributions that are long-tailed or heavy-tailed, both fairly common. Even one or two extreme scores can markedly increase the variability of the sample mean. Three alternative analyses that may yield more power have been used: Trimming, which reduces the influence of tail scores; transforming the data to a more normal shape, followed by regular Anova; and analysis based on the ranks of the data, which does not require normality (see Chapter 12).

3.3.4 UNEQUAL VARIANCE

Much of the concern expressed about unequal variance in different conditions is unnecessary. For randomized experiments, the most important reason is that unequal variance implies real treatment effects.

Randomized Experiments. Unequal variance is not usually a problem in randomized experiments. The main reason is simple: Unequal variance cannot occur unless there are real treatment effects. If subjects are assigned at random and the treatments have identical effects, then the population distributions for all treatment groups will be identical. Hence all groups will have equal true means and equal true variances.

If treatments do have differential effects, central tendency and variability both will generally be affected. Typically, however, means are affected considerably more than variances. With equal n, moreover, the α level is not much affected by unequal variance. Even when the true variances differ by a factor of 2 or 3, the effective α may change only from .05 to .06. With unequal variance, as with nonnormality, accordingly, the effective false alarm parameter of the overall F remains close to the nominal value specified by the investigator.

This conclusion, however, has an important limitation: It may not apply to analyses beyond the overall F. Confidence intervals, in particular, can be adversely affected by unequal variance (pages 93 and 97). Extensions of Anova to handle these cases are discussed in Section 12.5.

Nonrandom Groups. Natural groups, in contrast to randomized groups, will differ naturally in variability. One common example involves comparison of age groups in developmental psychology. In many tasks, younger children will be more variable. Anova that allows for unequal variance may be necessary, especially for two-mean comparisons and other follow-up tests (Section 12.5).

3.3.5 A WIDER NULL HYPOTHESIS

The Anova assumptions can be viewed from a different perspective, in which F is considered a joint test of all assumptions: the standard null hypothesis of equal means; the other two distributional assumptions (normal distribution and equal variance); and the independence assumption. Independence is critical, as already noted, but it can ordinarily be secured through experimental procedure and will be assumed to hold in what follows.

A statsig F, accordingly, implies violation of one or more of the three distributional assumptions: equal means, equal variances, and normal distributions. The null hypothesis of equal means is just one of these three assumptions. Yet we single it out, claiming that a statsig F implies unequal means, whereas logically a statsig F could imply nonnormal distribution or unequal variance. This asymmetrical treatment is justified because F is sensitive to unequal means and relatively insensitive to nonnormality and unequal variance.

This property of F is a piece of good fortune, one that could hardly have been anticipated. To appreciate just how fortunate this is, it may be noted that this same approach falls flat for testing the null hypothesis of equal variances. Most tests of variances are so sensitive to nonnormality as to be almost useless. If our null hypotheses had generally to refer to equal variances, as happens in some experiments, statistical analysis would have been frustrating. The actual outcome, however, justifies the asymmetrical treatment of the three distributional assumptions.

This justification can be pushed one step further by considering F as a test of the "wider hypothesis" of equal means *and* equal variances (see Fisher, 1960, pp. 44*ff*). In this wider null hypothesis, equal variance is no longer a statistical assumption, but goes hand-in-hand with equal means.

This wider null hypothesis is entirely sensible. Under random sampling or randomization, means and variances both must be equal, unless there are real treatment effects. Hence unequal variances imply real treatment effects, just as unequal means do, although the interpretation may differ in the two cases. Confidence intervals, as already noted, can be adversely affected by unequal variance. This wider null hypothesis, accordingly, ameliorates much of the concern with unequal variance in randomized experiments.

3.3.6 ROBUSTNESS

Violations of the assumptions may have two kinds of adverse effects, one on α, the other on β, or power. This point may be clearer by looking back at the two sampling distributions of F shown in Figure 3.1, page 63. Both of these sampling distributions rest on the assumption of equinormality (normality and equal variance). Their shapes will change under nonnormality and/or unequal variance. Suppose that nonnormality causes a rightward shift of the sampling distribution for H_0 true. Then more than α of the area under this shifted curve will lie to the right of F^*. The *operative* α will be larger than the *nominal* α; too many false alarms will occur when H_0 is true.

For typical experimental applications, fortunately, violations of equinormality have relatively little effect on the shapes of the two sampling distributions. This conclusion has been established by generating the two sampling distributions assuming nonnormal populations and/or unequal variance. Such sampling distributions typically differ little from those shown in Figure 3.1. This means that the operative α and β typically differ little from their nominal values obtained under the assumption of equinormality.

The F test, accordingly, has been called *robust*. This conclusion has been supported in decades of studies. Results from a recent study, distinguished by its use of eight nonnormal distributions likely to arise in applications of psychological test theory, are cited in the two following subsections.

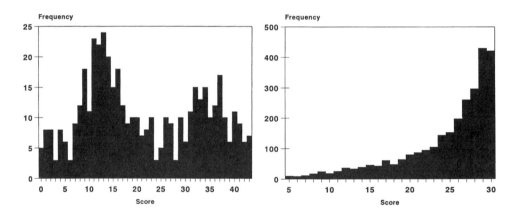

Figure 3.2. Anova is robust for both of these nonnormal distributions. (After S. S. Sawilowsky & R. C. Blair, 1992, "A More Realistic Look at the Robustness and Type II Error Properties of the t Test to Departures from Population Normality," *Psychological Bulletin, 111*, pp. 352-360. (Copyright 1992 by the American Psychological Association. Reproduced by permission.)

Robustness of α. Suppose your population has the bimodal, lumpy shape at the left of Figure 3.2. This distribution is far from normal and substantial α distortion might be feared.

To find out, Sawilowsky and Blair (1992) drew two random samples from this distribution, computed t, and compared it to t^* for the normal distribution. Since both samples were from the same distribution, H_0 is true, and t could be statsig only by chance. But since this distribution is nonnormal, the proportion of statsig ts will differ from α. How large will this distortion of α be?

This question was answered by repeating the whole procedure 10,000 times and counting the proportion of statsig ts. Ideally, this proportion will equal α. These proportions are shown at the left of Table 3.1 for α = .05. All entries are close to .05. Even with this markedly nonnormal distribution, α distortion is clearly small.

The same random sampling procedure was applied to the skewed distribution at the right of Figure 3.2. Here again, α distortion is negligible, as may be seen at the right of Table 3.1. Similar results were obtained for six other nonnormal distributions. The t test does quite well, therefore, and the same applies to the F test, for t and F are equivalent with two groups since $t^2 = F$.

TABLE 3.1

FALSE ALARM PARAMETER FOR
TWO NONNORMAL DISTRIBUTIONS

n_1, n_2	α:	Bimodal		Skewed	
		.05	.01	.05	.01
5, 15		.048	.009	.044	.010
10, 10		.052	.011	.050	.008
10, 30		.048	.010	.047	.008
20, 20		.052	.012	.047	.010
15, 45		.054	.012	.051	.009
30, 30		.051	.010	.049	.010
20, 60		.050	.011	.049	.011
40, 40		.049	.012	.053	.011
30, 90		.051	.012	.045	.010
60, 60		.055	.010	.051	.009

NOTE: Bimodal and Skewed refer to the two distributions in Figure 3.2. (After S. S. Sawilowsky & R. C. Blair, 1992, "A More Realistic Look at the Robustness and Type II Error Properties of the t Test to Departures from Population Normality." *Psychological Bulletin, 111,* pp. 352-360. (Copyright 1992 by the American Psychological Association. Reproduced by permission.)

Robustness of Power. Further work by Sawilowsky and Blair showed that power was little affected by nonnormality, even in the least favorable case of unequal sample sizes of 5 and 15. In this analysis, the bimodal distribution was duplicated with a constant added to all the scores. The means of the original and the duplicated distributions thus differ by the added constant.

One sample was drawn from the original distribution, the other from the duplicated distribution, and t was computed. This process was repeated 10,000 times for each of four different added constants. The observed proportion of statsig ts thus estimated the power of the t test for this nonnormal distribution. For comparison, the same process was also performed for a normal distribution. Relative to the normal distribution, power was roughly .03 less. Results were similar or better for the other seven nonnormal distributions studied by Sawilowsky and Blair. With equal n, moreover, power suffered relatively little even for a 4 to 1 ratio between the variances of the two distributions.

These results on robustness of power have one significant limitation. The F and t tests are the best possible when their assumptions are satisfied; no other test can have greater power under equinormality. The foregoing results extend the usefulness of these tests by showing relatively little distortion of α or β when the standard Anova assumptions are not satisfied.

But alternative tests may have greater power when equinormality does not hold. Robustness refers only to comparisons of the F test *with itself* under different assumptions about normality and equal variance. Among the alternative tests in Chapter 12, trimmed Anova shows good promise for increasing power.

3.3.7 CONTROLLING THE SHAPE OF THE DATA

The shape, or distribution, of the data can have substantial effects on the reliability of the means and on the power of the analysis. The investigator, however, often has considerable control over the shape of the data. The main determinants of shape of the data are decisions made at the middle levels of the Experimental Pyramid regarding task–procedure–measurement. Minor change at these levels sometimes has major impact in the data analysis.

One common nonnormal shape is *long-tailed* or *skewed*. Long tails should be anticipated when scores are unbounded, as with time to perform some reaction or task. Even with an easy task, occasional subjects may take unusually long time, producing a long tail. Skewing can occur even with bounded scores. An easy multiple choice task, for example, may yield bunching at the upper end of the scale and a tail toward the lower end.

A second likely nonnormal shape is the *heavy-tailed*, with relatively more cases in each tail than the normal curve. For a long time, the normal shape was enshrined as the empirical norm, a faith reflected in its misleading name of *normal*. Now it is thought that near-symmetrical distributions are often heavy-tailed, especially with groups of organisms.

Experimental control over the shape of the response distribution provides opportunities to increase power. Some learning tasks, for example, may be designed to measure either errors in a fixed number of trials or errors to some specified criterion. The latter measure, being unbounded, might be questionable with young children or patients because a few might persevere with some inappropriate strategy, yielding extremely high error scores. In the cited example of easy multiple choice tests, skewness could be reduced by making the test of intermediate difficulty. Among the many vital functions of pilot work, the importance of distribution shape should not be overlooked.

Even after the data are in, their shape can still be changed by applying a statistical transformation (Section 12.4). A long-tailed distribution of response times, for example, becomes more normal by taking reciprocals, that is, by transforming time to speed. Even more useful may be the trimmed Anova of Section 12.1.

The Experimental Pyramid implies that the shape of the data depends primarily on empirical determinants. Task, procedure, and measurement constitute an empirical transformation that determines the shape of the data. Statistical theory, in contrast, concentrates on statistical transformations after the data have been obtained. Although statistical transformations can be helpful, they involve only the tip of the Pyramid. For empirical investigators, the main concern over the shape of the data should instead be focused at the lower levels of the Pyramid in planning the investigation.

NOTES

3.2.1a. The values of F^* and t^* are standardly called *critical* values, but *critical* overstates their function and meaning, as though they derived from some external standard of validity. The present term, *criterial values*, which recognizes that they function as somewhat arbitrary decision criteria, is suggested as being more suitable.

3.2.2a. A glance at Fisher's formula for the F distribution is worthwhile, not for illumination but just to see that it really exists:

$$\text{Prob}\,(F) \; = \; cF^{\frac{1}{2}(v_1 - 2)}(v_2 + v_1 F)^{-\frac{1}{2}(v_1 + v_2)}.$$

In this equation, v_1 and v_2 are the df for numerator and denominator, respectively. The constant c is a complicated function of v_1 and v_2 that makes the area under this F distribution equal to 1.

The curve in Figure 3.1 labeled "H_0 true" was obtained from this formula: $\text{Prob}\,(F)$ is the vertical elevation of the curve, as a function of F on the horizontal axis. Different df give different curves of different shape.

Note that Fisher's formula does not depend on any empirical quantity, only on the df for numerator and denominator. This is why it has universal usefulness, for it does not involve the error variance or any other empirical quantity. With unequal variances, however, an empirical parameter is required, which markedly complicates the analysis. For a clear mathematical derivation of Fisher's formula, see Hoel (1962).

3.2.3a. A handy standard to judge whether an F reported in an article is large or small is $F(1, 60) = 4.00$ at $\alpha = .05$. And since $t = \sqrt{F}$, $t^*(60) = 2.00$. It will help to remember even this one value of F^*.

A larger frame of reference for F^* is given in the following table.

Denominator df:	10	20	60	∞
Numerator df = 1	4.96	4.35	4.00	3.84
Numerator df = 2	4.10	3.49	3.15	2.99

3.2.4a. The listed expression for the variance between the population means of A, $\sigma_A^2 = \sum \alpha_j^2 / a$, deserves two comments. Since population quantities are involved, we divide this sum of squared relative effects by the number of terms in the sum, namely, a. This contrasts with sample estimates, in which we divide by 1 less than the number of terms in the sum in order to get an unbiased estimate of the population quantity (Equation 2 of Chapter 2 and Equation 5b of this chapter).

Some writers eschew the symbol σ_A^2 on the ground that the population means are fixed, not random, and prefer a related symbol, $\theta_A^2 = [(a/(a-1)]\sigma_A^2$. This statistical nicety adds an unnecessary symbol.

3.2.5a. The formulas for hand calculation of Section 3.2.5 can be simplified one step further by using totals instead of means. Equation 11a can thus be rewritten as $SS_{between} = \sum Y_{j+}^2 / n_j - SS_{mean}$, where Y_{j+} is the total of the n_j scores in group j. Similarly, $SS_{mean} = Y_{++}^2 / N$, where Y_{++} is the total of all N scores.

3.3.1a. The potential nonindependence of subjects run in batches or small groups can be handled by including batches as a factor in the design (see Sections 14.2 and 15.1). It may be usually preferable, however, to run subjects one at a time, which will generally improve the quality of the response as well.

3.3.1b. The problem is that resetting the apparatus to the same nominal specifications will yield somewhat different actual settings each time and hence somewhat different results. Such setting error will be constant for a block of subjects. Hence this setting error will be confounded with whatever experimental conditions are given in this block. Differences between treatments applied in different blocks are thus artifactually too large because they include setting error in addition to any real effects. By the same token, the apparent error term will be artifactually too small.

This problem arises whenever any aspect of procedure is held fixed for a consecutive block of subjects. This confounding can be serious (Snedecor & Cochran, 1980, p. 282), but it can be avoided and even turned to good use by including blocks as a factor in the design (Section 14.2).

APPENDIX: HOW TO RANDOMIZE

Randomization provides a solid ground for experimental analysis. It provides a vital means to handle the twin problems of validity and reliability of the response. Virtually all statistics texts emphasize randomization as a basic principle; virtually none tell how to do it.

A.1 RANDOMIZATION PROCEDURES

How to randomize in practice is the concern of this section. The first three subsections present what may perhaps be called *standard randomization procedure* for the usual run of psychological experiments. Field studies often present complications, as noted later.

Subject Assignment Sheet. The standard way to randomize subjects across experimental conditions is to make up the *subject assignment sheet* before running the first subject. In one useful form, this sheet lists the sequence of conditions in a randomized order; this is the order in which they are to be run. The first subject to appear is run under the first listed condition, the second under the second listed condition, and so on down the list. The subjects may appear for the experiment in any arbitrary manner; randomization is accomplished by the construction of the list.[a]

This subject assignment sheet should ordinarily include a line or two to list subject's I.D., experimental condition, and date. Persons who run each subject should be identified. The completed sheet should be retained in the permanent file for the experiment.

Also included on the sheet, no doubt, should be space for comments on the subject's behavior. Such comments can be helpful for understanding unusual scores and thereby for improving experimental procedure in future work. In addition, this requirement encourages the experimenters to improve their observational skills and gain better appreciation of subjects' phenomenology. This is valuable for all of us, not only when we are graduate students.

With human subjects, the question–answer period at the end of the experiment can provide material for comments. One technique is to present selected experimental stimuli and ask subjects to explain their response. To be effective, these comments should be systematic for all subjects.

Randomizing Conditions. One way to randomize the sequence of conditions is to use Table A1 (page 809) or some other table of random numbers. With four treatments, for example, let the digits 1 to 4 stand for the four treatments. Enter the random number table by choosing a haphazard starting place, and use the chosen digit to determine the treatment for the first subject. Then proceed with successive digits, ignoring digits other than 1 to 4.

This procedure, as it stands, has an undesirable peculiarity. Ordinarily, randomization is constrained by requiring equal n across conditions. With two conditions, one will be filled up somewhat before the other; the last block of subjects will thus all be under one condition. Although this peculiarity is randomized across the set of all possible random assignments, it confounds possible temporal trend in each particular experiment. This can be minimized with block randomization (see next subsection).[b]

More extensive tables of random numbers are available (e.g., Fisher & Yates, 1963). Many computer packages also include random number generators. The small table presented here should be useful for many purposes because different experiments will begin at different locations. Alternatively, a mechanical randomizer may be used. For example, up to six conditions can be randomized by throwing a single die.

Block Randomization.   In block randomization, randomization is applied separately to successive blocks of subjects. To illustrate, consider two treatments randomized in blocks of four. Each successive block of four treatments then contains two instances of each treatment, randomly ordered among themselves. Each successive block is randomized independently of preceding blocks. Block randomization largely eliminates the peculiarity noted in the preceding subsection.

Block randomization is often simplest using random permutations of 9 and 16 numbers shown in Table A2 (pages 810 and 811). Blocks of size up to 16 can be handled with one listed permutation. Thus, three instances of each of four treatments could be randomized in a single block using the numbers 1 to 12.

Block randomization has an additional advantage: Blocks becomes a factor in the design. Systematic change in response over the course of the experiment will appear as systematic differences in successive block means. It is always desirable, therefore, to inspect the pattern of block means.

It might be further argued that blocks should always be included in a formal Anova. This seems desirable if substantial temporal trend is likely, especially if trend may differ across treatments. In some situations, moreover, evidence that temporal trend is small may buttress others' credence in your procedure.

I do not, however, recommend that blocks should always or even generally be included in the formal Anova. The main benefit comes from including blocks in the design, which balances block effects across treatments. Formal analysis of blocks may not be needed. If block effects are unimportant, a full factorial analysis with blocks will be mostly statistical clutter, mostly a source of false alarms. It would often seem enough to assess only the main effect of blocks, ignoring their interaction residuals in the Anova (see *Partial Analysis*, Section 18.4.3).

Treatment Randomization. With repeated measures on each subject, treatments may be presented in systematic order or in randomized order. Systematic order, as with a Latin square, seems advisable when carryover effects may be a problem or when position effects may be substantial (Section 14.3).

In some situations, however, position and carryover effects are expected to be small. Many studies of perception and judgment–decision fall in this class. One common procedure, accordingly, is to randomize the treatments separately for each subject.

Separate randomization for each subject is straightforward when a computer is used for stimulus presentation, using a random number generator for online randomization. With hand or mechanical presentation of stimuli, however, using a different presentation order for each subject could be pretty tedious. If order effects are expected to be small, a single stimulus sequence may suffice, presenting it in forward order for half the subjects, in reverse order for the other half, thereby balancing any linear trend.

With repeated measures, one can never be absolutely certain that position and carryover effects will not cause serious bias. It is easy to become compulsive about this issue and insist on the most meticulous design in every case. This would be a mistake, I believe, stemming from failure to appreciate the function of prior knowledge in experimental analysis.

I also believe, however, that position and carryover effects receive far less attention than they deserve. Better evidence to support the common practice of taking for granted that they are not important would be desirable.

Bad Randomizations. What should you do about a "bad" randomization? Suppose you notice on your subject assignment sheet that the first 12 subjects are in condition A_1 and the next 12 in condition A_2? This confounds conditions with any temporal trend. You might feel, however, that you must not tamper with the random assignment. My advice would be to recognize that you erred in not using block randomization and start over.

When some factor is anticipated to be relevant, it can often be incorporated in the experimental design. The temporal blocking of the previous paragraph illustrates this approach, as does Latin square design to handle position effects. Of special importance are individual differences, part of which may be controlled by subject stratification (Section 14.2).

For the most part, however, bad randomizations cannot be detected. They consist of assigning better subjects to one condition, poorer subjects to another. But "better" and "poorer" reflect individual differences that are largely unknown. Being unknown, they cannot be incorporated in the experimental design. Bad randomizations are thus inevitable. Statistical theory recognizes this: Bad randomizations mainly constitute the false alarms, an essential component of statistical inference.

A.2 RANDOMIZATION IN FIELD SITUATIONS

In field situations, randomization is needed even more than in standard laboratory studies, but is often more difficult, sometimes impossible. Two studies that took advantage of field conditions to accomplish randomization are cited in the first two subsections. More general discussion is given in the last two subsections (see also Anderson, 1982, Sections 7.2 and 7.3). These brief comments only highlight an important issue that deserves a book of its own.

Field Randomization in Smoking Prevention. Smoking is one of the two main preventable causes of sickness and death in the U. S. Many wish to give up smoking but find they are addicted, unable to quit. The telephone counseling program at the Cancer Center, University of California, San Diego, developed a counseling-by-phone program to help those who wish to quit, using funds from the Tobacco Tax Health Protection Act of 1989 passed by the voters of the state of California. A toll-free number was included in advertisements by the San Diego County antismoking campaign. Persons who called this number were screened on readiness to quit within one week plus absence of more serious problems such as psychiatric condition.

Persons who passed this screening test were assigned to one of three groups, based on the last two digits of their phone number. This assignment procedure was considered random on the reasonable assumption that the last two phone digits had no relation to the person's likelihood of quitting. Random assignment seemed ethical because there were many more applicants than could be treated.

The three treatment conditions were: (a) Self-help subjects, who were mailed a self-help quit kit; (b) one-session subjects, who received the quit kit plus one 50-minute carefully structured telephone session with a trained counselor; (c) six-session subjects, who received five additional telephone counseling sessions, of which three were within the first critical week after beginning the quit attempt.

Quit rates for the self-help, one-session, and six-session groups were 19%, 24% and 27% at three months and 5.4%, 7.5% and 9.9% at 12 months. With about 1000 subjects in each group, all effects were statsig by chi-square test. Although the 12-month success rates may seem small, they are reasonably impressive in this area. (They also indicate how difficult it can be to change human behavior.) Of special significance, telephone counseling is much more accessible than other treatment procedures. And it is much less expensive.

Subject attrition is a general problem in field studies. In this smoking study, about 14% of the subjects could not be contacted for follow-up evaluation, most because of disconnected phones or moving without leaving a forwarding address. A further problem in many field studies concerns the validity of the subject's self-reports, in this case, about abstinence. How these and other problems were handled is discussed in the original article (Zhu et al., 1996).

De Facto Randomization in Coronary By-Pass Surgery. A striking social effect on recovery from coronary by-pass surgery was unearthed in this study. The critical factor was whether the patient's roommate during the two days prior to surgery was post- or preoperative, that is, had already had or had yet to have his operation. Mean recovery days before hospital discharge were 7.7 and 9.1 for the post- and pre- groups. The 1.4 days faster recovery for patients who had a postoperative roommate before their own surgery may be appreciated more by noting that the first three postoperative days are generally spent in intensive care; rarely was any patient discharged earlier than 6 days. As another measure of value, hospital costs ranged up to 1000 dollars per day in 1987 and have since increased markedly.

Interpretation of this result depends on an assumption of de facto randomization. By hospital policy, patients were assigned beds in terms of bed availability. Bed assignment was a routine, clerical hospital procedure. With knowledge about hospital procedures, there was ample reason to believe that bed assignment had no relation to the patient's speed of recovery. With a keen eye for this field opportunity, not to mention an enormous amount of devoted labor over a 2-year period, these investigators opened up a cogent area for medical psychology (Kulik & Mahler, 1987; see further Kulik, Mahler, & Moore, 1996).

Randomization in Society. The importance of randomization in field studies has been emphasized by a long line of investigators. Among the first was Student's (1931) critique of the Lanarkshire nutrition experiment, which aimed to assess possible benefits from supplementing school food with milk. Remarkably for its time, the experimental design called for an effectively random assignment to experimental and control conditions, with 20,000 school children in 67 schools. Not unnaturally, but most unfortunately, the investigators did not quite trust the random assignment. They decided to guard against mischance: ''In any particular school where there was any group to which these [randomization] methods had given an undue proportion of well fed or ill nourished children, others were substituted in order to obtain a more level selection'' (quoted by Student from the original report).

This was a fatal mistake, said Student, especially as this adjustment was left to a head teacher in each school. At the start of the experiment, therefore, the two groups were far from equivalent: The no-milk control children were initially superior to the milk children by about three months' growth in weight and four months' growth in height. Since the experiment itself lasted only four months, these differences were relatively large. Presumably, the teachers substituted needier-looking children in the milk group.[a]

It might seem that such misassignment could be corrected by using the *gain* scores for height and weight. Such corrections are fraught with danger (Section 13.1.2). In this study, moreover, Student found evidence for a confound in the weight gain scores.

Student concluded that the Lanarkshire nutrition experiment, although "planned on the grand scale, organized in a thoroughly business-like manner and carried through with the devoted assistance of a large team of teachers, nurses and doctors, failed to produce a valid estimate of the advantage of giving milk to children" (p. 406). Student's conclusion has been reemphasized by Gilbert, Light, and Mosteller (1975), who evaluated many programs on social action and concluded that beneficial effects, if any, are generally small and are easily masked by bias. In general, therefore, attempts to match natural groups rather than randomize introduce confoundings that render the results sometimes wrong and generally inconclusive. They summarized (p. 150) by saying that failure to use randomized design is often "*just fooling around with people.*"

Randomization is often resisted in field studies. One reason is lack of understanding of the importance of randomization. Lay persons may be shocked by the idea of leaving this basic matter to chance (one reason for using block randomization). A second reason is fear of chance accidents, not uncommon even among persons with substantial statistical understanding (another reason for using block randomization). A third reason is that randomization requires care, time, and trouble that may be resisted. A final reason revolves around ethical concerns about assigning those who need help to a control condition. In medical investigations, accordingly, it may be difficult to get cooperation from hospital administrators and doctors.

The need for randomization is gaining increased acceptance in society, notably in the medical field. In the polio study of Section 10.1.1, it was a hard choice to assign children randomly to placebo and vaccine groups when there was reasonable expectation that more of the placebo children would develop paralytic polio. Sometimes, however, the reasonable expectation turns out to be wrong. In the diabetes study of Exercise 10.7, belated randomized experiments showed that the preferred medical treatment was causing more deaths than the placebo. Similarly, once-popular treatments of gastric freezing for duodenal ulcer (Miao, 1977) and internal mammary artery ligation for angina pectoris (Barsamian, 1977) were soon discontinued after randomized tests showed that they were at best ineffective.

When randomization is accepted, it should be made simple and foolproof. Systematic surveillance is essential to ensure that the randomization procedure is adhered to. Field studies are typically complex and involve personnel with diverse capabilities and motivations. The miscarriage of the Lanarkshire nutrition experiment is not a historical oddity. In his instructive summary of 12 social reform programs, Conner (1977) notes that the prescribed randomization was violated in every case in which it was not aggressively supervised by the investigator. Carelessness, unconscious bias, conscious fudging, and opinionated disadherence are ever-present threats that should be foreseen in developing experimental design and procedure.

Reporting Method of Randomization. How much detail should be reported about method of randomization depends on several considerations, including the importance of the issue and concerns that readers of the report may have about possible bias. With many laboratory experiments, as in judgment–decision and perception, bias seems unlikely. Treatment randomization, accordingly, could often be left to a computer. Subject randomization can also often be treated analogously, as with the cited study of smoking prevention.

When the possibility of bias will be a serious concern to others, it seems desirable to be completely explicit. This would be the case with many field experiments. In a survey of experimental tests of innovative surgical procedures, Gilbert, McPeek, and Mosteller (1977, pp. 140*ff*) advocate detailed reporting on how randomization was accomplished. In particular, they recommend using a published table of random numbers, together with written detail on exactly how it was used. This allows one public check on method. The desirability of such procedure is underscored by the study of controlled drinking in Section 8.1.6, which claimed to use randomization, but seemingly did not. Similarly, the detection of fraud in "rock solid" studies of extrasensory perception cited in Section 8.1.6 depended in part on discrepancies between the reported randomization procedure and the actual stimulus sequences.

It would seem even more important to report how the randomization was implemented. The need for strict control of implementation was indicated in Conner's article cited in the previous subsection. As Gilbert et al. say, "Many find it wise to assume that things that can go wrong in an investigation are likely to . . . . When the investigator carries out such quality control measures, they deserve careful reporting in much more than a phrase. *Care here offers one indicator of the quality of the investigation*" (pp. 141–142, italics added).

3A.1a. An error in the subject assignment sheet that produces unequal n can be a headache. Everyone makes such clerical errors. Having another person make an independent check of the subject assignment sheet seems advisable.

3A.1b. A subtle randomization artifact undid a crucial test of Estes' (1964) stimulus sampling-conditioning theory of learning. Estes argued that the observed discrepancies from the theory were not serious, merely preexperimental response tendencies that would extinguish with extended training. In the crucial experiment, however, the reinforcement sequences shifted every 48 trials, which would violate randomness and artifactually train in the very behavior predicted (Anderson, 1964a). This artifact was avoided by Friedman, Carterette, and Anderson (1968, p. 453), who found that the theoretical predictions "disagree with the data in almost every respect" (see Anderson, 1982, pp. 150-153).

3A.2a. Student's purpose in criticizing the Lanarkshire nutrition experiment was to show how future work could be improved. Besides insisting on randomization, Student pointed out how block-type design could factor out individual differences, thereby reducing error, and allowing a much smaller and less costly experiment.

EXERCISES FOR CHAPTER 3

NOTE. Exercises have varied levels of difficulty. Some ask for calculations that have precise answers. Others ask for conceptual interpretation or for personal research judgment and often do not have precise answers; these exercises address issues that are your main concern in actual research. Developing your research judgment is a continuing matter, for which these exercises are stepping stones.

1. Given these three groups of scores:

   group 1 $\{3, 4, 5\}$; group 2 $\{5, 6, 7\}$; group 3 $\{6, 7, 8\}$.

   a. Get s^2 for group 1 using pencil and paper.

   b. By visual inspection, say why the other two groups also have $s^2 = 1$.

   c. What principle underlies the rationale of (b)?

   d. Calculate $F = 7.00$ by hand, using hand formulas of Section 3.2.5.

(F and t ratios are reported to two decimal places, unless F is larger than, say, 20. Accurate F and t ratios often require at least four digit accuracy in interim calculations.)

2. Suppose the example of Section 3.2.3 had the scores $\{1, 3, 5\}$ and $\{8, 8, 11\}$.

   a. By visual comparison with the example, show that $MS_{within} = 3.5$.

   b. By comparison with the example, guess roughly at the value of F.

   c. Calculate F by hand and compare it to your guess in (b).

3. Growing up is as difficult as it is important, and we get no second chance. Research on parenting should thus be a preeminent concern of psychological science. This is far from true, which seems to me a grave criticism of our field.

   Some pioneer work has been done, however, to compare training programs for parents of children with developmental disabilities. Two parent training programs are compared in Figure 3.3. Each black bar represents one parent trained with a naturalistic procedure, which emphasized flexible interaction between parent and child, aiming especially to increase the child's motivation, as by allowing the child to participate in choice of activities. Each white bar represents one parent trained with a structured procedure, following precepts of standard learning theory, which emphasized giving the child well-structured tasks, clear instructions, and trial-by-trial reinforcement with reinforcers chosen to be functional for each child. The main training material was in a manual studied by each parent, who was monitored to a specified criterion of performance with their own child. Naive blind observers watched videotapes of parent–child interaction; they rated parent's affect from negative (0) to positive (5).

   a. By visual inspection of Figure 3.3, do you think the difference between training programs is reliable? Why *exactly* do you think so?

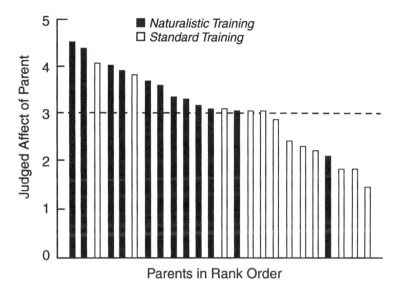

Figure 3.3. Parents of autistic children show more positive affect when training their child using naturalistic procedure (black bars) than procedure based on standard learning theory (white bars). (After Schreibman, Kaneko, & Koegel, 1991).

b. Mean affect is 3.55 and 2.72 for the two groups, with $n = 12$. $\sum Y^2 = 250.681$. Calculate F by hand. From Expression 2 on page 34, show that the 95% confidence interval for the mean difference has width ± .59. Interpret the results.

c. How much, if anything, does the statistical analysis of (b) add to the visual inspection of (a)?

d. What do you think of the communication power of Schreibman's graph?

4. Supplementary analyses are sometimes desirable on a published article. Suppose a journal article reports means of 3 for a control group, and 7, 9, 11 for three experimental groups, with $n = 8$. The reported $F(3, 28)$ is 8.00, so the author concludes the data show real differences. You wish to test differences among the three experimental groups. Use hand calculation with the formulas of Section 3.2.5.

a. Show that $MS_{error} = 11.667$.

b. Do Anova for the three experimental groups.

c. Discuss the relation between your analysis and that in the article.

5. By visual inspection, guess whether F for each of the following three data sets would be larger, smaller, or equal to the F for Exercise 1.

a. $\{103, 104, 105\}$; $\{105, 106, 107\}$; $\{106, 107, 108\}$.

b. $\{4, 5, 6\}$; $\{6, 7, 8\}$; $\{7, 8, 9\}$.

c. $\{-8, -7, -6\}$; $\{-6, -5, -4\}$; $\{-5, -4, -3\}$.

d. What principle underlies these examples? Why is this a good principle?

6. In Exercise 1, suppose you change one score by one point.

a. What score would you change to maximize F?

b. What score do you change to minimize F?

7. P says, "I'm not interested to test whether the effect is statsig; I just want to know how big it is." What circumstances—if any—do you think would justify P's attitude?

8. You are TA in the advanced undergraduate statistics course. The students are assigned to read the subsection on *Robustness of* α in Section 3.3.6. Three students come to your office confused about the meaning of "Ideally, this proportion will equal α" in the third paragraph. What do you tell them?

9. Those same three students return the next week, now confused about *Robustness of Power*. What, they ask, does it mean to say that "Relative to the normal distribution, power was roughly .03 less."

10. The Rev. Franklin Loehr (1959) has made a sincere, dedicated effort to place religion on a scientific foundation. Prayer is considered efficacious by many, but experimental evidence is scanty. Loehr saw prayer as an ideal field for experimental analysis. He used seeds of fast-growing plants (e.g., corn) and had devout persons pray over them as they germinated and sprouted. The response measure was the distance from the soil level to the tip of the highest leaf. Seeds were assigned at random to the prayer and no-prayer conditions. Care was taken to equalize moisture, light, and other environmental factors.

The results were claimed to show a reliable effect; the experimental plants showed more growth than the controls.

a. Why do you think fast-growing plants were selected?

b. One skeptic considered Loehr's design–procedure sound and the data analysis correct. Still, he scoffed that the statsig result must be a false alarm. Is this a reasonable reaction to a bona fide experimental analysis?

c. Rev. Loehr replicated the experiment and found again that the prayed-over plants did statsig better. In light of this replication, is there any reason the skeptic of (b) should not be at least moderately convinced of the positive power of prayer on plants?

d. Suppose the result was not near statsig, even with a large N. Of itself, without regard to background knowledge, how strongly would this negative outcome argue against the positive power of prayer on plants?

Note: Loehr's (1959) popular book gives little technical detail. Various reasonable precautions were said to have been taken and in at least one case the person who measured the plants was blind to their treatment condition. One curious claim was that negative prayer had greater effect than positive prayer. Technical articles are said to be published in *Religious Research*, but I have not read them. Galton (1872) found that people who were more prayed for (e.g., English monarchs) did not live longer, but the ingenuity of his inquiry does not mitigate the confounding. The apparent lack of experimental analysis of this issue seems remarkable.

11. Suppose three group means are 3, 5, and 7, with a total of 30 subjects. The error mean square is 9.

　　a. Use the hand formulas of Section 3.2.5 to show that F is 4.44 if there are 10 subjects in each group, and 3.00 if the subjects are divided 3, 10, and 17, for the three groups in the given order.

　　b. What moral does this exercise suggest?

12. After presenting both a hand calculation and a Minitab printout for a t test, Howell (1992, p. 171) points up a presumed advantage of Minitab, saying "Thus, whereas we concluded that the probability of a Type I error [= false alarm] was *less than* .05 [with the hand calculation], Minitab reveals that the actual probability is .0020." [Here .0020 is the p value on the Minitab printout.] Explain Howell's misconception (consider of H_0 false and H_0 true separately).

13. Consider the error variability, MS_{within}. Other things equal, increasing sample size will: (a) increase error variability; (b) decrease error variability; (c) neither of these two; it depends. (d) none of these.

14. You are TA in the undergraduate course on research methods, which is currently covering variance and confidence interval. One of your students comes to you saying, "My variance is negative, and I can't figure out what that means." How do you answer?

15. Every time you do an experiment, you are taking a random sample (at least ideally). Sooner or later, you are going to be hit with a "bad" random sample.

　　a. In terms of confidence interval, in what way(s) can a sample be "bad?"

　　b. What proportion of samples from a normal distribution will be "bad?"

　　c. Why not just throw out the "bad" random samples?

16. Write a one-page essay on the concept of placebo, using the index entries in the Subject Index.

Exercises on Random Assignment

r0. Some people claim that different groups of subjects should be carefully matched on relevant characteristics before beginning an experiment: "Leaving this critical matter to chance is utter madness; the proof of this madness is that the randomizers themselves admit that random assignment *guarantees* a proportion α of false alarms (given H_0 true)." This claim sounds pretty reasonable, don't you think? What can you add to support this claim?

r1. a. Construct a subject assignment sheet with 16 subjects in each of three conditions, using unblocked randomization. For purposes of this problem begin at the first entry in Table A1 of random numbers and proceed lexicographically. Let digits 1 to 3 denote the three experimental conditions; ignore the other digits. Record your stopping location by row and column.

   Include space on your subject assignment sheet for all information that is to be collected in the experimental session (see text).

   b. What seemingly nonrandom features can you detect in your sequence?

r2. Construct a subject assignment sheet with 10 subjects in each of 4 conditions, randomized in blocks of 8, using one permutation of 16 numbers in Table A2 for each block. In practice, the first permutation would be chosen haphazardly and subsequent permutations lexicographically. For this problem, however, begin with the first listed permutation and proceed lexicographically. For convenience, assign numbers 1 and 2 to condition A_1, numbers 3 and 4 to condition A_2, and so on, in each permutation. Ignore the remaining numbers.

r3. To her horror, Q realized at the end of her experiment that all seven subjects in her A_1 condition had turned out to be male, all seven in her A_2 condition female.

   a. Q had used a table of random numbers and made up a subject assignment before scheduling any subjects. Was her randomization procedure at fault?

   b. What should Q do now?

r4. Write down how to do a block randomization for Q in Exercise r3.

r5. You plan to run three groups of undergraduates from the subject pool, for which you post a sign-up sheet. You have no control over which subject appears at each specified time. How can you randomly assign subjects to conditions?

r6. Subject randomization might be done online manually, for example, by throwing a die or tossing a coin as each subject enters the laboratory. What objections might there be to this (assume block randomization is used)?

r7. Under *Bad Randomizations* in Section A.1, can rejecting the given "bad randomization" bias the treatment means?

r8. McGuigan (1993, pp. 69-70) cites the case of a "knowledgeable graduate student" who wished to compare speed of rat maze running for an experimental and a control group. It came out that he reached into the cage of rats and assigned the first rats that came to hand to the experimental group, the others to the control.

   a. What bias seems not unlikely with this subject assignment procedure?

   b. How serious do you consider this possible bias?

   c. What would be the simplest way to get randomized assignment?

   d. What are two morals of this example?

r9. Clinical research often has difficulties in getting randomized experimental and control groups. The *waiting list control* procedure (Kazdin, 1992, p. 124*ff*; Fowles & Knutson, 1995; see also Zhu, 1999) begins by asking those who apply for therapy whether they would participate even if treatment were delayed. Those who agree are randomly assigned to an experimental group, in which therapy begins at once, and a control group, in which therapy is delayed some specified time. An assessment of the controls just before their treatment is begun is compared to an assessment of the experimental group taken at the same time.

   a. What could go wrong with this waiting list control procedure?

   b. What alternative design might be workable?

PREFACE

Three topics are considered in this chapter that extend the Anova techniques of the previous chapter: confidence intervals, focused comparisons, and power.

Confidence intervals present the sample mean together with an estimate of its variability. A confidence interval is thus an ideal statistic; the interval is a better measure of central tendency than its middle point by itself. The interval summarizes the sample evidence in an efficient, useful way by including a visible index of uncertainty. This uncertainty is submerged in the F or t ratio, but brought out in the clear in the confidence interval.

Focused comparisons look for specific patterns in the data. Focused comparisons have two potential advantages: They can be more informative than the overall F; and they typically have greater power.

The simplest focused comparison is a comparison of two means. With more than two experimental conditions, a statsig F implies real differences but does not localize them. When grounded two-mean comparisons have been planned beforehand, therefore, the overall Anova should ordinarily be bypassed in favor of two-mean confidence intervals.

Another useful focused comparison is the linear trend, which looks for straight-line patterns in the data. In the example of Section 4.2, the linear trend reveals a real difference missed by the overall F. No less important, this trend analysis is informative about the pattern of treatment effects. Forethought in planning linear trend tests may increase the effectiveness of your experiment at little cost.

Power is critical. Without adequate power, an experiment lacks value as evidence; it is a waste, at best. Some experiments are doomed to failure because of inadequate power. Such failures can often be avoided by making a preliminary guesstimate of power. If this guesstimate is too low, power can be increased in various ways. Alternatively, a better experiment may be found.

Everyone considers power, in effect, when they guess how many subjects to run. These intuitive guesses often do well. Still, a simple formula is available that can often improve these intuitive guesses. This power formula is the ounce of prevention that avoids the pound of woe.

The most important aspect of power is not statistical, but extrastatistical— how to increase power. Power depends on empirical specifics, especially on procedures that reduce response variability. This aspect of power is discussed in the final section, *Nine Ways to Increase Power*.

Chapter 4

ELEMENTS OF ANALYSIS OF VARIANCE   II

Three further topics in analysis of variance are considered in this chapter. The first two concern focused analyses beyond the overall Anova of the previous chapter. With more than two groups, a statsig Anova indicates that the means are not all equal, but this does little to localize the differences. All might be different, or all equal but one. Ways to localize differences are discussed in the first two main sections.

The other topic is power. If your experiment lacks power to detect a real difference between treatments, it seems better to find out before you do it. How can you find out? The power formula in the last main section can help. Weak experiments can be made stronger or avoided.

4.1 CONFIDENCE INTERVALS

Confidence intervals go beyond the overall Anova to assess differences between two treatment conditions. The width of the interval gives visual information on the reliability of the difference, as well as on its size.

4.1.1 CONFIDENCE INTERVAL AS SIGNIFICANCE TEST

The confidence interval of Section 2.2 provides a significance test of a difference between the means of two independent samples. In Expression 2 of Chapter 2 (page 34), the standard deviation, s, equals the square root of MS_{within} from the overall Anova. The expression for confidence interval may then be rewritten in the following two equivalent forms, using either t^* or F^*:

$$\bar{Y}_1 - \bar{Y}_2 \pm \sqrt{2}\, t^* \sqrt{\text{MS}_{\text{within}}/n} \tag{1a}$$

$$\bar{Y}_1 - \bar{Y}_2 \pm \sqrt{2}\, \sqrt{F^*} \sqrt{\text{MS}_{\text{within}}/n} \tag{1b}$$

The df for t^* are $N - a$, the same as for $\text{MS}_{\text{within}}$ in the overall Anova; the df for F^* are 1 and $N - a$. The Anova uses the data from all groups to get a more reliable estimate of error. Note that $\sqrt{\text{MS}_{\text{within}}/n} = s_{\text{mean}}$ is the standard deviation **of the mean**, $\bar{Y}$, also called standard error of the mean—**not to be confused** with $\sqrt{\text{MS}_{\text{within}}} = s$, the standard deviation **of a single response**, Y.

If 0 lies outside the confidence interval, $\bar{Y}_1 - \bar{Y}_2$ is statsig different from 0. To see this, note that we have 95% confidence that the true mean difference lies inside the given interval. If 0 lies outside this interval, we have 95% confidence that the true mean difference is not 0. The confidence interval thus provides a significance test of the null hypothesis that $\mu_1 - \mu_2 = 0$. If $\bar{Y}_1 - \bar{Y}_2$ is statsig different from 0, of course, $\bar{Y}_1$ is statsig different from $\bar{Y}_2$. Confidence intervals for unequal n are given in Note 4.1.1b.[a, b]

4.1.2 "ERROR BARS" AS CONFIDENCE INTERVALS

Treatment means, especially in graphic form, are sometimes presented with *error bars*. In two-sided form, the error bar extends one standard deviation, s_{mean}, on both sides of the mean. This may be written

$$\bar{Y} \pm s_{\text{mean}} = \bar{Y} \pm \sqrt{\text{MS}_{\text{within}}/n}. \tag{2}$$

The half-bar is thus the unit of variability of the mean, a convenient way of exhibiting its uncertainty.

The error bar is actually a confidence interval, obtained by setting $t^* = 1$ in the confidence interval of Expression 1a. With 60 df, the two-sided error bar corresponds to 68% confidence. With fewer df, confidence is a little less.

When a graph is presented with error bars, visual assessment whether two means are statsig different is sometimes desirable. As a visual rule thumb, a distance of three half-bars between two means is borderline statsig. To see this, note that the error bar for a single mean, given in Expression 2, must be multiplied by $\sqrt{2}\, t^*$ to get a statsig confidence interval in Expression 1a. With 60 df for error, $t^* = 2.00$, so the distance between the two means would have to be $\sqrt{2} \times 2 = 2.8$ standard deviations, that is, 2.8 times the half-bar. With 16 df for error, the criterial difference increases mildly to 3.0 half-bars.

This standard of three half-bars may not be generally appreciated. Two means whose error bars do not overlap may be far from statsig different. To be statsig, the empty gap between the ends of their error bars should be another half-bar wide.

4.1.3 NULL HYPOTHESIS AS A RANGE: "ACCEPTING" H_0

Confidence intervals may sometimes be used to "accept" a null hypothesis. A narrow confidence interval that contains 0 gives confidence that any real effect is small. There is no need to claim that the real effect is null, of course, merely that it is small and, presumably, unimportant.

In empirical practice, as this argument emphasizes, the null hypothesis actually corresponds to a range around 0. Although the null hypothesis is stated as a point hypothesis that the true mean is exactly 0, this is a statistical formalism. Empirically, it only makes sense to consider the null hypothesis as a range rather than a point. Small effects usually have small importance. If the true effect is small, it might as well be 0 in most cases. Indeed, investigators ordinarily desire small effects to be nonstatsig because a statsig small effect is virtually a false alarm. The significance test is obliging on this score, for it gives low power for real effects in a moderate range around 0 (see power curves in Figure A7). Rightly understood, therefore, the null hypothesis logic is well suited to its job (see further Section 19.2.2 and Note 19.2.2a).[a]

This line of thought can sometimes be pushed further, to claim that an effect is unimportant even though statsig. What governs importance is substantive size, not statistical significance. The confidence interval delimits the likely numerical size of the effect. If this size is substantively small, the investigator may decide the true effect is not important. This argument rests on integrated use of statistical and extrastatistical inference, the former to delimit the likely size of the effect, the latter to evaluate substantive importance of effects within the delimited size range.

4.1.4 UNEQUAL VARIANCE

The confidence intervals of Expressions 1 and 2 take s, the estimated standard deviation of the population, equal to MS_{within} from the overall Anova. This procedure yields the most reliable s and hence the shortest confidence intervals. However, it assumes equal variance across conditions.

With unequal variance, confidence intervals based on MS_{within} can be seriously in error (see discussion of Table 4.1 on page 97). Unequal variance can be a problem when some design factor is a subject variable, such as age or clinical category; such subject groups may differ markedly in variability before the experiment begins. Even with random assignment, however, unequal variance can occur when different treatments have markedly different effects.

This problem can ordinarily be resolved by calculating MS_{within} from the one or two groups involved in the confidence interval. If two groups have considerably unequal variance, a reduction in df is needed (Section 12.5). Being based on less data, however, these individualized confidence intervals are less reliable and more susceptible to extreme scores.

4.1.5 CAVEATS ON CONFIDENCE INTERVALS

As invaluable as they are, confidence intervals have limited applicability. A confidence interval for three means, for example, does not exist; this is one reason why we need Anova. With multiple comparisons (pages 99*ff*), confidence intervals are not generally available. With repeated measures (Chapter 6), a single mean may have several different confidence intervals, depending on which other mean it is compared with; an error bar for a single mean may thus be meaningless. Other limitations are noted in *Incompleteness of Neyman–Pearson Theory* in Section 19.1.2 as well as in Note 19.2b.

Normality is assumed in the foregoing expressions for confidence interval. What needs to be normal, however, is not the population of Y values, but the sampling distribution of the mean, $\bar{Y}$. This normality holds in most applications by the central limit theorem. For a single mean from a very skewed distribution, however, relatively large samples are required for normality.

For the difference between two such means, in contrast, the skewness tends to cancel. Such confidence intervals seldom need qualification unless sample size and error variance both differ substantially between the two groups (see Section 12.5; see also discussion of Table 4.1, page 97).

Confidence intervals and error bars should be *defined in complete detail*. The data used in the calculation should be specified, together with the df and level of confidence. It should be clear whether a common error term has been used and whether the interval is for a single mean or difference between two means.

4.1.6 THE CONCEPT OF CONFIDENCE

Confidence is not probability. From a perspective that conceptualizes probability in terms of long-run frequencies, it is wrong to speak of the probability that the true mean lies within the particular confidence interval you obtain—either it does or it doesn't. However, you can say that 95% of the confidence intervals constructed in this manner will contain the true mean. Hence you may have 95% confidence that your particular one does. Usually, therefore, confidence may be considered subjective belief (Section 19.1.2).[a]

It would be far wronger to say that the probability a new sample mean will lie within the given confidence interval is 95%. It is virtually always less than 95%.

To appreciate this, suppose the sample mean chanced to be far from the true mean. Then the probability that a new sample mean would lie within this particular interval would be near zero. In practice, of course, we cannot know how far our particular sample mean lies from the true mean. Hence we cannot know the probability that a new sample mean will lie within the confidence interval for our particular sample mean.

4.2 FOCUSED COMPARISONS

Experimental studies are usually designed to test specific hypotheses. These hypotheses come first. Your plan for analyzing the data should embody your hypotheses. In some studies, the overall Anova is undesirable clutter, best avoided. In other studies, an initial overall Anova would need supplementary analyses to help localize the effects. Ways to go beyond the overall Anova, or even bypass it, are discussed in the first section. The associated danger of increased false alarms is taken up in the second section.

4.2.1 FOCUSED COMPARISONS

Visual Inspection. Visual inspection of the data, of individual scores as well as means, is the foundation of data analysis. Visual inspection of the pattern of means is the main basis for relating the data to the experimental manipulations and hypotheses. For certain hypotheses, visual inspection may be augmented through confidence intervals, which provide a visual measure of variability. Often no more is needed. Do not benumb your audience—and begrime your results—with unneeded statistical analysis when the data are clear as they stand.

Visual inspection also has a more basic function—a function no statistical test can fill. This function is to assess size and importance of the effects. Whether an observed effect is "small" or "large" is mainly an extrastatistical, substantive question. A substantive standard based on extrastatistical knowledge is needed to assess size, and even more to assess importance.

The fundamental importance of visual inspection gets short shrift in most statistics texts. This is understandable, for visual inspection leans heavily on extrastatistical considerations. Experienced investigators, however, treat visual inspection as an integral part of data analysis.

Many texts seek to fill this gap with statistical indexes of size and importance. One useful index is the power effect size, discussed in Section 4.3. Most of these statistical indexes, however, have little value; they obscure rather than illuminate (Section 18.1).

Subdesign Anova. *Subdesign Anova*, also called subset Anova, refers to Anova on some subset of conditions. As one example, you may have several experimental groups that are your main interest, together with a single control. The overall F, however, could be statsig merely because the control differs greatly from all the experimental conditions. The important analysis would be a subdesign Anova, restricted to the experimental groups.

Subdesign Anova would be the mainstay in some experiments. The treatment conditions may divide naturally into two subgroups, each of which needs separate analysis. An overall Anova might be better avoided. Plan the analysis beforehand to represent your experimental questions. Planning should be straightforward if you are clear about your purposes. If you are not clear, planning can be even more helpful.

Two-Mean Comparisons. The most useful focused comparison is between two means. Such comparisons may be made with a confidence interval, as already discussed. The confidence interval has the added virtue that its width exhibits the likely error of the mean difference.

Two dangers beset the use of two-mean comparisons. First, they can be seriously incorrect with unequal variance, as shown in the later discussion of Table 4.1. Second, making a number of two-mean comparisons can escalate α, an issue addressed in Section 4.2.2.

Linear Trend. When the independent variable is quantitative, or metric, the response is often a near-linear function of its metric value. Linear trend analysis, which focuses on this functional relation, has two potential advantages over the overall F: greater informativeness and greater power.

This twofold potential of linear trend is shown in the following numerical example. We vary drug concentration across four equal steps, with $n = 10$ subjects at each concentration. We expect the response to increase with drug concentration, and we find the four observed means are 1, 2, 3, 4, with $MS_{within} = 7.5$. Substitution in Equation 5a on page 61 of Chapter 3 shows that $SS_{drugs} = 50$, so $MS_{drugs} = 16.67$. Hence $F = 2.22$, rather less than the criterial value, $F^*(3, 36) = 2.89$. The overall F is thus not statsig.

The data, however, show a perfect linear trend; all of SS_{drugs} is concentrated in this linear trend. But the linear trend has only 1 df, so $MS_{drugs:linear} = SS_{drugs} = 50$. Hence $F = 6.66$, three times larger than before, and comfortably greater than the criterial $F^*(1, 36) = 4.13$. In this example, the linear trend is statsig, whereas the overall F is not (see also *Numerical Example* in Section 18.2.1).[a]

The linear trend test has a more important advantage: It is more informative. Even had the overall F been statsig, it would have said little about the pattern in the data. In this hypothetical example, it is true, a blind man could recognize the perfect linear trend, but Nature seldom yields such neat data.

A principle embodied in this example is that statistical analysis needs to be based on extrastatistical information. When you have good reason to expect a particular pattern of data, it is usually preferable to focus your analysis on that pattern. Without such expectation, the overall F would be preferable because it looks for all possible patterns. In the present example, the data pattern 2, 4, 1, 3, yields the same overall F, but a linear trend of zero.

Contrasts. *Contrasts* look for specified patterns in the data, as with the linear trend of the previous subsection. A contrast is a weighted sum of treatment means. If your experimental hypothesis predicts a pattern that can be expressed as a weighted sum, contrasts have potential advantages for you.[b]

By far the most common contrasts are the two-mean comparisons and the linear trend test of the preceding subsections. But two-mean comparisons are better done with confidence intervals, as already shown. And linear trend is better done with the linear regression analysis of Chapter 9. Other contrasts are not often useful.

Learning formulas for contrasts thus has minor importance, and is deferred to Sections 15.3, 18.2 and 18.3. These later discussions also point out some common misconceptions about contrasts for nonlinear trend, especially about orthogonal polynomials.

Unequal Variance. For two-mean comparisons, the error term is commonly taken as MS_{within} from the overall Anova. Unlike overall F, however, two-mean comparisons can be sensitive to unequal variance. To illustrate, consider four groups with equal n, and population means and variances given in Table 4.1.

TABLE 4.1

Group	A_1	A_2	A_3	A_4
Mean	1	2	3	4
Variance	1	1	3	3

The average variance of the four groups is 2, and this is what would be estimated by MS_{within} in the overall Anova. Using this overall error term would be disastrous for two of the six two-mean comparisons.

For the comparison between groups A_1 and A_2, the appropriate variance is 1, not 2. For this comparison, the obtained F would be half its correct value, a frightful loss of power.

For the comparison between groups A_3 and A_4, the appropriate variance is 3, not 2. For this comparison, the obtained F would be 50% larger than its correct value, causing far too many statsig results.

Although the overall F for all four groups is robust against the unequal variance, this clearly does not transfer to all follow-up tests. Confidence intervals for two-mean comparisons suffer the identical problem.

In practice, unequal variance is in one way less serious, in another way more serious than this example suggests. The 3 to 1 ratio of variances is high and would likely be noticeable so appropriate analyses could be made. However, a 1.5 to 1 ratio of variances would escape detection in typical experiments. Yet even this modest degree of unequal variance would seem barely acceptable distortion of α and β for the two-mean comparisons.

A simple approach is to use only the data from the two groups in question. This two-group F is robust and yields an appropriate error term. This error term has fewer df, however, a serious shortcoming with small n (see also Section 12.5). This dilemma has no simple solution, except for replication.

In randomized experiments, it should be reemphasized, unequal variance is not ordinarily serious for the overall F. Unequal variance cannot occur unless the treatments have real effects (Section 3.3.4, page 70). But follow-up analyses require caution. In some studies, the experimental groups may all have greater variability than the control. Two-mean comparisons among the experimental groups should then use an MS_{within} obtained from the experimental groups with the control omitted, or alternatively, just from the two groups in the given comparison. In some learning experiments, analogously, one group may learn to near-perfect, showing almost no variability.

With nonrandom groups, in contrast, unequal variance can be serious. A typical example appears in developmental studies that seek comparisons across age groups. Many experiments include such comparisons together with randomized experimental conditions within each nonrandom group. Caution is needed to ensure that the unequal variance among the nonrandom groups does not affect the analysis of the experimental conditions.

One-Tailed Tests. A *one-tailed test* allows only one direction of difference between two conditions; it corresponds to the experimental hypothesis that $\mu_1 < \mu_2$. The standard *two-tailed test*, in contrast, allows for a difference in either direction; it corresponds to the experimental hypothesis that $\mu_1 < \mu_2$ or $\mu_1 > \mu_2$. Anova yields a two-tailed test, as does the standard t test. In the graph of the t distribution, the standard criterial region consists of the lower and upper .025 tails. A one-tailed test would use a single tail as the criterial region.

Most writers disapprove of one-tailed tests but a few argue for them. One argument is that a one-tailed test is warranted when the direction of difference has been predicted beforehand. But then the criterial region contains only results that support the prediction; a contrary result could never be statsig. This practice seems unacceptable.

The only case in which one-tailed tests would seem appropriate is when only one direction of difference is relevant. This sometimes happens in applied studies. A new medical treatment, for example, will be adopted only if superior to the standard treatment; finding that it is worse seldom has practical value. If not, it seems pointless to test this possibility.

I concur that a one-tailed test is appropriate in such situation—but only if the ½ α level is used. The reason for the ½ α level is empirical pragmatics.

The pragmatic ground for the .05 level is that it has proved reasonably satisfactory in widespread use. However, empirical use of the .05 level differs in a significant way from its presentation in statistics texts. Most studies use two-tailed tests; one-tailed tests are infrequent. In most studies, however, a difference is expected in a predicted direction. Moreover, the results, if statsig, usually agree with prediction. In effect, therefore, most studies use a ½α tail, supplemented with an "insurance" of ½α in the opposite tail. That the .05 level has been satisfactory in practice rests on this pragmatic ground.

The standard value of α thus seems generally inappropriate for a one-tailed test. This α is much larger than warranted on pragmatic grounds. Relative to standard practice, this amounts to using an α close to .10. This practice stems from implicit belief that the .05 level is sanctified by some Higher Power, failing to appreciate the empirical earth on which it rests.[c]

4.2.2 THE PROBLEM OF α ESCALATION

Anova might seem unnecessary because the t test could be applied to every pair of groups. A study with four groups, for example, could be completely analyzed with six two-mean t tests. Multiple t tests, however, suffer a serious problem. Each test is an opportunity for a false alarm; more tests allow more false alarms. The false alarm parameter for the *family* of tests will thus be larger than the α used in each separate test.

This α escalation, as it may be called, can be surprisingly serious. Suppose you have three conditions and apply the t test to each pair of means using α = .05. If all three true means are equal, the probability that the t test between the largest and smallest sample means will be statsig is not .05, but nearly .13.

Anova was developed to provide a significance test for any number of conditions, not just two as with the t test. Anova thus tests the null hypothesis that all true means are equal. This notable achievement keeps the false alarm parameter at the prescribed level, regardless of the number of conditions.

The corollary shortcoming of overall Anova is that it does not localize differences with three or more conditions. Given a statsig overall F, follow-up analyses are needed to localize the difference as discussed in the preceding section on focused comparisons. With four or more conditions, these follow-up tests will inevitably be troubled by α escalation.

LSD Method. The threat of false alarms can be held down by beginning with an overall Anova. A statsig F implies real effects somewhere; seek to localize them with visual inspection and two-mean comparisons. This is Fisher's least significant difference (LSD) method.

The LSD method might seem foolproof. Since the overall F holds the false alarm parameter at the prescribed value, it would seem to protect the follow-up tests against α escalation. This protection is only partial, however, and its shortcomings should be understood by anyone who considers using it.

To see the limitation of the LSD method, suppose our concern is with four experimental treatments, which unknown to us have identical effects. For supplementary purposes, a fifth treatment is included that is certain to have a very different effect. This one very different treatment will produce a statsig overall

F, seeming to justify two-mean follow-ups. But the difference between the largest and smallest sample means for the four equal treatments will be statsig about .20 of the time. The operative α is thus .20.

When the null hypothesis is true only for a subset of conditions, as in this example, the LSD method gives full protection only for $a = 3$. This shortcoming is less a criticism than a caution about the LSD method. In this particular situation, the design requires a subset Anova of the four experimental conditions. If statsig, the operative α on two-mean, follow-up tests is at most .10 (Chapter 17). Some risk of α escalation then seems justifiable to localize these effects.

Multiple Comparisons. Various *multiple comparisons procedures* have been developed to hold down the threat of false alarms that accompanies multiple tests. Fisher's method of α splitting (also called the Bonferroni method) illustrates the *familywise approach*. If four tests are to be run, for example, the α of .05 may be split into four parts to get an α of .0125 for each individual test. For the family of four tests taken together, therefore, the effective α is at most .05. In other words, the probability of no false alarm in any of the tests is at least $1 - \alpha = .95$.

The basic principle of the familywise philosophy is that α is fixed for the family of all the tests taken together, regardless of their number. Hence the probability of even a single false alarm in all the tests of the family is at most α. Most texts on psychological statistics adopt a familywise philosophy, taking a hardline position that α must be held at some assigned level such as .05 for the family of all tests made in the experiment.

The trouble with the familywise approach is loss of power on the individual tests. The miss rate, β, increases because a larger F^* is required for each individual test. The dilemma of $\alpha-\beta$ tradeoff discussed in Section 2.3.5 is amplified when multiple tests are run.

I believe the familywise philosophy is mistaken for general use. The argument is simple. Suppose an α of .05 is appropriate for a study with two groups. Adding two more groups should not penalize the analysis of the first two by requiring that α be split to .025; that causes β to increase. This argument is elaborated in the *Parable of the Two Philosophies* in Chapter 17.

In some situations, it is true, even one false alarm would be fatal. Suppose three experimental medical treatments are tested against a standard treatment to see if the standard should be replaced. For this purpose, a familywise α seems essential. Of course, the significance test has limited relevance in this kind of situation. Replication and cost–benefit analysis would usually be required before making a decision to abandon the standard treatment.

The main danger from α escalation arises when numerous measures are taken and each is analyzed separately. With no real effects, each test is a chance for a false alarm. With so many chances, something is almost sure to be statsig.

For ordinary experiments in psychology, however, the problem of α escalation is not usually serious. One reason lies in background information, which leads to planned comparisons. A second reason is the principle of replication. These two reasons are discussed in the next two subsections.

Planned Comparisons. Many experiments embody specific hypotheses that should be tested in their own right. The principle advocated here is that comparisons planned in advance—and that have a reasonably firm a priori basis—may ordinarily be tested using the standard α for each.

"Planned in advance" and "reasonably firm a priori basis" are both essential conditions. The former means that the comparisons are decided upon before collecting the data, not after looking them over. The latter rules out the dubious tactic of blanket plans for numerous possible comparisons. These conditions also imply that the experimental hypotheses will typically have some prior likelihood of being correct, as with the foregoing example of linear trend.

This principle of using the standard α for each of a set of planned comparisons has reasonably wide acceptance. Some proponents are cited in Chapter 17, which also discusses some cautions in applying this principle. One caution is that incongruence between the planned comparisons and the actual pattern in the data will require fall-back to post hoc tests, which are tainted by the possibility of chance accidents (see *Post Hoc Tests* below).

Replication. Replication is a cure-all for α escalation. If the same result is statsig in two successive experiments, it is unlikely to be a false alarm.

Replication has become a norm in experimental psychology (Section 2.4.6, page 52). With replication, concern over false alarms largely disappears. With replication, accordingly, there is ordinarily little need to reduce the false alarm parameter to allow for multiple tests in typical psychology experiments.

Post Hoc Tests. The data should always be scrutinized for unexpected results; these may be the most interesting and important. But they may also be chance accidents, to which data snooping is quite vulnerable (see varied examples in Diaconis, 1985). The question is how to handle unexpected results.

In many experimental studies, in my opinion, a reasonable way to handle unexpected results is to give a confidence interval or significance test using the regular α, making clear that the test was done post hoc. Anything unexpected deserves to be pointed out, together with some indication of its reliability. Calling it post hoc gives the reader appropriate warning that it is only suggestive, an uncertain hint, not a claim for a real effect. If the result is minor, no more seems needed. If the result looks important, something the investigator would like to get credit for, it should be pinned down with additional work. With such replication, the α uncertainty of data snooping largely disappears. Further discussion is given in Section 17.4.3 (see also Note 4.3.5a).

4.3 POWER ANALYSIS

Power calculations are worthwhile. They provide guidelines on how many subjects you need. They can lead to desirable improvements in experimental design and in statistical analysis. And they help avoid wasting your time with experiments that have small chance of success. For these reasons, power calculations are becoming more common. Some grant agencies now require power calculations as part of grant applications.

4.3.1 POWER FORMULA AND EXAMPLES

Calculating power is easy. It begins with guesses about the true means of the treatment conditions, μ_j. Subtracting the overall mean $\bar{\mu}$ from each μ_j yields the relative effects, $\alpha_j = \mu_j - \bar{\mu}$. The standard deviation σ_A of these relative effects may be termed the *power effect size*:

$$\sigma_A = \sqrt{\sum \alpha_j^2 / a}. \tag{3}$$

Also needed is a guess about σ_ε, the standard deviation for error. The ratio of these two standard deviations yields the ***standardized** power effect size, f*:

$$f = \sigma_A / \sigma_\varepsilon. \tag{4}$$

The power index, ϕ, is then

$$\phi = f \sqrt{"n"}, \tag{5}$$

where "n" is the number of subjects per condition. With this value of ϕ, power may be read off the power curve for the appropriate df in Figure A7 (pages 816*ff*).[a]

Three Groups or Two? Reducing the scope of an experiment from three groups to two can increase power substantially. Suppose $\mu_j = 0, 1, 2$, for three groups, with $\sigma_\varepsilon = 1.8$ and $n = 8$. Then $\alpha_j = -1, 0, 1, \sum \alpha_j^2 = 2$, and Equation 3 gives $\sigma_A = \sqrt{2/3}$. From Equation 5, $\phi = (\sigma_A / \sigma_\varepsilon)\sqrt{8} = 1.28$.

  For this example, the numerator df $= 2$, so we should use a power curve from Figure A7. This figure shows two sheafs of curves, one for $\alpha = .01$, one for $\alpha = .05$. From the latter sheaf, we choose the curve labeled 20 df for denominator. Locating $\phi = 1.28$ correctly on the horizontal, we read off power on the vertical as approximately .46. This is surely too low.

  To increase power, consider omitting the middle group, distributing 4 of its 8 subjects to each remaining group. In this case, $\mu_j = 0$ and 2, so $\alpha_j = -1$ and 1, and $\sigma_A = 1$. These values yield $\phi = 1.92$. Since the numerator df $= 1$, we should use the power curve of Figure A7. From the 20 df curve, we read off power as .75, a substantial improvement over .46. Although omitting the middle group may be painful, this power analysis argues that it should be done.

Of course, the investigator might be able to increase n from 8 to 12 for all three conditions. This would seem preferable if 36 subjects are easily available, but they might not. In either case, the power calculation precipitates a change from an experiment that is not worthwhile to one that has a reasonable chance of success.

Minimum Effect Size. An alternative approach to power calculation is to decide on the smallest effect size that is important to detect if it is real. Power is then calculated for this effect size. This approach is often appropriate with remedial treatments, from medicine to education. Ordinarily, a new treatment is recommended only if it promises some minimum degree of improvement. A similar view is generally implicit in experimental analysis, as indicated in the earlier discussion of the null hypothesis as a range.

To illustrate, suppose some standard treatment has a mean effectiveness of 60 on a 0–100 scale, with a standard deviation of 12. You consider that a revised treatment that gave 10% improvement would be just worth the cost of changing from the standard treatment. Thus, you wish to detect a true difference of 6 (or more) points between the present and revised treatments.

On this basis, the two relevant treatment means are 60 and 66, which yields $\sigma_A = 3$ from Equation 3. Since σ_ε is given as 12, you obtain

$$\phi = \sqrt{n}/4.$$

With an n of 64, $\phi = 2.00$, and this yields power about .80. Power of .80 seems none too high, so some thought should be given to increasing it (pages 107*ff*).

In some situations, of course, 64 subjects per condition would be out of the question. You might still hope that the true effect was greater than 10%, which would allow fewer subjects, but hope is only hope. Alternatives are to reduce error variance, to use a more powerful design, as with repeated measures, or to seek a more powerful analysis, such as trimmed Anova (Section 12.1).

"Inconsistencies" in the Literature. Investigators generally feel obliged to comment on "inconsistent results" when their study fails to verify a statsig result previously published, or vice versa. Typically, the reader is led through a conjectural maze of differences in experimental detail between the two experiments. This is a serious matter, for many cases are on record in which some small detail has a big effect.

But such "inconsistency" must be common if power is less than .7 for either of the two experiments, even though both involve exactly the same real effect (Exercise 20). In such cases, the term "inconsistency" is misleading. Power calculations should thus be prerequisite to any discussion of such seeming inconsistencies. This advice is reinforced in the next subsection.

Are Statsig Results Reliable? The meaning of statistical significance can be better appreciated when it is realized that the power of an exact replication of a statsig result may be little better than .50. Suppose you wish to follow up some published result which is just statsig at your chosen α level. A first step would be a power calculation of an exact replication, taking the reported means and error variance as guesses about the true values. With two groups, you will obtain a power not far from .50 (Exercise 11).

Your power calculation thus reveals that marginally "significant" results are not notably reliable nor replicable. Replicability is a hallmark of science, but replicability of .5 seems dubious. A study with marginal results may deserve publication when it is expensive or involves an uncommon subject population. The same can hardly be said for a marginal result in a typical single experiment. This power argument supports the increasingly common editorial requirement of multiple related studies for published articles.

A further problem is that the power calculation in the first paragraph over-estimates power. The reason is that the reported means and variance are unreliable empirical estimates of the true values, whereas the power formula assumes perfectly reliable estimates. If this unreliability is taken into account, the power estimate is somewhat low. This is discussed by Gillett (1995), who presents a way to handle it. As a practical matter, it may be simpler to adopt a rough rule of increasing projected sample size by, say, 20% in such applications.[b]

Small Effects. Inspection of the power curves of Figure A7 indicates low power for small effects, unless n is large. If the true effects are zero in Equation 3, then $\phi = 0$, and the power curve has a vertical elevation of .05. This point is not properly power, of course, but it may be included as the limit point of the power curve. This point for $\phi = 0$ does not appear on the power curve, however, but is off the page far to the left. The first plotted point on this power curve is at $\phi = 1.2$. Even with this much larger ϕ, power is at most .40.

Low power for small effects seems usually desirable. Usually, an investigator does not want small effects to be statsig. Large effects are generally more important and worthwhile. This argument is reinforced by the practical consideration that minor confounding variables are present in most experiments. Observed differences between treatment means will thus include real treatment differences plus small effects from confounding variables. These confounded effects can often be ignored relative to large treatment effects, but they are dangerous with small treatment effects.

This reasoning reinforces the argument of Section 4.1.3 that the null hypothesis is properly considered a range rather than a single point. If the true effect is small, a statsig result is kissing cousin to a false alarm. The significance test thus does a responsible job by providing low power for small effects.

Alternative Definition of Power Effect Size. For two groups, an alternative definition of standardized power effect size is often used, namely,

$$d = \frac{|\mu_1 - \mu_2|}{\sigma_\varepsilon}. \tag{6}$$

The advantage of d is that the numerator equals the difference between the two means. From Equations 3 and 4, in contrast, $\sigma_A = \frac{1}{2}|\mu_1 - \mu_2|$. Hence $d = 2f$. Further discussion of the concept of effect size is given in Section 18.1.

This d index of effect size is useful in signal detection theory (Section 20.3) as well as in meta-analysis, which seeks to summarize evidence about the effect of some experimental manipulation across a number of different published studies. Numerous meta-analyses have been reported, ranging from effectiveness of computer-based instruction to care programs in pregnancy. Since different studies use different response measures, summarizing them is easier if they can be made comparable. This is the reason for dividing by σ_ε in Equation 6. Each d is thus expressed in terms of its standard deviation, and in this limited but useful sense, ds are roughly comparable across studies that use different measures or have different variability.

Some texts present power formulas in terms of d. This is unnecessary, since Equations 3–5 hold for two groups as well as for more than two. There seems little reason to learn two sets of power formulas when one will do it all. Keep in mind, however, that "effect size" in the literature often refers to d, not σ_A nor f.

4.3.2 POWER AS GUESSTIMATE

Power calculations are *guesstimates*. To use the power formula, as already noted, you must make guesses about the true means and error variance. The power calculation quantifies the guesses you put into the formula; it cannot improve their accuracy.

The key to useful power calculations thus lies in your guesses about effect size and error. These guesses will ordinarily be based on previous work, both published and pilot. The better your feel for the behavior, the better will be your guesstimate of power.

Keep in mind that empirical estimates are notably more variable for σ_ε than for the μ_j. Accumulation of information about error variability should thus be a continuing concern. This is another reason why it is important to report estimates of error variability.

More than one power calculation, using somewhat different guesses, is often desirable. The main reason is to assess how sensitive the power guesstimate is to your guesses about σ_A and σ_ε. If optimistic and pessimistic guesses both yield high power, the proposed study looks promising. If they disagree, however, it may be advisable to seek ways to increase power before proceeding.

The term *guesstimate* is used to emphasize that the power formula does not ordinarily yield an estimate in the usual sense, that is, the sense in which the sample mean is an estimate of the population mean. The values of μ_j in the power formula are usually guesses, as already emphasized. The true means in any situation are unknown; they might be nearly equal so actual power would be negligible. The power calculation thus represents the guess and hope of the investigator. This is no criticism of the power formula, of course, which seeks to help you by making your guesstimate more precise and informative.

4.3.3 COMMENTS ON POWER

Power calculations require attention to effect size and to error variance, both of which tend to be vague to many researchers, especially to those in early stages of developing their skills with experimental analysis. Results are not all-or-none, but graded in size. Increasing the size of an effect through experimental procedure can facilitate future work. Decreasing error variability can be even more useful. A calculation that indicates low power can be a blessing. Not only does it help you avoid likely failure from a weak experiment, but it forces your attention on improving quality of your research. Since power calculations are so easy, they deserve extensive use.[a]

Power of .80 is generally considered acceptable, although justification for this choice is obscure. Power of .50 is surely too low for general use, but power of .90 seems considerably more comfortable than .80—with 9 to 1 odds of success rather than 4 to 1. The final standard, of course, involves not just the probabilities of hits, misses, and false alarms, but more importantly, their costs and benefits. Costs and benefits, however, must be determined on extrastatistical grounds. Here again, statistical inference, at the top level of the Experimental Pyramid, is integrally bound up with empirical substance at lower levels.

One cost is associated with results that promise to be important or controversial. Such results may be expected to trigger follow-up studies by other workers, which would be largely lost labor if the original result was a false alarm. Higher power, especially replication, seems desirable in such cases. The most notable dry holes, however, arise from faulty method, not false alarms. One example is the somatotype investigation of Section 1.2.3 (page 13); others appear in Chapter 8 on confounding.

A second cost is the expense that would be required to increase power, say, from .80 to .90. This expense might more efficiently be used to run a second experiment. Indeed, lower power may be desirable for experiments in a series. In this case, results in the same direction will buttress one another across experiments even if they are marginally statsig. If the experiment must stand alone, however, my personal feeling is that power of .80 is uncomfortably low.[b]

4.3.4 NINE WAYS TO INCREASE POWER

If the power calculation suggests that power is too low, it can be increased. Figure 2.1 is reproduced here as Figure 4.1 to show the false alarm–power situation graphically. The false alarm parameter α is the area to the right of F^* under the curve labeled "H_0 true." The power, $1 - \beta$, is the area to the right of F^* under the curve labeled "H_0 false." Moving F^* leftward will increase power—at the expense of increasing α.

It seems better to increase power by shifting the curve labeled "H_0 false" to the right. The power formula is a statistical recipe for such shifts. Increasing σ_A will shift "H_0 false" to the right with no effect on "H_0 true." Decreasing σ_ε does the same. Increasing n will shift "H_0 false" to the right, and also shift the right tail of "H_0 true" to the left. We now consider how to accomplish these changes experimentally.

1. Decrease Error Variance. By far the best way to increase power is to decrease error variance. This goes beyond significance tests per se to provide more precise estimates of effect size, as revealed in tighter confidence intervals.

A good way to reduce variability is through good method: clarity of instructions, reliable apparatus, uniform procedure, task–subject congruence, and so on. Good method also helps improve the quality of the data.

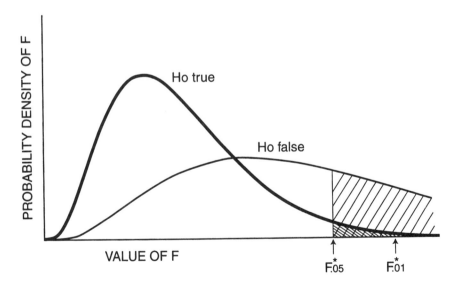

Figure 4.1. Two sampling distributions of F ratios: H_0 true (heavier curve); H_0 false (lighter curve). Vertical axis plots probability density of each value of F listed on horizontal axis. Points labeled F^* cut off .05 or .01 of the area under curve for H_0 true.

In many tasks, the main component of error is individual differences. If their effects cannot be reduced by design changes, they may still be reducible through good procedure as well as by screening out extreme cases.

2. Increase Effect Size. Increasing effect size certainly seems a desirable way to increase power. This is easier said than done. The most obvious way requires a stronger experimental manipulation, which is often not feasible. Indirect ways of attaining the same end are included in points 7-8 following.

3. Increase n. The most obvious way to increase power is to increase n. This seems generally less desirable than decreasing error variability or increasing effect size. These latter two ways are good in themselves, whereas increasing n is often bad in itself. Increasing n entails added cost. This added cost goes beyond the experiment in question, for it would also apply to follow-up studies while doing nothing to put the behavior under better control.

4. Weaken α. A cheap way to increase power is to use a weaker α. Weaker α may be justified in certain situations. As one example, preliminary screening tests sometimes use $\alpha = .10$ to avoid passing by some potentially important treatment. A second example occurs in single subject analysis with a considerable number of subjects, in which the single subject analyses are employed to classify subjects into distinctive subgroups. In both these situations, the weak initial α is fortified by the subsequent analysis.

Usually, however, weaker α is bad policy. Weaker α potentiates more false alarms, whose followup may be costly in wasted work. In general, as in the two cited examples, the choice of α should be determined by cost–benefit analysis, not by desire for power per se.

5. Change Analysis. Changing the statistical analysis sometimes yields very substantial increases in power. The linear trend example of Section 4.2.1 (page 96) illustrates the potential gain in power by switching from the overall Anova to the linear trend. The general principle is that an analysis will be more powerful the more closely it is matched to the pattern of the real effects. The better your substantive knowledge, therefore, the more power you can expect.

6. Change Design. Changing the experimental design can also increase power. Substantial increases can be obtained from designs that extract individual differences from the error term, especially blocking designs, analysis of covariance, repeated measures designs, and single subject designs. Some advantage may be obtainable from adding any design factor that controls a source of extraneous variation, such as day-to-day shifts in apparatus sensitivity.

A different tactic is to use fewer conditions, which allows a larger n per group. At the same time, the effect size, σ_A, may even increase. Both advantages are illustrated in the first power calculation of Section 4.3.1. Reducing the scope of a study is an unpleasant but common necessity.

7. Change Task. Still another way to increase power is to change the experimental task, whether by minor improvements or by major revision. Benefit may come in two ways, from an increase in effect size or a decrease in variability.

Development of more sensitive tasks should be of continual concern, especially in extended research programs. The validity of the response measure is primary, of course, but reliability and effect size are also important. Your personal observation of subjects' task behavior is important for task development.

8. Transform Response. Response transformation can sometimes increase power substantially with little cost. Power gain from transforming a skewed distribution to normal shape is illustrated in Exercise d1 of Chapter 12. A general discussion of response transformation is given in Section 12.4.

The task itself is a response transformation. As one example, numerical judgments of stimulus magnitude may be obtained with two methods, rating or magnitude estimation. Magnitude estimation, however, is relatively more variable, both within and between subjects. In general, as in this example, the distribution of response, as well as its relative variability, can be markedly affected by minor aspects of task and procedure. Task validity is more important than power, of course, but the power problem deserves due consideration.

Your task–procedure is a transformation from a response complex in the organism to a typically one-dimensional observable measure. Different task–procedures may tap into the same response complex to yield different observable response measures, as with rating and magnitude estimation. The experimental task is a tool that the investigator tries to shape in desired directions. The most important shaping criterion is to avoid confounding, but reliability and power are also important criteria.

9. Reduce Extreme Scores. Extreme scores decrease power because they increase the error variance disproportionately. Although the value of reducing extreme scores has already appeared in points 1, 6, and 8, this issue deserves emphasis because of its great importance.

The most important defense against extreme scores is through empirical procedures that make the task clear and meaningful to the subjects. A second defense is through screening out likely extreme subjects or through a shift to repeated measures design. Still a third defense is with the trimming procedure of Section 12.1, which seems promising.

4.3.5 PLAN YOUR DATA ANALYSIS BEFOREHAND

Why do statisticians so frequently admonish empirical research workers to plan their analysis *before collecting the data*? Why not wait to see how the data come out? It's often hard to think beforehand about exactly what analyses will be needed. With the data at hand, the problem becomes more concrete and real.

Why Plan? The most important reason for planning is to reduce oversight. An extreme but actual case is the investigator who got so carried away with his experimental treatment for autistic children that he simply overlooked the need for a control group. A more common outcome is a realization that your planned controls do not rule out certain plausible confounds or alternative interpretations. An ounce of forethought can save that pound of regret.

A second reason for planning is to estimate power, that is, the likelihood of a positive result. As noted earlier, a preliminary calculation showing inadequate power gives the opportunity to improve your plan by increasing power, thereby avoiding costs of a wasted experiment. A power calculation can be cheap insurance, but it requires explicit statement of what hypotheses are to be tested.[a]

A common refrain of consulting statisticians is that their main function is often simply to get investigators to be explicit about what they seek to find out. Relative to that, they say, the statistical contribution is often less important. This statement may reflect experience in such areas as medicine and education. Experimental psychologists are usually clear about what they are after. Surprisingly many, however, do not make preliminary power calculations.

Investigators typically take considerable care in planning their experiment. These plans consider what experimental treatments to study, especially which ones allow discriminative tests between competing theories, what procedure to use, what response variable to measure, and what confounds to avoid. The fruit of all this effort lies in the data analysis; it deserves no less planning.

How To Plan. One way to plan is to hypothesize two sets of results, one ideal, the other containing likely problematic or nonideal outcomes. Make up a set of condition means, together with a plausible error variance. Calculate Anova for these hypothetical results to see if they support the interpretation you favor.

Something of this kind is necessary for a power calculation. It also helps avoid oversight, of course, and it sharpens your intuitive feel for good design.

Another way to plan is through pilot work. This yields real data, not colored by enthusiasm and hope. More important, it puts the investigator in direct contact with the behavior, an invaluable guide to planning.

If You Don't Plan, Replicate. Planning to replicate can be an agreeable way to plan. Available knowledge may be too meager to allow reasonable guesses about the outcome, either because the task is new or because the experiment is complex. In such cases, a set of real data to work over can provide a concrete, realistic framework for planning a replication experiment.

Planning should not be overdone. Much cannot be foreseen. Plans that work out as expected may reflect great insight—or that nothing new is being learned.

NOTES

4.1.1a. The advantages of confidence intervals over standard t and F tests have been noted by many (e.g., Cochran & Cox, 1957, p. 5). In psychology, Grant (1962), Cohen (1988), Loftus (1993), and Reichardt and Gollob (1997), among many others, have been strong advocates of confidence intervals.

4.1.1b. With unequal n, the confidence interval for the difference between two independent means is

$$\bar{Y}_1 - \bar{Y}_2 \ \pm \ t^* \sqrt{\mathrm{MS}_{\mathrm{within}} \left[1/n_1 + 1/n_2 \right]}. \tag{6}$$

Note that the square root term is the standard deviation of the mean difference. You can check that this expression reduces to Expression 1a when $n_1 = n_2$.

4.1.3a. A seeming peculiarity of the significance test is that an observed difference between two means may be statsig but opposite to the true difference. Rejecting H_0 only implies that the true means are not equal, not which is greater. The obvious solution is to decide direction by visual inspection. When the true difference is very close to zero, visual inspection will lead to an incorrect directional conclusion with probability very close to $\frac{1}{2}\alpha$. This has been reified as "Type III" error to distinguish it from the Type I error (false alarm) of claiming a real effect when the true effect is exactly zero. There is no way to avoid this possibility when the real effect is small.

This issue has been discussed at length by Leventhal and Huynh (1996). They argue for a directional version of the null hypothesis, but this differs little from standard practice based on visual inspection. Their main finding is that standard power calculations yield slight overestimates in selected extreme cases.

In the range view of the null hypothesis, Type I error includes Type III error as a special case. If the true effect is substantial, on the other hand, a wrong directional conclusion is improbable.

4.1.6a. A coin toss helps clarify the difference between confidence and probability. Before we toss the coin, the probability of heads is $\frac{1}{2}$. Now we toss the coin but do not look at the outcome. The outcome, however, is either heads or tails; there is no longer a chance element, which is essential to probability. In the frequentist view, our ignorance about the outcome is not probability.

But we may have 50% confidence in heads; even odds on the outcome is a fair bet. Confidence is thus a valid guide to action (see *Confidence, Probability, and Belief*, Section 19.1.2, page 607).

4.2.1a. Usually, the linear trend will be superior to the overall F. However, the numerical example in the text unduly favors the trend test because these data are perfectly linear. If the data depart substantially from linearity, the overall F might have more power, although it would be less informative (see further Sections 18.2 and 18.3).

4.2.1b. In a *contrast*, the weights must sum to zero. This can always be accomplished by subtracting the mean weight from each weight; the pattern remains unchanged. The weights for the linear trend example would thus be $-1.5, -.5, +.5, +1.5$, obtained by subtracting the mean of 2.5 from the listed values, 1, 2, 3, 4 (Section 18.2).

4.2.1c. This pragmatic argument is supported by Anova with more than two groups, for which one-tailed tests do not exist. Consistency requires the same effective α with three groups as with two and this requires using $\frac{1}{2}\alpha$ with one-tailed tests.

Several articles on pros and cons of one-tailed tests are reprinted in Kirk (1972). Those against the practice are clearly apprehensive that one-tailed tests weaken the effective α level, but none seem clear about the pragmatic ground of the two-tailed test.

4.3.1a. A handy approximate power formula—*16* s-*squared over* d-*squared*—may be worth memorizing. To get power of .80 at $\alpha = .05$ for two groups requires approximate group sizes of

$$n = 16s^2/d^2, \tag{7}$$

where $s^2 = MS_{within}$, and $d = \mu_1 - \mu_2$ is the hypothesized difference between the means (Lehr, 1992). A similar formula is given by Dallal (1992).

4.3.1b. Detailed, practical statistical analyses of bias in power guessestimates and the importance of confidence bounds are given by Taylor and Muller (1995, 1996) and Muller and Pasour (1997), who also cite software available by e-mail.

4.3.3a. Extensive treatment of power is given by Cohen (1977, 1988), who has been zealous in urging the importance of power. In particular, Cohen has emphasized the power problem considered under *"Inconsistencies" in the Literature* (page 103). An easier source is Kraemer and Thiemann (1987).

Cohen (1962) also argued that much psychological research is woefully deficient in power, but his argument was a non sequitur. Mulaik, Raju, and Harshman (1997, p. 83) point out that Cohen did not actually estimate power for the experiments he surveyed; all may have had ample power (see Note 18.1.2b).

4.3.3b. Two arguments for using .80 as the desirable level of power were presented by Cohen (1977, 1988). The first argument is that power values of .90 and higher would require impracticably large samples for most current research in social–personality fields. This argument may have some merit, but it could equally well imply that most such research is hardly worth doing and that new tasks and methods should be developed to get greater power.

Cohen's second argument is that .80 power at $\alpha = .05$ yields a miss to false alarm ratio of .20 to .05, or 4 to 1, and that this 4 to 1 ratio accords with the feeling that a false alarm is four times as serious as a miss. By this reasoning, a false alarm 12 times as serious as a miss would justify a power of .40, which seems upside down.

4.3.5a. A related reason for planning is that tests suggested by the data are tainted by chance. If you run four groups, it might seem attractive to test the two with the biggest difference. This difference, however, has 20% chance of being statsig when all true means are equal. Post hoc tests are often in order, but planned tests provide much stronger evidence.

EXERCISES FOR CHAPTER 4

1. In what way does the significance test of the difference between two means deal with the following questions? (After Freedman, Pisani, & Purves, 1998.)

    a. Was the experiment well designed?

    b. What is the substantive meaning of the result?

    c. Is the difference important?

    d. What is the size of the difference?

    e. Is the difference due to chance?

2. a. In what ways could a very large effect fail to be statsig?

    b. In what ways could a very small effect be statsig?

    c. In what ways could an unimportant effect be highly statsig?

3. Exercise 1 of Chapter 3 considers three groups of scores:

        group 1 $\{3, 4, 5\}$; group 2 $\{5, 6, 7\}$; group 3 $\{6, 7, 8\}$.

    a. Get the error bar for group 2 using information from the given exercise and assuming an overall Anova. Does this error bar indicate a statsig difference between groups 2 and 3?

    b. Graph the data including error bars with each mean.

    c. Get 95% confidence interval for a single mean.

    d. Get the 95% confidence interval for the difference between every pair of means. What inferences may be drawn from these confidence intervals?

    e. The foregoing data were obtained in a physiological study of emotional arousal by Q, who gave higher levels of a stressor to the higher-numbered groups. Q argued that the difference between groups 2 and 3 was real. What was her argument?

4. Anova between an experimental and a control group yields F just a trifle greater than F^*.

    a. Where does 0 lie with respect to the confidence interval about the difference between the two means?

    b. Consider the confidence interval for the mean of the experimental group taken alone. Where does the control mean lie with respect to this interval?

5. What are the differences between a real effect and a statistically significant effect? Be precise.

6. An article claims a statsig difference between two means on the ground that "$\bar{Y}_1$ was statsig greater than 0, whereas $\bar{Y}_2$ was actually negative."

    a. Use confidence intervals to show the error in this reasoning.

   b. Conceptually, what confusion is embodied in the given claim?

7. Higher power implies: 1. Greater likelihood of a statsig result. 2. More reliable means. 3. Narrower confidence intervals. 4. Greater likelihood that H_0 is false.

   a. Are any of these four answers correct?

   b. Which do you consider the best answer?

8. For the experiment you are presently planning, what experimental procedures can you use to decrease error variability?

9. Every sample contains some truth about the population mean as well as some error. How does the confidence interval quantify truth and error conjointly?

10. Uncle Norman's **Golden Marble Test**.

"In my office," says Uncle Norman, "I have an urn with 19 *lead* marbles, one of **gold**. For a modest fee, I will test your null hypothesis by drawing one marble at random." The decision rule is:

> **Gold** marble: Reject H_0.
>
> *Lead* marble: Do not reject H_0.

"The beauty of my test," exclaims Uncle Norman, "is that it maintains α at .05—regardless of the shape of your distribution! No assumption of normality or equal variance is needed!"

   a. Does Uncle Norman's test really maintain α at .05 regardless?

   b. What else is wonderful about Uncle Norman's Golden Marble Test!!

   c. In terms of the 2 × 2 decision table of Figure 2.2, what is *statistically* inadequate about Uncle Norman's test?

   d. Explain the fatal statistical flaw in Uncle Norman's Golden Marble Test in terms of the two curves of Figure 4.1.

   e. What is the moral of this exercise?

11. *A statsig result may not be too reliable.* In an experiment with two groups of 32 subjects, $\bar{Y}_1 = 3.02$, $\bar{Y}_2 = 1.00$, $MS_{error} = 16$.

   a. Show that 0 is just outside the 95% confidence interval, a statsig result.

   b. Show that power of an exact replication is near .50, not even close to .95.

   c. Perhaps the result of (b) is peculiar to this numerical example. Manufacture another yourself, with smaller n and different error variance. Set $\bar{Y}_1 = 1$, and choose $\bar{Y}_2$ so that $t = t^*$. Then calculate power of exact replication.

12. In the numerical example of power for minimum effect size:

   a. Show that $\alpha_1 = -3$, $\alpha_2 = 3$.   b. Verify that $\phi = \sqrt{n}/4$.

13. You are planning an experiment and wonder how many subjects to use. Your guesses about the true means of your four experimental conditions are 4, 6, 9, and 15. Your guess about the error variance is 100.

    a. Calculate power for $n = 9$ and $n = 16$ at $\alpha = .05$.

    b. What n do you need to get power of .90?   c. Repeat (a) for $\alpha = .01$.

NOTE. Power calculations require visual interpretation of closely spaced lines in the power charts, which is not easy. My answers are only approximate, but accuracy is not critical since the power calculations yield only guesstimates for a proposed experiment, not used as a published result.

14. The lead article in *Sex Roles* (1992, Vol. 37) concluded about a hypothesized result: "These differences were not statistically significant because the sample size was too small." Comment.

15. A journal article reports a statsig Anova for four groups of 12 subjects, with means of 1, 5, 7, and 8, with $F = 3.86 > F^* = 2.84$.

    a. Find the error half-bar for a single mean.

    b. Find the 95% confidence interval for a difference between two means.

    c. Which of the six possible two-mean comparisons would have 0 outside of the confidence interval for their difference?

    d. Find power of an exact replication, taking the given sample data as population values.

    e. What qualification on the results of this power calculation are indicated by the outcome of (c).

    f. Suppose A was a metric variable, with increasing levels for the four groups in the order listed. What could be added to the conclusion of (c)?

16. (After Tversky & Kahneman, 1971.) One of your students has performed a difficult, time consuming surgical experiment with 20 rats, with numerous physiological measures. Although her results are generally inconclusive, one before–after comparison yields a $t = 2.70$, which is highly significant. This result is surprising and could be of major significance.

    Considering the large number of statistical tests, you recommend replication. Your student replicates with another 20 rats. The result is in the same direction, although the t of 1.21 falls short of the criterial value of 2.09. Discuss the appropriateness of each of the following courses of action.

    a. Your student should combine the data of the two experiments and publish the result as showing acceptable standards of evidence.

    b. She should report the two experiments separately in the same paper, presenting the second as a replication of the first, and treating the combined results as showing acceptable standards of evidence.

    c. She should run another group of (how many?) animals.

d. She should try to explain the difference between the two experiments.

e. What alternative course of action would you suggest?

17. Intuitively, what will happen to the "H_0 true" curve in Figure 4.1 if:

a. the treatment effect is increased?   b. error variance is decreased?

c. sample size is increased?

18. Intuitively, what will happen to the "H_0 false" curve in Figure 4.1 if

a. the treatment effect is increased?   b. error variance is decreased?

c. sample size is increased?

19. You are TA in an honors course on research method. One of your student teams finds in their course experiment that the confidence interval for $\bar{Y}_1 - \bar{Y}_2$ excludes 0. "Therefore," they write, "we can be 95% confident that an exact replication of this experiment would yield a confidence interval that also excluded 0."

a. How does Section 4.1.6 disagree with them?

b. How do power considerations relate to this?

20. P and Q conduct parallel experiments, both of which involve the same real effect, and both of which have power of .7.

a. What is the probability their significance tests will be "inconsistent."

b. Why is this not as bad as it sounds?

21. Statistics has many uses in industry. Here we consider a simple example from *Mathematical Methods in Reliability Engineering* (Roberts, 1964), in which you must purchase a certain part from one of two vendors. The parts fail after a time, so you wish to select the vendor who manufactures the most reliable parts. In your tests, you find that 9 parts from vendor A have a mean life of 42 hours with a standard deviation of 7.48 hours; 4 parts from vendor B have a mean life of 50 hours and a standard deviation of 6.48 hours. Assume price and other considerations are equal. (With thanks to Jaynes, 1976.)

a. In principle, what should you do?

b. Roberts says you should use a *t* test, and adds:

> If, at this juncture, you are tempted to say, without further ado, "I shall choose B. His product exhibits a longer mean life with somewhat less scatter in the data," I can only suggest that you turn back to the beginning of this chapter and start over; or perhaps statistics is not for you!

What do you say to Roberts?

22. What factors will change β without changing α?

23. Q had a keen hypothesis that pain could be reduced by distracting attention.

She measured the time subjects would keep their hand immersed in ice water until it became "too painful." A voice-actuated computer game, rock music, and a no-distraction control were tested. Her experimental procedure was impeccable, but the results were not statsig ($\alpha = .05$).

Nothing daunted, Q tried again, thinking she just had not used the right distraction conditions. She did more pilot work, talked with the subjects to understand their phenomenology of pain, and worked up a new set of distraction conditions that seemed more effective. Still not statsig.

"Third time's the charm," said persevering Q. Sure enough, her third experiment got a statsig result. "I knew my hypothesis was true," cried Q, "I just had to find the right distraction conditions!"

  a. Why do the first two failures taint the success of the third experiment?

  b. Statistically, why is Q's effective $\alpha \geq .1426$?

  c. What should Q do now?

  d. What is one moral of this exercise for journal policy?

24. Referring to α escalation, one prominent text states "When the number of [null] hypothesis tests increases, so does the probability of a Type I error [= false alarm]" (pp. 177, 169). Explain to these authors their conceptual error.

25. Verify the text statement that the means 2, 4, 1, 3 show zero linear trend.

26. In the next to last paragraph on page 100, justify the assertion that "For this purpose, a familywise α seems essential."

27. Some proportion of random samples from a normal distribution will yield confidence intervals that do not contain the population mean. Can this proportion be decreased by

  a. Increasing n?   b. Decreasing MS_{error}?   c. Increasing real effect?

28. Yes or no: The miss rate β should not be made as small as possible.

29. Why is the 95%/99% preferable to the 99%/95% confidence interval? Why cannot this dilemma be resolved by choosing a compromise confidence level of, say, 97.5%?

30. Verify the "visual rule of thumb" in Section 4.1.2.

31. You teach the undergraduate honors course in research method, in which you explain that a statsig result is unlikely if there is no real effect. You notice, however, that many of your students mistake this to mean that a statsig result implies a real effect is likely. How do you handle this?

PREFACE

Multiple determination is a central problem in every science. The effect of any one variable may depend on context and situation, that is, on what other variables are operative. Many experiments seek to isolate and study single variables. To understand perception, thought, and action, however, requires analysis of how multiple variables act in concert.

Factorial design provides a systematic approach to multiple determination. Although factorial design seems prosaic, it turns out to have important advantages, illustrated with the P–Q comparison of Figure 5.1. Factorial design, accordingly, has become a mainstay of experimental analysis.

A conceptual discontinuity is involved in the shift from a single variable, studied in previous chapters, to two (or more) variables, taken up in this and following chapters. This discontinuity stems from the necessity to make some assumption about the joint, integrated action of the two variables.

Analysis of variance bridges this discontinuity in a crude but often useful way. Its main assumption is that the two variables add; any difference between this additivity assumption and the actual data is handled by the brutal, Procrustean method of calling the difference a residual and including it in the Anova model. There is thus an ad hoc residual for every combination of the two variables, that is, for every cell of the factorial design. Sometimes these residuals, also called interactions, are meaningful, but more often they are not. This troublesome issue is broached in the discussion of Figure 5.4 but is mainly deferred to Chapter 7.

Virtually all material of the previous chapters on one-way design transfers directly to factorial design. This includes formulas for SSs, MSs, and Fs, confidence intervals, and power. Novel, however, is the concept of *factorial graph*, which facilitates visual inspection as illustrated in Figure 5.3.

Chapter 5

FACTORIAL DESIGN

Multiple determination is an axiom of life sciences. Behavior cannot be understood in terms of single variables. The classic Experimental–Control paradigm, basic though it is, misses the importance of multiple determination.

A conceptual discontinuity occurs between one and two variables. With two variables, some assumption about their integrated action becomes necessary. Each separate variable may have its own effects, but the observed response depends on their joint action. Each may modify the other's effects, moreover, so possible *inter*actions must be allowed. To extend experimental analysis to multiple determination thus requires new ideas. Such new ideas appear with factorial design.

5.1 TWO–FACTOR DESIGN

5.1.1 LOGIC OF FACTORIAL DESIGN

Scientific Method. *Factorial design*, developed extensively by R. A. Fisher in conjunction with analysis of variance, represented a fundamental advance in scientific method. Factorial design has become a basic tool for experimental analysis of multiple determination.

Previously, as Fisher observed, exposition of scientific method had emphasized the rule of varying just one variable at a time. This rule seemed sensible because it ensured that any effect would have an unambiguous causal interpretation. As a consequence, however, multiple determination was typically studied in unsystematic, often haphazard ways.

Fisher, in contrast, argued for varying two or more variables simultaneously. If only variable A is varied, variable B does not usually disappear, but remains at some fixed value. Results so obtained might not generalize to some other value of B. The A effect could even reverse itself at a second value of B, as sometimes happens.

Factorial design attacks multiple variables. Generality of the A effect can be assessed by comparing effects of A across different levels of B—and vice versa. Indeed, the factorial graph is a visual picture of the separate and integrated effects of both variables, illustrated previously in the blame experiment of Figure 1.3 and in the mother love experiment of Figure 5.2 below.

Statistical analysis revealed hidden power. This factorial approach is more cost-effective than one-variable design. Moreover, analysis of variance can help dissect the separate and integrated effects of the variables.[a, b]

Advantages of Factorial Design. Factorial design can yield more information at less cost than single variable design. To illustrate, suppose investigator P follows the rule of one variable at a time. In his first experiment, P compares levels A_1 and A_2 of variable A at some fixed level, B_1, of variable B. Wishing to assess generality of this result, P runs a replication experiment comparing A_1 and A_2 at some other fixed level, B_2. This pair of experiments is diagramed at the left side of Figure 5.1.

Investigator Q runs exactly the same four conditions, but all in a single experiment. Her design is diagramed at the right of Figure 5.1. It might seem that P and Q have done equivalent work. In fact, Q's design is triply superior.

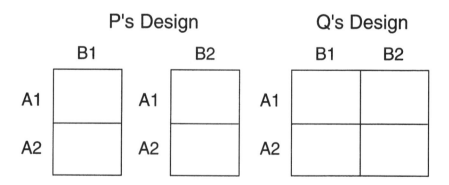

Figure 5.1. Two one-way designs and one two-way design.

First, Q's design allows a valid comparison of the effects of B_1 and B_2. In contrast, P's design confounds B with the inevitable changes from the first to the second experiment—improvements in procedure; changes in subject population; different research assistants; shift in apparatus sensitivity; and so forth. In P's design, any real effect of B is inextricably entangled with such uncontrolled variables. Very possibly this confounding is not serious—but this is uncertain. Q avoids this danger by varying both variables simultaneously.

Furthermore, P's confounding also clouds the generality of the observed results for variable A: Does A have similar effects at each level of B? Q can test this directly; P has a problem. To see the problem with P's design, suppose A had opposite effects in his two experiments. This would be a striking result, but P could not be sure whether it was caused by variable B or by some confounded variable, such as listed in the previous paragraph. P might object, claiming that there was no particular reason to suspect such confounding. His argument is not unreasonable, but it does not escape the confounding. Even if A showed similar effects in both experiments, this similarity might itself result from known and unknown differences between the two experiments. Q's design avoids this confounding; it allows a straightforward causal interpretation.

Finally, Q's design is more efficient. To illustrate, suppose P runs 20 subjects in each condition, whereas Q runs only 10. To compare the two levels of A, however, Q may average across the two levels of B to obtain an effective n of 20 for each mean—the same as for each of P's experiments. P obtains some advantage from his replication, it is true, but this is clouded by the confounding already discussed. In short, Q gets more information at less cost.

To this, Q may add that if P wanted to assess the generality of the A effect, he should have replicated her 2×2 design twice, once under the conditions of each of his two successive experiments—with ns of 10. This would be better in every way.

This three-point comparison illustrates why factorial design is one of the great inventions. Fisher went much further, however, to provide a general method of analysis for factorial data.

Factorial Design and Factorial Graph. A two-factor design may be represented as a row–column matrix, in which the rows represent the levels of variable A and the columns represent the levels of variable B. Each cell of the matrix thus represents one treatment combination, denoted A_jB_k for cell jk in row j, column k. A design with a rows and b columns is called an $a \times b$ design. Thus, Q's design in Figure 5.1 is a 2×2 design.

A 3×4 design is shown in Figure 5.2. The left half shows the *factorial data table*. The three rows correspond to the three levels of variable A; the four columns correspond to the four levels of variable B. There are thus $3 \times 4 = 12$ experimental treatments; each is a combination of one level of A and one of B. The entry in cell jk is the mean of n responses to treatment combination A_jB_k.

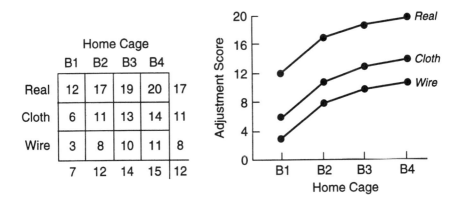

Figure 5.2. Factorial data table and factorial graph for 3×4 design.

To make this concrete, imagine that the A variable corresponds to the three kinds of mothers (wire, cloth, and real) in Harlow's experiments with infant monkeys. The four columns represent different types of home cage rearing conditions, varied in physical and social stimulation. The data represent social adjustment of the monkeys after they have grown to adolescence. For the sake of this illustration, suppose we are so fortunate as to have 24 infant monkeys to assign to the 12 experimental conditions.

The *factorial graph* is shown at the right of Figure 5.2. The column treatments, B_k, may be spaced on the horizontal axis in any convenient way, usually with equal spacing, as in this example. The vertical axis represents the response measure. Each entry in the first row of the design is plotted above the corresponding column stimulus, and these points are connected to form a data curve for row 1. This process is repeated so that each row of data forms a separate curve.

The factorial graph is thus a direct transcription of the factorial data table.

5.1.2 ANOVA MODEL FOR TWO-FACTOR DESIGN

With two variables, the primary consideration is how they are integrated to produce the observed response. The standard statistical assumption is that the two variables have mainly additive effects.

Idea of Factorial Analysis. The main concern in factorial analysis is usually with the effects of each variable separately. In the factorial table of Figure 5.2, the top row may be considered a one-way design, with B varied across four levels, and A held fixed at level A_1. These four cell entries show a steady increase in home cage effect, with an indication of diminishing returns.

The second row of the table replicates the first row, except that A is now held fixed at level A_2. Similarly for the third row. This factorial pattern of replication reveals how well the effects of B generalize across different levels of A.

The *main effects* of B are the column means, listed at the bottom margin of the table. The main effects of A, similarly, are the row means, listed at the right margin of the table. These two main effects have main importance.

In fact, each main effect corresponds to a one-factor design. Both could be analyzed with the methods of Chapter 3. To analyze the main effect of A, ignore the B variable and treat the data as three groups of eight infant monkeys, each group representing a different mother condition. To assess the main effect of B, ignore A and treat the data as four groups of six infants, each raised in one home cage condition. This would yield two F ratios, each testing the null hypothesis for one variable.[a]

One major question remains. Does the effect of B depend on the level of A? The main effects just considered are blind and deaf to this question—because each variable has been averaged over the other.

To answer this question, we compare the pattern of data between different rows. Since each row of data corresponds to one curve in the factorial graph of Figure 5.2, this graph gives a straightforward visual answer. The three row curves are parallel; all three curves show the identical pattern of observable effect. Hence the main effect of B also has the same pattern, for it is just the average of the three rows.

The parallelism also means that A and B have additive effects. Comparison of the two lower curves shows that a cloth mother is 3 points better than a wire mother in each column. It is as though cloth adds 3 adjustment points— regardless of home cage environment.

The parallelism–additivity pattern illustrated in these hypothetical data cannot generally be expected. In any actual experiment, the effect of A may depend on the level of B, perhaps in a way that requires qualification of the main effect of A. Even the main effects may be obscured by error variability. Analysis of the data thus requires the Anova model, to which we now turn.

Conceptual Anova Model. Conceptually, the Anova model begins in the simplest way. The response to the treatment combination in any cell is represented as a sum of row and column effects:

$$\text{cell mean} = \text{row effect} + \text{column effect.}$$

Of course, this additive rule will rarely give a perfect fit to the cell means. Deviations from additivity are handled by the Procrustean method of including a *residual* in each and every cell. In words,

$$\text{cell mean} = \text{row effect} + \text{column effect} + \text{residual.}$$

The row and column effects give the best fit of an additive, row + column model to the cell means. The residuals, as their name implies, are just what is left over. Since each cell has its own residual, the model fits perfectly—for every set of data. This achievement, of course, shows that the Anova model is purely statistical, not generally a model of substantive process.

The model must also represent the variability of the individual responses in each cell. This is done exactly as in Chapter 3. In words,

individual response = cell mean + error.

These word equations define the conceptual character of the Anova model.

Population Model. To put the conceptual Anova model into algebraic form involves a bar–dot notation: An overbar signifies an average over rows and/or columns; a dot subscript signifies which variable has been averaged over. Let μ_{jk} denote the cell mean in cell jk, that is, in row j, column k. Then $\bar{\mu}_{j.}$ denotes the mean of all the μ_{jk} in row j, averaged across columns. Accordingly, $\bar{\mu}_{j.}$ is called the *row mean* for row j. Similarly, the *column mean* $\bar{\mu}_{.k}$ is the mean of all the μ_{jk} in column k, averaged down rows. The overall mean is the average of all the μ_{jk}, denoted $\bar{\mu}$, the two dot subscripts being omitted. Finally, Y_{ijk} denotes the response for individual i in cell jk, and ε_{ijk} represents the "error."

With this notation, the last word equation may be written

$$Y_{ijk} = \mu_{jk} + \varepsilon_{ijk}.$$

Incorporating the second word equation yields the full Anova model:

$$
\begin{aligned}
Y_{ijk} &= \bar{\mu} && \text{(overall mean)} \\
&+ (\bar{\mu}_{j.} - \bar{\mu}) + (\bar{\mu}_{.k} - \bar{\mu}) && \text{(row + column)} \\
&+ (\mu_{jk} - \bar{\mu}_{j.} - \bar{\mu}_{.k} + \bar{\mu}) && \text{(residual)} \\
&+ \varepsilon_{ijk}. && \text{(error)}
\end{aligned}
\tag{1a}
$$

You can check this last equation by showing that the μ terms all cancel except for μ_{jk}. The reason for writing the model in this tautological form is that each term on the right has a meaning and function.

Additivity. The heart of the Anova model lies in the second line of Equation 1a. This is the sum of the row and column effects. These are *relative effects*, expressed as deviations from the overall mean.

To illustrate, suppose that all row treatments had identical effects. Then the row means $\bar{\mu}_{j.}$ would all be equal to one another, and hence all equal to $\bar{\mu}$. Hence all $(\bar{\mu}_{j.} - \bar{\mu})$ would be zero. Nonzero relative effects thus represent real differences in effects of different row treatments. Similarly, nonzero $(\bar{\mu}_{.k} - \bar{\mu})$ represent real differences between effects of different column treatments.

The Anova model arbitrarily forces this additive, row-plus-column representation onto the data. This is useful because experience has shown that the integrated effects of two variables can usually be approximated as a sum of their separate effects. The substantive integration process may itself be additive, as in Figure 5.3 (page 131). On the other hand, the additive representation will misrepresent the data in some cases (see left panel of Figure 5.4, page 134).

Residual. The third line of Equation 1a gives the *residuals*, one for each cell. Each residual is the deviation of the cell mean from the additive, row-plus-column model. That is, the residual in each cell is just what is left over after the row and column effects have been subtracted from the cell mean:

cell residual = cell mean − overall mean − row effect − column effect;

$$\text{cell residual} = \mu_{jk} - \bar{\mu} - (\bar{\mu}_{j.} - \bar{\mu}) - (\bar{\mu}_{.k} - \bar{\mu}).$$

This cell residual, as may be seen, equals the third line of Equation 1a.

Error. The error terms in the last line of Equation 1a represent the variability in the data. With independent groups design, all subjects in cell jk receive the same experimental treatment. Hence the individual differences among their responses is a measure of chance variability. Just as with the one-way designs of Chapter 3, therefore, these error terms serve as the yardstick for assessing whether the treatments produce real effects.

The error term will be denoted with the subscript *error* instead of the subscript *within* used in previous chapters. The *within* subscript was used to emphasize that the error yardstick consisted of individual differences within a group of subjects treated alike. The concept of error variability is more general, however, so this shift in terms is introduced at this point.

Deviation Scores. Each line of Equation 1a can be considered a *deviation score*. Accordingly, Equation 1a may be rewritten in the more compact form

$$Y_{ijk} = \bar{\mu} + \alpha_j + \beta_k + (\alpha\beta)_{jk} + \varepsilon_{ijk}. \tag{1b}$$

$$\alpha_j = (\bar{\mu}_{j.} - \bar{\mu}),$$

$$\beta_k = (\bar{\mu}_{.k} - \bar{\mu}),$$

$$(\alpha\beta)_{jk} = (\mu_{jk} - \bar{\mu}_{j.} - \bar{\mu}_{.k} + \bar{\mu}),$$

$$\varepsilon_{ijk} = Y_{ijk} - \mu_{jk}.$$

The row deviations, α_j, sum to zero, exactly as with the one-way design of Chapter 3. Similarly for the column deviations, β_k. The symbol $(\alpha\beta)_{jk}$ is a mnemonic for the cell residual, and does not imply multiplication of α and β. These cell residuals also sum to zero, in each row and in each column.

The *raison d'être* of the Anova model appears in these deviation scores. This point was foreshadowed in the previous discussion of the relative effects of variable *A*, now abbreviated as α_j. If every level of *A* had the same effect, all α_j would be zero. The α_j thus measure real effects of *A*, much as in Chapter 3.

The β_k, similarly, measure real effects of variable B. These α_j and β_k are the *main effects* in the model for the population.

The residuals $(\alpha\beta)_{jk}$ are also deviation scores, but they differ in kind from main effects. These residuals are also called nonadditivities because they represent the deviations from the additive, row + column model. Sometimes they are useful warnings about possible lack of generality of main effects.

The ε_{ijk} are a third kind of deviation score. They represent variability, whereas the first two kinds represent treatment effects. The Anova model puts variability to good use as a yardstick for real effects.

Sample Model. The population model of Equation 1a is a conceptual framework for representing each score as a sum of effects. For data analysis, this idealized population model must be transposed to the sample domain. To do this, replace the population parameters in Equation 1a by sample estimates:

$$
\begin{aligned}
Y_{ijk} \; &= \; \overline{Y} &&\text{(overall mean)} \\
&+ (\overline{Y}_{j.} - \overline{Y}) + (\overline{Y}_{.k} - \overline{Y}) &&\text{(row + column)} \\
&+ (\overline{Y}_{jk} - \overline{Y}_{j.} - \overline{Y}_{.k} + \overline{Y}) &&\text{(residual)} \\
&+ (Y_{ijk} - \overline{Y}_{jk}). &&\text{(error)} \qquad (2a)
\end{aligned}
$$

This sample model has the more compact form, parallel to Equation 1b, of

$$Y_{ijk} = \hat{\mu} + \hat{\alpha}_j + \hat{\beta}_k + (\hat{\alpha\beta})_{jk} + \hat{e}_{ijk}, \qquad (2b)$$

where the "hat" denotes a sample estimate. In this hat notation, $\hat{\alpha}_j = (\overline{Y}_{j.} - \overline{Y})$, and so forth. These sample estimates are our clues about real effects.

5.1.3 ANOVA FORMULAS FOR TWO-FACTOR DESIGN

The analysis of variance rests squarely on the foregoing Anova model. Each term on the right of Equation 2a has a specific meaning in the data analysis because each term is a deviation score that represents one effect.

Thus, $(\overline{Y}_{j.} - \overline{Y})$ denotes the deviation of the sample mean of row j from the overall mean. It estimates the relative effect, $(\overline{\mu}_{j.} - \overline{\mu})$, in the population. Large values of $(\overline{Y}_{j.} - \overline{Y})$ in the sample argue for a real effect in the population.

The question is whether these sample deviations are "large enough" to be considered definite evidence for real effects.

To answer this question, proceed in the same way as with one-way design in Chapter 3. Square and sum each set of deviations to get a sum of squares (SS). Convert each SS into a mean square (MS) and thence to an F ratio. Each F tests for some specified effect. That's it in a nutshell; details follow.

Sums of Squares. Each SS is a sum of *squared deviations*:

$$SS_A = nb \sum_{j=1}^{a} (\bar{Y}_{j.} - \bar{Y})^2. \tag{3a}$$

$$SS_B = na \sum_{k=1}^{b} (\bar{Y}_{.k} - \bar{Y})^2. \tag{3b}$$

$$SS_{AB} = n \sum_{j=1}^{a} \sum_{k=1}^{b} (\bar{Y}_{jk} - \bar{Y}_{j.} - \bar{Y}_{.k} + \bar{Y})^2. \tag{3ab}$$

$$SS_{error} = \sum_{i=1}^{n} \sum_{j=1}^{a} \sum_{k=1}^{b} (Y_{ijk} - \bar{Y}_{jk})^2. \tag{3e}$$

Each SS represents one term in the Anova model of Equation 1b, as shown by the deviation scores. Thus, the deviations $(\bar{Y}_{j.} - \bar{Y})$ in Equation 3a are sample estimates of the α_j, the relative effects of A. Similarly, the deviations in Equations 3b and 3ab are estimates of the β_k and the $(\alpha\beta)_{jk}$, respectively.

Each SS has a meaning. SS_A represents the differences among the A means, exactly as with one-way design in Chapter 3. Similarly for SS_B. These SSs represent the main effects of the two experimental manipulations.

Can the cell means be represented simply by adding the effects of A and B? Or does the effect of A depend on the level of B? This question is addressed by SS_{AB}, which consists of the deviations from additivity.

Are these SSs large enough to be considered real? To answer this question, they must be compared with chance, that is, with error variability. This error variability is given by the deviation scores in Equation 3e—these are the differences between subjects treated alike. Hence they represent error variability, just as with one-way design.

These comparisons yield the F ratios, obtained in the next two steps.

Mean Squares. To get the MSs, divide each SS by its df.

$$MS_A = SS_A/(a-1). \tag{4a}$$

$$MS_B = SS_B/(b-1). \tag{4b}$$

$$MS_{AB} = SS_{AB}/(a-1)(b-1). \tag{4ab}$$

$$MS_{error} = SS_{error}/ab(n-1). \tag{4e}$$

***F* Ratios.** To get F ratios, divide each MS by MS_{error}.

$$F_A = MS_A/MS_{error}. \quad df = (a-1)/ab(n-1) \tag{5a}$$

$$F_B = MS_B/MS_{error}. \quad df = (b-1)/ab(n-1) \tag{5b}$$

$$F_{AB} = MS_{AB}/MS_{error}. \quad df = (a-1)(b-1)/ab(n-1) \tag{5ab}$$

Null Hypotheses. These three F ratios test the three corresponding null hypotheses.

$$H_0: \quad \bar{\mu}_{1.} = \bar{\mu}_{2.} = \ldots = \bar{\mu}_{a.}. \tag{6a}$$

$$H_0: \quad \bar{\mu}_{.1} = \bar{\mu}_{.2} = \ldots = \bar{\mu}_{.b}. \tag{6b}$$

$$H_0: \quad \mu_{jk} = \bar{\mu}_{j.} + \bar{\mu}_{.k} - \bar{\mu}, \quad \text{for all } j \text{ and } k. \tag{6ab}$$

These null hypotheses may be written more compactly in deviation form.

$$H_0: \quad \alpha_j = 0 \quad \text{for all } j. \tag{7a}$$

$$H_0: \quad \beta_k = 0 \quad \text{for all } k. \tag{7b}$$

$$H_0: \quad (\alpha\beta)_{jk} = 0 \quad \text{for all } j \text{ and } k. \tag{7ab}$$

All this calculation is done by computer. You need to understand what the computer is doing, however, to interpret its output. This problem of interpretation is deferred to Section 5.2.

Three Rules for Degrees of Freedom. Three universal rules govern the df associated with each MS in Equations 4 and each F ratio in Equations 5.[a]

(1) For any main effect, the df equals the number of levels minus one.

(2) For any residual, the df equals the product of the df for the corresponding main effects.

(3) For the error term, the df equals the total number of scores minus the number of treatment conditions.

Use these rules to check your computer printout. The likelihood of error is not in the computer, but in what you tell it to do. A 3×4 design, for example, may mistakenly be entered as a 4×3 design. Journal reviewers use such checks on articles submitted for publication.

These rules follow the rationale of Chapter 3 that each df represents one unit of information. Although A has a levels, the relative effects α_j contain only $(a - 1)$ units of information; if we know $(a - 1)$ of the α_j, we can calculate the last one because the α_j sum to zero. Hence the last α_j carries no new information. The relative effects of A thus constitute $a - 1$ units of information, so A has $a - 1$ df.

Similarly, B has $(b - 1)$ df. Straightforward extension of this rationale shows that the AB residual has $(a - 1)(b - 1)$ df.

The rule for error df also follows the rationale of Chapter 3. In each cell, the error is determined by the deviation scores in that cell. If we know $(n - 1)$ of these deviation scores, we can calculate the last one, again because the deviation scores sum to zero. Each cell thus yields $n - 1$ df for error. Pooling over all ab cells yields $ab \times (n - 1)$ df, which verifies the third rule.

Overall Mean. The overall mean, $\overline{Y}$, in Equation 2a allows a test of the null hypothesis that the overall mean $\overline{\mu}$ is 0. This test may be of interest if Y is a difference score. In fact,

$$SS_{mean} = nab\,\overline{Y}^2. \tag{3m}$$

This SS_{error} has 1 df, so $SS_{mean} = MS_{mean}$; dividing by MS_{error} yields F_{mean}. This F tests the null hypothesis

$$H_0 : \overline{\mu} = 0. \tag{7m}$$

Unless this test has substantive interest, it is omitted from the Anova table.[b]

The overall mean falls into the same pattern as the other terms of the Anova model. Indeed, the overall mean may also be considered as a deviation score, namely, a deviation from zero. With the inclusion of F_{mean}, the df for all the systematic sources (rows, columns, residuals, and overall mean) add up to ab, the number of cell means in the design. All the information units have been used up; the pattern of the Anova model is complete.[c]

Hand Calculation for Two-Way Design. Equations 3 are unfriendly for hand calculation. Deviations scores are used in these equations because they are conceptually meaningful. They lead to decimal numbers, however, which slow the calculation and potentiate errors. Simpler, more efficient formulas are given in the appendix, in case you need them. To illustrate these hand calculations, the appendix also includes a numerical example.

5.1.4 STATISTICAL CONSIDERATIONS

Assumptions. The discussion of statistical assumptions for one-way designs (pages 68-75) applies without change to designs with two or more factors. The scores in each cell are assumed to be an independent random sample from some population, all these populations being normal with equal variance but possibly unequal means. The overall F, as indicated in Chapter 3, is robust against nonnormal distribution and, with equal n, against unequal variance.

Unequal variance can be a problem mainly in two cases. First, using the overall MS_{error} for two-mean comparisons and other follow-up tests involves the dangers illustrated with Table 4.1 (page 97). Instead, it may be necessary to use the MS_{error} estimated from just those groups used in the test. Second, very unequal natural variability may occur with subject variables, with different ages of children, for example, or different types of aphasia. Even the overall F is not robust against extremely unequal variances (see further Section 12.5).

The assumption of equal n in all the foregoing equations deserves comment. Although one-way Anova with unequal n is straightforward, factorial Anova with unequal n has a peculiar complication. Avoid this complication if you can get equal n. If not, consult Section 15.4.

Expected Mean Squares. The common sense of the F ratio may be seen by looking at the expected values of the four mean squares of Equations 4:

$$E(\text{MS}_A) = \sigma_\varepsilon^2 + [bn/(a-1)] \sum \alpha_j^2 ; \qquad (8a)$$

$$E(\text{MS}_B) = \sigma_\varepsilon^2 + [an/(b-1)] \sum \beta_k^2 ; \qquad (8b)$$

$$E(\text{MS}_{AB}) = \sigma_\varepsilon^2 + [n/(a-1)(b-1)] \sum (\alpha\beta)_{jk}^2 ; \qquad (8ab)$$

$$E(\text{MS}_{\text{error}}) = \sigma_\varepsilon^2 . \qquad (8e)$$

For each of the first three sources in Equations 8, the second term on the right is greater than 0 to the extent that there are real effects, that is, to the extent that the corresponding null hypothesis is false. If all α_j are zero, for example, MS_A and MS_{error} have equal expected value. Hence F_A will tend to be near 1 when H_0 is true, larger than 1 when H_0 is false. Similar statements hold for the other two systematic sources.[a]

Normality is not required; these expected values hold regardless of the shapes of the distributions. They also hold with unequal variance but equal n. In this case, σ_ε^2 is interpreted as the mean error variance across the several groups. This means the expected value of F is practically independent of the two statistical assumptions. This independence mirrors the well-known robustness of the overall Fs of Equations 5.

5.2 INTERPRETING FACTORIAL DATA

Visual inspection has the primary role in understanding data, especially with factorial design. Although it is customary to speak of interpreting the Anova, this is misleading. What needs interpreting is the pattern in the data—in relation to the experimental design. For this, Anova has a subordinate role.

The primacy of visual inspection tends to be passed over, in part because it is often taken for granted, in part because formal statistics has greater salience. In part also, visual inspection typically rests on substantive knowledge that eludes formal statistics.

5.2.1 FACTORIAL STRUCTURE

The row × column structure of factorial design is well suited to visual analysis. This factorial structure represents a constructive form of replication that can help assess both reliability and generality of treatment effects.

Generality and Reliability. The pattern in the factorial table/graph is a direct picture of the effects of the experimental variables. Each row represents effects of the column variable, B; these effects are exhibited as one curve in the graph. A flat curve thus represents zero effect of the column variable.

Row and column are treated symmetrically in the table. In the graph, however, row effects appear as vertical separations between the row curves. This visual representation of row and column effects was illustrated with Figure 5.2.

At the same time, the table/graph helps assess generality of the row and column effects. In Figure 5.2, each row represents a one-way design for the column variable, with a fixed level of the row variable. The shape of this row curve thus shows effects of B. Similar shape of two row curves is visual evidence for generality—that the column variable has similar effects regardless of the level of the row variable. The row factor in the design thus provides replication for the column variable. And vice versa. This twofold form of replication is a notable property of factorial design.[a]

Furthermore, the factorial graph can often give a visual indication of reliability. This stems from the replication property just noted. If the several row curves show similar pattern with little irregularity, it may provisionally be concluded that error variability is small. Much irregularity, although it may reflect lack of generality, suggests large error variability. This visual indication of error variability often shows the essential results, as illustrated next.

Psychophysical Illusion.   The usefulness of visual inspection with factorial graphs is illustrated in Figure 5.3, an experiment on the size–weight illusion. Subjects lifted cylinders of varied gram weight, listed as curve parameter, and varied height, listed on the horizontal axis. They judged felt heaviness of each cylinder on a 1–20 scale.

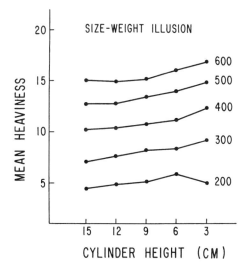

Figure 5.3. Parallelism supports addition rule: Heaviness = Size + Weight. Subjects judge heaviness of cylinders varied in gram weight (curve parameter) and cylinder height (horizontal axis). (After N. H. Anderson, *Methods of Information Integration Theory*, Academic Press, 1982.)

The factorial graph shows the mean heaviness judgments for the $5 \times 5 = 25$ weight–size combinations. The pattern in the graph represents the separate effects of the two variables as well as their joint, integrated effect.

The illusory effect of the size variable is clear in the upward trend of the top curve. All five points represent a 600-g cylinder, but smaller cylinders feel heavier. The height variable shows diminishing returns, as shown by the left-ward flattening of the curve.

Very similar patterning appears in each other curve. Hence the illusory effect depends on height alone, regardless of gram weight. The parallelism of these curves supports the hypothesis that the two variables are integrated by an additive process: felt heaviness = size + gram weight.[b]

This additive rule argues against the once-favored density interpretation, namely, that the illusory effect appears because subjects really judge density, not heaviness. Since density depends on the ratio, weight ÷ size, the density hypothesis implies nonadditivity.

Visual inspection shows one deviant point at the lower right. Two inter-related visual cues lead to recognizing this deviance. First, this point departs considerably from the prevailing pattern of parallelism. Second, all the other points show small deviations from parallelism, which serves as a visual measure of error variability.

The deviant point in Figure 5.3 underscores the usefulness of visual inspection with factorial design. These data show less variability than is usual, but they demonstrate how the factorial graph can sometimes furnish a visual index of error variability. Often, just looking at the factorial graph gives the best understanding of the data.

This experiment, it may be added, illustrates a tool for studying consciousness. The observed response measures the conscious sensation of heaviness. This conscious sensation is an integration of two nonconscious effects: of the gram weight and of the size. By virtue of parallelism, the vertical elevations of the curves represent the pure effect of gram weight; each successive 100 g adds progressively less subjective heaviness.

In this way, the effect of size has been factored out of the conscious sensation to reveal the nonconscious effect of gram weight. In fact, a plot of the vert-ical elevations of the curves as a function of gram weight is the long-sought psychophysical function, validated by the success of the additive model. Fac-torial design thus helped resolve the classical problem of measuring sensation, nonconscious and conscious (Section 21.2, *Functional Measurement Theory*).

Visual Inspection and Anova. Anova is an important supplement to visual inspection. Trends that seem clear to the investigator may be questionable to the reader. The investigator's visual inspection may be unduly influenced by hope and desire or suffer perceptual bias.[c]

Moreover, Anova goes beyond visual inspection to use within cell information, thereby obtaining a much superior measure of variability. This allows construction of confidence intervals, a further aid to visual inspection. Such statistical aid is more needed with smaller designs. In a 2×2 factorial graph, in particular, visual inspection of the four means can hardly assess reliability of main
effects, much less of deviations from additivity.

5.2.2 USING THE OVERALL ANOVA

A two-way design is a union of two one-way designs, one for A, one for B. All
discussion of the previous two chapters thus transfers directly to the main effects
in factorial designs. The residuals, however, present a new problem, namely,
the problem of describing integrated action of two variables. Statistics attacks
this problem by imposing an additive model; the residuals are what is left over.

Main Effects. Statsig F_B is evidence for real differences between the column
means, that is, evidence that the column treatments had different effects.
Interpretation of F_B is almost the same as for one-factor designs in Chapter 3.
In fact, if A is ignored, the design reduces to a one-factor design. If MS_B is calculated for this one-factor design using Equations 5 of Chapter 3, it will be
identical with the MS_B calculated for two-factor design using Equation 3b
above. The discussion of localizing a statsig F in Chapters 3 and 4 thus applies
directly to localizing main effects in factorial design.

An important complication arises with two-factor design. The main effects
of B are *averages* over the A variable. This may be seen in Equation 3b, which
assesses the deviations among the column means, $\overline{Y}_{.k}$. These column means are
averaged down the rows; the column means are the mean row. The pattern in
the mean row may differ from that in the individual rows; it will differ unless
the row curves are parallel. The main effect of B may thus misrepresent the
basic cell means. The same holds for A.

Main effects should not be taken at face value, therefore, without visual
inspection of the complete factorial data pattern. This inspection can be aided
by the test of F_{AB} on the residuals.

Residuals. F_{AB} for the residuals helps assess generality of main effects. Given
a main effect of A, the question is whether this effect holds uniformly for all
levels of B.

To answer this question, look at the pattern in the factorial graph. Parallelism of the row curves means that B has the same observable effect at every level
of A; nonparallelism means that B has different observable effects at different
levels of A.

Parallelism also means that the residuals are zero. Since F_{AB} is calculated
from the residuals, parallelism means that F_{AB} is zero. F_{AB} is thus a test of
parallelism and hence a test of generality of main effects. Statsig F_{AB} implies

real nonparallelism and hence that B has different effects at different levels of A. Caution is then needed in assessing generality.

Unfortunately, F_{AB} has limited usefulness. It may fail to be statsig from low power, especially because it is a global, overall test, not sensitive to specific trend, such as fanning of the row curves. On the other hand, it may be statsig, yet require little qualification of the main effects. To understand what F_{AB} means in any particular case, it is necessary to look at the factorial graph or table. This important matter is illustrated next.

Interpreting Residuals. In Figure 5.4, each panel gives the factorial graph for a 2×2 design. All three panels exhibit effects of both variables—together with a substantial deviation from parallelism. The question is whether and how this nonparallelism requires qualification of the main effects.

To begin, we show that the residuals are identical in all three panels in Figure 5.4. One row curve is the same in all three panels; the other row curve is shifted up or down by a constant. This vertical shift changes only the main effect of A; the amount of nonparallelism stays the same. Since the residuals represent deviations from parallelism, all three panels have identical residuals. Hence F_{AB} for residuals will be identical in all three cases.

Each graph, however, requires a different interpretation. The left panel shows a crossover, which requires severe qualification of the main effects. In fact, A has zero main effect; the two row means, which correspond to the middle points on the two row curves, both equal 13.5. Ignoring error variability, the null hypothesis for A is true in this case, but it is misleading: A has opposite effects at different levels of B. The main effect of A is misleading because it averages out these opposite effects. In this case, F_{AB} is a cogent warning.

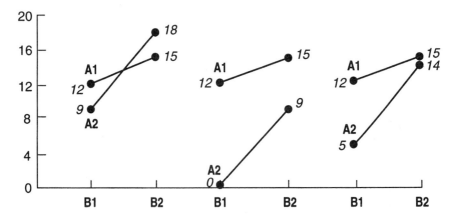

Figure 5.4. Three 2×2 graphs with identical interaction residuals.

Crossovers are not common, but they do occur. In cognitive algebra, a crossover is prized as a critical test between adding and averaging models (e.g., Figure 21.5, page 707). In applied psychology, crossovers have been conjectured when B is a subject variable. Thus, a teaching method more effective with well prepared students may be less effective with poorly prepared students. This is a practical problem for students and instructors in the first-year graduate design–statistics course because the students usually differ widely in background knowledge and aptitude. An experimental example with praise and blame for grade-schoolers is cited in Note 5.2.2a (see also Section 7.4.2).[a]

The center panel of Figure 5.4 shows a different but equally clear situation. Here A_1 is superior to A_2 at both levels of B. Unlike the left panel, little qualification of main effects is required. The amount by which A_1 is superior to A_2 does depend on B, it is true, but this will usually be unimportant. The same applies to the B variable, not only here, but also in the left panel. Although F_{AB} is exactly the same as in the left panel, it means little.

A more perplexing situation is given in the right panel. Here A_1 is superior to A_2 at both levels of B. The amount of superiority, however, is small at B_2. If this small difference is not statsig, how should it be interpreted?

One interpretation is that nothing definite should be said about the generality of A effects. Although A_1 is definitely superior to A_2 at B_1, this superiority has not been sufficiently demonstrated at B_2. On this hardline argument, the main effect would be considered misleading.

An alternative interpretation is to argue for overall superiority of A_1. The small superiority at B_2 is the best estimate of the real effect, and is consistent with the large superiority at B_2. If A_1 and A_2 represent different magnitudes of the same variable, it may be reasonable to expect the same direction of effect, regardless of the level of B.

Interactions. The foregoing residuals are generally called *interactions*. The neutral word *residual* has been adopted in this book because *interaction* carries illegitimate surplus meaning that has caused widespread misunderstanding. Many texts state that main effects are not meaningful when interactions are statsig. This statement is incorrect for three reasons. The first reason was shown in the center panel of Figure 5.4, in which the interaction residual was large, but no qualification of main effects was required: A_1 was superior to A_2 and B_2 to B_1.

Second, an interaction residual may be merely an illusion of the response scale. Third, an interaction residual may be merely an artifact of the arbitrary row-plus-column Anova model. Interactions differ qualitatively from main effects in these two basic ways, as will be discussed in Sections 7.2 and 7.3.

The term *residual* is precise. It avoids the illegitimate surplus meaning of the term *interaction*. Further discussion is deferred to Chapter 7.

Of course, an interaction residual predicted from grounded theory is welcome support for the theory. And any statsig residual is a warning to study the factorial graph. Usually, however, Anova interactions are smoke without fire.

5.2.3 CONFIDENCE INTERVALS

The discussion of confidence intervals of Section 4.1 transfers essentially unchanged to factorial design. Keep in mind, however, that confidence intervals generally have different lengths for cell, row, and column means.

Confidence Intervals. For any single mean, $\bar{Y}$, the confidence interval is

$$\bar{Y} \pm t^* \sqrt{MS_{error}/"n"}, \tag{9}$$

where t^* is the criterial value of t and "n" is the number of scores in the mean. For the difference between two means, the confidence interval is larger by $\sqrt{2}$.

The value of "n" is nb for a row mean because each row mean is the average of n scores in each of b cells. For a column mean, similarly, "n" = na. For a cell mean, of course, "n" = n. Confidence intervals for row means are thus

$$\bar{Y}_{j.} \pm t^* \sqrt{MS_{error}/nb}; \tag{10}$$

$$\bar{Y}_{j.} - \bar{Y}_{j'.} \pm \sqrt{2}\, t^* \sqrt{MS_{error}/nb}. \tag{11}$$

To get the $100(1 - \alpha)\%$ confidence interval, use the criterial t^*_α.

A bad blunder is to confuse nb and na and even n, which can produce a huge error in the confidence intervals. The uniform rule is that the divisor of MS_{error} is the number of scores in the given means. This follows from the square root law of sample size for s_{mean}, the standard deviation of the mean (Equation 2.7c).

Error Bars. An error bar is a particular confidence interval. It is obtained by setting $t^* = 1$ in the above formulas. The error bar thus has a width of $2s_{mean}$. For large samples, the error bar is the 68% confidence interval. The difference between two means must be about three half-bars to be statsig (Section 4.1.2).

Confidence intervals can be confused in two ways. One is whether they stand for a single mean or the difference between two means. The other is the level of confidence. Error bars in published graphs usually seem to be 68% confidence intervals for single means. Confidence intervals specified as such in the text, on the other hand, usually seem to be 95% confidence intervals. Good reporting requires explicit specification of what was done in each application.

Error Term. Usually, MS_{error} for confidence intervals is taken from the overall Anova. When the equal variance assumption holds, this error term is appropriate for each and every confidence interval. It uses all the data to get a more stable estimate of variability.

With unequal variance, however, each confidence interval may require an individualized error term, based only on the data from the one or two groups in question. Using the overall MS_{error} can cause serious trouble when variances differ across conditions, as previously shown in the discussion of Table 4.1 (page 97). For experimentally manipulated variables, there is not usually much reason for concern. However, subject variables such as diagnostic category of patients can show substantial differences in variance.

5.2.4 BEYOND OVERALL ANOVA

A statsig F_A implies real effects but does little to localize them. All levels of A might have different effects or only one. Usually, therefore, further analysis beyond the overall Anova is needed. Besides confidence intervals, some other techniques may help understand the data.

Visual Inspection. Visual inspection is typically more useful with factorial design than with one-way design. In many cases, it will suffice to show a statsig main effect and interpret its pattern by visual inspection. If the pattern is critical for some issue, of course, more objective assessment will often be necessary. But to belabor the obvious with a significance test reveals a slave to statistics.

Contrasts. Contrasts for main effects may be made using the procedures for one-way designs of Chapter 4. The most common contrasts are two-mean comparisons. These are most informative in the form of confidence intervals, as in Expression 11 above.

Linear trend tests on main effects may also be useful. Some computer programs include them as an option. Alternatively, and perhaps preferably, regression analysis may be applied, as noted under *Contrasts* in Section 4.2.1.

More complex contrasts among cell means have occasional uses (Section 18.2). For example, the interaction residual in a 2×2 design can be expressed as a contrast among the four means. The value of this contrast measures the deviation from parallelism (Note 7.5.1a). As another example, linear trend of the residuals may be more informative and more powerful than the overall F_{AB}.

Subdesign Anova. It is sometimes desirable to analyze a subdesign of the full factorial design. The A conditions may fall into two classes, for example, that deserve separate consideration. This may be done by splitting the full design into the two indicated subdesigns and applying Anova separately to each. An overall Anova may then be superfluous.

Subdesign Anova may be useful when A is a subject variable, such as age or patient category. Thus, a developmental study might plan one analysis for two or more younger age groups and another for two or more older ages. In both cases, the subdesign has the same factorial structure as the full design, but with fewer levels of the age variable.

Simple Effects. *Simple effects* refer to effects of a single row or single column. Simple effects thus refer to a special kind of subdesign in which only one factor is varied. To assess the simple effects of A at B_1, for example, apply the hand formulas of Section 3.2.5 to the means of the first column to obtain $SS_{A \, at \, B_1}$. Alternatively, give the data of the first column to the computer, but recompute F using MS_{error} from the overall Anova. This F tests the null hypothesis that the true means in the first column are all equal.

This simple effects approach was implicit in the foregoing discussion of interpreting residuals in Figure 5.4. The question whether the statsig residual required qualification of the main effects was addressed by looking at the simple effects of A at each level of B. With only two levels of each variable, analysis with simple effects is often useful.

On the whole, however, simple effects have limited usefulness. These limitations deserve comment since some texts present simple effects as an automatic default, to be employed instead of testing main effects when F_{AB} for residuals is statsig. The main limitation is conceptual. Simple effects refer to one-way designs; they are only indirectly related to the residuals, which are inherently a factorial, multivariable concept.[a]

Multiple Comparisons. A final means to go beyond the overall Anova is by using some technique of multiple comparisons. Multiple comparisons may be needed when a reasonably firm a priori base for planned tests is lacking, especially when α escalation from multiple tests is of concern.

Multiple comparisons has been discussed in Section 4.2.2 and more detail is given in Chapter 17. Multiple comparisons may be applied directly to the row or column means, treating them as one-way designs. For elucidating residuals, however, multiple comparisons are not very useful.

Planned Tests. Tests planned to assess specific hypotheses would usually be done instead of overall Anova. In principle, planned tests are more powerful and more informative. This tactic was illustrated with the linear trend analysis of Section 4.2.1.

5.2.5 POWER

Power for main effects in factorial designs can be calculated using the formulas for one-way designs. The main effect for A is treated as a one-way design with a levels. The formulas of Section 4.3 then apply, keeping in mind that "n" for the power index ϕ in Equation 5 of Chapter 4 is the number of scores in each A mean. Thus, "n" = bn for rows in a two-factor design.

The same approach applies to factorial designs with more than two factors, which are taken up in the next section. For a three-factor design, the "n" for the A main effect would be bcn.[a]

5.2.6 PLAN AHEAD

I recommend a dry run Anova, after the pilot work and before the experiment proper. Write down a factorial table of expected means, together with a plausible value for error variance. Do the Anova and interpret the data in relation to your conceptual framework. Two dry runs may be desirable, one with the data you hope to get, another with likely alternative data. A dry run provides opportunity to detect shortcomings easily overlooked in the optimistic enthusiasm of setting up the experiment.

Investigators often spend large amounts of time studying the literature, devising a clean task, constructing tests or apparatus, and doing pilot work to debug the procedure, but neglect a dry run or even a power calculation. The cost is small; the potential benefit is great.

There is an alternative: Plan to replicate. The initial experiment serves as a wet run for the replication, more valuable although more costly than a dry run.

5.3 THREE-FACTOR DESIGN

Studies with more than two factors are common in psychological research. In the mother love experiment of Figure 5.2, for example, an obvious third factor is the sex of the infant monkey. In the blame experiment of Figure 1.3, additional variables besides intent and damage would include reparation, such as material recompense or apology, extenuating circumstances, such as provocation, as well as age and gender of the subject children.

All ideas and procedures presented for two-factor design transfer directly to multifactor designs. The main issues of multiple determination appeared as soon as the second variable was added; no further discontinuity occurs when a third variable is added.

Three aspects of three-factor design are taken up in the next three sections. First, visual inspection increases in importance because several factorial graphs are involved, as shown in Figure 5.5 on the next page. Second, the three-factor extension of the Anova model is presented and its conceptual structure explained. This essentially repeats the treatment for two-factor design, but with one interesting complication. Third, the only formulas needed are for confidence intervals, and these are virtually the same as with two-factor design.

5.3.1 ILLUSTRATIVE THREE-FACTOR DESIGN

A design with three factors, *A*, *B*, and *C*, may be viewed as a set of two-factor, *AB* designs, one for each level of *C*. A graphic representation is useful, as with the 3 × 4 × 2 design of Figure 5.5. The left and center panels at the top show two *AB* designs, one for each level of the third variable, *C*. These two panels

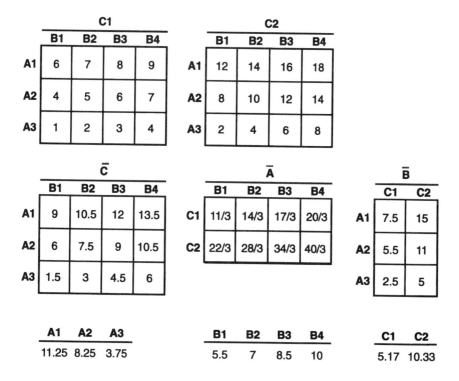

Figure 5.5. Three-factor design. Main effects in bottom layer; two-way data tables in middle layer; three-way data table in top layer.

constitute the basic design, which has $3 \times 4 \times 2 = 24$ experimental conditions. The entries in each cell are means for n subjects.

For the mother love experiment, C_1 and C_2 could denote male and female infants. For the blame experiment, C_1 and C_2 could represent two ages of children. In each of these examples, the three-factor design may be viewed as a replication of the two-factor, AB manipulation across two different subject populations. More commonly, C represents a third experimental manipulation, as with two levels of extenuation in the blame experiment.

Interpreting a three-factor design may usefully begin with visual inspection of the main effects, tabulated in the bottom layer of Figure 5.5. These have main importance in most experiments, just as with two-way designs.

The next step would usually be to inspect the patterns for the variables taken two at a time. These two-factor tables are shown in the middle layer of Figure 5.5. The mean AB pattern is shown in the left middle panel, in which the entries are averages over the levels of C. Similarly, the center middle panel represents the mean CB pattern and the right middle panel represents the mean AC pattern. These two-way patterns usually provide the most meaningful picture.

The data of Figure 5.5 were constructed from the algebraic model, $Y = (A + B)C$. The response in each cell of the design is thus the sum of A and B, multiplied by C. Because A and B are additive, the data should exhibit parallelism when averaged over C. Just such parallelism can be seen in the left middle panel. This reflects the parallelism in the two separate AB panels in the top layer for the complete three-factor design.

In contrast, the CB table in the center middle panel shows a linear fan. This mirrors the multiplication operation of the model used to generate these data; the entries in the second row are twice those in the first row. A linear fan pattern also appears in the AC table.

Figure 5.5 illustrates one standard procedure for interpreting three-factor experiments. With real data, of course, the real patterns will be obscured by error variability. Often, therefore, visual inspection needs to be supplemented by analysis of variance. To this end, the Anova model for three-factor design is considered briefly.

5.3.2 ANOVA MODEL FOR THREE-FACTOR DESIGN

Analysis of variance for three-factor design rests on the additivity assumption already employed for two-factor design. The Anova model begins by finding the best fit to the cell means using a sum of the three main effects. All deviations from this additive model are represented by including residuals.

The main complication in going from two-way to three-way design is that additivity has three facets, for it applies separately to each pair of variables. This was seen in Figure 5.5, in which additivity held for A and B, but not for A and C, nor for B and C. Accordingly, there is a separate, independent set of residuals for each pair of variables. This threefold additivity is the main concern of the following discussion.

Let Y_{ijkm} denote the score of the ith subject in cell jkm of the design. All n subjects in this cell receive the same treatment, (A_j, B_k, C_m). In terms of deviation scores, the Anova model for the population is

$$
\begin{aligned}
Y_{ijkm} \;=\; & \bar{\mu} && \text{(overall mean)} \\
& + \; \alpha_j + \beta_k + \gamma_m && \text{(main effects)} \\
& + \; (\alpha\beta)_{jk} + (\alpha\gamma)_{jm} + (\beta\gamma)_{km} && \text{(two--way residuals)} \\
& + \; (\alpha\beta\gamma)_{jkm} && \text{(three--way residual)} \\
& + \; \varepsilon_{ijkm}. && \text{(error variability)} && (12)
\end{aligned}
$$

The main effects in the second line of Equation 12 are the marginal means in deviation form. For example, $\alpha_j = (\bar{\mu}_{j..} - \bar{\mu})$ denotes the relative effect of level j of variable A. This is the same as with two-way design, except that two other variables must be averaged over, not just one. This double averaging is indicated by the double dot subscript. The other two main effects are defined similarly. Except for this double averaging, main effects have the same character as with two-factor design.

The AB residuals in the third line of Equation 12 have the same character as the AB residuals for two-way design. The only difference is that they apply to the two-way table of means averaged over the third variable, C. Thus,

$$(\alpha\beta)_{jk} = \bar{\mu}_{jk.} - \bar{\mu}_{j..} - \bar{\mu}_{.k.} + \bar{\mu}.$$

These residuals represent deviations from two-factor additivity. If any pair of variables has additive effects, their residuals will all be zero.

Three-factor design actually yields three sets of two-way residuals, one for each pair of factors. All have similar character, being deviations from additivity. Thus, nonzero AC residuals will appear graphically as nonparallelism in the AC data table. This point may be seen in Figure 5.5. Here A and B have additive effects, and the two-way, $A \times B$ table is indeed parallel. The other two-way data tables exhibit nonparallelism because C does not add to but multiplies with A and also with B.

Deviations from additivity may, or may not, require qualification of the main effects. This issue has already been discussed with Figure 5.4, and that discussion applies also to two-way residuals with three-factor design. Thus, the nonzero AC residuals in Figure 5.5 require little qualification of the main effects of A or C: A_1 is uniformly superior to A_2, and A_2 to A_3; similarly, C_2 is uniformly superior to C_1. The amount by which C_2 is superior to C_1 depends on the level of B, it is true, but such dependence usually has minor interest.

A novel feature of three-factor design is the three-way residual, in the fourth line of the model equation. Up to this point, the model has represented each cell mean as a sum: three main effects plus three two-way residuals. The three-way residuals represent what is left over in each cell.

Some experimental studies of cognitive algebra are designed to produce specified patterns of residuals. In the data of Figure 5.5, the algebraic structure of the model, $Y = (A + B) \times C$, implies the three-way residuals are all zero. On the other hand, the three-factor multiplication model, $Y = A \times B \times C$, implies a fanning pattern in every factorial graph. In cognitive algebra, as these examples illustrate, three-way residuals serve a theoretical diagnostic function. Analogous predictions of specific patterns of three-way interactions occasionally appear throughout psychology.

But often, if not typically, three-way residuals lack meaning. Some reasons are the same as already given with two-way residuals. A further complication will be given in the more extensive discussion of Chapter 7.

5.3.3 ANOVA FORMULAS FOR THREE-FACTOR DESIGN

The population model of the previous section is basic to understanding what Anova is up to with three-factor design. Calculational formulas are not presented here as this is done by computer. For most purposes, only formulas for confidence intervals are needed, and these are essentially identical to those for two-way design.

Confidence Intervals. Confidence intervals follow the rule illustrated previously with one- and two-factor design (Sections 4.1 and 5.2.3). The general formula for a single mean is

$$\bar{Y} \pm t^* \sqrt{MS_{error}/"n"}. \tag{13}$$

Three-factor design yields three levels of means. A cell mean, at the lowest level, is based on n scores, whereas a row mean, at the highest level, is based on nbc scores. A mean based on more scores is more reliable, of course, so it has a shorter confidence interval. Thus, we have

$$\bar{Y}_{111} \pm t^* \sqrt{MS_{error}/n} \, ;$$

$$\bar{Y}_{11.} \pm t^* \sqrt{MS_{error}/nc} \, ;$$

$$\bar{Y}_{1..} \pm t^* \sqrt{MS_{error}/nbc} \, .$$

For a difference between two means, both based on $"n"$ scores, the confidence interval is $\sqrt{2}$ times larger than for a single mean:

$$(mean_1 - mean_2) \pm \sqrt{2} \, t^* \sqrt{MS_{error}/"n"}. \tag{14}$$

With equal variance, MS_{error} in the foregoing formulas would be taken as the error term from the overall Anova (see *Error Term* in Section 5.2.3).

Degrees of Freedom. A valuable check on your computer output is with degrees of freedom. The df follow exactly the same three rules listed with two-way design. By rule 2, the AB residual has $(a - 1)(b - 1)$ df, regardless of how many other variables are in the design. By the same rule, the ABC residual has $(a - 1)(b - 1)(c - 1)$ df.

The df for all systematic sources, mean included, should add up to the number of cells in the design. These rules apply equally to designs with more than three factors. They are useful, not to say advisable, as a check that you have instructed the computer properly.

5.3.4 MORE THAN THREE FACTORS: PARTIAL ANALYSIS

Multiple factors often arise as minor task variables that need to be balanced in the experimental design. In a study of rats learning a T-maze, for example, the two arms of the T-maze, being in different spatial locations, may be confounded with ambient noise, illumination, and odors, all powerful stimulus cues to rats. Even without such external cues, some rats have strong position preferences. Standard procedure is to balance experimental conditions across the two arms of the T, thereby controlling all possible confounding factors, unknown as well as known. In effect, the two arms become an additional factor in the experimental design.

Similar balancing problems are ubiquitous. Two or more experimenters may run the rats, more than a single T-maze may be used, and the rats may be run at different times of the day. Also the study may use successive shipments of rats, perhaps from different breeders. Since these factors may influence the results, it is desirable to balance them over experimental conditions. Even a design with just two main experimental conditions may include several minor variables that need balancing. This automatically makes them factors in the design, leading to a high-way factorial design.

High-way designs, unfortunately, introduce numerous high-way interaction residuals. Thus, a five-way design has 26 different residuals, which could be tedious to interpret. Most of them, moreover, would probably be unimportant, as with the two-way residual in the center panel of Figure 5.4.

With many high-way designs, a procedure of *partial analysis* seems appropriate: Make an a priori decision not to assess specified higher-way interaction residuals. In an extreme form of partial analysis, the Anova would include only the main effects of each variable and the low-way residuals for the primary experimental variables. A five-factor design with two primary and three minor variables would thus have five main effects but only one residual to consider, not 26. The interpretation of the data is thereby much simplified.

Justification for partial analysis is given in Section 18.4.3. Here it may be noted that many investigators carefully balance minor variables without realizing they are thereby using a factorial design. Having balanced a minor variable, it seems generally desirable to assess its main effect. Partial analysis does this without suffering under numerous interaction residuals of dubious meaning.

NOTES

5.1.1a. The development of factorial design is principally due to pioneering work in the 1920s by R. A. Fisher (1960, pp. 93-94):

> In expositions of the scientific use of experimentation it is frequent to find an excessive stress laid on the importance of varying the essential conditions *only one at a time*. . . . to study the effects of this single factor, is the essentially scientific approach to an experimental investigation. This ideal doctrine seems to be more nearly related to expositions of elementary physical theory than to laboratory practice in any branch of research. . . .
> The modifications possible to any complicated apparatus, machine or industrial process must always be considered as potentially interacting with one another, and must be judged by the probable effects of such interactions. If they have to be tested one at a time this is not because to do so is an ideal scientific procedure, but because to test them simultaneously would sometimes be too troublesome, or too costly. In many instances, as will be shown in this chapter, the belief that this is so has little foundation. Indeed, in a wide class of cases an experimental investigation, at the same time as it is made more comprehensive [by including multiple determinants], may also be made more efficient . . . [so that] . . . more knowledge and a higher degree of precision are obtainable by the same number of observations.

Seventy years later, however, we read:

> One-factor-at-a-time experiments and similar "common sense" design strategies continue to be prevalent in industrial experiments in spite of the strong emphasis in statistics courses that these design strategies should be avoided. In justifying the avoidance of such design strategies, technical criteria such as design efficiency and confounding . . . routinely are overlooked by experimenters in industry. (Gunst & McDonald, 1996, p. 44.)

Actually, factorial design may be considered an ideal form of varying one variable at a time. Each row in a two-factor, $A \times B$ design varies only B, for one fixed level of A. Each additional row is thus a systematic replication of the B effect, but at a different level of A. From this perspective, factorial design conjoins the rule of one-variable-at-a-time with the principle of replication.

5.1.1b. Three distinct concepts are usually conglomerated under factorial design. One is the design itself, a rectangular matrix illustrated in Figure 5.2, which possesses advantages in estimation and generalization of main effects. Second is the Anova model of Equation 1a, which provides a conceptual model of multiple determination. Third is the analysis of variance, a flexible tool for detecting trends in the data.

5.1.2a. Treating main effects as one-way designs yields correct values of SS_A and SS_B. The error term from these analyses, however, would be inflated because it includes SS_{AB}. The two-way Anova excludes SS_{AB} and so yields correct MS_{error}.

5.1.3a. The term *degrees of freedom* comes from a geometric representation of the data in N-dimensional space. Each observation corresponds to one dimension in this space, and hence to one spatial degree of freedom. To some statisticians, this geometric representation is a helpful way of thinking. Fisher could visualize his theorems in this way, so he often did not bother to give a formal algebraic proof, distressing statisticians who lacked this geometric facility.

5.1.3b. To test the null hypothesis that the overall mean equals any constant, C, use $SS_{mean} = nab\,(\bar{Y} - C)^2$.

5.1.3c. For publication, the SS column, being redundant, is omitted. The source labeled *Mean* is also omitted unless it has empirical interest, as with difference scores. The letters denoting sources are generally replaced by mnemonic names that specify the empirical nature of the source. When only a few F ratios need to be explicitly cited, these may be included in the running text, the complete Anova table itself being omitted. Of course, the article should ordinarily give the means, in tabular or graphic form, together with measures of error variability.

5.1.4a. Because the expected value of a ratio does not equal the ratio of the expected values, the expected value of F when the null hypothesis is true differs from 1. This peculiarity of mean ratios is important for ratio scores with a variable denominator.

An example comes from a once popular theory that claimed that tasks begun but not completed set up a tension that caused them to be remembered better than completed tasks. In some early studies, the response measure was the number of incompleted tasks recalled divided by the number of completed tasks recalled. The investigators thought they had demonstrated their hypothesis by showing that the mean ratio exceeded 1. Unfortunately, this will happen even when there is no real difference between the two types of tasks. Under this null hypothesis, each ratio of 4 to 2, say, will be matched by a ratio of 2 to 4. The mean of 4/2 and 2/4 is not 1, but 1.25. This ratio bias will show an effect where there is none. Difference scores yield a valid test.

5.2.1a. A subtle conceptual issue is hidden behind statements that parallelism in the factorial graph implies generality—that A adds the same amount regardless of the level of B. This assumes an outcome view, in which the observable response is taken at face value. In this outcome view, parallelism is prima facie generality. In a process view, the matter is very different. In a process view, in fact, parallelism may imply lack of generality, a measurement issue deferred until Chapter 7.

5.2.1b. Properly speaking, this additive equation for felt heaviness refers to the subjective values of the physical levels of size and gram weight (see Chapter 21).

5.2.1c. Visual inspection of factorial graphs can suffer from the illusion of nonparallelism shown in Figure 5.6. The lines are parallel but appear closer together toward the right; the perception of interline distance is influenced not only by vertical separation, but also by perpendicular distance between the curves. It is sometimes necessary, therefore, to measure the vertical separation between curves with a millimeter rule.

5.2.2a. Blame and praise are prominent social reinforcers, still an open field of opportunities for experimental analysis. A classroom study of 124 fifth-grade children by Thompson and Hunnicut (1944) illustrates opposite reinforcer effects depending on personality. The teacher gave each child a sheet of paper filled with rows of digits. On signal, the children crossed out all instances of a specified digit as fast as they could for 30 s. Then the teacher toured the class, writing P for poor or G for good on each child's paper. This was repeated for six trials, on the last of which all children were marked G.

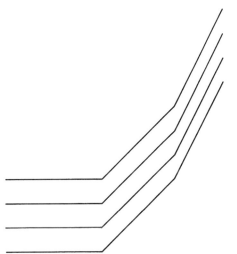

Figure 5.6. Illusion of nonparallelism. (From N. H. Anderson, *Methods of Information Integration Theory*, p. 50. Academic Press, 1982.)

Reinforcement was independent of actual performance. The P and G children had been specified beforehand and got the same treatment every trial. The P children were thus blamed no matter how hard they tried (perhaps a fitting preparation for life, which dispenses overplus of blame and is niggardly with praise).

Praise and blame had virtually equal effects, both substantially greater than a control class that received no verbal feedback. In addition, the children had been classified as introverts or extroverts on a personality test. These two personality groups, however, had nearly equal mean scores.

These two main effects seem simple and straightforward. But they concealed a large crossover in the factorial graph: For introverts, praise was better than blame; for extroverts, blame was better than praise. The data of the previous paragraph were the marginal means of the 2 × 2 design, which severely misrepresented the data.

This example illustrates the potential value of factorial design. Also, it illustrates the potential value of incorporating individual differences into the experimental design—and the potential danger of not doing so.

5.2.4a. A practical limitation of simple effects is lower power, since they are based on only a fraction of the data. In a 4 × 4 design, for example, simple effects are based on only 1/4 of the data.

5.2.5a. Power for F_{AB}, the test of the residuals, uses the power effect size formula

$$\sigma_{AB} = \sqrt{\sum\sum(\alpha\beta)^2_{jk}/[(a-1)(b-1)+1]}. \qquad (15)$$

The rest of the calculation follows Equation 5 of Chapter 4. Power for the overall residual may be useful in 2 × 2 and other small designs. For larger designs, it would usually be more pertinent to assess power for contrasts or other specified patterns of residuals.

APPENDIX: HAND CALCULATION FOR FACTORIAL DESIGN

This appendix presents hand formulas for two-way factorial design, together with a numerical example, These hand formulas are sometimes useful in follow-up analyses of published articles. Reading an article that gives some main effect F, for example, you may wish to make a specific two-mean comparison using a confidence interval. The two means are given, but not the error term. To reconstruct the error term, compute SS_A from the A means in the article using Equation 16a below. Thence get MS_{error} using Equation 5a (e.g., Exercises 8 and 18). Of course, the following formulas can also be used to do Anova by hand from your own raw data.

Hand Formulas for SSs for Two-Way Design.

$$SS_{mean} = nab\,\bar{Y}^2; \tag{16m}$$

$$SS_A = nb\sum_{j=1}^{a}\bar{Y}_{j.}^2 - SS_{mean}; \tag{16a}$$

$$SS_B = na\sum_{k=1}^{b}\bar{Y}_{.k}^2 - SS_{mean}; \tag{16b}$$

$$SS_{AB} = n\sum_{j=1}^{a}\sum_{k=1}^{b}\bar{Y}_{jk}^2 - SS_{mean} - SS_A - SS_B; \tag{16ab}$$

$$SS_{error} = \sum_{i=1}^{n}\sum_{j=1}^{a}\sum_{k=1}^{b}Y_{ijk}^2 - SS_{mean} - SS_A - SS_B - SS_{AB}. \tag{16e}$$

Numerical Example for 2×3 Design. The above formulas follow a uniform schema, simple once understood. To illustrate, consider the following 2×3 design, with $n = 2$ subjects per cell. Bold face numbers are marginal means.

0, 2	1, 3	4, 6	**2.667**
3, 5	4, 6	7, 9	**5.667**
2.5	**3.5**	**6.5**	**4.167**

The first step is to get the SSs. From Equation 16m,

$$SS_{mean} = 2\times2\times3\times4.167^2$$
$$= 208.367.$$

From Equation 16a,

$$SS_A = 2 \times 3 [2.667^2 + 5.667^2] - SS_{mean}$$
$$= 235.367 - 208.367$$
$$= 27.000.$$

From Equation 16b,

$$SS_B = 2 \times 2 [2.5^2 + 3.5^2 + 6.5^2] - SS_{mean}$$
$$= 243.000 - 208.367$$
$$= 34.633.$$

From Equation 16ab,

$$SS_{AB} = 2 [1^2 + 2^2 + 5^2 + 4^2 + 5^2 + 8^2] - SS_{mean} - SS_A - SS_B$$
$$= 270 - 208.367 - 27.000 - 34.633$$
$$= .000.$$

By Equation 16e, the first step in obtaining SS_{error} is to square and sum the individual scores. This sum of squares equals 282. From this, subtract the four lower-order SSs already calculated. This yields

$$SS_{error} = 12.000.$$

This SS_{error} has 6 df, one for each cell in the design.
Divide each SS by its df to obtain the MSs:

$$MS_{mean} = 208.367;$$
$$MS_A = 27.000;$$
$$MS_B = 17.316;$$
$$MS_{AB} = .000;$$
$$MS_{error} = 2.000.$$

Finally, divide the mean squares for the four systematic sources by the error mean square to get the F ratios:

$$F_{mean} = 208.36; \quad df = 1/6.$$
$$F_A = 13.50; \quad df = 1/6.$$
$$F_B = 8.66; \quad df = 2/6.$$
$$F_{AB} = .00; \quad df = 2/6.$$

From Table A5, $F^*(1, 6) = 5.99$ and $F^*(2, 6) = 5.14$. Both main effects are thus statsig, but not the residual. That $SS_{AB} = 0$ could be foreseen because the two rows of data differ by 2 in each column, being graphically parallel.

The 95% confidence intervals for the difference between two means have length ± 2.00 for rows and ± 2.45 for columns. Thus, A_1 differs from A_2, B_3 differs from B_2 and B_1, while the difference between B_2 and B_1 is uncertain.

Learn the Schema, Not the Formulas. The SSs in Equations 16 obey a uniform schema:

> Square and sum the means for the effect in question.
> Multiply by the number of scores in each mean.
> Subtract lower-order SSs.

By incorporating this schema into your knowledge system, you will not need to rely unduly on the written formulas, for they merely embody the schema. This is the same schema as in Section 3.2.5.

More on the Hand Formulas. Four other aspects of Equations 16 also have some conceptual interest. First, Equation 16e may be rewritten

$$\sum_{i=1}^{n}\sum_{j=1}^{a}\sum_{k=1}^{b} Y_{ijk}^2 = SS_{mean} + SS_A + SS_B + SS_{AB} + SS_{error}.$$

The left side is the sum of all squared scores; the five components of this sum on the right side are meaningful in terms of the experimental design. Thus, the total Sum of Squares on the left side is broken down—analyzed—into the five meaningful components. Analysis of variance is really analysis of Sums of Squares.

Second, Equations 16a and 3a both yield SS_A but with a different subtraction. Subtracting the mean $\overline{Y}$ from each score in Equation 3a is equivalent to subtracting SS_{mean} from the sum of squared row means. This correspondence is carried to a higher level in the equations for SS_{AB} and SS_{error}.

Third, the multipliers in front of the summation signs follow the same uniform rule already seen with Equations 3. Each multiplier equals the number of scores in the means being summed. In Equation 16a, each row mean $\overline{Y}_{j.}$ is an average of nb scores (n scores in b cells), so the multiplier is nb. In Equation 16ab, each cell mean $\overline{Y}_{jk}$ is an average of the n scores in cell jk, so the multiplier is n. This rule even holds for the invisible multiplier of 1 in Equation 16e.

This multiplier rule appears because each equation is actually a triple sum, over i, j, k. This triple sum is explicit in the last equation and implicit in the others. Thus, the row means for SS_A in Equation 16a have been averaged over the column index k; hence summing over columns is equivalent to multiplication by b. Similarly, summing over the subject index i is equivalent to multiplication by n.

Fourth, Anova for factorial designs is really repeated application of Anova for one-way designs. To get SS_A, ignore B and treat the data as a groups of nb scores. This is just what Equation 16a does. To get SS_B, ignore A and treat the data as b groups of na scores, just as in Equation 16b.

Now treat the design as a one-way design, with ab groups to get SS_{total} and SS_{error}, just as in Section 3.2.5. From this, $SS_{AB} = SS_{total} - SS_A - SS_B$. This is just what Equation 16ab does.

The formulas of one-way Anova thus suffice for two-way Anova. The same applies to factorial design with three or more variables.

EXERCISES FOR CHAPTER 5

1. A two-way factorial graph can be plotted in two complementary ways: With levels of the column stimuli on the horizontal or with levels of the row stimuli on the horizontal. Although both ways are equivalent, one may be more intuitive than the other.

   a. Plot the complementary form of the factorial graph of Figure 5.2. Which do you consider more useful?

   b. Plot the complementary form of the factorial graph in the left panel of Figure 5.4. Which way do you consider more useful?

   c. Do the same as in (b) for the center panel of Figure 5.4.

   d. Compare both forms of the two-way, AB data table of Figure 5.5.

2. Piaget claimed that young children are unable to integrate two informers. Instead, they *center*, that is, they judge using only one of two given informers. Piaget considered centration to be a pervasive characteristic of cognition up to age 6 or even older. For the Intent × Damage design described in relation to Figure 1.3, draw factorial graphs, labeled appropriately, that show the following patterns of behavior:

   a. Centration on Damage.

   b. Centration on Intent.

   c. Blame = Intent + Damage.

   d. Blame = Intent × Damage.

   e. Accident-configural integration: Blame independent of amount of damage if damage is accidental; otherwise, Blame = Intent + Damage.

   f.* Centration on the larger of Intent and Damage.

3. Plot the two-way factorial graph for the following means.

2	11	6	7
7	17	10	12

   a. Relying on visual inspection, guess which sources in the Anova will be substantial, which will not.

   b. What features of your graph are clues to the variability of the data?

   c. What can Anova add to this visual inspection?

4. In the left panel of Figure 5.4, the two levels of A have quite different effects. Yet the text says "The null hypothesis for A is true in this case." What's going on?

5. For the data table of Figure 5.2:

   a. Use the hand formulas of the Appendix to this chapter to show that $SS_{rows} = 336$ and $SS_{columns} = 228$.

   b. By visual inspection, say what $SS_{residual}$ will be.

6. Do Anova for this 2×3 data table ($n = 2$) and interpret the results.

    1, 2   3, 4   5, 6

    1, 2   1, 2   1, 2

If you had a reasonably firm expectation that the observed data would turn out as shown in this table, what alternative analyses would you plan?

7. For the numerical example in the Appendix to Chapter 5:

   a. Verify the calculation using a computer.

   b. Using Expression 11, show that the 95% confidence interval for the difference between the two row means is 3 ± 2.00. Does this agree with the F test? Which, if either, is preferable?

   c. Why does the confidence interval for column means listed in the Appendix differ in length from that for row means?

   d. Show that the error bar for a cell mean is ± 1.00.

   e. How does this error bar relate to the standard deviation of a cell mean?

   f. How does this error bar relate to the standard deviation of the population of scores?

8. You need to follow up a published study with a 3×2 design that reports A means of 1, 2, 3, B means of 1.35 and 2.65, $F_A = 3.33$, $MS_{error} = 3.60$, $n = 6$.

   a. First, use the hand formulas of the Appendix to check whether $F_A = 3.33$ is consistent with the other cited figures. As a first planning step, you calculate power for main effect of A in an exact replication, taking the given data at face value.

   b. Show similarly that power for B is about .50.

   c. What do you do about your follow-up?

9. In the next to last paragraph under *Advantages of Factorial Design* in Section 5.1.1, evaluate Q's suggestion that P replicate her 2×2 design twice is "better in every way"? List Sources and df for this Anova.

10. In a survey of his work on interpersonal attraction, Aronson (1969, p. 159) presented two hypotheses derived from a rationale of anxiety reduction:

Hypothesis 1: "If a beautiful woman were to evaluate a male subject favorably, she would be liked better than a homely woman who evaluated him favorably."

Hypothesis 2: "If a beautiful woman were to evaluate him unfavorably, she would be liked *less* than a homely woman who evaluated him unfavorably."

Aronson concluded "The results confirmed our predictions: There was a significant interaction—the beautiful-positive evaluator was liked best, but the beautiful-negative evaluator was liked least" (p. 161).

These quotes refer to an experiment by Sigall and Aronson (1969), in which male subjects were told that a first-year graduate student in clinical psychology would test them as part of a department-wide program. This person was actually a personable female undergraduate, blind to the purpose of the experiment, made up to appear attractive for a random half of the male subjects, unattractive for the other half. She gave each subject the California Psychological Inventory, spent seven minutes in an alleged "examination" of the completed form, and gave the subject a favorable or unfavorable evaluation of his personality according to a predetermined schedule, regardless of his answers. She then left and the experimenter obtained the subject's responses to some questions on a -5 to $+5$ scale that were emphasized to be totally anonymous.

Mean ratings of liking for the confederate were as follows ($n = 12$).

Female	Attractive	Unattractive
Favorable	3.67	1.42
Unfavorable	1.08	1.17

For the interaction, $F(1, 44) = 7.87$.

    a. Are the two quoted hypotheses of equal interest?

    b. Does visual inspection of the data table confirm both quoted hypotheses?

    c. Does the significant interaction confirm the quoted hypotheses?

    d. How did the authors err in doing the factorial Anova?

    e. Should this experiment have been published?

10a. In the Sigall–Aronson data of the preceding exercise, show that the 95% confidence interval for Hypothesis 2 is .09 $\pm$ 1.19. What does this mean?

11. Using the three rules for degrees of freedom, show that the df for all systematic sources, including mean, add up to the total number of treatment means:

    a. for a two-way design;   b. for a three-way design.

12. a. Plot a two-way factorial graph for the following means. Relying only on visual inspection, give your judgment about which sources are substantial, which are not.

    b. What features of the figure are clues to the variability of the data?

    c. What can Anova add to this visual inspection?

7	21	36
14	23	30
19	24	26

13. You have a 2×3, $A \times B$ design with entries of 12, 18, 25 in the first row. Construct entries for the second row such that the only nonzero sources are:

    a. B.

    b. AB residual.

    c. B and AB residual.

    d. Give a verbal argument to show that it is not possible to find a second row such that only A is nonzero.

    e. Prove (d) algebraically.

14. Above Equation 3a, the text asserts each SS is a sum of squared deviations.

    a. Explain what these deviations are in Equation 3a.

    b. What is the substantive significance of these deviations?

    c. Do the same for Equation 3e.

    d.* If the factorial plot is parallel, show that all deviations in Equation 3ab are zero.

15. In the last paragraph of Section 5.2.1, justify and/or fault the statement that visual inspection of the four means in a 2×2 factorial graph "can hardly assess reliability of main effects."

16. In a 4×3 design, suppose the A values are 1, 2, 4, and 8, and the B values are 0, 1, and 3. Assume an additive model so that each cell entry equals the sum of the corresponding values of A and B.

    a. Plot the factorial graph. Prove that the curves are parallel.

    b. Do (a) with A values of α_1, α_2, α_3, α_4, and B values of β_1, β_2, β_3.

17. You are TA in the undergraduate honors class in animal behavior. In the term paper experiment, one of your students writes: "My obtained F was greater than the criterial F^* for $\alpha = .05$. Therefore, I may reject the null hypothesis and conclude that the population means are significantly different. I realize, of course, that this conclusion has a 5% chance of being wrong."
Grade this answer constructively.

18. Sometimes you need the error term from published data to get a confidence interval not presented in the article, for example, or to make a power calculation. In the numerical example in the Appendix, suppose you were given the row means, 2.667 and 5.667, each on 6 scores, together with their F of 13.50.

    a. Get MS_{error} from this given information.

    b. Estimate power for the row effect in an exact replication.

19. Construct data for a $2 \times 3 \times 2$ design with all effects zero except:

    a. A and B.   b. BC.   c. A and AB.

(It may help to sketch a factorial graph, then translate it into numbers.)

20. With $n = 2$, Figure 5.5 is based on 48 scores. Each score is one unit of information, so the total df is 48. Where do these 48 df appear in the Anova?

21. a. Make up a realistic set of data for the 2×2, praise–blame experiment of Note 5.2.2a that satisfies the indicated pattern.

    b. Introvert/extrovert was not an experimentally controlled variable in this experiment. Instead, it was a score on a personality test. Perhaps the effect is due not to personality, but to some confounding characteristic of the subjects that is correlated with the personality test. Discuss whether confounding with motor skill seems a likely explanation of these results. What data did the investigators measure, not included in the note, that would bear on this issue of alternative explanations?

22. In your experiment, based on a 3×4 design, with $n = 3$, you have an a priori theoretical hypothesis that all cells with A fixed at A_1 have equal true mean. How do you use Anova to test this?

23. In the previous exercise, you have an a priori hypothesis that all cell entries with B fixed at B_1 are zero. How do you test this?

24. For power calculations for three-factor design (Section 5.2.5) with n subjects in each cell, what are the values of "n" for the three main effects? For the AB residual?

25. People construct situation models that integrate specific information from the situation at hand with nonspecific world knowledge to use for goal-directed action in the situation. How to analyze the structure of such situation models is a central theoretical problem. With spatial situations, such mental models involve priming gradients whose structure can be studied using response times.

In the following experiment, subjects began by thoroughly memorizing a diagram of a rectangular laboratory building with 10 rooms, each containing two to four named objects. Next, they read a narrative of some 20 sentences that served to motivate the situation confronting a protagonist in the laboratory; this was followed by a motion sentence in which the protagonist moved from a *start room* to a *goal room* (e.g., "Then he walked from the storage room into the lounge"). These motion sentences required the protagonist to move through one or two unmentioned *path rooms* between the start and goal rooms.

Finally, subjects read a probe sentence that referred concretely to a memorized object in one of the one or two unmentioned path rooms through which the protagonist would have had to move to get to the goal room from the start room.

The response measure was the reading time for this probe sentence.

Previous work had established that reading time depended on the location of the object along the protagonist's path; the motion sentence induced a priming gradient such that reading time increased steadily with distance *backward* from the goal room in which the protagonist had finished his motion.

Two hypotheses about the distance gradient were tested. Under the standard *Euclidean distance hypothesis*, the distance was the actual physical distance. Under the *categorical distance hypothesis*, the distance would depend on the number of rooms, but not on the physical distance, contrary to the Euclidean hypothesis. Previous studies had confounded these two variables.

Three variables were manipulated in a 2^3 design relating to the room in which the object in the probe sentence was located. *Room size* (short, long) was expected to have an effect under the Euclidean distance hypothesis, no effect under the categorical distance hypothesis. *Room division* (divided, undivided) was expected to have an effect under the categorical distance hypothesis, no effect under the Euclidean distance hypothesis. *Near-far* referred to the Euclidean distance between the goal room and the object, which was expected to have no effect under the categorical distance hypothesis.

    a. Evaluate the two hypotheses by visual inspection of Figure 5.7.

    b. What can Anova add to this visual inspection?

26. You have a $3 \times 4 \times 2$ design, with $n = 5$.

    a. Write out Source and df for the Anova table.

    b. You have a theoretical hypothesis that all cells with A fixed at A_2 and with C fixed at C_1 have equal true means. How do you test this?

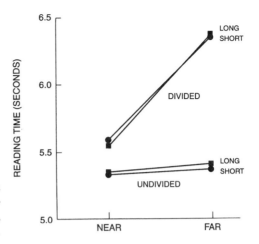

Figure 5.7. Reading times in experiment on organization of spatial mental models. (After Rinck, Hähnel, Bower, & Glowalla, 1997).

26. You have a $3 \times 4 \times 2$ design, with $n = 5$.

    a. Write out Source and df for the Anova table.

    b. You have a theoretical hypothesis that all cells with A fixed at A_2 and with C fixed at C_1 have equal true means. How do you test this?

27. This exercise has two goals. One is practice in estimating the main effects, α_j, β_k, and the residuals, $(\alpha\beta)_{jk}$, from factorial data. More important is to illustrate that the residuals may lack psychological meaning (see also Exercise 7.5).

    a. For the following 3×4 table of cell means, use visual inspection to localize the interaction residual. Assume error-free data.

1	2	3	4
3	4	5	6
6	7	8	3

    b. Use Equation 1b to show that $\alpha_j = -1.83$, .17, and 1.67, and that $\beta_k = -1.00$, .00, 1.00, and .00.

    c. Use the expression for $(\alpha\beta)_{jk}$ in Equation 1b to show that all 12 Anova residuals are nonzero. What is the moral of this demonstration?

28. In Figure 5.1, suppose A had a statsig effect in the same direction in both replications for both P and Q. They both interpret this to mean that the A effect holds for both levels of B. In what way is Q's interpretation on firmer ground?

PREFACE

Psychological process has its locus within the individual organism. Ideally, therefore, each subject would be tested under all experimental conditions. The main benefit is substantive: Comparisons across conditions are more cogent because the main effect of individual differences is factored out, not confounded with conditions, as in the independent groups designs of previous chapters. To study patterning in response, moreover, within-individual comparison may be essential.

A secondary benefit is also obtained: The error term is markedly lower, which yields shorter confidence intervals and greater power. Such *repeated measures design* is the focus of this chapter.

A complication with repeated measures design is loss of independence: Response to any two treatments is correlated across subjects. Because of this dependence, the error term used in previous chapters is no longer correct. Fortunately, the Anova model is readily extended to handle this dependence. Unfortunately, this extension is sensitive to the sphericity assumption on which it rests. Almost miraculously, a simple adjustment has been found that allows valid significance tests even when sphericity is violated.

All material of previous chapters transfers essentially unchanged to repeated measures design. The main novelty is that each analysis or comparison generally requires its own personal error term. Instead of a single error term, as in previous chapters, multiple error terms are often required. This complication is more than repaid, however, by the greater informativeness and greater power of repeated measures design.

Chapter 6

REPEATED MEASURES DESIGN

Using each subject in a number of experimental conditions has two attractions: one statistical, one substantive. The statistical attraction is that error variability is lower because subjects are their "own controls." Comparison of treatments A_1 and A_2 compares two scores from each subject. The main effect of each subject cancels in the difference, thereby freeing the comparison from the main effect of individual differences.

Using different subjects in different conditions, as in previous chapters, confounds individual differences with conditions. Although randomization resolves this confounding, it does so at the high cost of putting the individual differences in the error term. MS_{error} typically runs several times smaller in repeated measures designs. Confidence intervals are correspondingly shorter and power is greater. From this statistical standpoint, comparing the same subject across different conditions is most desirable.

More important is the substantive consideration that psychological process has its locus within the individual. Many investigations focus on the pattern of response across a set of stimuli, but this pattern may be irretrievably confounded with individual differences in response to given stimuli. To study response pattern, therefore, within individual comparison is desirable, perhaps essential.

Response pattern was the concern in the blame experiment of Figure 1.3, page 27 of Chapter 1, which showed the factorial graph of blame as a function of actor's intent to harm and amount of harm done. In this task, different individuals may show different judgment patterns (e.g., Figure 11.3, page 318). A group graph would hardly be meaningful; repeated measures is essential.

Analogous concern with response pattern is common in every area of psychology, most notably in perception, but also in diverse other areas from person cognition to operant psychology. Such response patterns are ideally studied with repeated measures.

Often, of course, there is no alternative to using different subjects in different conditions. In Harlow's mother love experiments, for example, an infant monkey nursed on a wire mother is irreversibly changed by its rearing; it cannot be recycled back to infancy to see how it would develop with a cloth mother.

Analogous irreversible changes are common in many areas, such as learning, physiological psychology, and marriage–family life, as well as in many medical experiments. This chapter, however, is mainly concerned with stable state tasks, in which the treatments do not have lasting effects (*Order Effects*, page 164).

All material of previous chapters transfers to repeated measures design virtually without change. No new concepts are needed. Moreover, the same formulas given in Chapters 2-5 apply also with repeated measures.

One major statistical complication does arise: Responses to any two treatments are correlated across subjects, and this correlation must be incorporated into the Anova. Happily, this can be accomplished with two easy variations on the Anova of previous chapters.

6.1 SUBJECTS × TREATMENTS, $S \times A$ DESIGN

This section considers a single experimental variable, A. Each subject (S) is tested at all a levels of A, with one response at each level. The data thus form a row × column, subjects × treatments ($S \times A$) factorial design.

6.1.1 ILLUSTRATIVE $S \times A$ DESIGN

Anova for the $S \times A$ design is simplicity itself. Consider the $S \times A$ design of Table 6.1, with three subjects tested at each of four treatments.

TABLE 6.1

ILLUSTRATIVE SUBJECTS × TREATMENTS, $S \times A$ DESIGN

	A_1	A_2	A_3	A_4
S_1	5	8	8	7
S_2	3	7	5	3
S_3	1	3	2	2

This is a two-way, $S \times A$ factorial table. The Anova formulas of Chapter 5 may be applied directly to obtain MSs for the three sources: S, A, and SA.

The error term for A is the SA residual, as will be shown later. Hence

$$F_A = \frac{\text{MS}_A}{\text{MS}_{SA}}. \qquad \text{df} = (a-1)/(n-1)(a-1) \qquad (1)$$

This F ratio is interpreted as in previous chapters. If F_A is statsig, the null hypothesis of equal treatment effects may be rejected. Everything is exactly the same as in Chapter 5, except for the error term in the denominator of F.

6.1.2 ANOVA MODEL FOR $S \times A$ DESIGN

The justification for the F test of Equation 1 rests on the Anova model. Let Y_{ij} be the score for subject i in condition j. Then the Anova model is

$$Y_{ij} = \bar{\mu} + S_i + \alpha_j + (S\alpha)_{ij} + \varepsilon_{ij}. \tag{2}$$

This parallels Equation 5.1b for factorial design, with β replaced by S. Here, however, the ε_{ij} represent within subject response variability.[a]

This equation reveals the advantage of repeated measures design. With two treatments, F_A tests the difference between their means. This is equivalent to a test of the difference scores for each subject, $(Y_{i1} - Y_{i2})$. From Equation 2, this difference score is

$$
\begin{aligned}
Y_{i1} - Y_{i2} &= \bar{\mu} + S_i + \alpha_1 + (S\alpha)_{i1} + \varepsilon_{i1} \\
&\quad - \bar{\mu} - S_i - \alpha_2 - (S\alpha)_{i2} - \varepsilon_{i2} \\
&= (\alpha_1 - \alpha_2) + [(S\alpha)_{i1} - (S\alpha)_{i2} + \varepsilon_{i1} - \varepsilon_{i2}].
\end{aligned}
$$

S_i has canceled out; the difference between treatment means, $(\alpha_1 - \alpha_2)$, is thus freed from the main effect of individuals. This cancellation illustrates the principle of repeated measures design. The term in brackets represents the error variability, which requires our next attention.[b]

6.1.3 ERROR VARIABILITY

The error term with repeated measures is the subject–treatment residuals, MS_{SA}. It has a different character from the error term for independent scores of previous chapters. Three aspects of this error term are considered here.

Subject–Treatment Residuals as Error. Because subjects is a factor in the design, the corresponding sum of squares, SS_S, is factored out in the Anova, thereby reducing the error. The magnitude of this error reduction can be seen in any particular case by comparing MS_S with MS_{SA}. MS_S is the main effect of individual differences; it corresponds to the error term that would be obtained if different Ss were run at each level of A. In contrast, MS_{SA}, the error term for repeated measures, is usually several times smaller than MS_S.

These two error terms can be visualized in the factorial graph of Figure 6.1. The data points are from Table 6.1; the parallel curves represent predictions from the row + column, subject + treatment model, $S + A$. There is one curve for each S; their vertical elevations correspond to the main effect of S. This main effect appears as S_i in Equation 2 and as MS_S in the Anova.

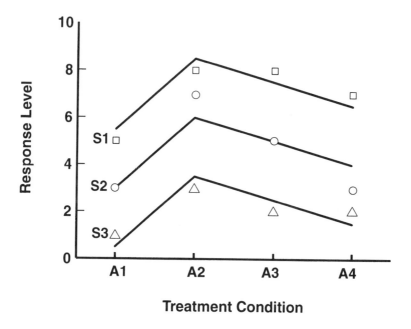

Figure 6.1. Responses of three subjects under four conditions (from Table 6.1). Parallel curves are best fits of additive model, Subjects + Treatments. Deviations between data points and line for each separate subject constitute the error term, MS_{SA}, in Equation 1.

The repeated measures error term consists of deviations between the curve and data points for each S. These deviations are the residuals from the additive, subject + treatment model. These *subject–treatment residuals*, also called subject–treatment interactions, appear as $(S\alpha)_{ij}$ in Equation 2 and as MS_{SA} in the Anova.

The key point is this: Deviations of the points from the curves in Figure 6.1 (= MS_{SA}) are much smaller than the vertical distances between the curves (= MS_S). In this example, $MS_{SA} = 2/3$ and $MS_S = 25$, respectively. The error term would thus be $25/(2/3) = 37$ times larger for an independent subjects design than for a repeated measures design. This advantage is exaggerated in these artificial data, but it is very real in practice.

The reason why MS_{SA} is the appropriate error term for A may also be seen in Figure 6.1. Suppose the residuals from the curve for each S are small. Such regularity indicates a very similar pattern of A effects for every S. Seeing such regular pattern across subjects gives confidence that it is real.

On the other hand, suppose the residuals from the curve for each S are large. This means the response to A is highly variable from one S to another. Seeing such irregularity in the A effects casts doubt on their reality. In this way, the residuals from the additive, $S + A$ model make sense as an error yardstick to assess the main effect of A.

Expected Mean Squares. The verbal rationale for the error term in the preceding subsection can be formalized with the expected values of the mean squares:

$$E(\text{MS}_{\text{mean}}) = \sigma_\varepsilon^2 + a\sigma_S^2 + na\,\bar{\mu}^2; \tag{3a}$$

$$E(\text{MS}_S) = \sigma_\varepsilon^2 + a\sigma_S^2; \tag{3b}$$

$$E(\text{MS}_A) = \sigma_\varepsilon^2 + \sigma_{SA}^2 + n\sigma_A^2; \tag{3c}$$

$$E(\text{MS}_{SA}) = \sigma_\varepsilon^2 + \sigma_{SA}^2. \tag{3d}$$

The last two MSs are the important ones. Note that their expected values differ only in the term $n\sigma_A^2$. If A has null effects, so that all $\alpha_j = 0$, then $\sigma_A^2 = 0$. In this case, MS_A and MS_{SA} both have equal expected value, so their ratio, F_A, will tend to be near 1. To the extent that the null hypothesis is false, σ_A^2 will be greater than 0, MS_A will tend to be larger than MS_{SA}, and F_A will tend to be larger than 1.[a]

A complete statistical analysis must show that the sampling distribution of F_A given by Equation 1 follows the F distribution of Chapter 3, under the null hypothesis. This involves statistical assumptions discussed at the end of this chapter. Given these assumptions, F_A may be interpreted the same way as in previous chapters.[b, c]

Replication Within Subjects. In some situations, each S can be tested under each condition more than once. Such replication provides a useful measure of response consistency within subjects. If many subjects varied considerably in their responses to the same treatment, this would raise a natural concern about shortcomings in task and procedure. Similar concern would arise if most subjects showed consistent behavior but two or three did not. Such deviance might be in the two or three subjects, of course, but it might reflect residual shortcomings in task and procedure. When practicable, therefore, replicating the design for each S seems desirable (see also Chapter 11).

Within subject replication has two additional advantages. First, comparisons between successive replications allow checks on order effects (see further *Order Effects*, next page). Second, replication facilitates single subject analysis, which can be important in following up the group analysis. Follow-up analysis of single subjects can be vital when different individuals exhibit different response patterns. Single subject follow-up analysis can also help improve task–procedure (e.g., Farkas, 1991, Note 2, p. 89).

Investigators sometimes hope that replication within subjects will substantially increase the reliability of their data. Regrettably, this is not often true. Replication would reduce the effective response variability within subjects, which is σ_ε^2 in the error term of Equation 3d. However, replication has no effect on the main component of error, namely, σ_{SA}^2, which measures individual differences in response to the same treatment. Moreover, the df for F do not increase; the test of A is made on the mean response for each S, regardless of whether this mean is based on one, two, or more scores.[d]

6.1.4 BOX'S df ADJUSTMENT

A df adjustment developed by Box (1954) is almost mandatory with repeated measures design. This adjustment compensates for violations of the statistical assumption of sphericity (see Section 6.5.1). All computations to get the F ratio remain identical. The sole difference is that numerator and denominator df are both multiplied by a fraction ε, which measures the deviation from sphericity. These reduced df are used to determine F^* in standard statistical packages (see Section 6.5.2). No adjustment is needed with 1 df tests.

6.1.5 ORDER EFFECTS

The most serious problem with repeated measures design is empirical, not statistical. If two treatments are given each subject, one treatment must come second. The first may influence the response to the second through warmup, practice, learning, interference, adaptation, assimilation, contrast, fatigue, and so on. Such *order effects* are confounded with treatment effects.

Order effects are sometimes negligible and easy to handle. Rarely, of course, is it advisable to give the treatments in the same order to every subject. In some cases, however, it would suffice to give the treatments in one order to half the subjects, in the reverse order to the other half. In other cases, a number of different random orders could be used, perhaps different for every subject.

This approach to order effects may be illustrated with the blame task cited in the introduction to this chapter. An initial instruction–practice period is used to establish a stable frame of reference for each subject. Once this is established, order effects should be minimal and could be handled with the simplest balancing procedure. Similar tactics are used in many experiments on perception and judgment–decision throughout psychology.

A more systematic approach is to balance treatments across serial position, so that each treatment occurs equally often as first, second, third, and so on. Such *Latin square* designs can be extremely useful for controlling temporal trend. Latin square designs can be analyzed with a simple extension of the repeated measures Anova of this chapter, and deserve the attention of all who use repeated measures (see Section 14.3).

A different approach is to interpolate a washout or baseline treatment between successive experimental treatments. Members of a taste panel, for example, may wash their tongues with distilled water between successive tastes of foods or wines to eliminate carryover effects. Operant tasks and medical studies, similarly, sometimes interpolate a standard treatment, intended to return subjects to a standard baseline of response between successive experimental treatments. This baseline method may be essential when each treatment takes days or weeks. This approach is discussed further in Chapter 11 on single subject design, which contains additional discussion of order effects.

Difficult decisions sometimes arise. A design with independent subjects may be very costly, whereas a repeated measures design may be at risk of confounding from order effects, potentially serious, but about which little definite is known. In such situations, the repeated measures design may seem a worthwhile risk, but designed to include checks on the confounding. This kind of problem is discussed in more detail in Section 14.4 on within-versus-between subjects design.

Order effects always deserve careful consideration. In many classes of tasks, they are no more than a minor nuisance and can be handled in the simple ways already indicated. Effective tactics differ widely across situations, however, so detailed discussion is deferred to the cited sections. In this chapter, order effects will not be considered further.[a]

6.2 MULTIPLE REPEATED MEASURES

Repeated measures may be made on more than one variable. The Anova follows the rationale already given for the $S \times A$ design.

6.2.1 $S \times A \times B$ DESIGN

Both A and B are repeated measures variables in the $S \times A \times B$ design. Each subject goes through all ab treatment combinations of the $A \times B$ factorial design. The Intent × Damage design for the blame task in Figure 1.3 (page 27) is actually an $S \times A \times B$ design, with A = Intent, B = Damage.

The complete design for Figure 1.3 is thus a three-way factorial, with subjects as the third factor. The SSs, MSs, and dfs for this three-way design are computed in the standard way, exactly as in the previous chapter. The general Anova format is shown in Table 6.2, which includes some hypothetical results.

This $S \times A \times B$ design is novel in having three error terms. Each systematic source has its own error term, namely, its residual (interaction) with subjects. In Table 6.2, accordingly, $F_A = \text{MS}_A/\text{MS}_{SA} = 72/8 = 9.00$. In the same way, $F_B = \text{MS}_B/\text{MS}_{SB} = 4.00$ and $F_{AB} = \text{MS}_{AB}/\text{MS}_{SAB} = 2.00$.

TABLE 6.2

ANOVA TABLE FOR $S \times A \times B$ DESIGN

Source	df	df	SS	MS	F
Mean	1	1	240	240	10.00
S	$n-1$	6	144	24	
A	$a-1$	2	144	72	9.00
SA	$(a-1)(n-1)$	12	96	8	
B	$b-1$	3	48	16	4.00
SB	$(b-1)(n-1)$	18	72	4	
AB	$(a-1)(b-1)$	6	12	2	2.00
SAB	$(a-1)(b-1)(n-1)$	36	36	1	

NOTE: Algebraic formulas for df are not ordinarily included in published papers.

Also shown in Table 6.2 is a test of the mean, MS_{mean}/MS_S. This F of 10.00 tests the null hypothesis that the overall mean, $\bar{\mu}$ in Equation 2, is zero. This test is useful when the data are difference scores, for example, or other contrasts, such as linear trend. Usually, however, this null hypothesis has no interest and is omitted.

Four MSs in Table 6.2 involve subjects. These show two trends common in repeated measures designs. Most obvious is that MS_S is several times larger than MS_{SA} and MS_{SB}. This reflects the fact that MS_S represents the main effect of subjects, which is nearly always much larger than subject–treatment residuals. The other trend is that MS_{SA} and MS_{SB} are both larger than MS_{SAB}. This reflects a rule of thumb that two-way residuals, to the extent that they are not mere response variability, are larger than three-way residuals.

Interpretation of repeated measures Anova is the same as with independent scores Anova in Chapters 3–5. In both cases, Anova is testing for systematic differences among the treatment means. Thus, F_A tests the main effect of A, specifically, the null hypothesis that the a marginal means for the A treatments are equal. Similarly for F_B. Finally, F_{AB} tests the null hypothesis that the AB residuals are all zero, that is, that the $A \times B$ factorial graph is parallel. These tests on the data means are interpreted exactly as in Chapter 5.

6.2.2 MULTIPLE VARIABLES

More than two repeated measures variables are readily possible. Judgments of blame for a harmful action, for example, depend on two primary determinants: the intention behind the action and the amount of harm done. Additional variables abound. Extenuating circumstances and atonement by the harmdoer, for example, would both be expected to reduce blame. This would yield a four-factor design with subjects as a fifth factor.

In these multi-variable designs, each systematic source has its own error term, a principle already illustrated in Table 6.2. With four variables, there are $2^4 - 1 = 15$ systematic sources, and hence 15 error terms. In general, the error term for any systematic source is its residual with subjects, as in Table 6.2.

The operating manual for your statistical package will show how to tell the computer which variables are repeated measures. The computer will select the correct error terms. Check the printout to catch errors in your instructions. The first check is on the df, which should follow the rules of Section 6.3.2 below. No less important is a check that the main effect means make sense. Always get a complete printout of the raw data for your permanent file.

6.3 MIXED DESIGNS

Repeated measures variables may be mixed with independent scores variables in the same design. In one common application, subjects fall into different natural groupings, such as age groups in developmental studies. To study development of intuitive physics, for example, each child could be given varied trials in a task based on integration of speed and distance (e.g., estimating how much time animals of varied natural swiftness, such as turtle and cat, will take to run a given distance, as in Figure 20.1) or on Piaget's conservation problem (how much water is contained in a glass as a function of its height and diameter). Different children, however, would usually be used at different ages. Mixed design is also common with variables that produce irreversible changes.

Anova for mixed designs is a straightforward conjunction of previous procedures. The repeated measures variables are called *within subjects* variables; variables with different subjects at each level are called *between subjects* variables. The prototype design, with one within and one between variable, is considered next.

6.3.1 $(S \times A) \times G$ DESIGN

In the $(S \times A) \times G$ design, A is a within subjects variable and G is a between subjects variable. This design should be visualized as a set of $S \times A$ factorials, as in Table 6.1, one for each level of G. Each subject serves at every level of A, but only one level of *G*. At each level of *G*, therefore, are *n* different subjects. Comparisons of the *G* means thus require a between subjects error. Comparisons of the *A* means, in contrast, require a within subjects error. The Anova table, accordingly, includes separate **Between** and **Within** subtables, shown in Table 6.3.

The Anova of Table 6.3 is straightforward. The main concern is to understand the error terms in the two subtables.

The main effect of *G* is just a comparison of the *G* means, averaged over *A*. Averaging over *A* yields a single score for each subject. With a single score per subject, the independent scores analysis of Chapter 3 applies directly. This is shown in the Between subtable, where S/G denotes the between subjects variability. The $S/$ notation is used to emphasize that different subjects appear at each level of *G*, and that the SS and df are pooled across levels of *G*. Thus, $MS_{S/G}$ is equivalent to MS_{within} of Section 3.2.1, and so provides the error term for MS_G.

The main effect of *A* is a little more complicated because it involves averaging over different subjects at different levels of *G*. To understand this analysis, consider a single group, G_1. These *n* subjects constitute an $S \times A$ design that could be analyzed by itself. This would test effects of *A* at G_1, with MS_{SA} as the error. This procedure could be repeated for G_2, and so on. Each group thus yields one MS_{SA} but these all have the same expected value. Hence they may be pooled to get the error term for *A*. Pooling is done by adding the several SS_{SA},

TABLE 6.3

ANOVA TABLE FOR $(S \times A) \times G$ MIXED DESIGN

Source	df	df	MS	*F*	*F**
Between					
mean	1				
G	$g-1$	2	35	3.50	4.26
S/G	$g(n-1)$	9	10		
Within					
A	$a-1$	3	16	8.00	2.96
AG	$(a-1)(g-1)$	6	6	3.00	2.46
SA/G	$g(n-1)(a-1)$	27	2		

adding their df, and dividing to get the pooled MS_{SA}, denoted by $MS_{SA/G}$. This error is used both for A and for the AG residual.

A numerical illustration is included in Table 6.3, which assumes four different subjects in each of the three G conditions, each subject tested at all four levels of A. The between and within error terms stand in the ratio of 10 to 2, indicating the greater sensitivity of repeated measures designs foreshadowed in Table 6.2.

This difference in error terms needs to be considered when designing the experiment. To get equal power, between effects must be substantially larger than within effects. A few subjects may suffice to study within effects, but considerably more may be needed to make the between manipulation worthwhile.

An interesting property of the mixed design is that G, the between variable, also appears in the Within subtable in the form of the AG residual. Since AG involves one within and one between variable, it might seem that it would require some average of between and within error terms. What happens, however, is that the main effect of subjects is factored out by the $S \times A$ design separately at each level of G. At each level of G, therefore, the A effect is freed from the main effect of subjects; these A effects may be considered one column in the $A \times G$ factorial data table. The AG residual, being a test of parallelism, involves comparisons between these columns. Since the main effect of subjects has been factored out of each column, comparisons between columns are also freed from the main effect of subjects.[a]

6.3.2 HIGHER-WAY MIXED DESIGNS

Multiple between subjects variables and multiple within subjects variables may be included in the same design. Anova for such designs follows the pattern already indicated. The following rules provide checks on computer output (n denotes the number of subjects at each level of the between variables). These rules are undigestable verbatim, but they stem from a uniform schema, which is what you should assimilate.

> The Between subtable includes all between variables, $G, H, \ldots$, together with all their residuals (interactions).
> The Between subtable has a single error term, $MS_{S/}$, which is used as the denominator of the F ratio for all the sources in this subtable.

> The Within subtable includes all within variables, $A, B, \ldots$, together with all their residuals (interactions).
> Each of these within sources also has residuals (interactions) with every source in the Between subtable; all these are also included in the Within subtable.

> Each repeated measures source has its own error term, namely, its residual (interaction) with subjects. This same error term is also used for all the residuals (interactions) of this source with every systematic source in the Between subtable.

The df for main effect of any systematic source is one less than the number of levels of that source (excepting the mean with 1 df).

The df for main effect of subjects is $n - 1$ times the product of the number of levels of each between variable (see df for S/G in Table 6.3 and similarly for S/GH in Table 6.4).

The df for any residual (interaction) is the product of the df for the corresponding main effects.

The total df in the Between subtable equals the total number of subjects.
The total df in the Within table equals the total number of scores, minus the total number of subjects.

The schema underlying these rules is more easily grasped by example. Table 6.4 illustrates this schema for the $(S \times A \times B) \times G \times H$ design, with two within and two between variables. This table shows a single error term, S/GH, in the Between subtable. The Within subtable shows three error terms:

> SA/GH for A and its residuals with G and H;
> SB/GH for B and its residuals with G and H;
> SAB/GH for AB and its residuals with G and H.

The df follow the rules just listed.

TABLE 6.4

ANOVA TABLE FOR $(S \times A \times B) \times G \times H$ DESIGN

Source	df	Source	df
Between		**Within** (cont.)	
Mean	1	B	$b - 1$
G	$g - 1$	BG	$(b - 1)(g - 1)$
H	$h - 1$	BH	$(b - 1)(h - 1)$
GH	$(g - 1)(h - 1)$	BGH	$(b - 1)(g - 1)(h - 1)$
S/GH	$(n - 1)gh$	BS/GH	$(b - 1)(n - 1)gh$
Within			
A	$a - 1$	AB	$(a - 1)(b - 1)$
AG	$(a - 1)(g - 1)$	ABG	$(a - 1)(b - 1)(g - 1)$
AH	$(a - 1)(h - 1)$	ABH	$(a - 1)(b - 1)(h - 1)$
AGH	$(a - 1)(g - 1)(h - 1)$	$ABGH$	$(a - 1)(b - 1)(g - 1)(h - 1)$
AS/GH	$(a - 1)(n - 1)gh$	ABS/GH	$(a - 1)(b - 1)(n - 1)gh$

Simpler and complexer designs may be handled analogously. With only one between subjects variable, for example, all sources involving H would disappear in Table 6.4. With only one repeated measures variable, all sources involving B would disappear.

Interpretation of these higher-way mixed designs follows the same principles as for simpler designs. Statsig main effects have their usual meaning. Each pair of variables yields a two-way residual, and this assesses deviations from parallelism in the corresponding two-way factorial graph. These overall F tests may need supplementation, an issue taken up next.

6.4 BEYOND OVERALL ANOVA

To understand the pattern of results may require specific tests in addition to—or instead of—the overall F. Most important, of course, is visual inspection. Other statistical analyses may also be helpful, some of which are considered in this section. First, however, the problem of unequal correlation must be considered.

6.4.1 MULTIPLE ERROR TERMS

In general, each repeated measures test requires its own error term. This rule is a consequence of the likelihood of unequal correlation between treatments. To illustrate, consider two-mean comparisons among four treatments with unequal correlation. Let the correlations be $\rho(A_1, A_2) = \rho(A_3, A_4) = \frac{1}{2}$, and $\rho = 0$ for the other four treatment pairs. Assume equal σ^2 for all treatments. The variance of each two-mean comparison may be calculated from the general formula for the variance of a difference score, $Y_1 - Y_2$:

$$\sigma^2_{(Y_1 - Y_2)} = \sigma^2_{Y_1} + \sigma^2_{Y_2} - 2\rho\,\sigma_{Y_1}\,\sigma_{Y_2}. \tag{4}$$

Assume equal variance so $\sigma^2_{Y1} = \sigma^2_{Y2} = \sigma^2$. Substitution of the given values of ρ into this formula then shows two different comparison variances:

$$\sigma^2_{(A_1 - A_2)} = \sigma^2_{(A_3 - A_4)} = \sigma^2; \tag{4a}$$

$$\sigma^2_{(A_1 - A_3)} = \sigma^2_{(A_1 - A_4)} = \sigma^2_{(A_2 - A_3)} = \sigma^2_{(A_2 - A_4)} = 2\sigma^2. \tag{4b}$$

MS_{SA} from overall Anova is an average of these two variances—markedly too large for the first two comparisons, considerably too small for the last four. The operative α would thus differ widely from the nominal α. Even with equal variance, unequal correlation can produce seriously unequal error terms.

Unequal correlation seems generally likely. Two similar treatments, for example, are more likely to affect each subject similarly than two dissimilar treatments. Even if the null hypothesis of no *mean* difference is true, unequal correlation is readily possible.

Thus, every two-mean comparison generally requires its own error term. The same rule applies to any other within test that follows up the overall Anova.

6.4.2 TWO-MEAN COMPARISONS AS SUBDESIGN ANOVA

After visual inspection, comparisons of two levels of a variable are the most useful planned or supplemental tests. To make two-mean comparisons, simply apply Anova to the subdesign produced by omitting the data at all other levels of that variable. The correct error term is thus produced automatically, based on just the data being analyzed, in accord with the foregoing rule.

In the $S \times A$ design of Table 6.1, for example, suppose a comparison is desired between A_1 and A_2. Treat this as a design with just these two conditions; give the computer just the data of the first two columns ($a = 2$).

This same procedure holds for more complex designs. To compare two A conditions in any design, apply Anova to the subdesign that omits all levels of A except the two in question. In this Anova, the main effect of A has 1 df and tests between the two given A means.

This procedure may give you more than you desire, for it includes all the other design factors as well. Indeed, this Anova has the very same sources as the overall Anova, but with 1 df for A instead of $a - 1$. Because fewer data are involved, a likely consequence is that statsig sources in the overall Anova will be nonstatsig in the subdesign Anova. Less likely but still possible is that a nonstatsig source in the overall Anova will be statsig in the subdesign Anova. Although the subdesign Anova can sometimes be informative, reconciling it with the overall Anova seems likely to be mainly a nuisance. When the purpose of the test is solely to compare the two means, it seems reasonable to act accordingly and officially ignore the accompanying tests.

A minor modification may be appropriate for comparing two means of a between subjects variable. Consider a comparison of G_1 and G_2 in an $(S \times A) \times G$ design. The foregoing subdesign Anova would yield an error term based on only those subjects in the two given conditions. However, the error term from the overall Anova would be appropriate—and more reliable as it has more df—if the equal variance assumption is warranted (see Section 3.3.4). This error term may be used to recompute F and to get a confidence interval for the difference between the two means.

6.4.3 CONFIDENCE INTERVALS

To get a confidence interval for the difference between two means of a within subjects variable, use the same formula as with a between subjects variable (Expression 1 of Chapter 4), but with ε-adjusted df for t^*:

$$\bar{Y}_1 - \bar{Y}_2 \ \pm \ \sqrt{2} \, t^* \sqrt{\text{MS}_{\text{error}}/"n"} \tag{5}$$

As always, "n" equals the number of scores in each mean. The proper MS_{error} is needed, but this may be obtained as indicated in the previous section. Getting confidence intervals is thus straightforward.

Unfortunately, as already noted, every pair of means requires its own MS_{error}. Hence the width of the confidence interval will differ for every two-mean comparison, in marked contrast to between subjects variables. Worse yet, the same mean will generally have several confidence intervals, of different widths, depending on which other mean it is compared with. This multiplicity of confidence intervals complicates the description of the data.

For visual inspection, a rough simplification may sometimes be appropriate, using each separate within subjects error term with ε-adjusted df for all corresponding two-mean comparisons. This may sometimes be justified when it simplifies visual inspection of the main trends in the data. This rough approach is not a substitute for assessing significance, of course, to which the rule of separate error terms applies.[a]

For single means, confidence intervals and error bars require a between subjects error to get an interval that will include the true mean with specified confidence. This differs sharply from the case of a *difference* between two means, for the difference score factors the main effect of subjects out of the error. This within subjects error term would yield a much-too-narrow confidence interval for a single mean.

6.4.4 ASSUMPTIONS FOR TWO-MEAN COMPARISONS

Minimal statistical assumptions are needed for two-mean comparisons with repeated measures. With only two scores per subject, unequal correlation cannot arise. Unequal variance, moreover, is automatically taken into account because the Anova in effect analyzes the single difference score.

Normality is reasonably assured by the central limit theorem in most applications. Although the separate scores may be more or less nonnormal, this will usually cancel in the difference score.

The only remaining assumption is that the subjects constitute a random sample from some population (see *Generalization From Handy Samples*, page 177). Other than this, statistical problems are minimal. This freedom from assumptions may more than compensate for the reduced df.

6.4.5 PLANNED TESTS

If specific tests are planned prior to collecting the data, they would ordinarily be made without regard to the overall Anova. The principle of planned comparisons (page 101) applies equally repeated measures designs: Any reasonably firm a priori hypothesis may ordinarily be tested using the standard α level without adjustment for multiple tests.

Unless the a priori hypotheses are reasonably well-grounded, however, relying on them is risky. If they are not in tune with nature, they will hardly elucidate the data. Furthermore, their failure taints subsequent, alternative analyses.

It may be more prudent, therefore, to begin with an overall Anova, intending to follow this with supplemental tests to localize any statsig effect. The most useful supplement is visual inspection and nothing more may be needed. If more formal analyses are employed, it may or may not be desirable to decrease the α level in the spirit of multiple comparisons (Section 4.2.2).[a]

Decision about α level depends on empirical cost–benefit analysis. Many discussions of multiple comparisons seem predicated on a belief that the false alarm parameter has a sacrosanct value. If even a single false alarm would be fatal—as is sometimes the case—a familywise multiple comparisons procedure should certainly be used. On the other hand, a statsig overall F indicates real effects and the investigator has a duty to try to localize them. Using the regular α for supplemental tests may thus be warranted even though this increases the opportunity for false alarms.

Replication cures all. Post hoc tests in one experiment may be turned into planned tests for a replication. If a result is statsig in the replication, it provides even greater confidence than if the replication alone had been done. With replication, the complications and worries of α escalation virtually vanish.

6.4.6 SIMPLE EFFECTS

Simple effects refer to subdesigns in which only one variable varies, the others being fixed at one of their levels (Section 5.2.4). In a two-way design, effects of A at B_1 would be simple effects. In a three-way design, similarly, effects of A at B_1 and C_1 would be simple effects.

Simple effects are readily analyzed as subdesigns: Ignore the data from all but one level of specified factors. In a two-way design, simple effects of A at B_1 correspond to the first column of the AB data table. All that is necessary, therefore, is an Anova on this one-way subdesign. Simple effects in three-way designs may be tested with similar subdesign Anova.

Simple effects are not often useful, for reasons given in Section 5.2.4. A further limitation with mixed designs is that simple effects of a between subjects variable require a between subjects error term, which will hardly illuminate its interaction residual with a within subjects variable.

6.4.7 POWER

Power calculations for repeated measures are simple with two-mean comparisons. Effect size, σ_A, would be calculated from Equation 4.3 with $a = 2$. An empirical estimate of σ_ε in Equation 4.4 could be obtained from pilot data for the two conditions or from previous data. To such data, apply repeated measures Anova to get the two-mean MS_{SA}; its square root estimates σ_ε in Equation 4.4. Equation 4.5 then completes the power calculation.

This two-mean approach bypasses two major difficulties with power calculations for more than two conditions: The error term for any such calculation depends on the pattern of intercorrelations among all conditions; the df require an adjustment for nonsphericity. To take account of these two difficulties is not easy. Both difficulties disappear for two-mean comparisons.[a]

6.5 STATISTICAL ASSUMPTIONS

The main statistical problem in repeated measures analysis concerns non-independence, or correlation, among the scores. In Table 6.1, a subject low/high on one treatment tends to be low/high on another. Scores for any two treatments are thus correlated across subjects. The independence assumption used in previous chapters no longer holds; it must be replaced with some assumption about the intercorrelations.

6.5.1 SPHERICITY ASSUMPTION

The assumption made about the intercorrelations is called *sphericity*. In its simplest form, sphericity is equal variance and equal correlation: population variances equal for all treatments; population correlations equal for each and every pair of treatments. Sphericity is actually more general than this, but the greater generality has minor practical importance and will be ignored here.

If sphericity is satisfied, together with the other assumptions of Section 6.5.3 below, then the sampling distribution of F under H_0 follows Fisher's formula. Hence Table A5 may be used to obtain the criterial value, F^*.

But sphericity generally cannot be expected. In many situations, probably most, sphericity will be violated because of unequal correlation. Perceptual tasks, for example, may show serial correlation with short intertrial intervals; responses are more highly correlated on successive than on nonsuccessive trials. Serial correlation is a natural consequence of carryover effects from one treatment to the next and also of drift in the subject's state.

Anova is not robust against violations of sphericity. Fortunately, nonsphericity can be handled with Box's ε adjustment.

6.5.2 BOX'S ε ADJUSTMENT

If sphericity is violated, the sampling distribution of F under H_0 is shifted to the right. Hence the effective false alarm parameter, which equals the area to the right of F^* will be greater than the nominal α specified by the investigator. This shifted distribution, miraculously, turns out to be approximately distributed as F with reduced df. Specifically, if the standard df for numerator and denominator are both multiplied by a fraction, ε, the corresponding F^* will yield very nearly the correct α. The value of ε ranges from a maximum of 1 (no adjustment) to a minimum of $1/(a - 1)$, depending on how badly sphericity is violated.

With ε adjustment, the df listed in the printout are only nominal, serving as error checks in the manner previously noted. To determine F^*, the computer should use the reduced df. The program then prints out the "tail probability," or p value, which is the area under the sampling distribution of F for the reduced df, to the right of the obtained F. If $p < \alpha$, the result is statsig.

The value of ε is estimated from the data and called $\hat{\varepsilon}$. This estimate is conservative, so the actual α will be somewhat less than the nominal α. A separate adjustment is associated with each error term in the Within subtable. In Table 6.4, for example, three separate ε adjustments are required.

No ε adjustment is needed for main effects of repeated measures variables that have two levels. This is because the Anova effectively tests the one difference score between the two levels. For this same reason, no ε adjustment is needed for two-mean comparisons or other contrasts. For between subjects variables, of course, no ε adjustment is needed because the Between Anova is performed on a single score per subject. Finally, the alternative $\tilde{\varepsilon}$ adjustment, which is available in some packages, appears to be in error.[a, b]

The ε adjustment seems generally preferable to multivariate analysis of variance (Manova). Although Manova has been advocated by various writers on the ground that it rests on a less stringent form of sphericity, Anova with ε adjustment appears to be a little superior in most cases. Anova is also simpler.[c]

6.5.3 OTHER STATISTICAL ASSUMPTIONS

Normality and Equal Variance. Analyses in the Between subtable are robust against nonnormality and unequal variance in the same way as with independent scores in previous chapters. This holds automatically because the between analyses deal with just a single score for each subject, namely, the average over all repeated measures.

For analyses in the Within subtable, unequal variance is subsumed under nonsphericity and can be handled by the ε adjustment. About effects of nonnormality with repeated measures, little seems known. My guess is that nonnormality is substantially less a problem than with independent scores. Normality of the $(S\alpha)_{ij}$, which is most important for F_A, is facilitated because these are deviations from the additive, $S + A$ model. The effect of one deviant score is not localized in one cell, therefore, but diluted across all cells of the design. Indirect support for this guess appears in Myers et al. (1982), who did a simulation study with dichotomous responses of 0 and 1, a highly nonnormal distribution, and found that ε-adjusted F did quite well. The shortage of information on this question seems surprising by contrast with the numerous studies of nonnormality with independent scores.

Generalization From Handy Samples. Anova rests on an assumption of randomness, specifically, that the subjects, or observations, are a random sample from some well-defined population. Rarely is this true. Nearly always, subjects are a handy sample from some vaguely defined population. With independent subjects, effective randomness can be achieved by random assignment of subjects to treatments (Section 3.3.2, page 69). But this is not possible with repeated measures. Hence we lack statistical warrant for claiming a real effect even in our handy sample.

In my opinion, extrastatistical inference is the foundation for repeated measures design. The essential assumption is that the treatment means and the error term for our handy sample are similar to what we would get in a population to which we wish to generalize. This assumption rests entirely on extrastatistical judgment. Qualitatively, the repeated measures error term makes sense for such extrastatistical generalization, as indicated in *Subject–Treatment Residuals as Error*. Statistical theory goes further to provide quantified results based on an idealized assumption of random sampling. Empirically, however, our inferences depend on extrastatistical judgments of similarity between our empirical situation and the idealized statistical situation.[a]

NOTES

6.1.2a. I realize it is notational impropriety to intrude a Latin letter amidst these Greek letters for population quantities. However, the appropriate Greek letter, σ, is reserved for other purposes. The most common usage is π, for person. However, S is more mnemonic and agrees with its common use as a subscript for SSs and MSs.

6.1.2b. The subject–treatment residuals, $(S\alpha)$, and the within subject response variability, ε, are confounded in the error term in brackets. These two components of the error cannot be separated with only one replication of each treatment for each subject. For convenience, the error term will be called the subject–treatment interaction residual even though it includes within subject response variability.

6.1.3a. The asymmetry between the expected mean squares for the two main effects, S and A, in Equations 3b and 3c arises because subjects is considered a random factor, treatments a fixed factor (Section 15.2). This random–fixed difference produces a corresponding asymmetry in the residuals $(S\alpha)_{ij}$. Since S is random, the residuals depend on which subjects were sampled; a different sample of subjects would yield different residuals. We cannot require that the residuals sum to zero across subjects in each column, therefore, only that their expected value across subjects is zero in each column. Hence the column means, that is, the main effect of A, contain a component of variability that represents these random residuals; this appears in Equation 3c as σ_{SA}^2.

Since A is fixed, however, we may require that the residuals sum to zero in each row, that is, across treatments for each subject. Hence the row means, that is, the main effect of subjects, do not contain an analogous residual component—as shown by Equation 3b.

Equations 3 make sense even though subjects are generally a handy sample rather than random. Any given treatment will have different effects for different subjects. With a random sample, subject–treatment residuals constitute a proper measure of error variability for statistical generalization. These residuals are our best estimate of error for generalization from a handy sample; in either case, we must recognize that a given treatment will have different effects for different subjects.

6.1.3b. Some texts distinguish between ''additive'' and ''nonadditive'' models for repeated measures Anova. In this view, the model of Equation 2 is nonadditive; the additive model assumes that all residuals $(S\alpha)_{ij}$ are zero. This additive model, however, seems wholly unrealistic; different treatments must be expected to have different effects on different subjects. This must generally be true even if the treatments have equal true means. One text reaches the opposite conclusion that the additive model ''appears to be more realistic'' because it satisfies the sphericity assumption, which the nonadditive model is unlikely to do (Winer, Brown, & Michels, 1991, p. 271). This unrealistic view in a generally able text sacrifices psychology to statistics.

6.1.3c. Strictly speaking, it is incorrect to say that repeated measures design controls individual differences. It controls only the main effect of subjects, as shown by Equations 3. It does not control the subject–treatment residuals; these constitute the main component of error, σ_{SA}^2 in Equation 3d. The advantage is great, of course, since the subject main effect is generally much larger than the subject–treatment residuals.

6.1.3d. If all treatments were replicated for each S, each cell in Table 6.1 would have two or more scores. Assuming replications are independent, the within cell variability would estimate σ_e^2. This MS_{error} could be used to test MS_S and MS_{SA}, as shown in Equations 3. These two tests, however, usually have little interest; individual differences in response to treatments may generally be taken for granted.

6.1.5a. I suffered an unexpected order effect in my first personal experiment in psychology. I used a task of probability learning, in which subjects predicted which of two events would occur next in a sequence of trials. The two events had unequal frequencies, which the subjects were to learn, but were otherwise random. Accordingly, I used a random number table to construct a random sequence for each condition.

One random sequence was as good as another, I thought, so I made only one for each of the several frequency conditions. But just for reassurance, I used a second random sequence in one condition. The two gave sharply different results—kaput!

An order effect is inherent in this learning task. Given that different stimulus sequences yield different results, a sample of stimulus materials would be necessary (see *Stimulus Samples*, Section 1.4.3, page 22).

6.3.1a. The fact that the AG interaction residual has a within subjects error in Table 6.3 is a potential opportunity to increase power on the between variable. Because of the lower within error, the AG residual may be statsig even though G is not. Real AG residual imply real effects of G. Inclusion of a within factor may thus provide useful information on a between variable, especially with small n, as with Harlow's mother love experiments. Of course, this potential advantage is qualified by the greater difficulties of interpreting statsig residuals (Chapter 7).

6.4.3a. The tactic of using a single error term for all two-mean within subject comparisons has been advocated by Loftus and Masson (1993), mainly to allow a single confidence interval for all such comparisons. This tactic seems inappropriate. Although a single confidence interval may simplify exposition of the data, as indicated in the text, it is no substitute for correct analysis with correct error terms. Thus, one empirical assessment found radically different error terms for different trend components (Anderson, 1982, Note 2.2.2b, pp. 106f).

6.4.5a. Most of the multiple comparison procedures used with independent scores (Chapter 4) do poorly with repeated measures because they do not allow a different error term for every two-mean comparison. If a strict familywise α is desired, it can be obtained with Fisher's α splitting, with the error term calculated separately for each test. In fact, some texts recommend only the α splitting (Bonferroni) procedure. Familywise methods that are more generally applicable are given in Keselman, Keselman, and Shaffer (1991) and in Keselman (1994).

It is interesting to note that Fisher's LSD method is similarly applicable, subject to the objections noted in Section 4.2.2. The overall F is handled by the ε adjustment. If that is statsig, follow-up tests would be made using an error term calculated specifically for each test, but with the same α. Amid the thickets of statistical articles on multiple comparisons, Fisher's two original procedures appear to be the only ones that retain general usefulness with repeated measures designs.

6.4.7a. For a multivariate approach to power with repeated measures, see Maxwell and Delaney (1990, pp. 568–575), who provide a useful discussion with tables of sample size needed to obtain power of .50, .80, and .95. The power problem has been studied extensively by Muller (e.g., Taylor & Muller, 1995; Muller, et al., 1992); the latter reference cites software for power calculations, available by e-mail. The two-mean approach cited in the text may be more practicable in most applications.

6.5.2a. An error in the published formula for the alterative $\tilde{\varepsilon}$ adjustment proposed by Huynh and Feldt (1976) has been reported by Lecoutre (1991), who presents a corrected formula. Some computer packages incorporate the published formula, which is correct only when there are no between subjects variables.

6.5.2b. In relation to ε adjustment, "Greenhouse–Geisser" has two different referents. Greenhouse and Geisser (1959), observing that the minimum value of ε was $1/(a-1)$, pointed out that an observed F statsig with these minimum df would certainly be statsig with Box's $\hat{\varepsilon}$. In those days of mechanical calculators, this was a useful way to avoid a tedious calculation of $\hat{\varepsilon}$. This minimim ε adjustment no longer has much use, except for evaluating older publications, for which ε is not determinable.

Unfortunately, "Greenhouse–Geisser" is also used to refer to Box's $\hat{\varepsilon}$ adjustment, which they extended to more complex designs (e.g., BMDP2V). Some caution is thus needed in interpreting this term when it appears in a published article. This case also illustrates the importance of reporting what statistical package and program were used in the data analysis.

6.5.2c. Although strong preference for multivariate analysis of variance over ε-adjusted Anova has been expressed in numerous articles and books, ε-adjusted Anova actually seems superior for most experimental applications. In their meta-analysis of this literature, Keselman, Lix, and Keselman (1996, p. 275) concluded: "For balanced [equal n] designs, the usual F and $\hat{\varepsilon}$ adjusted F tests . . . were generally robust to moderate degrees of covariance heterogeneity [nonsphericity], whereas the multivariate procedures were slightly more affected." To this substantive advantage may be added the practical advantage that ε-adjusted Anova does not require learning a whole new statistical apparatus (see further Section 18.4.2).

6.5.3a. Some texts address this roadblock to statistical generalization of repeated measures data by saying that a statsig result can be statistically generalized to a population "just like" the handy sample. This argument invokes a meretricious statistical halo that obscures the essential empirical logic.

Statistically, no random sample is "just like" its parent population. The function of the randomness assumption is to avoid bias, to quantify error, and thereby allow generalization from the sample to the population—despite their many random differences. Empirically, we have no interest in a population "just like" our handy sample, but rather in a population "similar to" the handy sample, similarity being a hopeful judgment based on extrastatistical considerations.

This fundamental role of extrastatistics is clear in generalizing across species, as from Harlow's monkeys to human infants. It is no less important in generalizing from humans to humans.

With independent subjects design, it is true, randomization allows a statistical generalization to the handy sample, which could be considered a "just like" population. But this randomization argument is not applicable with repeated measures designs.

In empirical science, it is obvious that generalization is mainly extrastatistical. Statistical significance is merely a needed sign that the data have some minimum reliability. The halo of statistical significance should not conceal the more important empirical considerations needed for substantive inference.

Statisticians say little about extrastatistical generalization. Statistics texts in empirical science unfortunately follow suit. Effective application of statistical inference requires that it be subordinated to and integrated with extrastatistical inference, as discussed with the Experimental Pyramid of Chapter 1. This difficult problem faces the student and the instructor. It should be the foremost concern of those who write the texts.

EXERCISES FOR CHAPTER 6

1. You are TA in the undergraduate honors class on research method. The instructor asks you for a two-paragraph writeup to be given to the class to show advantages and disadvantages of repeated measures design. What do you write?

2. In your undergraduate class on research method, one pair of students worked together to develop person descriptions consisting of a photograph of a male college student (the row factor) and a pair of his personality traits (the column factor) for a study on person cognition. Each factor is varied across three levels: low, medium, and high attractiveness.

   Female college students judge how much they would be interested in a date with each of these males. Both students perform the same experiment using the same person descriptions, but each runs a separate group of 16 subjects from the standard pool. Each subject judges all nine person descriptions twice in randomized order. Their mean responses are as follows.

Stud.-1: 11	25	45	Stud.-2: 7	21	53
17	34	51	25	30	47
24	38	55	20	46	51

   a. Plot the factorial graph for each student. In what way do the two sets of data agree? In what way do they disagree?

   b. The two graphs presumably should show the same pattern. Hence the cited disagreement raises suspicion about one or the other set of data.

   (i) What is suspicious about the data of Student 2, and why?
   What feature of the Anova would shed light on this question?

   (ii) Argue instead that Student 2 shows the true picture.
   What feature of the Anova would shed light on this question?

3. a. Show that $F_A = 7.50$ for the data of Table 6.1 by hand calculation.

   b. What does this tell you?

4. Assume sphericity for the data of Table 6.1. Using your analysis from the previous exercise, get a confidence interval for difference between A_1 and A_2.

5. Intuitive physics of 5-year-olds is shown in the following table for two tasks. Right panel shows judgments of amount of liquid in glasses as a function of the height of liquid and diameter of glass (cm).
Left panel shows judgments by same 5-year-olds of area of rectangles as a function of height and width (cm). Equivalent response scale in both tasks.

   a. Graph these data and get the main implications by visual inspection. See

Exercise 2 of Chapter 5.

b. Suppose a $2 \times 3 \times 3$, Task $\times$ Height $\times$ Width Anova is run on these data (treating diameter of glass as width). By visual inspection, aided as needed by pencil and paper, say whether each Anova source would have an F ratio that is large, medium, or small (near 1).

c. Parts a–d of Exercise 5.2 suggest four possible hypotheses for this task of intuitive physics. How can Anova test them?

Rectangle height				Glass height			
Width	07	09	11	Diam.	2.5	5.0	7.5
11:	11.4	14.7	17.7	8.5:	3.1	10.2	16.1
9:	7.4	11.7	13.9	7.5:	4.2	11.8	17.3
7:	4.2	7.2	10.4	6.5:	4.2	12.4	16.7

(Data after Anderson & Cuneo, 1978, Figure 1.)

6. What specific experimental procedures would you use to reduce each of the two components of the error term, MS_{SA}, in Equation 3d in a repeated measures study of (a) rats learning to run a straight runway for food reward and (b) 7-year-old children in the blame study of Figure 1.3 of Chapter 1?

7. Some people live dismal half-lives because they suffer never-ending, chronic pain that little can be done about. You hope to show that your joint use of hypnosis plus drug is superior to either hypnosis or drug alone. You use a repeated measures design, with volunteers from a pain clinic whom you have screened to be reasonably hypnotizable. You are successful: The combined treatment is superior to either one alone, with a statsig F and a respectable effect size.

    a. What may you conclude about the effect on individual subjects?

    b. How can you amplify your design to get firmer evidence on individuals?

    c. Is it appropriate to screen subjects as indicated?

8. You have an $(S \times A) \times G$ design, with $n = 8$, $a = 4$, and $g = 5$.

    a. Write out Sources and numerical values of df. Check that the sum of your df is correct.

    b. How can you get a confidence interval for G_1 versus G_2?

    c. How can you get a confidence interval for A_1 versus A_2?

9. In the experiment of Figure 5.7 in Exercise 25 of Chapter 5, each subject went through all 2^3 experimental conditions, a repeated measures design.

    a. Although small, the difference between divided and undivided path rooms for the near path looks perhaps longer than chance. How would you get a confidence interval to test this difference?

b. Suppose you obtain a similar confidence interval for the far path. How do you think its width would compare with that of (a)?

10. You are writing up the experiment of Table 6.2 for publication. You notice that the F of 2.00 in Table 6.2 is close to statsig at $\alpha = .05$. How do you handle this? Indicate whether follow-up tests on these data might be useful.

11. On page 163, the text states that "σ_A^2 will be greater than 0, [and] MS_A will tend to be larger than MS_{SA}." Why does the first clause assert "will be" while the second clause says only "will tend to be"?

12. You are in your second year as assistant professor, busily pursuing the program of research you began with your Ph.D. thesis. Glancing at the latest issue of the main journal in your field, you notice an article that seems to blow your research program to the moon. Your first thought is to replicate this experiment, adding what you consider an essential control. Your first step for replication is a power calculation. The report gives means of 5 and 1 for the two critical conditions, each with 32 subjects, and an F of 4.00.

    a. From the given data, show that an exact replication would yield power about .50.   b. Now what do you do?

13. In Section 6.4.3, why does a confidence interval for a single mean require a between subjects error whereas a confidence interval for the difference between two means uses a within subjects error?

14. There is a numerical relation between the df in the Between subtable and the df in the Within subtable in the $(S \times A) \times G$ design of Table 6.3.

    a. Can you discover it?   b. Can you explain it?

15. Yuval Wolf (2001) presented a version of the blame experiment of Figure 1.3 to 20 juvenile delinquents, half of whom had records of violence, half of whom did not. He hypothesized that the violent subgroup would place more weight on harm, less weight on intent than the nonviolent subgroup.

    a. Draw a factorial graph showing the hypothesized pattern.

    b. How should this hypothesis appear in the Anova?

16. The ab conditions of an $S \times A \times B$ design are presented once to each subject in a separate randomized order for each subject, and then a second time. This replication (R) factor may be added as another factor in the design.

    a. Write down the Anova source table, indicating appropriate error terms.

    b. Suppose the two replications are entirely equivalent, with no order effects, differing only from within subject variability. What does this mean for the terms involving R and S?

17. Q gave preliminary practice to avoid practice effects in her repeated measures design, but she still planned to avoid possible confounding by balancing treatments across serial position. Alas, her research assistant gave all the treatments in the same order.

    a. This use of only one order of presentation does not invalidate the Anova test of the observed means. Why not? What does it invalidate?

    b. What results, if any, might be salvageable?

18. (Transposed from Fisher, 1958, p. 126.) The world-famous San Diego Zoo seeks to create natural surroundings for animals from around the world. Breeding and rearing these animals is one of its specialities, but it faces many problems because each species generally has unique dietary needs about which little may be known. Diet experiments are difficult with some species, moreover, because only a few animals may be available to test different diets.

    Consider an animal that usually has two offspring at a time. Diets D_1 and D_2 are randomly assigned to the two members of the first birth at the zoo. The weight gain of the infant receiving diet D_2 is 90 g greater. This experiment is repeated some months later when the second birth occurs. This time diet D_2 has an 80 g advantage.

    a. Is the effect statsig?

    b. Suppose the second replication had yielded a 110 g advantage for D_2, so its mean advantage is almost 20% larger. How much does Anova say this larger effect increases your confidence in a real effect? Explain.

    c. What possibly important variable was omitted in this design? How would you handle it?

19. The *additive-factor method* introduced by Sternberg (1969, 1998) seeks to dissect a response into successive, independent stages. The overall reaction time (RT) will then be the sum of the separate RTs for successive stages. If successful, this method can give unique insight on serial organization of responses.

    Consider a simple task thought to consist of two stages. Seek two variables, each of which you hope will influence the duration of one stage, with no influence on the duration of the other stage. Manipulate these two variables in factorial design. If all goes as hoped, the durations of the two stages will be additive. This additivity will be observable as parallelism in the factorial graph.

    One such experiment (Sternberg, 1969, Exp. V) used three variables, each at two levels to obtain a $2 \times 2 \times 2$ repeated measures design with $n = 5$. The stimuli were numerals presented visually and the response was a spoken numeral. The three variables were: *Stimulus Quality*: Numerals presented *intact* or *degraded* with visual *noise*. *Stimulus–Response (S–R) Mapping*: Response was the numeral itself or the numeral plus 1. *Number of Alternatives*: Number of stimuli was two or eight, and similarly for number of responses.

a. On intuitive grounds, two of these variables may be expected to affect separate stages and so have additive effects on RT. Which are they?

b. One variable may be expected to affect both stages in (a). How so?

c. Each subject received extensive preliminary training and then was given seven experimental sessions. The following table gives the means for this experiment. Plot them in a graph with two levels of one variable on the horizontal, thus obtaining a graph with four curves, representing two 2 × 2 designs. Of the three possible choices of which variable to use on the horizontal axis, which do you think is most informative and why?

d. Use visual inspection to interpret Sternberg's mean RTs in terms of his theoretical formulation.

e. For any 2 × 2 design, the deviation from parallelism may be expressed as a single number, namely, the double difference (interaction residual)

$$(\bar{Y}_{11} - \bar{Y}_{21}) - (\bar{Y}_{12} - \bar{Y}_{22}).$$

Show that this double difference is 2.2 ms for the Stimulus Quality × S–R Mapping design, averaged over Number of Alternatives.

f. The standard deviation (error half-bar) for the deviation from parallelism of (e) was 3.5 ms. Show that the 95% confidence interval is 2.2 ± 9.7 ms.

g. Since this is a repeated measures design, each analysis requires its own error term. In fact, the error half-bar for Number of Alternatives × S–R Mapping was 12 ms. Why do you think this error half-bar is so much larger than the 3.5 ms for (e)?

h. Find the 95% confidence interval for the nonadditivity of (g); interpret.

i. One 2 × 2 design remains. Do you expect the error half-bar for this interaction to be larger, smaller, or about the same as the two already given?

j. Suppose nonadditive effects of Stimulus Quality and S–R Mapping had been found. Why would it still be possible to maintain that stimulus encoding and response selection are distinct and independent processes?

	Two stimuli		Eight stimuli	
	R = S	R = S+1	R = S	R = S+1
Intact	329.6	348.8	371.4	472.4
Noisy	357.6	379.8	424.2	526.4

	Two & eight stimuli	
	R = S	R = S + 1
Intact	350.5	410.5
Noisy	390.9	453.1

(Mean reaction times in ms, after Sternberg, 1969, 1998. See further Section 11.4.4.)

20. To your dismay, you find in writing the report of your experiment on belief integration that you need to show that individual differences are real. This need is unusual, as everyone takes individual differences for granted, but your theoretical interpretation hinges on this point.

   a From the material on page 163, construct a conservative test of individual differences.

   b. If you had foreseen this need, how could you have designed the experiment to get an appropriate test?

21. (With thanks to G. Keppel.) Perception of the external world is critical for all organisms: To locate food; to avoid predators; to seek warmth; and so on. A major task of comparative psychology is to study the diverse information processing systems of different organisms.

   Desert iguanas, like other reptiles, are thought to use odors to guide their actions. They extrude their tongue to pick up airborne molecules, which they convey to the olfactory Jacobson's organ in their mouth. Tongue extrusion makes a good response measure and was used in the following inquiry into how iguanas perceive the external world (Pedersen, 1988). This kind of experiment can enlarge our appreciation of evolutionary processes that have shaped organisms' tools for information perception and goal-seeking.

   The stimulus manipulation was a pan of sand placed in the test cage in which a single iguana lived for the seven days of the experiment. Five sources of sand were used in a repeated measures design: (1) clean sand; (2) sand from the iguana's home cage; (3) sand from a different iguana home cage; (4) sand from the home cage of western whiptail lizards, which often forage in close proximity to iguanas, although with minimal interaction; and (5) sand from the home cage of kangaroo rats, whose burrows iguanas favor for their own homes and whose droppings they apparently consume. Tongue extrusions were counted from a videotape of the 30 min following placement of the test pan of sand, with one test session per day. Subjects were 10 iguanas collected in the desert near Twenty-Nine Palms, California.

a. Pedersen preceded the five test sessions with two preliminary sessions. The first preliminary session was just after each iguana had been transferred from its home cage to the test cage, where it lived for the duration of the experiment. The second was at the same time on the following day. Why not begin the experiment at once?

b. The five test conditions for each subject must be run in some order. How would you handle this?

c. Pedersen considered the home cage condition as a control and planned to compare it with each of the other four conditions. Discuss the relative merits of planning these four comparisons versus planning to make the overall Anova.

d. The four comparisons planned by Pedersen in (c) are not independent. In particular, a substantial sampling error in the home cage condition would throw off all four comparisons en bloc. How might this danger have been reduced?

e. Pedersen presented mean response for each sand condition as a vertical bar, together with the standard deviation of the mean of the 10 responses (error half-bar, or standard error of the mean) as a line projecting upward from the bar. Why is this error bar not appropriate for this repeated measures design? What alternative measure of variability would you suggest?

f. One iguana made no tongue extrusions under any test condition. This iguana seems extreme as overall mean response ranged from 6.0 in the home cage sand condition through 9.4 in the whiptail lizard sand condition to 23.1 in the kangaroo rat sand condition. Discuss the pros and cons of excluding this iguana from the analysis. What decision would you make?

g. The comparison of kangaroo rat sand with home cage sand was comfortably statsig, but none of the other three comparisons tested by Pedersen came close. Suppose this condition had also been nonstatsig; in that case, would you consider the experiment publishable?

h. These 10 iguanas are obviously not a random sample from any larger population. Yet they presumably have some generality. Based on the given information and your own background knowledge, what two considerations do you think are most important for generalization?

i. Keppel (1991, p. 365) used these data to illustrate the potential of specific comparisons, or contrasts, saying, "A rich variety of comparisons can be examined with this experiment . . . . of perhaps greater interest [than Pedersen's four comparisons with clean sand as control] are comparisons between conditions representing different odors—for example, home cage versus other iguanas, other iguanas versus lizards and kangaroo rats, lizards versus kangaroo rats, and so on. Certain complex comparisons may also be interesting: clean sand versus all other conditions combined, home cage and other iguanas combined versus lizard and kangaroo rat combined, and so on."

Make the best argument you can that the main interest in this experiment is with the sizes of the effects, and that the significance tests suggested by Keppel have relatively little value.

NOTE: The raw data are included in the Instructor's Manual. It is instructive to do repeated measures analysis on the raw data with and without the nonresponsive iguana. I am indebted to Geoffrey Keppel, who secured the raw data and included them in his text, and to Joanne Pedersen for permission to use these data. I wish to apologize to Geoff Keppel for criticizing his emphasis on contrasts, as his text is at the top in integrating statistics into empirics.

PREFACE

The term "interaction" in Anova carries illegitimate surplus meaning that has inflicted needless mystification and confusion on generations of graduate students, who have searched for meaning in the word "interaction," meaning that is not there. Contrary to prevailing opinion in current texts, Anova interactions are often artifacts or illusions. Even when real, they are often unimportant. Understanding interactions depends on understanding two problems— **model** and **measurement**.

The *model problem* is that the Anova model is arbitrary, not substantive. Anova interactions are defined as discrepancies from the arbitrary row-plus-column model of Anova. But this addition model does not usually represent psychological process. Even more must discrepancies from this arbitrary model lack substantive meaning.

For process analysis, interaction seems properly defined as nonconstancy of parameters of some substantive model. Models with constant parameters, however, may show Anova interactions (e.g., Figure 7.3). The same data may thus show zero interaction in the substantive model, nonzero interaction in Anova.

The *measurement problem* is that an observed interaction may be an illusion of the response scale. With a nonlinear response scale, an interaction in the observed data may disappear or even reverse direction in terms of the true linear response scale (Table 7.1). Few response scales in psychology are known to be linear; interactions should therefore be interpreted cautiously in studies oriented at process analysis.

Main effects, as shown in the text, are largely untroubled by these two problems, at least with randomized experiments.

Interactions can be useful, most notably when some theory predicts an interaction of specified shape. Crossover interactions, in which variable A has opposite effects at different levels of variable B, are always interesting. And in general, any interaction between major variables deserves scrutiny. The fact remains, however, that much ado about interactions is nothing.

188

Chapter 7

UNDERSTANDING INTERACTIONS

A *little learning* is a dang'rous thing;
Drink deep, or taste not the Pierian spring:
There shallow draughts intoxicate the brain,
And drinking largely sobers us again.

Alexander Pope

Interaction is a fundamental issue in psychology; it goes beyond the separate effects of two variables to consider their joint action. Historically, concern with interaction preceded analysis of variance and continues independently in a variety of ways.

Anova, however, seemed to promise unique assistance for studying interaction processes. Anova provides *statistical interactions*, called *residuals* in previous chapters. The face meaning of a two-way residual—that the effect of variable *A* depends on the level of variable *B*—was thought to be a direct reflection of interactive process. The term *interaction* presumably originated from this face meaning.

But *interaction* carries surplus meaning from English language connotations, meaning that is inappropriate and misleading with Anova. Often, perhaps mostly, statistical interaction means very little.

For this reason, the term *residual* is used to denote Anova "interactions" in this book. In this chapter, however, the customary term will be employed.

Why statistical interactions often lack meaning is essential to their understanding. Current texts are near-unanimous in misunderstanding interactions. They fail to recognize two pitfalls. First, an interaction may be an illusion of a nonlinear response scale, devoid of substantive reality (pages 193*ff*). Second, an interaction may be an artifact of the Anova model—not a property of the data, but a distortion by a model that misrepresents the data (pages 196*ff*).

7.1 FUNCTIONS OF INTERACTIONS

Interactions are sometimes useful. Discussions of such usefulness have appeared in Chapters 5 and 6, but it seems appropriate to summarize them before taking up the pitfalls that threaten the user.

7.1.1 CROSSOVER AND NONCROSSOVER INTERACTIONS

Crossover and *noncrossover* interactions are qualitatively different and require separate consideration. For crossover interactions, also called *disordinal*, variable *A* has opposite effects at different levels of variable *B*. Although not common, crossovers are important, as illustrated with the opposite effects paradox on page 199, and with the comparisons of within subjects and between subjects design cited in Section 14.4.3.

Most observed interactions are noncrossovers: Variable *A* has the same directional effect at different levels of *B*, but its size differs. The following discussion, unless otherwise indicated, is limited to noncrossovers.

7.1.2 PATTERN ANALYSIS

Interactions are sometimes useful in testing hypotheses about patterns in the data. Occasional reports appear in the literature in which the theoretical analysis predicts a specific two-way or even three-way interaction pattern. Finding the predicted pattern, buttressed by a statsig interaction, is heart-warming support for the theory (e.g., Note 7.5.1b).

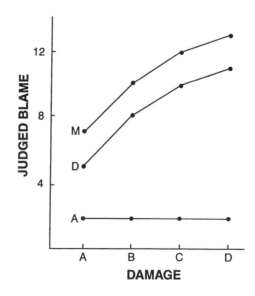

Figure 7.1. Configural effect shown by nonparallelism in factorial graph. Blame judgments by subgroup of accident-configural subjects, slightly idealized after Leon (1980). (M, D, and A denote malicious intent to harm, displaced aggression, and accidental harm.)

Cognitive algebra makes similar use of interactions. The multiplication model, for example, implies an interaction showing a specific pattern, namely, a linear fan. This use of interactions was illustrated in the discussion of Figure 5.5 (page 140) and is considered further in Chapter 21 (see Figure 21.6, page 714).

Interactions may also be useful for process analysis. One example appeared in Figure 1.3, reproduced here as Figure 7.1. The parallelism of the top two curves suggests that blame for a harmful act is an additive integration of the two determinants: intent (curve parameter) and damage (horizontal axis). The non-parallelism of the bottom curve was reliable, with a statsig interaction in the actual data; visual inspection indicates that damage has negligible effect when the damage is accidental. However, understanding this interaction pattern depended on extrastatistical information, including verbal reports of subjects.

7.1.3 GENERALITY OF MAIN EFFECTS

Interactions are warnings that main effects may lack generality. This matter was previously discussed in relation to Figure 5.4, reproduced here as Figure 7.2. All three panels show equal interactions, but their implications differ.

The crossover interaction in the left panel of Figure 7.2 shows that variable A has opposite effects at the two levels of variable B. This represents a strong lack of generality of main effects.

The center panel of Figure 7.2 shows the same size interaction as the cross-over in the left panel, but its implications are very different: A_1 is substantially superior to A_2 at both levels of B. The amount of this A_1 superiority does depend on B, but the direction is the same. For most purposes, therefore, this interaction requires little or no qualification of the main effects.

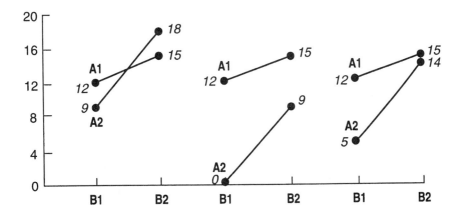

Figure 7.2. Three 2×2 graphs with identical interaction residuals.

A more problematic case is in the right panel of Figure 7.2, where A_1 is only a little better than A_2 at B_2. If this difference is not statsig, qualification may be needed as noted with Figure 5.4. For present discussion, however, suppose this difference is statsig. Then the interpretation depends on the empirical situation. As one example, suppose B_1 and B_2 represent low and high levels of subject aptitude for some learning task, A_1 and A_2 represent different methods of instruction. Evidently, A_1 should be used for all learners. Its advantage is greater with low aptitude, it is true, but it is better with high aptitude as well.

Similar reasoning may apply when A and B are both experimental manipulations. Showing the same directional effect may suffice as evidence for operation of a theoretical process. Not often, indeed, would a theory predict a constant, additive effect for any manipulation.

The interaction may be pertinent, however, for outcome studies in which the response has "cash value." The right panel of Figure 7.2 indicates that the beneficial effect of A_1, relative to A_2, will be small if treatment B_2 can be implemented. Cost–benefit analysis would be needed to calculate the optimum treatment. Cost–benefit analysis usually requires responses measured in cash value, of course, which are common in agriculture (Cochran & Cox, 1957) and engineering (Montgomery, 1997). In psychology, however, cash value measures are not frequent.

These remarks reaffirm the discussion originally given with Figure 5.4. For interpreting main effects, interactions have limited usefulness, a conclusion reemphasized in the following discussions of models and measurement.

7.1.4 MODELS AND MEASUREMENT

Confusion about interactions stems in part from confusion between outcome and process (Section 1.2.2). The statistical Anova interactions rest on an outcome orientation. But understanding these interactions usually requires a process orientation that may well lead to a different conclusion. The process orientation requires a substantive, extrastatistical orientation because interactions depend on two theoretical issues of process: *model* and *measurement*.

The standard Anova model defines two-way interactions as residuals from an *addition model*, row + column. This model is imposed arbitrarily, and may not be congruent to the integration process. Meaning and interpretation of interactions are entwined with the substantive validity of the imposed model. If this imposed model lacks substantive validity, deviations from it will not generally be meaningful. This dependence of interactions on an arbitrary model is explored in Section 7.3.

Interactions are sensitive to the *measurement scale*: The size and even the sign of an interaction depend on the response scale. Two investigators studying the same behavior could use different response scales, both reasonable, and get interactions in opposite directions. This response scale issue is taken up next.

7.2 MEASUREMENT THEORY AND INTERACTIONS

Interactions may be illusions. The standard interpretation of interactions in statistics texts is that "the effect of one variable depends on the level of the other variable." Such interpretations can sound impressive, as though they reveal *inter*action between the variables. Unfortunately, the interaction may be an illusion produced by a nonlinear response scale. Three aspects of this problem of response measurement are considered next.

7.2.1 INTERACTION DEPENDS ON RESPONSE SCALE

The illusory quality of interactions is not an esoteric statisticality, but a real everyday problem. To illustrate, consider two investigators, P and Q, who cooperate in an experimental study, observing the same behavior, a rat that runs a one-meter straight alley for food reward. They use a 2 × 2 design, with Hi and Lo levels of hunger motivation and Hi and Lo levels of food reward. Present concern is with asymptotic response, after enough trials are given so the rats have stablized their behavior.

P measures seconds to run the alley; his data are shown in the left of Table 7.1. An interaction is evident. Reward has a three-times larger effect when motivation is low than high. P argues that under high hunger, the rats are running almost as fast as they can, even for small reward. Hence increasing the reward has little effect. This makes psychological sense.

TABLE 7.1

INTERACTION DEPENDS ON RESPONSE SCALE

		P Reward			**Q** Reward	
		Hi	Lo		Hi	Lo
Motivation	Hi	2	3		3/6	2/6
	Lo	3	6		2/6	1/6
		Time			Speed	

NOTE: After Anderson (1961b).

Q measures speed in running the alley, which may be taken as the reciprocal of P's time score. Her data, shown in the right panel of Table 7.1, are parallel. There is no interaction: Reward has the same effect, regardless of hunger motivation.

Who is right, P or Q? At a behavioral level, the time and speed measures are equally valid and both are in common use. Physically, time and speed are both linear (equal interval) scales, with true zero points. They are nonlinearly related, however, so they necessarily yield different interactions.

We cannot tell whether P or Q is right. Without a linear psychological scale of response, one interaction is no better than the other. Without a theory of psychological measurement to validate the response scale, an observed interaction may well be devoid of meaning.

Two general truths appear in this example. First, size and even sign of an interaction depend sensitively on the measurement scale for the response. Second, there is usually no definite criterion to decide which response measure is linear. This problem of response measure requires further discussion.

7.2.2 TWO LEVELS OF RESPONSE MEASUREMENT

The foregoing measurement analysis raises a conceptual distinction between two levels of response measurement, observable and unobservable. If the observable response has intrinsic validity (and if the standard Anova model is appropriate), interactions are directly meaningful. But if the response serves as an indicator of something beyond itself, then interactions are subject to the measurement problem.

Observable responses with intrinsic validity appear in applied psychology. Worker output under different working conditions is a response with cash value. In auto safety programs, similarly, repair bills or number of accidents are measures with cash value. In such currency, the measurement scale has observably equal units so interactions may be taken at face value. This level of measurement is often at issue in studies aimed at outcome validity.

Most experimental studies, however, seek process validity. The observable response is not usually of primary interest in itself; implicitly or explicitly, it is treated as a measure of some unobservable state of the organism. In the P–Q example of Table 7.1, the rat's response lacks cash value; time and speed are both measures of some unobservable concept of response strength. In learning studies, similarly, the response measure might be number of errors in a fixed number of trials or number of trials to some specified criterion of learning. Both measures are useful indicators of some unobservable concept of difficulty of learning, but neither can be said to be a linear scale thereof.

From the perspective of measurement theory, therefore, an observed interaction may be an illusion. Despite being observable, it should not be considered a "fact" except in the most minimal sense. The observable "fact" in P's data is "this difference is greater than that difference." This "fact" may be falsified by legitimate transformation of the response measure, as Q's data show.

This observable–unobservable distinction points up a prevalent ambiguity. Anova interactions involve observable data. Typically, however, interpretation of the result refers to some unobservable response or construct. Most workers deal mainly with main effects, for which this observable–unobservable distinction is not ordinarily important.

But this distinction is critical for interaction—as just illustrated in Table 7.1. Conceptual clarity requires explicit awareness of the difference between the two levels of response measurement.

To resolve this ambiguity requires a *linear scale*, that is, a scale on which the observable response is a linear function of the unobservable state of the organism. Validated linear scales can be obtained with functional measurement theory under certain conditions (Chapter 21). Unless the response measure is linear, however, interpretation of interactions should cautiously recognize that they may be only illusions, devoid of substantive significance.

Interactions may be meaningful, despite this measurement ambiguity. Standard response measures are more than rank orders; they typically have some degree of metric information. Accordingly, they may be considered semilinear scales (Section 19.3.1, page 632). An observed interaction thus deserves serious consideration, especially when it has been predicted theoretically.

Nevertheless, the measurement problem is serious for everyday research. Time and speed measures are both in common use, but they show very different patterns in the data, illustrated in Table 7.1. A second example comes from judgments of quantity, for which the two methods of rating and magnitude estimation have been widely used. Both methods are plausible, yet they yield very different results (Figure 21.2, page 694, and Figure 21.8, page 730).

7.2.3 MEASUREMENT SCALES AND MAIN EFFECTS

Main effects are not scale-sensitive in the manner of interactions. This point deserves reemphasis because most research is concerned with main effects, not with interactions. Interactions are scale-sensitive because they compare *differences* at different locations on the response scale. Barring crossover, the relative size of such differences can be inverted by a monotone transformation, as suggested with the foregoing time–speed example. In the statement that the effect of A is greater at B_1 than at B_2, "greater" would turn into "lesser."

Main effects, in contrast, deal directly with different locations on the response scale. With random assignment, main effects are not usually reversible by monotone transformation. Hence the issue of linear scale is seldom pertinent for main effects. Indeed, a nonlinear scale may yield more power and so be preferable. This issue is discussed under *Scales and Statistics* in Section 12.2.4 (page 361) and under *Anova With Monotone Data* in Section 19.3.3 (page 635).[a]

7.3 MODEL THEORY AND INTERACTIONS

The psychological concept of interaction depends on psychological theory of multiple determination. Anova interactions are often irrelevant because the row-plus-column Anova model is not a model of psychological process.

The conceptual issue concerns how multiple determinants are integrated. This problem of integration model is more subtle than the measurement problem, but no less important. To concentrate on this integration problem, the measurement scale will be assumed linear in the following discussion.[a]

7.3.1 CONCEPT OF INTERACTION

Interaction may be defined in two ways, both of which rest on an integration model. The Anova definition of Chapter 5 rests on the row-plus-column addition model. In this model, zero interaction means that A has the same (additive) effect, regardless of the level of B. This definition might seem almost unexceptionable, more a fact than a definition.

But the Anova model is not a model of psychological process. Few empirical studies in any field claim that separate variables are integrated by a process of addition. The interactions, however, are defined as deviations from this row-plus-column, Anova model. If this model lacks substantive significance, the deviations from the model must even more lack substantive significance.

The alternative conception of interaction refers to a substantive model, including various nonadditive models. Interaction is then defined in terms of the substantive parameters of this model. Zero interaction refers to constancy of the model parameters; interaction refers to changes of model parameters across experimental conditions.

This substantive conception of interaction may not seem too meaningful when first encountered. The next three sections, accordingly, illustrate it with three concrete examples, each empirically grounded.

7.3.2 PROPORTIONAL CHANGE MODEL

Many experiments are concerned with changing behavior. Often, the possible change is limited by some maximum or ceiling. For example, consider a message that advocates a favorable belief on some issue. Subjects who already hold favorable beliefs cannot change very much, whereas subjects with less favorable beliefs can change more. If this result is obtained, however, it is questionable to conclude that the message was more effective with the subjects who were less favorable initially.

Instead, a proportional change model may apply: Amount of change is proportional to possible change. Figure 7.3 shows initial response levels of 20 and 60 for two groups, both of whom receive the same treatment. This treatment

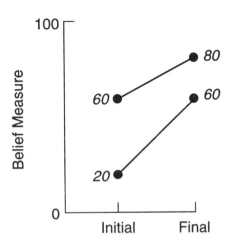

Figure 7.3. Nonparallel data correspond to zero interaction under proportional change model. (After Anderson, 1961b, 1963.)

moves each group halfway toward a maximum response level of 100. The final response levels are thus 60 and 80.

The data in Figure 7.3 are nonparallel. Anova would yield an interaction, and it may seem genuine because the response scale is linear by assumption. At face value, this means that the treatment was more effective with the initially less favorable group.

The proportional change model, however, implies that the treatment was equally effective with both groups. It changed both the same proportion of the possible change, in this case a proportion of ½. This change proportion is the model parameter, and it is constant. In terms of psychological process, there is no interaction.[a]

The proportional change model has been supported with belief change, with learning, and with other tasks (Chapter 21). Anova interactions are then more or less beside the point. Although true of the surface behavior measure, they are false at the underlying conceptual level.[b]

Two levels of discourse appear in this example: process and outcome. The process level is represented in the proportional change model. The Anova model, in contrast, operates at the outcome level of the observed data. The Anova model cannot be said to be wrong; a statsig interaction says that the observed change in one group differs from that in the other. This fact, however, refers to a different level from the conceptual change process. In the proportional change model, the constant change parameter means no interaction.

7.3.3 MULTIPLICATION MODEL

Multiplication models have been widely hypothesized in psychology. The Expectancy × Value schema, for example, has appeared in theories of animal behavior, personality, and judgment–decision. The same multiplicative structure appears in the statistical concept of expected value:

$$\text{Expected value} = \text{Probability} \times \text{Value}.$$

Many writers have conjectured that cognition obeys an isomorphic model, but with the three terms of this equation interpreted in subjective metrics. In a typical experimental test, the subject judges the worth of a gamble that yields a specified reward with specified probability. A factorial design is used, with specified levels of Probability and Value as rows and columns.

This multiplication model implies that Probability amplifies Value; the factorial graph will show the pattern of a linear fan. Data that follow this model will yield an interaction in Anova. But this does not mean that Probability and Value "interact" in any psychological sense. They do act jointly, it is true, but joint action is not *inter*action, regardless of whether the joint action is addition or multiplication.

True interaction would occur if the (subjective) Probability changed, depending on the level of Value. It has been conjectured, for example, that the same information about probability of an event will be evaluated differently, depending on whether the event has positive or negative consequences. The multiplication model, however, assumes the contrary, namely, that each level of Probability corresponds to a constant parameter in the multiplication model, independent of Value. Under the given conjecture, predictable deviations from the linear fan pattern would be expected. Such deviations could properly be interpretable as interactions.

This point may be seen in a different way. Suppose the row-plus-column model was replaced by a row-times-column model. This would seem appropriate in physics, for example, because most physical laws are multiplicative. Residuals from the row-times-column model would be zero. The Anova interactions would be nonzero because the row-plus-column Anova model is substantively inappropriate and misrepresents the physical law.

Multiplication models have also been found in psychology. Indeed, Subjective Expected Value does exhibit the linear fan pattern (Figure 21.7, page 715). So does the proportional change model of Figure 7.3. The additive Anova model misrepresents these psychological processes.[a]

The multiplication model reemphasizes the distinction between statistical and substantive interaction. It also reemphasizes the desirability of calling statistical interactions by their proper name of residuals, a name makes explicit their dependence on a model.[b]

7.3.4 OPPOSITE EFFECTS PARADOX

The *opposite effects* paradox underscores the conceptual problem involved with the notion of interaction. This paradox refers to the finding that the same informer stimulus can have positive or negative effects, depending on which other stimuli it is combined with. Opposite effects seems clearly to imply configural interaction, as though the meaning and value of the given stimulus were affected by the other stimulus.

Configurality, however, requires a reference standard. A result can be interpreted as configural only by showing that it differs from what would have been obtained had no configurality been operative. Opposite effects seems paradoxical because it violates our implicit expectation, namely, that any nonconfigural model implies that a given stimulus must have the same directional effect, regardless of what other stimuli it is combined with.

But opposite effects can also be interpreted in terms of averaging theory, without appeal to interactive process. The idea is simple: A medium value stimulus will average up a low value stimulus, average down a high value stimulus—thereby producing positive and negative effects in the two respective cases. Under the averaging model, the configural interpretation of opposite effects becomes unwarranted. Hence also an averaging process could account for the crossover in the left panel of Figure 7.2.

The implication is the same as just discussed for the multiplication model. Nonparallelism (= Anova interaction) can occur even though the parameters that represent the variables have constant, fixed value. Even without psychological interaction, therefore, the algebraic structure of the averaging model can yield residuals from additivity. These residuals vanish if the averaging model is fitted to the data.[a]

This interpretation of opposite effects in terms of averaging is not conjectural. The averaging model has been well supported in many areas of psychology. In fact, averaging appears to be a primary process of information integration (see Chapter 21). The main point here, however, is to reemphasize how misleading the standard conception of interaction can be.

7.3.5 NONADDITIVE PATTERN

An interesting pattern of data appears in Table 7.2. In this 2×2 design, three entries are equal, one is different. Anova, however, splits this one real difference into three equal SSs: for row, column, and interaction. Splitting one real effect into three different parts seems a poor way of describing these data. Statistically, moreover, it is inefficient. This is not a fault of Anova, only of persons who unthinkingly apply the addition model where it does not belong. A curious published example was given in Exercise 5.10.

TABLE 7.2

PROCRUSTEAN PROCLIVITY OF ANOVA

0	0
0	4

NOTE: After Anderson (1961b).

How such data patterns should be analyzed depends on prior knowledge and expectation. If the cited pattern was a reasonably firm, a priori prediction, an appropriate analysis would test the mean of the one different cell against the pooled mean of the other three, supplemented by subdesign Anova on the other three cells. This Anova comes from extrastatistical knowledge, however, not from a habit of applying factorial Anova (see also Exercise 13).

The data pattern in Table 7.2 might represent true interaction. Nonzero response occurs only when A and B are both at their second level, as though each is needed to make manifest the potential of the other. This interactive interpretation would seem reasonable in some situations, but it cannot be taken for granted. The same pattern can be produced by the foregoing multiplication model, with values of 0 and 2 for Probability and for Value.

A further aspect of this example appears if we assume a single nonadditive cell in a factorial design. The factorial graph will then be parallel except for this one discrepant cell. The interaction residuals, however, will be nonzero in every cell of the design. Anova fractures this one-point discrepancy into ab parts in an $a \times b$ design; every cell contains an interaction residual. These ab parts clearly do not represent any substantive process. Instead, they demonstrate the nonsubstantive character of the Anova model (Exercise 5).

This example reemphasizes the general principle that factorial Anova rests squarely on the arbitrary addition model of Equation 5.1. It is remarkable that this arbitrary model is so widely useful. But it is not a panacea. It imposes a conceptual framework on the data that is sometimes very misleading.[a]

7.4 INTERACTIONIST THEORIES

Interactionist theories, as their name implies, emphasize interactions among multiple determinants. Interactionist theories have natural appeal, but they have been disappointing. Their big shortcoming is their lack of concepts and methods to analyze how the multiple determinants are integrated. Three interactionist domains are considered here because of their relation to statistical interactions in analysis of variance.

7.4.1 INTERACTIONIST THEORIES IN PERSONALITY

Interactionist theories of personality begin with a primary assumption of inter-action between person and situation. This interactionist view differs fundamen-tally from traditional theories, which focus primarily either on person or on situation. The former seek a typology of traits and motivations to describe indi-vidual persons; the latter study effects of situational determinants on behavior. Even taken together, these two traditional approaches are too narrow—behavior results from *inter*action. Behavior cannot be any simple function of person and situation because person and situation *inter*act. This interactionist argument is persuasive in itself. It becomes more persuasive in view of the continued inabil-ity of the two traditional approaches to account for much of personality.

The difficulty is to put teeth into the interactionist argument. It is always easy to criticize any approach and point toward promising new directions. To fulfill such promises is not so easy. For interactionist theories, fulfilling the promise requires methods to measure person, situation, and their interaction.

In the personality domain, many interactionists thought that analysis of variance provided an effective method with statistical Person × Situation interactions. Consider rows as persons and columns as situations, with each per-son serving in every situation in a Person × Situation factorial design. The dif-ferential effect of situations across persons would then be captured in the Person × Situation interaction terms. These statistical Person × Situation interactions seemed just what was needed.[a]

Unfortunately for interactionist theory, these Person × Situation interactions are mostly meaningless. Two main reasons, measure and model, have already been discussed; a third reason is given in Note 7.4.1b. In particular, the validity of the interactions depends on the assumption of true linear measurement scales—for each individual. There is ample reason to disbelieve this assumption in personality research and little to support it. A more effective application of Anova to study Person × Situation interaction seems possible with personal design (Section 11.5.4, pages 335-336).[b]

7.4.2 INTERACTIONIST THEORIES IN EDUCATION

In educational psychology, many workers also adopted an interactionist approach. The underlying idea, of long-standing attractiveness, is that instruc-tion will be more effective when tailored to abilities and aptitudes of individual learners. Different instruction methods may thus be preferable, depending on the initial aptitudes of the subjects. This view has received a certain cachet under the name of Aptitude × Treatment Interaction (ATI) research.

Aptitude × Treatment interactions in education, however, face the problems just noted for personality theory. In particular, interactions may be an illusion of nonlinear response scales. In educational psychology, in contrast to personality theory, this problem of nonlinear response was recognized. Some workers, accordingly, held that only crossover interactions should be recognized, as in the praise–blame study of Note 5.2.2a. Such crossovers, however, have been elusive in educational psychology; a better instructional method is usually better across all aptitude levels.

Other workers have held that noncrossover interactions should be taken seriously. These interactions may be genuine, it is true, and may contain useful clues for improving instruction. But it is also true that noncrossover Aptitude × Treatment interactions may not have much relevance; the same treatment may be superior across all aptitude levels, as already discussed with the center and right panels of Figure 7.2. What is best for one is best for all. Even if genuine, therefore, an interaction may be nugatory.[a]

7.4.3 INTERACTIONIST THEORIES IN SOCIAL COGNITION

Numerous theories of social cognition began with one or another postulate of cognitive consistency (e.g., *assimilation, balance, congruity, dissonance,* and so forth) as a foundation for general theory. Their theme was that the mind strives for consistency; inconsistent informer stimuli will interact to reduce the inconsistency. A good deed by a disliked person, for example, might be reinterpreted as stemming from ulterior motives or discounted as unintentional.

Cognitive consistency is an attractive principle. Logically, consistency seems the first principle of rational thought and action. Psychologically, inconsistency resolution seems ubiquitous, as in rationalization and ego defenses.

The first experimental test with factorial Anova, however, showed a fatal flaw in the consistency theories. Inconsistency resolution, if it occurs, will produce predictable interactions. These interactions were not found (see e.g., factorial graph of Figure 11.2, page 317). A related class of theories of social cognition that tried to interpret each Anova interaction in three-way designs as a psychological process is cited in Note 7.3a.[a]

7.4.4 MULTIPLE DETERMINATION

Multiple determination is a fundamental problem in psychological science. Behavior generally depends on multiple determinants, sometimes in complicated ways (e.g., Note 7.6.3a). Statistical interactions can sometimes help assess these dependencies, especially for outcome-oriented investigations.

For analysis of interaction process, however, statistical interactions are flabby tools. To develop theories of multiple determination, it seems essential to establish psychological integration models. Establishing such integration models, as Section 7.2 indicates, is integrally bound up with psychological measurement theory, an issue considered in detail in Chapter 21.

7.5 HIGH-WAY INTERACTIONS

Two new problems arise with three- and higher-way interactions. First, they become increasingly difficult to describe and interpret. Whereas two-way interactions have a simple geometrical interpretation as deviations from parallelism, higher-way interactions do not. Second, the number of interactions increases exponentially with the number of factors.

7.5.1 INTERPRETATION OF THREE-WAY INTERACTIONS

A three-factor design yields three two-way interactions, AB, AC, and BC. Their interpretation is much the same as for the two-way interaction in a two-way design. Thus, nonzero AB interaction corresponds to nonparallelism in the two-way, AB factorial graph.

In addition, there is a three-way interaction, ABC. It has warning functions about two-way interactions somewhat like those that two-ways have about the one-way main effects. Specifically, each two-way interaction is an *average* over the third variable. Statsig three-way interaction means that each two-way factorial graph has a different pattern at different levels of the third variable. This may—or may not—require qualification of two-way interactions. The essential considerations are analogous to those in the foregoing discussion of two-way interactions and main effects.

Describing Three-Way Interactions. Zero three-way interaction has no simple graphic shape, unlike zero two-way interaction. Three-way interactions are qualitatively more complicated, therefore, and hence less useful.

Zero two-way interaction implies shape similarity; the curve for each level of A has the same shape across different levels of B. This shape similarity appears as parallelism in the factorial graph. Three-way interactions, in contrast, show no such simple shape property. The ABC interaction can be zero even though the two-way AB graph has visibly different shape across different levels of C.

This shape complication is illustrated in Figure 7.4. Each panel shows two AB graphs, one for each level of C. In the upper left panel, both AB graphs have identical shape. In this case, of course, the three-way interaction is zero.

In all four panels, the left AB graph is the same, but the right AB graph has different shapes. Yet all four panels show zero three-way interactions. This shows that three-way interactions lack any simple shape interpretation.

When each factor has only two levels, as in these examples, each interaction can be expressed numerically as a difference. The two-way interaction in the left 2×2 graph in each panel is the double difference: $(3 - 0) - (4 - 3) = 2$. The two-way interaction in each right 2×2 graph can be expressed similarly as a double difference; inspection shows that this double difference also equals 2 in each right graph.

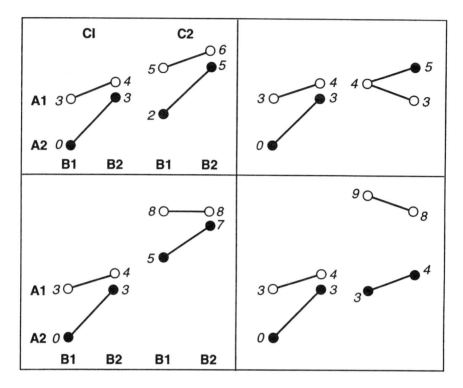

Figure 7.4. Zero three-way interaction does not imply simple shape similarity. Zero three-way interactions appear in all four panels. Each panel has same left-hand graph, but the right-hand graph has different shape in all four panels. Only in the upper left panel do the two graphs have the same shape.

The three-way interaction is a triple difference, namely, the difference between the double differences for the left and right graphs in each panel. Since both these double differences equal 2 in each panel, the three-way interaction equals 0 in each case. The left and right graphs in each panel show numerically equal deviations from parallelism, but very different shapes. Hence a zero three-way interaction need not correspond to any simple graphic shape.[a]

Zero two-way interaction is prized because it means that the observed effect of each variable is an additive constant, the same regardless of the level of the other variable. This reflects the parallelism property. The message of Figure 7.4, however, is that zero three-way interaction has no such simple meaning. Three-way interactions lack a clear baseline like parallelism. This lack of baseline can markedly complicate their interpretation. Higher-way interactions become progressively more complicated.

Three-way interactions are sometimes useful. Verifying a predicted three-way interaction can be good support for a theoretical hypothesis. In some cases, also, the pattern of the associated two-way interactions will clarify the meaning of the three-way, as with the configural effect of Note 7.5.1b. In general, however, three-way interactions are arbitrary statisticalities that may well not mean much of anything.[b]

Localizing Three-Way Interactions. Lacking extrastatistical information, three-way interactions cannot be localized. In any panel of Figure 7.4, suppose that a single one of the eight data points is displaced by $+1$. Since each panel exhibits zero three-way interaction, this one-point displacement will produce a nonzero three-way (see Note 7.5.1a).

Now suppose you are given these altered data and told to make the three-way interaction zero by finding and moving the displaced point back to its original position. Your task is impossible. The three-way can be made zero again by a change of ± 1 in any one of the eight data points. For all you know, any one of these eight changes could reflect the original state of affairs. In short, the three-way interaction is not localizable.

In practice, your situation may be worse. A real three-way interaction will not generally be localized in a single point, as in the foregoing example. Instead, it will be distributed across several data points. Without extrastatistical information, three-way interactions are uninterpretable.

In practice, of course, some extrastatistical information is usually available. Your data points are not arbitrary, as in Figure 7.4. They should exhibit some sensible relation to your experimental manipulations and to other extrastatistical information, as with the accident–configural blame schema of Figure 7.1. In some studies, moreover, the experimental hypothesis predicts a specific pattern of three-way interaction; an example appears in the configural effect of Note 7.5.1b. If you find an unanticipated three-way interaction, however, don't be disturbed if you can't localize or interpret it. What is disturbing is that several different interpretations may be equally good.

7.5.2 HIGHER–WAY INTERACTIONS

A four-factor design yields four three-way interactions, plus a four-way interaction. A five-factor design yields 10 three-way, 5 four-way, and 1 five-way interactions. Each added factor thus adds one higher level of complication.

Also, the number of interactions exponentiates. With k factors, there are $2^k - 1 - k$ interactions. Six factors yield 57 interactions. Of these, three might be expected statsig by chance. Finding seven statsig would suggest that some were real, but leave uncertain which was which. The expected three false alarms prejudice the meaningfulness of whatever results are statsig.

A design with many factors may thus seem a can of worms. An investigator may balk at balancing some minor procedural variable on the ground that adding one more factor to the design may almost treble the number of interactions and the number of potential false alarms.

An alternative is *partial analysis*: Include the minor variable, but delete its higher-way interactions from the Anova model. In this way, partial analysis secures the advantage of balancing minor variables without suffering under the higher-way interactions (see further Section 18.4.3).

7.6 PERSPECTIVE ON INTERACTIONS

Psychological interactions and statistical interactions are tenuously related, two very different concepts. This chapter has shown that, contrary to popular opinion, statistical interactions have very limited usefulness for understanding psychological interactions. The three main reasons are summarized in the first section. Psychological interactions have fundamental importance, of course, an issue discussed in two following sections.

7.6.1 STATISTICAL INTERACTIONS

Statistical interactions have very limited usefulness for empirical analysis. The three main reasons are:

Interactions may be an illusion of the response scale.
Interactions may be an artifact of the additivity assumption.
Even if real, interactions may be unimportant.

In short, "interactions" are a crude statistical device, occasionally useful, often a nuisance, often misleading.

Much mischief lies in the term "interaction." This term carries an illicit process implication, as though the two factors were in some dynamic relation. This is not generally true. This illicit implication can be avoided by abjuring the term *interaction* and using *residual*, which is neutral and correct.

7.6.2 PSYCHOLOGICAL INTERACTIONS

Two different kinds of psychological interaction should be distinguished: organism–stimulus and stimulus–stimulus. *Organism–stimulus interaction* is a biological universal; each organism must evaluate the everchanging stimulus surround through its own perceptual–cognitive apparatus. Individual differences in stimulus effects are obvious in affective preferences for foods, friends, and leisure activities, and even in everyday perceptual activities, such as seeing the world around us.

These organism–stimulus interactions have fundamental importance. But from the Anova standpoint, as just shown, these organism–stimulus interactions appear even with a single stimulus. A main effect of organisms can thus demonstrate organism–stimulus interactions, as with preferences for foods or prescriptions for glasses.

Quite different are the interactionist theories in personality and education that focus not on main effects, but on Anova interactions (Section 7.4). As to personality, Person × Situation interactions are mainly meaningless for the three given reasons. This fruitless effort only emphasizes how prevailing unclarity about statistical interactions has misdirected study of psychological process.

As to education, Aptitude × Treatment research is centered on outcome analysis so Anova interactions are pertinent. Despite its promise, Aptitude × Treatment research has had little success. A different direction, oriented toward process analysis, may have some usefulness.

Stimulus–stimulus interaction occurs when the combined effect of two stimuli differs from what it would have been in the absence of interaction; this reference standard may be implicit, but it is necessary. The problem, of course, is to define and determine this reference standard of no interaction.

Clear cases of stimulus–stimulus interaction seem to operate in perceptual illusions, as with the size–weight illusion of Figure 5.3 (page 131; see similarly color contrast of Figure 11.6, page 324). In these cases, a physical reference standard of no interaction is available, so a main effect suffices to exhibit the illusion. The integrated action of the two stimuli may nevertheless follow an addition rule, showing no Anova interaction, as in both of these illusions.

For most stimulus–stimulus combinations, however, an observable reference standard of no interaction is lacking, as with the cognitive consistency theories of Section 7.4.3. A process model, coupled with a linear response scale, can provide a reference standard. Thus, the postulate of cognitive consistency was neatly disproved by the constancy of the parameters of the averaging model.

Stimulus–stimulus and organism–stimulus interaction are both fundamental. They are not easy to analyze, however, as shown by the failures of the three attempts in Section 7.4. Process models for stimulus integration have had some success, however, as with the size–weight illusion and with studies of person cognition noted in Chapter 21, which pursues this line of inquiry.[a]

7.6.3 PROCESS AND OUTCOME

The present discussion of Anova interactions emphasizes once again the process–outcome distinction of Section 1.2 (pages 8*ff*). The standard approach to Anova interactions rests on an implicit outcome perspective, in which the response is taken at face value. A process perspective, in contrast, requires understanding the two issues of model and measurement.

This implicit outcome perspective has obstructed analysis of multiple determination. The term "interaction" is often applied when the outcome is found to depend on numerous determinants in complicated ways. One example is the venerable problem of primacy–recency in serial belief integration. In this area, as in many others, the aggregate of experimental studies was a disordered jumble; each new attempt to impose order led to more disorder. With primacy–recency, however, a process approach has revealed order at a deeper level, beyond the scope of outcome analysis. Such results argue for a shift in perspective on analysis of multiple determination.[a]

The Anova emphasis on multiple determination is well taken; no psychological problem has greater importance. Anova interactions are not often useful, unfortunately, because they rest on the arbitrary addition model and because they are oblivious to the measurement issue (see further Chapters 20 and 21).

7.6.4 STATISTICS TEACHING

It is a symptom of the state of statistics teaching that little of the foregoing discussion is to be found in current texts. Interactions receive extensive, almost adulational treatment, with little or no indication to the reader that they may well be illusions, artifacts, or, if real, unimportant. Many texts assert flatly that main effects are not meaningful when interactions are statsig. One text, unusually able, devotes upward of 10 pages, including a flow diagram with 34 boxes, to show how to interpret a single three-way interaction. Some texts do assert that Anova assumes a linear (equal interval) response scale, without realizing that this has little bearing on tests of main effects but is critical for interactions.

The foregoing considerations, I think, are hardly controversial. Nearly all have been in the literature for some decades. Why have they not been incorporated into current teaching?

One part of the answer is the prevailing outcome perspective, which ignores the two problems of measurement and model. The measurement problem has not been considered serious, despite repeated criticisms over four decades, probably because it is not usually serious with main effects, which are robust against nonlinear response scales (see *Semilinear Scales* in Section 19.3.1). Anova interactions, in sharp contrast, are extremely sensitive to the measurement scale, as shown in Table 7.1. This measurement problem gets virtually no discussion in current texts. The same holds for the model problem, illustrated with the proportional change model of Figure 7.3, which is also well known.

Another part of the answer is that statistics teaching has fixated on the top level of the Experimental Pyramid of Figure 1.1 of Chapter 1. The lower, empirical levels are more important; learning statistics needs to be subordinated to and integrated with these empirical levels. Developing texts and exercises for this purpose is not easy. This book is just one step in this empirical direction.

NOTES

This discussion of interactions is based on Anderson (1961b), which discussed the twin issues of interaction model and response measure illustrated in Table 7.1 and Figure 7.3. These issues were pursued further in Anderson (1962b, 1963). Useful discussion has been added by Bogartz and Wackwitz (1971) and reemphasized by Bogartz (1976), Harris (1976), and Loftus (1978).

7.2.3a. Although $Y_1 > Y_2$ is invariant under strictly monotone transformation, this is not necessarily true for means. Artificial examples can be constructed in which $\bar{Y}_1 > \bar{Y}_2$ in the original scores, but $\bar{Y}_1 < \bar{Y}_2$ in the transformed scores (Anderson, 1961b; Maxwell & Delaney, 1985). This logical possibility has little practical importance.

7.3a. The psychological inadequacy of the Anova model has also appeared in a number of theories in social and personality psychology that were founded on an assumption that each main effect and each interaction in a three-way factorial design had a direct psychological interpretation. Statistical interactions were taken as direct measures of psychological interaction. Anova thus seemed a key to revealing psychological process.

All this work, however, rested on the gratuitous assumption that the Anova model was a valid process model. And on the arbitrary assumption that the measured response was a true linear scale (see e.g., Anderson, 1969, 1972b, 1977, 1979b, 1982, Section 7.11); see also Section 7.4.

7.3.2a. Some attempts to study rate of forgetting have suffered from misuse of Anova interactions. Consider successive forgetting tests for two groups that have learned to different levels. The forgetting curves for the two groups will typically be nonparallel, with the group initially higher decreasing faster. This produces an Anova interaction, which some workers have interpreted as different rates of forgetting. A proportional change model seems more appropriate by the same reasoning as given with Figure 7.3. However, the proportional change model with equal rates of forgetting predicts nonparallel curves and hence an Anova interaction (see similarly Exercise 10).

The critical issue is to find a process model for forgetting. The proportional change model is restrictive since it requires the forgetting rate to be constant over time. A more general *shape function* model (Anderson, 1963) has shown promise, especially in cogent extensions by Bogartz (1990a,b), who discusses related models, and by Paul (1994), who discusses statistical analysis (see also Wixted, 1990).

7.3.2b. The proportional change model says that the actual change in response produced by a given stimulus is proportional to the possible change:

change in response $= Y_1 - Y_0 = w(\psi_1 - \psi_\infty)$ or $Y_1 = Y_0 + w(\psi_1 - \psi_\infty)$,

where Y_0 denotes the response before the given stimulus, Y_1 denotes the response after the stimulus, w denotes the change parameter, ψ_1 denotes the value of the given stimulus, and ψ_∞ denotes asymptotic response. In Figure 7.3, w was ½ for both groups.

7.3.3a. The algebraic form of an integration model need not be isomorphic to the integration process. In particular, success of the multiplication model for Subjective Expected Value (Figure 21.7) does not necessarily mean that the subject multiplies the two informers. An alternative process is that Value is positioned on an internal metric line, and the interval between 0 and Value is fractionated according to the Probability (Graesser & Anderson, 1974). Another alternative to multiplication appears with the Adverb × Adjective model, which appears to follow a nonalgebraic process (Anderson, 1974c, Section 7.9; see further Anderson, 1996a, pp. 402*ff*).

7.3.3b. This dependence of statistical interaction on the choice of integration model is discussed further in Anderson (e.g., 1961b, 1972b, 1982, Sections 7.10, 7.11, and 7.13) and in Hoaglin, Mosteller, and Tukey (1991, Chapter 1).

7.3.4a. In the averaging model, the effective, or relative, weight of each informer depends on the weights of all the other informers. In this sense, effective weight is configural. But this same process holds also with equal weighting, for which the averaging model implies parallelism, that is, no statistical interaction.

7.3.5a. This stumbling block of reification of interactions as psychologically meaningful may be illustrated with Rosenthal and Rosnow's (1985) discussion of the following 2 × 2 table, which shows mean change in attitude by conservatives and liberals in response to two communications, A and B.

Communication	A	B
Conservative	2	2
Liberal	5	1

After commenting on the main effects in the Anova, Rosenthal and Rosnow say

> Finally, we might state − *but it would be wrong*! − that the significant interaction . . . demonstrates that liberals were more strongly influenced by [communication] A than by B while conservatives were unaffected by the type of [communication] (p. 5).

The authors continue

> The interaction actually shows that conservatives and liberals reacted in exactly opposite ways to the two types [of communication] (p. 8).

But the first row of the table shows identical scores for conservatives under the two conditions. How can Rosenthal and Rosnow exclaim that it is wrong to say so?

Both quoted statements arise from reifying "interactions" as real phenomena. Application of the Anova model to the given data shows that the interaction residuals, $(\alpha\beta)_{jk}$, are ±1; the factorial graph of these residuals shows a pure crossover. If the interaction residuals are reified, conservatives and liberals do show equal and opposite response to the two types of propaganda. This is the basis for the two quoted statements. Since the Anova model defines interaction in terms of the $(\alpha\beta)_{jk}$, Rosenthal and Rosnow thought that the data had to be interpreted in these same terms.

Their misconception is transparent. Had only conservatives been run, no objection could arise to the statement that they were "unaffected by the type of [communication]." This is a data fact—the conservatives had identical scores under the two conditions. This fact cannot be changed by including the liberals. This fact cannot be changed by Anova.

Essentially the same misunderstanding of interaction appears in Levin and Marascuilo (1972) in their discussion of so-called Type IV errors. Contrary to both pairs of authors, the interaction test is only useful to the extent that it helps interpret the actual data. Both pairs of authors sacrifice the data to a cruel straitjacket of statistics; see similar critiques by Games (1973) and Meyer (1991).

The point at issue appeared in the discussion of Figure 7.2. All three 2 × 2 graphs have identical interactions; the factorial graph of the residuals will necessarily exhibit the same pure crossover in all three cases. Substantive interpretation, however, is quite different for the three graphs. Only in one graph is it a fact that one variable has opposite effects depending on the level of the other variable.

You may wonder how the four cited men, all prominent in psychological statistics and research method, could err so egregiously. The reason is that interpreting a statsig interaction usually requires comparisons of cell means that involve main effects as well as interaction residuals. From a purely statistical view, this may seem questionable on the statistical argument that this interpretation of the interaction depends on something besides the interaction residuals. The fallacy of this statistical argument becomes apparent when it leads to the absurd conclusion that "conservatives and liberals reacted in exactly opposite ways."

The root of the problem is that the Anova model is arbitrary, not substantive. It is remarkably useful, but it dissects the data in an arbitrary way that can readily misrepresent substantive significance, especially as regards "interaction." Anova should be an aide and servant to common sense, not a slavemaster.

7.4.1a. On the dominant role of statistical Person × Situation interactions, see Bowers (1973), Ekehammer (1974), Magnusson and Endler (1977), Magnusson (1990), and Mischel (1973). Although this approach has been criticized for reliance on variance components, the more basic issue that the twin problems of model and measurement render such interactions meaningless has gone virtually unrecognized. Here again, the confusion stems from applying the outcome orientation of standard Anova to an issue of psychological process (see also following note).

7.4.1b. A further measurement problem with Person × Situation interactions also needs consideration. An apparently insuperable obstacle is that meaningfulness of Person × Situation interactions requires that all subjects have equivalent units for the response scale. The interaction would be invalid, speaking analogically, if some subjects used an inch unit, others a centimeter unit. To see this, suppose a Person × Situation factorial graph exhibited parallelism, with zero interaction. Since we generally cannot know whether different subjects have equivalent units, we must allow that a meaningful factorial graph would require changing response unit for some subject.

But changing response unit changes the slope of the curve for that subject; this destroys the parallelism. If we observe a Person × Situation interaction, therefore, we cannot know whether it is genuine, merely a reflection of different personal units, or some combination of the two. Even with true linear scales with known zero points for each individual, therefore, Person × Situation interactions may still be meaningless.

A different approach to person–situation interaction has used Anova with single subjects. The two problems of model and measurement can be resolved with functional measurement theory (Chapter 21). The problem of unit comparability can be bypassed by studying response patterns for individuals. Two applications in person cognition are cited in Section 11.4.1 (see also *Personal Design* in Section 11.5.4).

7.4.2a. Aptitude × Treatment Interaction (ATI) is the theme of Cronbach (1975) and of Cronbach and Snow (1977, pp. 33, 492-495), which is a valuable reference for research methodology on instruction. Regrettably, ATI research has been disappointing; the sought-for crossovers have been scarce. Cronbach and Snow argue that noncrossovers should be taken seriously, but noncrossovers mean that the same instructional treatment is superior across all aptitudes (see discussion of right panel of Figure 7.2.) The later overview by Snow (1989) remains optimistic but the evidence is certainly unimpressive. Snow's concluding invocation of higher-order interactions emphasizes but does not mitigate the failure to establish useful two-way interactions.

This may be an overly pessimistic evaluation of an outstanding program of research in an area of highest social importance, but alternative approaches deserve consideration. In this area, interaction is generally defined as unequal slopes of the regression lines for the effect of each Treatment as a function of Aptitude. This limits the characterization of individuals to crude group scales of aptitude. Personal design (Section 11.5.4) with a handful of subjects that focuses on process rather than outcome (see e.g., Karpp & Anderson, 1977) may yield better insight than the brute force of the ATI approach, in which 100 subjects per treatment is considered more or less minimal.

Of course, the potential of individualized instruction is hardly in doubt. In studying a textbook, for example, different individuals naturally progress at different speeds and with different attention to the material on each page. Computerized instruction is often personalized analogously, requiring mastery of one segment before proceeding to the next. It does not follow, however, that individuals of different aptitudes will do best with different texts or programs, as ATI research has assumed.

7.4.3a. Cognitive consistency is an important issue, but not easy to study. Some methods are discussed in Anderson (1981, Chapter 3).

7.5.1a. When all factors have just two levels, main effects and interactions can be expressed as single numbers. For the 2×2 design, these are double differences:

$$\hat{\kappa}_A = (\bar{Y}_{11} + \bar{Y}_{12}) - (\bar{Y}_{21} + \bar{Y}_{22});$$

$$\hat{\kappa}_B = (\bar{Y}_{11} + \bar{Y}_{21}) - (\bar{Y}_{12} + \bar{Y}_{22});$$

$$\hat{\kappa}_{AB} = (\bar{Y}_{11} - \bar{Y}_{12}) - (\bar{Y}_{21} - \bar{Y}_{22}).$$

The ± 1s in these three contrasts follow the natural pattern. Thus, $\hat{\kappa}_A$ is the sum of the two means in the first row minus the two means in the second row.

These formulas have the advantage that they express the size of the effect as a number on the response scale itself, not as an SS. Similar patterns of ± 1s apply to multi-factor designs. Thus, the three-way interaction in a 2^3 design is the triple difference:

$$\hat{\kappa}_{ABC} = [(\bar{Y}_{111} - \bar{Y}_{121}) - (\bar{Y}_{211} - \bar{Y}_{221})]$$

$$- [(\bar{Y}_{112} - \bar{Y}_{122}) - (\bar{Y}_{212} + \bar{Y}_{222})].$$

Note that the first line refers to level C_1, the second to level C_2 with reversed signs. In Figure 7.4, the first line of this triple difference refers to the double difference in the left panel, the second line to the double difference in the right panel.

7.5.1b. Configural Effect Revealed Through Anova Interaction. That three-way interactions can be useful may be illustrated with their role in establishing a certain configural effect, namely, that a dimension of difference between two stimuli is more important than a dimension of equality. Such configural effects have been conjectured by a number of investigators, but definite evidence has been elusive.

In this experiment, a pair of informer stimuli was presented on each trial, each informer characterized by values on the same two dimensions. Subjects made an integrated response, based on the four given pieces of information.

Some of the paired stimuli presented on each trial were equal on one dimension and unequal on the other. By hypothesis, the dimension of difference will be weighted more than the dimension of equality in the integrated response. This configural effect implies crossover interactions in specific 2 × 2 subdesigns of the complete four-way design. These two-way interactions canceled because of the symmetry in the design. Instead, they revealed themselves as three-way interactions (Anderson & Farkas, 1975).

Mellers (1985) claimed that the interactions reported by Anderson and Farkas (1975) were not real, but could be removed by a monotone transformation of the response. Accordingly, Mellers interpreted these data as support for a difference model rather than the ratio model of decision averaging advocated by Anderson and Farkas.

But Mellers' claim is invalid, for it is mathematically impossible to remove crossover interactions by monotone transformation. This mistake could have been avoided since the crossover was a direct implication of the observed pattern of interactions, replicated in Farkas and Anderson (1979; see further Anderson, 1991d).

7.6.2a. Organism–stimulus interaction occurs at the valuation operation in the information integration diagram of Figure 21.3, whereas stimulus–stimulus interaction would occur at the subsequent integration operation. These two operations have been shown to be independent in certain cases, which provides a tool for quantifying organism–stimulus interaction.

7.6.3a. The term "interaction" is often used to indicate that results depend on multiple determinants in complicated ways, as with primacy–recency in serial belief integration (Anderson, 1996a, pages 339-342), with judgment of quantity by young children (Exercise 6.5), with base rate effects in judgment–decision theory (Figure 19.1), and in the "poopout" effect—the puzzling disappearance of a learned shock-avoidance response under continued reinforcement, which was found to have "a complex dependence on sex of rat, strain and stock of rat, and kind of avoidance task . . . with bimodal distributions of avoiders and nonavoiders" (Anderson, 1982, p. 53).

In these and many other cases of multiple determination, Anova interactions are not often much help. On the contrary, the standard approach of manipulating variables usually leads to a jumble of outcomes. Science needs a more basic approach that focuses on processes that govern how the multiple determinants are integrated into a unitary response. Although avoidance decrement remains unexplained, information integration theory has had some success with the other examples. Algebraic models for stimulus–stimulus integration have provided an effective way to quantify organism–stimulus interaction as well as context–stimulus interaction (Section 21.6.2).

EXERCISES FOR CHAPTER 7

1. Plot the following two data tables for a $3 \times 3 \times 2$ design.

a. By visual inspection, say which main effects are/are not substantial.

b. By visual inspection, say whether the AB residual is/is not substantial.

c. Do (b) for the ABC residual.

d. Make rough visual estimates of the marginal row and column means, and plot each as two curves in a 2×3, CA or CB design. By visual inspection of these graphs, say whether these residuals are substantial or not.

	C_1			C_2		
	B_1	B_2	B_3	B_1	B_2	B_3
A_1	7	21	39	20	32	48
A_2	14	23	30	26	36	41
A_3	23	24	25	32	34	36

2. In Table 7.2:

a. Get the three systematic SSs for the factorial Anova, assuming $n = 1$.

b. Assuming the observed pattern mirrors the true pattern, in what two ways is the factorial Anova bungling the data analysis?

3. Suppose you had expected the blame judgments of Figure 7.1 to come out as they did. How would you plan to analyze the data?

4. Use computer Anova to show that SS_{AB} has the same value for all three of the 2×2 graphs in Figure 7.2. Comment.

5. In Exercise 27 of Chapter 5, suppose the 6 in cell 24 is changed to deviate from the parallelism pattern in the same way as the entry of 3 in cell 34. Find the interaction residuals in column 4. Comment.

The next five exercises consider empirical situations that involve the two basic issues in understanding interactions: *model* and *measurement*. Some require background information that makes them longer.

6. In the experiment of Table 7.1, P and Q are disturbed by their disagreement about the interaction. Their first step is to check for mistakes in the recorded data. Sure enough, the time of 6 s is really 5 s.

a. Does this change affect the direction of P's interaction?

b. Does this change introduce an interaction in Q's data?

c. Psychologically, what does each interaction mean in this experiment, taking each at face value?

d. What is the moral of this exercise?

7. Apply the equation for the proportional change model given in Note 7.3.2b to verify the arithmetic given with Figure 7.3.

8. This exercise refers to the Rosenthal–Rosnow data in Note 7.3.5a. From Equation 5.2a, the expression for the interaction residual in any cell of a two-way design is   [cell mean − row mean − column mean + overall mean].

   a. Use this expression to show that the interaction residuals in the Rosenthal–Rosnow data are +1 or −1.

   b.* Show that any 2 × 2 table with nonparallel data will yield a pure cross-over for the factorial graph of interaction residuals. How does this relate to the interaction df?

9. The multiplication model, Behavior = Expectancy × Value, has been conjectured in diverse areas of psychology. But valid tests have been elusive. Potential for model test with factorial Anova is indicated in this exercise.

   a. Assume numerical values of four levels of Value, two positive and two negative, and of three levels of Expectancy. Plot the factorial graph, with Value on the horizontal. How does the shape of this graph reflect the multiplication operation?

   b.* Suppose that an outcome with negative Value causes subjects to change their Expectation. How will this interaction appear in the factorial graph?

10. (After Bogartz, 1976.) To test whether younger children are more distractible, Hale and Stevenson (1974) presented 5- and 8-year-olds with a task of short-term visual memory, both with and without distractors. This is a 2 × 2 design, with two levels of age and two of distraction.

   For 8-year-olds, mean scores were 6.43 and 5.65 without and with distraction. Corresponding scores for 5-year-olds were 3.94 and 2.88. (Perfect score was 12.)

   The problem is to compare the distraction effect between age groups; this comparison is complicated by the large main effect of age. Hale and Stevenson compared the two differences: $(6.54 - 5.65) = .89$ and $(3.94 - 2.88) = 1.06$. The difference between these two differences is the Age × Distraction interaction, which was not statsig. Since this experiment had used 72 children at each age, the authors considered they had adequate power to conclude that both age groups were equally distractible. Their design seemed an ingenious way of factoring out the large main effect of age on memory.

   But Bogartz (1976) pointed out that their interpretation rested on an implicit—and dubious—theoretical assumption, namely, that the distraction process obeyed an additive model. Suppose instead that the proportional change model applies, so that the decrement due to distraction is proportional to the level of memory under no distraction. Then equal proportional distraction would yield nonzero Anova interaction and zero Anova interaction would correspond to unequal distraction proportions.

a. Why was it important to have a substantial main effect of distraction?

b. Why does the main effect of age have secondary interest in the theoretical analysis? Exactly what interest does it have?

c. Assume with Bogartz that the distraction effect follows a proportional change model. Let w denote the proportion by which memory decreases from the nondistraction to the distraction condition. If $w = .20$, show that this proportional change model implies a nonzero Anova interaction (nonparallelism) when this distraction proportion is equal across age.

d. Generalize (c) to allow any value of w.

e. Construct a numerical example to show that zero Anova interaction implies greater distractibility for 8-year-olds under the proportional change model. Show that this result is general, not peculiar to your example.

f. Give a tentative interpretation of the cited data in the light of the foregoing considerations.

11. This exercise illustrates a not uncommon situation in which an interaction is claimed, but the evidence falls critically short.

An interesting field study by Ellsworth and Langer (1976) sought to show that the effect of staring depended on the social situation. Specifically, their hypothesis was that staring "may function as a stimulus either to approach or to avoidance depending on the context" (p. 117). (All quotes from their article.)

Their unwitting subjects were female shoppers just inside or outside a large department store, who had no idea they were in an experiment. Each shopper was told by one experimental assistant, A, that another experimental assistant, B, in view close by, needed help. Two variables were manipulated in a 2 × 2 design. **Ambiguity:** A indicated to the shopper either a *clear* condition (saying that B had lost her contact lens and needed help) or an *ambiguous* condition (saying that B was not feeling well and needed help). **Staring:** B either stared at the shopper or looked at the ground. Of main interest were ratings on a 0–4 scale by a blind observer of how much the subject helped B. For example, a shopper subject "who appeared to hesitate but went no further" was rated 1.

a. The main hypothesis was that "the difference in the amount of assistance offered to the two types of victims [clear or ambiguous] was expected to be greater when the victim stared" (p. 118); "The hypothesis was confirmed: There was no main effect of staring. More help was elicited in the clear condition than in the ambiguous, but the difference between these two conditions only reached significance when the victim [B] stared" (p. 117). Does this result provide adequate evidence for the conclusion?

b. The authors also state that "The Stare × Ambiguity interaction was nonsignificant, $F(1, 44) = 1.76$" (p. 120). How does this bear on the conclusion quoted in (a)?

12. In the upper left quadrant of Figure 7.4, left and right panels have the same shape. Suppose the upper left point is displaced upwards one unit, from 3 to 4.

    a. Express the three-way interaction as a triple difference to show that the one-unit change makes it nonzero.

    b. Show that the three-way interaction can be made zero again by a one-unit change in any of the eight data points.

    c. What does this imply about interpreting observed interactions?

13. You do a 2 × 2 experiment, planning a regular factorial Anova. Unexpectedly, the entries in the first row are 2 and 1, those in the second row 1 and 9.

    a. Why does the factorial Anova seem inappropriate for this data pattern?

    b. Suggest an alternative analysis and discuss pros and cons.

14. Suppose the four levels of B are 1, 2, 3, and 4; that A has one constant effect if $B < 2.5$, another constant effect if $B \geq 2.5$; and that the response equals the sum of the values of A and B. For simplicity, assume zero error variability.

    a. How will this process appear in a factorial graph?

    b. In what way would Anova misrepresent the specified process?

15. In a Person × Situation design, suppose persons and situations are perfectly additive—except for one deviant person.

    a. Extrapolating from Exercise 27 of Chapter 5, say how Anova will misrepresent these data.

    b. How could visual inspection reveal the truth?

16. In a 2^3 design, construct hypothetical data with all effects zero except:

    a. A.   b. A and B.   c. AB residual.

    d. ABC residual.   e.* AB, AC, and BC residuals.

Note: Simplify by using cell entries of $+1$ and -1 except use also 0 for (b). (Trial and error will yield plenty error on (e); use Equation 13 of Chapter 5.)

17. What is your psychological interpretation of the configural effect shown in Figure 7.1?

PREFACE

Confounding is a primary problem of experimental analysis. Most arguments in the literature revolve around issues of confounding, that is, alternative interpretations of an observed result. Much of the thought that goes into planning an experiment is concerned with how to avoid or control confounds.

Confounding is a basic connection between empirics and statistics portrayed in the Experimental Pyramid of Chapter 1. Confounding depends first on choice of task and response measure, second on experimental design. A statsig result is only a minimal first step; the important question is what it means. What it means hinges on questions of confounding at each lower level of the Pyramid.

Some important functions of statistics appear in dealing with confounding. These functions depend on empirical judgment melded with concepts and techniques of statistics. To make statistics an organic part of empirical investigation depends on empirical appreciation of confounding.

This chapter includes a broad collection of examples of confounding, chosen to illustrate common difficulties that need consideration when planning an experiment. One purpose of these examples is to help develop a bird's-eye perspective on confounding.

Among these examples are some in which psychological science went astray. Careless or even culpable neglect of confounds has sometimes led to fruitless controversy, to wasted effort by many workers, and to untruths in introductory texts. These lessons from the past can help us increase effectiveness of our future work.

These examples also illustrate that knowledge about confounds is a basic part of knowledge in any field. Some variables initially considered important turn out to be irrelevant; unsuspected variables are sometimes found to be important. The worth and quality of your work depend first on a good choice of problem and second on your knowhow about confounds and ways to deal with them. Such knowhow is part of the cumulative knowledge in each field.

The last part of this chapter discusses five ways to deal with confounding. Four of these concern experimental procedure and experimental design. The fifth is theory control, which can sometimes handle confounds not tractable with experimental manipulations.

Chapter 8

CONFOUNDING

Confounding is an ever-present problem in scientific inference. The placebo effect in medicine is a classic example, in which a beneficial outcome can be produced by an inert treatment that has no effect per se. Whatever real medicinal value a treatment may have is thus overlaid by—confounded with—this placebo effect.

Confounding means that an observed effect could be due to more than one cause. In the placebo example, giving a medicine carries a suggestion that it should be beneficial; this suggestion is often beneficial of itself. Medicine and suggestion are thus confounded. Accordingly, a positive outcome is not generally adequate evidence for a genuine effect of the medicine per se.

Four complementary, overlapping perspectives on confounding are useful. *Stimulus confounding* is the most common perspective in experimental analysis. Stimulus confounding arises from differences between the conceptual variable we wish to manipulate and the concrete physical situation we actually manipulate. The physical situation always involves other variables besides our intended variable. Our observed result may stem from these other variables, not from our intended variable.

Response confounding means that the observed response is, or may be, a compound of two or more response processes. Response confounding is a primary concern in observational studies, commonly discussed in terms of validity. Response confounding may be extrinsic, as with remediable ambiguity in a test question, or intrinsic, as when a one-dimensional measure is used to represent a multidimensional concept.

Response confounding is also important in experimental analysis. Extrinsic response confounding may arise from unclarity in instructions or task (Section 14.1.2) or startup effects from inadequate task familiarization (Section 14.4.1). Intrinsic response confounding may appear as side-effects of some stimulus manipulation or with response complexes (e.g., *Dynamic Systems* in Section 8.1.6). Stimulus confounding itself may be considered confounding of response to separate stimulus variables. Thus, a placebo reaction could be viewed as a confound of responses to the medicine and to suggestion. The stimulus perspective is popular because of the experimental focus on stimulus manipulation.

Response confounding is more important, however, for the meaning of the data depends entirely on the meaning of the response. Too often, experiments with verbal instructions fail to include adequate checks that the subject's understanding is what the experimenter presumes (see further Section 14.1.2).

Conceptual confounding, although not distinct from stimulus and response confounding, is more concerned with ambiguity in conceptual terms. One example is confounding of substantive and statistical meanings of "interaction" and "significance," discussed in previous chapters.

A general source of conceptual confounding lies in the objective–subjective duality in psychological science. An objectivist view is fostered by the experimentalist emphasis on stimulus manipulation. This view is reinforced by the pervasive tendency to utilize structure in the external world as a base for development of psychological theory. This externalist approach appears in the failed attempts to solve the problem of psychological measurement in fields as far apart as psychophysics and cognitive development. And in memory theory, externalist confounding led to the monolithic conception of memory as accurate reproduction of given material, to the neglect of more important functional conceptions of memory (pages 723*f*).

Statistical confounding represents a perspective based on experimental design and data analysis. Every chapter of this book may be viewed in terms of the confounds it addresses. Thus, the confounding of individual differences with treatments in the designs of Chapters 3–5 is controlled by randomization (Section 8.2.3, page 247). Again, the confounding of position with treatments in repeated measures designs (Chapter 6) can be controlled with Latin square design (Section 14.3). Some of these confounds can be handled with educated common sense, as with factorial design, but others cannot be well understood without statistical theory.

Research judgment is the foundation for dealing with the confounds that accompany every experimental situation. In each situation, some confounds are known to be important, some negligible, and some uncertain or even unknown. Choice of task and response measure embody empirical judgment about confounds. Nowhere is our debt to our predecessors greater than in the development of our knowledge and research judgment about confounds.

8.1 CATEGORIES OF CONFOUNDING

Much confounding depends on empirical issues and details that are specific and peculiar to each substantive area and to different tasks and measures within each area. General guidelines thus have limited effectiveness. I have tried to impose some order on a heterogeneous field with the categories of confounding taken up in the following sections. I have relied on specific cases as more effective than abstract warnings.[a]

8.1.1 SUGGESTION AND PERSONAL BIAS

Thought and behavior are sometimes surprisingly susceptible to suggestion as well as to personal bias. These two confounds are considered in the following two subsections.

Placebo Effect. The placebo effect is too well-known to require much discussion, but it does provide an instructive introduction to the issue of control. Suppose the effect of medication is measured with a before-after difference score. To control for temporal confounds, a control group that does not receive the medication is measured similarly. A statsig difference in favor of the experimental group implies a real benefit.

This implication is correct, but not sufficient. The significance test applies only to the top level of the Experimental Pyramid of Figure 1.1, page 3. The meaning of this result must refer to the lower levels of the Pyramid.

A second extraneous variable is confounded in this example: suggestion. People who receive medication expect a benefit. This expectation underlies many "miracle cures." To attribute the result to the medication per se, the control group must receive the same suggestion.

Still a third extraneous variable must be considered. If the persons who administer the treatments know which is which, their expectations can influence the subjects. Such expectations can also bias recording of the data and decisions about doubtful or borderline cases. This can be a real problem with personnel who have their own ideas about which treatment is best. "Double blind" procedure may thus be essential, in which the experimental personnel as well as the subjects do not know which treatment is which.

This placebo example reemphasizes the minor role of significance tests and the major role of the lower levels of the Experimental Pyramid. The big problems come after the significance test. The big problems involve substantive inference based on extrastatistical considerations.

The placebo issue also reemphasizes the process–outcome distinction of Section 1.2.1. The control problems refer to the process interpretation of the observed effect. From an outcome perspective, placebo effects are positive and hence sometimes desirable. A good "bedside manner" is well-known to have worthwhile medicinal effects. This is one reason why the placebo problem remains a live issue in medical science.[a]

Personal Bias in Somatotype Theory. A notorious example of personal bias appeared in "somatotype theory," which claimed impressive correlations between body type and personality (Sheldon & Stevens, 1942). Three dimensions of body type had been defined in terms of physical body measurement by Sheldon. Simplified, these three body types were: *endomorphic*, or fat; *mesomorphic*, or muscular; and *ectomorphic*, or thin. To these corresponded three dimensions of personality: *viscerotonic*, characterized by sociability and love of comfort; *somatotonic*, characterized by vigorous bodily activity and social assertiveness; and *cerebrotonic*, nonsocial repressors whose motivational structure is antithetical to the first two.

A key idea was that every person could be represented by a *somatotype*— a profile of three numbers, based on the physical measurements for the three dimensions of body type. This somatotype profile was claimed to predict and explain an analogous personality profile for the three personality dimensions.

Somatotype theory created a sensation. The long-elusive concept of personality now appeared to have a simple, objective biological foundation. The investigators attributed their success to the development of the three-dimensional profiles. The reported correlations between each of the three body types and the corresponding personality dimension were astonishingly high: .79, .82, and .83. Nothing like this had ever been seen before. These correlations, as the investigators emphasized, are as high as could be expected if the two profiles measured the same thing at different levels.

Laboriously, and painfully, other investigators found that they could not replicate the reported results. It really was painful, partly because of the considerable wasted work, but especially because of concern that their failure to replicate resulted from their own shortcomings. Only gradually, as news of failures to replicate spread through word of mouth, did it become evident that the reported results must be false.

The cause was failure to control personal bias. Sheldon and Stevens knew each subject's body type when they classified his personality. Although they recognized the possibility of personal bias, they claimed they were very careful and dismissed personal bias as not operative. Regrettably, they made no attempt to assess it. In fact, the reported results were only an artifact of their desires. All the follow-up work was wasted.

In every science, suggestion and personal bias have created problems. Examples in physical science are cited by the chemist Wilson (1952), who says:

> No human being is even approximately free from these subjective influences; the honest and enlightened investigator devises the experiment so that his own prejudices cannot influence the result. Only the naive or dishonest claim that their own objectivity is sufficient safeguard. (p. 44.)

8.1.2 CONFOUNDING WITH STIMULUS MATERIALS

Stimulus materials are sometimes confounded with the experimental variable. Sometimes this confounding is innocuous, sometimes fatal. The problem is that the observed results may be peculiar to the stimulus materials, not the result of the variable it was intended to represent. The following examples are cited in part as case histories, in part because theoretical conclusions drawn from the original work still have some currency.

"New Look" in Perception. The controversial "new look" in perception in the 1950s revolved around claims that motivational factors could have strong influences on perception. The precipitating experiment asked 10-year-olds to adjust the size of a circular disc of light to match the size of a stimulus disc held in their hands. The experimental stimuli were coins; the control stimuli were gray, featureless cardboard discs of equal size.

The general hypothesis was that a desired object will be "perceptually accentuated." The coins, being desired objects, will thus be perceived as larger than the cardboard controls.

The data seemed striking confirmation of this hypothesis. Coins were overestimated by as much as 30%; the controls were estimated at virtually their actual size (Bruner & Goodman, 1947). This large effect in a simple perception of size argued for potent effects of motivation. Many investigators hastened to pursue this exciting claim.

But the claim was false. The pitfall was confounding. The control discs control only for size; they do not control for the numerous other differences from the coins. The coins were brighter than the controls; such brightness difference was well known to increase apparent size considerably. This alone invalidated the experiment. Furthermore, the coins and controls also differed in hue, texture, figuration, and tactile cues. Every one of these confounded variables was previously known or subsequently shown to influence size judgments, perhaps some kind of record for number of confounded variables.[a]

Little was learned from the extensive follow-up work on this coin study. The results of successive studies grew increasingly confused and inconsistent. In the end, a few hardy investigators were able to demonstrate reliable, though small, effects by conditioning value to initially neutral discs. By then, however, experimental interest had largely extinguished.

These coin-type studies, it seems fair to say, were largely wasted effort that should have been avoided. Rudimentary knowledge of visual perception would have shown the importance of brightness and figuration. Even had this matter been overlooked in the enthusiasm for the initial experiment, it should have been looked into before submitting it for publication.[b]

Prototypes as Organizers. The concept of *prototype* has been popular in attempts to study cognitive organization. One prominent hypothesis is that prototypes have psychological reality and act to organize the processing of given stimulus fields. But clear evidence of such organization can be elusive. Two kinds of confounding vitiated the following much cited study.

In this study, subjects received a list of 10 trait sentences about some person (e.g., *Laura is energetic, Laura is friendly*). They were told to form an impression of the person and to remember the traits for a later memory test. Lists were given about one extraverted person and one introverted person. Subjects were not explicitly informed about this list organization, it being assumed they would discover it themselves (Cantor & Mischel, 1977).

The memory test presented traits from the original list as well as new traits not previously seen. Subjects rated their confidence that each trait was or was not in the original list. The new traits were of two kinds. Some were extravert or introvert, as in the original list; others were unrelated to the personality type of the original list. Thus, the new traits for Laura included both extravert and unrelated traits. These new traits provided the critical data.

The theoretical hypothesis assumes that the subject develops a prototype of the person in the original task (e.g., Laura is an extravert). In the later memory test, this prototype is assumed to make the new extravert traits seem more familiar than the new unrelated traits. This theoretical prediction seemed to be verified in the familiarity ratings.

But a fatal confounding with stimulus materials was present. The new extravert traits necessarily differ from the new unrelated traits. Any observed difference in response may thus stem from adventitious differences in these particular traits. As unbelievable as it may seem, no balancing of any kind was used. A single subset of extravert traits and a single subset of unrelated traits were used in the memory test. These extravert traits could be more familiar in themselves than the unrelated traits, merely from arbitrary choice of the investigator. Indeed, scrutiny of the data supports this artifact interpretation.[c]

A deeper confounding was also present. No prototype was needed to produce the predicted result. The individual traits in the original extravert list would be more similar to the extravert traits than to the unrelated traits in the test list. Unorganized memory for these individual traits could thus produce the higher familiarity ratings. The operation of a prototype was merely assumed; the same data would be expected even without operation of any prototype. This experiment was merely meaningless.

Stereotypes as Organizers. Stereotypes about groups of people are one form of cognitive organization and many studies have tried to show that stereotypes influence processing of new information. The following well-run study shows that unsuspected confounding can happen to anyone.

In this study, subjects were first given one of two stereotype expectancies: That all men in a certain group tended to be "more intellectual than average" or else "more friendly and sociable than average." They then received one behavior sentence about each of 50 men in the group and were later tested for recall memory of the sentences (Rothbart, Evans, & Fulero, 1979).

The 50 sentences included some that were consistent with the given stereotype, others that were inconsistent. Recall was better for consistent sentences. This result had been predicted from the theoretical hypothesis that the initial stereotype expectancy would facilitate memory encoding of the consistent sentences and/or inhibit memory encoding of the inconsistent sentences. This careful study seemed clear evidence that stereotypes influenced memory encoding.

Overlooked was a confound; the numbers of consistent and inconsistent sentences were unequal. When this confound was removed, recall was slightly better for inconsistent sentences (Hastie & Kumar, 1979).

This pair of studies illustrates an important aspect of normal science. Confounding variables cannot always be foreseen. Every experiment aimed at process analysis must rest on some assumption that certain variables are unimportant. It can be unpleasant to find out that an unsuspected confound undercuts one's own published work but this is part of normal scientific advance.

Perceptual Contrast and Assimilation. Optical illusions are fascinating with their compelling demonstrations of how our trusted visual sense can go so wrong in such simple situations. The earliest experimental psychologists studied these illusions with the high hope that such malfunctions of the perceptual system would provide unique insight into its operation.

All illusions embody multiple determination: Perception of some *focal stimulus* is influenced by some *contextual stimulus* in the illusory figure. In the line–box illusion of Figure 8.1 (next page), the focal stimulus is the centerline; the flanking boxes are the context. The illusion is dramatized by the vertical alignment, which was the traditional form of presenting the illusion.

Two basic illusory processes in vision were discovered over a century ago. *Contrast* means that perception of the focal stimulus moves away from the context stimulus; a medium stimulus may thus look larger next to a small stimulus, smaller next to a large stimulus. *Assimilation* is opposite to contrast; perception of the focal stimulus moves toward the context stimulus. Both processes have general importance, for they appear in other senses as well as in more cognitive judgments of everyday life.

The line–box illusion was considered a case of contrast. Big boxes seem to make the centerline look smaller; small boxes make it look bigger.

In fact, the illusion is a case of assimilation. In the experimental test of Figure 8.1, the subject saw just a single line–box figure and drew a line equal to the apparent length of the centerline. The data curve at the right of the figure shows that apparent length of the centerline increases to a peak and then decreases as

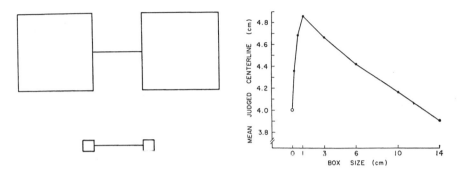

Figure 8.1. Line–box illusion, shown in left panel. Right panel shows magnitude of illusion as a function of box size. (After J. E. Clavadetscher & N. H. Anderson, 1977, "Comparative judgment: Tests of two theories using the Baldwin figure," *Journal of Experimental Psychology: Human Perception and Performance*, *3*, 119-135. Copyright 1977 by the American Psychological Association. Reprinted by permission.)

box size is varied from small to large. But all box sizes, except perhaps the very largest, produce a longer apparent centerline, as shown by comparison with the open circle for the no-box control.

Why was the line–box illusion traditionally considered a contrast effect? The reason appears in the data curve of Figure 8.1. Although the small and large boxes both make the centerline look longer, this assimilation effect is greater for the small boxes than for the large boxes. When both figures are presented together, as was traditional, the difference captures attention. Confounding the effects of the two box sizes produced the apparent contrast.

For almost a century, apparently, no one had run the no-box control. The contrast interpretation seemed clear and was consistent with work on other illusions. Indeed, the authors cited in Figure 8.1 did this experiment to test between two contrast models for optical illusions. The no-box control, included as part of the variable of box size in a factorial design, revealed the confound.

Optical illusions, contrary to their initial promise, have failed to reveal much about perception. A major problem is that most illusions involve both assimilation and contrast. With two processes acting in opposite directions, it is easy to explain almost everything and correspondingly harder to prove almost anything (but see Note 18.3.2b for Clavadetscher's two process theory).

Perception Versus Cognition in Infants. Remarkable innate capabilities in infants have been revealed in the last few decades. A key technique compares looking time to familiar and novel test stimuli subsequent to an initial familiarization phase. Numerous studies have shown that looking time increases as a function of the difference between the familiarization stimulus and the test stimulus. Time spent looking at test stimuli thus provides clues about how infants actually see the stimulus field on the familiarization trials.

In the example of Figure 8.2, 6-month-old-infants are first familiarized through repeated presentations of both events at the top. The short/tall rabbit is first stationary at the left, then moves rightward, vanishing behind the screen where it stops; after a certain time, a second rabbit concealed behind the screen moves rightward into view. This familiarization is assumed to set up a perceptual representation of a single rabbit pursuing a trajectory.

The two test events at the bottom are identical except for the window, which makes it physically impossible for the tall rabbit to move across without being seen. The infants looked longer at the impossible event. This was interpreted to mean that these infants had generated a representation of the rabbit pursuing a trajectory; reasoned that the tall but not the short rabbit would have to appear in the window before it could appear at the right; and were thus surprised because it had not appeared in the window. The increased looking time was taken to result from this disconfirmed expectancy. Striking innate cognitive capabilities are implied in this interpretation (Baillargeon & Graber, 1987).

Familiarization Events

Short Rabbit Event

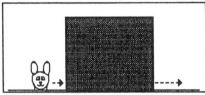

Tall Rabbit Event

Test Events

Possible Event

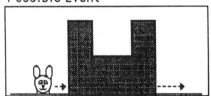

Impossible Event

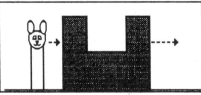

Figure 8.2. Schematic representation of familiarization and test conditions used by Baillargeon and Graber (1987). The short/tall rabbit is first stationary at the left, then moves rightward, vanishing behind the screen where it stops; after a certain time, a second rabbit concealed behind the screen moves rightward into view. (From R. S. Bogartz, J. L. Shinskey, & C. J. Speaker, 1997, "Infant looking time: The event set × event set design," *Developmental Psychology*, *33*, 408-422. Copyright 1997 by the American Psychological Association. Reproduced by permission.)

One possible confound was noted by Bogartz, Shinskey, and Speaker (1997), who suggested that the infants restricted their attention to a horizontal slice of the stimulus field corresponding just to the rabbit's head. If so, the window will not be noticed with short rabbit events, but it could have a novelty effect with the tall rabbit events. Such a novelty effect would increase looking time, as already noted. This is a purely perceptual process, however, not requiring the cognitive capabilities indicated in the previous paragraph.

This possible confound may seem untestable, and insightful design and analysis were needed to pin it down. Such a design was developed by Bogartz et al., and a substantial window effect of 12 s looking time was obtained.

Bogarts' study introduced a novel, potentially important approach to the study of infant abilities. The key was the development of a mathematical process model that could fractionate the overall looking time into components from several specified processes. This model was operationalized with the factorial design shown in Figure 8.3 of Note 8.1.2d. The model parameters, page 252, representing the separate processes could thus be measured. Some parameters were not statsig, evidence that the corresponding process was not operative. By this means, the cognitive process hypothesized in the original experiment was found wanting. Other parameters were statsig, as with the cited window effect, which supported the alternative, perceptual interpretation.[d]

This example also illustrates one source of scientific progress. Unsuspected confounds appear because science is always advancing into the unknown. In retrospect, confounds often seem obvious, even embarrassing, but they are a normal part of progress. In this case, the original study made a positive contribution by provoking the objection about confounding, which led on to the associated theoretical model and experimental design.

8.1.3 PROCEDURE CONFOUNDING

Potential confounds lurk in every aspect of procedure. The first case, of spontaneous generation of life, remains relevant today. The second case illustrates how a faulty methodology can have long-lasting consequences.

Spontaneous Generation of Life. In the mid-1700s, the idea that living things could come into existence spontaneously was widely accepted by the general public and by scientists as well. As one English naturalist learnedly observed, "To question that beetles and wasps were generated in cow dung is to question reason, sense, and experience." But although this belief in spontaneous generation was in tune with the prevailing outlook on insects and like creatures, it rested only on casual observation.

It was a notable event, therefore, when Joseph Needham presented experimental proof for spontaneous generation of animalcules, as the recently discovered microbes were then called. His experiment was simplicity itself.

Boil mutton gravy for 10-15 min, put it in a flask, and cork it tightly. The heat will kill any animalcules or their eggs that might be in the gravy; the cork will keep any from getting in later. To make doubly sure, Needham put the sealed flask in hot ashes for further heating. Yet a few days later, the microscope showed swarms of animalcules in the gravy—hard experimental proof of spontaneous generation. Animal matter was not necessary; a soup made of almond seeds would do as well. For this and subsequent work, Needham received the high honor of election as a Fellow of the Royal Society.

But the brilliant, flamboyant Italian naturalist, Lazzaro Spallanzani, saw two possible confounds in Needham's procedure: Some animalcules might have survived the 10–15 min boiling; also, animalcules might later have entered through the cork. Accordingly, he repeated the experiment but sealed the flasks by melting the glass neck. Then he boiled them for varying lengths of time. Sure enough, animalcules were found in flasks boiled 10-15 min, as Needham had done, but none in flasks boiled for an hour. Furthermore, animalcules were found in another set of flasks sealed only with corks, no matter how long they had been boiled. These results, however, attracted little attention.

In fact, spontaneous generation became more firmly entrenched through support from Count Buffon, an exceptionally able and respected naturalist. "You have put your finger on the very source of life," Buffon told Needham, "the very force that creates life." This life creating force they called the *Vegetative Force*, a momentous discovery that soon became a familiar concept throughout educated circles in England and Europe.

Against this glittering theory, Spallanzani's experiment had little effect. It was mainly ignored by Needham and Buffon (a still-common tactic in science). But Needham made one polemical slip; he couldn't resist one passing jibe at Spallanzani. The boiling heat applied for an hour so weakened the Vegetative Force, he said, that it could no longer make the little animals. In other words, Needham claimed a confounding in Spallanzani's procedure.

Had Needham said nothing about Spallanzani's experiment, he would have been a happier man. His passing remark gave Spallanzani an opening to renew his criticism. He developed additional controls to reject Needham's objection that excess heat weakened the Vegetative Force.

To these new experiments, Needham now objected that the heating destroyed the elasticity of the air inside the flasks; which elasticity was essential for operation of the Vegetative Force. Once again, Spallanzani developed controls to rule out this elasticity objection.[a]

This case from early biological science remains relevant because it embodies everyday thinking of scientists. The natural reaction to an experiment that disagrees with one's theory is to scrutinize it for confounds. They are generally easy to find, and seldom as airy as those raised by Needham. At the same time, experiments that seem to support an idea that is expected to be true are often accepted without serious scrutiny. Somatotype theory (page 222) was readily believed because it embodied standard stereotypes about personality of fat, muscular, and thin people. The prototype experiment (page 224) prospered despite glaring defects because people thought it ought to be true.

We take pride in our hard-headed experimental approach and speak approvingly of the stubborn fact that slays the grand theory. Not infrequently, however, the grand theory smothers the disagreeable fact. These problems have no simple solution, but awareness of history can give a useful perspective.

How Not To Study Child Development. Much work on child development has followed up groundbreaking investigations of Jean Piaget. The case of moral development (Piaget, 1932/1965) is considered here, in part as an extreme example of confounding, in part because Piaget's methodology is still advocated and used by some workers. Moreover, since Piaget relied on this same methodology throughout his work, understanding this confounding is important for understanding his general theory.

Two main claims by Piaget are of concern here. His first claim was that judgments about deserved punishment showed an age trend from focus on objective factors (specifically, the amount of damage caused by an action) to subjective factors (specifically, the intention behind the action). His second claim was for *centration*, namely, that children in the preoperational stage, up to 5 or 6 years of age, cannot integrate the two determinants of damage and intention. Instead, they *center* on one or the other, and judge the action solely by it.

Piaget's standard method required children to choose one of two given stimuli. For moral judgment, he told about two story children, one who had caused considerable damage fortuitously or even with good intention, the other who had caused negligible damage but as the result of an ill-intentioned act. One pair of Piaget's stories was:

> There was once a little girl who was called Marie. She wanted to give her mother a nice surprise, and cut out a piece of sewing for her. But she didn't know how to use the scissors properly and cut a big hole in her dress.

> A little girl called Margaret went and took her mother's scissors one day that her mother was out. She played with them for a bit. Then as she didn't know how to use them properly she made a little hole in her dress. (p. 122.)

The subject children were then asked to say which story child was naughtier. Following this, Piaget questioned the children about the reasons for their choice. The following discussion is based largely on the careful, detailed analysis of Piaget's method by Leon (1976, 1980).

Several confounds appear in the quoted pair of stories.

1. The Margaret story does not portray an ill-intentioned act, contrary to Piaget's statement about the intended structure of these stories.

2. The link between intent and damage is at best indirect. The damage is caused by the child's clumsiness.

3. The pair of stories present a complex of information that the subject child is presumed to have in mind when deciding which story child is naughtier. This complex of information could overload the children's memory so that the effective stimulus differs from the nominal stimulus. Such memory overload could masquerade as centration. It would of course be confounded with age.

4. Order effects are possible. The second story might cause the first to partly disappear from memory. Such order effects might interact with age, as already indicated. Also, as later investigators have pointed out, intent always precedes damage, and this order affects the results.

5. A more difficult confounding is also present. Following Piaget, the main concern was to study developmental trends in relative importance of intent and damage informers. What is manipulated, however, are specific, concrete instances of these two concepts. The results might be peculiar to these specific instances, not to intent and damage per se.

Because of these confoundings, Piaget's first conclusion about developmental trend in relative importance of damage and intention lacks validity. The same applies to most follow-up work. The claimed developmental trend is eminently plausible, but proving it is subtly difficult (see *Concept–Instance Confounding* below).

Centration, Piaget's second claim, was considered a basic inability of young children to integrate separate informers. Although sensitive to each informer separately, they cannot combine or integrate them. First claimed in moral development, centration was extended to general knowledge of the external world and became a primary characteristic of Piaget's preoperational stage.

In fact, the concept of centration is an artifact of Piaget's choice methodology. One confounding, pointed out by various investigators, is that a yes–no choice between the two story children is logically incapable of demonstrating centration. Thus, a choice of the story child who caused more damage cannot imply that intent has no effect, as centration requires. An alternative explanation is that the child integrates both informers but the net resultant happens to be greater for the story with greater damage.

Actually, Piaget's main evidence for centration was not the choice itself, but the child's verbal response when questioned about the reasons for the choice. But this questioning contains a serious confound noted by Leon. Having chosen the story with the greater damage, say, the child naturally emphasizes damage as the reason for the choice. Referring to intent would be contrary to the choice. Piaget's methodology almost forces the appearance of centration in the verbal response, especially at younger ages. This confound was fatal.

A more effective methodology was used by Leon. Intent was specified by explicit statements causally linked to the action. Instead of an all-or-none choice of the naughtier of two story children, subjects judged naughtiness of a single story child on a continuous, graphic scale, thus eliminating two of Piaget's confounds. Also, factorial design was used, illustrated in Figure 1.3, for which centration implies specific factorial patterns (Exercise 5.4). Indeed, Leon went beyond showing that young children can integrate intent and damage to discover that this integration obeyed algebraic rules.

Along with many others, I consider Piaget one of the great psychologists. He discovered numerous fascinating empirical facts about children's thinking—he did this by going to the children to examine their reactions in clever experimental tasks, especially tasks about knowledge of the external world, which was his main concern. In his hands, his choice-plus-questioning methodology led to striking achievements. We should be grateful for the good and prune out the bad.

Unfortunately, many who pursued Piaget's pioneering discoveries foundered on his methodology. The same choice methodology just illustrated with moral development was Piaget's standby in his diverse studies of cognitive development, most notably development of commonsense physics about the external world. This methodology remained popular despite its defects, of which the centration artifact is only a symptom. The distorted conceptual frameworks that have grown from this work have hindered psychological science.[b, c]

8.1.4 CONCEPTUAL CONFOUNDING

Two kinds of conceptual confounding have been prominent in earlier chapters. One is confounding of process generality and outcome generality as goals (Section 1.2.1). This conceptual confounding can readily lead to confounding in task, design, and procedure that undercuts both kinds of generality.

Another kind of conceptual confounding involved Anova "interactions." The common language meaning of interaction was confounded with its quite different statistical meaning. At the same time, the observable response measure was confounded with its unobservable referent. This twofold confounding has been discussed in Chapter 7.

Four other cases of conceptual confounding are considered in the following subsections. The first expands on a confounding that appeared in the preceding discussion of Piaget's methodology. The second concerns the classic issue of the definition of the stimulus. The third bears on one problem of interpreting rating judgments. The fourth considers the issue of meaning invariance.

Concept–Instance Confounding. Concept–instance confounding was one issue under *Stimulus Samples* on pages 22-23, in which the problem was to generalize from a sample to some population of stimuli. Concept–instance confounding is most egregious when results from a single stimulus exemplar are assumed to hold for the concept, as in the foregoing example of prototypes.

Concept–instance confounding crops up in many places. The pitfall is that the difference in response to the levels of a variable may be small or large, depending on arbitrary choice of levels. It is often convenient to ignore this dependence and speak simply of the effect of the variable. But sometimes this is a fatal error, as noted next.

The question of which of two variables is more important has been asked by investigators in several different areas, from judgment–decision to perception. In developmental psychology, this question bears on the developmental issue of which concepts appear earliest and which other concepts are derivative from these. Such questions of relative importance may be unanswerable, however, because the concept is confounded with its specific levels.

This question has already appeared in the foregoing claim by Piaget of a developmental trend from reliance on objective damage to reliance on subjective intent in judgments of punishment. To see the confounding, consider a 2 × 2, Intent × Damage design in which subjects rate deserved punishment for single story children. Some workers have interpreted the main effects of Intent and Damage as measures of their relative importance. Each main effect, however, represents the difference between two specific instances of the concept. The importance of the concept itself is qualitatively different from the difference in effect of two specific instances of that concept.

Intuitively, the concept of relative importance is natural and attractive. Workers who recognized the confounding naturally thought some way to compare relative importance must be possible. This is not true, regrettably, although theory control can solve the problem in some situations (Section 18.1.4).

Objective and Subjective Stimuli. The objective stimulus manipulated by the investigator is conceptually different from the subjective stimulus perceived by the organism. In many cases, fortunately, these two conceptual levels have a straightforward correspondence. When this is not true, trouble can arise.

A fertile ground for such confounding appears in concepts of *bias* and *distortion*, as with the foregoing issues of motivated perception and stereotypes. Evaluation of a job applicant, for example, may be influenced by gender, ethnic, or age stereotypes. A popular interpretation is that the given information is biased, distorted, or reinterpreted through the action of the stereotype. Implicit in this interpretation is an objectivist view that there is one correct meaning of the given information. Deviations therefrom are accordingly attributed to bias, distortion, or reinterpretation.

But the essence of any stimulus ultimately lies within the organism. Perception of a physical stimulus is a constructive process, as Helmholtz argued long ago, but to label construction as distortion is a misconception. Different subjects have different knowledge systems. Hence they will evaluate the same objective stimulus in different ways. To interpret this valuation process as bias or distortion is a conceptual confounding.[a]

Frame of Reference. Many tasks involve judgments that are comparative or relative. Even *good–bad* is partly relative. King Lear had horribly cursed his eldest daughter Goneril for dismissing 50 of the 100 knights in his entourage. Now he finds that his second eldest daughter Regan will allow only 25 knights. He speaks to Goneril, comparing her to Regan:

> Those wicked creatures yet do look well-favoured
>
> When others are more wicked. Not being the worst
>
> Stands in some rank of praise. I'll go with thee;
>
> Thy fifty yet doth double five and twenty,
>
> And thou art twice her love.
>
> *King Lear* (II.4, 249-253)

The response to any one stimulus may thus depend on a frame of reference partly determined by other stimuli.

This problem of frame of reference arose in attempts to extend the contrast–assimilation effects found with sensory stimuli to cognitive realms. Analogous effects were obtained with cognitive stimuli, promising evidence for unification of sensation and cognition. These effects, unfortunately, were found to be confounded with response bias, not true shifts in stimulus value.

In one representative study, subjects rated goodness of each of 11 successive personality traits that described a certain person. The first seven traits were clearly "good" for one group of subjects, clearly "bad" for another group. The final four traits, of neutral value, were the same for both groups.

The theoretical hypothesis was that sensory-type adaptation would occur as the first seven traits were presented. The last of the seven good traits would thus seem closer to neutral than the first; similarly for the seven bad traits. By comparison to this adaptation level, the neutral traits would seem somewhat negative to the "good" group, somewhat positive to the "bad" group.

This difference was observed in the ratings of the two groups. It was interpreted to imply that the neutral traits had different meaning and value to the two groups. This study was one of many that sought to exploit the mass of exact work on perception as a foundation for theory of social judgment.

In fact, the effect seems only an artifact of the frame of reference. With the rating response, it is known that subjects tend to spread their responses over the whole scale. The initial responses in the "good" group will thus tend to spread down below the neutral point; initial responses in the "bad" group will tend to spread up above the neutral point. When the first neutral trait is given, therefore, it must be rated below neutral by the "good" subjects, above neutral by the "bad" subjects.

This difference in response reflects the verbal frame of reference. The responses must differ even if the underlying feeling is identical. No real change in word meaning or value need be involved. With this design, the frame of reference artifact is confounded with any meaning–value change. This study is one of many that overlooked this artifact.[b]

This example is interesting because real changes in meaning–value do occur in some situations. People get habituated to bad situations, for example, which become less aversive. It can be exceptionally difficult, however, to deconfound the response artifact from any real change in meaning–value.

Meaning Invariance Versus Meaning Change. The hypothesis that people strive for consistency and actively reduce inconsistency is attractive, and it has been the primary postulate in a number of theories. These theories claim that when informer stimuli are integrated, they change one another's meanings so as to produce a more consistent, unified whole. Inconsistencies would thus be smoothed out by such change of meaning.

An early consistency theory was the Gestalt position of Asch (1946), who asked subjects to judge persons described by several personality traits. In one experiment, Asch asked subjects to list synonyms of the trait *calm* in two otherwise different descriptions. Different synonyms were given, which Asch interpreted to mean that *calm* had different meanings in the two descriptions.

Instead, the synonyms could have been produced in reaction to the other traits in the description. This confounding was clearly present; some of the responses were direct synonyms of the other traits, not of *calm* itself.

Similar confounding undercut nearly all of Asch's results. Similar confounding troubles much published work on cognitive consistency. Such confounding renders the results inconclusive.[c]

Meaning invariance is thus a viable alternative to Asch's claim of meaning change. The problem is to develop a valid test between these two interpretations. Such a test was obtained with theory control (Section 8.2.5). The cognitive consistency theories predict nonparallelism in an appropriate factorial design. But parallelism is obtained, illustrated in Figure 11.2, page 317. This outcome infirms the consistency theories and supports the alternative hypothesis of meaning invariance. Meaning invariance is fairly general, having been found in other areas, such as psycholinguistics (see Chapter 21).

8.1.5 FAILURE TO RANDOMIZE

The principle of randomization comes close to being an absolute for experimental analysis. Failure to randomize opens the door for confounding to walk in.[a]

The Case of the Molded Plastic. An interesting failure to randomize appeared in a study of strength of molded plastic. Hot plastic was injected into a mold, pressed for 10 seconds, then removed. This was then repeated using 20 seconds pressing time, then 30 seconds, and so on. After all the samples had cooled, their strength was measured. The data showed a lovely curve of increasing strength as a function of longer pressing time (Wilson, 1952/1990, p. 55).

The research supervisor, however, objected because randomization was not used; pressing time was confounded with order of pressing. This was a doctrinaire objection, apparently, without any specific hypothesis about how the confounding might have bad effects. Bad effects there were, however, for replication using randomized order showed essentially no relation between plastic strength and pressing time. Once the confounding was recognized, it was quickly tracked down. Plastic strength depended on the temperature of the pressing mold, which had steadily increased over successive trials.

Balancing Treatments Over Time. In *"Why randomize?"* Greenberg (1951) cites a medical study that employed repeated presentations of experimental and control conditions in the alternating order:

$$E\ C\ E\ C\ E\ C\ \ldots\ E\ C.$$

This might seem adequate to balance temporal trends, since E and C follow each other equally often except once in the long sequence. The slight asymmetry from starting with E would hardly seem a problem because numerous presentations were used.

The asymmetry begins to look more serious, however, if imaginary parentheses are placed around the treatment pairs:

$$(E\ C)\ (E\ C)\ (E\ C)\ \ldots\ (E\ C).$$

Suppose there is a temporal trend so that the response decreases by the amount d over the time between successive trials. Then E is favored over C by the amount d in each and every parenthesis. The *mean* difference is not increased by the multiple presentations, but its reliability and likely statistical significance will be. A similar argument applies if there is differential transfer between C following E and E following C. This design is thus dangerously flawed. In actual fact, a serious confounding was present in this medical study.[b]

Elimination of Subjects in Activation Theory of Emotion. A deliberate violation of random assignment arose in a study of the once-popular hypothesis that all emotions involve the same basic substrate of activation, differing in emotional quality only to the extent that they are distinguished by verbal labels (Schachter & Wheeler, 1962). This study involved three groups in which emotional activation was induced by drug injections: epinephrine activation, chlorpromazine depressant, and saline control. The response measure was emotional reaction to a slapstick film. But, contrary to the activation hypothesis, the epinephrine–saline difference was not statsig.

It was observed, however, that six of the 20 epinephrine subjects showed little indication of activation in ancillary measures included for this purpose. These subjects should not count, it was argued, because an effect should theoretically be found only in activated subjects. Hence these subjects were eliminated. This done, the difference was statsig.

This reasoning sounds plausible. Reactions to epinephrine vary across individuals. If these six subjects experienced little activation, they were simply irrelevant to the test of the theoretical hypothesis. Eliminating subjects violates the randomization, however, and this makes it suspect.

In fact, this elimination of subjects destroys the experiment. To illustrate the danger, suppose that the six subjects who did not report activation symptoms were stolid types who would have generally lower scores on the response measure of emotion. Indeed, eliminating them is what yielded the statsig results. But corresponding to these six subjects are another six in the control group expected to be similarly stolid with lower scores. The subject elimination would thus produce a serious bias in favor of the theoretical hypothesis.

We cannot know whether this confound was present, of course, but its plausibility undercuts the experiment. It is, of course, only one concrete example among other possible confounds.

The investigators did well to scrutinize the data in this detail. The outcome could have encouraged them to do a replication, obtaining a valid and more powerful test through preliminary screening of subjects not activated by epinephrine. Without replication, publication seems unwarranted.

This example bears on psychology of scientific progress. The cited theory of emotion rested essentially on the above experiment and one other. In this latter experiment, some results disagreed with the theory; all the other results failed to support the theory. But, after more or less plausible post hoc elimination of one-third of the subjects, the data fell "neatly in line with theoretical prediction" (Schachter & Singer, 1962, p. 396). It is not surprising that attempts to replicate have been unsuccessful; the main claimed results were artifacts of data analysis.

Curiously, this activation theory of emotion was widely embraced, and became a standard "fact" in introductory texts. Despite failures to replicate, the theory still has adherents. It agreed with what many people wished to believe at the time, personal biases that short-circuited serious evaluation of the data analysis.[c]

8.1.6 SUNDRY CONFOUNDING

Confounding Wins Nobel Prize. When the French physicist, Becquerel, heard of Roentgen's discovery of X-rays emitted by a fluorescent spot on a cathode-ray tube, he wondered whether phosphorescent minerals might also emit X-rays. Accordingly, he wrapped a photographic plate in black paper to keep out light, placed a crystal of phosphorescent material on top and exposed it to sunlight, which caused the crystal to phosphoresce. Sure enough, when the photographic plate was developed, there was an image of the crystal, formed by rays emitted by the crystal. This striking result was quickly published.[a]

Extending this work on a later day, Becquerel took his preparation outside only to find that clouds had come in to obscure the sun so the crystal did not phosphoresce. He returned the preparation to a dark drawer and resumed his work on a sunshine day. Although he had every reason to use his preparation from the dark drawer, he cautiously made a new preparation. Then for no particular reason, he developed the old plate together with the new. To his astonishment and dismay, the old plate showed an intense image of the crystal. His published paper was in error.

Becquerel quickly pursued this matter. He found that the intense image on the old plate was due to a trace of uranium in the phosphorescent crystal. Serendipitously, he had discovered radioactivity. For his work pursuing this clue, he shared the 1903 Nobel Prize with Marie and Pierre Curie. I wish all my readers similar alertness and similar skill when Nature taps on your door.

Desirable Confounding. For outcome generality, confounding may be desirable. In World War II, a meat shortage was accompanied by a surplus of sweetbreads, animal organs that had high nutritional value but were generally disliked in America. To help alleviate the meat shortage and improve the diet, Kurt Lewin was asked to develop a way to persuade housewives to serve more sweetbreads. In one condition, actually Lewin's control condition, a lecturer presented a group of housewives a solid case for the real nutritional advantages of sweetbreads over standard cuts of meat. In the other, experimental condition, similar material was presented, but the housewives also discussed the matter among themselves. In addition, Lewin asked for a personal commitment by asking these women to raise their hands if they planned to serve sweetbreads to their family within the next month.

A subsequent test indicated that the second treatment was more effective. For process generality, this might be unsatisfactory because the treatment confounds the personal discussion and the commitment variables (among others). But in this case, results were what counted. Lewin sensibly put multiple factors into the experimental group. Similar situations not infrequently arise with other issues of social action.[b]

Organ Slippage. Medicine supplies numerous examples of confounding, organ slippage being a dramatic example. When X-rays were introduced early in this century, doctors observed with consternation that the liver and other organs appeared too low in the body in the X-rays of many patients. This disease was named *organ slippage*; many surgical operations were performed to correct it.

Unfortunately for these patients, this disease existed only in the doctors' imagination. Their conception of organ location had been obtained from cadavers, which were horizontal. When X-rayed, however, people were in the vertical position, so their organs naturally hung lower.[c]

Examples from Physics. Apparatus confounding is often serious, as much in physical science as in psychology. Wilson (1952) cites other examples besides the case of plastic strength mentioned earlier. The Nobel physicist Feynman contributed another example when he refused to believe a critical photograph of the decay trace of an antiproton, insisting it must be an apparatus artifact. This was resolutely denied by those who constructed and used the apparatus. The disagreement was settled when Feynman deduced from the trace pattern that a metal bolt must be at a specific position in the apparatus, where it was indeed found (see Gleick, 1992, pp. 305*f*).

Clever Hans, the Mathematical Horse. "Hans, how much is 2/5 and 1/2?" Mr. von Osten asked his horse, Clever Hans. "9/10," replied Hans, tapping his right hoof 9 times to indicate the numerator, then 10 times for the denominator. In answer to "What are the factors of 28?," Hans tapped 2, 4, 7, 14, and 28. Besides such mathematical abilities, which even some graduate students might envy, together with ability to understand spoken and written German, Hans had musical ability. He would nod *yes* to consonant chords, *no* to dissonant chords, and even tap which note should be omitted to change dissonance to consonance.

Many skeptics, including experts on animal behavior and magician's tricks, came burning to expose Hans—and left believers. Intense scrutiny of von Osten revealed no signals or unwitting cues from him to Hans. Hans' intelligence seemed proven beyond doubt when it was found that his abilities remained even when his master was not present.

Hans' performance thus argued for high conceptual abilities in animals. Von Osten had taken four arduous years to train Hans, starting with very simple problems, and using carrots as reinforcers in an early demonstration of the efficacy of operant conditioning. Hans' performance seemed equivalent to that of a 13–14-year-old human. Even granted that Hans might be a Newton among horses, his performance suggested that animals possessed intelligence and rationality far beyond what anyone had previously suspected. This new view of the animal mind fueled passionate debate and Hans became the rage in Germany around 1904, celebrated in popular couplets, songs, picture postcards, even children's toys.

Hans was indeed exceptionally clever—but with no trace of mathematical, linguistic, or musical ability. He had learned to start and stop tapping in response to unwitting movements of the questioner, movements so slight that it was only with great difficulty that they were recognized. Overcoming numerous obstacles, including opinionated interference from von Osten and bites from temperamental Hans, this explanation was established by Oscar Pfungst (1911), who showed Hans a simple addition question on a slate he held in front of himself so he did not know the question. Hans could not answer correctly when no human present knew the answer. This failure implicated some signal cue, but it was still difficult to determine what it could be. In part due to Pfungst's perspicacity, in part to plain luck, the signal cue was found to be very slight movements, hardly as much as 1 mm, of the head, or even a slight motion of the eyebrows or nostrils of the questioner.[d]

Pfungst went further. Returning to his psychological laboratory, he began to play the part of Hans, at which he quickly became adept. Of 25 persons, naive to the purposes of the experiment, who served as questioner, silently thinking of some simple problem in addition, for example, 23 gave unwitting, slight movements when Pfungst had reached the correct number of taps. In another set of experiments, Pfungst could tell the questioners which one of four words they intended to silently think about even before the trial started. Similar abilities are sometimes found among mind readers and fortune tellers.[e]

Analogous confounding can occur in some psychological experiments. Experimenters' hypotheses can influence their interaction with subjects and produce the behavior they desire. Observers' expectations and stereotypes can influence what they see and bias their recording and reading of data. This and related problems have been studied by a number of investigators in social–personality (see contributors to Rosenthal and Rosnow, 1969). A substantial portion of work in these areas, it should be noted, is of poor quality (see Barber, 1976; Barber & Silver, 1968a,b; Kruglanski, 1975; Rosenthal, 1968).

Dynamic Systems. Behavior changes continuously over time. The much-studied conditioned reflex is only a momentary event in a dynamic system. The sound of the bell may cause Pavlov's dog to salivate, but this does not explain the dynamics of eating, neither why the dog starts eating nor why it stops eating.

One major class of dynamic systems has an optimal state, together with a control system that acts to rectify deviations from optimal state. If your food control system were disabled, for example, you might gain weight weight almost without limit or starve to death unless you forced yourself to eat. Luckily for most of us, the "wisdom of the body" keeps it in pretty good order.

But this wisdom of the body needs scientific study. Where is the food control system located? What information does it monitor? How does it work?

A provocative clue was found in the 1940s: Brain lesions in the ventromedial hypothalamus of rats induced overeating and obesity; lesions in the lateral hypothalamus reduced food intake and caused weight loss. These results suggest a "satiety center," in the ventromedial hypothalamus, which is activated by information in the blood and/or nerves; it operates by inhibiting a "hunger center" in the lateral hypothalamus. This two-center idea explains the effects of both types of lesions; and it leads on to search for the information signals that activate the satiety center. No less important, the results point to localization of function in the brain.

Further study, however, showed that ventromedial lesions produce a syndrome of behavioral, metabolic, and physiological changes: high aggressiveness; increased insulin response; decreased sympathetic activity; and finicky eating. Indeed, these rats overeat only if the food is highly palatable and easily obtained. In short, ventromedial lesions produce a confounded syndrome of effects, whose separate analysis is still in progress.

This example of confounding is included here for several reasons. First, hunger is a basic dynamic system that can be objectively studied. Second, and most important, it calls attention to dynamic systems, vital in every domain of psychology, wide-open if forbidding fields for pioneers. Third, it illustrates the need for analogous experimental analysis of such simplistic, amorphous concepts as learning, memory, belief, and so on. Fourth, it reemphasizes the ever-present difficulty of knowing whether your experimental manipulation does what you wish it to do—and nothing else.[f]

Fraud.   Fraud is not usually considered a likely confound, but it does occur. The experiments by Soal and Goldney (1943) were long considered rock-solid evidence for mental telepathy. An agent in one room, silent and concealed behind a screen, was the only person to see the target picture (one of five animals) on each of a long sequence of trials. The agent concentrated on each picture, attempting to transmit its identity by mental telepathy to the subject in the next room. On the other side of the screen, the assistant who called out the trial number to the subject had no cue about which target picture the agent was looking at. On each trial, the subject wrote down the first letter of one animal's name to indicate which picture he thought the agent had been looking at on that trial. Outside observers monitored some sessions but all were apparently impressed that the controls were airtight.

The subject did substantially better than chance with three different agents. Although few experiments on extrasensory perception have used adequate precautions, this one seemed completely convincing.

It seemed surprising, therefore, when Price (1955) raised the question of fraud in the Soal–Goldney experiments. Clearly, said Price, there are two possibilities: Either this is a genuine instance of extrasensory perception; or fraud was involved. To credit the former explanation, we must rule out the latter. But fraud was easily possible, said Price, and he went on to list six methods that could have been used. Price did not allege fraud. He said, however, that he would remain skeptical about extrasensory perception until an adequate experiment had been performed. For this, he was denounced as "irresponsible" by two authorities not involved in extrasensory perception (Meehl & Scriven, 1956).

In fact, fraud was involved, although this came to light almost accidentally. In the randomized list of digits for presenting the stimulus pictures on successive trials, Soal had interpolated dummy digits, a single stroke, which could be left as "1" or altered to "4" or "5" to fit the subject's actual response. This fraud was uncovered in clever statistical detective work by three successive sets of investigators who studied the "random" sequences used for stimulus presentation, all of which had been prepared by Soal. Fraud is now accepted, even by adherents of extrasensory perception.

Nor was this an isolated instance. J. B. Rhine, a persuasive apostle of extrasensory perception with a substantial experimental laboratory at Duke University, published in 1974 a paper discussing 12 assistants who had been implicated in fraudulent manipulation of results. Then a few months later, he published another instance of fraud by an "able and respected colleague and trusted friend." Further detail may be found in Markwick (1978), Colman (1987, Chapter 7), and Hansel (1980), on which this subsection is based.[g, h]

Controlled Drinking. Alcohol abuse is an extremely serious social problem. Treatment is obstructed because alcoholics typically have strong denial defenses. Attempts to moderate the level of alcohol consumption have had very limited success, which left many workers convinced that the only hope for chronic alcoholics is complete abstinence.

It seemed a splendid development, accordingly, when success was reported for an experimental study on controlled drinking by Sobell and Sobell (1973, 1978). Chronic alcoholics in a California state hospital were assigned either to a control treatment, oriented toward total abstinence, or to an experimental treatment, oriented toward controlled drinking. After discharge from the hospital, telephone follow-ups were done to assess long-term effects of the treatment. The interviewer assessed the number of days of "functioning well" (abstinence or controlled drinking). The experimental, controlled drinking group appeared to be better. This result was highly acclaimed.

Credibility of this study is undercut by deficiencies in experimental procedure. For example, the second-year follow-up assessments were made by one of the authors, who had a personal concern with establishing the efficacy of controlled drinking. Even the rudimentary precaution of having a blind assistant spot check these assessments was apparently not taken. Such precaution would seem essential, especially because the telephone interview and the response measure were unusually susceptible to personal bias. That such personal bias can be serious has long been known; one example was cited in the earlier case of somatotype theory. This confounding undercuts the credibility of the results.

This concern about personal bias is underscored by erroneous statements about procedure in the cited report. Thus, the 1978 report states repeatedly that follow-up interviews were made monthly, but this was later found to be untrue. In the second-year follow-up, for example, the frequency of interviews ranged irregularly from 1 to 17, with a median of 6, and with four patients with 3 or fewer interviews. Again, the original report claims that random assignment was used, whereas statistical analysis showed strong evidence of nonrandom assignment (Exercise 12.b2). Indeed, an investigating committee of the Sobells' study stated that "They simply didn't do what they said."

More serious is that independent investigation of these same subjects by Mary Pendery (Pendery, Maltzman, & West, 1982) revealed a very different picture. As one example, consider the six controlled drinking subjects ranked highest in the third-year follow-up, which had claimed that all six were "functioning well" on every day of that year. In sharp contrast, Pendery et al. found that four of the six had engaged in excessive drinking during that year (their Table 3). Here is what they say about one of these subjects:

> Subject states that "the third year included some of my worst drinking experiences." In August 1972, "after drinking more than a fifth of liquor per day, I went to the San Bernardino Alcoholism Services for help. I was having shakes and other withdrawal symptoms and was very sick physically. By then, a physician told me I had alcohol cirrhosis of the liver." A record of the subject's application for treatment there, his wife's statement, documentation of subsequent hospitalization for alcoholism treatment, and continued deterioration of his health are consistent with his self-report. (p. 173.)

Pendery, et al. concluded that

> Most subjects trained to do controlled drinking failed from the outset to drink safely. The majority were rehospitalized for alcoholism treatment within a year after their discharge from the research project. (p. 169.)
>
> (From M. L. Pendery, I. Maltzman, & L. J. West, 1982, "Controlled drinking by alcoholics? New findings and a reevaluation of a major affirmative study, *Science, 217,* 169-175. Copyright 1982 by American Association for Advancement of Science. Reprinted by permission.)

Although this report produced a "storm of controversy," not to mention extreme unpleasantness for the authors, the conclusion that controlled drinking is neither effective nor ethical with chronic alcholics has since been widely adopted, even by many who initially criticized this report.[i, j, k]

Within Subjects Design. A model of scientific cooperation and scientific integrity is considered in this subsection. A potential confounding in a published study was called to the authors' attention through a pilot study by a person at another university. Working cooperatively, these investigators showed that the confounding was real, an outcome that illustrates a need for caution in using within subjects design.

The role of organization in long-term visual memory was at issue. In the initial session, half the subjects saw eight scenes with objects arranged in "real-world" locations; the other half saw the same objects arranged haphazardly. In the memory test, subjects saw four identical copies and four transformed copies of each original scene from the initial session, each copy representing a different transformation. They judged each scene "same as" or "different from" the original scene (Mandler & Ritchey, 1977).

This experiment was based on a neat idea for studying memory organization by using various transformations: addition or deletion of an object; replacement by a conceptually similar or dissimilar object; and so forth. Such transformations could provide an analytical tool for delineating the fundamental but still poorly understood structure of memory organization.

The question of confounding arose with the four different transformed copies of each one of the original scenes. In the memory test, the transformed copy presented second is similar to the first transformed copy except in one respect. Subjects who recognized this similarity-and-difference could realize that this scene must also be different from the original scene, thereby getting a correct response. This clue is amplified for the remaining two transformed copies. Even with no memory of the original scene, subjects could still get a good score. This potential confounding was found to be real in the cooperative study between the two universities, which entailed some qualification of the original conclusions (Mandler & Read, 1980).

This case illustrates an everpresent danger with repeated measures, namely, that transfer from early trials can confound response to later trials. In the present case, within subject design could have been used by testing each subject on only one transformation of each original scene using Latin square design (see Exercise 14.b16).

This case is a model of responsible science. For each of us, unforeseen confounding can undercut our published work; this is part of normal progress. The original authors set a role ideal with their arduous, unpleasant follow-up experiment to settle the ambiguity in the original study and place this on record to avoid possible trouble to other investigators.

8.2 CONTROL OF CONFOUNDING

In a literal sense, *control* is deliberate manipulation of variables. Any observed effect can then be reasonably attributed to the manipulation. This form of control constitutes the foundation of experimental science.

In practice, however, control usually means to balance, hold constant, eliminate, or otherwise rule out the influence of extraneous variables, especially confounds that may accompany the manipulation. In this sense, the concept of control is an integral component of the Experimental Pyramid of Chapter 1, woven into every chapter of this book. To complement the foregoing discussion of categories of confounding, five kinds of control are discussed briefly here.

8.2.1 PROCEDURE CONTROL

The most important form of control is control of procedure—how the experiment is actually conducted. A well-designed experiment is not enough; it must also be well-executed. On the integrity of the procedure depends the integrity of the data (see further Anderson, 1982, Chapter 1).

Procedure control is paramount in test theory. Reliability and validity, the two primary goals, have to be achieved with concrete test items. Numerous examples have shown how hard it is to weed out items that will be misunderstood or confusing to an occasional testee. Procedure control is even more important in test administration. Some life decisions, about remedial schooling and therapeutic programs, for example, are made on the basis of tests. Administering a test should not be left to careless or poorly trained persons. Excellent discussions of these issues are given by Cronbach (1990, Chapter 3), who illuminates with borderline cases that can arise in practice.

Experimental psychology, in contrast to test theory, largely takes procedure control for granted. Statistics texts emphasize random assignment, for example, but rarely discuss *how* to randomize. Undergraduate texts on research method cover many useful topics but often say little about procedure control: How to write instructions, how to do pilot work, how to hold a rat, speak to a child, debrief a subject, and so forth.[a]

Procedure control is difficult to discuss because much depends on specifics of each area and task. Considerations vital in one area are often irrelevant in another. The following brief comments on three particular issues from my own experience may help focus attention on the general problem.

Subjects should not generally be run in batches, in my opinion, but one by one. Batch running is attractive because a lot of subjects can be run quickly, by taking time from a regular class or by signing up a batch of subjects in an empty room. But some subjects are sure to be inattentive in the batch situation and others are sure to be confused. This compromises the data. This is not simply a matter of greater variability but of systematic bias. Batch running sacrifices control of procedure—sacrificing the data (Anderson, 1982, pp. 31*ff*).

As one example, the representativeness heuristic stemmed from poor procedure (Kahneman & Tversky, 1972). This heuristic asserts that subjects make inferences from single samples almost entirely in terms of the sample proportion, regardless of sample size and population proportion. Their results seemed to support their claim. Results obtained by Leon and Anderson (1974), however, disagreed sharply with the representativeness heuristic (page 640).

The simplest explanation of this disagreement is that Kahneman and Tversky failed to make the task clear to their subjects. Subjects were run in a couple minutes in a large classroom batch. That the task was not clear is shown by the fact that 10% of their subjects gave unusable data and were eliminated. When 10% of the subjects are clearly confused, not much confidence can be placed in the other 90%. It seems likely that subjects understood the task simply as one of judging the sample proportion. In fact, the initial disproof of the representative heuristic just cited has been extensively supported in later work.[b]

A second suggestion is that research supervisors should routinely sit as a pilot subject for their assistants in each experiment for which this is possible. My own practice falls short, I must confess. I always go over successive pilot data for each experiment in detail with my assistants, but I somehow shirk serving as a pilot subject. When I have done so, however, I have often been taken aback at how many aspects of procedure they can be insensitive to. Many experimental tasks seem more or less robust against casual procedure, but some are not. Some of the inconsistencies that trouble the literature may reflect casual differences in procedure.

A third suggestion is that verbal instructions need careful attention. This issue, together with related issues of procedure, is discussed in Section 14.1.2.

8.2.2 DESIGN CONTROL

Experimental design has many uses for experimental control. Foremost is control of individual differences, a central concern because individual differences are a primary source of variability. Common controls are with repeated measures design (Chapter 6) and single subject design (Chapter 11), although these designs introduce dangers of confounding from transfer and other order effects (Section 14.4). Alternatives for control of individual differences that do not require repeated measures are block design (Section 14.2) and analysis of covariance (Chapter 13).

Other forms of design control focus on extraneous variables, epitomized in the placebo control of medicine. Such control groups do not actually control any extraneous variable. Instead, they represent effects of that variable, a baseline for comparing the response of the experimental group. Placebo control, in particular, does not control suggestion in the experimental group but instead seeks to equalize it in the control group. Comparison of the two groups then measures the experimental effect, free from the effect of suggestion.

Blinding is intended to implement the placebo control. Suggestion would not be equalized if subjects knew they were getting the control rather than the experimental treatment. Double blinding may be necessary to control persons who administer the treatments as well as those who record and analyze the subjects' reactions.

A second experimental group sometimes allows better control than a standard, no-treatment control. Instead of the experimental and placebo treatments, two or more experimental treatments would be tested. This tactic of treatment-control group may be useful when social–political considerations argue against a no-treatment control. If a clinical treatment is expected to be beneficial, withholding it may be ethically or politically problematic. If a social treatment holds out promise, subjects may not participate if they think they might end up in the control group or they might behave adversely if they think they have.

In many situations, moreover, a good case can be made for the promise of two or more different treatment conditions. In studies oriented at outcome, rather than process, this tactic of comparing different experimental treatments may be more useful than a no-treatment control. Among other advantages, it provides opportunities to seek continued improvements in the treatment.

A rather different application of design control can be useful when some confounded variable is expected to have negligible effects. Instead of trying to eliminate the variable or hold it constant, it is manipulated across two or more levels. A small effect then supports the view that no serious confounding is present. This control by systematic manipulation can be markedly simpler and markedly more effective than other forms of control.

Finally, Fisher's development of factorial design deserves emphasis as an innovative form of control: control by joint variation. With one-variable design, other variables are controlled by holding them constant at some fixed level, possibly null. This leaves it uncertain how far the results will generalize to other levels of the other variables. Factorial design not only gives information about more than one variable but also about their joint, combined action. This information bears on the two basic issues of generality (Section 1.4) and multiple determination (Section 1.5). This is a notable capability, although complicated by the twin problems of model and measurement discussed in Chapter 7 and pursued further in Chapters 20 and 21.

8.2.3 CONTROL BY RANDOMIZATION

Although randomization may seem an odd form of control, that is its essential function. Assignment of different subjects to different treatment conditions confounds subject differences with treatment differences. Randomization does not actually control subject differences, of course, but rather ensures that there is no systematic bias. That is its control function. Randomization thus becomes a foundation for more formal analyses, such as confidence intervals.[a]

A notable feature of randomization, as Fisher pointed out, is that it controls unknown factors that might affect the response. We tend to accept this as we are told, not recognizing how remarkable it is. A priori, controlling for any unknown factor might seem impossible.

Of course, randomization needs to be maintained throughout the conduct of the experiment. Random assignment of subjects to conditions is not enough. It would hardly do to assign at random, but then run all the experimental subjects first, followed by all the controls. This confounds conditions with any and all changes over time. Similarly, it could be risky to have one assistant run the experimental group and another the control group.

Randomization may also be used to control procedural variables such as order of presentation. With the line–box illusion of Figure 8.1, for example, the set of stimulus figures was presented to each subject in a different random order. For single subject design, this randomization procedure has the further advantage that it ensures independence of responses, thereby allowing standard Anova (Section 11.2).

Stimulus materials may be similarly controlled by randomization. With a handy sample of stimuli, a different stimulus could be randomly assigned to each subject. This confounds subjects and stimuli, but the variability among the subject–stimulus combinations is used as the error term. An alternative is to define a population of stimulus materials and use a random sample, perhaps treating this as a random factor in the design (Section 15.2).

8.2.4 CONTROL BY ELIMINATION

A confounding variable can sometimes be controlled by eliminating it. Elimination is one goal of procedure control. Adjusting subjects to the task helps eliminate misunderstandings that can cause confounding reactions. Similarly, running subjects individually rather than in batches helps eliminate wandering attention and carelessness. No less important is smooth, practiced performance by the experimenter in the conduct of the experiment.

A different kind of elimination arises in repeated measurements, in which effects of one treatment may carry over and confound the response to the next treatment. Passive elimination of carryover consists of allowing enough time for the effects of one treatment to disappear before presenting the next. Active elimination consists of interpolating a standard, baseline treatment after each successive experimental treatment to bring the subject back to a standard state before the next treatment (see further Chapter 11).

A more clever form of elimination is with masking. An apparatus may emit clicks or other sounds that serve as cues to subjects, much as the body movements of Clever Hans' master. An effective way to eliminate apparatus sounds is to bathe the subject in gray noise, for which purpose commercial noise generators are available. This does not actually eliminate the apparatus sounds, but buries them in the ambient noise field. You can test this auditory masking by standing next to a running faucet while someone speaks to you from the next room.

Visual masking has been used to control effective duration of short visual stimuli. Although duration of the physical stimulus can be controlled exactly, an afterimage may persist. The subjective stimulus thus has some uncertainly longer duration that the physical stimulus. To control the subjective stimulus, a visual nonsense figure may be flashed on the same retinal location as soon as the experimental stimulus is turned off, masking the afterimage.

8.2.5 THEORY CONTROL

The idea of theory control is to incorporate the confounding variable in a mathematical model. This model is then used to fractionate out effects of the confounded variable, leaving an unconfounded response. In some situations, theory control is more effective than other forms of control. Moreover, theory control can handle some situations intractable to other forms of control.

Anova Model. The common additive model can be useful to control confounding. One application appears with position effects in Latin square design (Section 14.3). Since the treatments have to be given in some temporal order, treatment effects are inevitably confounded with position effects from practice, maturation, fatigue, and so forth.

If the treatments are balanced across position, the Anova model can fractionate the main effect of position out of the data. This position effect is not only deconfounded from the treatment effect, but measured in its own right.

Factorial design may be similarly viewed as having a control function. This is clear when a minor variable is controlled by balancing it in the experimental design. In repeated measures design, the subjects factor controls the main effect of individual differences. Something similar applies with major variables in factorial design. The main effects of each are deconfounded from those of the other, as already discussed.

Anova as theory control is limited by reliance on the assumption of additivity (Chapter 7). In many applications, however, approximate additivity may suffice to obtain adequate control for interpretation of main effects. Moreover, the interaction residuals can provide warnings about deviations from the additive model that may affect the interpretation.[a]

Signal Detection Theory. A showcase example of theory control of confounding comes from the theory of signal detection. Confounding from expectation is a problem with *yes–no* judgments in perception. In a test of absolute odor thresholds, for example, the stimuli are very faint, on the verge of perception. Judgment about presence or absence of such faint stimuli is readily influenced by expectation. Attempts at control by elimination through the use of no-odor "catch trials" have not been too satisfactory.

Memory research faces a similar problem. Recognition confidence may be substantially influenced by nonmemory factors of suggestion and expectancy. Such nonmemory factors are important in studying validity of eyewitness testimony, for example, and whether hypnosis can improve memory recall.

In the theory of signal detection, expectancy factors are included in a mathematical model of the response process. Instead of trying to hold expectancy constant or eliminate it, it is systematically manipulated. The model then allows its effects to be fractionated out, leaving a purified measure of sensory acuity or of memory (see further Section 20.3).

Cognitive Algebra. Exact algebraic rules have been found in many areas of psychology (Chapter 21). Among other uses, these algebraic rules can provide theory control of confounding.

One application appears with the size–weight illusion. Apparent heaviness of a lifted weight is influenced through expectancy based on visual size, as was seen in Figure 5.3 (page 131). The traditional control was by elimination, placing the weights behind a screen so they could not be seen.

Theory control of the visual cue was obtained with the additive model, size + weight, demonstrated by the parallelism of Figure 5.3. The size– expectancy effect is thus fractionated out, leaving a pure measure of the sensory effect of the weight stimulus itself.

This model goes further to dissect the conscious sensation of heaviness into two nonconscious components, one for each stimulus determinant. It does this by shifting focus from the original sensory question to the more general question of how sensory and cognitive cues are integrated. This integration rule, aside from its own interest, gave a superior answer to the sensory question.[b]

NOTES

An exemplary book on confounding is the methods book of Underwood and Shaughnessy (1983), especially for its invaluable sets of exercises. Although these exercises are limited by their framework of traditional verbal learning and memory, this book deserves emulation in every field.

The undergraduate text, *Experimental Psychology*, by Solso, Johnson, and Beal (1998), is based on the theme that students learn best by concrete example. Numerous case examples are used to illustrate concepts of experimental method. These are expanded with 16 short articles reprinted from diverse fields, each with running commentary and with exercises for students. The material on the nature of experimental design and on control is well done and avoids the historical and philosophical didactics that deaden many texts. Although aimed at undergraduates, this book should be a useful resource for graduate classes; see also Ware and Brewer (1988), cited on page 778.

Among undergraduate texts concerned with experimental psychology, Levin and Hinrichs (1995) and Shaughnessy and Zechmeister (1997) are worthwhile. Useful texts more oriented toward social and field research include Jones' (1996) fine book, Aronson, Ellsworth, Carlsmith, and Gonzales (1990), and an admirable book by Light, Singer, and Willet (1990), concerned with observational studies of higher education.

I believe methods texts are a concern of the whole field, and deserve vigorous discussion and debate. Anyone who writes a text puts in enormous efforts, but seldom is there useful feedback. How to improve is a central question—and responsibility—yet virtually nothing is known about how. Many undergraduate methods texts suffer from over-involvement in statistics. At the graduate level, methods texts are almost nonexistent; what the unfortunate students get instead is statistics texts (see Chapter 23).

8.1a. Questions of confounding become acute when randomization is lacking, a domain considered in Sections 13.2, 15.5, and 16.2.

8.1.1a. Placebos can have considerable beneficial effect. A dramatic example is given in Robert's (1995) survey of five medical/surgical treatments that showed promise in initial uncontrolled studies but were later abandoned as ineffective. The success rates in these initial studies thus reflect placebo power. With a total of 6931 patients, the outcomes were 40% "excellent," 30% "good," and 30% "poor."

Sanford (1994) cites the example of slipped-disc patients who suffer chronic pain not alleviated by bed rest. Nevertheless, double-blind studies showed a favorable response rate of 47% to placebo, remarkably high compared to the 70% for a medical treatment. Both cited articles present instructive overviews of the complex of medical, ethical, and experimental problems raised by the placebo effect.

8.1.2a. Bill McGill told me that the original study on overestimation of coin size (Bruner & Goodman, 1947) was severely criticized by Bruner's colleagues over the egregious confounding. Bruner's sole follow-up (Bruner & Rodrigues, 1953) failed to replicate; control discs of metal were overestimated only slightly more than the coins. (Their post hoc claim of greater *relative* overestimation for coins than for metal discs seems questionable empirically and irrelevant theoretically.)

This controversy over motivated perception ramified into theory of stereotypes. A review of this literature, together with an integration-theoretical approach, is given in Anderson (1991h, pp. 217-221, 228-231).

8.1.2b. The long-term impact of slipshod science is shown by the citation of Bruner and Goodman's coin study as a "classic experiment" in the twelfth edition of a prominent introductory text (Zimbardo, 1988), with no indication that others, including Bruner himself, had failed to replicate these results. See similarly the following discussion of prototypes and the later discussion of activation theory of emotion.

8.1.2c. Similar stimulus confounding also vitiates the follow-up study by Cantor and Mischel (1979), which claimed better recall for person descriptions ostensibly organized around a consistent extravert or introvert theme than for mixed descriptions. Here again the conceptual variable was confounded with a single subset of stimulus traits.

Here again, evidence is lacking to show that subjects had actually developed the prototype; the evidence actually indicates otherwise, in which case the hypothesized effect would be impossible. And here again, Cantor and Mischel's own data suggest that this confound was real and could account for the results. Indeed, the replication by Tsujimoto (1978) disagrees with their interpretation (see Anderson, 1991h, pp. 227-228).

8.1.3a. The concept of spontaneous generation of life proved extremely resilient. Another century passed before it was finally laid to rest by Pasteur (Nicolle, 1961, Chapter 4). This example reflects the slow advance of science into biology and medicine.

8.1.3b. Piaget's choice task methodology has been fatal to others, as with Siegler's (1976, 1981) choice methodology for studying cognitive development and with Maloney's (e.g., 1985, 1988) related work on teaching college physics. As one example, Siegler reaffirmed Piaget's conclusion that the concept of time was mastered only at the late age of 10 or 12 years. In sharp contrast, the methodology of information integration

Within Subjects

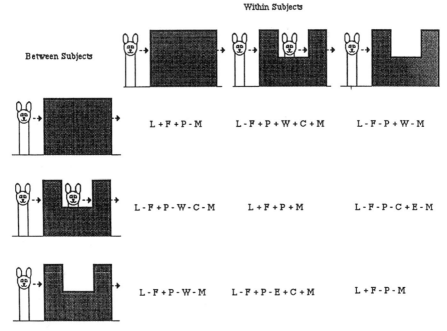

8.1.2d. Figure 8.3. Design and model for assessment of infant perception/cognition. A separate group of infants receives familiarization with one of the three stimulus situations shown as rows of this factorial design (see text). Each infant is tested with all three column stimuli. Entry in each cell represents the theoretical prediction of overall looking time; each letter represents one possible component process. Thus, W is added if no window is present during familiarization but is present in the test; subtracted if the reverse; and omitted if no window change occurs, as in the diagonal cells. (For completeness, the other parameters are: L = general level; F = familiarity effect; P = possibility effect; C = effect of change in face or motion; E = effect of change of rabbit in window to rabbit not in window or vice versa; and M = effect of amount of face or motion on test trial. The operative model was diagnosed as L + C + W; the possibility parameter P was not statsig, which infirms the cognitive interpretation cited in the text.) (From R. S. Bogartz, J. L. Shinskey, & C. J. Speaker, 1997, "Infant looking time: The event set × event set design," *Developmental Psychology*, *33*, 408-422. Copyright 1997 by the American Psychological Association. Reproduced by permission.)

theory demonstrated a true concept of time at least as early as 5 years (see Figure 20.1, page 651).

Piaget–Siegler methodology was adopted by Maloney (e.g., 1985, 1988) to study teaching of college physics. Maloney claimed that even college students have extremely poor capabilities for thinking in terms of functions involving mass, time, distance, and speed. Here again, information integration theory revealed an entirely different picture (Exercise 10.16).

8.1.3c. An interesting confound with stimulus materials arose when Diane Cuneo and I applied information integration theory to Piaget's famous conservation task. Young children say the same liquid is more when poured from a wide into a narrow glass, in which it rises to a higher level, This well-corroborated behavior is a nonconservation response, not recognizing that amount cannot change, something adults consider self-evident. Piaget claimed children *center* on height, unable to integrate diameter.

Centration was generalized to be a general characteristic of young children in Piaget's theory. Although they could attend to the separate dimensions of a stimulus, height and diameter in the present case, they were unable to integrate them.

To study development of the concept of conservation, we asked children to rate amount of liquid in glasses, using a Height × Diameter factorial design. The diameter effect could be a sensitive index of the effects of various techniques of teaching the idea of conservation. As a supplementary task, the same children rated area of rectangles (amount of cookie) in a Height × Width design (see Exercise 6.5).

The 5-year-olds showed no effect of glass diameter, just as though they were centering on height, strong agreement with Piaget. But equally strong disagreement with Piaget was found with the rectangles, which not only showed no centration, but instead an additive integration, Height + Width. This addition rule undercuts Piaget's claim that centration is a general characteristic of young children's thinking.

The inconsistency between these two tasks took us seven further experiments to iron out. Our final conclusion was that the apparent centration is peculiar to liquids in containers. This is presumably overlearned from everyday life, in which liquid height is a vital cue for drinking from containers. The conclusive experiment showed that when the container was taken away, leaving only the contents, the children did show a diameter effect. This work also led to a new outlook on children's judgments of quantity, as well as a new theory of conservation (Anderson & Cuneo, 1978; see also Anderson & Wilkening, 1991; Wilkening & Anderson, 1991; Bogartz, 1994b).

8.1.4a. This difference between the constructivist conception of the stimulus and the bias–distortion view is discussed in Anderson (1991h, pp. 195*ff*).

8.1.4b. This study of judgments of personality traits is reported in Berkowitz (1960). The same artifact pervades Helson's (1964) theory of adaptation-level (see further Anderson, 1981, Section 4.1; 1982, pp. 9*ff*).

8.1.4c. Asch (1946) presented several lines of evidence to support his hypothesis of meaning change, but only one does not suffer the confounding cited in the text. This exception is a primacy effect, in which the same set of traits yields different response when presented in forward and reverse orders. This primacy effect, however, has been shown to result from attentional factors, not meaning change (see Anderson, 1981, Chapter 3). Primacy may also stem from the basal–surface structure of attitudes and belief (Anderson, 1996a, pp. 147*ff*).

8.1.5a. Failure to Randomize. Three experiences of my own concerning failure to randomize may be of interest.

UNINSTRUCTED RESEARCH ASSISTANTS. My first year in graduate school, my major professor assigned me and one other student to run subjects in an eyelid conditioning experiment. I had some classwork to do, so I asked the other student to get started, saying that I would begin my share of the subjects the following week. The conditioning involved a very unpleasant puff of air to the open eye and the other student suffered from subjects' complaints. To avoid these complaints, he ran subjects only in the least aversive conditions. This would confound experimental conditions with experimenter, with time of quarter, and with possible apparatus changes over time. When I arrived to begin my part, accordingly, we started over. This confounding probably would have been unimportant in this task, but it would be poor workmanship.

The purpose of this example is to suggest that research supervisors should be vigilant with their assistants (see also Note 14.1.1c). I feel my major professor was at fault. He should have told us to begin by drawing up a random assignment schedule, perhaps submitting it for his approval. He had published basic papers in design–analysis and would never have thought of using nonrandom assignment himself (see also last paragraph under *Randomization in Society* in the appendix to Chapter 3). I mention this incident because my impression is that not a few research supervisors are lax in monitoring their assistants, a duty that is part of their teaching as well as their research.

HAPHAZARD ASSIGNMENT. A student once came to me for help in the analysis of data on sexual performance of male rats (truly enviable) he had carried out under the direction of his major professor. Several levels of a single independent variable had been used and he wished to apply Anova, especially a trend test. Unfortunately, the assignment of rats to conditions was totally haphazard. Some rats had been used in several conditions, some in only one. The number of rats in each condition varied irregularly. The best that could be done was to compare two conditions at a time, and even this was statistically queasy.

Confounding did not seem serious from substantive considerations and the results were probably reasonable indicators of the true effect. However, proper design would have avoided the pall that must afflict this article (Beach & Whalen, 1959).

Furthermore, proper design would have yielded markedly shorter confidence intervals. One silent advantage of statistics courses is that they instill a knowledge system that almost automatically avoids many naive mistakes.

DELIBERATE NONRANDOM ASSIGNMENT. In the third example, I served as action editor on a Ph.D. thesis in social–personality submitted for publication. The main experimental condition involved a deception that was revealed to the subjects after the experiment was over. The investigator feared that word of this deception would spread through the subject population, possibly undercutting the experimental manipulation. With the advice and consent of his thesis committee, therefore, he ran the control condition first and then the experimental condition. The time period to complete the experimental condition was thus reduced, thereby reducing the possible extent of contamination.

This failure to randomize was a serious mistake. In this task, temporal trends could readily have influenced the results. The given procedure confounded these temporal trends with the experimental–control conditions. The danger that knowledge of the deception would spread through the subject population seemed small in itself and presumably could have been adequately handled by a request for secrecy. What contamination might occur could dilute the effect but would not be expected to have any other serious consequences. I felt sorry to reject the paper, especially since the student's thesis committee bore major responsibility. The problem could have been resolved through replication with proper randomization (Exercise 14.a9).

8.1.5b. Another case of confounding of treatments with time is cited by Wilson (1990, p. 54). Further discussion is given in "Why Randomize" by Kempthorne (1977).

8.1.5c. On the confounding in Schachter's experiments on emotion, see Anderson (1989, p. 143). The cogent, early critique by Plutchik and Ax (1967) has been virtually ignored.

8.1.6a. Fluorescence and phosphorescence both refer to radiation from materials subjected to external stimulation. They differ in that fluorescence ceases with cessation of the external stimulation, as with a fluorescent lamp, whereas phosphorescence continues for a time, as with your TV screen (turn it off in the dark).

8.1.6b. I am indebted for the Lewin example to a source I have been unable to relocate.

8.1.6c. Organ slippage was reported in the TV program, *NOVA: Pioneers of Surgery*, previewed by Wagner (1988).

8.1.6d. The case of Clever Hans had a sad ending. Von Osten had invested his life in this project. He had complete confidence in his theory of animal abilities, quite unaware that Hans was reacting to these minimal cues. But the evidence was simple and irrefutable. It seems he did not long survive this disappointment.

8.1.6e. An ingenious, in-class teaching demonstration developed by Marshall and Linden (1994) simulates the Clever Hans effect with a white rat, Hanzel by name. In answer to questions from the class (e.g., "Is 5 the square root of 25?" and "Is the moon made of cheese") Hanzel pressed or did not press a bar, thereby activating a YES or a NO sign after 4 s delay. The pedagogical value of this demonstration is enhanced because half the class seems half-persuaded of Hanzel's intelligence and because the skeptics contribute by tracking down the hidden cue (an ultrasonic dog whistle manipulated by the instructor). Marshall and Linden suggest that this empirical approach is superior to the traditional approach of teaching critical thinking in terms of a series of abstract, learned steps because their approach involves active involvement with hypothesis testing, systematic manipulation, and other essentials of research method. I heartily agree.

8.1.6f. This section on eating dynamics is based on Martin, White, and Hulsey (1991).

8.1.6g. The fraud by students in Rhine's laboratory no doubt arose from pressure to get positive results. Similar pressures operate on everyone, especially investigators seeking grant funds to keep a project going and their personnel supported. Outright fraud is rare, but questionable behavior is not.

8.1.6h. When I was in graduate school, an article claiming to demonstrate telekinesis was submitted to the *Journal of Experimental Psychology*. The editor passed it around to a number of graduate students for scrutiny. It appeared to be extremely careful work, and no one found any fault. Although the result was weak, the editor accepted it for publication (McConnell, Snowdon, & Powell, 1955). None of us believed it, but no one thought that our beliefs should censor contrary results obtained in a careful study.

8.1.6i. The decision by *Science* to publish the report by Pendery, Maltzman, and West (1982) was sharply questioned in a letter to the editor by 10 editors of clinical-research–oriented journals. The editor replied:

In the absence of criticism of experiments and replication of results, the integrity of science would be destroyed. The overwhelming majority of scientists understand this, and most cooperate with those who challenge the validity of their work. The behavior of the Sobells with respect to the research report by Pendery *et al.*, was unprecedented in my experience of more than 20 years as editor.

The Sobells, in writing, threatened us with legal action while we were in the initial phase of considering the paper. Shortly after, we received a letter from their attorney. Under such circumstances, prudence dictates that contact between the principals cease and that one deal with the matter through attorneys.

The report that we published in our 9 July issue was very carefully edited. It was extensively reviewed, including evaluation by an expert statistician. Painstaking efforts were made to ensure an absence of comment about the integrity of the Sobells. We required that assertions made about patients' histories be documented by court records, police records, hospital records, or affidavits. The final draft was checked repeatedly, sentence by sentence, to ensure that supporting evidence was available. In crucial instances, two or more independent documents corroborated statements made.

For years the Sobell paper of 1972 went virtually unchallenged. Their work received a large play in the media. Attempts by Mary Pendery to examine the basic data and to follow up on patients' subsequent histories were impeded by repeated legal action by the Sobells. The avenue of a technical comment has been and remains open to the Sobells. They have not so far availed themselves of it. (P. H. Abelson, 1983, Editorial comment on controlled drinking study. *Science, 220,* 555-556. Copyright 1983 by American Association for Advancement of Science. Reprinted by permission.)

8.1.6j. Despite the sharp adverse reaction to the "new findings" of Pendery et al. (1982) for the controlled drinking experiment, their "reevaluation" now seems to have been silently accepted by many of their harshest critics (see Rivers, 1994, p. 202). As one example, Nathan (1986, p. 44) concluded that "The consensus among informed observers is that alcoholism treatment with controlled drinking as a prime treatment goal is neither efficacious nor ethical when offered to chronic alcoholics."

8.1.6k. Kohn (1997) incorrectly indicates that the report by Pendery et al. accused the Sobells of fraud. No hint of any such statement appears in this report, as is clear in the just quoted comment by the editor of *Science.*

Independent of this report, one of the authors later raised the issue of fraud (Maltzman, 1989, 1992). Maltzman actually had a good case criticizing the procedure used in the controlled drinking experiment, but he showed extremely bad judgment in raising the issue of fraud. Worse yet, he diverted attention from the strong case of Pendery et al. against the reported efficacy of controlled drinking. One consequence appears in the cited misstatment by Kohn. Another appears in the extreme reluctance of later articles that admit the failure of controlled drinking to even cite the report by Pendery et al.

8.2.1a. An instructive example of procedure control comes from work on conditioning of foot flexion in dogs by a highly respected experimentalist, described in his presidential address to APA's Division of Experimental Psychology:

I had some serious difficulties with the first dog I tried to condition. I was shown how, I was told how, and I had read how. At the end of several training sessions the dog was not giving any conditioned responses, so at the next session I increased the intensity of the shock. There were still no conditioned responses, so I again increased the intensity of the unconditioned stimulus. On a given trial, the animal struggled, and chewed through the strap that provided for attachment of a lever to the right foot, the foot that was to be conditioned to the bell-conditioned stimulus. I got some leather, cut it, and riveted it together to make a new strap. When this was attached to the lever and to the dog's foot, I continued the training session. It was not many trials before the animal responded to the bell again by chewing the strap in two. Shortly thereafter my career as a psychologist was giving way to that of harnessmaker, and the dog had a stable conditioned response of chewing a strap in two at the sound of a bell. When I sought advice, it was pointed out to me that I was using a shock of too great intensity, the lever strap was too long, the head stock was too high, a collar clip was not being used, and the belly strap was adjusted too loosely. . . . With the appropriate changes in these experimental conditions, further application of the training procedure resulted in elimination of the conditioned chewing response and quick establishment of a stable, clearly defined conditioned flexion response to the sound of the bell. (pp. 227-228.) (W. J. Brogden, 1951, "Some theoretical considerations of learning," *Psychological Review*, *58*, 224-233. Copyright 1951 by the American Psychological Association. Reprinted by permission.)

Good data depend on good procedure in every field of psychological science.

8.2.1b. Unfortunately, a good deal of the extensive work on the representativeness heuristic, reviewed by Koehler (1996), is difficult to interpret because of similarly casual concern with procedure (see also Anderson, 1996b).

8.2.3a. Repeated measures design includes a kind of control over subject–treatment interactions, for these are included in the error term.

8.2.5a. Innumerable published articles have used regression models to "control" differences between nonrandomized groups that differ preexperimentally. Such "control" is generally specious, merely wishful thinking (Sections 13.2, 15.5, and 16.2).

8.2.5b. Theory control may help avoid a drawback with the traditional *simplification strategy* of developmental psychology. Failure of children to perform a certain conceptual task may result from lack of auxiliary abilities required by the task, as with the memory demands in Piaget's choice task (pages 230*ff*). A natural reaction is to simplify the task so as to minimize the need for auxiliary abilities.

Implicit in this simplification strategy is an assumption that concepts are autonomous entities that can be revealed in pure form by stripping away the auxiliary abilities. "An alternative, almost opposite view is possible. In this view, concepts begin as tenuous aspects of particular skills. Only gradually and only partially do they evolve into autonomous existence" (Anderson, 1983, p. 262). In this alternative view, simplification strategy is self-defeating, for it throws out the concept along with the auxiliary abilities (see also Anderson & Wilkening, 1991, pp. 25, 33).

Complication strategy seeks to manipulate the levels of auxiliary ability in order to assess their effects. Complication strategy can sometimes be conjoined with theory control in the form of a theoretical model to factor out the auxiliary abilities.

PREFACE

Prediction is the strong point of *regression analysis*. In admitting graduate students, some departments utilize predictive power of the GRE. Similar predictive formulas are often used to sort out those more likely to succeed in particular jobs or to benefit from certain medical treatments. These statistical prediction formulas are typically superior to expert judgment, and less costly to boot.

The term *regression* merely means curve fitting, usually a straight line curve. This regression exhibits the response measure, Y, as a function of the predictor variable, X. The slope of this line reflects how strongly Y depends on X, so this slope is the main concern. Thus, a slope of 0 means that X has no predictive power for Y.

Statistically, regression analysis can be seen as an extension of Anova that uses a metric predictor variable, X, in place of the experimental variable, A, of previous chapters. The slope of the regression line, which is usually the main concern, can be determined, together with its confidence interval.

The two big problems with prediction are extrastatistical: To find good predictor variables; and to find a valid measure of the criterion to be predicted. The GRE is not actually a strong predictor of success in graduate school. Moreover, success in graduate school is not easily measured, and however measured may have little relation to the final criterion—life after graduation.

Regression can also be used in experimental studies, especially when the stimulus variables are quantitative or metric. With metric stimulus variables, regression analysis offers marked simplification of factorial design. Also, linear trend analysis is markedly simpler with regression formulas than with the linear contrasts of Anova that are generally recommended.

The correlation coefficient is a byproduct of regression analysis. It can be useful in specialized domains, as in test theory. The correlation coefficient suffers surprisingly many flaws, however, that severely limit its usefulness.

Causal analysis is the weak point of regression analysis. Regression–correlation is often used to attempt causal interpretation from uncontrolled, observational data. A good deal of what is reported in the media and even in professional journals is unwarranted inference based on regression analysis of uncontrolled data. The many well-known pitfalls are glossed over with lip-service cautions or simply ignored. Causal analysis with observational data has high importance, but effective work requires unusually high expertise, both statistical and extrastatistical.

Chapter 9

REGRESSION AND CORRELATION

Prediction is a strong point of regression analysis, already illustrated with prediction of success in graduate school in Section 1.5.1 (page 25). Regression analysis has valuable capability to utilize observational data, as in this example, not requiring experimental control. Multiple predictor variables can be teamed for better results with little more trouble than a single predictor. This simplicity contrasts with factorial Anova, in which each added variable expands the bulkiness of the factorial design. This usefulness of regression analysis reflects the empirical prevalence of linear trends with quantitative, metric variables.

With experimentally controlled variables, regression analysis can also be useful. Many experimental variables are metric: amount of reward, concentration of drug, length of word list, time intervals, and so forth. By utilizing the stimulus metric, regression can extract more information than factorial Anova. Simpler, nonfactorial designs also become feasible.

For causal analysis with observational data, regression has limited usefulness. A number of health problems, for example, have been traced back to their causes using observational data. Such results are more commonly presented as correlations, derived from the regression. Causal analysis is a weak point of regression with observational data, however, as shown by the well-known pitfalls of correlation.

9.1 ONE–VARIABLE REGRESSION

In one-variable regression, the data come in the form of Y–X pairs, one pair for each subject: Y is the response measure; X is the predictor measure. Thus, X might be grade point average in college, and Y success in graduate school. The problem is to find a formula that uses information in X to predict Y.

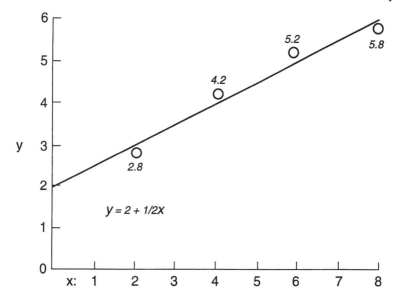

Figure 9.1. Regression line for set of four data points.

It helps to visualize the data as a graph showing Y as a function of X, as in Figure 9.1. Each subject or case is represented as one point, with Y on the vertical, X on the horizontal. The line in Figure 9.1 is the *linear regression*, the main concern of this chapter.

9.1.1 LINEAR REGRESSION

Regression finds a curve that comes as close as possible to all the data points. By far the most useful curve is the simplest, namely, a straight line: a line-ar regression.

Linear Regression Equation. A *linear regression* is a straight line curve. Its equation is

$$Y = b_0 + b_1 X. \tag{1}$$

In Figure 9.1, visual inspection indicates the regression line should pass through the Y values 3, 4, 5, and 6, for the four successive values of X.

The *slope* of the regression line is denoted by b_1 in Equation 1. If X increases by 1 unit, then Y increases by b_1 units. Looking at Figure 9.1, you can see that $b_1 = \frac{1}{2}$.

If $b_1 = 0$, the best-fit line is horizontal. In this case, $Y = b_0$, regardless of X. A horizontal regression line means that X has no predictive power.

The *Y-intercept* in Equation 1 is the value of Y when $X = 0$—where the line intercepts the vertical Y axis. When $X = 0$ in Equation 1, $Y = b_0$; the line intercepts the Y axis at $Y = b_0$. Figure 9.1 shows that $b_0 = 2$. In most applications, b_0 has little substantive interest.

The regression line is a kind of average of all the Y values of Figure 9.1. Unlike the ordinary mean, however, this average is not a single point, but a function that represents the relation between Y and X.

Prediction.   Prediction may be illustrated with the example of Figure 9.1. With the values of b_0 and b_1 just given, the linear regression is

$$Y = 2 + \tfrac{1}{2}X.$$

To predict for a new case from the same population, measure X_{new} and substitute in this regression. If $X_{new} = 2$, for example, $Y_{new} = 3$.

Prediction should generally be restricted to the range of X values in the original data. In the present example, it would be dangerous to predict for X_{new} values much less than 2 or much greater than 8. The danger arises because, in practice, the $Y–X$ relation is likely to change outside the given range.

9.1.2 FORMULAS FOR LINEAR REGRESSION

Visual inspection was enough to find the linear regression for Figure 9.1. Ordinarily, however, b_0 and b_1 must be calculated from formulas. These formulas involve the Sum of Squares from Equation 3.3, together with a similar Sum of Products.

Covariation.   Regression analysis is concerned with how Y *covaries* with X; some measure of the amount of *covariation* is needed. The first step is to define the *Sum of Products* of the Y and X deviation scores:

$$\mathrm{SP}_{YX} = \sum_{i=1}^{n}(Y_i - \bar{Y})(X_i - \bar{X}). \tag{2}$$

Note that this Sum of Products is similar to the Sum of Squares of Equation 3.3. If Y was changed to X in the above equation, we would get the Sum of Squares for X, denoted more simply by SS_X.

The Sum of Products measures how strongly Y depends on X. If Y and X are directly related, subjects high on X will tend to be high on Y. For subject i, therefore, a positive value of $(Y_i - \bar{Y})$ will tend to be paired with a positive value of $(X_i - \bar{X})$, and their product will be positive in Equation 2. Negative values of $(Y_i - \bar{Y})$ will tend to be paired with negative values of $(X_i - \bar{X})$, so their product will also be positive. A direct relation between Y and X will thus yield a positive Sum of Products.

If Y and X are unrelated, however, the sign of $(Y_i - \bar{Y})$ is unrelated to the sign of $(X_i - \bar{X})$. A positive $(Y_i - \bar{Y})$ will tend to be paired equally often with positive and negative values of $(X_i - \bar{X})$. Positive and negative products will tend to cancel so the Sum of Products will be zero, except for chance.[a]

The Sum of Products is thus a measure of the strength of the Y–X relation. Being a sum, however, it is larger for larger samples. To make it independent of sample size, we need to take the average. As with the sample variance, this averaging is done by dividing by $N - 1$, the number of data points minus 1. This average is called the *covariance*:

$$\text{Covariance} (Y, X) = \frac{1}{N-1} \text{SP}_{YX}. \qquad (3)$$

The *covariance* thus parallels the *variance*. If Y was replaced by X, Equation 2 would yield the Sum of Squares for X, and Equation 3 would yield the variance of X. The covariance is thus truly a co–variance.

Prediction Formulas. To use the regression equation, we need b_0 and b_1 for any given set of data. The formulas for these two regression coefficients are

$$b_0 = \bar{Y} - b_1 \bar{X}; \qquad (4a)$$

$$b_1 = \frac{\text{SP}_{YX}}{\text{SS}_X}. \qquad (4b)$$

In this formula for b_1, the numerator is given by Equation 2. The denominator is the Sum of Squares for X, defined as in Equation 3.3.

With these two formulas, prediction with linear regression is simplicity itself. Get a sample of cases from some population and use Equations 4 to get b_0 and b_1. Substitute the values of these two regression coefficients into Equation 1. For any new case, measure X_{new} and use Equation 1 to predict Y_{new}. Such applications are common in hiring employees, making medical diagnoses, and other forms of prediction.

Numerical Example. The data of Figure 9.1 are used to illustrate linear regression in Table 9.1. To get SS_X by hand calculation, we use the easier hand formula for the Sum of Squares from Section 3.2.5.

$$\text{SS}_X = \sum X_i^2 - N\bar{X}^2$$
$$= 120 - 4 \times 5^2$$
$$= 20.$$

We also need the sum of products, SP_{YX}. For this, there is also an easy hand formula, with similar form:

TABLE 9.1

ILLUSTRATIVE REGRESSION ANALYSIS

X_i	Y_i	X_i^2	$X_i Y_i$	$\hat{Y}_i$
2	2.8	4	5.6	3
4	4.2	16	16.8	4
6	5.2	36	31.2	5
8	5.8	64	46.4	6
20	18.0	120	100.0	(sums)

$$SP_{YX} = \sum Y_i X_i - N\bar{Y}\bar{X}$$
$$= 100 - 4(4.5 \times 5)$$
$$= 10.$$

From Equations 4, the two regression coefficients are

$$b_1 = \frac{SP_{YX}}{SS_X} = \frac{10}{20} = \tfrac{1}{2};$$

$$b_0 = \bar{Y} - b_1 \bar{X} = 4.5 - \tfrac{1}{2} \times 5 = 2.$$

The regression line is thus

$$Y = 2 + \tfrac{1}{2}X.$$

The last column of Table 9.1 gives predicted values, denoted by $\hat{Y}$. The *deviation* for case i, $(Y_i - \hat{Y}_i)$, is the deviation between the prediction line and the data point. In this example, each deviation equals .2 in magnitude.

Historical Example. A historical linear regression appears in Galton's pioneering studies of heritability, which showed that tall/short fathers tended to have tall/short sons, with b_1 near $\frac{1}{2}$. You can use Galton's equation to predict expected height of your own sons, with $\bar{H}_{father} = 69.5$ inches:[b]

$$H_{son} = \bar{H}_{father} + \tfrac{1}{2}(H_{father} - \bar{H}_{father}). \tag{5}$$

Galton's equation shows that a father two inches taller than average (H_{father} = 71.5 inches) can expect to have sons one inch shorter than himself. Symmetrically, a father two inches shorter than average can expect to have sons one inch taller than himself. The father–son relation could not be perfect, with $b_1 = 1$, for then all sons would have the same height as their fathers.[c]

In 1890, Galton's results were a revelation—quantitative order in the seemingly meaningless welter of individual differences. Galton's equation is only correlational, of course, and does not prove any genetic influence on height. It is logically possible, for example, that height is determined entirely by diet and that sons tend to follow the diets of their fathers. Proving heritability requires evidence of different character, as with Mendel's experiments on peas, in which genetic and environmental factors could be controlled.

A curious aspect of Galton's result is *regression to the mean*: Sons tend to be closer to the mean, $\overline{H}_{father}$, for both tall and short fathers, as Equation 5 shows. Similar regression to the mean has been observed with other characteristics, notably with intelligence. This regression to the mean is an inevitable consequence of imperfect correlation. Without understanding of statistics, it is an attractive mistake to conclude that the whole population is converging on a universal mediocrity. Closely related is the insidious *regression artifact*, discussed in Section 18.4.5.

Galton's studies provoked considerable work on statistical theory of relationships that hold for a population of people or other cases. Such relations apply to the population, as with the father–son heights of Equation 5, rather than any individual case. To handle such population relations required new statistical methods. Physical laws are $Y–X$ relations, of course, but typical physical laws hold for the individual case. Methods of data analysis from physical science were thus of limited help in this new area. Needed ideas and techniques were gradually worked out over the next several decades, especially by Karl Pearson and R. A. Fisher. As a historical misfortune, Galton's term *regression* came to refer to the statistical curve fitting itself, although this curve fitting has essentially nothing in common with his regression to the mean. In statistics, *regression analysis means curve fitting*, nothing more. Linear regression, our main concern in this chapter, just means fitting a straight line to the data.

9.1.3 STATISTICAL ANALYSIS

A basic question is whether X has predictive power: Is the observed $Y–X$ relation anything more than chance? Subject to assumptions discussed later, this issue may be addressed with Anova and confidence intervals.

Anova for Regression. The predictive power of X is measured by how much of the Sum of Squares for Y is predicted by the regression equation. This SS_{pred} is obtained as follows.

Let $\hat{Y}$ be the value predicted by the regression equation. For subject i,

$$\hat{Y}_i = b_0 + b_1 X_i. \tag{6a}$$

Substitution from Equation 4a yields

$$\hat{Y}_i - \bar{Y} = b_1 (X_i - \bar{X}). \tag{6b}$$

The term on the left, $\hat{Y}_i - \bar{Y}$, is that part of Y_i predictable from knowledge of X_i. If $b_1 = 0$, X has no predictive power. In this case, Equation 6b says the best that can be done is to predict the Y mean for every subject: $\hat{Y}_i = \bar{Y}$.

Predictive power is nonzero only to the extent that $\hat{Y}_i - \bar{Y} \neq 0$. Accordingly, the Sum of Squares for prediction is

$$SS_{pred} = \sum (\hat{Y}_i - \bar{Y})^2. \tag{7a}$$

By virtue of Equations 6b and 4b, Equation 7a may be written

$$
\begin{aligned}
SS_{pred} &= b_1^2 \sum (X_i - \bar{X})^2 \\
&= b_1^2 \, SS_X \\
&= \frac{SP_{YX}^2}{SS_X}.
\end{aligned}
\tag{7b}
$$

SS_{pred} has 1 df because it is obtained using just one regression coefficient, b_1. Thus, b_1 measures the predictive power of X for Y.

Of course, chance alone will make SS_{pred} greater than zero. To show real predictive power, we must show that SS_{pred} is greater than could reasonably be expected by chance. This requires a measure of chance alone, that is, an error term.

This error term is commonly taken as the deviations of the observed data points from the regression line. This makes sense because these deviations represent the unpredictable part of Y:

$$\text{deviation}_i = Y_i - \hat{Y}_i. \tag{8a}$$

The Sum of Squares for these deviations is

$$
\begin{aligned}
SS_{dev} &= \sum (Y_i - \hat{Y}_i)^2 \\
&= \sum [(Y_i - \bar{Y}) - (\hat{Y}_i - \bar{Y})]^2 \\
&= SS_Y - SS_{pred}. \qquad N - 2 \text{ df}
\end{aligned}
\tag{8b}
$$

In words, the deviation SS equals the total SS minus the predicted SS, as of course it ought. Since 2 df are used to estimate the two regression coefficients, b_0 and b_1, $N - 2$ df remain for the deviations.

TABLE 9.2

ANALYSIS OF VARIANCE FOR REGRESSION

Source	df	SS	MS	F
a. General form				
Mean	1			
Regression	1	SP_{XY}^2/SS_X		
Deviation	$N-2$	$SS_Y - SP_{XY}^2/SS_X$		
b. For Table 9.1				
Mean	1			
Regression	1	5.00	5.00	62.5
Deviation	2	.16	.08	

The rest is straightforward Anova. Each SS is divided by its df to yield an MS. The ratio of these two MSs yields F:

$$F = \frac{MS_{pred}}{MS_{dev}}. \qquad 1/(N-2) \text{ df} \qquad (9)$$

This Anova is in Table 9.2, which shows a statsig Y–X relation.

Confidence Interval for Slope. The standard deviation of the slope coefficient b_1 is obtained from the Anova as

$$\text{standard deviation}(b_1) = \sqrt{MS_{dev}}/\sqrt{SS_X}. \qquad (10)$$

For any sample statistic, the confidence interval is obtained by multiplying its standard deviation (standard error) by t^* Hence the confidence interval is

$$b_1 \pm t^* \times \text{standard deviation}(b_1). \qquad N-2 \text{ df} \qquad (11)$$

If 0 lies outside this confidence interval, b_1 is statsig different from 0. This will happen if and only if the Anova shows a statsig F in Equation 9.

Confidence Band for Regression Line. The regression line itself requires a confidence *band*, not an interval. This band, however, is not a pair of straight lines, above and below the regression line. The reason is that the regression line is more uncertain at the ends than in the middle. The confidence band is thus narrowest at the center and widens steadily away from the center.

To appreciate this, note that a data point at the center of the X values has no effect on the slope; it affects only the vertical elevation of the entire line. A data point near one extreme, however, has strong leverage on that end of the line, and hence a strong effect on the slope. For the same reason, prediction for a new case is less reliable the farther X_{new} is from the center, $\bar{X}$. The customary formulas have little general interest and are not included here.[a]

Trend Analysis by Regression. Regression analysis provides a simple, flexible way to do the trend tests noted in Chapter 4. The levels of A are metric in trend analysis, and these metric values are taken as the X values in the regression equation. SS_{pred} from the linear regression is identical with the Anova SS for linear trend (see further Section 18.3.1).[b]

This regression analysis is markedly easier than the Anova trend analysis. It automatically takes account of unequal numbers of subjects in each treatment condition. Also, it automatically takes account of unequal spacing of the levels of the treatment variable. Both complications can be handled with special formulas for the Anova linear trend, but the regression analysis is much simpler. A further advantage of the regression trend analysis is that it yields the slope coefficient, b_1, which is empirically meaningful.

Regression With Repeated Measures. In some experimental applications, each subject serves under all levels of some metric variable X. A linear regression may be run for each separate subject to obtain a slope coefficient b_1 for each subject.

Since b_1 equals the slope of the best-fitting straight line, it measures the $Y-X$ relation for each subject. Hence b_1 is a meaningful response score in its own right. Apply Anova to these slope scores; F_{mean} tests the null hypothesis that the true mean slope is zero. If some additional variable A is manipulated in the design, F_A will assess whether these slope scores depend on A.

Do the regression separately for each subject. A common mistake is to fit the regression line to the group means, perhaps under the misconception that the end product will be more reliable. If the regression line is indeed linear, the same line will be obtained either way. But only the individual fits can provide a confidence interval, test for linearity, or allow other statistical analyses. With nonlinear regression, moreover, fitting the group means will introduce bias (Anderson, 1982, Section 4.3, p. 186; Lorch & Myers, 1990).

Relation Between Anova and Regression. Anova and regression are closely related. Indeed, the statistical analysis of regression, as already seen, employs analysis of variance. The equivalence of these two methods just noted for trend analysis reemphasizes their close relation.

Historically, Anova and regression have been considered distinct, having been applied to different classes of problems. Regression analysis was developed to handle metric predictor variables, especially when uncontrolled, as in Galton's work on heritability. Anova was developed to handle nonmetric variables, especially when experimentally controlled. Different specialized formulas were developed for these two classes of problems.

These different formulas were important in a previous era, ending around 1970, when a major part of teaching and learning statistics was drill in accurate calculation, using machines that added and multiplied with clackety mechanical gears. Current computer packages make these differences between formulas much less important for the general user. Indeed, computational formulas developed for regression can be applied also to nonmetric variables, and are especially useful for Anova with unequal n.

In a deeper statistical sense, regression analysis and Anova are twins. Both are special cases of the general linear model (Section 18.4.7). The differences in the common computational formulas are only simplifications to accommodate nonmetric variables in Anova and metric variables in regression.

Anova and Regression as a Team. Regression analysis has a valuable capability for utilizing individual differences. In standard prediction situations, in particular, the prediction equation is simply a summary of the trend in the individual differences.

This capability can be used to improve Anova for experimental studies. With nonrepeated measures, Anova consigns all individual differences to the error term. Part of these individual differences, however, may be predictable by measuring some correlated variable for each individual. In an experiment comparing three different kinds of exercises for teaching undergraduate research method, for example, final performance might be partly predictable from a pretest of relevant knowledge. This predictable part of individual differences can be fractionated out, reducing the error term and yielding a more powerful Anova of the experimental treatments (see *Analysis of Covariance*, Chapter 13).

9.1.4 ASSUMPTIONS FOR LINEAR REGRESSION

Assumptions for linear regression mostly parallel those for Anova in Chapter 3, including the always vital assumption of independence of Y. Regression involves the additional assumption of linearity, however, which can cause trouble, directly, and indirectly too, as noted in the next two subsections.[a]

Violations of Linearity. If Y and X are not linearly related, predictions from the linear regression will be biased. This bias can be serious for new cases that lie outside the range of the cases utilized in estimating b_0 and b_1. Within the range of given cases, however, predictions based on the linear model will be satisfactory for most predictive purposes (see e.g., Figure 9.3, page 278).

In principle, nonlinearity can be addressed by adding nonlinear components to the regression model. For example, a quadratic regression could be used:

$$Y = b_0 + b_1 X_1 + b_2 X_1^2.$$

This approach may be useful when X is experimentally controlled. The variability in Y is then often small relative to the range of X, allowing the nonlinearity to reveal itself. Uncontrolled X, however, is often as variable as Y, as with heights of father and son in Galton's equation. With uncontrolled X, the scatter of the data points usually overwhelms any real nonlinearity.

Unequal Variance. With unequal variance, cases near an end of the X range can have undue influence on the slope of the regression line. In regression analysis, equal variance means that the variance of Y is the same for every X. In practice, however, cases near an end of the X range are more likely to be extreme and produce unequal variance. These end cases have greater leverage on the slope than cases near the center.

To illustrate this threat from unequal variance, suppose the values of X are 1, 2, 3, the corresponding true values of Y are also 1, 2, 3, and the respective variances are 0, 0, and 100. Although these variances are unrealistic, they illustrate a common problem. The true slope coefficient is 1, of course, and so is the expected value of b_1. Any sample value of b_1, however, will depend heavily on the random sample value of Y for $X = 3$. Since the standard deviation is 10, Y values more extreme than 3 ± 10 would not be unlikely, yet these two sample values would yield b_1 values of $+6$ and -4, respectively.

This example illustrates that data with higher variance can unduly influence the regression line. This is troublesome when, as is often the case, the higher variances appear toward the extremes of the range of X. Nonnormality, although not usually a serious problem of itself, tends to occur in conjunction with unequal variance, which is more serious in regression analysis.

Detecting Violations of Assumptions. Violations of the assumptions are often hard to detect. The first line of protection is to minimize violations through good procedure to get clean data. With patient groups, a screening test could help eliminate extreme cases and reduce error variance to boot. A second line of protection is statistical. In some cases, transformation (Chapter 12) may help deal with extreme scores, which are usually the main problem. More effective may be one of the methods for robust regression in Section 9.1.7.[b]

Standard statistical advice is to look at the deviations from prediction, also called residuals, which should be printed out by your computer program. This is a good idea—second to looking at the data themselves. If the residuals show any pattern, some assumption is violated. Systematic trend in the residuals would suggest nonlinearity, possibly amenable to nonlinear regression, or unequal variance, possibly reducible with transformation. On the whole, however, statistical methods to detect violations of assumptions are by no means satisfactory, especially with small samples (see further Draper & Smith, 1981, Chapter 3; Mosteller & Tukey, 1977, Chapter 16).

Random Sample. The most basic assumption in regression–correlation is randomness. All statistical results rest on the assumption that the data are a random sample from some well-defined population. Rarely will this be true. Typically, the data are a handy sample from some poorly defined population.

Prediction for new cases, accordingly, must rest on extrastatistical judgment. The investigator must rely on a judgment, implicit if not explicit, that the new cases are "similar" in "relevant" respects to the handy sample used to estimate b_0 and b_1 in the prediction equation.

As a concrete example, consider Galton's equation for heights of fathers and sons. I expect Galton's equation should have considerable generality, even though it comes from a handy sample of long-dead Englishmen. I expect it should hold for Englishmen of today, as well as for Canadians and Chinese. I also expect that a similar equation holds for mothers and daughters. I trust you will consider my expectations reasonable although they rest on a mass of background knowledge that would be hard to make explicit. I have no expertise in this area, so I may well be wrong. But the expert's expectations also rest on extrastatistical judgment about "similarity" in "relevant" respects.

Indeed, generality of Galton's equation is limited by population differences in $\overline{H}_{\text{father}}$. In particular, Englishmen have been getting taller over time, presumably because of better childhood nutrition and health care. It would thus be necessary to determine $\overline{H}_{\text{father}}$ for each given population. I assume, however, that the value of b_1 would remain approximately the same.[c]

As a second example, consider the use of the GRE for predicting performance in graduate school (Section 1.5.1). It seems reasonable to expect that GRE will be similarly useful in other American universities and for other departments besides psychology, and that the regression will perform at least as well as an admissions committee (see Section 16.1.3). These expectations, however, are largely extrastatistical.

From this empirical perspective of handy samples, the primary problem with predictive regression is extrastatistical. Statistical theory can be useful, if not essential, in finding the formulas for b_1 and its confidence interval, and especially in finding ways to reduce the influence of extreme scores, as with the robust methods of Section 9.1.7. The main need for research on regression analysis, however, is to study extrastatistical generalization.[d]

This empirical perspective suggests that teaching regression–correlation should change direction. Current texts are fixated on formulas and significance tests. The importance of extrastatistical inference is slurred over or ignored. Ignoral has some justification because extrastatistical considerations differ across areas and require some substantive expertise. The consequence, however, has been to misdirect attention away from the primary problem.

9.1.5 BEYOND ONE-VARIABLE LINEAR REGRESSION

The basic ideas of regression analysis have been presented using Equation 1, a one-variable linear regression. This simple linear regression is widely useful. Two extensions also deserve mention.

The most important extension is to prediction situations with more than one predictor. With graduate school admissions, GRE and GPA were both useful predictors. A little more predictive power was obtainable by including quality of applicant's undergraduate school as a third predictor variable. Analysis with multiple predictors is considered in Chapter 16, *Multiple Regression*.

The other extension is to substantive models that involve nonlinear terms, such as X^2 or e^{-X}, which occur in some engineering applications. In psychology, nonlinear terms have appeared in signal detection theory, reaction time models, and in the averaging model of cognitive algebra. These applications are largely outside the scope of this book, but some discussion is given in Section 16.1.5 on measurement theory in multiple regression, in Chapter 20 on mathematical models, and in Chapter 21 on psychological measurement theory.

9.1.6 SIDE EXCURSION: THE METHOD OF LEAST SQUARES

Technical aspects of statistical theory have a simple illustration with regression analysis. One of these levels involves the method of least squares, which is also the basis for standard Anova.

Definition of Best Fit.   In linear regression analysis, we seek a best fitting straight line, one that comes as close as possible to all the data points. This simple goal raises a nonsimple problem: How shall we define "as close as possible?"

An obvious definition of "as close as possible" is one that minimizes the sum of the absolute deviations. Consider a line with arbitrary values of b_0 and b_1. This line yields a predicted value, $\hat{Y}_i = b_0 + b_1 X_i$ for each data point. The deviation from prediction is $Y_i - \hat{Y}_i$, which equals $Y_i - (b_0 + b_1 X_i)$. The best fitting line is one with values of b_0 and b_1 such that the sum of *absolute deviations* is minimal:

$$\sum | Y_i - (b_0 + b_1 X_i) | = \text{minimum.} \tag{12a}$$

Granted this definition of best fit, the problem remains to calculate which values of b_0 and b_1 actually yield the minimum. The statistician seeks simple formulas that will be useful to you and me.

Unfortunately, simple formulas have not been found. In fact, no simple formulas exist. To find the best values of b_0 and b_1 requires extensive calculation that was close to prohibitive in the precomputer age (see Section 9.1.7).

An alternative definition of best fitting line is one that minimizes the sum of *squared* deviations. Accordingly, it is called *least squares*. This definition not only leads to simple formulas, but also has desirable statistical properties.

The Method of Least Squares.   In least squares analysis, we wish to choose b_0 and b_1 so that the sum of squared deviations is minimal:

$$SS_{dev} = \sum [Y_i - (b_0 + b_1 X_i)]^2 = \text{minimum}. \tag{12b}$$

The Y_i and X_i are given data, so SS_{dev} involves just two unknowns, b_0 and b_1.

Since SS_{dev} is a quadratic function of b_0, it has the shape of a parabola. The minimum value of SS_{dev} is at the bottom of the parabola. At this minimum, the tangent line to the parabola is horizontal, with zero slope. This is our clue: Apply calculus.

The derivative of any function gives the slope of its tangent line. Accordingly, we differentiate SS_{dev} with respect to b_0, then set this derivative equal to 0:

$$\frac{dSS_{dev}}{db_0} = \sum 2[Y_i - (b_0 + b_1 X_i)](-1) = 0.$$

Simplification yields

$$\sum Y_i = \sum (b_0 + b_1 X_i) = N b_0 + b_1 \sum X_i.$$

Hence

$$b_0 = \bar{Y} - b_1 \bar{X}. \tag{13}$$

This least squares derivation proves Equation 4a for the Y-intercept, b_0.

A similar derivation holds for b_1:

$$\frac{dSS_{dev}}{db_1} = \sum 2[Y_i - (b_0 + b_1 X_i)](-X_i) = 0.$$

Simplification yields

$$\sum Y_i X_i = b_0 \sum X_i + b_1 \sum X_i^2.$$

Substituting for b_0 from Equation 13, applying Equation 2 and the two hand formulas given in the numerical example yields

$$b_1 = \frac{SP_{YX}}{SS_X}. \tag{14}$$

This least squares derivation proves Equation 4b for the slope coefficient, b_1.

This derivation illustrates one reason for the great popularity of least squares. The derivatives of the squared terms are linear functions of b_0 and b_1 so the estimation equations are readily solved. This solution is unique because the parabola has only one minimum point. Similar results hold for regression with multiple variables.

Least Squares for Anova. The method of least squares is also the basis for the Anova formulas of previous chapters. For two-way factorial design, the parameters $\bar{\mu}$, α_j, β_k, and $(\alpha\beta)_{jk}$ in Equation 5.1b are chosen so that the sum of squared deviations is minimal:

$$SS_{dev} = \sum_{i,j,k} [Y_{ijk} - (\bar{\mu} + \alpha_j + \beta_k + (\alpha\beta)_{jk})]^2 = \text{minimum}.$$

Calculus may be applied as above, and this leads to the simple formulas in Chapter 5.

Statistical Properties of Least Squares. Remarkably, the method of least squares has highly desirable statistical properties. First, it yields unbiased estimates of the true model parameters–without any statistical assumptions of normality and equal variance. If equal variance does hold, the confidence intervals for these parameters are the narrowest possible based on linear functions of the data. And with normality, significance tests based on the F distribution are valid. Some of these optimal properties were not discovered until the work of Fisher, over a century after least squares was independently introduced by two renowned mathematicians, Gauss and Laplace, around 1800.

However, least squares analysis is sensitive to extreme scores. If the tails of the data distribution are "heavy," containing a higher proportion of scores than the normal distribution, other methods can do better. Statisticians have accordingly sought more robust methods, three of which are noted next.

9.1.7 ROBUST REGRESSION

Several robust methods of regression have been developed that are less sensitive to nonnormality than least squares. None lead to simple formulas; all require extensive calculation. Recently, however, they have been developed for practical use and some computer programs have become available. A clear summary oriented to applications is given by Birkes and Dodge (1993), on which this section is based.

Least Absolute Deviations. The method of least absolute deviations has already been defined in Equation 12a. The problem is to calculate best values of b_0 and b_1. It is not hard to show that a best fitting line must pass through two of the data points. Given this, a simple though tedious calculation is available. First, find b_0 and b_1 for the line through a given pair of data points, which is easy. For this line, calculate the sum of absolute deviations (Equation 12a), which is straightforward. Do this for every possible pair of data points, which is a lot of calculation. Choose whichever has the lowest sum of absolute deviations. This exhaustive method will always work although somewhat less exhausting methods are available.

M-Regression. A simple form of M-regression provides a compromise between least squares and least absolute deviations. In effect, it uses Equation 12a for large deviations, thereby reducing the influence of extreme scores; it uses Equation 12b for small deviations, thereby benefiting from optimal properties of least squares. This approach has been generalized to allow more complex definitions of best fit.

Rank-Weighted Regression. This method begins by calculating the slope of the line through each and every data pair of data points. The median of these slopes could be taken as the slope of the best-fitting line. It is superior, however, to use a weighted median, weighting each deviation by its rank so larger deviations get larger weight. Like M-regression, this rank-weighted regression can be considered a compromise between least squares and least absolute deviations.

Reliability. A good method for fitting a regression line must do more than estimate the parameters, b_0 and b_1, that minimize deviations from prediction. These two parameter estimates should also reliable, especially with nonnormal data.

All three of the foregoing methods are robust in that they yield more reliable estimates of the regression coefficients than least squares when applied to data with heavy tails. Furthermore, all three methods yield confidence intervals and significance tests for the regression slope, at least for large samples. These methods may also be extended to handle multiple predictor variables.

Birkes and Dodge discuss the relative merits of the three foregoing methods, as well as two others. Their analyses suggest that M-regression and rank-weighted regression are both effective with extreme scores and do almost as well as least squares with normal distributions. The method of least absolute deviations is about equally effective with extreme scores but considerably poorer if the data are normal.

Comment. If you seldom use regression analysis, it may not be worth while to learn how to do robust regression, unless you expect very nonnormal data, or unless the analysis has special interest, as with coital frequency in Note 9.1.4b. However, if you expect to do regression analyses in a succession of studies and if extreme scores appear at all likely, robust methods may well repay your efforts to understand and implement them. Birkes and Dodge recommend using more than one method jointly on each set of data. You can have more confidence if they agree and you obtain a warning sign if they disagree. Their advice seems sound. The best method in any situation is likely to depend on situational specifics and only become clear with comparative results over a series of studies. Within each given situation, simulation studies would seem needed to assess bias and reliability, especially with small or medium samples.

9.2 CORRELATION

In teaching correlation, two different goals must be considered. One is preparation for professional use of correlation analysis, in test theory, for example, or with observational data. For this, specialized texts and specialized courses are required. This goal cannot be achieved in texts like this one, which are mainly concerned with experimental analysis. Many comparable texts, in fact, give no coverage of correlation or regression.

The other goal is to prepare students who will not make regular use of correlation analysis to understand articles and reports based on such analysis. The following brief discussion is oriented toward this goal.[a]

9.2.1 CORRELATION COEFFICIENT

Is it possible to describe the *strength* of the relation between Y and X with a single number? One measure of strength is the b_1 regression coefficient, which equals 0 when there is no relation and increases in magnitude as the relation grows stronger. But b_1 also depends on the unit of the X scale, which seems inappropriate since the unit is wholly arbitrary. If you measure X in centimeters, say, and I measure X in inches, our b_1 coefficients for the same data will differ by about 4 to 10.

It seems desirable, accordingly, to seek a measure of the strength of the $Y-X$ relation that does not depend on the unit of X or of Y. The correlation coefficient, denoted r, claims to have this virtue although, as we shall see, this claim has strong qualifications.

Definition of Correlation Coefficient. The squared correlation may be defined as the ratio of predictable variance to total variance:

$$r^2 = \frac{SS_{pred}}{SS_Y}. \tag{15}$$

The correlation is thus obtained from the foregoing regression Anova.

Unlike b_1, r^2 is independent of the units of the variables. This raises hope that you can compare your r^2 with other values of r^2 in the literature without concern about comparable units.

Also, r^2 always lies between 0 and 1. It is 0 for a null relation and 1 for a perfect relation. This gives a simple framework for interpreting the size of r^2.

Most people use the correlation coefficient, r, instead of r^2. This is obtained by square rooting r^2 and prefixing the sign of b_1. Thus, r includes the sign of the Y–X relation and lies between -1 and $+1$. Some writers, however, complain that r is misleading. At face value, an r of .30 represents a relation half as strong as an r of .60. In terms of predictable variance, however, the relation is only one-fourth as strong. Indeed, a correlation of .30 means that less than a tenth of the variance in Y is predictable from X.

Statistical Significance. Whether a given r is statsig can be determined by looking in special tables that give the criterial values, r^*. The df are $N - 2$, since 2 df have been used up in estimating the two regression coefficients.

Alternatively, the statistical significance of r^2, and of r, is equivalent to the statistical significance of F in the regression Anova (Equation 9). Statsig F implies statsig r.

9.2.2 CORRELATION HAS LOTS OF PITFALLS

Correlation has lots of pitfalls for the unwary. All summary statistics have pitfalls, of course, for any attempt to represent a mass of data with a single number is bound to misrepresent something. The correlation coefficient, however, seems extreme in this respect.

The fact is that the problem of measuring the strength of a Y–X relation has no simple solution. The regression coefficient and the correlation coefficient both have advantages and disadvantages. Effective use of regression–correlation depends on understanding these advantages and disadvantages.

Correlation Depends on Range. The correlation is often misleading because it depends on the range of X. In the left panel of Figure 9.2, $Y = X$, with variability added in a systematic manner. This yields $r^2 = .72$. The right panel shows the same data, but over a truncated range of X; r^2 drops sharply to .38.

But the Y–X relationship is not changed by the truncation. The slope of the regression line is the same in both panels. Furthermore, the mean magnitude of deviations is also the same, namely, 1.2. These two measures, slope and

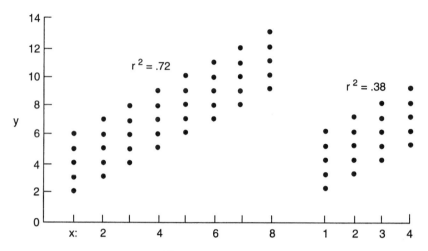

Figure 9.2. Range of predictor X variable affects magnitude of correlation. The correlation drops from .72 in the left panel to .38 in the right panel, although the true $Y-X$ relation remains unchanged.

magnitude of deviations, are meaningful in terms of the actual data. Both of these measures concur that truncating the range has not changed the $Y-X$ relationship. The correlation is thus misleading.

The correlation is misleading because it does not actually measure the $Y-X$ relation. Instead, it measures the predictable proportion of SS_Y as shown in Equation 15. When the range is truncated, the error variance remains constant, but SS_Y decreases. Hence the predictable *proportion* of SS_Y decreases.

By itself, therefore, a correlation of .4 is hardly meaningful. It is large if the X range is small, small if the X range is large.

The classic example of this range effect is the correlation between IQ score and school performance. This r^2 decreases steadily from around .65 in elementary school to perhaps .10 in college. But this decrease does not mean that the IQ–grade relationship is different in college; a decrease must occur simply because the lower IQ range does not appear in college. In general, correlations are meaningful only by reference to the predictor range.

Correlation Depends on Reliability. A second shortcoming is that correlation depends on unreliability in Y and X. The same true $Y-X$ relation may thus yield different correlations.

Correlation refers to the predictable proportion of Y, as shown in Equation 15. The less reliable is Y, the less is its predictable proportion, and this sets an upper bound to the correlation. Analogously, unreliability in X is useless for predicting Y; the less reliable is X, the less must be its predictive power.

The dependence of correlation on reliability and range has long been known. It has an important consequence: Different correlations may not be comparable unless it has been shown that their Y measures have equivalent reliabilities and equivalent ranges. This is often difficult.[a]

Correlation as Artifact of Subgrouping. Taller is better for your bank account! The correlation between height and income is substantial for adult Americans, even more substantial in other countries.

This height–wealth correlation arises because many women are housewives, with no paying job and hence no income. Also, women are generally shorter than men. A substantial correlation is thus guaranteed. If height and income were correlated separately for each gender, the correlation would be very small. The substantial correlation comes about only if the two groups are pooled.

This example is serious; almost any group of people includes many diverse subgroups. A correlation for the group may not hold for any subgroup. Conversely, a substantial correlation within subgroups may be lost in the group. Unfortunately, many of these subgroupings may be unknown and unsuspected. This thin-ice problem troubles personality theory, for example, and especially sociology, which deals with large, heterogeneous groups.

If subgroups are well-defined, separate regressions may be run for each, as with male–female. But these subgroups may themselves be heterogeneous, with further subgroupings based on ethnic, religious, socioeconomic, and other variables that may not be well-defined or measurable. This subgrouping problem is very real, illustrated in *Gender Bias?* in Section 10.2.2 (page 299).

Weak Inference With Correlation. Many writers over the last 2500 years have conjectured that cognition follows exact mathematical models. Satisfactory tests of these conjectures have been elusive. One approach has used correlation, seeking to show very high correlations between predictions from a model and actual behavior. Although very high correlation might seem strong support for the model, it is often no support at all.

The pitfall is that high correlation can be obtained from a model that is seriously incorrect. To illustrate, consider an experimental test of the once-popular hypothesis that social attitudes are formed by addition of stimulus information. Subjects received biographical information about U.S. presidents and made an attitudinal judgment of their statesmanship. The addition hypothesis implies that this attitude is the sum of the information values of the separate paragraphs. Predictions from the addition model are plotted in the right panel of Figure 9.3 as a function of the observed attitudes. If the addition model holds, all data points should lie on the straight diagonal except for random scatter due to unreliability. The observed scatter is small, and the correlation of .98 between predicted and observed seems pretty impressive. Judged by these correlation statistics, the theoretical addition model seems to do very well.

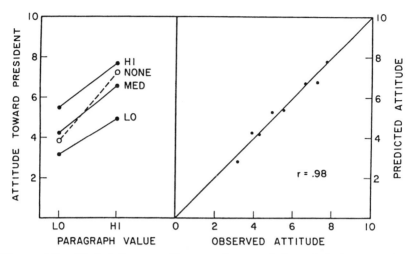

Figure 9.3. Weak inference with regression–correlation. Attitudes toward U.S. presidents disobey addition model, obey averaging model. Right panel plots predictions of the addition model as a function of the observed attitudes for eight attitude messages. Tight scatterplot and high correlation of .98 obscure and conceal the crossover visible in the factorial graph at left, which disconfirms the addition model. Averaging theory, in contrast, predicts both the parallelism of the solid curves and the crossover of the dashed curve in the factorial graph (see similarly Section 20.2.3). (After Anderson, 1973b.)

In fact, the addition model does very ill. Since the information paragraphs were presented according to a factorial design, the addition hypothesis predicts parallelism in the factorial graph. This graph is far from parallel, as shown in the left panel. The dashed curve shows a crossover interaction, sharply contrary to any form of addition model. The high correlation seems to say that the data support the addition model; the data themselves say no.

How can a model that is so bad seem so good? *Weak inference.* Correlation and scatterplot obscure and conceal serious faults of the model; they are weak inference statistics. Anova represents strong inference, for it reveals the important patterns in the data (Section 20.2.3).

Regression Coefficient Versus Correlation Coefficient. Some writers argue that the correlation coefficient should be abandoned, that the regression coefficient, b_1, is a better measure of the Y–X relation. This regression coefficient has meaning in terms of the metrics for Y and X, as in Equation 5 for heights of fathers and sons. Hence b_1 expresses the strength of this relation in substantive terms. That the correlation is unit-free actually seems a disadvantage when X has meaningful units. Moreover, b_1 is independent of the range of X, as shown in Figure 9.2. As a measure of effect size, therefore, the regression coefficient has notable advantages over the correlation coefficient (Tufte, 1970).

The correlation coefficient seems well suited, however, for prediction situations in which the variance of Y corresponds to prevailing individual differences. The variance of Y then constitutes the prediction problem, as in test theory. Hence r^2 has context-relevant meaning as predictive power, both in its own right and in comparison to other predictors. The regression coefficient does not seem as useful in such situations.

Correlation and Causation. The dictum that *correlation does not imply causation* has been illustrated with so many striking examples in introductory texts that further discussion may seem unnecessary. The temptations of causal interpretation are strong, however, and seemingly irresistible in fields that rely heavily on observational data, as with sociology or political science. Even psychologists, however, often interpret correlation as causality with no more than routine, lip service qualification. A standard tack is insinuate causality without explicitly claiming it.

For example, demonstrating a positive correlation between marriage satisfaction and frequency of sexual intercourse might seem superfluous. The authors of this published paper, although evidently aware of the illogic, nevertheless managed to suggest that more sex might improve distressed marrages. Psychologically, the opposite should be expected.[b]

The dictum, nevertheless, is overdone. Causation implies correlation, so correlation can be a useful clue to causation. Vaccination for smallpox, a terrible killer in Washington's army of the revolution, arose from Jenner's observation that milkmaids seemed immune to smallpox, which he guessed was due to their having experienced the milder cowpox. Correlational data continue to be important clues to causality in medicine and health psychology, and in other areas such as environmental science. Sometimes, moreover, auxiliary evidence supports a causal interpretation, as in meaningful relations between pipe–cigar–cigarette smoking and location of cancer.

For most psychological and social situations, however, multiple determinants are jointly operative. Simple, one-variable causal relations, such as in smallpox, typhoid fever, and various other diseases, are not common in the psychological field. Causal analysis with uncontrolled data is thus a minefield (see further *Ancova With Nonrandom Groups* in Section 13.2, *Quasi-Experimental Design* in Section 15.5, and *Multiple Regression* in Section 16.2.).[c]

Process Validity and Outcome Validity. The distinction between outcome validity and process validity of Section 1.2.1 is acute in correlation analysis. Causal interpretation typically seeks process validity. Any claim for process validity must address the confounding issue of the previous subsection.

Prediction, however, involves outcome validity. For purposes of prediction, correlation *is* outcome validity. Causal linkage is unnecessary. This practical value of correlation may need reemphasis to offset the foregoing criticisms with respect to process validity.

NOTES

9.1.2a. For simplicity of exposition, this paragraph assumes that Y and X have symmetric distributions.

9.1.2b. The slope coefficient of ½ in Galton's equation comes from a more extensive follow-up by Pearson and Lee (1903), who obtained a stronger relation than Galton.

9.1.2c. Regression equations are misleading because they ignore the error of prediction. In Galton's father–son equation, sons of the same father usually differ considerably in height. The correlation is only .5; the scatterplot has a lot of scatter that almost obscures the relation. Freedman, et al. (1998, p. 172) comment, "It was a stroke of genius on Galton's part to see a straight line in the chaos." The predictive power of GRE for success in graduate school is even smaller, although not less than that of an admissions committee.

9.1.3a. Formulas for the confidence band for a regression line, and for the confidence interval for any predicted value, are given in many texts (e.g., Myers & Well, 1991; Snedecor & Cochran, 1980). I have adopted the symbol, X_{new}, from Myers and Well.

9.1.3b. *Pure Error Through Within Cell Replication.* The regression error term obtained from Equation 8b differs from the Anova error term of previous chapters because it includes systematic deviations from linearity as well as pure error. A pure error term can sometimes be obtained that requires no assumption about the form of the regression equation. Suppose X is controlled experimentally and that two or more independent cases are run at each value of X. Since these cases are treated alike, their variability is pure error. This variability may be pooled across all values of X_i to obtain a single pooled error term that is independent of the form of the regression model. In fact, the values of X may be considered the levels of a one-way Anova. If this error term is used, the linear regression is identical to the linear trend of Chapter 4.

9.1.4a. Assumptions for regression differ somewhat, depending on whether X is *fixed*, as when experimentally manipulated, or *random*, as with father's height in Galton's equation and with most observational data. In practice, these different assumptions lead to the same results. In either case, linearity and independence imply that b_0 and b_1 are unbiased estimates of the population parameters, β_0 and β_1. Confidence intervals and significance tests are also the same.

9.1.4b. Extreme cases can be extremely serious in regression analysis. Kahn and Udry (1986) reanalyzed data considered in a previous report that had claimed surprising conclusions about age changes in marital coital frequency, showing that these conclusions were largely due to eight extreme cases out of 2063 couples, four of which were thought to be keypunch errors in the archival data. When a few extreme cases make a big difference, including them will misrepresent the main population.

9.1.4c. The main generalization that can be hoped for from a predictive regression is that the predictor variables will retain some usefulness in other situations. The values of b_0 and b_1 would usually have to be calibrated anew for each new situation.

9.1.4d. I have found little information on the fundamental problem of extrastatistical generalization from regression analysis. Mosteller and Tukey (1977), however, emphasize importance of searching out the real sources of variability.

9.2a. Some graduate texts do include a couple chapters on correlation. These invariably take the form of a cut-down specialist course, oriented around numerous formulas. This is not adequate to learn professional analysis. Snowed under with formulas, moreover, students learn relatively little to help them understand correlation in published articles.

9.2.2a. A clever attempt to study cognitive organization in person cognition ran aground on the two foregoing pitfalls that correlation depends on range and on reliability. Subjects were read 12 trait adjectives that described a person. They were then instructed to write down all the adjectives they could recall (the recalled adjectives) and also to write down any other adjectives they thought might describe the person (the inferred adjectives). Finally, they judged the person on likableness.

The theoretical hypothesis was that the cognition of the person was developed through dynamic cognitive interaction among the given trait adjectives. Under this hypothesis, the inferred adjectives were generated as part of this cognitive interaction and had a causal role in the response. The problem was to demonstrate this hypothesized causal relation.

This causal claim seemed to be supported. The likableness of the person correlated .47 with a sum of good–bad values of the recalled adjectives; this increased to .67 when the sum included both the recalled and the inferred adjectives. This substantial increase was claimed to show that the inferred adjectives did indeed have a causal role in the person cognition.

This causal claim is unwarranted. Suppose to the contrary that the inferred adjectives had no role in the person cognition. As one alternative hypothesis, the inferred adjectives could be merely synonyms of the recalled adjectives already written down, added to satisfy the task demand. Including them, however, may be expected to increase the range of the predictor as well as its reliability. Both effects would increase the correlation. Because of this twofold confounding, no causal interpretation is warranted.

The inferred adjectives may well have had a causal influence because subjects wrote them down as instructed before they judged the person. Any such effect, however, is inextricably confounded with the two correlation pitfalls (Anderson, 1982, p. 321).

9.2.2b. The correlation between sex and marriage satisfaction was reported by Howard and Dawes (1976).

9.2.2c. Insinuating causality from correlation seems stock in trade in a number of areas. Most statistics about diet and exercise in the media rest on correlations. So does a surprisingly large proportion of professional medical opinion.

A different example comes from a study of development of predation in newborn spiders. Spiders are entirely carnivorous and newborn spiderlings, completely on their own, suffer considerable mortality before catching their first prey. "In all, 52% of the spiderlings achieved success, and this first catch virtually ensured their subsequent success in prey-catching attempts. . . . It seems that spiderlings learn quickly." (Forster, 1982, p. 169.) This quotation implies that "this first catch" caused the "subsequent success," whereas both may have been caused by a better constitution.

EXERCISES FOR CHAPTER 9

1. a. Use the regression equation given for Figure 9.1 to predict Y for new cases, with $X_{new} = 0, 2, 5$, and 12.

    b. Which of these predictions is most/least reliable?

    c. Will all predictions for new cases lie on the regression line?

2. Justify the statement: "In Figure 9.1, visual inspection indicates that the regression line should pass through the Y values of 3, 4, 5, and 6 for the four successive values of X."

3. a. Use hand calculation to show that the standard deviation, or error half-bar, for b_1 for the data of Table 9.1 is .063. Use calculations given in the text.

    b. Find the 95% confidence interval for b_1.

4. a. Graph these data and find the linear regression by visual inspection.

$$X = 2, \quad Y = 5.8$$
$$X = 4, \quad Y = 5.2$$
$$X = 6, \quad Y = 4.2$$
$$X = 8, \quad Y = 2.8.$$

    b. How is this example related to Figure 9.1 in the text?

5. Under *Unequal Variance* in Section 9.1.4, verify that the Y values of 3 ± 10 would yield b_1 values of -4 and 6.

6. Graph $Y = b_0 + b_1 X$ over the range from -10 to 10 for:

    a. $b_0 = 0$; $b_1 = -2, -1, 0, 1$, and 2.

    b. $b_0 = -2, -1, 0, 1$, and 2; $b_1 = 1$.

    c. Explain the pattern in (a) and in (b).

7. If Galton had studied the relation between heights of mothers and daughters, what do you guess he would have found?

8. Do-it-yourself example of subgrouping artifact in correlation.
(No calculation is needed or wanted; a graph will suffice.)

    a. Consider two subgroups of three cases each. Make up simple artificial data with zero correlation within each subgroup, but a positive correlation for the group as a whole.

    b. Show similarly how a substantial positive correlation within each of two subgroups could vanish in the group as a whole.

9. An article reports a correlation of .31 for Y and X. In terms of variance, how much predictive power does X have? What does this mean in practical terms?

10. One point can make a big difference in regression. Run two regressions for the following data, one for the first 8 data points, the other for all 9, and compare them. What is the moral?

X	1	3	5	6	7	8	10	12	18
Y		10	11	10	12	12	10	11	10	19

11. In a psychophysiological study of emotion, investigator R measured X and Y for each of 6 subjects on each of 2 days. He reported a 95% confidence interval for b_1 of 2 $\pm$ 1.86 on 10 df. He argued that this statsig Y–X relation verified his own theory of emotion and infirmed the James–Lange theory of emotion (that the conscious emotion is not the cause of the emotional reaction, such as fight, flight, or freeze, but a consequence). Why does R have only 5 df? What is his actual confidence interval?

12. The speed of a ball rolling to the bottom of Galileo's inclined plane is proportional to the square root of the height from which it started to roll. You wish to test whether human cognition follows this physical law. In your experimental situation, you show subjects a ball at various elevations on an inclined plane; they predict how fast it would be rolling at the foot of the incline if it was released to roll freely down. Subjects respond on a graphic rating scale. In the instruction period, a few actual ball rolls are shown to calibrate their response scale. Each subject receives three trials at each of six elevations (Karpp & Anderson, 1997).

   a. Why would it be obtuse to test the null hypothesis that the initial height of the ball affects subjects' responses?

   b. Why would it be a mistake to fit a regression line to the data for all the subjects together?

   c.* For plotting the data, why does Galileo's law of falling bodies suggest an advantage from using $\sqrt{height}$ on the horizontal axis instead of height?

13. What causes your feelings of hunger? Are there hunger receptors like receptors for vision and taste? If so, where are they?
   Cannon hypothesized that hunger is caused by stomach contractions. His devoted student, Washburn, trained himself to swallow an uninflated rubber balloon with a rubber tube that led out through his esophagus and mouth. Cannon then inflated the balloon inside Washburn's stomach. Stomach contractions would increase air pressure in the balloon, which were recorded on an apparatus not visible to Washburn. Sure enough, when Washburn reported hunger pangs, the apparatus recorded stomach contractions. Cannon concluded that stomach contractions caused the feeling of hunger.

a. Washburn's stomach supported Cannon's hypothesis in this classic study. What is the main objection to this evidence?

b.* What alternative approaches can you suggest as further tests of Cannon's hypothesis?

14. Table 9.3 lists four sets of data ingeniously constructed by Anscombe (1973). Run a computer regression and get plots for each set.

TABLE 9.3

FOUR SETS OF REGRESSION DATA

Case	Y_a	Y_b	Y_c	X_{abc}	Y_d	X_d
1	8.04	9.14	7.46	10.0	6.58	8.0
2	6.95	8.14	6.77	8.0	5.76	8.0
3	7.58	8.74	12.74	13.0	7.71	8.0
4	8.81	8.77	7.11	9.0	8.84	8.0
5	8.33	9.26	7.81	11.0	8.47	8.0
6	9.96	8.10	8.84	14.0	7.04	8.0
7	7.24	6.13	6.08	6.0	5.25	8.0
8	4.26	3.10	5.39	4.0	12.50	19.0
9	10.84	9.13	8.15	12.0	5.56	8.0
10	4.82	7.26	6.42	7.0	7.91	8.0
11	5.68	4.74	5.73	5.0	6.89	8.0

NOTE: First three sets of Y all have same X values, listed in the fourth data column. From Anscombe (1973). Reprinted with permission from *The American Statistician*. Copyright 1973 by American Statistical Association. All rights reserved.

a. What is striking about this example?

b. What is the moral of this example?

15. In terms of the variance of Y, justify the statement under Equation 1 that "A horizontal regression line means that X has no predictive power."

16. A single group of subjects is run, each subject serving at four levels of a metric variable A. A regression line is fitted to each subject's data to obtain a slope value b_1 for each subject.

    a. You are told to apply Anova to these slope scores. What do you do?

    b. Suppose three independent groups of subjects were run, each at one level of variable B. How would the Anova change? How would it be interpreted?

    c. Compare this analysis with the alternative of a repeated measures Anova of the $(S \times A) \times B$ design.

17. For repeated measures regression, how would you find the confidence interval for the mean b_1, averaged across subjects?

18. Suppose the regression line has slope of 0. Then it says to predict $Y_{new} = \bar{Y}$, regardless of X. What property of the mean makes this a best prediction?

19. Below Equation 2, the text states "Hence a positive value of $(Y_i - \bar{Y})$ will tend to be paired with a positive value of $(X_i - \bar{X})$." Does this work in the case in which all X_i are negative? (Try a numerical example with three data points.)

20. Under *Unequal Variance* in Section 9.1.4, show that variances of 0, 100, 0 for $X = 1, 2, 3$ produce zero variance in b_1. What practical implication follows from the contrast between this case and that cited in the text?

21. Let $Y = 2, 1, 6$ for $X = 1, 2, 3$. Graph the data and use visual inspection to find the best-fit linear regression using least absolute deviations.

22. Show that Galton's equation implies regression to the mean (a) with a numerical example and (b) algebraically.

23. In Note 9.2.2c, how might you test between the two hypotheses (a) experimentally and (b) with observational data?

24. Verify the derivations of Equations 6b, 7b, 13, and 14.

PREFACE

All-or-none, categorical data are common: male or female; married, divorced, widowed, or single; success or failure; dead or alive. The basic data are frequencies of cases in each category.

Such categorical data are qualitative, not quantitative as has been assumed in previous chapters on Anova–regression. With Anova, scores were magnitudes of response for individual cases. With categorical data, in contrast, the "score" for each case is the category to which it belongs. Such category scores do not generally represent magnitude of any response measure, as illustrated with married–divorced–widowed–single.

A new statistical technique is needed to handle categorical data: *chi-square*. One principal application of chi-square is to compare the pattern of observed frequencies in the several categories with the null hypothesis of equal (or proportional) frequencies.

To illustrate, consider the study of smoking prevention cited in the appendix to Chapter 3. Three treatment conditions were used, each with about 1000 subjects. There were two response categories: successful quit attempt and relapse into smoking. Quit frequencies after three months were approximately 190, 240, and 270 for the three treatments. This looks promising. But perhaps chance alone could readily produce this difference. Is the observed difference in successes large enough to infer a real difference between these treatment conditions?

This question is answered by the chi-square test. Chi-square compares the observed frequencies with those expected under the null hypothesis of no difference between treatments.

Chi-square uses a single formula, quite simple, which applies universally. One simple rule suffices to get expected frequencies for the common two-way contingency tables, that is, tables of the form that describe the cited smoking data. This formula and this rule build directly on concepts developed in previous chapters.

Chapter 10

FREQUENCY DATA AND CHI-SQUARE

A new kind of data is considered in this chapter: *frequency data.* Cases are classified into one of various categories; the analysis looks at the frequency of cases in different categories.

The Experimental–Control paradigm is sometimes used this way. In the test of polio vaccine discussed below, the data are frequencies of polio cases in the vaccine and placebo groups. Frequencies of successes and failures are sometimes used in psychology, as in the experiment on smoking prevention cited in the preface to this chapter, and in several experiments in the Exercises.

Category data are qualitative, not quantitative. Each subject's "score" is the category to which they belong. This category is not typically a measure of amount or magnitude. Category data are thus very different from the numerical magnitude data used in Anova–regression.

Here is the key to analysis of category data:

Look at the pattern of frequencies across different categories.

In the polio example, this pattern is the simplest possible: the relative frequencies of polio in the vaccine and placebo groups. Since Anova–regression is not properly applicable to frequency data, some new statistical technique is required.

This new statistical technique is *chi-square.* It is analogous to analysis of variance, but considerably simpler for common applications.

The conceptual framework of previous chapters transfers directly to chi-square analysis. This will be illustrated in the following polio experiment. The null hypothesis is that the vaccine has no effect—that polio has the same frequency with the vaccine as with placebo. The chi-square test addresses this question: Is the difference between the observed frequencies and those predicted under the null hypothesis "large enough" to indicate an effective vaccine.

10.1 ELEMENTS OF CHI-SQUARE

Chi-square analysis is striking in its simplicity. One simple rule suffices to determine the frequencies expected under the null hypothesis for many common applications. This done, one simple chi-square formula applies in all cases. This approach is illustrated in the following test of polio vaccine.

10.1.1 THE HUGE POLIO EXPERIMENT OF 1954

Infantile paralysis—polio—was once a dreaded disease that left many children pathetically paralyzed. Franklin Delano Roosevelt, whose astonishing political career was almost cut down by severe polio paralysis, pushed the "March of Dimes," which collected funds to support medical research for a cure. Meier's (1989) popular account of the 1954 polio vaccine experiment includes interesting comments about experimental procedure in this huge field experiment.

The adjective *huge* is fitting because some 400,000 children were subjects in this experiment. A huge N was needed to get adequate power because polio is actually a rare disease. The main results are shown in this table.[a]

TABLE 10.1

EFFECTIVENESS OF POLIO VACCINE

Group	n	Polio	No Polio
Vaccine	200,745	57	200,688
Placebo	201,229	142	201,087

Did vaccination reduce the incidence of polio? The 57 polio cases in the Vaccine group are depressing, but this does seem considerably better than the 142 cases in the Placebo group. Taken by itself, the 57 − 142 difference seems substantial, well under half as much polio with vaccine.

But each group has some 200,000 children. Relative to this huge number, 57 and 142 are both very small. Perhaps the 57–142 split is just chance fluctuation. Some more objective assessment is necessary before recommending mass vaccination for all children in the U.S. To answer the question, we use the same significance test logic developed in Section 2.3.

If vaccination was ineffective, we would expect about equally many polio cases in the two groups. This is the null hypothesis of no effect. The question thus reduces to determining whether the observed 57–142 split, or one more extreme, has a probability less than α if H_0 is true. The usual .05 level is far too lax in this case, of course, and even .01 would seem too risky.

The intuitive idea for testing the null hypothesis of no effect has two straightforward steps. First, calculate what frequency would be expected in each of the four data cells of Table 10.1—if H_0 was true. Second, compare these expected H_0 frequencies with the observed frequencies in each cell. If the difference between observed and expected is "large enough," reject H_0 and conclude there is a real difference.

Statistical theory, conveniently for us, has shown how this intuitive idea can be given exact formulation. This is the chi-square test, taken up next.

10.1.2 FORMULA FOR CHI-SQUARE

The formula for chi-square is remarkably simple. Let O be the observed frequency in each cell; let E be the frequency expected if the null hypothesis is true. Then the chi-square statistic is

$$X^2 = \sum_{\text{cells}} \frac{(O - E)^2}{E}. \tag{1}$$

This is a universal formula, applying to all situations.

This formula makes sense. If the differences between the Os are merely chance, then O will equal E, on average. Larger values of $(O - E)$ are less likely if H_0 is true. Hence larger values of $(O - E)$ are stronger evidence for a real effect. These $(O - E)$ deviations are squared, just as in Anova, and for the same reason.

Of course, a given value of $(O - E)^2$ is weaker evidence when E is large than when E is small. To integrate evidence across cells with different Es, some way to adjust for E is needed. Happily for us, this adjustment is accomplished in the simplest way: Divide each $(O - E)^2$ by its E.

10.1.3 CHI-SQUARE SIGNIFICANCE TEST

Logic of the Chi-Square Test. The logic of the significance test for chi-square is identical with that for Anova in Section 2.3. Larger values of X^2 argue against the null hypothesis. If our observed X^2 is "large enough," we reject H_0 and claim definite evidence for a real effect. As with Anova, "large enough" means larger than could reasonably be expected by chance.

"Large enough" is quantified in the same manner as in Figure 2.1 for Anova, except the two curves have a chi-square shape, somewhat different from the F shape in Figure 2.1. One curve is the sampling distribution of X^2 under the null hypothesis. The formula for this "H_0 true" distribution makes it possible to calculate the criterial values listed in Table A6. The criterial value of chi-square is such that α of the area under this curve lies to its right. If our observed X^2 is larger than this criterial value, we reject H_0.

In practice, the criterial values are determined from a theoretical χ^2 distribution, which is only an approximation to X^2. This approximation is quite adequate when the Es are not too small (see below).

The concept of power also parallels that for Anova. If H_0 is false, the sampling distribution of X^2 will be shifted rightward, just as in Figure 2.1. Power is the area under this "H_0 false" distribution to the right of the criterion. The 2×2 decision table of Figure 2.2 also applies directly. Hits, misses, and false alarms have the same meaning for chi-square as for Anova.

This conceptual identity between F and X^2 is notable because the two differ in a fundamental way, namely, in the concept of error variability. In the Anova of Chapters 2 and 3, error variability is defined in terms of differences between subjects treated alike. These differences can be quantified because each subject has a numerical score, a measure of the magnitude of individual response.

The concept of error variability is equally necessary with categorical response: Some way must be found to quantify what can be expected by chance; this is necessary to determine what is "large enough." Our data, however, are only the number of individuals in each category. Accordingly, chance refers to the yes–no, binomial variability of each E value in the chi-square frequency table. Statistical theory shows that this idea leads to the X^2 formula of Equation 1.

Chi-Square Applied to the Polio Data. For the polio data, Equation 1 yields $X^2 = 36.1$ (see next section). This is larger than the criterial value of 10.83 for $\alpha = .001$. Accordingly, we may conclude that the frequency of polio differs between the vaccine and placebo groups.

Of course, this statsig effect does not allow us to conclude that the vaccine was effective. That requires scrutiny of the experimental procedure to assess threats from confounding.

One potential confound was bias in assignment of children to groups. The moral dilemma that faced the investigators is not uncommon in medical science. Is it ethical to assign children at random to the placebo group?

From the tabled data, it would appear that around $142 - 57 = 85$ children got polio that could have been avoided by vaccination. It was not known beforehand that the vaccine would be effective, of course, but there was enough evidence to warrant this extremely complex and extremely expensive experiment. The investigators considered various alternatives, but concluded that there was no good alternative to the random assignment that was used.

A second confound was nullified with double blind procedure. The medical personnel dealing with the children did not know which treatment had been given any child. This was essential to ensure unbiased classification, for there are other childhood diseases that are sometimes hard to distinguish from polio. Had the medical personnel been aware of the treatment for any given child, this could have influenced their classification and biased the results.

Had the vaccine been 100% effective, these careful procedures would not have been necessary. However, a substantial number of vaccinated children did get polio. Without careful procedure, the results would have been inconclusive.

10.1.4 CONTINGENCY TABLES

The polio vaccine data illustrate one kind of contingency table. The term *contingency* highlights the question: Are the frequencies in the columns *contingent on* the row classification? The null hypothesis is that column and row frequencies are noncontingent, that is, not correlated or not associated—knowing which row (column) a case is in tells nothing about which column (row) it is in.[a]

Proportionality Rule for Expected Values. The main problem with chi-square is to get the expected cell frequencies, the E values in Equation 1. These Es are calculated with the *proportionality rule*, illustrated in Table 10.2. The B variable was experimentally controlled, with **18, 12,** and **6** subjects in conditions B_1, B_2, and B_3, respectively. The response for each subject was classified as A_1 or A_2. Inspection of the data suggests that the proportion of A_1 responses depends on the B condition.

TABLE 10.2

NUMERICAL EXAMPLE OF CONTINGENCY-TABLE

	B_1	B_2	B_3	
A_1	9 (12)	12 (8)	3 (4)	24
A_2	9 (6)	0 (4)	3 (2)	12
Total	**18**	**12**	**6**	

The E values are calculated on the assumption that the null hypothesis is true—that the A response is unrelated to the B treatment. Therefore, the 24 subjects who gave A_1 responses should be divided *proportionately* across columns. *Proportionately* means in proportion to the number of subjects in each treatment condition. This proportionality principle represents the null hypothesis.

To apply the proportionality rule, note that 18, 12, and 6 subjects were assigned to B_1, B_2, and B_3, respectively. Hence the 24 subjects who responded A_1 should be distributed in the same proportion: 12, 8 and 4, if H_0 is true. These E values are listed in parentheses in the first row of data. By the same proportionality argument, the 12 subjects who responded A_2 should be distributed 6, 4, and 2. These E values are listed in parentheses in the second row.

Chi-Square Calculation. Given these Es, X^2 is obtained with Equation 1:

$$X^2 = \frac{(9-12)^2}{12} + \frac{(12-8)^2}{8} + \frac{(3-4)^2}{4}$$

$$+ \frac{(9-6)^2}{6} + \frac{(0-4)^2}{4} + \frac{(3-2)^2}{2}$$

$$= 9.00.$$

The df for a row × column contingency table are

$$df = (rows - 1) \times (columns - 1).^b \tag{2}$$

The 2 × 3 table thus has 2 df. From Table A6, the criterial value of chi-square on 2 df is 5.99 for $\alpha = .05$. The observed value of 9.00 is thus statsig.

Null Hypothesis. The null hypothesis deserves further consideration. It says that the row and column variables are unrelated—they show no *association*. In Table 10.2, therefore, the null hypothesis says that knowing which experimental condition (column) a subject is in tells nothing about which response (row) that subject will make.

Since the E values are calculated under the null hypothesis, they necessarily show no row–column association. If the Os agree with the Es, then they also show no association. If the Os disagree with the Es, they do show association. Association thus means that the cell frequencies in each row depend on, are contingent on, or are correlated with, the column variable. Reliable association is signaled by statsig X^2.

Confidence Interval. The variance of a proportion p_1 based on a sample of size n_1 is $p_1(1-p_1)/n_1$ by Equation 4 of Section 0.1.4. Hence the variance of the difference between two independent proportions is the sum of the two variances, $p_1(1-p_1)/n_1 + p_2(1-p_2)/n_2$. For large enough sample sizes, the normal approximation may be used to obtain the 95% confidence interval:

$$p_1 - p_2 \pm 1.96\sqrt{p_1(1-p_1)/n_1 + p_2(1-p_2)/n_2}. \tag{3}$$

This confidence interval could be used as a significance test for the proportion of polio cases in the vaccine and placebo groups of Table 10.1. The logic is the same as with the two-mean confidence interval of Section 2.2: If 0 lies outside the interval, we may have 95% confidence that $p_1 - p_2$ differs from 0, and hence that p_1 differs from p_2.

This confidence interval has two advantages over the chi-square test of significance: It shows the size of the effect directly in terms of the data proportions; and it exhibits the likely error of that effect. Although most texts present only the significance test, confidence intervals may be more meaningful and more useful with 2 × 2 tables or subtables.

10.1.5 ASSUMPTIONS OF CHI-SQUARE

Two assumptions are important for the chi-square test. First, expected cell frequencies must not be too small because the theoretical chi-square distribution, which is used to determine the criterial value for X^2, is only an approximation to the true distribution of X^2. This approximation is not adequate when the Es are too small. With too-small Es, the effective false alarm parameter differs from its nominal value.[a]

Opinions differ on how small is too small, but current opinion is more liberal. Rough rules for contingency tables, following Wickens (1989), are (a) all Es at least 2 or 3 with 1 df tests, at least 1 or 2 with more df; (b) N at least 4 or 5 times the number of cells; (c) larger samples needed with unequal marginal frequencies; to which may be added (d) larger Es needed with borderline X^2.

The second assumption of chi-square is that the data are independent random samples from the same distribution. For most applications, independence requires that each subject be counted only once; a second response from the same subject cannot be used. Doing so is *double counting*.

To illustrate the danger of double counting, consider 60 hypothetical female college seniors, each cross-classified on the basis of two characteristics: taller or shorter than average; and happier or less happy than average. The investigator believes that taller women are usually happier. The data are shown at the left of Table 10.3. The E for each cell is clearly 15, so

$$X^2 = \frac{1}{15}[3^2 + 3^2 + 3^2 + 3^2] = 2.40.$$

This chi-square is not statsig, not even close to the criterial value of 3.84.

TABLE 10.3

DOUBLE COUNTING VIOLATES CHI-SQUARE

	more happy	less happy		more happy	less happy	
taller	18	12	30	36	24	60
shorter	12	18	30	24	36	60
	30	30		60	60	

Now suppose that each subject is cross-classified a second time by an independent assessment. Suppose the classification is reliable, so the second classification essentially duplicates the first. Counting both assessments then doubles the frequency in each cell, shown at the right of Table 10.3. It is easy to show that this doubling of frequencies doubles X^2, which thus becomes 4.80, substantially larger than the criterial 3.84. But although 4.80 looks statsig, it is invalid because of the double counting.

The artifact of double counting is clear in this example. The second assessment of each subject added no information beyond the first; the right table contains no more information than the left table. The frequencies in the right table violate the independence assumption because the second measurement is perfectly correlated with the first.

Of course, independence is violated even if the second measurement is only partly correlated with the first, as in most actual cases of double counting. The essence of the independence assumption is that each case provides an equal unit of information. With nonindependence, a second score contributes less information than the first score. Such violation of the independence assumption destroys the validity of chi-square.

Double counting still occurs occasionally in published reports. A sure sign of double counting is an N in the chi-square test that exceeds the number of subjects. Some reports fail to present adequate information to check this, which raises a question about their validity.

Finally, it should also be noted that every case must appear in some cell of the table. In the polio example, it would not do to compare 57 with 142; the nonpolio cases must also be included. This requirement is not actually an assumption, but a precondition. Sometimes, however, it gets overlooked.

Power. The real problem with small Es is low power. This power deficiency has been obscured under extensive concern with the effect of small Es on the false alarm parameter. Ns as small as allowed by the cited rules are unlikely to have adequate power. A 70:30 split in a 2×2 contingency table is substantial, yet it yields power of only .45 with an N of 20.[b]

Unless there is good reason to expect a pretty large effect, it seems doubtful practice to use 2×2 contingency tables with Ns as small as 30. This point deserves emphasis because recent work on minimum cell sizes has encouraged use of smaller Ns. Unfortunately, this work has been concerned with the statistical false alarm parameter, with little regard to power. One objection to reporting experiments with low power is that claimed results will not readily be replicable (Chapter 4). A suggested prerequisite to such chi-squares is a preliminary calculation showing power of at least .75 for whatever effect size may reasonably be anticipated.

10.2 FURTHER ASPECTS OF CHI-SQUARE

10.2.1 CHI-SQUARE FOR ONE OR TWO VARIABLES

Indexes of Association. A statsig chi-square implies that the row and column variables are associated, or correlated. It says little, however, about the strength of that association. The foregoing confidence interval is an often useful index of effect size. It applies only to 2 × 2 tables or subtables, however, and it does not measure the association, or correlation, between the variables. Various other indexes of association have been proposed that allow larger contingency tables, but none is very satisfactory as a general purpose index. Two common indexes are noted here.[a]

The value of X^2 is not a good index because it depends on N, which is irrelevant to the strength of association. If you double all the cell frequencies, thereby doubling N, you double X^2. This suggests dividing X^2 by N; doubling N leaves X^2/N unchanged. This idea underlies Pearson's contingency index,

$$\phi = \sqrt{X^2/N}. \tag{4}$$

One shortcoming of this index is that its maximum value depends on the size of the table. Specifically, ϕ cannot be larger than the smaller of the number of rows and the number of columns, minus 1. Hence comparisons of ϕ across tables of different size is awkward. In particular, ϕ has a maximum of 3 for a 4 × 4 table, but a maximum of only 1 for a 2 × 4 subtable of this 4 × 4 table. One amendment is to adjust an $a \times b$ table for size by using

$$\phi' = \sqrt{X^2/N[\min(a, b) - 1]}.$$

Perhaps it is more sensible to recognize that table size is irrelevant to strength of association and avoid general use of this index.

A more useful index for 2 × 2 tables uses relative odds. In the polio table, divide the chance of getting polio without vaccine by the chance with vaccine. This odds ratio is 2.49, a direct measure of the effectiveness of the vaccine. The odds ratio is more meaningful in that it looks directly at the data. Its shortcoming is that it only applies to 2 × 2 tables or subtables. The ϕ index and relative odds are compared in Exercise 12.

The lack of a general purpose index of association strength was foreshadowed in the analogous discussion of r in Chapter 9. It reappears in the discussion of *Size and Importance* in Section 18.1. Indexes of association may be meaningful if they can be compared across many similar investigations. But too often, in my opinion, they are merely statistical busywork, busywork that diverts attention away from the actual proportions.

Goodness of Fit. Expected frequencies are sometimes obtained as theoretical predictions. As a simple example, coin tossing theoretically yields heads and tails in equal proportion. This differs from the foregoing contingency table, in which expected frequencies are calculated from the observed marginal frequencies. Tests of theoretical frequencies are sometimes called tests of goodness of fit to distinguish them from tests on contingency tables.

To illustrate goodness of fit, consider the sex of N infants born in a certain period in a certain hospital. To test whether Nature has a sex bias, take $E = \frac{1}{2}N$ for male and female. Reduce each $|O - E|$ by $\frac{1}{2}$ and use Equation 1 for the two cells to get X^2 on 1 df.[b, c]

As a more general application, chi-square can be used to test whether a distribution has some specified shape, for example, normal. The data are put into the form of a frequency histogram, which yields the O values. The normal distribution is fitted to this histogram using the sample mean and variance as estimates of the normal mean and variance. This fitted distribution is then used to calculate the theoretical frequency in each histogram interval, and these are used as the E values in Equation 1. The df are 1 less than the number of intervals in the histogram, minus 1 for each estimated parameter. The normal example has two parameters, mean and variance; df would be 3 less than the number of intervals in the histogram. Similar tests of goodness of fit can be applied generally; all that is needed is a theoretical basis for specifying the Es.

Single Subject Chi-Square. Goodness of fit for psychological process models may be testable in the manner indicated in the previous subsection. To illustrate, consider a two-choice decision task in which the signal information on each trial has some likelihood of coming from either of two specified sources. The subject judges which source the signal came from. The signal information is manipulated experimentally in factorial-type design but kept weak or noisy so the choice is probabilistic.

Theoretically, this choice task should obey the decision averaging model of cognitive algebra (Chapter 21). Goodness of fit could be tested by using the model to calculate the E values. This decision averaging model has the same form as the Bradley–Terry–Luce choice model. Chi-square analyses of this and other models are considered by Agresti (1996) and Wickens (1989).

Power is a serious problem with such choice tasks. Because model analysis typically seeks to accept the null hypothesis, large amounts of data are needed. Pooling data over multiple trials for more than one subject would be double counting, which violates independence. Single subject data are thus essential.

Single subject data, however, may violate independence through serial correlation of successive responses. In some tasks, independence may be obtained with treatment randomization. Other tasks may seek independence by interpolating a standard, baseline condition between successive trials in order to wash out the serial correlation (see further Chapter 11, *Single Subject Design*).

Anova in Place of Chi-Square. Chi-square has somewhat limited usefulness in laboratory experiments because the Ns are often not large enough to get adequate power. Anova is usually satisfactory with 8–15 subjects per condition because it capitalizes on the numerical magnitude information in the response. With yes–no responses from like numbers of subjects, chi-square may have too little power to be worth anything (Note 10.1.5b).

This problem of low power suggests seeking some way to restructure tasks to obtain a numerical response measure, which can provide higher power. Time to make a choice might be used instead of choice frequency, for example, or choices could be aggregated over a number of trials. A further advantage of Anova is its capability of analyzing repeated measures on the same subjects, which provides additional power and also more design flexibility.

Miscellaneous Comments. A few miscellaneous comments about chi-square deserve mention. First, the chi-square approximation is not adequate for N less than, say, 20. For 2 × 2 tables, exact tests for small N have been tabulated (Pearson & Hartley, 1966). These small tables have very limited practical value, however, because of low power (Note 10.1.5b).

Second, the "correction for continuity" for 2 × 2 contingency tables has largely been abandoned. It applies only for a very special case of contingency table. It is mentioned here because it was once considered essential in all cases, and often appears in the older literature. Since it acts to reduce X^2, any result statsig with this correction will remain statsig without it.

Third, power estimates are even more needed with chi-square applications than with Anova. A useful power chart is given in Wickens (1989, pp. 39, 395).

10.2.2 MORE THAN TWO VARIABLES

Frequency data often involve more than two variables. Polio is known to depend on parent's socioeconomic status, for example, and including this variable would require a three-way table in place of the foregoing two-way table. With three variables, chi-square analysis is notably more complex. Each pair of variables may, or may not, have an association, and each of these two-way associations may, or may not, depend of the level of the third variable.

Some situations cannot be understood with only two variables. Two variables that appear independent in a two-way table may appear associated when the same data are classified in a three-way format. Conversely, an association between two variables may disappear when a third variable is taken into consideration (see *Missing Variables* below). Unlike two-variable tables, moreover, the appropriate analysis with three or more variables may depend on whether the marginal frequencies are controlled by the investigator, as with the number of subjects in the vaccine and placebo groups, or uncontrolled, as with the height–happiness example of Table 10.3.

Log-Linear Models. *Log-linear models* have been developed to handle multiple variables. The name log-linear applies because taking logarithms transforms the proportionality rule that underlies the foregoing calculation of E values into a linear, or additive rule. Such log-linear models clarify the analysis of contingency tables with more than two variables.

Effective application of log-linear models requires a book of its own. The following discussion gives only an overview of their nature. The log-linear model for a two-way, $A \times B$ contingency table can be written

$$\text{log cell frequency} = \text{constant} + A \text{ effect} + B \text{ effect} \qquad (5)$$

$$+ \ A{-}B \text{ association.}$$

More formally,

$$\log \mu_{jk} = \lambda_0 + \lambda_{Aj} + \lambda_{Bk} + \lambda_{ABjk}. \qquad (6)$$

Here μ_{jk} is the true frequency in cell jk; λ_{Aj} is the effect of level j of variable A; λ_{Bk} is the effect of level k of variable B; λ_{ABjk} is the residual in cell jk.

The model of Equation 6 looks like the Anova model of Equation 5.1b, for it is a sum of three effects: row, column, and residual. And indeed the residual is calculated in exactly the same way; it is the residual from the row-plus-column model applied to the $A \times B$ table of the logs of the observed frequencies.

But although Equation 6 is similar in mathematical form to the Anova model, its substantive meaning is very different. The row and column effects are generally noninformative. Only the residual has general interest with frequency data; it embodies the association between A and B.

This difference between the log-linear model and the Anova model may be illustrated with the polio data of Table 10.1. The row variable is the number of children in the two groups; although this variable was controlled experimentally, it has no causal significance. The column variable is the number of children who did and did not contract polio; this variable has central importance, but it is the response measure, not a cause or correlate thereof as in Anova. All that is of interest is whether the row and column variables are associated, for this association measures the effectiveness of the vaccine. Quite opposite to Anova, therefore, the "main effects" have no interest, only the residual or "interaction." As this contrast indicates, analysis of typical frequency data differs essentially from analysis of numerical data.

An alternative test statistic is often used with log-linear models. This is the *likelihood ratio, L^2*:

$$L^2 = 2 \sum_{\text{cells}} O \log \left[\frac{O}{E} \right]. \qquad (7)$$

Here O and E are the observed and expected cell frequencies defined exactly as with X^2 in Equation 1. This L^2 statistic is approximated by a theoretical chi-square distribution with $(a - 1)(b - 1)$ df. Either L^2 or X^2 can be used for the same data, with X^2 perhaps preferable with small frequencies. The two will differ somewhat for the same data since each is a different approximation to the theoretical chi-square. A marginally statsig result with either should thus be taken with an extra grain of salt.

Gender Bias? Or Missing Variable? A *missing variable*—one operative in the processes that give rise to the data but not included in the data analysis—can confound the interpretation. This universal threat, as it may rightly be called, is illustrated for categorical data in the following investigation of gender bias in the University of California, Berkeley in the early 1970s. It appeared that 46% of male applicants were accepted to graduate school, but only 24% of female applicants. Some department must be gender biased in its admissions.

The engineering department naturally comes under suspicion. Representative data showed 50 male and 5 female applicants, of whom 30 males and 3 females were admitted. Acceptance rate was thus 60% for both genders.

Suspicion turns to the science departments. Representative figures showed 30 males and 10 female applicants, of whom 12 males and 4 females were accepted. Acceptance rate was thus 40% for both genders.

The bias must lie in the humanities departments! Who would have suspected this? Representative figures showed 20 male and 85 female applicants, of whom 4 males and 17 females were accepted. Acceptance rate is much lower in humanities, which get little grant money to support research assistants. But the given figures show 20% acceptance for both genders.

To sum up: No bias was present in the individual departments. Strong apparent bias appeared when the data were pooled over departments, as you can readily verify using the given data. This apparent bias resulted from missing variables: Higher female application rate in humanities together with lower acceptance rate, variables that are missing in the pooled data.[a]

One aspect of progress in science concerns missing variables, either uncovering them or showing that they can be ignored. Missing variables are a special threat in behavioral sciences, which deal with heterogeneous subject populations, as in the foregoing investigation of gender bias (see also Note 5.2.2a, page 146, and *Missing Variable Confounding* in Section 16.2.1, page 503). Similar threats appear in experimental studies, as shown by some examples of confounding in Chapter 8. An important part of the empirical lore needed to become expert in any field consists of background knowledge about variables that can be ignored and those that cannot.

NOTES

Wickens (1989) gives a good treatment of multiway contingency tables. His basic chapters require study, but seem essential for anyone who wishes to do serious work with frequency data. Usefully different perspectives appear in Fleiss (1981) and in Agresti (1996), who give many illustrative sets of data as well as helpful exercises.

10.1.1a. The polio cases in Table 10.1 include both paralytic and nonparalytic cases listed in Meier's (1989) Table 1. The frequencies of paralytic cases were 33 and 115 in the Vaccine and Placebo groups, respectively.

10.1.4a. *Homogeneity and Independence.* Contingency tables are mainly of two kinds. In one kind, one variable (row or column) represents different groups of subjects, as with the polio vaccine experiment, and the other variable represents the subject classification. The null hypothesis says that the proportion of each class of response is the same for each group—that the groups are *homogeneous.*

In the other kind of contingency table, there is only a single group. Row and column variables represent two characteristics of the same subjects, as with the height–happiness example of Table 10.3. The null hypothesis says that the two subject characteristics are uncorrelated, or *independent.*

For two-way contingency tables, fortunately, the X^2 test is exactly the same for both homogeneity and independence. With more than two variables, however, homogeneity and independence may yield different E values and hence different values of X^2 for the same numerical data. This is one complication that arises with more than two variables.

10.1.4b. The chi-square distribution was introduced in 1900 by Karl Pearson, the major figure in the early development of statistics. Pearson, however, thought that the df for a contingency table equaled rows × columns − 1. In Pearson's view, a 2 × 2 table would thus have 3 df, not 1. When Fisher solved this statistical problem, obtaining Equation 2, Pearson gave him a hostile reception, quoted by Agresti (1996, pp. 251*f*):

> I hold such a view [Fisher's] is entirely erroneous . . . . pardon me for comparing him with Don Quixote tilting at the windmill; he must either destroy himself, or the whole theory of probable errors.

To which Fisher replied (rather mildly for Fisher; see Fisher, 1956, pp. 2-3):

> If peevish intolerance of free opinion in others is a sign of senility, it is one which he [Pearson] has developed at an early age.

Pearson's substantial contributions to the early development of statistics would shine more brightly today had he been more tolerant, for Fisher was mercilessly correct. Agresti concludes his historical survey of chi-square (p. 265) by saying:

> And so, it is fitting that we end this brief survey by giving yet further credit to R. A. Fisher for his influence on the practice of modern statistical science.

10.1.5a. The theoretical chi-square distribution (χ^2) is almost as important as the normal distribution in statistical theory. In fact, χ^2 is distributed as the square of a unit normal variable. The χ^2 distribution thus appears in Anova: Under the null hypothesis, numerator and denominator of the F ratio have (independent) χ^2 distributions.

10.1.5b. To support the claim that N of 20 is generally too small with a 2×2 contingency table, suppose we expect a substantial effect, with true proportions of 70:30 and 30:70 in the two rows. Following Wickens' (1989) treatment yields power about .45 relative to the null hypothesis of 50:50 proportions. This seems considerably too low. Yet 70:30 versus 50:50 seems rather larger than one could often expect. An N of 30 would yield power of .57, also too low. A different approach leading to a similar conclusion is given by Overall (1980).

10.2.1a. *Agreement and Disagreement.* Sometimes useful is the *kappa* index of agreement-disagreement developed by Cohen (see Agresti, 1996; Wickens, 1989), which attempts to correct for the chance level of agreement between two classifications. Kappa may sometimes be useful as a descriptive index of agreement–disagreement. Rarely would a significance test be needed to show that two classifications agree better than chance. And rarely will it be necessary to show that two methods do not agree perfectly.

In contrast, a significance test for disagreement is sometimes needed. If voters are polled at two successive time points, for example, changes in opinion would appear as disagreements between the two responses. Systematic change would appear as a difference between the frequency of changes in the two directions. Chi-square can be adapted to test disagreement (Exercise 16).

10.2.1b. When testing goodness of fit with two categories, as in this example of relative frequencies of male and female births, a "correction for continuity" should be used. This correction consists of reducing the magnitude of each $|O - E|$ by $\frac{1}{2}$ before squaring. The effect is to reduce X^2. This correction improves the accuracy of the chi-square approximation in this case. This application of chi-square is equivalent to the normal deviate z test for a binomial proportion, which uses the same correction.

For 2×2 contingency tables, this correction for continuity is gradually being abandoned because it does more harm than good except in very special cases. It was long considered necessary, however, and is common in published papers.

10.2.1c. Male births are more frequent than females, about 106 to 100. Males are less healthy, however, so the numbers equalize around age 18. Most other species also show near equality of males and females.

Few people stop to wonder about this curious fact, but it is puzzling. The mother is the main support of the young in most species. Only a few males are necessary to perpetuate the species. For the good of the species, therefore, it might seem that evolution should select for females.

Fisher, who also did fundamental work in genetics, did stop to wonder about the near-equality of the sexes. He showed that this near-equality follows from Darwinian theory, which takes survival of the individual as the motor of evolution, not survival of the species (see Gould, 1980, Chapter 6).

10.2.2a. This discussion of gender bias in graduate admissions at UC Berkeley is based on Bickel, Hammel, and O'Connell (1975), reprinted with discussion in *Studies in Public Policy* (Fairley & Mosteller, 1977). The numerical example given in the text, which I have used for many years in my classes, comes from a secondary source that I regret I have not managed to relocate. Similar examples are cited in Wagner (1982).

EXERCISES FOR CHAPTER 10

Please do all calculations using only hand calculator. This will help you understand the basic *proportionality rule* for getting expected values.

1. The discussion of the polio data implies that a statsig X^2 is not adequate evidence that the vaccine was effective. Why not? What general principle does this illustrate?

2. In the polio experiment:

   a. Why should a preliminary power calculation be made?

   b. What criticism might be made of the N in this experiment?

   c. By analogy to Section 4.3 on power for Anova, guess what item of information is needed for a power calculation for chi-square.

3. In one of the final tests of Clever Hans, the mathematical horse of Chapter 8, Hans was instructed to perform a simple arithmetic task, such as adding two numbers. On each trial, Mr. von Osten would whisper one of the numbers in Hans' ear, following which Professor Pfungst would whisper the other number. On some of these trials, one or both men knew the answer; on these trials, Hans got 29 right and 2 wrong. On other trials, neither man knew the answer; on these trials, Hans got 3 right and 28 wrong (Pfungst, 1965, p. 37.)

   a. What is the null hypothesis in this 2×2 contingency table?

   b. Is chi-square really applicable with these small frequencies of 2 and 3?

   c. Show that $X^2 = 43.66$.

   d. Show that the 95% confidence interval is .84 ± .14.

   e. Is this chi-square test really needed?

4. In the field study of smoking prevention in the Appendix to Chapter 3, 19%, 24%, and 27% of the cases in the three treatment conditions had not smoked at the three-month mark. Assume each group had exactly 1000 subjects. Show that $X^2 = 18.26$.

5. A clinical trial (= experiment) extending over several years showed that breast cancer was developed by 216 of 6707 women on placebo control, and by 115 of 6681 women on the drug tamoxifen. Should the Food and Drug Administration approve tamoxifen for prescription by doctors?

6. In a field experiment in a nursing home, one group of residents received a treatment that emphasized their responsibility to make their own choices and control their own lives. A comparison group received a treatment that emphasized the responsibility of the staff to care for them and make them happy

(see further pages 465*f*). The hypothesis was that the first treatment would increase the residents' sense of personal control, with beneficial health effects.

"The most striking data were obtained in the death rate differences between the two groups" in the 18-month follow-up—only 7 of 47 subjects in the first treatment had died compared to 13 of 44 in the second treatment, which the authors claimed was statsig, "($p < .01$)" (Rodin & Langer, 1977, p. 899).

    a. Check their claim.   b. What is the moral of this exercise?

7. Adult-onset diabetes produces high levels of blood glucose because of deficiencies in glucose metabolism. It was widely held that lowering blood glucose to normal levels would reduce cardiovascular complications. The drug tolbutamide lowers blood glucose to normal levels and was routinely prescribed by many physicians. An objective test of efficacy of tolbutamide would be a large undertaking in a long-term study using double-blind, randomized design. Despite the high cost, an experimental study was considered desirable and it was performed with cooperation of a dozen medical clinics.

In addition to the placebo and tolbutamide groups, two groups received insulin, a standard treatment for diabetes. These two groups were expected to be fairly similar. Each group had a little over 200 patients as subjects. Deaths from cardiovascular disease were expected to run about 5% during the study.

    a. Are the expected numbers of deaths in each cell of the contingency table large enough to justify chi-square?

    b. Suppose the X^2 on 3 df for the overall data turns out to be statsig. What does this tell you? What does this not tell you? (See Section 4.2.)

    c. You wish to compare the tolbutamide group with the two insulin groups, ignoring the placebo group. The two insulin groups are expected to show similar results. Give two possible formats for the contingency table. Which one would you plan to use?

    d. Suppose the University Group Diabetes Program, which performed this study, had asked you to plan the statistical analysis for the data on cardiovascular deaths. What tests would you plan as essential? What supplementary tests, if any, would you consider desirable?

8. In the previous exercise, there were 10 cardiovascular deaths of 215 patients in the placebo group, 26 of 230 in the tolbutamide group, 13 of 223 in one insulin group, and 12 of 216 in the other.

    a. Consider two comparisons: tolbutamide with the placebo; and tolbutamide with the two pooled insulin conditions. Guess at the X^2 for each test, relative to the criterial X^2 of 3.84 on 1 df.

    b. Calculate chi-square for (a). (For the first, $|O - E| = 7.39$ in each cell.)

    c. This tolbutamide study was "received by some critics with a hostility which has no discernible scientific basis'' said Cornfield (1971, p. 1676) in his reply to critics (published in *Journal of the American Medical Association*, 1971, *217*, 1676–1687; well worth reading for several reasons). What is your conjecture about the origin of this ''hostility?''

d. What is the moral of this exercise?

9. You wish to compare three types of dyslexic children on ability to solve a certain kind of verbal problem. Each child receives three problems, which are scored success or failure. You had planned to apply chi-square to the frequencies pooled over all three problems, but now you realize that would involve double counting. Accordingly, you limit the chi-square to just the first problem, but this falls somewhat short of being statsig, p just under .10.

a. You notice, however, that the same trend appears in both other problems so you do a chi-square on each of them. They also yield p-values a bit under .10. ''Aha!'' you think, ''the probability that all three have $p \le .10$ is $.10 \times .10 \times .10 = .001$, by the multiplication rule of Chapter 0. So this result is evidently real.'' What is the flaw in this argument?

b. It's awful to have three responses when the chi-square analysis allows only one and wastes the information in the other two. How can you restructure the analysis to use all the data?

c. What alternative response measure might avoid this difficulty?

d. How much information do you get from a problem so easy/hard that all/none of the children solve it? What follows?

10. Show that pooling the three sets of figures on graduate admissions cited in *Gender Bias?* in the last subsection of this chapter yields the cited overall admission rates for males and females.

11. A medical survey of thyroid and heart disease in Whickham, England in 1972–1974 used a one-in-six sample of the electoral rolls. A follow-up 20 years later obtained the following survival data for all women in the original survey who had at that time been classified as smokers or having never smoked. (After Appleton, French, & Vanderpump, 1996.)

	Smoker	No-smoker
Dead	139	230
Alive	443	502

a. Summarize the sense of this table with two numbers. At face value, what do these two numbers imply?

b. Would it be valid to apply a chi-square test to these data?

c. The observed outcome may seem contrary to other knowledge. What missing variable might account for the observed pattern?

12. Suppose the 199 polio cases in Table 10.1 had been distributed 3 and 196. Calculate both $\hat{\phi}$ and the odds ratio and compare them with the values for the 57-142 split given in the text. Comment.

13. **Median Test.** Chi-square may be used as a *median test* for data that can be rank ordered. To illustrate the median test, consider the rank order of admission of the 40 patients in the study of controlled drinking listed in Exercise b2 of Chapter 12. Dichotomize the 40 subjects at the median admission time. Apply chi-square to test whether the greater proportion of Control subjects admitted in the second half is real.

14. How does *The Case of the Molded Plastic* in Section 8.1.5 illustrate the threat of missing variables?

15. In Section 10.2.1, explain why N is irrelevant to the strength of association. What is N relevant to?

16.* Cases occasionally arise that look like a two-way contingency table, but require a different analysis. Here is one such case (Karpp & Anderson, 1997).

Two methodologies have been used to study whether peoples' intuitive judgments of physical tasks have the same form as the physical law. One is the Piaget–Siegler choice methodology described in Section 8.1.3 and Note 8.1.3b; the other is the functional measurement methodology of Chapter 21. The cited experiment tested whether the two methodologies agree in their diagnoses of cognitive knowledge systems.

Subjects judged how fast a cart of specified *mass* released from a specified *height* on an inclined plane would be moving when it reached the bottom. Subjects responded to a set of mass–height combinations constructed to provide the diagnostic information needed for each methodology.

Of the 40 subjects, 3 were diagnosed as centerers by functional measurement, and these 3 were diagnosed the same by the choice methodology. The remaining 37 subjects were all diagnosed as integrators by functional measurement but only 8 were diagnosed as integrators by the choice methodology, the other 29 being diagnosed as centerers.

    a. What is the null hypothesis for comparing the two methodologies?

    b. Make a 2×2 table with rows corresponding to the two diagnostic methodologies, columns to the two diagnoses (integration, centering). Why would it be inappropriate to apply chi-square considered as a test of homogeneity or of independence (defined in Note 10.1.4a)?

    c. What statistical test would you apply?

17. "A given value of $(O - E)^2$ is weaker evidence when E is large than when E is small" (Section 10.1.2). Intuitively, why is this true? Justify it with a formula from Chapter 2.

PREFACE

Single subject design and analysis is an ideal. The primary advantage is maximal congruence between observation and phenomenon, that is, between the level of Measurement and the levels of Behavior and Phenomena in the Experimental Pyramid of Chapter 1. In addition, single subjects can be more readily studied over many sessions, which may reveal phenomena never seen in the common one-session experiments.

Two classes of designs have been used in single subject research. One class is *treatment randomization design*, in which the various treatments are presented to the subject in random order. Treatment randomization has the priceless advantage that it can yield independence of scores. All the methods of previous chapters then become applicable.

The other class is *serial observation design*, which involves repeated presentation of one treatment at a time to the subject. In the simple A-B design, for example, a series of trials under treatment A is followed by a series of trials under treatment B.

Analysis of serial observation data faces two difficult problems: *reliability* and *validity*. In the given A-B design, the first question is whether the A-B difference is reliable. The answer obviously involves comparison of the mean difference between treatments to the variability within treatments.

This reliability question is troubled by possible nonindependence of observations in the form of serial correlation between successive responses. Nonindependence typically makes the data look more reliable than they really are. This is even more a problem for visual inspection than for formal statistics.

The second question is validity: Can the A-B difference be attributed to the treatment conditions themselves, or are there likely confounds? The A-B design has two obvious major confounds: confounds with shifts in the external environment; and confounds with order effects in the subject, such as learning, adaptation, treatment-specific transfer, and illness. Various methods have been developed to deal with these confounds, especially repeated A-B series and baseline treatment interpolated between successive experimental treatments.

Although single subject design is widely used and essential in diverse areas, it has been completely neglected in graduate statistics texts. With this neglect has gone corresponding neglect of the foregoing methodological problems. Not much is known about serial correlation, in particular, despite its importance. This chapter aims for better integration of empirics and statistics in this vital area of experimental analysis.

Chapter 11

SINGLE SUBJECT DESIGN

Single subject design and analysis is an experimental ideal. An individual is studied under a number of conditions, and the analysis is performed on the data of this individual. The main advantage is substantive: maximal congruence with psychological phenomena. A collateral advantage is that longer-term investigations may be practicable, unfolding phenomena barely present in the common one-session experiment. There is also the statistical advantage that error variability will be even less than with repeated measures design.

Single subject design has always been a mainstay in perception. One reason is that many perceptual phenomena can be embodied in stable state tasks, so that responses under one condition are not confounded with order effects from previous conditions. One subject can thus provide a complete data pattern across all experimental conditions. Many studies use just two or three subjects, with results presented separately for each. Many results can be generalized on the basis of extrastatistical, background knowledge about similarity of sensory–perceptual process across individuals.

Single subject design has also been useful in diverse other areas. Among these are classical and operant conditioning, judgment–decision theory, physiological psychology, behavior modification, and medical science. Also notable are studies of unusual individuals, such as language disorders caused by brain damage that shed light on the multiple functional components of language.

A pall hangs over single subject design and analysis. This topic goes virtually unmentioned in current graduate statistics texts. Whole areas of experimental analysis that could benefit from this approach make little use of it. You can check yourself how very few single subject studies appear in any issue of any journal published by the American Psychological Association.[a]

On the other hand, areas that have emphasized single subject research have mostly been averse to formal statistics. As a consequence, the potential of single subject design has been markedly underutilized.

Two quite different kinds of experimental situations appear in single subject research. One kind allows treatments to be presented in random order. Treatment randomization gives strong leverage on reliability and validity.

The other kind relies on multiple, successive responses to one treatment at a time. Confounding from order effects then raises difficulties for validity and reliability both. These two problems, accordingly, are considered briefly in the first main section. The two kinds of experimental situations are then taken up, followed by some empirical examples of each.

11.1 VALIDITY AND RELIABILITY

Validity and reliability, the two basic problems of empirical analysis, are as important with single subject as with multiple subject studies. These two problems have been discussed in relation to the Experimental Pyramid of Chapter 1, but unique aspects arise with single subject design.

Temporal confounding and *serial correlation* are of primary concern. These two problems are inherent in single subject data. Statistical analysis does not create these problems; it does give tools to help recognize and deal with them.

11.1.1 VALIDITY

Temporal confounding is a primary problem with single subject research. Any two treatments differ in time and order of presentation; external temporal effects and internal order effects are thus both confounded with treatment effects. Such confounding affects the meaning and validity of the results.

External temporal factors include events in the environment that influence the behavior. If treatment B follows treatment A, any difference in response may be due to some environmental factor: drift or shift in experimental procedure, happenstance events in the environment, and so forth. Any and all such external factors, known and unknown, confound the A−B comparison.

External factors can, in principle, be handled with replication over successive time periods, as in A-B-B-A- . . . design. Consistency of the A-B difference over successive time periods argues against external influences.[a]

Position effects and *carryover effects* may also produce temporal confounding. These order effects are usually undesirable and need to be controlled through procedure and design. Such internal factors are considered in more detail under Latin squares (Section 14.3) and within−between design (Section 14.4). Similar considerations apply to many single subject studies.[b]

11.1.2 RELIABILITY

A critical reliability problem in single subject analysis concerns independence of observations. Reliability is measured by variability between data points. With independent data, the difference between any two data points is a direct measure of unreliability. With nonindependent data, however, the difference between two data points gives a biased estimate of unreliability.

Nonindependence is a serious concern because of the likelihood of *serial correlation*, that is, correlation between successive responses. One source of serial correlation is assimilation or contrast across successive trials. Trial-to-trial assimilation appears in various tasks of psychophysics and judgment–decision, for example, even though subjects are otherwise in a stable state. Thereby the response on one trial is positively correlated with the response on the previous trial.[a]

A rather different source of serial correlation may be called local drift. This refers to organismic changes in response level that extend over two or more successive observations but fluctuate unsystematically over longer periods. The subject's attention may drift away and snap back; mood and motivation may wax and wane. The state of the subject is thus more similar across successive trials than nonsuccessive trials. This induces serial correlation in the observed behavior even though there is no systematic trend.

Serial correlation violates independence. Each new observation is partly implicit in the preceding observation. To see the consequence, suppose the response is plotted as a function of successive trials. With a high positive correlation, responses on successive trials will be highly similar. The data look less variable, so to speak, than the behavior they represent.

Visual inspection has no way to allow for the serial correlation. Instead, visual inspection tends to treat successive responses as independent. With positive serial correlation, visual inspection sees the data falsely as too reliable. The usual formula for variance does the same, of course, thereby producing confidence intervals that are falsely too short.

At the same time, any happenstance influence on one trial may partly carry over to successive trials. To visual inspection, a one-trial external influence may seem a systematic effect lasting several trials. A visually convincing trend in the graph of the data may thus be an artifact of the serial correlation, not a real effect of treatment.

Serial correlation can be controlled in two main ways. One way is with treatment randomization, which can break up the serial correlation to obtain independence. The other way is to minimize serial correlation through experimental procedure, as with ample time between observations or by interpolating a baseline treatment between successive experimental treatments. These two approaches are taken up in the next two main sections.

Figure 11.1. Line–box illusion. Apparent length of centerline is affected by flanking boxes. For experimental analysis, just one of the two line–box figures is presented; the subject draws a line equal to the apparent length of the centerline. Contrary to century-long belief, the illusion involves assimilation, not contrast. The boxes make the line look longer, not shorter (see Section 8.1.2).

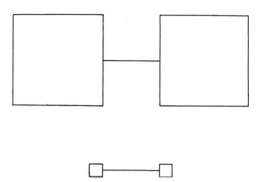

11.2 RANDOMIZED TREATMENT DESIGN

In randomized treatment design, treatment conditions are given in randomized order. The line–box illusion of Figure 8.1 is reproduced in Figure 11.1 as an example from visual perception. Although two line–box figures are shown here to dramatize the illusion, only one was presented in the experimental task, in which the subject drew a line equal in length to the apparent length of the centerline. A three-factor design was used to vary the sizes of the two flanking boxes and the length of the centerline. All stimulus combinations from this design could be presented in random order within each replication. For a given subject, factorial graphs would show how the apparent length of the centerline depends on the separate and integrated effects of the two boxes. Similar treatment randomization is used in many other perceptual tasks as well as in tasks of judgment–decision in diverse fields (e.g., Figures 11.2 and 11.9). Although such investigations often use repeated measures design with multiple subjects, single subject design may sometimes be preferable (Section 11.5.3).

11.2.1 TWO BENEFITS OF TREATMENT RANDOMIZATION

Treatment randomization has two important potential benefits. It can deconfound treatments from temporal position effects and even from some carryover effects, markedly easing questions about validity. Also, it can make treatment responses independent, markedly easing reliability analysis.

Temporal Position Effects. The first potential benefit of treatment randomization is to nullify confounding from position effects. If you present treatments to the subject in the same lexicographic order that you list your data for the computer, you embrace temporal confounding. Response to early and late levels of a variable could differ because of learning, fatigue, and other internal factors. External events could cause similar confounding.

Such confounding tends to be nullified with treatment randomization. Temporal effects are randomized across treatments so the treatment means are unbiased. Of course, the position effects do not disappear. Instead, they are randomized into the variability of the treatment means. The logic is identical to that for random assignment of subjects to conditions.

Independent Observations. Treatment randomization also helps ensure independence of different responses to the same treatment. Suppose instead that all replications of a given treatment are given in one consecutive block. Independence could then be violated by trial-to-trial assimilation, for example, which would induce positive serial correlation in the sequence of responses to each treatment (see also Note 3.3.1a, page 76). Something similar would occur if the treatments were given in any systematic order, say, from low to high.

To appreciate how randomization produces independence, consider the responses to two replications of a given treatment. Since their location is randomized in the sequence of trials, knowing the response to one tells us nothing about the error in the response to the other; they are statistically independent. With independence, differences between responses to the same treatment provide a valid estimate of error variability and valid confidence intervals. An early experimental application of randomized treatment design is the study of person cognition in Figure 11.2 (page 317).

Limitation of Treatment Randomization. Treatment randomization may not be effective with small numbers of treatments and trials. To illustrate, consider two treatments, A and B, each presented twice. The random order, A-A-B-B, which has probability 1/6, confounds treatments with temporal change. With this order, practice or adaptation can make B appear more different from A than it really is. Serial position effects are randomized out over all six possible orders, it is true, but the investigator is stuck with whatever confounding may accompany the one particular order selected. Such treatment-independent temporal effects can, however, be randomized out over a long sequence.

Treatment-specific carryover effects are more serious, as when one treatment affects response to some specific other treatment. Treatment randomization may dilute the confounding but does not nullify it.

When the number of treatment conditions and the number of trials are small, systematic order is usually needed, for example, ABBA. Systematic design can help balance and assess position and carryover effects, as with Latin squares.

11.2.2 ANALYSIS OF RANDOMIZED TREATMENT DESIGNS

Independence of observations is the main requirement for applying the basic concepts of Chapter 2. The law of sample size and the central limit theorem have the same efficacy for data from single subjects as from independent subjects. Confidence intervals are justified in the same way.

Moreover, the Anova–regression techniques of Chapters 3–5 and 9 apply without change: the Anova models; formulas for SSs, MSs, and Fs; formulas for confidence intervals; and power calculations.

Besides independence, the equinormality assumption also needs consideration. Normality, on the whole, may be better satisfied with single subject data than with group data. The same applies with the equal variance assumption.

Of course, equinormality may be badly violated in some situations. Aversive tasks may yield extreme scores, for example, and time scores may be skewed. Techniques of Chapter 12 may then be needed, especially trimming. Personal experience and pilot work with the task at hand are, as always, the basis for prudent choice of analysis.

11.3 SERIAL OBSERVATION DESIGN

Treatment randomization is not always appropriate or even possible. In some operant studies, a single treatment may last a month and hardly be repeatable. Some studies in behavior modification and medical science have only two treatments, one of which represents the normal, pre-treatment situation. Validity and reliability both present difficulties.

11.3.1 A-B-TYPE DESIGN

The term *A-B-type* refers to designs that present a sequence of trials under treatment A, followed by a sequence of trials under treatment B. A-B-type includes the simple A-B design as well as A-B-A, A-B-B-A, and other such designs. This section comments briefly on the validity problem.

Temporal Confounding in A-B-Type Design. In the simple A-B design, a single treatment B is initiated at some time point, subsequent to some comparison treatment A. In a prototypical application, A represents the normal situational condition before the experimental treatment. In general, however, A and B may be experimental treatments of equal importance.

A sequence of observations is assumed to be available under both A and B conditions. Our task is to scrutinize the pattern of these two sets of data to assess reliability and validity of the observed difference in the A and B effects.

The validity question, whether B does better than A, might seem unanswerable; B is completely confounded with any and all temporal factors. Suppose, however, that a graph of the behavior as a function of time shows a flat trend over a longish sequence of A observations, followed by a sharp change when B is introduced. This is prima facie evidence for a B effect. Given a long, flat trend under A, it seems unlikely that the behavior would change just when B was introduced unless B had a real effect.

In practical affairs, the simple A-B design is sometimes all that is available. If your child's health/behavior problem is improving under some treatment, you would hardly demand a control treatment. A-B design is thus common in medicine and behavior modification, as well as in everyday life. A-B design also occurs naturally with laws or regulations intended to improve some undesirable state of affairs, such as environmental pollution and teaching in the universities.

One difficulty with simple A-B design is that real effects are often not clear-cut. Temporal confounding is thus a serious threat, a threat that can be reduced with stronger designs. The next strongest is the A-B-A design, obtained by terminating B and reverting to A. If the behavior also reverts, the case for a B effect is strengthened. The A-B-A design also gives some protection against temporal trend. Additional periods of A and B provide additional protection.

Baseline Procedure. *Baseline procedure* is a form of control intended to produce a standard state between successive experimental treatments. Baseline conditions are common for minimizing carryover effects in perception. In olfactory studies, for example, one baseline condition requires subjects to smell their own elbows between trials with the experimental stimuli. Each of us has a personal odor, as any bloodhound can tell, and smelling our own elbow is an effective way to readapt to a standard state. Analogous procedure may be useful with the choice and rating responses widely employed in cognitive domains. Interspersing a standard stimulus may absorb carryover effects and also firm up the frame of reference for the judgment–decision. Baseline conditions are also common in medical science, where they are called *washout* conditions.

Many operant studies use treatment schedules that produce systematic, cumulative changes in behavior. Accordingly, a standard baseline schedule may be introduced after each experimental schedule to return the subject to a standard state before proceeding. If A and B_j denote the baseline and experimental treatments, the design would be A-B_1-A-B_2-A- . . . Effectiveness of baseline procedure cannot be taken for granted, of course, but needs justification in each kind of situation.[a]

11.3.2 SERIAL INDEPENDENCE

With serial observation data, reliability must usually be estimated from trial-to-trial variability in response. This estimate is biased when serial correlation is present. In experimental analysis, the best hope is usually to avoid or minimize serial correlation.

Serial Independence Assumption. Analysis is straightforward if successive responses are statistically independent. To illustrate, consider an A-B design with n independent responses in each condition. To test whether the mean response differs in the two conditions, apply the Anova of Chapter 3. Statsig F implies a reliable mean difference.

The reasonableness of the independence assumption depends on situational specifics. With only a single observation in each session, serial correlation may well be negligible. If a number of A observations are taken in a single session, on the other hand, serial correlation is a real possibility. Even in this case, however, interpolation of a standard treatment between successive experimental treatments, as in the cited example of elbow smelling, may reduce any serial correlation to acceptably small size.

Zero Serial Correlation in Behavior Modification?   Serial correlation may not be much problem in many behavior modification studies. Single subject A-B-type design is common in this area, as in the later examples of behavior modification with children. On the face of it, of course, serial correlation seems likely. In part because of this expectation, standard statistical methods have been avoided.

Little empirical evidence was available, however, because the number of observations per period has typically been no more than 10, far too few for adequate power to assess possible serial correlation. Instead, the problem was considered serious on the general feeling that behavior should be more similar on successive than on nonsuccessive observations. Positive serial correlation was thus considered normal, and proposals to use Anova were harshly criticized.

Huitema (1985) cogently proposed that the question of serial correlation should be studied empirically. Accordingly, he considered all articles from the first 10 years of the *Journal of Applied Behavior Analysis*, the premier journal in this field. Of these, 441 studies reported data that could be used to calculate a serial correlation. On the expectation of positive serial correlation in even a good fraction of these studies, the mean of all 441 serial correlations should be positive. This mean should have a narrow confidence interval, moreover, based on such a large N.

Contrary to expectation, the actual mean was slightly negative for the data of the initial, baseline phase. This absence of serial correlation was supported by similar results from subsequent treatment phases. Huitema did find evidence for a small proportion of positive serial correlations and a somewhat larger proportion was reported by Matyas and Greenwood (1996) for the subsequent seven-year period in the same journal.[a, b]

On the whole, these analyses suggest that serial correlation may not often be a problem in behavior modification and that Anova–regression techniques will often be applicable. Regrettably, little information on the empirical conditions that do and do not produce serial correlation is available. Serial correlation seems likely with short intertrial intervals, and has been explicitly studied in psychophysics. More generally, when drift in the subject's state has a longer period than the interval between trials, it will induce serial correlation. With a single observation per day, however, negligible serial correlation seems a reasonable hope.

Unfortunately, criticisms of Huitema's efforts have obscured the importance of obtaining longer sequences of observations to allow reliable estimates of serial correlation in different kinds of experimental situations. Such data could be collected in some empirical situations without too much trouble if their importance was recognized. Likely determinants of serial correlation are of special concern, such as intertrial interval, type of task, and interspersed baseline treatment. Obtaining a solid data base on serial correlation is an urgent need for methodology of serial observation design. This need is no less for visual inspection than for confidence intervals and power estimates.[c]

Serial Correlation as Substantive Phenomenon. Serial correlation embodies behavioral processes. It tells us something about the organization and structure of behavior. From this standpoint, serial correlation is not a statistical complication, but a phenomenon of potential importance.

Huitema's evidence on negligible serial correlation thus has deeper importance. It indicates that the prevailing expectation about serial correlation rested on a misconception about the organization and structure of behavior. Lack of knowledge about serial correlation reflects lack of knowledge about what controls behavior.

11.4 ILLUSTRATIVE SINGLE SUBJECT EXPERIMENTS

Illustrative single subject investigations from five areas are presented in the following sections. These include randomized treatment design and serial observation design, as well as one time series of field data.

11.4.1 PERSON COGNITION

When Thales, the ancient Greek philosopher, was asked "What is the hardest thing?" he replied, "To know thyself," a view well supported throughout modern psychology. If self-cognition is hard, cognition about other persons would seem still harder.

One perennially attractive hypothesis holds that person cognition is configural. Our cognition of another person, our spouse, for example, is developed by integrating multiple informers over the course of time. This cognition seems clearly unified, not a reproductive memory list, but an organized, functional system of knowledge. Such organization suggests that each new informer is interpreted in relation to what is already known. Its effective meaning is not fixed, it would seem, but configurally dependent on other informers. With concrete examples of experimental stimuli, such meaning change becomes overwhelmingly convincing to common sense.

This configural view appeared in numerous approaches that postulated one or another principle of cognitive consistency. The guiding idea was that the mind shuns inconsistency, strives for consistency (see numerous consistency theories in Abelson et al., 1968). Cognitive consistency promised to be a sovereign principle, a foundation for unified theory of cognition.

This principle of cognitive consistency implies *meaning change*: The informer stimuli interact and change one another's meanings in order to make a more consistent, unified whole. Quite different is the hypothesis of *meaning invariance*: The informers are integrated with no change of meaning.

Anova provides an easy, cogent test of the hypothesis of meaning change. Single subject Anova allows for individual differences in meaning of the stimulus informers; idiosyncratic changes in meaning are not averaged away as could happen with a group analysis.

In the initial experiment, each of 12 subjects received sets of 3 personality trait adjectives that described a hypothetical person. They judged how much they would like the person on a 1–20 scale. The 27 person descriptions were constructed from a 3^3 design, with Lo, Med, and Hi adjectives as the levels of each factor. To assess stimulus generality (Section 1.4.3), six different stimulus designs were used, each with a different selection of adjectives, with two subjects in each stimulus design. Subjects were run individually for five successive days. Each day began with eight warmup descriptions, followed by the 27 experimental descriptions in random order. Treatment randomization made the responses statistically independent, thereby allowing single subject Anovas, which were performed on the data of the last three days.

Visual inspection and Anova provide simple, direct tests of the hypothesis of meaning change. Suppose the meaning of each adjective does change depending on which other adjectives it is combined with. Then its effect on the response will differ from one cell to another in the design. Being thus variable, the effect of a given adjective cannot be an additive constant. Instead, systematic deviations from parallelism will be obtained. This will appear in Anova as nonadditive interaction residuals.

On the other hand, suppose each adjective has a fixed, invariant meaning. Suppose also that the adjectives in each person description are added or averaged to determine the likableness of the person. Then the interaction residuals are zero in principle and the factorial graphs should exhibit parallelism.

Two-factor graphs for the first two subjects in this experiment are shown in Figure 11.2, together with illustrative trait adjectives. Both subjects show parallelism. Parallelism disconfirms the cognitive consistency theories en bloc because they imply nonparallelism. Parallelism supports the averaging model— together with the hypothesis of meaning invariance (see also Figure 20.2).

Most subjects showed similar parallelism, and this visual inspection was supported by the single subject Anovas. The pooled interaction residuals, with

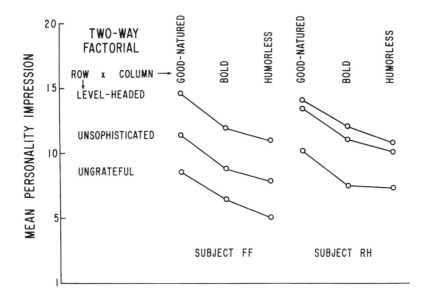

Figure 11.2. Parallelism pattern supports nonconfigural, adding-type rule in person cognition. Subjects judged likableness of hypothetical persons described by two trait adjectives listed in the Row × Column design: row adjectives of *level-headed, unsophisticated,* and *ungrateful*; column adjectives of *good-natured, bold,* and *humorless.* Each of these 3 × 3 = 9 person descriptions corresponds to one data point. (Data averaged over third trait for simplicity; see Figure 1.4 of Anderson, 1982.) (N. H. Anderson, 1962, "Application of an additive model to impression formation," *Science, 138,* 817-818. Copyright 1962 by American Association for Advancement of Science. Adapted with permission.)

20/54 df, have high power to detect deviations from the prediction of the averaging model. This initial application of functional measurement thus disconfirmed an entire class of cognitive consistency theories in a simple, effective way. This disconfirmation was constructive, for it revealed unexpected organization of cognition—the first established algebraic law of thought— together with meaning invariance as well as independence of the processes of valuation and integration (see **V–I** independence in Section 21.3.3, page 700).

Blame Schema. Blaming and avoiding blame are prominent in social–personal dynamics, but have received little scientific study. Pioneering work by Piaget (1932) led him to conclude that young children cannot integrate the two main determinants of blame, namely, the intent behind a harmful act and the amount of harm. Instead, they center on one or the other determinant and judge solely on that. This doctrine of *centration* was later extended to Piaget's main field of commonsense physics and became a central concept in his theory. Unfortunately, Piaget's primary method suffered severe confounding (pages 230*ff*).

These confoundings were avoided by Leon (1976, 1980), who asked children to judge how much punishment a story child deserved who had interfered with workmen painting a house. Each story presented one of three levels of the intention that the story child had to cause harm, and one of four levels of physical damage. Children at five age levels, from first to seventh grade, judged each of the 12 stories on a graphic rating scale. Each child thus provided a factorial graph, which allowed diagnosis of individual integration schemas.

The majority of children followed the algebraic blame schema of Figure 1.3:

Deserved punishment = Intent + Damage.

This algebraic integration schema disproves Piaget's centration hypothesis (Exercise 5.2). It goes beyond this to show that children have cognitive abilities qualitatively different from those recognized in Piagetian theory.

Some children showed certain other integration schemas. Spontaneous verbalizations had indicated that some children thought no punishment should be given when the damage was accidental. Being clumsy, young children have a personal interest in this schema. Accordingly, all children were selected who

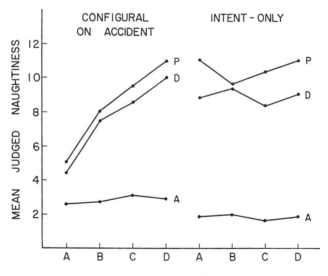

Figure 11.3. Schema diagnosis for single subjects in moral judgment. Two forms of the blame schema: intent-only schema in right panel; accident-configural schema in left panel. Children judged deserved punishment for harmful action by a story child, given the *intent* behind the action and the *damage* it caused. Curve parameter indicates level of intent: A = accident; D = displaced aggression; P = purposive damage. Increasing levels of damage on horizontal axis, A, B, C, D. Schemas diagnosed from pattern in individual factorial graphs, here pooled over subgroups of subjects. (After Leon, 1976, 1980.)

showed at most a one-point difference in their judgments of the two stories with least and most damage, both accidental.

Visual inspection of the individual factorial graphs of these 43 children revealed three distinct response patterns, corresponding to three distinct integration schemas. Six children followed an intent-only schema, shown in the right panel of Figure 11.3. The large separation between these curves indicates a large effect of intent; their flatness indicates a very small effect of damage. Another eight children had a similar pattern (not shown), but with a little larger effect of damage.[a]

An accident-configural schema was exhibited by the other 29 children, shown in the left panel of Figure 11.3. The flatness of the bottom curve shows that these children disregarded damage when it was accidental. However, the near-parallelism of the two top curves shows that these same children averaged, Intent + Damage, when the act had some deliberate intent behind it. This accident-configural schema appeared at all ages, including a few adults.

Leon's seminal study illustrates the importance of individual analyses. It also illustrates a cognitive methodology with notable advantages over the choice methodology popularized by Piaget.[b]

11.4.2 BEHAVIOR MODIFICATION

Operant conditioning techniques have been applied to a wide spectrum of behavior problems, especially with children. Among the advantages of operant techniques are their flexibility and the power of reinforcement over behavior. Two examples of single subject analysis are cited here.

Aggression in Retarded Children. Sam was a mentally retarded, nonverbal 9-year-old, who understood only simple commands. He was referred by his teacher because he met all attempts at instruction with aggression (pinching, hair-pulling, and scratching). Drugs and a special diet had been ineffective.

The rationale for this study began with the hypothesis that Sam's aggressive behavior functioned as a means to escape aversive demand situations. A further hypothesis was that the aggression could be controlled with positive reinforcers (Carr, Newsom, & Binkoff, 1980).

This study is instructive because, among other reasons, it illustrates the development of an effective task—the foundation of experimental analysis. Some behavioral task must be found that will elicit Sam's aggression but also elicit correct responses that can be reinforced. In addition, personal reinforcers must be found to suit Sam's idiosyncracies.

The behavioral task was a buttoning board that had been used in Sam's classroom. At the beginning of each daily 10-min session, Sam was handed a buttoning board and every 10 s was told to do one button. Although this demand typically elicited aggression, it was nearly always performed.

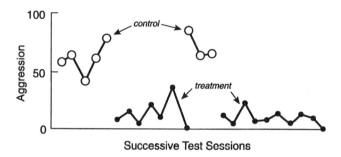

Figure 11.4. Positive reinforcement decreases aggression. Aggressive responses by Sam in 10-min daily sessions in aversive task. Open circles represent performance of simple, aversive motor task under classroom task situation; filled circles represent same situation plus positive reinforcers. (After Carr, Newsom, & Binkoff, 1980.)

In addition, pretesting was needed to establish effective reinforcers for Sam. One potato chip and a music box turned on for 4 s by the experimenter were two that were selected. These reinforcers have the advantage of not interfering unduly with the opportunity to emit aggressive behavior.

Sam and the experimenter sat in two facing chairs, 40 cm apart, so Sam had easy opportunity to aggress against the experimenter. One or two observers, seated separately, recorded frequency of aggression.

Two conditions were used in the A-B-A-B design of Figure 11.4. The control A condition consisted of demands to button a button, which received brief verbal praise just as in Sam's classroom instruction. The experimental B condition consisted of the same treatment plus one of the cited reinforcers. Successive data points represent successive days.

The data of Figure 11.4 speak for themselves: Aggression is high during the control condition and drops immediately when the personal reinforcers are used. The serial independence assumption seems reasonable in this situation so a formal Anova could be applied to supplement the visual inspection. Of course, a formal test is patently not needed here.

Figure 11.4 presents one of two experiments with Sam. The published paper also included two experiments with Bob, a 14-year-old so aggressive that the experimenter had to wear protective clothing and could only tolerate a 5-min session. This case was further complicated by the lack of positive reinforcers; Bob had an eating problem and no interest in music. To see how the investigators succeeded in extinguishing Bob's aggressive behavior and shaping him into an instructable person, see Carr et al. (1980, Experiment 4).

Attention-Deficit Disorder.   About 1.5 million children in the U.S. suffer from attention-deficit disorder. These children often have poor literary skills and may have trouble following teacher instructions. Special education services are often required.

About half of these children are treated with stimulant medication, most commonly with methylphenidate (Ritalin). The drug effects, however, are thought to be more or less task specific and idiosyncratic, both between and within children. The optimal dose level, moreover, does not seem predictable. Instead, the operative dose is typically determined by reports of parents and/or teacher, which is not too satisfactory. Parents and teachers are likely to judge on docility, not on what the children learn, as noted long ago by Binet in his pioneering studies of intelligence.

An experimental approach to the problem of determining optimal dosage was presented by Stoner, Carey, Ikeda, and Shinn (1994). One response measure was the number of words read aloud in the classroom situation from a passage of a school text. Such curriculum-based assessment, as it is called, has been extensively developed and has many attractive properties. Among these are simplicity, reliability, suitability for repeated administration, as well as face ecological validity.

Both subjects were rural children who had been referred to a university clinic by their family physician. A double-blind procedure was used. Following a coded schedule, each morning's dose was administered by the parents, who had been involved in the decision to perform the experiment. Performance was measured 1 to 2 hr later in school, at which time the drug effects were thought to be maximal. Besides the reading measure, an analogous arithmetic measure was also used. Many careful, thoughtful details of procedure are passed over here.[a]

The outcome of this experiment is illustrated in Figure 11.5, which presents reading scores for 32 school days for Bill, a 13-year-old 8th-grader. The article presents a similar graph for Bill's arithmetic performance as well as graphs for the other subject, who got a different sequence of dosage levels.

Visual inspection of Figure 11.5, in my opinion, shows no evidence for treatment effects. The response is about as high for the placebo as for the 10 mg and 15 mg doses. Response to the 5 mg dose is considerably higher, but it also shows high variability and the difference is visibly unreliable. Indeed, the later follow-up under 5 mg actually shows lower performance than the placebo.

The authors took a more positive view, presenting their data to the parents and physician as a basis for selecting a dosage level for continued treatment. Their published paper includes some cautionary comments about the threat of temporal confounding and about high variability, it is true, but the other three graphs in this article were about equally negative.

This study illustrates the need for standard statistics in the field of behavior modification, especially at the design stage. In this study, a power calculation

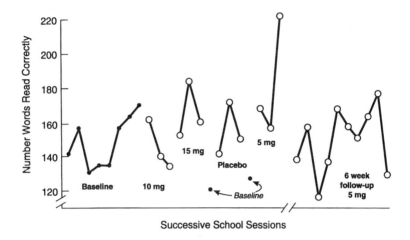

Figure 11.5. Methylphenidate medication evidently fails to help attention-deficit child. Each data point represents number of words read aloud from standardized text in classroom situation. No medication in baseline treatment (filled circles); 5, 10, and 15 mg indicate daily dosage of medication; placebo is a comparable dose with 0 mg medication. (After Stoner, Carey, Ikeda, & Shinn, 1994; see also Note 11.5.5b.)

would surely have shown that the given design had little chance of success (Exercise 12c). Moreover, a Latin square design would have been much more effective. And since the literature had shown inconsistent results, visual inspection could not have been expected to be adequate.

Standard statistics seems readily applicable in this case. With one trial per day, serial correlation could be expected to be near zero. Positive serial correlation would yield an effective α somewhat larger than its nominal value, which might be tolerable in this situation. Taking advantage of standard statistics, to paraquote the authors on the need for replication of their study "holds promise for contributing to improved outcomes for the hundreds of thousands of children who are prescribed stimulant medication annually" (p. 111).

11.4.3 PERSONALITY AND CLINICAL PSYCHOLOGY

Single subject design, especially randomized treatment design, should be central in personality–clinical psychology. But "These designs are rarely taught in research training in clinical psychology despite their potential for widespread use" (Kazdin, 1992, p. 470). The one chapter in Kazdin's edited book that focuses on this issue is a light overview of serial observation design (Hayes, 1992). Little more is found in Hersen, Kazdin, and Bellack (1991).

The work on behavior modification constitutes a resource for clinical applications, which also aim at behavior modification. Much is there to be learned, both dos and don'ts, as from the two foregoing studies. Indeed, the discussions cited in the previous paragraph rest largely on methods developed in behavior modification, which is much neglected in personality–clinical.

Another resource comes from judgment–decision theory, illustrated with the studies of person cognition in Figures 11.2 and 11.3. Such randomized treatment design with single subjects seems almost totally neglected in personality–clinical, yet it offers unique advantages.

The lack of progress in personality–clinical psychology has been repeatedly bewailed by Meehl (e.g., 1990, pp. 229-230, Meehl's italics):

> *Null hypothesis testing of correlational predictions from weak substantive theories in soft psychology is subject to the influence of ten obfuscating factors whose effects are usually (1) sizeable, (2) opposed, (3) variable, and (4) unknown. The net epistemic effect of these ten obfuscating influences is that the usual literature research review is well-nigh uninterpretable.*[a]

Meehl explicitly considers only "soft psychology," dealing with "nonmanipulated factors." His main obfuscating factor is the "crud factor," essentially that "everything correlates to some extent with everything else" (p. 204), which makes analysis of causal process almost impossible. This lack of progress contrasts sharply, it may be added, with impressive recent progress in developmental psychology, psycholinguistics, perception, behavior genetics, neuroscience, and some other fields that employ experimental analysis.

A new way of thinking is needed in personality–clinical psychology. The root of the problem lies in a conceptual framework that leads to the "bunch of nothing" that Meehl decries (see Note 11.4.3a).

Personal design has promise for studying many personality processes (Section 11.5.4), including knowledge of other persons (Figure 11.2), blame, excuses, and other ego defenses (Figure 11.3), as well as phobias, emotion, self-esteem, and other facets of personality. Personal design seeks to embed the experimental task within the experiential framework of the individual. It is suitable to longer-term studies of individuals, as in many studies in perception and in judgment–decision, and it has capabilities for true measurement of personal affect and value, including nonconscious aspects of personality (Chapter 21). The difficulties in embarking on this new way of thinking are outweighed by the potential. The outcome may be modest but it will be real, not Meehl's "bunch of nothing."[b, c, d]

11.4.4 PERCEPTION AND JUDGMENT–DECISION

Single subject design is natural and appropriate in many tasks of perception and judgment–decision. Surprisingly few, however, utilize single subject Anova.

Color Contrast. In color contrast, one hue induces its complementary hue. A gray field adjacent to a red field appears tinged with green, the complementary hue to red. Even more striking, a green field adjacent to a red field appears greener. Such *contrast effects* misrepresent physical reality but provide important information on the operation of the visual system. Contrast is also found with affective senses and seems to be a fairly general adaptive process.

A single subject study of red–green contrast is shown in Figure 11.6. The subject saw two small, adjacent color fields, *test field* and *inducing field*, each varied independently from red to green in five steps. The subject rated the test field (horizontal axis) on a scale from "red 9" to "green 9." Each curve represents one inducing field, which produced contrast. Each point is the mean of 10 judgments for Subject K.F.P.

The main conclusion is that color contrast follows an exact additive model. It might seem that a red inducing field would have less effect on a red test field than on a gray or green test field. Instead, the effect is constant, as shown by the parallelism of the solid curves.

Also of interest are the implications for psychophysical measurement. The parallelism of the solid curves indicates that the rating response is a true linear scale of subjective hue (see *Parallelism Theorem* in Chapter 21). Furthermore, since the solid curves are straight lines, it follows that the physical hue scale for the test field on the horizontal is also a true linear scale of subjective hue. This physical hue scale was defined in terms of activation of red and green cones, but

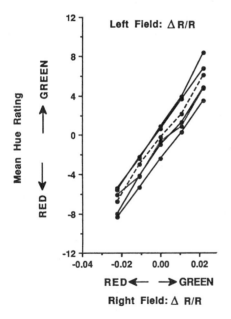

Figure 11.6. Additivity of red–green contrast. Hue judgments plotted as a function of hue of judged test field (horizontal axis) and hue of contrast-inducing field (curve parameter). Parallelism of solid curves implies that the apparent hue of the test field is the sum of its own proper hue and the contrast hue from the inducing field. (Dotted curve represents baseline response to test field by itself; its greater slope provides evidence for secondary induction. Scale on horizontal is relative activation of red cones, with the total (red + green) luminance held constant. Data for K.F.P. From Stefurak (1987; see Anderson, 1996a, pp. 290*ff*).

whether it was a true linear scale of subjective sensation was not known. This application of functional measurement theory illustrates a novel link between objective physical measures and subjective psychological measures.

Our Knowledge of the External World. A primary goal of psychological science is to understand how an organism develops knowledge of the external world. As noted elsewhere (Anderson, 1996a, pp. 281*f*):

> We live in two worlds together. One is the external physical world, in which our bodies move and function. Within our bodies is a very different world, a world of everyday sights, sounds, and other sensory–perceptual experience. We take it for granted that this internal psychological world mirrors the physical world. . . .
>
> Everyday theory of perception assumes we have direct contact with the external world. We think, without really thinking, that the eye somehow transmits little images of the external world to our conscious apprehension. The reason we see objects and motions is simple: That's what's there. . . .
>
> This naive theory of direct perception has persuasive arguments in its favor. Perception seems effortless and immediate. Simple arithmetic and memory tasks often give us trouble, but perceiving complex scenes does not. . . .
>
> Of course, this commonsense theory of direct perception is not correct. This became clear when systematic study of the sensory systems was begun. The sensory nerves do not transmit little images. Instead, they transmit neuroelectrical impulses, a biological computer code. Everyday consciousness is totally unaware of nature's engineering marvels by which our sensory systems convert physical energy, such as light, into neuroelectrical impulses—and from this computer code of the nerves construct this fantastic internal world of three-dimensional shapes, motions, and chromatic magnificence.

What are nature's engineering marvels? One is neurons sensitive to specific physical features, such as orientation of the contour lines of an object. Certain single neurons will fire in response to a vertical line, for example, but not to a horizontal line. Indeed, orientation assessment is one of the most important components of vision. Detection of such visual features is thought to occur very early in the chain of visual processing, at a preattentive stage that does not require focusing of attention.

A curious result is at issue in the following study (Shiu & Pashler, 1992). Subjects improved on a difficult task of discriminating angular orientation of a line—without feedback about correctness. However, this improvement only occurred if the subjects attended to orientation; it did not occur if subjects were trained to judge these same lines in terms of brightness. Over the first two experiments, moreover, there was little transfer to a new, equivalent position in the retinal field. The learning thus appeared to occur locally in the retina and the topographically connected regions of the brain.[a]

Data from one subject in Experiment 2 are used here to illustrate aspects of single subject design in perception. The main purpose was to verify the suggestion of Experiment 1 that accuracy improved even when subjects received no accuracy feedback. Subject P.P. received 12 blocks of 40 trials each day, under instructions to identify which of two lines with slightly different tilt had been presented on each trial. No feedback about correctness was given.

The results are shown in Figure 11.7, which plots percentage correct on successive days. A linear trend test over days 1–5 yielded a comfortably statsig result. This verified the suggestion of the previous experiment that learning occurred without feedback. This learning is not some initial adjustment to the task for it occurred mainly on later days.

Transfer tests were given on alternating trial blocks on days 6 and 7. The two open circles at the top right of Figure 11.7 show mild continued improvement on the training task itself. The most notable transfer is the large decrement shown by the lower filled circle, for trials on which the line angle was changed by 90°, a curious result that seems to have remained unexplored. In addition, the statsig difference between the two data points for day 7 shows substantial decrement from merely changing the position in the visual field at which the test line occurs. Together, these two results imply that the learning did not represent a focusing of attention.

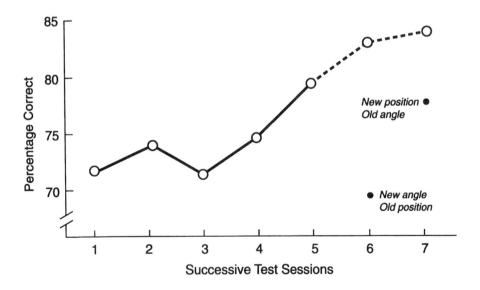

Figure 11.7. Visual discrimination learning under no feedback. (Shiu & Pashler, 1992.)

Three subjects were run, of which P.P. showed the slowest improvement over days. This slowest subject was chosen here to reemphasize limitations of the common one-session experiment.

To buttress the visual inspection, some measure of error variability is needed to assess reliability of the visible trends. The base for analysis was the unit score, namely, percentage correct in each block of 40 trials. This yielded 12 scores per day. A days × blocks Anova yielded a statsig linear trend over days.[b]

Additive-Factor Method in Perception/Cognition. Sternberg's (1969) additive-factor method is an ingenious application of factorial design to dissect the sequence of processes that lead from a given stimulus to a response. Further, it illustrates a class of perceptual/cognitive tasks that may require joint use of individual and group analysis.

Donders' subtraction method, published exactly one century before Sternberg, was a historic attempt to dissect components of stimulus–response processing. Donders measured reaction time to a given stimulus with and without insertion of an additional component. The difference in reaction time, he argued, measured the time required for the inserted component.

The critical assumption of Donders' subtraction method is that the inserted component does not alter the times for processes that precede or follow it. This assumption is more or less uncertain, and there is no way to test it. As a consequence, Donders' method has seen only sporadic use.

This difficulty is resolved with Sternberg's additive-factor method, previously described in Exercise 6.19. The subject sees a numeral either intact or degraded with visual noise (Stimulus Quality) and is to respond either with the numeral itself or with the numeral + 1 (Stimulus-Response Mapping). If these two variables influence independent stages in the overall response process, they will be additive. Observed parallelism in this 2 × 2 design would thus support stage independence of the two manipulated factors.[c, d]

Data for two of the five subjects are shown in Figure 11.8. The two dashed curves for each subject represent the case in which the numeral on each trial could be 1, 2, . . . , 8. Visual inspection indicates little deviation from parallelism. The two solid curves for the condition in which the numeral was either 1 or 8 show a little nonparallelism, but hardly enough to worry about. These individual graphs show the same pattern as the group data previously presented in Exercise 6.19.

The main concern here is to compare advantages of single subject and repeated measures design and analysis. Sternberg gave extensive preliminary training to bring subjects to a near-stable state and collected ample data that would have allowed individual Anova. Many studies in perception/cognition present similar opportunities.

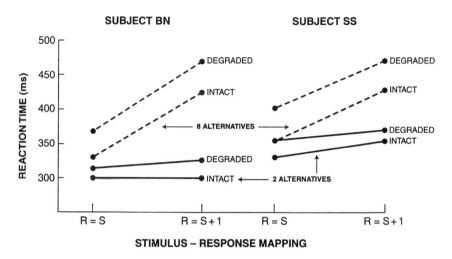

Figure 11.8. Test of additive-factor method. Parallelism of paired dashed lines and paired solid lines for each subject supports additivity of processing times for Stimulus Quality and Stimulus–Response Mapping. (After Sternberg, 1969.)

Advantages of group analysis are that only one Anova is required and that the error term for each Anova source is composed of the corresponding inter-actions with subjects (Table 6.4). If subjects were a random sample from some population, this error term would warrant statistical generalization of the sample results to the population. Subjects are virtually always handy samples, of course, but this same error term subserves extrastatistical generalization, as argued under *Generalization From Handy Samples* in Section 6.5.3 (page 177).

Single subject Anova has advantages of greater sensitivity. The error term contains only response unreliability of each individual; the repeated measures error is larger because it also includes the subject interaction residuals. Group analysis may thus obscure pertinent aspects of the individual behavior, espe-cially an occasional deviant individual. In this regard, single subject analysis may actually be more effective for extrastatistical generalization.[e]

The relative usefulness of group and individual analysis will no doubt differ across situations. One useful strategy is to design the experiment so both may be done—and to do both.

Two design problems illustrated in Sternberg's experiment concern indepen-dence and order effects. As in many studies of perception/cognition, subjects need some trials to readapt to each condition. Each condition may be given in a consecutive block of trials, therefore, with the response measure for each condi-tion being the mean over a terminal subblock. These means should satisfy the independence assumption in many tasks.

Of course, position effects from fatigue and other factors may still be present. Although such position effects will often be small, it may be prudent to balance them and measure their magnitude. Latin square design (Section 14.3) appears well-suited to this purpose and is explored in Exercise 14b.

Fundamental Violation of Classical Utility Theory. That "more is better" is a basic principle of utility theory, widely used in economic theory and in judgment–decision theory. Some form of this principle appears in the sure-thing axiom and in the dominance axiom, both of which have been central in attempts to develop general theory.

The ubiquitous averaging process of cognitive algebra, however, implies that more may be worse. If a positive object is added to another positive object, the overall value may actually decrease. A well-planned study by Schlottmann (2000) showed that this averaging process held for children at two age levels.

Schlottmann's results are in Figure 11.9. Compare the dashed curve (the judged value of the low, medium, or high chance to win the skipping rope alone) with the solid curve labeled *medium* (for the same chance to win the skipping rope together with a medium chance to win the marbles).

Utility theory requires the dashed curve to lie below all the solid curves; even a low chance of winning the marbles is worth something and so should raise the dashed curve at every point. Utility theory is disordinally violated by the crossover of the dashed and solid curves for both ages of children.

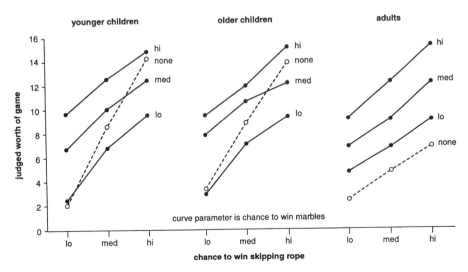

Figure 11.9. More may be worse, contrary to classical utility theory. Crossover of dashed and solid curves for both ages of children shows that adding one positive object to another may actually decrease the value of the two together. (After Schlottmann, 2000.)

Instead, the crossover of the dashed and solid curves implies that children averaged: The medium chance to win the marbles averages down the high and averages up the low chance to win the skipping rope. Adults, in contrast, integrate by adding in this task, as shown by the location of the dashed curve below and parallel to all the solid curves.

The near-parallelism of the three solid curves in Figure 11.9 supports an exact integration rule, either adding or averaging. These solid curves come from the two-factor design that combined each of the three chances to win the skipping rope with each of the three chances to win the marbles. The near-parallelism thus suggests an exact algebra of subjective utility at all age levels (see *Parallelism Theorem* in Chapter 21).

Schlottmann's application of functional measurement is cited here to illustrate a common class of situations in which a few subjects are not enough, unlike previous examples of this section, yet individual analyses are important. The double difficulty is that children's judgments are more variable than adults and that relatively few judgments can be obtained before they lose interest (see also last paragraph of Section 11.5.2, page 335). Schlottmann obtained two replications for each child, but even two replications requires experimenter skill to maintain children's interest and motivation. Because many subjects were used, an overall repeated measures analysis was used to summarize the main trends. This was supplemented with visual inspection of the factorial graph for each subject, together with single subject Anovas reported in verbal summaries. At each age level, all individuals exhibited similar patterns. In fact, the dashed curve lay below the solid curves for all 16 adults, but for none of the 32 children at each age group. Such agreement across children is notable in this hard task and should not be expected in general (e.g., Figure 11.3).[f]

11.4.5 OPERANT MATCHING LAW

In "matching behavior," subjects adjust their response rates to match relative rates of reinforcement. Matching behavior has been extensively demonstrated with two-choice tasks, both in probability learning with humans and in concurrent operant schedules with pigeons.[a]

In operant theory, this "matching law" is usually expressed in terms of observable quantities as

$$\frac{R_1}{R_2} = \frac{S_1}{S_2}, \qquad \text{(observable matching law)}$$

where R_1 and R_2 denote response rates on the two alternatives, and S_1 and S_2 denote corresponding rates of reinforcement. Tests of this matching law are straightforward because all four terms are directly observable.

But this matching law rests on a strong implicit assumption that the two choices yield equivalent reinforcements. This will not generally be true. Reinforcements on the two choices may differ in amount, for example, or in quality. It is desirable, accordingly, to allow different values for each reinforcer. Since these values will in general be unknown, they are denoted by ψ instead of S. This psychological version of the matching law may be written,

$$\frac{R_1}{R_2} = \frac{\psi_1}{\psi_2}. \qquad \text{(psychological matching law)}$$

This psychological matching law has been declared tautological on the argument that values of ψ_1 and ψ_2 could always be found to make the data fit the law.

In fact, a strong test of the psychological matching law can be obtained with functional measurement theory. With $R = R_1 / R_2$, the equation may be written as a multiplication rule, $R = \psi_1 \times \psi_2^{-1}$. By the linear fan theorem (Chapter 21), varying the two reinforcers in a factorial design should yield a linear fan.

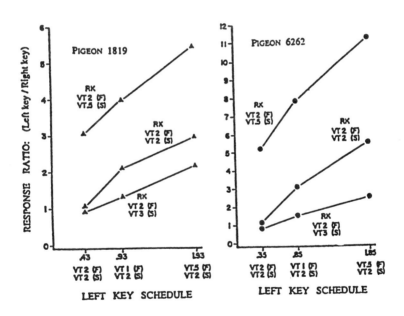

Figure 11.10. Linear fan pattern supports psychological matching law; also measures food and shock in common units. Factorial design presents conjoint, response-independent, variable-time (VT) schedules for food (F) and shock (S). Three schedules for left key listed on horizontal axis; three schedules for the right key (RK) listed as curve parameter. (After J. Farley and E. Fantino, 1978, "The symmetrical law of effect and the matching relation in choice behavior," *Journal of the Experimental Analysis of Behavior*, *29*, 37-60. Copyright 1978 by the Society for the Experimental Analysis of Behavior.)

Just such linear fans appear for the two pigeons of Figure 11.10, taken from the careful, arduous experiment by Farley and Fantino (1978). Joint food–shock reinforcement was used for each choice alternative. The ψ value of each was varied across three schedules to yield the 3×3 design indicated in the figure. Functional measurement theory goes beyond verifying the psychological matching law to provide validated scales of the ψ values. In this tour de force, Farley and Fantino were thus able to express food and shock in equivalent units, a milestone in attempts to unify positive and negative reinforcement.[b]

11.4.6 TIME SERIES

One example of serial observation data from a field study is included here to point up the importance of nonexperimental field research. This is a time series, typical of data on many social issues. In this case, the "subject" is the entire population of North Carolina.

Do Seat Belts Reduce Accidents? This example has multiple purposes. First, it illustrates a large class of social issues that lie outside the scope of traditional experimental analysis. These issues require a different perspective.

Second, this example illustrates an enlightened state legislature that recognized the need to evaluate the effects of their laws. Third, it illustrates the value of forethought to broaden the data base, as with the preliminary program of observations on actual seat belt usage. Fourth, it underscores the need to develop and verify statistical theory for time series within specific empirical contexts.

Foresighted provision for an evaluation of effectiveness was included in the 1985 law passed by the State of North Carolina, which required wearing seat belts for front seat occupants of passenger cars and light duty trucks and vans. A well-designed probability sampling study began assessing frequency of seat belt wearing three months before the law took effect. Beginning 1 October, 1985, violators were issued warning tickets for 15 months. Beginning 1 January, 1987, violators were subject to 25-dollar fines (Reinfurt et al., 1990).

A *time series* graph, showing seat belt usage at successive monthly times, was dramatically clear: 25% in the pre-law baseline period; an immediate jump to a stable 45% in the warning period; and an instant jump to near 80% at the beginning of the fine period, with a slow decline to about 65%.

But was this increase in belt usage effective in reducing accidents? Accident data were available from police records, which provided a baseline period back to 1981. Visual inspection of this times series showed perhaps a mild decline in vehicle accidents from baseline in the warning period, with a more definite mild decline in the fine period. Although this time series was quite irregular and complicated by a pronounced seasonal decline at year end, visual inspection seems fairly persuasive.

Visual inspection was supplemented by a statistical time series analysis, which was used to forecast what would have happened without the law. Comparing these forecasts to the observed data yielded an inferred reduction of 5.4% for the warning period and 14.6% for the fine period. Both inferred reductions were statsig, suggesting the law had substantial social benefits.

But these two values, 5.4% and 14.6%, are not real data. They come from forecasts, obtained from the time series, about what would have happened had no law been passed. These forecasts rest on the empirical validity of the model employed in the time series, which could hardly be considered solidly established. How far the time series statistics can be trusted is thus uncertain. This exemplifies a difficulty common with observational data.

In the present investigation, however, a comparison time series was at hand. This gave the corresponding percentages for rear seat occupants, who were not required to wear seat belts. The corresponding analysis of this time series showed a 10.2% decrease, nearly as large as the 14.6% for the front seat occupants. This comparison clouds the main analysis and leaves the results less convincing. At the same time, it emphasizes the value of forethought to obtain such comparison time series.[a]

11.5 METHODOLOGY IN SINGLE SUBJECT DESIGN

Much methodology is area- and task-specific. Methods and procedures have many differences across person cognition, behavior modification, visual perception, judgment–decision, and field studies, for example, as illustrated in previous sections. Each area needs its own single subject methodology.

Some issues of method, however, are common across areas. Foremost is independence, already discussed. A few additional issues of single subject methodology are taken up in the following sections.

11.5.1 GENERALIZING WITHIN SUBJECTS

Generality for a single subject has both internal and external aspects, which parallel the distinction between internal and external validity of Section 1.2. External generality refers to other situations and other times for the same subject. Present behavior may not generalize to other situations because they differ from the present situation in some relevant way. Present behavior may not generalize to future (or past) times because the organism changes over time, whether in fluctuations of health and motivation or in systematic changes of maturation and experience.

Assessment of external generality can be assisted with experimental design. Stimulus generality (Section 1.4.3) can be studied by including stimulus materials as a factor in the design, as in the study of person cognition of Figure 11.2.

Some information on temporal generality can be obtained with designs that can assess position and carryover effects, and especially through replication of the experiment over time. For the most part, though, external generality depends on extrastatistical judgment about stability of the behavior and about similarity of the experimental situation to other situations.

Internal outcome generality refers to the reliability of the present behavior. In one sense, the present behavior is a fact so no question of reliability arises. In a more useful sense, each present response is considered to include variability from causes specific to the moment of response. The pertinent question, accordingly, is whether treatment differences are larger than could be expected from this momentary variability.

This question of internal outcome generality is illustrated in the two studies of behavior modification cited in Section 11.4.2. In one of these, the treatment difference is clearly reliable. In the other, it is clearly not.

Internal outcome generality is prima facie a statistical question: mean differences relative to variability. Although this comparison can sometimes be made by visual inspection, as in the two behavior modification studies, it is essentially statistical in nature. At the same time, as just noted, visual inspection rests on a more or less implicit substantive model involving momentary variability.

11.5.2 GENERALIZING ACROSS SUBJECTS

Most studies of single subjects seek to generalize to a population of subjects. Even the behavior modification examples, concerned with treatment of particular children, were expected to be relevant to treatment for other children.

Response pattern thus becomes a primary concern. Individuals will surely differ in magnitude of response but may still show very similar patterns. Individual analysis is often necessary to assess individual patterns, which can be obscured by averaging over individuals.

Commonality of response pattern across individuals, however, differs between substantive areas. In some areas, virtually all subjects are expected to show similar response patterns, with individual differences appearing merely as amount or magnitude parameters. Two or three subjects may then suffice, with data presented separately for each. This approach is common in perception, as illustrated in three studies discussed earlier, and in operant tasks.

In other areas, individuals may be expected to differ in response pattern. The study of person cognition of Figure 11.2, for example, used 12 subjects for this reason. As it happened, most subjects in the experiment of Figure 11.2 showed the parallelism pattern. With judgments of blame, however, several different response patterns are found, as was illustrated in Figure 11.3, and the same may happen even in intuitive physics (Karpp & Anderson, 1997).

Diagnosis of individual differences in response pattern presents two practical problems. The first is to get enough data for adequately firm pattern diagnosis for each individual. The second is that a fairly large number of subjects may be required to get even two or three instances of less common patterns. In the blame example, the Intent-only pattern occurs in perhaps one subject in 10. If only one subject showed this pattern, its reliability and validity would seem uncertain. A total of 30 subjects would not seem too many to be reasonably sure of getting two or three in this subgroup. This, however, yields an overplus in the modal subgroup. In such situations, it could be helpful to develop a procedure to screen out subjects likely to exhibit common patterns.[a]

11.5.3 SINGLE SUBJECT OR REPEATED MEASURES ANOVA?

With data from a number of single subjects, repeated measures Anova may be useful in addition to, or even instead of, multiple single subject Anovas. A single group analysis is more compact and simple than many individual analyses. The repeated measures Anova also bears on the question of generality since the error term consists of individual differences in the form of subject–treatment interaction residuals. One useful technique is to present graphs based on repeated measures analysis together with tabular or verbal summaries of the individual analyses (e.g., Figures 11.3 and 11.9).

Many experiments in perception and cognition that could be treated in single subject manner are instead studied with repeated measures design. The line–box illusion on page 310 is a typical example. Many workers in these areas adopt repeated measures design without considering the potential of single subject design.[a]

11.5.4 PERSONAL DESIGN

Single subject design culminates in *personal design*, in which the task and/or stimuli are personalized to the individual subject and the analysis allows for personal values. Personal design thus aims to embed the experimental task within experiential knowledge systems of the individual. Such embedding has twofold advantage: It maximizes the meaning and relevance of the experimental task; and it can tap into well-established psychological processes.

The foregoing study of aggressive behavior is a prime example of personal design, for it was personalized through choice of task and reinforcers for each child. Both foregoing studies of person cognition were personalized in that the analyses took full account of personal meanings of the stimuli.

Individual differences are prominent in human affairs. Affective differences are substantial even in so biological an activity as eating. Individual differences in attitudes underlie virtually all social thought and action: marital roles of wife and husband, parent–child interaction, work, friendship, and so on.

This basic fact of individual differences lies as a quagmire in the path of psycho-logical science. Three main strategies for navigating this quagmire have been tried. The experimental strategy sought to capitalize on the power of experimen-tal method for causal analysis. The dominant experimental approach, however, was predicated on an assumption about general laws of behavior that would hold across individuals and even across species. Too often, this experimental strategy relied on standard group design that consigned individual differences to the sta-tistical error term, thus burying much that needed study.

The strategy of differential psychology did focus squarely on individual differ-ences, but with methods of correlation and personality tests that have little power for cognitive analysis. Strategies of phenomenology, ranging from the historical school of introspection to case histories in the psychoanalytic tradition and to con-temporary action theories, have given primary attention to the person. These stra-tegies are severely limited, however, because much of everyday cognition is not accessible to phenomenological scrutiny. Whereas the dominant experimental approach failed to take adequate account of the individual, phenomenological approaches generally lack the analytical power needed for theory of social cognition.

What is needed is a strategy that can combine experimental control with phenom-enology. This is the aim of *personal design*, which uses experimental method to study the individual at the individual level. (Anderson, 1990, pp. 243-244.)

The experimental and phenomenological approaches cited in this quotation are often called *nomothetic* and *idiographic*, respectively. Personal design unifies the nomothetic search for general laws with the idiographic recognition of individual differences in values. Such unification is illustrated in the study of person cognition of Figure 11.2, which demonstrated generality of the integra-tion rule across subjects at the same time that it measured and used the personal values of the stimuli. The nomothetic conclusion rested squarely on the idiographic capability.

Personal design usually requires a considerable number of responses from each individual, often assumed to be in a stable state, which limits its applicabil-ity. Within its limits, however, personal design may be useful in bringing exper-imental analysis to areas not ordinarily considered experimental, such as mar-riage and family life. Personal designs constructed around focal incidents or emotions in an individual's life may provide new methods for social and personality–clinical psychology (Notes 11.4.3b,c,d).[a]

Personal design can help bring experimental method to all social sciences: anthropology, economics, history, law, political science, psychotherapy, religion, and sociology, unifying them with psychology. . . Although personal design has obvious limitations, it may be uniquely useful in providing experimental leverage for disciplines traditionally deemed nonexperimental. (Anderson, 1996a, p. 45.)

11.5.5 FUNCTIONS OF STATISTICS

Visual inspection is always necessary and sometimes sufficient. It is unscientific, not to say unseemly, to muddle the exposition with statistical busy-work. But more objective methods are sometimes essential to assess reliability of the data patterns. Visual inspection and Anova are complementary tools. Both help you understand the data.[a]

The more important functions of statistics are at the lower levels of the Experimental Pyramid discussed in Chapter 1. The standard stereotype of statistics as significance tests obscures these more basic functions.

One function of statistics concerns independence, important for both classes of single subject design. Thus, treatment randomization is important regardless of whether the data are analyzed by visual inspection or formal test. With serial observation design, assessment of variability perforce relies on some conceptual model of the behavior, although this model is often left implicit and uncertain. Visual inspection generally makes an implicit assumption of independence and lacks capability to allow for serial correlation. Formal statistics is essential for understanding and helping to deal with serial correlation.[b]

A second function of statistics concerns description. As one example, the after-minus-before difference score seems the obvious measure of change, but this seeming hides surprising, sometimes fatal shortcomings that are only revealed through statistical analysis (Section 13.1.2). Statistical theory has many such uses: understanding selection–regression artifacts (Note 11.3.1a and Section 18.4.5); avoiding inappropriate measures of effect size and importance (Section 18.1); decreasing operative variability through trimming (Section 12.1); and so on.

Another function of statistics concerns power. All experiments rest on some assumption that they have adequate power; statistics can help decide how far this assumption is justified. The need for power calculation has been illustrated in the foregoing study of attention-deficit children.[c, d]

Perhaps the most important functions of statistics appear in experimental design. One example is the Latin square, especially squares balanced for carry-over effects. In this case, formal statistical analysis is essential to estimate means for treatment and carryover effects and to get confidence intervals. Statistical understanding of these and other designs is especially important for single subject studies.

One source of trouble is that single subject research has often originated with tasks and phenomena for which visual inspection was enough. A negative attitude toward more formal statistics often developed that hindered later work as better methods became increasingly needed. A prime example is psychophysics, which still suffers from certain methods that were once at the forefront but are now largely obsolete. One sign of this backwardness may be seen in the paucity of single subject Anova in the psychophysical literature.

Behavior modification, although the most articulately averse to formal statistics, is the main area that has given concerted attention to single subject methodology. Several books have been written, all of which can be read with profit, as they attack real problems that are also important in other areas. These books, like the present book, represent an empirical direction in design and analysis. Methodology consists in cumulative experimental procedure, not static precepts, but evolving knowledge systems.[e]

Each area faces its own special problems and needs to develop its own single subject methodology. Methodology is a continual concern of active investigators, and beginners in a field can profit from attention to issues of design and procedure in published articles. Much methodology, however, remains task- and area-specific lore. Efforts to crystallize such lore and make it useful to workers in other areas would be helpful.

> *Methodology* is a bad word to many. Most investigators are truly concerned with methods, of course, but the term *methodology* suggests a dogmatic stance on standardization of procedure and correct data analysis. It connotes involvement in niceties and complexities of apparatus and especially statistics that are generally barren, often useless digressions, sometimes active hindrances to productive inquiry.
>
> Properly considered, however, methodology is an organic part of substantive inquiry. Necessarily so, for the validity of methods derives from the empirical results that they bring in. . . . Knowledge is not divorced from the methods by which it was acquired; those methods themselves constitute an integral part of knowledge. (Anderson, 1982, p. 349.)

NOTES

For helpful comments on drafts of this chapter, I am indebted to Ted Carr, Joe Farley, Etienne Mullet, Laura Schreibman, Saul Sternberg, Ben Williams, and Wendy Williams.

11a. Indeed, the Task Force on Statistical Inference set up by the American Psychological Association to review current statistical practice and recommend guidelines refers to single subject [single-case] experiments as "nonstatistical" (see reply by the Task Force to comments on their preliminary report in the August, 2000 issue of *American Psychologist*, p. 965, center column, last full paragraph). In fact, single subject Anova has been around for decades (e.g., Figure 11.2, page 317).

11.1.1a. Standard notation uses A-B to denote one or more presentations of treatment A followed by one or more presentations of treatment B. The designations, A-B-A, A-B-B-A, and so forth, have obvious meanings.

11.1.1b. In some tasks, of course, position effects and carryover effects are the main interest. Learning across successive trials, for example, constitutes a position effect; the position effect is the learning curve. Transfer to a subsequent treatment constitutes a carryover effect. Learning and behavior modification are thus intended to produce position and carryover effects.

11.1.2a. The simplest serial correlation, also called a first-order autcorrelation, is between successive responses. This may be calculated with the regression–correlation analysis of Chapter 9, with X_i the response on trial i and Y_i the response on the following trial. To visualize this, write the sequence of responses in a row; beneath each response, write the response on the following trial. The first row is X_i, the second row is Y_i; the serial correlation is computed with Equation 9.15. Criterial values for significance tests and confidence intervals, however, need special tables. Higher-order autocorrelations may be calculated for responses separated by more than one step, These correlations are standard tools for diagnosing the structural model underlying the serial correlation.

11.3.1a. Operant baseline can introduce a criterion artifact. Each treatment schedule may require tens of days, and the required duration of each baseline schedule may depend on the preceding treatment. A fixed number of baseline sessions may be too few for some treatments, too many for others. It is common, accordingly, to continue the baseline treatment only until the behavior returns to some criterion of standard performance. This criterion potentiates the well-known regression artifact. If additional post-criterion trials are added, response on these trials will differ systematically from response on the criterion trials in the direction of the previous level of response (Section 18.4.5). This artifact may not be serious with a stringent criterion, but this is uncertain.

This artifact can be avoided by including a fixed number of sessions beyond the criterion. The response on these post-criterion trials is largely free of the artifact.

Such post-criterion trials are also needed to ensure valid comparisons among the experimental treatments. Ideally, it is true, baseline procedure returns the behavior to a constant standard state. When many sessions are given under one schedule, however, it is questionable whether the effects can ever be completely undone. The criterion procedure allows no valid test of the essential baseline assumption; instead, it confounds the hidden criterion artifact with the experimental treatment.

Post-criterion trials, in contrast, would allow a valid assessment of trends across successive baseline periods. In some cases, moreover, they could adjust for such trends to allow comparisons across successive experimental treatments.

11.3.2a. Although Huitema's (1985) Herculean effort should have been welcomed, the reaction was remarkably negative (see critiques cited in Huitema, 1988). In every critique, the central objection was that the small number of observations in each separate study yielded very low power. This objection was mistaken; this power problem had been foreseen by Huitema and he saw how to resolve it by considering the aggregate of studies. If the true correlation was generally positive in the 441 studies, the mean of the 441 serial correlations would have been positive. That was why he went to the great labor of reading and analyzing the data from all 441 studies; had each separate study had adequate power, a small random sample would have sufficed. More recently, Matyas and Greenwood (1996) have given a sensible discussion of the issue, together with additional data that suggest more serial correlation than obtained by Huitema, although markedly less than had generally been expected.

11.3.2b. Two complications with Huitema's analysis should be noted. First, under the null hypothesis, the expected value of a sample serial correlation based on N observations is not zero, but $-1/(N-1)$ (Huitema & McKean, 1991). Under the total null hypothesis of zero true serial correlation in all 441 studies, the expected mean of the observed values would be approximately $-.10$, whereas the actual value was $-.01$.

Second, Huitema sought to get information on individual cases by standardizing each serial correlation on the assumption that this would yield a unit normal distribution under the total null hypothesis. A statsig overplus of data in either tail of the distribution would then suggest that some cases had nonzero serial correlation. This procedure was also followed by Matyas and Greenwood, who discuss some problematic aspects of the standardization formula. It was on this basis that the excess of positive serial correlations noted in the text was obtained.

A more informative alternative would correlate the observed serial correlations with likely determinants, such as intertrial interval. This approach makes direct, empirical use of all the data, not just extreme cases, and is potentially more revealing.

11.3.2c. Two other techniques that have been suggested for serial observation design are time series and randomization statistics. The logic of time series is to identify the structural model underlying the observations, as in mathematical learning theory and in much economic analysis. To identify the structural model, however, requires 50-100 trials as a minimum, more than will often be available.

The other technique is randomization statistics (Section 12.2.1), which does not require normality. Anova is simpler, however, and far more flexible, especially for single subject experiments. Anova provides an easy formula for confidence intervals, which may require extensive calculation with randomization theory. Anova is readily extended to repeated measures, which do not permit random assignment. Also, of course, Anova is reasonably robust against violations of equinormality.

Some writers have criticized Anova because of its difficulties with serial correlation while simultaneously pushing randomization tests. But randomization tests also require independence as their basic assumption. And whereas Anova can assess serial dependence and in some cases allow for it, randomization statistics seems helpless.

11.4.1a. Leon did a repeated measures Anova for each subgroup, subsequent to the schema diagnosis for individual subjects (see similarly Shanteau & Anderson, 1969).

11.4.1b. Systematic development of Piaget's choice methodology by Siegler (e.g., 1976) went deeper into the morass, incorrectly claiming that children centered and failed to integrate in several tasks of intuitive physics (see Wilkening & Anderson, 1982, 1991; see also Figure 20.1). Siegler's choice methodology was applied in several studies about teaching college physics with equally incorrect results (Exercise 10.16). Superior methodology was already available that would have avoided this wasted work.

11.4.2a. General procedure in this experiment on attention-deficit children seemed thoughtful and cogent. Evidence for positive effects of methylphenidate comes from a careful, intensive study by Rapport et al. (1987), who presented both group and individual data for 42 children. These individual data were thought to indicate that drug effects are somewhat idiosyncratic across children as well as tasks (see Note 11.5.5c).

11.4.3a. Meehl (1990) continues his criticism of "soft psychology" by citing the general reaction to his analysis of the reason for lack of progress.

> My experience has been that most graduate students, and many professors, engage in a mix of defense mechanisms (most predominantly, denial), so that they can proceed as they have in the past with a good scientific conscience. The usual response is to say, in effect, "Well, that Meehl is a clever fellow and he likes to philosophize, fine for him, it's a free country. But since we are doing all right with the good old tried and true methods of Fisherian statistics and null hypothesis testing, and since journal editors do not seem to have panicked over such thoughts, I will stick to the accepted practices of my trade union and leave Meehl's worries to the statisticians and philosophers." I cannot strongly fault a 45-year-old professor for adopting this mode of defense, even though I believe it to be intellectually dishonest, because I think that for most faculty in soft psychology the full acceptance of my line of thought would involve a painful realization that one has achieved some notoriety, tenure, economic stability and the like by engaging, to speak bluntly, in a *bunch of nothing* (p. 230, bolding added).

11.4.3b. My concern about the conceptual framework that guides research in clinical psychology coalesced when I became involved in studies of judgment–decision in marriage in the late 1970s. Despite the overwhelming social importance of marriage and family life, despite the great opportunities for clinical research, despite the importance of family therapy, clinical branches of psychology departments showed near-zero interest in marriage at that time. This concern was sharpened by one participant at an APA symposium who declared that to go into marital therapy the first thing to do was to throw away everything you had learned about clinical psychology. Working through the problem, the classical approach, was sure to aggravate the trouble. Instead, the goal should be to forget the past and move forward (Anderson, 1991e).

11.4.3c. The paucity of single subject experiments in personality–clinical psychology contrasts dramatically with the idiographic emphasis on the uniqueness of the individual. Meehl's criticisms of significance tests and hypothesis testing miss the main problem. The main problem is that the hypotheses being tested stem from an ineffectual conceptual framework, symptomatized in his "crud factor." What is needed is a shift to a conceptual framework oriented toward experimental analysis with single persons.

11.4.3d. Configural judgment in personality–clinical psychology has been much claimed but little demonstrated. Integrated judgments based on two clinical behavior items showed differential weighted averaging with naive subjects (Anderson, 1972b), but perhaps expert judges would be truly configural. Information integration theory provides effective methods for analysis of configurality (see e.g., *Weak Inference* in Section 20.2.3, *Linear Response Methodology* in Section 21.6.1, and *Interactionist Theories* in Section 7.4). Functional measurement allows for personal values of individual judges, going beyond mere demonstration of configural judgment to analyze configural process.

11.4.4a. Although subject P.P. in Figure 11.7 does show some apparent transfer to the "new position, old angle" condition, the other two subjects in this experiment showed very little. Little transfer was also found in the first experiment, which used a substantial N. I am indebted to Ling-Po Shiu for furnishing these data.

11.4.4b. The days × blocks interaction residual was used as the error term, a practice that is buttressed by the curious finding of little trend within days. Two explanations were considered for the contrast between the learning trend across days and the lack of trend within days: Synaptic consolidation over the course of several hours, and within day fatigue, with some expressed preference for the latter.

11.4.4c. The logic of Sternberg's additive-factor method seems compelling. As with all theories, however, some alternative may hold instead. In fact, it appears that reasonable alternatives very different in nature can also yield additive results (see Miller, van der Ham, & Sanders, 1995).

11.4.4d. Additive factors can also produce linear fan patterns in some tasks, as illustrated in Shanteau's (1991) application of functional measurement to a list-search task.

11.4.4e. For experiments that seek to establish a null hypothesis, as with Sternberg's additive-factor method, it may be suggested that only individual analysis is completely satisfactory. Consider an investigation that seeks to affirm a null hypothesis, say, $X = 0$. In principle, X is zero for each individual subject, so $E(\mathrm{MS}_{SX})$ and $E(\mathrm{MS}_X)$ should both equal the individual response variability. In many studies of perception/cognition, an estimate of individual response variability with adequate df will be easy to get, so there is no need to use MS_{SX} as error as Sternberg did (Exercise 14a).

If the null hypothesis is false, on the other hand, then MS_{SX} will be too large and tend to obscure a nonzero X, especially because it will usually have few df and low power. Individual differences in the size of X will thus tend to obscure themselves. Testing MS_{SX} against MS_X is also a test of the model.

11.4.4f. A natural question with Schlottmann's study of utility theory in Figure 11.9 is whether the children understood the task. Schlottmann showed that even the younger children had good understanding of probability, of expected value, and of addition of goods. Also, her instructions and procedure were exceptionally thoughtful in bringing out the normative, additive nature of the task.

11.4.5a. Probability matching in humans was a central topic in the early days of mathematical learning theory. Conditioning models of simple mathematical and conceptual form predicted the observed matching. But matching refers only to the mean response. When the stimulus–response dependencies in the response sequence were analyzed, they disagreed severely with the mathematical models—the matching was found to be "fortuitous" (Anderson, 1960a, p. 92; see further Note 20.4.1a, page 677f).

11.4.5b. The operant study by Farley and Fantino (1978) cited in Figure 11.10 was the first application with animal subjects of the linear fan analysis for multiplication models that was introduced by Anderson and Shanteau (1970). Other applications of linear fan analysis to animal experiments are given by Hawkins, Roll, Puerto, and Yeomans (1983), Roberts (1987), and Gibbon and Fairhurst (1994).

11.4.6a. The investigators presented a more positive view of the effectiveness of seat belts, taking the inferred reduction in accidents pretty much at face value. They do not mention that the comparison times series for rear seat passengers clouds the issue.

11.5.2a. Other examples of individual analysis of response pattern include Anderson and Butzin (1978), Carterette and Anderson (1979), Cuneo (1982), Falk and Wilkening (1999), Karpp and Anderson (1997), Léoni and Mullet (1993), Lopes (1976a), Shanteau and Anderson (1969, 1972), Silverman and Paskewitz (1988), Surber (1985), and Wilkening and Anderson (1991). Assessing the generality of these individual patterns across time and task, as in Dozier and Butzin (1988), is a prime need.

Schlottmann's ingenious analysis of individual behavior patterns in phenomenal causality deserves special mention (see Schlottmann & Anderson, 1993). Schlottmann established a solid base of individual data and used the averaging model to estimate the weight each individual placed on different informers. These measured weights, leveraged with a prescient instructional manipulation, revealed five response strategies that could never be seen in the data themselves.

11.5.3a. I am surprised by the paucity of single subject Anovas in perception. In fact, I had trouble finding experimental illustrations. I should appreciate information about other applications in this area, and in other areas as well.

11.5.4a. A few comments relevant to single subject design in personality–clinical psychology are given for emotion in Anderson (1989) and for ego defense in Anderson (1991j). Personal design is discussed in Anderson (1990). Marriage and family life are considered in Anderson and Armstrong (1989) and Anderson (1991e). Of special interest and high potential are the studies of self-experimentation reported by Roberts and Neuringer (1998).

11.5.5a. The need for visual inspection of individual data with group experiments is nicely illustrated in Farkas (1991, Note 2, p. 89). In this way, Farkas uncovered an unclarity in stimulus materials that he rectified in his subsequent thesis experiments.

11.5.5b. *Behavior dynamics* is a fundamental problem in psychology. Behavior is typically a continuous evolution over time and space, as in goal-oriented movements and in language interaction. The diverse attempts to study dynamics of perception, thought, and action may benefit from closer linkage with one another. Minor contributions have been made with algebraic models of serial integration, including sequential dependencies and serial curves of learning, memory, and belief (e.g., Anderson, 1982, Section 3.6).

11.5.5c. The question of power for the study of Figure 11.5 may apply generally to studies of drug therapy with attention-deficit children. Current belief that drug effects are person-specific and/or situation-specific (Note 11.4.2a) may reflect inadequate power, not real differences (see *"Inconsistencies" in the Literature* in Section 4.3.1, page 103).

11.5.5d. The question of power is highlighted by the small number of observations typical of the studies of behavior modification summarized by Huitema. It seems doubtful that many of these studies had adequate power, even with zero serial correlation, to serve as more than pilot work. Yet not a few could readily have obtained an adequate number of observations. This point reemphasizes the theme that statistics has its main value in planning the investigation.

11.5.5e. Reference books on single subject design include Barlow and Hersen (1984), Franklin, Allison, and Gorman (1996), Kratochwill and Levin (1992), and Lattal and Perone (1988). Many chapters in these books can be helpful. Nearly all have focused on operant tasks, one of the very few domains that has given systematic attention to methodology of single subject design. Single subject experiments in perception, cognition, psycholinguistics, and personality/social, for example, often allow randomized treatment design. Systematic methodology is largely undeveloped, however, although modest progress has been made in information integration theory (Chapter 21).

Contributors to Franklin, Allison, and Gorman give useful coverage of statistical topics, including power and serial observation. Chapters in other books, however, not infrequently show shortcomings in statistical understanding that compromise some of their conclusions. It is common to read, for example, that standard statistics is only applicable to group data; in fact, single subject Anova has been around for decades.

One consequence of this negative attitude toward statistics has been neglect of needed groundwork for single subject analysis, most notably with the problem of serial correlation, but also with treatment randomization designs and balanced designs, such as Latin squares. A vital first step would be to obtain longer sequences of observations, which would be feasible in some situations, but which has not been done, in part because the need for doing so has not been appreciated. Finding determinants of serial correlation, which is clearly needed to get the problem under control, has hardly begun.

The total ignoral of single subject design in graduate statistics texts may be partly due to narrowness in previous presentations of single subject methodology. Although these presentations have made important contributions to serial serial observation design, only one that I have read recognizes single subject design with treatment randomization. Some identify single subject design with the rise of operant psychology in the 1930s, seemingly unaware that single subject design has been common for over a century in perception and learning. Some argue that group design and single subject design have an "intractable divergence" or are even "fundamentally incompatible" (see Baron & Perone, 1998).

There are important differences between single subject and group design, as this chapter shows, but the principles of design and analysis are the same in both.

EXERCISES FOR CHAPTER 11

NOTE: For the following exercises, assume independent scores even in serial observation design unless otherwise indicated. Independence always needs careful consideration; it is assumed here in order to focus on other problems.

1. You run four single subjects. Three show a substantial effect, comfortably statsig. The fourth shows nothing. You submit these results for publication, including four single subject Anovas. Among other editorial reactions, one reviewer requests a repeated measures Anova for all four subjects. The Editor indicates a revision should be acceptable, without remarking specifically on the repeated measures analysis.

    a. While you're fretting about how to handle the revision, your assistant rushes in, crying, "I've done the repeated measures analysis. Shall I show you the results right now?" How should you reply?

    b. What do you conclude about the reviewer's request?

    c. Suppose you conclude the repeated measures analysis requested by the reviewer is not appropriate. With your revision, you include a letter to the Editor that explains your reasoning. Nevertheless, the Editor makes this analysis prerequisite to publication. Now what do you do?

2. Construct a *very simple* conceptual example in which an A-B design suffers a total confounding that is revealed with an A-B-A design. Include a numerical, error-free example in graphic form.

3. The preface to this chapter, considering whether the A-B difference is reliable in an A-B design, asserts "The answer obviously requires comparison of the mean difference between treatments to the variability within treatments."

    a. Why exactly is *this* comparison *required*? (Of course, "mean" could be replaced by "median," for example, but this statisticality is ignored here.)

    b. Do you think the word "obviously" is justified?

4. To test relative efficacy of two therapy regimens (drug plus exercise) for a patient suffering chronic pain, a hypothetical patient–physician team used an A-B-A-B design. Each period was long enough to wash out effects of the previous period. Mild serial correlation seemed not unlikely so the response measure was taken as the mean over the last three observations in each period. At the end of the four successive periods, the response measures were 14, 19, 12, 17 (larger numbers mean greater pain).

    a. By visual inspection, guess how close $F(1, 2)$ will be to the criterial 18.5.

    b. Do the Anova and interpret the result.

    c. Suppose this patient is a member of your family, not conversant with statistical analysis. In light of (b), what do you advise?

d. Assuming this outcome is real, are there any confounding factors that would seem a *serious* concern for the interpretation?

e. What, if anything, does this Anova add to visual inspection?

5. Of the A-B design, Section 11.3.1 states "Given a long, flat trend under A, it seems unlikely that the behavior would change just when B is introduced unless B had a real effect."

a. What is the rationale for this statement?

b. What is the null hypothesis in this test? Be precise.

c. Can this null hypothesis be false if A and B have identical effects?

6. In an A-B-A design with 6 (independent) observations in each period:

a. How do you get a confidence interval for the difference between the mean of the two A periods and the mean of the B period? How many df?

b. What can be concluded from this confidence interval? What cannot?

7. In the numerical example of the 2×3 design in the Appendix to Chapter 5, suppose these scores had been obtained from a single subject, using treatment randomization to obtain independence, rather than 12 independent subjects, randomly assigned.

a. What changes would be required in the Anova?

b. What can be said about the generality of the results assuming subjects are (i) a random sample and (ii) a handy sample?

8. You run a single subject in a simple A-B design. Assume no confounding is present so the A-B difference can be interpreted at face value. How do you decide how many trials to run in each period? How does this apply to the experiment of Figure 11.5?

9. In subsequent studies of the blame schema of Figure 11.3, each of a substantial number of subjects received two randomized replications of the design.

a. Write out the Anova table (Source and df) for a single subject in this task.

b. Of what interest are the main effects?

c. Of what interest is the interaction residual?

d. What argument can be made for using $\alpha = .10$?

e. Is visual inspection useful for schema diagnosis in this case?

10. P plans a serial observation design in which he expects a small gradual increase in response level over the course of his experiment as well as a substantial difference between effects of A and B. P presents this plan to your research group, saying he intends to use an A-B-A design with equally many trials in each period. He plans to compare the mean of the B period with the pooled mean of the two A periods.

  a. Suppose there is a linear trend over trials. Will this confound P's results? (A numerical example may be helpful.)

  b. Do you think P's design and plan are reasonable?

Exercises 11a–11b concern the experiment of Figure 11.4; Exercises 12a–12d concern the experiment of Figure 11.5. Although visual inspection seems sufficient for these data, they are used here to illustrate Anova for serial observation design. Serial independence is assumed, as seems not unreasonable since sessions were at least one day apart. Read the data approximately from each figure, and make a neat table. Omit the last point in both sets of filled circle data in Figure 11.4.

11a. a. Do Anova on periods 2 and 3 of Figure 11.4 (with six and three data points, respectively). Interpret this result.

  b. Show that the 95% confidence interval for the mean difference between these two sets of scores has width near ± 15.6 (Note 4.1.1b for unequal n).

  c. Can you guess from visual inspection why the last point of each set of filled circle data was omitted? (Note 11.3.1a.)

11b. In Figure 11.4, the use of only three sessions in the second set of open circle data suggests the investigators noticed that the behavior had returned to its original level and decided on this basis to resume the experimental treatment.

  a. What is the advantage of this approach?

  b. What artifact endangers this approach (see Note 11.3.1a)?

  c. How could this danger have been avoided?

12a. In Figure 11.5, how does visual inspection show no statistical test is needed between placebo and 6-week follow-up (3 and 10 observations)?

12b. In Figure 11.5, do Anova for the four dosage levels (placebo, 5, 10, and 15 mg) using the data from the four sets of three data points. Find 95% confidence interval between largest and smallest means. Interpret the outcome.

12c. a. Do a power calculation for the difference between the 5 mg and placebo conditions, using the mean square error of 490 from the previous exercise. What does this mean to you?

  b. How large a difference between means would be needed to get power of .80 for the comparison of (a)?

12d. Methylphenidate has a half-life in the body of 4-6 hr and is thought to be completely eliminated within 24 hr. On this basis, design an experiment for Bill (Figure 11.5) based on a Latin square (Section 14.3), including pertinent details of procedure. Discuss pros and cons of this design.

13. In Figure 11.7, percentage correct responses on successive blocks of 40 trials were as follows for two conditions on day 6:

        Old position, old orientation: 83, 88, 85, 85, 83, 78;

        Old position, new orientation: 65, 68, 80, 63, 70, 70.

a. Get the error half-bar for a single mean and give its meaning.

b. Get a confidence interval for the mean difference and interpret.

c. What two hints does visual inspection of these data suggest?

14a. a. How does Sternberg's additive-factor method of Section 11.4.4 avoid the cited shortcoming of Donders' method (see also Exercise 6.19)?

b. The main effects are obvious. Don't belabor them with a significance test. But say why a small main effect would be undesirable.

c. How does the nonadditivity of Number of Alternatives with Stimulus Quality and with Stimulus–Response (S-R) Mapping support and buttress the interpretation that the latter two variables are additive?

d. Comparison of the RTs with two and eight alternatives might be safest if based on only the same numerals from the latter as from the former. Which two numerals would you use in the two alternative condition?

e.* The two-way nonadditivity of Number of Alternatives with S-R Mapping was 80.9 ms—over three times larger than two-way nonadditivity of Number of Alternatives with Stimulus Quality. Why does this not imply that Number of Alternatives is more important for the S-R Mapping process than for the Stimulus Quality process? (See *Concept–Instance Confounding* in Section 8.1.4, page 232).

14b. Latin square design is underutilized in perception/cognition. Suppose the Latin square of Table 14.3 is used for a single subject in Sternberg's additive-factor experiment of the previous exercise. Consider just the case of two alternatives. The 2×2, Stimulus Quality $\times$ S-R Mapping design then has four conditions, which are assigned the letters A_1, A_2, A_3, A_4, in Table 14.3. In a single session, the subject receives a block of trials at each of these four conditions, given in the order specified by the first row of the square, next in the order specified by the second row of the square, and so on. The primary response is the mean reaction time over a terminal subblock of each block of trials, the initial trials being omitted as warmup adjustment to the given condition.

The Anova at the right side of Table 14.5 may be applied, with $a = g = 4$ and $n = 1$. With a single subject, of course, some sources will have different meanings than indicated in the discussion of Table 14.5 for different subjects.

a. Position effects refer to progressive changes in response level over successive trials. What two sources in the Anova table at the right of Table 14.5 would represent position effects in the given Latin square?

b. What would be the likely origin of a position effect? How large would you expect position effects to be in Sternberg's experiment?

c. Suppose treatments have no effect but that the response level is 1 on the first trial and increases by 1 on each successive trial. What is the numerical relation between the Position and Sequence effects? Would you expect the same qualitative relation to hold generally?

d. The four treatments form a 2 × 2 design so $SS_{Treatments}$ on 3 df can be broken down into three parts. What do these three parts measure?

e. The *AG* term in the right panel of Table 14.5 corresponds here to the interaction of treatments with Sequences (rows). This term is used as the error term for all sources (including Sequences), that is, as an estimate of the response variability of this subject under the same experimental conditions. Why is this error term expected to be a little too large?

f. Suppose the experiment was run in four sessions, with just one row of the square in each session. What, if anything, would change in the analysis?

g. Why can $MS_{SA/G}$ be used to test sequences?

15. In Schlottmann's study of utility theory in Figure 11.9, the adult group did not violate utility theory; for them the dashed curve lay below and nearly parallel with the solid curves. Accordingly, the disordinal violation of classical utility theory in Figure 11.9 might be considered immature behavior by children. How do you think Schlottmann answered this question in her Discussion?

16. In a 4 × 4 study of perception of cold temperature, you give each treatment once to a single subject. You had planned to replicate, but this experiment is arduous and time-consuming and the subject could only with reluctance be persuaded to complete the first replication.

a. How can you get an approximate significance test for the main effect of each variable?

b. What disadvantage does this test have? How serious do you consider it?

c. Suppose you had replicated four of the treatment conditions before the subject quit. What good would this do you?

17. In the first paragraph of this chapter, what justification can be found in the Anova model of Equation 2 of Chapter 6 for the assertion that "error variability will be even less than with repeated measures design"?

PREFACE

Nonnormality is likely to widen confidence intervals and decrease power. The robustness of Anova applies mainly to the false alarm parameter, α. Power, in contrast, can be seriously affected by nonnormality.

The real trouble is **extreme scores**; they contribute disproportionately to error variance. Nonnormality is a problem mainly because it is usually accompanied by extreme scores. Distributions that have longer or heavier tails than the normal distribution are common in practice; these tail scores increase the error variance disproportionately.

Avoiding extreme scores depends first on empirics: experimental task, experimental procedure, and response measure. Better instructions, for example, will reduce the likelihood that an occasional subject will misunderstand the task and yield an extreme score. Similar considerations apply to every aspect of experimental procedure. Choice of response measure can have marked effects on the shape of the data distribution—which should be a primary concern in planning any investigation.

After the data are in, the shape of their distribution can still be changed statistically. *Trimming* seems the most useful statistical technique to deal with extreme scores. This is one of numerous ''robust'' techniques, distinguished from the others by a formula for the variance that makes for easy use.

Three alternatives to trimming are also considered: response transformation, outlier methods, and distribution-free rank tests. Time scores, for example, often have long right tails; transforming time to speed tends to normalize the data and increase power. Statistical tests for outliers are nonrobust, useful only in very special situations. Distribution-free tests of the ranked data appear inferior to Anova of these same ranks.

Unequal variance can have adverse effects on overall Anova, especially if coupled with unequal n. Available evidence suggests that extensions of Anova to handle unequal variance with more than two groups are sensitive to nonnormality and so not very useful. Even when applicable, moreover, overall Anova does little to localize the effects and explicate the data pattern.

Accordingly, an alternative to overall Anova with unequal variance is advocated in this book: Focus on two-mean comparisons at the outset. To this end, formulas are given for confidence intervals that allow unequal variance and unequal n as well.

Chapter 12

NONNORMAL DATA
AND UNEQUAL VARIANCE

Serious loss of power may result with nonnormal distributions. If all distributions were normal, the mean and standard deviation of Chapter 2 would be ideal statistics. This point may be emphasized by comparing mean and median. Both are equal in a normal population, and either could be used to estimate central tendency from a sample. But statistical theory shows that the median is more variable from sample to sample. The sample mean has a shorter confidence interval, in other words, one reason for preferring it over the median.

With a nonnormal population, in contrast, the sample mean may be more variable than the median. Even one or two extreme scores can have crippling effects on the confidence interval that represents the mean.

The first line of protection against extreme scores lies in experimental procedure. This extrastatistical issue deserves emphasis before we proceed to statistical techniques. Your expectation about the shape of the data is important in planning your experiment. Small changes in experimental procedure sometimes markedly reduce the likelihood of extreme scores. And it goes without saying that the data should always be inspected for extreme scores.

Of the statistical procedures for dealing with extreme scores, the trimming method of Section 12.1 may be far and away the best. Although as yet little used, it appears to be safe and effective.

Three other ways to deal with nonnormality have been developed by statisticians. Outlier rejection techniques have specialized applicability and do not seem robust (Section 12.3). Transformation to make the data more normal is sometimes helpful, although not a general purpose tool (Section 12.4).

A different tack is taken with distribution-free tests, which handle extreme scores by reducing the data to ranks. Hence no assumption is needed about the specific shape of the population (Section 12.2). Distribution-free tests are largely limited to one-way designs, however, for which it may be preferable to apply regular Anova to the ranks themselves.

12.1 TRIMMING

The idea behind *trimming* is simple. Extreme scores can adversely influence the reliability of the sample mean—*throw them out!* Statisticians have found legitimate ways to do something akin to this.

12.1.1 TRIMMED MEAN AND VARIANCE

Trimming has a simple logic. Consider a symmetrical distribution, but trim off equal right and left tails. By symmetry, the trimmed and untrimmed distributions have the same mean. Hence trimming does not bias the sample mean.

The great advantage is that the trimmed mean is less variable than the untrimmed mean with heavy-tailed distributions. The tail scores, which contribute disproportionately to the variance, have been trimmed away.

The critical problem is to find a formula for the sample variance of the trimmed mean. This variance is essential to get a valid confidence interval. Without a confidence interval, the trimmed mean lacks meaning.

Almost miraculously, this variance problem has a simple solution.

Trimmed Mean. To show how trimming is done, consider a single group, denoted j, with n independent scores. Line up the scores in numerical order, with Y_1 the smallest, Y_n the largest. Choose a trimming proportion p and adjust it a little so that $np = k$ is an integer. Trim the k lowest scores and the k highest scores. Calculate the *trimmed mean*, $\bar{Y}_{Tj}$, from the remaining $n - 2k$ scores:[a]

$$\bar{Y}_{Tj} = \frac{1}{n - 2k}[Y_{k+1} + Y_{k+2} + \ldots + Y_{n-k-1} + Y_{n-k}]. \quad (1)$$

Error Variance. The error variance for the trimmed mean follows a simple rule. Replace each trimmed score in the lower tail by a copy of the smallest untrimmed score; do analogously in the upper tail. There are thus k extra copies of the smallest untrimmed score and k extra copies of the largest untrimmed score. Include all these copies when—and only when—computing SS_{error}.

The first step in computing SS_{error}, therefore, is to get the mean of all scores, copies included. This mean is denoted by $\bar{Y}_{Wj}$:[b]

$$\bar{Y}_{Wj} = \frac{1}{n}[(k+1)Y_{k+1} + Y_{k+2} + \ldots + Y_{n-k-1} + (k+1)Y_{n-k}]. \quad (2a)$$

This $\bar{Y}_{Wj}$ is used only for computing the sum of squared deviations, $SS_{error, Wj}$. For group j, the hand formula from Equation 2.4 is:[c]

$$SS_{error, Wj} = (k+1)Y_{k+1}^2 + Y_{k+2}^2 + \ldots$$

$$+ Y_{n-k-1}^2 + (k+1)Y_{n-k}^2 - n\bar{Y}_{Wj}^2. \quad (2b)$$

To get the error MS, divide the error SS by the *trimmed df*: $(n - 2k - 1)$.

$$\text{MS}_{\text{error, } Wj} = \text{SS}_{\text{error, } Wj}/(n - 2k - 1) = s^2_{Wj}. \tag{2c}$$

Accordingly, the error half-bar for the trimmed mean is $s_{Wj}/\sqrt{(n - 2k)} = \sqrt{\text{MS}_{\text{error, } Wj}/(n - 2k)}$; see similarly Expressions 4 and 5 below.

Comment on Trimming. Trimming throws away the tail scores only in calculations involving treatment means and df. These tail scores still influence the variance of the trimmed mean. This influence is taken into account by including their copies in Equation 2b for $\text{SS}_{\text{error, } Wj}$.[d]

It's wonderful luck to have a simple formula for the variance of the trimmed mean. Statisticians have explored several dozen similar schemes, some of which can be better than trimming, but virtually all are complicated to use.

12.1.2 TRIMMED ANOVA

The foregoing formulas for trimmed mean and variance can be employed with analysis of variance. Trimmed Anova is available on some statistical packages. One-way Anova and confidence intervals are straightforward extensions of material in Chapter 3 and are given here.

Trimmed Anova. One-way trimmed Anova is the same as in Chapter 3, except for two changes. First, SS_{error} is obtained from Equation 2b, which takes account of the copies of the trimmed scores. From Equation 2c, therefore,

$$\text{MS}_{\text{error}} = \sum_{j=1}^{a} \text{SS}_{\text{error, } Wj}/a(n - 2k - 1); \tag{3a}$$

Second, SS_A is obtained using only the scores in the trimmed samples:

$$\text{SS}_A = (n - 2k)\sum_{j=1}^{a} \overline{Y}^2_{Tj} - a(n - 2k)\overline{Y}^2_{T.}; \tag{3b}$$

$$\text{MS}_A = \text{SS}_A/(a - 1); \tag{3b}$$

$$F = \text{MS}_A/\text{MS}_{\text{error}}. \qquad df = (a - 1)/[a(n - 2k - 1)] \tag{3c}$$

Here, as elsewhere, the size of the trimmed sample determines the error df.

Confidence Intervals. To get the error bar, or standard deviation, of the trimmed mean for any group, use the same formula as in Chapter 4:

$$\overline{Y}_{Tj} \pm \sqrt{\text{MS}_{\text{error}}/(n - 2k)}, \quad \text{(standard deviation of trimmed mean)} \tag{4}$$

where MS_{error} is taken from Equation 3a.

Confidence intervals for a single mean follow the corresponding formula:

$$\overline{Y}_{Tj} \ \pm \ t^* \sqrt{\mathrm{MS_{error}}/(n-2k)}, \tag{5}$$

where t^* is the criterial value of t on $a(n-2k-1)$ df. To get a confidence interval for the difference between two trimmed means, multiply by $\sqrt{2}$, just as with untrimmed means in Chapter 4. Accuracy requires ns of at least 7.

Numerical Example. The trimming formulas are illustrated in Table 12.1, with $k = 2$ scores trimmed from each tail. The trimmed scores are listed just below the untrimmed scores for each condition. Thus, the second row of data for A_1 shows two copies of 2 and two copies of 6. Similarly, the second row of data for A_2 shows two copies of 6 and two copies of 10.

$\mathrm{SS_{error}}$ is obtained by including these copies, as indicated in Equations 2a and 2b. These formulas yield $\mathrm{SS_{error,\,}}_{Wj} = 26$ for both conditions. Summing these yields $\mathrm{SS_{error}} = 52$, as listed in the table.

Note well that the copies contribute no df. $\mathrm{MS_{error}}$ requires that $\mathrm{SS_{error}}$ be divided by the *trimmed df*. Further, the operative sample size for confidence intervals is the size of the trimmed sample (Equations 4 and 5).

The trimming benefit is visible in the confidence intervals. Comparison of the two boldface entries shows that trimming reduced the likely error of the mean from 5.64 to 3.72. This increase in precision is free.

The trimmed scores are not really thrown out. They are replaced by the copies, and these copies are included in computing $\mathrm{MS_{error}}$. Omitting the tail scores makes the sample mean less variable with heavy-tailed distributions. This variability is quantified by the formula for $\mathrm{MS_{error}}$.

Power and False Alarms for Trimmed Means. Trimmed F yields greater power with heavy-tailed, symmetric distributions. This may be illustrated with one simulation condition from Lee and Fung (1985), which used a 15% trimmed mean and a power index $\phi = 1.5$ (Equation 4.5). One mildly nonnormal distribution showed power of .80 for trimmed F compared to .70 for untrimmed F. The more nonnormal the distribution, the greater the advantage of trimming; for one quite nonnormal distribution, power was .62 and .17, respectively. Trimming really can make a silk purse from a sow's ear.

With a normal distribution, not much is lost by trimming. For $\phi = 1.5$, the simulation yielded trimmed and untrimmed power of .63 and .69, respectively. For other values of ϕ, the power loss was considerably smaller than .06.

When the null hypothesis was true, trimmed Anova kept false alarms under good control. With normal distributions, the simulation showed an effective α near .05 for 15 combinations of number and size of groups, including unequal n. With quite nonnormal distributions, trimmed F was conservative, yielding effective αs of .03 or .04. This was better than untrimmed F, however, which yielded effective αs around .02.[a]

TABLE 12.1

NUMERICAL EXAMPLE OF TRIMMING

Two groups, A_1 and A_2, with $n = 9$.
Two scores trimmed in each tail of each group.

A_1: Untrimmed: 0 1 2 3 4 5 6 7 17 $\sum Y^2 = 429$

      Trimmed: 2 2 2 3 4 5 6 6 6 $\sum Y^2 = 170$

A_2: Untrimmed: 2 5 6 7 8 9 10 10 24 $\sum Y^2 = 1035$

      Trimmed: 6 6 6 7 8 9 10 10 10 $\sum Y^2 = 602$

Untrimmed sample means are 5 and 9; trimmed sample means are 4 and 8.
The Anova calculations are as follows.

Untrimmed: $SS_{error} = [429 - 9 \times 5^2] + [1035 - 9 \times 9^2] = 510$

                $MS_{error} = 510/16 = \mathbf{31.88}$

                   $SS_A = 9[5^2 + 9^2] - 18[\frac{1}{2}(5 + 9)]^2 = 72$

        $F(1, 16) = 2.26.$

Trimmed: $SS_{error} = [170 - 9 \times 4^2] + [602 - 9 \times 8^2] = 52$

                $MS_{error} = 52/8 = \mathbf{6.50}$

                   $SS_A = 5[4^2 + 8^2] - 10[\frac{1}{2}(4 + 8)]^2 = 40$

        $F(1, 8) = 6.15.$

Confidence intervals for mean difference:

Untrimmed $4 \pm \sqrt{2} \sqrt{F^*(1, 16)} \sqrt{31.88/9} = 4 \pm \mathbf{5.64}$ $[F^*(1, 16) = 4.49]$

Trimmed $4 \pm \sqrt{2} \sqrt{F^*(1, 8)} \sqrt{6.50/5} = 4 \pm \mathbf{3.72}$ $[F^*(1, 8) = 5.32]$

Comparison of **5.64** with **3.72** shows that trimming yields markedly more
reliable estimates of the population means from the same data.

12.1.3 PRACTICAL TRIMMING

Trimming should be helpful with situations in which occasional extreme scores may appear. Trimming was effective in the numerical example because it greatly reduced the influence of the extreme high score in each group. Symmetry allows heavy tails, now considered empirically common, which can have adverse effects in regular Anova.

Trimming appears effective even with asymmetrical data (Wilcox, 1994). In this case, the trimmed sample mean is a biased estimate of the population mean. If all conditions have the same shape, however, this bias will be the same for each condition mean and so will not affect comparisons between conditions. It may be worthwhile, however, to seek a preliminary transformation to make the data more symmetrical.

How Much To Trim? The optimal trimming proportion depends on the form and amount of nonnormality; the more nonnormal, the greater should be the trimming. Lee and Fung (1985) suggest a general purpose trimming proportion of 15%. This value fits well with their simulation study, based on $a = 4$ groups with $n = 20$. Other statisticians have suggested trimming proportions as high as 25% or 30%, but these statistical studies have used arbitrary nonnormal distributions, chosen for statistical convenience, that offer little empirical guidance.

Empirically, Rocke et al. (1982) found that 20% trimming did noticeably better than 15%, and 25% even better, for 20 data sets from 18th and 19th century astronomy and for 47 data sets from a 1976 volume of a journal of analytical chemistry. Since the optimal trimming proportion will no doubt differ across empirical areas, it is desirable to accumulate evidence for specific areas and specific tasks.

Recommendations. Trimming shows great promise and should have wide usefulness. If you think trimming might help you, it's easy to try out. Get some past data and apply the above formulas, or preferably, a statistical package. Alternatively, make up a few sets of hypothetical data that embody the shape of distribution you expect or fear. The merits of trimming will appear in comparing the confidence intervals for the trimmed and untrimmed data, as in the foregoing numerical example.

The need for trimming must be anticipated. To apply trimming after inspecting your data taints your results, just as would throwing out an extreme score (see further *Outliers*, Section 12.3).

If you employ trimming, I suggest you report auxiliary information on how well it worked, thus providing a guide to help others decide whether to trim, and how much. Besides error bars for trimmed and untrimmed means, error bars for alternative degrees of trimming would seem desirable. These analyses will be more useful if accompanied by information about the shape of the data.

12.2 DISTRIBUTION-FREE STATISTICS

Distribution-free statistics, sometimes called *nonparametric statistics*, assume that all populations have the same shape, but make no assumption about specific shape. In particular, they do not assume normality. They do assume equal variance and independence, however, just as with Anova.

Rank-type distribution-free statistics are considered here. If the measured data are metric, reaction time in seconds, say, or rating of date desirability, these numbers are lined up in increasing order. Then each number is replaced by its rank. The analysis is done on these ranks.

Ranking reduces the effect of extreme scores. Consider the highest score in a sample. The farther out it lies, the more it would run up the variance. With Anova, this one score could wipe out any statsig effect in the other scores. As a rank, however, it is just 1 larger than the next score, no matter how great the metric difference between them. Extremeness is thus much diminished.

A deeper advantage of ranking is to avoid any assumption about the shape of the distribution. Although all groups are assumed to have the same shape distribution, this shape may be anything. The specific shape is made irrelevant through the transformation to ranks. Accordingly, these tests are called *distribution-free*.

Rank tests can provide substantially more power than Anova with some nonnormal populations. With normal populations, surprisingly, they have nearly as much power as Anova. They have been fairly popular, therefore, and numerous statistical procedures have been developed.

The following presentation gives a simple approach to rank statistics, using the rank transform method of Conover and Iman (1981; Conover, 1999):

Transform the data to ranks and apply regular Anova to these ranks.

12.2.1 RANDOMIZATION THEORY AND RANK TESTS

The essential idea of ranks tests appeared first in randomization theory, the distribution-free approach introduced by Fisher. Since randomization theory has additional conceptual and practical interest, it is described briefly first.

Randomization Theory. To illustrate the logic of randomization theory, consider the difference, $\overline{Y}_{\text{diff}}$, between two sample means with subjects assigned randomly to the two treatment conditions. The question is whether this observed $\overline{Y}_{\text{diff}}$ is ''large enough'' to indicate a real difference.

Suppose the two treatments have identical effects. Then the measured score for each subject will be the same, regardless of which condition the subject is assigned to. *Hence the $\overline{Y}_{\text{diff}}$ for every possible random assignment can be calculated from the observed scores in the one random assignment actually used.* This aggregate constitutes the sampling distribution of $\overline{Y}_{\text{diff}}$ for H_0 true. The criterial region consists of those 5% of the $\bar{Y}_{\text{diff}}$ that have the largest magnitude, disregarding sign. If the observed $\bar{Y}_{\text{diff}}$ is one of these, reject H_0.

No assumption is needed about the shape of the distribution. Under the null hypothesis of identical effects, independence and randomization imply that all treatments have identical distributions, including equal variance. Randomization tests are thus the prototype of distribution-free analysis.

In practical applications, regular Anova usually provides a good approximation to false alarm rates from randomization analysis. This is valuable because randomization tests require massive computation. In principle, $\bar{Y}_{\text{diff}}$ must be calculated for every possible random assignment, which is often a huge number. In practice, it suffices to use a random sample of, say, 5000 random assignments, but this is still tedious. This approach has been pursued in detail for a variety of experimental designs by Edgington (1987).[a]

Randomization theory also has a notable conceptual advantage: It places statistical inference on an empirical foundation, namely, "the physical act of randomization," as Fisher put it. Together with independence, which is needed to ensure that all random assignments are equally probable, this physical act is a rational foundation for statistical inference for one-way designs.[b]

Rank Tests. The logic of rank tests is the same as randomization theory. The sole difference is that the data are first reduced to ranks, thereby reducing the influence of extreme scores. With two groups, $\bar{Y}_{\text{diff}}$ then refers to the difference in mean ranks (or equivalent statistic).

Traditional rank tests yield a chi-square value that provides an approximate significance test. This chi-square approximation avoids the massive computation needed for the foregoing randomization tests of the raw data.

Anova on ranks, however, yields a usually better approximation than chi-square. This rank transform Anova is presented next.

12.2.2 RANK ANOVA FOR ONE VARIABLE

Rank analysis is satisfactory only with a single variable. Standard tests such as Kruskal–Wallis H require that n be at least 10 for each group, although exact tables may be used for small n. The two cases of one-variable design— independent scores and repeated measures—are taken up next.

Rank Anova for Independent Scores. The first step in rank Anova for a one-way design with independent scores is to rank the scores from 1 to N in order of their magnitude. With tied scores, assign mean ranks (see Exercise b3). This ranking is done without regard to treatment condition. If two treatments have similar effects, their rank scores will be similar. If one has greater effect, it will tend to have higher ranks. Accordingly, we wish to test the null hypothesis of equal mean rank.

This test can be made with standard Anova. Treat the ranks as numbers and calculate SS_{within} and $SS_{between}$ exactly as in Chapter 3. Then the test statistic is

$$F_{ranks} = \frac{MS_{between}}{MS_{within}}. \qquad (a-1)/(N-a) \text{ df} \qquad (6)$$

The subscript *ranks* is used here only as a reminder that standard Anova has been applied to the ranks rather than to the original numerical scores. The criterial F^* is obtained from Table A5 exactly as in Chapter 3. This rank Anova can yield more power than standard Anova with long-tailed distributions.

Rank Anova appears to do as well or better than the three standard distribution-free tests for independent scores. These are the Kruskal–Wallis H test, the Mann–Whitney U test, and the Wilcoxon rank-sum test, all of which are essentially equivalent. Since the latter two apply only to the special case of two groups, there seems little point to learn about them, at least for empirical workers. They are mentioned here because they are cited in the literature.[a]

Rank Anova for Repeated Measures. With repeated measures, begin by ranking the treatments from 1 to a separately for each subject or case. A superior treatment will tend to have higher mean rank across subjects. Calculate SS_A and SS_{SA} just as for the $S \times A$ design of Section 6.1.1, except using the ranks as scores. The test statistic is the same as in Chapter 6:

$$F_{ranks} = \frac{MS_A}{MS_{SA}}. \qquad (a-1)/(a-1)(n-1) \text{ df} \qquad (7)$$

Here again the subscript *ranks* is only a reminder that standard Anova has been applied to the ranks rather than the original numerical scores.

I believe that Box's ε adjustment should be used, just as with regular Anova for repeated measures. If pairs of treatments have unequal correlation with the original numerical scores, the same should be true for the ranks. As yet, however, I have not found any article that mentions this matter.

The customary distribution-free test for a repeated measures variable is the Friedman test (for $a > 2$). The Friedman chi-square is conservative but "grossly inaccurate for small sample sizes" (Iman & Davenport, 1980, p. 593). F_{ranks} is somewhat liberal, but kept α below .065 for $n > 6$ subjects in their simulations.

For $a = 2$, a different ranking procedure provides more power. Get the difference score for each subject or case, rank these in terms of their absolute value, and then prefix each with the sign of the difference. The null hypothesis, which assumes a symmetrical distribution, is that mean of these signed ranks is zero. The traditional test is the Wilcoxon signed-ranks test. It is simpler and apparently at least as effective to apply regular Anova to the ranks and test F_{mean} (see Conover, 1999).

Rank Tests for Factorial Design. Factorial design has always been problematic for rank tests. The problem is that ranking can transform main effects into interaction residuals. To see this, suppose the raw data have zero interaction, shown by parallelism in the factorial graph. Nonlinear transformation of the vertical response axis will generally destroy the parallelism, producing an apparent interaction where there was none before. Since ranking is a nonlinear transformation, it can transform main effects into interactions, which seems generally inadvisable.[b]

To avoid this problem, alignment procedures have been developed to eliminate effects other than the one to be tested. An alignment test for a two-way interaction, for example, would begin by subtracting the row and column means of the original measured data from each score in each cell of the design. The subtraction eliminates both main effects to yield a residual score, which represents the interaction. These residuals are ranked and analyzed as already indicated. A variety of alignment procedures have been proposed, but none seems too satisfactory (see e.g., Harwell, 1991; Mansouri & Chang, 1995).

12.2.3 HOW USEFUL ARE DISTRIBUTION-FREE RANK TESTS?

Rank tests lack versatility. Even a simple two-way design presents the problems already indicated. More complex designs, such as Latin squares, are even more problematic. As noted previously (Anderson, 1961b, p. 307):

> It thus seems fair to conclude that parametric tests [= Anova–regression] constitute the standard tools of psychological statistics. In respect of significance level and power, one might claim a fairly even match. However, the versatility of parametric procedures is quite unmatched and this is decisive. Unless and until nonparametric [= distribution-free] tests are developed to the point where they meet the routine needs of the researcher as exemplified by the above designs, they cannot realistically be considered as competitors to parametric tests.
>
> One of the reasons for the popularity of nonparametric tests is probably the current obsession with questions of statistical significance . . .

After 40 more years of statistical study, rank tests still lack versatility.

A principled objection to rank statistics comes from the Experimental Pyramid of Chapter 1. The measurement transformation from the behavior to numbers is central in empirical analysis. A continuing goal of science is to improve our scales of measurement, making them more linear. The logical gulf between a pure rank order and a linear scale is empirically filled with semilinear scales that contain worthwhile metric information (Section 19.3.1). Statistical analysis should utilize this information and seek to improve empirical measurement. Rank statistics turns away from this goal, fixating on significance tests. Rank statistics thus ignores a basic concern of science to improve its methods of measurement.[a, b]

12.2.4 SCALES AND STATISTICS

An erroneous measurement-theoretical argument for using ranks instead of numbers for one-way design has been urged by a number of writers. The premise is that few psychological variables are known to be measured on true linear (equal interval) scales. Hence only rank-order information can be trusted, that is, greater than–less than relations. Anova, in contrast, takes the numbers at face value, as though a unit interval in the numbers was also a unit interval in the psychological scale. This seems to go beyond the data and therefore cannot be trusted.

A typical expression of this view is given by Siegel and Castellan (1988). Referring to the t and F tests, they assert that "The variables must have been measured on *at least* an interval scale, so that it is possible to *interpret* the results" (p. 20). This assertion is incorrect. With randomization, all groups in a one-way design have identical distributions under the null hypothesis of no treatment effects—regardless of the scale of measurement. If these distributions have equal means on the true linear scale, they will necessarily have equal means on any other scale, including whatever scale is actually used.

Anova can thus provide a valid test of the null hypothesis of equal true means, even with an arbitrary monotone response scale. Anova may not be advisable if the distributions are not normal, but nonnormality is a qualitatively different issue. This issue is discussed further in *Anova With Monotone Data*, Section 19.3.3.

12.3 OUTLIERS

Outliers can be a serious problem. Some clinical cases may be uncooperative, and the same holds with children and even with the white rat, which includes docility among its numerous experimental virtues. Outliers may also result from errors in recording and transcribing data. In any experiment, no matter how carefully done, some subjects or some scores may not belong to the population under study.

Ideally, outliers should be detected and eliminated. This is not easy. An extreme score may excite suspicion, but demonstrating that it is a genuine outlier depends jointly on substantive and statistical considerations that are typically uncertain.[a]

The term *outlier* is used here to denote a subject or score that does not belong to the population under study. An *extreme score*, in contrast, may belong to the population under study. This distinction is important because extreme scores, in contrast to outliers, should not generally be eliminated. Some writers, however, do not make a definite distinction.[b, c]

12.3.1 STATISTICAL OUTLIER THEORY

Statistical outlier techniques are not generally robust and so have limited usefulness. To appreciate this nonrobustness, consider a sample from a normal distribution that may be contaminated by at most one high outlier. The sampling distribution of the single highest score can be determined under the normality assumption. The upper tail of this sampling distribution is the criterial region. If the highest score lies in this region, it is treated as an outlier.

In this normal example, the test statistic is $(Y_{ex} - \bar{Y})/s$, where Y_{ex} is the highest score (Barnett & Lewis, 1994). If the population is indeed normal, the probability is .05 that the most extreme test score in a sample of size 15 will exceed 2.41. With $\alpha = .05$, accordingly, a score more extreme than 2.41 will be considered an outlier and rejected.

But this test seems very sensitive to nonnormality. If the population has a long upper tail, test scores greater than 2.41 will be substantially more frequent than .05. These cases will be wrongly rejected as outliers. This will wrongly decrease the error variance, thereby yielding too-short confidence intervals and too many statsig results.

Numerous other outlier rejection tests have been proposed, some that allow more than one possible outlier, some that allow specific nonnormal distributions. Nearly all rely on some assumption about the exact shape of the distribution; all these suffer the same problem of being sensitive to deviations from the assumed distribution.

This nonrobustness for outlier tests contrasts sharply with the robustness of regular Anova, which stems from the central limit theorem of Chapter 2. This theorem applies to the group means in regular Anova, but not to the single extreme scores in outlier analysis, even less to extreme cases in regression analysis (Note 9.1.4b).

Outlier techniques are thus more or less limited to situations in which extensive data are available to pin down the shape of the operative distribution. The classic example is astronomical observations, the cradle of outlier theory. A modern example is industrial quality control. But for most psychological applications, it seems fair to say that too little is known about distribution shape to allow much confidence in using statistical outlier rejection techniques.[a]

Outlier-type logic is sometimes used to establish a cutoff criterion. Thus, a cutoff may be set at, say, three standard deviations from the mean. Some such criterion may be reasonable, even when the distribution is not normal, but it suffers because the probability of so large a deviation is sensitive to sample size. Barnett and Lewis (1994, p. 223) comment that with a normal distribution, a value "three standard deviations above the mean is not significant (at 5%) in a sample of size 60, *is* significant (at 1%) in a sample of size 15, and can never occur in a sample of size 10. So much for the three standard deviations rule!"

12.3.2 PRACTICAL OUTLIER THEORY

Robust statistics is an effective alternative to outlier rejection. The ease with which elimination of extreme scores can be rationalized is a good reason against doing so. Instead of seeking to identify and eliminate outliers, choose a procedure that is relatively insensitive to them. This avoids the likely bias with outlier rejection techniques noted in the previous section.

The trimming procedure of Section 12.1 is thus recommended when outliers seem a threat. When outliers can be identified without error, they should of course be eliminated. Subject populations are seldom so well defined, however, that any one subject can assuredly be said to not belong. Trimming has the strong additional advantage that it can also reduce harmful effects of less extreme outliers that would elude the outlier rejection technique.

In experimental psychology, the main method for detecting outliers is empirical research judgment. Research judgment underlies the use of cutoff scores, as with reaction time measures. Research judgment appears when subjects are eliminated for "failure to understand instructions" and similar reasons. In these cases, of course, substantive information is available besides the extremeness of a score. Thus, a long reaction time may be considered an outlier not merely because it is extreme but also because attentional processes are expected to produce such scores.

Despite its high importance, methodology for extreme scores in psychological research is in a primitive state. Elimination of subjects seems often justifiable, but guidelines for doing so are generally casual or nonexistent. Systematic concern with this issue is desirable, beginning with surveys of articles that report subject elimination in various areas. Related discussion is given in Section 14.1.1, *Screening Subjects and Dropping Data.*[a]

12.4 TRANSFORMATIONS

Measurement is a transformation between two worlds: the real world of phenomena and a symbolic world of concepts and theory (see Section 1.1.3 on the Experimental Pyramid, page 4). This measurement transformation is empirical; it resides in the investigator's choices of task, procedure, and measurement device. These choices rest on substantive considerations of meaning and validity of the response measure. The information content of the data is mainly determined by these choices.

Also, of course, the information content of the data depends on statistical properties of the distribution of response. In particular, the width of a confidence interval depends heavily on the more extreme scores in the tails of the distribution. A small change in task–procedure sometimes has a big influence on the shape of the data. A learning task, for example, may be run a fixed number of trials or, alternatively, to some specified criterion of learning. The latter measure, being unbounded, could be risky with children or clinical groups, in which an occasional nonlearner may appear.

As a second example, judgments of magnitude or amount may be obtained with two methods: rating or magnitude estimation. Magnitude estimation, however, yields extreme scores as well as unequal variance across the response range. In general, effects of task–procedure on the shape of the data should be kept in mind when planning the experiment.

Even after the data have been collected, their shape may be changed with a purely statistical transformation. Worthwhile increases in effective information content can sometimes be obtained with little cost.

Statistical transformations are the main concern here. The discussion assumes independent groups, with a single score for each subject. Most of this, however, applies also to single subject studies, as with various reaction time tasks. The following sections consider the main transformation criteria, specific transformations, and pros and cons of using transformations.

12.4.1 CRITERIA FOR TRANSFORMATION

The main function of transformation is to decrease the effective variance, thus shortening confidence intervals and increasing power. Five common criteria for transformation are noted in the following subsections.

Extreme Scores. Extreme scores are usually undesirable, for substantive as well as statistical reasons. One substantive concern is that extreme scores may stem from extraneous processes. A long reaction time, for example, may arise from inattention, not from the process of interest. An extreme subject, similarly, may not belong to the population under study.

A more serious substantive concern is that an extreme score may stem from some shortcoming of procedure. The task may contain some ambiguity, for example, that trips up an occasional subject. Such problems can degrade the quality of the data and their information content.

The main line of protection against extreme scores is experimental task and experimental procedure. Task clarity deserves first consideration, including tasks for animals and young children. It is invaluable to develop an intuitive appreciation of how subjects view the task, especially by serving as a subject yourself. Other relevant considerations are mentioned in Section 8.2.4 on confounding, in Section 14.1.1 on eliminating subjects and data, and in Section 14.1.2 on writing instructions. Together, task, procedure, and measurement device constitute the empirical transformation that determines your data.

The statistical concern is that extreme scores increase variability and decrease power. Most of the specific transformations discussed below act to reduce influence of extreme scores.

Normality. Reducing nonnormality has been the most common transformation criterion in the statistical literature. Many tasks yield skewed distributions with a long tail. Transformations can pull in a long tail to get a more normal shape. Common examples are the reciprocal and log transformations given later.[a]

Equal Variance. Equalizing variance has also been studied as a criterion for transformation. In some tasks, the variance of the response varies directly with its numerical value. This pattern may be expected when higher levels of a stimulus variable have larger effects, as with stimulus intensity, work load, or in reaction time experiments. If the standard deviation is proportional to the mean, log-type transformation tends to equalize variance as well as improve normality.

Eliminating Interaction Residuals. A rather different transformation criterion is to reduce nonadditivity. This approach may decrease error terms that consist of interaction residuals, as with random factors, especially subject–treatment residuals in repeated measures design (Section 18.4.6).

Maximize F. A bulldozer approach to increasing power is to seek a transformation that maximizes F. This could be attempted, for example, by trial-and-error choice of the power exponent in the power transformation given below.

The danger is that maximizing F takes advantage of chance fluctuations in the data. The false alarm parameter may be inflated. This danger can be avoided by using preliminary data to develop a fixed transformation, perhaps with one free parameter, for standard use in subsequent work.

Response Linearity. One additional transformation criterion may be noted: To obtain a linear (equal interval) scale for the response measure. Linear scales are the primary focus of psychological measurement theory (Chapter 21) and a near-essential for testing mathematical models (Chapter 20).

Most theories of psychological measurement rely on choice data, and so require some statistical transformation to obtain linear response scales. However, empirical transformation to linearize the measured response is notably more effective (Section 21.6).

Multiple Criteria. A transformation that satisfies one criterion will also often satisfy others. This is by no means sure, however, and a gain on one may be overweighed by a loss on another.

An example appears with magnitude estimation, for which variability increases steadily for larger response. Hence a log-type transformation will act to equalize variances; normality will also be improved. At the same time, nonparallelism in a factorial experiment may be largely eliminated, as in Figure 21.8 of Note 21.2.2a. In this case, an empirical transformation was effective, namely, the rating response also shown in this figure. Actually, the main goal in this experiment was to obtain a linear scale of sensation, a goal supported by the successful parallelism of the integration model with the rating response.

12.4.2 STATISTICAL TRANSFORMATIONS

Most of the common transformations are summarized in the following subsections, except for rank transformation, which has been discussed in Section 12.2. Most of these transformations can be implemented with a single transform command to the computer. Accordingly, it is easy to try out various transformations to see how they work on a made-up set of likely data before finalizing your experimental design.[a]

Reciprocal Transformation. The reciprocal transformation replaces each score by its reciprocal. This pulls in a long right tail, making the data more normal. Studies that measure time, for example, often have long right tails. These long times have much less influence on the variance when the data are transformed to reciprocals.

The reciprocal time score is often meaningful as a speed. In some tasks, indeed, the speed measure seems closer to a true linear scale than the time measure. Frequency scores can analogously be transformed into rate scores. In this view, the reciprocal transformation is more empirical than statistical.

Log Transformation. With a long-tailed distribution, a transformation is sought that will pull in the tail scores more strongly the farther out they are. One of many that do this is the log transformation, for it equalizes the intervals between 1 and 10 and between 10 and 100. Such transformations have a double benefit, reducing undue influence of extreme scores at the same time as they increase normality. A log-type transformation will also equalize variance when treatments have multiplicative rather than additive effects.

Power Transformation. The pth power transformation is given by

$$Y' = Y^p, \tag{8}$$

where Y and Y' are the original and transformed scores. The power transformation is flexible and general; different values of the power exponent p yield a continuous family of transformations, of which three may be noted.

With $p = -1$, the foregoing reciprocal transformation is obtained. With $p = \frac{1}{2}$, a square root transformation is obtained, which is appropriate when Y is the frequency of some infrequent event. With p near 0, the power transformation has effects like a log transformation. Indeed, the limit of the power transformation as p approaches 0 is linearly equivalent to the log transformation.

The optimal value of p may need to be chosen by trial and error. Thus, normality could be increased by choosing p to minimize some index of skewness. Additivity could be increased by choosing p to minimize the interaction F.

Arc Sine Transformation. The arc sine transformation applies when the data come in the form of percentages or proportions. The transformation consists of replacing each proportion π by the angle whose sine is $\sqrt{\pi}$. Although this may seem odd, it follows from the criterion of equalizing the variance, $\pi(1 - \pi)$, for binomial proportions. No transformation is needed if most of the observed proportions lie between .25 and .75. A good discussion with a numerical example is given by Snedecor and Cochran (1980).[b]

Cutoff Transformations. A cutoff transformation eliminates scores below, or above, some cutoff criterion. Cutoffs are common with reaction time measures, which are generally agreed to suffer from outliers that arise from extraneous processes. Cutoffs are also used, in effect, when subjects are eliminated for unsatisfactory task performance, such as not learning in a learning task (see also Section 14.1.1).[c]

Trimming. Trimming may also be considered a transformation. Since trimming assumes symmetric distributions, it is a valuable supplement to the foregoing transformations, which mostly assume skewed distributions. Alternatively, it may be desirable to begin with a statistical transformation to get more symmetrical distributions, and then apply trimming. Trimming may thus supplement or even supersede the classical transformations considered above.

12.4.3 COMMENTS ON TRANSFORMATIONS

Choosing a Transformation. Decisions about transformation should be made before the data are collected. Enough prior information will usually be available to indicate whether the data will be skewed, say, or heavy tailed. This should suffice to indicate at least roughly the form of the desired transformation.

It seems advisable to sketch a graph of how you expect the data distribution to look while still in the planning stage. This graph may be supplemented by trying out various transformations on a made-up set of likely data.

Some transformations contain a transformation parameter, such as the exponent p of the power transformation, and it is common practice to estimate this parameter from the data at hand. The sources I have consulted seem unconcerned that this increases the effective α; presumably this increase is small with a single parameter and not-too-small n. It may be preferable, however, to use existing data to fix an a priori value for the transformation parameter.

Comparing Transformed and Untransformed Data. How can one determine how much a transformation has helped? Confidence intervals cannot be compared directly between the transformed and untransformed data, except for trimming. A log transformation, for example, will make the standard deviation much smaller, but it will also make the mean effect much smaller.

This question can be answered with the F ratio; the transformation that yields the larger F has greater power. Different transformations on the same data may thus be compared directly. Any one data sample, of course, may be misleading in this respect.

To get an intuitive feeling for what transformations do, try out several on some convenient data of your own. It is easy to compare several pth power transformations, for example, because each one requires only a single transform command. Of course, a histogram or box plot of transformed data for each group should be secured and appreciated.

How Transformations Work. An effective transformation is one that increases the power index ϕ in Equation 4.5, as emphasized by Levine and Dunlap (1982, 1983). Ostensibly, most transformations aim at some different goal, to get more normal data, for example, or to equalize variance. These goals are mainly means to the end of increasing ϕ.[a]

12.4.4 PROS AND CONS OF TRANSFORMATIONS

Statistical transformation can be invaluable in certain situations. Except for trimming, however, statistical transformation does not seem a general purpose tool. The two following subsections list some pros and cons.

When Not To Transform. As a working suggestion, statistical transformations other than trimming should be used conservatively. One concern is that the original response scale sometimes has a natural meaning whereas the transformed scale may be hard to understand. A graph showing proportions is generally meaningful, for example, but not a graph showing arc sine transformed proportions.

Some writers express concern because transformations change interactions in factorial design (see the time–speed example in Table 7.1, page 193). This concern, however, seems to stem from reification of interaction residuals, not realizing that they may be illusions of a nonlinear response scale or artifacts of the additive Anova model (Chapter 7). Indeed, a transformation that reduces interaction can be beneficial by increasing power on main effects.

In some cases, of course, interactions have conceptual significance so transformation is undesirable. Some models of cognitive algebra (Chapter 21) predict deviations from additivity that ought not be transformed away. Thus, the linear fan pattern of Figure 21.7 reveals that subjects follow the multiplication rule, Expectancy × Value, but this linear fan would be destroyed by using any of the standard transformations.

With mathematical models of reaction time, similarly, time is the natural response metric and transformation could misrepresent the pattern of response. Ulrich and Miller (1994) showed that the common cutoff transformation distorted patterns of linearity and additivity predicted from theoretical models of reaction time (Note 12.4.2c). The same would apply with Sternberg's additive-factor analysis of reaction times (Section 11.4.4).

When To Transform. Statistical transformations may be routine in some situations, especially with long-tailed distributions. Examples include the common use of speed instead of time scores, and rates or proportions instead of frequencies. Speed and rate are directly meaningful, of course, and may be considered more empirical than statistical transformations.

Statistical transformation should be seriously considered when data are expensive or scarce. Any modest increase in power can be worth a lot, especially in a continuing research program. Developing a standard transformation in initial work would seem close to obligatory for getting shortest confidence intervals in later work.

Simulation studies of transformation need situation-specific application. Simulation assesses statistical properties of the transformation by random sampling of numerous hypothetical data sets under various assumptions about the shape of the response distribution, likely frequency of outliers, and so forth. Classical statistics of transformations has concentrated on closed mathematical expressions, as with the foregoing power transformation. As a consequence, this classical approach is somewhat limited for practical applications.

The benefit of—and need for—simulation appears in a detailed study of reaction times by Ratcliff (1993), who considered a good dozen transformations. Each transformation was applied to data generated from various distribution shapes, including outliers, thereby allowing comparison of power. Ratcliff's results indicate that the common practice of using a fixed cutoff to eliminate long reaction times may be acceptable but is not optimal. Interestingly, the reciprocal transformation was close to optimal across a range of conditions.

Finally, the primacy of empirical over statistical transformation may be emphasized once again. All measurement is a transformation; the meaning and content of this transformation are primarily determined by the investigator's choices of task and procedure. These choices also affect the shape of the data and the amount of information it conveys, especially the width of confidence intervals. The most effective statistical analysis is founded on extrastatistical choices of task and procedure.

12.5 ANOVA WITH UNEQUAL VARIANCE

The following discussion suggests that, with more than two conditions, unequal variance should usually be handled by focusing on two-mean comparisons instead of overall Anova. One reason is that the main problem with unequal variance comes in attempts to localize effects.

This point may need emphasis because standard discussions of unequal variance have focused on overall Anova. The usual finding that overall Anova is reasonably robust may not be particularly relevant because the overall Anova does not localize effects. Localization requires follow-up analyses, but these are often invalid if the overall error term is used.

This danger with follow-up analysis was seen in the discussion of Table 4.1; the error term from the overall Anova was seriously incorrect for some of the two-mean comparisons. Confidence intervals suffer in the same way. For Table 4.1, standard deviations for the three mean differences, $(\bar{Y}_4 - \bar{Y}_3)$, $(\bar{Y}_4 - \bar{Y}_2)$, and $(\bar{Y}_2 - \bar{Y}_1)$, differ in length in the ratio $\sqrt{3} : \sqrt{2} : 1$. An error bar or confidence interval for any one mean may thus be more or less misleading for comparing it with another mean.

Visual inspection suffers similarly. With equal variance, it often suffices to begin with an overall Anova and complete the analysis with visual inspection, supplemented with one representative confidence interval. With unequal variance, however, visual inspection tends to mislead from assuming that each mean is equally variable.

The first following section addresses some practical considerations that are generally applicable when unequal variance may be a concern. The second section gives formulas for two-mean comparisons with independent scores.

12.5.1 ANTICIPATING UNEQUAL VARIANCE

Unequal variance should be anticipated when planning the experiment. The first line of protection is to minimize unequal variance through experimental procedure. The second line of protection is to plan the analysis before collecting the data. When unequal variance can be anticipated, adverse effects can often be ameliorated by planning appropriate data analysis.

Planned Comparisons. From a statistical perspective, planning can help deal with two threats from unequal variance: α escalation and low power.

The problem of α escalation arises from attempts to localize effects by using two-mean comparisons. This may require α splitting or some other multiple comparisons procedure (Chapter 17), which decreases the two-mean α level at a cost of power. There is considerable agreement, however, that α adjustment is not necessary if the comparisons have been planned beforehand on reasonably firm ground (Section 4.2.2).

Lower power arises in two ways. First, each two-mean comparison will usually require its own error term, based on the data of just the two conditions being compared, which has fewer df than the overall error. Second, these df must be further reduced to allow for unequal variance. What might seem adequate sample size with equal variance may thus be inadequate with unequal variance.

Experimental and Observational Variables. With random assignment, as noted previously, unequal variance can arise only if the experimental treatments have different effects. As a rule, treatments have their primary effect on means, with relatively smaller effects on variances. If the variance differences are large enough to be of concern, the mean differences will usually be large, perhaps not even in need of a formal test.

Of course, exceptions do occur. Aversive stimuli may elicit opposite reactions, such as fleeing or freezing, in different individuals. Opposite reactions can increase the variance while balancing out in the mean. Again, a control group with no treatment effect may be considerably less variable than any of several experimental groups. As a third example, floor–ceiling effects may entail lower variance for conditions near the floor or ceiling.

Observational variables, not under experimental control, are more problematic. Different age groups of children may show large differences in variability on language measures, for example, and the same holds for different categories of language disorder. The main concern in such situations is often to get good estimates of the magnitude of the variable, represented by the confidence interval around each group mean. When variability differs across groups, correct confidence intervals must be based on the separate variability within each group.

Significance testing is often irrelevant with observational variables. Often the response measures some phenomenon of intrinsic interest, as with vocabulary size, in contrast to experimental data that measure the effect of some controlled manipulation. Measurement of the observational phenomenon, in terms of the center and width of a confidence interval, thus has primary concern. A significance test may obscure the main point.

Problems can arise when an observational variable and an experimental variable are combined in a two-way design. MS_{error} from the two-way Anova may then be seriously misleading if used in confidence intervals. Trimmed Anova deserves consideration in such cases, as it tends to equalize variances.

Most discussions of unequal variance express generalized concern without regard to this experimental–observational distinction. Some present examples of extremely unequal variance from observational data as though these were typical. Such discussions have little relevance to experimental studies.

Assessing Unequal Variance. To judge whether unequal variance is large enough to worry about is usually difficult. Visual comparison of variability between groups is not too helpful because the sample variance is rather variable. With equal true variance, sample variances can readily differ by 2 to 1. Standard statistical tests for unequal variance are not much help. One shortcoming is their lack of robustness against nonnormality.

A more serious shortcoming is that statistical tests for unequal variance answer the wrong question, namely, whether the differences are statsig. The right question is how large the differences are; and whether this is large enough to worry about. A *no* answer to the statsig question is less than helpful when the test has low power, as is perhaps common with usual group sizes. A *yes* answer does not tell whether the difference is large enough to worry about.

In my view, accordingly, diagnosing unequal variance in typical psychological investigations must rest mainly on empirical knowledge. Empirical knowledge can, I believe, be a fairly good guide in many situations. This guide, however, deserves continual development, through reporting and collating data on variability.

12.5.2 ANALYSIS WITH UNEQUAL VARIANCE

Confidence Intervals for Two-Mean Comparisons. Confidence intervals for a difference between two means that have unequal variance may be obtained in the usual way, except that a df adjustment is necessary. With independent scores, the variance is additive:

$$\sigma^2_{(\bar{Y}_1 - \bar{Y}_2)} = \sigma^2_{\bar{Y}_1} + \sigma^2_{\bar{Y}_2}.$$

Since $\sigma^2_{\bar{Y}} = \sigma^2_Y / n$, the standard deviation of the mean difference is

$$\text{standard deviation}\,(\bar{Y}_1 - \bar{Y}_2) = \sqrt{[\hat{\sigma}^2_{Y_1} / n_1 + \hat{\sigma}^2_{Y_2} / n_2]}, \tag{9}$$

where each $\hat{\sigma}^2$ equals MS_{error} from the data of the corresponding group. This standard deviation is the error half-bar for $(\bar{Y}_1 - \bar{Y}_2)$.[a]

To get a proper confidence interval, we need the value of the criterial t^*, which depends on the df. The df are not $(n_1 - 1) + (n_2 - 1)$, as would be the case with equal variance. To appreciate why, consider the extreme case of zero variance for Y_2. Then the variance of the difference equals the variance of $\bar{Y}_1$, and so has only $n_1 - 1$ df. Adding more observations of Y_2 increases n_2 but adds no information; it does not increase the number of information units, that is, the df. Something similar happens whenever one group has smaller variance. Each observation from the group with the larger variance provides 1 df, in effect, whereas each observation from the group with the smaller variance provides only a fractional df.

For the special case of two groups with equal n, a formula for effective df proposed by Brown and Forsythe simplifies to

$$df = (n - 1) \frac{[s_1^2 + s_2^2]^2}{s_1^4 + s_2^4}, \tag{10}$$

where s_1^2 and s_2^2 are MS_{error} for the two separate groups. This df decreases from $2(n - 1)$ for equal variance to $(n - 1)$ as the variances become more unequal.

Equal n seems usually desirable, one reason being greater robustness. It may seem attractive, when unequal variance is expected, to assign larger n to the condition with the larger variance. This does decrease the error term of Equation 9, but only mildly for a variance ratio as large as 3 to 1. If much greater variance ratios are expected, unequal n may perhaps be worth considering, at least with larger N.[b]

Overall Anova for More Than Two Groups. The Brown–Forsythe and Welch tests are widely recommended as extensions of overall Anova to handle unequal variance with more than two groups. With normal distributions, they keep α under better control and provide more power than regular F.

Nonnormal distributions, however, undercut both tests. Simulations with the normal and four nonnormal symmetric distributions by Lee and Fung (1983) concluded that the Brown–Forsythe and Welch tests "perform poorly except under normality. Under long-tailed [= heavy-tailed symmetric] distributions, they are conservative and have very low power" (p. 137).[c]

Accordingly, neither test may be generally useful. This conclusion rests in part on the expectation that unequal variance will usually be accompanied by nonnormality.

Trimming. Trimming may have as much potential, perhaps more, with unequal variance as with equal variance. By decreasing the influence of the tail scores, the trimmed variances may be expected to be more equal.

Trimmed versions of the Brown–Forsythe and Welch tests, both available in BMDP, may deserve consideration, as they seemed to perform fairly well in the cited study. As already suggested, however, two-mean comparisons may be generally preferable to overall Anova between all the means.

Repeated Measures. With repeated measures, two-mean comparisons with unequal variance are handled straightforwardly. Because of likely nonsphericity, each two-mean comparison ordinarily requires its own error term. Each such comparison is equivalent to a test of the corresponding difference score, which automatically takes account of unequal variance.

NOTES

12.1.1a. The integer adjustment is not necessary but simplifies the exposition.

12.1.1b. For the curious, this procedure of replacing the trimmed scores by copies is called Winsorizing, after the statistician Charles Winsor; this is why the subscript W is used. Winsorized Anova, using the Winsorized mean in place of the trimmed mean, seems less desirable than trimmed Anova (Barnett & Lewis, 1994, pp. 79-81).

12.1.1c. The hand formula of Equation 2b is convenient for hand calculation. Conceptually, however, SSs are better understood as squared deviations, as in Equations 3.3 and 3.4a. In deviation form,

$$SS_{Wj} = (k+1)(Y_{k+1} - \bar{Y}_{Wj})^2 + (Y_{k+2} - \bar{Y}_{Wj})^2 + \ldots$$
$$+ (Y_{n-k-1} - \bar{Y}_{Wj})^2 + (k+1)(Y_{n-k} - \bar{Y}_{Wj})^2.$$

12.1.1d. If trimming actually threw out the trimmed data, as some have said, it would seem pretty dubious. These scores are not thrown out, however, but taken into account in calculating the variance. The conceptualization of the mean as an interval of likely error thus harmonizes with trimming procedure.

Other robust techniques seek to do better by giving lowered weight to more extreme scores in calculating the sample mean. Special computer programs are required, but these may be worth looking into if data are expensive.

12.1.2a. Simulation studies, especially by Karen Yuen Fung, are the main practical basis for the utility of trimming. Simulation can only assess a few of the many possible distributions, of course, so users may need to conduct their own simulations using distributions they actually encounter. This caution applies especially with asymmetrical distributions, for which limited results are available.

12.2.1a. Edgington's (1987) treatment of randomization theory considers only significance tests, not confidence intervals or power calculations.

12.2.1b. Randomization as a rational, empirical base for statistical inference has been systematically developed by Kempthorne (see 1977 and references therein). Randomization tests, unlike rank tests, do not sacrifice all metric information in the data.

12.2.2a. The equivalence of rank Anova, Kruskal–Wallis H test, Mann–Whitney U test, and Wilcoxon rank-sum test is a consequence of the monotone relation between their respective test statistics. In principle, therefore, an exact criterial value can be determined for each test, and the reject–do not reject decisions will be identical for each test (Conover, 1999).

In practice, the formula for the distribution of each of these rank test statistics is only an approximation to its true distribution. In practice, therefore, the α levels are more or less in error. Conover and Iman (1981) and Conover (1999) cite simulation studies and claim that rank Anova usually does best. A marginally statsig F_{ranks} may better be discounted, however, unless perhaps the other rank tests give similar results.

12.2.2b. The rank transform procedure was suggested by Conover and Iman (1981) for factorial as well as one-way design, but this is clearly inappropriate. Being nonlinear, rank transformation will generally make additive data nonadditive. If the original data show zero interaction, therefore, the transformed data will generally show nonzero interaction. Transformation to remove interactions is often desirable, but not the reverse.

The rank transform method for factorial design has been strongly criticized on grounds of statistical theory as well as extensive simulations because it does not keep false alarms under control for interactions (e.g., Akritas, 1990; McKean & Vidmar, 1994; Sawilowsky, Blair, & Higgins, 1989; Thompson, 1991). This work seems a labored way to arrive at an obvious consequence of nonlinearity of the rank transform.

12.2.3a. I suspect that trimming will be generally superior to rank tests. The main trouble usually comes from extreme scores whereas the central region of the data contains useful metric information that ranking throws away. Trimming protects against extreme scores while utilizing the metric information in the central region. Rank tests protect against extreme scores by abandoning the metric information in the central region.

Trimming has the collateral advantage that it encourages development of ways to reduce the likelihood of extreme scores through empirical improvements in measurement methods, thereby increasing the information content of the data. Rank tests, in contrast, are oblivious to extreme scores and to the problem of measurement. Simulation studies to compare trimming and rank tests are highly desirable. As yet, however, I have not located any.

12.2.3b. An eloquent, refreshing approach to distribution-free statistics is given by Cliff (1996), who stresses the importance of confidence intervals and, more generally, descriptive statistics, over significance tests. Cliff's book thus differs markedly from other books on distribution-free statistics, which largely seek to mimic classical statistics based on normal theory and are mainly concerned with significance tests. Cliff's book deserves consideration by anyone interested in the distribution-free approach.

I feel, however, that Cliff's approach suffers the same limitations cited in the text and in the previous note: lack of versatility; loss of metric information from the use of ranks; and nonconcern with improving methods of measurement.

12.3a. Legal questions of illegitimate birth are used to illustrate outlier theory by Barnett and Lewis (1984, pp. 2*f*). In the case of *Hadlum* v. *Hadlum* in 1949, Mr. Hadlum claimed adultery by Mrs. Hadlum on the ground that she had given birth 349 days after he had left England to serve his King and country. The average human gestation period is about 280 days, compared to which 349 days does seem extreme. The judges, however, ruled that it was not scientifically impossible. Two years later, the House of Lords set 'the limit' at 360 days.

Barnett and Lewis gave me the impression that the judges, and the House of Lords as well, needed education in statistical outlier theory. I changed my mind after chancing to learn of birth weights of 22 lb 8 oz for one boy in Italy and one in South Africa (*Guiness Book of World Records*, 1990), to be compared with a (U.S.) mean and standard deviation of 7.1 and 1.1 lb. Birth weights of these two boys were thus an astonishing 14 standard deviations distant from the mean. Although statistical outlier theory might say these two birth weights are impossible, common sense concurs with the conclusion of Section 12.3.1 that seldom is enough known about shapes of empirical distributions, most especially in the tails, to warrant use of outlier rejection techniques.

12.3b. Barnett and Lewis (1984, Section 2.3; see similarly 1994) consider outliers to arise from contamination: "We shall consider in some detail different forms of contamination model, or *outlier generating model*, which have been proposed and studied" (p. 35). Under this definition, also used here, an outlier is not a proper member of the population. They also use a different definition, however, saying "We shall define an outlier in a set of data to be *An observation (or subset of observations) which appears to be inconsistent with the remainder of that set of data*" (p. 4). This latter definition conflates a symptom with the disease. This apparent inconsistency reflects the uncertainty and ambiguity in the concept of outlier, amply discussed by Barnett and Lewis.

12.3c. Trimming is sometimes considered an outlier technique, although it is essentially different. Trimming does not identify and eliminate outliers, that is, scores that do not belong. Instead, it reduces the influence of tail scores, regardless of whether they are outliers. Trimming is thus appropriate with extreme scores that are not outliers, and with difficultly detectable outliers mentioned in the following note.

12.3.1a. A second difficulty facing outlier theory is that harmful outliers may be almost undetectable. This gloomy conclusion was reached by Tukey (1960), who studied effects of a low probability "contaminant" that had the same mean but higher variance than the primary normal distribution. Even with a probability as low as .01, the contaminant can markedly increase the expected variance for small samples, thereby decreasing power. Even in large samples, however, the contamination is masked by the tail variability of the primary distribution.

Tukey's analysis, however, has limited relevance. It assumes that contaminants have the same mean as the primary distribution. Typically, perhaps, outliers come from populations with markedly different means, which markedly increases their detectability.

12.3.2a. Outliers in the form of errors should be anticipated whenever data are generated or recorded by subjects, as with questionnaires, or by clerical personnel, as with hospital files, public records, and other archival data. Not infrequently, these outliers are gross errors that can be spotted by common sense (e.g., Note 9.1.4b).

12.4.1a. A major locus of nonnormality is extreme scores, which have three major sources: Ambiguities in task–procedure, such as inadequate control of attention or unclear instructions; heterogeneity of subject population; and the nature of the task, as with long-tailed distributions of time scores. All three can often be ameliorated with care in developing task–procedure.

12.4.2a. Classical transformations are presented clearly by Snedecor and Cochran (1980, Chapter 15), together with numerical examples. Of special interest is their citation of a study on how to select a transformation that satisfies multiple criteria. Emerson (1991a,b) and Emerson and Stoto (1983) give useful treatments.

12.4.2b. The arc sine test was employed in the article considered in Exercise 10.6, not the chi-square test that is asked for. Both tests yielded very similar results, of course, as noted in the Instructor's Manual.

12.4.2c. The usefulness of cutoff transformations to prevent power loss from reaction time outliers was verified both by Ratcliff (1993) and by Ulrich and Miller (1994, pp. 64f). Both articles also agree firmly on the need for detailed, explicit reporting on how outliers are handled. Cutoffs may thus be useful for comparing effects of different experimental treatments. But since the cutoff is a nonlinear transformation, it can distort the shape of the data, thereby distorting tests of mathematical models that predict the shape of the data, as Ulrich and Miller demonstrate.

12.4.3a. That transformation to remove skewness or unequal variance does not, of itself, have much effect on power was shown by Budescu and Appelbaum (1981) and other studies cited by Games (1983). These studies, however, held constant the standardized power effect size ϕ, also called the noncentrality parameter, in the power formula of Equation 4.5. Holding ϕ constant is necessary, of course, to test the effect of skewness or unequal variance per se. In most of these cases, it appeared that "the transformation does not systematically improve the operational power of the F test" (Budescu & Appelbaum, p. 70), a conclusion reasserted by Games. This result is interesting because standard transformations ostensibly aim to reduce nonnormality and/or unequal variance.

So why do applied statisticians recommend transformation? The answer is that in practice transformations act to increase ϕ, the standardized power effect size. This conclusion was demonstrated by Levine and Dunlap (1982, 1983), although for a rather narrow, special case.

An extension by Rasmussen (1989) reported good increases in power, together with negligible inflation of α, using the power transformation with p estimated from the data. The nonnormal data were all power transformations of normal data, however, which limits the generality of the results.

Rasmussen also claimed that transformation did not inflate α even with very small samples. This is hard to believe. Unfortunately, Rasmussen's article presents averages over sample size. He does cite a "packet of 20 tables available from the author" (p. 208) for separate sample sizes, but I have been quite unable to obtain these tables.

12.5.2a. The problem of two means with unequal variance has theoretical interest because it can be attacked in three very different ways, using the three theoretical frameworks of Section 19.1 (Kendall & Stuart, 1979). This problem is also salutary as a demonstration of the virtues and limits of the simple formulas with equal variance.

12.5.2b. Minimal variance for a difference score between two means with unequal variance is obtained by assigning cases to the two conditions in the ratio

$$n/N = (\sqrt{k} - 1)/(k - 1),$$

where k is the ratio of the larger to the smaller variance, n is the number of cases in the condition with the smaller variance, and N is the total number of cases for both conditions. This result may be derived by differentiating $[\sigma^2/n + k\sigma^2/(N - n)]$ with respect to n and solving the resulting quadratic. Note that a df adjustment would also be needed.

12.5.2c. The relative merits of the Brown–Forsythe and Welch tests have been assessed in simulation studies (see summaries in Maxwell & Delaney, 1990, pp. 697*ff*, and in Myers & Well, 1991, pp. 106*ff*). These studies, however, seem mostly irrelevant because they used normal distributions, which seem unlikely with substantially unequal variance.

The Welch test did poorly with the skewed distributions used by Clinch and Keselman (1982), although the Brown–Forsythe test was satisfactory. Moreover, contrary to Levy's (1978) statement that the Welch test is robust against non-normality, his Table III showed overly high levels of α for a uniform and two long-tailed distributions, in some cases even with equal n. These results agree with the more extensive work of Lee and Fung (1983) cited in the text.

Empirical utility of the simulation literature is severely limited by the predilection for extreme cases of little practical relevance. The cited simulations have used extremely unequal variance, such as 6:2:1 and 50:10:1 for three groups and 9:4:4:1 and 27:9:3:1 for four groups. Such extremely unequal variances are rarely seen in experimental analysis. Usually, moreover, the group ns are very unequal, also rare in practice. Future simulation studies would be more useful if realistic cases were considered.

EXERCISES FOR CHAPTER 12

a. Trimming

a1. Consider the numerical example of trimming in Table 12.1.

    a. By visual inspection, show that A_1 and A_2 have equal trimmed variance.

    b. By visual inspection, how will the trimmed mean for A_2 change if the 24 is changed to 24,000,000?

    c. By visual inspection, how will the width of the confidence interval for the trimmed mean for A_2 change if the 24 is changed to 24,000,000?

    d. Use the calculations given in the table to show that the standard deviation of a trimmed mean is 1.14.

a2. In Table 12.1, suppose three scores were trimmed in each tail.

    a. In the trimmed Anova, which calculations would remain the same? Does this hold in general, or is it peculiar to these samples?

    b. What calculations would change?

a3. The following scores represent number of successful responses in 30 trials on verbal concepts by two groups of 7 dyslexic children, obtained by Q in her thesis research.

0	0	11	12	13	14	15	16
4	5	6	7	8	9	10	11

    a. Get F for the untrimmed data.

    b. Trim two scores in each tail and show that $F = 10.71$.

    c. Get the 95% confidence interval for the mean trimmed difference.

    d. What major empirical questions are raised by the two scores of 0?

a4. Q was uncertain about what trimming proportion to use. So she tried all three of .10, .20, and .30. All three yielded a barely statsig F.

    a. What should Q do?

    b. What should be Q's main concern in planning any replication?

a5. Draw a graph of a two-humped symmetrical distribution to show why the trimmed and untrimmed means have equal expected value.

b. Rank Tests.

b1. Two teaching techniques for parents of autistic children are compared in the graph of Exercise 3 of Chapter 3. Get ranks for the two groups from this graph and do rank Anova.

b2. The report claiming success of controlled drinking in Section 8.1.6 said that subjects had been assigned at random to the experimental and control groups. These subjects were recruited over a 10-month period as they entered the hospital. Here is the list of subjects in order of admission, (e and c denote experimental and control):

c e e e e c e e e e c e e e e c e e e e c c e e e e c c c e c c c c c c e c c c c .

a. By visual inspection, do you notice any apparent nonrandomness?

b. What null hypothesis will be tested by rank Anova? How exactly can the test of this null hypothesis assess departures from randomness?

c. Show that $F_{ranks} = 13.44$ on 1/38 df.

d. In light of given information, list one concrete reason why lack of random assignment might bias the results.

e. How would you have handled the random assignment?

b3. *Ranks for tied scores.* Tied scores are assigned the mean of their ranks. First rank all scores from 1 to N; for tied scores assign successive ranks. Then replace these ranks for each group of tied scores by the mean of their ranks. If two tied scores receive ranks 2 and 3 in the first step, assign both a rank of 2.5. If three tied scores receive ranks of 7, 8, and 9 in the first step, assign all three a rank of 8. **Check** that the sum of the final ranks equals $N \times (N + 1)/2$.
The following data illustrate this technique for handling ties.
(**Note:** The N is far too small to justify a rank Anova in practice.)

A_1: 6 9 9 7;
A_2: 4 7 6 4;
A_3: 2 4 3 3.

a. Show mean ranks are 10, 6.75, and 2.75 for the three respective groups.

b. Show that $F_{ranks} = 14.17$.

c. Outliers.

c1. P and Q were now living together, which caused them to think about family dynamics. Seeking experimental tasks to study these phenomena, they decided to compare two praise techniques that one marital partner could use to decrease duration of quarrels. Their pilot work showed one extreme duration, and they wondered how to handle such extreme scores in their main experiment. Q argued that these extreme scores were outliers and that they should use a screening measure to eliminate couples with distressed marriages. P argued that they should use trimming.

a. Discuss justification of each design alternative.

b. What procedure, not necessarily either of these, would you argue for?

c2. You have 10 difference scores and wish to test the null hypothesis that the true mean is zero. Here are the scores:

−2, −1, 1, 1, 2, 2, 3, 3, 4, 5.

a. Run regular Anova to test H_0: $\mu = 0$.

b. Show by trial and error that increasing the highest score, 5, to some larger number will (i) increase the size of the effect and (ii) lose the statsig F found in (a).

c. Discuss two implications of your demonstration.

d. Transformations.

d1. Consider the following data for two groups:

A_1: {1.67, 2.00, 2.50}; A_2: {3.33, 5.00, 10.00}.

a. Show that $F_A = 4.03$.

b. Apply a reciprocal transformation; find F_A. Comment.

d2. Consider the data of Table 7.1.

a. In light of Table 7.2 and Exercise 7.2, why might Q expect more power on main effects than P?

b. In light of his theoretical interpretation, why might P argue that his measurement scale is preferable even if it has less power?

d3. This and the two following exercises aim to help you develop foresight about what shape distribution to expect in your data. Draw a graph showing what shape of distribution you would expect in the following situations.

a. Random samples of one digit between 0 and 9, inclusive.

b. Random samples of size 5 from the 10 digits, 0 to 9, and take the mean.

c. Random samples of size 3 from the 10 digits, and take the largest.

d4. Sketch the shape of the distribution you expect for:

a. A final exam in second undergraduate course in research methods.

b. Number of trials to learn a 12-item, English–Spanish paired associates list by undergraduates with no Spanish background.

c. Running times for hungry rats learning a T-maze for food reward.

d. Reaction time in a "vigilance task," in which subjects monitor for very infrequent danger signals over extended periods of time.

e. Age of woman at her first marriage.

d5. Many distributions do not follow the bell-shaped normal curve. Draw a rough curve—well labeled—for a nonnormal distribution, together with your rationale, for some quantity from each of the following:

    a. Everyday life.

    b. Psychological research.

    c. Biology.

    d. Astronomy.

d6. Nonpositive numbers cause a problem for some transformations. A square root transformation, for example, is not meaningful with negative scores. Similarly, the log of 0 is $-\infty$, not a score anyone wishes to encounter in their data. Suppose you see that a transformation would be helpful but you have a few forbidden nonpositive scores. How can you apply a preliminary linear transformation to eliminate them?

e. Unequal Variance.

e1. In the third paragraph of Section 12.5, verify that the three standard devations stand in the ratio $\sqrt{3} : \sqrt{2} : 1$.

e2. In Equation 10 for effective df with unequal variance, suppose $n_1 = n_2 = n$.

    a. What do you think the df ought to be if $\sigma_1 = \sigma_2$? Verify your answer.

    b. Suppose $\sigma_1 \to \infty$. What will happen to df$'$. Give your intuitive rationale.

PREFACE

Analysis of covariance (Ancova) can reduce variability due to individual differences, thereby yielding narrower confidence intervals and greater power. Prime opportunities arise with experiments that compare effectiveness of methods to produce some change: change in health, behavior, attitude, or skill. The change score, after − before, may seem the natural measure; this change score seems to adjust for individual differences in the before score. But change scores turn out to be full of pitfalls. Ancova not only avoids these pitfalls, but gives a superior analysis.

Furthermore, Ancova is more general than the change score. Ancova can utilize any correlate of the main response measure, even correlates on a different dimension for which a change score makes no sense.

Ancova rests on a simple idea: Combine Anova and regression. Let X denote an individual difference variable and Y the response measure. Run a regression of Y on X and get Y_{pred} as shown in Chapter 9. Since Y_{pred} is predictable error variability, $(Y - Y_{pred})$ is less variable than Y alone, for it subtracts out that part of Y that is predictable from X. Take advantage of this lesser variability by (in effect) applying Anova to $(Y - Y_{pred})$.

This chapter aims at a conceptual understanding of Ancova. Formulas and calculations, accordingly, are largely passed over in order to discuss empirical issues. With randomized subject groups, Ancova has considerable potential that seems to have been relatively neglected. If you can find an individual difference variable that is correlated with your response measure, you can decrease your response variability and increase your power, often at little cost.

With nonrandom subject groups, matters are very different. Nonrandom groups differ systematically on individual difference variables before the experiment begins. These systematic differences are confounded with experimental treatments. Many writers assert that Ancova "controls" or "partials out" these individual differences, thereby removing otherwise deadly confounds. Such assertions have little truth. The second part of this chapter shows why Ancova generally fails to "control" with nonrandom groups.

Chapter 13

ANALYSIS OF COVARIANCE

Measuring relevant variables for each subject before beginning an experiment can have a double benefit. One benefit is statistical: lower error variability. The other benefit is substantive: information on how the experimental effect depends on individual differences.

Consider effectiveness of different maintenance schedules on health of premature infants. We would surely measure each infant's weight at the start of the experiment. In fact, *change* in weight is an obvious response measure. Intuitively, the change score seems to "correct" for the initial differences in weight for different infants. But change scores are unexpectedly treacherous. Change scores should usually be avoided in favor of analysis of covariance, which extracts the help and avoids the harm.

Analysis of covariance (*Ancova*) rests on a simple idea. In the experiment on infant health, much of the final weight would be predictable from the initial weight. This predictable component consists of individual differences that would go into the error term in an ordinary Anova or confidence interval. But this predictable component of individual differences can be removed with regression analysis. Removing this predictable component of individual differences reduces the variability of the response, yielding tighter confidence intervals. Ancova rests on this happy marriage of Anova and regression.

Other variables could also be measured for each infant, such as birth age, a nurse's judgment of prognosis, as well as mother's health and health practices. To the extent that any such *covariate* correlates with infant weight gain, it also can be used to reduce error variability. The change score idea is not applicable to these other covariates, of course, but Ancova is.

Ancova has been applied in two very different cases. Of primary concern here is the case of random assignment to experimental treatments, discussed in the first half of this chapter. By virtue of random assignment, otherwise uncontrolled subject variables, such as those just listed, can benefit the analysis.

To be worthwhile, Ancova requires covariates that correlate perhaps .40, if not more, with the primary response measure. Even with a correlation of .40, the covariate accounts only for 16% of the variance. Such covariates are sometimes found in randomized experiments with cases of language deficit, psychophysiological studies of emotion, social attitudes, health, education, and so forth. If you can find such a covariate, you may get substantial increases in power at little cost, together with information on individual differences. This benefit can be worth a lot when subjects are scarce or expensive. In randomized experiments, Ancova deserves more consideration than it seems to have received.

Ancova is sometimes applied in nonrandomized experiments, in which treatment groups differ preexperimentally. In the example of premature infants, the same maintenance schedule may be used for all cases in the hospital. The needed comparison group may be cases in a preceding time period. But this comparison has numerous confoundings—changes in the population of hospital users, changes in nurses and ward routine, in transient diseases, and so on. Such counfounded comparisons are tenuous. Contrary to popular misconception, Ancova cannot generally "control for," "partial out," or "hold constant" such preexperimental differences.

13.1 COVARIANCE WITH RANDOM GROUPS

The following discussion considers experiments in which subjects are assigned randomly to treatment conditions, and some covariate X is measured as well as the response measure Y.

13.1.1 ANCOVA MODEL AND ANALYSIS

The idea of covariance is simple. The original response Y is adjusted by subtracting that part of Y that is predictable from a linear regression on X. Graphically, Y_{adjusted} is the deviation of Y from the regression line. In effect, an Anova is done on Y_{adjusted}. To the extent that Y is predictable, Y_{adjusted} is less variable than Y, giving more power and shorter confidence intervals.[a]

Ancova Model. Let A_j denote the levels of a variable that is manipulated experimentally, just as in Chapter 3. Let X_{ij} denote the covariate for subject i in condition A_j and let Y_{ij} be the subject's response. If the covariate was ignored, the Anova model for this one-way design would be given by Equation 1b of Chapter 3 (with $\bar{\mu}$ omitted for simplicity):

$$Y_{ij} = \alpha_j + \varepsilon_{ij}. \qquad \text{(Anova model)} \qquad (1)$$

To this, the Ancova model adds a linear regression term representing that part of Y predictable from X, namely, $\beta_1(X_{ij} - \bar{X}_{..})$. The term $(X_{ij} - \bar{X}_{..})$ is the covariate in deviation score form; it is analogous to the treatment effect, α_j. The coefficient β_1 is the true regression coefficient, assumed equal across experimental conditions. This predictable part of Y follows Equation 6b of Chapter 9, with subscripts modified to allow for more than one group. The Ancova model may then be written

$$Y_{ij} = \alpha_j + \beta_1(X_{ij} - \bar{X}_{..}) + \varepsilon'_{ij}. \qquad \text{(Ancova model)} \qquad (2)$$

Comparison of Equations 1 and 2 shows that the Ancova error term, ε'_{ij}, is smaller than the Anova error term, ε_{ij}, by the amount that Y is predictable from X. If X is an individual difference variable, this predictable part of individual differences is removed from the error. Ancova thus provides an easy way to use auxiliary information about individual differences to increase power.

Graphically, the Ancova model prescribes a separate regression line for each A condition, all with equal slope, β_1. The model thus implies a set of parallel lines, separated vertically by the amounts α_j, which represent the main effect of A. The parallelism reflects the additivity of A and X assumed in Equation 2.

In the randomized experiment on premature infants, X and Y would be the infant's weight before and after experimental treatment. In this example, a large reduction in error variability would be expected. Ancova can be extended to include additional covariates, such as mother's food habits. These covariates could also provide helpful hints about causation.

Statistical Analysis. The computer fits the Ancova model of Equation 2 to the data, using the method of least squares (Section 9.1.6). It prints out an Ancova table, much like the ordinary Anova table. The calculations are a little complicated, not especially instructive, and are not detailed here. However, two aspects of the analysis deserve consideration.

The reduction in error is straightforward. $SS_{error(Y)}$ is obtained as in Anova. From this is subtracted the part that is predictable from X. Following Equation 7b of Chapter 9,

$$\text{reduction in } SS_{error(Y)} = SS_{pred(Y)} = b_1^2 \, SS_X. \qquad (3)$$

In addition, Ancova also adjusts the treatment means. This adjustment compensates for chance differences among the covariate means, $\bar{X}_{.j}$, produced by the random assignment. These differences, although chance, carry information because they are correlated with $\bar{Y}_{.j}$. Ancova takes advantage of this information by using the regression equation to adjust the means:

$$\bar{Y}_{.j(\text{adjusted})} = \bar{Y}_{.j} - b_1(\bar{X}_{.j} - \bar{X}_{..}). \qquad (4)$$

The magnitude of the adjustment, given by the second term on the right, depends on the regression slope, b_1, and on the difference between each covariate mean and their overall mean, as shown in the parentheses.[b]

To visualize this adjustment, imagine a separate regression line fitted to the data of each treatment group, all with the same slope, b_1. Slide the mean $\overline{Y}_{.j}$ for group j along its regression line until it lies just above the overall mean, $\overline{X}_{..}$. Its elevation is then the adjusted Y mean. These $\overline{Y}_{.j(\text{adjusted})}$ estimate what the Y means would have been had the X means been equal. This is the graphical equivalent of the Equation 4. This adjustment is justified by the random assignment, which implies that the true X means are equal for each group. This adjustment of means is a minor secondary benefit of Ancova. A numerical example is given in *Ancova Idealized* (Section 13.2.1).

SS_A is calculated from the adjusted means of Equation 4. This adjustment can decrease or increase the differences among the treatment means. The F will usually increase, of course, because the error will usually decrease.

Ancova Table. The Ancova F is obtained using the adjusted MS_A and MS_{error}. The df for MS_A are $a - 1$, just as in Anova. The df for MS_{error} are 1 less than in Anova because 1 df is used to estimate the regression coefficient, b_1.

The printout may include a variety of information: tables of adjusted and unadjusted means; comparisons among all pairs of adjusted means; significance test of b_1; standard deviations (= standard errors) for use in confidence intervals; and so forth. (These two-mean comparisons probably make no allowance for α escalation, Section 4.2.2.) You should also obtain graphs of Y versus X for each treatment condition for visual scrutiny.

You may wonder how much your covariate helped, if at all. One clue is to compare MS_{error} from Ancova with MS_{error} from Anova ignoring the covariate. If the covariate is useless, both MSs have equal expected value. Usefulness of the covariate may thus be assessed by how much it reduces the error.[c]

13.1.2 APPLICATIONS OF ANCOVA

Ancova may be viewed as a method for matching or equating groups on the covariate. In this respect, it is generally superior to difference scores. Also, it is often preferable to stratification or blocking on the covariate. A few additional practical issues are also taken up in the following subsections.

Avoid Difference Scores; Use Ancova. Difference scores are often attractive. Many investigations seek to produce a specific change: improved health, better appreciation of your spouse, and many others. It then seems natural to measure the response before and after treatment and analyze the change, $Y - X$; this change score is just what is at issue. Moreover, the change score subtracts out—and thereby seems to "correct" for—individual differences in X, the score before treatment.

In fact, analyzing the difference score is nearly always a mistake. One reason is that $Y - X$ will often be more variable than Y alone. To appreciate this danger, suppose that X and Y have zero correlation. By Equation 2.5, the variance of the difference score is then the sum of the variances, $\sigma_Y^2 + \sigma_X^2$. But the variance of the Y score alone is only σ_Y^2. Hence you would do far better to analyze the Y score alone.

You will suffer increased error if you use the difference score unless the correlation is sufficiently high ($\rho \geq .5$ when X and Y have equal variance). And even when ρ is larger than .5, Ancova will nearly always do better. This result illustrates once again how statistics can clarify data analyses that are nonobvious or even counterintuitive.

Ancova handles this situation with near-perfection. It has a skillful touch that reaches into X and extracts its predictive part, leaving behind the random noise that vitiates the difference score. This is not actually a miracle; it is accomplished by estimating the optimal predictive value of b_1 in the regression. The difference score, in contrast, is a special case of Ancova with b_1 ham-handedly set equal to 1.

In the cited case of zero correlation, the estimated b_1 will be near its true value of 0. The cost is only 1 df; the expected value of MS_{error} remains unchanged. With a correlation of .4 or more, you may expect your 1 df to be repaid by lower MS_{error}. Unless the difference score is logically necessary, or simply convenient, it is only beneficial when ρ is very near 1.

Blocking Versus Ancova. An alternative to Ancova is to use the covariate to stratify, or block, subjects before beginning the experiment. A standard procedure for blocking is to rank subjects on X, assign the top a subjects to block 1, the next highest a to block 2, and so forth. Within each block, the a subjects are assigned at random to the a treatments (Section 14.2).

Blocks thus becomes a second factor in the design, and two-way Anova may be applied. The SS for blocks represents individual differences, and this is fractionated out, thereby reducing MS_{error} in the same way as with Ancova. One advantage is that blocking allows categorical covariates, whereas standard Ancova requires a numerical covariate.

Which is superior, Ancova or blocking with Anova, assuming both are applicable? No great difference should ordinarily be expected. Ancova does somewhat better when its assumptions are reasonably satisfied. If the regression is purely linear, Ancova extracts 100% of the information in the covariate, at a statistical cost of only 1 df. Even as many as five blocks would extract no more than perhaps 85% of the covariate information and would cost 4 df just for main effect of blocks. If the regression is expected to substantially nonlinear, on the other hand, blocking may be a little better. Also, blocking is more robust; blocking reduces error empirically through the experimental design, whereas Ancova relies on a statistical model and its associated assumptions.

The most important consideration is practical, and it argues for Ancova. To randomize subjects across conditions within each block requires that X be measured for all subjects before running the first subject. This may be tedious, often infeasible. In psychophysiology, for example, X could be a resting state measure taken before the experiment starts. Even if it was feasible to get all subjects in for an initial session to measure resting state, it would usually be expensive and it would probably yield a lower $Y-X$ correlation.

Ancova, in marked contrast, has no trouble because X could be measured at the beginning of the experiment for each subject. In many situations, perhaps most, this practical advantage of Ancova over blocks Anova will outweigh any statistical considerations.[a]

Ancova With Factorial Design.   Ancova for factorial design is straightforward. No further assumptions are needed. The assumption of parallel regression lines, however, applies to all conditions in the design. This assumption may be doubtful when one factor has large effects. Also doubtful would be a subject factor, such as age groups in developmental psychology.

Multiple Covariates.   Ancova readily allows more than one covariate. Instead of predicting Y from the one-variable regression model of Chapter 9, the multiple regression model of Chapter 16 is used. Two or three weak covariates can thus be teamed to get worthwhile results, a useful option because good covariates are scarce in most experimental situations.

Statsig Covariate.   What does it mean if the groups show a statsig difference on the covariate, X? With random assignment, X can be statsig by chance through a "bad" random assignment. This is no sin; bad random assignments must occur with α probability. Ancova applies regardless.

In fact, the groups always differ on the covariate. Randomization only avoids bias; group means on the covariate are equal only on average. Sample differences in $\bar{X}_{.j}$ are real within each random assignment, regardless of whether they are statsig. The Ancova adjustment of these means in Equation 4 is only meaningful because these sample differences are real; otherwise the adjustment would be merely random noise stemming from unreliability of the measurements. In sum, Ancova is all the more useful with a bad random assignment, for it filters correlated badness out of Y.[b]

With nonrandom groups, of course, a real, nonrandom difference on the covariate must be expected; a significance test may have little point. The partial measure bias of Section 13.2.2 disables the Ancova adjustment.

Two Correlated Response Measures.   In a randomized experiment, suppose treatment effects are observed on two response measures, Y and Y', of which the former has primary interest. In particular, Y' may be some side effect of the treatment that confounds the causal interpretation.

In a study of instruction methods, to take a standard example, students who received a more effective method may also report having spent more time studying. This additional time may mediate the treatment effect, not some greater effectiveness of the method per se. In a study of drug effects on emotional arousal, as a second example, suppose heart rate is used as the measure of emotional arousal. Suppose the drugs have a side effect, such as heightened activity, that also affects heart rate, but through a different, nonemotional process. This side effect confounds the interpretation of the treatment effect.

In such situations, Ancova might seem attractive. Thus, Y' would be a measure of reported study time in the first example and a measure of activity in the second example. Ancova might seem justified by statements in statistics texts and journal articles that Ancova can "control" or "hold constant" the side effect, Y'. In this case, admittedly, the Ancova adjustment may take away part of any real treatment effect. But if what remains is statsig, the argument goes, surely it must be real.

Regrettably, Ancova seems seriously invalid for controlling the side effect. The main pitfall is substantive: Measured variables are usually partial measures. In the drug example, heightened activity is a complex variable that could be measured in various ways, none of which could be presumed to be *the* measure. What has not been measured, directly or indirectly, cannot be controlled because it is not in the analysis (see further Section 13.2.2).[c]

13.1.3 ANCOVA ASSUMPTIONS

The assumptions of Ancova include those of its two components, namely, analysis of variance and regression. Despite this pyramiding of assumptions, Ancova appears to be reasonably robust with random groups, except that extreme scores can distort the regression. Detailed discussion of assumptions is omitted here, except for the following comments on extreme scores and on the assumption of parallel regression lines.[a]

Extreme Scores. The main dangers with Ancova arise from extreme scores. Nonnormal distributions of Y scores can serious loss of power owing to extreme scores. Also, extreme scores, either in Y or X, can exert undue influence on the slope of the regression line.

The first line of protection against extreme scores is to minimize them with design and procedure. If extreme scores seem at all likely, it may be advisable to seek Ancova based on robust regression (Section 9.1.7).

Parallel Regression Lines. Standard Ancova assumes parallel regression lines, that is, that the true regression line has the same slope β_1 for every group. If the true slopes, β_{1j}, differ across groups, the adjusted means in Equation 4 will be biased because they use the same slope estimate for all groups. The amount of bias depends on $(\beta_{1j} - \bar{\beta}_{1.})$ and on $(\bar{X}_{.j} - \bar{X}_{..})$. With random assignment, both differences should usually be small so the bias should also be small. Furthermore, the bias tends to increase the error, yielding a conservative test.

Nonparallel regression lines may sometimes be a problem, of course, but Ancova can be extended to allow nonparallel regression lines. Formally, β_1 is replaced by β_{1j} in Equation 2. Mild statistical complications arise (Huitema, 1980, Chapter 13).

Nonparallel Regression as "Interaction." Nonparallel regression lines in Ancova correspond to "interaction" in Anova. To see this, visualize the covariance design as a factorial, $A \times X$ design, with A as the row factor and X as the column factor. The regression line for each experimental condition then corresponds to one row curve in the factorial graph. Equal slope of the regression lines is equivalent to parallelism in this factorial graph.

Some texts, accordingly, warn against interpreting or even testing the effect of the experimental A variable when the regression lines are nonparallel. Indeed, some statistical packages do not even include an option for Ancova with nonparallel regression. This advice is even more simplistic with Ancova than Anova. Understanding nonparallel regression in Ancova is similar to understanding "interactions" in Anova. Finding that the effect of A depends on X does not nullify and usually does not even qualify the main effect of A.

13.2 COVARIANCE WITH NONRANDOM GROUPS

Ancova is sometimes applied to nonrandom groups under the misconception that it will "control" or "hold constant," or "partial out" preexperimental differences between the groups. The benefit of a Head Start program given to disadvantaged children, for example, cannot be assessed by comparing their initial and final test scores; improvement would be expected in the natural course of development even if the treatment had null effect. A no-treatment group is needed to allow comparison of gains.

However, random assignment to conditions may be considered infeasible; instead, some nonrandom group is chosen as a comparison "control." Such nonrandom comparison groups differ systematically from the treatment group; in the Head Start studies, comparison groups are typically less disadvantaged. This systematic difference confounds the comparison of the two groups. Similar confounding is common with action programs, not only in educational settings, but also in industrial training, medical procedures, and health programs.

In this kind of situation, Ancova becomes tempting. The score on the initial test before treatment would be used as covariate, thinking that Ancova will "statistically control" the systematic initial differences between the groups.

Is it really possible to "statistically control" systematic preexperimental differences? In the Head Start example, these differences represent some years of intensive socialization in different families, different neighborhoods, with different playmates, and diverse other sociocultural influences. Can Equation 2, augmented with additional covariates, really "control," "hold constant," or "partial out" the effect of several years of uncontrolled sociocultural differences whose nature is largely unknown?

Of course not. What Ancova really does is considered next.

13.2.1 NATURE OF COVARIANCE ADJUSTMENT

Two Functions of Covariance Adjustment. Ancova has two quite different functions. With random groups, the principal function is to reduce error variance in the main response measure. Equalizing treatment groups on the covariate with Equation 4 is secondary, a minor nicety.

It's just the opposite with nonrandom groups. The big difficulty is that differences between groups, being nonrandom, are confounded with the treatment. Hence they undercut causal interpretation of observed effects. The principal desire, accordingly, is to "equalize" or "control" the treatment groups on the covariate. The hope is that this statistical "control" will somehow justify causal interpretation.

Ancova Idealized. Here is a numerical example to illustrate how Ancova adjusts the treatment means. Let $X = 1, 2, 3$ for the three subjects in experimental group E, and $X = 5, 6, 7$ for the three subjects in comparison group C. Assume for simplicity that Y and X are equivalent measures, for example, after and before scores on equivalent tests. Assume also that Y and X are perfectly reliable, with no error of measurement.

Suppose neither treatment has any effect, so that the Y scores equal the X scores. The Y means are thus 2 and 6, a big disadvantage for group E. In this example, of course, the apparent disadvantage of E is due solely to the preexperimental difference. The question is how Ancova handles this confounding.

Since $Y = X$, the regression line for each group has unit slope. Graphically, Ancova tells us to slide the Y mean for each group along its regression line so their X means coincide on the horizontal axis. This occurs at $\overline{X}_{..} = 4$. Hence the Ancova adjustment increases $\overline{Y}_{.E}$ by 2 points, decreases $\overline{Y}_{.C}$ by 2 points. The adjusted means are thus equal—as they should be since treatments had no effect. This graphical analysis may be verified with the formula of Equation 4. Ancova has thus provided a correct interpretation of the data.

Ancova can do even better. Suppose E has a real effect, changing the Y scores by the amount c for each subject. Then the foregoing analysis shows that $\overline{Y}_{.E} = 4 + c$, which differs from $\overline{Y}_{.C} = 4$. Any differential treatment effect will thus be preserved and revealed.

But this striking capability, regrettably, is seldom applicable to nonrandom groups. Two major pitfalls are discussed next.

13.2.2 TWO PITFALLS WITH NONRANDOM ANCOVA

Partial Measure Bias. An apparently fatal bias undercuts Ancova with non-random groups. In typical applications, the covariate is a partial measure of a complex variable; some determinants of the behavior are missing.

Socioeconomic status, often used with Ancova or multiple regression, is a prime example of a partial measure. Children's school progress is substantially correlated with parents' socioeconomic status. In a Head Start study, accordingly, it would seem essential to "control for" systematic differences on socioeconomic status between the treatment group and any nonrandom comparison group. But socioeconomic status is an amorphous concept with diverse aspects. It includes types of parents' jobs, family neighborhood, home ownership, and numerous other aspects. The crude 5-step scale in common use hardly begins to measure the amorphous mass of operative causal variables.

It is impossible to "control for" variables that have not been measured, indirectly if not directly. This partial measure bias appeared in the foregoing discussion of two correlated response measures. It reappears in multiple regression, and its seriousness is illustrated in *The Mystery of the Missing Cloud Cover* in Section 16.2.2 (page 506). Partial measure bias seems an impassable barrier to routine use of Ancova with nonrandom groups.

Unreliability Bias. Unreliability in the covariate biases the regression coefficient. This bias undercuts the covariance adjustment of the group means. Denote the measurement error in the covariate by ε' so the measured value of X equals its true value X', plus ε': $X = X' + \varepsilon'$. The linear regression used in Ancova fits a straight line to the observed data:

$$Y = b_0 + b_1 X + \varepsilon.$$

Substitution of $X = X' + \varepsilon'$ yields

$$Y = b_0 + b_1(X' + \varepsilon') + \varepsilon.$$

The ε' term causes a bias in b_1. On average, b_1 will be less that the true β_1. The algebraic relation is

$$E(b_1) = [\sigma_X^2/(\sigma_X^2 + \sigma_\varepsilon^2)]\beta_1, \tag{5}$$

where σ_X^2 is the variance of the measured X values. This equation shows that b_1 systematically underestimates β_1.

To see the consequence, look back at the numerical example for idealized Ancova in the previous section. In this example, the numerical values of X were the true values, and these yielded $b_1 = 1$, the true slope. In practice, however, X will be measured with error, so b_1 will be less than 1, as shown by Equation 5. This bias in the slope biases the Ancova adjustment of the treatment means.

In the foregoing numerical example, the regression line will tend to be too flat for both groups, with slope less than 1. After adjustment, the mean for group E will lie below that for group C (Exercise 2). Although the treatment had no real effect, Ancova will say it had a harmful effect. Even if it had some beneficial effect, it could still appear harmful. This bias in b_1 undercuts causal interpretation.[a, b]

Quasi-Experimental Design. The prototypical *quasi-experimental design* consists of two groups, an experimental group E, which receives a designated treatment, and a comparison group C, which typically gets no treatment at all. The prefix, *quasi*, refers to the lack of randomization. The two groups are nonequivalent, with systematic preexperimental differences. The foregoing Head Start example is a quasi-experimental design.

The typical goal is to show that group E changes more than group C, which is to be taken as evidence for the effectiveness of the experimental treatment. This causal interpretation is problematic, of course, because the treatment is confounded with preexperimental differences.

The term quasi-experimental was introduced by Campbell and Stanley (1966) in the belief that Ancova provided a valid "control" for preexperimental differences. It was soon recognized that Ancova did not have this capability, one reason being the bias in estimating β_1 discussed above. This misconception was floodlighted when initial evaluations of Head Start indicated harmful effects. Further discussion of quasi-experimental design is deferred to Section 15.5, which includes additional comments on Ancova.

A Misuse of Ancova. A common misuse of Ancova with nonrandom groups consists in showing that the treatment effect remains statsig even after the covariate has been included in the analysis. This outcome is then interpreted as demonstrating a true causal effect of the treatment. This interpretation is undercut by both foregoing biases. Most important is the partial measure bias, potentially deadly with any analysis of uncontrolled data. The statsig result may be caused, not by the treatment, but by unmeasured aspects of the concept referred to by X. Care is always needed to avoid reification, taking the *name* given to X as equivalent to the underlying concept X is intended to measure.

Also problematic is the alternative outcome, in which a statsig treatment effect disappears when the covariate is included in the analysis. This does not imply that the treatment has no causal effect. A causal treatment effect could vanish simply because Y is correlated with X, as in the earlier section on *Two Correlated Response Measures*.

13.2.3 SCIENCE WITH NONRANDOM GROUPS

Process analysis for groups that differ preexperimentally requires grounded substantive theory. Ancova is only a statistical formula, not substantive theory. The great utility of Ancova with random assignment disintegrates with nonrandom groups. Ancova is only an outcome model, not a model of psychological process.[a]

The adjustment of means in Ancova asks, in effect, how individuals in each nonrandom group would have behaved—had these individuals been different from what they actually are. But they are what they are: an intricate outcome of genetic differences and innumerable, diverse past experiences. To ask how they would have behaved if they were different from what they are is not empirically meaningful (Anderson, 1963). To revise their past history would require a Higher Power than Ancova.

Causal analysis with nonrandom groups has high social importance. Statisticians have given much attention to these problems, but the central difficulties are empirical. A quantitative model of psychological process, solidly grounded in empirical data, is generally necessary to justify comparison of nonrandom groups. Statisticians naturally focus on linear models, but the great usefulness of linear models for outcome analysis has obscured their great shortcomings for process analysis, illustrated with "weak inference" in Figure 9.3.

Without empirical grounding for the Ancova model as a process model, published statements that Ancova was used to "statistically control," "hold constant," or "partial out" uncontrolled variables are less than worthless. I think it fair to say that the great majority of empirical studies rest on little more than wishful thinking. Related discussions of quasi-experimental design (Section 15.5) and multiple regression (Chapter 16) suggest some ways to make headway on this fundamental problem of field science.

Comparing nonequivalent groups is sometimes possible with a theoretical model of behavior that has been empirically grounded. What may be compared across groups are parameters of the model. This model approach does not pretend to "equalize" or "control" the group differences. Instead, it seeks a comparison within a theoretical description of psychological process.[b]

This substantive model approach may be illustrated with signal detection theory (Section 20.3). The d' statistic does "control for" unequal frequencies of false alarms obtained under different conditions to yield a pure measure of sensory acuity. But this "control" is accomplished through a grounded substantive model of detection behavior, in which d' is a sensory parameter. The key idea is that d' is invariant across different conditions in the signal detection model. A similar example from cognitive algebra is shown in the size–weight experiment of Figure 20.3 (page 653).

NOTES

A good short treatment of analysis of covariance is given by Snedecor and Cochran (1980, Chapter 18). The book by Huitema (1980) is well-informed, thorough, and reasonably elementary. Among psychological texts, Maxwell and Delaney (1990) give an extensive discussion with a positive outlook on Ancova. Reichardt (1979) gives an illuminating discussion of Ancova with nonrandom groups, some of which is summarized in Section 15.5 on quasi-experimental design. I am indebted to Anthony Greenwald and Charles Reichardt for helpful comments on this chapter.

13.1.1a. Strictly speaking, Ancova is not simply Anova on the deviations from the regression line (Maxwell, Delaney, & Mannheimer, 1985). Intuitively, however, it is helpful to visualize Ancova in this way. Computer programs use a least squares analysis of Equation 2, which yields correct results.

13.1.1b. The adjustment of the means in Equation 4 assumes the regression is linear. With random groups, this linearity assumption is usually reasonable, even when the true regression is substantially nonlinear, because the $\bar{X}_{.j}$ will be relatively close together.

13.1.1c. A covariate may yield a worthwhile reduction in MS_{error} even though its true correlation with Y is only $\rho = .4$, too small to be dependably statsig at $\alpha = .05$. Hence a covariate may be retained for future use even though it is not statsig in the present application. One determinant in this decision is prior belief in the evidence value of the covariate, to which the evidence of the present experiment is subsidiary. In this situation, of course, a "false alarm" usually has low statistical cost and an α of .20 would seem often appropriate.

13.1.2a. Using blocks and Ancova together may be most effective. The historically first application of Ancova (Fisher, 1932) was used to illustrate a blocks-and-Ancova analysis by Snedecor and Cochran (1980, p. 371). Y was the current yield on 16 plots of tea bushes in Ceylon; X was yield in the previous year, prior to applying the four experimental treatments. In one set of these data, blocking reduced MS_{error} from 136 to 48; Ancova produced a further reduction to 27. Good design and analysis, at almost no cost, thus increased precision five-fold. Even 30% increases, which are more to be expected, will often be worthwhile (see similarly Maxwell and Delaney, 1990, pp. 395*ff*).

13.1.2b. Significance tests are not too meaningful for assessing differences on the covariate between randomized groups. The difference in any actual sample is real in that sample (barring measurement unreliability). Whether the group differences on X are statsig depends strongly on N, which is irrelevant to the issue.

13.1.2c. Ancova with a correlated response measure also suffers a statistical bias. Unreliability in X causes the sample regression coefficient b_1 to underestimate the true coefficient β_1. Causal interpretation requires a structural regression, whereas standard Ancova incorporates a predictive regression. When Ancova with the structural regression would equalize the adjusted Y means, the standard Ancova will not, and vice versa. The outcome is thus ambiguous regardless of whether Ancova leaves the differences statsig or nonstatsig. Standard Ancova is thus conceptually invalid, although correction for the unreliability may be possible (Note 13.2.2b).

13.1.3a. Two independence assumptions appear in Ancova. The first is independence among the Y scores. This is the same as in Anova (Section 3.3.1) and equally essential.

The second independence assumption is substantive rather than statistical, namely, that the experimental treatments do not affect the covariate. This treatment–covariate independence is not actually an assumption, for Ancova applies regardless. If treatments do affect the covariate, however, the means adjustment of Equation 4 will remove some of the treatment effect. This can happen if the covariate is measured after the experimental treatment has begun.

13.2.2a. The unreliability bias in the regression coefficient of Equation 5 can be seen to be negligible when the covariate is controlled experimentally to cover a much larger range than the response variability.

13.2.2b. In principle, the unreliability bias in b_1 can be corrected. This requires *structural regression*, based on β_1, which differs from ordinary *predictive regression*, based on b_1. Predictive regression makes opportunistic use of the covariate X to predict the criterion Y, untroubled by the unreliability bias.

Structural regression, in contrast, is concerned with the substantive relation between Y and X. This structural–predictive distinction parallels the process–outcome distinction of Section 1.2.1. Unreliability in the covariate distorts the $Y–X$ relation. Progress has been made in analysis of structural regression "errors in variables" analysis (Fuller, 1987) and in LISREL and related programs. This does nothing, of course, about the deadly partial measure bias (see further Section 16.2, page 504).

13.2.3a. Logically, the additive Ancova model, Subjects + Treatments, of Equation 2 could be a valid model of psychological process. Empirically, this seems unlikely. One objection is that it has no place for subject–treatment interaction residuals. A second objection is that subjects and treatments differ qualitatively.

This issue does not trouble Ancova with random groups, which only takes advantage of outcome predictive power in the regression, however limited this may be. For process analysis of nonrandom groups, however, focus on the discrepancies betwen model and reality is essential. This distinction is exactly the same as with weak inference in the discussion of Figure 9.3.

13.2.3b. The need for a substantive model of psychological process to justify Ancova for nonrandom groups is noted in Anderson (1963), which considers the problem of comparing rate of learning or other change between groups that begin at different levels. Substantive considerations led to a "shape function" method with a multiplicative form. Standard Ancova is invalid for it rests on an addition model (see further Paul, 1994; see also Bogartz, 1990a,b).

EXERCISES FOR CHAPTER 13

1. In the numerical example of *Ancova Idealized* of Section 13.2.1:

    a. Draw a graph to show how "the Ancova adjustment increases $\overline{Y}_E$ by 2 points, decreases $\overline{Y}_C$ by 2 points."

    b. Do the same assuming treatment E increases Y by a constant c for each subject.

    c. Redo (a) using Equation 4.

2. a. Repeat the graphic analysis of part (a) of the previous exercise to show how Ancova would reach wrong conclusions if the estimate of b_1 was lower than its true value, say $b_1 = .6$. Estimate graphically the apparent difference between E and C, and check using Equation 4. How does this relate to evaluation of Head Start programs?

    b. Repeat (a) assuming treatment E adds 1 point to each subject's score.

3. The error variances for Anova and Ancova, denoted σ_ε^2 and $\sigma_{\varepsilon'}^2$, respectively, obey the relation (Winer et al., 1991, p. 741):

$$\sigma_{\varepsilon'}^2 = \sigma_\varepsilon^2 (1 - \rho^2) \frac{df_{error}}{df_{error} - 1},$$

where ρ is the Y–X correlation. For moderate df, the df ratio at the right is close to 1. Ignore this term and plot a graph of the ratio of the two error terms as a function of ρ. How would you describe this trend? What does this mean for experimental design?

4. To calculate power for Ancova, use Equations 3-5 in Chapter 4 for Anova. Replace the error variance, σ_ε^2 in Equation 4, by the Ancova error variance from the previous exercise.

    P wishes to study emotional arousal in three kinds of stress situations, but is uncertain how many subjects to run. He guesses the true means are 1, 2, and 4, with an error variance of 6. He plans to measure arousal before and after the experimental stress, the before measure to be used as a covariate. Tentatively, P considers $n = 9$.

    a. Show that power is about .57, .64, .70, and .78 for $\rho = 0, .3, .45$, and .6. Comment.

    b. Guesstimate similarly the 95% confidence interval for difference between two means for each of the four correlations in (a). What problem do they raise for P?

    c. What changes in the experimental design might P consider?

5. In *Blocking Versus Ancova*, justify the statement that the resting state "would probably yield a lower Y–X correlation" if measured in an initial session before the experiment has been started.

6. Here are X and Y scores for two groups, each with four subjects assumed to have been assigned at random.

       group 1: X = 0, 2, 4, 6;

                      Y = 2.8, 4.2, 5.2, 5.8.

       group 2: X = 2, 4, 6, 8;

                      Y = 3.0, 4.4, 5.4, 6.0.

a. Which has the greater $\bar{Y}$?

b. Plot both sets of data and fit a separate regression line to each by eye, as illustrated in Figure 9.1.

c. By the randomization assumption, it makes sense to use Ancova. You can do this by eye: Slide the $\bar{Y}$ for each group along its own regression line until its $\bar{X}$ coincides with the overall $\bar{X}$ for both groups taken together. The adjusted Y means for each group can now be read from your graph.

d. Check your adjusted means from (c) against Equation 4.

7. The general formula for variance of a difference score is

$$\sigma_{Y-X}^2 = \sigma_Y^2 + \sigma_X^2 - 2\rho\,\sigma_Y\sigma_X,$$

where ρ is the Y–X correlation. Suppose Y and X have equal variance, $\sigma_X^2 = \sigma_Y^2 = \sigma^2$, as might be expected with before and after measures of the same quantity.

a. Show that $Y - X$ and Y have equal variance when $\rho = .5$.

b. Suppose that ρ is greater than/less than ½. Which yields lower variance: the difference score or Y alone?

c. Why exactly is it preferable to apply Anova to whichever of Y and $Y - X$ has smaller variance?

d. Why would Ancova with X as a covariate generally do better than Anova of the difference score?

8. In the before–after paradigm, some response is measured on equivalent scales before (X) and after (Y) treatment is given. You use this before–after paradigm to study belief change with two randomized groups, 1 and 2, using the difference score, $Y - X$. But your assistant brings you an Anova on the Y score; it seems the X scores have disappeared. You wonder whether the Anova of Y is

valid; perhaps the random assignment chanced to put more subjects with high X scores in one of the groups, a possibility that cannot now be checked.

  a. What null hypothesis is tested by your assistant's Anova of Y? Give answer in words and in symbols.

  b. What null hypothesis would be tested with an Anova of $Y - X$? Give answer in words and in symbols.

  c. Why are the two null hypotheses of (a) and (b) equivalent?

  d. Suppose your treatment has no effect. Do the two Anovas have the same false alarm parameter, or is one better?

  e. Suppose your treatment has an effect. Which Anova do you think has more power?

  f. What advantage would Ancova have over the change score?

9. Why do nonrandom but not random groups suffer from incapacity of one-dimensional covariates to represent multidimensional constructs?

10. Section 13.2.3 asserts that it is not generally meaningful to ask how non-random groups would behave if they were different from what they are. Why does this assertion not apply to random groups?

11. How does the numerical example in *Bias in Estimating* β relate to the Ancova comparison between nonrandom groups in the Head Start research?

12. In the cited experiment on premature infants, how might it be helpful to use a preliminary screening test? List potential benefits and disadvantages.

Preface

This chapter has two themes: *reducing error variability* and *order effects*. The main source of variability is usually individual differences, which can be handled in four ways: good procedure; screening out extreme scores; blocking on some individual difference variable; and using repeated measures. Repeated measures faces problems of order effects, but in many cases order effects can be handled with Latin square versions of standard repeated measures designs.

14.1. Screening Subjects and Writing Instructions. *Extreme scores* are a major headache. In empirical perspective, extreme scores may result from shortcomings in procedure, from real individual differences in the population, or from outliers that do not belong. In statistical perspective, extreme scores run up the error variance, widen confidence intervals, and decrease power.

The first line of protection against extreme scores lies in experimental procedures to prevent them. Most important, of course, are procedures to establish task–subject congruence. Also useful are procedures to screen out extreme subjects or scores.

14.2. Block Design. If subjects are stratified, or *blocked*, on some individual difference variable, these individual differences can be factored out, thereby reducing the error term. Although somewhat limited in range of applicability, blocking has more potential than has been realized, especially in the limiting case of analysis of covariance.

14.3. Latin Squares. Latin squares are useful extensions of repeated measures design, in which treatment position is included as a design factor. Latin squares balanced for previous treatment go further to provide some analysis of carryover effects, that is, treatment–treatment interactions. This class of designs has unrealized potential for experimental analysis.

14.4. Within Subjects Versus Between Subjects Design. Within subjects design is highly desirable, for substantive and statistical reasons both. But within subjects design can suffer from transfer or carryover from one treatment to the next. As a consequence, within subjects design sometimes yields very different results from between subjects design, in which carryover effects cannot occur. Decisions about which design to use depend mainly on extra-statistical knowledge about the situation at hand. A number of empirical examples are given to help focus attention on this basic design problem.

Chapter 14

DESIGN TOPICS I

Reducing variability is a major concern in planning an experiment, discussed with the Experimental Pyramid in Chapter 1. One reason is substantive: Reducing variability means getting the behavior under better control; better control generally improves the quality of the response. The other reason is statistical: Lower variability means greater power and tighter confidence intervals.

The first main section considers two practical aspects of controlling variability that deserve more consideration than they often get: *Screening extreme scores* and *writing instructions*.

Three classes of designs that can help reduce variability are considered in the last three main sections. *Block design* includes an individual difference variable as a design factor, and thereby removes it from the error term. *Latin square design* extends repeated measures design by balancing treatments across serial position. Finally, some dangers of using repeated measures are considered in the discussion of *Within Subjects and Between Subjects Design.*

Increasing validity goes together with reducing variability. The techniques for reducing variability in the first two main sections tend also to increase validity. Latin squares in the third main section seek the same goals by using repeated measures. Latin square designs improve on the repeated measures designs of Chapter 6 by providing ways to deal with order effects.

14.1 TWO DESIGN PROBLEMS:
SCREENING SUBJECTS AND WRITING INSTRUCTIONS

Two problems of design and procedure are considered here. Both address the problem of extreme scores, a major headache of experimental analysis.

One problem concerns eliminating subjects and/or data. The other problem concerns writing instructions. On these two intensely practical problems, the present discussion is limited and provisional.

14.1.1 SCREENING SUBJECTS AND DROPPING DATA

Extreme scores are usually undesirable. One reason is substantive: An extreme subject may be essentially different, not belonging to the population of interest. A second reason concerns procedure: An extreme score may result from some shortcoming of procedure. A third reason is statistical: An extreme score contributes disproportionately to the error variance.

Prevention is the first line of protection against extreme scores. Two aspects of prevention are taken up in the first two subsections. Three further subsections consider elimination of subjects and/or data. These comments are mainly oriented toward independent groups design.

Screening Tests. Screening tests can help prevent extreme scores and minimize subject loss. Subjects unable to perform adequately in the experimental task can sometimes be detected and screened out. Screening can be especially useful with child and patient populations. With screening tests, random assignment is ordinarily applied only to those subjects who pass the screening test.

In a published study of motor learning, one subject in one condition turned out to be a motor moron. The extreme score of this subject produced a high error variance which obscured certain results common to the other subjects. The investigator did the analyses with and without this subject and reported both in his writeup. This was acceptable to the journal reviewers and editor, and is one way to handle extreme subjects. A screening test, however, would have detected this subject, avoided the complication, and increased reliability.

Screening can have additional benefits. The score on a screening test can sometimes be used to stratify, or block, the subject population. In the motor learning study just cited, blocking would have reduced error variability. In the anagram experiment of Section 14.2.2 (page 410), the reduction in error from blocking was equivalent to doubling the number of subjects.

The instruction–practice period can sometimes be adapted for screening. Subjects who have difficulty with the task or who exhibit untoward behavior can be dropped from the formal experiment. Of course, dropping should be done in such a way that it does not hurt the subject's feelings.

Screening limits the population to which the results may apply. For studies aimed at outcome validity, this limitation may or may not be worth the gain in reliability. For process validity, limiting the population may increase validity as well as reliability.

Experimental Procedure. The quality and meaning of the data depend on the experimental task and procedure. Task and procedure are tools for attaining validity and reliability, as was emphasized with the Experimental Pyramid. Experimental procedure has primary effectiveness for reducing the threat of extreme scores.

A first principle of experimental procedure is to adapt the task to the subject. This principle may appear self-evident, but some research seems instead to force the subject into preconceived schemas and predetermined tasks. Also hindering recognition of this principle is that most studies rely on tasks and procedures developed in previous work. As beneficiaries of this previous work, we tend to take it for granted, not appreciating how much trial-and-error it often represents. Task–procedure development is a continuing process, however, as in revising old tasks for new uses.

The dual first principle is to adapt the subject to the task. As a rule, the task should be made clear and the subject should be at ease. This applies especially to animals and children, not just to the standard college sophomore. Sufficient practice is important. There are exceptions to this rule, of course, in studies of anxiety, say, or studies of the adaptation process itself. Usually, however, the initial phase of an experiment involves startup effects that degrade both reliability and validity of the response measure (Section 14.4.1, page 425).

A practical principle is smoothness and order in experimental procedure. The experimenter should be well practiced with the procedure before running the first regular subject. One reason is to reduce extraneous startup effects. No less important is to reduce mistakes and errors. With well-practiced procedure, moreover, the experimenter can give more attention to understanding the subject's perspective. Experimental procedure should thus be simplified and routinized. This holds especially for data recording.

Sometimes a shortcoming in procedure goes undetected in the pilot work and only surfaces after a dozen or so subjects have been run. This shortcoming may seem serious enough to deserve correction, yet not serious enough to start anew. One way to handle this is to adopt temporal blocking as standard in experimental design. A change in procedure can then be introduced at the end of any block (Section 14.2). The writeup should say something like "The following changes in procedure were introduced beginning with the bth block of subjects." The block effects provide a check on the change of procedure.

Subject Loss. Subject loss is not uncommon in some experimental situations. Young children may fail to understand the task or develop some idiosyncratic response strategy. In experiments involving surgery or drugs, some subjects may sicken or die. In a multisession experiment, some subjects may drop out.

Subject loss raises two issues of validity. The first is whether the loss is caused by the treatments. Children's failure to perform acceptably may occur mainly in a more difficult condition. Unsuccessful surgery may be more frequent in the experimental than in the control group. Such treatment-caused subject loss may bias the results because the lost subjects may differ systematically from those that remain. Losing or eliminating a subject then carries away part of the treatment effect.

The second validity issue is that any subject loss raises a question about the quality of the experimental procedure and hence about the quality of the response. One subject's failure to understand may reflect ambiguities and shortcomings in task–procedure that adulterate the quality of response of other subjects (see the study of probability judgment cited in Section 8.2.1, page 245).

Subject loss is not necessarily bad. It might be argued, perhaps, that some subjects should be lost. Perfection is seldom efficient. The good workman seeks a practical minimum of subject loss through screening tests and good experimental procedure. Although one should be alert to possible bias, especially with marginal results, subject loss is recognized as normal in many situations (Anderson, 1982, Section 1.2.5).

One rule, I believe, is generally considered absolute: All subject loss, elimination, or screening, must be recorded and reported. This information is necessary to evaluate the results. It is an essential part of the public record, just as with other aspects of procedure.[a]

Eliminating Subjects. Although eliminating an extreme subject is sometimes appropriate, it is never comfortable. Keeping a seemingly deviant score may bias the data, but so may eliminating it.

Robust statistics provides a happy solution. The trimming procedure of Section 12.1 can markedly reduce the variance inflation caused by extreme scores without actually eliminating them or introducing bias. Arguable decisions about individual extreme scores are not needed. Trimming is applicable in many situations with group data, where it is most needed. Trimming and other robust statistics are a second line of protection against extreme scores. Also pertinent is Section 12.3 on *Outliers*.

Eliminating Data. In repeated measures design, eliminating extreme scores for a given subject may sometimes seem desirable. One tactic is to monitor the response and repeat any trial that fails to meet some criterion. A second is to replace a seemingly deviant score by one derived from other responses to the same treatment, a tactic that may also be used with missing scores. Both tactics introduce possible bias from eliminating responses that are not really deviant. It may be preferable—perhaps—to keep the questionable responses, expecting to average them out in the overall analysis. The reader of the published report is thus saved the worry of deciding whether the elimination was justified.[b]

Still a third tactic is to give three replications of each treatment and use their median as the response. This minor tactic sticks in my mind because one investigator who really needed to use it had run only two replications.

Extreme Scores Can Be Helpful Clues. The positive potential of extreme scores should not be overlooked. In their positive mode, extreme scores represent some substantive phenomena, possibly more interesting than the main population. Well-known examples from introductory texts include lightning calculators, mnemonists, and persons with eidetic imagery (see also *Clever Hans: The Mathematical Horse*, page 239). Even the aforementioned motor moron might have repaid individual study. Extreme scores should not be dismissed, therefore, without pausing to see if they present an opportunity.

In their negative mode, extreme scores can be a useful warning signal of possible shortcomings of procedure. This negative usefulness of extreme scores relates to the principle of replication (Section 2.4.6, page 52). Improving procedure is a continuing process. Extreme scores in one experiment are a guide to improvement in the next. In particular, concern over bias from treatment-caused subject loss can often be eliminated through replication studies.[c]

14.1.2 INSTRUCTIONS, STIMULI, AND STIMULUS PRESENTATION

Clarity of instructions helps reduce individual differences in how subjects understand the task. Clarity decreases error variability, therefore, even in repeated measurements design. Even more important, instructions help define the task for the subjects, and thereby determine the quality of the response. The nonverbal component of instructions is basic, especially with animal subjects, but only verbal instructions are considered here.

Writing Instructions. An instructive example of response quality comes from a Bayesian urn task, in which subjects see a succession of beads, red or white, drawn from an urn. They are told to judge the probability that the urn has more red than white beads. Previous experiments had assumed that subjects were indeed judging probability. This assumption was certainly plausible, but it was incorrect. Meticulous work by Shanteau (1970) showed that subjects were actually doing something qualitatively different from the instructions, namely, estimating the proportion of red beads in the sample. Much previous work applying Bayesian ideas to judgment–decision thus lost its meaning. Whether this defect might have been detected earlier is hard to say, but this example shows that validity of instructions cannot be taken for granted.

In experimental psychology, how to write instructions has received little systematic attention. Yet it is important, as illustrated in the previous paragraph. The following discussion, based on my own experience with experimental studies of judgment–decision, is presented only as an example. These remarks are provisional, mainly intended to call attention to the general problem (see also Chapter 22, *Writing Articles*).

Two paragraphs from a previous discussion of how to write instructions may be quoted here (Anderson, 1982, p. 28):

> Most experiments on judgment aim to elicit a quality or dimension of judgment that is already natural to the subjects. With simple perceptual or social judgments, such as loudness or likableness, there is no reason to think that the meaning of the response is sensitive to the instructions. Nevertheless, some

meticulousness in instructions is always in order. One reason is to minimize the ever-present possibility of misunderstanding. A second reason is to detect the infrequent, but inevitable, subject who seems unable to perform even very simple tasks. A third reason is to provide a basis for the reader's confidence in the meaningfulness of the published results. A fourth reason is to be able to provide other investigators with adequate detail for replication . . . And a final reason is that the face validity of the response can be incorrect, as instanced in [the Bayesian urn task cited in the first paragraph of this subsection].

With child or patient populations, a more interactive mode of instruction is often needed. The experimenter monitors the subject's understanding at each stage of instruction and recycles through that stage, with suitable variation, until understanding is obtained. Such interactive instructions can also help by building rapport. Except perhaps for pilot work, however, instructions should always follow a prescribed written outline. When any degree of experimenter–subject interaction is involved, it may be desirable to record some examples on tape. These procedures help ensure that no research assistant will omit some important aspect. And, of course, they provide a sometimes necessary basis for replication, both within and between laboratories.

The introductory phase of the instructions has three steps. First, the general idea of the task is given simply and briefly. This provides a schema on which the subject can organize subsequent detail. Next, this schema is firmed up with one or two concrete, illustrative stimuli. Finally, the response scale is introduced. These three steps are illustrated in the verbatim instructions reproduced in a chapter note.[a]

The next phase checks on the subject's understanding. This may be done by presenting a few representative stimuli and checking that the subject's responses are sensible. Asking subjects to explain the task in their own words may also be helpful.

A set of practice stimuli is then presented. These help firm up the subject's set and increase the reliability of the response. A final check on understanding may then be obtained by asking subjects to explain how they arrived at their judgment for a few selected stimuli. Although their answers do not often reveal much about their judgment processes, they often expose shortcomings of instruction and procedure.

No detail should be mentioned until and unless necessary. Subjects are easily led astray by tangential detail, or by detail presented too early. This is why, for example, the actual response scale is not introduced until the general idea of the task has been made clear. Repetition of main points can be valuable, but care is needed to weed out nonessential details. This rule might seem superfluous, but it is a stumbling block for many graduate students, perhaps because they themselves have not sorted out what is not essential.

Instructions should be written, labeled, and dated. The experimenter should be sufficiently practiced to read the instructions in a conversational manner, looking more at the subject than at the typescript.

Writing Stimulus Items. Experimental treatments may have a verbal form, as in many experiments on judgment–decision or person cognition, in which the subject makes a judgment based on verbal stimulus informers. The meaning of the data depends entirely on subjects' understanding of these stimuli. Developing such verbal stimuli requires no less care than writing instructions, and many of the foregoing comments apply directly.

In test theory, concern with construction of stimulus items goes back a century to Binet's pioneering studies of intelligence. His work established validity as a central concern. In experimental psychology, this issue has received much less consideration. The work in test theory, however, has shown many pitfalls for the uneducated. Anyone who plans to use verbal stimuli should be familiar with the extensively developed methodology of test theory (e.g., Cronbach, 1990; Henrysson, 1971; Millman & Greene, 1989; Wesman, 1971).

Stimulus Presentation. In repeated measures design, experimental stimulus items should generally be presented one by one, under some form of experimenter control. The practice of having subjects proceed at their own pace through a booklet throws open the door to invalidity and unreliability. Some subjects are bound to be hasty, careless, or confused. If a booklet must be used, it seems advisable to put only one item on a page and have the subject turn pages on command, not self-paced. With computer presentation, similarly, some minimum time should ordinarily be programmed between successive stimuli and between stimulus and response unless otherwise indicated, as with reaction time tasks.

In test theory, extensive consideration has been given to proper administration of tests, eloquently described by Cronbach (1990, Chapter 3). This work is a model for experimental psychologists (see also Clemans, 1971).

14.2 BLOCK DESIGN

Block designs seek to control some source of variability by including it as a factor in the design. Such blocking, as it is called, has two potential benefits, one statistical, one substantive. The statistical benefit is increased reliability of the treatment means; the Anova removes effects of the blocking variable from the error. The substantive benefit concerns generality; effects of the experimental variable may be compared across the separate levels of the blocking variable.

In psychology, the most common blocking variable is individual differences. Accordingly, the logic of block design will be illustrated with individual difference blocking in the first two sections. Other blocking variables, especially successive time periods, are noted in the third section. The final section takes up several issues in block design.

14.2.1 LOGIC OF BLOCK DESIGN: INDIVIDUAL DIFFERENCES

The idea of *block design* is simple. Find an individual difference variable B that is expected to correlate with the response measure. Stratify, or *block*, subjects according to their B scores, e.g., High, Medium, and Low. Include these blocks as a factor in the design. The experiment is thus replicated across blocks.

With blocking, a one-way design becomes a two-way, $A \times B$ design. Within each separate block, subjects are randomly assigned to the A conditions. With equal n, the Anova table is

Source	df
A	$a - 1$
B	$b - 1$
$A \times B$	$(a - 1)(b - 1)$
S/AB	$ab(n - 1)$

B is here considered a fixed factor, so the last source serves as the error.

The main potential benefit is greater reliability of the treatment means. To appreciate this potential benefit, suppose the blocking variable was ignored. Then SS_{error} would be the sum of the SSs for the last three terms in the Anova table. This error is expected to be larger than the listed error, $MS_{S/AB}$, to the extent that B is correlated with the response. The stronger this relation, the greater will be the reduction in error.

The error reduction is accomplished by the design. In effect, the design matches subjects across treatments. This matching makes the treatment means more reliable. Anova merely reveals what the design has accomplished.

Blocking is only useful, of course, to the extent that the blocking variable is correlated with the response. MS_B need not be statsig to be useful, but its expected value should be considerably larger than that of the error term $MS_{S/AB}$. If not, power will likely be reduced from using up df for B and AB.

The B effect, being individual differences, may shed light on the nature of the task. In addition, the AB interaction residual provides information about the generality of the A effect across levels of B. This substantive benefit is illustrated in the following example on methods of language learning.

14.2.2 TWO ILLUSTRATIVE BLOCK DESIGNS

Methods for Language Learning. Children learn language aurally and only later transfer to visual reading. Should a foreign language be taught the same way? Or, having learned to read one language, would it be better to begin with visual learning for a second language?

To study this question, Pimsleur and Bonkowski (1961) had one group of subjects learn a list of paired associates with aural presentation, then relearn it with visual presentation, the A–V order. Another group learned the list in the opposite V–A order. The response measure was the number of trials to reach a criterion—summed over original learning and relearning. This clever learning–relearning procedure roughly equates the task for the two groups, yet allows any advantage of initial learning mode to reveal itself.

Subjects were UCLA students enrolled in Spanish II, blocked on their grade in Spanish I. Of the A–B students, a random half received the A–V order, half the V–A order. The C–D students were randomized similarly. The list of paired associates consisted of 10 nonsense dissyllables as stimuli, with common English color words as responses.

The A–V order was superior to the V–A order for both groups of subjects, as may be seen in the means of Table 14.1. At face value, the A–V superiority seems definitely greater for the poorer subjects, 7.00 compared to 2.42 for the better subjects. Visual appearance is misleading in this small design, however, for the interaction F was only 1.39.

TABLE 14.1

ANOVA WITH BLOCKING:
AUDIO-VISUAL VERSUS VISUAL-AUDIO PRESENTATION

Grade	Audio-Visual	Visual-Audio
A or B	9.15	11.57
C or D	11.71	18.71

NOTES: $n = 7$, $\sum Y^2 = 5572$. (After Pimsleur & Bonkowski, 1961.)

In this study, the main benefit of the blocking variable was substantive. By including blocks, the investigators showed that the same method was uniformly superior, both for better and for poorer students. The worth of this conclusion, of course, depends on showing that the blocking variable was relevant to the behavior. This was verified, F_{blocks} being even a little larger than $F_{methods}$.

TABLE 14.2

TWO ANALYSES FOR DATA OF TABLE 14.1

Without blocks					With blocks			
Source	df	MS	F		Source	df	MS	F
Methods	1	156	4.83*		Methods	1	156	5.88*
Error	24	32.37			Blocks	1	165	6.22*
					M × B	1	37	1.39
					Error	24	26.54	

* $p < .05$

The statistical benefit of blocking may be assessed by doing the Anova two ways, both with and without the blocks variable, shown in Table 14.2. Including blocks removes their effect from SS_{error}. Correspondingly, MS_{error} is reduced from 32.37 to 26.54, a 20% increase in efficiency. Although modest, a 20% benefit represents higher power and a more accurate estimate of the size of the method effect. In this educational application, however, the main benefit of blocking was substantive. Paul Pimsleur died young, but the "Pimsleur Method" for language learning is widely available on audio cassettes. You can sometimes see it impressively advertised in airlines magazines.

Multi-Purpose Blocking. A multipurpose blocking variable was used to test whether group interaction on a cooperative task would facilitate or interfere with performance. An anagram-type task was used, in which subjects wrote as many words as possible using the letters { a f l i y o b t }. Subjects were junior high students in a marginal neighborhood, who were run in all-male or all-female groups of 1, 2, or 3.

For blocking, a preliminary test using the letters { i w m r p a c o } was given in the students' English classes. Ability varied greatly, from 0 words to just above 20. The 20% who made no more than 5 words were screened out. The remaining 295 were stratified in 5 ability levels, which was included as a factor in the design. Within each ability level, 32 students were randomly selected for a total N of 160 (Anderson, 1961a).

The blocks variable thus had four purposes. First, it screened out the very poor students, who would mainly have added noise to the data. Second, it ensured that students in each group had comparable ability, which was expected to maximize any group facilitation. Third, it allowed assessment of how group facilitation might depend on ability level. Fourth, the blocking variable increased statistical efficiency by more than 100% through reducing MS_{error}, in effect doubling the size of the experiment.

The results showed neither facilitation nor interference. The teams performed about as well as nominal groups formed by pooling words produced by two or three individuals who worked alone, with duplicate words not counted. Previous work had claimed to show inferiority of real groups, even in a similar task. This claim, however, appeared to reflect a confound with a too-short time limit in the previous work. Analysis of word production as a function of time in the present experiment showed that the real groups were initially somewhat slower in generating words, a natural consequence of the team situation, but they reached the same total as the nominal groups. Because the N of 160 was effectively more than doubled by the block design, accepting the null hypothesis would seem reasonable for this type of task (Section 4.1.3, page 93).[a]

14.2.3 OTHER BLOCKING VARIABLES

Successive time periods is often useful as a blocking variable. If the number of subjects in each treatment is a multiple of four, for example, the experiment could be run in four successive blocks. Each block would constitute a complete replication of the experiment, with random assignment of subjects separately within each block.

With this blocking, possible temporal changes in the subject population are balanced across the experimental treatments (see Exercise 12.b2). The same balance holds for possible changes in experimental procedure, from increased skill of the experimenters, for example, or from apparatus wear. Furthermore, the main effect of blocks measures such temporal changes.

Such temporal blocking could be useful when the experiment involves some deception, as in certain experiments in social psychology, in which the deception is revealed to the subjects at the end of the experiment. Despite requests for secrecy, there is always concern that word-of-mouth report will gradually contaminate the subject population. A small block effect would provide concrete reassurance that this danger is not serious. Also reassuring would be small block × treatment residuals (see Note 8.1.5a).

Procedure can legitimately be changed partway through the experiment when temporal blocking is used. Shortcomings of procedure may surface after a number of subjects have been run. These may seem serious enough to change, but not serious enough to start over. Such procedural changes may be introduced at the end of any block; since randomization is applied separately in each block, no bias is introduced. Of course, comparison of the data before and after the change is needed to check whether the pattern of results has changed.

Other potential sources of variability can be treated similarly. In some experiments, subjects come from two or more sources. Including subject source as a factor in the design not only balances sources across treatments but also allows the source effect to be evaluated. Some long-term conditioning experiments with animals, to take a second example, use two or more similar

apparatuses to run two or more subjects simultaneously. Apparatus may then be
treated as a factor in the design, again with random assignment. In many cases,
the main value of using such blocking variables in the design is for reassurance
that they are not important.[a]

14.2.4 ISSUES IN BLOCK DESIGN

One issue in block design is whether to use it. This depends on assessment of
costs and likely benefits. Two or three other issues are also noted, including a
justification for treating blocks as a fixed factor.

Substantive and Statistical Benefits. The two potential benefits of block
design were illustrated in the foregoing experiment on language methods. The
potential statistical benefit is a reduction in the error. The potential substantive
benefit is information on the individual differences variable. Finding that the
better method was better for both good and poor students was welcome in this
application to education.

These benefits should not be taken for granted. Even a small benefit requires
a correlation of B with Y of at least .35, which may not be easy to find (Exercise
13.3). Methodology in any area should thus give attention to finding useful variables for blocking. This also contributes to the larger problem of understanding
individual differences.

Blocking has two costs. To allow random assignment, the blocking variable
must be measured before the experiment begins. In the language methods study,
the investigator had only to look in his grade book for Spanish I. In the anagram
study, the cost was moderate because the pretest was given to entire classes of
students in single short sessions. In other situations, however, measuring the
blocks variable can be expensive.

The second cost of blocking is df. This cost was minimal in the language
methods study, 1 df for main effects of blocks and 1 df for block–treatment residuals. A study with four treatments and four blocks, however, could use up 3 +
9 df for block effects.

More blocks extract more information from B, but at a swiftly diminishing
rate. As a rough guide, 2, 3, 4, and 5 blocks will extract up to 67%, 75%, 80%,
and 83% of the information available in the blocking variable. A two-block
design thus does surprisingly well and would seem often sufficient for error
reduction. More blocks is sometimes desirable, however, to get more detailed
information on how the response depends on the blocking variable.

Covariance Alternative. Analysis of covariance may be superior to block
design when B is quantitative, corresponding to X in Chapter 13. A major practical advantage is that covariance does not require measuring the B scores for
every subject before running the first; unlike blocks, covariance does not require
random assignment with respect to B. Hence B could be measured at the

beginning of the experimental session for each subject. A further advantage is that Ancova requires only 1 df and, assuming a linear relation, extracts more information than any number of blocks. Nonnumerical, categorical variables can be handled by reducing them to two categories, coded as 0 and 1, which can extract the larger part of the available information.

Ancova has the further advantage that additional blocking variables can be included at little more cost than measuring them. Two or three potential blocking variables can thus be teamed, each using only 1 df. Correlated blocking variables, which are troublesome for blocks factorial design, are straightforward with Ancova. With small-N studies, this approach can provide needed power. Because of these advantages, Ancova deserves serious consideration (see further Section 13.1.2).

Blocks as Fixed Factor. Blocks is treated as a fixed factor in the foregoing Anova table. Some texts treat blocks as a random factor (Section 15.2). In that case, the correct error term for the treatment effect would be the treatment × block residual (interaction).

I see no justification for the random factor approach with the kinds of blocking variables under consideration. In the language methods study, the two blocks, namely, A–B and C–D students, are not a random sample from any population of blocks. Generalizing the results to some larger population of blocks, the raison d'etre of random factor analysis, is not even meaningful. Most psychological applications are of this type.

Natural blocks, in contrast, could be treated as a random factor. With animal litters, one treatment could be assigned to each subject in a litter. This blocking reduces effects of genetic variability and of prenatal environmental variability as well. Litter is analogous to a single subject in a repeated measures design so the proper error term is the litter × treatment residual. This natural blocking differs in kind from that in the foregoing discussion.[a]

Matching Groups. Block design is one way of matching treatment groups. Within each block, subjects are matched by virtue of similar scores on the B variable. Individual differences between blocks are thus removed from the error term. Hence the treatment means are more reliable.

Matching subjects across treatment conditions is a frequent concern and is sometimes worthwhile. It is easy to go astray, however, despite, or perhaps because of, the simplicity of the idea of matching. Matching by taking a difference or change score can actually do harm by increasing error variance (Section 13.1.2). Matching to "equate" nonrandom groups runs afoul of the treacherous regression artifact (Section 18.4.5). A survey of all articles in Volume 51 (1958) of the *Journal of Comparative and Physiological Psychology* indicated that matching was not well handled (Anderson, 1959a). Forty years later, great improvement still seems possible.

Matched Pairs. Subjects sometimes come in natural pairs, as with twins. With two experimental treatments, random assignment would be performed separately within each set of twins. The difference score for each set of twins could be analyzed to test F_{mean}. As Student asserted in his critique of the Lanarkshire nutrition experiment (see Appendix to Chapter 3), 50 sets of twins would have provided as much power as the many thousands of children actually studied, at much less expense, and probably with greater validity.

Similar technique could be used with larger groups, as with litters of rats. Each group would be treated as a "subject" in a repeated measures Anova, a technique that allows more than two treatments. The $S \times A$ residual is the error term, as already indicated under *Blocks as Fixed Factor*.

It would usually be a mistake, however, to match pairs when there is no natural matching. To illustrate with the language methods study, suppose subjects were matched on their numerical grade in Spanish I. To do this matching, all subjects would be ranked on their grade, the two highest would form one pair, the next two highest a second pair, and so on. Within each separate pair, one subject would be randomly assigned to each treatment. This is equivalent to using 14 blocks, but now the interaction residual must be used as the error term. This error would generally be larger and have fewer df than the proper error term shown in Table 14.2 (see Note 14.2.4a).

Post Blocking. In *post blocking*, subjects are assigned at random without regard to any blocking variable. After the experiment is complete, however, an attempt is made to block. This practice is sometimes used in medical experiments, in which it is usually difficult or impossible to measure blocking variables for all subjects before the experiment begins. Fleiss (1986, Section 6.3) argues against post blocking in clinical experiments for several reasons, especially because there are "hundreds of background characteristics not only measurable but often actually measured on patients in clinical experiments, and it is not unusual for each of them to serve as the basis for post-stratification" (p. 165). The same argument of course applies to Ancova with numerous covariates. With such data dredging, α escalation will be severe.

Results of such post-blocking analyses are valid only under the principle of planned comparisons (page 101). The blocking variables must be specified beforehand and have a reasonably firm a priori basis. It may be desirable, of course, to try out other possible correlates of the behavior on a post hoc, exploratory basis. Although these lack definite value as evidence, they can serve as clues to be tested in future work. Alternatively, they can be tested with independent sets of data, as in *Split-Half Replication* (Section 16.1.2, page 490).

14.3 LATIN SQUARES

Order effects are a concern when each subject receives more than a single treatment. *Latin square* designs can help control and analyze order effects.[a]

14.3.1 ORDER EFFECTS: POSITION AND CARRYOVER

Two kinds of order effects may be distinguished. One kind is *position effects*. Response to later treatments may be affected by adaptation, practice, fatigue, attentional weariness, and so forth. Position effects are assumed to depend only on serial position within the sequence of treatments, independent of which particular treatments occurred at previous positions.

A different kind of order effect involves *carryover effects* from one treatment to a following treatment. Hangovers are an example from everyday life; psychophysical contrast and assimilation are examples from perception. In general, carryover effects refer to treatment-specific transfer, as with the attitude experiment cited in Section 14.3.3 (pages 420*f*). Carryover effects differ from position effects in that they depend on the particular treatment.

For most purposes, although not all, position and carryover effects are undesirable. Following the philosophy of the Experimental Pyramid, they should be reduced through experimental procedure. Position effects from practice can be reduced by presenting a practice session prior to the experimental treatments. Carryover effects can often be reduced by allowing more time between treatments (see also Sections 14.4.1 and 14.4.2, pages 425*f*).

But order effects can hardly be eliminated completely. Some will remain, and the experimental design should guard against confounding them with treatments. Even when order effects are expected to be negligible, moreover, showing so may still be desirable.

TABLE 14.3

TWO FORMATS FOR 4×4 LATIN SQUARE

	Position				Treatment			
	1	2	3	4	A_1	A_2	A_3	A_4
S_1:	A_1	A_2	A_3	A_4	1st	2nd	3rd	4th
S_2:	A_2	A_3	A_4	A_1	4th	1st	2nd	3rd
S_3:	A_3	A_4	A_1	A_2	3rd	4th	1st	2nd
S_4:	A_4	A_1	A_2	A_3	2nd	3rd	4th	1st

A natural design precaution is to present the treatments in different sequences to different subjects, as with the Latin square at the left of Table 14.3 on the previous page. Each of four subjects takes the four A treatments but in a different sequence, as indicated by the cell entries. Thus, subject 2 takes A_2 first, A_1 last, and so on. With this design, each treatment occurs exactly once at each serial position. This position balance is shown more directly by rewriting the Latin square in the format at the right of Table 14.3. A Latin square of any size is easily constructed with the cyclic patterning shown in this 4×4 square. Write the A_j in numerical order in the first row. To get the second row, push all the A_j one space leftward, pick up A_1 as it falls off the end, and put it in the last space. To this second row, apply this same procedure to get the third row, and so on.

The cyclic pattern just described balances position effects, but it is vulnerable to carryover effects. Since A_2 follows A_1 all three possible times, any carryover effect from A_1 is completely confounded with the response to A_2. Similarly for the other treatments. Balancing for carryover effects is considered later; present concern is solely with position effects. Accordingly, carryover effects will be assumed negligible unless otherwise noted.

14.3.2 ANOVA FOR LATIN SQUARE

The present discussion treats Latin squares as repeated measures designs. The Anova is identical with the repeated measures designs of Chapter 6, but with one added source to represent position effects.

A quite different application of Latin square is with nonrepeated measures, with a single score for each subject. This application, considered in Section 15.3.2 (page 456), involves rather different considerations that present some serious confounding problems. Unclarity about this distinction has led to unduly negative comments about Latin squares for repeated measures.

Anova for Single Latin Square. The single Latin square is an $a \times a$ square with one subject in each sequence of treatments. Although some computer programs can give the full Latin square Anova, the regular repeated measures Anova can be supplemented by an easy hand calculation.

In the numerical example of Table 14.4, the first step is to apply the repeated measures Anova of Table 6.1. The computer printout yields SS_A on 3 df and $SS_{[SA]}$ on 9 df. The subscript $[SA]$ is bracketed to indicate that this $SS_{[SA]}$ includes the SS_P for position, which must be calculated and subtracted out.

To get SS_P, run a one-way Anova on the position means as follows. First, get the means of the four scores at each position. These are the column means from the right half of Table 14.4. To these four means, apply the hand formulas of Section 3.2.5 (page 67) to get SS_P for position on 3 df, listed below the table. This SS_P is part of $SS_{[SA]}$ and may be subtracted to yield

TABLE 14.4

NUMERICAL EXAMPLE OF LATIN SQUARE

	Position				Position			
	1	2	3	4	1	2	3	4
S_1:	A_1	A_2	A_3	A_4	9	8	8	15
S_2:	A_2	A_3	A_4	A_1	14	15	16	15
S_3:	A_3	A_4	A_1	A_2	19	12	9	15
S_4:	A_4	A_1	A_2	A_3	20	8	16	22

$$SS_P = 4[15.50^2 + 10.75^2 + 12.25^2 + 16.75^2]$$

$$- SS_{mean} = 93.188$$

SS_{mean}	=	3052.562	
SS_S	=	92.688	
SS_A	=	86.188	$F_A = 6.54$
$SS_{[SA]}$	=	119.562	
SS_P	=	93.188	$F_P = 7.07$
SS_{SA}	=	26.374	$F^*(3, 6) = 4.76$

$$SS_{SA} = SS_{[SA]} - SS_P. \tag{1}$$

The df for SS_{SA} are the 9 for $[SA]$ minus the 3 for P; MS_{SA} is used as the error term to get F_A and F_P. To the extent that position effects are nonzero, MS_{SA} is expected to be smaller than $MS_{[SA]}$.

The several SSs for the data of Table 14.4 are listed below the table. You can readily verify them using the hand calculations of Section 3.2.5 or with a computer. In this artificial example, the position effect is as large as the treatment effect. In practice, large position effects might be accompanied by adverse carryover effects.

The general Anova table for a single $a \times a$ square is shown at the left of Table 14.5, with $N = a$. Do not use F_A from the computer printout. Instead, follow the numerical example and recompute F_A using MS_A from the computer printout and the error term MS_{SA} from your hand calculation. As in the numerical example, $SS_{SA} = SS_{[SA]} - SS_P$.

The ε adjustment from the printout should generally be used to determine the criterial F^* for repeated measures Latin squares, just as in Chapter 6. The proper df would thus be $\varepsilon(a - 1)$ and $\varepsilon(a - 1)(a - 2)$. For simplicity, this ε adjustment was not used in Table 14.4.

A single 4×4 square has only 6ε df for error, which is very small. A single 5×5 square has 16ε df for error, which seems marginal. In practice, accordingly, small Latin squares are generally run with replication.

Square Replication. Replication of a Latin square has the obvious advantage of increasing the amount of data. Instead of repeating the same square, however, it is usually preferable to use different squares. Since each square has different sequences of treatments, possible carryover effects have more opportunity to balance out across following treatments.

Two forms of replication are considered here. The first kind replicates by using a number of different squares, with only one subject in each sequence, for a total of N subjects. This is again a subjects × treatments design, but with N subjects, not just a. The Anova table, listed in the left of Table 14.5, is essentially the same as for the single square already discussed. The computer printout

TABLE 14.5

ANOVA FOR REPLICATED LATIN SQUARE

Source	df	Source	df
Between		**Between**	
Mean	1	Mean	1
Subjects (S)	$N - 1$	Sequences (G)	$g - 1$
		S/G	$g(n - 1)$
Within		**Within**	
Treatments (A)	$a - 1$	Treatments (A)	$a - 1$
		[AG]	$[(g - 1)(a - 1)]$
Position (P)	$a - 1$	Position (P)	$a - 1$
		AG	$(g - 2)(a - 1)$
SA	$(N - 2)(a - 1)$	SA/G	$g(n - 1)(a - 1)$

is supplemented by a hand calculation for SS_P from the a position means, exactly as with the single square. Subtracting SS_P from $SS_{[SA]}$ yields SS_{SA}, which is the error term for A and P.

The other kind of replication may also use more than one different square, but has more than one subject in each sequence. Sequences then becomes a between subjects factor; the basic analysis is that of the $(S \times A) \times G$, mixed repeated measures design of Table 6.3, with G representing sequences. This Anova table is at the right of Table 14.5, with g equal to the total number of different sequences and n equal to the number of subjects in each sequence.

The error term for all within sources is $MS_{SA/G}$, which is the error term used by the computer with $n > 1$. Accordingly, there is no need to recompute F_A. However, the computer output for SS_{AG} is really $SS_{[AG]}$ because it includes S_P. The computer's F_{AG} should thus be ignored. Instead, calculate SS_P from the position means, subtract it from $SS_{[AG]}$ to obtain SS_{AG}, and divide by the within subjects error to get F_P and F_{AG}.

Note that the left side of Table 14.5 is a special case of the right side, with $n = 1$ subject in each sequence. Sequences is then confounded with subjects. In the Between subtable, accordingly, sequences becomes identical with subjects and S/G disappears. In the Within subtable, similarly, SA/G disappears and AG becomes identical with SA.

This second form of replication has a seeming advantage of two additional sources, namely, the sequence effect in the Between subtable and the treatment × sequence effect in the Within subtable. Both sources are zero under the standard Latin square model (page 423). If either is statsig, that warns about carryover effects or other nonadditivities in the data. These warning signs are insensitive, however, the more so the larger the square. Even for the 4 × 4 square, therefore, the first form of replication may be preferable as it provides more opportunities for nonadditivities to balance out.[a]

Including Between Subject Variables. Between subjects variables can readily be included with a Latin square. In Harlow's mother love experiments, for example, suppose the monkeys were tested in several social situations when they reached adolescence. The social situations constitute a repeated measures variable, presented in Latin square order to balance position effects. The three mother conditions (real, cloth, and wire) are a between subjects variable. With one monkey in each sequence, the Anova follows the identical pattern already seen at the right of Table 14.5, except that G is now the mother variable, not the sequence variable.

In this example, the between infant error for MS_{mother} would be much larger than the within infant error for $MS_{situation \times mother}$. The mother test will lack power because few infants are likely to be available. The more sensitive test of situation × mother, however, may contain some information about how social adjustment depends on the mother variable. This interaction residual, accordingly, may be less a complication than substantive information. For this purpose, social situations with substantially different effects across mother conditions would be desirable.

14.3.3 EXTENSIONS OF THE LATIN SQUARE

Two extensions of the Latin square are considered here. One allows additional treatment variables; the other balances carryover effects.

Hyper-Latin Squares. The Latin square is interesting because it compresses three factors into a two-factor design. This compression can be amplified. The Latin square idea can thus be extended to include additional variables.

Table 14.6 shows the pattern for two variables, also called a Greco-Latin square. Each cell in the square represents a single treatment—a combination of one level of each of the two variables, A and B. By themselves, the A_j form a Latin square design; so do the B_k. Furthermore, each A_j occurs exactly once with each B_k, so A and B are statistically independent.

A Greco–Latin square can transform a between subjects variable into a repeated measures variable with very substantial benefits. An application to cognitive algebra of social attitudes may be used for illustration. In these studies, subjects judged statesmanship of U.S. presidents, each described by biographical paragraphs of standardized value (Low, Low-Medium, High-Medium, High). The primary treatments, the A_j, were combinations of paragraphs of different value that were constructed to test the averaging hypothesis for attitude integration (see Figure 9.3, page 278).

TABLE 14.6

4 × 4 GRECO-LATIN SQUARE

A_1B_1	A_2B_3	A_3B_4	A_4B_2
A_2B_2	A_1B_4	A_4B_3	A_3B_1
A_3B_3	A_4B_1	A_1B_2	A_2B_4
A_4B_4	A_3B_2	A_2B_1	A_1B_3

In the first row of this Greco-Latin square, the subject would respond to all four paragraph combinations, A_1 to A_4, in the order listed. But there is a difficulty: The same president cannot be used four times in succession; biographical information would carry over from one treatment to the next. If Theodore Roosevelt was presented a second time to the same subject, some information from the first presentation would remain in the subject's memory and influence the attitudinal judgment to the second.

This difficulty was resolved by using a different president at each serial position for each subject. Thus, B_1, B_2, B_3, and B_4 might be James Knox Polk, Grover Cleveland, Theodore Roosevelt, and Woodrow Wilson. In this way, each subject would form an attitude about each of four different presidents, each with a different treatment, A_j. Because the A_j had been standardized, they were comparable across presidents. In this way, the Greco-Latin square allowed a repeated measures design for the primary variable.

The power advantage can be substantial. In one application, a between subjects design would have required 510 subjects to get the same power as the 48 subjects actually used in a Greco-Latin square (Anderson, 1981, Section 1.3.2). Of course, constructing and standardizing the biographical paragraphs required considerable work. Once constructed, however, these paragraphs could be used in a number of experiments. Attitude research, which nearly always uses between subjects design, can be more efficient in this way.

Greco–Latin squares may also be used when both A and B are primary variables. For example, suppose a rat gets a short pulse of reinforcing electrical brain stimulation for bar pressing on an FI schedule. Amplitude and duration of stimulation could each be varied over 4 levels. Only 4 trials are required for each rat, instead of the 16 for the complete factorial.

Indeed, one more variable could also be balanced similarly, still requiring only 4 trials per rat. This seems the ultimate, for it uses all 15 df for main effects. Replication would ordinarily be needed to get an error term, but a single unreplicated square would estimate the main effects of all three primary variables, while balancing for position and rats.[a]

The Anova for the Greco–Latin square follows the pattern at the left of Table 14.5, except for the added B variable. The SS for B may be obtained by hand calculation in the same way as previously indicated for P. Accordingly, $SS_{SA} = SS_{[SA]} - SS_P - SS_B$. The same formula holds for replication with different squares.

There is a price for compressing multiple variables into hyper-Latin squares. If interaction residuals are present, they are confounded with main effects. Marginal main effects thus lack credibility. But for exploratory work, at least, a hyper-square could be economical.

Balanced Square for Carryover Effects.   With repeated measures, carryover effects are a natural concern. The cyclic square of Table 14.3 is undesirable because each treatment always has the same predecessor. Carryover from any one treatment will thus be confounded with one particular other treatment.

Such confounding can be ameliorated with a square balanced for previous treatment. A balanced 4 × 4 square is shown in Table 14.7 on the next page, in which each treatment follows each other treatment exactly once.

TABLE 14.7

BALANCED LATIN SQUARE

A_1	A_2	A_3	A_4
A_4	A_3	A_2	A_1
A_2	A_4	A_1	A_3
A_3	A_1	A_4	A_2.

To illustrate this balanced Latin square, consider a study of motor skill of commercial pilots, say, with four treatments: alcohol, tranquilizer, lack of sleep, and placebo. Suppose A_1 has a hangover effect that persists to the following treatment. In the cyclic square of Table 14.3, this carryover would be concentrated entirely on treatment A_2, confounding its comparison with A_3 and A_4. In the balanced square, carryover tends to be equalized across treatments. No less important, the carryover effect for each treatment can be measured. The numerical calculations, which are a little complicated, are given clearly together with a numerical example in Cochran and Cox (1957, Section 4.6a). Considerable simplification results if the last column of the square can be replicated so that each treatment also follows itself.[b]

Balanced Latin squares are little used in psychology. This is surprising; they are an obvious design for dealing with carryover effects, a natural concern with repeated measures. Even when carryover effects are expected to be negligible, moreover, documenting this for others by using a balanced square may be helpful. An algorithm for constructing balanced squares is given in Note 14.3.3c.[c]

14.3.4 MODEL AND ASSUMPTIONS FOR LATIN SQUARES

The Latin square is a special case of repeated measures design, in which treatments are balanced across position. The statistical assumptions for repeated measures Anova thus apply so the ε adjustment is generally needed.

Present concern, however, is not with these statistical assumptions, but with position and carryover effects. These effects are a concern with any repeated measures design, of course, but they are usually passed over lightly. The following considerations are thus pertinent to all within subjects designs.

Model for Latin Square. The three variables in the Latin square are subjects, treatments, and position, denoted by S, A, and P. A complete model would include all three interaction residuals involving the position term P, namely, SP, AP, and SAP. The three position residuals, however, cannot be determined in this design. The standard model handles this problem by assuming all three position residuals are zero. These two models may be written:

Complete Model: $Y = S + A + P + SA + SP + AP + SAP +$ error.

Standard Model: $Y = S + A + P + SA + \quad 0 \quad + \quad 0 \quad + \quad 0 \quad +$ error.

The standard model is the same as for the $S \times A$, repeated measures design, except for the added term for position. SS_P is determinate because position is balanced across treatments.

Position Residuals. The three interaction residuals for position will not generally be zero, as assumed in the standard model. The main concern is with SP, the subject × position residual. With any position effect, such as practice or fatigue, some subjects will be slow, some fast. These subject differences in position effect are subject × position residuals, and they can be substantial. The other two positions residuals, AP and SAP, would not ordinarily seem serious. One reason is that the AP residual should generally be a fraction of the main A effect, and SAP a fraction of AP.

An appreciation of how nonzero position residuals affect the Anova may be gained from inspection of the expected mean squares given by Myers and Well, listed in Note 14.3.4a. The key result is that the standard error term for repeated measures design is an acceptable error for treatment and for position. Its expected value should be a little large in most applications, yielding Fs that average a little small. Their result thus puts the Latin square on good ground.[a]

Carryover Effects. Even the complete model listed above does not allow for carryover from one treatment to the following. In the foregoing example of motor skill, tranquilizer effects might carry over to the following treatment. Anova for the balanced square of Table 14.7 may then be needed (see Note 14.3.3b). As a more complex possibility, the tranquilizer effect may carry over only to the alcohol treatment.

The seriousness of this carryover problem must be assessed in terms of extrastatistical knowledge about the situation at hand, together with careful scrutiny of the data at hand. The first line of protection, of course, is experimental procedure that minimizes possible carryover effects (Section 14.4.2). For squares larger than 2 × 2, partial protection is available from the balanced design illustrated in Table 14.7.

14.3.5 OTHER ASPECTS OF LATIN SQUARES

2 × 2 Latin Square. The 2 × 2 Latin square requires separate consideration. It presents two treatments in both possible orders: $A_1 A_2$ and $A_2 A_1$, with n subjects in each order. This design, also called a crossover design, is often useful when two treatments are to be compared. It is common in medical science, for example, in which A_1 might be a new treatment whose effectiveness is to be compared with a standard treatment or a placebo.

2 × 2 LATIN SQUARE

	1st	2nd	1st	2nd
Sequence 1	A_1	A_2	1	1
Sequence 2	A_2	A_1	1	8

The Anova follows the pattern indicated in the right half of Table 14.5.

The special problem with the 2 × 2 square concerns the interpretation of the sequence effect. This tests between the two row means, both based on the same two treatments, but differing in the order of presentation. A real difference can only result if the carryover effect differs for the two treatments. This is, in effect, a treatment–treatment interaction (see further Exercise b11).

A statsig sequence effect thus raises doubt about the main effect of treatments: At least one treatment has a different effect when it follows the other than when it comes first. What is the proper measure of treatment effects?

To see the difficulty, consider the extreme numerical example at the right of the above table, which shows a large superiority of 4.5 for A_1 versus 1.0 for A_2. The sequence effect is equally large, however, which implies differential carryover and caution about interpreting the treatment effect. In fact, both treatments have equal effect when given first.

Some writers argue that a statsig sequence effect precludes interpretation of the treatment main effect. Instead, the treatment effect should be tested using only the data in the first column. The within subjects design is not appropriate, in other words, and between subjects analysis is required (see also Section 14.4, next page). This argument certainly applies to the above numerical example.

This argument, however, may often be an overfearful failure to utilize the greater precision of repeated measures design. It is akin to the argument that main effects cannot be interpreted when the interaction residual is statsig. Differential carryover can sometimes be serious, of course, but judgment on this issue requires extrastatistical, task-specific knowledge.[a]

Position Effects. Visual inspection is always desirable with position effects. Any real position effect will likely be concentrated in the linear component, and this may be diluted in the overall F for position (see *Linear Trend*, page 96). Unfortunately, the linear component of position lacks a proper error term.

In many studies, prior experience will indicate that position effects will be relatively small. In such cases, it may be adequate to use the Latin square in order to obtain balance without troubling to calculate $SS_{position}$. Instead, just do the repeated measures of Chapter 6. This seems a sensible use of prior knowledge to simplify the analysis. A similar issue arises with block designs (Section 14.2) and more generally with partial analysis (Section 18.4.3).

Role of Latin Squares. Latin square designs have been criticized because interaction residuals can bias treatment means and significance tests. For Latin squares with independent groups, this bias can be serious (page 456).

For repeated measures designs, however, such bias seems much less serious. One reason is that all three interaction residuals in the complete model (page 423, top) involve position, and only the subject × position residual is likely to be sizable in most applications. Except for the 2 × 2 square, moreover, the balanced square is available to balance and measure one-step carryover effects.

Repeated measures designs always suffer potential threats from position and carryover effects. They may yield systematically different results from between subjects designs, as discussed in the next main section. Use of repeated measures designs thus depends heavily on extrastatistical considerations. They are exceptionally useful, however, and the Latin square is their best form.

Square Randomization. Standard advice is to select a Latin square for any experiment completely at random. For many purposes, I think it would suffice to begin with the cyclic square, illustrated in Table 14.3, as this is easily constructed. Next, permute the columns at random to remove the cyclicity. Then assign subjects to rows at random and assign treatments to Latin letters in the square at random. Otherwise, consult Fisher and Yates (1963).

A balanced square, of course, is not random but systematic. The columns should not be permuted because that would destroy the balance. It is still advisable, however, to randomize within this restriction in the manner just indicated.

14.4 WITHIN SUBJECTS AND BETWEEN SUBJECTS DESIGN

Repeated measures design, also called within subjects design, has both substantive and statistical advantages over between subjects design (Chapters 6 and 11). Within subjects design may suffer, however, from the order effects discussed with Latin squares in the preceding main section. Within and between design may thus yield different results, so the choice between them needs consideration. Much depends on situational specifics, as illustrated in Section 14.4.3.[a]

14.4.1 STARTUP EFFECTS

Any task involves initial adjustment and familiarization. The first trial for a rat in a T maze involves novel odors and sights, all fascinating to the rat. Exploration of these novel stimuli may interfere with the process under study. For any human subject, the very first experiment is also a novel experience, one that evokes various reactions not ordinarily relevant to the experimenter's purpose. Even well-practiced motor skills often show substantial warmup effects at the start of a new session.

A natural tactic is to use a startup phase to familiarize the subject with the task. This phase has the threefold purpose of reducing startup effects, increasing response reliability, and more important, increasing the validity of the response measure. With repeated sessions, a brief startup phase might be included with each later session.

Preliminary practice is usually desirable, although there are exceptions. In a between subjects learning task, some learning might occur in the startup phase and this might confound comparisons of learning across conditions. In a within subjects task, the startup phase might produce differential transfer when the first treatment varies across subjects.

14.4.2 SHORT-TERM SHIFTS

Short-term shifts include effects from one trial that may persist to the next trial or two. Among these are contrast and assimilation effects common in perception. Also included are other carryover effects stemming from fatigue, shifts in attention, and so on.[a]

Three tactics are common for handling short-term shifts. The first is to allow sufficient time between trials for them to dissipate. This may require only a few seconds for some tasks of perception and judgment but more than a day with alcohol or other drug treatments.

The second tactic is to interpolate a standard condition after each treatment to return the subject to a standard state before beginning the next treatment. This *baseline* or *washout* tactic is more appropriate with more persistent carryover effects (see also *Baseline Procedure* in Section 11.3.1, page 313).

The third tactic is to balance short-term effects across treatments. This may be done by treatment randomization (Section 11.2) or with Latin square design (Section 14.3). Latin squares balanced for preceding treatment are attractive because they allow one-step carryover effects to be measured.

14.4.3 INTERACTION

Within subjects design can suffer because of interaction between different experimental conditions. Some interactions are obvious, as just illustrated with short-term shifts. Others are less obvious and may not be suspected or uncovered for some time. Of the many diverse kinds of such interactions, five are cited here to help illuminate a general issue.

Interaction in Conditioning Studies. The same experimental manipulation often has much larger effects in within subjects than in between subjects design. This within–between difference in effect size has been found with intensity of the conditioned stimulus in classical conditioning and with magnitude of reward in instrumental conditioning.

In human eye-blink conditioning, for example, with soft and loud tones as conditioned stimuli and an aversive air puff as the unconditioned stimulus, Grice and Hunter (1964) found a crossover interaction. Percentage conditioned eye-blinks were roughly 23 and 66 for the soft and loud tones in the within condition, 39 and 46 in the between condition.[a]

Theoretically, this outcome disagreed with an interpretation in terms of associative conditioning, in which the effect of the conditioned stimulus derives from its absolute intensity. Also of theoretical interest, a biological interpretation in terms of a protective function of the conditioned blink seems inconsistent with the low blink rate to the soft tone in the within design. This pattern of data was one of an accumulation of results that were increasingly problematic for stimulus–response theories and helped lead to the current cognitive perspective.

Interaction in Verbal Learning. In verbal learning, a number of studies have found interaction between different levels of a stimulus factor that is varied within subjects. Such interaction is not possible when the stimulus factor is varied between subjects (see similarly *Within Subjects Design* at the end of Section 8.1.6, page 243).

As one possible interaction, subjects may concentrate on learning words of one kind more than another. Underwood (1983, pp. 157–161) cites a study of free recall of three lists of words, one list for each of three different groups. One list included only high frequency words, and one only low frequency words, thereby providing a between subjects comparison of high and low frequency. The third list included half high and half low frequency words, which provides a within subjects comparison of high and low frequency.

Ample evidence indicates that high frequency words, being more meaningful, should be learned faster. This prediction was verified for the between design: Mean recall was 10.9 and 8.9 words for the high and low lists, respectively. But the opposite effect was obtained for the within design, the corresponding means being 9.7 and 11.0.

One interpretation is that subjects quickly recognized the difference between the two types of words and decided to allot more time to the harder low frequency words. Regardless of the interpretation, this crossover interaction raises doubt about using within subjects design to study effects of meaningfulness.

A second possible interaction may arise from contrast between two different kinds of stimuli in a mixed list. Thus, verbal stimuli are better remembered when they elicit bizarre images than common images when both are given in a mixed list, but not ordinarily when separate lists are used (see review by Einstein & McDaniel, 1987). This does not appear to reflect differential allocation of time/attention, but requires a more complex theory (McDaniel et al., 1995). In this case, the within subjects process has substantive interest.

Stimulus Context Effects. Responses to the focal stimulus on any trial may be affected by context stimuli. In the color contrast study of Figure 11.5, the gray field looks greenish next to a red field, reddish next to a green field. A surprisingly strong assimilation effect appears with the line–box illusion of Figure 8.1 (page 226). Analogous effects can occur with conceptual qualities; a strong belief may seem more moderate when compared with one more extreme.

Adaptation is an important special case, in which the stimulus context may be a single stimulus presented repeatedly over trials. With perceptual stimuli, adaptation changes the neutral point of stimulus magnitude. You can check this sensory adaptation by putting one finger in hot water, an adjacent finger in cold water, observing how both temperature feelings fade away. Then putting both fingers in lukewarm water evokes a cool or warm sensation in the respective fingers, a consequence of the shift in the neutral points of sensation. Evidently, physical measurement alone cannot explain psychophysics. Similar adaptation can occur with conceptual stimuli.

If the context effect itself is the object of study, within design seems exactly appropriate, as with the two perceptual examples just cited. If the context effect is undesirable, within design may still be possible if it has short-term effects, using the three tactics of Section 14.4.2. If it has longer-term effects, however, between design may be necessary.

Optimal Conditions. Different optimality conditions may be found using within and between design. Height of desk or workbench is a prosaic but important determinant of comfort and productivity. Determining the optimal height is important because even a tiny effect would become huge when summed over hundreds of hours for each of thousands of workers.

In one study, productivity in a simple motor task was tested using a repeated measures design with six workbench heights, ranging from 18 inches below to 2 inches above elbow level. A strong, clear maximum was found for workbench height 6 inches below elbow level. This within design seems ideal, for subjects serve as their own controls.

Surprisingly, the optimal height depended on the range of workbench heights. A second group of subjects was tested with six heights, all 8 inches higher than those of the first group. For them, optimal height was about 4 inches higher than for the first group. The two groups thus yielded different conclusions about optimal working conditions (Kennedy & Landesman, 1963).

It seems that subjects learned a composite skill adapted to the range of all six treatment conditions. This interaction among the treatments pushed the optimal height toward the middle of the treatment range for each group. To determine a true optimum might thus require between design.

Frame of Reference in Judgments of Magnitude. Judgments of magnitude generally depend on some frame of reference that relates the range of stimuli to the response range. With the common 1–10, *least–most* rating scale, for example, subjects tend to distribute their responses across the whole scale, regardless of the range of stimuli. Such frame-of-reference effects may produce different results in within and between design.

As one example, consider judgments of likableness of persons described by sets of 2 or 6 personality traits, all traits of equal value within each set. Number of traits has large effects in within design, small effects in between design.

Which design yields a valid result? Between design tends to wash out any real effect of number of traits because of the relative nature of the *least–most* response scale. Within design eliminates this artifact because each subject has to make, in effect, comparative judgments based on different numbers of traits. This interpretation is buttressed by the commonsense consideration that if you like a woman and find out something new and good about her, you will like her even better. Two theoretical implications are given in the chapter note.[b]

Such frame-of-reference effects are ubiquitous. They are not surprising, of course, when the ends of the judgment scale are relative, as with *least–most*. However, similar effects occur when the ends are more definite, as in *bad–good*, or even with probability, which has absolute ends of 0 and 1. For a related confounding, see *Frame of Reference* in Section 8.1.4 (page 234).

14.4.4 CUMULATIVE CHANGE

Many tasks are characterized by cumulative change in response, notably with learning and memory. Some of these tasks clearly require between design; other tasks seem natural for within design.

Learning mirror reading or mirror writing, for example, could be studied only under one anxiety or drug condition. This learning effect is substantially irreversible so the same subject cannot be meaningfully run under another such condition. Many tasks of learning and memory are of this type.

The learning curve, on the other hand, can often be studied on a within subjects basis. Time on successive trials would generate the learning curve for each subject in the mirror reading example. Using a different group of subjects for each number of trials would be nonsensible.

In some cases, of course, measuring the response might interfere with the process under study. In an incidental learning task, the subject may be told to rate successive words on pleasantness and then, without warning, tested on memory for the words themselves. With the subject once alerted, further trials would not measure incidental learning.

A somewhat different example appears in studies of forgetting. To measure forgetting requires a recall trial, but this recall trial is a rehearsal opportunity and may be expected to retard future forgetting. Between design may then be necessary to study forgetting or interference as a function of time.

14.4.5 GENERALITY

The process—outcome distinction of Section 1.2 is important in choosing within or between design. The cited study of bench height is a prime example of outcome generality since the goal was to find an optimal height for business application. A within design might seem ideal in this case on the plausible expectation of no interaction among height conditions. The actual results are thus a pointed warning to keep alert to possible interaction among treatment conditions in within design.

An extreme stand against within subjects design was taken by Poulton (1973), who asserted that within design should only be used when it would yield the same results as between design. Poulton supports his stand by citing the bench height study, the centerpiece of a number of analogous studies in his article. However, Poulton's stand rests on unrecognized but severe restrictions on the domain of inquiry, especially his sole concern with outcome generality. Within design is clearly appropriate in some of the foregoing examples. In some cases, indeed, between design answers the wrong question.

For process generality, of course, design choice is governed by the processes that are of interest. Of the two cited studies of verbal learning, the meaningfulness interaction was considered an undesirable confound. However, the interaction involving bizarre images represented a phenomenon deserving of study. In the cited conditioning study, similarly, the within design was considered to reveal a process of intrinsic interest.

Even for outcome generality, moreover, the situation to which generalization is desired often represents within rather than between design. Many situations of everyday life are of within type, as with the foregoing example of effect of number of traits in person cognition.

Another example concerns inverse inference from sample to population, which is common to statistics and to theory of human judgment—decision. The representativeness heuristic (Kahneman & Tversky, 1972) claimed that subjects ignore population base rate and sample size, and judge solely on the basis of sample proportion. They failed to find a base rate effect, a result they took to support their heuristic. Leon and Anderson (1974), however, found a large base rate effect, contrary to the representativeness heuristic (see Figure 19.1). This latter study was criticized by Ward (1975) on the ground that it used within design whereas Kahneman and Tversky had used between design. Life, however, is a within design; each of us makes many inferences about causes of related outcomes or events. This view was reaffirmed by Fischhoff, Lichtenstein, and Slovic (1979), who corroborated Leon and Anderson (see also discussion of Figure 19.1 and Anderson, 1996a, p. 360, Note 12).

NOTES

14.1.1a. Unreported subject loss troubled some work on the "poopout effect," in which rats learn a shock-avoidance response but then gradually cease to avoid at the warning signal, instead waiting until the shock comes on to make an escape response (Anderson & Nakamura, 1964). Quite a few rats, however, did not learn the avoidance at all.

In writing up some subsequent experiments, we had considerable trouble relating our results to a published paper that reported avoidance conditioning but not any subjects that failed to learn. When I later saw one of the authors at a meeting, he said they actually had thrown out a lot of rats that had failed to learn. He seemed unaware that their failure to mention this subject elimination in their article might mislead others.

14.1.1b. An example of filling in missing responses arose in a functional measurement analysis of a mental search task by Shanteau (1991). Subjects began by thoroughly memorizing this serial list of eight four-letter words:

>   rice, lime, tuna, beef, fish, pear, cake, veal.

They were then asked various questions that had some, none, or all of the words as answers. Among these questions were:

>   Which have exactly two vowels?
>   Which have exactly two consonants?

Their task was to process the memorized list serially, speaking correct answers aloud.

The sequence of response times followed an additive model that demonstrated the independence of the two primary processes: memory retrieval; and the decision whether a given word was an answer. The decision processing times could be quantified with this model. As one interesting result, decision time for the listed consonant question was twice as long as for the vowel question although the two have identical answers.

Occasionally, a subject failed to speak a correct answer. In order to complete the data curve, the mean latency for the other subjects was substituted in these cases. Such missing responses occurred about 3% of the time in the later experiments, a frequency that seems not unreasonable for this particular task. Various checks indicated that this substitution procedure did not bias the results. Extremely long response times occurred about 1 time in 200 and were replaced in a similar manner.

This experiment is one of many in which within subject replication would be desirable. This would have eased the missing data problem and, more important, allowed assessment of individual differences through single subject analysis.

14.1.1c. The following example of extreme scores is a lesson in experimental procedure as well as the principle of replication. In this study, subjects had to evaluate each of a sequence of stimuli on a low-to-high rating scale. A substantial number of subjects switched their scale direction partway through, thus interchanging low and high. This switch was clear in the data because many stimuli were clearly low or high. My assistant had not monitored the subjects' behavior after they got started in the experiment and, because the subjects were being run under time pressure at another institution, transcribing responses was deferred until subject running was complete. Thus, the problem was not noticed until all 96 subjects had been run one by one. Because the switch was clear in the data, it was easy to detect and replace these subjects and this was done.

The response display was faulty, not subject-proof against this switching. Although there seemed no likelihood that this subject loss could produce any bias in this task, it had cast a shadow over the data. Accordingly, the experiment was replicated with another 96 subjects, using a subject-proof response display and procedure. This replication yielded virtually identical results (Anderson, 1971).

14.1.2a. The following illustrative instructions are from an experiment on the size–weight illusion, in which felt heaviness of objects of the same gram weight varies inversely with their size (see Figure 5.3, page 131). The response was made by a line-mark on a separate slip of paper for each trial. Note that the first paragraph sets up the schema for the task, without unnecessary detail.

> Your job in this experiment is to judge the heaviness of a series of blocks like these (show a couple). As you lift each block, you should judge how heavy it feels to you.
>
> Here is how you lift the blocks. I will place the block here on this platform. Then you lift it by pulling down on this handle. Pull the block up once briefly and let it down. Keep your eyes on the block as you lift it. Do not jiggle the block, but just lift it briefly and set it down. You have ample time to lift the block, but you should set it down before the buzzer sounds. If the buzzer comes on, that means you are taking too long.
>
> This is how you make your judgement. Just make a mark on this line. Mark near this end for the lightest weight; mark near this end for the heaviest weight. It is not important exactly where you mark, except that you should stay away from the ends of the line, even for the lightest and heaviest of the weights. For the other weights, mark at intermediate positions on the line so as to express how heavy each weight feels to you.
>
> These two blocks are the standards for the experiment. This one is the heaviest; this one is the lightest. (Have S lift each standard three times alternately; the first time you give each standard, point to the appropriate region of the line lying in front of S and say "This one should be marked around here," pointing about ½ or 1 inches from the light end, and 1 or 2 inches from the heavy end.)
>
> I'm going to start with a practice session. In this practice you should get used to the feel of the blocks, and how to make your judgements on the line. It will take you a while to get used to the task, so you should feel free to change the way you make your judgements until you find the way that is most suitable. Remember, there is no right or wrong way to answer; your job is simply to tell how heavy each block feels to you.
>
> All right, that ends the practice. Now there's a short rest before we continue.
>
> All right, now it's time for another break.

Verbatim instructions from two other experiments are given in Anderson (1982, Appendix A). A complex set of instructions, developed by Anne Schlottmann to study probability judgments in children, is reproduced in Anderson and Schlottmann (1991).

14.2.2a. For some years, I used this anagram experiment to illustrate block design in my design–statistics course because the 100$^+$% increase in efficiency is impressive. One of my students was so impressed that he blocked in his Ph.D. thesis on the von Restorf isolation effect (Erickson, 1963). Indeed, he blocked on two variables, which is very tedious. But neither blocking variable was related to the response measure, so his blocking effort was wasted. He was not pleased. Thereafter I switched to the language methods study, which gives a more modest indication of the likely benefit of blocking.

I should emphasize that this anagram experiment, although a good example of blocking, was an embarrassingly bad choice of problem because the task lacks generality.

14.2.3a. Block design has been widely developed in applied areas, in which blocks often arise naturally. Incomplete block designs can be useful when each subject (or block) can take only some of the experimental treatments (e.g., Cochran & Cox, 1957).

14.2.4a. The idea that blocks should be treated as a random factor arises from the *randomized blocks design* developed in agriculture, in which fertility gradients across a field can be a substantial source of variability. To reduce the effect of this variability, the field is divided into smaller blocks that can be expected to be more uniform in fertility. Each treatment is applied to one plot of ground in each block. Variability between blocks is thus removed from the error. Since there is typically no replication within plots, the block × treatment residual is necessarily used as the error. This is statistically appropriate because generalization across a population of blocks is desired. This blocks rationale is the same as with repeated measures, in which each subject is a block.

This randomized block approach has been taken over in some psychology texts without realizing that most subject blocking in psychology is conceptually different. That is why these texts begin with the case of one replication of each treatment in each block, a case that is generally undesirable in blocking on an individual difference variable, as in both examples of Section 14.2.2. For most psychological applications, however, the population consists of individual subjects; the blocks have no empirical reality as do agricultural blocks. Although Hays (1994, p. 560) attempts to bridge this gap with an artificial example to which the agricultural analysis would apply, his approach would be impossible in practice. Texts that give a correct treatment include Keppel (1991), Myers and Well (1991), and Maxwell and Delaney (1990), the last of which is also enthusiastic about the covariance alternative.

14.3a. Among psychological texts, Myers and Well (1991) give a good treatment of Latin squares for repeated measures. The more technical treatise by Jones and Kenward (1989) discusses uses of collateral data from washout or baseline treatments interpolated between regular treatments. Cotton's (1993) chapter on Latin squares is useful although not easy. Winer et al. (1991) and Kirk (1995) give considerable space to Latin squares for independent scores, which are discussed in Section 15.3.2.

14.3.2a. An alternative approach to replication with Latin squares is given by Myers and Well (1991, Table 11.7, p. 359), who consider replication with several different squares but with only one subject per sequence. They treat squares as a between subjects variable, rather than sequences as was done here. With a subjects in each square, the differences between different squares can be tested, following the Anova at the right of Table 14.5, with G as squares rather than sequences. But although the square term provides a warning about nonadditivities, this warning would seem too insensitive to be worthwhile. In effect, it tests for differences between squares in nonadditivities averaged over all a sequences of each square. Even the more sensitive sequence term in the present analysis would seem to lack power except for 2×2 and 3×3 squares.

Myers and Well also use two interaction terms involving square: position × square and treatment × square. The treatment × sequence effect, AG, in the right half of Table 14.5 corresponds to their treatment × square term. The corresponding position ×

sequence effect has been omitted to simplify understanding Table 14.5, but it could be added. Finally, Myers and Well treat square as random, whereas the present sequence term is considered fixed, in line with the rationale of Section 15.2.

14.3.3a. In the 4×4 Greco–Latin square illustrated in the text, the A_j and B_k represent orthogonal squares because each A_j occurs exactly once with each B_k. The following square takes this balance to the limit by adding a third variable C:

$$A_1 B_1 C_1 \qquad A_2 B_3 C_2 \qquad A_3 B_4 C_3 \qquad A_4 B_2 C_4$$

$$A_2 B_2 C_3 \qquad A_1 B_4 C_4 \qquad A_4 B_3 C_1 \qquad A_3 B_1 C_2$$

$$A_3 B_3 C_4 \qquad A_4 B_1 C_3 \qquad A_1 B_2 C_2 \qquad A_2 B_4 C_1$$

$$A_4 B_4 C_2 \qquad A_3 B_2 C_1 \qquad A_2 B_1 C_4 \qquad A_1 B_3 C_3$$

You can check that C is orthogonal to both A and B.

This hyper-Latin square reduces the $4^3 = 64$ cells of the three-variable, $A \times B \times C$ design to $4^2 = 16$ cells. Main effects of A, B, C, rows, and columns, are available as marginal means. These use all 15 df, so replication would be needed to get an error term. Any and all interaction residuals are, of course, completely confounded with main effects. Don't plan on this balance with 6 treatments; no 6×6 Greco–Latin square exists. As far as is known, however, the 6×6 case is a unique exception.

14.3.3b. Balanced squares are not a cure-all, for they deal only with the most common kind of carryover effect. Each treatment is assumed to have a one-step carryover effect, to the one following position, independent of what other treatment is at that position. Thus, balanced squares do not take specific account of treatment–treatment interactions.

Carryover effects in more complicated repeated measures designs have been explored by Cotton (1998). However, Cotton assumes without comment that all interactions involving subjects are zero, which seems wholly unrealistic. If treatments formed a two-way design within the square, each main effect should have its own error term, contrary to Cotton (e.g., his Table 5.3). Cotton's goal of developing a more general analysis of carryover effects has high importance, but the problem is not simple.

14.3.3c. *Algorithm for Constructing Balanced Latin Square.* To construct a Latin square balanced for effect of previous treatment, begin with row 1 as

$$1 \qquad 2 \qquad a \qquad 3 \qquad a-1 \qquad 4 \qquad . \quad . \quad .$$

Get row 2 by adding 1 to each number in row 1, and setting $a + 1 = 1$. Repeat for each successive row. For $a = 4$, this algorithm yields

1	2	4	3
2	3	1	4
3	4	2	1
4	1	3	2

If a is even, each treatment will follow each other treatment exactly once. Also, each sequence of treatments will appear in both forward and reversed orders.

If a is odd, two squares are required. The first is constructed as above, the second by reversing the sequences of the first. For $a = 3$, all six possible sequences are required. For $a = 5$, the algorithm yields 1 2 5 3 4 for the first sequence, 4 3 5 2 1 for the reversed sequence. The remaining rows follow the given rule.

14.3.4a. From Myers and Well (1991, p. 354), the expected mean squares for the complete Latin square model in present notation (their $\theta^2 = [(a-1)/a]\sigma^2$) are given in the following table. To get a valid F for treatments requires an error term that has the same expected mean square as MS_A except for σ_A^2. The SA term comes close; it includes every term in $E(\text{MS}_A)$ except σ_A^2. However, it also includes treatment × position term, σ_{AP}^2, and to this degree is larger than the correct error term. The observed F will be too small, therefore, the operative α will be less than its nominal value, and confidence intervals will appear wider than they should. As can be seen, the same applies to the position test.

Source	Expected mean square
S	$\sigma_\varepsilon^2 + [(a-1)/a]\sigma_{AP}^2 + [(a-1)/a]\sigma_{SAP}^2 + a\sigma_S^2$
P	$\sigma_\varepsilon^2 + \sigma_{SA}^2 + \sigma_{SP}^2 + [(a-2)/a]\sigma_{SAP}^2 + (a-1)\sigma_P^2$
A	$\sigma_\varepsilon^2 + \sigma_{SA}^2 + \sigma_{SP}^2 + [(a-2)/a]\sigma_{SAP}^2 + (a-1)\sigma_A^2$
SA	$\sigma_\varepsilon^2 + \sigma_{SA}^2 + \sigma_{SP}^2 + [(a-2)/a]\sigma_{SAP}^2 + [(a-1)/a]\sigma_{AP}^2$

This outcome is much better than could have been feared. The bias in F is on the safe side and may not be generally serious because treatment–position residuals seem unlikely to be substantial in most applications of Latin squares (in contrast to subject–position residuals). To the extent that σ_{AP}^2 is nonzero, there is some loss of power, but this should be more than compensated by the removal of σ_P^2 from the error term. Simulation studies to assess likely magnitude of these effects in realistic situations would be most desirable, especially with the balanced square.

An incidental implication of these expected mean squares is that power can be increased by reducing any position residual through empirical procedure. This further illustrates the lesson of the Experimental Pyramid for integrating statistical and extra-statistical considerations.

14.3.5a. Much argument has revolved around the 2 × 2 Latin square, especially in the medical literature, where it is called a crossover design (see further Cotton, 1989; Hills & Armitage, 1979; Exercise b11).

14.4a. Other comparisons of within and between subjects design are given in Dawes (1969), Greenwald (1976), Grice (1966), Poulton (1982), and Anderson (1982, Section 1.3); see also previous note.

14.4.2a. Contrast and assimilation are common in perception, but most studies are concerned with effects of stimuli presented simultaneously, as with color contrast (Figure 11.6, page 324) or length assimilation (Figure 8.1, page 226). Similar but weaker effects may occur when perceptual stimuli are presented on successive trials. A general adaptation–contrast effect was discovered by Beebe-Center (1932) and utilized as a base for a systematic theory of adaptation-level by Helson (1964). Contrary to Helson's theory, however, assimilation effects have been found with felt heaviness of lifted weights as well as with judgments of bizarre behavior of ward patients (Anderson, 1982, Section 1.1.5).

14.4.3a. Statistical Comparison of Within and Between Design. Comparison of treatment effects for within and between design presents a statistical problem of different error variability. The experimental variable has a within subjects error in the within design, a between subjects error in the between design. The former error is too small, the latter too large, to compare the effect of the experimental variable across the two designs. Some average of these two errors is needed.

To formalize this problem, consider the data as a factorial design, in which one factor is the experimental variable, the other factor is the type of design with two levels (within and between). The desired comparison is then the interaction term in this factorial. For the common case of two levels of the experimental variable, the interaction may be written as the double difference,

$$dd = (\bar{Y}_{B_1} - \bar{Y}_{B_2}) - (\bar{Y}_{W1} - \bar{Y}_{W2}). \qquad (2)$$

Subscripts B and W represent the between and within designs, and 1 and 2 represent the two levels of the experimental variable. Equation 2 is a contrast with unequal variances, which may be analyzed in the manner indicated in Section 12.5. Each term in the first parentheses has an error of $MS_{between}$; each term in the second parentheses has an error of MS_{within}. With n_b subjects in both between groups and n_w subjects in the within group, the confidence interval around the null hypothesis value of 0 is

$$dd \pm t^* \sqrt{2MS_{between}/n_b + 2MS_{within}/n_w}. \qquad (3)$$

Since large differences between the two error terms may be expected, the df adjustment of Section 12.5 is also required to obtain t^*.

An Anova analysis that allows more than two levels of the experimental variable is given by Erlebacher (1977, 1978). The first of these articles cites 15 studies that compared within and between design and observes that 10 of them "completely avoided the direct statistical test of the interaction" (p. 213). The cited study of eye-blink conditioning, it may be noted, used a valid although not quite optimal statistical analysis.

14.4.3b. Two theoretical implications stem from the finding that more information of equal value yields a more extreme judgment. At face value, this outcome supports an addition model of information integration and infirms the averaging model (see *Prior Information* in Section 21.4.1, page 706, and Exercise 21.c1). Also, the outcome disagrees with the representativeness heuristic (Kahneman & Tversky, 1972), which implies that amount of information has no effect (Anderson, 1991a, p. 113; see further Section 14.4.5).

EXERCISES FOR CHAPTER 14

NOTE: For the first group of exercises, labeled "a," assume independent scores.

a1. What should be done to avoid possible hurt feelings and distress by a human subject who is eliminated from the experiment for failing to meet some screening criterion?

a2. Under *Methods for Language Learning* (Section 14.2.2), explain the sentence, "This was verified, F_{blocks} being even a little larger than $F_{methods}$."

a3. Q included successive, temporal blocks in her design and found $F_{blocks} = 2.67$ on 3/16 df. What should she make of this?

a4. P used block randomization in six successive, temporal blocks in an experiment in which previous work clearly indicated that block effects were not substantial. P did not include blocks in his factorial Anova of the main treatment variables. By a priori plan, however, he did test the main effect of blocks, using the hand formulas of Section 3.2.5 to get SS_{blocks}, which he tested against MS_{error} from the overall Anova.

    a. What are two objections to P's test of the block effect?

    b. What would P say about these two objections?

    c. Suppose P found a large effect of blocks. Would that require any qualification of his main analysis?

    d. Do you think P erred in not including blocks in his factorial Anova?

a5. Design an experiment in your area in which you would use the initial phase to increase reliability and validity of the response measure. Specify exactly how you would expect each advantage to be realized.

a6. In the field study of smoking prevention cited in the Appendix to Chapter 3, the effect at 12 months was not large.

    a. How might the screening procedure be amplified to screen out more of the probable relapsers?

    b. What advantage might be expected from (a)?

a7. The last paragraph under *Screening Tests* states that limiting the subject population can increase process validity. Cite two different situations in which you could expect such increases.

a8. a. Find a published experiment in your area in which you would expect a benefit from blocking on individual differences in follow-up work. Specify the blocking variable, how you would measure it, and why you chose the number of blocks you did.

b.* Include a hopefully realistic guess of how much reduction in MS_{error} you would expect (Equation 15 from Chapter 9).

a9. How could you use block design to deal with the threat that knowledge of a deception might spread through the subject population in the third example of Note 8.1.5a?

b1. In Table 14.4: a. Verify the numerical values for each of the listed SSs.

b. Show that F_A would not be statsig had the position effect been ignored.

b2. Q tested five treatments in a Latin square, with two groups of five subjects, one experimental and one control.

a. Write out Source and df for her Anova table, ignoring the Latin square and treating this as an $(S \times A) \times G$, repeated measurements design.

b. Extend (a) to a Latin square analysis by including the position effect. Indicate what each Source means.

b3. Section 14.3.1 suggests beginning the experiment with the same practice session for all subjects in order to reduce the position effects during the experiment proper.

a. Cite a specific task in which this procedure would be inadvisable.

b. Cite a specific task in which this procedure would be advisable.

b4. The second paragraph under *Startup Effects* states that the preliminary phase has a "threefold purpose" (page 426). Describe a specific experimental task in your own field to illustrate how each purpose would be achieved.

b5. You use a 5 × 5 square but with two successive replications for each subject. You have at least three different choices for order of treatments in the second replication. What are their advantages and disadvantages?

b6. You give four treatments in succession to each subject. Unknown to you, all have equal true effect. The response changes, however, because there is a position effect. Suppose this position effect is entirely linear.

a. Show by numerical example (or better yet algebraically) that giving the treatments in the forward and reverse orders will balance out this linear trend.

b. Does similar balance hold for any number of serial positions?

c. Suppose the treatments have different effects. Do the forward and reverse orders still balance the linear position effect?

b7. You run four subjects in a repeated measures design with four treatments. Although there is good reason to believe position effects are negligible, you balance them with a Latin square. Now you wonder whether to use the repeated measures analysis of Chapter 6 or the Latin square analysis of this chapter.

a. How many df does the Latin square give you for error?

b. What is the advantage of including the position effect in this Anova?

c. What is the disadvantage of including the position effect in this Anova?

d. If position is not included in the Anova, is the position balance destroyed?

e. You consider increasing the error df by ignoring position and treating this as a simple repeated measures design. What do you decide?

b8. You wish to balance position effects in your experiment, in which each subject gets eight treatments. Unfortunately, apparatus limitations allow you to use only four sequences. How can you apply the Latin square idea to get partial position balance?

b9. You have a 2 × 3, repeated measures design in which each subject takes all 6 treatments. To assess position effects, you use a 6 × 6 Latin square to balance treatments across position. Write out Source and df for your Anova.

b10. You have three infant monkeys in each of Harlow's three mother love conditions, each infant to be tested in all of three social interaction situations using a Latin square.

a. Write out Source and df for the Anova table, ignoring the Latin square and treating this as an $(S \times A) \times G$, repeated measures design.

b. Extend (a) to a Latin square analysis by including the position effect. Indicate the error term for each source and what it would mean empirically.

b11. The 2 × 2 Latin square presents unique difficulties in interpretation. As one example, the position effect in a 2 × 2 Latin square is sometimes interpreted as an interaction between treatment and sequence. In an empirical study of drug effects on memory cited by Cotton (1989; see further Dawes, 1969; Hills & Armitage, 1979), placebo means were approximately 3.4 in the placebo–drug sequence and 4.6 in the drug–placebo sequence; drug means were 3.2 and 2.0 for the placebo–drug and drug–placebo sequences, respectively.

a. Plot these data as a 2 × 2 factorial graph, with drug and placebo on the horizontal axis, one curve for the placebo–drug sequence, and one curve for the drug–placebo sequence. Does this graph support a treatment × sequence interaction? At face value, what does this mean about transfer?

b. Replot these four means as a 2 × 2 factorial graph with drug and placebo on the horizontal axis, one curve for each position. Reinterpret by visual inspection.

c. Which of these two graphs seems to give a truer picture of the data? Or do both have equal validity? Justify your choice.

d. Suppose the placebo mean in the drug–placebo sequence was 4.2 instead of 4.6. How would this appear in the Anova of (b)? What would this mean for interpreting the data?

b12. Consider the following data for the Greco–Latin square of Table 14.6.

4	8	11	11
7	9	12	10
10	10	9	13
13	11	10	12

a. Show that SSs for rows, column, A, and B all equal 20.

b.* By what simple rule were these data generated?

b13. Assume treatment effects of 1, 2, 3, and 4 for A_1, A_2, A_3, and A_4, respectively, in a Latin square design. Also assume that A_4 has a carryover effect of 4, which is added to whatever treatment follows. Assume all other effects are zero in the Latin square model of Section 14.3.4.

a. Use the model to generate the 16 cell entries for the cyclic square of Table 14.3 and for the balanced square of Table 14.7.

b. Get treatment means for both squares; explain the difference.

c. Get position means for both squares and explain.

b14. A single subject is presented treatments using an $a \times a$ Latin square, so a responses are obtained for each treatment. The subject goes through the successive treatments in the first row, then in the second row, and so on.

a. You apply the Anova outlined in the left part of Table 14.5. What does Subjects in the Between subtable correspond to in this design? What does this term mean? How does this term relate to the position effect?

b. How would you test the treatment effect? Is the ε adjustment needed?

c. What would you do if only some rows of the square could be run?

b15. For each of the following situations, give your opinion whether a between subjects or within subjects design should be used, with justification.

1. Harlow's study of wire–cloth–real mothers.
2. Line–box illusion of Figure 8.1.
3. Effects of lesions in lateral and ventromedial thalamus (Section 8.1.6).
4. Methods of teaching psychology in high school.
5. Prototype experiment of Section 8.1.2.
6. Blame experiment of Figure 1.3.
7. Study of effects of motivation on perception of coin size in Section 8.1.2.
8. Rats tested with varied amounts of reward on one variable interval schedule.

b16. This exercise aims to bring out potential for adapting Latin squares to new situations. In the study of memory organization in the last subsection of Section 8.1.6, write out a Latin square you might use that would avoid the confounding and yet still allow within subjects design for comparing how much each of the four types of transformation degrades memory. Assume only four different original scenes were used.

a. Write out source and df. Say what each source would mean.
b. What would your response measure be for each scene?
c. What would your response measure be for the Anova?
d. What additional variable needs balancing within the Latin square?

PREFACE

Five issues in experimental design are considered in this chapter.

15.1. Nested Factors and Natural Groups. In one typical nested design, treatments are given to subjects in natural groups, as with classroom groups in education or hospital wards in medical science. Correct analysis requires that the error term be calculated from differences between group means. The practice of calculating the error term from differences between subjects is not valid because subjects within groups are not generally independent.

15.2. Random Factors. With a *random factor*, the factor levels are chosen at random from some population, of stimulus materials, for example, or therapists, or classroom groups. This helps obtain generality across the random factor. Indeed, random factor Anova can provide a statistical generalization from the random sample to the population, although this benefit may have unacceptable cost. It may usually be preferable, therefore, to use standard fixed factor Anova.

15.3. Reducing Design Size. Multiple factors must sometimes be included in a design, but multifactor designs tend to be large and costly, even infeasible. *Fractional replication* can reduce design size by using only a well-chosen fraction of the conditions in the complete factorial design. Fractional design, extensively developed by statisticians, has been underutilized by psychologists. The rationale is shown for a simple case and illustrated with an empirical study of serial belief integration.

For single subject analysis, Latin squares have unrecognized potential for reducing design size while balancing multiple variables. For independent groups, however, Latin square designs have limited usefulness.

15.4. Unequal *n*. When a factorial design has unequal n in different cells, the simple formulas of Chapter 5 are not applicable. This once confused issue is no longer a big problem because the complicated calculations for unequal n are now done by computer. It is suggested, however, that primary use be made of two-mean comparisons with confidence intervals instead of overall Anova.

15.5. Quasi-Experimental Design. In quasi-experimental design, treatments are given to groups that differ preexperimentally. Treatment effects are thus confounded with uncontrolled/unknown differences between groups. Common methods to ''control for'' or ''partial out'' uncontrolled variables are seldom justified. Field science with nonrandomized groups has high importance, but it requires high expertise.

Chapter 15

DESIGN TOPICS II

15.1 NESTED FACTORS AND NATURAL GROUPS

Two kinds of designs are considered in this section. The first is *nested design*, an interesting, often useful variant of factorial design. The second concerns designs with *natural groups* of subjects, one application of nesting.

The treatment is brief. Its purpose is to call attention to the conceptual structure of these kinds of designs. This will help you understand what an article is up to when it says it used nesting. You will also have one important check on the validity of a study in which subjects are run in groups.

By understanding the nesting idea, moreover, you will be able to recognize when this kind of design might be useful for your own purposes. In that case, you should consult a text that goes into detail on the many variants.[a]

15.1.1 NESTED FACTORS

Factor X is said to be *nested* in factor G if each level of X appears at only one level of G. This differs from the *crossed* factors in the usual factorial design, in which each level of X appears at all levels of G.

The difference between *nesting* and *crossing* appeared in the mixed repeated measures designs of Chapter 6: Subjects is nested in the between variable, crossed with the within variable. In the $(S \times A) \times G$ design, each subject appears at only one level of G, the between subjects variable. Hence S is *nested in G*; but S is *crossed with A* because each subject appears at every level of A.

This crossed–nested difference appears in the Anova model and table. If two factors are crossed, their interaction residual is meaningful, as with $S \times A$ in the $(S \times A) \times G$ design. In contrast, $S \times G$ has no meaning because S is nested within G. Accordingly, $S \times G$ does not appear in the Anova table.

15.1.2 NESTING IN NATURAL GROUPS

Natural groups are a design unit in some studies, not the individuals within each group. Each group is then only one "subject"—no matter how many individuals it contains. One reason is that individuals within a natural group may be expected to be more similar than individuals in different groups, whether from group selection or from common past experiences; an error term based on individual differences within groups will thus be too small. Also, using this error will confound treatment effects with preexisting differences between groups.

Natural groups are common in some areas. In educational studies, a school class is a natural group. In medical psychology, a ward or hospital may need to be treated as a single group.

To avoid the two difficulties referenced in the first paragraph requires more than one group for each treatment. Then the variability between groups treated alike can be estimated—this is the error variability needed for valid confidence intervals and significance tests.

Statistical Analysis. Let g denote the number of groups that receive each of the a treatments for a total of ag groups, with n subjects in each group. Let Y_{ijk} be the score of subject i in group j in treatment k. The Anova model is

$$Y_{ijk} = \text{individual } i + \text{group } j + \text{treatment } k. \tag{1}$$

Each score thus has three components: One represents the individual subject; one represents the group to which the subject belongs; and one represents the treatment given to all subjects in that group.

Equation 1 represents a doubly nested design: Subjects are nested within groups, since each subject appears in only one group. Similarly, groups are nested within treatments.

The basic analysis is on the group means. In this way, the natural variability between groups is included in the error term. The Anova is based on the following three formulas.

$$SS_A = ng \sum \bar{Y}_{..k}^2 - SS_{\text{mean}}. \tag{2a}$$

$$SS_{G/A} = n \sum \sum \bar{Y}_{.jk}^2 - SS_{\text{mean}} - SS_A. \tag{2b}$$

$$SS_{S/G} = \sum \sum \sum Y_{ijk}^2 - SS_{\text{mean}} - SS_A - SS_{G/A}. \tag{2c}$$

The equation for SS_A has the same form as Equation 3.10a (page 67) for one-way design. The treatment means, $\overline{Y}_{..k}$, are squared and multiplied by the number of scores in each mean, ng in the present case. From their sum is subtracted SS_{mean}, which of course equals $nag\overline{Y}_{...}^2$.

The second equation gives the variability between groups that get the same A treatment. It has similar rationale. Each group mean, $\overline{Y}_{jk}$, is squared, multiplied by the number of scores it contains, and summed. Subtracting SS_{mean} will yield the SS between all groups. This SS has two components: One is natural differences between groups treated alike; the other is differences between groups due to treatments, namely, SS_A. We subtract SS_A, accordingly, to obtain $SS_{G/A}$—the variability between groups treated alike. This is the proper error term for A, as shown by the expected mean squares in Table 15.1.

TABLE 15.1

EXPECTED MEAN SQUARES: NATURAL GROUP DESIGN

Source	df	df	E(MS)
A	$a-1$	1	$\sigma_\varepsilon^2 + n\sigma_{G/A}^2 + gn\sigma_A^2$
G/A	$a(g-1)$	4	$\sigma_\varepsilon^2 + n\sigma_{G/A}^2$
S/G	$ag(n-1)$	114	σ_ε^2

Inspection of the $E(MS)$ column in this table verifies that $MS_{G/A}$ is the proper error term for treatments. The null hypothesis implies $\sigma_A^2 = 0$ so MS_A and $MS_{G/A}$ have equal expected values. Accordingly, $F = MS_A/MS_{G/A}$ provides a valid test of the null hypothesis.

Error df. An unpleasant aspect of natural groups design is low df for error, illustrated in the second df column in Table 15.1. This numerical example assumes three groups in each of two treatments, with 20 subjects in each group. The df for A are only 1 and 4, even though 120 subjects were run.

This df problem is serious for studies with natural groups. As tempting as it is, using $MS_{S/G}$ as the error for treatments is invalid. Its $E(MS)$ is too small because the term in $\sigma_{G/A}^2$ is absent. MS_A could thus be statsig merely from natural group differences, so that $\sigma_{G/A}^2 > 0$, even though the treatment effect, σ_A^2, was nil. A watchful eye is needed in reading the literature because this problem is sometimes passed by. The error df should not be larger than the number of groups, without clear justification.

Error pooling is sometimes suggested, but this is not generally justified. Error pooling employs a preliminary test of $MS_{G/A}$ against $MS_{S/G}$. If $F_{G/A}$ is nonstatsig at a weak α, say $\alpha = .20$, SS and df are added for G/A and S/G to form a pooled error mean square. This pooled error is actually an average of

$MS_{G/A}$ and $MS_{S/G}$, each weighted by its df. Hence its expected value will usually be considerably smaller than the correct error term, $MS_{G/A}$.

Empirically, more or less substantial differences between natural groups can be expected. The preliminary test for pooling then takes improper advantage of those cases in which $MS_{G/A}$ chances to be small, thereby yielding too small an error and too high a false alarm parameter. Pooling would thus seem justified only with firm prior empirical evidence that natural group differences are small enough that the bias is outweighed by the gain in power (see further Section 18.4.4 on *Error Pooling*).[a]

There is an alternative to pooling. Experiments with natural groups are often expensive. If they are soundly designed and address an important problem, as with classroom education, publication would seem warranted almost regardless of the outcome.

Ad Hoc Groups. Subjects recruited separately but tested together in the same location may also show group effects. One reason is that variability in experimental procedure is confounded with groups. In some experiments, the mood or manner of the experimenter can influence the responses of the group as a whole, but mood and manner may vary from one time to the next. Happenstance in the environment or within the assembled individuals may act similarly. These confounds will masquerade as real differences between groups. The groups analysis of Table 15.1 may thus be necessary.

Testing subjects in ad hoc groups is not uncommon in social psychology, for example, or in judgment–decision; it yields a lot of data with a little of effort. This procedure is penny-wise, however, if group effects are at all likely. Hardly less serious is that ad hoc groups are prone to yield low-grade data because some subjects will almost inevitably be confused, inattentive, or careless. The response measure may lack validity (Section 8.2.1, page 245).

15.2 RANDOM FACTORS

A *random factor* is one for which the factor levels are chosen at random from some population. With recognition memory for visual scenes, results for any one scene may be peculiar to that scene. A sample of scenes would seem desirable, perhaps essential, for generality (Section 1.4.3).

Usually, of course, we choose our factor levels in some systematic way. These are called *fixed factors* and have been taken for granted in previous chapters. With a metric variable, such as substance concentration or stimulus duration, the stimulus levels would often be equally spaced. Many categorical variables, such as praise-blame in wife–husband interaction, would also be chosen systematically, not at random.

A visual scene, however, is a complex variable. Numerous different visual scenes could be used as stimuli. Generality of results obtained with a single scene would be questionable; multiple scenes would seem essential.

Similar considerations apply to stimuli in many areas, from language psychology to person cognition. Even two sets of stimulus materials would ameliorate the confounding from a single set.

Similar considerations also apply when some experimental person may have an impact on subjects' behavior. Examples include confederates in studies of social interaction, instructors in teaching studies, and therapists in behavior modification. Even two stimulus persons would ameliorate the confounding from a single person.

Choosing stimulus levels at random from some population has two advantages. One is that it avoids bias. The other is that results can be statistically generalized from the levels in the sample to the whole stimulus population. Such generalization is just the standard idea of statistical inference—applied to generalization across stimuli rather than across subjects.

Such statistical generalization has a price. Part of this price is that the error df will be too small unless the number of stimulus levels is relatively large. More seriously, the statistical generalization may be less effective than extra-statistical generalization.

15.2.1 FIXED, MIXED, AND RANDOM MODELS

Regardless of whether factors are random or fixed, all SS and MS calculations are identical. Only the error term differs; it may include variability in the random sample of stimuli as well as variability between subjects.

Error Terms. The proper error terms for two-way designs are shown in Table 15.2, where MS_{within} refers to variability between subjects treated alike, just as in Chapter 3. When A and B are both fixed, MS_{within} is the proper error term for all three systematic sources, as listed at the left of Table 15.2.

TABLE 15.2

ERROR TERMS FOR FIXED, MIXED, AND RANDOM MODELS

Source	A fixed B fixed	A fixed B random	A random B random
A	MS_{within}	MS_{AB}	MS_{AB}
B	MS_{within}	MS_{within}	MS_{AB}
AB	MS_{within}	MS_{within}	MS_{within}

When A and B are both random, the proper error term for both main effects is the interaction residual, MS_{AB}, as shown at the right of Table 15.2. The reason is that the random choice of factor levels constitutes a source of variability in both main effects. This variability must be taken into account in order to generalize from the two random samples to the two populations of factor levels. For two-way designs, fortunately, statistical theory has shown that this is accomplished by using the interaction as the error term.

For the mixed model in the center of Table 15.2, A is fixed and B is random. It may seem surprising that the error term for the fixed factor A is MS_{AB} whereas that for the random factor B is the smaller MS_{within}. This makes sense, however, because our test asks whether the A effect we observe for our particular sample of B levels generalizes to the population of B levels. This inference must allow for the variability in our sample of B levels. For the main effect of B, in contrast, our test only asks whether the observed B effect holds for the given fixed levels of A.

Actually, this mixed model has already appeared in Chapter 6 on repeated measures. In the $S \times A$ model of Equations 6.2 and 6.3, subjects was considered a random factor and treatments a fixed factor. The rationale for using MS_{SA} as error for MS_A given in Chapter 6 applies similarly for the general mixed model of Table 15.2.

With more than two factors, especially when stimuli is a nested factor, some sources may not have a proper error term. These cases can often be handled by adding and subtracting other MSs to obtain an estimate of the proper error term. These yield the "quasi-F" ratios that occasionally appear in the literature.[a]

Price of df. The df price for random factor analysis can be extreme. In a 2×2 design with $n = 8$, for example, fixed factor analysis yields 28 df for error, with $F^*(1, 28) = 4.20$. Random factor analysis, in contrast, yields only 1 df for main effect error, with $F^*(1, 1) = 161$. A larger criterial F^* is thus required; power is much lower. Unless the random factor has a considerable number of levels, random factor analysis may not mean much.

15.2.2 HOW USEFUL IS RANDOM FACTOR ANALYSIS?

Despite its promise of statistical generality, random factor analysis seems quite limited in usefulness. Not a few published experiments, it is true, are inconclusive because treatment effects are confounded with effects of a single exemplar of a stimulus population (e.g., *Prototypes* in Section 8.1.2, page 224). Proponents of random factor analysis have made a useful contribution by emphasizing the need for stimulus sampling. But random stimulus samples need not be treated as a random factor in the data analysis.[a]

Instead, stimulus levels may be treated as a fixed factor, even when chosen randomly. Evidence on generality is available in the data: Generality is supported or infirmed according as different stimuli yield similar or dissimilar effects. Evidence on stimulus generality may thus be obtained by visual inspection and by assessment of interaction residuals. Indeed, a large main effect of stimulus materials could itself be a cautionary sign.

Extrastatistical Generalization. Two major substantive problems trouble reliance on random factor analysis. The first is an asymmetry between subjects and stimuli. Most experiments, although not all, have central concern with the behavior of subjects but only peripheral concern with behavior of stimuli. Stimuli are usually chosen and developed as tools for analysis of psychological process. There is not usually some natural stimulus population to which statistical generalization is sought. Instead, the stimulus materials are circumscribed in many ways to implement the concerns of the investigator.

Moreover, extrastatistical considerations provide a basis for generalization. With equally spaced levels of a metric variable, for example, the fixed factor analysis holds only for the specific levels used in the experiment. But it would be misguided to choose the levels at random from some range, seeking thereby for a statistical generalization across that range. Visual curve fitting can provide far better generalization than random factor analysis.

Fixed factor analysis is superior to random factor analysis in this example because it supplements statistical inference with extrastatistical inference. For a factor with categorical levels, similar extrastatistical considerations could govern the selection of a representative sample and generalization therefrom. Such appeal to extrastatistical considerations may seem a shortcoming from a statistical perspective, but it's a big advantage of the empirical perspective.

Stimulus Heterogeneity. The other major substantive problem with random factor analysis is that stimulus populations to which random factor analysis is appropriate are often heterogeneous. Visual scenes, for example, may vary widely in complexity, familiarity, animacy, patterning, color, and diverse other characteristics. Generalization across such a heterogeneous population may not mean much. It would usually be more effective to classify potential stimuli in meaningful categories on the basis of extrastatistical knowledge (see Note 15.2.2a, page 475). These categories would be included in the design as a fixed factor. Even within a category, extrastatistical considerations could often be used to select a representative sample of stimuli.

Stimulus Generality. Random stimulus selection may be useful to avoid bias. To take an example from person cognition, Asch (1946) claimed a primacy effect: Stimulus traits in a person description had greater influence when they came early than when they came late. But only one of his two person descriptions showed primacy, which leaves both its reliability and its generality uncertain. In later work (Note 15.2.2b), 48 person descriptions were constructed using random selection of stimulus traits, and primacy was obtained in 43. By virtue of the random trait selection, which avoids bias, this preponderance of primacy demonstrates generality. This should not, however, obscure the potential importance of the five person descriptions that showed recency. The overall mean primacy may bury a pertinent issue.[b]

The emphasis on random factor analysis appears to stem in part from an implicit espousal of outcome generality rather than process generality (Section 1.2.1). Many studies, however, seek process generality. For this purpose, the stimulus population is not usually a natural given but a tool to be shaped by the investigator. For process generality, accordingly, fixed factor analysis seems usually appropriate.[c, d]

Stimulus generality is a fundamental concern in experimental design, one of the four kinds of generality discussed in Chapter 1. In some issues of semantic memory, the stimulus population of words is itself under study, so random factor analysis could be appropriate (Note 15.2.2a; see also Shoben, 1982). As in this example, random factor Anova provides a sometimes helpful tool for assessing stimulus generality. For many purposes, however, if not most, fixed factor analysis seems adequate and often superior.[e]

15.3 REDUCING DESIGN SIZE

Some designs are too big. They may require too much experimental time or too many subjects. It doesn't take much to get out of hand. Four experimental variables, each at three levels, yield 81 experimental conditions, which, with an n of 4, would require 324 subjects. Reducing design size may be essential. An obvious way to reduce design size is to use fewer levels of some variables or omit them altogether. This loses scope, however, so some alternative is desirable.

Methods for reducing design size have been much studied by statisticians. Two such methods are considered here: fractional replication and Latin squares for independent scores.[a]

15.3.1 FRACTIONAL REPLICATION

In *fractional replication*, design size is reduced by omitting selected cells from a complete factorial design. The basic idea may be illustrated with the following simple case.

Illustrative Fractional Replication. For illustration, we consider a half replicate of a 2^3 design, that is, a design with 3 factors, each at 2 levels. The full design has $2^3 = 8$ conditions, with 7 df: 3 for main effects and 4 for residuals.

A half replicate has only 4 conditions, with only 3 df. If we are clever about which 4 conditions we use, we can get independent estimates of all 3 main effects. Larger designs can be handled similarly.

TABLE 15.3

CONTRAST COEFFICIENTS FOR 2^3 DESIGN

	Cell number							
Effect	**111**	112	121	**122**	211	**212**	**221**	222
A	+	+	+	+	−	−	−	−
B	+	+	−	−	+	+	−	−
C	+	−	+	−	+	−	+	−
AB	+	+	−	−	−	−	+	+
AC	+	−	+	−	−	+	−	+
BC	+	−	−	+	+	−	−	+
ABC	+	−	−	+	−	+	+	−

This 2^3 design is shown in Table 15.3. The three-digit entries above the columns represent the 8 experimental treatments, with 1 and 2 denoting the two levels of each variable. Thus, 121 denotes treatment $A_1 B_2 C_1$, and so on. Each row in Table 15.3 defines one Anova source as a sum-and-difference of the 8 treatment means (see further below).

Suppose we can run only 4 of these 8 conditions. Which should we choose? Certainly not the first four; these all include A_1, none include A_2. No information on effect of A would be available. Selecting the first three and last one would overemphasize A_1, underemphasize A_2.

Instead, we want to choose two conditions that involve A_1 and two that involve A_2. Of course, we desire similar balance for B and C. One such choice is indicated in bold face. With these four conditions alone, we can estimate main effects for all three variables.

To get the main effect of A, add the mean, $\bar{A}_1$, of the two bold face $\bar{A}_1$ conditions and subtract the mean, $\bar{A}_2$, of the two bold face A_2 conditions:

$$\bar{A}_1 - \bar{A}_2 = \tfrac{1}{2}(\bar{Y}_{111} + \bar{Y}_{122}) - \tfrac{1}{2}(\bar{Y}_{212} + \bar{Y}_{221}). \qquad (3a)$$

In this equation, the third subscript shows that the two levels of C are balanced across A. Thus, C_1 occurs once with a + sign (first term on the right), once with a − sign (fourth term on the right). Similar balance holds for C_2. Hence the additive effect of C cancels, thereby freeing the main effect of A from confounding with the main effect of C. The same holds for the main effect of B.

Similar reasoning applies to the main effects for B and C.

$$\bar{B}_1 - \bar{B}_2 = \frac{1}{2}(\bar{Y}_{111} + \bar{Y}_{212}) - \frac{1}{2}(\bar{Y}_{122} + \bar{Y}_{221}). \qquad (3b)$$

$$\bar{C}_1 - \bar{C}_2 = \frac{1}{2}(\bar{Y}_{111} + \bar{Y}_{221}) - \frac{1}{2}(\bar{Y}_{122} + \bar{Y}_{212}). \qquad (3c)$$

Equations 3 thus show that we can measure all three main effects with the absolute minimum number of experimental conditions.

This reduction in design size has a price: Main effects are confounded with residuals. From Table 15.3, the bold face ± pattern for the BC residual is

$$\frac{1}{2}(\bar{Y}_{111} + \bar{Y}_{122}) - \frac{1}{2}(\bar{Y}_{212} + \bar{Y}_{221}). \qquad (3bc)$$

But this is the same as Equation 3a for $\bar{A}_1 - \bar{A}_2$. Thus, BC is completely confounded with A. The observed effect of A thus includes any BC residual, which renders it somewhat ambiguous. Similar confounding holds for the other two main effects. Of course, the complete confounding of this particular design is an extreme case.

Most fractional designs have only partial confounding; they provide some information on interaction residuals. A half replicate of a 2^4 factorial has 8 treatment conditions, which yield 7 df. Hence it can estimate the 4 main effects and still leave 3 df for residuals. These residuals can be chosen as those most likely to be real, thereby avoiding confounding them with main effects. This technique was used in the example of serial integration curves on page 455.

2^p Design. A 2^p design has p factors, each with 2 levels. With 2^p designs, every Anova source can be expressed as a sum-and-difference of cell means, illustrated in Table 15.3 for the 2^3 design. With 2^p design, therefore, fractional replication yields simple patterns of confounding.[a]

Statistical analysis is straightforward. Each sum-and-difference constitutes a contrast, which can be assessed with a confidence interval (Equation 4) or an F ratio. Independent scores and repeated measures require separate consideration.

Statistical Analysis: Independent Scores. To illustrate the statistical analysis for independent scores, consider the foregoing half-replicate of a 2^3 design. Equation 3a for $\bar{A}_1 - \bar{A}_2$ is a contrast, which may be rewritten as

$$\hat{\kappa}_A = \frac{1}{2}\bar{Y}_{111} + \frac{1}{2}\bar{Y}_{122} - \frac{1}{2}\bar{Y}_{212} - \frac{1}{2}\bar{Y}_{221}.$$

The confidence interval for any contrast is (Section 18.2, pages 559ff)

$$\hat{\kappa} \pm t^* \sqrt{\sum c_j^2} \sqrt{MS_{error}/n}, \qquad (4)$$

where n is the number of independent scores in each cell and the c_j are the contrast coefficients. Each $c_j = \frac{1}{2}$, so $\sum c_j^2 = 1$ in this case. These c_j are in normalized form (page 560), so $\hat{\kappa}$ has the same unit as the responses.

The null hypothesis is that the true mean κ_A is zero. If 0 is outside this confidence interval, A has a statsig main effect. To get MS_{error}, you can give the data to the computer as a one-way design with four conditions, ignoring the overall F. Virtually identical procedure holds for any main effect or any interaction residual in any 2^p fractional design (see Section 18.2.2, page 565).

Statistical Analysis: Repeated Measures. Suppose each subject responds to all the treatments in a fractional replication of a 2^p design. The key is to give each subject an individual score for each Anova source. This score is the sum-and-difference of that subject's treatment scores, using the $\pm$ pattern for the given source.

To illustrate, consider the foregoing half replicate of the 2^3 design, each subject serving in all four specified conditions. Subject i would be given an A score, just as in the preceding subsection:

$$\hat{\kappa}_{iA} = \tfrac{1}{2}(Y_{i111} + Y_{i122} - Y_{i212} - Y_{i221}).$$

Thus, $\hat{\kappa}_{iA}$ is the A main effect for subject i.

The null hypothesis is that the true mean of these $\hat{\kappa}_{iA}$ is zero. To test this, apply regular Anova to the $\hat{\kappa}_{iA}$ scores and use the resulting error term to obtain a confidence interval for the mean. Each other Anova source may be treated in the same way using the appropriate $\pm$ pattern from Table 15.3, page 451. Each source thus has its own error term, as is appropriate with repeated measures.

Removing Confounding in Fractional Replication. With repeated measures, the confounding in fractional replication can often be removed with little cost. The advantage is that a complete factorial design can be obtained even when time constraints allow each subject to take only a few treatment conditions. Even more striking, many tests have within subjects error terms.

Continuing with the 2^3 example, we assume two groups of n subjects. One group gets the four bold face treatments in the table, as already described. The other group gets the four light face treatments. Inspection of the $\pm$ patterns in Table 15.3 shows that the light face half replicate yields information on the main effects exactly equivalent to the bold face half replicate. Thus, the light face main effect for A is

$$\bar{A}_1 - \bar{A}_2 = \tfrac{1}{2}(\bar{Y}_{112} + \bar{Y}_{121} - \bar{Y}_{211} - \bar{Y}_{222}).$$

As above, the two means for $\bar{A}_1$ are positive, the two means for $\bar{A}_2$ are negative. The third subscript shows that the two levels of C are balanced across A and the second subscript shows the same balance for B.

For each bold face subject, calculate $\hat{\kappa}_A$ with the previous formula:

$$\hat{\kappa}_{iA} = \tfrac{1}{2}(Y_{i111} + Y_{i122} - Y_{i212} - Y_{i221}).$$

Each light face subject is similarly assigned a $\hat{\kappa}_A$ score as a sum-and-difference of the four light face treatments:

$$\hat{\kappa}_{i'A} = \frac{1}{2}(Y_{i'112} + Y_{i'121} - Y_{i'211} - Y_{i'222}),$$

where subscript i' denotes a light face subject.

A significance test for $\hat{\kappa}_A$, averaged over the two half replicates, may be obtained by treating the half replicates as two groups of n subjects. Then F_{mean} on $1/(2n - 2)$ df tests the null hypothesis that the true mean of κ_A is zero. Better yet, the error term may be used to construct a confidence interval. Similar procedure may be used with each other main effect.

Each main effect has a within subjects error. To see this, note that the main effect of each subject cancels in the $\hat{\kappa}_A$ score because, for each subject, two means have a + sign and two have a − sign. This holds for both the bold face and the light face subjects. Hence the main effect of each subject disappears from the variability among the $\hat{\kappa}_A$ scores.

No less notable, the confounding vanishes because the two half replicates form a whole replicate of the complete design. The confounding in the bold face half replicate is exactly canceled in the light face.

To illustrate this unconfounding, consider the BC residual. With the ± signs in Table 15.3, the BC contrast for the bold face subjects is

$$\hat{\kappa}_{iBC} = \frac{1}{2}(Y_{i111} + Y_{i122} - Y_{i212} - Y_{i221}).$$

For the light face subjects, similarly,

$$\hat{\kappa}_{i'BC} = \frac{1}{2}(Y_{i'211} + Y_{i'222} - Y_{i'112} - Y_{i'121}).$$

Adding these two expressions, the main effect of A cancels because the A subscript 1 occurs twice with a + sign in the bold face $\hat{\kappa}_{iBC}$, twice with a − sign in the light face $\hat{\kappa}_{i'BC}$. Similar cancellation occurs when the A subscript is 2. The mean of $\hat{\kappa}_{iBC}$ and $\hat{\kappa}_{i'BC}$ is thus unconfounded from the main effect of A—and vice versa. Every other Anova source is similarly free from confounding.

Furthermore, each two-way residual also has a within subjects error. The reasoning is the same as with main effects. In fact, confidence intervals and significance tests may be obtained in the same way as with main effects.

The three-way residual, however, has a between subjects error on $2n - 2$ df. Inspection of the bottom row of Table 15.3 shows that the four + terms come from the bold face subjects, the four − terms from the light face subjects. The main effect of subjects does not cancel, therefore, but goes into the error term for the three-way residual.[b]

General 2^p Design. The techniques for fractional replication, illustrated in the previous subsections, are readily extended to general 2^p designs. A 2^6 design, for example, can be run in 1/2, 1/4, or 1/8 replicate, allowing for estimation of all main effects, plus selected residuals. Design plans have been developed that confound main effects mainly with high-way residuals, which are typically expected to be negligible. With repeated measures, moreover, confounding can be removed in the manner already indicated.

A clear presentation of fractional replication and related designs is given in Cochran and Cox (1957), who present many specific designs, together with the confounding pattern (see also Note 15.3.1b). More extensive discussion is given by Montgomery (1997), with applications to engineering.

In psychology, fractional replication has been little used. Accordingly, an experimental application to serial belief integration is discussed next.

Serial Belief Curves Studied With Fractional Replication. Serial curves have been much studied in learning, memory, and belief formation. In belief formation, subjects receive a sequence of informers about some issue that they integrate to form a belief about that issue. One theoretical problem is to trace out the trial-by-trial integration of the belief, that is, to dis-integrate the final response into separate contributions from the informers at each serial position.

To get the serial curve of belief formation, a serial-factor design is used: Each serial position is a design factor; the informers at each position are the levels of that factor.

A prototypical task of belief integration is intuitive number averaging. In the experiment of Figure 15.1, the informers were two-digit numbers and subjects made an intuitive average of the given numbers. The two levels at each serial position were two numbers that differed by 17. With six serial positions, a complete design would require $2^6 = 64$ sequences, too many for a convenient within subjects design. Accordingly, a 1/8 replicate was used, so each subject judged only eight sequences.[c, d, e]

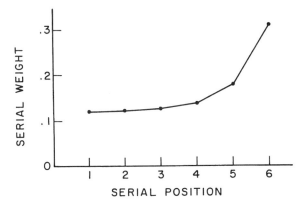

Figure 15.1. Recency in judgment–decision. Serial position curve for weight parameter in number averaging task. Subjects give intuitive average of sequence of six two-digit numbers. Final judgment is dis-integrated into six components, each representing the relative importance of the number at a given serial position. (After Anderson, 1964b.)

The psychological question is how the six informers are integrated to determine the final response at serial position 6. To answer this question, the final response needs to be dis-integrated into six components, one representing the effect of each separate serial position.

This serial belief curve is shown in Figure 15.1. The first point on the curve represents the weight of the first informer in the final response, and so on. Each weight is proportional to the corresponding main effect in the serial-factor design. The curve shows uniform recency; each later informer has higher weight. Subsequent work has generally corroborated this early finding of recency in judgment–decision.

Applications have been made in other areas besides judgment–decision. Work on attitudes has revealed two distinct components, basal and surface, in attitude structure. Work on memory has revealed a functional memory, distinct from the reproductive memory for the given informers.

15.3.2 LATIN SQUARES FOR INDEPENDENT SCORES

The Latin square idea used for repeated measures design in Section 14.3 can be used to reduce design size with independent scores. Two cases are considered in the following two subsections: independent groups and single subjects.

Latin Square for Independent Groups. With independent groups, each subject has only one score. There are no position or carryover effects to worry about, as with the Latin square for repeated measures. Instead, rows and columns can represent primary experimental variables. An example with three variables, A, B, and C, each at four levels, is shown here.

	B_1	B_2	B_3	B_4
A_1:	C_1	C_2	C_3	C_4
A_2:	C_2	C_3	C_4	C_1
A_3:	C_3	C_4	C_1	C_2
A_4:	C_4	C_1	C_2	C_3

There are only 16 cells in this design. Each cell represents one three-variable treatment combination. Thus, the top right treatment condition is $A_1B_4C_4$ and the bottom right is $A_4B_4C_3$. In a field study, for example, A might be four schools or neighborhoods, with B and C experimental variables intended to change food practices of mothers of young children. The square would be randomized as described in Section 14.3.5.

This Latin square reduces the complete $4 \times 4 \times 4$ design, which has 64 cells, to only 16 cells. This is a fourfold reduction in design size.

Furthermore, all three variables are completely balanced. Each level of any one variable occurs exactly once with each level of each other variable. The three main effects are thus statistically independent (orthogonal). Each main effect is thus free from confounding from the other main effects.

The Anova table follows, with n the number of scores in each cell.

Source	df
Mean	1
A	3
B	3
C	3
Residual	6
Error	$16(n-1)$

The calculations are straightforward. Ignore C and give the 4×4, $A \times B$ factorial data to the computer, which will print out SSs for A, B, AB, and the within-cell error. Of course, SS_{AB} is ambiguous because it includes the effect of C. However, SS_C can easily be obtained by hand from the four C means, exactly as with the position means of the example given in Section 14.3.2. Thence $SS_{residual} = SS_{AB} - SS_C$.

Even greater reduction in design size is possible. A fourth variable could be balanced by using a Greco-Latin square, illustrated in Section 14.3.3 (page 420). Indeed, a fifth variable can be balanced using a complete set of orthogonal squares (Fisher & Yates, 1963). In the latter case, the $4^5 = 1024$ cells in the complete factorial are reduced to just 16, with 3 df for each main effect.

The disadvantage of the Latin square is clear in the above Anova table. No specific interaction residual can be evaluated. But these residuals do not disappear; they are confounded with some listed source.

Statistical theory shows that each two-factor interaction residual is partly confounded with the main effect of the third factor, partly with the Residual. This Residual is thus an agglomeration of the several interaction residuals. Accordingly, a statsig or near statsig residual is a warning that the main effects may be biased estimates of the true means, and/or that the interpretation of the main effects may need qualification (Chapter 7).

This threat of confounding may be acceptable. Even with $n = 2$, the residual has 6/16 df, so a small Residual would provide some reassurance against confounding. Even if confounding is present, moreover, the pattern of the main effects may not be seriously affected. The advantage of smaller designs may thus be worth the risk of confounding, especially in preliminary work.

Regrettably, Latin square-type design is not too useful with independent groups of subjects. Aside from the confounding problem, each variable must have the same number of levels, which is often not desirable or even feasible. Fractional design and incomplete blocks are likely to be more useful.[a]

Latin Square for Single Subjects. Single subject Latin squares seem attractive for various experiments in perception and judgment–decision. Many percepts depend on integration of multiple stimulus cues, as with taste of foods or perception of distance. A proposed course of action, similarly, may involve multiple pros and cons that need to be integrated to judge its overall desirability.

With five stimulus cues, each at four levels, a complete factorial design would require $4^5 = 1024$ responses for a single replication. This could be reduced to as few as 16 responses as indicated in the previous subsection. If the integration is additive, the interaction residuals will be zero, and the Latin square design would be optimally efficient in assessing the main effects.

Independence of scores is essential. Accordingly, randomized presentation of stimulus combinations would seem necessary (Section 11.2, pages 310*ff*). Any position effects would then go largely into the error term and so should not be of much concern in many tasks. Possible carryover effects, however, could be more serious (page 423). The most attractive applications, accordingly, are to tasks in which the subject is in a fairly stable state across trials.

15.4 UNEQUAL *n*

Having unequal cell *n*s might seem a minor matter, but it has caused a lot of confusion with overall Anova for two-way design, stemming in part from approximate procedures used in precomputer days to avoid the extensive calculations needed for exact analysis. Exact analyses are now available in standard packages, but reliance on two-mean confidence intervals may be preferable.

15.4.1 STANDARD PARAMETRIC ANALYSIS

The *standard parametric analysis* rests on a simple principle: To accomplish the same goals as if the *n*s had been equal. Specifically, these goals are to estimate the same parameters and test the same null hypotheses as in the standard Anova model for equal *n*.

Unweighted Means. The main goal is to estimate the means. The first step is to put in each cell of the design the mean of whatever scores are in that cell (empty cells being disallowed). Each cell mean is thus an unbiased estimate of the true cell mean.

Each row mean is calculated as the *unweighted* average of the cell means in that row, that is, without regard to the number of scores in each cell. A cell mean based on a single score thus has the same influence on the row mean as a cell mean based on many scores. This might seem odd, but a little reflection shows that this is just what is wanted. Since each observed cell mean is an unbiased estimate of the true cell mean, the unweighted average of the observed cell means is an unbiased estimate of the true row mean.

Null Hypotheses. The unweighted mean for row j is

$$\bar{\mu}_{j.} = (1/b) \sum_{k=1}^{b} \mu_{jk}.$$

The null hypothesis for rows is

$$H_0 \text{ (rows)}: \quad \bar{\mu}_{1.} = \bar{\mu}_{2.} = \ldots = \bar{\mu}_{a.}.$$

The standard parametric analysis tests this null hypothesis, which is the same as with equal n, through its use of unweighted row means. Column means are treated similarly, by symmetry.

The interaction F also tests the same null hypothesis as with equal n. For a two-way design, therefore, this null hypothesis is equivalent to parallelism in the factorial graph of the unweighted cell means.

Error. The error term is estimated in the same way as with equal n: Calculate SS_{within} for each cell, sum over cells, and divide by the pooled error df, namely, $\sum\sum(n_{jk} - 1)$. Just this will be done if the data are presented to the computer as a one-way design with ab cells, or as a two-way design with unequal n. Assuming equal variance, this MS_{error} would be used in all analyses, including confidence intervals.

Exact Anova. Exact calculations for overall Anova require computer programs available on major packages. Nonmajor PC programs are not trustworthy (Dallal, 1988).

Even with a major package, be careful to check what your package program is doing. Major packages, some now available in PC form, allow at least three analysis options, including the standard parametric analyis, which is usually, but not always, the default. It seems advisable to check by using a published numerical example in which the same data are analyzed with all three options (e.g., Herr & Gaebelein, 1978; Fleiss, 1986, Section 6.4.2; Maxwell & Delaney, 1990, pp. 281–297; Myers & Well, 1991, pp. 555-563).[a]

Confidence Intervals. Confidence intervals are straightforward in principle, but they have a complication that leads to a messier formula than with equal n. Consider the unweighted mean for row 1:

$$\bar{Y}_{1.U} = (1/b)[\bar{Y}_{11} + \bar{Y}_{12} + \bar{Y}_{13} + \ldots + \bar{Y}_{1b}].$$

The complication is that the cell means in the brackets have unequal ns and hence unequal variances—which must be allowed for in the MS_{error} for the confidence interval.

The variance of this unweighted row mean equals $(1/b)^2$ times the sum of the variances of each cell mean in brackets, namely, σ^2/n_{cell}:

$$\text{Variance}\,(\bar{Y}_{1.U}) \;=\; (1/b^2)\,\sigma^2\left[(1/n_{11}) + (1/n_{12}) + (1/n_{13}) + \ldots + (1/n_{1b})\right].\,(5)$$

To get the sample standard deviation (standard error, or error half-bar) of $\bar{Y}_{1.U}$, replace σ^2 by MS_{error} and take the square root of the right side of Equation 5:

$$\sqrt{MS_{error}}\,(1/b)\left[(1/n_{11}) + (1/n_{12}) + (1/n_{13}) + \ldots + (1/n_{1b})\right]^{\frac{1}{2}}. \qquad (6)$$

Multiply by $\pm t^*$ to get the confidence interval.

To get the confidence interval for the difference between the means for rows 1 and 2, extend the one-mean confidence interval by including the cell ns for the second row:

$$(\bar{Y}_{1.U} - \bar{Y}_{2.U}) \;\pm\; t^*\sqrt{MS_{error}}\,(1/b)\left[(1/n_{11}) + (1/n_{12}) + (1/n_{13}) + \ldots + (1/n_{1b})\right.$$
$$\left. + (1/n_{21}) + (1/n_{22}) + (1/n_{23}) + \ldots + (1/n_{2b})\right]^{\frac{1}{2}}. \quad (7)$$

As a check, Expression 7 must reduce to Expression 5.11 when all cell ns are equal. The same pattern holds, of course, for any pair of row means, with a complementary form for columns.

Approximate Confidence Intervals. A useful approximation is to replace every cell n by the harmonic mean n_H of all the cell ns:

$$n_H \;=\; ab \;\div\; \sum_{j=1}^{a}\sum_{k=1}^{b} 1/n_{jk}. \qquad (8)$$

This n_H would be substituted for "n" in the expressions for confidence intervals given in Section 5.2.3 (page 136). This approximate analysis should be adequate at least as long as the ratio of largest to smallest cell n is no greater than 3 to 2.

With the harmonic mean, all confidence intervals have the same $\pm$ width. This single $\pm$ width can greatly simplify visual inspection. Important marginal results, of course, would require exact calculation.

The effect of the harmonic mean is to make all cells ns equal to n_H. A complete Anova could thus be done using n_H in the formulas given for equal n in Chapter 5, and this was common in precomputer days. This approximate Anova is remarkably good, as has been shown by Bogartz (see Note 15.4.1b).[b]

Besides approximate confidence intervals, the harmonic mean may also be used to calculate power. Since power is always a guesstimate, the n_H approximation should be quite adequate.

15.4.2 ALTERNATIVE ANALYSES

Two alternative options to the standard parametric analysis are considered in two following subsections. First, however, possible causes of unequal n need discussion, for this is relevant to the choice of analysis.

Five Cases of Unequal n. Appropriate analysis depends on why the ns are unequal. The main distinction is whether the unequal ns are independent of or are caused by the treatments. In the former case, the standard parametric analysis yields valid results. In the latter case, the lost subjects bias the observed means, which undercuts the interpretation under any analysis.

Case 1. Subject loss is accidental, unrelated to treatment. This happens. Belatedly, it may be found that some subjects accidentally received the wrong treatment, or that the apparatus malfunctioned, or even that some scheduled subjects were not actually run. Adding a replacement subject may be inappropriate because it would compromise the randomization, or it may be too late.

The essential point is that subject loss is unrelated to treatment. The observed treatment means are thus unbiased; they estimate the same true means as if no subjects had been lost. Standard parametric analysis is thus appropriate.

Case 2. Unequal n may be planned. More subjects may be assigned to a control condition, for example, when it is to be compared with several different experimental conditions. Again, one experimental condition may be expensive, in money or time, so relatively few subjects can be run. As long as subjects have been randomly assigned, however, no problem arises. The observed treatment means are unbiased estimates of the true means.

The Anova, it should be realized, is subsidiary in both the present and previous cases. It merely assesses the reliability of the observed means. Anova is more complicated with unequal n, but this is a technicality. What is important is that the treatment means are not biased by the unequal ns.

Case 3. Subject loss is caused by treatments. In a physiological study, surgery or drugs may cause death in certain treatment conditions. In a developmental study, the task may turn out to be too hard for some younger children. In an experiment with multiple sessions, one treatment may be onerous or boring, causing subjects to drop out before completing the experiment.

This is a touchy problem because the lost subjects take away part of the treatment effect. The observed treatment means may thus be biased and misrepresent the true means. Anova may be applied, of course, and it will do its assigned job of assessing the reliability of the observed treatment means. The problem is that these means may be misleading.

The direction of this bias in the means may sometimes be determinable, as in the developmental example. In some physiological studies, similarly, the poorer subjects will tend to be lost. The observed difference will be firmer or weaker, according as the bias is expected to decrease or increase the difference.

Case 4. Subject loss has uncertain cause. In some areas, subject attrition is a fact of life. Attrition is common in field experiments, but it can occur in many laboratory situations. A rat in a long-term operant study may sicken or die near the end. A child in a study of problem solving or moral judgment may become obstreperous or sullen. Often there is good reason to think that subject attrition is unrelated to the specific treatment, but this is always somewhat uncertain.

Subject attrition is a design–procedure problem, not essentially statistical. The problem is possible bias. This bias problem would remain even if the ns could be equalized by running additional subjects to replace the losses.

The possibility of subject attrition thus needs attention at the planning stage. The example of a task overly difficult for younger children might stem from inadequate pilot work. When subject attrition is expectable, special care in the initial stages of investigation is desirable. Pilot work is not sensitive to infrequent problems, however, and replication experiments with improved procedure may be needed to clear up ambiguities from subject attrition (see further Section 14.1.1 on eliminating subjects).

Case 5. The final case of unequal n is exemplified with organismic or demographic variables. With such observational variables, the ns often represent relative frequencies of subpopulations. The mean for the whole population should not give the same weight to a small as to a large subpopulation. In this case, standard parametric analysis is inappropriate. A weighted mean is usually appropriate, in which each subpopulation is weighted by its relative frequency.

Weighted Means Anova. To illustrate weighted means Anova, consider a study of attitude video games to persuade grade schoolers to like and eat more vegetables. Several kinds of games are developed to test which are most effective. A number of schools participate, yielding a two-way, Game × School design. The schools, however, differ markedly in size. Since the main concern is with the outcome generality of the stimulus materials, equal and opposite mean effects in a small school and a large school should not cancel, as they would with the standard parametric analysis. Instead, the cell means for the treatment games should be weighted by school size. The Anova of these weighted means is equivalent to that obtained by ignoring the school factor and treating the data as a one-way design with games as levels.

The full analysis would include a test of the interaction. This would provide a warning signal about differential stimulus effects across schools. This approach is advocated by Fleiss (1986), who is concerned with applications in clinical medicine in which one factor is a patient classification.

Additive Model (Model Comparison Approach). The other alternative to the standard parametric analysis is to assume an additive model, that is, a model with zero interaction residuals. The advantage is that this model yields estimated cell means more reliable than the observed cell means. A cell mean based on a single score, for example, would be relatively unreliable. Under the no-interaction model, however, that cell mean is the sum of the corresponding row and column effects. Hence that cell mean may be estimated using information from all cells in the same row or same column. This increased reliability can be substantial when the ns are very unequal, although it dwindles to zero as the ns approach equality.

This additive model analysis is usually presented as part of the *model comparison approach*, which begins with a test of the interaction. For a two-way design, the interaction test is the same as with the standard parametric analysis because it deals directly with the cell means, without averaging across unequal ns. If this is statsig, the main effects are not ordinarily tested under the model comparison approach. Only if this is not statsig, perhaps using a liberal α, would the main effects be tested.

This additive model analysis suffers when the interaction residuals are not truly zero. In that case, the row and column effects are confounded with the unknown interaction and with the pattern of cell ns. In effect, the row and column means themselves depend on the cell ns, as well as on the true means. Burdick and Herr (1980) give a 2×2 example in which the same true means yield (a) a positive row effect and a zero column effect with equal n; (b) an opposite row effect and a zero column effect with one pattern of unequal n; and (c) a zero row effect and a nonzero column effect with another pattern of unequal n. The same true means thus yield sharply different conclusions, depending on the cell ns. Furthermore, the preliminary interaction test is an unreliable safeguard, for the interaction may be substantial yet not statsig. This anarchy cannot happen with standard parametric analysis. Most texts, accordingly, advise against using an additive, no-interaction model.

Empty Cells. Empty cells, with $n = 0$, sometimes occur. Some combinations of row and column treatments may not be sensible, for example, or perhaps not even possible.

A simple analysis with empty cells is with the additive, row + column model, arbitrarily assuming all interaction residuals are zero. Standard parametric analysis cannot be used because it is impossible to estimate the interaction residual for any empty cell. The additive analysis may at least be useful for exploratory purposes.

This additive approach could go awry if the interaction residuals are substantial, especially if there is a crossover. A more piecemeal analysis may be helpful, in which the standard parametric analysis is applied to subdesigns with no empty cells (see further Searle, 1987, 1993).

15.5 FIELD SCIENCE AND QUASI-EXPERIMENTAL DESIGN

Field science refers to investigations "in the field," that is, in ongoing natural situations. Quasi-experimental design, a popular form of field investigation, is the main topic of this section.[a]

The following discussion of quasi-experimental design has two purposes. One is to dispel the mystification that surrounds the term *quasi-experimental*. A more important reason is to encourage readers to attack problems of field science. Awareness of these problems and opportunities can help laboratory science avoid barren ground.

15.5.1 IMPORTANCE OF FIELD SCIENCE

Some problems cannot be studied with standard laboratory experiments. Field investigations are needed instead. Many problems in educational psychology, for example, need to be studied in actual classrooms to get results that apply to actual classrooms. In general, field investigations seem necessary for most problems that involve changing human behavior in some substantial way.

Chemistry and physics have been remarkably successful as laboratory sciences. Laboratory experiments lead to engineered artifacts, such as machines and medicines. A steady stream of physical–chemical artifacts have been transforming society since 1800, at an ever-faster rate.

Human problems of attitudes and aptitudes, habits and skills, health and happiness, present very different difficulties for scientific study. Humans are complex systems functioning in complex social contexts. Artifacts for quick, error-free statistics can be manufactured for a few dollars, but they do little to aid learning how to utilize statistics when planning an investigation. Still more difficult is how to decide on a fruitful research problem. Beyond that lie problems of how to develop effective knowledge systems for everyday life of work, self-esteem, and family. Laboratory science is inadequate because the problem has changed from artifacts to functional social–cognitive systems.[a]

For human problems, field science is at least as important as laboratory science. Social–cognitive processes are complicated and poorly understood. Laboratory simplification often loses external validity, that is, generalization to the social–cognitive context. Indeed, laboratory science in psychology typically becomes involved in issues that have distant relevance to everyday life. Verbal learning is a stock example, but similar irrelevance is general, as with much research on attitudes and attribution in social psychology.

Such irrelevance is not, in itself, a criticism of laboratory studies, many of which have basic scientific interest. Some, moreover, can be helpful adjuncts to field science, as with certain issues of process (e.g., Anderson, 1982, Sections 7.2–7.7; Levin, Louviere, Schepanski, & Norman, 1983). They should not, however, obscure the necessity for field science.

15.5.2 EXAMPLES OF QUASI-EXPERIMENTAL DESIGN

In *quasi-experimental design*, an experimental treatment is given but a random-ized control is lacking. In one standard class of quasi-experimental designs, the experimental treatment E is given to one group of subjects and a comparison treatment C, often no treatment at all, is given to another, hopefully somewhat comparable group. Some response measure is obtained and we assume here that the E–C difference is statsig.

The critical question is: Can this E–C difference be attributed to the experi-mental treatment—or does it merely reflect preexisting differences between the two groups?

Three kinds of quasi-experimental design are noted in the following three subsections. In the nursing home example, the two groups seem reasonably comparable, but even so, treatment confoundings trouble the interpretation. In Head Start studies, the E and C groups have nearly always been nonequivalent to begin with and comparisons between them have generally been uninterpret-able. Finally, time series, which arise in many practical applications, seek com-parisons between two series of observations on the same case, one before and one after some treatment.

Personal Control and Wellness. Health and wellness may improve when peo-ple are more actively in control of their behavior and environment. This propo-sition was tested in a nursing home, in which elderly residents were well-cared for without personal effort (Langer & Rodin, 1976). A special talk by the nurs-ing home administrator to the assembled fourth floor residents, the experimental group, emphasized their personal responsibility for their own lives and everyday decisions; the corresponding talk to the assembled second floor residents, the control group, emphasized the responsibility of the staff to care for them and make them happy. After the talk, fourth floor residents were offered a choice of plants for them to take care of in their own rooms; second floor residents were handed a plant and told the staff would care for it.

The special talk and the personal choice of a plant for the experimental group were both intended to increase their feeling of personal control and thereby their wellness. Self-ratings of activity by the residents, a rating of alert-ness by a blind interviewer, and nurse's ratings of time spent in various activi-ties were obtained one week before and three weeks after the special talk.

The before–after change scores were generally positive for the experimental group, generally negative for the control group, the difference being statsig. At face value, even this weak, one-time environmental manipulation had definite effects on wellness. Although subject randomization was not used, residents on the two floors were thought to be fairly similar. This judgment was supported by the near-equivalence of the two groups on the before ratings.

Nevertheless, the lack of within-floor randomization caused serious threats to the interpretation, some of which are noted later and pursued in the Exercises. Despite these uncertainties, this pioneering study certainly seems meritorious. It would be expected to trigger follow-up studies that test both the empirical phenomenon and the theoretical interpretation in terms of personal control. In particular, a stronger experimental manipulation maintained over time would seem desirable (see also Exercise 10.6).

Compensatory Education. Preschool experience for disadvantaged children could hardly fail to have positive effects. Instead, the first major evaluation of the Head Start program found evidence of negative effects. How could this be?

The answer is that quasi-experimental design makes non-effects look like harmful effects when the experimental group is poorer initially. To evaluate the effect of an educational program, some comparison group is needed that does not receive the treatment. Comparison groups have typically been initially superior to the experimental group. It might seem that this initial difference could be adjusted by measuring change from pretest to postest. Statistical theory, however, shows that almost any attempt to adjust for initial differences can make even a positive effect look negative. Such adjustment procedures are considered in Section 15.5.4.

Time Series. A *time series* consists of a succession of observations on a single case or situation. The simplest example is a sequence of observations before and after introduction of some treatment. Interpreting such data presents two questions, one of reliability, one of validity.

The first question is whether the change is reliable. An obvious attack on this question is to treat the before observations as one group, the after observations as a second group, and compare the two means. This comparison is very treacherous because successive observations within each group are likely to be correlated, or nonindependent. Nonindependence can seriously bias visual inspection as well as Anova and distribution-free tests. Statistical procedures have been developed for analysis of some correlated time series, although they require many observations (see further Section 11.3, pages 312*ff*).

If the change is reliable, the second question concerns validity: Can the difference be attributed to the treatment? Any number of other causes may be at work; the same change could well have occurred even had no treatment been given. Lacking a control, this question can only be addressed through use of extrastatistical knowledge about the causal structure of the situation at hand.

Applied action programs often produce time series data. One class of examples is laws and regulations. Legislatures are prone to pass stiff laws about welfare limitations or mandatory jail sentences, for example, and government bureaus may set regulations on wearing seat belts or on teaching mathematics in the schools. But do these laws and regulations have the intended effects? They typically emerge from naive, often opinionated, beliefs about complex causality. It is desirable, therefore, to scrutinize the before–after time series to try to get some idea of effectiveness—and how to improve the laws and regulations.

A second class of time series includes individual life problems: health, work satisfaction, behavior problems of diverse kinds, and other aspects of personal life. Many life problems must be handled as single person time series, as with problems with your parents, spouse, children, and your self.

A short, clear introduction to time series is given by McCain and McCleary (1979), including an instructive reanalysis of armed robberies in Boston before and after passage of a strict gun control law. Examples of time series from behavior modification and highway safety are given in Sections 11.4.2 and 11.4.6. Here, however, time series will not be considered further.

15.5.3 THREATS TO INTERNAL VALIDITY

Threats to validity of quasi-experimental design have been given names and cataloged by various writers (see Cook & Campbell, 1979, Chapter 2), one list reaching a total of 35 threats. Most of these threats reduce to two: Treatment confoundings, illustrated in the following subsections; and measurement issues, mainly unreliability, discussed on pages 469ff.[a]

The present discussion aims only to give a general idea of the nature and problems of quasi-experimental design. Anyone who wishes to apply such design needs deeper understanding.

History. The term *history* denotes effects due to some extraneous event that occurs between pretest and posttest. The presence of such confounding in the nursing home study is suggested by the fact that, although the control group of second floor residents received a positive, sympathetic treatment, "71% were rated as having become more debilitated over a period of time as short as 3 weeks" (p. 197). Such rapid debilitation seems unlikely for long-term residents and suggests some alternative cause. A wave of colds on the second floor for example, or a death, or a new, unpleasant nursing attendant, could depress these residents as a group. The apparent superiority of the experimental group of fourth floor residents may have been an artifact of such confounding.

The history threat is especially serious when treatments are applied to natural groups, as with the two floors in the nursing home, or classroom groups in educational studies. The scores in each group may not be independent, but influenced by some common extraneous factor (Section 15.1.2, pages 444ff).

Differential Growth. Behavior develops at different rates for different individuals. If group C has a higher growth rate than group E, this may manifest itself as a harmful effect of the E treatment. This artifact is likely in Head Start and other studies of compensatory education, in which a Head Start C group is typically better than the E group at the beginning.

One reason to expect higher growth rate in a Head start C group is that their higher pretest scores may reflect higher growth rate in previous years. Higher growth rate could have various causes, such as better home environment. This higher growth rate is likely to continue during the treatment period. If the treatment had no effect, therefore, change scores would be larger for group C, making the treatment appear harmful.

A second reason to expect differential growth is the likelihood, for open knowledge systems, that growth rate increases with higher initial levels. The more you know already, the faster you can assimilate new knowledge. Thus, a school group that starts with a better vocabulary system may be expected to assimilate new knowledge faster. Hence an initial superiority of a comparison group to a disadvantaged group would increase over time in the normal course of events. If the experimental treatment has no effect, therefore, differential growth will make it appear actually harmful.

Other Treatment Confounding. Treatment confounding may also result from some nonblind aspect of procedure. In the nursing home example, the main treatment was presented by the home administrator, first in his special talk to each floor as a group, later in an individual visit to each resident, in which he reaffirmed the main points of his talk. Since the administrator was presumably aware of the investigators' hypothesis, this could affect the sincerity and effectiveness of his presentation. Indeed, his own preference for one treatment could have similar effects. Medical placebo studies indicate how serious such confounding can be. This confounding might have been avoidable by giving each resident a written version of the administrator's talk, together with an embedded questionnaire to ensure that they read it (Exercise 3).

A different kind of treatment confounding appears when treatments have multiple possible effects. The classic example is the placebo effect, in which treatments may operate through suggestion as well as medically. Also classic is the Hawthorne effect, akin to a placebo effect, in which it seemed that workers' productivity increased, not because of the experimental manipulation of lighting and other working conditions, but because of the attention given the workers. In experimental analysis, a primary problem is to develop controls for likely effects besides the process at issue.

Field experiments seem generally vulnerable to treatment confounding. The foregoing examples are only illustrative, far from complete (see further Chapter 8). Forethought is more than usually desirable, especially based on personal experience in the given situation (see "walk a mile in my shoes," p. 473).

15.5.4 ADJUSTMENT PROCEDURES

A variety of procedures have been proposed to adjust or correct for systematic initial differences between groups. Every one has serious shortcomings.

Matching. An obvious way to adjust for initial differences between groups is with *matching*. In the Head Start example, a vocabulary pretest could be given. Each disadvantaged child would then be matched with a nondisadvantaged child who had the same pretest score. Then the posttest vocabulary scores could be compared directly—so it would seem.

But matching is subject to a *regression artifact* (pages 582*ff*). Suppose the treatments for the two groups have equal effects. The posttest score for the matched disadvantaged group will nevertheless be lower, by virtue of the regression artifact. Even a positive effect of the Head Start treatment could thus appear harmful.

Matching is no longer much used. Unfortunately, procedures that have taken its place are subject to the same regression artifact, as discussed in the next two subsections (see further Anderson, 1982, Section 7.7).

Change Scores: Posttest – Pretest. As an alternative to matching, the change score, $Y - X$, might seem a valid response measure. Subtraction of the pretest X score seems to correct for any systematic difference between the groups.

The change score, however, is a clumsy form of analysis of covariance, in which the regression coefficient β_1 is arbitrarily set equal to 1 (Section 13.1.2, page 386). Hence the change score virtually guarantees a biased result.

This pitfall with change scores illustrates the necessity for statistical theory. To common sense, the change score appears highly desirable. Only through statistical theory do its shortcomings appear (see Harris, 1963).

Analysis of Covariance With Nonequivalent Groups. Analysis of covariance (Ancova) is often said to "control" or "correct for" initial differences between nonequivalent groups. Regrettably, this is not so. One reason is that unreliability in the covariate can produce apparent differences where none exist. Even the sign of a real effect can be changed.

To set out this artifact, suppose for simplicity that the pretest and posttest, X and Y, are equivalent. They might be identical behavioral measures or perhaps parallel forms of the same test. Both scores are measured for two nonequivalent groups and Ancova is applied with the hope that it will "control for" or "hold constant" the systematic initial difference between the two groups. It is enlightening to understand some of the considerations that blast this hope.

1. UNRELIABILITY. Unreliability in X biases the covariance adjustment. In the numerical example of Section 13.2.1 (page 391), both groups had equal true slopes, with $\beta_1 = 1$. If this true slope value is used, Ancova does a perfect job in adjusting the initial difference in X.

But in practice, β_1 will not be known. Instead, the estimated regression coefficient b_1 must be used. But b_1 is generally smaller than β_1 as shown in Equation 13.5. Hence the covariance adjustment is biased. Non-effects will appear as real effects; real effects may reverse direction.

The direction of this bias is simple. Suppose the treatment has no effect. If the treatment is given the better group, Ancova will falsely make it look helpful. If the treatment is given the poorer group, Ancova will falsely make it look harmful. This negative bias may mask a positive treatment effect, as seems likely with some Head Start programs.

2. FLUCTUATION. Some variables fluctuate over time, without systematic trend. Mood and motivation are obvious examples, but test performance also fluctuates from day to day. The X score may thus change for each individual over time even though there is no systematic trend.

Such fluctuation produces the same bias just indicated for unreliability. Although this may seem odd, the reason is simple enough. Because Y and X are equivalent measures, the Y score corresponds to the *final X* score, plus whatever effects the treatments have produced. Suppose that treatments have no effect and that the measures are perfectly reliable. Then Y and the *final X* would be identical and would show perfect correlation. But the *initial X*, which is what we actually use, differs from the final X because X fluctuates for each individual. Hence the operative correlation will be less than perfect—producing the same effect as unreliability.

3. STRUCTURAL CHANGE. Behavior typically involves multiple component processes. Reading, for example, is not unitary, but involves assemblage of diverse lexical, semantic, pragmatic, and functional processes. The same holds for virtually every significant activity, from motor skills to intellectual and interpersonal skills. Over the course of development, therefore, some components will increase in importance and others will decrease.

Ostensibly, X and Y are equivalent measures. Their psychological structure will differ, however, reflecting the structural change in component processes between pretest and posttest. Suppose again that the treatments have no effect and that both measures are perfectly reliable. Again, therefore, Y and the *final X* would be identical and show perfect correlation. The initial X, however, has lower correlation with Y because it has a different structure, which is differential across individuals. One effect of such structural change is thus analogous to the effect of unreliability.

These and other measurement problems are considered in depth in an illuminating chapter by Reichardt (1979), on which the present discussion is based. All these measurement problems arise also when Y and X are not equivalent measures, as was assumed for simplicity above. How serious these problems are depends on the situation; structural change would not be a factor in many short-term studies, with psychophysiological measures, for example.

Unreliability itself may be addressed with somewhat controversial adjustments. Unfortunately, the combined effect of these measurement factors may bias the result in either direction, depending on situational specifics. Even the likely direction of bias is thus often uncertain.

Partial Measure Bias. Partial measure bias may be fatal to any attempt to adjust for preexisting differences between nonrandomized groups. Such groups will generally differ in ways that are unknown or unmeasurable. The measures used for adjustment are then only partial measures. But what has not been measured, directly or indirectly, cannot be adjusted for.

To illustrate, consider a vocabulary score from a quasi-experimental Head Start study, intended for use in an adjustment with multiple regression or with Ancova. This vocabulary score stems from various knowledge systems the child develops through conversational interactions, especially in family and school, and through amount and kind of reading and TV. The vocabulary score is only a thin, one-dimensional reflection of the underlying knowledge systems. Two school groups with different knowledge systems will have different vocabulary scores. But no statistical technique that "equalizes" or "holds constant" the vocabulary score can do the same for the knowledge systems—and it is the knowledge systems that determine how much is learned.

An important distinction between random and nonrandom groups is underscored in this discussion of knowledge systems. With random groups, the vocabulary test score allows a valid test between treatment groups. That the vocabulary score is only a partial measure of the knowledge system is an opportunity to get a simple grip on a complex phenomenon. With nonrandom groups, however, the partial measure is inherently inadequate.

Multiple Regression and Ancova. Multiple regression, including partial correlation and Ancova, are often presented as methods for "controlling" uncontrolled variables. These methods have been popular because they promise valid comparisons between nonequivalent groups. These promises are broken by the artifacts already described. To say these methods "control" is wrong.

This fallacy is widely known—and widely ignored. More detailed discussion is given in Sections 13.2 (pages 390*ff*) and 16.2 (pages 501*ff*). In the Head Start program, as Campbell and Boruch (1975, pp. 241*ff*) show, multiple regression and partial correlation transform the initial inferiority of the disadvantaged group into a harmful effect of the Head Start treatment. A harmful effect is hardly credible, of course, which reemphasizes that multiple regression and partial correlation are invalid for "control."

Regression Discontinuity Design. One nonrandom groups design is valid and potentially important. The idea is to assign subjects to treatment and no-treatment groups solely on the basis of an initial X score. For example, remedial treatment could be given only to those who score below some specified cut-point on X. The great advantage of this design is that measurement unreliability causes no bias because the two groups are distinguished solely in terms of the measured X, not any underlying property that is measured with error.

Analysis of this regression-discontinuity design hinges on post-treatment behavior near the cut-point. Any treatment effect is expected to produce a discontinuity in Y score between subjects just below the cut-point, who receive the designated treatment, and no-treatment subjects just above the cut-point. A simple-minded test for discontinuity would be to fit two regression equations, one for each group. Both should be equivalent if the treatment has no effect. If the treatment does have an effect, they will differ in b_0. It should be emphasized, however, that analysis of regression discontinuity design is far from simple. The monograph by Trochim (1984) summarizes the extensive statistical and methodological work on regression–discontinuity design, including a valuable chapter on practical obstacles that arise in field implementation.

Regression discontinuity design may be politically feasible in situations in which cut-points are commonly used. The X score, it should be emphasized, may be a weighted sum of disparate components, including need, merit, affirmative action, political and personal considerations, or what you will. The essential requirement is that assignment to treatments be based solely on the X score, according to some prespecified rule. Unfortunately, exceptions to this essential requirement, often reasonable in themselves, are politically unavoidable in many social situations. This obstacle might sometimes be resolvable by including an evaluation of each case by concerned local persons as one component of the X score.

A superior design may be feasible. Instead of an absolute cut-point, randomized assignment would be used for a limited range of individuals around the cut-point. All individuals below the lower bound of the range would receive the treatment, none of those above the upper bound. But within this range, individuals would be randomly assigned to treatment and no-treatment.

This randomized subdesign resolves the questions that trouble even the regression discontinuity design. In particular, randomization may be applied after any exceptions have been excepted. Also, randomized design would be substantially more efficient and powerful (see Trochim, 1984, Chapter 3).

15.5.5 FIELD SCIENCE

Importance of Field Science. The importance of field science is matched by its difficulties. Current preoccupation with laboratory experiments has partial justification as a search for basic processes. Such experiments have certainly made us aware of the variety and complexity of thought and behavior, as may be seen by comparing one of the many remarkably fine introductory texts of today with those of 50 years ago. Unfortunately, this focus on phenomena readily amenable to laboratory study has obscured the great need for a complementary field perspective.

Many investigators, it is true, have concentrated on field studies. Even more prominent than quasi-experimental studies are those that use multiple regression (Chapter 16). Such work, however, is often done with inadequate understanding of the pitfalls, or even concern about them. Lack of competence can have far more serious consequences in field science than in laboratory studies.

Quasi-Experimental Design and Randomized Design. The term *quasi-experiment* was introduced by Campbell and Stanley (1966) in the mistaken belief that analysis of covariance would control for uncontrolled variables in nonrandomized design. Had this belief been correct, quasi-experimental design would have been a powerful tool for field studies. Of course, the pitfalls illustrated above were soon recognized. As Campbell and Boruch (1975, p. 203) observe, lack of randomization "invalidates most social experiments of a quasi-experimental design nature: that is, there is a profound underlying confounding of selection [initial group differences] and treatment" (see also Campbell, 1978, p. 303).

Quasi-experimental data can be effective when the causal structure of the situation is reasonably well understood. Many such examples are familiar from everyday life. When your toothache goes away after your dentist fills a cavity, there is little reason to think the ache disappeared of its own accord, independent of the treatment. On a grander scale, the astonishing recent advances in astronomy rest on a solid base of causal knowledge about observational data, especially about spectral emission and absorption lines of various chemical elements, which bring us information from other galaxies across vast reaches of space and time.

In social–cognitive contexts, however, causal structure is generally complicated and poorly understood. The vital first step, of course, is to obtain qualitative appreciation of the situation to be studied. A common complaint by those working in field situations, from schools to prisons, is that investigations designed by outside professionals typically rest on naive assumptions that have little relation to everyday reality. Field investigators should, as one field administrator said, "walk a mile in my shoes" before designing an investigation. Quasi-experimental studies can be invaluable pilot work for obtaining qualitative appreciation.

But for substantive conclusions, quasi-experiments are often unsatisfactory, often worthless. The shortcomings of quasi-experiments are well illustrated by the initial evaluation of the Head Start program. It is hard to believe that special schooling for disadvantaged children could actually be harmful, yet that was what this evaluation showed. This outcome should have been anticipated, as Campbell said; some of the artifacts illustrated above had long been known.

Head Start illustrates a far larger problem of education. The real problem is harder than merely showing Head Start is helpful. The real problem is to find what kind of Head Start treatment is most helpful. Parental involvement has been considered desirable, for example, but exactly how should this be done? Analogous questions arise with respect to the content of Head Start instruction.

This larger problem of education also arises with teaching in the schools and colleges. Society is spending huge sums on education with little knowledge about effectiveness—and little effort to find out. Progress on these questions seems improbable without large-scale randomized experiments in field settings (see also Notes 23.2a,b, page 781).

Summary View on Field Investigations. A summary view on field investigations may be reduced to three points. First, a field scientist should press to the limit and beyond to obtain randomized experiments. Randomized experiments are not as difficult as may appear, in many cases, and they provide inestimable benefits in validity. Campbell and Boruch (1975 p. 276) conclude their discussion of quasi-experimental design saying "Collectively, these biases . . . cumulate as powerful arguments for randomized assignment to treatment." Their chapter also includes an appendix summary of randomized field experiments of an educational nature, a useful guide for further work (see further Cook & Campbell, 1979).

In the same vein, Gilbert, Light, and Mosteller (1975) present an impressive, instructive collection of nearly 40 field studies. Despite the difficulties of organizing and implementing randomized field studies, such studies "have been done successfully in education, welfare, criminal justice, medical care, manpower training, surgery, and preventive medicine . . . valuable social and medical findings emerged" (p. 41). They reach the stern verdict that failure to use randomized design is often "*just fooling around with people*" (p. 150).

Second, field scientists have an obligation to be technically prepared. This includes thorough appreciation of the various "threats" to quasi-experimental design as well as thorough understanding of the pitfalls of multiple regression and Ancova. Randomized design has the great advantage that it can be used effectively with limited statistical knowledge. Without randomized design, much deeper understanding is required, both statistical understanding and substantive understanding. The argument of Chapter 13 may be repeated here: To compare nonrandom groups requires substantive theory that rests on firm empirical ground.

Campbell has suggested that psychology was not ready for the Head Start program. Thus, Campbell and Boruch (1975, p. 248) comment that "For Head Start . . . randomized assignment to treatment (by schools, residential blocks, classrooms, or pupils) would have been possible, had there been an awareness of the problems of inference that would result from nonrandom assignment." Much of this unreadiness seems to have been failure to use existing knowledge.

After all, the problems of nonrandomized field studies go back as far as Student's (1931) discussion of the Lanarkshire nutrition experiment (Chapter 3, Appendix, pages 81-82).[a]

Third, field studies are important and randomization is not always possible. The emphasis on randomized experiments is not intended to slight the potential value of quasi-experiments. The foregoing nursing home study seems useful, even though the results are less trustworthy than if some form of randomized design had been used.

Too often, however, field studies are uninterpretable, as with much of the Head Start program (see similarly *Premarital Cohabitation* and *Low Lead Controversy* in Section 16.2.2). Adequate technical preparation is essential to assess whether a given field study will be meaningful and/or to embed meaningful field studies within socially mandated programs.[b]

NOTES

15.1a. Kirk (1995, Chapter 11) considers hierarchical designs similar to the natural groups design considered in Section 15.1.2 (following page); see also Bogartz (1994, Chapter 6), Lindman (1992, Chapter 8), Myers and Well (1991, Chapter 10), and Winer et al. (1991, Sections 5.14 and 6.6).

15.1.2a. Establishing that natural group differences are small in some line of investigation would be desirable as it would allow pooling of $SS_{G/A}$ and $SS_{S/G}$. The only way to do this is through empirical assessment over a sequence of studies within a common experimental setting. To build up a knowledge base for pooling decisions, mean squares for all sources deserve to be reported. Even more important, it would seem, is development of procedures to reduce differences between groups, as with screening tests and clean procedure.

15.2.1a. Error terms for more complex mixed models, with both fixed and random terms, can be tricky, especially for confidence intervals. Schwarz (1993) commented in adverse detail on current texts and computer packages, and his article should be understood by anyone doing serious work with random factors. As one example, he says "Only an experienced [statistical] analyst should attempt the analysis of a mixed model using SPSS [Version 4.0]" (p. 56).

15.2.2a. The relevance of random factor analysis to language studies was pointed out by Coleman (1964) and amplified by Clark (1973), who used an example of comparing reading speed for nouns versus verbs, also adopted by Wickens and Keppel (1983). This example does not seem too pertinent because nouns and verbs are heterogeneous classes (consider, for example, the nouns *egg, spring, antidisestablishmentarianism, chair, heaven,* and *statistics*). It would seem essential to classify nouns and verbs into meaningful categories. Once that is done, however, the question of nouns-versus-verbs loses meaning. Different subclasses of nouns will give different results and there is no general way to obtain "comparable" subclasses of nouns and verbs (see also Cutler, 1981).

Instead, such classification suggests the need to study effects of word length, number of syllables, pronounceability, intersyllable interference, familiarity, breadth of meaning, and other factors, among which the noun–verb distinction seems minor, perhaps not even meaningful. This consideration reemphasizes the distinction between outcome and process generality. This critique is not peculiar to the noun–verb example; similar considerations apply generally for comparing different stimulus classes.

Moreover, random factor analysis is not practicable in many situations, for example, when some person is an important part of the stimulus situation. To get adequate df for error, random factor analysis would require a substantial number of persons, which is often not feasible. Similar considerations apply to some studies with longish textual materials rather than single words. A sample of two or three is a lot more comfortable than a sample of one, but a random factor analysis with two or three levels probably has too little power to be worth anything (Exercise 8). Fixed factor analysis, in contrast, provides more definite if less ambitious evidence on generality.

15.2.2b. This primacy effect in person cognition (Anderson & Barrios, 1959) is sensitive to procedural factors. It does not stem from some kind of fixation in the initial stage, contrary to a common interpretation, but rather from a labile decline of attention to later stimuli (Anderson, 1981, pp. 180-182; see also Anderson, 1991f, pp. 36-38).

15.2.2c. Outcome generality is an appropriate goal with applications of randomized block designs in agriculture; generality across a population of blocks is what is needed (Note 14.2.4a, page 433). In such practical applications, nil or opposite effects in a small minority of blocks would sometimes be natural to the field situation. The same would hold for many issues in applied psychology. In much psychological work, however, nil or opposite effects in a small minority of stimuli would have substantive interest.

15.2.2d. In personality theory, the question of relative importance of Person and Situation has been studied by treating both as random factors in a Person × Situation design. Random factor analysis then yields proportions of variance attributable to the two factors, which are taken as their relative importance. Such results seldom mean much for reasons given in Section 7.4.1 (page 201). A more basic objection is that this question of relative importance of Person and Situation is crude, not to say sterile.

15.2.2e. This discussion of random factors is based on Anderson (1982, Section 1.3.6). A different alternative to random factor analysis also deserves consideration. The appropriate level of analysis may be individual stimuli (Oden & Anderson, 1974, p. 147):

> Too often, psycholinguistic data are gross, qualitative differences, averaged over groups of propositions, and over groups of subjects as well. Such data can be very useful, but they also have severe limitations. Linguistic stimuli are complex and notoriously susceptible to confounding. Averages over groups of propositions may conceal important differences. Furthermore, since the same word often means different things to different people, averages over groups of subjects must also be treated with caution.

Psycholinguistic theory must be capable of handling the individual linguistic unit, at the level of the individual person.

15.3a. One additional method of reducing design size is occasionally useful. This may be called *coupling*, which refers to physical confounding of two or more variables (previously called *ganging*, Anderson, 1982, p. 45). Coupling A and B means that each level of variable A always occurs with the same level of B. Coupling thus yields a compound variable, $[AB]$. Any effect of $[AB]$ cannot be localized in either A or B.

Coupling can control minor variables. In a two-factor, $[AB] \times C$ design, the levels of A and B are jointly balanced across levels of variable C. Although the $[AB]$ effect cannot be further localized, this may not be important with two minor variables.

Coupling may also be used with major variables, for example, in applied studies that seek some beneficial treatment. A single treatment would be chosen that incorporates several possibly effective components, and this would be compared with a control. This two-condition design may be a cost-effective way to try out several possible treatments at once. A small effect would cast doubt on the effectiveness of every one of the treatments. A large effect would show the potential for more detailed analysis to localize its source. In some applied situations, of course, localization would not be important.

15.3.1a. Estimation in a fractional design can be clarified with the Anova model. For the illustrative 2^3 design, the Anova model with error omitted and interactions ignored is

$$Y_{jkm} = \bar{\mu} + \alpha_j + \beta_k + \gamma_m, \qquad j, k, m = 1, 2.$$

For the half replicate, the main effect of A is the contrast

$$\begin{aligned}
\bar{A}_1 - \bar{A}_2 &= +[111] &=& \quad + (\bar{\mu} + \alpha_1 + \beta_1 + \gamma_1) \\
&\quad + [122] && \quad + (\bar{\mu} + \alpha_1 + \beta_2 + \gamma_2) \\
&\quad - [212] && \quad - (\bar{\mu} + \alpha_2 + \beta_1 + \gamma_2) \\
&\quad - [221] && \quad - (\bar{\mu} + \alpha_2 + \beta_2 + \gamma_1).
\end{aligned}$$

All terms cancel except the α_j, leaving

$$\bar{A}_1 - \bar{A}_2 = 2(\alpha_1 - \alpha_2).$$

The main effect of A is thus estimated by the listed contrast.

This main effect, however, is confounded with the BC interaction residual. To see the confounding pattern, include the interaction residuals in the Anova model:

$$Y_{jkm} = \bar{\mu} + \alpha_j + \beta_k + \gamma_m$$
$$(\alpha\beta)_{jk} + (\alpha\gamma)_{jm} + (\beta\gamma)_{km} + (\alpha\beta\gamma)_{jkm}.$$

The contrast for the main effect of A thus becomes

$$\bar{A}_1 - \bar{A}_2 = \bar{Y}_{111} + \bar{Y}_{122} - \bar{Y}_{212} - \bar{Y}_{221}$$

$$= 2(\alpha_1 - \alpha_2)$$

$$+ (\alpha\beta)_{11} + (\alpha\gamma)_{11} + (\beta\gamma)_{11} + (\alpha\beta\gamma)_{111}$$

$$+ (\alpha\beta)_{12} + (\alpha\gamma)_{12} + (\beta\gamma)_{22} + (\alpha\beta\gamma)_{122}$$

$$- (\alpha\beta)_{21} - (\alpha\gamma)_{22} - (\beta\gamma)_{12} - (\alpha\beta\gamma)_{212}$$

$$- (\alpha\beta)_{22} - (\alpha\gamma)_{21} - (\beta\gamma)_{21} - (\alpha\beta\gamma)_{221}.$$

This simplifies considerably because the interaction residuals must sum to zero in each row and column. For the AB residuals, therefore, $(\alpha\beta)_{11} + (\alpha\beta)_{12} = 0$, so these cancel. Similarly, $(\alpha\beta)_{21} + (\alpha\beta)_{22} = 0$, and these also cancel. Hence the main effect of A is free of confounding with AB residuals. Similar cancellation holds for the four $(\alpha\gamma)$ terms for the AC residual. The foregoing equation thus reduces to

$$\bar{A}_1 - \bar{A}_2 = 2(\alpha_1 - \alpha_2) + (\beta\gamma)_{11} + (\beta\gamma)_{22} - (\beta\gamma)_{12} - (\beta\gamma)_{21}$$

$$+ (\alpha\beta\gamma)_{111} + (\alpha\beta\gamma)_{122} - (\alpha\beta\gamma)_{212} + (\alpha\beta\gamma)_{221}.$$

The four $(\beta\gamma)$ terms on the right represent the BC residual, which does not cancel. Similarly, the four $(\alpha\beta\gamma)$ terms on the right represent half of the ABC residual. These interaction residuals are confounded with the main effect of A.

Similar analysis holds for general 2^p fractional designs and leads to simple rules for confounding, cataloged in Cochran and Cox. More extensive catalogs of fractional replication designs are referenced in Anderson (1982, Note 1.3.7b).

15.3.1b. The present analysis of the 2^3 design in two half replicates differs from that of Cochran and Cox (1957, Section 6.11) in two respects. First, each main effect has a separate error term, whereas Cochran and Cox pool the three error terms and use this for all main effects and two-way residuals. Such pooling is inappropriate with repeated measures, for which each source should in general have its own error. Second, with random assignment of subjects, the "Replicates" factor of Cochran and Cox is equivalent to their "Error for ABC." In the present analysis, ABC thus has $2n - 2$ rather than $n - 1$ df. These differences arise because subjects in repeated measures designs differ substantively from "blocks" in Cochran and Cox. Similar considerations apply to other fractional designs considered in their book.

15.3.1c. Several details of the number-averaging experiment deserve mention. Each sequence had seven numbers, the last being a filler to avoid possible end-of-sequence effects on the response to the sixth number. To minimize carryover effects, subjects spent 15 s rating cartoons between each sequence of numbers. A different pair of two-digit numbers was used for the two factor levels at each serial position, with a difference of 17 in each pair. Using the same difference of 17 was intended to make the six main effects equivalent except for different weights at each serial position. A 6×6 Latin square design was used to balance number-pairs across serial positions. Number-pairs was not statsig, which supports the assumption that their subjective differences were equivalent. Subjects responded after each serial position, so a serial curve could be constructed for each serial position. It deserves emphasis, however, that the serial curve for any position requires response only at that one position.

One noteworthy aspect of experimental procedure concerned the stimulus presentation. In pilot work, my assistant, Ann Norman Atkinson, read the numbers aloud, using fellow graduate students as subjects. They could not do the task; the average of the previous numbers somehow seemed to float away. They were so embarrassed she had to promise not to reveal their names to me. I then told her to write each number on a slip so that each sequence was represented physically by a small packet of slips. Subjects were instructed to judge the average of each packet of slips, which were turned over one by one. With the task made concrete in this way, the difficulty vanished.

15.3.1d. The interpretation of the serial weight curve for the number-averaging experiment assumes that the intuitive averages by the subjects obeyed an averaging model. That they were instructed to average, however, does not mean that they did so. A test of the averaging model was included in the design in the form of a test for nonadditive interaction residuals (see next note). This test did not approach significance, which supports the averaging model. Serial curves have been obtained in many integration experiments, including functional memory (Anderson, 1996a, pp. 364*ff*).

15.3.1e. This 1/8 replicate of the 2^6 design was taken directly from Plan 6.A.4 of Cochran and Cox (1957). These 8 conditions yield 6 df for the 6 serial position effects, 1 df for interaction residuals. The likely locus of nonadditivity was between successive serial positions. The listed plan localized the 1 df for residuals primarily in the three successive pairs of serial positions, 1×2, 3×4, and 5×6, pooled, so it was exactly suited to this experiment. This interaction residual did not approach significance. Had interactions seemed more a threat, a 1/4 replicate would have yielded 9 df to test interaction residuals chosen to be sensitive to likely patterns of nonadditivity.

15.3.2a. A considerable number of experimental designs based on Latin squares for independent groups are given by Winer et al. (1991) and Kirk (1995).

15.4.1a. Lack of common terminology hinders decoding what options your package program is using for Anova with unequal *n*. I have used the terms *standard parametric analysis*, following Herr and Gaebelein (1978), and *additive model*, because they are meaningful. Fleiss (1986, pp. 172*ff*) and Maxwell and Delaney (1990, pp. 286*ff*) use *Type III* for the standard parametric analysis, together with *Type II* for the additive, model comparison approach, and *Type I* for the weighted means analysis. On the other hand, Myers and Well (1991, pp. 560*ff*) use Methods 1, 2, and 3 in place of Types III, II, and I.

15.4.1b. It seems widely accepted by applied statisticians that the harmonic mean is a good approximation to equal *n* as long as the *n*s are not too unequal, but surprisingly little information is available. Nearly all articles in the last two decades have constructed extreme cases to highlight differences between different approaches or as advocacy for one particular approach. Accordingly, they have used extremely unequal *n*s that are rarely seen in practice: 10 to 2, 25 to 2, and 9 to 1, in different articles. Such results have minimal value for experimental investigators.

A welcome exception is unpublished work by Bogartz (personal e-mail, 26 July, 1998), which showed that Anova with the harmonic mean did remarkably well. Bogartz did 10,000 random simulations for eight different sets of main effects in a 3×3 design, all with the same substantial interaction. In each design, three cells each had *n* scores, $n - k$ scores, and $n - 2k$ scores, in Latin square array. Values of *n* ranged from 10 to 25; values of *k* ranged from 1 to .2 *n*. In the worst case, therefore, the two smallest cells had 60% as many scores as the two largest cells. Anova was performed for each simulation using the harmonic mean of the cell *n*s as the common cell *n*.

Virtually no bias was found in α. Of the 112 cases in which a null hypothesis was tested, the mean α was .050; the mean deviation was .002. Of the five values of k for $n = 25$, there was no hint that α was related to the value of k.

15.5a. This discussion of field studies relies heavily on Campbell and Boruch (1975), Cook and Campbell (1979), Cook et al. (1992), Gilbert, Light, and Mosteller (1975), Hilton and Lumsdaine (1975), and Trochim (1984). A valuable elementary discussion is given by Light, Singer, and Willett (1990), which concentrates on planning research on higher education but gives useful coverage of all kinds of field situations. The undergraduate text by Jones (1996) is similarly useful. I wish to express my gratitude for a critique by Charles Reichardt.

15.5.1a. Another large class of field problems involves operation of governments. We take our form of government for granted, with inadequate appreciation of our founding fathers, whose prescience in prescribing a then-novel form of government that proved successful and adaptive contrasts so powerfully with the inhuman debacle of Stalinism that developed from Marx−Leninism in the former Soviet empire (Medvedev, 1989). Not that our own society lacks for difficult problems, as may be seen in the laws and regulations that stream from national, state, and local governments and from the courts. Foremost among these problems are education, on which knowledge seems woefully primitive, and family life, about which knowledge is mostly ignorance.

15.5.3a. Special names, such as *history*, have been given to these threats to validity of quasi-experimental design. These names may be useful as a checklist for those actively engaged in such work, but I have found them mainly an obscuring layer of verbiage. Most of these threats refer to treatment confounding or to measurement bias. What is most needed is development of case examples for education on assessing likely threats in specific situations.

15.5.5a. Further misdesign for Head Start was the original choice of IQ scores to measure treatment effects. A primary goal in the development of IQ tests has been to make them as independent as possible of school learning. A measure less sensitive to possible benefits from Head Start could hardly have been found.

15.5.5b. Study of nonrandom groups requires specialized training. A year of advanced course work on statistical issues seems minimal, with good understanding of Achen (1986), Bennett and Lumsdaine (1975), Cochran (1983), Cook et al. (1992), Cook and Campbell (1979), Huitema (1980), Mosteller and Tukey (1977), Reichardt (1979), Smith (1957), and Trochim (1984, 1986). Those who study nonrandom groups urge the social importance of the questions being asked. Does it not follow that they have corresponding social responsibility to be prepared to do a workmanlike job?

EXERCISES FOR CHAPTER 15

Exercises 1–7 and 19 pertain to the nursing home study of Section 15.5.2.

1. List three alternative explanations for the claimed improvement of the experimental group in the nursing home experiment of Section 15.5.2.

2. Suppose the experiment had been replicated using the first and third floors in the same way as was done for the second and fourth floors. What advantage would accrue?

3. An alternative method would be to assign the two treatments at random to individual residents within each separate floor. What are the advantages/disadvantages of within floor randomization?

4. An alternative design for the nursing home study would have given no specific talk or other treatment to second floor residents, but still make the same measurements as for the fourth floor residents. However, the control condition actually used was needed to control a confound in the experimental condition given the fourth floor residents that would affect the theoretical interpretation. What was this confound?

5. The main data were change scores between measures for each resident before and after the treatment.

   a. What is the advantage of this change score?

   b. What is the disadvantage of this change score (see Chapter 13)?

6. "Locus of control" is one of the few aspects of personality that has shown substantial correlations with performance in a variety of tasks. Locus of control refers to the degree to which people feel that they control external events or that external events control them. How might a preliminary measure of locus of control for each resident have been used in the nursing home study to:

   a. Decrease error variability? How much decrease would you expect?

   b. Increase substantive significance?

7. For a follow-up design for the nursing home study, assuming comparable facilities are available, what two changes would you consider most important?

8. This exercise aims to make concrete some isses in random factor analysis. The following experimental situation is typical of one class of situations in which random factor analysis has sometimes been misapplied.

   Subjects' responses may depend on personality characteristics of some person that are confounded with the treatment. Studies of social influence, for example, may use a confederate who has some essential role in the treatment. Similarly, effectiveness of marriage counseling will depend on the personality of the counselor. Again, expression of emotion in animals may depend on how the experimenter handles them.

To handle such confounding, it is often vital to use more than one confederate, counselor, or experimenter. For illustration, we may consider the study of social interaction discussed in Exercise 5.10, simplified for present purposes by ignoring the Favorable-Unfavorable manipulation. Suppose two confederates were used, together with an experimental variable in a 2 × 2, Confederate × Attractive-Unattractive design, with 12 subjects per cell.

a. What is F^* if confederate is treated as a fixed/random factor?

b. All MSs are the same, regardless of whether confederate is treated as random or fixed. What is changed in the Anova table?

c. What are two undesirable consequences of treating confederate as random?

d. Suppose F was statsig with confederate treated as a random factor. To what population do you think this result can be generalized?

e. If confederate is treated as fixed, what can be said about generality?

9. According to Section 15.1.2, individuals from the same natural or ad hoc group are likely to be more similar than individuals from different groups.

a. How does this statement manifest itself in MS terms?

b. How can you test this statement statistically?

10. Fractional replication design can be useful for studying long serial curves. To illustrate with a memory issue, consider judgments of frequency of occurrence, which some writers have claimed involves automatic processing unaffected by practice and experience. To measure the serial curve of frequency judgments, suppose a subject sees a rapid sequence of letters, followed by a single letter. The subject's task is to rate on a graphic scale the relative frequency of the single letter in the sequence.

In principle, a serial-factor design can be used, in which each serial position represents a factor with 2 levels, namely, presence or absence of the given single letter at that serial position. The main effects of this design measure the relative effect of each position on the response at the end.

In practice, fractional design seems essential. For 12 serial positions, which seems pretty minimal, a complete factorial design would yield $2^{12} = 4096$ sequences. With fractional replication, 16 sequences would suffice.

Further reduction in design size can be gained by coupling serial positions, so that each factor in the design is a block of successive serial positions, still with two levels, according as there are, say, 0 or 1 instances of the given single letter in that block.

To illustrate with a too-simple example, show how the fractional design in Table 15.3 could be used to get the serial curve of frequency memory for a single subject for 12-letter sequences, coupled in blocks of 4, with only 4 trials.

11. In Section 15.5.3, the subsection *Differential Growth* cites two reasons to expect higher growth rate for the C group in Head Start programs. Draw graphs to illustrate how each of these reasons will cause an experimental treatment that has no effect to appear harmful.

12. For *Differential Growth* in Section 15.5.3, draw a graph to show that if an ineffective treatment is given to the initially superior group, it will falsely appear to have positive benefits (Section 13.2).

13. Under *Error df* in Section 15.1.2, justify the statement that the expected value of the pooled error is generally smaller than the correct error term.

14. In the example of the half replicate of a 2^3 design considered in Table 15.3:

    a. Guess what is confounded with main effect of B; of C.

    b. Prove your guess using the ± signs in the table.

15. This question asks for *normalized* confidence intervals for fractional replication with independent scores. To normalize, divide the positive c_j by a constant so they sum to 1; do the same for the negative c_j; then the contrast has the same unit as the data (Section 18.2.1, page 560). Use Expression 4 to show that normalized confidence intervals are:

$$\hat{\kappa} \pm t^* \sqrt{MS_{error}/2n}, \text{ for a half replicate of a } 2^4 \text{ design.}$$

$$\hat{\kappa} \pm t^* \sqrt{MS_{error}/n}, \text{ for a quarter replicate of a } 2^4 \text{ design.}$$

$$\hat{\kappa} \pm \tfrac{1}{2} t^* \sqrt{MS_{error}/n}, \text{ for a half replicate of a } 2^5 \text{ design.}$$

16. Show that the confidence intervals given in Expressions 6 and 7 reduce to those given in Chapter 5 when all ns are equal.

17. For the Latin square in Section 15.3.2, verify that "Each level of any one variable occurs exactly once with each level of each other variable." List the index numbers for the 16 treatments in a three column array, headed by A, B, and C. Then it is easy to check that each combination of two index numbers occurs once and only once.

18. In the $(S \times A) \times G$ design, is A nested in or crossed with G?

19. In the nursing home study, what confound in the control condition actually used might undercut the theoretical interpretation in terms of increased feeling of personal control by individuals in the experimental group?

PREFACE

Multiple regression has two distinct uses with observational data: prediction of outcomes and interpretation of process. For prediction, multiple regression is efficient, effective, and makes optimal use of multiple predictor variables while avoiding certain biases that afflict human judges. In most prediction tasks, accordingly, multiple regression outdoes the experts.

Conceptually, multiple regression is extremely simple: *a weighted sum of predictor variables*. Confidence intervals and significance tests can be obtained with Anova, much as with one-variable regression in Chapter 9.

The two big problems in prediction are both extrastatistical: To find a good criterion and to find good predictors. Both problems may be illustrated with selection for graduate school. What is the criterion of good performance in graduate school? Good grades? Good thesis results? Productivity after the Ph.D.? Self-esteem and self-fulfillment in personal and professional life? Given the criterion, how can good predictors be found? Although both problems are empirical, regression can help.

For interpretation, in contrast to prediction, multiple regression suffers exceptionally serious confounds. *Missing variable confounding* refers to variables that have a causal effect but are not included in the regression equation. A missing variable can reverse the apparent causal influence of some other variable that is included. Causal effects of intercorrelated variables can readily be misunderstood if some have not been measured. Since nearly all variables in common use are partial measures, missing variable confounds are endemic.

Person–variable confounding is no less serious. Regression analyses usually rest on an implicit assumption that persons are completely interchangeable, that natural individual differences on some variable can be treated as though they were controlled experimentally. This assumption seems quite unrealistic.

The belief that multiple regression can "statistically control," "hold constant," or "partial out" uncontrolled variables underlies many, perhaps most, applications outside of prediction. "Statistical control" would be wonderful if it were true, but it is false. Person–variable confounding and missing variable confounding each falsify "statistical control."

Observational data can be useful clues. Causation does imply correlation, so correlation is a clue to causation. These clues, however, are untrustworthy and treacherous. Valid inference from observational data requires empirical knowledge about causation that is not often available. Conjoint observation and controlled experiment is needed as a base for determining when observational data allow trustworthy inference.

484

Chapter 16

MULTIPLE REGRESSION

This chapter is concerned with the common sense of multiple regression. One purpose is to indicate the potential of multiple regression analysis, together with some of its pitfalls. A second purpose is to provide a framework to understand published applications.

A new approach has been adopted. Formulas are largely omitted because few are needed to understand regression analysis. No attempt is made to teach regression calculations as this is better left to the computer. Instead, the discussion is concerned with conceptual understanding and practical applications.

16.1 MULTIPLE REGRESSION

Multiple regression is mainly useful for prediction, in personnel selection, for example, or medical diagnosis. Multiple regression has notable capabilities: It can pool predictive power of multiple predictor variables that may be quite different in nature; it is not fooled by mere face validity; it does not suffer from cognitive biases that afflict even experts; and it can learn from experience. In practice, multiple regression typically outpredicts expert judges.

A quite different use of regression analysis concerns interpretation and causal inference. One interpretational use is with controlled variables in experimental design. Multiple regression can have certain advantages over standard factorial Anova, especially in allowing simpler designs.[a]

The other interpretational use of multiple regression is with uncontrolled variables. The hope is that observational data can be made to yield causal inferences by "controlling for" or "partialing out" effects of uncontrolled variables. Such applications are minefields (Section 16.2, pages 501*ff*).

16.1.1 REGRESSION ANALYSIS

Multiple regression is a straightforward extension of the one-variable regression of Chapter 9. Instead of a single predictor variable, there are two or more. The model for multiple regression is simple:

Multiple regression is a weighted sum of predictor variables.

The weights are chosen to maximize predictive power. Formulas and calculations are straightforward extensions of those for one-variable regression.

The example of Section 1.5.1, predicting success in graduate school, used two predictors, GRE and GPA. Near optimal weights for GRE and GPA are 1 and 100 so[a]

predicted success = GRE + 100 GPA.

Multiple Regression Model. Let X_{ij} denote the value of predictor variable X_j for subject i, with Y_i the criterion value for that subject (see Exercise 14). Let b_j be the weight of X_j in the weighted sum of predictors.

In practice, we often know the values of the predictors, X_{ij}; these are typically measured characteristics of each subject or case. If we knew the b weights, we could predict Y_i. How can we determine what values of these b weights, also called regression coefficients, yield the best prediction?

The b weights must be determined empirically. This is usually done by using calibration data, in which the criterion Y_i is known for each case as well as the X_{ij}. The b weights are chosen to maximize the predictability of the known Y_i from the known X_{ij} in these calibration data.

The calibration data serve their purpose by providing estimates of the b weights. Once obtained, these b weights can be used to predict for cases whose Y is unknown. In the GRE–GPA example, calibration data were available from past graduate admissions; predictions were made for new applicants.

In what follows, we assume a set of calibration data, with p predictor variables. Our problem is to find the best b weights and test which predictors are useful, which should be eliminated. To formalize this problem, let $\hat{Y}_i$ be the value of Y_i that is predicted by using any given values of the bs:

$$\hat{Y}_i = b_0 + b_1 X_{i1} + b_2 X_{i2} + \ldots + b_p X_{ip}. \tag{1}$$

The best values of the b weights are those that minimize the deviations between the observed Y_i and the predicted $\hat{Y}_i$.[b]

Finding the best values of the bs may be done in the same way as for the one-variable regression model (Sections 9.1.2 and 9.1.6). Least squares technique chooses the bs to minimize the sum of squared deviations:

$$SS_{dev} = \sum_{i=1}^{N} (Y_i - \hat{Y}_i)^2 = minimum.$$

With p predictor variables, least squares yields $1 + p$ linear equations in the $1 + p$ unknown bs. Solving these equations to get the bs is straightforward, as illustrated in Chapter 9 with the two b weights, b_0 and b_1. With more predictors, the calculations become increasingly tedious but the computer never complains, and, even better, avoids the mistakes you and I would make.

Anova for Multiple Regression.   Part of Y_i is predictable from the X_j, namely, $(\hat{Y}_i - \bar{Y})$. Squaring this predicted part of Y_i and summing yields the SS for prediction:

$$SS_{pred} = \sum(\hat{Y}_i - \bar{Y})^2. \tag{2a}$$

This formula for SS_{pred} is exactly the same as for one-variable regression in Equation 9.7a. And similarly, in parallel with Equation 9.8b,

$$SS_{dev} = SS_Y - SS_{pred}. \tag{2b}$$

This SS for deviations from prediction is ordinarily treated as error variability.

The df for SS_{pred} equals p, the number of predictor variables; the df for SS_{dev} equals the number of data points, N, minus the number of bs estimated in the regression equation, namely, $p + 1$. Division by the df yields the MS. Finally, in parallel with Equation 9.9,

$$F = \frac{MS_{pred}}{MS_{dev}} \qquad df = p, \; N - p - 1 \tag{3}$$

tests the null hypothesis that the true b weights are all zero. A statsig F implies that the regression equation has real predictive power.

Multiple Correlation.   Each subject in the calibration group has an observed Y_i and a predicted $\hat{Y}_i$. These may be correlated, exactly as with one-variable correlation, to obtain an index of predictivity. Instead of calling this correlation r, however, it is called R; the capital letter emphasizes that $\hat{Y}_i$ is based on multiple predictors. Just as with a single variable, R^2 may be defined as the ratio of predicted to total variance:

$$R^2 = \frac{SS_{pred}}{SS_Y}. \tag{4}$$

R^2 is statsig if and only if the foregoing F is statsig.

As a descriptive statistic, R has the advantages and disadvantages previously indicated for r, plus others of its own. A notable advantage is that R pools the predictive power of all the separate predictors into a single overall index. This overall index allows for the redundancy (intercorrelation) among the predictors. This capability is essential, of course, for otherwise the common part of two correlated predictors would be counted twice, falsely inflating R.

However, R is biased: Its sample value tends to be larger than its true value. As a consequence, the regression is less effective in future prediction than appears in the calibration data, a *shrinkage* effect.[c]

Assessing Single Variables. A common concern is that some predictor variable may be adding little or no predictive power. Such variables should be eliminated. One reason for elimination is that they degrade the reliability of the b weights for other variables.

It is straightforward to test whether any given variable X_j adds predictive power. Run two regressions, first without, then with X_j. The increase in SS_{pred}—from without to with X_j—measures the predictive power added by X_j. This increase in SS_{pred} has 1 df; its F ratio tests the null hypothesis that the true $b_j = 0$, that is, that X_j adds nothing, *over and above* the other predictors.

These single variable tests are included in the computer printout as t tests for the b weights. For each predictor, the printout will include the value of b_j, its standard deviation, and the corresponding t ratio. This t ratio, which is equivalent to the F of the preceding paragraph, tests whether this single variable adds predictive power—over and above all the other predictors combined.

Relative Importance. Questions about relative importance of predictor variables seldom have a clear answer. This point needs emphasis because many investigators attempt to assess relative importance and often mistake the b weights as measures of importance.

One complication is that the b weight for any one predictor depends on all the other predictors. In particular, the b weight for X_j in a multiple regression may differ markedly from its b weight in a one-variable regression using X_j alone. In the one-variable regression, the b weight depends solely on the relation between X_j and the criterion. In the multiple regression, in contrast, the b weight depends also on the relation of X_j to every other predictor. In particular, a variable that is a good predictor by itself may add little when assessed as one of a group. Hence the b weight for any variable is usually ambiguous about the importance of that variable.[d]

A treacherous complication is that the b weight for any variable may depend on relevant variables not included in the regression equation. A predictor uncorrelated with Y can thus have a nonzero b weight. The regression analysis can cleverly take advantage of the correlation of this irrelevant variable with a relevant variable not included—a notable advantage for prediction.

For interpretation, in contrast, this cleverness is a confound. It is clearly misleading if an irrelevant variable has a positive b weight. Even more misleading is some variable that has a positive b weight when it should be negative; a life-and-death example is given in the subsection, *Mystery of the Missing Cloud Cover*, page 506.

With observational data, therefore, the b weight of a variable is an uncertain clue to its importance. Standardization does not solve this problem, and most texts discourage the use of standardized b weights. Other complications are discussed in Section 18.1, which shows that importance, although a seemingly straightforward concept, is actually elusive and often not meaningful.[e,f]

Assumptions: Fixed and Random Predictors. Assumptions for multiple regression are similar to those for one-variable regression. Prediction requires no more than independence of the Y_i, together with approximate correctness of the linearity assumption of Equation 1. Equinormality is not required.

Significance tests do assume normality and equal variance. Somewhat different normality assumptions are required for fixed and random predictors, much as with one-variable regression. Given these assumptions, Anova tests are obtainable, as well as various kinds of confidence intervals.

Observational data are likely to violate assumptions, especially from extreme scores and outliers (e.g., Note 9.1.4b, page 280). The preventive/curative measures discussed for one-variable regression are even more important for multiple regression. Robust regression to handle extreme scores (Section 9.1.7) may be even more useful with multiple regression.

16.1.2 PREDICTION WITH MULTIPLE VARIABLES

Prediction embodies a simple principle: *Like mirrors like.* Two persons similar on the predictors tend to be similar on the criterion. Multiple regression implements this prediction principle in a simple way, for it is just a weighted sum of predictors. The main statistical problems revolve around estimating the b weights, and even these can sometimes be bypassed with unit weighting.

The two big problems come before the regression analysis: Finding a valid criterion, and finding useful predictors. Both problems are largely extrastatistical. Regression analysis can help, however, especially with the predictors.

Small Sets of Predictors. It is often natural to begin with an overplus of predictor variables so as not to miss something important. For future prediction, however, it is generally desirable to select a small subset of best predictors.

How can we find a small subset of best predictors? Three selection procedures are available on standard statistical packages. *Forward selection* begins by running all p one-variable regressions to select the best single predictor. Next, this best single predictor is used in a two-variable regression with each remaining predictor. The second predictor that adds the most to SS_{pred} is retained. These two predictors are then run in three-variable regressions to find the third that adds the most. And so on. The computer will continue this forward selection until the contribution of the best added predictor falls below some specified stopping criterion.

Backward elimination proceeds in the opposite direction. First, an overall regression is run using all p predictors. Next, p regressions are run, each omitting one predictor; the one whose elimination loses the least predictive power is then eliminated for good. This elimination process is then repeated with the remaining $p - 1$ predictors; and so on.

Stepwise regression expands forward selection to include a backward elimination at each step. This can reveal a best subset that would be missed by the other two procedures. As a simple example, some predictor, fairly good in itself, may be largely redundant with two other predictors that are not as good separately, but better when combined.

Selection Bias. All three selection procedures just described are seriously biased. The regression treats all chance accidents in the given sample as genuine; hence it looks better than it really is. Whenever a selection procedure is used, the significance levels provided by the computer are more or less meaningless. Whenever any selection is performed, the b weights and R^2 furnished by the computer are biased and untrustworthy.

This selection bias is clear with forward selection. Consider six worthless predictors, each uncorrelated with the criterion. Any given one has α probability of yielding a statsig correlation. The best of the six obviously has much better than α probability. *Combining the best two of six will do still better.* The final R^2 will thus generally be much larger than its true value of zero.

Similar bias afflicts all selection procedures. The amount of bias is uncertain because it depends on the number of predictors and their intercorrelations. However, extreme bias can occur in realistic situations.

Cross-Validation. Selection bias can be resolved by *cross-validation*. This requires a pristine sample of cases, not previously used or touched. Those variables selected in the initial selection stage are used in a new regression with this pristine sample; This regression yields unbiased estimates of b weights. The importance of cross-validation is well-recognized in test theory, but is simply ignored in many observational studies.

Because of these biases, regression analysis should ordinarily be considered a stepwise investigation, planning to make successive improvements with independent sets of data. Valid analyses cannot generally be obtained from a single set of data.

Split-Half Replication. Replication for cross-validation is not always possible. Medical and educational studies, for example, may be large operations that involve considerable time and expense. Repeating the study is often not feasible. Cross-validation is still possible, however, by splitting the complete set of data into two or more subsets, one subset to be used at each successive stage in the validation process. Splitting should be anticipated in planning, especially to ensure adequate sample size for each subset of data.

Validity requires that analysis at any stage be completely independent of data to be used at a later stage. Mosteller and Tukey (1977, p. 38) suggest that the cases used at any stage be measured only after completion of the previous stage, as would often be possible in test theory. If split-half replication is required, then the data to be used at a later stage should be kept unlooked-at in a locked safe until the earlier stage is definitely terminated.

Post Hoc Analysis. Post hoc analysis tends to make data look better than they are. Nowhere is this danger greater than in multiple regression.

Post hoc analysis can occur in various forms. First and most common are the three selection procedures discussed previously. Second, the cutting point for categorical variables, young–old, for example, may be selected to obtain ''better'' results. Third, ''extreme'' cases may be thrown out.

Post hoc analysis can be important in searching for clues in the data. This can help increase the predictive power of the regression equation. The danger, of course, is that post hoc analysis is biased by chance variability in the data sample.

There is an honest way to utilize post hoc analysis without incurring its danger: *cross-validate.* Post hoc analysis is desirable and legitimate—when it can be cross-validated. Data analysis, like life, is a continuing learning experience. If the analysis can be improved, it should be. But post hoc analysis always has problematic validity, most especially with multiple regression. Post hoc analysis yields tainted evidence; its proof lies in corroboration in an independent set of data.

It seems appropriate to ask that published regression analyses state explicitly what analyses were planned beforehand and acknowledge all post hoc decisions in the data analysis. Some published reports show fairly clear signs of post hoc decisions, but often this is not acknowledged (e.g., Note 16.2.2e). Such reports can be seriously misleading.

Replication, including split-half analysis, seems generally essential. Replication is coming to be the norm in experimental articles. In observational studies, the replication principle is even more important. In most cases, at least split-half replication is feasible and then perhaps mandatory.

Correlated Predictors. Adding a good predictor can have bad consequences. If the added predictor is highly correlated with another predictor, it will add little predictive power. But the estimated b weight of the other predictor will become much more variable, having a much larger standard deviation. Some computer programs give warnings about high predictor correlations, also called *multicollinearity.*

It hardly seems desirable, of course, to exclude a predictor just because it is highly correlated with another predictor. Among the remedies that have been suggested, the simplest and almost best is to add highly correlated predictors to form a single composite predictor, perhaps after equalizing their ranges as with unit weighting in the next subsection.

Unit Weighting. The simplest mode of multiple regression is to just add the predictor variables to get a single predictor. No formulas are needed. No *b* weights need be estimated. This *unit weighting*, as it is called, often yields results nearly as good as least-squares regression weights, at least as long as the predictors are not negatively correlated among themselves. Of course, the efficacy of unit weighting depends on having good predictors to begin with.

With unit weighting, each predictor should be multiplied by a constant to roughly equalize their effective ranges (or standard deviations). In graduate school admissions, adding GPA to GRE would be useless because GPA has an effective range around 1 point, whereas GRE has an effective range over 100 points. In this case, the foregoing unit weighting formula, GRE + 100 GPA, was adopted at the University of Oregon, where this approach was developed (Dawes, 1971; Goldberg, 1977).[a]

Less Is More. People think behavior is more predictable than it actually is. Multiple correlations of .3 to .4, so common in personality, attitude, or behavioral research, may thus be taken as shortcomings of the predictors. "I can easily see how to improve this test," it is often thought, or "Surely by including additional predictors, I can account for more than 16% of the variance." This aspiration stems from one of several cognitive illusions that beset applications of regression analysis.

For observational data, as a rule of thumb, three modestly good predictors are the most one can usually hope for. One reason is redundancy, or intercorrelation, among the predictors. A predictor that is good in itself will add little if it is largely redundant with other predictors. Given two modestly good predictors that are fairly independent, it is often hard to find a third that adds much and usually difficult to find a fourth.

This point may be illustrated with the foregoing example of graduate student admissions. The original regression included a third variable, namely, quality of undergraduate school, which by itself is a reasonably good predictor. But quality of school adds little over and above GRE and GPA. Most of its predictive power is already contained in GRE. It was later eliminated, accordingly, thereby obtaining a more convenient formula.[b]

Predictor improvement should, of course, be a basic concern in any continuing line of investigation. An investigator should always be alert to opportunities to improve the validity, reliability, and economy of the predictors, and even more of the criterion. These loci of improvement, however, are quite different from increasing the number of predictors.

The Criterion Problem. The other big problem in prediction is to find a valid criterion. This criterion issue is more important, clearly, than finding predictors. This is a substantive issue for which regression methods are not much help, so the criterion problem is slighted in statistics texts. Criterion validity, however, is the central issue in regression analysis with observational data.

It might seem that a valid criterion is readily available by measuring the person's behavior. This is appropriate in some situations, as with mortality rate for surgical procedures or even with parole decisions. In most jobs, on the other hand, assessing performance is notoriously difficult. As one example, ratings by supervisors often suffer from limited information about performance. Also, stereotypes may introduce bias for or against social subgroups, and halo effects may cause less likable persons to get lower ratings.

A deeper level of the criterion problem may be illustrated with learning and teaching. The surface level is how well given material is learned. Below this is the level of what should be learned. The ultimate criterion presumably consists of knowledge systems that will be relevant some years after graduation. This surely applies to graduate school. Little seems known about such knowledge systems, but I suspect they have tenuous relations with specific course content, at least in social sciences and humanities, and certainly in psychological statistics (see preface to Chapter 23, page 764).

16.1.3 EXAMPLES OF PREDICTION STUDIES

Job Choices. Multiple regression is one means of achieving the goal of the utilitarian philosophers: The greatest good for the greatest number. We will be happiest when working at jobs for which we are well suited. But how can we determine what these jobs are? "The hardest thing is to know yourself" (Thales, c. 580 B.C.). Modern test theory can help us know ourselves.

Many high school students wonder where to look when they enter the job market. Each job requires a different mix of multiple abilities. A machinist, for example, requires perceptual skill and motor dexterity not needed by an accountant or beautician. Job performance and job satisfaction depend on a match between your own aptitudes and abilities and those required by the job.

What *are* the job-relevant aptitudes and abilities? This question is difficult, but reasonable progress has been made. An enormous amount of work on test construction has led to the development of the General Aptitude Test Battery (GATB), designed for administration by inexperienced testers and to testees with poor English. The GATB includes nine tests, which may be reduced to three groups, roughly describable as verbal–numerical, spatial–perceptual, and psychomotor dexterity (see e.g., Cronbach, 1990, pp. 394*ff*).

These test scores constitute a personal profile of aptitude–ability. This personal profile may be compared to a corresponding job profile to assess degree of match. The job profiles may be obtained by giving the same tests to people who are employed in that job or by rational analysis of job requirements. Job performance tends to be better when the personal profile matches the job profile.

The GATB is given to over a million people a year. Some are students, who may be steered toward a class of jobs consistent with their profile or counseled toward development of some particular strong or weak point in their profile. Others are job applicants, whose test scores will help employers select those more likely to do well in specified jobs.

Multiple regression and related techniques are used throughout the development and application of the GATB. In developing a test battery, the foregoing selection procedures would be used to find a best set of predictors and to assess predictive power. In applying the test battery, employers could use Equation 1, with the X_j being the applicant's test scores. Each job has its own b weights; the b weight for verbal–numerical tests would be high for an accountant, for example, but not for a beautician.

The traditional method of selecting people for jobs was the personal interview. Personnel offices of some major companies still rely on members who pride themselves on their ability to size up people in a brief personal interview. Although it is hard to believe, repeated studies have found that the validity of judgments based on unstructured interviews is not merely low, but virtually zero. Somewhat better results are obtained with structured interviews, in which the interviewer follows a list of specific questions to be asked.

Many issues of job choice remain open. Although the GATB is one of the best tests, its predictive power is disappointing. Massive efforts have gone into constructing tests of ability; further work in this direction seems unlikely to add much predictive power. One reason for low predictive power may be that your abilities are not fixed and static, but change and develop continuously over your lifetime. On-the-job learning has high importance but seems relatively neglected in traditional test theory. Similarly neglected are personality variables, such as motivation and work attitudes, which are central in performance on any job (Washington, 1901/1963).

Clinical Versus Statistical Prediction: I. A pioneering study of clinical versus statistical prediction concerned achievement of freshman at the University of Minnesota (Sarbin, 1943). Two predictors were used: percentile rank in high school and score on a college aptitude test. The criterion was GPA at end of the first quarter in the university. The b weights for the two variables were derived from calibration data of previous years.

Professional counselors also made predictions, but they had additional information besides the two cited variables. Included were tests of aptitude, personality, an eight-page individual record form, and a personal interview with each student. This interview would seem well-suited for assessing such important variables as motivation and general adjustment.

For women, the clinical and statistical methods yielded nearly equal correlations of .69 and .70, respectively. For men, the clinical method did somewhat poorer, as shown by respective correlations of .35 and .45.[a]

It thus appears that the clinical interview added no predictive power beyond that available in the two regression variables. This hardly seems credible in view of the cited potential of the interview. Nevertheless, this negative outcome has been corroborated repeatedly.

Sarbin pointed out, moreover, that the statistical method is much cheaper. This cost advantage has been further emphasized by Dawes (1971) and Goldberg (1977) in relation to admissions to graduate school. Dawes points to the potential time savings by the admissions committee, estimated at 10 minutes per application for each member of the admissions committee. This time cost is large; even in 1971, above 7 million applications had to be processed for all graduate fields in the U.S.

Dawes also takes note of students' costs of submitting applications to schools where they have little chance of being admitted. He suggests that each department list its b weights and cutoff criterion in its admissions materials. Students could then calculate their own regression score and use it in their decision whether to apply.[b]

Clinical Versus Statistical Prediction: II. The relative accuracy of expert human judgment and statistical prediction equations is of concern in many areas: hiring for all kinds of jobs; various kinds of clinical diagnosis and treatment; diagnosis of medical pathology; parole decisions; and many others. This issue appeared in Sarbin's pioneering study cited in the previous subsection, and it was dramatized by Meehl (1954), who surveyed some 20 published clinical–statistical comparisons and concluded that the statistical method was as good or better in all but perhaps one case. This conclusion has been solidified in subsequent work. The 136 studies surveyed by Grove and Meehl (1996) showed that "in around two fifths of the studies the two methods were approximately equal in accuracy, and in around three fifths the actuarial method was significantly better" (p. 295).

Grove and Meehl lament that "Despite 66 years of consistent research findings in favor of the actuarial method, most professionals continue to use a subjective, clinical judgment approach when making predictive decisions" (p. 299). They discuss 17 common objections to the statistical method and conclude that these objections arise mainly from "poor education" (p. 318).

Unfortunately, the focus on comparing clinical and statistical methods, however useful in itself, has slighted more important issues. One is training in judgment skills. Surprisingly, available studies suggest that naive judges do nearly as well as experienced judges (see Dawes, 1994; Garb, 1989, 1998; Oskamp, 1962). Among the suggested reasons why experience does not improve accuracy is that feedback about accuracy is typically minimal. Goldberg (1968), however, found no improvement over the course of several hundred cases with explicit accuracy feedback. Other training methods might be more successful.

Clinical Analysis. A related issue concerns the potential of human judges to be sensitive to cues from face-to-face interview, for example, that would elude standard tests. This issue involves the distinction between valuation of single informers and integration of multiple informers, emphasized by Sawyer (1966). The prediction equation only integrates the given values of given informers. In one sense, it begins after the main job, namely, finding and measuring the predictors, has been done. Sawyer suggests that Meehl's sole focus on the integration problem neglected the main virtue of the clinical method, namely, in valuation or measurement.

One way to test this potential of clinical judgment is to include it as an additional predictor in the multiple regression. This was done in the foregoing study by Sarbin, who found negligible improvement. Sawyer's review is somewhat more optimistic about clinical judgment. Despite its fundamental interest, both for outcome and for process analysis, this line of inquiry has not received much attention (see Garb, 1994).

Also of interest are the cognitive processes by which people deal with multiple informer cues. This issue has been muddled because of the primary focus on outcome in the form of accuracy. Process analysis requires an essentially different approach, as noted next.

Cognitive Analysis of Clinical Judgment. Experts typically claim their judgments are configural, that they take account of pattern or interaction among different informers. In this configural view, the meaning of any one informer depends on its relations with other informers. This configural view has been a default argument that expert judgment *must* be superior to statistical judgment.

Diametrically opposed to the interactive, configural view is the hypothesis that cognitive integration obeys a nonconfigural, linear model. This linear model has the same algebraic form as the regression model of Equation 1. This regression model is additive; the effect of any one variable is constant, regardless of the values of the other variables. If subjects did make configural judgments, the additive model should fail to fit them.

This configural–nonconfigural controversy differs fundamentally from the clinical–statistical controversy of the previous subsections. The clinical–statistical issue concerns the outcome question of objective accuracy. The configural–nonconfigural issue, in contrast, concerns the cognitive processes that underlie human judgments, without regard to their accuracy.

Perhaps the first adequate test of the hypothesis of configural judgment is the study of person cognition that was shown in Figure 11.2, page 317. Contrary to popular expectation, the results supported a nonconfigural, addition rule.

Present relevance of this study of person cognition is the functional measurement methodology that it introduced for studying clinical judgment. This methodology did not suffer the fatal flaws of multiple regression methodology that had vitiated previous studies of this issue. This methodology allows single subject analysis within the value system of the individual judge. Thus, it has attractive potential for cognitive analysis of clinical judgment.[c]

16.1.4 EXPERIMENTAL DESIGN
ANALYZED WITH MULTIPLE REGRESSION

Data from factorial designs may be analyzed with multiple regression programs. Metric information in the stimulus variables can thus be put to good use. This approach has been illustrated with trend tests in Chapter 9. Applications to process models are noted in Section 20.1.1.

Regression Model and Anova Model. The regression model may be viewed as a special case of the factorial Anova model of Chapter 5. The stimulus variables are now assumed to be metric, however, and this metric is exploited in the regression analysis. For a two-way design, factors A and B correspond to predictors X_1 and X_2, respectively. The X_1 value for every Y score in cell jk of the design is the known metric value of A_j ; the X_2 value for cell jk is the known metric value of B_k. This correspondence of the factorial and regression models may be written

$$Y = \bar{\mu} + \alpha_j + \beta_k + (\alpha\beta)_{jk} + \text{error}; \qquad (5a)$$

$$Y = b_0 + b_1 A_j + b_2 B_k + \text{deviation}. \qquad (5b)$$

These two models show two obvious differences. One is that the nonadditive terms $(\alpha\beta)_{jk}$ in the Anova model, otherwise known as interaction residuals, have no counterpart in the regression model. With more than two variables, moreover, the regression model maintains its simple additive form, whereas the nonadditive terms in the Anova model become increasingly numerous.

The other difference is that the main effect of A is represented by the α_j in the Anova model, but by b_1 in the regression model since the A_j values are known. Instead of testing the overall F_A, the regression analysis tests the linear trend, measured by the slope parameter, b_1. This trend test on 1 df will often be more powerful than the main effect test on $(a-1)$ df, as illustrated in *Linear Trend* in Section 4.2.1 (page 96).

Because of these two differences, the multiple regression requires only three parameters, namely, the three b weights of Equation 5b. Equation 5a for the Anova model, in contrast, requires ab parameters, one for each cell of the factorial design. This greater simplicity of the regression model stems in part from its reliance on the metric information in the Xs, in part from its neglect of the nonadditive interaction residuals.

A notable advantage of this regression approach is that a complete factorial design is not needed. Unequal cell ns are taken in stride and empty cells are allowed. As an extreme case, regression analysis could be applied to a two-way design, but with data for only one row and one column. Such capability could be invaluable when data points are expensive or otherwise difficult to obtain. Thus, a medical study might seek information about four variables, each with three levels. A single replication of a complete factorial design would require 81 experimental conditions. A regression analysis, in contrast, could be done with no more than 12 conditions, with only one observation in each condition.

This advantage of regression analysis has several costs. Equation 5b does not give information on nonlinear trends; it ignores interaction residuals by confounding them with main effects and/or putting them in the error; and it may yield biased estimates of the b weights. These complications can be overcome by extending the model, but each extension has a price. The simple model, fortunately, is widely adequate.

Extensions of the Regression Model. The foregoing regression model can be extended to include nonadditive terms. Most common is a product term such as $X_1 X_2$, which is the linear × linear trend component of the $X_1 \times X_2$ "interaction." This can be an efficient 1 df test of nonadditivity that capitalizes on the metric information in X_1 and X_2.

An important extension allows categorical variables in place of continuous variables. With just two categories, such as female–male, simply call the two categories 0 and 1 and use these as numerical X values. With more than two categories, special coding schemes are required (e.g., effect coding, dummy variable coding; see Edwards, 1985; Pedhazur & Schmelkin, 1991). Carried to its limit, this categorical analysis transforms the regression model of Equation 5b into the full Anova model of Equation 5a. The two analyses of course yield equivalent results (see further Note 20.1.2a).

Anova Versus Multiple Regression. Some writers set an opposition between Anova and multiple regression. This opposition has focused on a surface difference in terms of computing formulas. Conceptually, both are applications of the general linear model of statistical theory (Section 18.4.7).

Computing formulas for Anova are very simple for one-way design, even with unequal n, and for factorial design with equal n. This was the original base for their popularity, which continues because equal n holds in most experimental applications. Associated with this, Anova has a deeper simplicity that facilitates understanding of more complex designs, such as Latin squares. In this deeper simplicity, the Anova source table embodies the causal structure of the experimental design.

Regression formulas are useful for linear trend analysis, as previously noted. For factorial design with unequal n, moreover, the simple Anova formulas do not apply, and the analysis requires solution of a set of linear equations for which multiple regression programs are designed. But statistical Anova programs now take unequal n in stride. In introductory treatments, therefore, teaching somewhat complicated details of effect coding or dummy variable coding seems obtuse. What is important is understanding how unequal n affects the interpretation (see *Unequal n*, Section 15.4). This is as much a problem in regression as in Anova.

A real issue does underly the opposition between Anova and multiple regression. This is the difference between observational data, which characterize typical applications of regression analysis, and experimentally controlled data, which characterize typical applications of Anova. This difference is not statistical, however, but reflects prevailing practice in two main classes of empirical investigations. This difference is critical for studies that seek to go beyond prediction to understanding (Section 16.2).

16.1.5 MEASUREMENT THEORY IN REGRESSION ANALYSIS

Two measurement issues are important in regression analysis. One is whether is Y is measured on a linear (equal interval) scale. The other concerns similar linearity of the scales for the Xs. Both measurement issues are essential for understanding the concepts of interaction and nonlinearity in regression analysis (see Chapter 21 and Anderson, 1982, p. 181).[a]

"Interactions." "Interactions" are essentially the same in regression and Anova. In both, statistical interactions are defined as deviations from additivity. The usual regression test for interaction extends the additive regression model of Equation 5b by including the product term X_1X_2:

$$Y = b_0 + b_1X_1 + b_2X_2 + b_{12}X_1X_2 + \text{deviation.} \tag{6}$$

If inclusion of the product term increases predictive power, the data show nonadditivity. Although commonly considered an "interaction" with substantive significance, this is a likely artifact.

Chapter 7 on *Understanding Interactions* in Anova applies to regression analysis with little change. The key lies in the distinction between the observable response measure Y and the underlying concept that Y is presumed to measure. Suppose the underlying concept, denoted by ρ, is an additive function of X_1 and X_2. But suppose Y is a nonlinear measure of ρ. Then Y will be a nonadditive function of X_1 and X_2; hence the regression will exhibit a statistical interaction. This interaction is not real, however, merely an artifact of the nonlinear measurement scale for Y.

To illustrate, suppose $\rho = X_1 + X_2$. This true relation is additive, with no interaction. But suppose $Y = \rho^2$. Then the observable data follow the equation

$$Y = X_1^2 + 2X_1X_2 + X_2^2.$$

This equation contains the nonadditive cross product term, $X_1 X_2$, which will appear in the regression analysis of the observed data. Ostensibly, this is an interaction. But this interaction is not real because ρ is additive. This interaction appears in the observed data only because the scale for Y is not a linear scale of the concept ρ that Y is supposed to measure.

Of course, if Y was known to be a linear scale, observed interactions would be real, at least within the assumed model. Rarely, however, do regression studies provide evidence for scale linearity.

To this, it should be added that even real interactions often have minor substantive significance. The discussion of Figure 7.2 (page 191) for Anova interactions applies equally to regression interactions. The term "interaction" is just as misleading with regression as with Anova. *Residual* is more precise and avoids the surplus meaning of "interaction."

"Nonlinearities." Some regression analyses include nonlinear functions of the predictor variables, such as X_1^2. Often thought to have substantive meaning, these nonlinearities may merely be artifacts of the measurement scale.

Such artifactual nonlinearity appeared in the above equation. The nonlinear terms, X_1^2 and X_2^2, lack substantive reality. They appear merely because Y is a nonlinear scale of ρ (see Exercise 15).

Artifactual nonlinearity can also appear if any X is measured on a nonlinear scale. Since typical applications include no way to determine whether the Y and X scales are linear, the term "nonlinear" is typically ambiguous.

Outcome and Process. The foregoing discussion of interaction and nonlinearity is one more manifestation of the outcome–process distinction of Section 1.2.1. Outcome applications seek to maximize predictive power. This can sometimes be done by including such terms as $X_1 X_2$ or X_1^2 in the regression equation. If they increase predictive power, they are useful regardless of any substantive meaning.

Process interpretations, in contrast, must face the measurement problem. Typical discussions of "interactions" rest on an assumption that nonadditive terms somehow have substantive meaning. Instead, as already noted, they may merely reflect nonlinearity in the measurement scale for Y.

The same applies to nonlinear components. A statement that some nonlinear component accounts for $p\%$ of the variance is often thought to somehow have substantive meaning (see also Section 18.3.2, pages 567*ff*). This is incorrect if the nonlinear component is only an artifact of nonlinearity in the measurement scale for Y.

Multiplication Model. Some regression analyses use a multiplication model rather than an addition model. Examples include the well-known Expectancy × Value model of judgment–decision theory and the Motivation × Incentive model of behavior theory. The regression equation may be written

$$Y \;=\; b_0 \;+\; b_{12} X_1 X_2 \;+\; \text{deviation.} \tag{7}$$

Popular attempts to test multiplication models have used a regression method that seems natural and straightforward but is in fact inefficient or even invalid. This regression method begins by obtaining separate estimates of the values of Y, X_1, and X_2, following the typical regression approach. These estimates are substituted into Equation 7 to see whether it is verified. A one-variable regression may be used to determine b_0, which allows for an arbitrary zero point in the scale for Y, and b_{12}, which effectively equalizes the scale units across the three variables.

This method rests on an extremely strong measurement assumption, namely, that X_1 and X_2 are measured on linear scales with known zero points. Rarely will this measurement assumption be true in life sciences. Some writers, accordingly, concluded that the multiplication model was not generally testable.

Happily, functional measurement theory provides a valid test without need for zero point scales, illustrated with the Expectancy × Value experiment in Figure 21.7, page 715. No less important, this study also showed how functional measurement could establish true linear scales (see linear fan theorem in Section 21.5). This functional measurement capability provided the first conclusive analyses of the Expectancy × Value and the Motivation × Incentive models.

16.2 INTERPRETATION WITH OBSERVATIONAL DATA

The distinction between process validity and outcome validity of Chapter 1 is prominent with observational data. Multiple regression can make effective use of observational data for prediction, which is concerned with outcome validity. But a variable can be useful for prediction without understanding why. The phase of the moon, for example, was known to be a predictor of tidal height long before Newton developed a causal theory of gravitational attraction.

In contrast, interpretation with observational data is typically problematic, often impossible. Process analysis with observational data is beset with pitfalls. Regression analysis can still be of use, nevertheless, not least by revealing these pitfalls. The most dangerous pitfall, however, is not in regression analysis itself; the pitfall is the common misconception that multiple regression provides "statistical control" of uncontrolled variables.

16.2.1 MULTIPLE REGRESSION IS NOT STATISTICAL CONTROL

Many writers assert that multiple regression "controls," or "holds constant," or "partials out" uncontrolled variables. Such phrases seem to justify some causal interpretation. It would be wonderful if this were true, but it is false. Regression equations *do not* *control or hold constant* in any substantive sense.

The Misconception of Statistical Control. To understand the misconception that multiple regression can "statistically control" uncontrolled variables, consider the two-variable regression model

$$Y = b_0 + b_1 X_1 + b_2 X_2 + \text{deviation.} \tag{8}$$

If X_2 is changed to $X_2 + 1$, then Y changes to $Y + b_2$—regardless of X_1. Hence b_2 seems to measure the effect of X_2 on Y—with X_1 held constant. By the *assumed* additivity, the X_2 effect is the same for each and every X_1. At face value, therefore, it seems as though the regression model assesses the effect of X_2 while "holding X_1 constant," that is, while "statistically controlling" X_1. For if X_1 is constant, the observed effect seemingly must be due to X_2.

Under this misconception, multiple regression is a statistical substitute for controlled variables in randomized experiments. In a two-way design, the first row shows the effect of B with A held constant at A_1; the second row shows the effect of B with A held constant at A_2; and so on. Thus, the effect of B is assessed while A is indeed held constant, that is, controlled. But this control is empirical, not statistical, obtained through experimental manipulation.

This misconception underlies "statistical control" in multiple regression. This rationale is thought to have the causal implication that b_2 measures the true effect of X_2, freed from possible confounding with X_1. This rationale is also thought to have the causal implication that changing X_2 for a person to $X_2 + 1$ will change their Y to $Y + b_2$. This rationale is unwarranted. Two fundamental flaws are discussed in the next three subsections.

Person–Variable Confounding. Confounding of persons and variables generally vitiates causal interpretation of regression analysis. In typical regression analyses, different cases represent different persons. This fact gives a peculiar meaning to "statistical control." The usual interpretation of "statistical control" is that a change in X_1 for a given person would change Y for that same person in the manner specified by the regression equation.

Such interpretation of "statistical control" is not often valid. The misinterpretation arises from reifying the regression model as though it was a process model. In the main class of psychological applications,

the regression model describes a sample of different individuals.

These individual differences constitute the structure of the regression model. The regression model says:

> If person A has scores of X_1, X_2, and Y,
> and if person B has scores of X_1 and $X_2 + 1$,
> then person B will have a score of $Y + b_2$.

"Statistical control" amounts to nothing more than this.

"Statistical control" thus says nothing about what would happen if X_1 was somehow different for person A. Instead, "statistical control" is accomplished by switching persons. "Holding X_1 constant" says only that persons A and B happen to have the same X_1. "Holding X_1 constant" says nothing about causal effects. "Holding X_1 constant" refers to some other person; some other person with the same X_1 and a different X_2 has a predictably different Y. This person–variable confounding confounds most attempts to use regression analysis for causal inference.

This failure of "statistical control" was foreshadowed in the example of Chapter 9 on marital satisfaction. The finding that couples who have more sex also have greater marital happiness is descriptive of a collection of individuals with surprisingly diverse sexual preferences and practices. Beyond this, the regression model says nothing about any individual. On the contrary, validity of this causal interpretation is belied by the thought that scheduling more sex for distressed couples would do harm, not good.

This marriage example is exceptional in that our background knowledge discredits the regression analysis. More commonly, the regression analysis will reach a plausible conclusion, but the evidence is not better. In applications of regression analysis, person–variable confounding is endemic.

Missing Variable Confounding. A "missing" variable is one that is operative in the data situation but missing from the regression equation. Technically, this is called misspecification. Missing variables can bias the b weights of those variables that are included in the regression equation. This bias can be fatal.

To understand this missing variable confounding, suppose the regression equation includes some irrelevant variable, with no effect on the criterion. Its true b weight is thus zero. But suppose this irrelevant variable is correlated with some missing variable that is correlated with the criterion. Then the irrelevant variable will have a nonzero b weight—as though it somehow had causal influence.

A striking real example of a missing variable appears later in the *Mystery of the Missing Cloud Cover* (page 506). In this example, background knowledge saved the day. Typically, however, background knowledge will not be adequate to save the investigator. More often, perhaps, statistical analysis of observational data will seem consistent with background knowledge, as in *Gender Bias?* at the end of Chapter 10.

In social and personality areas, the missing variable pitfall seems generally severe. An R of .50 is quite high, yet this leaves up to three-fourths of the variance attributable to missing variables. The danger is not removed but re-emphasized by showing that assiduous efforts have failed to unearth additional useful predictors.[a]

One common class of "statistical control" arguments is notably susceptible to the missing variable pitfall. The argument is based on a regression analysis in which some variable shows a statsig b weight even after the other regression variables have been "controlled." The argument runs thus: "Part of the effect was explainable by the other variables, but the relation remained statistically significant even after these were controlled." The conclusion, often implicit, is that this relation is causal. No such conclusion is warranted; the statsig b weight may stem from some missing variable (see also Note 16.1.1f).

Partial Measures. Psychological variables are typically complex, poorly defined, and only partly measurable. Intelligence, for example, has diverse aspects; it is a system of knowledge. It cannot, in principle, be reduced to one or even several test scores. Even a seemingly simple variable such as vocabulary is a complex that is crudely represented in our partial measures.

Multiple regression deals with the measured test scores. Even if it could "statistically control" for these test scores, this would not control for the operative knowledge systems. Much of the causal determinants must thus be considered "missing variables." If $R < .60$ ($R^2 < .36$), what is missing is more important than what is not.

Sociological variables are virtually always partial measures, dangerously inadequate to represent social reality. Education, for example, is typically measured by number of grades completed. In reality, education is a complex variable that depends on school quality, state educational finances, sociocultural influences from past and present, and so on. To measure education by number of grades completed seems hopelessly inadequate for substantive interpretation. Multiple regression cannot "control" what is not measured.

It might be argued that what is not measured is represented by a swarm of minor factors that cancel out and do not bias the regression. This wishful thinking may be true in some situations, but serious evidence is lacking. The great utility of quantified measures in giving us a partial grip on complex phenomena should not blind us to their great limitations.[b]

Additivity. The additive structure of the regression model seems itself to invalidate common claims of "statistical control." Additivity involves a strong presumption: *Active manipulation of* X_1 *does not change* X_2. If a change in X_1 causes any change in X_2, the regression model misrepresents the process.

This additivity assumption seems generally unlikely. Observational variables often have substantive components in common, reflected in nonzero correlations between them. Almost inevitably, a change in one will produce changes in the other. This argument discredits many applications of regression analysis for "statistical control."

Error of Measurement. Standard regression analysis is statistically inadequate to represent substantive process. The statistical flaw is that unreliability in the measured variables biases the estimates of the *b* weights.

This bias does not trouble the prediction applications cited in Section 16.1. This bias does trouble interpretation, however, as illustrated in the later case of *Employment Discrimination and Reverse Regression*. In the *Low Lead Controversy*, similarly, unreliability produces biases and too-narrow confidence intervals (Greene & Ernhart, 1993), yet nearly all published reports on lead effects have failed to allow for unreliability.

This bias from error of measurement was explained in Section 13.2.2 on Ancova and discussed further in Section 15.5 on quasi-experimental design. Considerable statistical work has been devoted to develop regression methods that can deal with error of measurement, including structural equation models. However, person–variable confounding and missing variable confounding remain formidable obstacles.

Null-Control. One special case of regression analysis may warrant causal interpretation. Since causation implies correlation, absence of correlation suggests absence of causation. This logic may be called *null-control*. Null-control logic is illustrated in *Taxes and Education* in the next section.

Null-control logic is not definitive; a causal variable may have a near-zero *b* weight because of some missing variable. But although a missing variable can readily produce a nonzero *b* weight for a noncausal variable, a delicate balance would be required to cancel the *b* weight of a causal variable.

In practice, therefore, a regression that yields a negligible *b* weight for some predictor variable can thereby provide definite, though not definitive, evidence that the predictor has negligible causal effect. Null-control requires adequate power to demonstrate that the effect is negligible, of course, as shown by a narrow confidence interval for the *b* weight.

Causal, Structural Equation Models. Causal models claim to extract causal information from correlational data. This strong claim, together with available computer programs (e.g., LISREL), have made these models widely popular. Structural equation models have two advantages over multiple regression, to which they are statistically similar. One is ability to handle unreliability in the predictor variables. Hence they can remove the bias in the *b* weights that plague multiple regression, Ancova, and quasi-experimental design. The other advantage, more important, is ability to deal with latent variables, as with factors in factor analysis, inferred to underlie the measured responses.

Unfortunately, structural equation models suffer two major problems. First, they have the same two confoundings as multiple regression: person–variable confounding and missing variable confounding. Second, positive conclusions depend entirely on prior knowledge of a correct causal model.

Both problems are deadly serious in typical applications. The variables are generally vague and poorly defined, such as gender, attitudes, stereotypes, education, socioeconomic status, and intelligence. Missing variables are endemic. Most critically, causal knowledge is limited and vague.

Is there evidence that applications of structural equation models are more than wishful thinking? In my limited excursion into this literature, I have yet to find serious evidence in psychology or in sociology. Strong negative opinions have been expressed by experts, including Freedman (1987, 1991), Mason (1991), and Rogosa (1987). Breckler (1990) found that many quite different models could account for the same data, a continuing problem in the literature (MacCallum & Austin, 2000). Causal mathematical models have been established in experimental psychology, as with signal detection theory (Chapter 20) and the averaging model of information integration theory (Chapter 21). These causal variables, however, were under experimental control.[c]

Conjoint experimental and observational data seems essential to establish a firm base for the causal models. If such conjoint tasks can be developed, they may provide a base for determining what kinds of situations do and do not allow causal analysis of observational data.[d]

16.2.2 CASE EXAMPLES OF MULTIPLE REGRESSION

The purpose of the following examples is to suggest kinds of situations in which multiple regression is and is not useful for interpretation with observational data. As a rule, extrastatistical knowledge about the causal structure of the situation is necessary for interpretation, as in the first example.

Mystery of the Missing Cloud Cover. Missing variables can lead to misinterpretation. A dramatic example comes from a regression analysis intended to improve bombing accuracy, which was notoriously poor in World War II (cited by Mosteller & Tukey, 1977, p. 318). Accuracy was assessed from aerial photos subsequent to each run by a bomber group. Among the multiple predictors were amount of enemy fighter opposition, as well as altitude and speed of bombers over target. The last two were important because they could be controlled in future bombing runs to increase accuracy. Lower altitude means greater accuracy, of course, as does lower speed, but also greater danger from antiaircraft fire and enemy fighters.

Astonishingly, the regression equation said that bombing accuracy *increased* with amount of enemy fighter opposition. Surely this could not be correct. To those knowledgeable in regression analysis, this suggested the operation of some missing variable, correlated with both accuracy and fighter opposition. With this clue, the missing variable was found: amount of cloud cover.

Missing variables may easily pass unsuspected. The bombing example is atypical in yielding a *b* weight so contrary to background knowledge. Most missing variables will not yield suspicious results, yet may severely bias the *b* weights. A weak causal variable may thus appear to have a strong effect. Indeed, as just illustrated, the causal sign of a variable may even get reversed.

This example illustrates one kind of situation in which regression analysis of observational data can be helpful. Foremost is the background knowledge about the causal structure of the situation, which led to selection of relevant variables for the initial regression analysis, as well as to recognition of the missing variable. In this situation, it would seem sensible to employ the regression results to help set speed and altitude standards in future runs, even while recognizing that the results are by no means definitive.

Taxes and Education. School districts brought suit against the State of Washington, asking for more money. Substantial increases in per pupil tax support had been approved during a halcyon period, 1950–1975, but further increases were halted by a complex of social–economic factors. This plunged the school districts into unprecedented and chronic budget crises, as they faced recurrent confrontations with teachers' unions and steadily increasing material costs. Accordingly, the school districts brought suit under the provision of the state constitution that ''It is the paramount duty of the state to make ample provision for the education of all children residing within its borders.''

But the state itself was under financial pressure. It had greatly increased school funding in the previous 25 years; further tax increases were unpopular. How could the state defend itself?

The state rested its defense on the claim that increased funds could not be shown to increase school achievement. This claim was based on regression analyses. The ''subjects'' were 88 school districts; *Y* was the mean score for all students in each district on statewide math and language achievement tests.

Three classes of predictor variables were used in this regression. Background variables such as education level and socioeconomic status of parents showed statsig *b* weights. So did peer group variables, such as percentage of minority group students in each school district. In contrast, the *b* weights for school resource variables, such as class size and teacher salary, were not statsig. The statisticians for the state testified that ''If additional resources were spent in traditional ways (more teachers, more administrators, smaller classes), the data are consistent with . . . negligible effects on educational outcomes'' (Pincus & Rolph, 1986, p. 275).

This regression seems moderately convincing. Causation causes correlation: If better funding led to increased achievement, the *b* weight for resource variables should have been statsig. The only serious objection by plaintiff was that the regression analysis could have been more extensive. Similar regressions had been done in other states, however, all tending to the same conclusion.[a]

This example illustrates null-control logic. The focal result is a negligible *b* weight. If resource variables had causal effects, this *b* weight should have been positive. It is hard to imagine a missing variable that would nullify a positive *b* weight for school resource variables. This reasoning is thus markedly simpler than interpreting a nonzero *b* weight, which may result from many causes, including missing variables.

Employment Discrimination and Reverse Regression. Laws and government regulations are making headway against gender discrimination in hiring, salary, and promotion. But proving discrimination in any organization is typically difficult, as in *United States Department of the Treasury v. Harris Trust and Savings Bank*. The U. S. Department of the Treasury charged Harris Bank with salary discrimination against females. For employees hired within a certain time period, female salary seven years later was 40% less than male salary (Conway & Roberts, 1986).

Some of this salary differential, however, reflects lower qualifications of the females: Only 27% had formal education beyond high school compared to 74% of the males. When education level was added to gender in a multiple regression, the female shortfall was almost halved, falling from 40% to 23%. Harris Bank could plausibly argue that other missing variables could account for this 23%.

Furthermore, the causal variable in job performance is not the four-step scale of education level actually used in the regression. This four-step scale is only a crude, partial measure of qualifications. Two persons with high school diplomas, for example, might have quite different qualifications. Education level is used because it is easily measured and because it correlates with qualifications, which are not easily measured. Education level is a partial measure, in other words, insufficient as an explanatory variable.

Moreover, education level introduces a bias. As an indicator of qualifications, it is somewhat unreliable. This unreliability causes its *b* weight to be too small (see similarly Section 15.5). As a consequence, any discrimination would seem worse than it was. The statistical consultants for Harris Bank would point this out to the defense lawyers, who would hammer it home in their cross-examination of statistical witnesses for the plaintiff.

This unreliability bias can be avoided, in this particular case, by interchanging *Y* and *X* to obtain a *reverse regression*. The traditional regression compares salary between gender for given education level; reverse regression compares education level between gender for given salary. Since salary is known exactly, the unreliability problem disappears.

This reverse regression has a simple logic. If discrimination is operative, females will have higher education level than males with the same salary. In fact, this gender difference was negligible.[b]

Social attitude theory certainly implicates discrimination. The stereotype of women as less able and less suited for certain jobs has a long cultural history and remains socially real. This stereotype is inevitably one determinant of decisions about hiring and promotion. It cannot fail to have some effect (Anderson, 1991h). The suit against Harris Bank has the general social benefit of causing other institutions, banks especially, to scrutinize their hiring–promotion practices in order to avoid fractious ensnarlment with the federal bureaucracy. But perhaps this is a dubious means to a good end.

Personal Health. "Eat healthy" is a fine slogan, but what exactly does it prescribe? Different foods have different benefits. If we eat more of one, we will eat less of another. What is an optimal diet?

One line of evidence comes from observing what people do eat and correlating this with incidence of various diseases. The term "limey" originates in this way from the British practice of carrying a barrel of limes at sea to prevent scurvy. Today medical researchers look for less obvious correlation clues.

One such clue is that people who eat more fruits and vegetables, especially carrots and yams, have less cancer and heart disease. But people who eat more fruits and vegetables differ in many, many ways, including education, income, and other health practices. Multiple regression to "control" such uncontrolled variables is popular; masses of nutrition advice rests on such evidence. In view of the foregoing discussion, however, such "control" rings hollow.

More satisfactory evidence comes from biochemistry. Carrots and yams are rich in beta carotene, from which the body manufactures vitamin A. Vitamin A reduces the effects of free radicals produced by the body, which are known to be causative in cancer. Animal studies, moreover, have shown that extremely low levels of beta carotene are quite harmful. On these grounds, nutritionists and doctors would seem justified in recommending that diet be supplemented with vitamin A, especially for persons at high risk for heart disease and cancer.

The only way to be sure, however, is with randomized experiments with humans. Such experiments are huge operations. Upwards of 10,000 subjects must be monitored over several years across several hospitals. One of the many prosaic but essential problems is to measure noncompliance of subjects with the diet. The third study cited in the next paragraph listed 124 professional personnel, with small armies of technical and clerical staff going unmentioned.

Nevertheless, a few such experiments have been done—with negative results. One study used 29,000 older participants and found that angina pectoris, a mild symptom of heart disease, was slightly increased by beta carotene. Another, with 22,000 physicians, found neither benefit nor harm from 12 years of beta carotene supplementation, either for heart disease or for death from all causes. Still a third found statsig harmful effect of beta carotene.[c]

This case shows that randomized experiments are important even when the correlational clues are buttressed by knowledge about causal process. Although such experiments are expensive, they have potential benefit for every person now on the globe and for generations yet unborn.

Premarital Cohabitation. Is cohabitation before marriage useful preparation for subsequent marriage? Or is it harmful? The correlation is negative: Cohabiting couples who subsequently marry report lower marital satisfaction than noncohabitors. But this correlation cannot answer the question. Cohabitors and noncohabitors are different kinds of people; the negative correlation might stem from other differences between them. More religious people, for example, are less likely to cohabit and they report higher marital satisfaction.

It thus seems necessary to "control" for religion to determine whether cohabitation is truly harmful. Of course, many other personality variables would also need to be "controlled." Among these associated variables are sex-role attitudes, previous marriage, socio-economic status, wife–husband difference in age, and so on.

Thirteen such associated variables were measured in the best of the cohabitation studies (DeMaris & Leslie, 1984). Cohabitation was treated as a categorical variable, with values of 1 and 0 for cohabitors and noncohabitors. The correlation between cohabitation and marital satisfaction was negative, $-.17$ for husbands, $-.21$ for wives.

Premarital cohabitors are thus less satisfied when they subsequently marry, but this may reflect other variables than cohabitation itself. Accordingly, the investigators ran a multiple regression "controlling for religious preference; number of previous marriages; education; father's occupation; presence of children; and heterogamy of age, education, and religious activity" (p. 82). They found that "even after controlling for variables that might produce spurious effects," the correlation was still negative and, for wives, still statsig.

In my opinion, this regression analysis is worthless. Squaring the cited correlations shows that only .03 to .04 of the variance in marriage satisfaction is related to cohabitation. With so small an effect, untangling complex causal structure is impossible. There is no hope of making adequate allowance for unknown missing variables or partial measures. Furthermore, the person–variable confounding means that "controlling for" differences between cohabitors and noncohabitors does not actually address causal interpretation. Although this study was thoughtful and well-done, especially in considering a nonstudent population, it seems completely inconclusive.

This study has been included here for two reasons. First, it is typical of a vast literature in sociology, health, and some areas of psychology, that relies on multiple regression for "control." This multiple regression approach is undeniably attractive, for it claims to provide causal conclusions from observational data. The many pitfalls, although long known, receive mainly lip service or are simply ignored. Many writers carefully avoid explicit claims about causality, but insinuate them implicitly, especially through such terms as "control" of uncontrolled variables.

Second, this study is the first of three exemplary applications in the introductory text in the Sage series by Schroeder, Sjoquist, and Stephan (1986), who state that "Since people who do or do not cohabit may differ in other ways that might also affect marital satisfaction, it was necessary to control for these factors by including other variables in the regression equation" (p. 35) in order to determine effect of cohabitation.

The cited text is typical. Virtually all texts characterize multiple regression in similar misleading terms of "statistical control," "holding constant," and "partialing out." Warnings about pitfalls are always included, but they are muddled by the prevailing emphasis on formulas and by the desire to indicate that what is being taught is worth learning.[d]

Low Lead Controversy. Do low levels of lead in blood cause harm? In the 1960s, it became clear that high levels of lead in children's blood were causing neurological problems and mental retardation. Some of the evidence was observational, as with an outbreak of lead poisoning in Baltimore during the Great Depression that was traced to burning old battery cases for fuel. This and other evidence left little doubt that many children had been harmed by lead from the environment, especially from leaded household paint and leaded gasoline. Congress and governmental agencies accordingly made laws and regulations to disallow lead in household paint and to mandate unleaded gasoline.

The present question is whether very low levels of lead have harmful effects. A number of investigators have said *yes*, and have advocated more stringent laws and regulations to reduce environmental lead. Other investigators have disagreed, saying that the evidence is dubious, that any effect is at most small, and that other toxic substances in the environment are more serious health hazards and need prior attention.

A review of evidence is given in the Social Policy Report by Tesman and Hills (1994), issued by the Society for Research in Child Development. Evidence involves comparison of IQ, or other scores, for two groups of children who differ in levels of lead. This lead difference, however, is confounded with many factors that also affect IQ. Higher lead is more likely in children of lower family socioeconomic status, for example, because they tend to live closer to sources of lead contamination, such as residues from leaded gasoline and from pre-1977 house paint. But family socioeconomic status is correlated with children's IQ, which confounds the lead comparison. As another confound, higher lead is more likely in children of lower IQ mothers, perhaps because these mothers are less concerned with their children's cleanliness and hygiene.

To "control" these confounds, many researchers turn to regression analysis. The authors of this review follow along. Of one such study, they say "Controlling for possible confounds, i.e., family social class, maternal education and IQ, life events, and blood lead history, . . . " (p. 5). It seems agreed, however, that if low lead has an effect, it is small, perhaps 1 or 2 IQ points. With so small an effect, observational data cannot hope to unravel an obviously complex causal pattern. "Controlling for possible confounds" is entirely illusory.

This low lead review illustrates a not-uncommon case in which commendable social concern leads to slanted treatment of the evidence. The tenor of this review appears in the second sentence, which states "Only recently has it been known that even low levels of lead exposure may have serious effects on children's development" (p. 1). Far from being known, this matter is quite uncertain. The review relies heavily on work by Needleman and associates, especially Needleman et al. (1979), but this work has been strongly criticized by Ernhart, by Scarr, as well as by three investigating committees. This criticism, however, is dismissed in a footnote by saying "In March 1994 the Office of Research Integrity, serving DHHS, cleared Needleman of any misconduct and ruled that although the research contained numerous errors and misstatements, these 'did not necessarily alter the conclusion' (p. 13)." If Needleman's research contains numerous errors and misstatements, it should hardly be relied on. Nor should the cited criticisms of this research be virtually ignored.[e, f, g]

16.2.3 COMMENTS ON REGRESSION ANALYSIS

Observation and Experiment. Observation and experiment should go hand in hand. The best foundation for experimental analysis is observation to develop phenomenological appreciation of subject, situation, and task. Observation is more important than experiment in that it is a primary source of hypotheses. The value of experiments in *testing* hypotheses tends to obscure the more basic problem of *generating* hypotheses to be tested (see McGuire, 1997).

Observational data may contain useful information about causal process, as with various early medical discoveries (Shryock, 1947). One example is inoculation–vaccination for smallpox, a dreaded killer in Washington's army of the revolution. This means of prevention was triggered by Jenner's observation that milkmaids, who were subject to milder cowpox, seemed immune to smallpox. Similarly, the role of rat fleas as carriers of bubonic plague, the Black Death of the middle ages, was pinned down through a combination of observation and experiment, although at a surprisingly late date around 1900.

Observational data can be effective in simple causal situations, when a single causal factor has a major effect, as in the cited medical discoveries. Interpretation is markedly more difficult when multiple correlated causes are operative. Correlations can still be useful clues, however, because causation usually implies correlation.

Ideally, an observational situation allows conjoint experimental analysis. The potential of regression analysis for uncovering uncertain clues about complex causation often requires follow-up experimental analysis for validation. Such conjunction of observation and experiment can exploit the uncertain hints of regression analysis, as with *Personal Health*, page 509.

Experimental Pyramid. Substantive interpretation depends on all levels of the Experimental Pyramid of Chapter 1. Substantive inference is thus primarily extrastatistical. This theme of extrastatistical inference is even more important for observational than for experimental studies.

The importance of substantive causal knowledge in applications of multiple regression is clear in the foregoing examples. The most promising applications are to physical systems, as with the case of bombing accuracy. Even with physical systems, however, multiple regression is treacherous. As Box, Hunter, and Hunter (1978, p. 495) warn in their book on statistical analysis in engineering, "Broadly speaking, *to find out what happens when you change something it is necessary to change it.*"

With social systems, in contrast, prior causal knowledge is typically meager, as with premarital cohabitation and taxes—education. Multiple causes are the rule, moreover, and predictability is low, both of which complicate interpretation (see similarly Mosteller & Tukey, 1977, Section 13G).

It seems pertinent to question whether a great proportion of multiple regression analysis in social and medical science should ever have been published. The dangers and pitfalls have long been known, but they have been systematically ignored. Writing on the related topic of quasi-experimental design, Achen (1986, p. 11) says:

> Surprisingly, among social scientists only policy analysts have been much concerned with the statistical weaknesses of the experimental designs they are compelled to use. Caveats about nonexperimental inference recur endlessly in the policy analysis literature . . . Outside the policy community, however, no one appears to be much concerned. Other social scientists, carrying out essentially the same statistical procedures on similar data, simply ignore the problem.

Most researchers, says Achen, simply apply regression anlysis with little concern for the critical assumption of no misspecification (= missing variable confounding). Unfortunately, worthless regression analysis seems to have achieved autonomous status, maintained by mutual interest groups of investigators, reviewers, and grant agencies, and nurtured by current texts (see page 511).[a]

One remedial measure would be to disbar such terms as "statistical control," "holding constant," and "partialing out." Much of the meaninglessness produced by multiple regression stems from surplus meaning of such terms. These terms are in general substantively incorrect, so disbarring them seems desirable. Instead, the investigator should be required to demonstrate the substantive validity of the model used in the regression.

I sympathize with persons who have been taught that multiple regression is a means of "statistical control." It took me longer than I care to think to see through the smoke and mirrors. Disbarring such terms would prevent much confusion. Disbarring such terms would focus concern on the central issue of causal analysis.

A second remedial measure would be to orient teaching toward development of extrastatistical judgment. Good choice of problem is the primary determinant of accomplishment. Extrastatistical judgment is needed to evaluate whether a given application of regression analysis is reasonable or ill-advised. Current texts concentrate on how to do regression analysis. Far more important is when—and when not (see also Note 16.2.2d).

Most texts do warn that substantive theory is generally prerequisite for process analysis with multiple regression. These warnings, however, are obscured under the mass of statistical detail, by such phrases as "statistical control," and especially by students' implicit assumption that what is being taught must be worth learning. At best, these warnings are little help because little is said about what constitutes adequate substantive theory.

One issue of substantive theory concerns the standard additive regression model. Experimental studies can assess the validity of this model, as illustrated in Chapter 20. This approach, however, is never considered in regression texts.

An alternative approach is to reorient learning–teaching toward the extrastatistical research judgment needed for effective use of multiple regression. To develop such judgment requires a collection of real-life applications, both well-taken and ill-taken, together with the extrastatistical considerations. The foregoing examples are a step in this direction, but systematic group effort is needed by experts in statistics and empirics of multiple regression.

NOTES

Among texts on regression analysis, Pedhazur (1982) gives perhaps the best understanding of the pitfalls. Mosteller and Tukey (1977) is excellent though more advanced. *Regression analysis by example* (Chatterjee & Price, 1991) is a helpful guide to applications of regression analysis, emphasizing graphical methods with primary concern for revealing pattern in the data rather than significance tests. The exposition is built around numerous data sets, selected to illustrate particular techniques and problems.

16.1a. As in Chapter 9, regression analysis refers to situations with metric variables, typically with uncontrolled observational data. Although multiple regression can be used with experimentally controlled data and with nonmetric variables (Section 16.1.4), such applications are not frequent in psychology. This usage mirrors prevailing application as well as Scheffé (1959, pp. 192-193). As an alternative, regression could denote procedures for fitting any statistical model to given data and Anova could denote procedures that use SSs to get the error terms for confidence intervals and significance tests.

16.1.1a. The formula, GRE + 100GPA, differs slightly from that used by Goldberg (1977), in part because GRE here refers to the mean verbal plus quantitative score.

16.1.1b. The population model for multiple regression may be written

$$Y = \beta_0 + \beta_1 X_1 + \beta_2 X_2 + \ldots + \text{error},$$

where the β_j are the population values of which the b_j are sample estimates. For simplicity, this population–sample distinction is not made explicit in the text.

16.1.1c. Computer programs include an adjustment for shrinkage. This adjusted R^2 is sensitive to the statistical assumptions, however, and may not mean much.

16.1.1d. In the special case in which the predictor variables are independent (*orthogonal*), the b weights are also independent. Then the b weight of any predictor depends only on its relation to the criterion, not on the other predictors. This special case applies to some controlled experiments (but see Section 18.1), but has little practical relevance with observational data, for which predictors are typically nonindependent.

16.1.1e. Standardized b weights are obtained by standardizing the Xs. To standardize X_j, divide the X_j score for each subject by the standard deviation of the X_j scores for all the subjects. With standardization, each predictor variable has a standard deviation of 1, regardless of the units before standardization. Accordingly, standardization is sometimes thought to mean that the variables are on a common scale—and that their b weights are comparable. This can hardly be correct. One reason is that the standard deviation of individual differences on a measuring scale has no likely relation to the scale unit, (see also Section 18.1.4). The main consequence of standardization is that "the potential for self-delusion is greatly increased" (Pedhazur & Schmelkin, 1991, p. 422).

16.1.1f. An alternative attempt to assess contribution of a single predictor is with *partial correlation*, which is a correlation that represents the contribution of a given predictor— over and above all effects of other predictors, which are thus said to be "partialed out."

The main use of partial correlation is a misuse. In a typical use, X_1 remained statistically significant even after the effects of the other predictors had been "partialed out." The implication is that X_1 has some causal effect in its own right, distinct from the other variables. This implication is not justified, one reason being the missing variable problem. "Partialing out" is just another form of the fallacy of "statistical control."

16.1.2a. The multiple regression has no trouble adding GPA to GRE because the b weights equalize the effective units of these two variables. With unit weighting, however, a multiplier of GPA is needed for this purpose. This multiplier may be chosen as a convenient round number because predictive power is insensitive to the exact value.

16.1.2b. Psychologists have been so concerned with predicting, controlling, and explaining behavior that they have slighted the robust phenomenon of unpredictability. Why behavior is so unpredictable is interesting, important, and deserves study per se.

Also of interest is the cognitive illusion that behavior is fairly predictable. One reason is that this belief is largely postdiction. In any given situation, each of several possible outcomes may be quite plausible. The postdictive plausibility of the actual outcome then masquerades as predictability (see Anderson, 1991i, p. 128).

16.1.3a. These correlations seem high for this situation, at least for the women. One reason is that the University of Minnesota had a very liberal admissions policy, together with a high flunkout rate. As a consequence, the ranges of the predictors and the criterion were all substantial. Considerably lower correlations would be expected at the University of California, for example, which admits only about the top tenth of high school graduates. This range effect is one reason that r is not generally a good measure of the strength of the Y–X relation (Chapter 9).

16.1.3b. Dawes (1971) reports that the Oregon prediction formula correlated .38 with faculty judgments of performance in graduate school. Sternberg and Williams (1997), however, report much smaller correlations and question the usefulness of GRE (see also *The Criterion Problem* in Section 16.1.2).

16.1.3c. To look for configurality in clinical judgment, a faulty application of multiple regression was adopted by a number of investigators. In a typical study, the predictor variables were the same as in any of the tests between clinical and statistical prediction. The criterion, however, was the subject's own judgments. If the subject's judgments were indeed configural, the additive regression model should fail to fit them.

High correlations were obtained between the regression predictions and the subject's personal judgments. As a non sequitur, these high correlations were taken to mean that the subject's integration *process* was additive. It was not recognized that markedly nonadditive processes can readily yield correlations greater than .95 in applications of the kind in question. A proper test of the additive regression model requires a test of the deviations from additivity. The regression–correlation methodology was a form of weak inference (see *Weak Inference*, Section 9.2.2, pages 277*f*).

In contrast, the study of person cognition cited in the text applied Anova, thereby obtaining a valid test of the configurality hypothesis (Anderson, 1962a). Subsequently, the need to use Anova instead of multiple regression (see Section 20.1) was recognized by Hoffman, Slovic, and Rorer (1968). They failed, however, to recognize the critical issue of linearity of the response scale (Anderson, 1969).

16.1.5a. Measurement theory in regression analysis is discussed in Anderson (1972b, 1982, Sections 4.3 and 7.10–7.11). The seriousness of nonlinear scales is emphasized by Busemeyer and Jones (1983). Detailed discussion of interaction effects in multiple regression is given by Jaccard, Turrisi, and Wan (1990), although with limited recognition of the measurement problems.

16.2.1a. More precisely, missing variable confounding refers to variables correlated either with the criterion response or with the treatment. An example from developmental psychology (Scarr, 1985) concerns two predictor variables, namely, control and discipline exerted by mothers on $3\frac{1}{2}$–4-year-old children, measured in two observational situations. In a two-variable regression, greater control and greater discipline implied higher scores on both of two criteria namely, child's IQ and child's communication skills. A causal relation seems plausible—if only mothers would just exert more control and discipline, their children would improve intellectually. Scarr commented "As the editor of a developmental journal, I receive many papers of this sort" (p. 504).

But the picture changed when mother's vocabulary score was added as another predictor in a causal regression model. Vocabulary score carried the main predictive power for both criteria; control and discipline carried little predictive power. Their predictive power in the two-variable regression appeared to reflect their correlation with the missing variable of mother's vocabulary score.

16.2.1b. The problem of partial measures goes deeper than missing variables. Some determinants of behavior are qualitative, at best only partly quantifiable.

16.2.1c. Although not denying the cited criticisms of causal models, Blalock (1991) argued that there is really no *constructive* alternative, as least in sociology. But there is a constructive alternative, even in sociology—developing a foundation of psychological theory (see following note and *Personal Design*, Section 11.5.4, page 335).

16.2.1d. Numerous books have been written on structural equation models (e.g., Pedhazur & Schmelkin, 1991). All seem to acknowledge that extrastatistical knowledge is critical for valid model analysis; none seem to show serious justification that this knowledge exists. Those who write the books and teach the courses naturally emphasize the great need and the positive potential of causal analysis of observational data. What is still missing is good evidence that this potential has some actuality.

16.2.2a. In *Taxes and Education*, the judge ruled against the school districts on the main count, but did approve extra funding for certain special programs.

16.2.2b. The reverse regression in *Employment Discrimination* is subject to question, indicated in commentaries following the chapter by Conway and Roberts (1986). Conway and Roberts argue that the appropriate regression depends on substantive theory of employer behavior. Traditional regression would be appropriate if the employer considers the qualification of an individual applicant and selects a fitting salary; reverse regression would be appropriate if the employer considers a group of candidates and selects those with the best qualifications. Their argument further illustrates that causal inference from correlational data requires substantive foundation of causal knowledge.

16.2.2c. The three cited studies on beta carotene supplementation are Rapola et al. (1996), Hennekens et al. (1996), and the Alpha-Tocopheral, Beta Carotene Cancer Prevention Study Group (1994). Given the cited biochemical knowledge, it is natural to discount the harmful effect reported in the third study as a false alarm. In a fourth study, however, further evidence of harmful effects was found (Omenn et al., 1996).

16.2.2d. A third reason for including this cohabitation example is to point up the issue of sterile and fruitful research issues. Even if all of the small effect was causal, it would have little practical value, for premarital cohabitation has massive sociological momentum. The issue thus seems sterile.

Fruitful research issues are dying for attention. One alternative issue concerns effective ways to improve marital satisfaction and, more generally, learning–development in the family. Learning in family life, among wife, husband, and children, is surely a fertile field, one in which observation and experiment can make important contributions, both separately and jointly, especially for developing effective techniques for family learning.

16.2.2e. In the low lead controversy, Ernhart and Scarr sought to check the data analyses in the reference study by Needleman et al. (1979). To do this, they obtained court-approved access to the original data and analyses, but this was obstructed by Needleman, even to the extent of a lawsuit (Ernhart, Scarr, & Geneson, 1993; Needleman, 1993b; Scarr & Ernhart, 1993; see also Ernhart, 1993; Ernhart & Scarr, 1993; Needleman, 1993a; Scarr, 1993a,b, 1994). They did get 1½ days partial access to these records, abruptly terminated by Needleman, and this yielded enough information for them to uncover the following problems (Ernhart, Scarr, & Geneson, 1993, p. 78):

> Exclusion of the data of 40% to 50% of the 270 children who were tested. Exclusions were related to the likelihood of finding significant effects.
>
> No consideration was given to the risk of Type 1 error, given the very large number of variables analyzed. Results of analyses that did not support the hypothesis were not reported.
>
> Early analyses in the dated computer output included data for the full sample of the 270 children who had been tested. The initial analyses of covariance, which included age and other covariates, showed little in the way of statistical significance. These were followed by others that moved toward the results that were published. The progression of analyses contributed to a sense of deliberateness in a shift to misleading results.

Suit was brought to force Ernhart and Scarr to destroy their records from this 1½ days partial access to Needleman's data. In his ruling, Chief Judge Bruce Jenkins wrote:

> There is something inherently distasteful and unseemly in secreting either the fruits or seeds of scientific endeavors. This is especially true here, where there appears to be little professional or economic justification for the order sought by the plaintiff. . . . The only harm or prejudice asserted by Dr. Needleman appears to be the risk of academic criticism and potential misuse of his data by others. Exactly how this misuse will occur is not clear. This is insufficient justification for the relief sought by plaintiff. Plaintiff's motion is therefore DENIED. (As quoted in the cited reference, p. 77.)

For a similar case, see Note 8.1.6i.

16.2.2f. A committee of experts from psychometrics and biostatistics appointed by the United States Environmental Protection Agency (1983) found serious shortcomings in the Needleman et al. (1979) reference study. The Committee added that subsequent reanalyses of these data ''cannot be accepted as providing credible or reliable estimates of quantitative relationships between Pb exposure and neuropsychologic deficits in children'' (p. 40). Further, ''the Committee knows of no studies that, to date, have validly established (after proper control for confounding variables) a relationship between low-level Pb exposure and neuropsychologic deficits in children'' (p. 41). It may be added that a Hearing Board established by Needleman's home institution, the University of Pittsburgh (1992), found that Needleman had engaged in ''deliberate misrepresentation.''

16.2.2g. The sterile–fruitful issue of Note 16.2.2d arises also in the *Low Lead Controversy*. Here again, the effect appears to be so small that neither standard regression nor structural equation models can establish causality. Further reductions in environmental lead, as advocated by some lead researchers, would be difficult and costly. It seems more effectual to change the behavior of the threatened population.

Surprisingly, but not uncommonly, children eat flakes of paint, which is dangerous with older, leaded paint. Other children play on paint covered surfaces and eat without washing their hands. A couple of studies cited in the review sought to teach cleanliness to mothers and children with substantial reported reductions in lead level. Another behavioral approach comes from the suggestion that lead effects may be reduced by eating fresh vegetables. Educating mothers, and children, about cleanliness and nutrition could be more worthwhile than further reductions in environmental lead. Similar observations are made by Scarr (1994) and in the statistical review of the literature by Pocock, Smith, and Baghurst (1994).

Nutrition and cleanliness behaviors should, moreover, have far wider benefits than reducing lead level. They should improve general health and contribute to social competence and self-esteem.

16.2.3a. Observational data may be all that are available on some important social issues. Multiple regression has an advantage over uninformed opinion that fails even to look at available evidence or argues from selected examples to support some partisan view. Nevertheless, regression is subject to serious dangers, as with its mistaken use to establish busing as a means for ethnic integration (Mosteller & Moynihan, 1972; Pedhazur, 1982), and with the *Low Lead Controversy* cited in the text. As suggested in the summary comments of Section 15.5, high expertise in statistical theory and in empirical practice seem an essential prequisite to field studies with observational behavior that seek to demonstrate causality.

On extrastatistical grounds, it may be possible to justify the additive regression model as a causal process model for some empirical situations. In particular, it might sometimes be possible to rule out missing variable bias on the basis of empirical understanding of the causal structure of this situation. The danger of this approach, however, is indicated in the *Mystery of the Missing Cloud Cover* (page 506). Although the causal structure seemed reasonably clear, one critical variable was overlooked and only noticed because its omission led to a counterintuitive result.

What is needed is systematic study of multiple regression in realistic applications. Almost the only way to assess validity is through conjoint observation-plus-experiment. Although only possible in limited situations, such conjoint analysis seems essential to assess what regression really does in field situations. With conjoint studies, the experimental analysis can provide a needed validity criterion for the regression analysis, allowing specification of conditions under which regression is and is not likely to be meaningful. Until such work is done, regression analysis of observational data seems little more than wishful thinking (see also Note 15.5.5b).

EXERCISES FOR CHAPTER 16

1. In the Oregon admissions procedure, it might be objected that this prediction equation would be unfair to applicants from minority groups.
How do you suppose they handled this matter?

2. In relation to *Missing Variables Confounding*:

    a. Why might height have a large b weight for predicting childrens' vocabulary size if age was missing?

    b. Do you think one is a better predictor than the other?

    c. Do you think one is more causal than the other?

    d.* Can effects of age and height be separated?

3. In *Mystery of the Missing Cloud Cover* in Section 16.2.2, explain:

    a. How heavier fighter opposition could cause lower bombing accuracy.

    b. How the cloud cover variable could produce the counterintuitive result.

4. The *Mystery of the Missing Cloud Cover* of Section 16.2.2 shows that a missing variable can have fatal consequences. Experimental studies, of course, typically manipulate only a few variables. Numerous variables are thus missing from the design.

    a. In what way are randomized experiments not troubled by missing variables?

    b. In what ways are randomized experiments troubled by missing variables? Cite specific experimental illustrations from previous chapters.

5. Under *Cognitive Analysis of Clinical Judgment* in Section 16.1.3:

    a. Justify the statement "If subjects did make configural judgments, the additive model should fail to fit them."

    b.* Make up a factorial design using trait adjectives to describe persons and select row and column adjectives that you think will produce configural response, that is, responses that depart in some systematic direction from additivity. Make up and plot hypothetical data.

6. In *Taxes and Education* (Section 16.2.2):

    a. Give two plausible interpretations of the statsig b weight for background variables.

    b. What relevance does the statsig b weight for background variables have to the cited interpretation of the nonstatsig b weight for resource variables?

7. One of the three studies on effects of beta carotene (vitamin A) on cancer cited under *Personal Health* in Section 16.2.2 found a statsig harmful effect.

The article discussed this finding and concluded "In spite of its formal statistical significance, therefore, this finding may well be due to chance." Is this a proper way to gloss over a statsig finding?

8. a. How does the sex–marital satisfaction example of page 503 relate to the subsection on *Person–Variable Confounding*?

  b. Hypothesize a similar example in an area of interest to you.

9. Under *Clinical Versus Statistical Prediction I* in Section 16.1.3, Sarbin's test of clinicians' skill suggested that clinical judgments added little to the regression prediction.

  a. Outline the steps needed to demonstrate this conclusion.

  b. Is this a fair test of clinical expertise?

10. Show how the issue of gender bias in the last subsection of Chapter 10 can be conceptualized in terms of correlation produced by a missing variable.

11. Aptitude–treatment interactions have been a central concern in educational psychology on the plausible ground that the most effective procedure for teaching depends on the aptitude of the learner. Let X denote the aptitude, Y the amount learned. Consider an experiment with two treatments (e.g., *Methods for Language Learning* in Section 14.2.2).

  a. How will an aptitude–treatment interaction appear graphically?

  b. How will an aptitude–treatment interaction appear in one-variable regression analysis?

  c. Referring to a comparison of regression lines between treatment conditions, Pedhazur and Schmelkin (1991, p. 547) say that "In short, *a conclusion that there is no significant difference between the b's* [of the one-variable regressions] *is tantamount to a statement that there is no interaction between the treatments and the attribute* [attribute refers to aptitude of subject]." Comment.

12. Suppose you are using a regression with unit weighting, these weights being given. How can you test whether some one of the given variables can be eliminated without undue loss?

13. "A variable that is a good predictor by itself may add little when assessed as one of a group." (From *Relative Importance* in Section 16.1.1.)

  a. Verify this quote for the extreme case of a three-variable regression based on X_1, X_2, and $X_3 = X_1 + X_2$ (all intercorrelations positive).

  b. Based on (a), why does this quote apply generally?

  c. How did this issue apply to the prediction equation for success in graduate school?

14. Write down two-variable linear regression equations for the following four sets of four data points using graphs and visual inspection only. Comment.

a. X_1	X_2	Y		b. X_1	X_2	Y
1	2	1		1	2	5
2	2	2		2	2	6
3	2	3		3	2	7
4	2	4		4	2	8

c. X_1	X_2	Y		d. X_1	X_2	Y
1	1	1		1	5	1
2	2	2		2	6	2
3	2	3		3	7	3
4	1	4		4	8	4

15. The discussion of nonlinearities in Section 16.1.5 implies that artifactual nonlinearity can also appear if any X_j is measured on a nonlinear scale. Demonstrate this by considering the case of $Y = \psi_1 + \psi_2$, where ψ_1 and ψ_2 are linear scales of the concepts that X_1 and X_2 are supposed to measure. Assume that X_1 is a linear scale, with $X_1 = \psi_1$, but that X_2 is a nonlinear scale, with $X_2 = \sqrt{\psi_2}$. For simplicity, assume also that X_1 and X_2 are uncorrelated.

16. (After Box, 1966.) In various chemical reactions, temperature of the reacting solution is one determinant of yield, or efficiency, of a manufacturing operation. To optimize yield, the human operators may be instructed to hold the temperature within narrow limits, taking appropriate action whenever the temperature strays outside these limits. Suppose the question now arises whether the true optimum for temperature lies outside these limits. To answer this question, observational data are collected under normal operating conditions, including temperature and yield, and subjected to multiple regression.

  a. By analogy to one-variable regression, why will the temperature–yield correlation be small?

  b. Why will there not be a corresponding effect on the b weight for temperature?

  c. Granted that the expected value of the b weight for temperature will not be affected from holding temperature within a narrow range, what bad thing will happen to the estimated value of the b weight?

17. R and r are both correlations between Y and $\hat{Y}$. For a two-variable regression, why can't R be given a negative or positive sign as with r in Chapter 9?

18. You have five predictor variables and you wish to test whether X_4 and X_5, taken together, add statsig predictive power, over and above the first three

predictors. How do you think this test would be made (extrapolating beyond the information in the text)?

19. How can you explain the large difference in the predictive correlations for women and men cited in *Clinical Versus Statistical Prediction I* ?

20. You have a 3 × 5 factorial design, but all the data points have been lost except for row 1 and for column 1. The entries in row 1 are 1, 2, 3, 4, 5; the entries in column 1 are 1, 2, 3.

   a. Apply the two-variable regression model of Equation 5b, with the error term omitted to obtain estimates of the lost data. Give the 3 × 5 table.

   b. On what assumption does the validity of these estimates depend?

21. To illustrate some difficulties of interpreting regression *b* weights as measures of importance, consider the formula for b_1 in a two-variable regression:

$$b_1 = \frac{\rho_{Y1} - \rho_{Y2}\,\rho_{12}}{1 - \rho_{12}^2} \times \frac{\sigma_Y}{\sigma_1}.$$

Here ρ_{Y1} and ρ_{Y2} are the correlations between the criterion Y and the two predictors, X_1 and X_2; ρ_{12} is the correlation between the two predictors; and σ_Y and σ_1 are standard deviations of Y and X_1.

   a. Show that b_1 can be zero even though ρ_{Y1} is not zero. Could this be a serious problem in practice?

   b. Show that b_1 can be nonzero even though ρ_{Y1} is zero. Could this be a serious problem in practice?

   c. Interpret the *Mystery of the Missing Cloud Cover* (Section 16.2.2) in terms of this equation for b_1.

PREFACE

Every investigation with more than two conditions faces two linked hazards: escalation of false alarms and loss of power. Each comparison of two means is an opportunity for false alarm. Four conditions yield six two-mean comparisons—six opportunities for false alarms. Hence the effective α for this family of six comparisons is greater than the α used for each single test—not .05 but .20. This familywise α escalates rapidly with more conditions.

You can hold α down to whatever you want—at a price. The price is loss of power, that is, β increase. This is the α–β tradeoff dilemma of Chapter 2.

Two polarized philosophies have developed for dealing with this α–β trade-off dilemma. Each philosophy is mainly concerned with avoiding one of the two hazards. The *familywise philosophy* postulates that α should be set at some fixed value, regardless of the number of conditions. Necessarily, therefore, power decreases with more conditions. The *per comparison philosophy*, seeking to lessen such loss of power, allows larger α with more conditions.

The per comparison philosophy is advocated in this chapter for most work in experimental psychology. Current texts, in contrast, increasingly follow the familywise philosophy. But although some situations do require familywise analysis, these are not common in experimental psychology. The per comparison philosophy is founded on empirical common sense, as shown in the *Parable of the Two Philosophies.*

Extrastatistical considerations have an essential role with multiple comparisons. Among these are the guideline of *planned comparisons* and the principle of *replication*, which do much to provide reasonable control of α and β. This guideline and this principle are accepted by most empirical investigators.

Empirical judgment is the primary basis for handling multiple comparisons, not statistical techniques. Empirical judgment underlies the cost–benefit analysis necessary to deal with the α–β tradeoff dilemma. Above all, empirical judgment is needed in planning the design and analysis, especially in relation to the guideline of planned tests and the principle of replication. This chapter, accordingly, sets the issue of multiple comparisons within the framework of the Experimental Pyramid of Chapter 1.

Chapter 17

MULTIPLE COMPARISONS

A perplexing problem arises when multiple conditions are studied in an experiment. Multiple tests are then usually required; each test could err by producing a miss or a false alarm. The data analysis may thus suffer from multiple misses, multiple false alarms, or both. Statisticians have produced a variety of procedures to handle such situations, but all require hazardous compromise between the threat of misses and the threat of false alarms.

This chapter presents a commonsense approach that incorporates two empirical guidelines—planned comparisons and replication—as part of a per comparison philosophy.

17.1 THE TWIN PROBLEMS OF α AND β

17.1.1 THE PROBLEM OF α ESCALATION

When an investigator makes more than one test in a given experiment, the effective α escalates. This problem of α escalation is serious. With only two conditions in your experiment, you have only one test so no problem arises. But now suppose you add a third condition and test between the largest and smallest of the three means. Since the .05 level holds with two conditions, it might seem that adding a third would not have much effect, at worst perhaps an effective α of .075. In fact, this test between the largest and smallest means has an effective α of almost .13, more than 2½ times larger. Even with small experiments, the effective α for a *family* of tests taken together can be markedly greater than the α used for each separate test.

Of course, you can completely nullify the harmfulness of α escalation by studying only real effects. If your null hypotheses are all untrue, false alarms are impossible—α escalation does not touch you. If you are well grounded in your field, you will have a pretty good idea of what will pan out. You could do your lifetime of experiments without a single false alarm.

But this solution is not generally applicable. A pharmaceutical firm, for example, may test dozens or hundreds of compounds for potential therapeutic activity, expecting that nearly all will fail. They need protection against false alarms. To them, α escalation is serious. A similar predicament holds with many questionnaires. Multiple questions about health practices, for example, may furnish numerous correlations with each of numerous measures of health and illness. False alarms galore can be expected with so many tests. Similar α escalation may appear in studies that use multiple response measures.

For academic research, of course, planning to study only sure bets seems inadvisable. If you are so sure about a real effect, you may not learn much by demonstrating it. Important discoveries are more often made where knowledge is uncertain. To explore new territory requires taking risks, including risks of false alarms. The problem of α escalation thus needs closer consideration.

17.1.2 DEALING WITH α ESCALATION

Two procedures for dealing with α escalation were proposed by Fisher. These are considered in this section, in part for their usefulness, in part because they are forerunners of the two general classes of procedures for multiple comparisons studied by contemporary statisticians.

Anova as α Control. The problem of α escalation was addressed by Fisher with analysis of variance. Student's t, then brand new, could only handle two conditions at a time. Multiple conditions might thus require separate t tests between each and every pair of means. Such multiple tests allowed α escalation in the manner already described.

Fisher's F, however, allowed any number of conditions. Hence α could be set at .05 (say) for the overall H_0 that all true means were equal. If there were no real differences, the chance of false alarm was fixed at .05. Follow-up tests would still be needed to localize a statsig result, but a statsig overall F would indicate that there were real results to localize.

This technique is called Fisher's Least Significant Difference (LSD) procedure. Given a statsig overall F, follow-up tests could be made with two-mean comparisons (Chapter 4). Each such test would also be made at $\alpha = .05$. This is sometimes called the protected LSD procedure, as though the overall F protects the follow-up tests. But this protection holds only for three conditions.

With four conditions, suppose A_1 and A_2 have equal true means greatly different from A_3 and A_4, which also have equal true means. The great difference will produce a statsig overall F. Four of the two-mean comparisons will also be correctly called statsig. However, the null hypothesis is true for the two remaining comparisons, between A_1 and A_2 and between A_3 and A_4. Both are potential false alarms. If all two-mean tests are run, the false alarm parameter for this family of tests will not be α, but nearly 2α. The familywise α is held down by the overall F but not completely (Exercise 15; see also Section 4.2.2, page 99).

Fisher α Splitting Procedure. Fisher also suggested a second procedure, which may be called α *splitting*, commonly but less mnemonically known as the Bonferroni procedure. With two independent tests, an α of .05 would be split between them; each would be made with α set at .025. This family of two tests would thus have a familywise α just under .05.[a]

This α splitting technique can be extended to any number of tests. With five tests, for example, each could be made with $\alpha = .01$. Then the familywise α is definitely no larger than the chosen .05.

17.1.3 THE PROBLEM OF β INCREASE

Familywise α control has a heavy cost: β *increase*. When α is reduced for each test, the miss rate, β, necessarily increases. Hence power, $1 - \beta$, is lowered for each separate test. As a consequence, α splitting may lose so much power that the experiment is not worth doing. This problem of power loss necessarily afflicts all procedures that set α for the family of tests.

This α–β tradeoff dilemma is not new. It appeared in the discussion of α–β tradeoff for single F tests in Section 2.3.5 (page 46). But with multiple tests, the α–β tradeoff dilemma is more acute.

This α–β dilemma is not a shortcoming of statistical theory. The dilemma stems solely from making multiple tests. Statistical theory helps us understand the dilemma and to deal with it more effectively.

17.1.4 TWO PHILOSOPHIES OF MULTIPLE COMPARISONS

The α–β dilemma with multiple tests has been much studied by statisticians. Since the dilemma itself is polarized, it is no surprise that two polarized philosophies have developed, one more concerned with α, the other with β.

Familywise Philosophy. The *familywise α philosophy* postulates that α must be held at its prescribed value, typically .05, for the family of tests taken all together, regardless of the number of tests. This familywise philosophy is nicely exemplified by Fisher's α splitting procedure.

In the α splitting procedure, the α for each single test is lowered as the number of tests in the family increases. All familywise procedures do the same because they require that the overall, familywise α be constant, regardless of the number of conditions. As a necessary consequence, familywise procedures lose power as more conditions are added.

Per Comparison Philosophy. The *per comparison philosophy* is more concerned with power—holding down the miss rate, β. The investigator who adds conditions to an experiment should not be penalized by loss of power. Adding conditions should help, not hurt. This is the per comparison *principle* (not to be confused with per comparison error rate or with specific per comparison procedures). This principle appears in the following parable.

Parable of the Two Philosophies. To compare the two philosophies, consider investigator P, who runs an experiment with the two conditions, A_1 and A_2, with $n = 16$. His data yield means of 1 and 2, with an error mean square of 1.80. This yields $F(1, 30) = 4.44$, comfortably beyond the criterial F^* of 4.17. Pleased with this outcome, P writes up the results, and his paper is accepted for publication.

One of the reviewers, however, suggested that the interpretation of the result would be clarified by running two other conditions, A_3 and A_4. P sees the merit of this suggestion and runs these two conditions, again with $n = 16$. The means are 1 and 2, with an error mean square of 1.80, just as in the first experiment. This result is also statsig, and in due course it also is published.

Investigator Q did identical work at the same time in another laboratory, and got identical results. Q thought ahead, however, realized the importance of conditions A_3 and A_4, included all four in a single experiment, and tested the same two two-mean comparisons. Her results were identical to those of P—*but they were not statsig.* You can understand Q's feelings when she saw P's first publication—and how her feelings intensified when she saw P's second publication. "How can this be," thought Q furiously, "how *can* this be?"

The answer is that Q had been schooled in the familywise philosophy. So she split α to .025 for both two-mean comparisons, between A_1 and A_2 and between A_3 and A_4. This gives a familywise α of .05, as already indicated. With α = .025, the criterial value of $F(1, 60)$ is 5.29, substantially larger than her observed Fs of 4.44 for each comparison. True, P also adhered to the familywise philosophy, but he ran only two conditions in each experiment, so he could use α = .05 in both.

Q did better work than P. She has more power, as shown by the error df. Also, such post hoc comparisons as A_1 versus A_3 are facilitated because they were run under the same experimental conditions. In P's experiment, in contrast, such comparisons are confounded with the inevitable differences between experiments done months apart (see analogously the discussion of Figure 5.1, page 120). As a matter of social efficiency, moreover, other workers would find it time-effective to read one publication by Q rather than two by P. Evidently Q is suffering because she did better work.

Should Q suffer for doing better work? Yes—if you adopt the familywise philosophy. Should P be reinforced for doing poorer work? Yes—if you adopt the familywise philosophy.

This parable of P and Q embodies an essential argument of the per comparison philosophy, emphasized especially by Duncan (1955). Adding conditions to your design usually improves its scope and informativeness. Why should you suffer for doing so, as the familywise philosophy requires?

17.1.5 TWO GUIDELINES ON MULTIPLE TESTS

Good control of the twin hazards of α escalation and β increase can be obtained with two guidelines noted briefly in Section 4.2.2: *planned comparisons* and *replication*. These are discussed in the next two subsections.

Planned Comparisons. Comparisons planned in advance—with a reasonably firm a priori basis—may be tested without any α adjustment for multiple tests; all may use the standard α level. This guideline is widely accepted (e.g., Cliff, 1996, p. 149; Cochran & Cox, 1957, p. 73; Estes, 1991, pp. 18-19; Fisher, 1960, p. 59; Hochberg & Tamhane, 1987, p. 6; Keppel, 1991, p. 165; Snedecor & Cochran, 1980, p. 232; and Winer, 1971, p. 196). Although it seems to transgress the familywise philosophy, it is sufficiently convincing that it has been accepted by some, though by no means all advocates of that philosophy.

The rationale for this guideline was indicated in the parable of P and Q. Since Q had explicitly planned her two tests in advance, she should not have used the familywise procedure. Both of her tests should have used $\alpha = .05$, the same as for P. This same guideline applies to factorial designs, which implicitly specify a separate F test for each main effect (see also Note 17.2a). In part, this guideline rests implicitly on the per comparison principle that adding conditions should not cause undue loss of power.

The first proviso, *planned in advance*, means that the comparisons are decided on before collecting the data. The second proviso, *reasonably firm a priori basis*, rules out blanket plans to make all possible two-mean comparisons or other passel of tests. In general, only a small number of comparisons will have a reasonably firm a priori basis. This basis may be empirical, from pilot work or a previous study; practical, to compare specific treatments in applied settings; or theoretical, deriving from some conceptual hypothesis. Keep in mind, of course, that each planned comparison is one possible false alarm, whether it be a source in a factorial design or a two-mean comparison.

Keep also in mind that planned comparisons can lead you into a mire. Planned comparisons intended to bring out an expected pattern are likely to bog down with an unexpected pattern. A shift to post hoc tests may then be necessary, with corresponding loss of confidence (see *Post Hoc Tests*, page 101). Too late, some procedure of multiple comparisons may then appear to have been a better choice, providing needed flexibility in place of the greater power presumed for the planned comparisons. Unless the planned comparisons have a sufficiently firm basis, therefore, it seems unwise to predicate them as the basis for analysis.

Multiple tests allow multiple chances for false alarms. This is a prestatistical fact of life that holds even if each test represents a different experiment. It holds somewhat more strongly when multiple tests are made within a single experiment, as with factorial design. The guideline of planned tests suffers this same threat. This guideline is an empirical rule of thumb, which attempts to strike a working compromise for the $\alpha-\beta$ tradeoff dilemma.

Replication. Replication is the sovereign medicine for α escalation. If the same result is statsig in two successive experiments, it seems unlikely to be a false alarm.

Replication has become standard in much experimental psychology (Section 2.4.6, pages 52*f*). This being so, it should be recognized in planning the data analysis. Ordinarily, each experiment must be analyzed individually. Among other reasons, replication typically involves changes in design and procedure, so successive experiments may not be readily comparable in statistical terms. Integrating results across two or three replication experiments, accordingly, must usually be done on an extrastatistical basis. Virtually all discussion of α escalation, however, has been in purely statistical terms, which obscures the paramount importance of replication.

It follows that the familywise philosophy is not generally appropriate when replication is planned. The familywise philosophy implicitly assumes that the single experiment must stand on its own. In its concern over possible false alarms in the single experiment, it sacrifices power to detect real effects. Replication provides far better protection against false alarms than any statistical procedure.

When replication is planned, a liberal false alarm policy may be desired in the initial experiment to avoid missing promising leads. Furthermore, the results of the initial experiment may justify the use of planned comparisons in the replication experiment, as discussed in the first guideline. When replication is planned, therefore, Student–Newman range procedure of Section 17.2.2 or even Fisher's LSD procedure deserve consideration.

A worthy feature of the replication approach is that the danger of false alarm in the initial result is shouldered by you, the investigator. Unless your replication is statsig, you may have lost your added investment. It is not enough to get a replication result in the same direction; that will happen half the time by chance. Before replication, therefore, a power calculation is desirable. As we saw in Chapter 4, the power of an exact replication of a just statsig result may be only .50. Even less power may obtain with a just statsig result found with the LSD procedure, for example, because of possible α escalation. Sometimes, of course, you would expect increased power from improvements in procedure, especially from reduction in error variability. You pay the price for replication, and you must make your own cost–benefit decision.

17.2 FAMILYWISE PROCEDURES

The term *family* refers to a set of tests that might be made. One common family is the set of all possible comparisons of two means in a one-way design. Other families could compare each of several experimental conditions with a control, or test specific differences predicted by a theory.[a]

A *familywise procedure* keeps the probability of one, *or more*, false alarms no higher than the prescribed value of α—for all the tests in the family taken together. Reversely, the probability of no false alarm among all the tests of the family is at least $1 - \alpha$.

17.2.1 FISHER α SPLITTING PROCEDURE

The α splitting procedure, already described, is simplicity itself. With K tests in the family, use α/K as the false alarm parameter for each test. Then the family-wise false alarm parameter will be at most $K \times \alpha/K = \alpha$.

To see the rationale, suppose the K tests are independent, all with H_0 true, with α split into K equal parts. For any one test, with H_0 true, the probability of a false alarm is α/K, and the probability of no false alarm is $1 - \alpha/K$. Since the tests are independent, the corresponding probability of no false alarm in the entire family of tests is the product of the separate probabilities, that is, $(1 - \alpha/K)^K$. Hence the probability of one-or-more false alarms is

$$1 - (1 - \alpha/K)^K, \quad \text{which can be shown to be at most } \alpha.$$

The α splitting procedure actually yields a familywise α less than that prescribed. With five independent tests, $1 - (1 - .05/5)^5 = 1 - .99^5 = .049$, not enough less than .05 to worry about. If the tests are not independent, α splitting is more conservative.

The α splitting procedure has notable flexibility. It may be used with any test statistic, including chi-square and correlation. Splitting need not be equal; if more power is desired for one particular test, it may be assigned a larger part of α. Confidence intervals for two-mean comparisons can be obtained with Expressions 1 of Chapter 4 (page 92), using the t^* or F^* for the split α (not for α itself). Splitting is not limited to two-mean comparisons; the K tests may also include trend tests and subset Anovas with more than a single df.[a]

Confidence dwindling goes hand-in-hand with α escalation, as may be illus-trated with α splitting. Confidence refers to the family of tests rather than the separate tests. With $\alpha = .05$ for a family of five tests, each individual test would be made with $\alpha = .01$. This does not entitle you to 99% confidence in anything. If all five tests are statsig, you may have 95% confidence that none is a false alarm. If just one is statsig, your allowable confidence is also 95%. Although each test was made with $\alpha = .01$, this includes protection against false alarms in the other tests. You are entitled to 95% confidence that there is no false alarm in the entire family—and hence entitled to the same confidence in any one test of the family. The cure for confidence dwindling is replication.

17.2.2 RANGE PROCEDURES

To illustrate the range logic, suppose you have a groups of subjects and wish to test between all possible pairs of means. Line up the means in rank order, as illustrated below. Begin by testing the overall range, that is, the difference between the largest and smallest means. If this overall range is not statsig, no two-mean difference can be statsig.

If this range is statsig, continue in the same way: Test the subrange between the largest and second smallest, and the subrange between the smallest and the second largest. And so on. Stop when any subrange is not statsig; no means within that subrange can be statsig different. Statistical details are given below.

A notable feature of this range logic is that each statsig difference localizes an effect. This avoids the ambiguity of the overall F, which may fail to localize any two-mean difference. Of special value, this range procedure partly lifts itself by its bootstraps. If any range is statsig, this information can be incorporated to provide a more powerful test at the next step. These two features have made the range concept a popular foundation for multiple comparisons.

Studentized Range Statistic. The range approach was pioneered by Student and Newman, who introduced the q statistic, now called the *Studentized range*:

$$q = \frac{\overline{Y}_{max} - \overline{Y}_{min}}{\sqrt{MS_{error}/n}}. \tag{1}$$

The form of q is similar to Student's t, except that the denominator is the standard deviation of a single mean. Hence $q = \sqrt{2}\, t$ for $a = 2$ conditions.

Conceptually, however, q differs from t because the two particular conditions in the numerator of Equation 1 are not specified a priori; instead, they are determined from inspection of the data. Hence the expected value of q increases as more conditions are added.

This important idea may be understood by considering a number of conditions, all with equal means. Get sample means for two of these conditions, and then add a third. This third mean will sometimes be less than, or greater than, both of the first two; the range of the three will then be larger than the range of the two. This is only a chance fluctuation, of course, since the true means are actually equal. But the q statistic embodies these chance fluctuations, so its sampling distribution steadily widens as more conditions are added.

To use the q statistic, therefore, requires knowledge of its sampling distribution under the null hypothesis of all equal true means. The criterial value $q*$ is then chosen so that the chance value of q from Equation 1 has greater magnitude than $q*$ just α of the time. With 40 df for error, the values of $q*$ are 2.86, 3.44,

3.79, and 4.04 for a = 2, 3, 4, and 5, respectively (see Table A4a, page 814). If the observed value of q exceeds q^* it is statsig.

What do you do next? The obvious tack is to continue in the same way, testing next the difference between the largest and second smallest means, and so on. To pursue this tack, however, requires a decision about what α level is to be used in these successive tests. Different statistical solutions have been proposed, the first being that of Newman.

Student–Newman Procedure. The range statistic used by Student and Newman has been most popular in later theory, and similar mechanics of calculation are used in other tests. Accordingly, Student–Newman procedure (commonly called the Newman–Keuls procedure) is illustrated here. It turns out, however, that it is not a strict familywise procedure.[a]

Suppose we have 5 groups of 9 subjects with means lined up in order:

A	B	C	D	E
1	4	15	17	20.

We assume MS_{error} = 144 on 40 df. The first step is to apply the Studentized range test to the largest mean difference, E – A:

$$q = \frac{\bar{Y}_{max} - \bar{Y}_{min}}{\sqrt{MS_{error}/n}} = \frac{20 - 1}{\sqrt{144/9}} = \frac{19}{4} = 4.75.$$

For a = 5 conditions and 40 error df, q^* = 4.04, as already listed. Since $q > q^*$, the difference between A and E is statsig.

The next two largest mean differences are E – B and D – A. The q values for these two subranges are calculated in the same way, yielding 4.00 and 4.00. The value of q^* is reduced, however, because these two subranges include only 4 means. For a = 4 conditions, q^* = 3.79, as already listed. Both qs are larger than q^* and thus statsig.

At the next step, there are three subranges, each with three means: C – A, D – B, and E – C. These are treated similarly, but with q^* = 3.44.

As this illustration shows, the criterial q^* is adjusted at each step. This adjustment follows a simple rule: q^* is chosen to set the false alarm parameter at the prescribed α—for the number of means in the subrange being tested. If the overall range is statsig in the first step, the null hypothesis that the largest and smallest true means are equal is rejected. At most four true means can be equal, therefore, so only this less stringent null hypothesis need be considered. Hence we can use a less stringent q^* because the range distribution will be narrower for four means than for five. This step-by-step decision tactic allows progressively smaller differences to be statsig at successive steps, as shown by the progressively smaller values of q^* already listed.

Testing stops when any subrange is not statsig. No differences within that subrange can be statsig. In the foregoing example, E − C is not statsig, so the two-mean comparisons, E − D and D − C, may not be tested. C − A is statsig, however, which allows tests of the C − B and B − A comparisons.

The final outcome is a separation of the means into subsets. Two means are statsig different only if they belong to no common subset. Some seeming ambiguity may thus arise. Suppose five means yielded the three subsets, {A, B, C}, {B, C, D}, and {E}. Then E differs from all the others and A differs from D. No other differences are statsig in this example.

A Familywise Pitfall. It might seem that Student–Newman procedure yields a familywise α. If all true means are equal, then $\bar{Y}_{max} - \bar{Y}_{min}$ will be nonstatsig with probability $1 - \alpha$. If this range is not statsig, no further tests are allowed. This range will falsely appear statsig with the prescribed α, but only in this case can some other mean difference be statsig. Although you may get more than one false alarm in some experiments, $1 - \alpha$ is still the probability of no false alarm—if all true means are equal.

This argument, however, overlooks the pitfall previously noted for Fisher's LSD test. As before, consider two widely separated pairs of equal true means. Tests that involve one mean from different pairs will be statsig, as is appropriate. Stepwise testing will proceed until the tests include means from only one pair. At that point, each pair yields an independent chance for false alarm. For this pattern of means, accordingly, the familywise α is not .05 but .0975. In short, Student–Newman procedure does not maintain a familywise α in the customary sense that was illustrated with α splitting.[b]

Newman–Ryan Procedure. A modification of Student–Newman procedure was originated by Ryan to obtain a strict familywise α. The sole difference is a more stringent q_1^* except at the two initial steps. Specifically, for a subrange that includes p means, the false alarm parameter is set at[c]

$$\alpha_p = \alpha, \quad p = a, \ a - 1;$$
$$\alpha_p = 1 - (1 - \alpha)^{p/a}, \quad p < a - 1. \tag{2}$$

The second equation yields a smaller false alarm parameter for shorter subranges. This specification of the false alarm parameter is more stringent than Student–Newman procedure, which sets $\alpha_p = \alpha$ for all p.

To illustrate, consider $a = 5$ means and a familywise α of .05. The first test for the overall range of 5 means would use q^* for $\alpha = .05$, exactly as with Student–Newman. The subsequent test for the two subranges of 4 means would also be the same. The two procedures diverge for subranges of 3 means. Student–Newman would continue using q^* for $\alpha_3 = .05$. In contrast, Newman–Ryan would choose q^* so that $\alpha_3 = 1 - .95^{3/5} = .030$, by Equation 2. For any subrange of 2 means, similarly, $\alpha_2 = .0253$. By using smaller α for shorter subranges, the α escalation does not exceed the prescribed α for the family.

If a familywise α is desired, Newman–Ryan procedure has much to recommend it. It employs the step-by-step decision tactic of Student–Newman in a way that is close to optimal. Other, more complicated procedures can provide a little more power and would be worth considering for an extended research program or a single expensive study (see *Multiple F Tests*, pages 541*f*). Newman-Ryan is available on standard statistical packages, however, and is easy enough by hand.

Tukey Procedure. Tukey procedure begins the same as Student–Newman, by calculating q from Equation 1. If $q > q_*^*$ the range is statsig. For any other mean difference, apply Equation 1 to calculate q. If this $q > q_*^*$ this mean difference is also statsig. Tukey procedure uses the same q^* at every step. This yields a familywise α—regardless of the pattern of true means.[d]

Tukey procedure, however, has limited usefulness because it uses the same q^* throughout. Newman–Ryan procedure, in contrast, uses a smaller q^* for shorter subranges. With $a > 3$, therefore, differences must be larger to be statsig with Tukey procedure, which thus has less power. Step-by-step procedures such as Newman–Ryan are called adaptive because they use the original Student–Newman idea of exploiting information at each step to increase power at subsequent steps.

Scheffé Test. The Scheffé test has two notable properties. First, it is much more general than the foregoing procedures of two-mean comparisons, for it maintains a familywise α on the family of all possible 1 df contrasts, including trend tests. Thus, you could compare the two largest with the three smallest means, using $c_j = 1/2, 1/2, -1/3, -1/3, -1/3$. Furthermore, these contrasts may be selected through post hoc inspection of the data. The Scheffé test is not strictly post hoc, however, for it is valid only if it has been explicitly selected beforehand.

The second notable property of the Scheffé test is that it has almost no practical value. The price of its great generality is great loss of power. If only two-mean comparisons were at issue, for example, Newman–Ryan procedure would be markedly more powerful. Trend tests would generally be few in number, better assessed with α splitting to get a familywise α. The same holds for other contrasts.

Despite this practical irrelevance, the Scheffé test is acclaimed in virtually every text presentation of multiple comparisons. One prominent text calls it "very popular" and "widely used." No doubt there are actual situations in which the Scheffé test would be optimal, but I have not yet seen one. I mention this as one more illustration of the lack of integration of empirics and statistics.[e]

Chapter 17

17.3 PER COMPARISON PROCEDURES

Per comparison procedures set α for a single comparison and allow this α to escalate when multiple comparisons are made. But with $a = 4$, the six possible two-mean comparisons escalate α from .05 to .20. Virtually everyone agrees this is too much.

Per comparison theory thus faces the perplexing problem of setting a good compromise for α escalation. Except for far-sighted work of Duncan (1955), this problem has been largely avoided by statisticians. However, Duncan's proposed rule for α escalation seems too liberal.

17.3.1 MULTIPLE COMPARISONS RATIONALE

The rationale for multiple comparisons given by Duncan seems essentially that of the foregoing *Parable*. Common usage agrees that P was justified in using $\alpha = .05$ for each of his two separate experiments. Since Q did identical work, she also should use $\alpha = .05$ for each separate test. Q received bad teaching to use α splitting. Q's data should not be penalized because she ran all four conditions in a single experiment; hers was superior design. This rationale is accepted by a substantial number of investigators, previously cited, who allow a per comparison α for planned comparisons.

It seems gradually being recognized that the familywise α of .05 is too stringent for one-way designs with considerably more than two conditions. Some advocates of the familywise approach have accordingly recommended familywise α as large as .20 and .25, which implicitly accords with the per comparison philosophy. This larger α should of course depend on the number of conditions, but no rule for this dependence is given. Duncan, in contrast, faced this problem and presented a rational rule.

17.3.2 TWO RULES FOR α ESCALATION

Duncan's Rule for α Escalation. Duncan's rationale for α rested on a cost–benefit analysis for hits and false alarms. With a conditions, $a - 1$ independent tests are possible, one for each df. Each test adds independent information, so the investigator should be willing to pay an additional price in risk of false alarms with more conditions. Duncan assumed that each false alarm would add a fixed cost, two false alarms being twice as costly as one, and so on. This additive loss function, embedded in a Bayesian type analysis, implied that the false alarm parameter should increase by the rule

$$\alpha_p = 1 - (1 - \alpha)^{p-1} \qquad \text{(Duncan's rule)} \qquad (3)$$

As above, α_p is the false alarm parameter for a subrange that includes p means. For two adjacent means, α_2 is usually taken as .05, as with Student–Newman procedure. For p = 3, 4, and 6, however, α_p = .0975, .1425, and .2262, respectively. The q value for each test is calculated from the same formula as for Student–Newman procedure, but a special table of $q*$ is required. For the overall range, therefore, Duncan uses a more liberal α than Student–Newman, in line with the foregoing rationale.

Duncan's rule has been fairly popular and is available in major computer packages. It is losing favor, however, in part because the maximal false alarm parameter seems disquietingly high, as with .2262 for six conditions, and in part because many writers now advocate a familywise philosophy. As a consequence, Duncan's qualitative arguments have been obscured. Thus, Miller (1981, pp. 88f) rejects Duncan's α_p rule of Equation 3 on the ground that the additive loss function is inappropriate. Given a family of comparisons, "The statistician wants to prevent *any* false statements under nullity [null hypothesis], and one or several incorrect statements should be regarded with just about the same amount of disfavor" (see similarly Hochberg & Tamhane, 1987).

Miller's argument stems from a conceptualization of multiple comparisons that has statistical tractability at the expense of empirical relevance. Contrary to Miller, several false alarms would seem markedly more serious than one in most experimental applications. Miller takes for granted that multiple comparisons involves situations in which one false alarm is fatal so more are no worse. Such situations do exist, but they are not frequent.

Miller makes a second criticism of Duncan's procedure on the ground that the hypotheses in a multiple comparisons test are not generally independent or unrelated in a substantive sense and that Duncan's procedure thus confounds statistical with substantive independence, an argument seconded by Hochberg and Tamhane (1987, p. 70). This extrastatistical criticism seems well taken—applicable generally to multiple comparisons procedures. It does not, however, disagree with the per comparison principle that the maximal possible false alarm parameter should increase with the number of conditions, although not necessarily as much as Duncan assumes.

One-for-Two Rule. The per comparison principle may be more acceptable if coupled with some more conservative rule for α escalation. One alternative in the same spirit would allow a unit increment in the false alarm parameter for each *two* added groups. This would yield

$$\alpha_p = 1 - (1 - \alpha)^{p/2} \quad \text{(one-for-two rule)} \tag{4}$$

For p = 3, 4, and 6, this one-for-two rule yields α_p = .0741, .0975, and .1425, respectively, considerably less than for Duncan's rule.

This rule of one df for each two conditions seems reasonable. The first two conditions yield 1 df. Two additional conditions ought to be equally valuable.

Student–Newman Procedure. Student–Newman procedure is not strictly a per comparison procedure because it uses the standard α at every step. In contrast, per comparison approaches set a reference α for the final step of comparing two adjacent means, and use an escalated α to test the overall range at the first step. The α for the overall range at the first step thus depends on the number of means.

This point may be illustrated for four conditions by comparing Student–Newman procedure with the one-for-two rule. For both, the final step of comparing subranges of two adjacent means would use the customary α, say, .05. For the first step, which compares the smallest and largest means, the two respective αs are then .05 and .0975. The one-for-two rule thus has more power than Student–Newman procedure. Both, however, have the same familywise α of .0975.

17.4 PROBLEMS IN MULTIPLE COMPARISONS

Several other problems of multiple comparisons require comment.

17.4.1 VALIDITY CONDITIONS FOR MULTIPLE COMPARISONS

The Anova assumptions of Chapter 3 are also required in multiple comparisons procedures. These assumptions will not be reconsidered here (see especially the discussion of unequal variance in Table 4.1, page 97).

Two other conditions are required for a valid outcome. First, which procedure to use must be decided before looking at the data. Otherwise there will be a tendency to select a procedure favorable to the observed pattern.

Second, the family of tests that might possibly be made must also be specified beforehand, even though only a few of these tests may actually be performed. In some cases, the family is implicit in the procedure, as with the family of all pair comparisons in Student–Newman procedure. With α splitting, however, the tests must be explicitly itemized beforehand.

17.4.2 FAMILYWISE SITUATIONS

Some situations require familywise α. As a prototypical example, consider a test of whether any of several new medical treatments should replace a standard current treatment. In this situation, any false alarm is undesirable; two are hardly worse than one. Hence the α level should not be allowed to increase as the number of new candidate treatments increases. This example epitomizes the familywise premise that the number of false alarms greater than one is largely irrelevant. This is why familywise procedures define the false alarm parameter in terms of one-*or-more* false alarms.

Tests of theoretical hypotheses sometimes require a familywise procedure. The Yerkes–Dodson "law," for example, asserts that performance increases to a maximum as motivation increases, but then decreases as motivation becomes higher than optimal. A number of other theories also predict inverted-U curves. In experimental tests, the ascending segment of the curve is typically clear.

The critical question is whether the final segment of the curve shows a real downtrend. Typically, the final segment is irregular and its trend uncertain. A comparison of the highest point and the last point of the final segment is clearly biased; it capitalizes on what chances to be highest.

A valid test can be obtained with multiple comparisons. Specify beforehand the segment of the curve over which the downtrend is expected. Then compare all pairs of means on this specified segment using a familywise α, as with Newman–Ryan procedure. Any statsig two-mean decrease implies a real decrease, which supports the inverted-U shape (see similarly Note 18.3.2b).[a]

A difficult α–β tradeoff dilemma arises in screening potentially useful drugs against carcinogenic side-effects (see Shaffer, 1995; Westfall & Young, 1993). From 15 to 50 different tissue sites may be monitored for cancer in experimental animals, with cross-site correlations positive but low. It is important to detect real carcinogenic effects at any site, which argues for a liberal false alarm policy. On the other hand, an α of .05 for each test would yield a familywise α upward of .50; numerous expensive false alarms would be possible and probable. Replication is expensive, even infeasible; a single study may consume two years with a substantial N and extensive laboratory analyses. This kind of situation has no easy solution.

Studies that make numerous tests are obviously susceptible to false alarms. One example comes from a study purporting to show that dietary supplement of vitamins and minerals raised nonverbal IQ scores by several points in just three months. Confidence in this claim begins to vanish upon learning that 87 comparisons were made between experimental and control groups, of which only seven were statsig, little more than chance (see critique by Blinkhorn, 1991; see also Exercise 18.e2).

This last example raises a general problem. With numerous comparisons, a strict familywise approach has so little power as to be nearly worthless. One possible solution is to choose beforehand a small set of important comparisons and apply a familywise procedure to these. Perhaps this small set should be specified in writing before looking at the data. Other comparisons could be made post hoc and presented as exploratory hints. On the whole, however, replication may be the only solution (see also split-half replication below).

This brief list of situations is included to indicate the extreme diversity of concerns that empirical workers face in dealing with the α–β tradeoff dilemma. Instructive examples are given by Hochberg and Tamhane (1987, pp. 12-16) and Shaffer (1995). Westfall and Young (1993, Chapter 7) devote 50-some pages to a variety of practical applications, including some data analyses based on their promising bootstrap approach.

For many of these situations, a per comparison approach seems out of place. Although such situations are not frequent in experimental psychology, they do arise in other areas. The present advocacy of per comparison philosophy should be understood in the context to which it is directed, namely, the ordinary run of experimental studies.

17.4.3 SPLIT-HALF REPLICATION

Replication, a cure-all for α escalation, is not always possible. Medical records, census surveys, and other historical data, for example, may be limited to archival records. Large-scale questionnaire studies, similarly, may be nonreplicable for lack of funds or opportunity.

In such situations, a split-half form of replication can be obtained by splitting the available data, doing initial data dredging on one part, checking validity with the other part. In discussing a similar procedure for multiple regression, Mosteller and Tukey (1977) recommend intensely that data dredging of the first part be done in total ignorance of data in the second part (Section 16.1.2, page 491).

Even replication has a limitation when numerous tests are made. Suppose data dredging yielded 20 statsig results, of which only 2 remained statsig (.05) in the second analysis. Obviously, not much credence can be placed in these two results. It would thus seem desirable to apply extrastatistical considerations to prune the data dredging considerably before proceeding to the second stage. For example, only results that appear important would be retained for assessment in the second analysis. The pruned results need not be completely abandoned; they could be retained in a secondary class and those that remain statsig in the second analysis presented under a suitable label, such as *Post Hoc Hints*. With enough data and numerous tests, split-third replication may be advisable.

17.4.4 FURTHER PROBLEMS WITH MULTIPLE COMPARISONS

Multiple Measures. Radical α escalation can occur when multiple measures are made for each subject or case. Each measure that is tested separately provides additional opportunity for a false alarm. Combinations of several measures may also be tested, which yields additional α escalation, especially from combining measures that lean in the same direction. Still further escalation can be produced by considering subgroups of subjects, classified according to age, gender, socioeconomic status, and so forth. This kind of data dredging has been automated with selection procedures built into standard statistical routines, especially multiple regression.

Questionnaire studies generally include multiple items, with many opportunities for data dredging, as with personality inventories. Health, similarly, has numerous medical and psychological aspects that may be of concern. Such investigations often face difficult problems of α escalation (see quote in *Post Blocking*, page 414). In some of these situations, Manova could help by reducing the multiple measures to one (Section 18.4.2, pages 575*ff*).

Multiple comparison procedures have limited usefulness with multiple measures. To impose a familywise α would often destroy the exploratory potential of data dredging. Often, moreover, the family of possible data dredging analyses is more or less unlimited and cannot be specified beforehand.

The exploratory potential of data dredging can be preserved: *Replicate*.

Replication is standard in test construction, which ordinarily goes through several stages of item analysis and validation. Replication should similarly be standard in studies involving multiple measures, split-half replication at a minimum. Replication may be inconvenient or difficult, but without replication the work may well be worthless.

Post Hoc Analysis. The data should always be scrutinized for unexpected results; these may be the most interesting and important. But they may also be chance accidents, to which data snooping is especially vulnerable. The initial chapter by Diaconis in *Exploring Data Tables, Trends, and Shapes* (Hoaglin, Mosteller, & Tukey, 1985), is a cautionary of such statistical accidents that betrayed those who reported them as real. This book also gives enlightening perspective on real problems of exploratory data analysis in diverse domains very different from experimental psychology (Section 4.2.2, pages 99*ff*).[a]

Factorial Design. Main effects in factorial designs are readily amenable to multiple comparisons procedures. The row means, for example, would be treated as a one-way design, all but this one factor being ignored. With this analysis, Anova would only be used to get an overall MS_{error}. Each main effect is usually treated as a separate family, so the effective α for the experiment as a whole would escalate with the number of factors (Note 17.2a).

To localize interaction residuals, familywise α is ill-suited. A statsig residual, F_{AB}, implies that the measured effect of factor A depends on the level of B. To localize this dependence requires comparisons among cell means. Even a modest 3×4 design has 12 means, which yields 66 two-mean comparisons alone. Splitting .05 into 66 parts yields an α less than .001 for each comparison, so stringent as to make the tests practically powerless. The number of necessary comparisons can be reduced in various ways, but none is especially satisfactory. Of course, interaction residuals present more basic difficulties of meaningfulness, discussed in Chapter 7.

Multiple F Tests. Some multiple comparisons procedures use F instead of the Studentized range, q. This can give more power because F utilizes information in the entire pattern of means. Whereas the range between the largest and smallest depends only indirectly on the intervening means, F depends directly on all the means. Accordingly, multiple F tests may be expected to be more powerful. Moreover, they take unequal n in stride.

Unfortunately, multiple F tests are not simple to use. Localization depends on interrelations among Fs for subranges of means of all sizes, from a down to 2. Calculations are complicated and multiple F procedures have not been available in standard packages. However, investigators who routinely require familywise procedures and who need every last bit of power may wish to consider these tests, especially the Peritz procedure (Hochberg & Tamhane, 1987; Shaffer, 1995; Toothaker, 1991).

Confidence Intervals. Confidence intervals are problematic with multiple comparisons. With four equal true means, the ordinary t test between the largest and smallest means at $\alpha = .05$ actually has probability .20 of being statsig. Equivalently, the usual 95% confidence interval provides only 80% confidence for this particular comparison, although more confidence for means less far apart. In general, confidence dwindles with multiple comparisons in the same way that α escalates.

With α splitting, familywise confidence intervals can be obtained as noted in Section 17.2.1. These are *simultaneous* confidence intervals, which allow $(1 - \alpha)$ confidence that all intervals contain their true values. However, few multiple comparisons procedures allow simultaneous confidence intervals (Note 17.2.2d). Owing to statistical complications, confidence intervals for stepwise range procedures have not been developed.

Some visual indication of error variability is generally desirable, but the usual confidence intervals will be misleading; they will imply statsig results not justified with any of the foregoing procedures. Accordingly, I suggest presenting error bars, that is, one standard deviation of the mean or mean difference, as a helpful descriptive statistic.

17.4.5 THE TWO PHILOSOPHIES

How to handle the $\alpha-\beta$ tradeoff dilemma with multiple comparisons procedures depends on costs and benefits of hits, misses, and false alarms in each particular situation. Familywise philosophy seems questionable for general use because it assumes that more than one false alarm is little or no worse than one (see foregoing quote from Miller) and because it takes no account of benefits and costs of additional hits and misses. Familywise philosophy thus rejects the per comparison principle that adding conditions should ordinarily increase the false alarm parameter to balance costs of added misses and benefits of added hits.

Worst Possible Null Hypothesis. Fear of the worst case governs the familywise philosophy. However unlikely this worst case may be, it causes loss of power on other cases that may generally be expected in empirical practice.

With six conditions, Student–Newman uses the same α (.05) throughout. In contrast, Newman–Ryan uses progressively smaller α for shorter subranges, thereby guarding against the worst possible null hypothesis, namely, three pairs of equal true means. With widely separated pairs, both procedures will find the real effects. With less widely separated pairs, Newman–Ryan has less power on the real effects because it uses a smaller α for three and two means (.0253 and .0170, respectively). More seriously, the progressively smaller α loses power for every case but the worst possible. This shortcoming afflicts all familywise procedures.

The more liberal Student–Newman procedure seems the more reasonable in that the later steps will be reached only if the earlier steps have revealed real differences, in particular, the first and second steps for which both procedures use the same α. Granted that some real differences exist, further localization may be desirable even with some further risk.

Guarding against the worst possible case is essential in some situations, already discussed in Section 17.4.2. For most experimental studies, however, the attendant loss of power seems dubious compensation (see also recommendation by Miller in Note 17.2.2b).

Planned Comparisons. The guideline of planned comparisons provides some common ground for the two philosophies. Each factor in a factorial design obviously represents a planned comparison. This is recognized by most familywise advocates, who treat each main effect as a separate family.

This per factor α seems reasonable. Consider a 2×2 design, with a major variable plus a minor variable, such as subject gender, which is balanced in the design. Not many argue for a strict familywise approach, which would split α into three parts, one for each main effect and one for the interaction residual. Power on the major variable should not be reduced because the minor variable is included. The standard α is also appropriate for the minor variable, and would be no less appropriate if the second variable was major.

In the foregoing parable, Q had four conditions. Anova on these four conditions would be inappropriate, of course, because Q had two specific hypotheses. A range test would be similarly inappropriate. Q naturally went straight to her two planned comparisons. I see no reason she should split her α, any more than with the factorial design just considered. This guideline of planned comparisons is accepted fairly widely, as already cited.

As a less clear-cut case, consider four experimental conditions, all of approximately equal interest, so that all two-mean comparisons should be allowed for. Making t tests on all six pairs of means escalates α from .05 to .20, which seems hardly acceptable. An overall F can indicate real differences, but provides limited localization. A range procedure, however, begins with one two-mean comparison and opens the way to further localization.

But these four conditions were chosen by some plan, no less than with the cited 2 × 2 design. It seems inconsistent, therefore, to accept the guideline of planned comparisons for the factorial design, with a combined false alarm parameter of nearly 3α, but deny it totally by allowing only one family for the one-way design. Student–Newman procedure and the one-for-two rule hold the false alarm parameter to a maximum of 2α, the same as for the combined main effects in the two-way design.

Per Comparison Principle. The per comparison principle states that an increase in the number of experimental conditions should be accompanied by an increase of overall α. This principle is generally accepted if the added conditions appear in a separate experiment, as with P in the foregoing parable. This principle is also accepted by many for planned comparisons in a single experiment, as with factorial design or with Q's design in the foregoing parable.

In fact, the guideline of planned comparisons is justified by this per comparison principle. Usually, additional planned tests add conditions to the design. Planned tests thus represent experimental labor to obtain relevant data, not post hoc snooping through data already at hand.

The same principle should apply to a one-way design in which the investigator desires to compare every pair of means. But this extension is denied by the familywise philosophy, which postulates that α must be set for the family of all possible two-mean comparisons, and which therefore imposes a smaller α, sometimes much smaller, on individual tests of interest. Some less stringent α–β compromise seems desirable, for example, the one-for-two rule.

It deserves reemphasis that each condition in a typical experiment represents a substantial investment and represents a definite plan. It is not as though another question was added to a questionnaire. In typical experiments, therefore, the per comparison principle seems appropriate even though the analysis relies on a range procedure for the family of all two-mean comparisons.

Familywise α. The important difference between the two philosophies is whether adding more conditions should usually be accompanied by an increase in the maximal possible false alarm rate. The per comparison philosophy says *yes*; the familywise philosophy says *no*, often qualified by treating each planned test as a separate family.

Some familywise advocates qualify even further by proposing familywise α as high as .25 (e.g., Hochberg & Tamhane, 1987, p. 11; Keppel, 1995, pp. 179f; Toothaker, 1991, p. 85). This proposal stems from realization that a familywise α of .05 loses too much power at later steps in range procedures. The critical shortcoming of these proposals is the failure to give any rule for how this α should depend on the number of conditions. A familywise α of .25 may be appropriate with eight means, but surely not with four.

If a larger familywise α is to be used, its size should obviously depend on the number of conditions. But recognizing the need for such a rule is equivalent to recognizing the per comparison philosophy.[a]

Experimental Analysis. Cost–benefit analysis of possible false alarms, hits, and misses is essential for prudent behavior with multiple comparisons. Such analysis is implicit in the standard practice of using separate α for each main effect in factorial designs and similarly for the guideline of planned comparisons. Cost–benefit analysis is the essential rationale for the per comparison principle that adding conditions should ordinarily increase the familywise α.[b]

The problem of multiple comparisons is limited in most experiments because even six levels of a variable is unusual, whether for a one-way design or main effect in a factorial design. With three conditions, it is certainly wrong to make all two-mean comparisons with the standard α. But no α escalation occurs in this case if a statsig F is followed by all two-mean comparisons (Exercise 13). Variables with more than three levels are often ordered or metric, and a linear trend may obviate any need for pairwise comparisons.

Thus, multiple comparisons procedures only become relevant with four or more unordered factor levels. With four levels, Student–Newman procedure and the one-for-two rule both hold the familywise α to .0975, which seems reasonable on the per comparison principle. With six levels, both have familywise α of .1425, about half the .25 suggested by cited advocates of familywise philosophy. Experiments with more than six unordered levels are rare.

Serious problems of α escalation do arise in some classes of investigations. This has already been indicated with multiple measures, questionnaire studies, data dredging, and so forth. In these cases, unfortunately, familywise procedures are often ineffectual because of low power. The main guiding light is the principle of replication, which deserves attention by statisticians.

17.4.6 SUMMARY RECOMMENDATIONS

The guideline of planned comparisons and the principle of replication suffice to handle most problems with multiple comparisons that arise in experimental analysis. Beyond that, two recommendations may be made. First, to obtain a strict familywise α for all possible two-mean comparisons, Newman–Ryan seems a practical best for the reasons given earlier. If only a few tests are planned, however, α splitting may give more power. Variant procedures can offer small advantages, especially multiple F procedures, but these may not be worth the time to learn and evaluate.

Second, a per comparison approach seems appropriate for most experiments that require multiple comparisons. Student–Newman has practical virtue. For those who agree with per comparison philosophy, Duncan's rule or its more conservative one-for-two modification deserve consideration.

NOTES

17.1.2a. The α splitting procedure is credited to Fisher by Emerson (1991a, p. 184), Hochberg and Tamhane (1987, pp. 3-4), and Kendall and Stuart (1976, p. 44).

17.2a. The term *family* does not have a satisfactory definition, a basic ambiguity in the familywise philosophy. As one example, each main effect in a factorial design is commonly considered a separate family since each may represent a quite different variable. A 2×2 design would thus have two families, each allotted its own α, plus a third family for the interaction residual. The effective α for the four conditions is thus close to 3α. Statisticians have largely ignored this α escalation by restricting attention to one-way design. Even with one-way designs, however, the term *family* is vague because each planned comparison may be treated as a separate family. Exactly what the familywise approach means is thus somewhat vague.

17.2.1a. The α splitting procedure for a family of two-mean comparisons can be improved as follows. Order the K comparisons by numerical magnitude and test the largest at α/K. If this is statsig, test the second at $\alpha/(K-1)$. And so on. See Holm's sequentially adaptive procedure in Kirk (1995, p. 142) and Toothaker (1991, pp. 63-65).

17.2.2a. Newman (1939, pp. 20-21) gives warm credit to Student for the idea and practice of testing the range. Calling this Student–Newman procedure thus seems appropriate. Essentially the same procedure was published in 1952 by Keuls (see Hochberg & Tamhane, 1987, p. 66; Miller, 1981, p. 81), which does not seem to justify calling it the Newman–Keuls test, as is often done.

17.2.2b. Student–Newman procedure is recommended in Miller's (1981, p. 88) statistical monograph, even though it does not yield a familywise α:

> The Newman–Keuls [Student–Newman] levels provide a high degree of protection for the entire null hypothesis (viz., α), and this is the multiple range test this author favors. Moreover, it does not suffer from the overconservatism of the Tukey test caused by utilizing just a single critical value.

This recommendation by a prominent exponent of familywise procedures deserves mention because Student–Newman procedure has been harshly critized by quite a number of psychologists who advocate strict familywise procedures.

17.2.2c. Ryan's modification to make Student–Newman procedure a true familywise procedure received minor refinements by others, and these are included in Equation 2. This procedure has thus acquired variant names in different statistical packages.

17.2.2d. Tukey procedure allows a $(1-\alpha)$ confidence interval for the largest-minus-smallest mean difference. A confidence interval of the same width for any smaller mean difference will provide no less confidence. These latter intervals are too wide, of course, which reflects the conservatism of Tukey procedure. Student–Newman and Newman–Ryan procedures could be used to construct simultaneous confidence intervals in exactly the same way, using q^* from the first step in place of t^* in Expression 2 of Chapter 2. These are similarly too large at later steps and may fail to show statsig differences obtained by these procedures.

17.2.2e. Numerous multiple comparisons procedures are detailed by Kirk (1995, Chapter 4) as well as by Toothaker (1991), who also reviews power studies. Dunnett's test deserves mention for it provides a familywise α for comparing each of several experimental groups with a single control.

17.4.2a. Even with a small number of means, familywise α may be required to test theoretical predictions. The example of Anderson (1982, pp. 218f) is of interest since it may be the only test of the double cancellation property of conjoint measurement (Notes 21.6.3a,b) that used appropriate statistical analysis instead of weak inference.

A second example appears in Estes' (1991, pp. 50f) attempt to test a hypothesis of skewed-U shape for short-term serial memory: Correct recall over four serial positions should be highest at the last position, next highest at first position, and lowest at second position: $P_2 < P_3 < P_1 < P_4$. A valid test is given by α splitting; all three inequalities should be statsig at the $\alpha/3$ level.

Estes' analysis was inappropriate. He tested the contrast defined by the comparison coefficients $c_j = 1, -2, -1, 2$ (Section 18.2), which embody the hypothesized skewed-U shape. The fatal flaw is that patterns inconsistent with the theoretical hypothesis will also yield a nonzero contrast. The straight-line pattern of means, 40, 50, 60, 70, yields $\psi = 20$, although no dip appears at second position; the pattern, 40, 60, 50, 70, yields $\psi = 10$, although this pattern violates two of the three predicted inequalities.

Estes' approach failed to test goodness of fit, but instead relied on weak inference (Sections 20.2.2 and 20.2.3, pages 655ff). The theoretical hypothesis specifies the rank order of all four means; a one df contrast is necessarily inadequate.

17.4.4a. "Internal analysis" is an especially treacherous form of post hoccery. A flagrant example appeared in Schachter's activation theory of emotion, which rested almost entirely on two experiments, both of which failed to support the theory until post hoc, "internal analysis" was used to eliminate substantial proportions of discordant subjects (see last subsection of Section 8.1.5, page 237).

17.4.5a. Some writers have argued for the familywise approach on the ground that it provides a known α. This argument is misleading. The familywise α is only an upper bound, operative only for the worst possible null hypothesis. In any particular case, the operative α may be much less.

Furthermore, per comparison procedures also have a familywise α, namely, their α for the worst possible null hypothesis. But this familywise α depends on the number of conditions, thus avoiding this shortcoming of familywise philosophy.

17.4.5b. Implicitly, familywise philosophy rests on the cost–benefit rationale that false alarms beyond the first have zero cost. The proposals to use an α as high as .25 are an awkward reaction to this overstringent rationale.

Attempts to develop cost–benefit rationale are reviewed in Chapter 13 of Hochberg and Tamhane (1987), but all these assume an additive loss function, just as in Duncan (1955). The one-for-two rule for α escalation implies a cost-benefit rationale that each false alarm beyond the first costs half as much more. This rationale takes account of Miller's criticism of Duncan's additive loss function on the ground that added conditions generally involve some substantive redundancy.

EXERCISES FOR CHAPTER 17

1. How can a single experiment produce multiple false alarms? Multiple false alarms *and* multiple misses?

2. In the numerical example of Student–Newman range test, verify that the final outcome is the separation of the means into the following three subsets, each of which contains means that are not statsig different.

$$\{A, B\}, \quad \{B, C, D\}, \quad \text{and} \quad \{C, D, E\}.$$

   a. Which two-mean comparisons are statsig?

   b. You notice that the means seem to fall into two clusters, $\{A, B\}$ and $\{C, D, E\}$. Use the formula in Note 4.1.1b to get 14.83 ± 7.38 as a 95% confidence interval for the difference between the means of the two clusters. How much confidence do you have that this clustering is real?

3. You test four experimental conditions but the overall Anova falls somewhat short of statsig. However, your research assistant points out that your four experimental conditions form a clear a priori rank order and suggests that a linear trend test would be most effective. What do you do?

4. a. Show that the one-for-two rule of Section 17.3.2 yields $\alpha_3 = .074$ for $a = 3$ conditions. Compare with Student–Newman procedure.

5. In the familywise test of inverted-U shape (Section 17.4.2):

   a. What is the null hypothesis? Why is this null hypothesis appropriate?

   b. What is the familywise α if H_0 is true?

   c. Suppose the expected maximum condition had not been specified beforehand, but selected by inspection of the data. Why exactly would this invalidate the analysis? What modification is needed in this case?

   d. Would you have any preference between Newman–Ryan and Tukey procedures for this question of inverted U shape?

6. With one-way design, a statsig range always demonstrates a two-mean difference, whereas a statsig F says only that not all true means are equal with little information about which means differ from which. Hence a range procedure such as Student–Newman might seem preferable to the overall F. Although the range procedures may have a little less power in most situations, they go beyond the overall F to say which means differ from which.

   So: Why not make range procedures standard and forget about overall Anova? As a bonus, much material of previous chapters could be omitted; learning statistics would be much easier. What reason can you see for retaining the overall F for one-way designs?

7. You have a 3×4 design for which it is important to make two-mean comparisons for each main effect.

    a. Is it valid to ignore main effect Anovas and instead apply a range procedure to each main effect? What are the pros and cons?

    b. Range procedures are not useful with interaction residuals. Do you think it is valid to use the range procedure for main effects, and then use the overall Anova to test the interaction residuals?

8. In your undergraduate honors course in experimental analysis, one of your student teams reports a term experiment with four conditions, $n = 11$, in which a test between the largest and smallest means is statsig, $t = 2.37$, compared to $t*(40) = 2.02$. This test seems clearly post hoc to you. In fact, their report explicitly says that the test was made by selecting the largest and smallest means because that was where a real difference was most likely to be!

    a. What is the operative α level of their analysis?

    b. Using $q = \sqrt{2}\, t$, how large would their t have to be to be statsig?

    c. How do you handle this in grading their paper?

9. Justify the assertion "Obviously, not much credence can be placed in these two results" (last paragraph of Section 17.4.3.)

10. Justify "When α is reduced for each separate test, the miss rate, β, necessarily increases" in Section 17.1.3.

11. P planned six comparisons of which only one was statsig. Why do the five nonstatsig comparisons cast doubt on the one statsig? How should P handle this matter?

12. The critical first step in judging whether Hamilton or Madison had written the disputed papers in *The Federalist* (Section 19.1.3) was to find features of writing style that discriminated between the two in essays of known authorship. Why is there a problem of α escalation here? How would you handle it?

13. Show that Fisher's (protected) LSD procedure maintains a familywise α for $a = 3$. (Consider all three possible combinations of equal and unequal true means.)

14. With five experimental conditions, each with $n = 9$, Q applies Student–Newman range procedure and obtains $q = 3.97$ for the largest mean difference. What will she do now?

15. In the pitfall with Fisher's LSD procedure cited in Section 17.1.2, why is the false alarm parameter for the family nearly 2α?

Preface

Everyone recognizes the need to go beyond the significance test, especially to assess size and importance of effects. Unfortunately, most of the popular statistical indexes for assessing size and importance of effects not only fail to illuminate but actually obscure the data. This is not surprising since size and importance usually need to be assessed in empirical, extrastatistical terms. This issue is discussed in Section 18.1 on size and importance and continued in Section 18.3 on curve shape.

One useful way to go beyond the significance test is with the mean-plus-confidence interval. Section 18.2 presents this approach to analysis of contrasts designed to test specific effects.

Section 18.4 takes up the following seven topics.

1. *Concept of Validity.* This section relates the discussion of validity begun in Section 1.2 to two major positions, one from test theory, one from quasi-experimental design. Neither position suffices for experimental analysis.

2. *Multivariate Analysis of Variance.* Multivariate analysis of variance is a needed tool to handle multiple different measures on each subject. For common repeated measures designs, however, ε-adjusted Anova is generally preferable.

3. *Partial Analysis.* Valuable simplification of multi-factor design can be obtained by using extrastatistical knowledge systems to strike out most of the high-way statistical interaction residuals.

4. *Pooling.* Pooling interaction terms with error is sometimes appropriate when done a priori, but only in exceptional circumstances when done post hoc.

5. *Regression Artifact.* The ubiquitous, insidious regression artifact needs to be understood by everyone; see especially the Exercises.

6. *Multiplication Model for Repeated Measures.* With repeated measures variables, transformation of the data has a twofold potential benefit: Transformation can increase the size of the effect and also decrease the error term.

7. *General Linear Model.* All most of us need to know about the general linear model in 1½ easy pages.

Chapter 18

SUNDRY TOPICS

18.1 SIZE AND IMPORTANCE OF EFFECTS [a]

If the data analysis shows evidence for a real effect, natural next questions are: How big is the effect? How important is it? A significance test can provide evidence that the observed effect is real, not merely response variability, but this is a minor aspect of understanding the data.

Statistics texts, accordingly, have felt a need to go beyond tests of significance to consider size and importance. Numerical statistical indexes have been developed in attempts to answer these two questions.

Unfortunately, most indexes proposed to measure size and importance have little value. Size and importance are primarily substantive issues; to evaluate size and importance generally requires some substantive standard of comparison. Statistical indexes find it awkward or impossible to incorporate substantive standards. Instead of clarifying, they often obscure the data.[b]

Three kinds of size–importance indexes have been considered. The obvious kind looks at mean differences, and this kind is naturally useful. The second looks at percentages of variance, and the third refers to a mathematical model. These three are considered in Sections 18.1.2 to 18.1.4, following a preliminary overview in terms of the process–outcome distinction.

18.1.1 PROCESS AND OUTCOME

The process–outcome distinction of Section 1.2.1 gives a useful perspective on the size–importance issue: A small effect can be important, both for process and for outcome. But importance must be assessed in substantive, extra-statistical terms, although for different reasons in the two cases.

Outcome Studies. A typical outcome study uses a measure with intrinsic outcome validity: frequency of auto accidents; cure rates for a drug; effectiveness of care programs in pregnancy on babies' health. These measures have cash value, so to speak, a relevant yardstick for assessing effect size.

Small outcome effects can be important when they add up over a large population. A small effect in a single subject may be a large effect for the population. A small increase in cure rate for a rare disease remains a small effect, but a small increase in babies' health becomes a big effect when summed over many babies. Meaningful measures of size and importance must thus be interpreted in terms of empirical application.[a]

Process Studies. Process studies require a different framework for evaluating size and importance. A key point is that experimental situations are often contrived to isolate and reveal some process. One of many examples is infants' adaptation to visual patterns, measured by time spent looking at subsequent test patterns. Such studies have revealed remarkable perceptual organization, previously unsuspected, at very young ages. A few seconds looking time may be a small effect, but it can have high importance as an indicator of innate perceptual organization (e.g., Note 8.1.2d, page 252).

Process studies, as this example illustrates, often focus on some delimited task that satisfies criteria discussed in relation to the Experimental Pyramid of Chapter 1. Other examples include Pavlov's salivary reflex, Skinner's bar press, single-neuron recording, response times in search tasks, the trait adjective task in person cognition, and many, many more.

The importance of process findings is to be found in a network of empirical results and conceptual interpretation. Assessing size and importance is thus largely conceptual, dependent on substantive knowledge systems for the domain under study. Statistical indexes often obscure this central problem.

18.1.2 MEAN VALUE INDEXES

Mean Difference. The natural—and best—index of size for typical experimental studies is the differences between means. Assessment of size and importance should focus on the table or graph of means. The pattern of means reveals the effects of the experimental manipulations; this pattern is the base for understanding the substantive meaning of the data. Such understanding requires a substantive, empirical framework to interpret the pattern of means.

Confidence Interval. An observed mean difference, $(\overline{Y}_1 - \overline{Y}_2)$, is an unreliable estimate of the true difference, $(\mu_1 - \mu_2)$. It is often desirable, therefore, to supplement the mean difference with its confidence interval, which allows better assessment of the true difference.

The mean-plus-confidence interval is also a helpful clue about power. If 0 is just outside the confidence interval, the result is just statsig, which means that power of an exact replication is about .50 (Exercise 11 of Chapter 4).

Standardized Power Effect Size. Power calculations require an index of empirical effect size for any number of means. This need is served by the standard deviation of the means:

$$\sigma_A = \sqrt{\sum (\mu_j - \bar{\mu})^2 / a} = \sqrt{\sum \alpha_j^2 / a}. \tag{1}$$

Thus, σ_A is an average of the differences among the treatment means, expressed in terms of the relative treatment effects, α_j. With just two means, Equation 1 yields $\sigma_A = \frac{1}{2} | \mu_1 - \mu_2 |$.

Power calculations must take account of error variability, of course, as in the power formula of Equation 4 of Section 4.3, page 102:

$$f = \frac{\sigma_A}{\sigma_\varepsilon}. \tag{2}$$

This f index may be called the power effect size or, more correctly, the *standardized* power effect size.

Note that standardization changes the empirical index of Equation 1 into the statistical index of Equation 2. Whereas σ_A has the same unit as the measured behavior, the unit of f is unreliability (standard deviation, σ_ε). Standardized power effect size should not be confused with empirical effect size, for the two are measured on conceptually different scales.

Alternative Definition of Standardized Power Effect Size. For the special case of two means, the formula

$$d = \frac{| \mu_1 - \mu_2 |}{\sigma_\varepsilon} \tag{3}$$

is sometimes used for the standardized power effect size. Since $d = 2f$, d can be used for power calculations in place of f. The f index is more useful, of course, for it applies to two or more groups, whereas d applies only to two.

Keep in mind, however, that "effect size" in the literature usually refers to d rather than f. Keep also in mind that the unit of d is unreliability, so d is not really the size of the effect, which is $| \mu_1 - \mu_2 |$.

The d statistic is popular in *meta-analysis*, which seeks to summarize results from a considerable number of studies of some particular question, as in *Clinical Versus Statistical Prediction* in Section 16.1.3. Direct comparison of mean effects across studies is not often sensible, one reason being that the response measure is likely to have different units in different studies. One investigator may use a 1–100 rating scale, another a 7-step scale. Dividing each sample mean difference by its own standard deviation is a crude but useful way of making different studies roughly comparable. Except for such applications, the d index suffers much the same shortcomings as the ω^2 index discussed on pages 556f.[a, b, c]

Relative Range: *RR*. Magnitude indexes of importance will be illustrated with the *relative range, RR*, in part because of its simplicity, in part because it has occasional usefulness.

In a row–column design, let R_A be the range of the main effect of A, that is, the difference between the largest and smallest row means. Similarly, let R_B be the range of the column means. These ranges can be considered measures of the total effects of these two variables. The *relative range* for A is defined as

$$\text{Relative Range} = RR_A = \frac{R_A}{R_A + R_B}. \tag{4}$$

The denominator on the right equals the total range, or total effect, summed over the two variables. Hence RR_A is the proportion of the total effect due to A. If a third variable is included, R_A and R_B may change, but RR_A will remain the same. A variant definition would take the denominator to be the sum of the ranges for all the variables.

Factorial design is not necessary. For two variables, three conditions would suffice, based on the maximum and minimum levels of the two variables. Observational data may be treated similarly. Moreover, *RR* is defined solely in terms of the response measure; no stimulus measurement is required.

Indexes of relative magnitude are arbitrary in that they depend on arbitrary choices of the levels of the variables. Two investigators could reach opposite conclusions about relative importance because they used different ranges for A and B (see next subsection).

Nevertheless, magnitude indexes may be useful when the variables have some natural or customary range. Stimulus concentration, for example, has a natural range from 0 to at most 100%. In most investigations, preference values for foods would have a limited range from slightly negative to quite positive. In such situations, the relative range can be meaningful within the practical framework defined by the natural ranges.

A Problem of Reification. Magnitude indexes sometimes suffer reification, in which the specific levels of the variable are taken as the variable itself. If $RR_A > RR_B$, it is easy to fall into thinking A is more important than B. To see the pit, consider a 2×2 design. The effect of A, R_A, is the difference between the two marginal means for A_1 and A_2. This effect will be small or large according as the effective values of A_1 and A_2 are chosen close together or far apart. The same holds for B. Any finding about relative importance of A and B as *variables* reflects arbitrary choice of their *levels*. The reification consists of treating the specific levels of the variables as the variable itself.

This reification may be illustrated with developmental studies of blame. A popular hypothesis is that *damage* caused by the action will be more important to younger children than the *intent* behind the action. Some tests of this hypothesis have compared the differential effect of two levels of damage with that of two levels of intent. Whichever difference is greater for a given child is said to reveal which variable is more important for that child.

Any result is arbitrary, of course, for it depends on the arbitrary choices of the two levels of each variable. The concept of a variable is distinct from the levels of that variable. It is convenient to speak of the effect of the variable itself, and often this is harmless. For assessing relative importance, however, the reification is fatal (see *Concept-Instance Confounding* on pages 232*f*).

This limitation seems inherent in magnitude indexes; variables are necessarily confounded with their particular levels. Although useful in special situations, magnitude indexes do not allow conclusions about relative importance of variables per se. A weight definition is needed (pages 557*ff*).

18.1.3 PROPORTION OF VARIANCE STATISTICS

A second kind of size–importance index takes the variance of the behavior as a standard of comparison. Anova–regression can be applied to partition the total variance, SS_Y, into components from several sources. The relative effect of a given variable may then be defined as the proportion of the total variance that it accounts for. With two or more variables, proportion of variance statistics are similar to the foregoing relative range statistic; they differ in using variance in place of range. They suffer similar arbitrariness.

Proportion of Variance: r^2. The squared correlation measures the proportion of variance in the criterion, Y, that is accounted for by the predictor, X. This was shown in Equation 9.15:

$$r^2 \;=\; \frac{SS_{pred}}{SS_Y}.$$

Both r^2 and r are independent of the units in which Y and X are measured. Their size may thus seem directly meaningful as an index of the strength of the relation between Y and X.

The correlation index has serious flaws, however, for it depends on factors irrelevant to the strength of the Y–X relation. If the range of X is small, for example, r^2 will be small even though the Y–X relation is near-perfect. In some situations, r and r^2 refer to variance that has substantive meaning as a measure of association within a specific context, as in test theory. In many situations, however, if not most, r and r^2 mean little (see further Section 9.2, pages 274*ff*).

Proportion of Variance: R^2. With multiple predictor variables, the squared multiple correlation equals the proportion of variance accounted for by all the predictors (Equation 16.4):

$$R^2 \;=\; \frac{SS_{pred}}{SS_Y}.$$

This R^2 index can be useful in certain outcome-oriented studies, in which the total variance in some observational situation is a natural focus of interest. Moreover, the benefit added by an additional predictor can be assessed by how much it increases R^2. In test theory, accordingly, and in practical prediction, the R^2 statistic is often useful.

For assessing importance of individual predictors, however, R^2 is not generally useful. Among other reasons, the predictors are typically intercorrelated. The correlation of a single predictor with the criterion is thus not a good indicator of its usefulness in a multiple regression. And within the multiple regression, there is no meaningful way to define the independent contributions of intercorrelated predictors.

Measures of Association. Studies with observational data often rely on measures of association, usually correlation indexes, such as r and R. These can be viewed as descriptive measures of effect size and sometimes are natural and useful indexes. All have serious limitations, however, some of which have already been cited. See further the advantages of the regression coefficient over the correlation coefficient noted on page 278 as well as *Indexes of Association* for two-way frequency tables on page 295.

Proportion of Variance: ω^2. The seeming usefulness of R^2 with observational data has suggested that something similar could be used with variables that are experimentally manipulated. This approach led to the so-called ω^2 statistics. One common definition of ω^2 is by direct analogy to R^2. In a two-way design, accordingly,

$$\omega_A^2 \;=\; \frac{\sigma_A^2}{\sigma_A^2 \,+\, \sigma_B^2 \,+\, \sigma_{AB}^2 \,+\, \sigma_{error}^2}. \tag{5}$$

The denominator is just SS_Y, the total variance, the same as in the foregoing equation for R^2. It and σ_A^2 can be estimated from the Anova MSs.

One shortcoming of this definition is that ω^2 for A depends also on the other variable, B. If the two levels of B are chosen close together (far apart), A could account for a greater (lesser) proportion of the variance than B. Two investigators who used the very same levels of A but different levels of B could thus reach opposite conclusions about relative importance of A and B. This ambiguity of ω^2 reflects concept–instance confounding, already discussed under *A Problem of Reification* (page 554).

Some texts define ω^2 differently, relative to error variance alone. This definition may be written

$$\omega_{effect}^2 \;=\; \frac{\sigma_{effect}^2}{\sigma_{effect}^2 \,+\, \sigma_{error}^2}. \tag{6}$$

Comparing ω^2_{effect} for two effects is an obtuse way to compare their size. It is simpler and more meaningful to ignore the error variance and compare $\hat{\sigma}_{\text{effect}}$ for the two sources. Better yet, compare the mean differences themselves. And to compare the size of an effect to the error, it is simpler and more meaningful to use confidence intervals or the standardized power effect size.[a, b]

Bad Statistics. The ω^2 statistics, in my opinion, darken the problem they seek to illuminate. Desiring to go beyond tests of significance, many texts have emphasized ω^2 and similar statistical indexes. Students thus get the idea that it adds something meaningful to their papers to include percentages of variance accounted for. Nearly always what is added is only statistical clutter that obscures the meaning of the data. Size and importance must generally be defined in substantive terms, within an empirical, extrastatistical framework (see similarly Bogartz, 1994a, pp. 389*ff*). Omitting ω^2 statistics will help the reader understand the empirical significance of the actual data.

The ω^2 statistics are a symptom of deep trouble: overemphasis on the top level of the Experimental Pyramid, underemphasis on lower levels. The way to go beyond significance tests is not more statistics, but more extrastatistics.[c]

18.1.4 WEIGHT MEASURES OF IMPORTANCE

A quite different approach to assessing size and importance employs a framework of mathematical models in which a value parameter represents size and a weight parameter represents importance.

Model Framework. Underlying the intuitive concept of weight is an intuitive mathematical model, in which the weight parameter acts as a multiplier of the value parameter. The difficulties in establishing a valid weight measure of importance become clearer when this model is made explicit. Consider the additive model

$$Y = w_1 X_1 + w_2 X_2,$$

in which w_1 and w_2 are weights that act as multipliers on the values of X_1 and X_2. In this model framework, w_1 and w_2 represent importance of X_1 and X_2, as distinct from the particular levels of X_1 and X_2.

Unit Confounding in Weight Indexes. Weight definitions of importance seek a weight parameter that applies to the variable, regardless of its particular levels. A prototypical case is the b weight in a linear regression. Unlike the correlation coefficient, the b weight is essentially independent of the range of X. Any reasonable choice of levels of X will yield essentially the same b weight. Weight definitions avoid the confounding of the variable with its levels that undermines magnitude indexes.

Most weight definitions, however, suffer a different confounding—from the unit of the scale in which the variable is measured. Temperature, for example, may be measured in Celsius or Fahrenheit. The *b* weight will differ by a factor of 9/5 in the two cases. Two persons could thus come to opposite conclusions about relative importance of temperature and some other variable from comparing their *b* weights, depending on which temperature scale they used.

This temperature example illustrates a general problem. Many psychological measures, such as belief, motivation, or meaningfulness, have arbitrary units. Weights for different variables can be compared only if their units are equivalent, but these units will usually be unknown and unknowable.

Standardized Weights. To avoid the unit confounding of the previous subsection, various proposals have been made to standardize the weights. In one form of standardization, the weight for each variable is divided by the standard deviation of the levels of that variable. This standardization is attractive because the result is independent of the scale unit for the variable. Celsius and Fahrenheit scales would thus yield the same standardized weight.

But this standard deviation depends on the arbitrary choice of particular levels of the variable. Standardization thus suffers the objections already noted.

Another form of standardization uses the standard deviation of some subject population on each variable to standardize the weight for that variable. The most common case is standardized *b* weights of multiple regression analysis. Standardization is intended to avoid the arbitrary units that make unstandardized weights difficult to compare, but it introduces an arbitrary unit of its own. Indeed, the standard deviation of X_1 depends on individual differences that affect X_1 but not Y, individual differences that seem irrelevant to the importance question at issue. This standardization does not solve the unit problem, therefore, but obscures it.

Understanding Regression *b* Weights. In typical applications of multiple regression, the *b* weights suffer additional shortcomings as measures of importance. One unsolvable difficulty is that two correlated variables have a common part and there is no meaningful way to divide this common part between them.

A different difficulty comes from person–variable confounding. In the additive regression model of Equation 16.8, b_1 represents the coefficient of X_1 "with the other variables held constant." But X_2 is held constant only by confounding it with persons (see *Person-Variable Confounding*, page 502).

In graduate school admissions, for example, GPA has substantial correlation with GRE. The regression equation cannot undo reality and change GRE while holding GPA constant for any person. Instead, it changes the person, thereby confounding the variable with real individual differences. This confounding of variables with individual differences can be useful for prediction for a population of individuals, but is generally misleading for process analysis.

Valid Measure of Weight. To get a valid measure, the weight w must be separated from the value X. In the foregoing additive model, w and X act inseparably as a product. This underlies the unit confounding. The model clarifies the problem by showing that this unit confounding is not generally resolvable within an additive framework.

Valid measures of weight are possible, however, with the averaging model of cognitive algebra. The averaging model can provide functional measures with a common unit for different variables, separately for value and for weight. Qualitatively different variables can be compared on importance, regardless of their specific levels (Section 21.4.3, page 710). Where it applies, averaging theory can define and quantify a true measure of psychological importance.

18.2 CONTRAST ANALYSIS

A *contrast* represents some hypothesized pattern or trend in the means of the treatment conditions. Because a contrast focuses on a specific pattern, it can be more informative than the overall table of means. It can also provide a more relevant and more powerful test than overall Anova. The most common contrasts are the two-mean comparisons and linear trends of Section 4.2.1. More general contrasts have occasional uses and the rationale is given here.

18.2.1 CONTRAST FORMULAS

Independent scores are assumed in the following discussion. A similar approach holds with repeated measures, considered in the last subsection.

Definition of Contrast. A contrast, κ, is a weighted sum of treatment means. It is defined by a set of contrast coefficients, c_j, one for each treatment mean, whose sum is zero. In practice, these c_j are chosen to represent some pattern or trend anticipated in the data. These coefficients are applied to the treatment means to yield the weighted sum

$$\hat{\kappa} = \sum c_j \bar{Y}_j = c_1 \bar{Y}_1 + c_2 \bar{Y}_2 + \ldots + c_a \bar{Y}_a; \qquad \sum c_j = 0. \quad (7)$$

This equation implies that $\hat{\kappa}$ will be nonzero to the extent that the $\bar{Y}_j$ follow the same pattern as the c_j. The magnitude of $\hat{\kappa}$ thus measures the degree to which the observed data follow the hypothesized pattern.

Significance Test for Contrasts. The question whether $\hat{\kappa}$ differs reliably from 0 is readily answered with Anova. The sum of squares for $\hat{\kappa}$ is

$$SS_{\hat{\kappa}} = \frac{n\,\hat{\kappa}^2}{\sum c_j^2} = \frac{n(\sum c_j \bar{Y}_j)^2}{\sum c_j^2}. \quad (8)$$

All contrasts have 1 df, so $SS_{\hat{\kappa}} = MS_{\hat{\kappa}}$. The error term is MS_{error} from the overall Anova, assuming equal variance. Accordingly,

$$F_{\kappa} = \frac{MS_{\hat{\kappa}}}{MS_{error}} \qquad\qquad df = 1/df_{error} \qquad (9)$$

tests the null hypothesis that the true value of κ is 0:

$$H_0: \kappa = \sum c_j\mu_j = c_1\mu_1 + c_2\mu_2 + \ldots + c_a\mu_a = 0. \qquad (10)$$

Confidence Intervals for Contrasts. For contrasts, the standard deviation (= standard error), or error half-bar is

$$\sqrt{\sum c_j^2} \sqrt{MS_{error}/"n"}, \qquad (11)$$

where $"n"$ is the number of scores in each treatment mean. To get the confidence interval, multiply the standard deviation by t^*:

$$\hat{\kappa} \pm \sqrt{\sum c_j^2}\ t^* \sqrt{MS_{error}/"n"}. \qquad (12)$$

As a check on this formula, consider a two-mean comparison between $\bar{Y}_1$ and $\bar{Y}_2$. To express this as a contrast, choose the c_j as

$$c_1 = 1, \qquad c_2 = -1, \qquad \text{all other } c_j = 0.$$

Since these c_j sum to zero, they define a contrast. By Equation 10, they test the null hypothesis

$$H_0: \kappa = \mu_1 - \mu_2 = 0.$$

For this two-mean contrast, $\sqrt{\sum c_j^2} = \sqrt{2}$. Expression 12 thus yields the same two-mean confidence interval as Expression 1 of Section 4.1.1.

Normalization. The width of the confidence interval depends on the choice of the c_j. To make the confidence interval comparable to the measured data requires normalization. To normalize, reduce the contrast to a difference between two weighted means as follows. Multiply the positive c_j by a constant so their sum is 1. Thus normalized, the positive c_j constitute a weighted mean of the corresponding $\bar{Y}_j$. Treat the negative c_j similarly. The contrast is then a difference between two weighted means of measured scores and its confidence interval has the same unit as the measured scores.

If only a significance test is wanted, normalization is not necessary. The corresponding confidence interval, however, has an arbitrary unit that compromises its meaning. Although the unnormalized contrast can always be normalized later, beginning with the normalization will avoid not unlikely confusion.[a]

Numerical Example. To illustrate contrast analysis, consider the numerical example of linear trend of Section 4.2: Four groups of 10 subjects with means of 1, 2, 3, 4 for four equally spaced levels of the treatment variable, and MS_{error} = 7.5. For a linear trend, the c_j must have a linear pattern and sum to zero. The customary c_j are −3, −1, 1, 3, which we normalize to get

$$-3/4, \quad -1/4, \quad 1/4, \quad 3/4.$$

Accordingly,

$$\hat{\kappa} = (-3/4) \times 1 + (-1/4) \times 2 + (1/4) \times 3 + (3/4) \times 4 = 2.5.$$

$$SS_{\hat{\kappa}} = 10 \times (2.5)^2 / [(3/4)^2 + (1/4)^2 + (1/4)^2 + (3/4)^2] = 50.$$

$$F_{\kappa} = 50/7.5 = 6.66.$$

This F of 6.66 for linear trend is greater than $F^*(1, 36) = 4.13$, whereas the overall F of 2.22 was less than $F^*(3, 36) = 2.89$. The linear trend does better because it focuses on the actual pattern in the data.

Power. When contrasts are planned, power should ordinarily be calculated for them rather than for the overall Anova. The power formulas of Section 4.2 may be utilized, almost without change. Normalization is not necessary.

The size of a contrast is $\kappa = \sum c_j \mu_j$. Its standard deviation (Equation 4.3) is

$$\sigma_{\kappa} = \sqrt{\kappa^2 / a} = \sqrt{(\sum c_j \mu_j)^2 / 2}. \tag{13}$$

For contrasts, $a = 2$, that is, 1 more than the 1 df for the contrast, regardless of the number of means involved.

The error standard deviation for a contrast must include the c_j:

$$\sigma_{error:\kappa} = \sqrt{\sum c_j^2} \, \sigma_{\varepsilon}, \tag{14}$$

where σ_{ε} would be estimated by $\sqrt{MS_{error}}$.

The ratio of the standard deviations of the two previous equations yields the standardized power effect size of Equation 4.4:

$$f = \sigma_{\kappa} / \sigma_{error:\kappa}. \tag{15}$$

The value of n remains equal to the size of each group. The power index is given by Equation 4.5:

$$\phi = f \sqrt{"n"}. \tag{16}$$

This power index may be used exactly as illustrated in Section 4.3.

That a linear trend could be statsig even though the overall F was not statsig was shown in the foregoing numerical example. This example may be reused to illustrate the power advantage of the linear trend test. For the overall F, Equation 4.3 yields the standard deviation of the effect sizes,

$$\sigma_A = \sqrt{[(1-2.5)^2 + (2-2.5)^2 + (3-2.5)^2 + (4-2.5)^2]/4}$$
$$= \sqrt{1.25}.$$

Hence $f = \sigma_A/\sigma_{error:\kappa} = \sqrt{1.25}/\sqrt{7.5}$ and $\phi = f\sqrt{"n"} = \sqrt{12.5/7.5} = 1.29$. From Figure A7, the overall $F(3, 36)$ has power slightly over .50.

For the linear trend $\sigma_\kappa = \sqrt{2.5^2/2} = 1.768$ from Equation 13, and $\sigma_{error:\kappa} = \sqrt{20/16}\sqrt{7.5} = 3.062$ from Equation 14. Hence $\phi = [1.768/3.062]\sqrt{10} = 1.83$. From the power curve of Figure A7, this contrast yields power slightly over .70. To get equal power with the overall F would require 50% more subjects. The advantage of the trend test is not merely more power, of course, but more precise information about the pattern of the effects.

Unequal Spacing and Unequal n. If the levels of the treatment variable are spaced unequally, the c_j for the linear trend should show the same spacing:

$$c_j = A_j - \bar{A}. \tag{17}$$

Since each c_j is a deviation from their mean, their sum is zero. Normalization may be done as already indicated. Unequal n is covered in Note 18.2.1b.[b]

Orthogonality. Two contrasts are *orthogonal*, or statistically independent, if the products of their coefficients sum to zero. Let c_j and d_j be the coefficients for two contrasts. Orthogonality holds if

$$c_1 d_1 + c_2 d_2 + \ldots + c_a d_a = \sum c_j d_j = 0. \tag{18}$$

This equation means that the c_j and d_j are uncorrelated—that they represent unrelated, independent patterns.

Comparisons that are not orthogonal are not independent. The null hypotheses they test are correlated; false alarm, or real effect, in one comparison will partly reappear in any correlated comparison. At one time, accordingly, nonorthogonal contrasts were deemed inadmissible by some writers.

At present, however, nearly everyone agrees that contrasts should be dictated by substantive considerations. If your experimental hypotheses lead to nonorthogonal contrasts, you should test them, but keep their nonindependence in mind. Orthogonality, although important in statistical theory, has limited relevance for experimental analysis.

Repeated Measures. A contrast on a repeated measures variable A reduces the a scores for each subject to a single contrast score, κ_{iA}. These single scores may then be treated as a response measure in their own right.

For example, consider a test for linear trend of A in an $S \times A$ design with a single repeated measures variable. The c_j are the coefficients for linear trend, and κ_{iA} measures the degree to which subject i exhibits a linear trend. In fact, κ_{iA} is proportional to the slope of the best-fit straight line for that subject's data. The a scores for each subject are thus reduced to a single slope score.

Do an Anova of the κ_{iA}; F_{mean} tests the null hypothesis of no linear trend. To get a confidence interval, apply Expression 12, with MS_{error} from this Anova and n the number of subjects. If normalized c_j are used, the confidence interval will have the same unit as the data. Any contrast, not just linear trend, may be treated in exactly similar manner.

This analysis may be extended in two ways. First, a between subjects variable G may be added, yielding an $(S \times A) \times G$ design. Since the contrast reduces the A scores for each subject to a single score, the design is reduced to a one-way design with independent scores. As above, F_{mean} tests the null hypothesis that the mean contrast, averaged over groups, is zero. Statsig F_A implies real differences between groups—localized in the contrast pattern.

As a second extension, suppose a within subjects variable is added, yielding an $S \times A \times B$ design. At each level of B, the contrast reduces the A scores for each subject to a single score. The design thus reduces to an $S \times B$ repeated measures design, which may be analyzed in the standard way:

$$F_{\text{mean}} = \text{MS}_{\text{mean}}/\text{MS}_S;$$
$$F_B = \text{MS}_B/\text{MS}_{BS}.$$

Unless B has only two levels, the ε adjustment would usually be needed.

Each separate contrast generally requires its own error term with repeated measures. This occurs automatically with the foregoing procedure because a separate Anova is done with each separate contrast (see Note 18.4.2c).

18.2.2 APPLICATIONS OF CONTRASTS

When should you use contrasts? The answer is simple: Use contrasts when your experimental hypothesis specifies a pattern that can be expressed as a weighted sum of treatment means (with weights that sum to zero). These weights are the c_j for a contrast that represents the degree to which the data follow the specified pattern (e.g., Table 18.1, next page).

The plain truth is that contrast analysis has limited use. The most common contrasts are two-mean comparisons, but these are better done using confidence intervals. Next most common are linear trends, but these are usually better done with regression analysis. Other uses of contrasts are infrequent, except for factorial designs in which each factor has just two levels. With such designs, each main effect and interaction residual can be expressed as a sum-and-difference of cell means, that is, as a contrast. Each contrast is a number that equals the size of one effect, which is more meaningful than the corresponding SS, and it leads directly to a confidence interval, which is more meaningful than the corresponding F. This class of designs is considered in the following two subsections.

2 × 2 Factorial. Contrasts provide an interesting view of factorial designs with factors at two levels. To illustrate, consider a treatment for chronic pain, a grim, grinding fact of life for a substantial number of people. This treatment is to be tested with two types of chronic pain from surgical scar tissue, Pain-1 and Pain-2. We assume felt pain is measured at specified times after giving the treatment. Since pain can show strong placebo effects, we must include a placebo control. This design yields four groups of subjects, listed in the following table.

TABLE 18.1

Group

	Treatment–P1	Placebo–P1	Treatment–P2	Placebo–P2
$\kappa_{treatment}$	+1	−1	+1	−1
$\kappa_{medical}$	+1	+1	−1	−1
$\kappa_{residual}$	+1	−1	−1	+1

The ±1s in each row are the c_j for testing one specific hypothesis.

The contrast in the first row is most important. It tests the null hypothesis that the treatment has no effect. The first two c_j, (+1, −1), represent the (treatment − placebo) difference for Pain-1 condition; the second two c_j do the same for Pain-2. The contrast, $\kappa_{treatment}$, is thus the treatment effect summed across the two pain conditions.

The second row, similarly, is the contrast for the difference between pain response for the two medical conditions, summed over drug and placebo. This contrast would probably have limited interest since the two medical conditions differ naturally.

The contrast of the third row has a different nature. It tests the null hypothesis that the treatment effect is equal for both medical conditions. As the ± signs show, it subtracts the (treatment − placebo) difference for Pain-2 from the (treatment − placebo) difference for Pain-1. If this contrast is statsig, it may suggest the treatment is more effective for one medical condition than the other.

The design in Table 18.1 is actually a 2 × 2 factorial; the three contrasts correspond to the three sources in the overall Anova. The first two contrasts represent the main effects of treatment and medical condition, respectively. The third contrast represents the interaction residual. This analysis in terms of contrasts has the advantage over the overall Anova that it leads more directly to confidence intervals using Expression 12 above.

Normalization may be advisable. To normalize, replace each 1 by ½ in Table 18.1. Each contrast, and its confidence interval, will then have the same unit as the measured data. The 1s in each row of Table 18.1 give a valid significance test, but they yield a numerical value of the contrast that is twice the main effect.

Fractional Replication and 2^p Designs. The contrast analysis of Table 18.1 in the previous subsection is readily extended to 2^p designs, that is, designs with p factors, each at two levels. Index the levels of each factor by 1 and 2. In each cell of the design, the treatment combination can be denoted as a sequence of 1s and 2s, successive digits representing the levels of $A, B, C, \ldots$. In three-factor design, for example, 121 and 211 represent the cells with treatment $A_1 B_2 C_1$ and $A_2 B_1 C_1$, respectively.

Each main effect and interaction can then be represented as a contrast on the 2^p means. Each contrast must have some c_j in every cell. For any main effect, set $c_j = +1$ for a cell that contains level 1 of that factor, and set $c_j = -1$ for a cell that contains level 2. For any interaction, multiply the c_j for the corresponding main effects in each cell.

For the AB interaction of a 2^3 design, for example, the c_j for cell $A_1 B_2 C_1$ would be $(+1)(-1)$ and the same for cell $A_1 B_2 C_2$. The complete set of contrasts was given in Table 15.3 (page 451).

To get error bars and confidence intervals, normalization is recommended. To normalize, replace each 1 by $1/2^{p-1}$. Then $\hat{\kappa}$ has the same unit as the measured data, and so does its confidence interval.

Contrast analysis is useful for fractional replication (Section 15.3.1), in which only a fraction of the 2^p cells of the full design are used. In the experiment of Figure 15.1 (page 455), a complete curve of serial belief formation was obtained with only eight of the 64 cells of the full design. Each point on this serial belief curve equaled the numerical value of the contrast for the main effect of the corresponding serial position in the serial-factor design.

18.3 TREND ANALYSIS AND CURVE SHAPE

Many treatment variables are ordered or metric. They contain quantitative information that can be utilized in designing experiments and interpreting data. Metric information is obvious with many sensory stimuli, for example, air temperature, sound energy, and sucrose concentration. Metric information is far more general, of course, as with age in developmental psychology, number of trials in learning studies, interstimulus intervals in perception, and so forth. Variables that lack a physical metric may still have a psychological metric, as with rated values of pleasantness of foods and likableness of persons.

Metric variables are extremely useful in planning investigations. We often use a few selectively spaced levels of a metric variable, expecting to interpolate between them to find the overall trend. Seldom do we pause in gratitude for our good fortune that the typical response shows a smooth curve without jags or jumps. This is one of many examples of the silent role of extrastatistical knowledge in experimental design and in data analysis.

Metric variables can also be used to improve the analysis of the data. Linear trend, as already indicated, can be more informative and more powerful than overall Anova. Nonlinear trends can give some information, unfortunately very limited, about curve shape.

18.3.1 TWO TECHNIQUES FOR TREND ANALYSIS

Trend analysis may be done in two ways, with the regression analysis of Chapters 9 and 16, and with the contrasts considered in the previous section. For most purposes, the regression analysis is easier and more informative. This advantage of regression has not been generally recognized, in part because of a mistaken belief that nonlinear contrasts are generally useful.

One purpose of the following discussion, accordingly, is to point up the superiority of trend analysis by regression. An associated purpose is to show why nonlinear trends are not often useful. Equal n and equal spacing are assumed unless otherwise indicated.

Trend Analysis by Regression. Trend analysis is easy using a computer program to perform the linear regression of Chapter 9: The values of the predictor variable, X_1, are the metric values of the treatment variable; the criterion Y is the measured response.

As one advantage, regression analysis gives the slope of the best-fit straight line, namely, b_1. To get b_1 requires an extra formula when contrast analysis is used. Also, the regression printout includes the standard deviation or even a confidence interval for b_1 and takes unequal spacing of the X_1 levels in stride. Both of these also require an extra formula when contrasts are used.

Nonlinear trend components can also be obtained with multiple regression. The direct way, using $X_2 = X_1^2$, $X_3 = X_1^3$, and so on, suffers because the successive powers of X_1 are highly correlated. The aggravations of this multicollinearity can be much reduced by using $X_2 = (X_1 - \bar{X})^2$, $X_3 = (X_1 - \bar{X})^3$, an approach that is improved in Winer et al. (1991, pp. 207*ff*). To be independent in terms of SS (but not b), trend components should be extracted one by one: linear, quadratic, and so on. Else part of the linear trend may be included in the quadratic, and so on. Alternatively, the values of $X_1, X_2,$ and X_3 may be taken as the orthogonal polynomial coefficients described on the next page.

Trend Analysis by Contrast. The customary approach presents trend analysis in terms of contrasts. This approach was illustrated with the linear trend example under *Power* on page 561. This contrast approach usually employs orthogonal polynomials, illustrated below, so the SS for each trend component is independent of the others. Orthogonal polynomial c_j for quadratic, cubic, and higher trends are listed in a standard table, given in most texts, although these only apply with equal n and equal spacing.[a]

Three Goals With Trend Analysis. The main value of trend analysis is to increase power, as with the earlier example of linear trend. Power can sometimes be increased by testing the linear and quadratic trends together, which is done automatically with a two-variable regression. For significance testing, accordingly, regression analysis seems superior to contrast analysis.

A second goal of trend analysis is to obtain a prediction equation, which is sometimes desired in practical applications. For this purpose, regression analysis is clearly superior to contrast analysis.

Still a third goal of trend analysis is to describe the shape of the curve. Unfortunately, polynomial trends have little value for elucidating curve shape. Curve shape is an ambiguous concept that is taken up next.

18.3.2 CURVE SHAPE AND NONLINEAR TREND

You help the reader if you describe the curve shape of your data by visual inspection. Only in special cases, however, is it useful to seek a more quantitative analysis of curve shape. This point needs emphasis because most current texts present nonlinear trends, especially orthogonal polynomials, as valuable standard tools.

One purpose of this section, accordingly, is to show why nonlinear trend tests are not usually helpful. The first subsection considers power, the next several consider the concept of curve shape. The final subsection relates curve shape to measurement theory.

Nonlinear Trend and Orthogonal Polynomials. Nonlinear trend is usually presented with *orthogonal polynomials*. The term *orthogonal* means that these polynomial trends are statistically independent, having no SS in common. With four levels of the stimulus variable, for example, the SS can be split into three orthogonal components, corresponding to the linear, quadratic, and cubic trends. With equal spacing between levels and equal n, the ostensible shapes of these polynomial trends are mirrored in their respective c_j coefficients:

linear: $-3, -1, +1, +3$;

quadratic: $+1, -1, -1, +1$;

cubic: $-1, +3, -3, +1$.

Visual inspection of these c_j shows that the linear component represents a straight line, the quadratic a bowl shape, and the cubic a snake shape. All three trends are contrasts, since their c_j sum to 0. All three trends are orthogonal, moreover, as may be shown with Equation 18.

Quadratic and cubic trends could thus be tested in the same way as the linear component by using Equation 9 or Expression 12. More simply, the three sets of c_j could be used as three predictors in a three-variable regression. The three b weights are independent by virtue of the orthogonality. Orthogonal polynomials can be extended to cover any number of stimulus levels. For five levels, the linear and quadratic c_j are $\{-2, -1, 0, 1, 2\}$ and $\{2, -1, -2, -1, 2\}$.

It might be thought that nonlinear trend would increase power. This function is so handsomely fulfilled with the linear trend that good dividends from nonlinear trend are also expected. This expectation, however, is generally disappointed; in most applications, the SS is mainly in the linear component. Experiments that yield mainly nonlinear curves are rare.

Curve Shape. At face value, trend analysis represents the curve in terms of specific shape components, especially the linear, quadratic, and cubic polynomial components. Such shape analysis might seem a fine way to go beyond the test of significance to say something more substantive about the data.[a]

It would be nice if this belief was correct. Unfortunately, polynomial trends have very limited value for describing curve shape, even at a surface level. A symptom can be seen in the simplest case, $Y = X^2$. This is a pure quadratic, yet most of its variance lies in the linear component for $X \geq 0$ (Exercise c3; see similarly U-shaped curves in the next subsection).

Only the case of linear trend is unambiguous. If the trend is completely linear, neither unequal n nor unequal spacing will induce any nonlinear trend. Statsig nonlinear trend is thus a sign of real nonlinearity.

This nonambiguity of linear trend is fortunate because some theories imply perfect linear trend. Thus, certain list-search theories predict that search time is a linear function of list length (e.g., Shanteau, 1991; Sternberg, 1966). In cognitive algebra, similarly, the multiplication model predicts purely linear trend in the statistical interaction term (Chapter 21). In such cases, quadratic/cubic trends might provide the most powerful test of deviations from theoretical prediction. In both examples, it should be noted, the stimulus and response metrics have theoretical grounding that makes curve shape meaningful.

U-Shaped Curves. The problem of U-shaped curves, which arises in various empirical domains, illustrates a not uncommon misconception about nonlinear trend analysis. The Yerkes–Dodson "law," for example, asserts that performance is an inverted-U function of motivation, first increasing as motivation increases from low levels and then decreasing as motivation exceeds an optimal level. Pinning down such U shapes is generally difficult.[b]

Typically, the ascending arm of the inverted U-curve is not in doubt. The critical question is whether there really is a peak followed by a downturn. Typical empirical results show a small, ragged decrease. Assessing the reliability of this decrease is often complicated by the fact that the stimulus level that would produce the peak is uncertain. In most cases, it is difficult to reject the alternative hypothesis of no downturn but instead a steady final level or even a small continued increase.

Some texts have claimed that the U-shape question can be answered by testing the quadratic trend. The c_j for the quadratic trend exhibit a U shape, they argue, and that's exactly what is being sought in the data.

This argument is not correct. What the quadratic actually assesses is U shape in the residuals from the linear trend; this can be substantial even with a curve that increases steadily. For example, the curve {0, 6, 10, 12} increases steadily with no downturn. Yet this curve has a strong nonlinear component, which is entirely in the quadratic trend. In general, therefore, the quadratic trend says nothing about U shape.[c]

Misuse of Trend Analysis. Statsig linear trend does not imply that a straight line describes the data; nonlinear components may also be present. It would be misleading to suggest that the hooked curve {1, 3, 5, 4} has a linear shape. It has a substantial linear component, however, with $SS_{linear} = 6.05n$, nearly 70% of the total SS of $8.75n$.

To demonstrate a real effect, nevertheless, the linear trend test may be most powerful even when the curve is nonlinear. Common examples are curves that show ceiling or floor effects, for example, {1, 3, 5, 5}. For these four means, the linear trend is the most powerful test for real effects. It would be misleading, however, to conclude that the curve is linear.

Pointless tests represent a different kind of misuse of trend analysis. One example is attempts to supplement the linear trend with pairwise comparisons, thinking to obtain a more detailed description of the data. However, if extra-statistical considerations imply a steady trend and the linear trend is statsig, then all pairwise differences should be real. The pairwise tests cannot then shed additional light, for a nonstatsig pairwise difference would merely reflect low power. These tests are not simply irrelevant, but misleading clutter.

Two other cases of pointless trend analysis deserve mention. Listing percentage of variance accounted for by linear and specific nonlinear curve components is generally pointless because, among other reasons, these percentages depend on arbitrary choice of the range of the treatment variable. Even more pointless is testing for nonlinear trend in curves that clearly cannot be linear. When the response is limited by floor/ceiling effects, for example, any real effect must show floor/ceiling curvature. A significance test is then generally pointless because a nonstatsig result would merely mean inadequate power.

Curve Shape With Multiple Variables. Curve shape is usually considered a one-dimensional relation between the response and a single treatment variable. This one-dimensional conception of shape is limited because multiple determination is the norm. With two variables, the response forms a surface. Surface shape seems more pertinent than curve shape.

Surface shape is implicit although disguised in the standard two-way factorial graph. An alternative is a three-dimensional plot with two horizontal axes, one for each variable. In this form, a factorial graph with parallel straight lines would be a plane surface.

Three treatment variables produce a three-dimensional shape in four-dimensional space, which is hard to visualize. Two-way factorial graphs can provide helpful partial pictures of such multidimensional shapes. Higher-way interactions are seldom informative about shape (see discussion of Figure 7.4, page 204). Present concern, however, is with one-dimensional curve shape, the subject of the next subsection.

Measurement Theory and Curve Shape. Curve shape depends on two metrics, one for the stimulus variable, one for the response measure. Unless both metrics are linear scales, perhaps with known zeros, the visible curve shape may be ambiguous, not to say misleading.

This measurement problem is clear with the stimulus metric. To appreciate this ambiguity, suppose the graph of the observed response is an increasing straight line. Unless the stimulus scale is linear, nonlinear transformation of the horizontal axis would be needed to make it so. But transforming the horizontal axis will change the observed shape. Hence the observed shape may not mean much; the only definite conclusion is that the true curve is steadily increasing.

The same argument applies with the response metric. If the response measure is only monotone, the true response function could have virtually any shape. The sole restriction is that it change direction, up or down, only when the observed response does.

Despite these difficulties, observed curve shape may be useful in communication. In sensory–perceptual areas, for example, a convenient stimulus metric may be in general use. Within this framework, statements about curve shape have a conventional meaning useful in practical communication.

It should also be recognized that psychological scales are often semilinear (page 632). Even if they are not perfect linear scales, they may have far more metric content than a bare rank order. From this extrastatistical view, the surface pattern of the data can provide useful clues about reality. Surface pattern should not be dismissed merely because it is uncertain. This same consideration arose with interaction residuals in Chapter 7. You help the reader, therefore, with visual description of your graphs and tables.

18.3.3 STIMULUS METRICS

Pragmatic Stimulus Metrics. Pragmatic spacing of treatment levels, selected to yield approximately equal increments in response, is usually desirable. Equal intervals on the physical metric for the treatment variables may be less effective. Pragmatic metrics can lead to more meaningful curve shape as well as more powerful trend tests.

Studies of drugs and other substances, for example, often manipulate concentration in geometric steps (e.g., 2%, 4%, 8%, 16%). This geometric stimulus spacing often produces an approximate arithmetic increase in response, which is efficient. In graphing the data, accordingly, the geometric steps are usually spaced at equal intervals on the horizontal axis.

Linear trend analysis can capitalize on such pragmatic metrics. In the concentration example, the four levels would be considered equally spaced, in effect a logarithmic scale of the stimulus variable. Hence the X_j in the regression for the linear trend would be taken as 1, 2, 3, 4, not 2, 4, 8, 16. If the curve of response is more linear with the pragmatic metric, more SS will be concentrated in the linear component, thereby increasing power.[a]

Rank and Rating Metrics. Linear trend analysis may be applied with stimuli that are only rank-ordered, lacking any physical metric. Different food reinforcers, for example, could be ranked on preference value. Photographs of potential dates could be ranked on attractiveness. These ranks could then be taken as the stimulus metric.

Alternatively, and perhaps preferably, the stimuli might be prerated on a scale of 1 to 6, say, and these ratings used as the stimulus metric. With such preliminary information, treatment levels could be selected to cover the effective range at roughly equal steps. A linear trend test would be straightforward. Simply take the ratings as the stimulus values and proceed as above.

These rank and rating metrics are pragmatic. There is no great reason to expect them to be true linear scales, but semilinearity usually suffices. Even a rough ranking can increase the effectiveness of the experiment. This example illustrates again the principle of utilizing empirical knowledge as an organic part of statistical analysis.

18.4 SEVEN TOPICS

18.4.1 CONCEPT OF VALIDITY

The purpose of this section is to relate the discussion of validity in Section 1.2 to two major positions on this concept, to both of which the present position is indebted. Both positions originate in less experimental areas, especially studies in field settings and studies that depend on tests of ability, personality, and so forth. Their orientation and structure are thus somewhat different from the position given here, which is more concerned with experimental analysis.

The *word* validity is much less prominent in experimental analysis than in domains that rely heavily on tests as measures, domains such as educational psychology, personality theory, diagnosis and placement, and various branches of applied psychology. Test validity is critical in these domains. With tests of intelligence, aptitudes and skills, personality traits, social attitdes, and how well teachers do their job, the validity question, "Does your test measure what you claim?" has primary importance.

In experimental analysis, validity is no less important, but it is normally discussed with different words, especially *confounding*. It is usually clear that the response measure has the quality attributed to it. Typical experimental measures are percentage correct in a memory test, reaction time to a signal, success or failure in solving a problem, and ratings of grayness, pain, or blame. Such experimental measures have empirical validity that is lacking with measures of intelligence, attitudes, or teaching effectiveness.

What is problematic in typical experimental studies is whether the response measure is confounded with determinants that undercut the interpretation. In the example of placebo control, the measure of pain is not ordinarily in question. What is in question is confounded causes such as suggestion. This experimental perspective on validity has justification in that the quality of the response measure can usually be validated through experimental manipulations and on other grounds. Validity in experimental analysis thus has a different character than in domains that rely on tests as measures.

Validity Diagram. The discussion of validity in Section 1.2 centered on the two polarities in the validity diagram, reproduced here in Figure 18.1.

The *outcome–process* polarity relates to two very different research goals, one oriented toward practical applications, the other toward analysis of psychological process. The difference between these two approaches usually appears in the role played by the response measure.

In typical outcome research, the response measure is important in its own right, either directly or as a surrogate for another that is. In typical process research, the response measure is important as a measure of some underlying process. A Head Start program would employ outcome measures such as

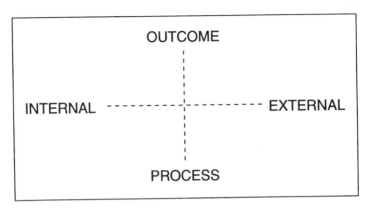

Figure 18.1. Validity Diagram.

vocabulary score or social adjustment, whereas typical learning studies would employ process measures such as number of saliva drops in dogs, bar press rate in rats, percentage correct in recall of nonsense syllables, or positron emission in the frontal lobe.

In the *internal–external* polarity, internal refers to validity within the situation in which the result was obtained, whereas external refers to validity of the obtained result in other situations. Internal validity is in part a matter of statistical inference; external validity relies mainly on extrastatistical inference.

The concept of validity provokes argument (Note 18.4.1a, page 592), so a comment on the nature and function of the present validity diagram may be useful. Its main function is to help clarify the goals of an investigation as a guide to more effective work. The outcome–process polarity is important because attempts to pursue both process and outcome usually entail compromises in design or procedure that compromise both goals (Section 1.2.2). The internal–external polarity involves problems of generality (Section 1.4) and emphasizes the prime importance of substantive, extrastatistical inference. These polarities operate at each level of the Experimental Pyramid (Chapter 1).

Validity is provisional and a matter of degree. To say that a statistical test is valid means that certain statistical assumptions seem adequately satisfied, that the data are not overly nonnormal, for example, or that ε adjustment is used in repeated measures design. Similarly, a measure of learning or belief may be valid for its purposes even though it is only a partial measure of the concept at issue (Section 1.2.4). In the same way, to take a final example, a validational test of a mathematical model or of an associated measurement scale does not yield absolute proof, only reasonable support in tests that could have failed (Chapters 20 and 21).

Two Alternative Positions on Validity. One alternative to the present position is that of Cook and Campbell (1979), who employ an internal–external distinction, stemming from earlier work by Campbell and Stanley (1966), somewhat similar to that used here. However, they conceptualize both internal and external differently from Section 1.2.[a]

Cook and Campbell split internal validity into statistical conclusion validity and internal validity proper. The former corresponds to the present concept of internal outcome validity, but the latter differs from the present internal process validity in two related respects. First, internal process validity involves construct validity, whereas Cook and Campbell treat construct validity as almost synonymous with external validity. Second, Cook and Campbell consider internal validity proper to be atheoretical. In contrast, the present internal process validity concerns the theoretical interpretation of the given result.

One implication is that, in contrast to the position of Cook and Campbell, randomization does not generally handle threats to internal process validity. This difference is illustrated with the placebo effect; it is not nullified by random assignment of subjects, but it confounds the process interpretation. In the present view, most threats to internal validity need to be handled through experimental design, especially control conditions.

Cook and Campbell split external validity into construct validity and external validity proper. The former appears to correspond to the present process validity, although their list of threats to construct validity (pp. 64-70) reflects their concern with field settings and nonrandomized experiments. The latter, external validity proper, is in principle defined in terms of sampling from determinate populations. This definition is totally inadequate for psychological theory. Generalizing from animals to humans is just one example of external validity that cannot be reduced to sampling from determinate populations.

A second major position is more bound up with the idea of construct validity, introduced formally by Cronbach and Meehl (1955). This approach harmonized with the demise of logical positivism, which sought to define concepts in terms of empirical operations. Positivist views arose from a philosophy of science that lacked contact with scientific reality. In a positivist view, "intelligence is what intelligence tests measure," a definition not accepted by Binet nor by most subsequent workers. Intelligence is a construct, as are learning, motivation, attitude, and most measured entities. The concept of construct validity thus gave explicit expression to long-standing practice. In the present position, construct validity may be considered a form of process validity.

Following the introduction of construct validity, a variety of other kinds of validity were proposed. This work is reviewed by Messick (1989), who gives a scholarly overview from the perspective of test theory. In Messick's view, there is now some consensus that validity should be considered unitary; all validity is construct validity, although it may have different aspects.

This unitary view seems so general as to lose usefulness. The polarity between outcome and process validity of Section 1.2 is real; so is the polarity between internal and external generality. Although the two poles of each distinction lie on a continuum, as shown in Figure 18.1, this does not make them unitary. They differ in quality and kind.

Both positions just considered have a critical problem that has been little recognized. Both rely on statistical "interactions" to conceptualize generalization to other persons and settings (Cook & Campbell, 1979; Cronbach & Snow, 1977). Statistical interactions, however, suffer two serious shortcomings. First, interactions, being defined as deviations from an arbitrary additive model, are themselves arbitrary, with uncertain substantive significance and validity. The reliance on the additive model stems from a corresponding concern with outcome validity rather than process validity. Second, without grounded theory of psychological measurement, these statistical interactions may be measurement artifacts of questionable meaning and validity (Chapter 7).[b]

This reliance on interactions arose because both positions are outcome oriented. Outcome orientation is natural in field settings (Cook & Campbell, 1979) and educational settings (Cronbach & Snow, 1977). Even within an outcome orientation, however, the additive model may be inappropriate.

Neither approach had much alternative, of course, since both are basically nontheoretical. They lack theory of cognitive process, the base for the substantive model needed to define interactions in psychological terms. And lacking substantive theory, they lack a theory of scales of measurement, also needed to define interactions. Both cited books are first-rate, it should be emphasized, required reading for workers in these areas. Their discussions of validity are useful, but their outcome orientation is too narrow for psychological theory.

18.4.2 MULTIVARIATE ANALYSIS OF VARIANCE

The term *multiple measures* refers here to several variables measured for each subject, especially variables that are not directly comparable. Heart rate, galvanic skin response, and finger blood volume, for example, might be measured for each subject in a psychophysiological study of emotion. A between subjects design may be used, in which different groups of subjects receive a different experimental treatment intended to affect emotional state. This between subjects manipulation of emotion is the focal concern.

Multiple measures differs from the repeated measures of Chapter 6. Repeated measures includes the same response under different experimental conditions. Multiple measures includes different responses under the same experimental condition, for which repeated measures Anova makes no sense. In the emotion example, numerical comparison of heart rate and galvanic skin response would not generally be meaningful.

To handle multiple measures, therefore, requires a new approach, namely, *multivariate analysis of variance* (*Manova*). Although Manova is outside the scope of this book, its rationale and relevance are presented briefly.[a]

Multiple Measures. Multiple measures might be handled with a separate Anova on each. Two objections arise, one statistical, the other substantive.

The statistical objection is twofold: loss of power and escalation of α. If each variable contains some useful information, combining them should yield more information than any one alone. Separate Anovas lose some joint information. The α escalation occurs because each separate Anova has a separate chance to yield a false alarm. Although α escalation may not be too serious with just two or three measures, some studies use many more (see Section 17.4.4 and *Selection Effects* in Section 0.3.2, page 799).

The substantive objection is that multiple measures reflect psychological structure. In some cases, the multiple measures may be different aspects of some single underlying state, as perhaps with health of premature infants considered in the introduction to Chapter 13. If so, it may be desirable to combine them into a single variable that best represents that state. In other cases, the underlying state will have more complex structure that cannot be represented by a single variable. To explore this issue, the pattern among the multiple measures needs to be scrutinized.

Manova can help with both objections. The essential idea is simple. In effect, Manova yields a weighted sum of the separate variables that maximizes differences between groups. Each separate measure is weighted to the degree that it contributes to this discrimination, making allowance for intercorrelations between the measures. The multiple measures are thus condensed into a single composite measure that is maximally sensitive to the experimental manipulation. This notable tool yields F ratios for main effects, interaction residuals, two-mean comparisons, and other contrasts. In each case, the null hypothesis asserts no difference on any of the separate variables. Manova thus provides a joint test of all the variables at once.[b]

For a continuing research program, Manova may be useful initially to determine an optimum set of variables and weights to be employed in later studies. This weighted sum is then a single response measure, to which ordinary Anova may be applied.

Homemade Manova is an easy, instructive way to try out this approach. Assign a priori weights to each variable to represent your own feelings about their relative importance. Apply ordinary Anova to this weighted sum and compare p values with the separate Anovas of each separate variable to see how much you have gained. Although I speak without experience in this area, I suspect that choosing weights that extract most of the available information will often be easy (see *Unit Weighting* in multiple regression, page 492). The main danger would seem to come from including useless variables, but these are detectable through separate Anovas or through successive elimination of non-contributing variables. If your homemade Manova looks promising, learning the Manova program on some major statistical package may be worthwhile. Actually, your homemade Manova may be best because a priori weights avoid loss of power from unreliability in estimated weights.

The optimal weighted sum provides only a one-dimensional representation of the psychological structure of the weighted measures. Perhaps this suffices; perhaps all the variables reflect a single underlying construct. But perhaps your experimental manipulation and measures tap into a multidimensional construct. Manova has some potential for deeper analysis of structure, a fundamental issue for psychological theory.

Multiple measures have been little used in general experimental psychology except in certain kinds of physiological studies. The current fixation on single response measures may be missing important facets of psychological structure. Issues of structure have been much studied in test theory, especially with factor analysis of abilities and intelligence, and an overview of the extensive work on test construction may help indicate advantages and limitations of a multivariate approach (see e.g., Anastasi & Urbina, 1997; Cronbach, 1990). All these approaches, however, take for granted a multidimensional, spatial representation that has little place for dynamic processes.

Repeated Measures. Manova can also be applied with repeated measures, but this seems seldom advisable. Regular Anova with ε adjustment seems generally preferable (Chapter 6). Although Manova makes a weaker assumption about sphericity, the ε adjustment takes account of deviations from sphericity. With repeated measures, therefore, Manova is not necessary and seems less useful.[c]

The relative worth of Manova and ε-adjusted Anova has been considered by a number of investigators. Manova is slightly less robust, tends to be more powerful with large n, less powerful when n exceeds a by less than perhaps 10 or 15, as is fairly common in experimental work. Indeed, Manova is not even applicable when $n < a$, whereas repeated measures Anova is. On the whole, Anova with ε adjustment appears superior with repeated measures designs.[d]

18.4.3 PARTIAL ANALYSIS

Factorial design sometimes seems a curse, not a blessing. Five factors yield 26 statistical interactions, most of which would defy interpretation. It is usually difficult to localize a higher-way interaction, and the attempt is disheartened by the thought that statistical interaction may well be an artifact of the Anova model or an illusion of a nonlinear response scale (Chapter 7). Eliminating minor variables from the design might thus seem more than desirable.

Yet five factors, and more, can readily occur in tasks that require balancing of procedural variables that have minor substantive interest. In a study of visual memory, suppose the subject views a sequence of pictures and is later tested with choices between pairs that contain one old picture from the given sequence and one new picture not seen before. Even if type of picture is not of much interest, several types may be desirable to assess stimulus generality. Type would then become a variable in the design. Different samples of pictures within each type may need to be balanced across the major experimental variables. Subject gender should probably be balanced in the design, and perhaps subjects should be blocked using a pretest of visual memory (Section 14.2, pages 407*ff*). It may also be worthwhile to measure the serial position curve of memory by using a Latin square to balance pictures over serial position. To these minor variables are added the major variables of primary interest, all tending to a high-way factorial design. This problem of multiple variables is common in some areas of investigation.

Such situations, with a number of minor variables, present a dilemma. A full factorial analysis may suffocate on statistical interactions. Fear of suffocation may lead to the alternative of ignoring minor variables. But although ignoral can often be rationalized by arguments that such variables should have little or no effect, it does not seem the best way to handle the matter. More acceptable would be to balance the minor variables but omit them from the Anova. This last choice is often appropriate, but partial analysis provides a better solution.

Rationale of Partial Analysis. The idea of *partial analysis* is straightforward. Include all appropriate factors in the design; test only main effects, plus a small number of selected interactions; do not test most high-way interactions.

Partial analysis is one form of extrastatistical inference; it acts by incorporating prior knowledge into design–analysis. Suppose two experimenters are used in a standard experiment on memory or perception and balanced in the design. Prior knowledge about such tasks would often indicate that experimenters should have little effect. Hence a statsig interaction involving experimenters could be dismissed as a likely false alarm. Granted this, there seems little advantage to testing it in the first place. On the contrary, it would cast a pall over other statsig effects (Section 7.5.2, page 205).

The full factorial Anova model is not sacred, neither statistically nor empirically. A model with 26 interactions is an empirical monstrosity. The choice of statistical model should be governed by substantive considerations at the lower levels of the Experimental Pyramid. Partial analysis is a simplification of the full Anova model, based on prior substantive knowledge.

Four-way interactions, it seems safe to say, are seldom interpretable. One reason is the difficulty of localization, even greater than for three-way interactions (see discussion of Figure 7.4, page 204). Furthermore, the interaction may be an artifact or an illusion, as already noted. And even if real, it need not require any particular qualification of the data. Without a priori reason, therefore, it hardly seems worthwhile to include four-way interactions in the model, especially those that involve a minor variable. Similar arguments apply to many three-way interactions.

Some statistical packages allow specified interactions to be deleted from the Anova model. This option, however, pools these terms with error which seems inadvisable unless the error has less than, say, 10 df (see Section 18.4.4, next page). Partial analysis does not assume that the ignored interaction residuals are zero, but rather rests on empirical judgment that they are small and unimportant. A full Anova would be performed, accordingly, but the specified terms would in principle be pooled into an untested residual.

Safety Features of Partial Analysis. Partial analysis has the danger that some pertinent high-way interaction will be overlooked. This danger does not seem serious, in part for the reasons just mentioned, in part because partial analysis contains safety features. The main safety feature is two-way interactions, which should usually warn about complications in the data. In particular, an unexpected two-way interaction between a minor and major variable suggests there may be some inadequacy in the conceptual framework behind the study or in the experimental task and procedure. Task and procedure may need reconsideration, with an eye to designing a replication experiment.

Indeed, even the main effect of a minor variable can serve a similar warning function. A statsig effect of experimenters in the foregoing example would suggest that the procedure was not under control. This would be of concern, regardless of experimenter interactions in the Anova.

The theme of Chapter 7 may deserve reemphasis. Statistical interactions, contrary to their name, have little basis in substantive theory. They are arbitrary parts of an arbitrary statistical model. The great usefulness of this statistical model should not obscure its great limitations. Two-way interactions have a simple form and are sometimes useful. Higher-way interactions are increasingly arbitrary and increasingly meaningless.

Suggested Guidelines on Partial Analysis. To crystallize the foregoing discussion, the following guidelines are suggested for experiments with many factors. Include all factors in the design, but limit the analysis as follows:

1. Main effects of all variables.
2. Low-way interactions of major variables.
3. Two-way interactions of a major and a minor variable.
4. Any interaction possibly pertinent or of concern to the reader.
5. Decide a priori which interactions will be assessed.[a]

Partial analysis aims to improve experimental design, to simplify data analysis, and to facilitate communication of results. Experimental design is improved by including minor variables in the formal design, a practice that becomes more attractive when it does not impose a heavy penalty of struggling with statistical interactions that may well lack meaning or pertinence. This simplifies the data analysis, of course, as well as writing up the results. More detailed exposition, including application to an experiment on verbal learning, is given in Anderson (1968).[b]

18.4.4 ERROR POOLING [a]

Some designs yield uncomfortably few df for error. It may be possible, however, to *pool* some "doubtful" source with the error. Pooling follows its name: Add the SSs for the doubtful and proper error sources to get a pooled SS; add the df similarly; divide to get the pooled MS_{error}.

The potential advantage of pooling is a more reliable error term and thereby shorter confidence intervals and more power from the same data. With less than 6 error df, each added df can be worth a lot, so pooling is attractive. Thus, $F^*(1, 5) = 6.61$, whereas $F^*(1, 6) = 5.99$ is 10% smaller and confidence intervals would be 5% shorter. Above 6 df, pooling becomes steadily less important; each added df has progressively smaller benefit. Above 10 or 12 df, pooling may not be worth the worry of deciding whether it is justified.

Pooling is dangerous, of course, when the true variance of the doubtful source differs from that of the proper error. The operative α may be biased and/or power may be lost. To reduce these dangers, a preliminary test for equality of the two pooled variances is often advocated, using a weak α (e.g., .25). Only if this preliminary test is not statsig are the two sources pooled.

I believe the preliminary test is seldom an adequate safeguard. In one class of situations, the doubtful term has true variance less than or equal to that of the proper error, as with some random factor designs. An example appeared with the natural groups design of Table 15.1: The proper between groups error had only 4 df; pooling the doubtful between subjects error would add 114 df! But pooling in this situation suffers the clear danger of yielding a too-small error and a too-high operative α.

This class of situations was studied by Bozivich, Bancroft, and Hartley (1956), which is the source of the much cited recommendation to use $\alpha = .25$ in the preliminary test. But this recommendation assumes that the investigator is "reasonably certain" (p. 1040) that the ratio of the two true variances is not much greater than 1.5, a strong assumption that is not often mentioned and not often justified. It may be added that Bozivich et al. assume at least 14 df for the proper error, which limits their results to cases in which pooling is hardly worth worrying about. In his rather different approach, Hines (1996) concludes that pooling is only safe in practice when the proper error df is large enough that the possible benefit would be small.

In a second class of situations, the doubtful error has true variance greater than or equal to that of the proper error, as is typical with fixed factor design. The preliminary test then gives some protection against pooling when the doubtful variance is large but it also biases α upwards by eliminating cases in which the doubtful term has a high sample variance even though its true variance is close to that of the true error. This class of situations was studied by Mead, Bancroft, and Han (1975), who conclude that power gain is "generally negligible" (p. 800) unless the doubtful error has substantially more df than the true error, which would not typically happen in practice. Similarly, Hines (1996, Section 6) advises against pooling except in one special case that is subsumed under a later comment.

Pooling based on the preliminary test seems generally inadvisable in either of these two classes of situations. Undue inflation of α is a real danger in the first class because the needed prior information about the two pooled variances will seldom be "reasonably certain." Loss of power is quite possible in the second class of situations.

A different qualm about the preliminary test is that all work on pooling has assumed normal distributions. But most tests for equal variance, Bartlett's test being most common, are sensitive to nonnormality and can hardly be trusted. Not less seriously, perhaps, nonnormality will impact the operating characteristic of the preliminary test in unknown ways.

Never pool in repeated measures designs. Bogartz (1993; see also Bogartz et al., 1997, p. 411) considered the case of the $(S \times A \times B) \times G$ design, with two within factors and one between. With few subjects, there are usually few df for $S \times A$, the error term for A. It is then tempting to pool $S \times A \times B$ with $S \times A$, and perhaps even pool $S \times B$ as well, and this has sometimes been done. But Bogartz' simulations show that the preliminary test does not prevent too many false alarms—not even when $S \times A \times B$ and $S \times A$ have equal true variances. When $S \times A \times B$ has smaller variance, as may generally be expected, the false alarm bias is even more serious. Repeated measures designs thus follow an absolute rule: *Never pool.*

Pooling is sometimes done on an a priori basis, without making any preliminary test. A classic case is a factorial design with $n = 1$ and hence no proper error term. Interaction residuals may then be pressed into service as a conservative error term. A 4×4 design would thus allow 9 error df. A similar case of pooling high-way interactions in a 2^p design is noted by Hines (1996).[b, c]

A more common case may be illustrated with a $2 \times 2 \times 3$ design with $n = 2$. This would yield 12 error df, which is adequate if not comfortable. In addition, it is desired to balance a minor variable with two levels, such as right-left position. This minor variable is expected to have a small main effect and negligible interactions. Balancing this minor variable, however, is equivalent to adding a fourth factor to the design, reducing n to 1, leaving no df for error. It might thus seem inadvisable to include the minor variable in the design.

In such case, however, it seems reasonable to balance the minor variable but test only its main effect. Its interaction residuals could all be pooled to get an error on 11 df. This kind of pooling follows the rationale of the previous section on *Partial Analysis*. It is pretty well limited, of course, to situations in which the true variance of any pooled term is not less than that of the proper error. Then the only risk is possible loss of power, a risk the investigator may consider advisable.

Pooling can be worthwhile when data are expensive or scarce. To justify pooling, situation-specific simulation seems essential and should not be an undue burden with present PCs. The approximate df will be known, which makes the task much simpler than the cited studies, which tried to cover wide ranges of df for the three sources. Two or more real effects need to be considered, of course, to assess significance level and power. In addition, it would seem vital to simulate with at least one plausible nonnormal distribution.

An honest alternative to pooling is to publish the data without regard to statistical significance. This seems justified with well-executed studies that are expensive or important. An empirical alternative is to take additional precautions to reduce error variability through experimental procedure. This empirical alternative is rarely discussed by statisticians although its potential dwarfs that of any statistical pooling procedure.

18.4.5 REGRESSION ARTIFACT

Many investigators have fallen into the black pit of the *regression artifact*. The most prominent class of regression artifacts stems from unreliable scores. To illustrate, consider one result from a once-influential research program on special training to increase children's IQ. Children with lower IQ scores on the initial test generally scored better when retested after the training; this gain was attributed to the stimulating effects of the training program. True, children with higher IQ scores on the initial test generally scored poorer the second time; but this loss was interpreted to mean that superior children did not find the program challenging and lost interest.[a]

In fact, both results are exactly what is expected if the program has no effect whatsoever. To see why, consider two individuals whose true score is exactly at the boundary between the two groups. Unreliability in the observed scores may place one in the lower group, the other in the higher group. If no real change occurs, the expected score on the second test is identical with the original true score. Hence the lower scorer will do better the second time; and the higher scorer will do poorer (on average). Similar reasoning applies to subjects with true scores near the boundary (Exercise d4). Only if we understand the statistical concept of unreliability—and how it interacts with the classification into lower and higher—can we avoid this black pit.[b, c]

Matching subjects, which seems an attractive way to equate nonequivalent groups, can also introduce a regression artifact. To test the efficacy of a medical, educational, or behavioral treatment, for example, the (after − before) change score is not generally safe because change is likely even with no treatment. Yet a randomized control may be hard to obtain. In this situation, it seems attractive to match each subject in the treatment population with a subject in some comparison population so that both subjects have the same pretest score. This matched comparison group then serves as the "control" group.[d]

Such matching virtually guarantees a regression artifact when the populations differ initially. Perhaps the best-known of innumerable examples is the initial evaluation of the Head Start program to improve IQ and vocabulary of disadvantaged children. This evaluation showed harmful effects: The comparison group, which received no special treatment, improved more than the disadvantaged group, which received the extensive supplemental education. This apparent harm was no doubt a regression effect.

A regression artifact would enter because the comparison children were chosen from a less disadvantaged population with generally higher IQ and vocabulary scores than the disadvantaged population. To match, it was necessary to select lower scorers from the comparison population. This selection includes subjects whose scores are low by chance; these subjects are guaranteed to score higher on average upon retest, as shown in the third preceding paragraph.

Such matching is now rare. Unfortunately, it has been replaced by multiple regression (Chapter 16) and Ancova (Chapter 13), which suffer similar artifacts. Although billions are spent each year on Head Start, evidence on effectiveness remains scanty (Sections 15.4 and 16.2). Even more scanty are experimental results on how to improve effectiveness.

Regression artifacts can occur within a single person. In chronic illness, for example, the person's condition fluctuates up and down over time. Down times, of course, are when people are most likely to seek treatment. Apparent improvement is thus virtually guaranteed by the regression artifact—but it is attributed to the treatment. This artifact is so well-known it is surprising to read that it was quite overlooked in Seligman's (1995) report on effectiveness of psychotherapy. Indeed, the data that Seligman subsequently furnished to disprove the artifact actually supported it.[e]

Matching might seem simple when change scores can be used. If X and Y are the initial and final scores, the change score, $Y - X$, seems to adjust or correct for individual differences on X. This change score is so natural and obvious that it may seem to present no threat. In fact, change scores are subject to a regression effect, illustrated in the previous paragraph. In addition, change scores can throw away power (Section 13.1.2, pages 386f). Change scores are surprisingly tricky, and statistics has made valuable contributions to understanding their use and misuse (see contributors to Harris, 1963).

As a final comment on this first class of regression effects, similar artifacts can occur even when the initial and final tests are perfectly reliable. The essential condition is that their correlation be less than unity. Imperfect correlation will generally occur when the two tests measure different concepts, of course, because the rank order of individuals will generally differ on the two concepts. But even when the two tests measure the same concept, the psychological structure of this concept may change over time. Reading comprehension, for example, may advance from phrases to sentences or from sentences to paragraphs; perceptual reading skills may become better organized. With such structural changes, the rank order of individuals will generally change, yielding an imperfect correlation. Such structural change produces the same regression artifact as unreliability, even with perfectly reliable scores (see Section 15.5.4, page 470).

A second class of regression effects arises when subjects are given continued trials until they meet some criterion. Use of a criterion is common in learning studies and may not cause any problem. When the criterion method is used to equate groups, however, it can be fatal.

To illustrate, consider the question whether younger children, who learn more slowly in certain tasks, also forget more slowly. If all subjects received the same number of trials, faster learners would begin the forgetting phase at a higher level, which could confound the measure of forgetting. It thus seems necessary to equalize initial learning. Accordingly, subjects may be run to a criterion of, say, one perfect repetition of a paired associates list. This use of a criterion is a form of matching that seems to equalize initial learning of slow and fast learners, thus allowing direct comparison of their forgetting. But because of unreliability, the observed score on the criterial trial is higher than the true score. This may be demonstrated by running one more trial past the criterial trial; the score will generally be less than perfect. The problem is that the magnitude of this regression effect will likely differ for the two groups. Hence they are not really equated.[f]

Many operant studies use a criterion. The observed performance on the criterial trial differs systematically from the true performance. This bias may not cause a problem, but then again it may (Note 11.3.1a).

To sum up, regression artifacts should be suspected whenever: An attempt is made to equalize or correct for individual differences; subjects are matched; a criterion is used; or subjects are classified or categorized on the basis of their performance. No artifact may be present, of course, and may not be a problem even if it is. But keep your weather eye open to avoid falling into the black pit of the regression artifact.

18.4.6 ALTERNATIVE MODEL FOR REPEATED MEASURES

This section presents an alternative to the Anova model for the repeated measures designs of Chapter 6. Different concepts of error variability are used in repeated measures design and independent groups design. This difference suggests an alternative statistical model for repeated measures, which in turn suggests an opportunity to increase power at little cost.

The Anova model for repeated measures of Chapter 6 assumes that subjects and treatments have additive effects. Each treatment, in other words, has the same main effect for every subject. However, deviations from additivity are also included in the model—these deviations are the subject–treatment interaction residuals. These deviations constitute the error term for treatments.

A plausible alternative assumption is that treatments amplify individual differences. Amplification corresponds to multiplication rather than addition. If this alternative assumption is true, or partly true, then the standard repeated measurements model is placing part of the treatment effect in the error term, a twofold loss of power. Salvaging this power may be possible by replacing the addition model of Anova with a multiplication model.

Nature of Error Variability. Error variability is conceptualized differently with repeated measures in Chapter 6 than with independent groups in Chapter 3. With independent groups, variability was an empirical fact, measured by observable differences between subjects treated alike.

With repeated measures, error variability is not an empirical fact. Instead, it is defined as residuals from the additive, subjects + treatments model. This error variability is not an observable, therefore, for it depends on an arbitrary statistical model that may be questioned on psychological grounds.

Of course, residuals from the additive, subjects + treatments model make sense as an error term. If treatments have real effects, subjects usually show a common pattern. Each subject may be represented as one row in the factorial $S \times A$ graph, with levels of A on the horizontal axis (see Figure 6.1). The row curve for each subject suggests a real effect to the extent that it is not horizontal. We gain confidence in a real effect to the degree that the curves for different subjects show a common pattern, that is, to the degree they are parallel (and not horizontal). The greater the individual irregularities from this common pattern of parallelism, the less confidence we have in a real effect. Error variability may thus be measured in terms of deviations from parallelism—that is, as residuals from the subjects + treatments model.

As this discussion shows, an important function of the additive model, subjects + treatments, is to define common pattern. Common pattern determines both the measure of the treatment effect and the measure of error variability. Common pattern, however, is definable in other ways that may be better.

Multiplication Model for Repeated Measures. If treatments amplify subject differences, a different Anova model for repeated measures may be appropriate. In Table 18.2a (next page), the scores for subject 2 run about twice those for subject 1. Common pattern would thus seem better defined in terms of a multiplication model, that is, as a fan of lines rather than as parallel lines.

A smaller error term will be obtained by using the more appropriate model to define common pattern. In the data of Table 18.2a, the additive Anova model

TABLE   18.2

COMPARISON OF ADDITION AND MULTIPLICATION MODELS

	A_1	A_2	A_3	A_4
a. Raw data				
S_1	1.3	2.1	3.1	4.3
S_2	2.1	4.3	6.3	8.1
b. Residuals, addition model				
S_1	.85	.15	−.35	−.65
S_2	−.85	−.15	.35	.65
c. Residuals, multiplication model				
S_1	−.10	.10	.10	−.10
S_2	.10	−.10	−.10	.10

yields $F(3, 3) = 8.72$, less than $F^*(3, 3) = 9.28$. Let's extend the additive Anova model (Equation 6.2) by adding the multiplicative term $S_i \times \alpha_j$:

$$Y_{ij} = \bar{\mu} + S_i + \alpha_j + S_i \times \alpha_j + (S\alpha)'_{ij} + \varepsilon_{ij}. \qquad (19)$$

This multiplicative term may be estimated from the residuals of the additive model. The remainder residuals, here denoted by primes, are the residuals from the extended addition–multiplication model of Equation 19. These remainder residuals constitute the error term. This error term will be smaller to the extent that the multiplication term is nonzero.

This extended model gives a better description of the data in Table 18.2a. In this example, the multiplication model can be fit by visual inspection, treating the levels of A as equally spaced and fitting a separate straight line to each subject's data. By eye, the straight line for subject 1 should pass through the points 1.2, 2.2, 3.2, 4.2. The residuals from the multiplication model are .10 in each cell. Subject 2 is treated similarly.

The residuals from the two models are very different. For the addition model, the mean magnitude residual, shown in Table 18.2b, is .50. For the multiplication model, the corresponding residual from Table 18.2c is only .10.

In each Anova model, the error term is obtained by squaring and summing the residuals and dividing by the df. All statistical assumptions are assumed to hold. The multiplication model has only 2 df for error, however, 1 less than for the addition model. This 1 df has been used to extract the multiplicative component out of the residuals from the addition model. The error mean square decreases substantially—from .86 for the addition model to .04 for the multiplication model. For the multiplication model, accordingly, the main effect of A yields $F(3, 2) = 187.50$, comfortably greater than $F*(3, 2) = 19.16.$[a]

The multiplication model has thus conferred a double benefit: a more informative description of the data, together with lower error. Lower error means greater power and tighter confidence intervals.

More Power From Transformation to Additivity. The standard additive model, subjects + treatments, has been pretty much taken for granted. It may suffer from conservative bias, however, as in the foregoing example, yielding an overly low treatment effect and overly wide confidence intervals. Some way to avoid these two losses is desirable.

Replacing the addition model model by a multiplication model does not seem attractive. Aside from added statistical complexities, an ε adjustment may not be available for the multiplication model.

Instead, the data can be changed by transformation toward additivity. The error residuals from the additive model depend on the response scale, as was shown in the time–speed example on page 193. If the data include a multiplicative component, a log-type transformation may make them more additive. A very large benefit is obtained in the example of Table 18.2 (Exercise e3).

This transformation approach is fairly general, applicable to other forms of nonadditivity. It requires nothing new, for it relies on the familiar repeated measures Anova of Chapter 6. It retains the ε adjustment. And it is readily implemented, as discussed under *Transformations*, Section 12.4. It should be helpful when treatment differences are amplified across subjects, but whether it will be generally useful in practice remains to be seen.

18.4.7 GENERAL LINEAR MODEL

Much of statistical theory rests on the *general linear model* (*GLM*), which includes Anova and regression models as special cases. Professional statisticians rely on the GLM because of its formal simplicity and because it provides a unified treatment of Anova–regression as well as multivariate analysis.

The two-factor Anova model of Chapter 5 illustrates the GLM:

$$Y_{ijk} = \bar{\mu} + \alpha_j + \beta_k + (\alpha\beta)_{jk} + \varepsilon_{ijk}. \tag{20}$$

The L in GLM merely means that it is a linear, or additive, function of the parameters in the model equation. In the Anova model, the parameters represent the main effects and the interaction residuals. These parameters are estimated from the data to determine the SSs for the Anova table.

This parameter estimation uses the method of least squares, described in Section 9.1.6. Larger factorial designs have numerous parameters, however, which is a calculational burden. Even a modest 3×4 design has 12 parameters, and this leads to 12 simultaneous linear equations in 12 unknowns. Standard solution procedures in terms of matrixes and determinants have been developed.

The mathematical method for solving a set of simultaneous linear equations uses matrixes. In matrix form, the GLM is simple and compact:

$$\boldsymbol{Y} = \boldsymbol{XA} + \boldsymbol{\varepsilon}. \tag{21}$$

Here $\boldsymbol{Y}$ is an $N \times 1$ matrix of the known data, $\boldsymbol{A}$ is a $p \times 1$ matrix of the p unknown parameters, $\boldsymbol{X}$ is an $N \times p$ matrix of constants chosen to represent the structure of the design and the parameters, and $\boldsymbol{\varepsilon}$ is an $N \times 1$ matrix of errors. This matrix equation is just shorthand for p simultaneous linear equations in p unknowns.

To apply this matrix formulation to data analysis requires some coding of the parameters; this coding is needed to determine the design matrix $\boldsymbol{X}$. Four coding methods have been used. With effect coding, the parameters are just those of the Anova model. For some purposes, however, dummy coding or orthogonal contrast coding may be more convenient. Perhaps the simplest of all is cell means coding, in which the parameters are just the cell means. Kirk (1995, Chapter 6) gives a reasonably clear treatment if you wish to know more.

Many computer programs are based on the GLM, as with Anova with unequal n or with multiple regression. To use these programs, of course, you need know nothing about this. In psychology, matrix methods are essential in factor analysis and other forms of multivariate analysis. In experimental analysis, however, matrix methods are seldom needed.

A wonderful feature of factorial Anova is that the SSs can be calculated from the simple formulas of Chapter 5 as long as the ns are equal. There is no need to solve the simultaneous linear equations using matrixes and determinants; nor any need to learn technical details of the GLM.

This is about all most of us need to know about the GLM. Some situations require learning about coding schemes and other technical detail, as in Bogartz' innovative use of regression models for process analysis (Note 8.1.2d). These situations are not common, however, and may be reserved to special courses.

NOTES

18.1a. This discussion of effect size and importance is based on Anderson (1982, Chapter 6).

18.1b. The need for empirical rather than statistical framework is striking with the issue of effect size. Numerous writers have extolled the virtue of going beyond the significance test to report some measure of effect size. This theme seems totally persuasive—until one looks at the measures of effect size that have been proposed. They smother the empirical effect under an additional blanket of statistics.

A total of 40 measures of effect size were collected from the literature by Kirk (1996) and are listed in his Table 1. Notably absent from this list are the most important indexes: the mean, the one-variable regression coefficient, and their confidence intervals. This state of affairs is a symptom of the pervasive orientation that fixates on statistics to the neglect of empirics.

Questions of size and importance have no easy answer because they are basically extrastatistical issues. They need to be addressed in empirical terms, within the framework of each experiment. Focus on statistical indexes obscures the real issue. See further *Importance Indexes and Self-Estimation Methodology* in Chapter 6 of Anderson (1982) as well as Anderson and Zalinski (1991). Also of interest are Kruskal and Majors (1989) and Wright (1988).

18.1.1a. That small effects can cumulate across many instances to be important for outcome analysis has been emphasized by numerous writers, including Gilbert, Light, and Mosteller (1975), Yeaton and Sechrest (1981), and Abelson (1985). Prentice and Miller (1992) point up importance of small effects in process analysis.

18.1.2a. The *d* index of Equation 3 is not a general measure of effect size because effect size is a substantive concept that must be understood in extrastatistical terms. The same *d* of .50 would mean different things in experiments on person cognition, verbal memory, animal learning, and even in two different experiments within any of these fields. Cohen (1988) covers over this substantive problem by classifying *d* values of .20, .50, and .80 as "small," "medium," or "large." This arbitrary classification obscures the prime importance of interpreting the mean difference—in its unstandardized form—within its own empirical framework.

18.1.2b. A much-cited non sequitur that published empirical reports generally have inadequate power was initiated by Cohen (1962) on the basis of his small-medium-large classification of effect sizes cited in the previous note. This claim was a non sequitur because, as Mulaik, Raju, and Harshman (1997) point out, Cohen did not calculate power from the data of any empirical report.

Instead, Cohen tabulated sample size for each report. This sample size was used to estimate power for the three cited *hypothetical* effect sizes of .20, .50, and .80 using Equation 3 (or formulas for comparable measures of effect size such as *r*). Cohen found that power averaged just under .50 for a "medium" effect size. He arbitrarily assumed that a "medium" effect size was the norm for empirical studies and so concluded that published experiments generally lack power.

Cohen's conclusion of inadequate power is a non sequitur because his analysis says nothing about power of any actual study, only about hypothetical studies with a "medium" effect size. Cohen's non sequitur was replicated by Sedlmeier and Gigerenzer (1989), who concluded that Cohen's warning had had no effect on increasing power in studies published subsequently. But every one of the 70 articles considered by Cohen might have had a "large" effect and hence power over .80 (see Table 3, p. 150, in Cohen, 1962). Were his non sequitur true, not many of these articles would have been published.

18.1.2c. An interesting nonmetric index of effect size is the probability that an observation in group A exceeds an observation in group B. This probability may be estimated by a simple counting procedure, and has been used in signal detection theory as an area estimate of d'. This estimate is equivalent to the Mann–Whitney U, normalized by dividing by the product of the ns of the two groups (see Note 20.3.3c, page 679). This index should be useful in a variety of tasks, although it neglects the response metric.

18.1.3a. The ω^2_{effect} of Equation 6 may also be seen as a clumsy form of the standardized power effect size of Equation 2. It may be rewritten as

$$\omega^2_{effect} = \left[\frac{\sigma^2_{effect}}{\sigma^2_{error}}\right] \div \left[\frac{\sigma^2_{effect}}{\sigma^2_{error}} + 1\right].$$

The numerator, which reappears in the denominator, is just the square of the standardized power effect size of Equation 2.

18.1.3b. For repeated measures designs, ω^2 is vitiated by multiple error terms. Consider one between and one within variable, each with two levels, that have identical effects—in terms of the means. Yet ω^2 will generally be much smaller for the between variable because it has a much larger error term. Any two within variables, since they have different error terms, are troubled similarly. It seems only sensible to forget ω^2 and compare the mean differences themselves, flanked by their confidence intervals.

The flaw is that equal differences in terms of the means become unequal in terms of the effect size index. A similar flaw afflicts most indexes of effect size because they standardize the actual effect. With standardization, error variability becomes the scale unit. Standardization is necessary to estimate power, of course, but standardized power effect size differs qualitatively from substantive effect size.

18.1.3c. *Note on p Value.* The p value is obviously not a measure of effect size, for it depends on N. For any nonzero effect size, the p value can be made arbitrarily small by increasing the sample size. A confidence interval is superior, for it exhibits the effect in its true form, namely, as an interval of uncertainty on the same scale as the measured data (with normalization, Section 18.2.1).

Neither is the p value a good index of power. This was seen in one exercise of Chapter 4, which showed that a difference between two means just statsig with $p = .05$ would have power about .50 in an exact replication.

As commonly used, the p value is a meretricious statistic. Not only does it not answer the size–importance question, but it obscures recognition that this question is primarily extrastatistical. One reason for popularity of the p value is the strong feeling that it speaks directly to the probability that the null hypothesis is false. This feeling is a cognitive illusion; the probability that the null hypothesis is false has no necessary relation to the *p* value (Section 2.4.3).

18.2.1a. Other texts do not normalize in this way, as may be seen in the standard use of integers for linear, quadratic, and other trend components. Integers simplify hand calculations, it is true, and they couple directly with the overall Anova because of the cited cancellation. But the confidence intervals will not be comparable to the measured data. With primary emphasis on confidence intervals in this text, rather than significance tests per se, normalization seems generally desirable.

18.2.1b. Contrasts With Unequal *n*. With unequal *n*, the means in Equation 7 have unequal reliability. Accordingly, Equation 8 for $SS_{\hat{\kappa}}$ changes to

$$SS_{\hat{\kappa}} = \hat{\kappa}^2 / (\sum c_j^2 / n_j) = MS_{\hat{\kappa}}.$$

The confidence interval for unequal *n* is changed similarly:

$$\hat{\kappa} \pm \sqrt{\sum (c_j^2 / n_j)} \ t^* \ \sqrt{MS_{error}}.$$

Equations 7, 9, and 10 remain unchanged; MS_{error} from the Anova is still used to get F_κ.

18.3.1a. Trend analysis is more complicated when the levels of the treatment variable are unequally spaced or when the *n*s are unequal for different levels. If orthogonal polynomial contrasts are desired, the c_j must be recalculated for each new application. With these orthogonal c_j, the linear, quadratic, and higher order trends are independent so the SSs are also independent, with no overlap.

18.3.2a. Psychology has a long tradition of seeking quantitative relations. In an earlier era, it was widely thought that curve shape was a direct, empirical road to understanding. Much attention was given to methods for analyzing curve shape in situations with metric variables. Statistical analysis of curve shape is mainly useful, however, only for testing theoretical shape predictions, as now seems generally realized. The emphasis on curve shape in current statistics texts seems a relic from this past era.

18.3.2b. U-shaped curves were critical in Clavadetscher's (1991) two process theory, assimilation-plus-contrast, for geometric illusions. Although both perceptual assimilation and contrast have been known to be central in geometric illusions for over a century, nearly all theories have avoided the problem of how these two processes are integrated and instead have sought pure cases in which only one process was operative. This seemed sensible, for the two processes have opposite effects, which makes it easy to explain almost anything. One process theories, however, have done poorly.

Clavadetscher demonstrated both processes in the Ebbinghaus illusion, in which a medium center circle seems larger/smaller when surrounded by a ring of smaller/larger context circles. On perceptual–cognitive grounds, Clavadetscher hypothesized that both assimilation and contrast are operative, but that assimilation is effective only over short distances between center circle and surround, whereas contrast maintains its effectiveness at much greater distances. With larger surround circles, assimilation will make the center circle look larger, contrast will make it look smaller. When this surround is close, assimilation and contrast have opposite effects, and the net illusion is small. As surround–center distance increases, assimilation decays rapidly, contrast decays slowly, so the center circle looks progressively smaller. Only at rather large distances does contrast also decay and the center circle increase to its normal apparent size.

Just this U shape was obtained, which supports Clavadetscher's two process theory and disconfirms both one process interpretations. In this case, a linear trend test was used to show that the rising limb of the U shape was reliable.

18.3.2c. This misconception that an inverted-U curve can be diagnosed with a quadratic trend appears in Keppel (1991, pp. 156*ff*) and in Myers and Well (1991, pp. 205*ff*). Both texts consider data about stimulus generalization of a conditioned galvanic skin reflex. The conditioning trials used a single conditioned stimulus. Generalization was then assessed by presenting test stimuli smaller or larger than the conditioned stimulus.

Theoretically, response to the test stimuli should be maximal for the conditioned stimulus itself and fall off on either side, although more slowly on the larger side because of greater stimulus magnitude. Unfortunately, the quadratic trend is not a valid test of this inverted U shape, as shown in the text (see similarly Anderson, 1963, p. 169). Hence some alternative method is necessary to analyze curve shape.

The main concern in the cited examples was to establish that the generalization curve decreased for test stimulus values larger than the conditioned stimulus. A valid test is straightforward because the peak point on the generalization curve was predicted to be at the value of the conditioning stimulus. A true inverted-U shape would thus manifest itself as a downtrend for larger values of the generalization stimulus. Perhaps the most powerful test would assess the linear component over the latter segment of the curve. An alternative would be a two-mean comparison procedure with a familywise α over the latter segment of the curve (Section 17.4.2).

18.3.3a. This logic might be pushed further by seeking stimulus transformations that maximize the linear trend. SS_{linear} is not overly sensitive to the stimulus metric, however, so attempts to fine tune the stimulus metric are in order only when power is greatly needed. Otherwise, seeking a minor statistical improvement would not be worth the increased problems for the reader in digesting the published report.

18.4.1a. Campbell's definition of internal validity has been considerably criticized (e.g., Cronbach, 1982) and has shifted over time, now being called "local molar causal validity." Cook (1991) compares the different conceptions of internal and external validity that have been presented by Campbell and by Cronbach. This difference seems to stem in large part from Campbell's disenchantment with quasi-experimental design and subsequent emphasis on randomized experiments (e.g., Campbell & Boruch, 1975), in contrast to Cronbach's concern with nonexperimental investigation, especially in education. This experimental–nonexperimental difference has great importance and it seems unfortunate that it has become focused on the word "validity," especially as this obscures the prime need of conjoint observational and experimental analysis to determine kinds of situations that are and are not amenable to observational analysis.

18.4.1b. Not a few effects have complicated dependence on multiple determinants, a fact strongly emphasized by Cronbach (e.g., 1975), who conceptualizes such dependence in terms of Anova interactions. This Anova conceptualization is ill-fitting because it rests on an arbitrary addition model (Section 7.3) and an arbitrary response measure (Section 7.2). Complex multiple determination is important, but representing each determinant as a factor in an Anova design is not an effective routine method to reveal the pattern of dependence (Note 7.6.3a). In fact, the interaction approach has not been very effective in Cronbach's systematic application to educational psychology (Note 7.4.2a).

18.4.2a. A reasonably elementary, nonmathematical treatment of Manova is given by Hand and Taylor (1987; see also Crowder and Hand, 1990), who include treatment of eight sets of data, together with printouts from three major statistical packages. As a historical note, Fisher opened the road to Manova with his work on discriminant functions.

18.4.2b. The essential test statistic for Manova is not actually F, but the "characteristic roots" of a certain matrix of sums of squares and cross-products. This matrix is a generalization of the SSs and SPs of regular Anova–regression. Once obtained, the characteristic roots may be transformed to an approximate F ratio. There are actually four somewhat different statistics based on characteristic roots, of which the Pillai–Bartlett trace is perhaps the most generally useful (see Hand & Taylor, Sections 4.3 and 4.4). However, Wilk's Λ and (for two groups) Hotelling's T^2 are more popular.

18.4.2c. Most writers on Manova recommend its use for repeated measures instead of Anova. The main argument has been that Anova somehow impels the use of a common error term for all contrasts (e.g., Keselman & Keselman, 1993, p. 127; Maxwell & Delaney, 1990, p. 594; for an exception, see Harris, 1993, page 257). This argument is not correct. The need for separate error terms, shown in Grant's (1956) pioneering paper on trend tests for repeated measurements, is now generally recognized.

Some older texts have recommended using a single error term. Current opinion, however, follows Grant with few exceptions.

One exception is Rosenthal and Rosnow (1985, p. 52; see similarly Rosenthal, 1987, p. 161), who say "Each of our contrasts was tested against the same error term against which we tested the overall effect of occasions. Under most circumstances, that is probably the wisest choice of error term for each contrast." But correct error terms for different contrasts may differ by 4 to 1 and more (Anderson, 1982, pp. 106f, Note 2.2.2b); using the same error term for all thus seems unwise.

The proper error term for any repeated measures contrast consists of the individual differences in that contrast score, κ_{iA}. In general, individual differences will be larger the larger the effect of the stimulus variable. Since different contrasts will generally embody effects of different magnitude, their proper error terms will generally be unequal. Even with equal variance, moreover, unequal error terms can result from unequal correlations.

18.4.2d. An overview of 17 simulation studies of effects of violations of assumptions for $(S \times A) \times G$ designs by Keselman, Lix, and Keselman (1996, p. 275) concluded

> For balanced {equal n} designs, the usual F and $\hat{e}$ adjusted F tests . . . were generally robust to moderate degrees of covariance heterogeneity [nonsphericity], whereas the multivariate procedures were slightly more affected by departures from this assumption.

This outcome supports the recommendation of Chapter 6 to use ε-adjusted Anova.

18.4.3a. Decision about which interactions will be ignored should of course be written down beforehand. These decisions may be facilitated by dry run Anovas with hypothetical means, one set with the results you hope for, one or more other sets with results you fear may occur. If you are not yet proficient with factorial design, inspection of the factorial graphs of ignored interactions may be instructive and reassuring.

18.4.3b. Partial analysis technique was presented as the first article in the first issue of *Behavior Research Methods and Instrumentation.* It used for illustration a six-factor experiment on the von Restorff isolation effect in paired associates learning, in which only the one variable of stimulus-versus-response isolation had basic interest (Erickson, 1963). The other five variables included two secondary control variables and three minor procedural variables. None of these could have been omitted without diminishing the quality of the experiment. The recommended partial analysis reduced the number of tested interactions from 57 to 5.

Partial analysis embodies the principle of incorporating substantive knowledge in the experimental design and in the data analysis. As concluded in the original article:

CONCLUDING COMMENT

Statistical analysis should be viewed in its place in the complete experimental process. Partial analysis depends on personal judgment, and different investigators may arrive at somewhat different analyses of the same set of data. Although this may seem objectionable, the really critical role of personal judgment is in problems of procedure and design. The investigator who brings an additional variable under control may thereby be doing good and sufficient service even when evaluating only its main effect. (Anderson, 1968, p. 6.)

18.4.4a. Any pooling procedure must be explicitly specified before the data are collected, except of course for strictly post hoc exploration. Otherwise it is hard to avoid slanting the procedure to fit chance patterns in the data. A pooling procedure may include data-contingent decisions, it is true, but the procedure itself must be prespecified.

18.4.4b. An experimental example of a priori pooling of interactions involving minor variables appears in Anderson and Whalen (1960).

18.4.4c. A quite different kind of pooling that occurs with random factors should also be noted. Some sources do not have a proper error term in certain random factor designs. Instead, an error term is obtained by adding/subtracting mean squares for two or more sources. This approach yields "quasi-F" ratios, which appear to work fairly well.

18.4.5a. This example of regression artifact is taken from McNemar's (1940) detailed critique of an extensive research program that had claimed dramatic changes in IQ (see Wellman, Skeels, & Skodak, 1940).

18.4.5b. Teachers may experience this same fallacy if they compare grades on midterm and final. Students with poorer midterm grades tend to improve on the final—a tribute to the teacher's effectiveness. Those with higher midterm grades tend to do relatively poorer on the final—no doubt because they got overconfident and slacked off. (After Wallis & Roberts, 1956, p. 262.)

18.4.5c. A quasi-realistic class demonstration of this regression artifact is given by Karylowski (1985). This demonstration involves student participation, requires little statistical background, and simultaneously illustrates the distinction between true score and unreliability as error score.

18.4.5d. Matching of nonequivalent groups is very different from matching followed by random assignment to treatment conditions. Matching followed by random assignment not only avoids bias but can also decrease error variability and provide information on individual differences (see block design in Section 14.2).

A survey of all articles in the *Journal of Comparative and Physiology Psychology* for 1958 showed that matching was poorly handled at that time (Anderson, 1959a). The following 40 years have not shown great improvement.

18.4.5e. Seligman (1995) sought to assess effectiveness of popular forms of psychotherapy using mail questionnaire self-reports obtained by *Consumer Reports*. But Brock, Green, Reich, and Evans (1996, p. 1083) point out "One glaring omission in Seligman's (1995) own list of flaws was regression towards the mean." This artifact would produce apparent improvement where none existed, as noted in the text. To Seligman's (1996) presentation of new data to deny this objection, Brock, Green, and Reich (1998, p. 62) conclude that "A closer examination of these new data . . . reveals that the a priori possibility [of regression artifact] was an a posteriori reality."

18.4.5f. A valid way to "equate" groups is sometimes available by incorporating the effect to be equated in a mathematical model that allows it to be factored out. Such theory control appears in the "shape function method" for comparing shape of learning and other curves noted in Anderson (1963, 1996a, pp. 379*f*). This idea of theory control underlies signal detection theory and psychological algebra considered in Chapter 20; see also Section 8.2.5, pages 249*ff.*

18.4.6a. This $F(3, 2)$ tests the same SS_A as the addition model, but uses the error term from the multiplication model. Alternatively, SS_A could be pooled with the SS for the multiplicative component to obtain the total SS explained by the multiplication model. But even though these data are very nearly multiplicative, most of the systematic variation is in the additive main effects. As a consequence, pooling reduces MS_A, thereby reducing the $F(3, 2) = 187.50$ to $F(4, 2) = 156.25$. This decreases power because $F*$ is nearly the same in both cases. In this example, therefore, the main advantage of the multiplication model is to reduce the error term. Practical applications would have more than two subjects, so MS_A could be expected to be relatively larger.

The visual fitting of a separate curve for each subject of Table 18.2 applies only in this special case. To assess the multiplication model would generally require the linear fan analysis of Section 21.5.1. This problem is bypassed here with the recommended tactic of transformation toward additivity.

(This capability of the additive model to nearly fit multiplicative data is one more illustration of the usefulness of Anova in practical applications, and its minimal bearing on problems of "interaction.")

EXERCISES FOR CHAPTER 18

a–c. Exercises for Sections 18.1–18.3.

a1. Consider *The Mystery of the Missing Cloud Cover* in Section 16.2.2. How does the negative b weight for fighter opposition bear on the distinction between process and outcome for assessing importance discussed under *Understanding Regression* b *Weights*?

a2. a. The bigger the real effect, the bigger is the expected F, and the smaller is the expected p. Thus, F and p might seem good indexes of effect size. Argue instead that F and p are poor indexes of effect size because both depend on the number of observations.

a3. P and Q do identical experiments, each using different random samples from the same population. P gets $p = .009$; Q gets $p = .032$. Who is better off if:

    a. H_0 is true?   b. H_0 is false?

a4. Multiple regression has been used to assess relative importance of stimulus informers. Mehrabian (1972) showed photographs of women's facial expressions intended to communicate *liking, neutrality*, or *disliking*, paired with recorded voices of women saying "maybe" intended to communicate the same three feelings. The three levels of each variable were assigned values of -1, 0, 1, and used in a two-variable regression analysis. The b weights were 1.50 for face, 1.03 for voice. These b weights were treated as indexes of importance; facial expression was thus considered 50% more important than voice tone.

    a. What is the argument to treat the b weights as measures of importance?

    b. What is the fatal flaw in the argument of (a)?

    c. With a 3×3 design, could Anova measure relative importance?

a5. Suppose the additive model holds so that each cell mean can be written as $\alpha_j + \beta_k$ (ignoring error and the overall mean). Show that the row means may be written as $\alpha_j + \bar{\beta}$. Show that the sum of the ranges for the row and column means equals the range of the cell means. Relate this to the relative range index of Equation 4.

a6. a. From Equation 1, show that $|\mu_1 - \mu_2| = 2\sigma_A$ for two groups.

    b. From (a) and Equations 2–3, show that $d = 2f$.

a7. P and Q have been independently funded by an international pharmaceutical corporation to develop a chemical intended to decrease family quarreling and increase family happiness. Both report success, but the development costs, especially getting FDA approval, are so huge that only one can be developed.

To decide which one, the corporation secures an independent evaluation of each chemical, compared with a placebo control, $n = 31$ families, with equivalent response measures for each chemical. The results show 99% confidence intervals of 8 ± 8 for P, 4 ± 4 for Q.

   a. What are the p values for P and Q? What do they imply/not imply?

   b. Does it make any difference which chemical the corporation decides to develop? If not, why not? If so, which one?

b1. Why *should* the c_j in a contrast sum to zero? To answer this question, assume the null hypothesis is true and see what will happen if the c_j do not sum to zero. First consider the case of $a = 2$ conditions.

b2. Use the comparison coefficients of Table 18.1, page 564, to show that the interaction residuals are identical in all three panels of Figure 5.4.

b3. You wish to test the mean of two groups against the mean of three other groups, all with equal n. Give the normalized c_j and write the expression for the confidence interval.

b4. Given $Y = 1, 3, 5, 5$, for $X = 1, 2, 3, 4$, with $n = 6$ and $MS_{error} = 8$.

   a. Show that the power for linear trend of this curve is .75.

   b. Show that the power for the overall F is .57.

   c. Plot the curve. What is the moral of this exercise?

b5. From Equation 12, show that multiplying all c_j by a positive constant k increases the width of the confidence interval by a factor of k. Is it good or bad for the confidence interval to change width like this?

b6. Justify the statement of the text that normalization of contrasts with a 2^p design requires a divisor of $1/2^{p-1}$.

b7. You have a quantitative model which predicts that $\mu_1 - \mu_2$ equals some nonzero constant, c. How do you test this hypothesis?

c1. In *Rank and Rating Metrics*, what is the advantage of rating over ranking?

c2. Consider the cubic curve, $Y = X^3$. Suppose $X = -1, 0, +1$. How much of the SS lies in the linear component? (Plot a graph; no calculation is needed or wanted.) What is the purpose of this exercise?

c3. Consider the pure quadratic curve, $Y = X^2$, with $X = 0, 1$, and 2. Show that the total SS is $8.667n$, of which 92% lies in the linear component, only 8% in the qadratic component (the quadratic c_j are $1, -2, 1$). What is the moral?

c4. Subjects receive four trials per day in an emotional adaptation task, using one emotional arousal condition each day. Each subject serves under three different emotional arousal conditions on three successive days. You wish to study adaptation of arousal, as it occurs within and between arousal conditions.

a. Suppose you plan to use the overall repeated measures Anova (Chapter 6). Write out Source–df and say which sources test your hypotheses.

b. In looking at your answer to (a), you wonder whether you should pass by the overall Anova and instead test linear trend. What do you think?

c. Before you decide to plan any analysis around the linear trend of (b), you feel you had better be sure you can actually make this calculation. Show how to use the contrast analysis of Section 18.2.1. It may help to begin with a numerical example.

d. What other variable needs to be controlled in this design?

c5. Given $Y = 1, 5, 7, 8$ for $X = 1, 2, 3, 4$, with n observations in each condition. Graph this curve, fit a straight line by eye, and guess what proportion of SS_A will be in the linear component. Check your guess by calculating the two SSs. Comment.

c6. Find a published curve in some area of interest to you. Suppose the response measure is only a monotone scale. Graph two other curves of quite different shape that would result from monotone transformation of these data and discuss whether the interpretation would differ in the three cases. How much reason do you have to think that the published curve is more valid than your two alternatives?

d. Exercises on Regression Artifact

d1. College students tend to have children less intelligent than themselves.

a. Why is this guaranteed by statistics?

b. What are its implications for your own parenting?

d2. In Chapter 9, Galton's equation showed that sons of taller/shorter fathers tended to be shorter/taller—closer to the population mean in both cases. Some writers have argued that the population as a whole is moving toward the mean, with increasing homogeneity over successive generations.

a. What will happen if we compare the heights of taller (shorter) sons with the heights of their fathers?

b. What does your answer to (a) suggest about systematic regression to the population mean over successive generations?

c. What does the hypothesis of systematic regression imply about the differences between the distributions of height across successive generations? What statistic is appropriate for empirical tests?

d3. (After Wallis & Roberts, 1956, pp. 258-261.) Many sports fans are avid connoisseurs of sports statistics. Bill McGill suspects major league batters are becoming mediocre, with the good ones becoming poorer, the poor ones better. As one illustration from the 1954 baseball statistics, Willie Mays (Giants) led the major league with a batting average of .345, whereas Ted Williams (Giants) came in last at .222. Sure enough, one year later, Mays dropped to .319 and Williams rose to .251.

Bob Boynton, on the other hand, suspects the good get better and the poor get poorer. He looked at the same two years as McGill. To illustrate, Kaline (Tigers) led the major league in 1955 at .340, whereas O'Connell (Braves) trailed at .225. Sure enough, one year earlier, in 1954, Kaline and O'Connell averaged .276 and .279, respectively.

a. Give a psychological rationale for McGill's hypothesis.

b. Give a psychological rationale for Boynton's hypothesis.

c. Boynton and McGill recognize that their results look contradictory. Of course, they realize anything can happen with selected examples. To know what is really going on, you must look at the mean scores for all above average players, and for all below average players. They do this. What do they find? And why?

d4. In the second paragraph of Section 18.4.5, give the reasoning of "Similar reasoning applies to subjects with equal true scores near the boundary."

d5. An alternative way to evaluate Head Start would be to match each Head Start child with a comparison child of same age, gender, and socioeconomic status. Both groups would be tested on vocabulary, say, or IQ. The great advantage is that this matching can be done after the Head Start program has been completed, thereby allowing a test in later years for permanence of the Head Start effect. How can the regression artifact undercut this comparison?

d6. In the example of comparing slow and fast learners in Section 18.4.5, justify the statement "But because of unreliability, the observed score on the criterial trial is higher than the true score." How could this be tested empirically?

d7. (After Rulon, 1941.) Whether progressive education does better than conventional instruction has been of concern to many investigators. In the absence of randomized experiments, some investigators have sought to compare different groups by matching subjects. One such study compared two groups: One group had conventional education through the first four grades; the other group spent the third and fourth grades in a program of progressive education. The assiduous investigator matched the two groups of children on six variables: mental age, chronological age, physical ability, social qualities, home surroundings, and educational achievement. The question was how these two groups compared at the end of the fifth grade. "In every [academic] subject it was found that the group with the background of progressive education did better than the group with the conventional background."

   a. How could the regression artifact enter here?

   b. How does this example differ from the Head Start comparisons cited in the text and other exercises?

   c. The question of effective education has highest importance. What way can you suggest to avoid the ambiguity of the matching method?

e. Exercises on Section 18.4.

e1. The editor of *Psychophysiology* asks you to review a submitted article on emotion, in which the investigators measured heart rate, galvanic skin response, and finger blood volume for each subject. Two groups of subjects were run to test a theoretical prediction from functional theory of emotion. You consider their experimental procedure to be sound and their theoretical logic seems reasonable. The Anovas show $p < .20$ for each of the three measures. "Although these separate tests are not statsig," say the investigators, "they are all in the predicted direction. The chance that all three are simultaneously less than .20 is $.20^3$, which equals .008. This seems definite evidence for a real effect."

The editor has asked you for a review that can be forwarded to the authors. Do you recommend acceptance, revision, or rejection?

e2. The test whether vitamin–mineral treatment would raise nonverbal IQ cited in Section 17.4.2 was meritorious in using several measures of nonverbal IQ. But the data analysis was shameful, for it tested each measure separately.

   a. Why was it meritorious to use several measures of nonverbal IQ?

   b. Why was the data analysis shameful?

   c. How could Manova help?

e3. For the data of Table 18.2a, verify the MS_{error} cited in the text and use it to show that $F(3, 3) = 8.72$. Do a log transform and apply Anova. Discuss the implications of these two analyses.

e4. Justify the assertion of the text in Section 18.4.6 under *Nature of Error Variability* that "We gain confidence in a real effect to the extent that the curves for all the subjects show a common pattern."

e5. You have a 3×5, single subject design with two replications, using treatment randomization to obtain independence. You plan to give preliminary practice and you are confident that any residual practice effect will be negligible. However, you anticipate that other investigators in your field will be concerned about practice effects. Accordingly, you decide to present the first and second replications in succession, using treatment randomization separately within each replication. Differences between the two replications will then prrovide a measure of practice effects.

    a. Write out Source–df for Anova, treating replications as a third factor with two levels. What is disconcerting about this Anova?

    b. An alternative design would randomize all 30 trials en bloc, without regard to successive replications, which therefore would disappear as a factor in the design. What advantage does this have? What disadvantage?

    c. How could you apply partial analysis?

e6. Some reports have followed a statsig Manova with separate Anovas on the separate measures. To the objection that the separate Anovas allow false alarm escalation (Section 4.2.2), they point out that Manova maintains the assigned α, and claim that this justifies the follow-up tests. This claim is examined here.

    Suppose that four measures were used, one with a huge difference between groups, the other three with zero difference between groups. For simplicity, assume all four measures are uncorrelated and independent.

    a. What is the probability of a statsig Manova?

    b. What is the probability of a false alarm on the separate Anova of each useless measure?

    c. What is the probability of a false alarm on at least one of the Anovas on the three useless measures?

    d. How will the above answers change if all three useless measures are perfectly correlated?

e7. In the fourth paragraph of Section 18.4.4, justify the statement about a clear danger of a too-small error term. Why is pooling dangerous in this situation?

PREFACE

Three conceptual issues are considered in this chapter. The first is how probability should be conceptualized in statistical theory. Should probability be defined in terms of objective considerations that can command agreement for different individuals? Or should it include subjective belief, which must differ for different individuals?

The main line of statistics in this century has an objectivist foundation. In this framework, probability is typically defined in terms of observable frequencies of chance events. This objectivist framework underlies the content and presentation of standard texts.

Recently, however, subjectivist schools have been vigorously developed, the most popular being the Bayesian school. In these frameworks, probability is defined in terms of personal belief. This subjectivist view has challenged the foundation and the very way of thinking of the objectivist school.

It is becoming clear that the subjectivist approach is viable and fills a real need. In applied settings, it has notable advantages for incorporating auxiliary information in making judgments and decisions, some of which seem intractable with the objectivist approach. These applications, however, generally require very considerable expertise, illustrated with the three case examples of Bayesian analysis given on pages 613–618.

For experimental psychology, these theoretical controversies are of minor practical concern. With the common fixed factor designs, subjective Bayesian analysis with a noninformative prior leads to the same numerical results as traditional Anova. Also, Neyman–Pearson theory of confidence intervals and power has been smoothly assimilated into the original Fisherian framework, as Neyman and Pearson intended, and is now taken for granted.

The second conceptual issue concerns the significance test. It has been viewed very differently in the three theoretical schools of statistics considered in the first main section. Also, it has been harshly criticized from many empirical directions. Section 19.2 presents a pragmatic view, showing how the significance test performs a useful function in empirical science (pages 624*ff*).

The third conceptual issue concerns psychological measurement theory, especially the concept of linear (equal interval) scale. Some writers have argued that a linear scale is an absolute prerequisite for Anova. Their argument is mistaken (Section 19.3, pages 630*ff*). With randomization, valid tests require only a monotone scale. Randomization thus justifies most uses of Anova in experimental analysis.

Chapter 19

FOUNDATIONS OF STATISTICS

Inference from effect to cause—*inverse inference*—is the main concern of this chapter. Inverse inference is a canonical form of scientific thinking. Our hypothesis predicts a certain effect under certain conditions. We set up these conditions empirically; if we observe the predicted effect, we take this as evidence for our hypothesis.

Of course, this inverse inference, from effect to cause, does not prove our hypothesis. The same effect might result from some other cause.

Statistics provides one tool for inverse inference, a tool that allows for the possibility that the effect was caused by chance. According as our observed effect is unlikely or likely to occur by chance alone, we do or do not consider it supportive evidence for our hypothesis. This argument is just common sense; the virtue of the significance test is to make it quantitative.

But this commonsense argument about chance has a serious limitation. It takes no account of other evidence, which is generally available. This other evidence must also be integrated to determine the credibility of our hypothesis.

How should this other evidence be integrated? This question is especially problematic when, as is usually true, the other evidence involves subjective belief rather than objective observations.

Two answers have been pursued in statistical theory. One answer is that statistics should confine itself to observables; subjective evidence must be handled in some extrastatistical manner. The second answer is that statistical theory has an effective way to handle subjective evidence—and that excluding it would cripple the statistical field.

There is a lot to be said for both answers. And an awful lot has been said, for the question lies at the foundation of statistics. Fortunately, the main sense of the controversy is interesting and clear, without reference to the subtleties and polemics. Even more fortunately, nearly all material covered in previous chapters remains applicable regardless of the theoretical differences of opinion.

19.1 FOUNDATIONS OF STATISTICS

The sample mean should be conceptualized as an interval of uncertainty, as discussed in Chapter 2. Ideally, it would seem, we could specify the probability that the true mean lies within any given interval, including the common 95% interval as a special case.

Can this ideal be realized in practice? Our sample gives us one particular interval; the true mean is either in this interval or it is not. How can the concept of probability apply to this one particular sample?

This question is a thread running through the following three sections, each of which presents a different answer. Two of these answers seem viable, namely, the confidence interval presented earlier in this book, and the Bayesian belief interval.

The difference between these answers stems from fundamental differences in the definition of probability. A familiar approach defines probability in terms of long-run frequencies of events. This frequentist definition appears in the exercises in calculating probabilities for coin tossing, dice throwing, and card dealing used in introductory textbooks. Such gambling problems were the origin of the theory of probability.

This frequentist foundation has been extensively developed. It is epitomized in the concept of sampling distribution, illustrated in Figure 2.1, and it underlies the classical approach to Anova–regression. It has also been applied in fields as disparate as genetics and quantum mechanics, in both of which probability is fundamental. This frequentist foundation appears in the approaches of Fisher and Neyman–Pearson discussed on the following pages.

One reservation with the frequentist view concerns probability of unique events. We have personal expectancies that our experiment will yield good results, that our grant application will be funded, and so on. Such expectancies have some claim to be treated as probabilities. We do treat our expectancies as probabilities in our everyday judgments. When we balance expected costs and expected benefits of alternative research problems, for example, we are using our personal expectancies as probabilities of the costs and the benefits.

Of course, long-run frequencies hardly make sense with unique events. To treat expectancies as probabilities requires some kind of subjective probability.

Some statisticians and philosophers, accordingly, have sought subjective theories of probability. They seek a mathematical formulation that will subsume frequentist theory and also handle unique events. Developing a unified statistical theory on this subjectivist base faces varied difficulties, but substantial progress has been made.

To psychologists, this subjective approach should seem attractive. Indeed, some writers have argued that Bayesian theory, which is the most popular of these subjectivist approaches, also governs human cognition.

19.1.1 FISHER'S FOUNDATION

More than any other person, R. A. Fisher made "significance testing" a focal concern in empirical sciences. Curiously, Fisher's conception of significance testing is now generally considered inadequate.

This point is curious because of the astonishing success of so much else of Fisher's work. As Neyman (1961, pp. 146*ff*) observed in his article entitled, "Silver jubilee of my dispute with Fisher," Fisher's early work "was concerned with the theory of experimentation of which he is the indisputable founder and leader." This theory of experimentation required "solving certain very difficult distributional problems" in which "Sir Ronald has no rivals." And on the foundations of statistical theory, Fisher's papers "left an indelible imprint on statistical literature."

The "theory of experimentation" refers to to factorial design, analysis of variance and covariance, Latin squares, and other practical methods considered in this book. Above all, it refers to randomization, which succeeded against opposition that even yet has not died away. Moreover, Fisher developed these practical methods hand-in-hand with a truly impressive foundation of theoretical statistics. This foundation includes not only the difficult distributional problems, but also such basic and insightful concepts as sufficiency, likelihood, and information. These methods and concepts have proved their value in every field of science, even in the humanities (see disputed authorship on pages 616*f*). They carried with them the practice of significance testing.

Significance Testing. Fisher's conception of significance testing centered on the null hypothesis: "Every experiment may be said to exist only in order to give the facts a chance of disproving the null hypothesis" (Fisher, 1960, p. 16). Statistical analysis, accordingly, had the function of evaluating the strength of the sample evidence against the null hypothesis.

Fisher's view may be illustrated with the F ratio of Chapter 3 for testing the difference between two means. The sampling distribution of F is derived under the assumption that H_0 is true. The upper tail of this sampling distribution is taken as the criterial region. If the observed F lies in this region, the result is said to be "statistically significant."

Fisher's logic seems straightforward. If F is statistically significant, either H_0 is false or a rare event has occurred. With such a result, therefore, we (provisionally) reject H_0.

But Fisher's "rare event" logic is missing an essential element—the location of the criterial region is not statistically specified. Any other 5% region would define a "rare event" just as well as the upper 5% tail. In this simple case, common sense tells us to choose the upper 5% tail. This choice, however, involves an implicit appeal to specific alternatives to the null hypothesis, which are not recognized in Fisher's theory.

It is not nitpicking to criticize Fisher's logic for not including the concept of alternative hypothesis. Fisher sought a complete theory, and a complete theory must have an explicit role for alternative hypotheses, not leaving the selection of the criterial region to common sense. However, Fisher reacted quite negatively when Neyman and Pearson formalized the concepts of alternative hypothesis and power (see below; see also Kruskal, 1980).

Fisher may have thought that his concepts of fiducial interval and fiducial probability finessed concern about alternative hypotheses. This concept, accordingly, is taken up next.

Fiducial Interval and Fiducial Probability.   For a sample mean from a normal distribution, a fiducial interval is calculated exactly as is a confidence interval. In this case, although not generally, the fiducial and confidence intervals are numerically equal.

Conceptually, however, the two intervals differ fundamentally. Specifically, a 95% fiducial interval is one that contains the true mean with .95 probability. Confidence intervals do not allow such probability statements.

The concept of fiducial probability is attractive because it refers to our one particular interval. In the confidence interval approach, probability applies only to a population of possible confidence intervals; to our one particular interval, only the subjective concept of confidence applies (see *Confidence, Probability, and Belief* on the next page).

From the fiducial standpoint, concern with explicit alternative hypotheses dwindles away; fiducial probability intervals can deal with alternative hypotheses in passing. If we do wish to test some alternative hypothesis, we need only check whether the hypothesized mean lies outside the fiducial interval. But without regard to significance testing, the fiducial interval claims to be a valid probability statement about the location of the true mean.

A notable attraction is that fiducial probability depends only on the evidence from the given sample. Fiducial probability makes no appeal to other evidence, in particular, to prior belief in any alternative hypothesis. The sample evidence can thus be quantified as probability without injecting a subjective element of prior belief. Fiducial probability thus seemed conceptually superior to confidence, as Fisher vigorously maintained. Fiducial probability also seemed conceptually superior to Bayesian probability, the most popular versions of which do rest on a subjective element of prior belief.

Unfortunately, the concept of fiducial probability is not conceptually viable. Explorations of the fiducial approach have led to internal inconsistencies and to apparently unresolvable problems. Today it is widely agreed that the concept of fiducial probability cannot be salvaged. It was sustained in part by its evident attractiveness and the plausibility of its agreement with the simple t test and other special cases, and in part through Fisher's determined advocacy, his stellar achievements, and his fearsome reputation.[a]

19.1.2 NEYMAN–PEARSON THEORY

Neyman and Pearson sought a firm statistical basis for the concept of significance test employed by Fisher. Their major achievements were systematic development of the two concepts of confidence interval and power.

Hypothesis Testing and Power. In Neyman–Pearson theory, significance testing is conceptualized in terms of decision between alternative hypotheses. To illustrate, consider the null hypothesis, H_0: $\mu = 0$, and the one-sided alternative hypothesis, H_A: $\mu > 0$. Two kinds of error are possible: *false alarm* (rejecting H_0 when it is true) and *miss* (failing to reject H_0 when it is false).

How can statistics help us cope with these two kinds of error? The Neyman–Pearson rule was to fix the false alarm parameter α at some acceptable level and choose the criterial region to minimize the miss parameter β, thereby maximizing power. In this way, the concepts of alternative hypothesis and power, both officially neglected in Fisher's theory, are explicitly incorporated within Neyman–Pearson theory.

Neyman–Pearson theory thus filled a gap in Fisher's conception of significance testing: The choice of the criterial region is determined by maximizing power. In the foregoing example, the criterial region would consist of the upper tail of the sampling distribution of t. It can be proved that this choice maximizes power on H_A, regardless of the specific value of μ—a uniformly most powerful test. Such tests, however, are not usually possible.

Fisher's theory of significance tests, as already noted, does not specify the location of the criterial region; the lower 5% tail would define a "rare event" equally well. Using the lower tail in this example would be stupid, of course, and everyone would follow common sense and use the upper tail. But common sense only applies in some simple situations and in any case, common sense is not statistical theory. Neyman–Pearson theory formalizes common sense by introducing concepts of alternative hypothesis and power. Neyman–Pearson theory can thus handle more complex situations in which common sense fails.

Confidence, Probability, and Belief. Confidence may be considered belief, but not probability. *Before* you do your experiment, the probability is .95 that the confidence interval you will get will contain the true mean. *After* you have done the experiment, however, you have one particular confidence interval; either it contains the true mean or it doesn't. Statistically, the probability is 1 or 0. You don't know which, but don't confuse your ignorance with probability.

The logic of confidence intervals, as Neyman and Pearson emphasized, is that the *method* of constructing them will produce correct answers $1 - \alpha$ of the time. If you use the confidence method, the long-run probability that any one interval will contain the true mean is $1 - \alpha$. Hence you are entitled to $1 - \alpha$ confidence that any one particular interval will contain the true mean.

This distinction between confidence and probability stems from a frequentist conception that defines probability in terms of long-run frequencies of events. *Probability* refers to a population of possible confidence intervals; *confidence* refers to one specific, given confidence interval.

Extrastatistically, however, confidence may be treated as a measure of belief. Ordinarily our actions will be the same with 95% confidence as with 95% probability. To illustrate, suppose you take one sample from a normal distribution and construct a 95% confidence interval for the mean. The true mean is known to God, Who offers you a fair bet whether the true mean is outside your one particular confidence interval. What should you request as fair odds? Surely 19 to 1 odds is fair, just as if the matter was probabilistic. Confidence thus leads to the same behavior as would probability.

Confidence may thus be considered personal belief. Personal belief is extra-statistical, outside Neyman–Pearson theory, to be sure, but it is part of everyday scientific inference—to which Neyman and Pearson intended their theory should be a useful adjunct. Indeed, it seems fair to say that Neyman–Pearson theory quantifies the personal belief provided by the evidence.[a]

Interpretation of confidence as belief has been emphasized by Mosteller and Tukey (1968, p. 181):

> The nonmathematical implications of 95% confidence limits call for action at least resembling that corresponding to a 95% degree of belief that the parameter does fall in the interval. When there is no extra information about the parameter, and when typicality and absence of selection do not seem to need challenge, there seems to be nothing wrong with attaching such a degree of belief to the confidence interval; in fact, it is hard to see why there should be serious concern.

Neyman–Pearson and Fisher.   Fisher criticized Neyman and Pearson stridently, arguing that they had confused two conceptions of probability, one treating probability in terms of long-run frequencies, the other treating probability as belief. But this confusion was just what Neyman and Pearson sought to avoid with their distinction between probability and confidence.

Initially, indeed, Neyman and Pearson thought they were clarifying Fisher's conception of significance testing. This seemed reasonable because confidence intervals and fiducial intervals were equal numerically in the initial applications in *t* test situations. In later work, as when unequal variances were allowed, the two approaches led to different results. It then became clear that Fisher was pursuing a quite different approach.

Power is a key concept in the Neyman–Pearson approach. Power, however, depends on the size of the effect. Hence power entails the associated concept of alternative hypothesis. The concept of confidence is impressive as a surrogate for probability that allowed treatment of the individual case with a long-run, frequentist conception of probability.

Neyman and Pearson thus provided a fundamental advance over Fisher, for the concept of power is basic in experimental analysis and in statistical theory. Moreover, their work harmonized well with the Anova–regression framework developed by Fisher, fiducial probability excepted. Today, we use the Fisher–Neyman–Pearson blend as a matter of course, and wonder at Fisher's hostility (see Kruskal, 1980).[b]

Incompleteness of Neyman–Pearson Theory. Costs and benefits are essential considerations in any decision between H_0 and H_A. In particular, costs of false alarms underlie the choice of α. The .05 level common in scientific work may not be stringent enough for practical social decisions. In the polio vaccine experiment of Section 10.1, for example, a false alarm would have entailed a useless program of vaccination for every child in America. If no other evidence was available, one might think that even $\alpha = .001$ would be too risky.

Costs and benefits are not explicitly included in Neyman–Pearson theory. They certainly play a role in planning the experiment, not only in choice of α, but also in sample size and other design details that determine power. Neyman and Pearson deliberately left out costs and benefits, however, in part because they are subjective and will differ across individuals. Leaving out costs and benefits did not deny their importance, but it was attractive in an attempt to build an objective theory. The importance of costs and benefits was recognized, however, and Neyman (1961) speaks highly of modern statistical decision theory, which addresses this problem.

A different incompleteness concerns technical troubles that beset confidence intervals: More than one method may be possible for constructing "best" confidence intervals; in some cases, confidence intervals are meaningless or nonexistent; and in some cases, beloved of critics, the confidence interval may be known to be incorrect simply from looking at the data.[c]

These technical troubles, however, have little relevance to everyday experimental analysis. Most data analysis is well served by simple confidence procedures of the kind presented in earlier chapters.

A possible incompleteness is that Neyman–Pearson theory does not include any concept of prior belief; only evidence from the given sample is considered. This lets the sample speak for itself, which seems attractive for statistical inference in science. Two investigators with different prior beliefs can thus agree on the analysis of a given set of data. Both have the further problem of integrating the evidence from this sample with their prior belief, but this integration problem is deliberately left outside of Neyman–Pearson theory.

In this way, Neyman and Pearson harmonized the conception of sample mean as an interval with an objective view of probability. Their treatment of prior belief agrees with the pervasive, fundamental importance of extrastatistical judgment, discussed with the Experimental Pyramid. Bayesian theory, in contrast, seeks to incorporate personal prior belief into statistical theory.

19.1.3 BAYESIAN THEORY

Since Bayesian theory is unfamiliar to most psychologists, the following discussion is longer than for Fisher and Neyman–Pearson. Three empirical applications are included to illustrate the unique potential of the Bayesian approach.

Bayesian theory adopts a subjective conception of probability as rational belief. The 95% Bayesian *belief interval* thus represents probability about the location of the true mean. The conceptual difficulty that Neyman and Pearson handled with the concept of confidence is instead resolved by a radical change in the definition of probability.

Subjective probability leads to statistical theory different in many ways from classical frequentist theory. The conceptual difference between confidence interval and belief interval is a sign of differences that ramify throughout statistical theory and practice. The Bayesian approach is more effective in many empirical situations, for it can exploit collateral information that lies outside the Fisher–Neyman–Pearson framework.

Happily, Bayesian and Neyman–Pearson theory yield essentially similar analyses for most common experimental problems. Accordingly, you may continue to apply the classical methods presented in this and other texts without anxiety (see *Anova and Bayesian Theory* on page 613).

Bayesian Theory. Bayesian theory can be written in a simple symbolic form:

$$\text{Posterior probability} \; = \; \text{Prior probability} \circledast \text{Evidence}, \qquad (1)$$

where $\circledast$ symbolizes an integration operator. Consider estimating a population mean from sample data. *Prior probability* represents our belief about the location of the mean before obtaining the *Evidence*, that is, the information extracted from the sample. *Prior probability* and *Evidence* are integrated to produce *Posterior probability*, that is, our belief about the location of the mean after integrating the Evidence.

Belief probability is not anarchic, as it might seem, for it is subject to the universal laws of probability theory, just as frequentist probability. Thus, if your Posterior follows a normal distribution, its standard deviation determines the 95% Bayesian belief interval by the same formula as for the 95% confidence interval. Your Prior belief may be any arbitrary personal opinion, it is true, but your Posterior belief must obey the Bayesian formula of Equation 1 for integrating the given Evidence with your Prior. Two persons may have very different Priors but they will converge on the same Posterior with Evidence from repeated samples (assuming they evaluate the Evidence in the same way).[a]

Bayes' theorem itself is a noncontroversial result from the early years of probability theory. When the Prior in Equation 1 is based on objective frequencies, everyone agrees that Bayes' theorem applies, as illustrated with the algebraic formula of Note 19.1.3h, page 639. Allowing subjective Priors might thus seem a straightforward extension of frequentist statistics.

Instead, subjective probability leads to statistical theory fundamentally different from classical frequentist theory. This difference appears in the way the two approaches treat randomness. In Neyman–Pearson theory, the true mean is a fixed property of the population and each possible random sample generates a confidence interval. Hence the confidence interval is random.

Bayesian theory conditionalizes the analysis on the given sample. It is illegitimate to consider what might have happened with other possible samples. The data analysis must be based solely on what did happen, never on what might have happened. The belief interval must be fixed, therefore, since it is based on the sample actually obtained. Instead, the "true mean" is random. A 95% belief interval thus contains the "true mean" with probability .95.

To highlight this issue, suppose you have a sample from a normal distribution so that confidence interval and Bayesian belief interval are numerically equal. You must allow the possibility that you have a "bad" sample, for which the interval does not contain the true mean. Neyman and Pearson argue that it thus makes no sense to say that your one particular interval contains the true mean with probability $1 - \alpha$; that's why they introduced confidence as a distinct concept from probability.

Bayesians also say nothing about the probability that your one particular interval contains the true mean. Instead, they redefine probability to refer to your belief about the true mean, given the evidence of your one particular sample. This is entirely legitimate. Remarkably, it turns out to have notable statistical advantages, both technical and conceptual, over the classical approach. It does run into trouble, however, because it does not recognize Fisher's principle of randomization.

Objections to Bayesian Theory.   One objection to Bayesian theory is ideological. Some writers insist that probability can only be defined in frequentist terms. This objection is dwindling away as Bayesian theory shows its usefulness.

A second objection is that subjective prior probability intrudes personal bias into the results. The same data can thus lead to different conclusions for different people. Strong personal belief about the outcome of an experiment could yield shorter Bayesian intervals and seemingly more reliable results. Such objections led to general rejection of the Bayesian approach in the latter part of the last century that continued well into this century.

This second objection is also dwindling away. A principal reason revolves around *noninformative priors*. A noninformative prior seeks to avoid personal bias by assigning equal prior probability to each possible value of the mean. Bayesian analysis with noninformative priors yields the same results as classical theory in a major class of applications. Such agreement could hardly have been foreseen, but it relieves much of the concern that personal bias will intrude into the data analysis (see next two subsections).

Furthermore, subjective judgment is essential in some problems. In many real-life decisions, costs and probabilities have to be estimated on the basis of expert knowledge. Frequentist probabilities, however desirable, are often not obtainable. Subjective probability thus opens a way to utilize expert judgment in statistical analysis.[b]

A third objection to Bayesian theory is that the sample data are taken as fixed and given. All the statistical analyses are predicated on the face value of the given data. It is inadmissible to consider other sets of data that might have occurred by random sampling. The principle of random assignment, in particular, is alien to the Bayesian framework.

This Bayesian alienation from random assignment seems startling, almost incomprehensible, from the classical perspective. Bayesians themselves are uncomfortable about this and have sought various ways to accommodate randomization (see page 619). This matter is interesting as one illustration that developing a unified theory in statistics faces difficulties analogous to those found in empirical science.

Noninformative Priors. A simple example of a noninformative prior would be a flat distribution over some finite interval, with equal probability for each value in the interval. The following normal prior, although not quite as simple, shows an important similarity between Bayesian and classical theory.

Suppose you have prior information about the true mean of some population. You wish to improve this estimate by integrating information from a sample, following Equation 1. Suppose your prior can be represented as a normal distribution, with mean μ_{prior} and variance σ^2_{prior}. Thus, μ_{prior} is your prior belief about the likely value of the true mean. The informativeness of your prior is measured by σ^2_{prior}—smaller variance represents stronger belief and more informativeness. A very weak belief corresponds to a very large σ^2_{prior}, representing a widely spread-out distribution that would be nearly noninformative about the location of the population mean.

Given a normal prior and a sample from a normal population, Bayesian theory implies that the posterior is also normal. The posterior mean is the average of the prior and sample means, each weighted inversely by its variance; high variance thus means low weight. Formally,

$$\mu_{posterior} = W \times \left[\frac{\mu_{prior}}{\sigma^2_{prior}} + \frac{\mu_{ev}}{\sigma^2_{ev}} \right], \tag{2}$$

where μ_{ev} and σ^2_{ev} are the mean and variance of the sample evidence and $W = \left[1/\sigma^2_{prior} + 1/\sigma^2_{ev} \right]^{-1}$.

Equation 2 shows the point. A nearly noninformative prior has nearly zero influence; the posterior is determined almost entirely by the sample evidence. To see this, note that $\mu_{prior}/\sigma^2_{prior}$ is nearly zero when σ^2_{prior} is very large. The same holds for $1/\sigma^2_{prior}$ in the weight W. If these two terms are ignored, the posterior mean equals the sample mean, as it must in the absence of prior information. For a strong belief, on the other hand, σ^2_{prior} would be small and your prior would have greater influence on your posterior.

For much scientific work, noninformative priors seem reasonable. For many practical problems, on the other hand, informative priors can be valuable for utilizing expert judgment and collateral information. Informative priors become increasingly useful as the concern of the investigation shifts from hypothesis testing to parameter estimation. Estimation is illustrated in the later example of whale census, which seeks a best estimate of the size of the bowhead whale population, not a test of any hypothesis.

Classical statistics, it may be noted, also leads to Equation 2—when the prior is given in objective, frequentist form. Even stronger agreement between classical and Bayesian statistics appears with Anova, as indicated next.

Anova and Bayesian Theory. The Anova results of Chapter 3 can also be obtained from Bayesian theory. This equivalence results when a noninformative prior is used, as shown in the landmark book by Box and Tiao (1973, Section 2.9). In particular, the Bayesian belief interval and the Neyman–Pearson confidence interval are numerically equal in these analyses.

To empirical investigators, like you and me, this equivalence is a relief. It means that the fireworks between the two approaches can be left to those concerned with higher levels of statistical theory.

This equivalence of the two approaches is only partial. It does not extend to repeated measures designs, for example, because subjects is treated as a random variable. In general, Bayesian theory cannot match the simplicity and versatility of classical statistics for a wide range of common applications.

This simplicity and versatility was Efron's (1986) main answer to the rhetorical title of his article, "Why Isn't Everyone a Bayesian?" In contrast to the simplicity and versatility of standard Anova–regression, "Bayesian theory requires a great deal of thought about the given situation to apply sensibly" (p. 1). None of the five commentators on Efron's paper disagreed. One of them, Chernoff (1986), seconded Efron by noting that "Fisherian theory provides relatively simple, effective tools, the robustness of which seems apparent in circumstances in which the Bayesian and decision theorist may find it difficult to operate" (p. 5).[c]

Nevertheless, the Bayesian approach is attractive for many statistical problems, especially some that resist analysis with confidence intervals. Prominent among these are nonexperimental situations, illustrated next.

Applications of Bayesian Theory. To appreciate Bayesian theory, familiarity with empirical applications is essential. The conceptual simplicity of the Bayesian formula of Equation 1 and of Equation 4 on page 615 conceals often-serious difficulties and complications. Such difficulties are not a criticism or shortcoming; on the contrary, Bayesian theory allows a principled attack on many problems that seem intractable with classical statistics. Without some familiarity with such applications, however, the simplicity of Equations 1 and 4, and the standard numerical illustrations of these equations, fail to convey the character and value of the Bayesian approach.

The following three examples illustrate kinds of problems to which Bayesian theory has been applied. The difficulties and complications are touched on lightly, mainly to indicate their existence and nature. Further appreciation of the applied side of Bayesian statistics can be gained by skimming the collections of diverse applications in *Case Studies in Bayesian Statistics* (Gatsonis et al., 1993) and in *Bayesian Biostatistics* (Berry & Stangl, 1996).

Two notable features of Bayesian theory appear in all three examples. First, all three are concerned with unique events in nonexperimental situations. Second, the Evidence value of the data depends on some substantive probability model. This probability model is needed to get the two conditional probabilities for the likelihood ratio LR of Equations 3 and 5 below. In the first example, of disputed paternity, the probability model derives from genetic theory. In the second example, of disputed authorship, the negative binomial probability model for word frequency was selected to fit empirical calibration data. As these examples indicate, Bayesian statistics takes more intimate cognizance of substantive considerations than classical statistics.

1. BAYES'S THEOREM ON THE WITNESS STAND. Disputed paternity is a subspecialty of law, common enough to warrant a two-volume reference book, now in its fourth edition. This issue has vital interest to the child, the mother, and the alleged father, as well as to society at large (Berry & Geiser, 1986).[d]

For present purposes, disputed paternity is interesting as a situation in which classical statistics seems ineffectual, but Bayesian statistics furnishes a simple analysis based on objective measurements of blood factors. Two kinds of evidence are used in paternity suits, the first being testimony from plaintiff, defendant, and witnesses. Thus, counsel for the defendant seeks to deny or minimize the frequency of sexual intercourse between defendant and plaintiff and to maximize plaintiff's promiscuity.

The other kind of evidence is from blood factors, especially red-blood-cell antigens, which, being inherited, are clues to paternity. Accordingly, blood samples from child, mother, and alleged father are analyzed in a specialized commercial laboratory. Elementary genetic theory then allows calculation of the probability that any child of this man and this woman would have each blood factor this particular child actually possesses.

If this conditional probability is zero, as happens not infrequently, that ends the case. If this probability is high, however, it is logically—and biologically—possible it would be even higher for some random man. In that case, it would seem evidence for rather than against the defendant. For comparison, therefore, the laboratory also furnishes a similar conditional probability for a random man from some relevant population.

Let H_0 be the hypothesis that the defendant is the true father, and H_A the alternative hypothesis that some random man is the true father. Also, let Data denote the measurements on one specific blood factor for this mother and child. Then the two specified conditional probabilities may be written as the two *cause → effect* relations

$$\text{Prob(Data} \mid H_0) \quad \text{and} \quad \text{Prob(Data} \mid H_A).$$

Note that Prob(Data $\mid H_0$) is the conditional probability that a child of this mother would have the specific blood factor possessed by this child—**if** the defendant was the true father. The second probability refers similarly to the random father.

What we want, however, is something entirely different, namely, the inverse inference, or *cause ← effect* relation

$$\text{Prob}(H_0 \mid \text{Data}).$$

This is the probability that the defendant is the true father—**given** the Data.

This inverse inference requires two steps. The first step is to form the *likelihood ratio* of these two conditional probabilities:

$$\text{LR} = \frac{\text{Prob(Data} \mid H_A)}{\text{Prob(Data} \mid H_0)}. \tag{3}$$

The LR is the discriminative Evidence value of the given blood factor. An LR of 1 is nondiscriminative since it means that the evidence is equally likely under both hypotheses. Small LRs argue that the defendant is the true father. To integrate the Evidence from several independent blood factors, simply multiply their individual LRs to get a single overall LR.

It is tempting to take a small LR, less than .01, say, as the probability that H_0 is true, that is, that the defendant is the true father. Doing so would be a logical error, the same as that discussed in relation to the p value in significance testing (Section 19.2.3). The given cause → effect relation cannot imply the cause ← effect relation that we seek unless we introduce a Prior probability for H_0.

The second step, therefore, is to introduce a Prior probability and apply Bayes' theorem. This application can be written in an especially useful form if we switch from *probability* of H_A versus H_0 to *odds* of H_A to H_0. Then Bayes' theorem can be written in a conceptually simple form as [e]

$$\text{Posterior odds} = \text{Likelihood ratio} \times \text{Prior odds}. \tag{4}$$

Prior odds may be considered as the juror's belief based on the oral testimony of plaintiff, defendant, and witnesses. The Likelihood ratio is determined from the blood sample evidence, its numerical value being given by the commercial laboratory.

As an ideal, jurors would have private computer displays on which to rate their provisional belief following the oral testimony. This belief probability could be indicated by marking a point, or an interval, on a line on the display. (A graphic rating may avoid confusion likely from the methods discussed by Berry and Geisser, 1986). A mark at the midpoint would thus represent a feeling of equally strong testimony on both sides. This provisional belief represents the Prior belief, or Prior odds, in Equation 4.

The blood sample evidence would then be presented and the Likelihood ratio explained. Then the computer would do the multiplication of Equation 4 and present each juror a private readout of their Posterior probability.

In practice, the blood sample evidence does seem to be presented last. By then, after the legal wrangling and cross-examination nitpicking, this objective, quantitative evidence will no doubt be welcome. Some commercial laboratories misuse statistics and present the Likelihood ratio, slightly transformed, as the probability of paternity. This involves a hidden assumption that the Prior probability that H_0 is true equals ½. In any case, the integration of the oral evidence and the blood sample evidence is left to the cognitive algebra of the individual jurors.

2. BAYES'S THEOREM AND DEMOCRACY. We take our democracy for granted, little appreciating how novel and politically fragile it was 200 years ago. At that time in history, many judicious people doubted that society could be stable without a king and thought that a government "of the people, by the people, and for the people" was all too likely to perish from the earth, as it almost did in our secession struggles.

A key historical event was the ratification of our Constitution, which established a strong federal government, superior to the separate states. Ratification was strongly opposed and barely succeeded. Much credit for this success is given *The Federalist*, the collection of short essays published in the newspapers over the name of "Publius," following a then-common practice of pseudonymity. *The Federalist* is now a core document of our political history.

For most of these essays, the specific author is known to be Alexander Hamilton or James Madison. For 12 essays, however, the specific author has been disputed by historians, with the weight of opinion inclining toward Madison as opposed to Hamilton.

Statistics provides an ahistorical approach to the authorship question, relying on internal evidence within the essays themselves. The idea is simple. Scrutinize those essays known to have been written by Hamilton and those known to have been written by Madison for features of writing style that differ between them. Use these discriminating features to determine authorship of each disputed essay.

Two statistical methods may be used to analyze such discriminating features. The classical method uses the linear discriminant function, introduced by Fisher for categorical classification, a common problem in classification of biological species, for example. This classical method is applied in one chapter of Mosteller and Wallace (1964, 1984), who were mainly concerned to explore and develop an alternative Bayesian approach.

Before any statistical analysis can be applied, however, discriminating features must be found. The first attempt was a flat failure. Tedious pre-computer word counting yielded mean sentence lengths for Hamilton and Madison of 34.55 and 34.59 words, respectively. Clearly, sentence length is not a discriminating feature.

Discriminating features were eventually found in the form of 30 function words, including *also*, *by*, and *this*. *Also* gives no more than fair discrimination, with overall frequencies per 1000 words of .31 and .67 for Hamilton and Madison, respectively. Although the ratio of relative frequencies is higher than 2 to 1, the absolute frequencies are low so a 2000-word essay might well have no instance of *also*. To determine authorship for individual essays, it was thus essential to integrate evidence value across the 30 words to get adequate discriminative power.

For a given disputed essay, let n_{also} denote the observed frequency of *also*. Calculate the probability that this n_{also} would be observed if Hamilton wrote a paper of equal length, and similarly for Madison. The ratio of these two conditional probabilities is the *likelihood ratio* introduced in the paternity example:

$$LR_{also} = \frac{\text{Prob}(n_{also} \mid \text{Hamilton})}{\text{Prob}(n_{also} \mid \text{Madison})}. \tag{5}$$

In an essay of 2000 words, 2 occurrences of *also* would have lower likelihood for Hamilton that for Madison, yielding LR_{also} less than 1. A similar LR may be calculated for each other word in this essay.

The evidence from all 30 words, assuming word independence, may be integrated by multiplying their separate LRs to obtain an overall LR, just as with the blood factors in the paternity example. Bayes' theorem may then be applied in the same way to yield

Posterior odds = LR × Prior odds.

The Prior odds may be based on the historical evidence, which inclines toward Madison. A conservative choice is Prior odds of 1 to 1, corresponding to Prior probability of ½. Bayes' theorem then yields the Posterior odds. These were overwhelmingly in favor of Madison on all but perhaps one essay.

The difficult statistical problem has been passed over, namely, how to calculate the evidence value, or likelihood ratio, for each word. This requires calculating the two conditional probabilities in the likelihood ratio of Equation 5. In the paternity example, these two probabilities could be calculated from genetic theory. In the present example, this calculation requires a probability model that specifies the probability of each possible number (0, 1, 2, 3, . . .) of occurrences of each given word for each author. Each word is infrequent, as illustrated with *also*, so the classic probability model is the Poisson distribution. The Poisson, however, did not fit well to the observed frequencies for essays of known authorship. Instead, a more general distribution, the negative binomial, was found to do reasonably well. The negative binomial, however, has two unknown parameters for each word for each author, parameters that have to be estimated from the essays of known authorship. To solve this estimation problem, Mosteller and Wallace introduced a second Bayesian analysis, which they consider the core of their study. This analysis fitted the negative binomial distribution to estimate the two conditional probabilities in the likelihood ratio of Equation 5 for each word.

This value of this work goes far beyond this historical question, for it illustrates a battery of statistical issues and techniques that have general interest and applicability, especially for empirical applications. Mosteller and Wallace (1964) comment that "Even by 1963, very few life-sized problems have employed Bayesian methods for their solution, and far fewer involve substantial analyses of data" (p. 2). Their meticulous, pioneering study was a harbinger of the current cascade of Bayesian analyses.

3. BAYESIAN THEORY CAN COUNT THE FISH IN THE SEA.*͟ Bowhead whales were hunted to near-extinction by 1914, when hunting was prohibited by international agreement, Eskimos partly excepted. The bowhead population showed weak recovery, however, and the International Whaling Commission became concerned that even the several dozen allowed the Eskimos each year were too many (Raftery & Zeh, 1993).

Reliable census data were needed, no easy task with whales. Fortunately, the main stock of bowheads migrates each spring through the water-ice channels off Point Barrow, Alaska, where they are confined to a narrow stretch between the solid shore ice and the solid arctic ice pack. Here two perches were built on the shore ice, from which observers could spot whales as they surfaced to breathe in their migration.

With two perches, a vital question could be answered: How many whales passed the first perch without surfacing to be seen? Observers at the first perch would radio the second perch, about 10 km away, for each spotted whale. By discounting these in their own spotting, the second perch observers could apply a fairly straightforward probability model to estimate how many whales had passed the first perch without surfacing to be seen. Adding the seen and unseen whales yields the total number for the given observation period.[g]

In the Bayesian analysis developed over several years by Raftery and Zeh, a Prior distribution of the number of whales was determined from certain auxiliary data, including aerial survey. A complex, biologically grounded model was developed to describe the probability distribution of whale sightings, analogous to the negative binomial distribution in the previous example. With this model, the Evidence value of the whale sightings for the 1988 migration could be determined. The Prior and Evidence were then integrated by a complex, computer-intensive form of Equation 1 to determine the Posterior distribution of number of whales.

The 95% Bayesian Posterior belief interval ranged from 6400 to 9200 whales, asymmetrical, with a mode at 7500. The Whaling Commission could thus use the 6400 figure as a safe minimum for future decisions.

This Bayesian analysis, although far from simple in actual use, has many advantages over classical analysis, itemized by Raftery and Zeh (1993, pp. 166-168). Among these are the abilities to utilize information in the auxiliary data and the ability to incorporate uncertainty about the tracking algorithm and about the model parameters in the Posterior distribution. In addition, the variance of the Posterior could be analyzed into several sources of uncertainty, thereby guiding improvements in future censuses. It was thus found that the major source of variance in the Posterior was the amount of time that no observer was operating, a valuable result for planning future work.

So thorough and cogent were Raftery and Zeh that the International Whaling Commission, an apparently conservative and contentious body, decided to adopt their census procedure. Similar work may be helpful in enumerating endangered species and related environmental problems.

This example has general significance because it is concerned with estimation, not with hypothesis testing as were the two previous examples. With estimation problems, it is often desirable to incorporate every bit of prior knowledge and auxiliary evidence to improve the reliability and accuracy of the estimate. In psychology, estimation rather than hypothesis testing is common in perception and psychophysics. In general, estimation becomes increasingly central as a field progresses.

Bayesian Theory and Randomization. The principle of random assignment, fundamental in experimental design, is conceptually alien to Bayesian statistics. These two opposed views of randomization appear in the conceptualization of sample: random in classical statistics, fixed in Bayesian statistics. Hence the classical confidence interval is random; the true mean is considered a fixed parameter. The Bayesian belief interval, in contrast, is fixed; what is random is belief about location of the true mean. This is why the probability that (= belief that) the true mean lies in the given interval is meaningful. Belief distributions replace the sampling distributions used in classical theory.

But conceptualizing the sample as fixed disallows consideration of other samples that might have been obtained; Bayesians express horror over the idea that a conclusion should be made by reference to data that did not occur. Randomization is alien in Bayesian theory, therefore, because randomization conceptualizes the given sample as one of a population of possible samples. As Berger (1984, p. 84) says, "The Bayesian conditional viewpoint argues against making *any* use of the randomization mechanism."

The vital role of randomization becomes clear when inferences from nonrandom groups are considered, as with Ancova in Section 13.2 and quasi-experimental design in Section 15.5. In fact, the importance of randomization is increasingly recognized in Bayesian applications, as in Box's (1983) plea for ecumenism in statistics and in Spiegelhalter, Freedman, and Parmar (1996).

Analogous other problems stem from the Bayesian doctrine that the sample must be taken as fixed. In particular, the danger of capitalizing on chance outcomes in the actual sample has appeared repeatedly in this book. But this danger can only be recognized by reference to outcomes from possible samples not actually drawn. This danger is not recognized in the Bayesian rule that the data analyses must be conditional on the face value of the given data.

The problem of α escalation with multiple comparisons is another example of this danger of capitalizing on chance (Chapter 17; see Berry, 1988). The same issue arises with cross-validation (Efron, 1986), outlier theory (Barnett & Lewis, 1984, Chapter 12; 1994, Chapter 9), and even regression to the mean (Section 18.4.5). Bayesian theory has some capability for taking account of chance outcomes in terms of the prior distribution as well as the data generating model. Some attempts have been made, but they seem to let in awkwardly by the back door sampling variability that should be welcome at the front door.

Is Cognition Bayesian? That human cognition obeys Bayes' theorem has been argued by a number of investigators, in psychology as well as in statistics. This claim is attractive since Bayesian theory centers on a subjective concept of probability. This claim is also harmonious with the predominant *normative* perspective, which believes that human judgment–decision should be conceptualized and studied in terms of optimal rules, especially Bayesian rules.

Furthermore, the Bayesian rule represents learning from experience. With experience treated as evidence, the symbolic Bayesian integration rule of Equation 1 may be written

$$\text{Posterior belief} = \text{Prior belief} \circledast \text{Experience}. \quad (6)$$

Integration of our Experience with our Prior belief represents learning. An algebraic formula for this Bayesian integration is given in Note 19.1.3h.

Some investigators have claimed that Equation 6 is more than an analogy, that everyday human cognition obeys this mathematical Bayesian model. This claim is incorrect, however, as may be seen with the experimental study of Figure 19.1. Subjects judged probability that a given sample of red and white beads had come from one of two urns, each with known, complementary, red:white bead proportions. The two urns represent two hypotheses, analogous to the two authors in the foregoing example of disputed authorship.

For the left 60:40 curve in the figure, the subject saw two urns, with 60:40 and 40:60 proportions of red and white beads. The four points on the curve give the judged probabilities that samples of 1, 2, 3, and 4 red beads had come from the 60:40 rather than the 40:60 urn. The upward trend shows that larger samples produce more extreme beliefs, although rather less extreme than probability theory requires. The right 60:40 curve shows very little trend for mixed red:white samples, although these mixed samples show a (red − white) difference of 1, 2, 3, and 4, from left to right, just as with the left curve.[h]

Bayesian theory predicts that both 60:40 urn curves should be identical. Because the 60:40 and 40:60 urns have complementary red:white proportions, the evidence value of the sample depends only on the (red − white) difference, regardless of sample size. This prediction is far from true; the two 60:40 curves are far from identical. The nonidentity of the two 80:20 curves and of the two 90:10 curves disagrees similarly with Bayesian theory.[i]

Instead, the data follow the decision averaging model from information integration theory (see Note 19.1.3j and Section 21.4). Bayesian cognition also fails with the prediction from integration theory that the same information can have opposite effects (see Figures 11.9, 20.4, and 21.5, pages 329, 656, and 707). Opposite effects raises doubt about the sure-thing principle itself. Shanteau's (1975) "water-down effect" (subsequently renamed the "dilution effect") shows similar opposite effects in a Bayesian urn task.[j]

Incompleteness of Bayesian Theory. Bayesian theory is fundamentally incomplete because it lacks a grounded theory of psychological measurement. Belief must be measured to apply Bayesian theory; invalid measures of prior belief can hardly yield valid statistical analysis. To get valid subjective measures requires psychological measurement theory. It may seem odd that a mathematical theory should be dependent on an empirical discipline. This dependence, however, is entailed by the subjectivist conception of probability.

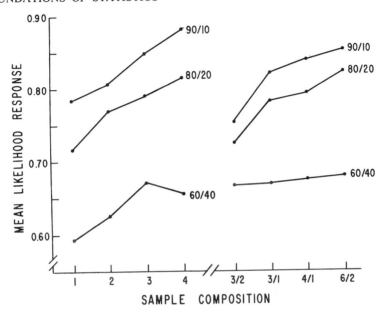

Figure 19.1. Judgments in Bayesian two-urn task disobey Bayesian model. Subjects see samples from an unknown one of two given urns of known composition. They judge probability that the sample came from the urn with more red beads. Left panel shows judgments for samples of 1, 2, 3, and 4 red beads, listed on horizontal axis; right panel shows judgments for samples of 3:2, 3:1, 4:1, and 6:2 red:white beads. Each curve represents data for paired complementary urns, e.g., 60:40 and 40:60, for which Bayesian theory implies that the probability depends only on the (red − white) difference in the sample. Hence each curve at left should be identical with the corresponding curve at right, because the net number of red beads in the sample is the same, point by point. Note that mixed samples have opposite effects at low and high urn disproportions. (From M. Leon & N. H. Anderson, 1974, "A ratio rule from integration theory applied to inference judgments," *Journal of Experimental Psychology, 102,* 27-36. Copyright 1974 by the American Psychological Association. Reprinted by permission.)

This measurement difficulty is serious for some applications; the observed measure of personal prior probability may be severely biased. The later discussion of Figure 19.2 (page 634) shows how two common methods for measuring response give sharply different results even with so simple and concrete a sensory quality as grayness. For all that is known, measures of subjective probability in common use may show equally large bias.

Of course, such dependence on human judgment is avoided as much as possible by Bayesian statisticians. Nevertheless, prior probability must be obtained as a human judgment in many areas, especially in business and other nonexperimental settings. Associated judgments of costs and benefits may also be required. These applications have generally relied on makeshift methods of measurement that are known to suffer serious bias.

Such measurement problems have received extensive discussion (Hogarth, 1975; von Winterfeldt & Edwards, 1986; Winkler, 1967). None of this work, however, has resolved the basic measurement question: Is the observed response a veridical measure of the person's true state? Indeed, most work has ignored this question of validity (Anderson & Zalinski, 1991).

A grounded theory of psychological measurement is now available that can address this validity question. This functional measurement theory has had some success in measurement of belief as well as of costs and benefits in statistical decision theory (see Chapter 21).[k]

19.1.4 SCIENTIFIC INFERENCE

Scientific inference, not statistical inference, is the central concern in empirical science. Scientific inference involves many diverse extrastatistical considerations, discussed with the Experimental Pyramid of Chapter 1. This empirical fact of empirical life is obscured in the statistical field and needs reemphasis to finish off this discussion of statistical inference.

Two Levels of Inference. Two levels of inference are required in many empirical investigations, one concerned with *reliability*, one with *validity*. Reliability is the focus of significance tests and confidence intervals: Can the observed outcome reasonably be attributed to chance? Or should some alternative, nonchance explanation be provisionally adopted? This reliability question may be called a Level R inference, deciding about two hypotheses, H_0 and H_A:

Level R: H_0: outcome caused by chance;

H_A: outcome caused by nonchance.

The second level of inference is concerned with validity. Assuming that chance has been provisionally ruled out at level R, the investigator may now wish to consider substantive causes: Can the observed outcome reasonably be attributed to a specific process hypothesized by the investigator? Or is it likely that the cause was some confounded process?

In the standard placebo example, one causal explanation is that the treatment had genuine medicinal power, another that the outcome was instead caused by suggestion. This may be called Level V inference, reflecting its concern with validity rather than reliability:

Level V: H_E: outcome caused by hypothesized process;

H_C: outcome caused by confounded process.

Statistical Inference. Statistical inference is primarily concerned with reliability, that is, with inference at Level R: whether H_A rather than H_0 caused the observed outcome. Two probabilities are necessary for this inference: That the given outcome would occur if H_0 alone was operative; and that the given outcome would occur if H_A was operative. Statistical formulas can supply the first probability. But the second probability typically depends on extrastatistical, substantive knowledge of the investigator. Only by using such extrastatistical knowledge can the relative probability of H_A rather than H_0 be determined (see *Scientific Inference Involves Prior Knowledge*, page 628).

Bayesian theory incorporates the needed extrastatistical knowledge; this appears in the investigator's prior probability. In principle, therefore, Bayesian theory has no difficulty with inference at Level R.

The Prior represents subjective knowledge, however, so it is not allowed in Neyman–Pearson theory. Neyman–Pearson theory does not deny the importance of Level R inference, of course, but treats this as partly outside the scope of statistical theory. This strategy can also be seen in Fisher's "rare event" logic, which Neyman and Pearson developed more completely.

Statistics applies to observed outcomes, at Level R, so it is not much help with process analysis at Level V. The essential difficulty is extrastatistical, namely, to judge likelihood of the outcome relative to the substantive hypothesis, H_E. This validity question involves judgment about confounding processes. This and other validity questions are the main concern of the investigator, far more important than the reliability question. This point reiterates the theme of extrastatistical inference, discussed with the Experimental Pyramid of Chapter 1.[a]

Decision Averaging Model. The decision averaging model of cognitive algebra may govern human inference at both Level R and Level V. At each level, the inference may be represented as a compromise between competing response tendencies that represent plausibilities of two (or more) alternative hypotheses. Algebraically, the decision averaging model has the form of a relative ratio, shown in Equation 2c of Chapter 21.

This decision averaging model did quite well in the Bayesian two-urn task of Figure 19.1, as shown in a different view of these same data in Note 19.1.3j. It has also done well in other tasks with analogous psychological structure; see index entries in Anderson (1996a). This model may thus provide a cognitive theory of statistical inference (see *Cognitive Alternative to Bayesian Theory* in Anderson, 1996a, pp. 331*ff*).[b]

19.2 FUNCTION OF SIGNIFICANCE TESTS

The statistical significance test has been roundly criticized by numerous writers. One critic remarked on

> the current obsession with questions of statistical significance to the neglect of the often more important questions of design and power. Certainly some minimal degree of reliability is generally a necessary justification for asking others to spend time in assessing the importance of one's data. However, the question of statistical significance is only a first step, and a minor one at that, in the overall process of evaluating a set of data. To say that a result is statistically significant simply gives reasonable ground for believing that some nonchance effect was obtained. The meaning of a nonchance effect rests on an assessment of the design of the investigation. (Anderson, 1961b, p. 307.)

This was not the first criticism of significance tests and it was far from the last. A good deal of later criticism, however, has concluded that significance tests have little value and are dysfunctional in practice. This strong conclusion stems from confusion about empirical science and confusion about statistics.[a, b]

The function of a significance test is modest and limited (Section 2.4). In one prototypical application, the investigator has an empirical hypothesis that one treatment has greater effect than another and obtains sample means in the predicted direction. A natural concern is that this observed difference might stem from chance variability in the data, even though the two treatments had equivalent effects.

This concern about chance outcomes is addressed by the significance test. It assumes no real difference—the null hypothesis—and calculates the probability that a difference as large as or larger than that observed could then occur, that is, by chance alone.

The investigator hopes the significance test will indicate the observed result to be unlikely by chance alone. This outcome is taken as support for the empirical hypothesis—and as warrant for asking the scientific public to pay attention to these data and this hypothesis.

The idea of a significance test is thus merely common sense. It provides a reasonably objective way to allow for prevailing variability in the data. The scientific public is entitled to some minimal warranty about the reliability of the outcome. This is why reviewers and editors ordinarily require that results be "statistically significant" for publication. Without such minimal indication of reliability, the scientific public should not ordinarily be obligated to spend time on assessing deeper problems of confounding and validity in the experiment nor to discuss it in their own papers.

This view of the nature and function of the significance test seems to me to represent a standard view in empirical science. It embodies a harmonious unification of ideas from Fisher and from Neyman–Pearson, little troubled by the sharp philosophical difference between fiducial probability and confidence discussed in Section 19.1.

19.2.1 MISUSE OF SIGNIFICANCE TESTS

Much of the criticism of significance tests concerns their misuse. Two much-criticized misuses are noted here (see also *Before and Beyond Significance Tests*, Section 2.4, pages 47*f*, and *"Accepting* H_0*"* in Section 4.1.3, page 93).

Statistical Significance Is Not Enough. A significance test is not enough by itself. Some index of likely error is essential, such as a standard deviation or confidence interval. Assessment of power may also be desirable. And certainly some appreciation of the shape of the data distribution is needed, in part to assess the assumptions of the statistical test, but mainly for better understanding of the task–behavior.

Even more important are the extrastatistical considerations that determine what the result means. First among these is possible confoundings (Chapter 8). The significance test cannot protect against substantive shortcomings of procedure; it is concerned with reliability, not with validity. Scientific inference, in contrast, depends primarily on validity considerations.

Something is wrong when data analysis begins and ends with a significance test. It is no criticism of the significance test to say more is needed; it is a criticism of the investigator who fails to provide the needed more.[a]

Statistical Significance Is Not Substantive Significance. A statistically significant result may have little value, scientific or practical. Small, unimportant effects may be "highly significant" with a large N. And trivial large effects are sometimes gilded with "significance" from a statistical test.

The confusion of statistical and substantive significance may stem in part from identification of the statistical nonnull hypothesis with the substantive hypothesis. Rejection of the statistical null hypothesis supports the statistical nonnull hypothesis—and this is ordinarily taken to support the substantive hypothesis. Conceptually, the two are quite different, as shown in the Experimental Pyramid of Chapter 1. Statistical hypotheses are localized in the top layer of the Pyramid; substantive hypotheses originate in the bottom layers of the Pyramid. Connecting the two requires a substantive chain of reasoning that connects through the middle layers of the Pyramid.

The need for this substantive chain of reasoning through the middle layers of the Pyramid is well recognized. It appears in every question about confounding, the main source of arguments in the literature. Assessing importance of a result also depends on substantive considerations. Malpractice of treating statistical significance as substantive significance is real, but it is no more a criticism of significance tests than medical malpractice is a criticism of medicine.

"Significant" is a misleading term, as various writers have said, because it evokes common language meanings unwarranted by the technical meaning. Banishing the term "significant" from data analysis would be therapeutic. The present neologism of "statsig" is a stopgap, pending a better phrase.

19.2.2 CLARIFICATION OF SIGNIFICANCE TEST ISSUES

Published criticisms of significance tests involve a number of conceptual issues that deserve comment. The following discussion considers typical experimental studies that compare two or more treatments.[a]

Significance Tests Are Always Made.[b] A responsible investigator makes a statistical test by the very act of reporting a comparative result. Implicitly, if not explicitly, he or she usually implies there is reasonable evidence that the result is real, not merely chance. This is the essence of the significance test.[c]

This assertion of evidence value may be made by visual inspection and common sense, without any formal statistical analysis. It still functions as a significance test. If the result is indeed obvious to the reader, it should not be belabored with a formal statistical test.

Within its domain, however, the formal statistical test has no equal. Visual inspection, however invaluable, sometimes shows serious biases and shortcomings. Even when the results seem obvious, moreover, the statistical test has an objective nature that is helpful in scientific communication, giving the reader/listener something more solid than the opinion of the writer/speaker.

In standard usage, "significance test" refers only to formal, statistical procedures. Accordingly, this usage will be employed in the further discussion. Before proceeding, however, it deserves reemphasis that every investigator has responsibility to indicate reliability of results. However this may be done, it has the essential function of a significance test.

H_0 as an Interval. In empirical science, the null hypothesis functions as an interval, not as a point (Section 4.1.3, page 93). In the statistical formalism, it is true, H_0 is typically a point hypothesis of exactly zero effect. In practice, however, it operates as an interval.[d]

The rationale is straightforward. Small effects are not generally of interest. Finding a small effect statsig is ordinarily akin to a false alarm. The significance test might perhaps be faulted if it was unduly sensitive to small effects, but it is not. Inspection of power curves shows that power is little greater than α for a considerable interval around zero unless N is very large. Empirically, it is to such an interval that H_0 refers.

All conceptual models embody certain idealized assumptions, assumptions that will never hold exactly in application. The proper concern is robustness— are the conclusions relatively insensitive to violations of the assumptions?

In practice, the significance test is usually robust against small deviations from the point null hypothesis, one reason for its usefulness.

The question addressed by the significance test could thus be phrased more appropriately as: Can this observed result be reasonably attributed to chance in conjunction with a small effect? This phraseology seems awkward, however, and not really necessary.

This conception of H_0 as an interval needs emphasis because one continually reiterated criticism of the significance test is that the null hypothesis is virtually never true—and hence no significance test is needed to reject it. This criticism evaporates when H_0 is considered an interval. The criticism took the formalism of the null hypothesis blindly, failing to comprehend how statistics functions in empirical science.[e]

Significance Tests Have Decision Functions. The significance test can help with scientific decisions. The individual investigator must decide whether to follow up a given experiment. With faith or hope in the experimental hypothesis, a p near .10 or even .20 may be sufficient encouragement to continue. Given the faith or hope, such a decision may be reasonable. Of course, a p of .10 indicates inadequate power. In its mild manner, the significance test is recommending that you decrease error variability or develop some alternative task–procedure.

Editors, similarly, must make all-or-none decisions about publication. They have a duty to help protect the scientific public from weak experiments. For this purpose, also, the α criterion serves a useful function. The attacks on significance testing generally failed to recognize these decision functions.

Significance Tests Are Not All-or-None. Taken literally, the significance test seems to impose an absolute decision criterion: reject—do not reject. But whether p is a little smaller or larger than the criterial α should surely not make so sharp a difference. This argument is often presented as evidence of illogic in significance testing. But few investigators are all-or-none absolutists. The significance test is an aid to thinking, not a substitute. Many texts sensibly recommend that a p near .05 be considered suggestive or tentative. In any case, "Do not reject" does not entail acceptance of the null hypothesis.[f]

All-or-none decisions are often required. Among these, already discussed, are investigator decisions whether to follow up an obtained result and editor decisions whether to publish a submitted paper. The .05 level is a useful screening device. This simple-minded device performs this difficult function reasonably well because most empirical workers apply it with common sense.

False Alarm Bias. Some critics voice concern over false alarm bias in the publication process. Since false alarms appear to be real effects, the argument runs, they tend to get published and accumulate in the literature. The conclusion, often left implicit, is that such false alarm accumulation is a fault of the significance test. Abolishing such tests, the critics imply, would eliminate the problem.

This argument fails to recognize the real problem. The risk of false alarms stems from variability in the data. This is a fact of empirical life, one that existed before formal significance tests were developed. Informal significance tests, visual inspection in particular, suffer the identical problem. Standard significance tests have the social function of reining in too-enthusiastic investigators. Contrary to the criticism, they hold down false alarms.

Scientific Inference Involves Prior Knowledge. The standard significance test seeks to let the data speak for themselves—independent of the investigator's prior belief and desire. Different investigators will interpret the same result in different ways, reflecting their different prior beliefs. Failure to establish a predicted effect may be treated as a flaw in the theory by a critic, but as due to low power or some shortcoming of procedure by an adherent of the theory.

It seems often desirable, therefore, to assess data in a way that does not depend on the investigator's prior beliefs. This property seems appropriate for most scientific work, for it facilitates harmonious communication over a given set of data between investigators with different prior beliefs. Integrating the information from the data with prior belief is thus a separate problem for each investigator.

The significance test, however, only suggests that chance by itself is not a likely cause. *This does not imply that some other cause is likely.* We make this inference because we have prior belief in some alternative cause—that's why we did the experiment. To let the data speak for themselves, the significance test leaves causal inference to the investigator (see next subsection).

Prior belief operates at every stage of experimental analysis. Prior belief begins with the experimental question or hypothesis. Prior belief and knowledge govern the numerous decisions about task, stimuli, subjects, and response measures. Prior knowledge is vital in experimental design to avoid confounds. Prior knowledge is important in the data analysis itself, as in choosing a trend test instead of the overall F or in choice of α in planned comparisons. Even the credibility of the statistical result depends on prior knowledge about robustness. Prior belief is interwoven throughout experimental analysis, as emphasized by the Experimental Pyramid in Chapter 1.

Why the Significance Test Works. The significance test, it seems to me, owes its success to extrastatistical knowledge. As experimentalists, we generally have some prior knowledge or we wouldn't be doing the experiment. Furthermore, our prior knowledge has substantial correlation with reality. Hence our experimental hypotheses have substantial likelihood of being correct; correspondingly, our null hypotheses have substantial likelihood of being false.

Suppose instead that our experimental hypotheses had little relation to reality, so that nearly all were false. Nearly all our null hypotheses would then be true. Our occasional statsig results would be mostly false alarms. Fisher's logic of "rare events" would have minimal value. A statsig result would require replication before any trust could be placed in it. A statsig result would definitely not warrant rejection of the null hypothesis, as Fisher claimed.[g]

Bayesian theory seems little better off even though it allows prior opinion. Given that the experimental hypotheses have little relation to reality, a noninformative prior seems called for. But under normality, a noninformative prior yields the same results as classical theory in many applications.[h]

In practice, we do usually give more or less credence to a statsig result. The justification for this practice, I suggest, is extrastatistical. We typically have prior evidence for our experimental hypothesis. Even though this extrastatistical evidence is not included in the formal statistical inference, it is an integral component of our scientific inference. This aspect of scientific inference can be seen in the common judgment that surprising results are less trustworthy and require replication.

19.2.3 SUMMARY COMMENT

The critics are certainly correct that the significance test is often misused. One reason is that a good deal of work is done by persons who were poorly taught. Some wield significance tests as though they were the Sword of the Lord; others cling to significance statistics as a security blanket because they lack confidence in their abilities with design and data analysis.

Second, many users of statistics are concerned with advocacy, to uphold or tear down some proposal, with opportunistic concern for objective evidence. Principal investigators of large research projects, as one example, need to justify continuation of grant funding to continue their mission and to support the personnel for whom they are responsible. Proponents of social action programs, Head Start, for example, or environmental issues, may be impelled by belief and faith in the greater good. Their prior belief easily leads to overemphasis on surplus meaning of *significance*; sometimes it leads to misuse of statistics.

A third reason is that integration of empirical and statistical considerations is not easy to teach. Empirical considerations, such as pros and cons of within subject design, involve knowledge systems that are not well-developed by the first year in graduate school. Perhaps the best way to combat the strong, natural tendency to teach statistics as self-contained is to develop case examples, real and hypothetical, that require students to exercise judgment rather than calculation. This idea underlies many Exercises in this book, but they are only one step in a direction that needs devoted study.

19.3 MEASUREMENT SCALES AND STATISTICS [a]

Psychology exhibits an astonishingly diverse array of conceptual qualities. Sensory experience alone includes sound, sight, taste, touch, pain, and sex, all very different in phenomenal quality. Motivation includes curiosity, play, hunger, thirst, warm–cold, fear, dominance–submission, and parental drive. Social interaction includes friendship, love, sorrow, and loneliness. Other domains are similarly multifarious.

Despite their diverse qualities, these concepts have one common aspect: They can often be treated as one-dimensional. One-dimensionality derives from the axiom of purposiveness—that behavior is oriented toward goals. Stimuli are evaluated in terms of approach and avoidance relative to an operative goal. This approach–avoidance axis is clear with affective senses, such as taste and warm–cold, which have evolved for goal-oriented functioning. This same approach–avoidance axis appears in the general good–bad polarity of everyday life. Granted its limitations, this one-dimensional representation confers a basic simplicity on complex domains.

Ability to capitalize on this one-dimensional simplicity resides in our measurement method. This view seems explicit in the common practice of measuring *how much* of a certain quality is found under given conditions.

These measurements, of course, are only verbal symbols, not the reality we seek to study. What we can learn depends on the relation between our number symbols and reality.

This measurement issue appeared in the Experimental Pyramid of Chapter 1 as the linkage between the real world of phenomena and a symbolic world of concepts and theory. Various aspects of this measurement linkage appeared in subsequent statistical topics, but only one is at issue here, namely, the problem of the *linear scale*.

One purpose of this section is to justify the main class of Anova applications with nonlinear scales of measurement. The contrary argument rests on a misconception described under *Anova With Monotone Data*, pages 635*f.* Preliminary discussion is needed, however, of scale types and measurement theory.

19.3.1 SCALE TYPES

Common usage allows three main types of quantitative measurement scales, here called *monotone, linear,* and *proportional.* Each scale type is defined by the functional relation between the measured numbers and the conceptual quantity being measured. We use R to denote the measured number and ρ to denote the conceptual quantity, which is typically not observable.[a]

It may be helpful to consider a concrete sensory quantity such as the white–black continuum of grayness shown in Figure 21.1 (page 693). In this figure, ρ would refer to your personal feeling of grayness, and R to some observable response, such as your rating of grayness on a scale of 1 to 20. The three types of measurement scale refer to different relations between R and ρ.

Monotone Scale. A *monotone* scale expresses relative magnitude: The scale numbers have the same rank order as the conceptual quantity. Thus,

$$R_1 < R_2 \text{ if and only if } \rho_1 < \rho_2. \tag{7}$$

Mathematically, Expression 7 says that R is a (strictly) monotone function of ρ.

Monotone scales are common in psychology. With the gray chips of Figure 21.1, for example, we can say which of two chips is lighter. With two sounds, similarly, we can generally say which is louder. In learning studies, to take a different domain, number of trials to reach some criterion is a common measure of learning rate.

The monotone scale fails when we seek to compare differences. Suppose $R_4 - R_3 > R_2 - R_1$. We should not say the first difference is greater than the second; this holds for the numbers, it is true, but it need not hold for the conceptual quantity the numbers measure. Hence we may not conclude that $\rho_4 - \rho_3 > \rho_2 - \rho_1$. Because of this limitation on comparing differences, analysis of multiple determination is extremely limited with a monotone scale.

Linear Scale. With a *linear scale*, the numbers are a linear function of the conceptual quantity. Mathematically,

$$R = c_0 + c_1 \rho, \tag{8}$$

where c_0 and c_1 are zero and unit constants.

Linear scales remove the cited limitation of the monotone scale. A comparison of two numerical differences is meaningful because it holds equally for the two corresponding psychological differences. Thus, it follows from Equation 8 that $R_4 - R_3 = R_2 - R_1$ if and only if $\rho_4 - \rho_3 = \rho_2 - \rho_1$. In a more common but less precise statement, equal intervals on the number scale correspond to equal intervals on the psychological scale.

Linear scales are basic in process analysis. With linear scales, psychological laws of multiple determination can be established (Chapters 20 and 21).

Proportional Scale. With a *proportional scale*, the numbers are proportional to the conceptual quantity. A proportional scale is just a linear scale with a known zero. The zero constant c_0 of Equation 8 is then 0 so

$$R = c_1 \rho. \tag{9}$$

The number 0, in other words, corresponds to the true zero on the conceptual scale of ρ.

Most physical scales are proportional scales. Length and mass, for example, have absolute zeros. The common Celsius and Fahrenheit scales of temperature are only linear scales, however, for their zeros are arbitrary. In psychology, the weight parameter of the averaging model may be estimated on a proportional scale with suitable design (Section 21.4).

Semilinear Scale. Most measurement scales in psychology are *semilinear*. They lie somewhere between a bare rank-order scale and a true linear scale. This semilinear character, as it may be called, is clear with sensory quantities. The classic decibel scale, which takes loudness as the logarithm of the physical scale of energy, is generally agreed to be roughly correct.

A second example of semilinear scale appears in the Munsell gray scale of Figure 21.1 on page 693. These gray chips appear to be approximately equally spaced along the psychological white–black continuum. It would be foolish to treat the Munsell gray values as a mere rank order, ignoring the semilinear information they incorporate.

A similar view may be applied to other quantities, such as pleasantness of smells and tastes, meaningfulness of words, and interpersonal feelings of affection and resentment. We often doubt that our measures of these quantities are true linear scales, but we are usually confident they are far better than bare rank orders. Confidence in degree of linearity can be overdone, as warned by the later example of magnitude estimation in Figure 19.2, but it represents a working part of our background knowledge.

Principle of Scale Typology. A simple principle underlies the foregoing scale typology: The name of the scale refers to the functional relation between symbol and reality. Thus, a scale is said to be *monotone*, *linear*, or *proportional*, according as the numbers are a monotone, linear, or proportional function of what is being measured.

This scale typology corresponds directly to the ordinal, interval, and ratio scales popularized by Stevens (1951):

> *monotone* corresponds to *ordinal*;
> *linear* corresponds to *interval*;
> *proportional* corresponds to *ratio*.

The present scale typology makes explicit the essential aspect of measurement, namely, the relation between the numerical scale of observable response and the typically unobservable scale of the conceptual quality.

This concept of measurement as a relation between the two worlds was not clear in Stevens' (1951) typology, which sought to define scale types in terms of observable quantities. Stevens' approach led to misconceptions that the scale type somehow resides in the measurement scale itself (see Anderson, 1961b, 1981, Section 5.4; Cliff, 1993, pp. 60, 64; Velleman & Wilkinson, 1993, p. 72). This misconception is avoided by making explicit that scale type is a functional *relation* between the symbolic and real worlds.[b]

The concept of semilinear scale has been little discussed. This is unfortunate because improving linearity of our scales of measurement should be a continuing endeavor. One obstacle has been the lack of linear standards against which to assess direction and degree of needed improvements. This obstacle can be removed under certain conditions by using functional measurement to provide a validational standard, as in the experiments summarized in Figure 19.2.

19.3.2 PSYCHOLOGICAL MEASUREMENT THEORY

Scale typology is a question, not an answer. The idea of the three scale types has long been part of general knowledge. Stevens' (1951) theme was that scale type limits the class of "permissible" statistics. Anova–regression would thus be permissible only with a linear scale. This theme begs the primary question, namely, how to determine whether a linear scale is operative in given situations. Stevens did attempt two criteria, but both failed. Stevens' (1951) original criterion failed because it was cast in terms of observable physical relations (Note 19.3.2a, page 644). Stevens' (1956, 1974) later criterion—that the method of magnitude estimation provided linear, even proportional scales—has failed numerous empirical tests. This issue requires more detailed comment.[a]

Rating and Magnitude Estimation. Some validity criterion is essential to assay scale type. This point may be illustrated by comparing the methods of *rating* and *magnitude estimation*. Ratings of sensations, feelings, and concepts can often be considered monotone scales. Whether they provide linear scales, however, is open to question. In fact, the rating method suffers biases that were long thought to destroy all hope for linearity.

In magnitude estimation, subjects judge the magnitude of their sensations by reference to a single standard stimulus. If the standard is called 50, for example, a sensation half as large should be called 25, one twice as large 100, and so forth. Magnitude estimation, Stevens asserted, yields true linear scales, even proportional scales.

Rating and magnitude estimation are fairly similar. Both ask for numerical judgments relative to standards, and subjects find both easy to use. The two methods differ mainly in that rating typically uses two standards, corresponding to the two ends of the rating scale, whereas magnitude estimation uses just the single standard. Despite this difference, the two methods might be expected to give fairly similar results.

In fact, the two methods disagree sharply, as shown in Figure 19.2 (next page). Subjects made grayness judgments of the Munsell gray chips shown in Figure 21.1 using both the rating method and the method of magnitude estimation. Figure 19.2 plots the magnitude estimations of each chip on the vertical as a function of the rating of the same chip on the horizontal. If the two methods agreed, the curve would be a straight diagonal line; this is far from true.

Figure 19.2. Magnitude estimation is biased and invalid. The curve represents magnitude estimations of grayness (lightness) of Munsell gray chips, plotted on the vertical, as a function of ratings of same chips, plotted on the horizontal. Equivalence of the two response measures would appear as a straight diagonal curve. The curve is far from the straight diagonal, which means that the two response measures are far from equivalent. Since ratings satisfy validational criteria for a true linear scale, the curve must reflect bias in magnitude estimation; see also Figure 21.8. (After N. H. Anderson, *Methods of Information Integration Theory.* Academic Press, 1982.)

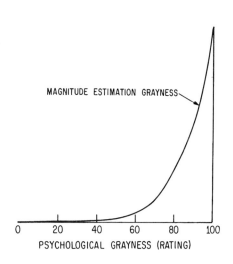

This sharp disagreement between rating and magnitude estimation means that at least one is not a linear scale. More generally, it reemphasizes that scale linearity cannot be taken for granted, for it may be badly violated even with such simple perceptual judgments.

Psychological Measurement Theory. A theory of psychological measurement is needed to adjudicate the difference between rating and magnitude estimation in Figure 19.2. Stevens (1956, 1974) made extremely strong claims that magnitude estimation provided true measurement. In fact, magnitude estimation has repeatedly failed empirical tests (see e.g., Note 21.6.3g, page 737). Magnitude estimation suffers more serious bias than any rating procedure.

A theory of psychological measurement has been developed that can adjudicate the controversy between rating and magnitude estimation. This theory is impartial. Both methods have equal opportunity to succeed. Both might fail. As it happened, the rating method succeeded through development of empirical procedures to eliminate its biases (Note 21.6.1a, page 733).[b]

19.3.3 SCALES AND STATISTICS

For statistical analysis, the monotone–linear distinction poses a basic problem. Many psychological scales are considered monotone, but few are known to be linear. Statistical analysis should be wary about treating numbers from a monotone scale as though they were from a linear scale.

This caveat applies especially to Anova–regression analysis. Anova relies on number *differences*; this appeared in the deviation scores in the SS formulas of Sections 3.2.1 and 5.1.3. With only a monotone scale, as already noted, two equal numerical differences may be unequal psychologically. With diminishing returns, 52 − 51 represents a smaller psychological magnitude than 2 − 1. Yet Anova treats both differences as equal. This seems dangerous; what is true of the numbers—and the Anova—may be false in reality.

The Distribution-Free Argument. Distribution-free statistics might seem ideally suited to psychological research. Rank statistics do not assume normality or any other shape of distribution (Section 12.2). They utilize only the rank-order information in the data; the specific shape of the distribution is irrelevant. Distribution-free methods were much studied by statisticians as less restrictive alternatives to classical theory based on normal distributions.

To some psychologists, however, distribution-free statistics were attractive for a different reason. Because the data are reduced to ranks for the statistical analysis, any monotone scale of the data will yield the same statistical results as any other. Hence any monotone scale will yield the same ranking as the true linear scale. With such statistical analysis, therefore, concern about linearity disappears. This invariance may not hold with Anova, as noted under *Interactions May Be Artifacts* on the next page. Rank-order statistics might thus seem to be uniquely suited for psychological measurement.

This argument was frequent in an earlier period when distribution-free statistics were under development. Some writers made strong arguments that linear scales were mandatory for using Anova–regression (e.g., Section 12.2.4, page 361). But despite its surface plausibility, this distribution-free argument is invalid as shown next.[a]

Anova With Monotone Data. Analysis of variance can be legitimate with data from a monotone scale. Consider a one-way design, with subjects assigned randomly to treatment conditions that do not differ in effect. The distribution of scores will then be identical in each condition; all groups will have equal means and equal variances—regardless of the response scale. Even with monotone scales, therefore, Anova can yield a valid test (Anderson, 1961b, 1976a).[b]

Whether Anova should be applied depends on normality, not on linearity. With normal distributions, Anova maintains α at the prescribed level and provides maximum power. With some nonnormal distributions, of course, distribution-free rank tests would be superior.

But normality, unlike linearity, is an observable property of the data. Normality has no necessary relation to linearity. A linear scale might well yield a highly nonnormal distribution while a monotone scale could yield normality. The monotone scale would then be preferable in terms of power as well as effective significance level.

Preference for a monotone over a linear scale may be illustrated with reaction time studies. Certain theories rest on an assumption that reaction times are additive across successive stages of processing; time is then the appropriate linear psychological scale. The reciprocal transformation, from time to speed, typically yields more normal data, however, so speed may be preferred for other purposes (see *Transformations*, Section 12.4).

Contrary to the foregoing distribution-free argument, therefore, Anova can be legitimate with monotone scales. In fact, Anova may be optimal. The distribution-free argument failed because it became trapped in words, ignoring experimental reality. Discussions of statistical analysis in other theories of psychological measurement became trapped in the same way. Randomization, fundamental on other grounds, here takes on an additional function.[c]

Interactions May Be Artifacts. With factorial design, different considerations apply to main effects and interaction residuals. For most practical purposes, the foregoing argument that one-way Anova is legitimate with monotone scales holds also for main effects in a factorial design. An interaction, in contrast, may easily be an artifact of a nonlinear, monotone scale. This issue was illustrated with the time–speed example in Table 7.1, page 190 of Chapter 7, *Understanding Interactions*. In that example, time and speed were both acceptable measures but they disagreed about the interaction. A nonlinear monotone transformation can make additive data nonadditive; and vice versa. Unless we know our scale is linear, presence or absence of interactions may mean little.

Interactions have a different character from main effects. Main effects are concerned with differences; hence monotone scales usually suffice. Interactions, in contrast, are concerned with differences of differences; hence linear scales are generally needed. In the left panel of Table 7.1, the interaction algebraically equals the double difference, $(6 - 3) - (3 - 2)$. But the two differences, $(6 - 3)$ and $(3 - 2)$, come from different locations on the time scale. If the time scale is only monotone, neither difference can be taken at its face numerical value. Indeed, this double difference is zero on the speed scale in the right panel of Figure 7.1. To rely on a double difference, barring crossover interaction, the response scale must be linear.

Semilinear Scales and Extrastatistical Inference. The issue of semilinear scales reemphasizes the need to integrate statistical into extrastatistical inference. Semilinearity is extrastatistical knowledge, generally unrecognized in discussions of scales and statistics. For everyday data analysis, semilinear scales give a provisional basis for comparing differences. Thus, the warning that interactions may be artifacts should not obscure their potential as uncertain clues to nonadditivity, especially when they have been predicted.[d, e]

Confidence intervals also illustrate the value of semilinear scales. Since confidence intervals are defined with a unit of variability, they can misrepresent reality to some extent if the measuring scale is nonlinear. Confidence intervals are useful, however, because the semilinearity of most empirical scales of measurement means they are usually approximately correct.

To improve scales of measurement is a continuing goal of empirical science. Among the many aspects of this endeavor, closer approach to linearity is an important one. Although the problem of linearity is basically substantive and extrastatistical, Anova–regression can provide unique assistance as shown in the discussion of psychological measurement theory in Chapter 21.

NOTES

19.1.1a. Few statistical issues have generated as much controversy as Fisher's concept of *fiducial probability*. In their concluding discussion comparing the three concepts of fiducial interval, confidence interval, and Bayesian belief interval, Kendall and Stuart (1979, p. 165) state

> There has been so much controversy . . . that, at this point, we shall have to leave our customary objective standpoint and descend into the arena ourselves. The remainder of this chapter is an expression of our personal views. We think that it is the correct viewpoint; and it represents the result of many years' silent reflexion on the issues involved, a serious attempt to understand what the protagonists say, and an even more serious attempt to divine what they mean.

19.1.2a. Usefulness of confidence as personal, extrastatistical belief seems to be ignored by Bayesians, who contrast the statistical concept of confidence with the Bayesian concept of personal, statistical belief.

The qualifications noted in the second sentence of the quotation from Mosteller and Tukey deserve comment. "Typicality," I take it, rules out samples considered to be biased. "Absence of selection" refers to the diverse dangers of sample selection that capitalize on chance outcomes listed in the later subsection, *Bayesian Theory and Randomization*. Similar qualifications apply to Bayesian belief intervals.

19.1.2b. Lehmann (1993) considers that the Fisher and Neyman–Pearson theories are complementary, not contradictory (aside from fiducial probability). The main difference is whether tests of composite hypotheses should be conditional, as Fisher later maintained, or unconditional, as Neyman and Pearson claimed. This issue, he says, cannot be decided by abstract principles, but depends on the empirical context of application.

19.1.2c. Examples in which the confidence interval may be known to be incorrect after the data have been collected are given by Jaynes (1976, p. 198) and by Mosteller and Tukey (1968, p. 181). These examples are not realistic, but they show that the concept of confidence interval is no panacea.

19.1.3a. A vital, hidden assumption in expositions of Bayesian theory is that all persons will evaluate the Evidence in similar way. In many real situations, however, Evidence is ambiguous and persons disagree even about its polarity. More Evidence can lead them to diverge rather than converge (see also following note).

This hidden assumption underlies Savage's (1962, pp. 20*ff*) "principle of precise measurement" (also called the "principle of stable estimation"), namely, that persons with different Priors will converge on the same Posterior with sufficient Evidence. This principle is intended to counter objections to including subjective belief in statistical analysis on the ground that subjective belief will be overwhelmed with sufficient Evidence. This assumption seems to have gone unquestioned, presumably because statisticians focus on situations in which the nature of the Evidence is clear, as with the two-urn task of Figure 19.1 (see also following note).

19.1.3b. The attractions of the Bayesian tack of utilizing prior belief and knowledge in statistical analysis should be weighed with the dangers. As one of many examples, the evidence for the Sheldon–Stevens theory of somatotypes of Section 8.1.1 was made entirely out of their prior beliefs. This example also undercuts the Bayesian claim that truth will emerge with sufficient data; the data themselves were produced from the prior beliefs (see previous note). Stevens' theory of magnitude estimation suffered in an analogous way (see also Note 21.6.3g).

19.1.3c. Standard Anova is so useful partly because the sample mean and variance are *sufficient* statistics for a normal distribution—these two numbers encapsulate *all* the information in the sample. Many distributions lack a simple set of sufficient statistics. In these cases, Bayesian theory may be superior to classical theory.

This practical usefulness of standard Anova–regression in preference to Bayesian methods appears in the reliance on Anova–regression by various proponents of the Bayesian approach. Thus, Box and Tiao (1973) made fundamental contributions to Bayesian theory, but the later book by Box, Hunter, and Hunter (1978) on engineering statistics relies solely on classical methods. Similarly, Lindman's (1992) first-year graduate text relies entirely on classical theory despite his coauthorship of a much-cited article on Bayesian statistics (Edwards, Lindman, & Savage, 1963) and his continued preference for a subjective conception of probability.

19.1.3d. This discussion of blood sample evidence is based on Berry and Geisser (1986), an instructive article that makes several criticisms of common court practice. One criticism relates to the appropriate choice of "relevant population" that defines the alternative hypothesis, H_A. If the child is Asian, for example, blood factor data obtained from a Caucasian or African–American population could be misleading.

The law, it may be noted, provides an interesting testing ground for statistical practice. Attorneys on each side are intensely motivated to uncover weak points in the analysis presented by the other side. Surprisingly, the picture of then-current practice given by the cited article suggests that defense attorneys have been snowed by statistics.

In the juror's judgment process, it may be noted, the concept of prior belief enters at two places. The second time is that considered in the text, a prior based on the oral testimony; this avoids the need to assume a prior probability, such as ½, in the Bayesian analysis. The first time is before any evidence has been presented. In this case, the Bayesian assumption presumably would be that jurors have noninformative priors, or perhaps nearly noninformative priors centered toward "not guilty." Experimental evidence on the value of the initial prior in juror judgment has been obtained by Thomas Ostrom (see Anderson, 1981, pp. 268f).

19.1.3e. To show the relation between probability and odds, let p and $1 - p$ be the probabilities that H_A and H_0 are true, respectively. Then the odds of H_A to H_0 are $p / (1 - p)$ to 1.

19.1.3f. You may have been taught that the whale is a mammal, not a fish. But listen to Herman Melville, a whaler in his youth, who deliberates this question: "Next, how shall we define the whale .... To be short then, a whale is a *spouting fish with a horizontal tail*" (*Moby Dick*, Chapter 32, bolding added).

19.1.3g. Among the multiple complications in this bowhead census, visual spotting extended only to about 4 km offshore, less in foul weather. Hydrophones were later installed to record bowhead vocalization, allowing triangulation to determine the location of whales. These location data improved accuracy, although at the expense of additional complexities. One complexity was the need to develop a tracking algorithm based on a substantive model of bowhead swimming behavior to decide whether successive vocalizations came from the same or different whales. A recent report claims that this particular population of bowheads is increasing, although other populations are not (Gerber, DeMaster, & Roberts, 2000, Figure 6).

19.1.3h. The two-urn task of Figure 19.1 provides an easy illustration of Bayes' theorem. Since we know the composition of the urn, we can easily calculate Prob(S | urn A) that any specific sample S came from urn A (or urn B). But what we wish to know is the inverse probability of the urn for a given sample— Prob(urn A | S). This inverse inference follows Bayes' theorem:

$$\text{Prob(urn A} \mid S) = \frac{\text{Prob}(S \mid \text{urn A}) \times \text{Prob(urn A)}}{\text{Prob}(S \mid \text{urn A}) \times \text{Prob(urn A)} + \text{Prob}(S \mid \text{urn B}) \times \text{Prob(urn B)}}.$$

The two urns have equal prior probability: Prob(urn A) = Prob(urn B) = ½. Bayes' theorem is not controversial when, as here, the prior probabilities of urn A and urn B can be taken as known, not subjective belief.

A sample of n red beads has probabilities of $.6^n$ and $.4^n$ of coming from the 60:40 and 40:60 urns, respectively. Substitution shows that Prob{urn 60:40 | n red} equals .60. .69, .77, and .84, for $n = 1, 2, 3$, and 4. The observed judgments in Figure 19.1 are substantially less, a result called "conservatism," discussed in the next note.

Subjects did follow the Bayesian prescription of judging on the basis of the difference, (red − white) in an auxiliary condition of Leon and Anderson (1974, Figure 3). This result is exceptional, however, and seems not to have been followed up.

19.1.3i. The experiment of Figure 19.1 also disproves the representativeness heuristic of Kahneman and Tversky (1972), which asserted that subjects judge solely in terms of the sample proportion, ignoring the composition of the urns. The representativeness heuristic thus implies that all three curves should be identical on the left side of Figure 19.1, and similarly for the right side.

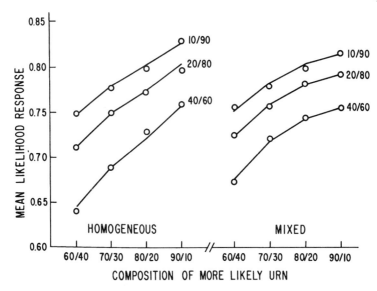

Figure 19.3. Decision averaging rule of information integration theory holds for Bayesian two-urn task. Open circles are data; curves are theoretical. Subject sees sample of beads drawn at random from one of two urns, each with specified numbers of red and white beads (listed on horizontal axis and as curve parameter, respectively.) Data points are mean judged probabilities that the sample comes from the more likely urn. Left panel averaged over four homogeneous samples (1, 2, 3, and 4 red beads); right panel averaged over four mixed samples (3:2, 3:1, 4:1, and 6:2 red:white ratios). (From M. Leon and N. H. Anderson, 1974, "A ratio rule from integration theory applied to inference judgments," *Journal of Experimental Psychology, 102,* 27-36. Copyright 1974 by the American Psychological Association. Reprinted by permission.)

But each set of three curves is far apart, showing strong effects of urn composition. The result of Figure 19.1, perhaps the first disproof of the representativeness heuristic, has been extensively confirmed.

This and other work on information integration theory provides a constructive alternative, well-grounded theoretically and empirically, that supercedes the heuristics approach. The representativeness heuristic is superceded by the decision averaging model (see next note); the anchoring–adjustment heuristic is superceded by the averaging model for serial belief integration (e.g., Figure 15.1, page 455); and the availability heuristic is superceded by functional memory (Anderson, 1996a, pp. 347*ff*).

19.1.3j. Although the Bayesian model failed in Figure 19.1, the decision averaging model from information integration theory did well. This is shown by the good agreement between theoretical curves and data points in Figure 19.3. Beyond this, the weights estimated from the model showed interesting dependence on stimulus variables.

19.1.3k. The need for theory of psychological measurement appears in Roberts' (1978, p. 12) discussion of Bayesian inference: "In assessing prior probabilities, skillful self-interrogation is needed in order to mitigate vagueness." Far more serious than vagueness is bias: The overt probability response may be an invalid measure of the person's true belief. This is not a subtle quibble; Figure 19.2 shows extreme invalidity of subjective judgments even with a concrete perceptual quality.

Attempts have been made to force persons to revise their judgments to be consistent, but these may merely amplify bias. Attempts have also been made to use payoff schemes that require optimal behavior to maximize outcome, but their validity depends on the dubious normative presumption of optimal behavior.

19.1.4a. It could be argued that the Bayesian rule is the optimal way to combine the subjective probabilities for H_E and H_C in Level V inference. To test this claim would require valid response measures of subjective probabilities (see previous note).

19.1.4b. The personal belief of the empirical investigator does involve integration of the various lines of evidence that bear on the validity of the interpretation. It could be argued that this integration should itself obey the Bayesian rule.

The decision averaging rule has been shown to hold for some tasks of belief integration, as in the Bayesian two-urn task of Figure 19.3. This decision averaging rule represents a compromise between opposing evidence, X and Y, with a ratio form, $X/(X + Y)$, analogous to the Bayesian rule in Note 19.1.3h. Even allowing subjective evidence values, however, cognition is not Bayesian in the urn task (Figure 19.1) nor does Bayesian theory allow opposite effects of the same information (e.g., page 707).

19.2a. Most points in the present discussion of significance tests have been made by previous writers, as with the treatment of the null hypothesis as an interval. Recent discussions and citations of previous literature are available in Oakes (1986, Chapter 2) and in the seven contributions to the summer, 1993 issue of the *Journal of Experimental Education*. Since the main draft of this section was written, additional discussions have been given by Hagen (1997), by contributors to Harlow, Mulaik, and Steiger (1997), and by six contributors to a special section, "Should Significance Tests Be Banned," in *Psychological Science*, January, 1997.

Summary of these and numerous other such articles is difficult because the same small handful of arguments keep being recycled, often in confused or incorrect form. The polemical fixation on evils of the significance test obscures the underlying problem, namely, the poor training of many researchers.

Reichardt and Gollob (1997, p. 278) remark in their positive, balanced treatment of confidence intervals that "Many of the criticisms of statistical tests are either false or exaggerated." Mulaik, Raju, and Harshman (1997, p. 74) say that many "arguments to do away with significance testing are based on criticisms of abusive misconceptions of the use and interpretation of significance testing by researchers. They can hardly be regarded as criticisms of significance testing properly understood and applied." As they say, Fisher, Neyman, Pearson, and other statisticians have been "critical of the very same abuses and misconceptions of significance testing that the current crop of critics of significance testing cite as evidence against significance testing" (see also Note 19.2.2a).

My reaction is that this literature has mainly attacked symptoms, often straw. The disease is lack of integration of empirics with statistics. Cure requires an empirical direction in teaching statistics, as discussed with the Experimental Pyramid of Chapter 1.

19.2b. Some writers imply that confidence intervals make Anova obsolete or that they apply to all problems. Both implications are wrong. Confidence intervals are sometimes suboptimal as significance tests, sometimes nonexistent, as with most procedures for multiple comparisons (Chapter 17). Confidence intervals apply only with one or two means; there is no confidence interval for three or more means. With three or more means, Anova is generally optimal for testing the null hypothesis of equal true means. With multifactor designs, the Anova table gives a compact, convenient summary, especially with repeated measures, in which the same mean may have multiple confidence intervals, depending on which other mean it is compared with (see *Caveats on Confidence Intervals* in Section 4.1.5, page 94).

19.2.1a. Not a few criticisms of the significance test implicitly assume that data analysis ends with a significance test. Such misfeasance is rare although it can be found; Snyder, Tanke, and Bersheid (1977) report no data, only Fs, ts, and ps.

19.2.2a. One frequent criticism of the significance test is that "it doesn't tell you what you really need to know," namely, "the probability that the null hypothesis is false." In empirical science, however, "what we really need to know" is usually something other than the probability that the null hypothesis is false.

In most applications, what we seek from statistics is reasonable evidence that chance is an unlikely cause of the observed result, together with an interval estimate of likely error. The confidence interval can give us this information although it does not tell us the probability that the null hypothesis is false.

But what we really need to know is extrastatistical—about confounding. Is the result caused by our hypothesized process or by some confound or peculiarity of the experimental situation? *This* is what we really need to know.

It deserves reiteration that most arguments in the literature concern empirical confounding, not statistical significance. Statisticians bypass empirical confounding as outside statistical theory; statistics books in empirical sciences do the same. Much of the criticism of significance testing stems from unfamiliarity with empirical science.

Bayesians are prone to the cited criticism because such probability statements are a showpiece of Bayesian theory. These probabilities, however, rest on prior probabilities that are subjective, open to more or less uncertainty and disagreement (Note 19.1.3b). This criticism also neglects to recognize that confidence and the confidence interval can be interpreted as subjective belief at an extrastatistical level (Note 19.1.2a).

In some situations, it is true, probability statements are exactly appropriate, as with the Bayesian examples of disputed paternity and disputed authorship considered in Section 19.1.3. For the most part, however, the argument that "what you really need to know" concerns the probability of the observed result rests on misconception about empirical science.

19.2.2b. The word "always" refers to comparative tests between two or more treatments, specified in the preceding paragraph. Some situations, of course, call for measurement of effect size without concern for a null hypothesis. In these situations, it is usually even more important to indicate reliability of the result, especially with an interval measure of likely effect size.

19.2.2c. A significance test may be considered any method for assessing whether an observed outcome can reasonably be attributed to chance. Visual inspection and confidence intervals may thus serve as significance tests, just as t and F. This point needs emphasis because some writers present confidence intervals as though they do not function as significance tests and/or as though they render significance tests irrelevant.

19.2.2d. The idea of treating the null hypothesis as an interval has been noted by various writers. Hodges and Lehman (1954) attempt exact treatment of the null hypothesis as an interval outside of which the results would be "materially significant." This becomes complicated even with two groups. Relative to this, the standard test is only approximate, but its simplicity and generality recommend it. The concern of Hodges and Lehman, shared by Grant (1962) and by Binder (1963), that extensive data make a significance test "embarrassingly powerful," reflects confusion between statistical and extrastatistical significance and fails to recognize the role of extrastatistical considerations in empirical science (see *Accepting and Rejecting Models* in Section 20.4.6).

19.2.2e. With a huge N, of course, a tiny effect will almost surely be statsig. But the confidence interval will show that the effect is tiny, presumably unimportant.

The *reductio ad absurdum* of the criticism that the point null hypothesis is never true was given by Meehl (1967), who argued that theories of "negligible verisimilitude" had probability approaching ½ of being confirmed as power is increased. Granted H_0 never true, the probability of a statsig result approaches 1 as power increases. Meehl assumed a directional prediction, which would have probability ½ of being directionally correct. As power increases, therefore, the probability of confirming the theoretical prediction will approach ½.

Paradoxically, therefore, increasing power appears to increase the confirmability of theories of "negligible verisimilitude." This state of affairs, says Meehl, contrasts lamentably with point predictions in physics in which increased power and precision make theoretical confirmation more difficult. Perhaps Meehl was pulling the philosophers' leg (this was published in *Philosophy of Science*), for a confidence interval will clearly reveal that the "verisimilitude" is indeed "negligible."

19.2.2f. Neyman and Pearson emphasize that "reject" and "accept" should not be taken literally.

19.2.2g. Fisher (1960, p. 58) considers that a statsig result does warrant rejecting the null hypothesis and taking the observed results to reflect real differences between experimental treatments. However, Fisher opposes reliance on prior belief, perhaps from reliance on his conception of fiducial probability.

19.2.2h. For the hypothetical situation in question, it might be argued that Bayesian theory could adopt a prior with a heavy weight on the null hypothesis. The individual investigator, however, would not be doing experiments at random, but with hope and belief in a real effect. This personal belief should be used in the Bayesian analysis. From this standpoint, the noninformative prior is conservative.

19.3a. This discussion of measurement scales and statistics is based on Anderson (1961b), which made three points. First, in a one-way design with randomization, Anova provides a valid test of the null hypothesis of equal means even with monotone measurement scales. Second, interactions in factorial design are not generally invariant unless the measurement scale is linear. Third, and most important, empirical analysis can and does make good use of what are here called semilinear scales.

Contrary to published misunderstandings, Anderson (1961b) did not claim that data analysis was independent of scale type. Quite the contrary; the need for linear scales to understand interactions was made dramatically clear with the time–speed example reproduced in Table 7.1 of Chapter 7. This article led onward to the development of functional measurement theory, which has had reasonable empirical success in solving the problem of the linear scale (see Chapter 21).

True, the cited article did claim that Anova was justified, even with a monotone scale, for one-way design with random assignment. But this is correct (see *Anova With Monotone Data*, page 635). The critics failed to recognize this virtue of random assignment.

19.3.1a. The present scale typology, *monotone–linear–proportional* and *semilinear*, was adopted in subsequent work on functional measurement theory. The essential ideas of these scale types have long been common knowledge.

The issue of semilinear scale has received little explicit attention despite its importance in experimental analysis. The difficulty is that semilinearity is not readily amenable to quantification. In some cases, however, existing scales can be assessed by comparison with linear scales derived from functional measurement theory. Magnitude estimation was shown to be invalid in this way in the experiments summarized in Figure 19.2.

19.3.1b. The term *linear scale* avoids the misleading implication of *equal interval scale* that intervals on the unobservable ρ scale may somehow be measured independently from the observable R scale. Were this so, the equal interval property would be directly testable. This may be so with physical scales, such as length, which can be defined in terms of additive units, but not for psychological scales.

Linearity may be established by success of the parallelism property of the addition model (see *Parallelism Theorem* in Chapter 21. Algebraic structures impose a metric on the unobservable ρ scale; this metric is a theoretical construct that represents reality and gives form to our intuitions about continuous quality. The "equal interval" concept is a consequence of linearity that has only analogical meaning and use.

19.3.2a. The time–speed example of Table 7.1 has historical interest as perhaps the first demonstration that the criterion originally given by Stevens (1951) for determining scale type was inadequate. Stevens' main concern was that the invariance of a statistic depended on the scale type, for scale type determined the class of permissible transformations. Thus, a median is invariant on a monotone scale, whereas a mean is not.

Without methods for determining scale type, however, such discussion of invariance is empty. Stevens' (1951) initial attempt to fill this emptiness relied on observable physical considerations, but these implied that both time and speed were interval, indeed, ratio scales. The time–speed example showed the lack of invariance, thereby demonstrating the failure of Stevens' original criterion (see similarly Anderson, 1981, Section 5.4; Cliff, 1993, pp. 60, 64; Velleman & Wilkinson, 1993, p. 72).

19.3.2b. The need for substantive theory as a foundation for psychological measurement also appears in the distinction between *response* measure, which is typically an observable, and *stimulus* measures, which are typically unobservable, as with the value and weight parameters in averaging theory. Indeed, the scale type of these parameters depends on the design; see uniqueness theorem in Anderson (1982, pp. 87*ff*).

19.3.3a. Stevens (1951) asserted that Anova and similar statistics were not permissible if the measurement scale was only monotone, not linear. This would nullify the bulk of psychological research, past and present, because most psychological scales are only monotone. A polarized literature evolved that has continued to this day. Stevens' position was adopted in the distribution-free argument cited in the text. Stevens' position has been reaffirmed by Townsend and Ashby (1984, p. 395), among many others, who asserted that: "If the strength of one's data is only ordinal [monotone], as much of that in the social sciences seems to be, then even a comparison of group mean differences . . . by analysis of variance is illegitimate." This assertion is incorrect, as shown in *Anova With Monotone Data*. This point had already been made in Anderson (1961b, 1976a). The fact that randomization justifies one-way Anova with monotone data shows that Stevens' assertions about permissible statistics are wrong.

19.3.3b. If treatments do have an effect, it is logically possible that the rank order of means is not invariant under monotone transformation of the individual scores (Anderson, 1961b). This logical possibility lacks practical relevance. A similar comment holds for main effects in factorial design.

19.3.3c. With nonrandom groups, of course, an observed mean difference can readily be an artifact of a nonlinear, monotone scale. This seems a minor concern, however, relative to the main difficulty with nonrandom groups, namely, confounding with preexperimental differences (see Section 15.5, *Quasi-Experimental Design*).

19.3.3d. Semilinear scales are basic in empirical measurement because they embody normal development of knowledge. This central aspect of science is denied by Stevens' scale typology. Semilinear scales are also denied by mathematical measurement theory, which insists on a near-absolute gulf between monotone and linear scales. For example, Townsend and Ashby (1985, p. 394) deny semilinearity in stating that "Meaningfulness is an all-or-none concept. Thus, a statement cannot be almost meaningful." On the contrary, semilinearity implies that statements can be approximate and meaningful. Adherence to Stevens' scale types obscured the empirical nature of science.

19.3.3e. The usefulness of semilinearity may be illustrated with an early finding of nonparallelism in information integration (Anderson, 1965). Although this nonparallelism was small and could readily have been dismissed as nonlinear response, instead it served as a clue to uncovering the ubiquitous averaging process.

This clue to the averaging process would have been not permissible under Stevens' scale typology. Conjoint measurement (Krantz, Luce, Suppes, & Tversky, 1971, p. 446) would have required that this clue be smothered under a monotone transformation. Instead, the averaging process provided a fundamentally new foundation for psychological measurement theory—on solid empirical ground (Notes 21.2a, 21.6.3a–21.6.3e).

PREFACE

Mathematical models can give unique insight into some issues, illustrated here with the addition model and a signal detection model. Model analysis can be simple, moreover, as both models demonstrate. Technicalities are minimized in order to concentrate on conceptual issues. Most of this discussion, accordingly, applies generally to other mathematical models.

The analytical power of the addition model is shown in three experimental applications in Section 20.1.3, itemized as follows:

- Cognitive development has been placed in a new perspective through revealing impressive cognitive capabilities in young children, qualitatively different from those of Piagetian theory (Figure 20.1, page 651).

- Meaning invariance is a fundamental result, one that unifies diverse areas from person cognition to psycholinguistics (Figure 20.2, page 652).

- In psychophysics, the addition model pinned down the elusive psychophysical law and also provided capability for true measurement of conscious and nonconscious sensation (Figure 20.3, page 653).

As these three examples illustrate, the concepts and methods of Anova−regression given in previous chapters turn out to be quite adaptable for studying substantive models of psychological process.

The model from signal detection theory resolved a general bias problem in choice decision tasks. Whereas previous approaches sought to minimize bias through experimental procedure, signal detection theory instead incorporated the bias in a mathematical model. This model could factor out the bias and even measure it. Initially applied to sensory psychophysics, this detection model provided a clear conceptual analysis of the threshold concept, revealed its inadequacy, and replaced it. This detection analysis has been extended to memory and other cognitive tasks, providing sensory−cognitive unification.

A new approach to signal detection is suggested, based on information integration. Algebraic structure of integration models becomes the base, not the statistical variability structure on which signal detection theory rests. This algebraic base emphasizes the use of continuous response measures, which have certain advantages over the discrete choice responses of signal detection theory. Of special interest is capability for analyzing suprathreshold data, which are outside the scope of detection theory.

Chapter 20

MATHEMATICAL MODELS
FOR PROCESS ANALYSIS

This chapter seeks to convey appreciation of how mathematical models can help study perception, thought, and action. Two classes of models are considered, both of which utilize statistics: Addition models, which can be handled with Anova–regression techniques of previous chapters; and signal detection models, which employ a simple application of the normal distribution.

Conceptual issues are the main concern so technical details are mostly bypassed. Much of the discussion thus applies to all mathematical models.

A collateral purpose is to point up a neglected potential of Anova–regression for process analysis. Despite their ubiquity in statistical analysis, Anova–regression models have not often been used in psychological theory. Some writers have asserted that Anova is useless for analyzing information processing. In fact, Anova has proved a powerful tool for revealing cognitive process and structure across many domains (e.g., Figures 20.1–20.3).

20.1 TWO MODELS FOR ADDITION PROCESSES [a]

Psychological addition/subtraction processes have been established in a number of empirical domains. In fact, there is good evidence for a general purpose adding-type rule of cognition. Because of its simplicity, the addition rule lays bare most problems of model analysis, especially the twin problems of psychological measurement and testing goodness of fit.

To fix ideas, consider children's judgments of time. A toy train runs down a track at a certain speed and enters a tunnel, hiding it from view. The child presses a buzzer when the train enters the tunnel and releases it to indicate when it should have reached a marked distance along the tunnel. The buzzer duration is the response measure.

Three hypotheses may be considered for this time judgment task. Most obvious is that the children have internalized the physical rule:

$$\text{Time} \;=\; \text{Distance} \div \text{Speed.} \tag{1a}$$

Children can learn this rule from their physical environment, so it seems plausible that older children may follow it.

Younger children, however, might employ a subtraction rule:

$$\text{Time} \;=\; \text{Distance} - \text{Speed.} \tag{1b}$$

This rule is qualitatively correct; the response is greater for greater distance and less for greater speed. This subtraction rule would not be surprising because young children appear to employ a general purpose adding-type rule in other tasks, including some for which the physically correct rule is multiplication.

Finally, Piagetian theory postulates centration—that younger children are generally incapable of integrating two determinants and judge on the basis of one alone. Assuming distance is the more salient, Piaget's centration rule would state that judged time is a direct function of the marked distance:

$$\text{Time} \;=\; \text{Distance.} \tag{1c}$$

In all three rules, Time, Distance, and Speed are considered to be the child's personal values, of course, not the physical values.

To test these three algebraic rules, consider a factorial design with three levels of physical distance and three levels of physical speed. Each child is familiarized with the task and then judges two successive replications of the nine stimulus combinations, presented in random order.

20.1.1 REGRESSION ANALYSIS

One way to analyze data from the foregoing task of time judgment is with the two-variable regression model of Equation 16.1, with X_1 = physical distance, X_2 = physical speed, and Y = the child's time judgment. With two responses in each cell, we can obtain a pure error term on 9 df. The computer will print out four MSs: for distance, speed, deviations, and error.

The subtraction hypothesis implies that the response in each cell is the sum of a row effect plus a column effect, with nothing left over. The deviation from the subtraction model, in other words, is zero in each cell of the design. A key term in the analysis, therefore, is $F_{\text{deviations}}$. The data provide evidence against or for the subtraction hypothesis according as $F_{\text{deviations}}$ is statsig or not. Accordingly, $F_{\text{deviations}}$ is said to test *goodness of fit* for the subtraction model.

The division model implies that $F_{\text{deviations}}$ should be statsig and that these deviations will show a fan pattern. Regression analysis can be extended to test goodness of fit for this division model, but this will not be considered here. Goodness of fit for the centration hypothesis is left to Exercise a1.

Regression analysis is especially simple because it utilizes the prior knowledge represented by the physical metrics for distance and speed. Although these physical metrics are not the child's metrics, which are based on perceptual apprehension, the b weights in the regression analysis adjust the X units to agree with the child's. It is only necessary that the child's metric be linearly related to the physical metric for each stimulus dimension.

The shortcoming of this regression approach has the same source as its advantages. The assumption that the child's values of Distance and Speed are linearly related to physical distance and speed used in the regression analysis will be more or less incorrect. Any departure from linearity will act to increase $SS_{deviations}$, tending to infirm the model. Regression analysis will thus tend to falsify a true model. With the regression model, in short, statsig $F_{deviations}$ is somewhat ambiguous.

20.1.2 ANOVA

A second way to analyze the time judgments is with Anova. The subtraction hypothesis implies that the factorial graph will be parallel, that is, that the true Anova residuals are zero in each cell of the design. If F_{AB} is statsig, this speaks against the model. F_{AB} thus tests *goodness of fit* for the subtraction model.

The division hypothesis implies that the factorial graph will exhibit a fan pattern. F_{AB} should be statsig, therefore, with SS_{AB} concentrated in 1 df. Extension of Anova to handle multiplication and division models is given under the *Linear Fan Theorem* of Chapter 21.

Anova avoids the shortcoming of the regression model; the physical metrics of the stimulus variables are not used. Instead, Anova finds the stimulus values for which the addition model does best; no other stimulus values can do better. If the subtraction model fails this Anova test, the foregoing ambiguity with the regression analysis does not appear.[a]

Furthermore, Anova can be applied with tasks that use symbolic stimuli because it does not require physical metrics of the stimulus variables. This advantage is illustrated next with an experiment on the foregoing task of time judgment to study conceptual structure in children.

20.1.3 ILLUSTRATIVE APPLICATIONS

Some psychological tasks do obey algebraic rules. Anova has unique usefulness for analyzing algebraic rules. To demonstrate this usefulness, three illustrative experiments are cited here.[a]

Cognitive Development. Developmental psychologists often comment that the structure and function of adult knowledge can hardly be understood without studying its origin and growth in children. How children learn about the external world is thus central in understanding human knowledge.

Intuitive physics has special interest because children get massive daily experience with certain physical laws. They thus have opportunity to internalize these laws. Many laws of physics have simple algebraic form, moreover, as already illustrated with time = distance ÷ speed, and this constraint from the external world might induce a corresponding cognitive algebra.

The foregoing task of time judgment was transposed from a classic experiment by Wilkening (1982). Wilkening's subjects made judgments about an animal fleeing over a footbridge from a fierce, barking dog. The three variables were time (how long the dog barked), distance (how far the animal fled), and speed (fleetness of the animal, represented by pictures of turtle, cat, and others). With this ingenious task, judgments could be obtained for each of the three variables, given values of the other two. In addition to the three separate judgments, therefore, their interrelations could also be studied.

For time judgments, which are of present concern, the animal was placed along the footbridge at a certain distance away from the dog. The child pressed a button that made the dog bark for as long as the child thought it would take the animal to run the indicated distance.

Time judgments for two ages are shown in Figure 20.1. The 10-year-olds in the right panel show a near-linear fan, which argues for a division rule. The 5-year-olds in the left panel show near-parallelism. At this younger age, children appear to integrate by the adding-type rule:

$$\text{Time} \; = \; \text{Distance} - \text{Speed}. \tag{1b}$$

This remarkable result demonstrates functional understanding of all three concepts at age 5. A more radical change of ideas about development of time concepts is hard to imagine. Previous work had claimed that a time concept did not appear until much later, over age 10 (Note 11.4.1b, page 340). The integration paradigm has been similarly helpful throughout developmental psychology.

The conceptual implications of this result are more important than the algebraic model itself. Two such implications are that children have conceptual understanding of time, speed, and distance, and that this understanding is metric. That this understanding is conceptual follows from the algebraic integration and the symbolic definition of speed in terms of the animal pictures. That this understanding is metric is manifest in the algebraic rule. That functional metric understanding occurs so early is also vital for understanding development of quantification. Both implications are important in understanding human knowledge of the external world. As this example illustrates, a prime virtue of mathematical models is ability to go beyond algebraic structure to qualitative, conceptual analysis of cognitive process.[b]

Meaning Invariance. Integration experiments have led to the counterintuitive conclusion that meanings of words often do not interact but instead have fixed meaning within a given context. Similar invariance is also found with other

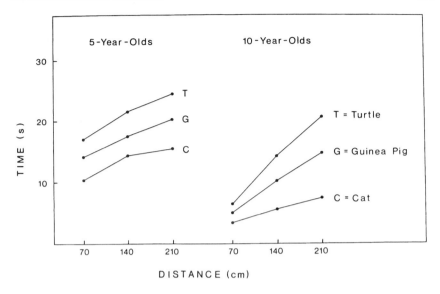

Figure 20.1. Addition and division processes in children's intuitive physics. Children judge time required by turtle, guinea pig, and cat to run 70, 140, or 210 cm. Judgments were made by producing an actual duration of a barking dog record. Parallelism in left panel shows that 5-year-olds follow subtraction rule, Time = Distance − Speed. Linear fan in right panel shows that 10-year-olds follow the psychophysical division rule, Time = Distance ÷ Speed. (After Wilkening, 1982.)

kinds of stimuli. Interactive views have been widely popular, as with the theories of cognitive consistency cited in Section 7.4. Similarly, experts often claim that their judgments are configural, that the meaning of any one informer depends on which others accompany it. These interactive views are introspectively persuasive, but they are mostly a cognitive illusion.[c]

Person cognition seems an ideal domain for finding strong interactions between informers. Construct person descriptions by combining informers in a row × column design. Suppose the meaning of the informer in row 1 changes because of cognitive interaction with the different column informers in different cells of row 1. Then the value of the row 1 informer will differ from one column to the next. Hence the data cannot be additive; the cognitive interaction has produced statistical interaction. Anova provides a powerful test—a test that makes allowance for personal meaning of individual subjects.

The interactionist view was disconfirmed in the first study of this type. The data were additive, as is apparent from the three-factor parallelism of the person judgments shown in Figure 20.2 (next page); see further *Parallelism Theorem* and associated discussion in Section 21.3. Graphs for two individual subjects were shown in Figure 11.2 (page 317), which gives additional detail.

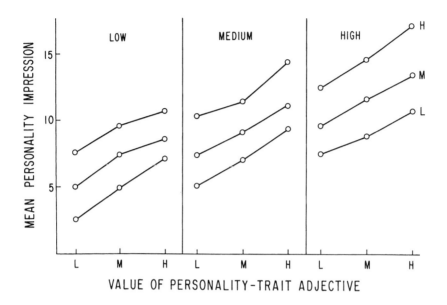

Figure 20.2. Parallelism supports meaning invariance, disconfirms interaction hypothesis in person cognition. Subjects judged likableness of 27 persons, each described by three personality adjectives in 3^3 design. L, M, and H denote adjectives of low, medium, and high value. Interaction hypothesis implies nonparallel curves, contrary to observed parallelism. Observed parallelism implies that person judgments are formed by averaging without interaction among the informers. (After Anderson, 1962a.)

Additivity implies meaning invariance. Contrary to the interactionist claim, each personality trait adjective has a fixed meaning, regardless of which other adjectives it is combined with. Not less important than meaning invariance is the associated implication of modularity, that the two operations of evaluating the individual stimulus informers and of integrating these values are independent (see **V–I** independence in Section 21.3.3, page 700).

This task of person cognition may also be construed as psycholinguistic function because of its use of verbal stimuli. Meaning invariance has also been demonstrated in other language tasks. Indeed, cognitive algebra may be a language universal (Anderson, 1996a, Chapter 12).[d]

Context in Psychophysics and Perception. Context plays a strange role in the field of perception. Although context typically has prominent effects on perception of focal stimuli, the study of context effects has remained largely task-specific, lacking generality. Indeed, one once prominent approach to psychophysics considered context effects a nuisance to be avoided.

Mathematical models may provide a general approach to context effects. A context effect need not be considered a nuisance. Instead, it can be a tool for theoretical analysis as well as a substantive phenomenon of intrinsic interest.

This model approach may be illustrated with the size–weight illusion shown in Figure 20.3. The upward slope of the top curve shows that perceived heaviness of a 600-g cylinder is greater the smaller its height, listed on the horizontal. Each other curve shows a parallel effect for lesser weights.

The popular interpretation of this illusion had been that subjects really judged density, not heaviness. But the density hypothesis corresponds to a division model, Size ÷ Weight, which implies that the curves in Figure 20.3 should form a fan. No sign of this fan pattern can be seen.

Instead, the curves are virtually parallel (except for one deviant point discussed in Section 20.4.6, page 675). Subjects appear to add the two informers. Presumably the effect of the size cue stems from an expectancy learned from the ecological correlation between size and weight.

The long-controversial psychophysical function concerns the dependence of subjective sensation on the physical stimulus. This experiment on heaviness sensation yielded perhaps the first validated psychophysical function. The vertical distances between successive curves are a linear scale of the sensory effect of gram weight; each added 100 g has diminishing effect on felt heaviness. The graph of these vertical distances as a function of gram weight is the psychophysical function—validated by success of the addition model (see *Parallelism Theorem*, pages 697*ff*).

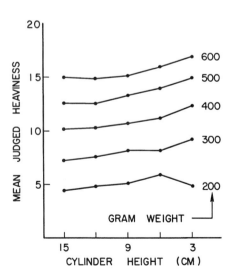

Figure 20.3. Size–weight illusion obeys adding-type model. Subjects judge felt heaviness of cylinders varied in height and gram weight. Observed parallelism implies that size and weight are integrated by adding-type rule. Vertical elevations of curves represent psychophysical function for gram weight. (After Anderson, 1970a.)

Other measurement aspects of this experiment also deserve mention. First, the effect of the weight in Figure 20.3 is preconscious. What reaches consciousness is an integrated resultant of preconscious effects of the two stimulus variables. Functional measurement thus fractionated the conscious sensation into its preconscious components and measured them. Second, the contextual cue, far from being a nuisance, was the key to validating the model—and thereby validating the measurement scales (Anderson, 1975).

All perception, thought, and action depend on context; multiple determination is a fundamental fact of psychological science. The three foregoing experiments demonstrate a new direction of attack with analytical power across three quite different areas of psychology.

20.2 PROBLEMS IN MODEL ANALYSIS

The addition model of the three foregoing experiments is a prototype of mathematical process models. Its simplicity makes it ideal for illustrating conceptual problems in model analysis. A few of these conceptual problems are taken up in the following sections.

20.2.1 PSYCHOLOGICAL MEASUREMENT

The central problem in analysis of algebraic models concerns psychological measurement. Actually, there are two measurement problems: one for the stimuli, the other for the response.

Stimulus Measurement. Stimulus measurement must allow for whatever personal values the subject attaches to the stimuli. In the train experiment of Figure 20.1, Distance and Speed are considered psychological terms, conceptually distinct from their physical counterparts. Wilkening was studying the processes underlying the child's judgments, not their outcome accuracy. The child's processes for integrating Distance and Speed cannot be determined without measuring the child's own values for Distance and Speed. This is clear with the symbolic speed stimuli used by Wilkening, which have no physical metric and whose meaning will differ from child to child.

One advantage of Anova is that it makes complete allowance for personal values. Separate measures of the stimulus values are not needed. Indeed, the critical prediction of parallelism can be assessed by visual inspection of the factorial graph. The functional values of the stimuli are implicit in this graph; these values are given explicitly by the marginal means of the factorial data table (Conclusion 2 of the parallelism theorem, page 698). If the model succeeds, therefore, it can furnish validated measures of stimulus values in the metric of each individual.

The validity of the stimulus values derived from the model depends of course on the validity of the model. Unless the model fits the data, the derived scales may not mean much. After the following subsection on response linearity, accordingly, three sections are devoted to this issue of goodness of fit.

Response Measurement. A linear response scale is desirable for most model analyses. In the train experiment, this linearity assumption requires that the observed duration of the child's buzzer press be a linear function of the child's underlying conception of duration. Response linearity may seem self-evident in this case because the response constitutes a duration. In the example of Figure 20.3, however, it is not self-evident that the rating response is a linear function of felt heaviness.

The parallelism observed in the three foregoing figures is prima facie evidence for response linearity. Unless the response scale was linear, a correct addition model would yield nonparallel data. A successful prediction thus provides joint support for the model and for response linearity. Further discussion of this fundamental issue is deferred to the parallelism theorem of Chapter 21 (see also Note 19.3.2b). In this chapter, response linearity is assumed in order to focus on other problems in model analysis.

20.2.2 GOODNESS OF FIT

The central question in model analysis is whether the model fits the data. Specifically, are the discrepancies between the model predictions and the data real? This is the question of *goodness of fit.*[a]

Anova provides a straightforward test of goodness of fit, both for addition and for multiplication models. The addition model implies that the interaction residuals are zero in principle and nonstatsig in practice, pages 673f. Accordingly, the factorial graph should be parallel for addition/subtraction models. Similarly, multiplication/division models imply a linear fan pattern (see *Linear Fan Theorem* in Chapter 21).

Goodness of fit requires attention at the design stage. Not a few studies have realized too late that their design could not actually test goodness of fit. One mistake is failure to provide for an estimate of error variability. This pitfall was avoided in the hypothetical experiment of Section 20.1 by using two replications so a within-cells error term was available to test the interaction residual.

20.2.3 WEAK INFERENCE

Weak inference refers to a rather common tactic that seems to test the model but does not really do so. Weak inference with correlation and scatterplot is illustrated in Figure 20.4 (next page). The data come from a test of the venerable hypothesis that consumers form preferences by adding values of relevant aspects of the product, in this case, durability and absorbency of diapers.

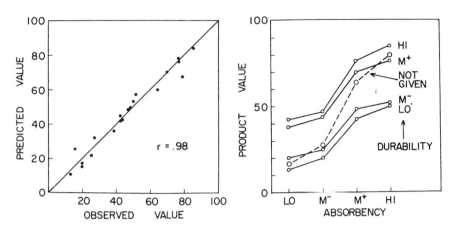

Figure 20.4. Weak inference and strong inference. Consumer preferences obey averaging model, disobey addition model. Weak inference statistics of correlation and scatterplot in left panel seem good support for addition model; predictions of addition model correlate .98 with the observed data. But these same data show a crossover in the factorial graph in right panel, which disconfirms any kind of addition process. Averaging theory predicts both the parallelism of the solid curves and the crossover of the dashed curve. Factorial graph and Anova reveal what the scatterplot and correlation conceal. (After Troutman & Shanteau, 1977; see Anderson & Shanteau, 1977, Figure 3.)

The left panel of Figure 20.4 shows predictions from the addition model plotted as a function of the observed preferences on the horizontal. The addition model implies that all the data points will lie on the straight diagonal, except for error variability. The points cluster very close to the diagonal, with little sign of systematic discrepancy. The correlation of .98 between predicted and observed is impressive. Judged by these correlation–scatterplot statistics, the addition model seems to do very well.

A very different picture of these same data appears in the right panel of Figure 20.4; here is shown the factorial graph. The addition model implies parallelism. This implication is contradicted by the crossover—a critical test that infirms the addition hypothesis and supports averaging theory (see *Opposite Effects Test* in Section 21.4.1, page 706).

The same data look very different in the two panels of Figure 20.4. The reason is simple: The left panel looks at the main effects—slurring over the non-additive discrepancy. The main effects are large, to be sure, but main effects say little about discrepancies from additivity. In the right panel, in contrast, the nonadditive discrepancy stands out.

A second example of weak inference is shown in Figure 20.5. The left panel plots judgments of expected Performance, given information about the person's Motivation and Ability. The linear fan pattern supports the hypothesized multiplication rule, Performance = Motivation × Ability. Comparison of the two equal-length vertical bars highlights the nonadditivity.

How does the addition model handle these data? Predictions from the Motivation + Ability model are shown in the right panel of Figure 20.5. If this addition model was correct, all the data points would fall on the straight diagonal, except for error variability. Clearly, the points do cluster close to the straight diagonal, with little sign of systematic discrepancy; predictions from the addition model correlate .99 with the data. Here again, correlation and scatterplot argue strongly for an addition model. But here again, correlation and scatterplot are blind to the real question.

Regression scatterplot and correlation are weak inference; they do not actually test goodness of fit. On the contrary, they obscure and conceal discrepancies from prediction. Factorial graph and Anova are strong inference, for they reveal the essential pattern in the data.

Weak inference also comes in other forms. The model may be shown to account for a high percentage of the variance, for example, or to leave only a small percentage of variance unexplained. Alternatively, some form of relative mean square discrepancy may be shown to be "small." Although sometimes

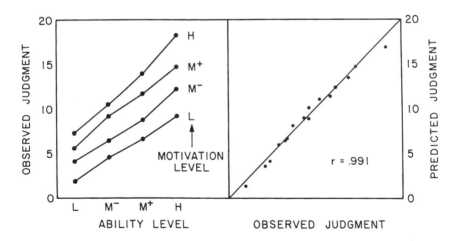

Figure 20.5. Weak inference and strong inference. Judgments of expected performance of persons characterized by their motivation and ability obey multiplication model, disobey addition model. Right panel plots predictions of addition model as a function of the observed values; tight scatterplot and high correlation of .99 seem to support the addition model. Same data shown in factorial graph in left panel exhibit nonparallel fan pattern. Fan pattern disconfirms addition model, supports multiplication model for social attribution: Performance = Motivation × Ability. (From N. H. Anderson, *Methods of Information Integration Theory.* Academic Press, 1982.)

helpful, all such statistical indexes fail the central issue of goodness of fit, that is, testing whether the discrepancies from the model are real.

Weak inference stems in part from confusion over the two goals of process and outcome. The addition model has great usefulness for outcome analysis and so became popular for practical prediction. This outcome-oriented way of thinking was carried over to questions concerning the process of integration, without realizing that such process questions required a new way of thinking. Whereas outcome is mainly concerned with main effects, process is mainly concerned with pattern.[a]

20.2.4 OUTCOME AND PROCESS

Experts in any field, be it personnel selection, clinical diagnosis, or everyday person cognition, typically believe their judgments are configural. They are sensitive, they assert, to patterns or configurations of informer cues; they interpret each informer in relation to the others. Because of this expertise, they believe their judgments will be superior to judgments made by a statistical regression equation, which relies on unthinking, nonconfigural addition.

Two questions arise, one of outcome, one of process. The outcome question is whether experts are in fact superior to the statistical equation. This outcome question has a straightforward resolution. If the experts are superior, they will show higher correlation with the criterion. The numerous studies of this issue show that, on the whole, experts do more poorly (e.g., Section 16.1.3).

A quite different question concerns the process underlying expert judgment. Are these judgments really configural, as the experts claim? Do the experts' verbal reports give a valid picture of their cognitive processes?

Many studies of this process question adopted the same technique just indicated for the outcome question. Accordingly, the statistical regression equation was fitted to the experts' judgments. This statistical model accounted for most of the variance in the experts' judgments; their judgments showed very high correlations with those predicted by the nonconfigural, addition model. It was concluded that experts' judgments were not really configural after all.

This conclusion was a non sequitur. A valid test for configurality must look at the discrepancies between the expert judgments and those predicted by the nonconfigural model. These discrepancies can be large even though the correlation is high. The correlation index is a weak inference statistic. Although useful for the outcome question, the correlation and analogous indexes noted in Exercise a7 were booby traps for the process question.

This identical point has already been illustrated in Figure 20.4. In both examples, the error stemmed from failure to realize that two qualitatively different questions were involved—outcome and process—and that different analyses were appropriate for each (see also Section 1.2.2).

20.3 SIGNAL DETECTION THEORY

Modern theory of signal detection is a "silver lining" theory. It turned a long-troublesome dark cloud inside out, transforming it into a tool for analysis and theory. The dark cloud was bias in judgments about presence or absence of signals obscured by noise. The traditional approach sought to reduce or eliminate bias through experimental procedure; signal detection theory took advantage of the bias by incorporating it within a mathematical model. Then the bias could be factored out mathematically leaving a pure measure of sensory acuity.

This model approach has been notably successful. Moreover, the model has been extended to many other areas. Although originally concerned with the narrow task of detecting sensory signals partially obscured in a noisy background, it has been extended to problems of recognition memory, speech discrimination, medical diagnosis, and others. It has thus helped unify sensory and cognitive analysis.[a]

20.3.1 OVERVIEW OF DETECTION TASKS

Modern theory of signal detection was developed by statistical decision theorists and communications engineers, who were concerned with extracting faint signals obscured by noise, as with the radio signals sent back by the Galileo space probe from planet Jupiter. It was then adopted by psychologists, who belatedly recognized that most of the essential ideas had been presented long before by Fechner and Thurstone.

Detection as Behavior. Signal detection pervades animal behavior, both of prey and predator. The mouse foraging on the forest floor at night is alert for slight unusual sounds. The owl has evolved keen hearing to detect the rustle of the mouse amid wind-caused noises, as well as soft feathers to decrease the sound of its attack flight. Insects, to take a different example, may detect mates at great distances with chemical signals called pheromones.

Our human sensory systems are a priceless evolutionary legacy that is well-adapted for survival in the physical environment and is equally important if less capable in the social and intellectual environments. We are proficient at sports, not surprisingly, and driving cars in heavy traffic. At other activities, such as doing statistics or having a happy marriage, our brains are no more than painfully adequate. Still, we should be grateful they are as good as they are.

Many problems of civilized life are detection problems. A radiologist inspects an X-ray to detect signals of cancer, for example, which are often not clear against the background "noise" of normal variability in organ appearance. The counselor taking a distress call on the suicide hotline seeks to detect the few likely suicide attempts among the great majority of callers who, however despairing, will not actually attempt suicide. The selection committee for a new assistant professor position searches for signals of research promise in the numerous application folders they evaluate. And all of us seek to detect the outline of our future in the confused shape of the present.

The 2 × 2 Decision Table. In the *yes–no* detection experiment, the subject receives a signal-plus-noise on some trials, noise alone on other trials, under instructions to say whether the signal was present on each trial. Faint, uncertain signals are presented that will be missed on some Signal-plus-Noise trials. Some Noise trials, moreover, may seem to contain a signal. The response is thus probabilistic, correct on some trials, incorrect on others.

The data from a yes–no experiment form the 2 × 2 decision table of Table 20.1. This table should look familiar; it's the same as Figure 2.2 for significance testing. Noise corresponds to H_0, Signal-plus-Noise to a real effect.

There is one big difference, however. The significance test is a one-shot affair, only a single trial. A yes–no experiment, in contrast, includes many trials—of both kinds. The Hit rate can thus be based on a considerable number of trials. The same holds for the other three rates in Table 20.1.

The Bias Problem. Our goal is to use the data of the 2 × 2 decision table to measure the subject's sensitivity to the signal. The obstacle we face is a criterion bias. The subject will be unsure on many trials and could call them either way. By using a more liberal criterion, the subject could get more hits—at the cost of more false alarms.

A traditional tactic was to tell the subject to call *yes* only if very sure; the Noise trials served as catch trials to ensure compliance. Sensitivity could then be measured by the number of hits as a function of signal intensity. But with this instruction, most subjects will use very conservative criteria, calling *no* unless very certain. The Hit rate will go down, the Miss rate will go up—and

TABLE 20.1

2 × 2 DECISION TABLE FOR SIGNAL DETECTION

		Stimulus	
		Noise	Signal
Decision	*yes*	False	Hit
Decision	*no*	O.K.	Miss

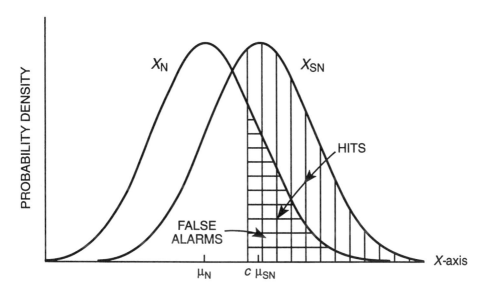

Figure 20.6. Conceptual diagram for signal detection theory. X_N and X_{SN} represent normal distributions of information values X of stimulus on Noise and Signal-plus-Noise trials, respectively. Subject is assumed to say *yes* or *no* according as the X value on any trial is greater or less than the criterion c.

the subject's true sensitivity will be underestimated. Not less seriously, the subject is still using a criterion, and small, hardly detectable changes in this criterion could have considerable effect on the Hit rate.

20.3.2 SIGNAL DETECTION THEORY

Signal detection theory (SDT) resolved the bias problem by incorporating bias in a theoretical model. This model can factor out the criterion—leaving a pure measure of detection sensitivity. Bias was transmuted into an analytical tool. Indeed, criterion "bias" can be reconceptualized as cognitive process rather than outcome accuracy, of keen interest in cognitive decision theory.

Signal Detection Model. SDT begins by representing the stimulus as an informer, X, which measures the amount of information about presence of a signal on each trial. On each trial, the physical stimulus is evaluated to yield a particular value of the informer variable X. This particular X value differs from trial to trial because of the random noise. Repeated Signal-plus-Noise trials thus produce a distribution of X values, shown as the X_{SN} distribution in Figure 20.6. Similarly, the X_N distribution in Figure 20.6 represents the probability of each particular value of X on Noise trials.

In auditory detection, for example, the signal could be a .1 s pure tone added to a 1 s white noise. The X dimension would be similarity between the stimulus and a memory image of the signal.

The decision rule is simplicity itself. The subject is assumed to adopt a criterion, c, and say *yes* or *no* on each trial according as the signal informer, X, is greater or lesser than c on that particular trial.

Note that $X < c$ on some SN trials in Figure 20.6. On these trials, the subject says *no*. This is a Miss in Table 20.1. And on some N trials, $X > c$, so the subject says *yes*, a False Alarm in Table 20.1. The criterion c thus governs the two error rates, exactly analogous to the criterial F^* in Figure 2.1.

In Figure 20.6, the effective strength of the Signal equals the distance between the means of the two distributions. A stronger signal corresponds to an SN distribution that lies farther to the right. A more sensitive subject is similarly represented by an SN distribution that lies farther to the right. Accordingly, the distance between the two means may be taken as a measure of sensory difference or of sensory acuity. This sensory measure is called d' so

$$d' = \mu_{SN} - \mu_N.$$

To quantify this conceptual picture, only a single assumption is needed: The SN and N distributions are normal with equal variance. From elementary properties of normal distributions (page 790), it follows that

$$d' = z_{Hit} - z_{False}, \qquad \text{(fundamental formula of SDT)} \qquad (2)$$

where z is the standard normal deviate (see below).

This *fundamental formula* of SDT has two notable properties. First, d' is constant—independent of the criterion. Second, d' is determined in terms of *observable* quantities; the two z scores are just the normal deviates for the observed proportions of Hits and False Alarms. This model has factored out the criterion, leaving a pure measure of signal sensitivity.

The fundamental formula, $d' = z_{Hit} - z_{False}$, follows directly from Figure 20.6 by using elementary properties of the normal distribution in Chapter 0 at the end of this book. Since the X_N and X_{SN} distributions are both normal, we may relabel the horizontal axis in terms of normal z scores. Accordingly, $z_{Hit} = \mu_{SN} - c$ and $z_{False} = \mu_N - c$. Both z scores have the same unit, by virtue of the assumption that both distributions have equal variance. Hence we may subtract one difference from the other. In this subtraction, the unknown c cancels, yielding the fundamental formula.[a]

If empirically valid, this SDT model is remarkable. It claims to measure the subject's sensitivity to the signal, freed from the subject's bias. It would thus be possible to test, for example, whether hypnosis will increase face recognition in eyewitness testimony about accidents or crimes. Subjects use a laxer criteria in the hypnotic state, but this criterion can be factored out mathematically by the model, leaving a pure measure of accuracy.

Goodness of Fit. Is the SDT model accurate? Does it provide an acceptable account of the Hit and False Alarm rates from a detection experiment? This is the question of *goodness of fit*.

Anyone can do a detection experiment, use the observed proportions to calculate z_{Hit} and z_{False}, subtract the two, and call this d'. But this d' may mean nothing unless the model has empirical validity.

What empirical predictions does SDT make that can be used to test goodness of fit? It makes the very strong prediction that d' is constant, independent of the criterion. No more is needed, accordingly, than to manipulate the criterion experimentally and compare d' across conditions. The criterion may be manipulated in various ways. One simple way is to tell the subject to adopt a lax criterion in some sessions and a strict criterion in others. The two criteria will yield quite different proportions of Hits and False Alarms. The data for each criterion will then yield a value of d'; both should be equal.[b]

The results of such tests are mixed. Often d' seems constant, but frequently it is not. Usually, d' decreases when the criterion is laxer, which can be explained by assuming that the SN distribution has greater variance than the N distribution. This explanation has some plausibility since the SN distribution includes both Noise and Signal variability.

But regardless of the explanation, nonconstant d' is embarrassing because it means that the theoretical measure of sensory acuity does depend on the subject's criterion. Moreover, nonconstant d' does not seem readily predictable. Fortunately, the model can be extended to allow nonconstant d' and still provide a reasonably satisfactory measure of sensitivity. This requires manipulation of the criterion in each experiment. In designing a detection study, therefore, criterion manipulation seems generally desirable, not to say essential (Macmillan & Creelman, 1991, p. 83).

This outcome illustrates a general moral about mathematical models. All models make simplifying assumptions, as with the SDT assumption of equal variance that underlies the prediction of constant d'. Failure of a model prediction need not require abandoning the conceptual framework if it can be attributed to failure of a simplifying assumption. In the present case, the basic conceptual framework can be retained, while allowing sensitivity to depend on the subject's criterion. The model can actually do better, as just indicated, by showing how a measure of average sensitivity can be obtained that will allow comparison across different experimental manipulations.

Measuring the Criterion. The SDT model yields a second benefit. It can measure the criterion, which might otherwise be hard or impossible. Since the criterion represents the subject's decision processes, this measurement capability leads into cognitive theory. Indeed, some studies of cognitive process may be more concerned to measure c than d'.

The criterion in Figure 20.6 may be measured as the average of the two z scores:

$$c = -\tfrac{1}{2}(z_{Hit} + z_{False}).\qquad(3)$$

The zero point for the c scale lies midway between the means of the two distributions. At this point, the Miss and False Alarm rates are equal so z_{Hit} and z_{False} are equal and opposite. The minus sign is used so that a laxer criterion (higher *yes* rate) yields a more negative value of c.

The c parameter is generally called *bias*, a term that stems from the dominant concern with outcome accuracy that has characterized SDT. From a process perspective, the term *bias* may be somewhat misleading.

ROC: Relative Operating Characteristic. If the criterion is varied experimentally for a given signal intensity, each level of the criterion will yield a z_{Hit} and z_{False} pair. Each pair may be plotted with z_{Hit} on the vertical, z_{False} on the horizontal. The curve connecting these plotted points is called the ROC, or relative operating characteristic. The ROC is widely used as a descriptive statistic, especially in comparing alternative detection models.

The detection model predicts the shape of the ROC: It should be a line parallel to the straight diagonal of zero sensitivity, on which $z_{Hit} = z_{False}$. This parallelism is equivalent to the constancy of d'. If the SN distribution has greater variance, however, the ROC will have flatter slope.

20.3.3 CONCEPTUAL ISSUES IN SDT

SDT illustrates the potential of mathematical models. It has provided a new way of thinking about the nature of sensory signals and the process of detection. The fundamental formula itself is only the tip of a conceptual iceberg.

The conceptual shift is away from the concept of threshold to the concept of criterion. This conceptual shift deserves emphasis, for it rests on the assumption that there is no hard and fast distinction between Noise trials and Signal-plus-Noise trials. Instead, the stimulus is processed in a similar way on every trial to yield a value of the informer, X, which varies on a continuous scale. This new way of thinking had to overcome considerable inertia that had developed with the concept of threshold.

Various other shifts in way of thinking flow from the shift from threshold to criterion. Most notable is that cognitive processes are considered an integral part of what had previously seemed a purely sensory domain.

Concept of Threshold. The concept of *threshold* arose as a natural explanation for nondetection of weak signals: Why should the same signal be detected on some trials, but not on others? A simple explanation was that the effective signal was variable, which was generally acknowledged, and that it had to exceed some critical threshold value to be detectable. If a signal does exceed the threshold, it is detected. Signals below the threshold simply do not get through the sensory system. Noise trials, in particular, would rarely if ever exceed the threshold. This threshold concept also seemed harmonious with the all-or-none character of neuronal action.

The threshold concept had been questioned by various writers, but the first effective alternative came with SDT. The concept of threshold does not appear in Figure 20.6. Instead, stimulus information is considered a continuous variable; the function of the threshold is taken over by the decision criterion.[a]

SDT Versus Threshold Theory. Once this alternative conceptualization had been made explicit, tests between threshold and no-threshold theory became clear. One test involves second guesses in which, for example, the signal is presented at random in one of four successive time intervals. The subject is to say which interval it was in—and then to make a second guess. Threshold theory says the second guesses must be at chance. SDT says second guesses will be above chance, as in fact they are. This is one of several discriminative tests, all of which disagree sharply with the traditional concept of threshold.

The second-guess task is qualitative, not quantitative. It does not depend on the foregoing SDT model for d', only on the concept of threshold. Hence it holds regardless of quantitative details of the detection process. Such qualitative tests are prized for their robustness.

Correction for Guessing. A threshold concept underlies various ''corrections for guessing'' that have been proposed independently in numerous areas and tasks. The essential assumption, often implicit, is that responding is all-or-none. The subject either does or does not detect the signal, or, in other tasks, does or does not recognize the word, remember the face, and so on.

The guessing hypothesis may seem almost self-evident. In the yes–no experiment, subjects sometimes say *yes* on Noise trials. A natural interpretation is that they are guessing; when no signal is given, what else could cause a *yes*? This guessing interpretation is reinforced by the fact that the proportion of false *yes* answers is readily manipulable, for example, by telling subjects to use a more/less conservative criterion.

Under the guessing hypothesis, some Hits will be guesses, not true detections. But a guessing correction can be made to reveal the true detection rate. The key is that all *yes* answers on Noise trials must be guesses, according to threshold theory. Hence the guessing rate can be measured—it is just the observable proportion of false alarms.

On Signal trials, some signals will exceed the subject's threshold. These represent the subject's true sensitivity; a more sensitive subject has a lower threshold. Some signals will fail to exceed the threshold, however, and on these trials the subject must guess. The observed Hits include those guesses that chance to be Hits, as well as the true detections.

Let s denote the subject's true sensitivity, that is, the proportion of Signal trials that are above threshold. The proportion of Hits obtained by guessing equals the False Alarm rate times the probability, $1 - s$, that the signal is below threshold. With HR as the observed proportion of *yes* responses and FAR as the guessing rate, elementary probability theory shows that the subject's true sensitivity is (Exercise b9)

$$s = \frac{\text{HR} - \text{FAR}}{1 - \text{FAR}}. \tag{4}$$

Analogous corrections for guessing have appeared in diverse areas, often without explicit recognition that an all-or-none, threshold concept is being invoked.[b]

In sharp contrast, SDT considers detection to be continuous, not all-or-none. The effective signal information, X, is a continuous variable. Unlike threshold theory, the all-or-none *yes* response is not considered a veridical measure of the underlying perception. Instead, the criterion imposes an all-or-none response on a perceptual continuum. Hence the correction for guessing is invalid.

Subliminal Perception. A concept of *subliminal perception* has often been invoked to argue for a threshold of consciousness. In particular, motivation may set up a threshold that blocks stimuli from consciousness, as in Freudian theory.

Provocative evidence comes from experiments in which subjects receive very brief visual presentations of affect-laden words, referring to taboo topics hypothesized to evoke some unconscious defense mechanism that blocks conscious recognition. In this task, subjects will report seeing no word on some trials, but then identify the presented word with above chance accuracy from a multiple choice. Since the above chance identification shows some perception of the stimulus, it would seem that the initial failure to recognize reflects a threshold set up by ego defense against threatening words.

SDT, however, not only disallows the concept of threshold, but has no place for the concept of consciousness. Instead, it explains the result in a manner analogous to that used with the second-guess task. Without going into detail on an intricate issue, it seems fair to say that SDT has held its own against subliminal perception (see Macmillan & Creelman, 1991).

Sensory Analysis With SDT. Before SDT, sensory measures were considered inevitably task dependent. There appeared little prospect that any approach would unify the disparate results that were obtained when the same stimuli were presented by different methods, such as yes–no, forced-choice, method of limits, and others. Even results from the same task would be difficult to compare across different laboratories. Conceptual unity could hardly be expected when different methods yielded noncomparable results.

This gloomy state of affairs has been much changed by SDT. Different tasks now yield comparable measures of sensitivity:

> Prior to this development [of SDT], it had become a commonplace that the prominent psychophysical procedures yield different values for the sensory threshold, and there was a tendency to regard the results of a psychophysical experiment as meaningless except in relation to the specific procedure used. It is now the case that half a dozen laboratories, which have been using the procedures and the measures associated with the theory of signal detectability in auditory experiments regularly obtain results that are within one decibel of one another. (Green & Swets, 1966, pp. 113-114.)

SDT has thus yielded greater unification within sensory analysis.

Such unification is a promising sign for psychological science, which often seems headed into ever-increasing fragmentation. When simple sensory tasks resisted unification, prospects for unification in other domains were not hopeful. The unification provided by SDT thus suggests one potential of mathematical models. Indeed, further unification of sensory and cognitive analysis also appears in SDT.

Cognitive Analysis With SDT. The decision criterion in SDT is cognitive, not sensory, for it is influenced by costs, payoffs, expectations, and like factors. By incorporating the decision criterion, SDT combined sensory theory and cognitive decision theory. Sensory analysis thus became more cognitive and cognition more sensory. This sensory–cognitive unification is underscored by the capability of SDT to measure the criterion, a cognitive concept.

Many promising cognitive analyses have appeared, with applications of SDT to speech perception, memory, and other areas. To illustrate, consider a task of recognition memory in which the subject is first presented one group of faces for familiarization, and later presented the same "old" faces mixed in with "new" faces in a yes–no recognition task.

The informer variable X is familiarity. The "new" faces are considered to constitute a distribution of Noise, the "old" faces a distribution of Signal-plus-Noise. The formula for d' may thus be applied directly to the data, as well as the formula for c. The subject's memory can thus be quantified across diverse conditions of learning and forgetting. This measurement tool has been much used in memory research.

Further Work in SDT. SDT has expanded far beyond the yes–no task and is still developing. One open issue concerns the difference between detection tasks, which were considered in the foregoing discussion, and classification tasks, in which the subject is to name or otherwise categorize the stimulus on each trial. Classification tasks yield lower sensitivity, a result conjectured to reflect variability of the memory for the signal.

Some uncertainties underlie even the foregoing yes–no model of SDT. Alternative theories have been proposed that employ a "low threshold," that is, a threshold that can often be exceeded by the noise. Again, various alternative explanations have been suggested for the nonconstancy of d', which remains a nagging puzzle. Indeed, the foregoing interpretation in terms of unequal variance does not seem consistent with failures to find a dependable relation between signal strength and ROC slope.

The two issues of the previous paragraph have general interest in that competing interpretations often make very similar predictions. Although these interpretations are conceptually quite different, they can hardly be distinguished with available empirical tasks. This outcome is not infrequent with mathematical models, and serves a warning against overinvolvement with particular models. Some problems can only be resolved by a conceptual shift.

SDT represented just such a conceptual shift. It showed how the traditional concept of threshold could be tested, and found that it was clearly inadequate. Despite the uncertainties that remain, unifying the concepts of decision criterion and signal sensitivity is an enduring contribution.

Information Integration Approach to Detection Theory. The addition model for information integration considered in Section 20.1 may be used to supplement SDT, perhaps even replace it. This approach aims at analysis of multiple determination, a fundamental area in which SDT has not done well.

To amalgamate the two models, apply the addition model to describe integration of information from two or more determinants. This yields an integrated information variable, X, to which standard SDT analysis is then applied. Factorial design allows application of the parallelism theorem illustrated in Figures 20.1–20.3. As one example, the prediction of constant d' corresponds to parallelism in a two-way design with signal strength and criterion as the two factors (Anderson, 1974a, 1982, Section 3.10).

Somewhat different is serial integration, in which each trial consists of a sequence of stimulus presentations. For example, the stimulus presentation at each position could have two levels, Noise and Signal-plus-Noise, manipulated in a serial-factor design like that in the number averaging experiment of Figure 15.1. One possible response dimension would be judgment of the average stimulus magnitude across all positions. The addition model allows a separate weight for each serial position to represent memory effects (Exercise a5). The parallelism theorem of Chapter 21 shows how this model can be tested and, if successful, used to estimate weights, just as in Figure 15.1 (page 455).

A very different integration approach uses algebraic structure to replace the statistical variability structure of Figure 20.6, which is the foundation of SDT. Algebraic structure has the potential of establishing linearity of a continuous response measure, which would be a powerful tool. With ratings of stimulus magnitude on each trial, for example, the distributions of Figure 20.6 would be visible in the data. A direct test of the common assumption of greater variance of the Signal-plus-Noise distribution may thus be possible.

Ratings are often used in detection experiments, but they are analyzed as categorical choice data (Note 20.3.2b). Nevertheless, they show that subjects are sensitive to metric information in weak sensory signals. With suprathreshold stimuli, ratings can be linear scales, as shown in Figures 20.1–20.3 and discussed further in Chapter 21. That ratings of near-threshold stimuli can be linear thus seems plausible although as yet apparently untested.

As a simple illustration, consider a task in which each trial presents two stimuli according to factorial design. Subjects judge, say, average magnitude of the two stimuli on a continuous graphic scale. The averaging task predicts parallelism. Observed parallelism supports response linearity. The main effects of the factorial design then constitute linear scales of stimulus magnitude. With just a monotone response, a scale-free measure of discrimination accuracy could be obtained through the Mann-Whitney U statistic.[c]

This integration approach is conceptually simpler than SDT and also more general. With a linear response, sensitivity can be measured directly as the difference between response on Signal-plus-Noise and Noise trials. This direct approach harmonizes with the SDT assumption that the underlying variable X is continuous, but obviates the roundabout way by which SDT reconstructs this continuous variable through the two unobservable distributions of Figure 20.6. A continuous response measure bypasses the unobservable distributions as well as the criterion. Also, it can yield a complete psychophysical function.

This integration psychophysics rests on algebraic structure instead of the unobservable statistical variability structure of SDT. The addition model, although unobservable in itself, has an observable signature in the form of parallelism, illustrated in Figures 20.1–20.3. Algebraic structure thus provides a base and frame for developing linear scales of response (Section 21.6.1).[d]

This integration alternative, if successful, has several advantages. One is usefulness in studying mixtures, cross-modal integration, and other forms of multiple determination (McBride & Anderson, 1991). Another is greater efficiency, especially important when the number of trials is limited, as with taste and odor. Still another is potential for analysis of single stimuli, as with speech identification or medical diagnosis, in which each stimulus has a discriminable identity but SDT requires pooling over a set of stimuli. Also of interest is the possibility of unified treatment of threshold stimuli with suprathreshold stimuli, which cannot be handled in detection theory.

Underlying all these possibilities is the shift in focus—from accuracy of outcomes to processes of valuation and integration. Multiple stimulus informers are ordinarily operative so integration is an ecological norm. Algebraic models have shown empirical promise in integration experiments in other areas. Integration models seem potentially useful in detection theory.

20.4 ISSUES IN MODEL ANALYSIS

A few general issues in model analysis are taken up in the following sections. These are less concerned with how, more with why and whither.

20.4.1 MODEL ANALYSIS

Some situations cannot be understood without mathematical analysis. This conceptual role of models appeared in the foregoing discussion of SDT, especially in the development of a valid measure of sensory acuity. Similarly, the issue of meaning invariance of Figure 20.2 required mathematical analysis, both to understand and to resolve. The same holds for the independence of the valuation and integration operations (Section 21.3.3, pages 700ff), even though this issue is essentially qualitative. Similar cases appear throughout this book.

Model analysis forces explicitness. Assumptions that may be barely noticed in a verbal treatment often become questionable when made explicit. The human mind has remarkable capabilities for envisaging an overall plan to reach some goal without working out details of successive steps. These successive steps often present unanticipated difficulties. A mathematical model may be seen as a more detailed working out of a conceptual formulation. Such qualitative, conceptual benefits can be helpful, even without quantitative detail.

A recurrent criticism of mathematical models is that they foster premature formalization. This danger afflicts every psychological domain—perhaps more seriously with nonmathematical formulations. Empirical paradigms and theoretical issues often acquire an inertia that carries them far beyond the limits of their usefulness. Memory research, for example, has fixated on reproductive memory, neglecting the functional memory of everyday life. In developmental psychology, some major programs have centered on stage concepts based on choice task methodology that radically misrepresented children's cognition (see Figure 20.1). The contemporary cognitive movement, as a third example, still gives only occasional, incidental attention to everyday life, that is, to functional cognition and affect.

A more serious criticism is that mathematical models often sacrifice the phenomena to the model. Some research programs gamble everything on tasks that lack intrinsic merit. Too often, failure of the model leaves behind nothing of value. *Focus on the phenomena* should, in my opinion, be considered a primary guide to conduct. If a phenomenon has intrinsic interest, experimental analysis can hardly fail to find something of value.[a, b]

20.4.2 MODEL STRUCTURE AND MODEL PARAMETERS

Structure is one aspect of process analysis. This structural aspect is well illustrated by the contrast between the traditional concept of threshold and the concept of criterion in SDT. Figure 20.6 thus represents a conceptual structure that is in some ways more basic than the model-derived d' parameter. This conceptual framework becomes more credible, of course, and more useful, when it is developed into an exact mathematical model that yields quantitative analyses, as with measurement of d'.

Psychological structure is central in algebraic models. Among the aspects of structure are meaning invariance, discussed with the experiment of Figure 20.2, and the associated implication that valuation and integration are independent operators. Other aspects of structure concern psychological reality of conceptual terms of the model, as with Time, Speed, and Distance in the developmental study of Figure 20.1, page 651.

A second aspect of process analysis concerns measurement. A mathematical process model contains parameters that measure certain aspects of the process. In SDT, the main parameter is d', the measure of sensory acuity, whose virtues have been indicated in the earlier quotation.

In psychological algebra, the parameters are the values and weights of the stimuli. The model can serve as a tool for measuring these values and weights. As one example of measurement, the vertical elevations of the curves in Figure 20.3 are, in effect, the elusive psychophysical "law" for heaviness sensation.

20.4.3 MULTIPLE DETERMINATION

Multiple determination is a fundamental problem for theory construction. This premise seems evident on the ground that virtually all perception, thought, and action result from multiple determinants. Understanding multiple determination is thus essential for general theory (Section 1.5).

Mathematical models provide unique advantages for analysis of multiple determination. This point was illustrated with signal detection theory in Figure 20.6. The subject's decision criterion, instead of being considered an undesirable bias, was incorporated as one of two determinants in the detection model. This model for multiple determination provided a simple resolution of a longstanding difficulty. It led to new insight, moreover, as with its conceptualization of signal information as continuous rather than all-or-none.

Information integration theory parallels signal detection theory in certain ways. In the size–weight illusion of Figure 20.3, for example, the contextual cue of size was incorporated into the integration model. Instead of being an undesirable bias from the stimulus context, this cue provided validational constraint for the integration model. Further, the effect of stimulus size could be factored out, leaving a pure measure of subjective heaviness. This parallels the factoring out of the criterion in SDT. This appeal to a context effect provided an effective solution to the century-old problem of measuring sensation. Other kinds of context can similarly be transmuted from undesirable complications to useful phenomena.

The functional measurement method of psychological algebra has a wider range of application than signal detection theory. It applies to many different kinds of judgments and decisions besides detection, as in the experiments of Figures 20.1–20.3. No less important, it allows suprathreshold continuous response, a fundamental realm outside the scope of signal detection theory.

Multiple determination has been a continual roadblock in psychology. The approach of cataloging a multitude of variables that affect some behavior, once considered an epitome of scientific inquiry, says little about joint action of the variables. The interactionist theories discussed in Section 7.4 emphasized the problem, but failed to provide effective methods to analyze interaction. Factorial design and Anova are useful, but their reliance on arbitrary non-additive terms in the Anova model reveals their inadequacy for understanding what interaction means psychologically.

The scope and focus of psychological research have been severely constricted by lack of capabilities for analysis of multiple determination. Without such capabilities, investigators had to find issues that could be studied with available tools. Much has been learned, but psychology has suffered continued fragmentation as more and more determinants have been found to influence behavior. The much-remarked proliferation of mini-theories stems from devotion to mini-questions. Unified theory requires a new way of thinking.

Mathematical models are no cure-all for analysis of multiple determination. They have many limitations that need not be noted here. They have unique capabilities, however, that are potentially useful in every area of psychology. Some appreciation of their nature will help you recognize such opportunities when they pass by.

20.4.4 OUTCOME AND PROCESS

Outcome studies and process studies typically involve discordant goals, and unclarity about goals is likely to lead to inconclusive work. This issue, discussed in Section 1.2.2, applies equally with mathematical models, as illustrated in the foregoing discussion of *Weak Inference* (pages 655*ff*). Such unclarity about goals is a common stumbling block in studies with algebraic models.

Regression and Anova models are primarily useful for outcome analysis. A regression model can be exceptionally useful for prediction. For process analysis, however, regression models have many pitfalls. One pit, already noted, is that the customary reliance on known metrics for the stimulus variables undercuts the validity of the test of goodness of fit. A second pit is weak inference, often visible as design inadequacies that fail to allow a proper test of goodness of fit. A truly treacherous pit comes in using regression models to "control" uncontrolled variables (Sections 13.2, 15.5, and 16.2).

The outcome character of the Anova model is clear in its arbitrary treatment of deviations from additivity. In the two-way design of Figure 20.3, the one-point deviation from parallelism produces an interaction residual in all 25 cells of the design. But 24 of these 25 residuals lack psychological meaning. In three-way design, moreover, the response in each cell may include four distinct nonadditive residuals. These residuals are arbitrary. They are imposed on the data by fiat, and seldom represent psychological process.

Sometimes Anova and regression are useful for process analysis, as indicated in Section 20.1. With addition and multiplication models, Anova is doubly useful, both for goodness of fit and for parameter estimation. We may be grateful that these statistical models are so useful for outcome analysis and that they can sometimes be pressed into service for process analysis.

20.4.5 CHECKLIST ON MODEL ANALYSIS

Many published tests of mathematical models have relied on invalid analyses. Such articles are generally difficult to evaluate, especially by readers not well versed in model lore. The following checklist may be helpful, not only in evaluating published work, but also in planning future work.

1. Was the model fitted separately for each subject or only for the mean data, averaged over subjects?

Separate fits are usually essential to test goodness of fit. This point was noted with the linear regression model for repeated measures in Section 9.1.3.

2. Were separate measures of the parameters used?

Use of separate parameter estimates requires explicit attention to invalidity and unreliability of those estimates (Note 20.1.2a). It is usually more effective to estimate parameters from the same data used to test goodness of fit.

3. Was goodness of fit tested?

Goodness of fit requires an explicit test whether the discrepancies from the model are statsig (Sections 20.2.2 and 20.2.3). Qualitative tests can be invaluable for disproving models (Note 20.2.2a), but confirming a model requires a significance test of discrepancies. Assessments that only show high agreement between the data and the predictions of the model are usually inconclusive weak inference. Strong inference requires assessment of the discrepancies.

4. Does the test of fit have satisfactory power?

Because model analysis usually seeks to "accept" the null hypothesis, weak experiments are a special danger. A separate power calculation for each new experiment may not be needed, of course, when similar previous studies can speak to the power question. Thus, the power of Anova in psychological algebra is indicated in the example of Figure 20.3, discussed on page 675, top.

This checklist should be used with care. A model analysis can be useful even though it fails to satisfy the first three criteria. The fact is, however, that not a few published model analyses have little value because of violations of one or more these criteria (see further Anderson, 1982).

20.4.6 ACCEPTING AND REJECTING MODELS

Accept/reject decisions about process models involve far more than a statistical test of goodness of fit. One point is that a good fit may be worth little if numerous other models make the same prediction, a severe problem with structural equation models for causal analysis (Section 16.2.1).

Qualitative tests are often advantageous. Thus, the opposite effects test for averaging versus adding (Section 21.4.1, page 706) requires only a monotone scale. Also, it rules out an entire family of addition models (Note 20.2.2a).

Conversely, nonstatsig discrepancy may not provide much support. This point reflects the unusual role of the statistical null hypothesis in model analysis. In standard experiments, the investigator usually aims to show a real effect—by rejecting the null hypothesis. Failure to reject is usually failure pure and simple; weak experiments are their own penalty. In model analysis, in diametrical contrast, the investigator usually desires to accept the null hypothesis, namely, that there are no discrepancies from the model. An experiment lacking power, with little value as evidence, may masquerade as success.

It is important, accordingly, to design the investigation so the data will have reasonable evidential value. The most satisfying solution, in many ways, is through replication. Finding no systematic discrepancy across several experiments speaks well for the model, even though no one may have high power by itself. Each may explore additional variables, moreover, giving a broader base to the interpretation. This replication approach is no less helpful for understanding possible discrepancies from the model. Systematic pattern in discrepancies across replications can help pin down their cause. This illustrates a general guideline: Potential for follow-up work should be a primary consideration when you choose the problem to which to devote the next portion of your life.

A third point is that a model need not be abandoned merely because it shows statsig discrepancies. This point is obvious with models for prediction and other outcome analyses. Thus, Figure 20.4 shows that an addition rule may give good predictions even though founded on an erroneous process assumption.

Even with process models, however, statsig discrepancies can sometimes be lived with. Any experiment designed to elucidate some process requires simplifying assumptions that will not hold exactly. Extraneous processes may also operate that produce discrepancies from the model predictions. Such discrepancies do not necessarily vitiate the value of the model for explaining the focal process.

On the contrary, an ideal model test may be one with statsig discrepancies that can reasonably be considered unimportant. That the discrepancies are statsig argues that the experiment had adequate power. If they can reasonably be attributed to violation of a simplifying assumption, this argues for the model.

Lest this rationale seem too dubious in the abstract, a concrete example has already appeared in the size–weight study of Figure 20.3. The overall parallelism of the curves in Figure 20.3 supports the addition model. The Anova, however, showed a discrepancy from the predicted parallelism, with a statsig interaction residual. Visual inspection shows that the discrepancy is localized in a single point, at the lower right. This was attributed to an end effect in the rating response, of a kind that had been observed in previous work. When this one point was omitted, the F for discrepancy was not close to statsig. The one discrepant point demonstrated the power of the Anova, thereby buttressing the support for the parallelism of the other 24 data points. The data were accordingly considered good support for the model.

Another illustration that statsig discrepancies do not necessarily vitiate the explanatory value of the model appeared with SDT. The basic prediction of constant d' has failed in a substantial number of experiments. This failure, however, may be reasonably attributable to failure of the simplifying assumption of equal variance for the Noise and Signal-plus-Noise distributions. And regardless of the explanation, SDT seems able to surmount this difficulty to obtain a useful average measure of sensory acuity.

20.4.7 CONTINUOUS DEVELOPMENT

Models are continually changing, just like other theories. Such evolution is characteristic of science, "the endless frontier." This fact is not always palatable, for the usual standard of success is successful prediction. A failed prediction should be instructive, however, even if not reinforcing, for it requires reconsideration of the ideas that led to the prediction.

Even the best models require development to handle new situations. This point was illustrated with SDT, which faces questions not yet adequately resolved. Information integration theory, similarly, has made limited progress with genuine interactions, such as discounting of inconsistent informers.

Even a model failure may be progress, providing insight into the phenomena. Some of the many abandoned formulations that strew the history of psychology have been stepping stones to better formulations. Mathematical models can speed up this evolution.

Scientific progress is an untidy evolution, a continuous flux of inconsistencies, uncertainties, zigzags, and blind alleys. It certainly differs from one traditional view, which likens scientific progress to a systematic building project, a steady accumulation of bricks of truth. The evolutionary view seems more realistic and can help make our efforts more effective.

20.5 MODELS AS BASE FOR UNIFIED THEORY

Mathematical models are a base for developing unified psychological science. These models are necessary as the only general way to handle the ubiquitous fact of multiple determination.

This point may be illustrated with the test of the interactionist theories shown in Figure 20.2 (page 652). These theories begin with one or another postulate that informers interact to change one another's value or meaning during the process of integration. This interaction hypothesis, strongly emphasized by the Gestalt psychologists, was overwhelmingly plausible in the task of person cognition in Figure 20.2.

But the parallelism pattern in Figure 20.2 disproved the interactionist theories en bloc. If the trait adjectives did interact, the effect of each row adjective would depend on which column adjective it was combined with. Its effect would not be constant, but would change from one column to the next. Hence the data could hardly be additive or parallel. This disproof of the interactionist theories is constructive, for it supports an alternative explanation for the integration process. This outcome transformed the problem of multiple determination. It opened up a potential base for unified theory, a potential that has been actualized (Chapter 21).

Meaning invariance (pages 700ff) is a basic conceptual implication, far more important than the integration model per se. This conceptual implication could not be established, however, without quantitative model analysis.

The parallelism pattern of Figure 20.2 is deceptively simple in two respects. First, parallelism depends on empirical reality of an adding-type rule for the integration. Second, parallelism also depends on having a linear scale for the response measure (see *Parallelism Theorem* on page 698).

Fortunately, adding-type models have been established by numerous workers on information integration theory. A few were shown in Figures 20.1–20.4; others are cited in the following chapter. This empirical reality provides a unique foothold on multiple determination.

Hardly less fortunately, empirical procedures were developed to obtain a true linear response measure from ordinary ratings. When this work began, the rating method was near-universally condemned as invalid, not a linear (equal interval) scale, and hence not usable in model analysis. But success was obtained—through development of simple experimental procedures to make the observed response a true linear scale (Note 21.6.1a, page 733). This is the base on which algebraic psychology was established.

Similar model analysis is essential for general theory. The reason is simple: multiple determination. Virtually all perception, thought, and action depend on integration of multiple determinants. Unified theory depends on capability for analysis of multiple determination. General analysis of multiple determination depends on mathematical models.

NOTES

20.1a. For convenience, the term *addition* will be taken to include both addition and subtraction operations; mathematically, subtraction is addition of a negative number. This usage does not imply psychological equivalence. The term *adding-type* will also include averaging models, although averaging differs from adding both mathematically and psychologically (Section 21.4, pages 705*ff*).

20.1.2a. This contrast between stimulus measurement in regression and in Anova illustrates a general problem in model analysis. A test of goodness of fit usually depends on securing the values of certain parameters in the model. These parameter values may be obtained in two ways: from the data at hand or from separate data. The first way is used in Anova, the second in regression. The first is usually preferable.

It might instead seem that separate parameter values would be superior; estimating parameters from the data and then using these parameters to "predict" those same data seems dubious. In fact, however, separate parameters suffers two shortcomings— invalidity and unreliability—both likely to be serious.

Invalidity can be avoided by estimating parameter values from the data at hand. This gives the model its best opportunity to fit the data. This is done in Anova, which avoids the ambiguity that troubles the regression analysis and provides a valid test of goodness of fit. A statsig discrepancy can thus be unambiguously attributed to the model itself.

Unreliability in the separate parameter values will generally introduce bias. This bias problem was illustrated with Ancova for nonrandom groups (Section 13.2). Without working familiarity with statistical theory of "errors in variables," reliance on separate predictor values is dangerous. Other difficulties with regression analysis of substantive models are noted in Section 20.2 and in Anderson (1982, Sections 4.3 and 6.1.1).

Regression analysis can be extended to estimate stimulus values in the same way as Anova, as noted in Chapters 9 and 16. Bogartz put this approach to good use in the study of infant perception/cognition of Note 8.1.2d. The present criticism concerns use of prior stimulus metrics without allowance for unreliability or invalidity.

20.1.3a. Except for Bogartz (1994a), the role of Anova for analysis of mathematical process models is completely ignored in statistics texts. This reflects the traditional focus on statistics to the neglect of empirics.

20.1.3b. What is most remarkable is that children can do these time judgments at all. This requires a complex assemblage: the imagined animal fleeing from the imagined dog across an imagined bridge at some imagined speed, and so on. This mental assemblage must be distilled into a quantitative judgment using an unfamiliar, symbolic response mode. The conceptual implications cited in the text are only one aspect of a fundamental issue of assemblage integration. One value of algebraic rules is potential for assemblage analysis (see *Assemblage Theory* in Anderson & Wilkening, 1991, pp. 20*ff*).

20.1.3c. The experiment of Figure 20.2 reaffirmed the long-known fallibility of verbal report, that people "tell more than they know." But contrary to Nisbett and Wilson (1977), individuals can give veridical self-reports. One illustration comes from Wright (1996), who used functional measurement theory to resolve two difficulties that had nullified previous attempts to disprove the thesis of Nisbett and Wilson that verbal reports reflect social norms, not self-knowledge. By providing a validity criterion for verbal report, functional measurement can help establish conditions under which phenomenology is and is not veridical (see also Anderson, 1982, pp. 288*ff*; 1996a, pp. 391*f*).

20.1.3d. The error of Simon's (1976) denunciation of Anova for analysis of cognitive process ("The variance analysis paradigm . . . is largely useless for discovering and testing process models to explain what goes on between appearance of stimulus and performance of response" [p. 261]) is well illustrated in Figures 20.1–20.3. Much was revealed about cognitive process in these experiments that could not otherwise have been determined (see also two previous notes). Indeed, the failure of verbal report protocols to recognize meaning invariance and **V–I** independence demonstrates a fundamental defect in Simon's primary method of inquiry based on protocol analysis. Simon's error stems from an extremely limited view of cognition that has no place for affect and emotion and little place for multiple determination (Anderson, 1982, p. 302, 1991a, p. 18).

20.2.2a. To *disprove* a model, qualitative tests are not only appropriate but often best. Examples are the opposite effects test shown on page 706, a strong disproof of addition models, and the second-guess task cited on page 665, a strong disproof of the classical threshold model. These qualitative tests also give some support to the alternative model, but strong support requires quantitative tests of goodness of fit.

In particular, quantitative analysis was essential to reveal meaning invariance and **V–I** independence (Section 21.3.3, pages 700*ff*). In general, quantitative analysis is essential to handle multiple determination.

20.2.3a. A review of weak inference by Anderson and Shanteau (1977, p. 1163), which included examples from three popular areas of judgment–decision, concluded:

> In each of these examples from decision theory, high correlations provided initially compelling support for the model in question. This led to further, often intensive, research on the psychological processes that were presumed to lie behind these models. Reanalysis and later evidence have shown that these correlations were deceiving. They did more to obscure than to reveal the underlying processes. As a consequence, much labor came to nothing.

One of these examples was the classic problem of subjective expected value, which is shown to follow a multiplication model in the study of Figure 21.7, page 715. Previous work, because it had relied on weak inference, had erroneously claimed that this integration process was additive. The other examples also showed that attempts to pursue process analysis with outcome tools was a mistake.

20.3a. Many other issues have been studied in detection theory, including other tasks besides yes–no, other definitions of bias, and several low threshold theories (Green & Swets, 1966; Macmillan & Creelman, 1991).

20.3.2a. Statistically, the normal distribution acts as a transformation from the observable response proportions to the theoretical z scale in SDT, exactly as in Case V of Thurstone's method of pair comparisons. By virtue of this transformation, the detection process becomes additive in the z metric. In SDT, the z scores theoretically are a true linear scale, with known zero, that is, a proportional scale. The validity of this scale of course depends on the validity of the SDT formulation.

20.3.2b. A less blatant criterion manipulation is with differential payoffs for Hits and Misses. Alternatively, the proportion of signal trials may be varied from 0 to 1, thereby manipulating the subject's expectancy and thereby also the criterion. The most efficient way may be indirect, with a rating response. SDT considers each successive step on the rating scale to represent a stricter criterion. Accordingly, the cumulative proportion of ratings less than or equal to a given rating provides a z_{Hit} - z_{False} pair, which taken together determine an ROC in an economical way.

20.3.3a. In common usage, the term *threshold* is a purely descriptive term for stimuli so weak that they elicit only a probabilistic response. This usage is general; it has nothing to do with the concept of literal threshold as a block to perception.

20.3.3b. An all-or-none threshold model and a continuous model are compared in Massaro (1991, pp. 274*ff*) for effect of sentence context on word recognition.

20.3.3c. A distribution-free measure of accuracy of discrimination between two stimuli, N and SN, can be obtained from continous response measures, including ratings, by estimating the probability that responses are less on N than SN trials. This equals the area under an ROC-type curve (with probability of hit and false alarm on vertical and horizontal, respectively). This area is often used instead of d' in signal detection studies.

Bamber (1975) showed that this area is estimated by the Mann-Whitney U statistic, normalized to lie between 0 and 1. This same idea was used by Herrnstein, Loveland, and Cable (1976) with pecking rate by pigeons in a naturalistic concept formation task.

Beyond independence, the only assumption is that both distributions have the same shape, regardless of what that shape may be. The criterion is controlled by treatment randomization. Only a monotone response is required and an error theory is available. All kinds of tasks of imperfect discrimination can be treated in this way.

This distribution-free method seems simpler and more powerful than standard SDT for analysis of discrimination accuracy. It seems surprisingly neglected.

20.3.3d. Macmillan and Creelman (1991, p. 226) comment favorably on the use of ratings in information integration theory, but imply that this approach does not apply to detection tasks. Actually, the article they cite did show how integration theory could be used in detection tasks, both with choice measures and with continuous response measures (Anderson, 1974a, pp. 246–249; see also Anderson, 1982, Sections 3.10 and 3.11). Their particular criticism of the rating method rests on an SDT conception of the rating process that remains conjectural; an alternative theory of the rating process is in terms of the decision averaging model of Equation 21.2c (page 708). In any case, their criticism seems avoidable with a continuous, graphic scale.

20.4.1a. This suggestion to focus on the phenomena stems in part from disappointment over my extensive work on stimulus sampling theory (Estes, 1964), which focused on matching behavior for two-choice human probability learning. Unfortunately, Estes' theory proved barren:

> As has been noted, the existing data indicate that there is much in the behavior that is neglected by the stimulus sampling models. Indeed, it would almost seem that what is neglected is just what is of most interest, and in this respect one must question the net usefulness of the theory. (Anderson, 1964a, p. 141; see also Note 3A.1b, page 83.)

The realm of probability learning, however, has not yielded very many substantive results. The concentration on theory led to neglect of what was of most interest in the behavior. . . . disappointingly little substance remains from all this work. (Anderson, 1982, p. 153.)

The concern that theory can lead one astray has been voiced by others, notably Skinner, who complained that the demise of a theory commonly took with it the associated empirical research. The cited case of probability learning supports Skinner's view, for little of this extensive work retains any value. For a large-scale illustration, compare the impact of Skinner's operant approach with that of Hull–Spence learning theory, which was predominant in the 1950s and which has now largely vanished.

Systematic discussion of guidelines for productive research problems is desirable. Skinner's view is a partial truth. Dustbowl empiricism, which has been the credo of some departments, is not an answer, for dust is unlimited. Moreover, Piaget changed the face of developmental psychology through his choice of experimental tasks, despite the incoherences and inconsistencies of his theory (Anderson, 1996a, pp. 243, 274; Anderson & Wilkening, 1991, pp. 37*f*).

20.4.1b. Sacrificing the phenomena is perhaps even more common in qualitative than quantitative theory. Prominent theories of social attribution, for example, were largely developed around extremely artificial tasks that provided little phenomenal nourishment, leaving the theories "stunted," to use the term of a major proponent. Similarly, developmental stage theories of moral judgment have been constructed around abstract moral dilemmas that have little relevance to everyday life and cannot be used at all below 10–12 years of age, the locus of much moral development (see Anderson, 1996a, Chapters 6 and 7; Hommers & Anderson, 1991).

The key to productive research lies in the choice of substantive problem. General guidelines for choosing a fruitful problem, however, seem largely nonexistent. This is one reason behind the continuing fragmentation of the psychological field.

My own preferred guideline, to focus on phenomena with intrinsic interest, emphasizes the importance of everyday life, a realm that has been surprisingly neglected in psychology. Psychology caricatures itself by the contrast between the immense mass of experiments on animal conditioning, for example, and the meager body of experiments on school learning, marriage and parenting, and affect of everyday judgment–decision, areas hardly recognized in most psychology departments.

Scientific research seems inherently wasteful, if that is an appropriate word. Many blind alleys must be explored; unsuspected confounds often emerge; ideas that are insightful in the light of prevailing knowledge often peter out or fall apart with further work. No algorithm can "look into the seeds of time and tell which grain will grow and which will not."

Nevertheless, historical inquiry into causes of failed effort should prove instructive for future work. Two prominent examples from this book may be noted. One is the class of situations in which cascades of research were precipitated by striking claims based on slipshod work that should never have been published. Several of these have been cited in Chapter 8 on confounding. Another is the class of unwarranted claims of "statistical control" of uncontrolled variables discussed in Sections 13.2, 15.5, and 16.2. Of related interest are the contrast between externalist and internalist strategies of Section 21.7.2 (page 725), and the contrast between categorical choice and continuous response as a base for psychological measurement theory (page 721 and Notes 21.6.3a–21.6.3f).

EXERCISES FOR CHAPTER 20

a. Exercises on Addition Model

a1. How can you test goodness of fit for Piaget's centration hypothesis for the time judgments of Equation 1c of Section 20.1 (see Exercise 5.2):

    a. with Anova?

    b. with standard regression analysis of Chapter 9 or 16?

    c. Which seems preferable?

a2. In Figure 20.3 on the size–weight illusion:

    a. Why would it be gauche to report the F for gram weight?

    b. Would it be gauche to report the F for size?

    c. Suppose the main effect for size was not statsig. How would this bear on the purposes of the experiment?

a3. Restate in your own words the reasoning of the last paragraph of *Cognitive Development* in Section 20.1.3, beginning "The conceptual implications of this result are more important than the algebraic rule itself."

a4. For the 3×3, Distance × Speed experiment considered in Section 20.1:

    a. Make up hypothetical data for a single subject that follow the postulated subtraction model exactly. Add an error of $\pm c$ in each cell, where c is a constant equal to about 10% of the range of data, choosing the ± sign at random for each cell. Make two replications. Apply Anova and comment.

    b. Make similar data for the physically correct division model and compare the factorial graphs for both sets of data by graphical inspection.

    c. Test the subtraction model with the data generated by the division model using visual inspection and also Anova. Comment.

    d. The cell means predicted by the subtraction model are equal to (row mean + column mean − overall mean). Apply this subtraction model to the division data of (b). Graph these predicted values as a function of the observed values and compute the correlation. Discuss in relation to Figure 20.5 and your analysis in (c).

a5. Serial belief integration can be studied using serial-factor design, in which each serial position constitutes a factor in the design. The main effect of each factor then measures the effect of the informer stimulus at the corresponding position. To illustrate the idea, consider three serial positions, each of which may present an informer of value 0 or 100, that is, against or for some belief issue. Subjects judge their belief only once, after all three informers have been presented, based on all the given information. Asssume that the response to sequence i is the weighted average, $\sum\limits_{i=0}^{i=3} \omega_i \psi_i \div \sum\limits_{i=0}^{i=3} \omega_i$, where ψ_i is the value of the informer at position i and ω_i is its weight. Subscript 0 indicates the initial belief, which can here be ignored (see further Exercise 21.c2).

There are eight possible sequences of informers, denoted by sequences of 0s and 1s. You get the following mean responses to the eight sequences:

1 1 1	90.91		0 1 1	72.73
1 1 0	54.55		0 1 0	36.36
1 0 1	63.64		0 0 1	45.45
1 0 0	27.27		0 0 0	9.09

a. Plot these data to verify that they satisfy the parallelism property.

b. If the averaging model holds, then the weight at each serial position is proportional to the main effect of that serial position. On this basis, show that the weights for the three successive positions stand in the ratio 2:3:4.

a6. Deservingness is a prominent social concept, especially in judgments about rewards and punishments. Two determinants of judged deservingness are what a person achieves and what the person needs. Design an experiment with children to test whether these two determinants are integrated by an adding-type rule, including reasonable amount of procedural detail. For example, children might be asked to role play Santa Claus in distributing toys at Christmas time. Make up hypothetical data and test the given model.

a7. Some writers attempt to assess goodness of a mathematical model in terms of the proportion of variance it accounts for. Most frequent is $r^2 = SS_{pred}/SS_Y$. Equivalently, $r = \sqrt{r^2}$ may be used, that is, the correlation between the observed values and those predicted by the model. An alternative is to use proportion of variance not accounted for, such as $1 - r^2$ or $RMSD = \sqrt{1 - r^2}$. If RMSD is less than .05 (or 5%), say, the model fit is deemed good.

a. For prediction and other outcome analyses, which of these two approaches seems preferable?

b. For analysis of integration process, which approach seems preferable?

c. For process analysis, why are both approaches questionable in light of Figures 20.4 and 20.5?

a8. The logic of placebo control rests implicitly on a rudimentary mathematical model, a form of theory control (Section 8.2.5).

a. Write down this model, defining your terms.

b. What empirical assumption is critical to this control?

c. How robust is this model against nonadditivity?

a9. In Figure 20.1, it might be argued that the parallelism for the 5-year-olds is an artifact—that half the 5-year-olds center on distance, half on speed.

a. Show by numerical example that this form of the centration hypothesis implies parallelism in the factorial graph of the mean data, averaged over children (disregarding response variability).

b. How can you analyze the data to test this artifact interpretation?

c. Give algebraic proof for (a), allowing an arbitrary proportion π of children to center on Distance, $1 - \pi$ on Speed.

a10. For the regression model of Section 20.1.1:

a. How many df are there for main effects of distance and speed?

b. Where do the 9 df for error come from?

c. How many df for deviations?

d. What are the two components of the deviations term?

b. Exercises on Signal Detection Model

b1. Discuss differences and similarities between Figures 20.6 for decision theory and Figure 2.1 for significance testing.

b2. Section 20.3.3 states that "the function of the threshold is taken over by the decision criterion."

a. What is the "function of the threshold?"

b. How does the concept of criterion differ from the concept of threshold?

c. What experimental manipulation cited under *Goodness of Fit* in Section 20.3.2 implies that the concept of criterion is necessary?

b3. To study memory under hypnosis, subjects were shown a videotape of an auto crash in their normal state. They were then tested with leading questions such as "Did you see the stop sign?" in both normal state and under hypnosis. These are called "leading" questions because the wording implicitly suggests that the correct answer is "yes." Actually, all questions were false. Subjects gave more "yes" answers under hypnosis than in their normal state. (For a review of this issue, see Klatzky & Erdelyi, 1985.)

a. Can we conclude that memory retrieval is poorer under hypnosis?

b. What fatal flaw disallows application of SDT to this experiment?

c. Suppose hypnosis has negligible effects on memory retrieval. How might this negative answer be important for the legal system?

b4. Explain the predictions of threshold theory and SDT for the second-guess choice task (page 665). Is the SDT prediction sensitive to constancy of d'? Is this good or bad?

b5. Suppose subjects make two responses in a yes–no task: first a *yes* or *no*, then a rating of confidence in the correctness of the yes/no. Show how these data can provide a qualitative test between SDT and high threshold theory.

b6. You and your dog participate in an olfactory discrimination task. Sketch a graph to compare N and SN distributions of Figure 20.6 for you and your dog.

b7. You obtain ratings in a standard SDT task for N trials and for SN trials. You plot a histogram of each set of ratings and notice that the SN ratings have a larger variance. "Aha," you think, "this is direct evidence for the hitherto untested assumption about the relation between these two variances that is frequently made in SDT."

    a. Why must your rating procedure yield a linear scale (Section 19.3.1) for this variance conclusion to be completely certain?

    b.* How could you test the linearity assumption?

b8. Verify d' and c for these three 2×2 tables, patterned after Table 20.1.

70	30		90	10		70	30
30	70		10	90		50	50

$d' = 1.048$ $d' = 2.564$ $d' = .524$

$c = 0$ $c = 0$ $c = -.262.$

b9. Derive the "correction for guessing" implied by threshold theory for the *yes–no* experiment to obtain the "true" hit rate (Equation 4 in the text).

b10. In applying SDT to recognition memory in Section 20.3.3, both the "old" and "new" faces are represented as distributions. Explain how the concept of a distribution of faces of varied familiarity applies to

    a. The set of "old" faces.   b. The set of "new" faces.

    c. In what conceptual way do these familiarity distributions differ from the distributions of X_N and X_{SN} for sensory signals in Figure 20.6?

b11. Do you think d' can provide meaningful measures of sensory acuity for nonverbal organisms? We can't just tell a bee, "Fly to whichever color chip looks bluer" or a bloodhound: "Bark if this odor [giving sample] is present in the next whiff of air." How can we get meaningful choice responses from nonverbal organisms?

    Will cross-species comparisons be meaningful?

c. Additional Exercises on Mathematical Models

c1. You wish to measure recognition familiarity for two classes of common English words for a certain type of aphasic patients in their normal state and under three experimental conditions. Application of SDT, however, faces two difficulties. Many familiarity values are above threshold, so SDT is hardly applicable. Even for the threshold choices, moreover, you would need many trials to get reliable frequencies of Hits and False Alarms.

Accordingly, you wonder whether the information integration approach discussed in the last subsection of Section 20.3.3 can be applied. You construct stimulus pairs using a 5×5 factorial design and ask subjects for two ratings of each pair: of the average familiarity and of the difference in familiarity of the two words in each pair.

a. Following the cited text discussion, how do you use the factorial data to get familiarity values for each stimulus?

b. It would be a lot simpler to obtain familiarity judgments of each stimulus separately. What is the advantage of getting judgments of pairs?

c2. You present the experimental plan of Exercise c1 to your research group. Someone points out that each word gets repeated presentations so its familiarity value may increase over trials.

a. What is the easiest way to test this possibility?

b. With the aphasic subjects, you decide you cannot take any chance about the objection of (a). This means you can present each word only once to each subject. How can you use the Latin square idea of Section 14.3 to get an efficient design?

c3. Ratings of familiarity can provide a more sensitive measure of memory than choice data. To illustrate, suppose we select two random samples of visual scenes from a large population and give familiarity training with one fraction to get a set of "old" stimuli, the other fraction serving as "new" stimuli (balanced across subjects to play safe). Later, we obtain familiarity ratings of half of each fraction under the subject's normal state and half under a certain medication. This yields a 2×2, repeated measures design. For each subject, we get $(\bar{Y}_{old} - \bar{Y}_{new})$ for each condition. Any effect of condition, positive, negative, or zero, will appear in the difference between these two differences.

The rating response provides a direct measure of memory, not requiring any assumption about normal distributions. Far fewer trials are needed than with yes–no choices.

a. What assumption is involved in this comparison? How serious do you consider it?

b.* How might this assumption be tested?

c4. Organisms may use two strategies to deal with a stimulus field. The integration strategy is to integrate the elements of the field into a unified whole, thereby utilizing all available information. Integration strategy requires substantial processing capacity, however, and a nonintegration strategy may be more cost-effective, responding in terms of just one salient element in the stimulus field.

One kind of nonintegration strategy arose with Piaget's centration hypothesis of Exercise a9. Here is a more complex centration strategy. Each individual child centers on factor A on some trials, on factor B on the other trials. You obtain continuous, numerical responses as before.

a. Show that the factorial plot, averaged over trials, will be parallel for each child (disregarding response variability), as though they added on each trial.

b. Show how to choose levels of A and B so that the distribution of response to some AB combination will differ under the nonintegration and integration hypotheses.

c5. An alternative to Sternberg's additive-factor model considered in Section 11.4.4 assumes that additivity is an artifact of all-or-none responding. In this "alternative pathways model" (Roberts & Sternberg, 1993), only one process is operative on each trial. If each of two variables in a factorial design affects just one of these two processes, the data will appear additive although the two factors do not add.

Much the same problem arose with a factorial experiment to test Piaget's centration hypothesis, as noted in the previous exercise. Show how the argument in that exercise can be transposed to test alternative pathways model.

c6. Many judgments are *comparative*: The focal stimulus is judged relative to some stimulus that serves as a comparison standard. A basic problem of processing order arises when the comparison standard has two or more dimensions. Are these separate dimensions integrated, and then the comparison is made to this integrated standard (IC order)? Or are separate comparisons made on each dimension, and then these comparisons integrated (CI order)?

The IC and CI processing orders have been empirically distinguished in certain applications, for example, in adaptation-level theory and in fairness theory. To illustrate the idea, let F denote the focal stimulus, C and D two dimensions of the comparison standard. Denote the comparison process by $/$, and suppose the integration follows an additive rule. The two orders may then be written

IC order: $F/(C + D)$.

CI order: $F/C + F/D$.

a. How can the algebraic structure of these two models be translated into an experimental test between them?

b. In Helson's (1964) theory, the adaptation-level is an integration of all relevant stimuli in the field, and the focal stimulus is compared to it.

Apparent length of the centerline in the line-box illusion of Figure 8.1 depends on some comparison of the centerline with the two flanking boxes. Show that Helson assumes the IC order. How would you test it against the CI order for the line-box illusion?

c7. As a check on the size–weight illusion of Figure 20.3, subjects could be asked to lift two weights in succession and judge their average heaviness. Consider a 5 × 5 design with gram weights of 200 to 600 g for each factor. Suppose the factorial graph exhibits parallelism.

a. From the discussion of Figure 20.3, what does this factorial graph say about the psychophysical function?

b. How exactly does (a) provide a check on the size–weight study? What could this suggest about the relation between nonconscious and conscious sensation?

c. What relation may be expected between the marginal means for the row and column factors?

c8. Problems of serial integration appear in every area of psychology. A plausible hypothesis in some such tasks is that the integration is a weighted sum or average of the values of the informer stimuli at successive serial positions. One example is the probability urn task, in which subjects revise their opinion about the composition of the urn as successive samples are drawn. To study serial integration task in this urn task, you present single red and white beads on successive trials, purportedly drawn at random. Subjects see only one bead at a time; at the end they make a numerical judgment of the probability that the urn contains more red than white beads.

a. What are the values of the two informers? Is it reasonable to think these values are independent of serial position?

b. You wish to get the serial weight curve for six serial positions. But this would require $2^6 = 64$ sequences, which you consider too many. How could you use fractional replication to reduce the number of sequences (see experiment of Figure 15.1)?

c. You wish to study serial position effects for sequences of 12 informers. If you use a complete serial-factor design, how many sequences are needed?

d. How can you get partial information on the serial position curve of (c) using the fractional design for 6 positions of Table 15.3 and Figure 15.1?

PREFACE

Two axioms are basic to construction of unified science of psychology. The **axiom of purposiveness** recognizes that behavior is goal-directed. Purposiveness is evident in our evolutionary heritage of sensory–motor systems—survival tools to approach and to avoid goals. The **axiom of multiple determination** recognizes that perception, thought, and action result from multiple influences, including changing motivations of the organism and a variable environment.

Each axiom corresponds to a capability of organisms. The first corresponds to capability for evaluating multiple aspects of the environment in relation to operative motivations. The second corresponds to capability for integrating these multiple values into a unified resultant, manifest in goal-oriented behavior.

General theory must possess the two corresponding capabilities: To measure values of aspects of the environment within the functional goal currency of individual organisms; and to analyze operative rules of value integration.

Both capabilities have been developed in information integration theory (IIT). A solution to the long-controversial issue of true psychological measurement was obtained in this way—functional measurement—distinguished from other measurement theories by empirical success.

Multiple determination has been found to obey simple algebraic rules in many areas, from person cognition through developmental psychology and judgment–decision to animal behavior. These algebraic rules allow measurement of functional, goal-relevant values for the individual organism.

The main value of algebraic psychology lies in conceptual implications, beyond the algebraic structure. One conceptual implication concerns independence of valuation and integration—a key to functional analysis. With this goes the implication of meaning invariance. A third implication is the functional conception of memory, quite different from the traditional conception of reproductive memory. In addition, functional measurement provides a ladder to go beyond algebraic models to study nonalgebraic and configural integration.

IIT is a general, unified theory that has been developed through empirical applications of functional measurement theory. IIT is general in being empirically grounded across diverse areas. IIT is unified in that the same concepts and methods apply in all these areas. Although incomplete in many ways, IIT offers a self-sufficient approach to functional cognition, an approach near the level of the perception, thought, and action of everyday life.

Chapter 21

TOWARD UNIFIED THEORY [*]

Unified theory of psychological science rests on two axioms:

> Axiom of purposiveness;
> Axiom of multiple determination.

Purposiveness reflects the evident fact that perception, thought, and action are directed toward goals. *Multiple determination* represents the evident fact that virtually all perception, thought, and action depend on multiple determinants. These two axioms are at once guides and cornerstones for construction of unified theory.

Instead of unification, psychology has become increasingly fragmented. The lack of unified theory has been overshadowed by the many fascinating recent developments, which have greatly extended our knowledge horizons, both in breadth and in depth. Ours is truly a golden age. But the excitement of these developments has increased the fragmentation in our field. The need for unified theory has been lost to sight.

The lack of unified theory reflects widespread nonconcern with the two axioms. The purposiveness of behavior was submerged in the era of conditioned responses, rote verbal learning, and psychophysical thresholds. The cognitive movement has expanded our conceptual horizons in many ways, but it has neglected value, emotion, belief, self, and other affective phenomena that are the heart of purposiveness. Multiple determination has been considered in particular situations, but mainly as specific context effects, seldom as general theory. This fragmented approach has had some notable successes, but it has led away from unified theory. Those who have been concerned with the two axioms have mostly failed to develop effective methods to deal with them.

---

[*] This chapter continues the theme of the previous chapter—the value of Anova-regression for studying psychological process.

Personal views are given on some controversial issues, especially on implications of the two axioms for directions in which to pursue unified theory. Detailed discussion of other views is not feasible here, but comments on other theories of psychological measurement are given in the notes to Section 21.6.3.

21.1 UNIFIED THEORY

21.1.1 AXIOM OF PURPOSIVENESS

Perception, thought, and action are goal-directed. Some goals are to be approached, for they favor survival. Other goals are to be avoided, for they are inimical to survival. The perceptual–central–motor processes that subserve such purposiveness are a showpiece of evolution.

Goal-directedness is an Archimedean lever for psychological science. Goals impose a one-dimensional character on perception, thought, and action. This one-dimensional representation is manifest in our everyday notions of amount and magnitude. This one-dimensional view also pervades psychological research; most experiments involve magnitude measures of stimulus and of response. This one-dimensionality constitutes a priceless simplification of reality, which is complex and essentially not dimensional. Purposiveness thus makes measurement central in psychological science—a door to unified theory.

21.1.2 AXIOM OF MULTIPLE DETERMINATION

General theory of multiple determination imposes a special requirement on psychological measurement. Linear (equal interval) or even proportional scales are essential. Without such scales, even direction of action cannot generally be predicted. Without true measurement, unified theory cannot be obtained.

The problem of the linear scale, however, has been controversial ever since Fechner's claim to have solved it in 1860. In the 1930s, a special committee of the British Association for the Advancement of Science pondered this matter and concluded that true measurement was impossible in psychological science. Few psychologists have accepted this pessimistic conclusion, but their attempts to resolve this measurement issue have generally failed.

Both axioms, however, can be solved jointly. Algebraic models of multiple determination have provided a working base and frame for true measurement of psychological quantities. In this way, algebraic models provide a foundation for unified theory.

21.1.3 INFORMATION INTEGRATION THEORY

The two axioms have been cornerstones for development of information integration theory (IIT). Purposiveness appears in the valuation operation $\mathbf{V}$ of Figure 21.3, page 696; multiple determination appears in the integration operation, $\mathbf{I}$.

This $\mathbf{V}$–$\mathbf{I}$ analysis is essential in principle, as already indicated. By a blessing of Nature, this approach has been reasonably successful in empirical application across diverse areas already illustrated in the previous chapter. The main ideas are given in this chapter.

21.2 FUNCTIONAL MEASUREMENT THEORY

Functional measurement theory has three main differences from other theories of psychological measurement. First is its focus on continuous measures of stimulus and response. This focus on continuous measures follows from the axiom of purposiveness. Nearly all other measurement theories have instead begun with discrete choice responses, hoping to use these as a base to construct the needed continuous measures.

There was a reason why other theories based themselves on choice response. As Thurstone pointed out long ago, continuous response measures, such as ratings, suffer nonlinear biases. They seem no more than monotone scales, and methods to linearize them were lacking. Choice data, based on greater than−less than judgments, thus seemed the only secure foundation for psychological measurement theory. But these choice theories have failed.

Second, functional measurement theory theory makes measurement derivative from substantive theory—a reversal of the traditional direction. Other theories sought to solve the measurement problem as a preliminary to substantive theory. Functional measurement makes measurement an organic part of scientific theory.[a]

Third, functional measurement theory has a solid empirical base. One application appeared in the study of person cognition of Figure 20.2 (page 652). This experiment infirmed the cognitive interaction theories and provided an empirical solution to the problem of true measurement of personal value of verbal stimuli. No less important, it demonstrated a simple method for true measurement of response.

21.2.1 THE PROBLEM OF THE LINEAR SCALE [a]

Psychological measurement theory has a primary concern whether scales are linear or only monotone. A linear scale is also called an "equal interval" scale—equal intervals on the symbolic number scale represent equal intervals on the scale of the psychological quality being measured. With a monotone scale, in contrast, the numbers have the same rank order as what is being measured, but equal number intervals are not generally equal psychologically (Section 19.3, pages 630ff, *Measurement Scales and Statistics*).

The Need for Linear Scales. Linear scales are essential for general quantitative theory. This need follows from the fact of multiple determination, a fundamental aspect of perception, thought, and action. Without linear scales, analysis of multiple determination is severely limited.

This point may be illustrated with compromise between conflicting forces, a common form of behavior. With only monotone scales of these forces, little can be said about the resultant of a conflict. With just two opposing forces, the greater will predominate, but nothing can be said about how much. With three opposing forces, even the direction of the resultant may not be predictable if only the rank order of their magnitudes is known (Exercise a8).

Linear scales are invaluable because pattern in the observed data is then a veridical picture of pattern in underlying psychological process. Such pattern analysis is neatly illustrated in the parallelism theorem and the linear fan theorem below. With nonalgebraic rules and configural integration, pattern analysis is even more important.

Two Attitudes Toward Numbers. Two opposite attitudes toward numerical response measures are common. The first takes numbers at face value, unthinkingly assuming a linear scale. Our everyday experience with numbers is mostly with physical scales, such as length and money. These are proper linear scales; the numbers correspond exactly with physical reality. We thus become habituated to taking numbers at face value, a habit that has negative transfer to psychological scales.

Most statistics texts also take numbers at face value, perhaps with passing reference to the problem of the linear scale. This tack has some justification, for the problem of linear scales is basically substantive, not resolvable at a statistical level. This tack also has negative transfer, however, as with the common failure to recognize that statistical interactions may be substantive illusions.

The opposite attitude toward numerical response measures argues that linear scales are generally impossible in psychology. The argument seems strong: Most scales seek to measure some unobservable concept (Figure 21.3, page 696); linearity is then a relation between the observable response scale and the unobservable concept. Assessing linearity thus seems impossible because this assessment rests on true measurement of the unobservable.

21.2.2 MEASUREMENT OF SENSATION

A concrete example will sharpen the measurement issue. To illustrate the difficulty in the clearest way, a simple perceptual continuum is used.

Grayness Seems Measurable. Many psychophysical sensations seem measurable in principle. This may be seen in Figure 21.1, which shows the Munsell scale of lightness, or grayness, as it will be called here. These gray "chips" portray a one-dimensional quality that we call grayness; given two chips, we can say which is lighter. Moreover, our sensation is evidently a continuous function of the physical reflectance listed by each chip. Our sensation of grayness thus has real existence as a one-dimensional quality. In principle, therefore, it should be measurable on a linear scale.

The problem facing psychology is to find a method for measuring magnitude of our grayness sensation. The outcome of one such method is exhibited in Figure 21.1. These chips were selected by a complicated process intended to

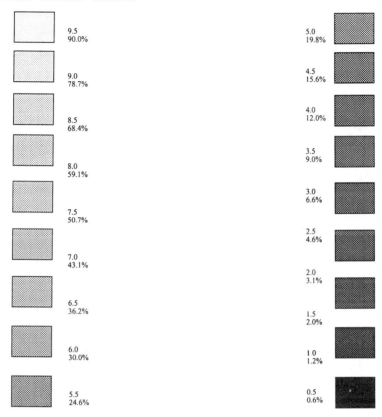

Figure 21.1. A steady progression of Munsell gray chips, from white to black; % R denotes percentage of incident light that is reflected from each chip. Munsell lightness values from 9.5 to 0.5. (Reproduced with permission of Munsell Corporation.)

produce equal differences in grayness between adjacent chips. Visual inspection suggests approximately equal differences, although this reproduction loses a lot of the original appearance.

Far more interesting than grayness are sensory pleasure and pain, belief, expectancy, interpersonal affects such as friendship and blame, and personal affects such as motivation and happiness. Grayness is considered here because it seems so clearly measurable. Unless we can measure grayness, we can hardly hope to measure these more interesting qualities.

A Roadblock to Measurement. There seems a simple way to measure grayness: Just ask people to give numbers that represent the magnitudes of their grayness sensations.

Two common methods may be used to measure grayness. One is the ordinary rating method. The whitest chip can be called 0, for least gray, and the blackest chip 100. Given these two standard stimuli, subjects would be instructed to rate the other chips in proportion to their experienced sensation.

The other method is magnitude estimation, which uses only a single standard, usually someplace in the middle of the stimulus range. Subjects are instructed to call the standard 50, say, and to assign 100 to a chip that seems twice as gray as the standard, 25 to a chip that seems half as gray, and so forth.

Rating and magnitude estimation are fairly similar. Both methods ask subjects to give numbers in proportion to their sensations. Subjects readily adapt to both methods. Indeed, subjects may use the two methods on alternate days with the feeling that their number responses are pretty correct with both methods. Although perfect agreement of the two methods is too much to expect, they ought to agree fairly well.

In fact, the two methods disagree violently. This is shown in Figure 21.2, which plots magnitude estimations for single gray chips on the vertical as a function of the ratings of these same chips on the horizontal. If the two methods were equivalent, the data would plot as a straight, diagonal line. The actual plot, as can be seen, is far away from the straight diagonal. The two methods thus give startlingly different results.

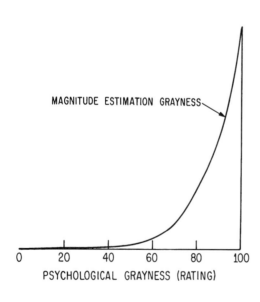

Figure 21.2. Magnitude estimation differs radically from rating. The curve represents magnitude estimations of grayness (lightness) of Munsell chips, plotted on the vertical, as a function of ratings of same chips, plotted on the horizontal. Equivalence of the two response measures would appear as a straight diagonal line. The curve is far from the straight diagonal; the two response measures are far from equivalent. Since the ratings satisfy validational criteria for a true linear scale, the deviation of the curve from the straight diagonal must reflect bias in magnitude estimation. (After N. H. Anderson, *Methods of Information Integration Theory.* Academic Press, 1982.)

Rating and magnitude estimation are thus highly nonlinear functions of each other. At least one of them, therefore, is a nonlinear function of grayness. Which—if either—is a linear scale?

To highlight this question, suppose you were informed that one of these two methods did yield a linear scale. How could you tell which one it was? Some *validity criterion* is needed.[a]

Physical Measurement Is Not Psychological Measurement. Some writers have argued that all measurement should be confined to observables. Only trouble, they say, can come from trying to measure unobservables. Stick to observables; unobservables may not even exist. This argument is understandable in view of the sharp difference between two plausible methods of subjective measurement that was shown in Figure 21.2.

But this objectivist view denies the psychological reality of the grayness sensation just seen in Figure 21.1. Physically, grayness does not exist. Physically, the chips differ only in physical reflectance value. These physical reflectances, however, differ greatly from the psychological grayness sensations.

To appreciate this difference between physical and psychological scales, note that the reflectance values of the two whitemost chips are listed as 90.0% and 78.7%. The difference of 11.3% physical reflectance is needed to produce this one step difference in psychological grayness. For the two blackmost chips, in stark contrast, the physical difference is only 1.1%. These reflectances are proportional to the amount of light energy that falls on your retina. Equal steps on the psychological scale of grayness sensation thus differ by a factor of 10 on the physical scale of light energy.

Psychological science requires psychological measurement. Physical measurement will not do. Grayness is a psychological reality, different from physical reflectance, qualitatively and quantitatively.

Psychological measurement, however, requires some validity criterion, as Figure 21.2 demonstrates. How can we determine whether our numbers are a valid linear scale of psychological reality?

21.2.3 FUNCTIONAL MEASUREMENT

A solution to the problem of the linear scale has been provided by functional measurement. Some basic concepts are presented in this section; methods for measurement are taken up in subsequent sections.

Integration Diagram. Functional measurement postulates that psychological scales are derivative from substantive laws, specifically, laws of multiple determination. The information integration diagram of Figure 21.3 portrays this class of laws. The organism is considered to reside in a multi-variable field of observable stimuli, denoted by S_A, S_B, . . . , at the left. These multiple stimuli are determinants of the observable response, R, at the right. Between the observable stimuli and the observable response intervene three processing operations: *valuation, integration,* and *action,* denoted by **V**, **I**, and **A**.

The valuation operator, **V**, extracts information from stimuli. In the integration diagram, it refers to processing chains that lead from the observable stimuli, *S*, to their psychological counterparts, ψ. Valuation may be as simple as perceiving the grayness of a chip in Figure 21.1 or as difficult as interpreting a remark by your spouse.

The integration operator, **I**, combines the several discrete psychological stimuli, ψ, into a unitary response, denoted by ρ. Integration thus represents multiple determination—the backbone of functional measurement.

The action operator, **A**, transforms the implicit response, ρ, into the observable response, *R*. This ρ → *R* distinction is clear with the grayness example: ρ would be your private feeling of grayness of a chip in Figure 21.1 and *R* your rating of grayness on a 1–100 scale. Or ρ could be a feeling of irritation with your spouse, and *R* a verbal retort, facial grimace, or sullen silence.

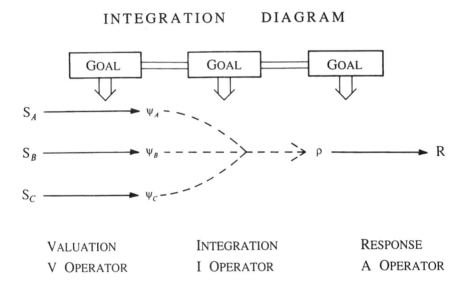

Figure 21.3. Information integration diagram. Chain of three operators, **V** – **I** – **A**, leads from observable stimulus field, {*S*}, to observable response, *R*. Valuation operator, **V**, transforms observable stimulus, *S*, into subjective representation, ψ. Integration operator, **I**, transforms subjective stimulus field, {ψ}, into implicit response, ρ. Action operator, **A**, transforms implicit response, ρ, into observable response, *R*. (After N. H. Anderson, 1970b.)

The Three Unobservables.   The three central entities in the information integration diagram are all unobservable. The integration operator, in particular, is generally beyond the reach of introspection.

The physical stimuli, S, are observable, but the corresponding psychological stimuli, ψ, are inside the body, often nonconscious. Thus, your grayness sensation for a chip in Figure 21.1 is not a public observable. It is real to you, I think, but this is your private sensation. I cannot experience your sensation, nor can you experience mine.

The implicit response, ρ, may be conscious, but it also is inside the body; the observable R may be severely biased as a measure of ρ, as was shown by the contrast between rating and magnitude estimation in Figure 21.2.

To illustrate, consider the simple addition model for two variables, A and B :

$$\rho = \psi_A + \psi_B.$$

Testing this model seems to require true psychological scales for the two stimulus terms on the right and for the response term on the left. If we had such scales, we could check whether the stimulus values add up to equal the response. Without such scales, we seem helpless.

This measurement problem is fundamental. Unless it can be solved, even the simple addition model—wrong or right—will remain generally untestable. And if this simple model cannot be tested, cannot be disproved, little hope appears for studying other models for multiple determination.

The problem of the three unobservables seems formidable. Attempts to divide and conquer have naturally been made, seeking to solve only one unobservable at a time. But these attempts were bound to fail; all three unobservables must be determined simultaneously.

In fact, nature has provided a remarkably simple solution for all three unobservables. The key is to capitalize on algebraic structure of the integration function, **I**. Algebraic structure is the foundation of functional measurement. This structural analysis is illustrated in the following parallelism theorem.

21.3 ADDITION MODEL

Functional measurement is most easily understood with the addition model. The same concepts and methods apply to the averaging and multiplication models considered later.

21.3.1 PARALLELISM THEOREM

The diagnostic sign of an addition model is a pattern of parallelism in the factorial graph. Suppose that two stimulus determinants are manipulated in factorial design. In cell jk, accordingly, the treatment is the stimulus combination

$\{S_{Aj}, S_{Bk}\}$, and the observed response is R_{jk}. The question is whether this response can be represented as a sum of the values of the two stimuli. The parallelism theorem answers this question with transparent simplicity.

Parallelism Theorem. The parallelism theorem employs two premises:

$$\rho_{jk} = \psi_{Aj} + \psi_{Bk}; \quad \text{(addition)} \tag{1a}$$

$$R_{jk} = c_0 + c_1\rho_{jk}. \quad \text{(linearity)} \tag{1b}$$

The linearity premise says that the observable response, R_{jk}, is a linear function of the implicit response, ρ_{jk} (c_0 and c_1 are zero and unit constants whose values can be ignored). From these two premises follow two conclusions:

Conclusion 1: The factorial graph will be parallel.

Conclusion 2: The row means of the factorial data table will be a linear scale of the ψ_{Aj}; similarly, the column means of the data table will be a linear scale of the ψ_{Bk}.

Conclusion 1 follows directly by substituting Equation 1a into Equation 1b:

$$R_{jk} = c_0 + c_1\psi_{Aj} + c_1\psi_{Bk}.$$

Thus, the two premises imply that the observable R_{jk} is indeed a sum of the unobservable stimulus values. Comparison with the Anova model of Equations 5.1 shows that the residual from additivity is zero. Granted the two premises, therefore, the factorial plot will be parallel. For Conclusion 2, see Exercise a10.

21.3.2 BENEFITS OF PARALLELISM

The parallelism theorem provides a simple and precise test of the addition model. Hardly more is necessary than to look at the factorial graph. Observed parallelism constitutes strong support for both premises of the theorem taken together. Hence it supports each of them separately. Observed parallelism thus helps attain a cornucopia of benefits:

1. additive integration;
2. linearity of the response measure;
3. linear scales of each stimulus variable;
4. stimulus invariance;
5. independence of valuation and integration.

The first three benefits correspond to the three unobservables. The first involves the integration model; the next two involve the two measurement problems: measurement of response and measurement of stimuli.

By virtue of these three benefits, therefore, the parallelism theorem solves the problem of the three unobservables in the integration diagram. Each of these three benefits requires comment.

Addition Rule. If the factorial graph exhibits parallelism, that obviously supports the premise of additivity. This is substantial support, as indicated under *Parallelism as Evidence* on page 703.

The true value of the parallelism theorem, of course, lies in the experimental investigations that demonstrate its empirical validity. Unless addition processes appear in nature, the theorem would have little value. A solid empirical foundation has in fact been obtained, after overcoming considerable complication caused by averaging processes.

Stimulus Measurement. Nothing need be known a priori about the stimulus values—the test of parallelism is made directly on the response. We manipulate the observable stimuli, S_{Aj} and S_{Bk}, and thereby also manipulate the corresponding unobservable stimuli, ψ_{Aj} and ψ_{Bk}. These unknown stimulus values become manifest in the observed response. The observed response thus provides measures of the functional values of the stimuli.

This stimulus measurement rests on Conclusion 2 of the parallelism theorem. This conclusion tells us that the row (column) means provide a linear scale of the row (column) stimuli of the design. These are true psychological scales— of the stimulus values that were functional in the observed behavior.

Response Measurement. Response linearity is important. Unless the response is linear, the data will generally be nonparallel even though the addition model is true. But observed parallelism supports the linearity of the response scale. The importance of this implication is hard to overemphasize.

Response linearity has been the crucial issue in psychological measurement theory. Everyone has desired linear response measures, but the validity problem seemed insurmountable: How can we tell whether R is a linear function of ρ when the latter is unobservable? The perplexity of this question is highlighted by the sharp disagreement between rating and magnitude estimation shown in Figure 21.2. This obstacle has been surmounted by the parallelism theorem, which provides a practicable validity criterion.

Response Generality. Generality is a prime attraction of response linearity. Linearity derives from empirical procedure. If response linearity can be established in one situation, similar procedures may be expected to yield linear response in other situations. In fact, the procedures developed for the rating method in functional measurement have proved useful across many domains. Even young children do well (see figures on pages 329, 651, and 707).

A general method for linear response has surpassing advantages. With a linear response, the pattern in the observable data is a veridical picture of the pattern in the unobservable process—a priceless advantage with tasks that do not obey an algebraic model or that involve configurality/interaction.

To illustrate, consider a deviation from parallelism. If it might merely be a nonlinearity in the response scale, its meaning would be uncertain. With a linear response methodology, however, such deviations can be treated as real and meaningful. New lines of inquiry open up, especially for studying nonalgebraic processes (see Sections 21.6.1, page 717, and 21.7.1, page 723).

21.3.3 COGNITIVE ANALYSIS

The parallelism theorem has unique capability for cognitive analysis. This capability has already appeared in the discussion of the first three benefits of observed parallelism. No less important are the last two benefits, conceptual implications that are discussed in the next two subsections.

Value Invariance. Parallelism implies that the stimuli did not "interact" with one another, but had fixed, constant values. The addition model includes a strong, implicit assumption of stimulus independence; Equation 1a assumes that S_{Aj} has a fixed value, regardless of which S_{Bk} it is combined with. If the row and column stimuli did interact to change one another's values, then the factorial graph would generally be nonparallel. Parallelism implies not merely additivity, but the deeper property of value invariance (see also Note 21.3.5a).

Value invariance argues against interpretations in terms of interactive or configural process that have been popular in every field, from judgment–decision through language processing to person cognition. With language, it was puzzling that *a few crumbs* were more numerous than *a few cookies*; language quantifiers seemed to interact with context in unpredictable ways. With person cognition, it was widely believed that the meaning of one informer in a person description was not constant, but changed, depending on its relations to other informers in that description. Cognitive algebra, however, revealed determinate, noninteractive processes (see figures on pages 652 and 701).[a]

V–I Independence. Parallelism also implies that **V** and **I** are distinct and independent operators. **V–I** independence has ecological economy. Values are sensitive to operative goals; they embody ever-changing motivational states. The same stimulus will thus have different values relative to different goals. Integration operations, in contrast, are relatively insensitive to motivational states. With this reliance on valuation to assess operative values as they depend on the immediate context, a few general purpose integration processes suffice to produce a wide spectrum of adaptive behavior.

V–I independence is buttressed by the contrast between the sensitivity of valuation and the insensitivity of integration to the operative goal or context. Interaction between context and individual stimuli reveals valuation as adaptive behavior, as just emphasized for goal as context. Once evaluated, however, the individual stimuli often show little interaction with one another as they are integrated. A conception of integration as pooling of activated features seems

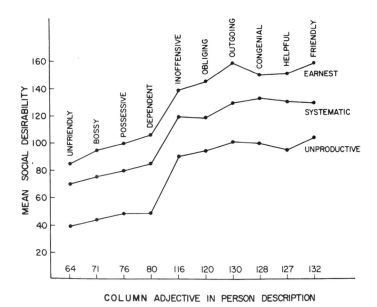

Figure 21.4. Functional measurement analysis supports meaning invariance, disconfirms hypothesis of meaning interaction. Each point is the mean of 12 judgments of social desirability of a person described by two trait adjectives, listed in the figure. Adjectives were combined in a row × column design. (From Anderson, 1974b,c.)

incompatible with independence of valuation and integration. This discovery of **V–I** independence reveals separate stages of information processing.[b]

Meaning Invariance in Person Cognition. An empirical foundation is essential to demonstrate the worth of parallelism analysis. Conjectures about addition laws have long been common in psychology, but they remained conjectures because measurement theory was not available to test them. Functional measurement has placed the addition model on solid empirical ground, within a general theory of information integration.

Functional measurement is illustrated with a study of person cognition in Figure 21.4. Subjects judged social desirability of persons described by pairs of adjectives listed in the figure. The observed parallelism supports the hypothesis that the adjectives are integrated by an adding-type law.

Four aspects of psychological measurement appear in this factorial graph. First, the parallelism is evidence that the rating method provides a true linear scale of response. Second, the numbers on the horizontal axis are a linear scale of the social desirability values of single adjectives, obtained as the column means of the factorial design (Conclusion 2 of parallelism theorem).

Third, the apparent affective bimodality is real, visible in the jump in each curve between *dependent* and *inoffensive*. The column adjectives thus form two clusters, four negative and six positive. Had only one curve been obtained, the jump could have been attributed to avoidance of a neutral point in the rating scale. But comparison of the three curves shows that the jump occurs at different places along the response scale while the curves maintain parallelism. The affective bimodality is genuine, therefore, and is considered to stem from a general approach–avoidance polarization of behavior.[c]

Fourth, these data imply meaning invariance; each adjective has a fixed value and meaning. *Systematic*, for example, has the same value in a *friendly* or *helpful* person as in an *unfriendly* or *bossy* person. Many writers have made strong claims to the contrary, adducing compelling phenomenological reports that the adjectives interact and change one another's meanings.

But such meaning change would generally produce nonparallelism. Thus, *systematic* and *unproductive* in the two lower rows would generally change by different amounts in each column because of different semantic–pragmatic relations with the column adjective. This would yield nonparallelism. The parallelism observed in this and related studies cast cognition in new light.

Overall, this experiment yields the foregoing five benefits of parallelism:

1. The adjective information is integrated by an adding-type rule.
2. The rating response is a veridical measure of the person cognition.
3. The subjective values of the adjectives are revealed in the factorial graph.
4. Each adjective has invariant meaning, the same in all person descriptions.
5. **V** and **I** are independent operators.

21.3.4 EMPIRICAL ADDITION MODELS

Parallelism has been obtained in numerous experimental studies reviewed elsewhere (Anderson, 1974a,b,c, 1981, 1982, 1991a,b,c, 1996a). A few are cited in this book: person cognition (pages 317, 652, and 701), social attitudes (page 278), psychophysical sensation (pages 324, 653, and 730), consumer judgments (page 656), young children's judgments of attractiveness of toys (pages 329 and 707) and of time (page 651). Most of these, however, are actually averaging rather than adding, as shown by the opposite effects diagnostic illustrated in figures on pages 278, 329, 656, and 707.

True addition processes have been revealed in a few experiments. A neat example is visible for the adults in Schlottmann's study of probability judgment shown in Figure 11.9 (page 329). The study of moral judgment summarized in Anderson (1996a, pp. 218*ff*) is of interest in that the same variable is added with a second variable, averaged with a third. Stefurak's study of red–green contrast in Figure 11.6 (page 324) not only demonstrated true addition, but also showed that a physiological scale defined in terms of relative activation of red and green cones was a true linear scale of psychological effect.

Parallelism analysis has been employed by Sternberg (2000, in press), with impressive reanalyses of data from published studies in diverse areas. For those studies with a "composite" response measure, response linearity is an empirical consequence of observed parallelism, by virtue of the parallelism theorem. These applications help solidify the functional measurement approach with non-symbolic, behavioral response measures (see also Note 21.7.1a, page 740).

21.3.5 PROBLEMS OF EVIDENCE

The parallelism theorem has the common *if-then* form of scientific hypotheses. Given the premises, the data must exhibit the prescribed pattern.

In empirical science, of course, we are not given the premises. Scientific reasoning goes in the inverse direction from *if-then*. We wish to make an inverse inference, from the observed data to the truth or falsity of the premises. Such inverse inference is always more or less uncertain (Section 19.1). One problem concerns unreliability in the data. Another concerns alternative explanations. These two problems are discussed in the two following subsections.

Goodness of Fit. Anova helps put the parallelism theorem on practical ground. Any set of data will contain response variability, so the observed factorial graph will never be perfectly parallel, even though both premises of the theorem hold true. The foregoing presentation has ignored response variability, but this must be included in empirical applications.

The first question, accordingly, is whether the deviations from parallelism are reliable or can reasonably be attributed to chance. This question, of course, is exactly what is addressed by the F for interaction residuals in Anova.[a]

Other issues must also be considered in empirical assessment of an addition model. These issues also pertain to other mathematical models and were discussed in the previous chapter (Section 20.4). The essential point here is that visual inspection of the factorial graph, supplemented with Anova, can provide an effective assessment of the data pattern and hence of the addition model.

Parallelism as Evidence. Observed parallelism is good support for the addition model, but not absolute proof. This issue may be clarified with Table 21.1 (next page), which relates the two premises of the parallelism theorem to the pattern in the factorial graph. If both premises are true, parallelism is guaranteed by the parallelism theorem. This is case 1 of the table.

If one premise is true and the other false, the observed data will be nonparallel. In case 2, additivity holds, so the factorial graph of the unobservable ρ would exhibit parallelism; but the transformation from ρ to R, being nonlinear, destroys this parallelism. In case 3, nonadditivity holds, so the factorial graph of the unobservable ρ would be nonparallel; since the transformation from ρ to R is linear, the nonparallelism in ρ will be preserved in R.

TABLE 21.1

PARALLELISM AND NONPARALLELISM

Case	Additivity	Linearity	Response Pattern
1	Yes	Yes	Parallelism
2	Yes	No	Nonparallelism
3	No	Yes	Nonparallelism
4	No	No	??

If only these three cases were possible, parallelism would be definitive: Parallelism would occur if and only if an addition model was operative. One additional case, however, remains to be considered.[b]

In the last case in the table, both premises are false. It is tempting to think the data will be nonparallel in this case also; falsity of either premise alone violates parallelism so falsity of both together might doubly violate parallelism. Logically, however, nonlinearity in the response might just offset nonadditivity in the integration to yield net parallelism. This may not seem likely, but it is certainly possible. Nor is such offsetting just a logical curiosity; an empirical possibility arose with the finding that young children judge area of rectangles by adding height and width (Exercise 6.5). Subject to this qualification, observed parallelism may be considered good support for both premises of the theorem jointly, and hence for each one separately.

Monotone Parallelism Theorem. The assumption of response linearity in the foregoing parallelism theorem is not necessary. The monotone parallelism theorem requires only monotone response.

The idea is simple. If the addition model holds but the response scale is only monotone, the observed data will be nonparallel. Because the addition model holds, however, some monotone transformation will make the data parallel. This monotone transformation can be found with available computer programs.

In effect, the observed response is a monotone coding of the unobservable response; it can be decoded by finding the monotone transformation needed to make the data parallel—thereby revealing the true linear scale. If the process is inherently nonadditive, of course, then the data cannot generally be made parallel by any monotone transformation. Only the assumption of additivity is needed—and additivity is testable (Note 21.3.5c, page 731).

It is a great convenience, of course, to have a linear response. Monotone analysis is much more complicated and much less powerful. In principle, however, response linearity is not necessary; only the algebraic structure of the integration is at issue. Indeed, response linearity is derivative from observed parallelism, as noted in the second benefit listed in Section 21.3.3, page 702. In such empirical applications, therefore, linearity is a result, not an assumption.[c]

Empirical Foundation. The main concern is whether the parallelism theorem holds empirically. No mathematical theorem can yield psychological measurement. Experimental analysis is essential. Unless adding-type processes operate in nature, the parallelism theorem will have minor value.

Fortunately, observed parallelism has been fairly common. Despite, or perhaps because of its simplicity, the parallelism theorem has been a valuable empirical tool (see other applications in Section 20.1.3).

However, the empirical usefulness of the parallelism theorem only appeared in an unexpected way. Most instances of parallelism represent averaging, not adding. But averaging can also produce nonparallelism, and this markedly complicated the theoretical development.

21.4 AVERAGING THEORY

Psychological measurement theory rests primarily on the averaging model, not on the addition model. The reason is empirical: Perception and cognition have been found to embody averaging processes in many tasks; true adding processes have been much less common.

The averaging model, however, obeys the parallelism theorem only in the special case of equal weighting. In general, the data will be nonparallel owing to differential weighting. This nonparallelism presented unusual difficulties, but it led to a firm foundation for psychological measurement theory.

21.4.1 AVERAGING MODEL

Averaging theory requires a distinction between *weight* and *value*. To illustrate, suppose you draw a sample from an urn of red and white beads in order to judge the percentage of red beads in the entire urn. Given a 3-red:1-white sample, your best guess is obviously 75% red. The same is true for a 6-red:2-white sample. Both samples thus have identical *value*. The larger sample, however, contains more information and so has greater *weight*.

In general, as in this example, weight represents amount of information. Value, in contrast, represents the level of response implied by that information.

Equal Weight Case. The equal weight condition means that all levels of a given design factor have equal weight. In a two-way design, all S_{Aj} have the same weight, ω_A, and all S_{Bk} have the same weight, ω_B. Equal weighting thus refers to levels within each factor; different factors may have unequal weight. The response to the stimulus combination $\{S_{Aj}, S_{Bk}\}$ is thus

$$\rho_{jk} = \frac{\omega_A \psi_{Aj} + \omega_B \psi_{Bk}}{\omega_A + \omega_B}. \tag{2a}$$

The numerator in this equation is just a weighted sum of values; division by the sum of weights converts the sum to an average.

The equal weight case of averaging is not distinguishable from the addition model of Equation 1a, at least with standard factorial design. In fact, this equivalence is a central property of the equal weight case—all benefits of the addition model listed in the previous section apply directly. To enjoy these benefits, experimental precautions to get equal weighting are.[a]

Psychologically, however, averaging and adding are very different. One sign of this difference appears in the following opposite effects test to discriminate between the two.[b, c]

Opposite Effects Test: Averaging Versus Adding. A critical test between averaging and adding may be obtained quite simply: Add a medium stimulus to a high stimulus and also to a low stimulus. If the medium stimulus is averaged, it will pull down the response to the high stimulus and pull up the response to the low stimulus. But if the medium stimulus is added, it will pull both high and low in the same direction.

One of many such tests is shown in Figure 21.5. The left panel plots children's judgments of how much they would like to play with pairs of toys in a 3×3 design. The parallelism of these three curves supports both the addition model and the equal weight averaging model.

The right panel of Figure 21.5 replots the "medium" curve from the left panel and adds the dashed curve, which represents judgments of the single toy listed on the horizontal. The crossover shows that the medium toy does have opposite effects. This crossover disconfirms adding and supports averaging.

This opposite effects test is *scale-free* in that it requires only a monotone response scale. Further, opposite effects disproves almost any version of the addition model, such as addition with diminishing returns. Hence the opposite-effects test is almost *model-free* as well.[d, e]

Prior Information. The organism may have relevant information before the experiment begins. Examples are expectancies in animals and beliefs and stereotypes in humans. The information presented by the experimenter is integrated in with this prior information, a form of learning. Prior information and belief, also called *initial state*, are essential concepts in IIT.[f]

As one illustration, the concept of prior information accounts for the fact that more informers of equal value typically produce a more extreme response. This fact has been taken to argue against the averaging hypothesis. If the response was based only on the average value of the given informers, so the argument goes, their number would have no effect.

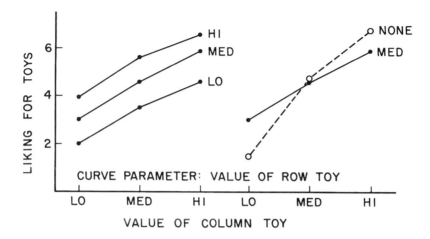

Figure 21.5. Opposite effects test supports averaging theory, infirms addition theory. Children judge worth of pairs of toys (solid curves) or single toys (dashed curve). Crossover of dashed and solid curves in right graph shows that the same medium toy has opposite effects: It increases total worth with a low toy, decreases total worth with a high toy. (From N. H. Anderson, *Foundations of Information Integration Theory*. Academic Press, 1981.)

However, the cited effect is readily understood in terms of averaging with prior information. When a high value informer is averaged with prior information of medium value, the response becomes higher. This incremental effect continues with diminishing returns with each added informer, thereby producing an informational learning curve. In this way, averaging theory has done well with serial curves of belief learning (Exercise c2).

Differential Weighting. In general, each stimulus may have its own weight as well as its own scale value. In the foregoing urn example, 3-red:1-white and 6-red:2-white have equal value, for both imply that the urn has 75% red beads. The larger sample, however, has greater weight. In general, weight represents amount of information in the informer, whereas value represents its implied magnitude of response.

In its general form, the averaging model allows each level of each factor to have its own weight as well as its own value. With differential weights and including prior information, the averaging model may be written

$$\rho_{jk} = \frac{\omega_{Aj}\,\psi_{Aj} + \omega_{Bk}\,\psi_{Bk} + \omega_0\,\psi_0}{\omega_{Aj} + \omega_{Bk} + \omega_0}. \tag{2b}$$

The subscripts on the weights indicate that each stimulus may have its own weight as well as its own value; different levels of factor A may thus differ in weight ω_{Aj} as well as in value ψ_{Aj}.

Weight and value of the prior information are denoted by ω_0 and ψ_0 in Equation 2b. In the equal weight case, the prior state has the same effect for every cell in the design. Prior state was ignored in Equation 2a since the predictions remain unchanged. In the differential weight case, however, the prior state must be included in the analysis.

Since the weight parameter represents effective amount of information, nonparallelism is expected to be fairly general, as is in fact true. Only with this general averaging model was it possible to make sense of the diverse occurrences of parallelism and nonparallelism. Indeed, verification of predicted patterns of nonparallelism produced by experimental manipulations was a key to establishing averaging theory on empirical ground. The most dramatic verification is the crossover illustrated in Figure 21.5, which manipulates weight by varying number of informers. The nonparallelism of the decision averaging model just below also reflects variation in weight of information.

Decision Averaging Model. An important special case of differential weighting arises in tasks that are polarized toward some all-or-none decision. In the urn task mentioned at the beginning of this section, suppose your task was different—to judge the probability that the urn contained more red than white beads. In this task, the 3-red:1-white sample should have a value of 1, not .75; given a sequence of 3-red:1-white samples, you should move closer and closer to a judgment that red was certainly more numerous than white. Analogously, a 2-red:3-white sample should have a value of 0. The *weight* of each sample will depend on the disproportion between red and white.

Consider a design in which A represents stimuli polarized toward 0, B represents stimuli polarized toward 1. With these stimulus values, and with $\omega_0 = 0$ for simplicity, Equation 2b reduces to the relative ratio of the weights,

$$\rho_{jk} = \frac{\omega_{Bk}}{\omega_{Aj} + \omega_{Bk}}. \tag{2c}$$

This *decision averaging model* may be viewed as a compromise between competing responses (Anderson, 1981, p. 66). It has done well in the Bayesian probability urn task of Figure 19.3 (page 640) and in other applications.

21.4.2 EMPIRICAL AVERAGING MODELS

The key difference between adding and averaging lies in the weight parameter. Adding models predict parallelism regardless of weighting; averaging models predict parallelism only with equal weighting, not with differential weighting. Such predictable deviations from parallelism thus provide a diagnostic, most simply with the opposite effects test already shown in Figure 21.5. To date, averaging has been common, true adding uncommon.

Experimental applications of averaging models appeared in various figures in this book, already cited under *Empirical Addition Models*. Many others are cited elsewhere (e.g., Anderson, 1981, 1996a). The present discussion, accordingly, considers how the averaging model can be useful in its main function, namely, study of qualitative, conceptual issues.[a]

Conceptual Implications of Averaging Theory. Conceptual implications of the averaging model are more important than algebraic structure. Several substantive implications are cited in Section 21.7.1 (pages 722*ff*); implications for measurement theory are noted in the next section. Three other conceptual implications are noted here to illustrate the potential of model analysis.

Comparing relative importance of two variables has typically run aground on concept–instance confounding (Section 8.1.4, page 232*f*). The averaging model can resolve this confounding by separating the importance weight of the variable itself from the particular values of the particular instances used to instantiate that concept in the experiment.

One instance of this confounding appeared in moral judgment, beginning with Piaget's claim of a developmental increase in importance of intent relative to harm done in judgments of deserved punishment for a harmful action. So plausible is this claim that few realized the fatal flaw in the evidence (pages 554*f*). This problem was resolved in a tour de force by Surber (1982), which may remain the only correct analysis of this developmental issue.

Cognitive reality of prototypes was affirmed in a striking thesis by Zhu (1991), who found that judgments based on a probability quantifier and base rate information followed an averaging model. By virtue of meaning invariance, therefore, the probability quantifiers could be considered well-defined prototypes, invariant across different base rate contexts.

Cognitive reality of prototypes had been strongly questioned by various context effects, for example, that *a few crumbs* are more numerous than *a few cookies*. At face value, *a few* seems to have different meanings depending on the context. Instead, Zhu's analysis explains such context effects in terms of direct integration of the context into the judgment, with an invariant value of the focal word itself. An analogous conclusion has been reached by Heit (1993) for effect of expectation on recognition memory (see similarly Exercise c9).

Zhu's analysis provides new depth for lexical analysis. Not only do the words have an invariant prototypical value, but they also have a weight parameter that represents their fuzziness. Both value and weight are quantifiable through the averaging model.

A third example comes from Schlottmann's cogent analysis of phenomenal causality (Schlottmann & Anderson, 1993). The averaging model revealed the operation of the same integration rule across different individuals. This

integration rule may correspond to Michotte's proposal of an invariant perceptual structure that embodies phenomenal causality.

Different individuals, however, showed distinctive patterns in their weight
parameters estimated from the averaging model. These patterns pointed to a
cognitive/experiential level in the valuation processing, outside the scope of
Michotte's view, but in line with the views of his critics.

Differential Weighting. Manipulation of the weights will produce predictable
patterns of nonparallelism, a tack that has produced strong support for averaging
theory. Several studies of this kind have manipulated reliability or credibility of
the information. Notable among these are Birnbaum (1976), Birnbaum, Wong,
and Wong (1976), Birnbaum and Stegner (1979), Kaplan (1971a), and Surber
(1981, 1985). Social attribution was shown to follow the averaging model in the
same way (Himmelfarb & Anderson, 1975), and Anderson and Jacobson (1965)
used a similar manipulation to study inconsistency discounting.

Decision Averaging Model. The decision averaging model did well in its first
application, which used a probability urn task (Leon & Anderson, 1974; see Figure 19.3). A model of similar form was developed independently in fuzzy
psycholinguistics by Oden (1974, 1978) and extended in the Oden–Massaro
fuzzy logic model of perception (Oden & Massaro, 1978; Massaro, 1987).

The decision averaging model has the form of a relative ratio, $X/(X + Y)$,
a ratio form employed by various investigators. Most of these formulations,
however, postulate yes–no type choice data (e.g., Luce, 1959). Hence they
apply only to threshold situations, just as with signal detection theory. The decision averaging model, in contrast, also applies to continuous response measures.
Hence it can handle suprathreshold tasks, as in the cited probability urn task.[b]

A further difference is that the decision averaging model is derived from
information integration theory. It is a special case of the general averaging
model of Equation 2b, in which the ψ values are dichotomous; the variable
parameters are the weights. The decision averaging model is thus part of a general theory, grounded empirically through functional measurement.

21.4.3 AVERAGING MODEL AND MEASUREMENT THEORY

The averaging model has provided a foundation for psychological measurement
theory. The main reason is its empirical ubiquity. Not many tasks that have
been conjectured to follow addition models have actually done so, but many
have followed the averaging model.

Moreover, the averaging model has unique capability for measuring both
importance weights and preference values. With suitable design, weights of all
stimuli can be measured on a common proportional scale, that is, a linear scale
with known zero and common unit. Similarly, stimulus values can be measured
on a linear scale with common zero and common unit. In this way, importance

of qualitatively different factors, such as approach and avoidance, can be quantitatively compared.[a]

Averaging theory thus implies that weight and value have equal conceptual status. This two-parameter representation is clear in the urn task already considered under *Decision Averaging Model*. This weight–value conception of measurement is necessary empirically, as demonstrated by the success of the averaging model in diverse substantive tasks. This weight–value distinction is another difference between psychological and physical measurement.

Other measurement theories rest on the traditional one-parameter, value representation. They cannot generally untangle weight and value, nor can they deal with differential weighted averaging. Traditional measurement theories are thus in principle inadequate for psychological measurement.

21.5 MULTIPLICATION MODEL

Multiplication models have been conjectured in many areas of psychology, most notably with various analogues of the statistical model for expected value. In statistical theory, the expected value of an event is its value multiplied by the probability that it will occur. A natural hypothesis is that cognition follows a similar model, but with subjective assessments of probability and value:

Subjective expected value = Subjective probability × Subjective value.

This SEV model could not be tested without subjective measurement scales. Some workers attempted to use objective parameters, but with little success. Some writers even proclaimed the problem insoluble. In fact, it was solved by the following linear fan theorem.

21.5.1 LINEAR FAN THEOREM

The basic tool for multiplication models is the linear fan theorem. A multiplication model manifests itself as a linear fan pattern in the factorial graph. The linear fan theorem is like the parallelism theorem, but faces a new obstacle.

Linear Fan Theorem. Two premises are required by the linear fan theorem:

$$\rho_{jk} = \psi_{Aj} \times \psi_{Bk} ; \quad \text{(multiplication)} \tag{3a}$$

$$R_{jk} = c_0 + c_1 \rho_{jk} . \quad \text{(linearity)} \tag{3b}$$

The linearity premise is the same as for the parallelism theorem, and it serves the same purpose. From these two premises follow two conclusions:

Conclusion 1: The appropriate factorial graph will be a linear fan.
Conclusion 2: The row means of the factorial data table will be a linear scale of the ψ_{Aj}; similarly, the column means of the data table will be a linear scale of the ψ_{Bk}.

The second conclusion is the same as in the parallelism theorem. However, the linear fan pattern of the first conclusion is obtained only with the "appropriate" factorial graph. This requires that the column stimuli be spaced on the horizontal axis in a special way, namely, in proportion to their subjective values.

This requirement for subjective spacing of the column stimuli reflects the algebraic structure of Equations 3, which imply that the response is a linear function of ψ_{Bk} with slope ψ_{Aj}. Suppose the S_{Bk} were indeed spaced at their subjective values, namely, ψ_{Bk}. The first row of data, $R_{1k} = c_0 + c_1 \psi_{A1} \psi_{Bk}$, would then fall on a straight line with slope $c_1 \psi_{A1}$; the second row, R_{2k}, would fall on a straight line with slope $c_1 \psi_{A2}$; and so on. Hence the factorial graph would be a fan of straight lines, if the multiplication model was true. If the multiplication model was false, however, the factorial graph would generally not be a linear fan. This linear fan test is simple—but it requires the subjective values.

The model analysis might thus seem impossible because the subjective values will generally be unknown. Some investigators tried to use objective, physical values instead. This worked poorly because subjective and objective value generally differ.

Fortunately, a bootstrap operation is possible. If both premises of the theorem hold, Conclusion 2 tells us that the column means of the data table are a linear scale of the subjective values of the column stimuli. With these subjective values, therefore, the linear fan will reveal itself. We need only space out the column stimuli on the horizontal axis at the values specified by the column means (see Figure 21.6, page 714).

In practice, we do not know whether the multiplication model holds. Provisionally, however, we may use the observed column means in the indicated manner. If both premises of the theorem hold, we will find a linear fan. The first application of this linear fan theorem provided the first general test of the foregoing SEV model, shown in Figure 21.7, page 715.[a, b]

21.5.2 BENEFITS OF LINEAR FAN PATTERN

The linear fan theorem provides a simple, precise test of the multiplication model. An observed linear fan pattern is good support for both premises of the theorem taken jointly. Hence it supports each premise separately. Just as with parallelism, an observed linear fan helps attain a cornucopia of benefits:

1. multiplicative integration;
2. linearity of the response measure;
3. linear scales of each stimulus variable;
4. stimulus invariance;
5. independence of valuation and integration.

The first three benefits correspond to the three unobservables in the integration diagram. The first involves the integration process; the next two involve the two measurement problems: measurement of response and measurement of stimuli. These three unobservables are essentially the same as with the parallelism theorem. In fact, most of the previous discussion applies directly here.

The last two conclusions are conceptual, qualitative rather than quantitative. Stimulus invariance means that stimuli paired in each cell do not interact to change value or meaning. For if the value of S_{Aj} did change from one cell to another, these changes would fracture the linear fan. And just as with the parallelism theorem, **V–I** independence implies that these two operators represent distinct stages in the chain of information processing from given stimuli to observed response in the integration diagram of Figure 21.3.

Conversely, obtaining a linear fan provides good evidence for both premises and thereby for all five listed benefits. The earlier section, *Problems of Evidence*, applies in its essentials also to the multiplication model.

21.5.3 LINEAR FAN EXAMPLES

Motivation × Incentive. The idea that motivation acts as a multiplier of incentive value is a long-standing conjecture in behavior theory. This conjecture could not be tested, however, owing to lack of measurement theory. Tests became possible with the linear fan theorem.

The simplicity of the linear fan theorem is illustrated with the hypothetical data in Table 21.2. This table shows a Motivation × Incentive design, with three levels of Motivation (slight, moderate, and great thirst) and four levels of Incentive (warm water, cold water, coke, and beer). The hypothesized integration model may be written symbolically as:

TABLE 21.2

AMOUNT PAID FOR DRINK AS FUNCTION OF
MOTIVATION AND INCENTIVE

| | Thirst Quencher | | | |
| | Water | | | |
Thirstiness	Warm	Cold	Coke	Beer
Slight	13	15	21	17
Moderate	15	21	39	27
Great	20	36	84	52
Mean	16	24	48	32

NOTE: From Anderson (1978).

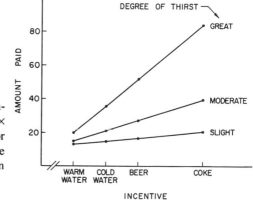

Figure 21.6. Linear fan analysis implies multiplication rule, Motivation × Incentive. Response is amount paid for each of four drinks under each of three levels of thirst motivation listed in Table 21.2. (From Anderson, 1978.)

Response = Motivation × Incentive.

The linear fan analysis is shown in the factorial graph of Figure 21.6, in which the data points are taken directly from the table. The three curves form a perfect linear fan. The Motivation × Incentive conjecture becomes testable in this way, and it has received some empirical support.

One odd feature appears in Figure 21.6: The incentives are unequally spaced on the horizontal axis. In fact, coke and beer have reversed their order from the table. Only with this subjective spacing of the stimulus values is the linear fan revealed. Conversely, the linear fan analysis reveals the stimulus values functional in the judgments.

The key idea for multiplication models was the realization that the needed stimulus values could be derived from the data. This spacing of the incentives is prescribed by the linear fan theorem. This spacing is determined by the column means, listed in the bottom row of the table. If all is well, these column means estimate the true values, by virtue of Conclusion 2 of the linear fan theorem. Their use is provisional, but justified by emergence of a linear fan.

Subjective Expected Value. An empirical test of the foregoing SEV model is shown in Figure 21.7. Subjects judged the worth of lottery tickets of the form

You have _____ chance to win _____.

Chances to win were indicated by the throw of a die, indicated on the horizontal axis; amount to be won is listed as curve parameter.

The data form a clear linear fan, which supports the SEV model. Note the unequal spacing on the horizontal axis, which shows that subjective probability differs from objective probability. The SEV model is basic to judgment–decision theory, of course, but previous attempts to assess it had failed from

Figure 21.7. Subjective expected value obeys multiplication rule. Subjects judged personal worth of lottery tickets with specified chance to win (horizontal axis) and specified amount to be won (curve parameter). Linear fan pattern implies multiplication. (After N. H. Anderson and J. C. Shanteau, 1970, "Information integration in risky decision making," *Journal of Experimental Psychology*, *84*, 441-451. Copyright 1970 by American Psychological Association. Reprinted by permission.)

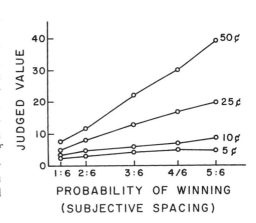

inability to measure subjective probability. Indeed, the best previous attempts had argued for an addition model. Only through the linear fan theorem was the multiplication model verifiable.

This functional measurement study was the first to present an effective, general method for analysis of multiplication models. By demonstrating the linear fan pattern empirically, moreover, it solved the classic problem of simultaneous measurement of subjective probability and utility; these are just the column and row means, respectively, of the factorial data table.

21.5.4 EMPIRICAL MULTIPLICATION MODELS

Linear fan analysis was originally developed to study the multiplication rule for subjective expected value. The first experimental application did well, as just demonstrated in Figure 21.7. At the time, it was feared that a ceiling effect might flatten down the top curve. That this did not happen was reassuring evidence for linearity of the rating method.

Numerous successful applications have followed. Among these are probability judgments with adults (Lopes, 1976b; Wyer, 1975; Anderson, 1981—see Exercise b8, Figure 21.10) and with children (Anderson, 1980; Schlottmann, in press; Wolf, 1995), fuzzy logic (Oden, 1977), psycholinguistics, (Borges & Sawyers, 1974; Oden & Anderson, 1974; see Anderson, 1996a, Figures 12.1 and 12.6, respectively), intuitive physics (Anderson, 1983; Karpp & Anderson, 1997; Wilkening, 1982), social attribution (Anderson & Butzin, 1978; Singh, 1991), motivation (Klitzner & Anderson, 1977), and snake phobia (Klitzner, 1977; see Anderson, 1981, Figure 1.17, p. 53).

Intuitive multiplication, illustrated with the SEV rule of Figure 21.7, seems a common human ability. It is considered a general purpose learned schema about objective structure of various tasks, not only with probability, but especially with intuitive physics and even with psycholinguistics. In some tasks, however, the linear fan pattern represents as-if rules that follow some process diferent from multiplication (Anderson, 1996a, pp. 66*f*).

An important extension of linear fan analysis is to behavioral response. Such response measures were used by Borges and Sawyers (1974), Lopes (1976b), and Klitzner (1977), although their subjects were human and the response measures could be considered symbolic.

Nonsymbolic behavioral response measures have great interest. The first was the linear fan for response times in a serial search task with humans by Shanteau (see Anderson, 1981, pp. 56*f*). Time production by 10-year-olds shows a linear fan in Figure 20.1. For animals, confirmation of the psychological form of the matching law with pigeons' key pecking by Farley and Fantino (1978), shown in Figure 11.10, and a different multiplication model for electrical brain stimulation reward with rats' bar pressing by Hawkins, Roll, Puerto, and Yeomans (1983), are historical firsts. Other applications are given by Roberts (1987), Gibbon and Fairhurst (1994), and Sternberg (2000, in press).[a]

21.6 PSYCHOLOGICAL MEASUREMENT THEORY

Without psychological measurement theory, analysis of multiple determination cannot get very far. Even the question whether the whole differs from the sum of its parts is not generally answerable if the parts cannot be measured. Since multiple determination is basic in perception, thought, and action, lack of linear scales has crippled psychological science.

A solution to the measurement problem has been presented in this chapter. Algebraic models of information integration provide a base and frame for psychological measurement, for both response and stimulus, as shown with the parallelism and linear fan theorems. In this functional view, measurement is derivative from empirical analysis of algebraic structure (Note 21.2a, page 729).

Standard statistical methods have been useful for studying algebraic structure. The parallelism and linear fan theorems both show how visual inspection of the factorial graph can diagnose empirical models. A more quantitative test is provided by the interaction residual from Anova, which in principle is zero for an addition model and concentrated in the linear × linear component for a multiplication model.

A successful model supports the linearity of whatever response scale was used. A successful model also provides linear scales of the functional stimuli. For addition and multiplication models, these stimulus scales are the marginal means of the factorial design. For nonlinear models, Anova can be extended to test goodness of fit with the replications method (Note 21.3.5c, page 731).

21.6.1 LINEAR RESPONSE METHODOLOGY

Linear response scales should be the primary goal of psychological measurement theory. This dictum follows from the axiom of multiple determination; process analysis of multiple determination depends on pattern in the data. If the response is linear, pattern in the observable data mirrors pattern in the unobservable process. If the response is not linear, the process pattern is exceedingly slippery to pin down; a mild example appears with the time–speed comparison of Table 7.1 (page 193).

This need for linear response measures is clear with the parallelism theorem. Without a linear response, the parallelism in the speed data of Table 7.1 does not signify additivity; and the nonparallelism of the equivalent time data in the left panel does not signify nonadditivity. Without a linear response, all monotone transformations of the data are in principle equivalent.

But with a linear response, the observed pattern is veridical. Observed parallelism implies additivity; and observed nonparallelism implies nonadditivity. A linear response makes the difference between night and day.

Response generality is fundamental. If methodology for linear response has been developed in one situation, the same method may reasonably be expected to succeed in other situations, as has been shown with the rating method.

Stimulus generality, in contrast, cannot generally be expected because stimulus values change with everchanging goals; the same stimulus will have different values relative to different goals. Functional measurement has aimed at response generality through its focus on continuous response measures. Traditional approaches to psychological measurement theory, in contrast, have fixated on stimulus scaling, with little or no recognition of the central problem.

Linear response methodology can, in principle, be developed with functional measurement theory. Response linearity, being a premise of both the parallelism theorem and of the linear fan theorem, is supported by observed patterns of parallelism and linear fan. Empirically, the rating method has been widely successful, and response rate has shown promise.[a]

Linear response methodology is important for studying nonalgebraic rules and genuine interaction, as well as stimuli that affect more than one process (e.g., Anderson, 1991a, pp. 254*f*). With a linear response, the pattern in the observable data is a veridical reflection of the pattern in the unobservable response. Linear response is no magic key for attacking these problems, but it can be uniquely helpful.[b]

Another important role for linear response methodology comes when factorial-type design is infeasible or impossible. A sensible way to choose the best of several alternative courses of action, for example, is to add up subjective estimates of costs and benefits of each alternative, planning to choose the one with the highest sum. But this rational rule depends squarely on valid subjective estimates of the costs and benefits. The alternative with the highest sum based on ratings might well have a low sum based on magnitude estimates, as indicated in Figure 21.2 (page 694).[c]

From this standpoint, algebraic laws are a ladder to higher theory, through serving as a base and frame for developing linear response methodology. This new theoretical framework allows progress on some previously intractable problems, such as serial belief curves and analysis of genuine interaction, and on some problems barely thought of, such as functional memory.

21.6.2 IN DEFENSE OF IIT AND FUNCTIONAL MEASUREMENT [a]

Various criticisms and limitations of functional measurement need comment.

Values Depend on Goal and Context. An incorrect criticism of information integration theory is that stimulus value depends on goal and context. Far from being a criticism, such dependence is an essential characteristic of IIT. The functional perspective and the axiom of purposiveness *mandate* that values depend on goal and context. Under different motivations, in particular, the same goal object will have different values (see index entries under *Valuation* in Anderson, 1996a). Functional measurement can, under certain conditions, measure such functional values.

This criticism reflects failure to distinguish between valuation and integration operations, **V** and **I**. The values placed on the separate stimuli are sensitive to the operative goal but not to one another. **V–I** independence thus reveals a fundamental difference between context–stimulus interaction in the valuation process and stimulus–stimulus interaction in the integration process.

That psychological stimulus values have functional dependence on goal and context deserves reemphasis. Psychological measurement differs from the stereotype derived from physics. Functional measurement theory embodies this goal-oriented dependence; it measures functional values, as its name implies.

Nonparallelism. A second incorrect criticism asserts that the averaging model implies parallel data. A number of writers have presented nonadditive or nonparallel data with the claim that this contradicts averaging theory. But differential weighted averaging yields nonparallel data, notably with the decision averaging model (Equation 2c). In fact, averaging theory has provided a unified account of most of the parallelism and nonparallelism observed in integration studies. Verification of predicted nonparallelism has provided strong support for averaging theory, as with the crossover of Figure 21.5.

Response Linearity. The most common concern about functional measurement is with response linearity. This concern is natural because the rating method, which has been employed in much of the empirical work, suffers well-known nonlinear biases. What is the evidence that the experimental precautions of Note 21.6.1a have eliminated such biases?

The answer is simple: Rating linearity has been established by the wide success of algebraic laws. This answer is epitomized in the parallelism theorem. Observed parallelism provides joint support for both premises, additivity and response linearity. Empirically, parallelism has been observed in numerous experiments across many areas of psychology. This is strong evidence for the response methodology (see further the nine lines of evidence summarized in Anderson (1996a, pp. 94-98, 105).

Statistical Assumptions. A measurement model must be verified by testing goodness of fit with actual data (Section 20.2). Visual inspection may suffice. The efficacy of visual inspection was shown with the factorial graph for size–weight integration shown in Figure 20.3; no Anova was needed to recognize this pattern of parallelism.

Some writers have questioned the use of Anova in functional measurement, raising doubt about the statistical assumption of equinormality (normal distribution and equal variance). But no statistical assumptions are needed with the parallelism theorem; the sample means are unbiased estimates of the population means. Hence the parallelism pattern of an addition model holds regardless of the shapes of the distributions. Visual inspection of the factorial graphs may thus suffice, as illustrated in Figures 21.4 and 21.5 and in Note 21.2.2a.

The linear fan pattern requires only that the two factors have uncorrelated effects; the linear fan pattern will then appear regardless of nonnormality and/or unequal variance. Here again, visual inspection may suffice, as in Figure 21.7.

Actually, equinormality seems well satisfied in typical applications of functional measurement, at least with the rating response. One reason is the use of end anchors to avoid response end effects (Note 21.6.1a, page 733). Unbounded response measures may not be equinormal, as with response times, but even this may not be serious for testing an interaction contrast. For most applications, in short, equinormality is not a serious concern.

Nonalgebraic Integration. Much integration must surely be nonalgebraic, not amenable to the three algebraic rules. This objection is certainly correct; it underscores the importance of algebraic laws as a base and frame for developing linear response methodology—an invaluable tool for analysis of nonalgebraic process and genuine interaction (Section 21.6.1, page 717).

Incompleteness. The top-down nature of IIT is a major locus of incompleteness. IIT begins with a search for regularity and law in patterns of observable behavior. This top-down strategy has the advantage of a solid grounding in primary phenomena of psychology, especially experiences of everyday life. Such observable patterns can be informative about deeper levels of information processing, already illustrated with value invariance, interaction, and cognitive reality of common language concepts (see further Section 21.7.1, pages 722*ff*). Two of many such open issues are noted here.

One incompleteness concerns the nature of the three operators, **V**, **I**, and **A**, in the integration diagram of Figure 21.3. Some valuation operators depend on sensory–perceptual processes, analysis of which can be aided with integration methods, as with Stefurak's study of red–green contrast in Figure 11.6 and with the size–weight experiment of Figure 20.3 (see also Anderson, 1974a). Other valuation operators depend on similarity of given informers to an ideal, for which an averaging process has shown promise (Anderson, 1974a, pp. 254-258; Lopes & Oden, 1980).

An integration rule must operate through some process. Averaging, for example, can be achieved by diverse processes, while multiplication may sometimes result from the fractionation process discussed with Figure 21.7. On these questions, not much is known (Anderson, 1996a, pp. 64-70).

The action operator, **A**, has great interest as part of the general problem of psychomotor behavior. Integration studies to date have been mainly concerned with empirical procedures to make **A** linear. The theory of the rating response that has emerged may have general interest. Rating is considered a compromise between two competing responses, corresponding to the two ends of the rating scale—a case of the decision averaging model of Equation 2c. Rating linearity is thought to derive from motor skills of the organism in local space. Similar response processes seem not unlikely in other motor tasks.

A basic incompleteness concerns *assemblage*, that is, the construction of an organized system for use in goal-oriented action. A notable example was discussed with children's judgments of time in Figure 20.1 (page 651). The integration rule, however, referred to operation of the entire assemblage. New tasks are needed to analyze separate components of the assemblage.

Assemblage may be considered a fundamental form of information integration, largely nonalgebraic in character. Assemblage is thus akin to concepts of plans, problem solving routines, and schemas that have been discussed by many writers. Few of these, however, allow even a Cinderella role for emotion and affect, pleasure and pain, which are life's heart's blood. Even fewer recognize the problem of psychological measurement, although quantification is inherent in purposiveness. IIT can cooperate in such investigations; algebraic integration rules and functional values constitute boundary conditions that must be obeyed by theories of deeper levels of analysis.

21.6.3 RELATIONS WITH OTHER MEASUREMENT THEORIES

Psychological measurement theory has been a contentious area; many theoretical positions have been advocated. Historical reasons have led most workers to approaches quite different from functional measurement. This section summarizes three distinguishing characteristics of functional measurement; some comparative comments are given in the notes.[a, b, c, d, e, f, g, h, i, j, k, l]

The most distinctive characteristic of functional measurement is its broad empirical base in a unified theory. Successful applications have been made in most areas of psychology (Anderson, 1996a). It seems fair to say that no other theory of psychological measurement comes close. The most popular alternatives have been mathematical measurement theories, which have received extraordinarily intensive study by many highly capable workers. But these mathematical theories have had virtually no empirical success; they are the "revolution that never happened" (Cliff, 1992, p. 186; see Note 21.6.3b).

A second characteristic of functional measurement is its emphasis on continuous response. Nearly all other measurement theories—Thurstonian pair comparisons, Coombs' (1964) unfolding theory, conjoint measurement (Krantz, Luce, Suppes, & Tversky, 1971)—take discrete choice data as basic in principle and disallow continuous response.

Algebraic laws have been discovered in numerous experiments in diverse domains of human psychology. These laws have been there all the time, waiting to be discovered. But they could not be discovered with measurement theories that relied on choice data. Instead, the algebraic laws were discovered in experiments that used continuous response measures. This work also made clear that a primary goal of psychological measurement theory is to develop linear response methodology for analysis of nonalgebraic processes (Section 21.6.1)

The averaging model is the third distinguishing characteristic of functional measurement. Averaging entails two basic differences from other measurement theories. One difference is that weight and value, ω and ψ, have equal conceptual status. The traditional conception of measurement as one-dimensional scales of value is inadequate in psychology. The other difference is that the averaging model can account for disordinal data, as with the crossover of Figure 21.5. Other measurement theories appear to have exceptional difficulty with such disordinality. Only by embracing disordinality could psychological measurement theory be developed.

21.7 UNIFIED THEORY

The two axioms—purposiveness and multiple determination—are a foundation for unified psychological science. Life is goal-directed; living consists of approaching and avoiding goals. But the many attempts to use purposiveness as a base for theory construction have not been very successful. Some writers banish the concept as teleological.

Purposiveness makes psychology radically different from physics. Nowhere is this difference greater than in the fact that values depend on goals. This goal-dependence means that algebraic models in psychology and physics are quite different in nature and function. Understanding this difference is essential for development of unified theory.[a, b]

21.7.1 CONCEPTS AND PROCESSES

Conceptual analysis of psychological concepts and processes is the main value of algbraic models. This point is easy to overlook; the quantitative structure of the models masks their qualitative implications. To counteract this stereotype, qualitative, conceptual consequences of algebraic models deserve comment.

Invariance. Invariance is a principal implication of an algebraic model, already illustrated for addition models under *Meaning Invariance in Person Cognition* (page 701). But although this result is prima facie quantitative, its main significance was qualitative, or conceptual. The algebraic model replaced an entire class of cognitive consistency theories, which had claimed ubiquitous interactions among stimulus informers.

This conceptual consequence restructured the issue of interaction. Valuation and integration were seen to be distinct processes, quite different from what had previously been thought. This restructuring also cast new light on the axiom of purposiveness.

Independence of Valuation and Integration. Independence of valuation and integration—$V-I$ independence—is a pivotal finding of IIT. This independence makes possible a unified treatment of the two axioms of purposiveness and multiple determination.

Purposiveness implies that values depend on momentary goals. Valuation is goal-directed, so the same informer will take on different values depending on the motivational state of the organism, whether deprived or satiated, for example. Because motivational states are continually changing, so are values. Measurement in psychology has a higher order of difficulty than in physics.

$V-I$ independence is a rock of constancy in the sea of changing values. Values for a given goal are invariant within many situtions. Hence they become measurable through an algebraic model, as shown by Conclusion 2 of the parallelism theorem and the linear fan theorem. Integration processes themselves may have considerable generality across different situations, as shown by the ubiquity of the three algebraic rules.

$V-I$ independence argues against theories which assume that informers activate stimulus elements and that integration occurs by pooling of these activated elements. If so, V and I would not generally be independent because of overlap among elements activated by different informers. This class of theories seems inconsistent with addition models and even more with multiplication models (e.g., Anderson, 1981, pp. 211f).

Reality of Concepts and Modules. Success of a model supports the reality of the concepts represented by the variables used in assessing the model. In the developmental study of intuitive physics of Figure 20.1, for example, the factorial pattern suggests that time, speed, and distance have psychological reality by age 5, if not earlier. This conceptual implication depends on but is more important than the algebraic model per se.

IIT has long emphasized the importance of algebraic models for helping to firm up our ideas about reality of psychological concepts. In particular, meaning invariance and $V-I$ independence, discussed in the two previous subsections, help support reality of the stimulus concepts of the model as well as reality of the response concept (Anderson, 1981, 1982).

Sternberg (2000, in press) has gone further to claim that if an addition or multiplication model holds, then the variables in the model correspond to independent "modules." If Sternberg is correct, then IIT has been demonstrating independent modules in virtually every area of psychology since the initial 1962 experiment of Figure 20.2.[a]

Interaction and Configurality. Interaction and configurality are fundamental issues in psychological science. The theme of interaction has been emphasized at least since the early days of Gestalt psychology, and similar concern may be seen in discussions of context effects in every field. Substantive concepts of interaction, however, have generally remained vague and ambiguous, partly from confusion with statistical Anova interactions (Chapter 7), but mainly from lack of tools for effective analysis (see Section 21.6.1).

One contribution of IIT was to demonstrate that many presumed interactions are not interactions. The foremost example is meaning invariance, as in Figures 20.2 and 21.4. Contrary to persuasive phenomenological evidence, the stimulus informers did not interact with one another.

Analogous results have been obtained in other work. What had seemed to be context–stimulus interaction is often instead direct integration of the context, independent of the focal stimuli. Examples include the positive context effect of Exercise c9, Zhu's (1991) clever studies on psycholinguistics, Heit's (1993) analysis of expectation effects in recognition memory, and other misconceptions about memory processing (Anderson, 1996a, pp. 377*ff*).

No less important, a conjoint empirical–theoretical base for analysis of interaction has been obtained. Conceptual clarification came through revelation of the fundamental distinction between stimulus–stimulus interaction, which is not frequent, and goal–stimulus interaction, which is a universal characteristic of purposiveness. Functional measurement gave this distinction a cutting edge by making goal–stimulus interaction quantifiable. This quantification of purposiveness opens a spectrum of new opportunities in psychological science.

Functional Memory. The function of memory is to bring past experience to bear on present action. The need for a functional conception of memory distinct from the traditional conception of reproductive memory was shown in an early IIT experiment, which found a dissociation between memory for the given list of verbal materials and a belief or judgment based on that same list.

This functional conception of memory is congruent with the axiom of purposiveness. A primary function of memory is to subserve the valuation operation, which evaluates present informers by reference to past experience. These values refer to operative goals, thereby making memory purposive and functional. The integrated resultant may itself be stored in memory for future use.

Much memory is thus memory of beliefs, attitudes, motivations, emotions, and affects that are resultants of past goal-oriented valuation—integrations of stimuli long forgotten. Belief and affect have little place in the monolithic conception of memory as reproduction of specified stimuli, with its canonical response measure of accuracy. But such concepts are central in everyday perception, thought, and action.

Functional memory is largely constructive, not reproductive. This conception agrees with Bartlett's early conception of memory as reconstruction and with similar constructivist leanings in recent memory research. This work, however, still remains imprisoned within a reproductive framework, partly from lack of theory to handle valuation—integration (Anderson, 1996a, Chapter 11).

Assemblage. Humans have remarkable abilities to deal with imaginary situations. This capability was noted in the discussion of the experiment of Figure 20.1 on Time = Distance − Speed. This task requires complex mental assemblage to represent an imaginary situation in a sensible imaginary way, capability that is present in metric form already at age 5. Most integration experiments with human subjects exhibit similar assemblage capabilities.

The algebraic rule can be a tool for investigating the fundamental problem of assemblage. On this issue, regrettably, little has been done (see index entries under *Assemblage* in Anderson, 1991c).

Stage and Continuity in Cognitive Development. The study of cognitive development leads naturally to stage-like conceptions. Long-term developmental changes typically appear qualitative rather than merely quantitative, exhibiting changes in structure rather than mere accumulation of amount. Stage language and concepts can thus be useful at a purely descriptive level.

Almost invariably, however, stage descriptions become reified as distinct entities, each claimed to have a unique organization that differs qualitatively from preceding and following stages. Without denying their rough usefulness for outlining developmental trends, stage concepts take on a rigidity that stifles analysis of continuity. Indeed, IIT has shown the falsity of Piaget's stages of cognitive development and raised doubt about Kohlberg's stages of moral development (Anderson, 1996a, Chapter 6).

These developmental integration studies have been constructive, for they revealed a very different picture of development. Also, they contributed a developmental methodology for analysis of continuity that can help set the stage intuitions on firmer ground.

Internal World and External World. Psychological science seeks to use the external world of observables to uncover structure and dynamics of the internal world of unobservables. This approach was epitomized in the problem of *The Three Unobservables* (page 697). Functional measurement theory has provided an effective attack on this problem, one that has worked reasonably well in many experiments.

In this functional approach, the structure of the internal world is the foundation for theory construction. This approach has been effective because algebraic models provide a solution to *The Three Unobservables.*

In diametrical contrast, reliance on the external world has been common in other formulations. Externalist strategy is attractive because it seems to provide something solid and definite to build on. Externalist strategy is explicit in some branches of behaviorism, which ignore or deny the internal world.

Externalist strategy is far more general, typically a taken-for-granted way of thinking that has often directed inquiry down sterile channels. Traditional memory theory is one example, as shown by its hallmark of reproductive accuracy as a response measure. Psychophysics is another example, in its ill-fated belief that Nature's laws would be found in the psychophysical function—the **V** operator in the integration diagram, which relates the external stimulus, S, to the internal stimulus, ψ. Instead, Nature's laws were found in the **I** operator.

Judgment–decision is a striking example of shortcomings of externalist thinking. Despite various efforts to introduce cognitive theory (e.g., Anderson, 1991i), this field remains dominated by the normative postulate that objective laws of probability and expected value are the essential base for theory construction. So powerful is this normative perspective that deviations from the objective laws have even been reified as psychological phenomena. A further symptom of this malaise appears in the makeshift methods of psychological measurement that remain common in the judgment–decision field.

Ironically, algebraic models have been a staple of the judgment–decision field, and many writers speculated that normative algebraic models had psychological counterparts, as with subjective expected value. Externalist strategy, however, prevented discovery of these algebraic laws; they were only revealed through internalist strategy. IIT showed that the cognitive model had the same algebraic form as the normative model in some situations (e.g., Figure 21.7, page 715), but not in others (e.g., Figure 21.5, page 707).

A rather different example concerns the child's development of knowledge of the external world of space, time, number, probability, and so on. This was the main concern of Piaget, who studied children's understanding of simple physical laws, such as time = distance ÷ speed. Reflecting this concern, Piaget was one of the few who recognized the importance of multiple determination and quantification. His entire theory, however, was dominated by his general assumption that development operates to bring the internal world into isomorphism with the external world. Under this isomorphism assumption, structure of the external world provided the framework for understanding development of the internal world. But the isomorphism assumption failed even more severely in developmental psychology than in judgment–decision theory.

Structure of the external world is a useful heuristic for exploring structure of the internal world; survival depends on some reasonable correspondence between the two worlds, as is manifest in the evolution of sense organs. As one example, this externalist heuristic led many writers to one or another form of the Motivation × Incentive rule, first shown to have empirical validity with the study of Figure 21.7 on subjective expected value.

But the structure of the internal world often differs from that of the external, physical world. This difference was shown with the Time = Distance – Speed rule of Figure 20.1, in the Height + Width rule for young children's judgments of rectangle area (Anderson & Cuneo, 1978; Exercise 6.5), and in various experiments on intuitive physics (e.g., Anderson, 1983; Cuneo, 1982; Wilkening & Anderson, 1991; Karpp & Anderson, 1997).

Values, moreover, are not generally determinable from the external world, not merely with social attitudes and moral beliefs, but even palatability of foods. Unified theory must embrace the axiom of purposiveness, which implies that values are central in perception, thought, and action.

Conscious and Nonconscious. Conscious report is an invaluable aid to analysis of the internal world. But conscious report is often nonveridical, often confidently nonveridical. Much of the internal world, moreover, is not accessible to consciousness.

Both limitations of conscious report can be ameliorated with integration rules. This point was illustrated with the size–weight integration of Figure 20.3. The parallelism pattern validated the verbal report as a true measure of conscious heaviness. Further, it provided a validated measure of the nonconscious effect of the physical weight, and of the visual cue to boot. Integration rules can dis-integrate conscious feeling into nonconscious components.

This example illustrates the potential of IIT for analysis of nonconscious determinants that underlie consciousness. One attraction of this approach is its capacity for determining conditions under which conscious report is and is not veridical, illustrated under *Interaction and Configurality* on page 723 (see also Note 20.1.3c, pages 677*f*). No less important is capability for studying the nature of consciousness through its relation to nonconscious determinants (Exercise 20.c7; see also Anderson, 1989).

Cumulative Science. IIT represents cumulative science. This work developed a unified set of concepts and methods that are empirically productive in nearly every area of psychology. Although incomplete in many ways, this integration-ist approach offers promise for further unification.

21.7.2 ALGEBRAIC PSYCHOLOGY

Why did it take so long to discover algebraic psychology? Algebraic laws have long been popular conjectures, perhaps the earliest being Aristotle's formula for justice (Exercise b6). The parallelism theorem is so simple it seems strange it was not exploited long ago. Only recently, however, have algebraic models in psychology been established on solid empirical ground.

The measurement problem was the primary obstacle to discovering algebraic psychology. Linear or proportional scales are essential, but such scales were widely considered not available, if not impossible, in psychology. This point was illustrated with the example of Figure 7.1, in which the two physical scales of time and speed could not both be linear scales of psychological process. Yet no criterion seemed available to determine which, if either, was correct.

The rating method was almost universally condemned because it was subject to well-known nonlinear biases. Although ratings suffice to demonstrate main effects, the biases cripple the study of response pattern, which is essential for algebraic psychology. Ironically, it was the rating method, cleansed of its biases, that provided the base for algebraic psychology.

The general reaction to this lack of linear scales was to begin with choice data. Choice of the larger of two stimuli is psychologically simple and requires no appeal to the magnitude of the difference. Use of choice data was begun by Fechner (see Link, 1994), amplified by Thurstone, and expanded with Coombs' unfolding method and, most notably, with Luce–Tukey conjoint measurement.

Unfortunately, choice data proved fundamentally inadequate. The numerous demonstrations of algebraic laws of the last 40 years have virtually all used continuous response measures. The traditional focus on choice data in psychological measurement theory has been a blind alley, one that seems to have blinded its adherents to the numerous successful applications of continuous response measures (but see Notes 21.4.2b and 21.6.3e).

Functional measurement reversed the traditional direction. The algebraic laws themselves are the base and frame for psychological measurement (Note 21.2a). Algebraic laws can provide linear scales of the response measure and also of the stimulus variables. This was the key that solved the measurement problem, opening a path to unified theory. This functional approach worked because Nature blessed psychology with algebraic laws—and because empirical procedures were found to remove the biases in the response measure.[a]

Conceptual implications are the primary value of algebraic laws. Although interesting in themselves, these laws are most important as tools for deeper analysis. This point, already discussed in Section 21.7.1, deserves reemphasis. Algebraic laws have made a working reality of the two axioms of purposiveness and multiple determination.[b]

21.7.3 UNIFIED FUNCTIONAL THEORY

IIT seeks to develop a unified functional theory. Unified theory must build on the two axioms of purposiveness and multiple determination. The first axiom implies that value is a central theoretical concept. The second axiom implies the need to discover laws that govern integration of multiple determinants. Together, the two axioms imply that value, especially affective value, must be measured on true psychological scales to attain unified theory.

A working solution to these two axioms has been obtained in IIT. Multiple determination has been found to obey exact algebraic laws in nearly every domain of psychology. These algebraic laws ground functional measurement methodology for true measurement of stimulus values and also of response. No less important, this approach can go beyond to help study nonalgebraic and configural integration of multiple determinants.

Phenomenology has been central in IIT. Most of the response and stimulus concepts have come from phenomenology of everyday life. Phenomenology is often considered suspect, in part because it seems vague and subjective, in part because it is subject to cognitive illusions. In contrast, standard response measures of reaction time and accuracy seem exact and objective.

But many phenomenological concepts are exact and objective, for they obey algebraic laws. Cognitive illusions can be taken in stride, as with the compelling illusion of meaning change in person cognition. Not least important, these measures of everyday concepts are more closely related to psychological reality than reaction time or accuracy.

Many writers have emphasized the centrality of purposiveness, but none developed methodology to address the two critical problems of valuation and integration. Without such methodology, psychologists had to take up issues and questions they could study with available tools. This tack led to ways of thinking that obscured the goal of unification. Although much has been learned, this work concentrated on specialized issues and controversies, thus increasing the fragmentation in our field (Anderson, 2000; Noble & Shanteau, 1999).

IIT aims at unification, with the two axioms as cornerstones. It has had some modest success. The same concepts and methods have provided a unified treatment in areas as far apart as judgment–decision, sensation–perception, learning–memory, language processing, developmental psychology, and social cognition. Promising applications have also been made to animal behavior.

IIT is incomplete in many ways, of course, but it is an open theory that can help explore many other issues. This openness can be seen in the wide range of areas that have been studied so far. Algebraic laws are not an end but a means. Work to date is only a beginning, it is true, but it is a true beginning.[a]

NOTES

Information integration theory (IIT) has been developed in collaboration with many students and colleagues. I wish to express my heartfelt appreciation to these men and women (see Anderson, 1996a, p. v) for their dedicated labors, and to compliment them for their enduring contributions to psychological science.

21.2a. "The uniqueness of FM [functional measurement] is in its realization that the hypothesized integration function could itself be used as the base and frame for scaling subjective values" (Budescu & Wallsten, 1979, p. 307).

Also unique to functional measurement is its extensive empirical foundation. When I introduced this functional approach (Anderson, 1962a,b), I realized that making measurement theory an integral part of substantive investigation represented a 180° conceptual shift from traditional approaches, which had viewed measurement as a preliminary to substantive inquiry. I also realized that the worth of this functional approach depended on establishing empirical validity of algebraic laws. With the blessing of Nature, such laws have been established. The true foundation of psychological measurement theory lies in such empirical investigations.

The necessity of empirical foundation is underscored by the averaging model, unexpectedly found to be the main integration rule in the empirical analyses. The traditional conception of measurement in terms of the single dimension of scale value was inherently too narrow. Measurement theory must recognize the coequal status of two scales of measurement—of weight *and* value.

21.2.1a. Proportional scales, which are needed in some applications (e.g., Exercise a7), are linear scales with a known zero. Linearity is the critical element; a needed zero can then often be estimated from the data.

21.2.2a. A validity criterion to assess whether magnitude estimation or rating yields a true linear scale has been provided by the parallelism theorem (pages 697*ff*).

In the experiment of Figure 21.8 (next page), subjects were shown two Munsell gray chips from Figure 21.1 and instructed to judge their average grayness. This *prescribed averaging model*, seemingly prosaic and uninteresting, has an important function—as a validity criterion for response linearity. Since subjects are told to average, the factorial plot may be expected to exhibit parallelism—if the response is a linear scale.

Judgments with magnitude estimation are shown in the right panel; these are radically nonparallel, as shown by the two equal-length vertical bars. Judgments with ratings are shown in the left panel; these are roughly parallel.

As far as one experiment may go, this one implies that magnitude estimation is biased and invalid (see further Notes 21.6.3g,h). Rating and magnitude estimation had equal opportunity; the parallelism theorem acted as an impartial judge of both methods. Magnitude estimation could have succeeded, but it failed. The rating method could have failed, but it succeeded.

21.3.3a. This and other applications of information integration theory to language processing are discussed in Anderson (1996a, Chapter 12).

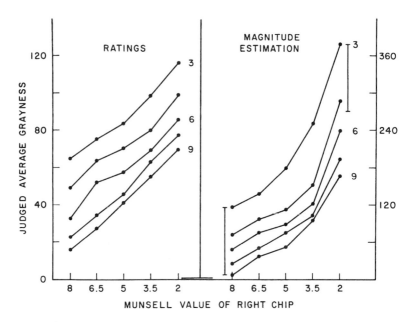

Figure 21.8. Rating passes validity test; magnitude estimation fails. Subjects judge average grayness of two gray chips, with Munsell values of right and left chips indicated on horizontal axis and as curve parameter, respectively. Parallelism in left panel supports validity of rating method; gross nonparallelism in right panel implies magnitude estimation is invalid. (After Weiss, 1972.)

21.3.3b. Gross inconsistencies among informers can produce discounting interactions, which violates *bV*–*bI* independence. Curiously, evidence from person cognition suggests that inconsistency discounting is mainly affective, not semantic, and mainly change in weight, not change in value (Anderson, 1981, Section 3.4), in agreement with the conception of functional memory. Incidental results suggest that weight rather than value changes may also be used to resolve inconsistency in semantic judgment (Anderson, 1996a, p. 389), although this issue seems largely unstudied.

21.3.3c. Similar bimodality has been observed in ratings of colors, odors, poems, and so forth (see Guilford, 1954). Guilford interpreted this bimodality as an artifact of distortion by the rater and the rating scale. Bimodality is real for person cognition, however, as shown by the functional measurement analysis of Figure 21.4. The axiom of purposiveness suggests that bimodality should be general, but this seems the sole empirical test.

21.3.5a. Statistical issues for parallelism analysis, including uniqueness, are discussed in Anderson (1982, Chapter 2). One uniqueness issue with addition models is that a linear interaction among the stimulus values is not detectable with factorial design (a problem that does not trouble multiplication models or compound addition–multiplication models). Interaction based on semantic or pragmatic interrelations will hardly be linear, but this issue did arise with the *positive context effect*—that the judged value of one informer shifts toward the values of the other informers with which it is combined (Exercise c9). This positive context effect has been shown to be a generalized halo effect, however, not change of meaning (Anderson, 1981, Section 3.2).

21.3.5b. For logical completeness, it would be desirable to show that no nonadditive model will yield parallelism (see also previous note). The averaging model with equal weighting does yield parallelism, but it is additive in this case. However, parallelism can be obtained as an artifact of averaging across subjects or trials (Exercise 20.a9).

21.3.5c. Analysis is far more difficult when monotone transformation is used. Goodness of fit is a critical problem. Not only does the transformation use up an unknown number of df, but the deviations from the fit are intercorrelated. Fortunately, goodness of fit can be handled with the replications method introduced by Leon and Anderson (1974; see further Anderson, 1982, pp. 194*f*). This replications method was successful with two studies of integration psychophysics that used monotone transformation (Anderson, 1976b; Carterette & Anderson, 1979). An interesting alternative approach to monotone analysis has been presented by Dixon (1998).

21.4.1a. One precaution to obtain equal weighting is to ensure equal attention to each stimulus informer (Note 21.6.1a). The importance of attentional factors on weighting has appeared in studies of primacy and recency observed with serial presentation.

Unequal weighting occurs naturally in some situations, especially when stimuli carry different amounts of information. To get equal weighting may require preliminary standardization, as with the personality adjectives and the biographical paragraphs about 17 U.S. presidents (Anderson, 1982, Appendixes B and C, respectively).

21.4.1b. The term *adding-type* is used to include averaging, adding, and subtracting.

21.4.1c. The differences between averaging and adding stem from the weight parameter, which makes averaging a hybrid configural–nonconfigural model. It is nonconfigural in that each informer has constant parameters, value and weight, the same regardless of what other informers is is being integrated with. These constant weights, however, are the absolute weights.

The effective weights are the relative weights, which are required to sum to 1. In Equation 2a, the absolute weight of A is ω_A; its relative weight is $\omega_A/(\omega_A + \omega_B)$. Averaging is thus configural in that the effective weight of each informer depends on the weights of all the others.

21.4.1d. The opposite effects phenomenon is an interesting illustration of one ambiguity of "interaction." Opposite effects constitutes a crossover interaction in Anova, which seems to imply value change. But this inference depends on an implicit assumption of additivity. The averaging process produces the crossover with no change of value. The relative weight does change, but this is built into the algebraic structure.

21.4.1e. The *sure-thing axiom*, once considered a cornerstone for judgment–decision theory, is infirmed by the averaging crossover of Figure 21.5. This counterexample has special interest since it does not involve any probabilistic element as with other arguments against the sure-thing axiom. A misconception in the earlier argument (e.g., Anderson, 1996a, Chapter 10) has been rectified by Schlottmann (2000), who has also replicated the experiment of Figure 21.5 under improved conditions (Figure 11.9).

21.4.1f. The concept of prior information was originally called *initial impression* or *initial state*. The present word *prior* indicates its similarity to the Bayesian concept of prior probability. Prior information is more general, since it refers to any dimension of response, probability being a special case.

732

21.4.2a. Busemeyer's (1991) discussion of algebraic models in intuitive statistics includes a striking analysis of covariation as averaging. Busemeyer presents a very general model that subsumes previous hypotheses as special cases, yet provides far more effective methods for data analysis. Busemeyer's work is an impressive demonstration of the power of mathematical models to crystallize and amplify common sense.

21.4.2b. *Support theory* (Tversky & Koehler, 1994) appears to follow the same algebraic model and the same measurement logic as the decision averaging model of IIT given in Anderson (1981, pp. 66, 77*ff*). The two weight parameters in the decision averaging model of Equation 2c represent amount or strength of information favoring the two response alternatives; this seems equivalent to the Tversky–Koehler concept of support for each alternative. The decision averaging model was explicitly developed in terms of a continuous response, unlike formally similar models for choice response, but like the support model.

Tversky has vigorously criticized functional measurement for its use of continuous response measures to analyze algebraic models. He has argued strenuously instead for reliance on ordinal, choice data (e.g., Krantz & Tversky, 1971a,b; see similarly Krantz, Luce, Suppes, & Tversky, 1971). With the support model, however, Tversky relies on continuous response measures, mirroring the logic of functional measurement. Indeed, the support model is notably similar to, if not identical with, the decision averaging model. This is a welcome vindication of functional measurement Anderson (1970b, 1971a), which he and his coauthors previously condemned (see also Notes 21.6.3d,e).

21.4.3a. This maximal uniqueness requires expanding a regular factorial design to include subdesigns that omit one or more factors (see uniqueness theorem in Anderson, 1982, Section 2.3.2). Iterative analysis is required, for which an AVERAGE program is available (Zalinksi & Anderson, 1991). Goodness of fit may be tested using the replications method for general nonlinear models (Note 21.3.5c). Parameter estimation may be biased, especially for the prior weight, but this bias does not trouble the test of goodness of fit (Zalinksi & Anderson, 1998).

An application in which subdesigns were physically impossible appears in the study of phenomenal causality by Schlottmann and Anderson (1993); each of the three variables was an integral physical component of the stimulus display. The level of uniqueness allowed by this design was sufficient for uncovering distinctive individual strategies in the valuation process, differences not visible in the data themselves (Note 11.5.2a).

21.5.1a. The key idea for analysis of multiplication models was that the column means of the factorial design could be used as provisional values of the column stimuli. This allowed a check on the hypothesized linear fan pattern. A linear measure of response is hardly less important, of course, but this is assessed conjointly with the model itself. Linear fan analysis was successful in its first empirical application (Anderson & Shanteau, 1970; see Figure 21.7, page 715), and in numerous later experiments.

21.5.1b. Detailed discussion of statistical issues for analysis of multiplication models, including uniqueness, is in Anderson (1982, Chapter 2). The linear fan pattern, unlike the parallelism pattern, assumes that effects of the factorial variables are independent, or at least uncorrelated, so that the mean of the product is the product of the means. Computer programs have been developed by Weiss and Shanteau (e.g., 1982).

21.5.4a. An important article by Roberts (1987) applied the multiplication model to a number of published studies that had used rate as a response measure. Roberts seemed unaware, however, of the extensive work on multiplication models that had followed introduction of the linear fan analysis by Anderson and Shanteau (1970; see summaries in Anderson, 1974a,b,c, 1978, 1981, 1982).

This previous work based on IIT and functional measurement had two advantages over Roberts (see also Note 21.7.1a). First, functional measurement theory had developed superior statistical analyses (Anderson, 1982). More basic, functional measurement had recognized the critical issue of response linearity and had resolved it, both in principle and in practice. Roberts simply takes for granted that the response measure is a true linear or proportional scale (Section 19.3.1).

Functional measurement theory, however, made explicit how validity of the response measure rests on success of the algebraic model, and explicated issues of uniqueness and of goodness of fit. This logic was shown with the linear fan theorem of Section 21.5.1. This functional measurement logic was applied in the analysis of multiplication models for response rate for the operant matching law by Farley and Fantino (1978) and for rewarding electrical brain stimulation by Hawkins et al. (1983). Roberts' work is an important addition to establishing response rate as a true psychological scale.

21.6.1a. Two simple procedures, together with one less simple, have been generally successful in obtaining linear measures with the rating method. Since ratings are comparative, a stable frame of reference should ordinarily be established before collecting data. The first procedure is to present *end anchors*, stimuli that are a little more extreme than the regular experimental stimuli. These end anchors define the range of the stimuli and begin setting up a correspondence between the subject's feelings and the external response range. The second procedure is to firm up this correspondence with practice on representative experimental stimuli (see further Anderson, 1982, Chapter 1).

A continuous, graphic rating scale avoids number preferences that can trouble the common 1–10 scale. Also, graphic scales are usable with young children; 4-year-olds and even 3[+]-year-olds with a gifted experimenter can do well (see Figure 8.4, p. 258, in Anderson, 1996a). This remarkable ability to use the rating scale in a linear manner is thought to derive from perceptual-motor skills in local space that are utilized in assemblage with the decision averaging model.

The less simple procedure is concerned with response quality. Instructions and practice should seek to ensure that each subject understands the nature and relevance of the stimuli and the nature of the response (see also Section 14.1.2 on writing instructions). This usually requires individual monitoring during practice as well as running only one subject or possibly two at a time.

21.6.1b. Self-estimation of weights and values (Anderson & Zalinski, 1991) can help with analysis of unique one-time situations (e.g., next note).

21.6.1c. This utilitarian principle of choosing the alternative expected to yield the greatest good is the essential idea of modern multiattribute analysis. The idea is simple. Represent each alternative as a set of independent attributes, measure the weight and value of each attribute, sum these weighted values, and choose the alternative with the greatest sum. You do something of this sort when you choose which research problem will have greatest probable payoff.

Multiattribute analysis is sometimes applied to large scale problems in society, government, and business. Many such applications rely on subjective estimates of weights and values by concerned persons or by experts. But unless these subjective estimates are valid, the multiattribute analysis may tell you to select a poor alternative. This threat is serious, as shown by the sharp difference between the two methods of rating and magnitude estimation in Figure 21.2. Oddly, one popular method for measuring weights has relied on magnitude estimation, which seems dubious.

Valid methods for subjective parameter estimation can be developed from functional measurement theory (see Anderson & Zalinksi, 1991; Wang & Yang, 1998; Zhu & Anderson, 1991). Such methods are vital for multiattribute analysis as well as for study of interaction and configurality (see also Note 21.2.1a).

21.6.2a. Only general criticisms of functional measurement theory are considered here. Other criticisms refer to particular tasks or particular substantive interpretations. For example, the disproof of the representativeness heuristic by Leon and Anderson (1974) has been criticized as an artifact of within subject design (see Anderson, 1982, pp. 51f; 1996a, p. 360). This class of criticisms is not considered here. The subtle matter of model–scale tradeoff is discussed elsewhere (e.g., Anderson, 1974a, 1996a, pp. 101f).

21.6.3a. Conjoint measurement, the main competitor to functional measurement, employed a similar idea of studying algebraic structure with factorial design. Luce and Tukey (1964) made an exciting contribution by showing that a numerical representation (like that of the parallelism theorem of Section 21.3.1) could in principle be derived using only ordinal, greater than–less than, choice data.

Measurement theory based on algebraic structure had also been advocated in Anderson (1962a,b), except that continuous response measures were allowed, bypassing the extreme difficulties with choice response. This functional measurement approach was empirically effective in Anderson (1962a) and in many later applications.

Functional measurement theory has been much criticized by workers in conjoint measurement for its reliance on continuous response. Krantz and Tversky (1971a), although admitting that observed parallelism supports an addition model, claim that the ordinal choice tests of conjoint measurement are markedly more effective (see similarly Krantz, Luce, Suppes, & Tversky, 1971). This claim underlay the enormous efforts on choice data by highly capable persons over the preceding and following decades. But this claim was amply disproved over the following 30 years by the empirical success of functional measurement and the empirical failure of conjoint measurement (see following note).

It deserves notice that some proponents of the ordinal approach have recently adopted continuous response measures (Notes 21.4.2b and 21.6.3e).

Ironically, one ordinal test has been invaluable in functional measurement, namely, the opposite effects test (e.g., Figure 21.5, page 707; see also Note 20.2.2a, page 678). But the opposite effects test revealed the prevalence of averaging rather than adding as the main integration rule. Opposite effects represents disordinal data, which seem outside the capability of the ordinal methods of conjoint measurement.

The averaging model, moreover, entails a shift from traditional conceptions of psychological measurement in terms of the single scale of value. A dual-scale conception is needed, with weight and value having coequal status.

21.6.3b. "The revolution that never happened" was used to characterize conjoint measurement by Cliff (1992, p. 186), himself a longtime advocate of conjoint measurement. The huge mass of work on conjoint measurement failed because it remained almost entirely mathematical, devoid of empirical base. Cliff's evaluation confirms Tukey's (1969, p. 88) admonition that the mathematical approach of conjoint measurement was all "theoretical in the less satisfactory sense of that word."

The empirical algebraic laws essential for genuine measurement are lacking in conjoint measurement. This lack of empirical fruition is the prime characteristic of the failure cited by Cliff (1992), in agreement with the more extensive evaluation of conjoint measurement in Anderson (1981, Sections 5.5 and 5.6.1; Louviere, 1988, pp. 14-27).

Functional measurement has been much criticized by workers on conjoint measurement theory and its extensions. Functional measurement succeeded, however, whereas conjoint measurement failed. Indeed, prominent advocates of conjoint measurement have recently adopted approaches that seem notably similar to functional measurement (see Notes 21.4.2b and 21.6.3e).

The true foundation of psychological measurement theory lies in algebraic laws that have been empirically established (e.g., Figures 20.1–3, Figures 21.4–5, and 21.7–10).

Functional measurement may thus be called the revolution that did happen.

21.6.3c. In their reply to Cliff's critique cited in the previous note, Narens and Luce (1993) acknowledge the lack of empirical fruition, saying that their axiomatic approach continues unable to study algebraic structure in actual data because it cannot handle response variability (randomness). Functional measurement, in contrast, has been allowing for response variability in the study of algebraic structure since 1962 with reasonable success (see also Note 21.3.5c). It thus seems precisely correct to say that the axiomatic approach has been a blind alley.

Narens and Luce also fault cognitive theory in general for lack of concern with structure of multiple determination. This criticism is well taken because multiple determination is fundamental for cognitive theory. They fail to recognize that a unified theory of functional cognition, empirically grounded in structural laws of multiple determination, had been developed in IIT (Anderson, 1981, 1982, 1991a,b,c, 1996a).

21.6.3d. Two basic differences between functional measurement and conjoint measurement are that functional measurement relies on:

1. Continuous response measures rather than choice response.
2. Empirical analysis rather than mathematical analysis.

Continuous response measures have provided effective methods for handling response variability, which is essential for empirical analysis. This capability has eluded the best efforts of workers on conjoint measurement. Lack of capability with continuous response measures is why the conjoint measurement revolution "never happened."

Continuous response also has greater psychological reality than choice response. Continuousness is a primary characteristic of sensory systems and motor systems that subserve purposiveness.

Empirical analysis is essential because functional measurement uses algebraic laws as base and frame for developing psychological measurement theory. Conjoint measurement relies even more strongly on algebraic laws. But unless such laws have empirical reality, the parallelism theorem and the linear fan theorem, and the analogous theorems of conjoint measurement, have minor value.

Such empirical laws have been widely established in the work on IIT. In contrast, conjoint measurement has centered on mathematical theorems about choice response that are now seen to have little usefulness. The true foundation of psychological measurement lies in empirical algebraic laws, such as have been established in IIT.

Continuous response measures are essential for analysis of nonalgebraic integration. Algebraic laws are a means to develop linear response measures—a ladder to higher levels of inquiry. Development of methodology for continuous response is thus a primary goal of psychological measurement theory (Section 21.6.1).

21.6.3e. An about-face may have appeared in Luce's position on psychological measurement. Whereas functional measurement has been dedicated to continuous response measures, Luce has been dedicated to discrete choice measures, both in his choice theory and in his extensive work on conjoint measurement and its extensions. About-face appears in Luce, Mellers, and Chang (1993, p. 115), who rely on continuous response measures and conclude that "Choice is viewed as a derived, not a primitive, concept."

IIT has provided the foundation for valid theory of psychological measurement, based on continuous response. Functional measurement theory is well developed theoretically and has proved empirically effective in numerous experiments in many areas of psychology. Choice as a derived concept is wholly harmonious with the emphasis on continuous response in functional measurement.

21.6.3f. As Cliff (1996, pp. 6, 89) has pointed out, the principle that true psychological scales can be obtained by monotone transformation to linearize the response to fit a theoretical model was proposed independently by Anderson (1962b) and by Shepard (1962a,b). These two approaches pursued different kinds of tasks and models. Shepard's nonmetric approach was mainly concerned with multidimensional scaling, a kind of factor analysis of structure of complex natural stimuli, whereas IIT was mainly concerned with empirical manipulation of multiple determinants to analyze structure of integration processes (Anderson, 1981, Section 5.6.5).

To obtain the monotone transformation, these two approaches also pursued different directions, one empirical, one statistical. Functional measurement pursued the empirical direction, placing primary emphasis on task–procedure as an empirical transformation of the concept being measured. If this empirical measurement transformation can be made linear through empirical procedure, psychological analysis will be much simplified, as demonstrated empirically in Anderson (1962a; see Figure 20.2, page 652). A primary goal has thus been to develop linear response methodology (Section 21.6.1).

The nonmetric approach of Shepard and his followers relied entirely on rank-order information in the data and on statistical transformation of the ranks to fit a metric model. Once highly popular, this nonmetric approach is no longer widely used.

Cliff, himself a proponent of nonmetric analysis, evaluates the failure of the "nonmetric revolution" as comparable to the failure of conjoint measurement (Note 21.6.3b). One reason given by Cliff for this failure of the nonmetric approach is that valid scaling depends on valid models. Yet, "In most applications, the models were models in the sense of toys, not models as serious attempts at description of reality" (Cliff, 1996, pp. 90-91).

The algebraic models of IIT, in contrast (e.g., Anderson, 1974a, p. 256), are serious attempts to describe reality of information integration. These models describe real laws in many areas. These laws provided a base and frame for true psychological measurement. These laws give teeth to the two axioms of purposiveness and multiple determination—the foundation for unified theory of cognition (Section 21.7, pages 721*ff*).

21.6.3g. The first failure of Stevens' method of magnitude estimation appeared in his own first experiments (Stevens, 1956); different loudness scales were obtained when different standard stimuli were used. Stevens gave no way to determine which was the true scale. Similar failures have attended nearly every effort to validate magnitude estimation (see Note 21.2.2a and detailed reviews by Anderson 1974a, Section IV.B.5; 1981, Section 5.4; see similarly Krueger, 1989).

The flaw in Stevens' method of magnitude estimation appears to be a diminishing returns effect in number usage. The number difference between 100 and 101, for example, is psychologically less than the number difference between 10 and 11. To compensate, the subject uses increasingly large number differences to indicate equal psychological differences. This diminishing returns in number usage is familiar from everyday life in which, for example, four dollars is a big difference in the cost of a compact disc but a small difference in the cost of a compact disc player.

A dramatic illustration of diminishing returns in magnitude estimation appears in Stevens' (1974, p. 375) conclusion that lightness (grayness) is a power function of physical energy with exponent of 1.2—convex upward. Figure 21.1 (page 693) implies an exponent near .3—convex downward, which is more realistic physiologically.

Functional measurement, as emphasized with Figure 21.8 on page 730, is neutral in the controversy between rating and magnitude estimation. Had magnitude estimation satisfied validity criteria such as parallelism, it would have been adopted.

Ironically, Stevens was almost the sole person prior to 1960 who sought to base psychological measurement on continuous response measures. He was oriented in the right direction; why did he fail to reach the goal?

Stevens failed because his total faith in magnitude estimation led him to slough off its repeated failures to satisfy validity criteria. Had Stevens taken these failures seriously, he could well have succeeded in revising his measurement procedure to eliminate the bias. Stevens' treatment of magnitude estimation is reminiscent of his work on somatotype theory (Section 8.1.1, page 222).

21.6.3h. In the field of psychophysics, functional measurement embodies a fundamental conceptual shift—a shift to *integration psychophysics*. The traditional conception of psychophysical law, vigorously reinforced by Stevens, is inherently incapable of handling integration of multiple determinants, which is fundamental to perception, thought, and action. Integration psychophysics is more effective, far broader, and honors a long tradition in psychophysical analysis (see Anderson, 1970b, 1975; McBride & Anderson, 1991). Integrationist views have found increasing favor among followers of Stevens (e.g., Algom, 1992; Kreuger, 1989; Marks, 1974; see Anderson, 1992, pp. 102-104).

The essential contrast between integration psychophysics and Stevens' approach is between *psychological law* and *psychophysical law*. These two laws appear as *bI* and *bV*, respectively, in the integration diagram of Figure 21.3. Stevens fixated on the psychophysical law of long tradition and denied the importance of integration of multiple determinants. Being a function of a single variable, however, the psychophysical law is inherently unable to establish response linearity or psychological measurement.

The psychological law, in contrast, being a function of more than one variable, does have capability to establish psychological measurement; this capability appears in the parallelism theorem and linear fan theorem. Indeed, the psychophysical law is just an issue of psychological measurement, being derivative from the psychological law, *bI* (Conclusion 2 of the two cited theorems).

This method for deriving the psychophysical law is effective. The psychophysical law for heaviness has been demonstrated in Figure 20.3. The psychophysical law for grayness is similarly derivative from Figure 21.8. By validating a linear response methodology conjointly with an integration operator, functional measurement resolved the controversy over psychological measurement begun by Fechner long ago.

21.6.3i. Functional measurement has been employed by Oden and by Massaro in their fuzzy logic studies of language processing and perception (see e.g., Oden, 1978; Massaro, 1987, pp. 23, 51). The basic model in their work has been a ratio model, similar to the decision averaging model of Equation 2c (see also Anderson, 1996a, pp. 356*f*).

21.6.3j. Gigerenzer and Murray (1987, pp. 91*ff*) make serious factual errors in their discussion of cognitive algebra and functional measurement. They wrongly state that "Out of all possible cognitive algebra hypotheses, only those that fit the linear, additive structure of the analysis of variance are even considered." Quite the contrary, the basic model of cognitive algebra—the averaging model—is in general nonadditive (see further Anderson, 1996a, pp. 276*f*).

Furthermore, configural and nonalgebraic cognition can be, and have been, studied with functional measurement (see *Linear Response Methodology*, pages 717*f*). Cognitive algebra has thus made major contributions to the study of nonalgebraic cognition.

"Cognition as intuitive statistics" is the title that Gigerenzer and Murray give their book. This theme had been successfully pursued in IIT for 20 years previously. Numerous careful experimental studies had revealed an exact cognitive algebra, not only in intuitive statistics (e.g., Figures 11.9, 15.1, and 19.3), but also in many other domains (e.g., Figures 11.2, 11.6, 20.1–5, 21.4–5, 21.7–10; see further Anderson 1974a,b,c, 1981, 1982). The scholarship in the book by Gigerenzer and Murry thus seems lamentable (see similarly Kahneman & Tversky, 1996).

21.6.3k. Additive units was the foundation for Campbell's (1928) theory of measurement in physics. To measure length of a rod, for example, lay out unit lengths end to end to cover the rod and count up these units. Mass may be determined similarly, by adding unit masses in a balance scale. Psychology lacks additive units. Many writers have accordingly argued that true measurement is not possible in psychology.

A different foundation for measurement is algebraic laws—the base and frame for functional measurement (Note 21.2a). Even in physics, this conception of measurement as derivative from algebraic structure may be preferable to Campbell's additive units.

21.6.3l. Sternberg (2000, in press) and Roberts (1987) adopt a position similar to that of functional measurement and IIT in their analysis of addition and multiplication models. Thus, the linear fan analysis used by Roberts (1987) is the same as that introduced by Anderson and Shanteau (1970)—the key was the scaling of the stimulus variables to reveal the fan pattern (see linear fan theorem, pages 711f). More generally, nearly all their statistical discussion had already been presented in functional measurement theory, summarized in Anderson (1982).

Both Sternberg and Roberts, however, seem to take for granted that the observed response is a true linear or proportional scale, without recognizing the underlying measurement issues. But a priori knowledge of the scale properties of the response does not generally exist. Instead, this knowledge derives from success of the algebraic model, as listed under the five benefits of the parallelism and linear fan theorems.

Sternberg and Roberts may have been misled by the special case of Sternberg's additive-factor method. This method *requires* time as the response measure. Additivity then becomes a diagnostic of separate stages. In general, however, scale properties of the response measure must be established empirically.

21.7a. IIT as unified theory may be compared with Newell's (1990) *Unified Theories of Cognition*, which is representative of a class of current theories quite different in nature. Newell's approach cannot lead to unified theory because it begins with a theoretical foundation that is fundamentally too narrow. In particular, it has no place for affective phenomena associated with the axiom of purposiveness. These affective phenomena pervade life. Construction of unified theory must begin with life; life cannot be breathed in afterwards.

Another fatal narrowness is Newell's (1992, p. 476) admission that his approach does not deal with quantification. With respect to uncertainty, in particular, he states that "Placing inside the human the mechanisms for doing an uncertainty calculus, say probabilities or fuzzy logic, *cannot be right*" (italics added). But surely this *is* right, as illustrated with subjective expected value in Figure 21.7, page 715. Quantification is an essential prerequisite for unified theory because quantification is a fundamental mode of perception, thought, and action.

As a pertinent example of the need for quantification, Newell cites as a special achievement that his system predicts developmental stages in Piaget's balance scale task that were claimed by Siegler (1976, 1981). But the fact is that Siegler's claim has been repeatedly shown to be an artifact of his Piagetian choice methodology. A completely different portrayal of cognitive development emerged from application of the functional measurement methodology of IIT (see Wilkening & Anderson, 1982, 1991).

21.7b. I wholeheartedly agree with Newell's concern for a unified approach to psychological science. I disagree, however, with his claim that the large collection of past results provides a base for unification. On the contrary, I believe most of these results will be left behind, forgotten side issues of little reach. This seems an inevitable consequence of neglecting the problem of psychological measurement—the foundation for analysis of multiple determination.

IIT does not overlook the kind of symbolic thinking considered by Newell. This kind of thinking is implicit in both the valuation and integration operations, as well as in the reality of the concepts embodied in these operations. Useful contributions have thus been made to language processing, judgment–decision, perception, and other areas. Much remains open, of course, especially with functional memory and with assemblage processes discussed in Section 21.6.2, but this line of inquiry is not closed off as Newell has done with affective phenomena and with quantification.

740

21.7.1a. Two basic ideas of IIT appear in Sternberg's (2000, in press) discussion of modular processes: *algebraic integration models* and *invariance*. Both ideas have been successful in numerous experiments in every area of psychology (Anderson, 1974a,b,c, 1981, 1982, 1991a,b,c, 1996a). Sternberg's chapter gives an impressive array of applications of addition and multiplication models, especially important because these experiments used nonsymbolic, behavioral response measures.

I disagree, however, with Sternberg's principal conclusion, namely, that success of a model implies that the processes affected by the design factors represent *modules*. Thus, Sternberg (in press, Table 3, see also p. 44) claims that additive effects in a factorial design is joint support for (a) an additive integration rule and (b) modularity of the processes influenced by the separate factor variables—a principal conclusion reiterated throughout his chapter. (This discussion is limited to what Sternberg calls "composite measures," that is, a single response measure to factorial stimulus combinations; his additive-factor method is excluded.)

I believe instead that modularity requires strong external evidence besides additivity. Indeed, modularity is not essential for additivity (e.g., Note 21.3.5a).

This issue of modularity may be clarified with a couple examples from published experiments. Judgments of area of rectangles furnishes two relevant considerations. Adults show a linear fan, in line with the physical rule of Height × Width. Sternberg's theory, accordingly, implies that height and width correspond to modules, an implication that has geometrical plausibility. But the operative integration process may be summation of unit areas; neither height nor width may be psychologically relevant. This nonmodular interpretation is plausible in that it also applies to irregular figures that have empty holes or more than one part. The observed linear fan may be only an "as-if" multiplication rule (e.g., Anderson, 1982, p. 298, 1996a, pp. 66*f*).

Young children, in contrast, show parallelism, an ostensible Height + Width addition rule (Exercise 6.5). Here again, an alternative interpretation is possible, namely, that they judge the perimeter as a single stimulus, noncognizant of height or width. The addition rule was plausible, of course, and was supported by finding addition rules in other tasks that obeyed a physical multiplication rule (e.g., Figure 20.1). But granted psychological reality of height and width, it does not follow that they correspond to modules (personal communication to Saul Sternberg, on the Big Laguna hiking trail, 2 June 2000).

In the initial experiment on person cognition, values of the personality traits were integrated by an adding-type rule, a result that supports invariance of these stimulus values. But the valuation operation is goal-dependent (Figure 21.3). The subject could judge the person on many different qualities, or dimensions; each would induce a different value for a given trait adjective. If valuation corresponds to a module, this module is only a temporary assemblage, constructed for the immediate goal.

Psychological reality of the variables of integration models has continually been of keen interest in IIT. Parameter invariance has been demonstrated in many, many other experiments on IIT. By virtue of invariance, a successful algebraic model buttresses the reality of the variables of that model, helping along the process of transforming concepts from everyday language into grounded scientific concepts. This work is most important for its conceptual implications about structure and process of perception, thought, and action (Section 21.7.1). Sternberg (2000, in press) does not discuss any work on IIT, which could have helped clarify his position.

21.7.2a. Establishing algebraic psychology was considerably more difficult than the simplicity of the parallelism and linear fan theorems suggests. One reason was uncertainty about empirical procedures that would yield linear scales, an uncertainty starkly clear in Figure 21.2, page 694. A deeper difficulty was that averaging is the most common integration rule, and in general averaging yields nonparallelism. That everything worked out so neatly is a blessing of Nature.

21.7.2b. A basic issue in functional memory concerns how mood, motivation, expectancy, and other such states operate in memory-based tasks. One popular hypothesis is that such states influence an encoding stage; a popular competing hypothesis is that such states influence a retrieval stage. Quite overlooked has been a third hypothesis, suggested in IIT, that the state operates as a distinct informer that is integrated as it stands (Anderson, 1996a, pp. 377*ff*), that is, as the initial state of the organism.

Analytical power on this issue may be available through averaging theory, which has potential for dis-integrating an integrated response to measure functional values of the separate stimuli. Thus, the third hypothesis implies no value change in the separate stimuli (see also Exercises c6 and c7).

The standard strategy of comparing competing hypotheses can be efficient in special cases in which just one hypothesis is correct. But often, perhaps typically, multiple processes are operative. Since standard strategy usually depends on artificial experimental conditions contrived to eliminate alternative hypotheses, such work is likely to lose meaning when more than one process is operative. Algebraic models have some capability for measuring separate effects of multiple processes.

21.7.3a. In IIT, algebraic models are chiefly tools to be used for further analysis. Hypothetico–deductive predictions about which model, if any, will operate in given situations have lesser interest. This point is nicely illustrated with the initial experiment on person cognition; any outcome would have been instructive. Had nonparallelism been obtained, it would have provided useful information about meaning change. As noted in an earlier discussion of inductive theory (Anderson, 1981, pp. 82):

> Many psychological theories claim to operate in the deductive mode. It is often considered to be the ideal, sometimes the only truly scientific way of thinking. Workers in the deductive mode often have difficulty comprehending inductive theory; to them, it appears formless and uncertain. To workers in the inductive mode, however, the deductive mode appears simplistic, not to say specious, beyond the local level. Among other reasons, what passes for deductive theory in psychology is typically an awkward form of inductive theory.
>
> For the plain fact is that deductive theories are rarely abandoned when their deductions fail. Instead, they are modified, first in their auxiliary simplifying assumptions, later in their basic conceptual assumptions. Deductive theories in psychology typically exhibit a short, initial period of deductive flourish, followed by slow, grudging acceptance of inductive change. Open acceptance of a more inductive approach as a basic research orientation would seem developmentally more truthful, not to say more efficient.
>
> Inductive theory views science not as formalized knowledge, but as living inquiry. . . . And it is more open to Nature, which continually reveals new riches to surprise and delight her students.

EXERCISES FOR CHAPTER 21

Exercises for Addition Model

a1. Can you average length by visual inspection? To find out, present two unequal lengths in 3×4 factorial design and judge average length of each of the 12 pairs. After practice trials, present the design twice to provide an error term for Anova. Do this experiment with two subjects, yourself and one other. Get verbal reports of how subjects think they did the task. For this exercise, use a 1–20 rating scale. To avoid end bias, use *end anchors* to be called 1 and 20, respectively (Note 21.6.1a). Analyze and discuss the data.

a2. In a 2×5 design, suppose the row stimuli have values 1 and 3, and the column stimuli have values 1, 2, 4, 8, and 16.

    a. Assume an addition model, calculate the cell entries for the factorial table, and plot these values, showing that they exhibit parallelism.

    b. In this same 2×5 design, suppose the row stimuli have values a and b, and the column stimuli have values v, w, x, y, and z. Assume an addition model and write down the entry in each cell of the factorial data table.

    c. How does the factorial table for (b) reveal parallelism?

a3. Conclusion 2 of the parallelism theorem says that the marginal means for each factor are a linear scale of the values of that factor. Check this numerically with the column factor for the numerical example of Exercise a2.

a4. With an additive model, the cell entries are completely determined by the marginal means. The formula for a two-way design is

    cell mean = row mean + column mean − overall mean.

Get marginal means for the data of Exercise a2 and check that this formula is correct. (As an optional exercise, derive this formula algebraically.)

a5. a. How, according to the parallelism theorem, do the data of Figure 20.3 relate to the subjective values of heaviness?

    b. The psychophysical function is the function relating the subjective value of some sensory dimension to the objective, physical magnitude. How does the measurement of (a) solve the problem of determining the psychophysical function for heaviness?

    c. Why go to this illusion to get subjective heaviness? Why not eliminate the illusion by concealing the weights behind a screen and ask subjects to judge heaviness of these unseen lifted weights?

a6. In Figure 21.4: a. Why is the parallelism essential to show that bimodality is real? b. Explain bimodality in terms of propensity to approach and avoid goals. c. Outline an experiment to test bipolarity with another stimulus class.

a7. An occasional pitfall in data analysis is to treat numbers at face value, as though they came from a proportional scale with a known zero. Usually, however, the zero point is unknown. Here is an example (Rosnow & Arms, 1968).

In a test between averaging and adding models for attractiveness of social groups, subjects made preliminary ratings of single faces on a 0–100 scale of friendliness. Then 50 was subtracted from each rating on the assumption that the midpoint of the rating scale was its true zero. These reduced ratings were used to construct paired groups, one with four faces, one with three, to yield specified differences in mean value and total value.

In one illustrative pair, the four faces in one group had values 17, 18, 17 and 16; the three faces in the other group had values 22, 19, and 22. Subjects were instructed to choose which group in each pair was more friendly.

a. What results did the authors predict from the two models?

b. What results are predicted by these models if the true zero of the scale in the initial face ratings is really 60?

c. Following the logic of Figure 21.5, how could you get a valid test between averaging and adding in this task of perception of social groups?

a8. You are in an ethical dilemma in which every action, including inaction, has both positive and negative consequences. Instead of drifting with events and hoping for the best, you decide to apply utilitarian calculus and choose the action you expect to yield most good or least bad. Utilitarian calculus requires that you assign a value to each consequence of a given action, weighted as appropriate by the probability of that consequence, and add these up to get the net value of that action. You choose whichever action has highest net value.

Assume for illustration that one specific action leads to three separate, independent consequences, with measured values of $+1$, $+4$, and -8. You assume an additive rule, which implies that the net value of this action is -3.

Stop! Perhaps your value scale is only monotone. Perhaps the true value, ψ, follows a law of diminishing returns relative to your measured value, S.

a. Suppose $\psi = \sqrt{|S|}$. Show that the true value of the action is positive.

b. What is the relevance of Figure 21.2 to this particular problem?

c. What is the relevance of Figure 21.8 to this problem?

a9. Prove Conclusion 1 of the parallelism theorem (assume errorless response). Use Equation 1 to express R_{1k}, the entries in row 1 of the factorial design, in terms of the ψ values. Do the same for R_{2k} and subtract.

a10. a. Prove Conclusion 2 of the parallelism theorem (assume errorless response). Use Equation 1 to get the column means.

b. Extend (a) to allow each level of each factor to have its own weight as well as its own value. Comment.

a11. Why does Figure 21.2 imply that at least one of rating and magnitude estimation yields a nonlinear scale?

b. Exercises for Multiplication Model

b1. In a 2×4 design, suppose the row stimuli have values 1 and 3, and the column stimuli have values 2, 3, 7, and 9.

a. Assume a multiplication model and calculate the cell entries for the factorial table. Plot these values to demonstrate the linear fan pattern, using the marginal means spacing prescribed by the linear fan theorem.

b. Repeat (a) assuming the column stimuli have values of 2, 7, 3, and 9.

c. In (a), the zero point constant, c_0, has been taken as 0, as though the response scale was a proportional scale (with known zero). In general, however, c_0 will be unknown. To see whether the linear fan theorem still holds with only a linear scale, include c_0 and repeat (a).

b2. In Table 21.2, suppose the Coke entry of 84 is changed to 54. Show that this deviation from the multiplication model produces a nonlinear fan graph.

b3. For the size–weight experiment of Figure 5.3, plot a factorial graph to show the pattern expected from the density hypothesis. Assume plausible subjective values for size and weight. How sensitive do you think the pattern in your graph is to your particular choice of subjective values?

b4. There are five forms of algebraic model with three variables. Four are

$$A + B + C; \quad AB + C; \quad A(B + C); \quad \text{and} \quad ABC.$$

a. You are given a three-way data table and told that it follows one of the four listed forms. How can graphs be used to diagnose which one?

b. What is the fifth form of three-factor model? How is it distinguishable from the others? (Note that $A + BC$ has the same form as $AB + C$.)

b5. Do language quantifiers function as multipliers? This exercise asks you to test this hypothesis empirically.

a. Get one subject, perhaps yourself, and obtain likableness judgments of persons described by adverb–adjective combinations. Use the four adverbs {slightly, fairly, quite, extremely} and the two adjectives {sincere and insincere} to obtain eight person descriptions. After practice (Note 21.6.1a), present two randomized replications, using a 0-20 or graphic rating.

b. Plot the data by spacing the four adverbs on the horizontal axis according to the judgments of the sincere person, averaged over the two replications. (This yields a perfectly straight line curve for the sincere person, an irregular curve for the insincere person.) What does the multiplication model predict about the curve for the insincere person?

c.* The factorial graph has one ascending curve, one descending. Their average is nearly flat, so the marginal means are unreliable estimates of the functional values of the adverbs. Yet both curves contain equivalent information about appropriate spacing of the adverbs on the horizontal. How can both be combined to get more reliable estimates?

Get these more reliable estimates, replot the data, and compare with (b).

d.* The adjectives have quantitative content in themselves; a *sincere* person is sincere to some degree. Show how your data can measure this implicit quantifier; just give the idea, using a graph.

b6. In Aristotle's view, fairness (justice) means that reward, or outcome O, should be proportional to work, or input I. For two persons, A and B,

$$O_A / O_B \;=\; I_A / I_B.$$

In recent times, an alternative model has been popular, based on the idea of piece-rate pay under which industrial workers get paid according to the number of pieces of work they accomplish. This piece-rate model states that

$$O_A / I_A \;=\; O_B / I_B.$$

A third model comes from information integration theory, by viewing the situation as a compromise between competing forces. The decision averaging model of Equation 2c implies

$$O_A / (O_A + O_B) \;=\; I_A / (I_A + I_B).$$

a. Intuitively, why might the comparison process be easier in Aristotle's model than in the piece-rate model?

b. Show that these three fairness models are algebraically equivalent and so cannot be distinguished empirically.

c. Each fairness model can be expanded to an unfairness model by taking the difference between the left and right sides. Aristotle's model becomes

$$U_A \;=\; \text{Unfairness to } A \;=\; O_A / O_B - I_A / I_B.$$

Consider a two-way, $O_A \times O_B$ design, with fixed values of I_A and I_B. Show how the pattern of the two-way factorial graph can distinguish between the three unfairness models.

d. All four factors were manipulated in the experiment of Figure 21.9, which shows the six two-factor graphs (see also Note 7.5.1b, page 213). Interpret these data patterns in terms of each unfairness model.

b7. Prove the two conclusions of the linear fan theorem.

b8. Optimal behavior follows algebraic models many judgment–decision tasks. Such models form a base for most major approaches to judgment–decision theory. An attractive hypothesis is that cognition obeys these same models, but with subjective values of the stimulus informers. Since the parallelism and

746

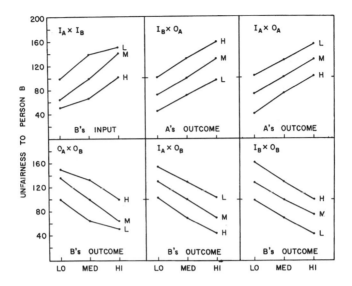

Figure 21.9. Processing structure in judgments of unfairness revealed in factorial data patterns. (After Anderson & Farkas, 1975; see further Farkas, 1991.)

linear fan theorems allow for subjective values, they can test this hypothesis, as was done with subjective expected value in Figure 21.7.

In one judgment–decision task, the subject sees two urns, each with a specified known proportion of red and white beads. One urn is picked with specified known probability, and one bead is drawn at random from that urn. Subjects judge the probability that the bead will be white.

    a. What algebraic model is implied by probability theory?

    b. Figure 21.10 shows the three two-factor graphs from an experiment that varied all three factors. How well do these data support the model?

c. Exercises for Averaging Model

c1. Giving more informers of equal value produces a more extreme belief; this is the *set-size effect*. This set-size effect is contrary to a simple averaging model, but can be explained by assuming that subjects average an internal informer, the *initial state* or *prior belief*, together with the given informers. Including this initial state, Equation 2a becomes

$$\rho_{jk} = \frac{\omega_A \psi_{Aj} + \omega_B \psi_{Bk} + \omega_0 \psi_0}{\omega_A + \omega_B + \omega_0}.$$

    a. Why is set-size effect contrary to averaging model without initial state?

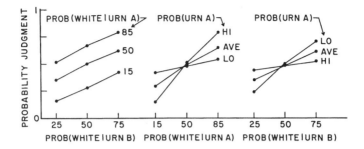

Figure 21.10. Addition–multiplication model for subjective expected probability confirmed by factorial graphs. Urn A has 15, 50, or 85 white beads in 100; urn B has 25, 50, or 75 white beads in 100. Choice of urn A over urn B is made with Hi, Ave, or Lo probability; one bead is chosen at random from the chosen urn. Plotted response is judged probability this chosen bead will be white. (From N. H. Anderson, *Foundations of Information Integration Theory*, Academic Press, 1981.)

b. Show how this explanation of the set-size effect works for the following numerical example: Each informer has value 100; prior belief has value 50; weights of 1 for each informer and for prior belief. Compare theoretical response to a single informer and a pair of informers of equal value.

c. Develop a general formula in place of the foregoing numerical example, assuming each informer has value ψ and weight ω. Set $\omega_0 = 1 - \omega$.

d. Extend the formula of (c) to allow n informers.

c2. This exercise continues Exercise 20.a5 on serial belief integration.

a. Show that prior belief has the same weight as the first serial position.

b. Use the given value parameters and the estimated weights to calculate an inferred belief for each informer sequence. Plot these as a horizontal *tree diagram*—as a set of eight curves, each with three data points for the three successive serial positions. It is common to base the tree at an assumed prior value for the initial state. The branch for sequence 101 would thus be 50, 75.00, 42.86, and 63.64.

c3. Assume plausible numerical values to illustrate that the averaging model can predict the data pattern for the toy experiment of Figure 21.5.

c4. An information integration approach to signal detection theory may be illustrated with the following task of recognition memory. First, subjects receive familiarity training with a considerable number of faces, words, or other stimuli. Recognition memory is then tested by presenting a group of, say, four stimuli in a simultaneous row, some "old," some "new." The four positions in the row may be considered a 2^4 design, with "old" and "new" as the two levels of each factor. Subjects rate familiarity of the group as a whole, assumed here to be an equally weighted average of the individual stimuli.

a. How plausible do you consider the averaging model for this task?

b. How can the averaging model of (a) be tested with the indicated design?

c. Suppose equivalent informers are used at each serial position. Ideally, all four main effects are equal. Why might you nevertheless expect larger main effects (i) at later (ii) earlier positions?

d. How could this approach be used to measure effect of varied numbers of presentations of the stimuli in the original familiarity training?

e. It would be a lot simpler to obtain familiarity ratings of single stimuli rather than of a group. How could success of the averaging model show that these single stimulus ratings provide a true linear scale?

c5. To extend the decision averaging model to n alternatives, ask subjects to divide a graphic scale into n parts, each part representing strength of one alternative. (a) How does this task relate to Equation 2c? (b) Get a consistency check with suitably chosen groups of two and three alternatives. (c) Discuss one testable alternative to the foregoing extension to three alternatives.

c6. Individual differences can be quantified and analyzed with averaging theory. In personality theory, *response dispositions* are tendencies to evaluate another person in certain ways, independent of specific information about that person. Some people tend to view others positively, some view others negatively. Martin Kaplan (1971a,b) argued that response disposition may be considered the initial state in the averaging model. Disposition, represented by $\omega_0 - \psi_0$ and measured with the Kaplan Checklist, is thus one informer, to be averaged with given informers about some person, real or hypothetical.

Give the averaging model for this task, assuming n given informers of equal weight, ω, and equal value, ψ. Let ω_0 and ψ_0 represent weight and value for subject's disposition. Derive predictions a–d (all verified experimentally).

a. For a fixed number of informer stimuli, a factorial design based on disposition and informer value will produce parallelism in the factorial plot.

b. Disposition effects will decrease as number of informers increases.

c. Disposition effects decrease as informer weight increases.

d. Subjects with positive dispositions will rate others more favorably.

e.* Outline an experimental test of the process underlying prediction (d).

f. An alternative hypothesis is that disposition affects informer values directly. Does this hypothesis make the same four predictions?

g.* Extend (e) to projective personality tests (e.g., Mischel, 1986, pp. 62*ff*), in which disposition affects response to ambiguous situations.

c7.* Besides dispositions (previous exercise), our knowledge systems contain other contents used in valuation of single stimuli, prior to integration. Can you find a way to study knowledge systems for ego defense, such as avoiding blame (Anderson, 1991j), or Freudian projection, using functional measurement to determine weight and value of given informer stimuli?

c8. In the task introduced by Schmidt and Levin (1972), subjects judge difference in likableness of two persons described by one or two trait adjectives. Let Diff_{A-B} denote the judged difference between two persons described by traits A and B, respectively; let Diff_{AX-BX} denote the judged difference between two persons described by the same A and B, plus the trait X, common to both. Assume each difference judgment equals the difference between the (implicit) judgments of the separate persons (Anderson, 1982, pp. 257f, Note 5.4h).

    a. Show that an addition model predicts that $\text{Diff}_{A-B} = \text{Diff}_{AX-BX}$, but that the averaging model with equal weights makes a different prediction.

    b. Show that the averaging model with equal weights implies that Diff_{AX-BX} is independent of X.

    c. Suppose that more negative X traits have greater weight. What trend in Diff_{AX-BX} is predicted by the averaging model?

    d. What experimental manipulation would you use to test prediction (d)?

c9. The *positive context effect* is a critical issue in the theory of information integration: If the informers in a set are related in some way, the judgment of an individual informer moves toward the value of the other informers.

In one typical experiment, subjects first form an impression of a person A, described by two favorable traits and one medium trait; they then rate the likableness value of the medium trait according to "How much you like that trait of that person." These judgments are repeated for person B, described by two unfavorable traits and the same medium trait.

The data show a strong positive context effect: The medium trait is rated substantially higher in person A than in person B.

    a. How can the meaning change hypothesis explain this effect?

    b. Alternatively, the positive context effect my be a generalized halo effect: The judgment of the medium trait is an average of its context-free value and the value of the person impression. The medium trait does not change value when the subject forms an impression of the person. Instead, the positive context effect results because the overall impression of the person acts on the post-impression judgment of the medium trait.

    Some words have a broad range of meaning (e.g., *nice*), others have a narrow range (e.g., *prompt*). Several investigators used this fact to test between meaning change and halo process as explanations of the positive context effect. What was their reasoning?

Preface

Communication is vital in science. We hope our grant application will make clear the importance of our proposed research to the grant panel. We hope the reviewers and editor will appreciate the contribution of the papers we submit and accept them for publication. We hope others will read our published articles and understand them.

Unclear writing will obstruct our hopes; clear writing will help attain them. Five principles of clear writing are discussed in the first part of this chapter.

Main Point Principle. Focus at once on the Main Point. Tell the reader where each paragraph is going by beginning with the Main Point. Use headers to flag the Main Point of each section and subsection. Don't let secondary and tangential material confuse the reader about your Main Point.

Revise Principle. Clear writing requires work. Initial drafts are generally fuzzy and ill-organized because our ideas are not yet clear. One benefit of writing is to make our ideas clear. Even after our ideas have become clear to ourselves, much revision is usually needed to make them clear to others.

Less Is More Principle. You will be successful if most readers dig out and appreciate your Main Point. Don't water down the Main Point with secondary and tangential points. Use headers to segregate secondary material from the Main Point.

Paragraph Principle. Ideally, each paragraph begins with its Main Point. This provides a schema for the reader to organize the subsequent arguments. And ideally, each paragraph ends with a restatement of its Main Point.

Reader Communication Principle. Write for the reader. What counts is how much gets communicated. This principle is self-evident, but it is hard to apply. Effective writing requires practice.

Tactics of Writing. The second part of this chapter gives various tactics of writing. These are organized around standard format for experimental articles. Two tactics deserve special mention.

First, the Less Is More Principle applies especially to statistics. As an antidote to statisticitis, try writing the first draft using only visual inspection. Second, use two-level organization to separate detail needed by the specialist from the Main Points needed by the general reader.

These principles and tactics are generally agreed on by those who write books on how to write. A number of these books, all of which offer excellent advice, are reviewed in a chapter note.

Chapter 22

PRINCIPLES AND TACTICS OF WRITING PAPERS

Writing papers helps develop your ideas. Nearly everyone feels greater understanding after having written a paper. In writing a Discussion section, you have
to think out implications of your results, showing how they relate to your own
theory, to other results, and to other interpretations. Such systematic thinking
leads to fuller appreciation of the problem you are studying.

A second function of writing is to communicate. We put a lot of heart and
soul into our research. We believe it makes a worthwhile contribution, one that
deserves attention. Accordingly, we expect others to read our published papers.

Most published papers, however, are read by few people. One reason is time
pressure. When you write a paper, you are competing for the reader's time.
Poorly written papers repel readers; well-written papers attract readers. Five
principles and a handful of tactics in the next two sections can make a big
difference to your status in the field.[a]

22.1 FIVE PRINCIPLES

The following five principles are basic to effective writing. They can be found,
in one or another form, in every discussion of how to write scientific articles.

22.1.1 MAIN POINT PRINCIPLE

The most important principle is to **begin** with the Main Point. The Main Point
sets up a schema with which the reader can organize the argument and details
that follow. This schema focuses attention on what is central and facilitates
dealing with what is auxiliary.

It may not be elegant to begin with "The purpose of this article is to . . . ,"
but it is effective communication. "The issue of X has been controversial . . ."
is better, but the Main Point should be clearly stated in the first paragraph and,
if possible, in the first sentence.

The Main Point Principle violates the natural progression from premise to
conclusion. A natural way is to begin with the premises and proceed by
reasoned arguments to the conclusion. This progression seems natural to the
writer who knows where the argument is headed. But to the reader who does
not, this progression can be difficult.

A corollary is to **end** with the Main Point. This tells the reader you have
arrived. It gives closure. Also, it leaves the Main Point freshest in memory.

Applied to the whole article, the Main Point Principle advises: Leave the
reader with one main idea to remember. Any article will contain a mass of
detail about method, results, and relations to the literature. Readers easily get
sidetracked by subsidiary ideas and the Main Point becomes confused and
entangled with secondary issues. It is enough if they remember the Main Point
well enough to refer back to the article as needed. Make sure the main idea
stands out stark and clear from the mass of surrounding details. In summary:

Begin with the Main Point. End with the Main Point.

22.1.2 REVISE PRINCIPLE

A useful rule for the first draft is "Don't get it right, just get it written."
Marshal your ideas in a preliminary outline. Then write as much as you can as
fast as you can. Get your ideas down in black and white, without worrying
about form or order.

Most papers require repeated revision. Initial revision begins at the higher
levels of organization. Don't worry over words, sentences, and paragraphs in
initial drafts; that's wasted time because they generally need extensive revision
as the overall organization clarifies.

The main problem in initial drafts is usually to work out one's ideas. One's
ideas, which had seemed so clear, somehow liquefy and become elusive upon
beginning to write. This experience arises because much thinking is not in the
form of words. To translate nonverbal thoughts into verbal form can be frustrating. At the same time, our ideas often rest on implicit assumptions that need to
be thought through and made explicit.

After having developed a reasonable draft, put the paper aside for a week or
so. When you resume, unclarities and tangential material will stand out better
and be easier to deal with.

Working out one's ideas, although often painful, is generally rewarding.
The best reward is to uncover unsuspected implications of the results or extensions of the theoretical framework. Writing a paper is an important process of
self-development.

22.1.3 LESS IS MORE PRINCIPLE

The principle that good writing is concise goes back at least to Roman times. It has been emphasized by those who write for a living, and is even more appropriate for scientific communication.

"Omit needless words!" Unnecessary words dilute meaning and impact. Tangential and secondary ideas sidetrack the reader and obscure the Main Point. The injunction just quoted was given in the *Elements of Style* by Strunk (1972, pp. ix*f*), who elaborated thus:

> Vigorous writing is concise. A sentence should contain no unnecessary words, a paragraph no unnecessary sentences, for the same reason that a drawing should have no unnecessary lines and a machine no unnecessary parts. This requires not that the writer make all his sentences short, or that he avoid all detail and treat his subjects only in outline, but that every word tell.

As E. B. White says in his revision of Strunk's book:

> There you have a short, valuable essay on the nature and beauty of brevity— sixty-three words that could change the world.

The Less Is More Principle applies generally, not just to omitting unnecessary words. Secondary ideas, speculations, and references obscure the Main Point. Most readers do well if they dig out and appreciate your Main Point. Secondary material tends to dilute the Main Point and sidetrack the reader. When secondary material is presented, segregate it from the Main Point.

22.1.4 PARAGRAPH PRINCIPLE

The paragraph is a primary unit of exposition. Each paragraph, as a rule, should contain one idea—and only one. Auxiliary ideas may be incorporated, of course, as part of the argument of the paragraph. At the end of the paragraph, however, the reader should have in mind one idea. This idea will usually be linked with ideas from preceding and following paragraphs, but it should have a distinct identity, just as a link in a chain.[a]

By the Main Point Principle, the first sentence of each paragraph should, if at all possible, state the Main Point of that paragraph. Beginning with the conclusion is effective communication. It leaves the reader clear about where the paragraph is headed; it provides a schema for organizing the argument of the paragraph on which the conclusion is based.

As a concrete example, a paragraph in the Results could begin "Figure 1 shows a pattern of parallelism, suggesting the operation of an adding-type model." The first paragraph of the Discussion could begin "The parallelism observed in the present factorial graphs supports the hypothesis of meaning invariance: Two or more verbal stimuli that are combined in a description of a person act independently, with no interaction between them."

The paragraph is as basic to written language as the sentence, but it is notably more difficult. Writing sentences comes fairly naturally; writing paragraphs does not. A paragraph requires a meaningful progression of thought that often requires repeated application of the Revise Principle, in part because the material resists linear ordering, in part because the writer is still clarifying the ideas.[b]

22.1.5 READER COMMUNICATION PRINCIPLE

What counts is whether your paper gets read and understood—how much gets communicated. The reader is the criterion. Aim at the reader.

Many people have difficulty with the Reader Communication Principle. One reason is lack of fluency, a lack with which I sympathize. Like many others, I find it hard enough in the first draft to get my ideas into rough meaningful form, without worrying too much about the reader. The Reader Communication Principle, however, is self-evident. It can be applied in revision, after the initial draft is written.

Have some reader in mind. This is essential in some sense, but not a few writers lack skills to look at what they write from an external view. They see what they intended to write, not what the words actually say to another person. I suggest aiming at a second-year graduate student, perhaps a specific person. Have him or her in the background in your initial draft and in the foreground in later drafts.

Discussions of how to write typically proclaim *Clarity* as a basic principle. Clarity is a grand ideal, but *be clear* is an injunction rather than a principle. We all aspire to be clear; what we need are the skills to attain clarity. The foregoing principles all aim at clarity. The tactics in the next section can help you develop your writing skills.

22.2 TACTICS OF WRITING

The writing tactics considered here are addressed to the typical empirical paper. Each following section, except the first and last, takes up one standard section of an empirical paper. Although these tactics are stated somewhat absolutely, they are meant to be applied flexibly. Every paper presents its own expositional problems that require judgment for their solution. To the extent that you master these tactics, you can proceed to develop the style most congenial to you.

22.2.1 TWO-LEVEL ORGANIZATION

A unique problem of exposition must be resolved in the typical empirical paper. It needs to be written at two distinct levels, one general, one specific.

The general level includes the main points: the purpose of the study, the idea of the task, the pattern of the data, and the theoretical implications. These main points are what you want your readers to understand and retain in memory.

The specific level includes the diverse details of task, procedure, and design. These details are necessary for the expert in your field to assess the quality of your work, the conceptual importance of your task, for example, and the likelihood of confounds that may trouble your interpretation. Analogous detail, sometimes extensive, may be needed in presenting the data analysis. These details are also needed for others to follow up your work.

The specifics interfere with the general. The specifics cannot be omitted because they determine the validity of your results. But readers are mainly interested in the general. Unless they find the Main Point interesting, the details are hardly worthwhile. Moreover, an article that requires readers to plow through a lot of detail will have few readers.

The primary tactic, therefore, is to write at two levels, the level of the main points and the level of details. Organize the paper so that those readers who wish to skim or skip the details can do so. Such two-level exposition, as it may be called, turns out to be easier than it sounds.

Two-level exposition depends on signals for skimming and skipping. The ubiquitous headers in scientific articles facilitate such two-level exposition. This two-level function is most apparent in Method, which you should expect readers to skim-skip at first reading. In Results, such headers as *Main Results* and *Supplementary Analyses* have similar expositional functions.

The first sentence of a paragraph can be a skip signal: ''The statistical analyses largely confirm the visual inspection;'' ''Some additional aspects of the data . . .'' and ''The results of P and Q might seem to differ from the present finding . . . '' are as much as many readers will need to read.

Such organizing devices can structure an article so the general reader can get the main point with minimal time and effort. The details are there, available if and when they become important to the reader. With such two-level organization, you can increase what counts, namely, the number of people who read your article and remember the Main Point.

22.2.2 METHOD

The Method section is a good place to begin writing your paper. You thus get on your way with the material that is most readily organized and most easily written.

An ideal Method, to exaggerate a little, is one that does not have to be read the first time through the paper. The first reading is usually at the general level, mentioned previously, whereas Method mostly involves the specific level.

Method, accordingly, should be organized for skimming and skipping. An initial paragraph that summarizes the task–procedure allows the reader to skim-skip to Results. The less Method you require your readers to read, the more readers you will have.

For the rest, organize the material with headers and subheaders. Headers serve a threefold function. They structure your exposition. They serve as signals for skimming and skipping. And they help readers relocate specific information that they may require at various points in Results or Discussion.

22.2.3 RESULTS

Begin with the Main Point. An ideal Results would begin ''Figure 1 shows the main results. The pattern of these data . . . '' Following paragraphs would fill out the visual inspection and substantive interpretation.

Many articles contain a number of results. Organize these results with headers, which have the three functions just listed in the previous section.

Figures should be explained. A well-made figure is largely self-explanatory, of course, through its labels and legend. But don't leave the reader to sink or swim. Guide the reader's visual inspection by explicit reference to experimental treatments represented by specific curves. Explain how the elevations and shapes of the curves reflect the experimental treatments. This explanation does not have to be complete, but it should ensure that the reader comprehends the main pattern of the data.

Tables need explanation more than figures. Many readers suffer wholistic dazzle when confronted by a table. Help them. Point to illustrative numbers to indicate how the table is organized and what trends it shows.

The Main Point Principle implies that formal statistics should ordinarily be deferred until the overall data pattern has been described. Beginning Results with something like ''A $3 \times 5 \times 4$ Anova was run, with repeated measures on the first two factors . . . '' is just horrible. In some cases, of course, including a confidence interval along with the means in the running text may be appropriate. Often, however, the statistical analyses require considerable detail. This detail should be largely deferred until the main pattern of the data has been made clear. A separate header, *Statistical Analysis*, is a good expositional device. With relatively simple analyses, it may suffice to begin a new paragraph with "The statistical analysis generally supported the trends noted in Figure 1."

Data are primary, statistics secondary. The Anova is not the data. Don't obscure the Main Point with secondary considerations.

The Less Is More Principle applies especially to statistics. The malign overplus of statistics common in current articles reflects lack of understanding, both of science and of scientific exposition, perhaps accompanied by apprehensive beginner's fears of reviewer criticism. As an antidote to statisticitis, I recommend writing the first draft of Results without any significance tests. At that point, you can see what statistical analyses need to be reported, what do not.

Sometimes, it is true, considerable statistical detail is needed. The design may be complex or the data may be analyzed in terms of some mathematical model. Sometimes, accordingly, considerable statistical analysis is necessary. For the most part, however, less statistics means more reader communication.

22.2.4 DISCUSSION

It is customary and helpful to begin Discussion with a more or less self-contained overview of the main findings. A reader who later returns to your article can thus get back online with minimum effort. Other readers will be delighted to skip directly from Abstract to Discussion. What counts, besides pride of workmanship in your published contributions, is what gets read.

The Discussion is the place to relate your main results to the literature. Other articles are thus considered in relevant context. This is one reason for minimizing references in the Introduction.

Some studies have secondary findings that must also be related to the literature. Often a good solution is to place such secondary discussion in Results, under an appropriate header. This avoids diluting Discussion with material that may have little interest to most readers.

Brevity in Discussion has much to be said for it. Some writers like to spin out possible implications of their results and directions for future work. This may be intensely interesting to the author, but will likely turn off the reader. Do not end Discussion in this way; end with the Main Point. You will have few enough readers who comprehend your Main Point; don't dim their understanding by diluting your strong points with weak points.

22.2.5 INTRODUCTION

Do the Introduction last.

An Introduction should fulfill its name by setting the reader on a clear path to what is to follow. Until you have written what follows, you are seldom sure what it will be. In writing Results, for example, relative importance of published articles may alter considerably as you work out the implications of your data. Or some supplementary analysis may be required that puts a new slant on the outcome. If you write your Introduction first, it is almost sure to be out of joint with Results.

Even more should Introduction be deferred until after Discussion has been written. Writing Discussion requires clarifying and extending your ideas. This often entails a shift in emphasis. Old ideas are seen in new light; new ideas may move to center place. Until you have finished your Discussion, therefore, you can hardly set the reader on a clear path to it, as your Introduction should do.

Be brief.

What is important are your results and the interpretation you put on them. Use the Introduction to set up your problem, to indicate why it is interesting, and to get the reader on to the Main point—your results and interpretation—as swiftly as you can.

An Introduction is not generally expected to be a review of the literature. The extensive literature reviews expected in dissertations are seldom appropriate for experimental articles; that is the function of review articles. Indeed, most references to the literature should be in Results and Discussion—contiguous to the relevant material. Do not repeat these references in the Introduction unless they are essential at that point.

Of course, longer Introductions are sometimes appropriate. In some cases, a fairly extensive theoretical development may be needed, as with certain controversial issues or with some mathematical models. In other cases, a fairly extensive review of the literature may be useful to the reader, as with a study of some uncommon issue. Unless there is a clear, definite need, however, the Introduction should be brief.

Apply the five principles.

The Main Point Principle counsels you to use the first sentence and paragraph to set up a schema the reader can use to organize and assimilate the subsequent material. The Less Is More Principle cautions against diverting attention from your main ideas with theoretical complications, tangential considerations, and peripheral references. The Paragraph Principle directs you to see each paragraph as a single organized unit of thought. The Reader Communication Principle, implemented with the Revise Principle, tells you to structure the Introduction to what the reader needs to move right on to Results and Discussion.

22.2.6 REFERENCES

References have two related functions: To guide the reader to relevant literature, and to give proper credit to previous workers.

Reader guidance may best be achieved by limiting references to those essential to the argument of the article. The survey of the literature expected in a thesis or a review article is out of place in the typical experimental article. A long list of references is often just window dressing—ersatz scholarship.

Giving proper credit is sometimes obscured under criticism. Any interesting question evokes differences of opinion. It is overly easy to pick fault with other studies and gloss over their contributions. Any experiment, no matter how painstaking, has limitations and insufficiencies. The natural tendency to focus on such limitations is easily overdone, especially because it makes one's own contribution seem more substantial. It is generally preferable, therefore, to commend previous workers and present one's own work as a complement and extension. In scientific research, as everywhere in life, the Golden Rule is: Give praise, not blame.

References should be correct. This self-evident rule is often not obeyed. Correctness requires checking the final list against the original sources word by word and number by number. For this, a xerox of the first page of every article is useful. Ideally, one person should read the original reference while a second person checks the file or hard copy. Each reference that has been checked should have a file note to this effect.

22.2.7 ABSTRACT

Abstracts get read. Much more than the articles themselves. This is your main opportunity to communicate. For some readers, your Abstract will tell them they need to read the full article. For many, your Abstract will be as far as they go, at least for the moment. Make the most of this opportunity.

Begin with the Main Point.

Don't cite statistical tests.

Give only essentials of design and procedure.

Apply the Less Is More Principle and the Reader Communication Principle. Strike out such noninformative statements as "Analysis of variance showed that . . . " and "Implications for further work were discussed." Don't try to give a complete summary; readers who are interested by the Abstract can read the full article.

22.2.8 NOTE ON UNCLEAR REFERENT

The problem of unclear referent is so troublesome that it deserves specific comment. Unclear referent is epitomized in "this." When writers use "this," they presume the reader knows what "this" refers to. Very often the reader will not know. The referent of "this" may be some general implication of the preceding discussion; or there may be more than one possible referent; or the reader may not have comprehended the argument; or "this" may paper over a hole in the argument. Such ambiguity does not trouble the writer because "this" is at the focus of immediate attention as the writer writes.

My suggestion is to go through a near-final draft and scrutinize each and every "this," especially "thises" that begin sentences. Replace most with the explicit referent. The explicit referent avoids possible unclarity. Also, it increases meaningfulness directly by placing the needed idea in the reader's mind just when it is needed.[a]

22.3 BETTER COMMUNICATION SKILLS

Some excellent books on scientific writing are available. All can be studied with profit, and I have summarized some in Note 22.3a to indicate special features that may be of interest. These books show striking agreement on principles and tactics.[a]

Writing skills develop slowly with practice. It is easy to agree on principles and tactics; the hard problem is to integrate them into your writing habits. One way is through revision, as you weed out your own infelicities.

The best way to learn to write, I believe, is through exercises: Multiple choice of selecting the best word to complete a phrase or sentence; awkward sentences that are to be rewritten; unclear sentences that need to be revised; disorganized paragraphs that need to be organized; and others.

The foregoing principles and tactics are no substitute for such exercises. The Paragraph Principle, for example, is simple to understand, hard to implement. One's ideas and sentences get tangled up and resist the linear structure demanded by clear writing. For most of us, learning by doing is slow going. A book of exercises can provide directed practice. However, I have found only one book that incorporates such exercises (Zeiger, 1991), and it deals with biomedical material that is not too meaningful to most psychologists. A similar book, oriented toward psychologists, would be invaluable.

I believe that every department of human sciences has an obligation to provide instruction in communication, teaching as well as writing. Effective communication is important for professional success and should not be left to happenstance, as it is at present. A regular class seems essential, in which students evaluate one another's writing. Such experience also makes it easier to appreciate and apply the principles and tactics presented in books on writing. Training for teaching is even more obligatory.

NOTES

22a. One reason for including a chapter on writing skills in a book on design and analysis is to emphasize that statistical analysis has secondary place in your Results section. Instead, the data and their plain meaning should dominate Results. The Less Is More Principle applies especially to reporting statistical analysis.

This chapter on writing also emphasizes that design and analysis are part of scientific communication. An article is a package of information. Design−analysis and exposition go hand in hand. Good design and good analysis facilitate good writing.

Writing skills, as essential as they are, are utterly neglected in most graduate schools. I have for many years included one lecture on writing in my design−analysis course, but one lecture can barely sensitize students to the issues. A graduate course in scientific writing would be far more effective than any book that relies on self-study.

22.1.4a. The Paragraph Principle is one case of a more general Unit Principle—that unitization of thought and idea is vital for communication. Other basic units are the Sentence and the Section.

The conception of *sentences* as units is integral to language structure, especially written language. Each written sentence has a beginning, indicated by a capital, and an end, indicated by a period. The capital prepares your mind to receive an idea; the period signals that the idea has now been presented. If the sentence is well-written, enough of that idea will have been communicated to allow you to proceed. Capital and period are basic inventions for organization of thought.

Sections as units are prescribed in the standard format for experimental reports: Abstract, Introduction, Method, Results, Discussion, and References. Further section levels may appear within each of these main sections, indicated by headers. Typical Method and Results sections contain two or three levels of header.

Section unitization has a twofold function. It helps the writer organize the exposition. Similarly, it guides the reader in assimilating the material. The importance of both functions is recognized and formalized in the standard use of headers and sub-headers in scientific communication.

22.1.4b. The Paragraph Principle is universally accepted. Zeiger (1991) uses the two useful terms of Topic Sentence, which corresponds to the present Main Point, and Supporting Sentences, which emphasizes that the paragraph is a conceptual unit, organized under the Topic Sentence.

22.2.8a. A note may be added on first-person style, which is more readable than impersonal style. "I think this result means . . ." is more alive and interesting than "The present interpretation of this result is . . . ."

One objection to first-person style is that most writers become self-conscious and awkward with "I" and "we." Their self intrudes between the reader and the material. With "I think that," the writer's opinion begins to displace objective content.

My own objection is that first-person style is just a cosmetic device. It diverts attention from more basic writing problems. Not one of the foregoing principles and tactics has any essential relation to first-person style. By removing your self from what you write, you can better understand what your words will be saying to your reader.

First-person style can be appropriate in a theoretical article and in other cases. Even in these cases, however, it may be advisable to defer use of first person until you have mastered an impersonal style.

First-person style in this book has two purposes. "We" is intended to involve the reader, who sits at my left hand as I write, whom I consider a partner in comprehending what is written. In this usage, "we" is fairly common in texts when it would not be in a journal article. "I" is used mostly to indicate a position on which there is, or may be, disagreement, or an opinion on an issue for which adequate evidence is not available.

22.3a.   Some excellent guides to scientific writing are available. Those cited here come in inexpensive paperback. The classic is *The Elements of Style* (Strunk & White, 1972) quoted in the text. Of special value are the sections entitled "Make the paragraph the unit of composition" and "Revise and rewrite." The two sections "Omit needless words" and "Avoid the use of qualifiers" are gems. Although this book is aimed at professional writers, its 78 pages are worthwhile for all who write.

A clear, sensible, and complete guide to science writing is *Writing Successfully in Science*, by O'Connor (1991), secretary-treasurer of the European Association of Science Editors, who thoughtfully considers how to write tables and figures before proceeding to problems of writing prose. Also included are chapters on submitting your paper, on presenting short talks and posters, and on grant applications and curricula vitae. Intended for all branches of science, the advice on length of Introduction deserves quotation: "One to three paragraphs should be enough for most journal articles" (p. 60).

Psychologist's Companion (Sternberg, 1993) goes beyond the experimental research paper to writing grant proposals and lectures. Chapter 6 is a useful discussion of the widely required style standards of the American Psychological Association. A strong beginning is made in Chapter 1 with "eight common misconceptions," one of which is quoted here:

> **Misconception 2:** *The important thing is what you say, not how you say it.* The second stage of discovery came when I found myself with just a few [student] papers to read, and plenty time in which to read them. Now, I thought, I can be fair both to students who write well and to those who do not. I was quickly disabused of this notion. I discovered that whereas it is usually easy to distinguish well-presented good ideas from well-presented bad ideas, it is often impossible to distinguish poorly presented good ideas from poorly presented bad ideas. (p. 2).

Scientists Must Write (Barrass, 1978) has been reprinted many times. Although aimed at more at physical sciences, it is well worth while for human sciences. Of special interest are four short chapters entitled "Think - plan - write - revise," "Thoughts into words," "Using words," and "Helping the reader." Also included are chapters on tables and a figures, and a final chapter on giving talks, including blackboard use.

The Craft of Research (Booth, Colomb, & Williams, 1995) is worth skimming for useful ideas, of which it has many. The term *research* in the title, however, mainly refers to library research, especially for term papers. Written by three professors of English, it has little direct relevance to scientific research. Its attraction is that the authors are intimately familiar with students' writing problems and present a well-articulated, common-sense approach. For the serious student, William's (1997) *Style: Ten Lessons in Clarity and Grace* deserves study.

The Maltese Falcon is widely praised for its literary style: simplicity, clarity, and precision. In this book, immortalized in film by Humphrey Bogart, Mary Astor, Sidney Greenstreet, and Peter Lorre, Dashiell Hammett brought his writing style to its peak, liberated the detective story to real life, and elevated it from pulp fiction to literature. Hanmett was much concerned with how to write, saying:

> Every writer who brings an idea to a blank sheet of paper is faced by the same primary task. He must set his idea on the paper in such form that it will have the effect he desires on those who read it. . . . Clarity is the first and greatest of literary virtues. . . . Simplicity and clarity . . . are the most elusive and difficult of literary accomplishments. (Quoted from Nolan, 1983, p. 65.)

Writing for Social Scientists (Becker, 1986) is a personalized account, based in part on Becker's own writing habits, in part on his classes on writing for graduate students in sociology. Although his personalized, narrative style is very different from the highly organized, topical style of the foregoing books, Becker makes many of the same points. Here are two quotes.

> I find unnecessary words by a simple test. As I read through my draft, I check each word and phrase to see what happens if I remove it. If the meaning does not change, I take it out. The deletion often makes me see what I really wanted there, and I put it in. I seldom take unnecessary words out of early drafts. I'll see them when I rewrite and either replace them with working words or cut them. (p. 81)

> Working as a book editor showed me a larger dimension of editing. I found that I could see an inner logic struggling to express itself in others' work more easily than I could see it in my own, just as I could see redundancy, fancy talk, and all the other faults in their prose more easily than in mine. (p. 99)

Becker advocates a plain style apparently uncongenial to a major trend in sociology, in which "classy" style tends to be professionalized (see his Chapter 2). Classy style is less a problem in psychology, but it does occur with classy terms of surplus meaning, most notably in personality theory and in the recent cognitive movement. The same malady, in different form, appears in the overdoses of statistics so common in psychology journals.

Perhaps the most effective book is *Essentials of Writing Biomedical Research Papers* (Zeiger, 1991). Detailed examples, both good and bad, are given for each topic: sentence structure, paragraph structure, the Discussion section, and others. Especially useful are exercises for the reader to correct. Most writing faults are common to all of us, but recognizing them in our own writing is hard. We tend to read what we intended to say, not what our words actually say. Correcting others' writing is illuminating, especially with examples selected to exhibit common faults. The author is a lecturer in scientific writing, a position every university should have, with a crisp, clear style. Regrettably, nearly all of Zeiger's examples deal with cardiovascular research, which detracts from their usefulness to psychological researchers. A parallel book oriented toward psychology is desirable.

Serve the Student should be the foundation and guide for educational systems. The measure of teaching is not what is taught, but what is learned. Teachers are coaches; their job is to coach students along their life paths of learning. Consonant with the cornerstone of **Serve the Student**, formal education should be conceptualized and organized as an organic part of lifelong learning.

Transfer is the goal of education. Instruction should facilitate development of knowledge systems and work skills that will be needed and useful in life. To be effectual, instruction needs to determine the structure and operation of knowledge systems in relation to life needs.

The foregoing principles are general; they apply to all teaching. What do they imply for the first-year graduate course in design and analysis? In this course, students need to develop abilities to understand data, design and conduct investigations, write reports of their investigations, and/or critically evaluate such reports by others. In short, they need to develop skills of scientific inference, whether in academic research or in the diverse applications of psychological science in practical affairs.

But scientific inference is primarily extrastatistical. The knowledge systems needed in scientific inference are mainly empirical, as was discussed with the Experimental Pyramid of Chapter 1. Statistical inference should thus be subordinated to and integrated with extrastatistical inference based on substantive knowledge systems. **Serve the Student** thus leads to an empirical direction in design and analysis.

This empirical direction is pursued in this book. Other texts, in contrast, are dominated by a statistical perspective appropriate for the statistics department, but ill-suited to an empirical department. Statistical concepts and techniques can be invaluable in empirical research, but they need to be learned—and taught—as organic parts of scientific inference.

This book is only a step in this empirical direction. The first-year course in design and analysis is a concern of the whole field. It deserves cooperation among those who teach statistics in every institution. It deserves cooperation from other faculty whose students take this course. Above all, it deserves massive empirical research on effective teaching and transfer. The main concern of this book is to facilitate development of the empirical perspective— as a guide along our personal paths of lifelong learning.

Chapter 23

LIFELONG LEARNING

Graduate school is one stage along our path of lifelong learning. Our goal should be to develop knowledge systems that will make our lives and work more effective and more rewarding.

Knowledge systems about interpretation of data and about design of investigations are central to accomplishment. Such knowledge is needed in every field of psychology. Such knowledge can also help with some problems of everyday life, both in work and in home life.

Understanding the structure and functioning of such knowledge systems is prerequisite for effective teaching, as measured by effective learning. Without such understanding, teaching and learning will be haphazard and doctrinaire.

23.1 EMPIRICAL DIRECTION

The theme of this book is that design and analysis are best learned within an empirical framework. This empirical direction requires both justification and elaboration: Justification for the substantial differences from comparable texts; elaboration because this book is only one step and needs further development.

23.1.1 STRATEGY OF THIS BOOK

The strategy of this book flows from the Experimental Pyramid, reproduced on the next page. Empirical inquiry is largely extrastatistical inference; statistical inference is a minor means to an extrastatistical end. The usefulness of statistical inference depends on how well it is subordinated to and integrated with scientific inference, that is, with extrastatistical knowledge systems.

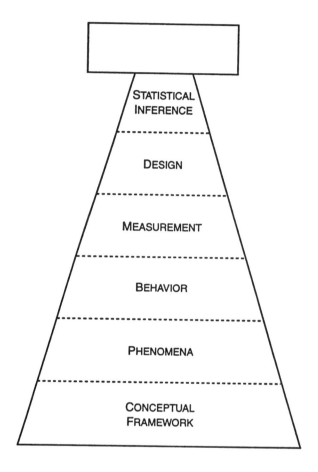

Figure 23.1. Experimental Pyramid.

Experimental Pyramid. The philosophy of this book is summarized in the Experimental Pyramid of Figure 23.1, previously discussed in Chapter 1. Two issues, generality and confounding, illustrate this empirical philosophy.

Generality is the most important aspect of scientific inference. Every investigator seeks to generalize results from some sample to a larger population. That such generalization can be made precise, under certain idealized assumptions, is an impressive and invaluable achievement of statistical theory.

Empirically, however, generalization rests mainly on extrastatistical considerations. Rarely do we have a random sample of subjects from a well-defined population. Often we generalize to a population quite different from our sample. Generalization from experiments with animals, for example, is common in introductory psychology texts, which discuss numerous studies with the white rat, monkey, and other animals that we believe shed light on human behavior. Other empirical facets of generalization are discussed in Section 1.4.

Confounding is hardly less important than generality. Controversies in the literature usually revolve around questions of confounding. Most questions of confounding, however, involve substantive, extrastatistical considerations, extensively illustrated in Chapter 8.

Statistical methods can make helpful, sometimes vital, contributions to problems of generality and confounding. These contributions require empirical judgment, however, in which the statistical considerations are integrated into the substantive structure of investigation.

Statistical Perspective and Substantive Perspective. In the standard statistical perspective, the data are taken as given; the function of statistics is to assess evidence value of the data. Concern with substantive considerations goes little further than the assumptions of the statistical techniques. This statistical perspective, natural in a statistics department, also dominates texts and courses on experimental design and statistics in empirical departments.

This statistical perspective has the great attraction that the same basic concepts and techniques apply in every field. By disregarding substantive considerations, statistical concepts and techniques can be presented in a uniform way in their purest logical form.

The big shortcoming of this statistical perspective is lack of transfer. In empirical science, statistical concepts and techniques have value only as they transfer into empirical practice. Transfer depends on substantive considerations, especially about pros and cons of possible designs and possible response measures. Learning to make such substantive judgments is harder than learning statistical assumptions and formulas. But for that very reason, substantive considerations need primary emphasis in statistics teaching.[a]

A related shortcoming of the statistical perspective is that many useful techniques are not really content-free. Within subject design is one example among many. The statistical techniques require only a short chapter. More important is the substantive issue whether within subject design should be used at all (pages 425*ff*). The great statistical advantages of these designs must be balanced against extrastatistical judgments about risks from confounding with position and carryover effects. The statistical arguments about how within subject data should be analyzed, whether with ε-adjusted Anova or with Manova, are trifling compared to substantive questions about position and carryover effects that may require elaboration of within subject designs, as with Latin squares or interpolated baseline treatment, or even recourse to between subject design. The standard emphasis on statistical assumptions obscures such design problems, which are prior to and more important than the Anova table.

These arguments for substantive perspective apply also to reading the literature. As one illustration, I have used the 2 × 2 data table of Exercise 5.10 for many years to illustrate a misuse of factorial Anova. This exercise seems clear since both experimental hypotheses are two-mean comparisons, both quoted verbatim and freed from surrounding verbiage. Yet not a few students are slow to appreciate that the data analysis should follow the experimental hypotheses; and that the interaction test in the original article is irrelevant and misleading. Indeed, the prevailing unclarity about statistical interactions (Chapter 7) reemphasizes the need for empirical framework in statistics instruction.

To learn statistics, therefore, the substantive perspective should be primary for empirical workers. The same should hold for teaching statistics.

Transfer. The main aim of teaching should be to facilitate transfer— integration of statistical concepts and methods into an empirical framework of substantive inquiry. Bypassing the transfer problem is insidiously tempting. Statistics so readily lends itself to treatment as a self-contained body of knowledge that it readily comes to be taught that way. It has an inner beauty, moreover, in its logical structure and in the steady march of derivations and formulas that conjure certainty from uncertainty. In social sciences, in which so much is uncertain and controversial, these derivations and formulas can be a fine security blanket. The effectiveness of this security blanket can be seen in the plethora of statistical analyses that begrime so many published articles.

A further reason to bypass the transfer problem is that each substantive area poses unique problems of design, task, and measure. Very different considerations arise in studying language development, visual perception, behavior modification, animal behavior, person cognition, functional memory, and the other diverse areas of our diverse field. How to teach design and analysis to students who will be working in so many areas without getting overinvolved in any one is a difficult problem. This concern agrees with that of *Informal Reasoning and Education* (Voss, Perkins, & Segal, 1991, p. xi):

> Until recently, the phenomenon of contextualized reasoning, as opposed to abstract mathematical or logical reasoning, has received very little theoretical attention from psychologists. Although interest is now growing, the studies undertaken to date have been limited to a narrow range of reasoning situations. As a result . . . we continue to know very little about reasoning as it occurs in many other important everyday contexts, both at school and at work.

Transfer—and the difficulty of obtaining it—have been concerns of psychology since Thorndike's work early in the last century. The first step, clearly, is to ascertain what abilities are important in the transfer activity. The present discussion, accordingly, seeks to focus attention on the role and function of statistics texts in an empirical field.

Textbook Versus Handbook. Virtually all current texts seek two goals that are hardly compatible: To be a textbook for first-year graduate students and to be a handbook for advanced researchers. These two goals require different content and different modes of exposition. Attempts to achieve both goals require compromises that undercut both.

A first-year text should help students acquire basic concepts and skills. This requires fairly detailed coverage of a modest range of content. Some of this exposition needs to be rather elementary, moreover, because a significant proportion of first-year graduate students in psychology have minimal background in statistical thinking.

A handbook is oriented toward advanced researchers. It is to be kept at hand as an external memory or to leaf through for some alternative technique. Many techniques need to be included that will not be used often or by many. Compact exposition is desirable, in part to achieve extensive coverage in allowable space, in part to allow researchers to leaf through efficiently. Both characteristics are undesirable in a first-year text.

Current texts compromise these two goals. Seeking to be intelligible to first-year students, they adopt a level of exposition overly dilute and limited for the handbook function. This mode of exposition uses up space, so much that is important in a handbook must be omitted.

For the first-year student, the compromise is more serious. Because the texts are written in part for the advanced researcher, they include far more material than first-year students can cope with. The level of exposition is often compromised for the same reason. Unable to assimilate all the material, uncertain of what is essential, the first-year student is not in a good learning position. A common tactic is to develop skills of finding a numerical example in the text that shows how to do an assigned exercise at the end of the chapter. This short-circuits the main goal of developing skills of research judgment for integrating extrastatistical and statistical considerations.

Handbook and textbook are both needed. Both functions will be better served, however, if they are separated. A good handbook would be invaluable, and some current texts are well on their way to performing this function.[b]

This book is oriented toward the textbook function. The core material is given in Chapters 1–12. This core is adequate for most applications.

To some extent, this book also serves a handbook function, partly in chapter notes, but mainly in the later chapters. In this way, more advanced topics such as Latin squares, block design, fractional replication, unequal n, random factors, contrasts, nesting, pooling, transformations, curve shape, covariance, multiple regression, and quasi-experimental design, can be covered without compromising the textbook function of the core.

My aim has been to show the potential of these advanced topics with a minimum of technicalities. Pros and cons of each topic receive considerable discussion, but mainly at the level of common sense. Formulas and calculations are mostly left to statistical packages.

Low-Math Approach. Formulas have been minimized. This low-math approach follows the empirical direction of the Experimental Pyramid, which exhibits the pervasive importance of extrastatistical aspects of scientific inference. This low-math approach also recognizes that statistical ideas are most effective in planning the experiment, before the data have been collected.

For understanding statistics, this low-math approach may also be optimal. Minimizing formulas makes it easier to understand their conceptual structure, which is not only more important than the formulas themselves, but is also more important in empirical analysis. This approach can thus facilitate integration of statistical method as an organic part of scientific investigation.

This low-math approach may omit too many formulas. Some situations require specialized techniques, as with nonnormal data, unequal variance, or nested designs. The danger of omitting too much is real, but I believe it is nothing compared to the danger of including too much. With empirical understanding, most experimental workers could do reasonably well with visual inspection alone, supplemented with a single formula for confidence interval. No amount of statistics can save the person who lacks empirical understanding.

Empirical direction should be primary for textbooks. To construct a path to this goal is difficult, however, a task that requires empirical analysis. Articles on statistical aspects of statistics are frequent in psychological journals, but those on conceptual–empirical aspects are few. Those on learning–teaching are even fewer.

This book aims in this empirical direction, beginning with the Experimental Pyramid in Chapter 1 and continuing especially in chapter exercises. It is only one step, however, on a long road.

23.1.2 CONTENT

Because of its base in the Experimental Pyramid, this book has different content from comparable books on design–analysis. Some of these differences have been noted in previous chapters. A brief overview is given here to highlight the direction that has been pursued.

Emphases. Visual inspection is a basic skill in experimental analysis. Visual inspection of raw data is important to fill out one's feeling for the behavior, especially with respect to extreme scores. Visual inspection, of tables as well as figures, is essential in relating the pattern of means to the experimental manipulations and hypotheses. Furthermore, visual understanding is important in constructing figures and tables for your own Results that will best communicate with your readers. Visual understanding is even more important to understand tables and figures in a published paper or scientific talk.

Statistical analysis should be an aid to visual inspection. A practical reason for emphasizing visual inspection is to help students to develop skills of intuitive appreciation of data patterns rather than slavish reliance on statistics. The confidence interval is a notable combination of the two.

Replication is central in experimental analysis and needs corresponding recognition in texts on design–analysis. Replication takes the edge off many statistical perplexities, such as marginal results, multiple comparisons, and post hoc analysis. Instead of inducing students to worry whether their p is .04 or .06, call them both marginal, in need of replication before they can be taken seriously. With replication, post hoc exploratory analysis can be encouraged.

Replication is neglected in statistics. One reason is that most replication is not literal, but involves improvements in procedure and/or changes in experimental variables. Hence each experiment must usually be analyzed by itself. Yet cross-experiment generality is in some ways more important than statistical analyses of single experiments. Such replication, which involves extrastatistical generalization, is taken for granted by experienced investigators. The replication principle seems essential for understanding how to use statistics.

A complete chapter on confounding has been included in the core. Most arguments in the literature are about confounding, not about statistical significance—about extrastatistical inference rather than statistical inference. In the view from the Experimental Pyramid, a general treatment of substantive confounding seems essential in a first-year text on design–analysis. Concrete examples of confounding have been used, as this seems more effective than abstract classification of heavily situation-specific knowledge. Many of these examples have immediate implications for experimental design, as with *Confounding With Stimulus Materials* and *Failure of Randomization*. The section on *Control of Confounding* considers some applications of standard statistics.

A separate chapter of the core is devoted to single subject design, which is vital in fields as far apart as perception, neuroscience, behavior analysis, judgment–decision, language, and social–personality. Single subject design has been even more neglected in statistics texts than statistics has been abjured by most who use such designs. This book aims to bring out the unrealized potential of standard design and analysis for single subject experiments.[a]

A handful of statistical concepts is enough. Most are given in Chapter 2 and in the refresher chapter at the end. The concept of sampling distribution is fundamental, of course, and can be made more intuitive in relation to the law of sample size. The central limit theorem is hardly less important, especially as the foundation for confidence intervals. To these concepts is added a superstructure dealing with variability assessment as a basis for estimation and decision. Although Chapter 2 is short, assimilating its content and meaning is a continuing task, only begun in our first graduate year. Spreading the exercises of Chapters 2-4 over the entire course may gain advantages of distributed practice.

Underlying all the foregoing emphases is the Experimental Pyramid: This Pyramid reveals the pervasive importance of extrastatistical considerations and the need for personal research judgment to subordinate statistics to empirics.

Models and Measurement. Multiple determination underlies all behavior. Understanding multiple determination depends on two issues: the integration model and the scale of response measurement. Standard statistics handles multiple determination in an arbitrary way, with the additive models of factorial design and multiple regression. As useful as these arbitrary models can be, they can also be severely misleading for understanding psychological process. This shortcoming is evident in the persistent confusion over "interactions" in factorial Anova and in the prevalent misconception that multiple regression somehow "controls" uncontrolled variables.

Some understanding of substantive models of multiple determination is essential to appreciate the uses and misuses of the arbitrary statistical models. This issue is covered for factorial Anova in Chapter 7 and for multiple regression in the second half of Chapter 16. In addition, Chapter 20 presents two simple classes of substantive models, signal detection theory and cognitive algebra, that have had some empirical success. The issue of psychological measurement, as important as models, is considered briefly in Sections 7.2 and 19.3 and more extensively in Chapter 21. More generally, these two issues of model and measurement show that statistics is not limited to the outcome questions that characterize typical applications, but can be essential to understand the psychological processes that underlie observed outcomes.

De-Emphases. A number of topics that have been stock fare in other texts have been de-emphasized in this book. This follows the theme of the Experimental Pyramid of Figure 23.1, which de-emphasizes the significance test by emphasizing the deeper importance of empirics. Further de-emphasis of the significance test is achieved through confidence intervals. Besides providing a visual indication of effect size, confidence intervals give visual appreciation of the response variability and constitute a visible reminder to reduce it.

The extraordinary emphasis on numerical calculations in virtually all other texts seems long obsolete. In the precomputer age, numerical calculations were a major part of data analysis. Drill in accurate calculation was an essential part of statistics teaching. Numerical examples were useful for drill and served also as refreshers for advanced researchers in their own data analyses. Today, thankfully, space previously needed for numerical examples can be better used to improve conceptual and substantive understanding. The same applies to exercises for students. Most numerical examples and exercises in this book use simple sets of numbers whose pattern can be appreciated by visual inspection.

More complex illustrative numerical examples are included with guidebooks for major statistical packages. Some of these can be adapted and explained by the course instructor, together with the various program options. The explanation should also indicate what is important in the printout, what is not, for these printouts contain far more information than is ordinarily needed. Because of the multiplicity of statistical packages, no attempt has been made to include such material in this book.

Contrasts have been largely omitted from the core. I included general contrasts in initial drafts of this book but later realized they are not often needed. In particular, the frequent claim for their usefulness in analyzing curve shape is mistaken (*Trend Analysis and Curve Shape*, pages 565*ff*). Two-mean comparisons and linear trend suffice for most purposes, and neither requires students to learn general contrasts. Two-mean comparisons can be made with a confidence interval or with Anova. Linear trend may be better done with a linear regression program, which does not require equal spacing or equal n. Discussion of general contrasts, accordingly, is deferred to Section 18.2.

Distribution-free statistics is handled by transforming the data to ranks and applying regular Anova. No new ideas are needed; no additional layer of formulas. The main concern with violations of standard Anova assumptions is that extreme scores can cause serious loss of power. Accordingly, I have emphasized the need to inspect the raw data for extreme scores—and the prior importance of avoiding extreme scores through experimental procedure. The attractive potential of trimmed Anova is also emphasized.

Except for confidence intervals and power effect size, indexes of size and importance are hardly mentioned in the core chapters, but instead are taken up in Section 18.1. Most such indexes impose a statistical answer on a substantive question; they obscure rather than clarify the data.

Many topics de-emphasized in the core chapters are considered in later chapters, as with contrasts, covariance, and unequal n. This later material is in topical form to allow different instructors to cover what they want and individual readers to locate what they might need. This later material also takes up various controversies.

Controversies. A number of issues are more or less controversial. Most of the first person "I"'s in the text are intended to signal a position on which there may be considerable differences of opinion. A few are noted here.

A separate chapter has been devoted to interactions in the hope of dispelling persistent misconceptions about this issue. This material is not new, but except for Bogartz (1994a) I have not found any text that shows much awareness of the issue. This situation underscores the dominance of the statistical perspective in other texts; the interaction issue is not statistical, but substantive, as already noted under *Models and Measurement* (preceding page).

In psychological measurement theory, the question of linear (equal interval) scales has long been contentious. An erroneous argument against Anova–regression is that these techniques require a linear response scale, which is seldom available. In fact, a monotone (ordinal) scale suffices with randomized one-way design (pages 634*ff*). Functional measurement theory, moreover, has had reasonable success in establishing linear response measures.

The issue of multiple comparisons has led to a polarization between two philosophies, familywise and per comparison. Current textbooks in psychology show increasing intolerance for any deviation from the familywise dogma that α must be fixed at some preassigned value, regardless of how many comparisons are made. Yet there are sensible reasons, as well as considerable agreement by eminent investigators, that some α escalation is allowable with planned comparisons. This issue is broached in Chapter 4 and pursued in a separate chapter, mainly as handbook guidance.

The foundations of statistics are intensely controversial among statisticians. The dominant frequentist school, based on objective definition of probability in terms of frequencies, has been giving ground to a subjective definition of probability as belief. These schools of thought are surveyed in Section 19.1, together with three empirical applications of Bayesian statistics to illustrate potential of the subjective approach. Fortunately, Anova for experimental psychology remains largely the same under either conception of probability.

Extrastatistical Inference and Personal Research Judgment. The litany of criticisms of significance tests cited in Section 19.2 contains grains of truth, but has mainly reinforced the stereotype of statistics as significance testing and has obscured its more vital functions. These vital functions come in choices of task, response measure, design, and in controls for confounding. These vital functions apply before the data are even collected.

Extrastatistical inference is primary in empirical science. This fact of scientific life inevitably gets obscured in statistics texts. I have sought to lessen this misplaced emphasis by structuring the first chapter around the Experimental Pyramid, by showing how statistics can help solve extrastatistical problems in planning an investigation, by including a core chapter on confounding, by emphasizing conceptual understanding rather than formulas and calculations, and by presenting exercises aimed at developing personal research judgment. This book, however, is only a step in this empirical direction.

Teaching: To Serve the Student. The most important controversy for a text on design–analysis concerns teaching: What to teach and how to teach it. The guiding principle is simple: **Serve the Student**.

This principle implies, I believe, seeking to help students learn what they are likely to need in later life. For first-year graduate students, the main needs may be summed up as ability to plan and conduct sound investigations, to evaluate the literature, and to apply similar scrutiny to evidence about affairs of everyday life.

Current texts are based on a very different idea; they treat statistics as largely autonomous and content-free. Formulas and numerical examples are presented as though they are the essence of statistics. I believe this approach is profoundly mistaken and miseffective, at least for social–behavioral sciences. I have tried to set out a different direction, based on the Experimental Pyramid.

Writing any text is a labor of love, perhaps more so for graduate level statistics than any other course. I wish to apologize for my negative comments on other texts for they all contain much good. Some contain a foundation for a good handbook. But they fail their primary function as first-year texts. A new direction needs to be pursued. I believe this book has made a worthwhile advance, but I am keenly aware how much remains to be done.

In any case, this book will serve a useful purpose if it provokes concern with the current mode of teaching. For the remarkable—truly astonishing—aspect of the controversy over teaching is how little there is.[b]

23.1.3 EXERCISES

Exercises embody dynamics of the learning process. Exercises are almost the most important part of any text.

Personal Research Judgment. Personal research judgment is the essence of research and application: Personal judgment governs your choice of problem, whether you choose one that is fruitful or one that is sterile; personal research judgment further determines how effective your attack on your problem will be. Exercises should mainly seek to help students develop their personal research judgment as integral components of their empirical knowledge systems.

Statistics can make unique contributions to personal research judgment. Conversely, personal research judgment is the primary ability for using statistics. In the main, personal research judgment is extrastatistical, grounded in empirics. For teaching statistics, therefore, the central issue is how to help students integrate statistics into empirical knowledge systems.[a]

How to construct exercises that will help students develop their personal research judgment is an important problem, about which little is known. The present exercises are intended as stepping stones in cooperative endeavor toward more relevant and more effective teaching–learning. A few specific goals are noted briefly in the following subsections.

Visual Inspection. Visual inspection is the most important skill for data analysis. Visual inspection is needed to assess patterns in the data and relate these patterns to empirical, background knowledge. In much experimental analysis, statistical inference is only a supplement to visual inspection.

Visual inspection is also important in communication. Graphic presentation is prominent in colloquium talks, conference reports, and journal articles. Graphic skills are as important for the person who wishes to communicate as for the person who tries to glean meaning from the message.

One class of exercises, accordingly, should aim to help students develop their skills of visual inspection. I have tried to construct such exercises in various ways, for example, with exercises that require judgment about reliable trends based solely on visual inspection. Confidence intervals are especially useful as visual indicators of effect size and reliability.

Statistical Concepts. A handful of statistical concepts is enough for most purposes in empirical science: Mean–variance and likely error, confidence interval, sampling distribution, central limit theorem, probability, significance test, power, and problems of post hoc tests. To these may be added the more empirical concept of additive model, which appears in Anova–regression with more than one variable. Various exercises are directed at helping readers further their development of these concepts.

Fortunately, these same concepts underlie all statistical analysis. Understanding of analysis of variance can thus transfer largely to regression analysis, chi-square, and other statistical procedures.

Problem Solving. Statistics is most useful in planning an investigation—a problem solving stage as shown in the Experimental Pyramid. One class of exercises, accordingly, should be oriented toward helping students develop personal research judgment for planning. Such exercises require students to work out alternative designs for a given situation, and to evaluate pros and cons of each. The pros and cons must be empirically embedded within the proposed situation. Repeated measures designs, to take one example, depend on empirical judgment about possible order effects that are often uncertain. Similarly, empirical judgments about confounding and generality determine the meaning and worth of the results.

Exercises to develop skills of problem solving are not easy to construct. Personal judgment is needed, not calculation with cookbook formulas. Such exercises can be hard for many first-year students, who may not have developed relevant background knowledge. One teaching tactic is to assign such exercises twice, with an intervening class discussion of preliminary answers.

Scientific Inference. Scientific inference is largely extrastatistical, based on substantive knowledge. Integration of design–analysis with empirical knowledge is thus a primary goal. Such integration is not easy, but I have tried to develop exercises that will help students in this empirical direction.

Also included are some exercises that involve evaluation of journal articles. Evaluating published articles or proposed research plans is an important skill, one that conjoins extrastatistical and statistical inference. Although exercises cannot generally represent the full complexity of such evaluations, they can help develop component skills. More such exercises would be desirable, but each one typically requires a fair amount of space to be at all realistic.

Exercises as Foundation for a Science of Learning–Teaching. Exercises should be considered professional contributions, I believe, deserving publication, criticism, and revision, much like current journal articles. Development of effective exercises should be a continuing process, a concern for all of us, just as with experimental issues. An exercise needs scrutiny from different points of view and testing with diverse groups of students. Cooperative endeavor, dedicated to experimental analysis, is needed to help develop collections of effective exercises for general use.

In this view, exercises are public knowledge, just as empirical results or theoretical ideas. This view applies not only to statistics and research methods, not only to psychology, but to textbooks in every field.

The goal of learning–teaching is transfer: Ability to apply what we have learned to problems we will encounter in future work. Effective learning–teaching depends on investigations to determine what knowledge systems we will need. Psychology stands apart from other fields in that some inkling of the nature of these knowledge systems has begun to emerge.

The learning process has fundamental importance to all of us. Cooperative endeavor is needed to improve our efforts. The need for combined efforts of different persons, who bring different perspectives and different skills to bear on an issue, appears continually in empirical research. The same surely holds for teaching–learning. This book has been written in this spirit.

23.1.4 UNDERGRADUATE STATISTICS

In order to **Serve the Student**, instruction should follow the principle of helping students develop knowledge systems that will be useful and needed in their life after leaving school. This principle underlies the empirical direction of this book, which is written for graduate students in psychology. Serving undergraduates involves very different considerations because relatively few will continue with graduate studies.

Education for Citizens. Undergraduate education in the social–behavioral sciences should emphasize knowledge systems that help students become better citizens—better spouses, better parents, better workers, better able to form opinions on everyday social–political issues, and better able to appreciate the humanities, sciences, and the natural world around them.

As education for citizens, few knowledge systems have such broad potential as research method. Evaluation of uncertain sample evidence underlies all perception, thought, and action. Vital concepts include the sample–population distinction, variability, and rudiments of experimental control. Simple skills with graphs, tables, and numbers are almost as important as reading.

Teaching emphasis should be qualitative, not quantitative, aimed at development of conceptual understanding. A single formula for confidence interval gives concrete actuality to the concepts and is ideal and sufficient for most data analyses these students will face. They should understand the opportunities and dangers of unplanned or post hoc tests, of course, but analysis of variance should certainly not be taught. Formulas should be strenuously minimized, with major emphasis on empirical understanding and visual inspection.

Do undergraduate texts on psychological statistics satisfy this principle of education for citizens? Far from it. Nearly all mimic the pattern of graduate texts. This pattern is inappropriate for undergraduates for several reasons, a misguided way to serve the students.

Teach Research Methods; Eliminate Undergraduate Statistics. Courses on research method are the best way to convey what undergraduates in social–behavioral sciences need to know about statistics. Statistics aims to quantify the information available in a sample, but does so within an idealized framework founded on random sampling. Far more important are extrastatistical considerations such as experimental control, placebo and other confounding, kinds of generality, generalization from handy samples, and so on. Such extrastatistical considerations are basic in research methods but tend to be actively avoided in statistics texts.

The big problem is transfer. The framework of research methods is explicitly concerned with transfer; in contrast, the framework of statistics centers on statistical formulas to the detriment of transfer.

There is just one remedy and it is simple: Eliminate undergraduate statistics courses; replace them with courses on research method. Courses on research methods can include what statistics is needed much more effectively.

This remedy echoes my book review of an undergraduate text, a review entitled by editor E. G. Boring *Statistics Wins 'and Student Loses*:

> The fault stems from an initial failure to consider and investigate the needs of the students in their future work. The desirability of this starting point and this goal is strongly suggested by what is known of transfer. Until there is an end of teaching statistics and a beginning of teaching the student, psychological statistics will remain one of the profession's principal misfeasances. (Anderson, 1960b, p. 313.)

Forty years have seen little improvement; undergraduate statistics remains one of the profession's principal misfeasances. Statistics texts, simply by being classified as statistics texts, can hardly avoid perpetuating this misfeasance. These texts are a crime against the students. To serve the student, these courses should be eliminated and replaced with research methods (see texts cited on page 258). Interesting efforts in this direction are in *Handbook for Teaching Statistics and Research Methods* (Ware & Brewer, 1988), which reprints about 90 very brief articles from *Teaching of Psychology*.[a]

23.2 LIFELONG LEARNING

We all strive for accomplishment. We pursue action and knowledge, in part for pleasure in exercising our abilities, in part to gain personal recognition, and in part to benefit society. We dream that, when our life has reached its summing up, what we leave behind us will have had some value.

An ideal road to accomplishment is through self-fulfillment. Develop a way of life that matches your interests and abilities. Some people are good with animals, some with children, some with perception of the external world, some with linguistic concepts, some with mathematical analysis, and some with social issues and interpersonal skills. By capitalizing on your strengths, you will accomplish more and be happier.

A major obstacle to self-fulfillment is the great overemphasis on academic research that pervades Ph.D. training, derivative from *Serve the Professor*. Even before arriving in graduate school, students are immersed in the view that the one ideal is scientific research, and that the only worthwhile goal is an academic job in a research university. But most Ph.D.s get nonacademic jobs or teaching jobs in nonresearch institutions. As a consequence, they often experience feelings of disappointment and failure. Their adjustment is additionally handicapped because the modal Ph.D. program quite ignores applied psychology and gives lip service to teaching.[a, b]

Of special significance is the growth of practical applications of psychological knowledge. These include not only such fields as education, health psychology, tests, man–machine systems, and family counseling, but also research units in business and government. Psychologists are in demand because psychology is the basic social science and because psychologists have better scientific training than other social scientists. Practical applications have the added appeal that they can make a real difference in society. Indeed, contemporary American society offers historically unparalleled opportunities for self-fulfillment.

There is a place for each of us. No other field is as broad and variegated as psychology. Many different ways of thinking are needed, even within a single area. The history of psychology is a continuing demonstration of the narrowness of our successive conceptual frameworks. Progress has been impressive, but in large part it consists of continually uncovering unsuspected new richness in the phenomena we study. Our time has unique potential as new phenomena are opened to investigation and old phenomena come under new scrutiny. Future generations will never have such opportunities as lie before us today. Future workers will look back on our era of boundless opportunity as

THE GOLDEN AGE OF PSYCHOLOGY.

NOTES

23.1.1a. Lack of transfer is manifest in the various research notes and articles about elementary misconceptions of statistics that are frequent even in trained psychologists.

23.1.1b. Two different kinds of handbook may be useful, one mainly concerned with design, the other with statistical arguments and derivations. *Experimental Design* by Cochran and Cox (1957) is an admirable illustration of the first kind, a classic in its field and still a valuable resource. Although much of the content is not especially useful in psychological research, the mode and level of exposition deserve careful consideration. Most notable is the paucity of equations and formulas. A comparable text in psychology would be invaluable.

A textbook of statistics proper, giving statistical arguments and derivations, would be useful for many empirical workers and as a reference book for instructors in design–analysis. Innumerable statistics texts have been written by statisticians, but mainly for statistic students and statisticians. Those with an empirical perspective are mainly oriented toward engineering and agriculture (e.g., Box, Hunter, & Hunter, 1978; Draper & Smith, 1981; Montgomery, 1997; Snedecor & Cochran, 1980). In psychology, considerable portions of Maxwell and Delaney (1990) and Myers and Well (1991) seem to me to have the right spirit and level for a handbook of statistics for psychologists.

23.1.2a. Not a few who use Anova disbelieve it can be applied to single subject data, testimony to the need for empirical direction in teaching statistics (Note 11a, page 338).

23.1.2b. Textbooks should be a collective responsibility of our social duty as teachers (Anderson, 1959a, 1960b, 1972a). Criticism is essential to improve teaching. Yet public criticism of teaching is negligible—in marked contrast to criticism given research articles. This contrast mirrors the relative importance accorded teaching and research.

For several reasons, unfortunately, the statistical orientation perpetuates and amplifies itself. Among these reasons is the common statistical reaction that the cure for poor empirical judgment in design and analysis is more statistics. The more statistics the students know, the argument goes, the better they will be able to deal with the innumerable empirical complications that arise. In actuality, I believe, the opposite is true; the real need is for research judgment. In writing the core chapters for this book, I realized, slowly and tortuously, how much standard material has marginal usefulness and how much standard exposition is marred by inappropriate goals.

What is needed is not more statistics, but less; less statistics and more empirics; less statistics and more extrastatistics. This book is a step in this empirical direction.

23.1.3a. The difference between the exercises in this and other texts is reflected in the absence of answers. Other texts generally include answers to many of the exercises, which is reasonable with numerical calculations, for the student still has to get the correct steps of the calculation. This practice has been followed here with some exercises on calculation by including answers as part of the exercise.

With exercises requiring thought and judgment, however, including answers would short-circuit the learning process. What matters is the mental activity involved in seeking an answer, not the answer itself. Indeed, a wrong answer may be quite instructive. Answers are included in the companion *Instructor's Manual*.

In our everyday work, personal research judgment is needed to construct different possible experimental plans and to evaluate their pros and cons. Exercises should seek to develop these judgment skills, which are quite different from standard exercises in calculation with cookbook formulas.

23.1.4a. One exception to this misfeasance in undergraduate statistics is the well-crafted text by Freedman, Pisani, and Purves (1998). It includes many well-chosen real examples that bring the ideas home, relying heavily on concrete, visual arguments with a minimum of algebra. Although written within a statistical framework, it is a model of how to Serve the Student. Also notable is Wallis and Roberts (1956), out of print, but still a resource and in some ways a model for statistics teachers.

23.2a. Serve the Professor underlies the orientation of major research universities, not *Serve the Student*. This orientation had some justification in a previous era, when professors subsidized the educational system by working long hours for low pay. Today, however, university professors get handsome salaries, together with extremely attractive working conditions.

The root cause of the present orientation is simple. The prestige scale for major universities is research: How much grant money do their professors receive? How much scholarly research have they published? How prominent are they in the status hierarchy in their field? These are central questions for the university administration in decisions about hiring, promotion, and salary.

This prestige scale distorts and obscures the social responsibility of the universities for systematic study of learning and teaching. With this orientation, *Serve the Student* gets mainly lip service.

Two litmus tests provide stark evidence of this disorientation of the universities. First, if the universities were oriented toward serving the student, research on education would have top priority. Every academic department would have faculty actively engaged in experimental analysis of teaching, especially investigating the nature of knowledge systems needed in later life and how to optimize transfer. Such persons are rare. Many men and women are devoted teachers, but they depend on personal intuition and what they learn is largely lost when they retire.

Second, all Ph.D.s hired for teaching positions would be required to have systematic training for teaching. Four years of substantive immersion in a field is a general minimum for substantive research; one year of similar immersion in learning to teach seems a minimum for beginning to teach. Students deserve no less. Yet such training is virtually nonexistent. The TA system is a failure of responsibility by the universities.

Universities operate to **Serve the Professor——Serve the Student** comes hindmost.

23.2b. How can students hope to reform our educational system? Students know little about what knowledge systems they will need in future, and can hardly realize that their instructors are almost equally in the dark.

Yet students can be effective in reforming the educational system—they can demand that every department, bar none, have faculty dedicated to research on teaching.

No other area of science has the importance of research on teaching. A lesson of science is that research improves the effectiveness of almost any activity. A lesson of history is that proposals for such improvement nearly always meet resistance from the status quo.

Just two numbers are necessary to analyze data from most experiments: **mean** and **standard deviation.** These two numbers resolve the basic difficulty that a sample mean is an uncertain estimate of the true mean of the population from which the sample is drawn.

Ideally, therefore, we desire an interval around the sample mean that is likely to contain the population mean. The *best possible* interval would be one that gives us specified, known confidence that it contains the population mean. This interval tells us the *likely error* of the sample mean.

The miracle of statistics is that it can give us the best possible. For example, an interval extending one standard deviation either side of the sample mean will contain the population mean with about 67% confidence in most applications. If you desire an interval that gives greater confidence, statistics can provide it. These *confidence intervals* provide a base for *significance tests*, which serve as evidence that an experimental treatment has had a real effect on behavior.

Two easy formulas are enough to get confidence intervals. With these two formulas, you can do much of your data analysis, sometimes all.

The confidence interval has an empirical lesson: *Reduce the variability of your data.* This variability determines the standard deviation, which in turn determines the width of your confidence interval, that is, the likely error of your sample mean. The lower the variability in your data, the lower is your likely error.

Reducing variability is mainly accomplished through experimental procedures. In addition, statistical techniques can provide inestimable aid. These two approaches, empirical and statistical, are stressed throughout this book. They embody the *Empirical Direction in Design and Analysis.*

Chapter 0

BASIC STATISTICAL CONCEPTS

How to design experiments and analyze data is the subject of this book. A small handful of statistical ideas and techniques is enough for most experiments. This chapter gives an overview of some basics.

0.1 BASIC STATISTICAL CONCEPTS

0.1.1 SAMPLE AND GENERALITY

Sample Principle. *Samples* are the base for all knowledge. In everyday life, judgments and decisions rest on evidence from samples, directly or indirectly. A test is a sample of your knowledge and abilities, as with a statistics exam or a test for driver's license. Blood and urine samples can help diagnose your health. What others think of you depends on samples of your behavior.

Samples are equally important in psychological science. Nearly every experiment you read about in any of your textbooks presents evidence from a small sample of subjects, as with the infant monkeys in Harlow's "mother love" experiments. All those experiments you yourself are destined to do will also use small samples.

This fundamental role of samples appears in all sciences. The study of stars and galaxies depends on tiny samples of light. Our knowledge of dinosaurs comes from hard-won samples of scattered fossils; the same applies to our knowledge about hominid precursors of *Homo sapiens.*

Generalization from Samples. A sample is seldom important in its own right. Instead, we use evidence from the sample to reach some general conclusion. No one is interested in those particular infant monkeys studied in Harlow's mother love experiments. Similarly, the peas from Mendel's small monastery garden were thrown out long ago, whereas Mendel's inspired interpretation of the statistical pattern of these peas lives on in modern theory of genes.

You also, in your own experiments, will seek generalizations from a small sample of behavior from a small sample of organisms. Generalization from samples has certain hazards. Unless you plan your experiment to deal with these hazards, your work may be inconclusive, wasted.

The science of statistics gives you tools to deal with two major hazards of samples: **Bias**—your sample may be unrepresentative and yield erroneous generalization; **variability**—different members of your sample may exhibit widely different behaviors, so even the main trend may be uncertain.

0.1.2 HOW STATISTICS DEALS WITH SAMPLES

Statistics begins with an idealized situation. We assume we have a *random sample* from some well-defined *population*. A random sample, in its simplest form, is one in which each member of the population has an equal chance of being selected for the sample.

One example of random sample appears in Table A1 of random numbers (page 809); each digit from 0 to 9 was selected with equal probability. Favorite examples in introductory texts are flipping coins and throwing dice because they so clearly and concretely give equal chance to each outcome. Election polls are the best-known empirical examples, and professional polling organizations go to considerable expense to secure a random sample of voters.

Random samples can deal with the two hazards of bias and variability. These two hazards are taken up in the next two subsections.

Random Sample Avoids Bias.   To achieve our goal of generalizing from the sample to the population, we desire a sample that is representative of the population. We wish to avoid biased, unrepresentative samples.

Bias refers to the *method* by which a sample is selected. A sampling method is biased if it yields samples that differ on average from the population. If you poll students in the introductory psychology class for their opinions on effective reforms for college teaching, your sample is biased in that these students are mostly sophomores and freshman. Juniors and seniors, whose opinions are based on more experience, will be underrepresented.

Random sample avoids bias. Because each member of the population has an equal chance of getting in the sample, there cannot be any *systematic* difference between sample and population. Although each sample will differ from the population in some way, these differences will be random, not systematic.

Many people are horrified at the thought of leaving the sample to random chance. ''We should use what we know about the population,'' they cry, ''to select a *representative* sample. You must be mad to leave this crucial matter to blind chance.''

This objection has two answers. The first is that when people try to select a representative sample, they invariably introduce bias; the cure may be worse than the illness. The second is that statisticians have developed ways to take advantage of what you know about the population while still avoiding bias. Thus, polling organizations use what they know about the population to stratify it and then take random samples within each stratum. Experimentalists may use the analogous procedure of block design (Section 14.2). Within each stratum or block, however, random sampling is essential to avoid bias.[a]

Random Sample Quantifies Variability. In life sciences, individual differences can be a primary obstacle to generalization. Every different sample will contain different individuals and hence yield somewhat different results. Every sample will thus differ more or less from the population.

But in practice, we have just one particular sample. What confidence can we have that the results for those individuals in our one particular sample will hold for the population?

These individual differences cannot be avoided; they are inherent in the situations we wish to investigate, as with the infant monkeys in the mother love experiments and even with Mendel's peas. Furthermore, little is usually known about these individual differences. Individual differences might thus seem an insuperable obstacle to generalization in psychological science.

Remarkably, statistics makes it possible to deal with variability, including the variability produced by individual differences. Statistics turns the sow's ear of variability into the silk purse of a *confidence interval*.

This statistical approach rests on plain common sense. What is remarkable is not this common sense, but that statistical theory has developed a simple, effective formula to quantify the uncertainty of samples.

0.1.3 SAMPLE EVIDENCE QUANTIFIED

Suppose we have a random sample from some population, with each case represented by some measured number. These numbers are usually a jumbled mass, whose main sense is hard to discern. Accordingly, we usually condense the sample to get two summary numbers, the *mean* and its *likely error*.

The sample mean is helpful as a single number that shows the central tendency of the sample. We use this sample mean as an estimate of the mean of population from which the sample was drawn.

The sample mean, however, is not reliable. Random chance could have given us many different samples, all with different means. The mean of our particular sample will be more or less in error about the population mean. *Without some indication of its **likely error**, the sample mean has no meaning.*

In this view, the sample mean is an interval of likely values of the population mean. *It is misleading to treat the sample mean as a specific number, without regard to its **likely error**.*

How can we determine the likely error of the sample mean? An obvious solution is to draw many samples and see how much their means vary from one sample to the next. But in practice we have only the one sample. Its mean could be close to the population mean or far away. How can we tell?

The answer to this question comes from common sense:

> *The likely error of the sample mean is proportional to*
> *an average of the differences between the numbers in the sample.*

If the sample numbers are close together, we expect the sample mean will be close to the population mean. If the sample numbers are widely scattered, we fear the sample mean may be far from the population mean.

This common sense can be made exact. The likely error of a sample mean can be quantified with a *confidence interval*. To get this confidence interval, we need a measure of "the differences between the numbers in the sample." This needed measure is the standard deviation, given next.

Variance and Standard Deviation. The variability among the numbers of a sample may be measured by the *sample variance*, s^2, defined by the formula*

$$s^2 = \frac{1}{n-1}\sum_{i=1}^{n}(Y_i - \bar{Y})^2. \tag{1a}$$

This formula applies to a sample of n numbers, Y_i, with mean $\bar{Y}$. This formula makes sense. Each term in parentheses, $(Y_i - \bar{Y})$, is the deviation of individual sample elements from their mean—a direct measure of variability.

The square root of the variance is the *standard deviation* of the sample:

$$s = \sqrt{s^2}. \tag{1b}$$

The standard deviation is also a measure of variability among the sample numbers. It has many uses, especially for confidence intervals.[a]

---

* $\sum$ **Notation.** Addition is the basic operation in statistics. The symbol $\sum$ (read "sum") is shorthand for addition. We denote a sample of numbers as

$$Y_1,\ Y_2,\ Y_3,\ \ldots\ Y_{n-1},\ Y_n,$$

and a representative number as Y_i. The sum of these n numbers is denoted

$$\sum_{i=1}^{n} Y_i = \sum Y_i.$$

The sample mean, $\bar{Y}$, is denoted by an overbar:

$$\bar{Y} = \frac{1}{n}\sum_{i=1}^{n} Y_i = \frac{1}{n}\sum Y_i.$$

Similar summation notation is used throughout statistics, as in Equation 1a for variance.

Nearly everything in this book can be understood with just two numbers: mean and variability, $\bar{Y}$ and s. This pair of numbers yields the confidence interval shown next in Expression 2, as well as Student's t test of Equation 3 below. This pair of numbers reappears in disguised form in the F test for more than two experimental groups (Chapter 3).

Confidence Interval. The *confidence interval* that represents the sample mean is the interval

$$\text{from} \qquad \bar{Y} - t^* s / \sqrt{n} \qquad \text{to} \qquad \bar{Y} + t^* s / \sqrt{n}. \qquad (2)$$

In this formula, s is the sample standard deviation from Equations 1. The value of t^* may be chosen from Table A4 (page 813) to provide 95% confidence that the population mean lies within this interval. This interval thus represents the likely error of the sample mean. (This result assumes a random sample of independent scores from a normal distribution; see below.)

Confidence intervals epitomize data analysis; they distill the sample information to obtain an interval that contains the population mean with specified confidence.

Step back a minute to consider the principle behind the confidence interval. You can never be absolutely certain the population mean lies inside your confidence interval. An occasional random sample will be very deviant and will not contain the population mean. You may, however, be 95% confident that the population mean lies within the interval you calculate with this formula.[b]

Numerical Example of Confidence Interval. To illustrate how to calculate a confidence interval for a single mean, consider the sample data

$$\{5, \quad 6, \quad 7, \quad 8, \quad 9\}, \text{ with mean } \bar{Y} = 7.$$

Equation 1a yields the sample variance

$$s^2 = \frac{1}{5-1}[(5-7)^2 + (6-7)^2 + (7-7)^2 + (8-7)^2 + (9-7)^2]$$

$$= 10/4 = 2.5.$$

Taking the square root yields the sample standard deviation

$$s = \sqrt{2.5} = 1.581.$$

To get the criterial value, t^*, look in Table A4 at the row for df, which equals $n - 1$ (sample size minus 1. In this example, df $= 5 - 1 = 4$. Table A4 shows $t^* = 2.78$ for $\alpha = .05$. The 95% confidence interval thus has half-width:

$$t^* s / \sqrt{n} = 2.78 \times 1.581 / \sqrt{5} = 1.97.$$

By Expression 2, the 95% confidence interval is thus 7 ± 1.97. If this were a random sample from a normal distribution, we could have 95% confidence that the true mean of the population lay in the range from 5.03 to 8.97. This is a fairly wide range, but we should not expect too much from so small a sample.

Confidence Interval as Significance Test. To illustrate the concept of *significance test*, consider the classic problem of comparing an experimental treatment E with a control treatment C. We assume a random sample of subjects from some population, each of whom receives both treatments. The two responses of subject i are denoted Y_{Ei} and Y_{Ci}. We wish to test whether treatment E is superior to treatment C.

The natural measure of effectiveness of treatment E is the difference between responses to the two treatments. For subject i, this difference score is

$$Y_{\text{diff}, i} = Y_{Ei} - Y_{Ci}.$$

Suppose the mean difference, $\overline{Y}_{\text{diff}}$, is positive and visual inspection shows that only a few individual subjects have negative difference scores. This evidence supports our experimental hypothesis that E is superior to C.

But can we be at all confident E is superior to C? Perhaps our positive result is a random fluke. Many other random samples might have been selected. These other samples would have different subjects who would have given different responses. Perhaps many of these random samples would have yielded an opposite effect. This may seem unlikely, but how unlikely is it?

This question exemplifies the sample–population distinction. What we wish to know about is the effect of E in the *population*; but our evidence is limited to the *sample*. Is it safe to generalize from our sample to the population?

Suppose our sample had three subjects. It would hardly be convincing if two of the three subjects showed positive results. Three of three would still seem weak evidence. But even a sample of 60 subjects seems tiny if the population has, say, 60 thousand people.

What we need is some objective way to decide whether the sample evidence is strong enough to decide beyond reasonable doubt that treatment E is indeed superior to treatment C. This decision procedure is called a *significance test*; it may be performed with the confidence interval.

To see how the confidence interval resolves our decision problem, construct the 95% confidence interval for the foregoing difference score, $\overline{Y}_{\text{diff}}$. We have 95% confidence that the population mean of the difference scores lies within this interval. Therefore, if 0 lies outside this interval, we have 95% confidence that 0 cannot be the population mean. In other words, we have 95% confidence that the two treatments differ in effectiveness. The difference is then said to be *statsig* (statistically significant).

Keep in mind that a statsig result is reasonable evidence, not proof. Possibly both treatments are equally effective, but one chances to be more effective in our particular random sample. If both treatments were actually equally effective, such a statsig difference would happen 5% of the time. Since 1 chance in 20 seems unlikely, we take a statsig result as reasonable evidence for a real effect in the population.

The t Test for a Single Sample. The significance test of the preceding sub-section is usually given in a different form, namely, as Student's t ratio,

$$t = \frac{\bar{Y}}{s/\sqrt{n}}. \tag{3}$$

The numerator of this ratio is just the sample mean; the denominator is the standard deviation of the sample mean. The t ratio thus expresses the size of the sample mean in units of its standard deviation, that is, in units of its variability.

Larger values of t are thus evidence that the population mean differs from 0. Our decision rule is:

> If the magnitude of t is "large enough,"
> decide that the population mean is not 0.

"Large enough" means that chance alone would rarely produce a t this large, conventionally only 5% of the time.

Student's great achievement was to make this decision rule precise—by deriving a formula for exact values of "large enough." These "large enough" values are the criterial values, t^*, listed in Table A4 (page 813), that are used in the confidence interval of Expression 2. If the value of t that you obtain from your data is larger than t^*, you have reasonable evidence that the population mean differs from 0. If you think 95% confidence is not enough, you can construct a 99% confidence interval by using $\alpha = .01$ in Table A4. Student's (1908) discovery heralded a new era in statistics.

To use Student's t ratio, all you need is Equation 3 and Table A4 (page 813).

The significance test provided by the confidence interval is exactly the same as the significance test provided by the t ratio. This follows because the same criterial value t^* is used in both.

The confidence interval is more informative than the t *test.* The t test gives a yes–no answer about statistical significance. The confidence interval adds information about likely error—the narrower the confidence interval, the more confident we are about the size of the true effect. Accordingly, confidence intervals are increasingly used instead of the t test.[c]

Comparing Two Experimental Conditions. Confidence intervals can also be constructed for experiments with independent groups of subjects, in which treatment E is given to one group of subjects, treatment C to a different group. Using different groups may be necessary to avoid practice effects that could *confound* the response to whichever treatment came second. Because each group consists of different subjects, the difference score is not applicable.

Fortunately, the same approach can readily be extended to provide a confidence interval for the difference between $\bar{Y}_E$ and $\bar{Y}_C$ for two different groups of subjects. The essential idea is the same (Chapter 2).

0.1.4 NORMAL DISTRIBUTION

Heights of adult American women are shown in the bell-shaped curve of Figure 0.1. The horizontal axis is height; the vertical axis is probability density. The elevation of each point on the curve represents the probability density that a woman chosen at random will have the corresponding height, indicated on the horizontal axis.

The main sense of this bell curve is that mean height is 63.5 inches and that most women are near average in height. Some will be tall, a few very tall.

This curve is a *probability distribution*; it shows how the relative probabilities of different heights are distributed across the range of heights. This bell shape, which is called a *normal* probability distribution, is fairly common and may be used for various practical purposes as illustrated here.[a]

Standard Normal Curve. A normal curve is completely determined by just two parameters: mean, μ, and standard deviation, σ. If we know μ and σ, we can calculate everything else. Such calculations are often easier if we use the standardized form of the normal curve. To standardize any score:

1. subtract the mean;
2. divide by the standard deviation.

The standardized scores then have a mean of 0 and a standard deviation of 1. They are commonly called z scores.

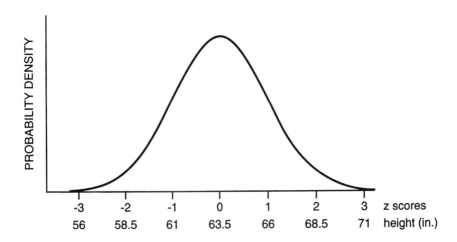

Figure 0.1. Normal distribution showing heights of adult American women in inches and in standard z scores. Shaded area under this normal curve is 16% of the total. Hence 16% of women are taller than 66.0 inches. Equivalently, 16% of the women have z scores greater than 1.

Suppose your girlfriend is 5 feet, 6 inches tall. You wonder what proportion of American women are taller than your girlfriend. Graphically, the answer is shown in the normal curve of Figure 0.1. The arrow denotes a height of 66.0 inches; the shaded, tail area shows what proportion of women are taller.

To find the exact value of this shaded area, standardize your girlfriend's height. First, subtract the population mean of 63.5 inches, leaving 2.5 inches. Then divide by the standard deviation of 2.5 inches to get $z = 1.00$.

Now look at Table A3 (page 812) which gives the tail area under the normal curve to the right of the given z score. For $z = 1.00$, the value .1587 represents the shaded area in Figure 0.1. In other words, 16% of women are taller than your girlfriend.

Standardization is useful because the single Table A3 can be applied to any and every normal distribution. Suppose you wonder how much your newborn infant weighs, relative to other babies. Means are 7.06 pounds both for males and females, with a standard deviation close to 1 pound (Hansman, 1970). Use these population values to get the z score for your own baby and then consult Table A3 (page 812). Every home should have a copy of this z table.

Finding Areas Under the Normal Curve. The z score method may be used to find any area under the normal curve. Consider a woman 5 feet, 2. She wonders what proportion of women she is taller than. To standardize, she subtracts the population mean, leaving -1.5 inches. Dividing this remainder by the standard deviation of 2.5 inches, she obtains her z score of -0.6.

Negative z scores are not listed in Table A3, but they are readily handled because the normal curve is symmetrical. Hence the area to the left of $z = -0.6$ equals the area to the right of $z = +0.6$. In the present example, therefore, the woman 62.0 inches tall is taller than 27% of the population.

These examples show that 68% of the z scores lie between -1 and $+1$. This $2z$ range is sometimes presented as a representative range in terms of the actual data. In the present example, accordingly, about two thirds of American women have heights in the 5-inch range between 61.0 and 66.0 inches.

Similarly, Table A3 shows that 95% of the z scores lie between -1.96 and $+1.96$. The z score of 1.96 corresponds to a tail area of .0250, so 2.5% of the scores are larger; by symmetry, 2.5% are less than -1.96. The remaining area thus comes to 95%. This is why $t* = 1.96$ in Expression 5 given next.

Binomial Data. Many events have just two outcomes, as with sex of newborn infants. Is it true, as you may have heard, that 106 boys are born to 100 girls? Does similar imbalance hold for other species?

To estimate a population proportion, we naturally use the proportion observed in some sample. Of course, the sample proportion, p, will differ from the population proportion, π, so we need to know the likely error of p. In short, we need a confidence interval around p.

To get a confidence interval for a proportion, p, we need the formula for its standard deviation. As long as sample size is small relative to population size,

$$\text{standard deviation}(p) \;=\; \sqrt{p/(1-p)}\,/\sqrt{n}. \tag{4}$$

Substitute this standard deviation for s in Expression 2. For large samples, $t^* = 1.96$. We thus get the 95% confidence interval:

$$p \;\pm\; 1.96\,\sqrt{p(1-p)}\,/\sqrt{n}. \tag{5}$$

Poll results are usually accompanied by a "margin of error"—one standard deviation of the proportion. How large a sample is needed to get a 2% margin of error in a close election between two candidates? From Equation 4 for standard deviation (p), we need to choose n so that $\sqrt{p(1-p)}\,/\sqrt{n} = .02$. Given that the election is close, p is near ½. Hence we solve the equation $\sqrt{\tfrac12 \times \tfrac12}\,/\sqrt{n} = \tfrac12 \div \sqrt{n} = .02$, finding $n = 625$.

Note that the population size does not appear in Equation 5, only sample size. A random sample of 625 voters will have the same margin of error for a close election for U. S. president as for governor of sparsely populated Nevada. This useful result illustrates how statistics can reveal facts that lie beyond the reach of common sense.

Normal Distribution and Experimental Analysis. The normal distribution is the base for confidence intervals and significance tests in experimental analysis. Expression 2 for the confidence interval and Equation 3 for the t test both assume the sample came from a population with a normal distribution.

Many populations are normal, it is true, but many are not. For example, the binomial distribution of the previous subsection is far from normal. Fortunately, the confidence interval from Expression 2 is applicable almost regardless of the shape of the population. This fundamental contribution of statistical theory is presented on the seven-step road in Section 2.2 of Chapter 2.

To generalize from sample data, statistical theory treats these data as a random sample. Random samples avoid bias and allow likely error to be quantified (pages 785*ff*). In typical experiments, subjects are assigned at random to different experimental conditions. By virtue of this *randomization procedure*, the data for each condition may be regarded as a random sample, thereby allowing confidence intervals and significance tests (see page 69).

Scientific generalization, of course, rests primarily on extrastatistical considerations, a fact that should not be obscured by statistics. Harlow's studies with infant monkeys, for example, are mainly interesting for what they suggest about human infants; such suggestions rely on extrastatistical knowledge. To show that an effect is "statistically significant" is only a first step, relatively minor, in understanding what it means. This issue of extrastatistical generalization is developed with the Experimental Pyramid in Chapter 1.

0.2 PROBABILITY

Probability thinking has fundamental importance in psychological science. The confidence interval of the previous section, which specifies the likely error of the sample mean, is one of many examples of probability thinking.

0.2.1 LAWS OF PROBABILITY

There are just a few laws of probability and they are essentially common sense. For a simple illustration of the probability laws, imagine a Probability Urn with 100 balls numbered 00 to 99. We consider a random process that selects one ball from the Probability Urn, each with equal probability. An *event A* consists of one or more balls, and A is said to occur if the random process selects any ball that belongs to A. The *probability of A* is then just the number of balls in A, divided by 100. Examples are: A consists of the numbers ≥ 95; A consists of numbers with exactly one digit equal to 2; and so forth. These two events have probabilities of .05 and .18.

The laws of probability are integration rules. They show how probability information is integrated across two or more events. Two basic integration rules involve AND and OR. Event **(A AND B)** consists of those balls common to A and B. Event **(A OR B)** consists of those balls in A, plus whatever additional balls are in B; a ball in both A and B counts only once.[a]

The OR Rule. The probability of (A OR B) is just the proportion of balls in A and B together:

$$\text{Prob}(A \text{ OR } B) \;=\; \text{Prob}(A) + \text{Prob}(B) - \text{Prob}(A \text{ AND } B). \quad (6a)$$

Prob(A AND B) refers to the overlap, those balls common to both A and B. This common part gets added twice, once in Prob(A) and once in Prob(B), so we must subtract it in the above equation.

An important special case of the OR rule arises when A and B are mutually **exclusive**, containing no balls in common. It is then impossible to get a ball in (A AND B), so Prob(A AND B) is zero. The above equation then reduces to the *addition rule for exclusive events*:

$$\text{Prob}(A \text{ OR } B) \;=\; \text{Prob}(A) + \text{Prob}(B). \quad (6b)$$

The Conditional Rule. It is often necessary to consider the probability of one event A, **given** that another event B has already occurred. This **conditional probability** is denoted Prob(A | B) [the symbol "| B" is read "given B"]. This probability is the *relative* proportion of balls in A that are also in B:

$$\text{Prob}(A \mid B) \;=\; \frac{\text{Prob}(A \text{ AND } B)}{\text{Prob}(B)}. \quad (7)$$

The numerator on the right is the proportion of balls common to both A and B.

This numerator is converted to a conditional probability by dividing by the proportion of balls in B, that is, Prob(B).

To illustrate, suppose that A consists of all numbers in the Probability Urn with exactly one digit equal to 2. Then Prob(A) = .18, as already noted. Now suppose B consists of the numbers from 00 to 49, so Prob(B) = .50. Counting shows that (A AND B) consists of 13 numbers, so Prob(A AND B) = .13. By the conditional rule of Equation 7, Prob(A | B) = .13/.50 = .26.

The AND Rule. We can get the AND rule by rewriting the conditional rule of Equation 7:

$$\text{Prob}(A \text{ AND } B) = \text{Prob}(B) \times \text{Prob}(A \mid B). \tag{8}$$

In words, the probability that a ball is common to both A and B equals the probability that the ball is in B, times the probability that **given** it is in B, it is then also in A.

A special case of the AND rule applies to independent events. A and B are **independent** if occurrence of one gives no information about occurrence of the other. Independence means

$$\text{Prob}(A \mid B) = \text{Prob}(A) \quad \text{and} \quad \text{Prob}(B \mid A) = \text{Prob}(B). \tag{9}$$

In terms of the Probability Urn, A and B are independent when the proportion of A balls within B is the same as in the rest of the Urn. If B consists of the numbers 00 to 49, for example, and A consists of even numbers, then A and B are independent. However, if A consists of all numbers for which exactly one digit is 2, A and B are not independent.

If A and B are independent, the two previous equations imply

$$\text{Prob}(A \text{ AND } B) = \text{Prob}(A) \times \text{Prob}(B). \tag{10}$$

This is the *multiplication rule for independent events*.

0.2.2 CONCEPT OF INDEPENDENCE

The concept of independence is needed throughout statistical theory. Every statistical analysis depends on some assumption of independence, which, in its simplest form, means that knowledge of one score gives no information about any other score. In particular, the confidence interval of Expression 2 is only valid if the individual Y scores are independent. The concept of independence thus requires special consideration.

A classic fallacy of intuitive statistics occurs with runs of events. If a fair coin comes up nine heads in a row, the well-known "gambler's fallacy" says it is more likely to come up tails the next time. A common rationalization appeals to "the law of averages." Heads and tails are equally likely, the argument goes, and must occur equally often in the long run. Hence the nine heads in a row must be evened out by more tails.

The standard refutation of this argument is that "the coin has no memory." With no memory of previous occurrences, the coin could not even out the nine heads with more tails, no matter how intensely it desired to do so. Some causal, physical process with a memory would be necessary to justify the given argument. The statement that "the coin has no memory" is a dramatic way of emphasizing that no such process is known or suspected.

Your main concern is to ensure that the data from your experiments do satisfy the independence assumption. Independence will be violated if one observation tells something about another. One obvious violation of independence occurs when two or more responses are measured for each subject. If one response is high/low for a given subject, this tells you the other response for this subject is also likely to be high/low. The responses are not independent, in other words, but correlated across subjects. In the E versus C experiment on page 788, each subject was in both conditions, so the two scores for each subject were not independent. This difficulty was handled by using difference scores, $Y_{Ei} - Y_{Ci}$, so each subject had only a single score, and these could be considered independent across subjects.

Independence may also be violated if subjects are run together in groups. Some event may occur that has similar effect on several subjects in one particular group, so their responses are not independent. Good experimental procedure, accordingly, usually requires that subjects be run singly, one by one.

Nonindependence means that observations are partly redundant, even more a difficulty for visual inspection than for statistical analysis. The independence assumption is not innocuous, therefore, but must be satisfied through empirical procedures. This is often easy, but should never be taken for granted.

0.3 PROBABILITY THINKING

The foregoing laws of probability can improve the effectiveness of your thinking, but only if you understand them intuitively. A few of the many ways in which probability thinking appears in experimental analysis are noted here.[a, b]

0.3.1 USEFUL PROBABILITY IDEAS

Sample Mean as an Interval. Probability thinking is essential to understand how to generalize from sample data. Different samples will give different means; any one sample mean will have more or less error as an estimate of the population mean. We should not think of the sample mean as a specific number, therefore, but as an interval that is likely to contain the population mean.

This common sense idea has been elaborated in statistical theory to quantify "more or less error." This is just the confidence interval of Expression 2, which quantifies the likely error of the sample estimate of the population mean.

Law of Averages. The law of averages, to continue the foregoing coin example, does not say that the *numbers* of heads and tails tend to equalize in the long run. What tends to equalize in the long run are the *proportions* of heads and tails.

Remarkably, this law of averages has a simple mathematical form, also called the square root law of sample size. This law of averages has already appeared in Equation 4 for the standard deviation of a proportion, namely, $\sqrt{p(1-p)} \div \sqrt{n}$. With $p = \frac{1}{2} = 1 - p$, the standard deviation of the *proportion* of heads in n tosses is

$$\text{standard deviation (\textit{proportion} of heads)} = \frac{1}{2} \div \sqrt{n}. \qquad (11a)$$

This standard deviation *decreases* steadily as sample size increases. For a sample of size 25, you can expect the proportion of heads to deviate from chance by .10, on average. For a sample of 100 (4 times larger), you can expect a deviation of .05 (2 times smaller). On average, the proportion of heads deviates from chance less and less for larger samples.

In sharp contrast, the *number* of heads deviates from chance *more and more* for larger samples. In fact,

$$\text{standard deviation (\textit{number} of heads)} = \frac{1}{2} \times \sqrt{n}. \qquad (11b)$$

For a sample of 25, you can expect the number of heads to deviate from chance by 2.5, on average. For a sample of 100 (4 times larger), this average deviation is 5 (2 times larger).

Base Rate. *Base rate* refers to the prevailing probability of some event in a given population. Base rate is thus a control standard to assess effectiveness of attempts to change that probability.

As a classic example, psychoanalysts used to point out with satisfaction that two thirds of their patients improved. But the base rate for improvement was itself two thirds (Meehl, 1954; Section 16.1.3). Two thirds of the patients improved regardless of kind of therapy, including no special therapy. One reason is that patients come for treatment when they feel especially down, temporary fluctuation that tends to improve with time. Although well known, this fallacy recurred in a recent major study (Note 18.5.4e).

Base rate is important in diagnostic tests because most produce some proportion of false alarms, signaling a defect where none exists. Even though a test is certain to detect every case with a defect, it may have little diagnostic value. If defects are rare, true alarms will also be rare. But every nondefect has a chance to be a false alarm. Because there are so many nondefects, the false alarms may far outnumber and swamp the true alarms (Exercise 18).[a]

Expected Value. Life is one gamble after another. We are not usually sensitive to this ubiquity of chance, partly because the probability of bad luck is small in most of our actions, partly because of a natural optimism of the human spirit. When we buy a used car, it is true, we are keenly aware it is a gamble because the probability of bad luck is substantial. Every car ride, however, is also a gamble even though the probability of accident is very small. Perhaps marriage should also be considered a gamble, seeing that half end in divorce.[b, c]

Probability and *value* are two essential properties of a gamble. The used car purchase not only has an apprehensive probability of turning out badly, but also usually represents a considerable sum of money. The net value of a gamble depends on both properties, probability and value.

How should we integrate these two properties of a gamble to determine its net value? The answer is by multiplication. This product defines the *expected value*—the average payoff if the gamble is played many times:

$$\text{Expected value} = \text{Probability} \times \text{Value}. \tag{12}$$

To illustrate, suppose you bet one dollar on red on the roulette wheel at Las Vegas. If the roulette ball bounces into one of the 18 red slots, the croupier pays you one dollar; if the ball bounces into one of the 18 black slots, you lose your dollar. This would yield an even bet, with expected value of 0; the casino would make no money and could not pay the croupier.

How can the casino pay the croupier? It adds two more slots on the roulette wheel (0 and 00). If the ball bounces into either of these slots, you lose.

You thus have 20 chances to lose but only 18 to win. Your expected value is

$$\text{Expected value} = (18/38) \text{ dollar} - (20/38) \text{ dollar}$$

$$= -5.26 \text{ cents}.$$

That the odds favor the casino is well known. If they didn't, the casino would go broke. Why people flock to casinos to flout the inexorable law of expected value has been much discussed in psychology of judgment–decision.

Expected value is a guideline to handle chance: Seek gambles with positive expected value, avoid those with negative expected value. Given a choice between two gambles, choose the one with larger expected value.

This guideline of expected value is important in your research. Each experiment you do is a gamble, with two possible bad outcomes: false alarm and miss. Statistics gives you quantitative tools to help deal with these two risks, as discussed in the next subsection.

False Alarms and Misses. Probability thinking is basic to using confidence intervals and significance tests. Consider the standard E versus C experiment. If the E − C difference is truly 0, a significance test using the 95% confidence interval will nevertheless claim a real difference 1 time in 20—a *false alarm*.

On the other hand, if there is a real E − C difference, the confidence interval may fail to detect it—a *miss*.

Two bad outcomes are thus possible, false alarms and misses. One way to deal with these two bad outcomes is to put one's head in the sand. This ostrich thinking is often adopted through ignorance. It brings a certain amount of bliss, it is true, but at the cost of wasted work in the form of false alarms and/or misses that could have been avoided.

Probability thinking can help you deal with the risks of false alarms and misses. Probability thinking makes clear that these two risks are inherent in dealing with sample data. Probability thinking goes further. It allows you to quantify the risk of false alarms; if you think 95% confidence is not enough, you can decrease this risk by using a 99% confidence interval. But doing so has a price: The risk of misses goes up. Techniques for dealing with this dilemma of two bad outcomes are taken up in Sections 2.3.5, 2.3.7, and 4.3.

For you, the bottom line is that the outcome of your experiment is partly a matter of chance effects in your sample. Some experiments have a good chance of success, some do not. Probability thinking can help you understand these chances—and quantify them—thereby helping you avoid the poor and choose the good. Even better, probability thinking can help you improve your chances if you apply it in the planning stage of your experiment.

This theme of foresight in planning an experiment appears repeatedly throughout this book. In the empirical perspective, experimental foresight is a primary function of statistics.

0.3.2 DEALING WITH DATA

Many complications can arise when dealing with data. Three are discussed in the following subsections.

Figures Always Lie. Data lie in many ways and for many reasons. One reason is that we typically deal with small samples from a large population. Necessarily, the sample will misrepresent the population to some extent. This misrepresentation is amplified when we summarize the sample with a single number, such as the mean.

The culprit is not the mean, of course, but the person who uses the mean without statistical understanding. Such misrepresentation can be reduced by using a confidence interval, which presents the mean in its true form—as an interval of likely error.

The mean can mislead in a very different way. Suppose we find the E treatment is statsig superior to the C treatment. It is easy to fall into thinking, without thinking, that E is better for every subject. But E may be worthless for some subjects. It may even be harmful for others. This problem is familiar in medicine, in which harmful side effects can occur, and do occur in some patients. Here again the culprit is not the mean, but the person who learns statistics without empirical understanding.[a]

Selection Effects. Subtle biases can arise from *selection effects* that take advantage of chance accidents in the data. One kind of selection bias can arise when more than one comparison is tested. Each separate comparison has a 5% threat of false alarm; this 5% threat is multiplied when multiple comparisons are made. This selection bias is rather common in health studies.

As an illustration, one study reported that dietary supplements of minerals and vitamins raised nonverbal IQ by several points in just three months, a notable accomplishment. A 95% confidence interval comparing the experimental and control groups showed that the difference was statsig (for the real case behind this partly hypothetical example, see page 539). But previous claims for increased IQ have not held up, many of them vitiated by experimental and statistical blunders. Accordingly, we scrutinize the Method section to check for possible blunders. There we read that seven measures of nonverbal intelligence were used in order not to miss any aspects of intelligence. Use of multiple measures was desirable in this case, but the analysis blundered. Separate tests were made on each measure, but only one yielded a statsig effect.

At this point, our confidence in the claimed result begins to evaporate. Suppose there is no real effect. Use of the 95% confidence interval then carries a 5% threat of false alarm. But each of the seven comparisons has a separate threat of false alarm. Although these seven threats are not independent, taken together they yield a false alarm threat usually much higher than 5%.

This kind of selection effect is a general problem because most investigations make more than one comparison (see further Section 4.2.2, pages 99*ff*). A related kind of selection effect deserves separate discussion in the next subsection, which includes a strategy for dealing with them.

Exploration and Replication. Personal inspection of your data is an essential part of scientific inference. One reason, among others, is that unexpected results may appear. Unexpected results may be more important than the expected. Notable discoveries have been made in this way (see e.g., *Confounding Wins Nobel Prize*, pages 237*f*).

But such exploration of the data suffers from likelihood of the selection effect discussed in the preceding subsection. You are sifting through the data for results that stand out, and some will stand out by chance.

How can you handle this danger of being sandbagged by chance results? The best answer is **replication.**

Exploration of the data is suggestive, but not conclusive. Test such suggestions with a new investigation. If the result replicates, it seems unlikely to be a selection effect or false alarm.

Replication is becoming increasingly required in empirical research. One reason is to avoid selection bias. No less important is that understanding any phenomenon generally requires a network of interrelated experiments. The *Principle of Replication* is thus as important for substantive as for statistical reasons (see further Section 2.4.6).

0.3.3 REDUCE VARIABILITY !

That data are variable is a basic fact of empirical science. Different samples from the same population will yield different results. This is why the sample mean should be considered an interval of likely error. Expression 2 on page 787 shows that this likely error is proportional to your variability, s. If you can reduce your variability, you will get narrower confidence intervals—and greater power to detect experimental effects.

How to reduce variability is a major concern of this book. Two general approaches are available: experimental and statistical. To foreshadow this concern with reducing variability, one aspect of each approach is discussed briefly in the next two subsections.

Experimental Procedure. The width of your confidence interval—your likely error—depends on your experimental procedure, especially task–subject congruence. To reduce likely error, the first line of attack is to establish task–subject congruence.

Your subjects enter a situation that to them is usually novel and unclear. Novelty and unclarity will evoke irrelevant reactions; these will increase the variability of your measured response. The first step, therefore, is to put each subject at ease. With children, ask about their favorite games, TV programs, and so on. When picking up a rat, gentle it on your arm to calm its terror in the grasp of this huge monster.

Subject–task congruence also requires that the task be clear to the subject. One or two subjects who fail to understand the task can yield extreme scores, producing a high value of s and hence a wider confidence interval. Task clarity is a major concern in books on test construction, in which the pervasive difficulties and treacherous pitfalls have been extensively documented (see Section 14.1.2 on writing instructions, pages 405f).[a]

Try to see the task as subjects see it. With verbal subjects, find out what the instructions mean to them while planning the experiment. Serve as a subject yourself. With nonverbal subjects, rats, monkeys, or human infants, personal appreciation is harder to get but no less important.

Pilot work is essential for subject–task congruence. Not only should subjects be adapted to the task, but the task should be adapted to the subjects. Every experiment should begin with successive stages of pilot work to improve task–subject congruence.

Learn from others. Ask your fellow students to fault your design, good practice for them and for you. Attend to questions and criticisms following your departmental colloquia. Study Method sections in published articles; these are repositories of lore that can help you avoid dismal mistakes and get cleaner data. The more you learn from others, the more you will learn from Nature.

Statistical Method. By far the largest source of variability in most experiments is individual differences. Consider the foregoing E versus C experiment, but with different subjects in each group. Each mean will depend on which subjects chance to be sampled for each condition. Different samples of subjects will yield different results because they contain different individuals. The E condition could appear superior merely because better subjects chanced to be in this condition.

Your first goal, accordingly, is to show that the E–C difference is reliable, not a likely chance outcome of individual differences. This is just what the confidence interval does for you. The standard deviation, s, in the confidence interval is composed mainly of individual differences in most experiments.

In some experiments, however, we can run each subject in both conditions. Subjects high/low on Y_E will generally be high/low on Y_C. Since our response measure is the *change*, $Y_{Ei} - Y_{Ci}$, the high/low differences between individuals cancel out. The standard deviation, s, is much reduced, therefore, and the confidence interval is much narrower.

This example illustrates repeated measures design, in which the same subject is measured repeatedly, under a number of successive conditions. Repeated measures designs are highly prized for lower variability, but they present certain difficulties. One difficulty is that practice is confounded with experimental treatments. If treatment C is given first, E second, practice alone may make E look better than C. How to handle this and other difficulties with repeated measures is a central issue in experimental design (see Chapter 6 and Sections 14.3 and 14.4).

The ultimate in reducing individual differences is single subject design, with sufficiently many observations to allow separate data analysis for each individual. Of course, the same individual will give different responses to the same stimulus on different trials, even in simple, repetitive tasks of reaction time or rating person descriptions. The data analysis, accordingly, must take account of variability *within* each individual. Standard statistical techniques can be applied to help deal with response variability within the individual, as well as with problems of confounding that arise from practice and other order effects. Statistical techniques are no less useful in dealing with independence, which is a central problem in single subject design. Single subject designs are common in a few fields, such as perception, behavior modification, and judgment–decision, but deserve broader use (Chapter 11).

0.4 SCIENTIFIC INFERENCE

Scientific inference is mainly extrastatistical. As empirical scientists, we seek empirical inferences from our data. In this endeavor, statistics is a helpful but minor aid. Statistics is mainly concerned with **reliability**; empirical science is mainly concerned with **validity**.

The narrowness of a confidence interval, for example, is a measure of the likely error—the reliability—of the sample mean. If 0 is outside the confidence interval for $\bar{Y}_E - \bar{Y}_C$, this is reasonable evidence that E and C had different effects. Such evidence for reliability of our result is generally prerequisite to making a public claim of a discovery.

Empirically, however, our central problem is not reliability, but validity. Granted that our result is real, what does it mean? Most controversies in science revolve around substantive meaning, not statistical significance. Validity is primarily substantive, outside the statistical domain.

This extrastatistical character of scientific inference is well illustrated with **confounding**. A standard example of confounding is the practice effect mentioned on page 789. Another is the classic placebo effect. Merely giving a medication carries the suggestion that it will be beneficial; this suggestion can be surprisingly beneficial, even though the medication is worthless. These two possible causes of an observed effect will be confounded unless we use appropriate experimental design and procedure. A significance test of the sample effect may be necessary, but it is far from sufficient.

Confounding is mainly extrastatistical, important enough for a separate chapter. Confounding, however, is only one aspect of scientific inference.

Scientific inference is discussed in terms of the Experimental Pyramid on page 3 of Chapter 1. Six levels of investigation are shown in this Pyramid, each of which involves a different facet of scientific inquiry.

The top level of the Experimental Pyramid is statistical inference, which includes concepts and tools such as confidence interval. The standard stereotype confines statistics to this top level, which applies mainly after the data have been collected. Empirical workers generally hope their their result will be "statistically significant," so this top level of the Pyramid comes to be seen as all-important, whereas it is least important.

In fact, the main value of statistics comes in the problem solving stage of planning the experiment, long before the data are collected. Statistics should be woven into your thinking at every level of the Experimental Pyramid. Empirics and statistics should be an organic harmony. Instruction should aim to help you along the learning road of empirics–statistics integration.

This aim underlies the "Empirical Direction" of this book.

NOTES

0.1.2a. A third answer to the proposal to select representative samples of subjects is that they are practically impossible to achieve. Individual behavior is highly unpredictable in novel situations.

0.1.3a. Although $MS_{error} = s^2$ is an unbiased estimate of σ^2, its square root, s, is not an unbiased estimate of σ. This bias is not ordinarily pertinent; in particular, it does not affect the t test or confidence intervals.

0.1.3b. The confidence interval will of course differ from sample to sample. However, 95% of the confidence intervals around the sample mean will contain the population mean. Hence you are entitled to 95% confidence that the confidence interval calculated from your one particular sample contains the population mean (see further *The Concept of Confidence*, page 94).

0.1.3c. The confidence interval also adds information about the size of the effect—measured jointly by the width of the confidence interval and the distance between the end of the interval and 0.

0.4.1a. *Formula for Normal Distribution.* Although the mathematical formula for the normal distribution is not needed to understand anything in this book, it is given here to show that it really does exist. For a normal distribution with mean μ and standard deviation, σ, this formula is

$$Y = \frac{1}{\sigma \sqrt{2\pi}} e^{-1/2 \left[\frac{X-\mu}{\sigma} \right]^2}. \tag{14}$$

This formula gives the probability, Y, of each value of X, as illustrated in Figure 0.1 where X is women's heights. In this formula, π denotes the ratio of the circumference of a circle to its diameter, and e denotes the base for natural logarithms.

This formula shows that all normal distributions have the same overall shape; they differ only in their mean, μ, and standard deviation, σ. The multiplier, $1/\sigma \sqrt{2\pi}$, makes the total area under the normal curve equal to 1, as it must be to be a probability distribution.

For the curious, this formula contains three famous numbers. Two are π and e, workhorse numbers that pop up everywhere in mathematics. Both are *transcendental* numbers, so called because they are not the roots of any polynomial equation with rational coefficients. $\sqrt{2}$ is an *irrational* number—not expressible as the ratio of two whole numbers—and hence not really a number to the ancient Greeks. The discovery that $\sqrt{2}$ was irrational caused a crisis in the Pythagorean religion analogous to, although lesser than, the crisis in the Catholic church caused by Galileo's discoveries.

0.2.1a. Probability theory also includes the NOT rule: $Prob(NOT\ A) = 1 - Prob(A)$.

0.3a. Runs of consecutive events present some interesting aspects of probability thinking. A couple has four girls in a row and are expecting their fifth child. Will it be another girl? Since height and other physical characteristics are correlated across siblings, it seems reasonable to expect the same for sex. On this plausible argument, the probability that the fifth child will also be a girl is greater than ½.

Actually, sex of successive children is independent—heads or tails. This sex independence was only discovered through empirical analysis, which is always necessary to decide whether two physical events are independent.

0.3b. To illustrate another important aspect of runs of events, consider all couples with six children. List the sex of the children in the order of their birth. Then

$$\text{Prob(B B B B B B)} = \text{Prob(B G G B G B)}.$$

This may seem counterintuitive on the ground that 6 boys is considerably less probable than 3 boys and 3 girls. This equation, however, specifies the *order* of birth. In fact, all 64 possible orders of 6 children are equally likely, including the two listed. The apparent contradiction arises because 20 of these orders contain 3 boys and 3 girls, whereas only one order contains 6 boys. (This argument assumes equal probability of female and male births, which is slighly inaccurate.)

0.3.2a. Some workers in judgment–decision theory have erroneously claimed that people take no account of base rate in their everyday judgments (e.g., page 640).

0.3.1b. A third reason we are insensitive to the ubiquity of chance is that we mistake our facile retrospective rationalization of causal coherence for prospective judgments of causal inevitability (Anderson, 1991i, p. 128).

0.3.1c. Much distress could be avoided and more happiness experienced if men and women received instruction in family life before and while living together. Courses on marriage and family life should be standard requirements in colleges and universities. What could be more important for personal happiness and social efficiency? This basic aspect of human life is largely ignored in academic psychology, a black mark on our field (Anderson, 1991e).

0.3.2a. Several popular books on misuses of statistics have been written. You owe yourself to browse at least one. They are written from varied points of view, so I suggest skimming in the library to find which are most meaningful to you. Here are some.

> *Flaws and Fallacies in Statistical Thinking* (S. K. Campbell, 1974).
> *How To Lie With Statistics* (D. Huff, 1993).
> *Misused Statistics* (2nd ed.) (H. F. Spirer, L. Spirer, & A. J. Jaffe, 1998).
> *Statistical Deception at Work* (J. Mauro, 1992).
> *On the Wild Side* (M. Gardner, 1992).
> *A Mathematician Reads the Newspaper* (J. A. Paulos, 1995).
> *How Numbers Lie* (R. P. Runyon, 1981).
> *Say It With Figures* (6th ed.) (H. Zeisel, 1985).
> *Statistics: A Guide to the Unknown* (3rd ed). (J. Tanur et al., 1989).

0.3.3a. Even more than for reducing variability, subject–task congruence is important for response quality. If different subjects understand the task in different ways, your response measure may be just a mess. More than once, it has been belatedly found that subjects told to do one thing were actually doing something rather different (see e.g., Shanteau's work on judgments of probability cited on page 405 and the result on unfairness in marriage in Anderson, 1996a, p. 178*f*).

EXERCISES FOR CHAPTER 0

1. In the numerical example of Section 0.1.3, suppose 9 is changed to 14.

   a. By visual inspection of Equation 1a, without actual calculation, do you think the variance will increase, decrease, or stay the same? Why?

   b. Use Equations 1 with hand calculation to show that $s = 3.536$.

2. Given the information of Figure 0.1 about heights of adult U.S. women, guess the mean and standard deviation for heights of adult U.S. men.

3. Consider the half-width of the confidence interval, $t * s / \sqrt{n}$.

   a. As n increases, other things being equal, what happens to the half-width?

   b. Intuitively, why does your answer to (a) make sense?

   c. As s decreases, other things being equal, what happens to the half-width?

   d. Intuitively, why does your answer to (c) make sense?

   e. For your present experiment, what can you do to decrease s?

4. In the numerical example of confidence interval in Section 0.1.3, suppose the numbers are difference scores, $Y_{Ei} - Y_{Ci}$, each subject in both treatments.

   a. Can we reasonably conclude treatment E is superior to C?

   b. Get the t ratio for the mean of this sample. Interpret it.

   c. Which do you prefer, confidence interval or t test? Why?

5. Under *Confidence Interval as Significance Test* in Section 0.1.3, explain in your own words the meaning of:

   a. "Therefore, if 0 lies outside this interval, we have 95% confidence that 0 cannot be the population mean."

   b. "In other words, we have 95% confidence that the two treatments differ in effectiveness."

6. You test E versus C with the same subjects in both conditions, and get difference scores of 0, 1, 2, 3, and 4 for your five subjects.

   a. What is the similarity between this sample and that in the *Numerical Example* (page 787) in the text?

   b. On the basis of this similarity, guess s for the given sample.

   c. What principle underlies your guess in (b)?

   d. On the basis of this similarity, find the 95% confidence interval for the mean for a significance test. Interpret.

   e. Get the t ratio for the mean (Equation 3) for a significance test.

   f. Which do you prefer, confidence interval or t test?

7. Use Equation 1a to calculate with pencil and paper the variances for these four samples with $n = 2$. Also get the standard deviations using Equation 1b.

　a. (1, 3}.　b. {1, 5}.　c. {1, 7}.　d. {1, 9}.　　[Variance for (d) is 32.]

　e. What progressions do these four cases exhibit?

　f. Use these progressions to predict mean and standard deviation for the next two samples in the progression.

　g. Do (f) for the variance.

8. Length and weight of normal term, newborn males in the U.S. follow near-normal distributions with means of approximately 19.5 inches and 7.1 pounds, and standard deviations of approximately .89 inches and 1.08 pounds.

　a. Find the range of lengths that includes 68% of the cases.

　b. Find the range of weights that includes 95% of the cases.

9. Consider two samples: {1, 3} and {1, 2, 3}. By visual inspection of Equation 1a, say which will have smaller variance. Or will both be equal?

10. Under *Law of Averages*:

　a. Verify that the standard deviation of the proportion of heads is .10 and .05 for samples of size 25 and 100, respectively.

　b. Verify that the standard deviation of the number of heads is 2.5 and 5 for samples of size 25 and 100, respectively.

11. Pollsters can get more accurate results with larger samples, but larger samples are more expensive. In the numerical example of Section 0.1.4, how large a sample is needed to cut the margin of error in half? What does this tell you?

12. You see a poll on TV saying that 56% of the voters favor the bond issue for wildlife conservation in your state, with a margin of error of 4%.

　a. How large was the poll?

　b. The bond issue needs a simple majority to pass. Taking this poll at face value, is the bond issue likely to pass?

　c. What statistical assumption underlies the validity of this poll result?

　d.* How can the statistical assumption of (c) be satisfied empirically?

　e. What clue suggests that the poll may not be too trustworthy?

　f. What empirical assumptions underlie the validity of this poll result?

13. a. Verify that a random number between 00 and 99, inclusive, has probability .18 of having exactly one digit equal to 2.

　b. Below Equation 7, verify "Counting shows that (A AND B) consists of 13 numbers."

  c. Show "Rewriting the conditional rule of Equation 7" yields Equation 8.

14. *Figures Always Lie* in Section 0.3.2 considers two ways in which data can lie. Give two other ways. (See also Note 0.3.2a.)

15. The OR rule of Equation 6 is often illustrated graphically. Draw a square to represent the set of all balls in the Probability Urn. Inside the square, draw two possibly overlapping circles to represent the balls in A and B, respectively. Let the area in circle A be proportional to the number of balls in A, and similarly for B. Show that adding areas can illustrate the two listed equations for the OR rule.

16. Surgeons were told that the annual rate for complications following a certain surgical procedure was 20%. For the current year, now half over, the rate was 14%. They were asked to predict the rate for the rest of the year.

  a. What dumb mistake did the surgeons make? And why?

  b. What is *your* prediction? And why?

(Note: This is a result from a published study, but I have not relocated it.)

17. Granted that a coin "has no memory," it is logically impossible for it to equalize the *numbers* of heads and tails, as noted in the text. How then can it equalize the *proportions* of heads and tails? You may be able to discover the principle by considering the following example. You toss a fair coin 300 times and observe 200 heads, 100 tails—100 more heads than tails.

  You decide to toss 300 more times. How many heads and tails should you expect in these additional 300 tosses? Considering all 600 tosses, what should you expect to happen to (i) the difference in number of heads and to (ii) the proportion of heads?

18. How base rate can fool uneducated intuition is illustrated in this example from Christensen–Szalanski and Beach (1982):

> In a city of 100,000 people, there are 7,000 people who have contracted disease K. A test for disease K is positive in 80% of the people who have the disease and negative in 80% of the people without the disease. The test is given to all the people in the city. In this city, what is the probability that a person with a positive test has disease K?

  a. The modal answer of the subjects was .80. Intuitively, do you think this is too low, too high, or about right?

  b. Calculate the number of those with disease K who will test positive.

  c. Calculate the number of those without disease K who will test positive.

  d. From these two calculations, find the probability that a person who tests positive has disease K.

  e. What is the moral of this example?

STATISTICAL TABLES

NOTE: Power charts are from Table 18 in E. S. Pearson and H. O. Hartley (Eds.), *Biometrika tables for statisticians* (1972, Vol. 2). New York: Cambridge University Press. Reproduced by permission of *the Biometrika Trust*.

TABLE A1

RANDOM DIGITS

09188	20097	32825	39527	04220	86304	83389	87374	64278	58044
90045	85497	51981	50654	94938	81997	91870	76150	68476	64659
73189	50207	47677	26269	62290	64464	27124	67018	41361	82760
75768	76490	20971	87749	90429	12272	95375	05871	93823	43178
54016	44056	66281	31003	00682	27398	20714	53295	07706	17813
08358	69910	78542	42785	13661	58873	04618	97533	31223	08420
28306	03264	81333	10591	40510	07893	32604	60475	94119	01840
53840	86233	81594	13628	51215	90290	28466	68795	77762	20791
91757	53741	61613	62269	50263	90212	55781	76514	83483	47055
89415	92694	00397	58391	12607	17646	48949	72306	94541	37408
77513	03820	86864	29901	68414	82774	51908	13980	72893	55507
19502	37174	69979	20288	55210	29773	74287	75251	65344	67415
21818	59313	93278	81757	05686	73156	07082	85046	31853	38452
51474	66499	68107	23621	94049	91345	42836	09191	08007	45449
99559	68331	62535	24170	69777	12830	74819	78142	43860	72834
33713	48007	93584	72869	51926	64721	58303	29822	93174	93972
85274	86893	11303	22970	28834	34137	73515	90400	71148	43643
84133	89640	44035	52166	73582	70091	61222	60561	62327	18423
56732	16234	17395	96131	10123	91622	85496	57560	81604	18880
65138	56806	87648	85261	34313	65861	45875	21069	85644	47277
38001	02176	81719	11711	71602	92937	74219	64049	65584	49698
37402	96397	01304	77586	56271	10086	47324	62605	40030	37438
97125	40348	87083	31417	21815	39250	75237	62047	15501	29578
21826	41134	47143	34072	64638	85902	49139	06441	03856	54552
73135	42742	95719	09035	85794	74296	08789	88156	64691	19202
07638	77929	03061	18072	96207	44156	23821	99538	04713	66994
60528	83441	07954	19814	59175	20695	05533	52139	61212	06455
83596	35655	06958	92983	05128	09719	77433	53783	92301	50498
10850	62746	99599	10507	13499	06319	53075	71839	06410	19362
39820	98952	43622	63147	64421	80814	43800	09351	31024	73167
59580	06478	75569	78800	88835	54486	23768	06156	04111	08408
38508	07341	23793	48763	90822	97022	17719	04207	95954	49953
30692	70668	94688	16127	59196	80091	82067	63400	05462	69200
65443	95659	18288	27437	49632	24041	08337	65676	96299	90836
27267	50264	13192	72294	07477	44606	17985	48911	97341	30358
91307	06991	19072	24210	36699	53728	28825	35793	28976	66252
68434	94688	84473	13622	62126	98408	12843	82590	09815	93146
48908	15877	54745	24591	35700	04754	83824	52692	54130	55160
06913	45197	42672	78601	11883	09528	63011	98901	14974	40344
10455	16019	14210	33712	91342	37821	88325	80851	43667	70883

Digits are random; grouped by 5s for convenience.
From *A million random digits* by permission of The RAND Corporation.

TABLE A2a

Permutations of 9 Numbers

1 7 5	8 7 6	3 1 7	5 8 2	7 3 5	4 9 8	5 7 6
4 2 9	2 9 3	2 6 9	9 4 7	6 8 2	3 2 6	1 4 2
6 8 3	1 5 4	8 5 4	1 3 6	9 4 1	7 1 5	8 9 3
9 7 4	1 7 3	9 5 4	5 3 4	3 8 2	9 1 3	1 2 5
8 3 6	9 6 4	2 6 8	8 6 1	6 1 5	8 7 5	7 3 8
1 5 2	2 8 5	1 7 3	9 7 2	9 7 4	4 2 6	6 4 9
7 6 1	2 8 9	5 9 2	9 6 7	9 7 4	5 2 1	1 3 6
9 8 5	1 7 3	1 4 3	1 3 8	6 8 2	9 3 4	5 8 4
2 3 4	6 5 4	6 7 8	2 4 5	3 1 5	7 8 6	9 7 2
2 1 9	6 7 5	6 1 9	3 6 1	3 6 5	9 2 1	2 4 3
3 7 5	4 9 8	3 2 5	5 4 9	1 9 8	6 7 8	5 8 7
8 6 4	2 1 3	8 4 7	7 8 2	7 4 2	5 4 3	9 6 1
4 3 9	7 4 5	9 5 3	8 1 5	8 6 2	6 5 8	9 6 7
8 6 7	8 3 2	6 4 7	3 2 4	9 1 4	7 3 1	8 4 5
2 1 5	9 6 1	8 2 1	6 7 9	7 5 3	4 2 9	2 3 1
6 5 7	2 3 1	6 4 7	4 2 8	5 7 4	5 1 3	2 9 6
2 3 8	4 9 5	3 8 2	6 1 3	2 3 6	7 8 9	1 5 4
1 9 4	6 8 7	5 1 9	5 7 9	1 8 9	4 2 6	8 3 7
6 3 8	9 5 4	6 8 2	6 9 5	3 2 6	6 5 1	3 1 7
2 7 1	8 3 7	7 3 4	8 1 2	8 7 4	9 2 3	6 9 5
4 5 9	2 6 1	9 5 1	3 7 4	1 9 5	4 7 8	2 8 4
3 6 8	8 7 5	6 4 3	5 6 2	9 7 3	5 2 4	8 1 2
2 5 1	1 9 3	9 7 1	8 3 4	6 1 4	3 6 9	3 9 7
4 9 7	2 6 4	8 2 5	7 9 1	5 8 2	8 7 1	6 5 4
1 5 7	1 7 6	3 8 1	2 7 6	2 3 9	9 8 6	6 5 4
3 2 4	2 8 3	2 9 5	8 5 4	6 4 5	1 2 7	8 2 9
8 9 6	4 5 9	7 6 4	3 1 9	1 8 7	5 4 3	7 1 3
2 1 5	8 1 2	9 6 2	4 7 2	8 5 2	2 6 9	5 6 9
6 8 4	6 7 4	1 3 8	6 3 9	1 3 4	4 7 1	8 3 1
9 3 7	3 5 9	7 5 4	5 8 1	6 9 7	3 5 8	4 2 7
9 8 1	6 5 9	4 3 1	8 1 7	9 1 3	3 4 2	3 6 2
6 7 3	3 7 1	6 7 8	9 6 4	4 2 6	5 7 8	7 9 5
4 2 5	2 8 4	5 2 9	2 5 3	5 7 8	6 1 9	8 1 4
3 6 8	9 8 5	5 6 2	2 1 3	8 2 5	9 5 4	3 4 7
5 4 9	2 4 7	9 1 8	6 9 5	6 9 4	2 1 7	1 5 9
7 1 2	1 3 6	7 3 4	4 8 7	1 7 3	6 8 3	2 6 8

NOTE: Each block is one permutation. From L. E. Moses and R.V. Oakford, *Tables of random permutations.* Reproduced by permission of Stanford University Press.

TABLE A2b

PERMUTATIONS OF 16 NUMBERS

```
 2 16  8 14     5 12  9 10    15  3 16 11    14 15  6 16     5  3 12  7     6  5 14 12
 9  3 10  6     1  2 11 16    10 12  9  2     1  4  2  3    15 13  2  9     7  3  2  9
 7  1  5 11    15 13 14  3     7  4 13  5    13  9 11  8     8 10  6  1    13  1 16 10
 4 13 15 12     7  8  4  6     8  1  6 14    10 12  7  5    14  4 11 16     8 11  4 15

14 11 15  7     5  1 10  8    12 14  3 10    13  4  2  6     2  9 15 10     9 10  5  8
 9 10  8  5    12  2  9  3     2  4 16  8    14  3 15 11     1  6 13 16    11  1 13 16
 2  6  1 13    11  6  4 14     5 11 13  1    10 12  1  5    12  4 11  3     7  4  6 15
 3  4 16 12    16 13  7 15     7 15  6  9     7 16  9  8     7  8 14  5    14  3  2 12

11  2 13  9     8 13  3  4    11  2  4 16     4  3  1  2     8 15 11  6     1 11  4 13
12 16 10  1     2  5 15 11    10  1  8 14    13  6  8 11    13  2  5 10     6 14 12 10
 6  4 15  8    10  1 12  7     3  7  5  6    10 12 15  7     9 14  3 12    15  7  3  8
 7 14  3  5    16  6  9 14     9 13 15 12    16  9 14  5     4  7  1 16    16  5  9  2

 1 15 12  2    11 14 15  1    14  3 11  6     7  9  4 14     8  2 11  9    14 12 11  4
 6  4  8  7    13  3  9 12     9  1  2 16    10 12 15  5     3  6 12  4     2  3  9 15
 5 16 13 10     7 10  2 16    12 10  5  4     6 13 16 11    10 14  1 15     8  7 13 10
 3 11 14  9     8  6  5  4    15  8  7 13     1  3  2  8     5  7 16 13     6 16  5  1

15  7  6  5     7 14 10  1    16  2  4  5     9  3  8 10     8 16  5  3    10  5  3 14
16 12  1 10     9 11  5 16     3 11 14  6     4 15  2 16    14 11 10  6     4 11 13  2
13  3 11  4     6  8  3  2    12  7 15  8    11 12  5  7     7  1  2 13    12  8 15  1
14  8  2  9    12  4 13 15    13 10  1  9     1 13 14  6    12  9  4 15     6  7  9 16

 9 14  7  1    12  2 15  3     9 16  4 10     6 10 12  4     4  3 10  9    14  8  6  2
13 10  5  8     5  9  1 11    14 15  1 13    11  5  7 16    15  6 11 16     4 11  5 13
12  6  2 11    10  4 16  8     3 12  7  6     2  8 15  3     5  2 14 12    12  3  9 10
15  4  3 16     7  6 13 14     8  5 11  2    14  9 13  1    13  1  8  7    15 16  1  7

15 11 12  6     9 12  3 15    15  4  9 13    12  2  7  3    14 11 12  9    10 15  4 13
 9 10 14  3     1 10  8 16     7 16  6 10     9 15  5  6     5 15 13  6     8  7 14 11
13  7  4  2    14  6  5  7     5 12  3  1    14  4  8  1     4  3 10  8     9 12  5  3
16  1  5  8     2 11 13  4     2 11 14  8    16 11 13 10     1 16  2  7     2  1  6 16

 7  5  3  6     7  4 12 14    12 10  7 13    10  8 16  2     2 11 10 13     7 16  3  4
15  2 12  1     9 15 13  8     4  3  2 14     7  5 12  4    12  3  6 16    12  9  5 14
11 16  9 14     2  3  5  6     6  8 16  9    14 15  1 13     9 14  7  5     6 11  1  8
 4 13  8 10    16 11  1 10    11 15  5  1     3 11  9  6     4  1 15  8    10 13 15  2

 3  7 16 12     4 10 15  8    13 12  9  2     3  7  8 13    15 11 13 10    15  8 13  4
 8  5 15  2    11 12  7  9    14  7  4  3    15  9 10  2     5  3  4  8    14  1 12  2
13  4 11  6     6 14  2  5    10  8  1 16    14  6 11  1     1  7  9 14    16 10  5  6
 9 14  1 10     3  1 13 16     5 11  6 15     5  4 16 12    12  6 16  2     3 11  7  9
```

NOTE: Each block is one permutation. From L. E. Moses and R. V. Oakford, *Tables of random permutations*. Reproduced by permission of Stanford University Press.

TABLE A3
STANDARD NORMAL z SCORES

z	Area	z	Area	z	Area	z	Area	z	Area	z	Area
.00	.0000	.50	.1915	1.00	.3413	1.50	.4332	2.00	.4773	2.50	.4938
.01	.0040	.51	.1950	1.01	.3438	1.51	.4345	2.01	.4778	2.51	.4940
.02	.0080	.52	.1985	1.02	.3461	1.52	.4357	2.02	.4783	2.52	.4941
.03	.0120	.53	.2019	1.03	.3485	1.53	.4370	2.03	.4788	2.53	.4943
.04	.0160	.54	.2054	1.04	.3508	1.54	.4382	2.04	.4793	2.54	.4945
.05	.0199	.55	.2088	1.05	.3531	1.55	.4394	2.05	.4798	2.55	.4946
.06	.0239	.56	.2123	1.06	.3554	1.56	.4406	2.06	.4803	2.56	.4948
.07	.0279	.57	.2157	1.07	.3577	1.57	.4418	2.07	.4808	2.57	.4949
.08	.0319	.58	.2190	1.08	.3599	1.58	.4430	2.08	.4812	2.58	.4951
.09	.0359	.59	.2224	1.09	.3621	1.59	.4441	2.09	.4817	2.59	.4952
.10	.0398	.60	.2258	1.10	.3643	1.60	.4452	2.10	.4821	2.60	.4953
.11	.0438	.61	.2291	1.11	.3665	1.61	.4463	2.11	.4826	2.61	.4955
.12	.0478	.62	.2324	1.12	.3686	1.62	.4474	2.12	.4830	2.62	.4956
.13	.0517	.63	.2357	1.13	.3708	1.63	.4485	2.13	.4348	2.63	.4957
.14	.0057	.64	.2389	1.14	.3729	1.64	.4495	2.14	.4838	2.64	.4959
.15	.0596	.65	.2422	1.15	.3749	1.65	.4505	2.15	.4842	2.65	.4960
.16	.0636	.66	.2454	1.16	.3770	1.66	.4515	2.16	.4868	2.66	.4961
.17	.0675	.67	.2486	1.17	.3790	1.67	.4525	2.17	.4850	2.67	.4962
.18	.0714	.68	.2518	1.18	.3810	1.68	.4535	2.18	.4854	2.68	.4963
.19	.0754	.69	.2549	1.19	.3830	1.69	.4545	2.19	.4857	2.69	.4964
.20	.0793	.70	.2580	1.20	.3849	1.70	.4554	2.20	.4861	2.70	.4965
.21	.0832	.71	.2612	1.21	.3869	1.71	.4563	2.21	.4865	2.71	.4966
.22	.0871	.72	.2642	1.22	.3888	1.72	.4573	2.22	.4868	2.72	.4967
.23	.0910	.73	.2673	1.23	.3907	1.73	.4582	2.23	.4871	2.73	.4968
.24	.0948	.74	.2704	1.24	.3925	1.74	.4591	2.24	.4875	2.74	.4969
.25	.0987	.75	.2734	1.25	.3944	1.75	.4599	2.25	.4878	2.75	.4970
.26	.1026	.76	.2764	1.26	.3962	1.76	.4608	2.26	.4881	2.76	.4971
.27	.1064	.77	.2794	1.27	.3980	1.77	.4616	2.27	.4884	2.77	.4972
.28	.1103	.78	.2823	1.28	.3997	1.78	.4625	2.28	.4887	2.78	.4973
.29	.1141	.79	.2852	1.29	.4015	1.79	.4633	2.29	.4980	2.79	.4974
.30	.1179	.80	.2882	1.30	.4032	1.80	.4641	2.30	.4893	2.80	.4974
.31	.1217	.81	.2910	1.31	.4049	1.81	.4649	2.31	.4896	2.81	.4975
.32	.1255	.82	.2939	1.32	.4066	1.82	.4656	2.32	.4898	2.2	.4976
.33	.1293	.83	.2967	1.33	.4082	1.83	.4664	2.33	.4901	2.83	.4977
.34	.1331	.84	.2996	1.34	.4099	1.84	.4671	2.34	.4904	2.84	.4977
.35	.1368	.85	.3023	1.35	.4115	1.85	.4678	2.35	.4906	2.85	.4978
.36	.1406	.86	.3501	1.36	.4131	1.86	.4686	2.36	.4909	2.86	.4979
.37	.1443	.87	.3079	1.37	.4147	1.87	.4693	2.37	.4911	2.87	.4980
.38	.1480	.88	.3106	1.38	.4162	1.88	.4700	2.38	.4913	2.88	.4980
.39	.1517	.89	.3133	1.39	.4177	1.89	.4706	2.39	.4916	2.89	.4981
.40	.1554	.90	.3159	1.40	.4192	1.90	.4713	2.40	.4918	2.90	.4981
.41	.1591	.91	.3186	1.41	.4207	1.91	.4719	2.41	.4920	2.91	.4982
.42	.1628	.92	.3212	1.42	.4222	1.92	.4726	2.42	.4922	2.92	.4983
.43	.1664	.93	.3238	1.43	.4236	1.93	.4732	2.43	.4925	2.93	.4983
.44	.1700	.94	.3264	1.44	.4251	1.94	.4738	2.44	.4927	2.94	.4984
.45	.1736	.95	.3289	1.45	.4265	1.95	.4744	2.45	.4929	2.95	.4984
.46	.1772	.96	.3315	1.46	.4279	1.96	.4750	2.46	.4931	2.96	.4985
.47	.1808	.97	.3340	1.47	.4292	1.97	.4756	2.47	.4932	2.97	.4985
.48	.1844	.98	.3365	1.48	.4306	1.98	.4762	2.48	.4934	2.98	.4986
.49	.1879	.99	.3389	1.49	.4319	1.99	.4767	2.49	.4936	2.99	.4986
.50	.1915	1.00	.3413	1.50	.4332	2.00	.4773	2.50	.4938	3.00	.4987

TABLE A4

CRITERIAL VALUES OF t FOR $\alpha = .10, .05,$ AND $.01$

df	.10	.05	.01	df	.10	.05	.01
1	6.31	12.71	63.66	18	1.74	2.11	2.90
2	2.92	4.30	9.92	19	1.73	2.09	2.86
3	2.35	3.18	5.84	20	1.72	2.09	2.84
4	2.13	2.78	4.60	21	1.72	2.08	2.83
5	2.01	2.57	4.03	22	1.72	2.07	2.82
6	1.93	2.45	3.14	23	1.71	2.07	2.81
7	1.90	2.36	3.50	24	1.71	2.06	2.80
8	1.86	2.31	3.36	25	1.71	2.06	2.79
9	1.83	2.26	3.25	26	1.71	2.06	2.78
10	1.81	2.23	3.17	27	1.70	2.05	2.77
11	1.80	2.20	3.11	28	1.70	2.05	2.76
12	1.78	2.18	3.06	29	1.70	2.04	2.76
13	1.77	2.16	3.01	30	1.70	2.04	2.75
14	1.76	2.14	2.98	40	1.68	2.02	2.70
15	1.75	2.13	2.95	60	1.67	2.00	2.66
16	1.75	2.12	2.92	120	1.66	1.98	2.62
17	1.74	2.11	2.90	∞	1.64	1.96	2.58

NOTE: Abridged from Table 12 in E. S. Pearson and H. O. Hartley (Eds.), *Biometrika tables for statisticians* (1966, Vol. 1). New York: Cambridge University Press. Reproduced by permission of *the Biometrika Trust*.

TABLE A6

CRITERIAL VALUES OF CHI SQUARE FOR $\alpha = .05$ AND $.01$.

df	1	2	3	4	5	6	8	10
.05	3.84	5.99	7.81	9.49	11.07	12.59	15.51	18.30
.01	6.64	9.21	11.34	13.28	15.09	16.81	20.90	23.21

NOTE: Abridged from Table 8 in E. S. Pearson and H. O. Hartley (Eds.), *Biometrika tables for statisticians* (1966, Vol. 1). New York: Cambridge University Press. Reproduced by permission of *the Biometrika Trust*.

TABLE A4a

CRITERIAL VALUES FOR STUDENTIZED RANGE FOR $\alpha = .05$ AND $.01$

Number of means

df	α	2	3	4	5	6	7	8
6	.05	3.46	4.34	4.90	5.30	5.63	5.90	6.12
	.01	5.24	6.33	7.03	7.56	7.97	8.32	8.61
7	.05	3.34	4.16	4.68	5.06	5.36	5.61	5.82
	.01	4.95	5.92	6.54	7.01	7.37	7.68	7.94
8	.05	3.26	4.04	4.53	4.89	5.17	5.40	5.60
	.01	4.75	5.64	6.20	6.62	6.96	7.24	7.47
9	.05	3.20	3.95	4.41	4.76	5.02	5.24	5.43
	.01	4.60	5.43	5.96	6.35	6.66	6.91	7.13
10	.05	3.15	3.88	4.33	4.65	4.91	5.12	5.30
	.01	4.48	5.27	5.77	6.14	6.43	6.67	6.87
12	.05	3.08	3.77	4.20	4.51	4.75	4.95	5.12
	.01	4.32	5.05	5.50	5.84	6.10	6.32	6.51
14	.05	3.03	3.70	4.11	4.41	4.64	4.83	4.99
	.01	4.21	4.89	5.32	5.63	5.88	6.08	6.26
16	.05	3.00	3.65	4.05	4.33	4.56	4.74	4.90
	.01	4.13	4.79	5.19	5.49	5.72	5.92	6.08
18	.05	2.97	3.61	4.00	4.28	4.49	4.67	4.82
	.01	4.07	4.70	5.09	5.38	5.60	5.79	5.94
20	.05	2.95	3.58	3.96	4.23	4.45	4.62	4.77
	.01	4.02	4.64	5.02	5.29	5.51	5.69	5.84
24	.05	2.92	3.53	3.90	4.17	4.37	4.54	4.68
	.01	3.96	4.55	4.91	5.17	5.37	5	5.69
30	.05	2.89	3.49	3.85	4.10	4.30	4.46	4.60
	.01	3.89	4.45	4.80	5.05	5.24	5.40	5.54
40	.05	2.86	3.44	3.79	4.04	4.23	4.39	4.52
	.01	3.82	4.37	4.70	4.93	5.11	5.26	5.39
60	.05	2.83	3.40	3.74	3.98	4.16	4.31	4.44
	.01	3.76	4.28	4.59	4.82	4.99	5.13	5.25
120	.05	2.80	3.36	3.68	3.92	4.10	4.24	4.36
	.01	3.70	4.20	4.50	4.71	4.87	5.01	5.12
∞	.05	2.77	3.31	3.63	3.86	4.03	4.17	4.29
	.01	3.64	4.12	4.40	4.60	4.76	4.88	4.99

NOTE: Abridged from Table 29 in E. S. Pearson and H. O Hartley (Eds.), *Biometrika tables for statisticians*, (1966, Vol. 1). New York: Cambridge University Press. Reproduced by permission of *the Biometrika Trust*.

TABLE A5

CRITERIAL VALUES OF F FOR $\alpha = .05$

	Numerator df					
Denom df	1	2	3	4	6	8
1	161	200	216	225	234	239
2	18.5	19.0	19.2	19.3	19.3	19.4
3	10.1	9.55	9.28	9.12	8.94	8.85
4	7.71	6.94	6.59	6.39	6.16	6.04
5	6.61	5.79	5.41	5.19	4.95	4.82
6	5.99	5.14	4.76	4.53	4.28	4.15
7	5.59	4.74	4.35	4.12	3.87	3.73
8	5.32	4.46	4.07	3.84	3.58	3.44
9	5.12	4.26	3.86	3.63	3.37	3.23
10	4.96	4.10	3.71	3.48	3.22	3.07
11	4.84	3.98	3.59	3.36	3.09	2.95
12	4.75	3.89	3.49	3.26	3.00	2.85
14	4.60	3.74	3.34	3.11	2.85	2.70
16	4.49	3.63	3.24	3.01	2.74	2.59
18	4.41	3.55	3.16	2.93	2.66	2.51
20	4.35	3.49	3.10	2.87	2.60	2.45
24	4.26	3.40	3.01	2.78	2.51	2.36
30	4.17	3.32	2.92	2.69	2.42	2.27
40	4.08	3.23	2.84	2.61	2.34	2.18
60	4.00	3.15	2.76	2.53	2.25	2.10
120	3.92	3.07	2.68	2.45	2.17	2.02
∞	3.84	3.00	2.60	2.37	2.10	1.94

NOTE: Abridged from Table 18 in E. S. Pearson and H. O. Hartley (Eds.), *Biometrika tables for statisticians* (1966, Vol. 1). New York: Cambridge University Press. Reproduced by permission of *the Biometrika Trust*.

COMMENT: This table should meet nearly all your needs for F.* One need is for chapter exercises, at least those done by hand. Unlisted values for denominator df in the first column can be found by interpolation. The other need, namely, for confidence intervals, may be met by using t* values from Table A4, which also includes values for $\alpha = .10$ and $.01$, for use with 90% and 99% confidence intervals. Neither table is generally needed for computer analyses because these generally print out the "p value." You need only compare this p with your prechosen α. Four decades ago, when most of us used mechanical calculators, more extensive tables were needed, including other α values besides .05. These relics of a past age can be still found in virtually all other texts should they become necessary.

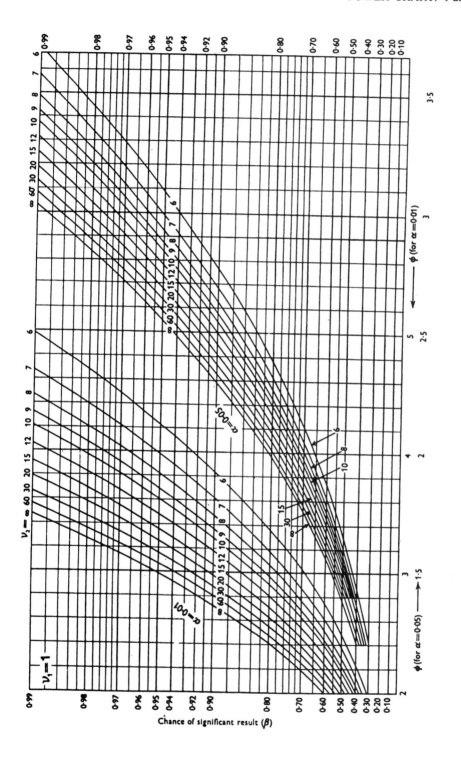

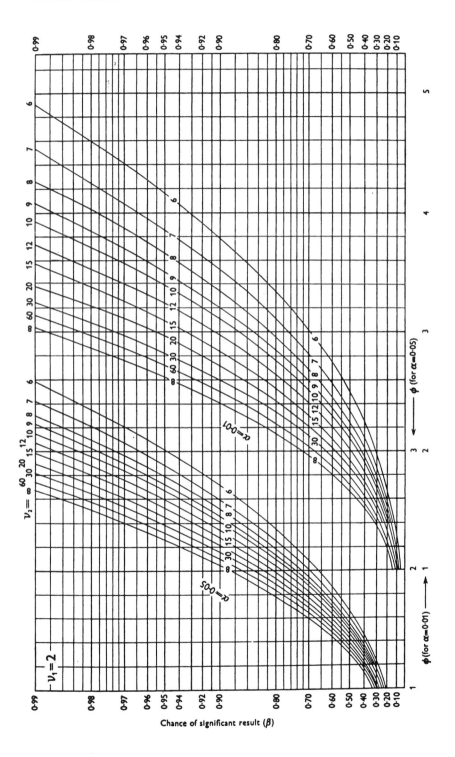

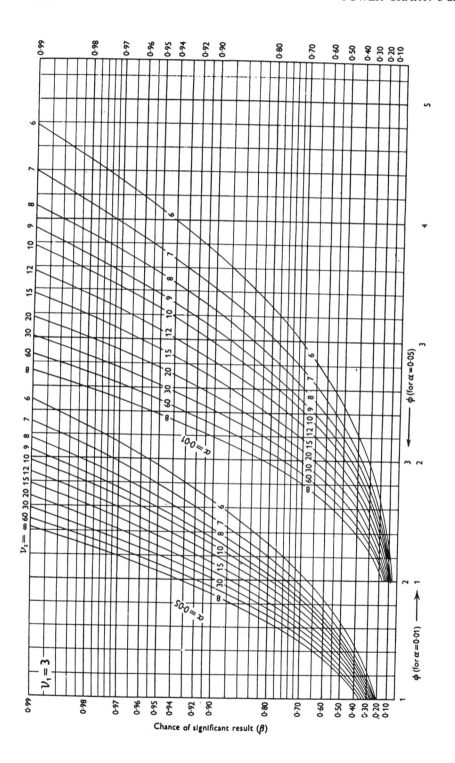

$v_1 = 3$

Chance of significant result (β)

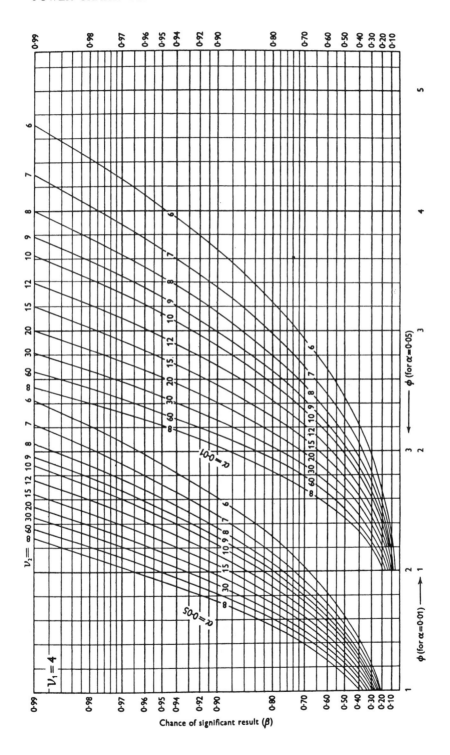

Chance of significant result (β)

REFERENCES

Abelson, P. H. (1983). Editorial comment on controlled drinking controversy. *Science, 220*, 555-556.

Abelson, R. P. (1985). A variance explanation paradox: When a little is a lot. *Psychological Bulletin, 97*, 129-133.

Abelson, R. P., Aronson, E., McGuire, W. J., Newcomb, T. M., Rosenberg, M. J., & Tannenbaum, P. H. (Eds.). (1968). *Theories of cognitive consistency: A sourcebook.* Chicago: Rand McNally.

Achen, C. H. (1986). *The statistical analysis of quasi-experiments.* Berkeley, CA: University of California Press.

Agresti, A. (1996). *An introduction to categorical data analysis.* New York: Wiley.

Akritas, M. G. (1990). The rank transform method in some two-factor designs. *Journal of the American Statistical Association, 85*, 73-78.

Algom, D. (Ed.). (1992). *Psychophysical approaches to cognition.* New York: North-Holland Elsevier Science.

Alpha-Tocopherol, Beta Carotene Cancer Prevention Study Group. (1994). The effect of vitamin E and beta carotene on the incidence of lung cancer and other cancers in male smokers. *New England Journal of Medicine, 330*, 1029-1035.

Anastasi, A., & Urbina, S. (1997). *Psychological testing* (7th ed.). Upper Saddle River, NJ: Prentice Hall.

Anderson, D. R., & Well, A. D. (1975). Hale and Stevenson's failure to find a developmental trend in the effects of distraction: A floor effect. *Journal of Experimental Child Psychology, 20*, 363-365.

Anderson, N. H. (1959a). Education for research in psychology. *American Psychologist, 14*, 695-696.

Anderson, N. H. (1959b). Test of a model for opinion change. *Journal of Abnormal and Social Psychology, 59*, 371-381.

Anderson, N. H. (1960a). Effect of first-order conditional probability in a two-choice learning situation. *Journal of Experimental Psychology, 59*, 73-93.

Anderson, N. H. (1960b). Statistics wins and students loses. Review of *Statistical analysis in psychology and education* by G. A. Ferguson. *Contemporary Psychology, 5*, 312f.

Anderson, N. H. (1961a). Group performance in an anagram task. *Journal of Social Psychology, 55*, 67-75.

Anderson, N. H. (1961b). Scales and statistics: Parametric and nonparametric. *Psychological Bulletin, 58*, 305-316.

Anderson, N. H. (1962a). Application of an additive model to impression formation. *Science, 138*, 817-818.

Anderson, N. H. (1962b). On the quantification of Miller's conflict theory. *Psychological Review, 69*, 400-414.

Anderson, N. H. (1963). Comparison of different populations: Resistance to extinction and transfer. *Psychological Review, 70*, 162-179.

Anderson, N. H. (1964a). An evaluation of stimulus sampling theory: Comments on Professor Estes' paper. In A. W. Melton (Ed.), *Categories of human learning* (pp. 129-144). New York: Academic Press.

Anderson, N. H. (1964b). Test of a model for number-averaging behavior. *Psychonomic Science, 1*, 191-192.

Anderson, N. H. (1965). Averaging versus adding as a stimulus-combination rule in impression formation. *Journal of Experimental Psychology, 70*, 394-400.

Anderson, N. H. (1968). Partial analysis of high-way factorial designs. *Behavior Research Methods & Instrumentation, 1*, 2-7.

Anderson, N. H. (1969). Comment on "An analysis-of-variance model for the assessment of configural cue utilization in clinical judgment." *Psychological Bulletin, 72*, 63-65.

Anderson, N. H. (1970a). Averaging model applied to the size-weight illusion. *Perception & Psychophysics, 8*, 1-4.

Anderson, N. H. (1970b). Functional measurement and psychophysical judgment. *Psychological Review, 77*, 153-170.

Anderson, N. H. (1971). Two more tests against change of meaning in adjective combinations. *Journal of Verbal Learning and Verbal Behavior, 10*, 75-85.

Anderson, N. H. (1971a). An exchange on functional and conjoint measurement. *Psychological Review, 78*, 457-458.

Anderson, N. H. (1972a). Is this book worth $1,000,000? Review of *Experimental principles and design in psychology* by H. D. Kimmel. *Contemporary Psychology, 17*, 132f.

Anderson, N. H. (1972b). Looking for configurality in clinical judgment. *Psychological Bulletin, 78*, 93-102.

Anderson, N. H. (1973a). Functional measurement of social desirability. *Sociometry, 36*, 89-98.

Anderson, N. H. (1973b). Information integration theory applied to attitudes about U.S. presidents. *Journal of Educational Psychology, 64*, 1-8.

Anderson, N. H. (1974a). Algebraic models in perception. In E. C. Carterette & M. P. Friedman (Eds.), *Handbook of perception* (Vol. 2, pp. 215-298). New York: Academic Press.

Anderson, N. H. (1974b). Cognitive algebra: Integration theory applied to social attribution. In L. Berkowitz (Ed.), *Advances in experimental social psychology* (Vol. 7, pp. 1-101). New York: Academic Press.

Anderson, N. H. (1974c). Information integration theory: A brief survey. In D. H. Krantz, R. C. Atkinson, R. D. Luce, & P. Suppes (Eds.), *Contemporary developments in mathematical psychology* (Vol. 2, pp. 236-305). San Francisco: Freeman.

Anderson, N. H. (1975). On the role of context effects in psychophysical judgment. *Psychological Review, 82*, 462-482.

Anderson, N. H. (1976a). How functional measurement can yield validated interval scales of mental quantities. *Journal of Applied Psychology, 61*, 677-692.

Anderson, N. H. (1976b). Integration theory, functional measurement and the psychophysical law. In H.-G. Geissler & Yu. M. Zabrodin (Eds.), *Advances in psychophysics* (pp. 93-130). Berlin: Deutscher Verlag der Wissenschaften.

Anderson, N. H. (1977). Some problems in using analysis of variance in balance theory. *Journal of Personality and Social Psychology, 35*, 140-158.

Anderson, N. H. (1978). Measurement of motivation and incentive. *Behavior Research Methods & Instrumentation, 10*, 360-375.

Anderson, N. H. (1979a). Algebraic rules in psychological measurement. *American Scientist, 67*, 555-563.

Anderson, N. H. (1979b). Indeterminate theory: Reply to Gollob. *Journal of Personality and Social Psychology, 37*, 950-952.

Anderson, N. H. (1980). Information integration theory in developmental psychology. In F. Wilkening, J. Becker, & T. Trabasso (Eds.), *Information integration by children* (pp. 1-45). Hillsdale, NJ: Lawrence Erlbaum Associates.

Anderson, N. H. (1981). *Foundations of information integration theory.* New York: Academic Press.

Anderson, N. H. (1982). *Methods of information integration theory.* New York: Academic Press.

Anderson, N. H. (1983). Intuitive physics: Understanding and learning of physical relations. In T. J. Tighe & B. E. Shepp (Eds.), *Perception, cognition, and development* (pp. 231-265). Hillsdale, NJ: Lawrence Erlbaum Associates.

Anderson, N. H. (1989). Information integration approach to emotions and their measurement. In R. Plutchik & H. Kellerman (Eds.), *Emotion: Theory, research, and experience* (Vol. 4, pp. 133-186). New York: Academic Press.

Anderson, N. H. (1990). Personal design in social cognition. In C. Hendrick & M. S. Clark (Eds.), *Research methods in personality and social psychology: Review of personality and social psychology* (Vol. 11, pp. 243-278). Beverly Hills, CA: Sage.

Anderson, N. H. (Ed.). (1991a). *Contributions to information integration theory. Vol. I: Cognition.* Hillsdale, NJ: Lawrence Erlbaum Associates.

Anderson, N. H. (Ed.). (1991b). *Contributions to information integration theory. Vol. II: Social.* Hillsdale, NJ: Lawrence Erlbaum Associates.

Anderson, N. H. (Ed.). (1991c). *Contributions to information integration theory. Vol. III: Developmental.* Hillsdale, NJ: Lawrence Erlbaum Associates.

Anderson, N. H. (1991d). Editor's Note 1. In N. H. Anderson (Ed.), *Contributions to information integration theory. Vol. II: Social* (pp. 90-94). Hillsdale, NJ: Lawrence Erlbaum Associates.

Anderson, N. H. (1991e). Family life and personal design. In N. H. Anderson (Ed.), *Contributions to information integration theory. Vol. III: Developmental* (pp. 189-242). Hillsdale, NJ: Lawrence Erlbaum Associates.

Anderson, N. H. (1991f). Functional memory in person cognition. In N. H. Anderson (Ed.), *Contributions to information integration theory. Vol. I: Cognition* (pp. 1-55). Hillsdale, NJ: Lawrence Erlbaum Associates.

Anderson, N. H. (1991g). Schemas in person cognition. In N. H. Anderson (Ed.), *Contributions to information integration theory. Vol. I: Cognition* (pp. 57-103). Hillsdale, NJ: Lawrence Erlbaum Associates.

Anderson, N. H. (1991h). Stereotype theory. In N. H. Anderson (Ed.), *Contributions to information integration theory. Vol. II: Social* (pp. 183-240). Hillsdale, NJ: Lawrence Erlbaum Associates.

Anderson, N. H. (1991i). A cognitive theory of judgment and decision. In N. H. Anderson (Ed.), *Contributions to information integration theory. Vol. I: Cognition* (pp. 105-142). Hillsdale, NJ: Lawrence Erlbaum Associates.

Anderson, N. H. (1991j). Psychodynamics of everyday life: Blaming and avoiding blame. In N. H. Anderson (Ed.), *Contributions to information integration theory. Vol. II: Social* (pp. 243-275). Hillsdale, NJ: Lawrence Erlbaum Associates.

Anderson, N. H. (1992). Integration psychophysics and cognition. In D. Algom (Ed.), *Psychophysical approaches to cognition* (pp. 13-113). Amsterdam: Elsevier Science.

Anderson, N. H. (1993). Nonconscious sensation and inner psychophysics. *Behavioral and Brain Sciences, 16,* 137-138.

Anderson, N. H. (1996a). *A functional theory of cognition.* Mahwah, NJ: Lawrence Erlbaum Associates.

Anderson, N. H. (1996b). Cognitive algebra versus representativeness heuristic. *Behavioral and Brain Sciences, 19,* 17-18.

Anderson, N. H. (1996c). Functional memory requires a quite different value metaphor. *Behavioral and Brain Sciences, 19,* 190-191.

Anderson, N. H. (1997). Functional memory versus reproductive memory. *Behavioral and Brain Sciences, 20,* 19-20.

Anderson, N. H. (27 November, 2000). Unified theory. (Chapter prepared for Festschrift for William McGuire).

Anderson, N. H., & Armstrong, M. A. (1989). Cognitive theory and methodology for studying marital interaction. In D. Brinberg & J. Jaccard (Eds.), *Dyadic decision making* (pp. 3-50). New York: Springer-Verlag.

Anderson, N. H. & Barrios, A. A. (1961). Primacy effects in impression formation. *Journal of Abnormal and Social Psychology, 63,* 346-350.

Anderson, N. H., & Butzin, C. A. (1978). Integration theory applied to children's judgments of equity. *Developmental Psychology, 14,* 593-606.

Anderson, N. H., & Cuneo, D. O. (1978). The Height + Width rule in children's judgments of quantity. *Journal of Experimental Psychology: General, 107,* 335-378.

Anderson, N. H., & Farkas, A. J. (1975). Integration theory applied to models of inequity. *Personality and Social Psychology Bulletin, 1,* 588-591.

Anderson, N. H., & Jacobson, A. (1965). Effect of stimulus inconsistency and discounting instructions in personality impression formation. *Journal of Personality and Social Psychology, 3,* 531-539.

Anderson, N. H., & Nakamura, C. Y. (1964). Avoidance decrement in avoidance conditioning. *Journal of Comparative and Physiological Psychology, 57,* 196-204.

Anderson, N. H., & Schlottmann, A. (1991). Developmental study of personal probability. In N. H. Anderson (Ed.), *Contributions to information integration theory. Vol. III: Developmental* (pp. 111-134). Hillsdale, NJ: Lawrence Erlbaum Associates.

Anderson, N. H., & Shanteau, J. C. (1970). Information integration in risky decision making. *Journal of Experimental Psychology, 84,* 441-451.

Anderson, N. H., & Shanteau, J. (1977). Weak inference with linear models. *Psychological Bulletin, 84,* 1155-1170.

Anderson, N. H., & Whalen, R. E. (1960). Likelihood judgments and sequential effects in a two-choice probability learning situation. *Journal of Experimental Psychology, 60,* 111-120.

Anderson, N. H., & Wilkening, F. (1991). Adaptive thinking in intuitive physics. In N. H. Anderson (Ed.), *Contributions to information integration theory. Vol. III: Developmental* (pp. 1-42). Hillsdale, NJ: Lawrence Erlbaum Associates.

Anderson, N. H., & Zalinski, J. (1991). Functional measurement approach to self-estimation in multiattribute evaluation. In N. H. Anderson (Ed.), *Contributions to information integration theory. Vol. I: Cognition* (pp. 145-185). Hillsdale, NJ: Lawrence Erlbaum Associates.

Anscombe, F. J. (1973). Graphs in statistical analysis. *American Statistician, 27,* 17-21.

Appleton, D. R., French, J. M., & Vanderpump, M. P. J. (1996). Ignoring a covariate: An example of Simpson's paradox. *The American Statistician, 50,* 340-341.

Aronson, E. (1969). Some antecedents of interpersonal attraction. In W. J. Arnold & D. Levine (Eds.), *Nebraska Symposium on Motivation, 1969, 17,* pp. 143-173. Lincoln, NE: University of Nebraska Press.

Aronson, E., Ellsworth, P. C., Carlsmith, J. M., & Gonzales, M. H. (1990). *Methods of research in social psychology* (2nd ed.). New York: McGraw-Hill.

Asch, S. E. (1946). Forming impressions of personality. *Journal of Abnormal and Social Psychology, 41,* 258-290.

Baillargeon, R., & Graber, M. (1987). Where's the rabbit? 5.5-month-old infants' representation of the height of a hidden object. *Cognitive Development, 2,* 375-392.

Bamber, D. (1975). The area above the ordinal dominance graph and the area below the receiver operating characteristic graph. *Journal of Mathematical Psychology, 12,* 387-415.

Barber, T. X. (1976). *Pitfalls in human research.* New York: Pergamon Press.

Barber, T. X., & Silver, M. J. (1968a). Fact, fiction, and the experimenter bias effect. *Psychological Bulletin Monograph Supplement, 70*(6, Part 2), 1-29.

Barber, T. X., & Silver, M. J. (1968b). Pitfalls in data analysis and interpretation: A reply to Rosenthal. *Psychological Blletin Monograph Supplement, 70*(6, Part 2), 48-62.

Barlow, D. H., & Hersen, M. (1984). *Single case experimental designs* (2nd ed.). New York: Pergamon.

Barnett, V., & Lewis, T. (1984). *Outliers in statistical data* (2nd ed.). New York: Wiley.

Barnett, V., & Lewis, T. (1994). *Outliers in statistical data* (3rd ed.). New York: Wiley.

Baron, A., & Perone, M. (1998). Experimental design and analysis in the laboratory study of human operant behavior. In K. A. Lattal & M. Perone (Eds.), *Handbook of research methods in human operant behavior* (pp. 45-91). New York: Plenum

Barrass, R. (1978). *Scientists must write*. New York: Chapman & Hall.

Barsamian, E. M. (1977). The rise and fall of internal mammary artery ligation in the treatment of angina pectoris and the lessons learned. In J. P. Bunker, B. A. Barnes, and F. Mosteller (Eds.), *Costs, risks, and benefits of surgery* (pp. 212-220). New York: Oxford University Press.

Beach, F. A., & Whalen, R. E. (1959). Effects of ejaculation on sexual behavior in the male rat. *Journal of Comparative and Physiological Psychology, 52*, 249-254.

Becker, H. S. (1986). *Writing for social scientists*. Chicago: University of Chicago Press.

Beebe-Center, J. G. (1966). *The psychology of pleasantness and unpleasantness*. New York: Russell & Russell. (Originally published 1932)

Benison, S., Barger, A. C., & Wolfe, E. L. (1987). *Walter B. Cannon: The life and times of a young scientist*. Cambridge, MA: Belknap Press.

Bennett, C. A., & Lumsdaine, A. A. (Eds.). (1975). *Evaluation and experiment*. New York: Academic Press.

Berger, J. O. (1984). The robust Bayesian viewpoint. In J. B. Kadane (Ed.), *Robustness of Bayesian analyses* (pp. 63-144) (includes commentary). New York: Elsevier Science.

Berkowitz, L. (1960). The judgmental process in personality functioning. *Psychological Review, 67*, 130-142.

Berry, D. A. (1988). Multiple comparisons, multiple tests, and data dredging: A Bayesian perspective. In J. M. Bernardo, M. H. DeGroot, D. V. Lindley, and A. F. M. Smith (Eds.), *Bayesian statistics* (Vol. 3, pp. 79-94). New York: Oxford University Press.

Berry, D. A., & Geisser, S. (1986). Inference in cases of disputed paternity. In M. H. DeGroot, S. E. Fienberg, & J. B. Kadane (Eds.), *Statistics and the law* (pp. 353-390). New York: Wiley.

Berry, D. A., & Stangl, D. K. (Eds.). (1996). *Bayesian biostatistics*. New York: Marcel Dekker.

Bickel, P. J., Hammel, E. A., & O'Connell, J. W. (1977). Sex bias in graduate admissions: Data from Berkeley. In W. B. Fairley and F. Mosteller (Eds.), *Statistics and public policy* (pp. 113-130). Reading, MA: Addison-Wesley. (Reprinted from *Science*, 1975, *187*, 398-404.)

Binder, A. (1963). Further considerations on testing the null hypothesis and the strategy and tactics of investigating theoretical models. *Psychological Review, 70*, 107-115.

Birkes, D., & Dodge, Y. (1993). *Alternative methods of regression*. New York: Wiley.

Birnbaum, M. H. (1974). The nonadditivity of personality impressions. *Journal of Experimental Psychology, 102*, 543-561.

Birnbaum, M. H. (1976). Intuitive numerical prediction. *American Journal of Psychology, 89*, 417-429.

Birnbaum, M. H., & Stegner, S. E. (1979). Source credibility in social judgment: Bias, expertise, and the judge's point of view. *Journal of Personality and Social Psychology, 37*, 48-74.

Birnbaum, M. H., Wong, R., & Wong, L. K. (1976). Combining information from sources that vary in credibility. *Memory & Cognition, 4*, 330-336.

Blalock, H. M. (1991). Are there really any *constructive* alternatives to causal modeling? *Sociological Methodology, 21*, 325-335.

Blinkhorn, S. (1991). A dose of vitamins and a pinch of salt. *Nature, 350*, 13.

Bogartz, R. S. (1976). On the meaning of statistical interactions. *Journal of Experimental Child Psychology, 22*, 178-183.

Bogartz, R. S. (1990a). Evaluating forgetting curves psychologically. *Journal of Experimental Psychology: Learning, Memory, and Cognition, 16*, 138-148.

Bogartz, R. S. (1990b). Learning–forgetting rate independence defined by forgetting function parameters or forgetting function form: Reply to Loftus and Bamber and to Wixted. *Journal of Experimental Psychology: Learning, Memory, and Cognition, 16*, 936-945.

Bogartz, R. S. (1993, August). On pooling error terms in repeated measures designs. Unpublished paper. University of Massachusetts, Amherst.

Bogartz, R. S. (1994a). *An introduction to the analysis of variance.* Westport, CT: Praeger.

Bogartz, R. S. (1994b). A window into children's minds. Review of *Contributions to information integration theory. Vol. III: Developmental* (N. H. Anderson, Ed.). *American Journal of Psychology, 107*, 449-453.

Bogartz, R. S., Shinskey, J. L., & Speaker, C. J. (1997). Interpreting infant looking: The event set × event set design. *Developmental Psychology, 33*, 408-422.

Bogartz, R. S., & Wackwitz, J. H. (1971). Polynomial response scaling and functional measurement. *Journal of Mathematical Psychology, 8*, 418-443.

Booth, W. C., Colomb, G. G., & Williams, J. M. (1995). *The craft of research.* Chicago: University of Chicago Press.

Borges, M. A., & Sawyers, B. K. (1974). Common verbal quantifiers: Usage and interpretation. *Journal of Experimental Psychology, 102*, 335-338.

Bowers, K. S. (1973). Situationism in psychology. *Psychological Review, 80*, 307-336.

Box, G. E. P. (1954). Some theorems on quadratic forms applied in the study of analysis of variance problems, II. Effects of inequality of variance and correlation between errors in the two-way classification. *Annals of Mathematical Statistics, 25*, 484-498.

Box, G. E. P. (1983). An apology for ecumenism in statistics. In G. E. P. Box, T. Leonard, & C-F. Wu (Eds.), *Scientific inference, data analysis, and robustness* (pp. 51-84). New York: Academic Press.

Box, G. E. P., Hunter, W. G., & Hunter, J. S. (1978). *Statistics for experimenters.* New York: Wiley.

Box, G. E. P., & Tiao, G. C. (1973). *Bayesian inference in statistical analysis.* Reading, MA: Addison-Wesley.

Bozivich, H., Bancroft, T. A., & Hartley, H. O. (1956). Power of analysis of variance test procedures for certain incompletely specified models, I. *Annals of Mathematical Statistics, 27*, 1017-1043.

Breckler, S. J. (1990). Applications of covariance structure modeling in psychology: Cause for concern? *Psychological Bulletin, 107*, 260-273.

Brock, T. C., Green, M. C., & Reich, D. A. (1998). New evidence of flaws in the *Consumer Reports* study of psychotherapy. *American Psychologist, 53*, 62-63.

Brock, T. C., Green, M. C., Reich, D. A., & Evans, L. M. (1996). The *Consumer Reports* study of psychotherapy: Invalid is invalid. *American Psychologist, 51*, 1083.

Brogden, W. J. (1951). Some theoretical considerations of learning. *Psychological Review, 58*, 224-233.

Bruner, J. S., & Goodman, C. C. (1947). Value and need as organizing factors in perception. *Journal of Abnormal and Social Psychology, 42*, 33-44.

Bruner, J. S., & Rodrigues, J. S. (1953). Some determinants of apparent size. *Journal of Abnormal and Social Psychology, 48*, 17-24.

Budescu, D. V., & Appelbaum, M. I. (1981). Variance stabilizing transformations and the power of the *F* test. *Journal of Educational Statistics, 6*, 55-74.

Budescu, D. V., & Wallsten, T. S. (1979). A note on monotonic transformations in the context of functional measurement and analysis of variance. *Bulletin of the Psychonomic Society, 14*, 307-310.

Burdick, D. S., & Herr, D. G. (1980). Counterexamples in unbalanced two-way analysis of variance. *Communications in Statistics: Theory and Methods, 9*, 231-241.

Burke, J. (1998). Connections. *Scientific American, 279*, 102-103.

Busemeyer, J. R. (1991). Intuitive statistical estimation. In N. H. Anderson (Ed.), *Contributions to information integration theory. Vol. 1: Cognition* (pp. 187-215). Hillsdale, NJ: Lawrence Erlbaum Associates.

Busemeyer, J. R., & Jones, L. (1983). Analysis of multiplicative combination rules when the causal variables are measured with error. *Psychological Bulletin, 93*, 549-562.

Campbell, D. T. (1978). Quasi-experimental design. In W. H. Kruskal & J. M. Tanur (Eds.), *International encyclopedia of statistics* (pp. 299-305). New York: The Free Press.

Campbell, D. T., & Boruch, R. F. (1975). Making the case for randomized assignment to treatments by considering the alternatives: Six ways in which quasi-experimental evaluations in compensatory education tend to underestimate effects. In C. A. Bennett & A. A. Lumsdaine (Eds.), *Evaluation and experiment* (pp. 195-296). New York: Academic Press.

Campbell, D. T., & Stanley, J. C. (1966). *Experimental and quasi-experimental designs for research.* Chicago: Rand McNally.

Campbell, N. R. (1928). *An account of the principles of measurement and calculation.* London: Longmans, Green.

Cannon, W. B. (1965). *The way of an investigator.* New York: Hafner. (Originally published 1945)

Cannon, W. B. (1969). Hunger and thirst. In C. Murchison (Ed.), *A handbook of general experimental psychology* (pp. 247-263). New York: Russell & Russell. (Originally published 1934)

Cantor, N., & Mischel, W. (1977). Traits as prototypes: Effects on recognition memory. *Journal of Personality and Social Psychology, 35*, 38-48.

Cantor, N., & Mischel, W. (1979). Prototypicality and personality: Effects on free recall and personality impressions. *Journal of Research in Personality, 13*, 187-205.

Carr, E. G., Newsom, C. D., & Binkoff, J. A. (1980). Escape as a factor in the aggressive behavior of two retarded children. *Journal of Applied Behavior Analysis, 13*, 101-117.

Carterette, E. C., & Anderson, N. H. (1979). Bisection of loudness. *Perception & Psychophysics, 26*, 265-280.

Chatterjee, S., & Price, B. (1991). *Regression analysis by example.* New York: Wiley.

Chernoff, H. (1986). Comment. *The American Statistician, 40*, 5-6.

Christensen-Szalanski, J. J. J., & Beach, L. R. (1982). Experience and the base-rate fallacy. *Organizational Behavior and Human Performance, 29*, 270-278.

Clark, H. H. (1973). The language-as-fixed-effect fallacy: A critique of language statistics in psychological research. *Journal of Verbal Learning and Verbal Behavior, 12*, 335-359.

Clavadetscher, J. E. (1991). Studies of a two process theory for geometric illusions. In N. H. Anderson (Ed.), *Contributions to information integration theory. Vol. I: Cognition* (pp. 217-257). Hillsdale, NJ: Lawrence Erlbaum Associates.

Clavadetscher, J. E., & Anderson, N. H. (1977). Comparative judgment: Tests of two theories using the Baldwin figure. *Journal of Experimental Psychology: Human Perception and Performance, 3*, 119-135.

Clemans, W. V. (1971). Test administration. In R. L. Thorndike (Ed.), *Educational measurement* (2nd ed., pp. 188-201). Washington, DC: American Council on Education.

Cliff, N. (1992). Abstract measurement theory and the revolution that never happened. *Psychological Science, 3*, 186-190.

Cliff, N. (1993). What is and what isn't measurement. In G. Keren & C. Lewis (Eds.), *A handbook for data analysis in the behavioral sciences; Methodological issues* (pp. 59-93). Mahwah, NJ: Lawrence Erlbaum Associates.

Cliff, N. (1996). *Ordinal methods for behavioral data analysis.* Mahwah, NJ: Lawrence Erlbaum Associates.

Clinch, J. J., & Keselman, H. J. (1982). Parametric alternatives to the analysis of variance. *Journal of Educational Statistics, 7*, 207-214.

Cochran, W. G. (1983). *Planning and analysis of observational studies.* New York: Wiley.

Cochran, W. G., & Cox, G. M. (1957). *Experimental designs* (2nd ed.). New York: Wiley.

Cohen, J. (1962). The statistical power of abnormal–social psychological research: A review. *Journal of Abnormal and Social Psychology, 65*, 145-153.

Cohen, J. (1977). *Statistical power analysis for the behavioral sciences* (rev. ed.). New York: Academic Press.

Cohen, J. (1988). *Statistical power analysis for the behavioral sciences* (2nd ed.). Mahwah, NJ: Lawrence Erlbaum Associates.

Coleman. E. B. (1964). Generalizing to a language population. *Psychological Reports, 14*, 219-226.

Colman, A. M. (1987). *Facts, fallacies and frauds in psychology.* London: Unwin Hyman.

Conner, R. F. (1977). Selecting a control group: An analysis of the randomization process in twelve social reform programs. *Evaluation Quarterly, 1*, 195-244.

Conover, W. J. (1999). *Practical nonparametric statistics* (3rd ed.). New York: Wiley.

Conover, W. J., & Iman, R. L. (1981). Rank transformations as a bridge between parametric and nonparametric statistics. *The American Statistician, 35*, 124-133.

Conway, D. A., & Roberts, H. V. (1986). Regression analyses in employment discrimination cases. In M. H. DeGroot, S. E. Fienberg, & J. B. Kadane (Eds.), *Statistics and the law* (pp. 107-168). New York: Wiley.

Cook, T. D. (1991). Clarifying the warrant for generalized causal inferences in quasi-experimentation. In M. W. McLaughlin & D. C. Phillips (Eds.), *Evaluation and education: At quarter century* (pp. 115-144). Chicago: University of Chicago Press.

Cook, T. D., & Campbell, D. T. (1979). *Quasi-experimentation.* Chicago: Rand McNally.

Cook, T. D., et al. (1992). *Meta-analysis for explanation.* New York: Russell Sage.

Coombs, C. H. (1964). *A theory of data.* New York: Wiley.

Cornfield, J. (1971). The University Group Diabetes Program. *Journal of the American Medical Association, 217*, 1676-1687.

Cotton, J. W. (1989). Interpreting data from two-period crossover design (also termed the replicated 2 × 2 Latin square design). *Psychological Bulletin, 106*, 503-515.

Cotton, J. W. (1993). Latin square designs. In L. K. Edwards (Ed.), *Applied analysis of variance in behavioral science* (pp. 147-196). New York: Marcel Dekker.

Cotton, J. W. (1998). *Analyzing within-subjects experiments.* Mahwah, NJ: Lawrence Erlbaum Associates.

Cronbach, L. J. (1975). Beyond the two disciplines of scientific psychology. *American Psychologist, 30*, 116-127.

Cronbach, L. J. (1982). *Designing evaluations of educational and social programs.* San Francisco: Jossey-Bass

Cronbach, L. J. (1990). *Essentials of psychological testing* (5th ed.). New York: HarperCollins.

Cronbach, L. J., & Meehl, P. E. (1955). Construct validity in psychological tests. *Psychological Bulletin, 52*, 281-302.

Cronbach, L. J., & Snow, R. E. (1977). *Aptitudes and instructional methods: A handbook for research on interactions.* New York: Irvington.

Crowder, M. J., & Hand, D. J. (1990). *Analysis of repeated measures.* New York: Chapman and Hall.

Cuneo, D. O. (1982). Children's judgments of numerical quantity: A new view of early quantification. *Cognitive Psychology, 14*, 13-44.

Cutler, A. (1981). Making up materials is a confounded nuisance, or: Will we be able to run any psycholinguistic experiments at all in 1990? *Cognition, 10*, 65-70.

Dallal, G. E. (1988). Statistical microcomputing—Like it is. *The American Statistician, 42*, 212-216.

Dallal, G. E. (1992). The 17/10 rule for sample-size determination. *The American Statistician, 46*, 70.

Dawes, R. M. (1969). "Interaction effects" in the presence of asymmetrical transfer. *Psychological Bulletin, 71*, 55-57.

Dawes, R. M. (1971). A case study of graduate admissions. *American Psychologist, 26*, 180-188.

Dawes, R. M. (1994). *House of cards: Psychology and psychotherapy built on myth*. New York: The Free Press.

DeMaris, A., & Leslie, G. R. (1984). Cohabitation with the future spouse: Its influence on marital satisfaction and communication. *Journal of Marriage and the Family, 46*, 77-84.

Dempster, F. N. (1988). The spacing effect: A case study in the failure to apply the results of psychological research. *American Psychologist, 43*, 627-634.

Diaconis, P. (1985). Theories of data analysis: From magical thinking through classical statistics. In D. C. Hoaglin, F. Mosteller, & J. W. Tukey (Eds.), *Exploring data tables, trends, and shapes* (pp. 1-36). New York: Wiley.

Dixon, J. A. (1998). Developmental ordering, scale types, and strong inference. *Developmental Psychology, 34*, 131-145.

Dozier, M., & Butzin, C. (1988). Cognitive requirements of ulterior motive information usage: Individual child analyses. *Journal of Experimental Child Psychology, 46*, 88-99.

Draper, N. R., & Smith, H. (1981). *Applied regression analysis* (2nd ed.). New York: Wiley.

Duncan, D. B. (1955). Multiple range and multiple *F* tests. *Biometrics, 11*, 1-42.

Edgington, E. S. (1987). *Randomization tests* (2nd ed.). New York: Marcel Dekker.

Edwards, A. L. (1985). *Multiple regression and the analysis of variance and covariance* (2nd ed.). New York: W. H. Freeman.

Edwards, W., Lindman, H., & Savage, L. J. (1963). Bayesian statistical inference for psychological research. *Psychological Review, 70*, 193-242.

Efron, B. (1986). Why isn't everyone a Bayesian? *The American Statistician, 40*, 1-11.

Einstein, G. O., & McDaniel, M. A. (1987). Distinctiveness and the mnemonic benefits of bizarre imagery. In M. A. McDaniel & M. Pressley (Eds.), *Imagery and related mnemonic processes: Theories, individual differences, and applications* (pp. 78-102). New York: Springer-Verlag.

Ekehammer, B. (1974). Interactionism in personality from a historical perspective. *Psychological Bulletin, 81*, 1026-1048.

Ellsworth, P. C., & Langer, E. J. (1976). Staring and approach: An interpretation of the stare as a nonspecific activator. *Journal of Personality and Social Psychology, 33*, 117-122.

Emerson, J. D. (1991a). Graphical display as an aid to analysis. In D. C. Hoaglin, F. Mosteller, & J. W. Tukey (Eds.), *Fundamentals of exploratory analysis of variance* (pp. 165-192). New York: Wiley.

Emerson, J. D. (1991b). Introduction to transformations. In D. C. Hoaglin, F. Mosteller, & J. W. Tukey (Eds.), *Fundamentals of exploratory analysis of variance* (pp. 365-400). New York: Wiley.

Emerson, J. D., & Stoto, M. A. (1983). Transforming data. In D. C. Hoaglin, F. Mosteller, & J. W. Tukey (Eds.), *Understanding robust and exploratory data analysis* (pp. 97-128). New York: Wiley.

Erickson, R. L. (1963). Relational isolation as a means of producing the von Restorff effect in paired-associate learning. *Journal of Experimental Psychology, 66*, 111-119.

Erlebacher, A. (1977). Design and analysis of experiments contrasting the within- and between-subjects manipulation of the independent variable. *Psychological Bulletin, 84*, 212-219.

Erlebacher, A. (1978). The analysis of multifactor experiments designed to contrast the within- and between-subjects manipulation of the independent variables. *Behavior Research Methods & Instrumentation, 10*, 833-840.

Ernhart, C. (1993). Deliberate misrepresentations. *Pediatrics, 91*, 171-173.

Ernhart, C. B., & Scarr, S. (1993). Rebuttal to reply on commentary. *The PSR Quarterly, 3*, 142-147.

Ernhart, C. B., Scarr, S., & Geneson, D. F. (1993). On being a whistleblower: The Needleman case. *Ethics and Behavior, 3*, 73-93.

Estes, W. K. (1964). Probability learning. In A. W. Melton (Ed.), *Categories of human learning* (pp. 89-128). New York: Academic Press.

Estes, W. K. (1991). *Statistical models in psychological research*. Hillsdale, NJ: Lawrence Erlbaum Associates.

Fairley, W. B., & Mosteller, F. (1977). *Statistics and public policy*. Reading, MA: Addison-Wesley.

Falk, R., & Wilkening, F. (1998). Children's construction of fair chances: Adjusting probabilities. *Developmental Psychology, 34*, 1340-1357.

Farkas, A. J. (1991). Cognitive algebra of interpersonal unfairness. In N. H. Anderson (Ed.), *Contributions to information integration theory. Vol. II: Social* (pp. 43-99). Hillsdale, NJ: Lawrence Erlbaum Associates.

Farkas, A. J., & Anderson, N. H. (1979). Multidimensional input in equity theory. *Journal of Personality and Social Psychology, 37*, 879-896.

Farley, J., & Fantino, E. (1978). The symmetrical law of effect and the matching relation in choice behavior. *Journal of the Experimental Analysis of Behavior, 29*, 37-60.

Fischhoff, B., Slovic, P., & Lichtenstein, S. (1979). Subjective sensitivity analysis. *Organizational Behavior and Human Performance, 23*, 339-359.

Fisher, R. A. (1932). *Statistical methods for research workers* (4th ed.). Edinburgh: Oliver & Boyd.

Fisher, R. A. (1956). *Statistical methods and scientific inference*. New York: Hafner.

Fisher, R. A. (1958). *Statistical methods for research workers* (13th ed., revised). New York: Hafner.

Fisher, R. A. (1960). *The design of experiments* (7th ed.). New York: Hafner.

Fisher, R. A., & Yates, F. (1963). *Statistical tables for biological, agricultural, and medical research* (6th ed.). New York: Hafner.

Fleiss, J. L. (1981). *Statistical methods for rates and proportions* (2nd ed.). New York: Wiley.

Fleiss, J. L. (1986). *The design and analysis of clinical experiments*. New York: Wiley.

Forster, L. (1982). Vision and prey-catching strategies in jumping spiders. *American Scientist, 70*, 165-175.

Fowles, D. C., & Knutson, J. F. (1995). Clinical research methods. In I. P. Levin and J. V. Hinrichs, *Experimental psychology* (pp. 295-330). Dubuque, IA: Brown & Benchmark.

Franklin, R. D., Allison, D. B., & Gorman, B. S. (Eds.) (1997). *Design and analysis of single-case research*. Mahwah, NJ: Lawrence Erlbaum Associates.

Freedman, D. A. (1987). As others see us: A case study in path analysis. *Journal of Educational Statistics, 12*, 101-128.

Freedman, D. A. (1991). Statistical models and shoe leather. *Sociological methodology, 21*, 291-313.

Freedman D., Pisani, R., & Purves, R. (1998). *Statistics* (3rd ed.). New York: Norton.

Friedman, M. P., Carterette, E. C., & Anderson, N. H. (1968). Long-term probability learning with a random schedule of reinforcement. *Journal of Experimental Psychology, 78*, 442-455.

Fuller, W. A. (1987). *Measurement error models*. New York: Wiley.

Galton, F. (1872). Statistical inquiries into the efficacy of prayer. *The Fortnightly Review, 68, 12-* new series, 125-135.

Games, P. A. (1983). Curvilinear transformations of the dependent variable. *Psychological Bulletin, 93,* 382-387.

Garb, H. N. (1989). Clinical judgment, clinical training, and professional experience. *Psychological Bulletin, 105,* 387-396.

Garb, H. N. (1994). Toward a second generation of statistical prediction rules in psychodiagnosis and personality assessment. *Computers in Human Behavior, 10,* 377-394.

Garb, H. N. (1998). *Studying the clinician.* Washington, DC: American Psychological Association.

Gatsonis, C., Hodges, J. S., Kass, R. E., & Singpurwalla, N. D. (Eds.) (1993). *Case studies in Bayesian statistics.* New York: Springer-Verlag.

Gerber, L. R., DeMaster, D. P., & Roberts, S. P. (2000). Measuring success in conservation. *American Scientist, 88,* 316-324.

Gibbon, J., & Fairhurst, S. (1994). Ratio versus difference comparators in choice. *Journal of the Experimental Analysis of Behavior, 62,* 409-434.

Gigerenzer, G., & Murray, D. J. (1987). *Cognition as intuitive statistics.* Hillsdale, NJ: Lawrence Erlbaum Associates.

Gilbert, J. P., Light, R. J., & Mosteller, F. (1975). Assessing social innovations: An empirical base for policy. In C. A. Bennett & A. A. Lumsdaine (Eds.), *Evaluation and experiment* (pp. 39-193). New York: Academic Press.

Gilbert, J. P., McPeek, B., & Mosteller, F. (1977). Progress in surgery and anesthesia: Benefits and costs of innovative therapy. In J. P. Bunker, B. A. Barnes, and F. Mosteller (Eds.), *Costs, risks, and benefits of surgery* (pp. 124-169). New York: Oxford University Press.

Gillett, R. (1995). The expected power of *F* and *t* tests conditional on information from an earlier experiment. *British Journal of Mathematical and Statistical Psychology, 48,* 371-384.

Gleick, J. (1992). *Genius: The life and science of Richard Feynman.* New York: Pantheon Books.

Goldberg, L. R. (1968). Simple models or simple processes? Some research on clinical judgments. *American Psychologist, 23,* 483-496.

Goldberg, L. R. (1977). Admission to the Ph.D. program in the department of psychology at the University of Oregon. *American Psychologist, 32,* 663-668.

Gould, S. J. (1980). *The panda's thumb.* New York: Norton.

Graesser, C. C., & Anderson, N. H. (1974). Cognitive algebra of the equation: Gift size = Generosity × Income. *Journal of Experimental Psychology, 103,* 692-699.

Grant, D. A. (1956). Analysis-of-variance tests in the analysis and comparison of curves. *Psychological Bulletin, 53,* 141-154.

Grant, D. A. (1962). Testing the null hypothesis and the strategy and tactics of investigating theoretical models. *Psychological Review, 69,* 54-61.

Green, D. M., & Swets, J. A. (1966). *Signal detection theory and psychophysics.* New York: Wiley.

Greenberg, B. G. (1951). Why randomize? *Biometrics, 7,* 309-322.

Greene, T., & Ernhart, C. B. (1993). Dentine lead and intelligence prior to school entry: A statistical sensitivity analysis. *Journal of Clinical Epidemiology, 46,* 323-339.

Greenhouse, S. W., & Geisser, S. (1959). On methods in the analysis of profile data. *Psychometrika, 24,* 95-112.

Greenwald, A. G. (1976). Within-subjects designs: To use or not to use? *Psychological Bulletin, 83,* 314-320.

Grice, G. R. (1966). Dependence of empirical laws upon the source of experimental variation. *Psychological Bulletin, 66,* 488-498.

Grice, G. R., & Hunter, J. J. (1964). Stimulus intensity effects depend upon the type of experimental design. *Psychological Review, 71,* 247-256.

Grove, W. M., & Meehl, P. E. (1996). Comparative efficiency of informal (subjective, impressionistic) and formal (mechanical, algorithmic) prediction procedures: The clinical–statistical controversy. *Psychology, Public Policy, and Law, 2*, 293-323.

Guilford, J. P. (1954). *Psychometric methods* (2nd ed.). New York: McGraw-Hill.

Gunst, R. F., & McDonald, G. C. (1996). The importance of outcome dynamics, simple geometry, and pragmatic statistical arguments in exposing deficiencies of experimental design strategies. *The American Statistician, 50*, 44-50.

Hagen, R. L. (1997). In praise of the null hypothesis statistical test. *American Psychologist, 52*, 15-24.

Hale, G. A., & Stevenson, E. E., Jr. (1974). The effects of auditory and visual distractors on children's performance in a short-term memory task. *Journal of Experimental Child Psychology, 18*, 280-292.

Hand, D. J. & Taylor, C. C. (1987). Multivariate analysis of variance and repeated measures. New York: Chapman and Hall.

Hansel, C. E. M. (1980). *ESP and parapsychology: A critical reevaluation.* Buffalo, NY: Prometheus.

Hansman, C. F. (1970). Anthropometry and related data. In R. W. McCammon (Ed.), *Human growth and development* (pages 103-154). Springfield, IL: Thomas.

Harlow, H. F. (1971). *Learning to love.* New York: Ballantine Books.

Harlow, L. L., Mulaik, S. A., & Steiger, J. H. (Eds.). (1997). *What if there were no significance tests?* Mahwah, NJ: Lawrence Erlbaum Associates.

Harris, C. W. (Ed.). (1963). *Problems in measuring change.* Madison, WI: University of Wisconsin Press.

Harris, R. J. (1976). The uncertain connection between verbal theories and research hypotheses in social psychology. *Journal of Experimental Social Psychology, 12*, 210-219.

Harris, R. J. (1993). Multivariate analysis of variance. In L. K. Edwards (Ed.), *Applied analysis of variance in behavioral sciences* (pp. 255-296). New York: Marcel Dekker.

Harwell, M. R. (1991). Completely randomized factorial analysis of variance using ranks. *British Journal of Mathematical and Statistical Psychology, 44*, 383-401.

Hastie, R., & Kumar, P. A. (1979). Person memory: Personality traits as organizing principles in memory for behaviors. *Journal of Personality and Social Psychology, 37,* 25-38.

Hawkins, R. D., Roll, P. L., Puerto, A., & Yeomans, J. S. (1983). Refractory periods of neurons mediating stimulation-elicited eating and brain stimulation reward: Interval scale measurement and tests of a model of neural integration. *Behavioral Neuroscience, 97*, 416-432.

Hayes, S. C. (1992). Single case experimental design and empirical clinical practice. In A. E. Kazdin (Ed.), *Methodological issues & strategies in clinical research* (pp. 491-521). Washington, DC: American Psychological Association.

Hays, W. L. (1994). *Statistics* (5th ed.). New York: Holt, Rinehart, and Winston.

Heit, E. (1993). Modeling the effects of expectations on recognition memory. *Psychological Science, 4*, 244-252.

Helson, H. (1964). *Adaptation-level theory.* New York: Harper & Row.

Hennekens, C. H., et al. (1996). Lack of effect of long-term supplementation with beta carotene on the incidence of malignant neoplasms and cardiovascular disease. *The New England Journal of Medicine, 334*, 1145-1149.

Henrysson, S. (1971). Gathering, analyzing, and using data on test items. In R. L. Thorndike (Ed.), *Educational measurement,* (2nd ed., pp. 130-159). Washington, DC: American Council on Education.

Herr, D. G., & Gaebelein, J. (1978). Nonorthogonal two-way analysis of variance. *Psychological Bulletin, 85*, 207-216.

Herrnstein, R. J., Loveland, D. H., & Cable, C. (1976). Natural concepts in pigeons. *Journal of Experimental Psychology: Animal Behavior Processes, 2*, 285-302.

Hersen, M., Kazdin, A. E., & Bellack, A. S. (Eds.). (1991). *The clinical psychology handbook* (2nd ed.). New York: Pergamon Press.

Hills, M., & Armitage, P. (1979). The two-period cross-over clinical trial. *British Journal of Clinical Pharmacology, 8*, 7-20.

Hilton, E. T., & Lumsdaine, A. A. (1975). Field trial designs in gauging the impact of fertility planning programs. In C. A. Bennett & A. A. Lumsdaine (Eds.), *Evaluation and experiment* (pp. 319-408). New York: Academic Press.

Himmelfarb, S. (1993). The measurement of attitudes. In A. H. Healy & S. Chaiken, *The psychology of attitudes* (pp. 23-87). Orlando, FL: Harcourt Brace Jovanovich.

Himmelfarb, S., & Anderson, N. H. (1975). Integration theory applied to opinion attribution. *Journal of Personality and Social Psychology, 31*, 1064-1072.

Hines, W. G. S. (1996). Pragmatics of pooling in ANOVA tables. *The American Statistician, 50*, 127-139.

Hoaglin, D. C., Mosteller, F., & Tukey, J. W. (Eds.). (1991). *Fundamentals of exploratory analysis of variance.* New York: Wiley.

Hochberg, Y., & Tamhane, A. C. (1987). *Multiple comparison procedures.* New York: Wiley.

Hodges, J. L., Jr., & Lehmann, E. L. (1954). Testing the approximate validity of statistical hypotheses. *Journal of the Royal Statistical Society, B, 16*, 261-268.

Hoel, P. G. (1962). *Introduction to mathematical statistics* (3rd ed.). New York: Wiley.

Hoffman, P. J., Slovic, P., & Rorer, L. G. An analysis-of-variance model for the assessment of configural cue utilization in clinical judgment. *Psychological Bulletin,* 1968, *69*, 338-349.

Hogarth, R. M. (1975). Cognitive processes and the assessment of subjective probability distributions. *Journal of the American Statistical Association, 70*, 271-294.

Hommers, W., & Anderson, N. H. (1991). Moral algebra of harm and recompense. In N. H. Anderson (Ed.), *Contributions to information integration theory. Vol. II: Social* (pp. 101-141). Hillsdale, NJ: Lawrence Erlbaum Associates.

Howard, J. W., & Dawes, R. M. (1976). Linear prediction of marital happiness. *Personality and Social Psychology Bulletin, 2*, 478-480.

Howell, D. C. (1992). *Statistical methods in psychology* (3rd ed.). Belmont, CA: Duxbury Press.

Huitema, B. E. (1980). *The analysis of covariance and alternatives.* New York: Wiley.

Huitema, B. E. (1985). Autocorrelation in applied behavior analysis: A myth. *Behavioral Assessment, 7*, 107-118.

Huitema, B. E. (1988). Autocorrelation: 10 years of confusion. *Behavioral Assessment, 10*, 253-294.

Huitema, B. E., & McKean, J. W. (1991). Autocorrelation estimation and inference with small samples. *Psychological Bulletin, 110*, 291-304.

Huynh, H., & Feldt, L. S. (1976). Estimation of the Box correction for degrees of freedom from sample data in randomized block and split-plot designs. *Journal of Educational Statistics, 1*, 69-82.

Iman, R. L., & Davenport, J. M. (1980). Approximations of the critical region of the Friedman statistic. *Communications in statistics, theory and method, A9*, 571-595.

Jaccard, J. J., & Fishbein, M. (1975). Inferential beliefs and order effects in personality impression formation. *Journal of Personality and Social Psychology, 31*, 1031-1040.

Jaccard, J., Turrisi, R., & Wan, C. K. (1990). *Interaction effects in multiple regression.* Newbury Park, CA: Sage.

Jaynes, E. T. (1976). Confidence intervals vs Bayesian intervals. In W. L. Harper & C. A. Hooker (Eds.), *Foundations of probability theory, statistical inference, and statistical theories of science, Vol. II: Foundations and philosophy of statistical inference* (pp. 175-213). Dordrecht, Holland: D. Reidel.

Jones, B., & Kenward, M. G. (1989). *Design and analysis of cross-over trials.* New York: Chapman and Hall.

Jones, R. A. (1996). *Research methods in the social and behavioral sciences* (2nd ed.). Sunderland, MA: Sinauer.

Kahn, J. R., & Udry, R. (1986). Marital coital frequency: Unnoticed outliers and unspecified interactions lead to erroneous conclusions. *American Sociological Review, 51,* 734-737.

Kahneman, D., & Tversky, A. (1972). Subjective probability: A judgment of representativeness. *Cognitive Psychology, 3,* 430-454.

Kahneman, D., & Tversky, A. (1996). On the reality of cognitive illusions. *Psychological Review, 103,* 582-591.

Kaplan, M. F. (1971a). Dispositional effects and weight of information in impression formation. *Journal of Personality and Social Psychology, 18,* 279-284.

Kaplan, M. F. (1971b). The effect of judgmental dispositions on forming impressions of personality. *Canadian Journal of Behavioral Science, 3,* 259-267.

Karpp, E. R., & Anderson, N. H. (1997). Cognitive assessment of function knowledge. *Journal of research in science teaching, 34,* 359-376.

Karylowski, J. (1985). Regression toward the mean effect: No statistical background required. *Teaching of Psychology, 12,* 229-230.

Kazdin, A. E. (Ed.). (1992). *Methodological issues & strategies in clinical research.* Washington, DC: American Psychological Association.

Kempthorne, O. (1977). Why randomize? *Journal of Statistical Planning and Inference, 1,* 1-25.

Kendall, M., & Stuart, A. (1976). *The advanced theory of statistics* (Vol. 3, 3rd ed.). London: Griffin.

Kendall, M., & Stuart, A. (1979). *The advanced theory of statistics* (Vol. 2, 4th ed.). London: Griffin.

Kennedy, J. E., & Landesman, J. (1963). Series effects in motor performance studies. *Journal of Applied Psychology, 47,* 202-205.

Keppel, G. (1991). *Design and analysis: A researcher's handbook* (3rd ed.). Englewood Cliffs, NJ: Prentice Hall.

Keselman, H. J. (1994). Stepwise and simultaneous multiple comparison procedures of repeated measures means. *Journal of Educational Statistics, 19,* 127-162.

Keselman, H. J., & Keselman, J. C. (1993). Analysis of repeated measurements. In L. K. Edwards (Ed.), *Applied analysis of variance in behavioral sciences* (pp. 105-145). New York: Marcel Dekker.

Keselman, H. J., Keselman, J. C., & Shaffer, J. P. (1991). Multiple pairwise comparisons of repeated measures means under violations of multisample sphericity. *Psychological Bulletin, 110,* 162-170.

Keselman, J. C., Lix, L. M., & Keselman, H. J. (1996). The analysis of repeated measurements: A quantitative research synthesis. *British Journal of Mathematical and Statistical Psychology, 49,* 275-298.

Kirk, R. E. (1972). *Statistical issues.* Monterey, CA: Brooks/Cole.

Kirk, R. E. (1995). *Experimental design* (3rd ed.). Pacific Grove, CA: Brooks/Cole.

Kirk, R. E. (1996). Practical significance: A concept whose time has come. *Educational and Psychological Measurement, 56,* 746-759.

Klatzky, R. L., & Erdelyi, M. H. (1985). The response criterion problem in tests of hypnosis and memory. *The International Journal of Clinical and Experimental Hypnosis, 33,* 246-257.

Klitzner, M. D. (1977). *Small animal fear: An integration-theoretical analysis.* Unpublished doctoral dissertation, University of California, San Diego.

Klitzner, M. D., & Anderson, N. H. (1977). Motivation × Expectancy × Value: A functional measurement approach. *Motivation and Emotion, 1,* 347-365.

Koehler, J. J. (1996). The base rate fallacy reconsidered: Descriptive, normative, and methodological challenges. *Behavioral and Brain Sciences, 19,* 1-54.

Kohn, A. (1997). *False prophets.* New York: Barnes & Noble.

Kraemer, H. C., & Thiemann, S. (1987). *How many subjects?: Statistical power analysis in research.* Monterey Park, CA: Sage.

Krantz, D. H., Luce, R. D., Suppes, P., & Tversky, A. (1971). *Foundations of measurement* (Vol. 1). New York: Academic Press.

Krantz, D. H., & Tversky, A. (1971a). Conjoint-measurement analysis of composition rules in psychology. *Psychological Review, 78,* 151-169.

Krantz, D. H., & Tversky, A. (1971b). An exchange on functional and conjoint measurement. *Psychological Review, 78,* 457-458.

Kratochwill, T. R., & Levin, J. R. (1992). *Single-case research design and analysis.* Hillsdale, NJ: Lawrence Erlbaum Associates.

Krueger, L. E. (1989). Reconciling Fechner and Stevens: Toward a unified psychophysical law. *Behavioral and Brain Sciences, 12,* 251-320.

Kruglanski, A. W. (1975). The human subject in the psychology experiment: Fact and Artifact. In L. Berkowitz (Ed.), *Advances in experimental social psychology,* (Vol. 8, pp. 101-147). New York: Academic Press.

Kruskal, W. (1980). The significance of Fisher: A review of *R. A. Fisher: The life of a scientist. Journal of the American Statistical Association, 75,* 1019-1030.

Kruskal, W., & Majors, R. (1989). Concepts of relative importance in recent scientific literature. *The American Statistician, 43,* 2-6.

Kulik, J. A., & Mahler, H. I. M. (1987). Effects of preoperative roommate assignment on preoperative anxiety and recovery from coronary-bypass surgery. *Health Psychology, 6,* 525-543.

Kulik, J. A., Mahler, H. I. M., & Moore. P. J. (1996). Social comparison and affiliation under threat: Effects on recovery from major surgery. *Journal of Personality and Social Psychology, 71,* 967-979.

Langer, E. J., & Rodin, J. (1976). The effects of choice and enhanced personal responsibility for the aged: A field experiment in an institutional setting. *Journal of Personality and Social Psychology, 34,* 191-198.

Lattal, K. A., & Perone, M. (Eds.). (1998). *Handbook of research methods in human operant behavior.* New York: Plenum.

Lecoutre, B. (1991). A correction for the $\tilde{\varepsilon}$ approximate test in repeated measures designs with two or more independent groups. *Journal of Educational Statistics, 16,* 371-372.

Lee, H., & Fung, K. Y. (1983). Robust procedures for multi-sample location problems with unequal group variances. *Journal of Statistical Computation and Simulation, 18,* 125-143.

Lee, H., & Fung, K. Y. (1985). Behavior of trimmed F and sine-wave F statistics in one-way ANOVA. *Sankhyā: The Indian Journal of Statistics, 47*-B, 186-201.

Lehmann, E. L. (1993). The Fisher, Neyman–Pearson theories of testing hypotheses: One theory or two? *Journal of the American Statistical Association, 88*, 1242-1249.

Lehr, R. (1992). Sixteen *s*-squared over *d*-squared: A relation for crude sample size estimates. *Statistics in Medicine, 11*, 1099-1102.

Leon, M. (1976). *Coordination of intent and consequence information in children's moral judgments.* Unpublished doctoral dissertation, University of California, San Diego.

Leon, M. (1980). Integration of intent and consequence information in children's moral judgments. In F. Wilkening, J. Becker, & T. Trabasso (Eds.), *Information integration by children* (pp. 71-97). Hillsdale, NJ: Lawrence Erlbaum Associates.

Leon, M., & Anderson, N. H. (1974). A ratio rule from integration theory applied to inference judgments. *Journal of Experimental Psychology, 102*, 27-36.

Léoni, V., & Mullet, E. (1993). Evolution in the intuitive mastery of the relationship between mass, volume, and density from nursery school to college. *Genetic, Social, and General Psychology Monographs, 119*, 389-412.

Leventhal, L., & Huynh, C-L. (1996). Directional decisions for two-tailed tests: Power, error rates, and sample size. *Psychological Methods, 1*, 278-292.

Levin, I. P. & Hinrichs, J. V. (1995). *Experimental psychology.* Madison, WI: Brown & Benchmark.

Levin, I. P., Louviere, J. J., Schepanski, A. A., & Norman, K. L. (1983). External validity tests of laboratory studies of information integration. *Organizational Behavior and Human Performance, 31*, 173-193.

Levin, J. R., & Marascuilo, L. A. (1972). Type IV errors and interactions. *Psychological Bulletin, 78*, 368-374.

Levine, D. W., & Dunlap, W. P. (1982). Power of the *F* test with skewed data: Should one transform or not? *Psychological Bulletin, 92*, 272-280.

Levine, D. W., & Dunlap, W. P. (1983). Data transformation, power, and skew: A rejoinder to Games. *Psychological Bulletin, 93*, 596-599.

Levy, K. J. (1978). An empirical comparison of the ANOVA *F*-test with alternatives which are more robust against heterogeneity of variance. *Journal of Statistical Computation and Simulation, 8*, 49-57.

Light, R. J., Singer, J. D., & Willett, J. B. (1990). *By design: Planning research on higher education.* Cambridge, MA: Harvard University Press.

Lindman, H. R. (1992). *Analysis of variance in experimental designs.* New York: Springer-Verlag.

Link, S. W. (1994). Rediscovering the past: Gustav Fechner and signal detection theory. *Psychological Science, 5*, 335-340.

Loehr, F. (1959). *The power of prayer on plants.* Garden City, NY: Doubleday.

Loftus, G. R. (1978). On interpretation of interactions. *Memory & Cognition, 6*, 312-319.

Loftus, G. R. (1993). Editorial comment. *Memory & Cognition, 21*, 1-3.

Loftus, G. R., & Masson, M. E. J. (1994). Using confidence intervals in within-subject designs. *Psychonomic Bulletin and Review, 1*, 476-490.

Lopes, L. L. (1976a). Individual strategies in goal setting. *Organizational Behavior and Human Performance, 15*, 268-277.

Lopes, L. L. (1976b). Model-based decision and inference in stud poker. *Journal of Experimental Psychology: General, 105*, 217-239.

Lopes, L. L., & Oden, G. C. (1980). Comparison of two models of similarity judgment. *Acta Psychologica, 46*, 205-234.

Lorch, R. F., Jr., & Myers, J. L. (1990). Regression analyses of repeated measures data in cognitive research. *Journal of Experimental Psychology: Learning, Memory, and Cognition, 16*, 149-157.

Lord Rayleigh. (1894). On an anomaly encountered in determinations of the density of nitrogen gas. *Proceedings of the Royal Society of London, 55*, 340-344.

Louviere, J. J. (1988). *Analyzing decision making: Metric conjoint analysis.* Beverly Hills, CA: Sage.

Luce, R. D. (1959). *Individual choice behavior.* New York: Wiley.

Luce, R. D., Mellers, B. A., & Chang, S-J. (1993). Is choice the correct primitive? On using certainty equivalents and reference levels to predict choices among gambles. *Journal of Risk and Uncertainty, 6,* 115-143.

Luce, R. D., & Tukey, J. W. (1964). Simultaneous conjoint measurement: A new type of fundamental measurement. *Journal of Mathematical Psychology, 1,* 1-27.

MacCallum, R. C., & Austin, J. T. (2000). Applications of structural equation modeling in psychological research. *Annual Review of Psychology, 51,* 201-226.

Macmillan, N. A., & Creelman, C. D. (1991). *Detection theory: A user's guide.* New York: Cambridge University Press.

Magnusson, D. (1990). Personality development from an interactional perspective. In L. A. Pervin (Ed.), *Handbook of personality: Theory and research* (pp. 193-222). New York: Guilford.

Magnusson, D., & Endler, N. S. (Eds.). (1977). *Personality at the crossroads: Current issues in interactional psychology.* Hillsdale, NJ: Lawrence Erlbaum Associates.

Maloney, D. P. (1985). Rule-governed approaches to physics: Conservation of mechanical energy. *Journal of Research in Science Teaching, 22,* 261-278.

Maloney, D. P. (1988). Novice rules for projectile motion. *Science Education, 72,* 501-513.

Maltzman, I. (1989). A reply to Cook, "Craftsman versus professional: Analysis of the controlled drinking controversy." *Journal of Studies on Alcohol, 50,* 466-472.

Maltzman, I. (1992). The winter of scholarly science journals. *Professional Counselor, 7,* 38-39, 41-43. (Reprinted in *Chronicle of Higher Education*).

Mandler, J. M., & Read, J. D. (1980). Repeated measurement designs in picture-memory studies. *Journal of Experimental Psychology: Human Learning and Memory, 6,* 400-406.

Mandler, J. M., & Ritchey, G. H. (1977). Long-term memory for pictures. *Journal of Experimental Psychology: Human Learning and Memory, 3,* 386-396.

Mansouri, H., & Chang, G.-H. (1995). A comparative study of some rank tests for interaction. *Computational Statistics & Data Analysis, 19,* 85-96.

Marks, L. E. (1974). *Sensory processes.* New York: Academic Press.

Markwick, B. (1978). The Soal–Goldney experiments with Basil Shackleton: New evidence of data manipulation. *Proceedings of the Society for Psychical Research, 56,* 250-277.

Marshall, M. J., & Linden, D. R. (1994). Simulating clever Hans in the classroom. *Teaching of Psychology, 21,* 230-232.

Martin, R. J., White, B. D., & Hulsey, M. G. (1991). The regulation of body weight. *American Scientist, 79,* 528-541.

Mason, W. M. (1991). Freedman is right as far as he goes, but there is more, and it's worse. Statisticians could help. *Sociological Methodology, 21,* 337-351.

Massaro, D. W. (1987). *Speech perception by eye and ear: A paradigm for psychological inquiry.* Hillsdale, NJ: Lawrence Erlbaum Associates.

Massaro, D. W. (1991). Language processing and information integration. In N. H. Anderson (Ed.), *Contributions to information integration theory. Vol. I: Cognition* (pp. 259-292). Hillsdale, NJ: Lawrence Erlbaum Associates.

Matyas, T. A., & Greenwood, K. M. (1996). Serial dependency in single-case times series. In R. D. Franklin, D. B. Allison, & B. S. Gorman (Eds.), *Design and analysis of single-case research* (pp. 215-243). Mahwah, NJ: Lawrence Erlbaum Associates.

Maxwell, S. E., & Delaney, H. D. (1985). Measurement and statistics: An examination of construct validity. *Psychological Bulletin, 97,* 85-93.

Maxwell, S. E., & Delaney, H. D. (1990). *Designing experiments and analyzing data.* Belmont, CA: Wadsworth.

Maxwell, S. E., Delaney, H. D., & Mannheimer, J. M. (1985). ANOVA of residuals and ANCOVA: Correcting an illusion by using model comparisons and graphs. *Journal of Educational Statistics, 10,* 197-209.

McBride, R. L., & Anderson, N. H. (1991). Integration psychophysics in the chemical senses. In N. H. Anderson (Ed.), *Contributions to information integration theory. Vol. 1: Cognition* (pp. 295-319). Hillsdale, NJ: Lawrence Erlbaum Associates.

McCain, L. J., & McCleary, R. (1979). The statistical analysis of the simple interrupted time-series quasi-experiment. In T. D. Cook & D. T. Campbell (Eds.), *Quasi-experimentation,* (pp. 233-293). Chicago: Rand McNally.

McConnell, R. A., Snowdon, R. J., & Powell, K. F. (1955). Wishing with dice. *Journal of Experimental Psychology, 50,* 269-275.

McDaniel, M. A., Einstein, G. O., DeLosh, E. L., May, C. P., & Brady, P. (1995). The bizarreness effect: It's not surprising, it's complex. *Journal of Experimental Psychology: Learning, Memory, and Cognition, 21,* 422-435.

McGuigan, F. J. (1993). *Experimental psychology* (6th ed.). Englewood Cliffs, NJ: Prentice-Hall.

McGuire, W. J. (1997). Creative hypothesis generating in psychology: Some useful heuristics. *Annual Review of Psychology, 48,* 1-30.

McKean, J. W., & Vidmar, T. J. (1994). A comparison of two rank-based methods for the analysis of linear models. *The American Statistician, 48,* 220-229.

McNemar, Q. (1940). A critical examination of the University of Iowa studies of environmental influences upon the IQ. *Psychological Bulletin, 37,* 63-92.

Mead, R., Bancroft, T. A., & Han, C-P. (1975). Power of analysis of variance test procedures for incompletely specified fixed models. *The Annals of Statistics, 3,* 797-808.

Medvedev, R. (1989). *Let history judge: The origins and consequences of Stalinism* (rev. ed.). (G. Shriver, Trans.). New York: Columbia University Press.

Meehl, P. E. (1954). *Clinical versus statistical prediction.* Minneapolis, MN: University of Minnesota Press.

Meehl, P. E. (1967). Theory-testing in psychology and physics: a methodological paradox. *Philosophy of Science, 34,* 103-115.

Meehl, P. E. (1990). Why summaries of research on psychological theories are often uninterpretable. *Psychological Reports,* Monog. Suppl. 1-V66, 195-244.

Meehl, P. E., & Scriven, M. (1956). Compatibility of science and ESP. *Science, 123,* 14-15.

Mehrabian, A. (1972). *Nonverbal communication.* Chicago: Aldine-Atherton.

Meier, P. (1989). The biggest public health experiment ever: The 1954 field trial of the Salk poliomyelitis vaccine. In J. Tanur (Ed.), *Statistics: A guide to the unknown,* 3rd ed. (pp. 3-14). Pacific Grove, CA: Wadsworth & Brooks/Cole.

Mellers, B. A. (1985). A reconsideration of two-person inequity judgments: A reply to Anderson. *Journal of Experimental Psychology: General, 114,* 514-520.

Melton, A. W. (1936). The end-spurt in memorization curves as an artifact of the averaging of individual curves. *Psychological Monographs, 47,* (Whole no. 212, 119-134).

Messick, S. (1989). Validity. In R. L. Linn (Ed.), *Educational Measurement* (3rd ed., pp. 13-103). New York: American Council on Education, and Macmillan.

Meyer, D. L. (1991). Misinterpretation of interaction effects: A reply to Rosnow and Rosenthal. *Psychological Bulletin, 110, 571-573.*

Miao, L. L. (1977). Gastric freezing: An example of the evaluation of medical therapy by randomized clinical trials. In J. P. Bunker, B. A. Barnes, and F. Mosteller (Eds.), *Costs, risks, and benefits of surgery* (pp. 198-211). New York: Oxford University Press.

Mischel, W. (1973). Toward a cognitive social learning reconceptualization of personality. *Psychological Review, 80*, 252-283.

Mischel, W. (1986). *Introduction to personality* (4th ed.). New York: Holt, Rinehart and Winston.

Miller, J., van der Ham, F., & Sanders, A. F. (1995). Overlapping stage models and reaction time additivity: Effects of the activation equation. *Acta Psychologica, 90*, 11-28.

Miller, R. G., Jr. (1981). *Simultaneous statistical inference* (2nd ed.). New York: Springer-Verlag.

Millman, J. & Greene, J. (1989). The specification and development of tests of achievement and ability. In R. L. Linn (Ed.), *Educational Measurement* (3rd ed., pp. 335-366). New York: Macmillan.

Montgomery, D. C. (1997). *Design and analysis of experiments* (4th ed.). New York: Wiley.

Moses, L. E., & Oakford, R. V. (1963). *Tables of random permutations*. Stanford, CA: Stanford University Press.

Mosteller, F., & Moynihan, D. P. (Eds.). (1972). *On equality of educational opportunity*. New York: Random House.

Mosteller, F., & Tukey, J. W. (1968). Data analysis, including statistics. In G. Lindzey & E. Aronson (Eds.), *The handbook of social psychology* (2nd ed., Vol. 2, pp. 80-203). Reading, MA: Addison-Wesley.

Mosteller, F., & Tukey, J. W. (1977). *Data analysis and regression*. New York: Wiley.

Mosteller, F., & Wallace, D. L. (1964). *Inference and disputed authorship: The Federalist*. Reading, MA: Addison-Wesley.

Mosteller, F., & Wallace, D. L. (1984). *Applied Bayesian and classical inference: The case of the Federalist Papers* (2nd ed.). New York: Springer-Verlag.

Mulaik, S. A., Raju, N. S., & Harshman, R. A. (1997). There is a time and a place for significance testing. In L. L. Harlow, S. A. Mulaik, & J. H. Steiger, (Eds.), *What if there were no significance tests?* (pp. 65-115). Hillsdale, NJ: Lawrence Erlbaum Associates.

Muller, K. E., LaVange, L. M., Ramey, S. L., & Ramey, C. T. (1992). Power calculations for general linear multivariate models including repeated measures applications. *Journal of the American Statistical Association, 87*, 1209-1226.

Muller, K. E., & Pasour, V. B. (1997). Bias in linear model power and sample size due to estimating variance. *Communications in Statistics—Theory and Method, 26*, 839-851.

Myers, J. L., DiCecco, J. V., White, J. B., & Borden, V. M. (1982). Repeated measurements on dichotomous variables: Q and F tests. *Psychological Bulletin, 92*, 517-525.

Myers, J. L., & Well, A. D. (1991). *Research design and statistical analysis*. New York: HarperCollins.

Narens, L., & Luce, R. D. (1993). Further comments on the "nonrevolution" arising from axiomatic measurement theory. *Psychological Science, 4*, 127-130.

Nathan, P. E. (1986). Outcomes of treatment for alcoholism: Current data. *Annals of Behavioral Medicine, 8*, 40-46.

Needleman, H. L. (1993a). Letter to Editor. *The PSR Quarterly, 3*, 48-52.

Needleman, H. L. (1993b). Reply to Ernhart, Scarr, and Geneson. *Ethics and Behavior, 3*, 95-101.

Needleman, H. L., Gunnoe, C., Leviton, A., Reed, R., Peresie, H., Maher, C., & Barrett, P. (1979). Deficits in psychologic and classroom performance of children with elevated dentine lead levels. *The New England Journal of Medicine, 300*, 689-695.

Newell, A. (1990). *Unified theories of cognition*. Cambridge, MA: Harvard University Press.

Newell, A. (1992). Précis of *Unified theories of cognition*. *Behavioral and Brain Sciences, 15*, 425-492. (Multiple book review.)

Newman, D. (1939). The distribution of the range in samples from a normal population, expressed in terms of an independent estimate of standard deviation. *Biometrika, 31*, 20-30.

Neyman, J. (1961). Silver jubilee of my dispute with Fisher. *Journal of the Operations Research Society of Japan, 3*, 145-154.

Nicolle, J. (1961). *Louis Pasteur.* Greenwich, CT: Fawcett.

Nisbett, R. E., & Wilson, T. D. (1977). Telling more than we can know: Verbal reports on mental processes. *Psychological Review, 84*, 231-259.

Noble, S., & Shanteau, J. (1999). Information integration theory: A unified theory of cognition. (book review). *Journal of Mathematical Psychology, 43*, 449-454.

Nolan, W. F. (1983). *Hammett: A life at the edge.* New York: Congdon & Weed.

Oakes, M. (1986). *Statistical inference.* New York: Wiley.

O'Connor, M. (1991). *Writing successfully in science.* New York: Chapman & Hall.

Oden, G. C. (1974). *Semantic constraints and ambiguity resolution.* Unpublished doctoral dissertation, University of California, San Diego.

Oden, G. C. (1977). Integration of fuzzy logical information. *Journal of Experimental Psychology: Human Perception and Performance, 3*, 565-575.

Oden, G. C. (1978). Semantic constraints and judged preference for interpretations of ambiguous sentences. *Memory & Cognition, 6*, 26-37.

Oden, G. C., & Anderson, N. H. (1974). Integration of semantic constraints. *Journal of Verbal Learning and Verbal Behavior, 13*, 138-148.

Oden, G. C., & Massaro, D. W. (1978). Integration of featural information in speech perception. *Psychological Review, 85*, 172-191.

Omenn, G. S., et al. (1996). Risk factors for lung cancer and for intervention effects in CARET, the beta-carotene and retinol efficacy trial. *Journal of the National Cancer Institute, 88*, 1550-1559.

Oskamp, S. (1962). The relationship of clinical experience and training methods to several criteria of clinical prediction. *Psychological Monographs: General and Applied, 76*, Whole 547, 1-27.

Overall, J. E. (1980). Power of chi-square tests for 2 × 2 contingency tables with small expected frequencies. *Psychological Bulletin, 87*, 132-135.

Paul, L. M. (1994). Making interpretable forgetting comparisons: Explicit versus hidden assumptions. *Journal of Experimental Psychology: Learning, Memory, and Cognition, 20*, 992-999.

Pearson, E. S., & Hartley, H. O. (1966). *Biometrika tables for statisticians* (3rd ed.). New York: Cambridge University Press.

Pearson, K., & Lee, A. (1903). On the laws of inheritance in man. *Biometrika, 2*, 357-462.

Pedersen, J. M. (1988). Laboratory observations on the function of tongue extrusions in the desert iguana (*Dipsosaurus dorsalis). Journal of Comparative Psychology, 102*, 193-196.

Pedhazur, E. J. (1982). *Multiple regression in behavioral research* (2nd ed.). New York: Holt, Rinehart and Winston.

Pedhazur, E. J., & Schmelkin, L. P. (1991). *Measurement, design, and analysis.* Hillsdale, NJ: Lawrence Erlbaum Associates.

Pendery, M. L., Maltzman, I. M., & West, J. W. (1982). Controlled drinking by alcoholics? New findings and a reevaluation of a major affirmative study. *Science, 217*, 169-175.

Pfungst, O. (1965). *Clever Hans* (R. Rosenthal, ed). New York: Holt, Rinehart and Winston. (Originally published 1911)

Piaget, J. (1965). *The moral judgment of the child.* (M. Gabain, Trans.). New York: Free Press. (Originally published 1932)

Pimsleur, P., & Bonkowski, R. J. (1961). Transfer of verbal material across sense modalities. *Journal of Educational Psychology, 52*, 104-107.

Pincus, J., & Rolph, J. E. (1986). How much is enough? Applying regression to a school finance case. In M. H. DeGroot, S. E. Fienberg, & J. B. Kadane (Eds.), *Statistics and the law* (pp. 257-287). New York: Wiley.

Plutchik, R., & Ax, A. F. (1967). A critique of *Determinants of emotional state* by Schachter and Singer (1962). *Psychophysiology, 4*, 79-82.

Pocock, S. J., Smith, M., & Baghurst, P. (1994). Environmental lead and children's intelligence: a systematic review of the epidemiological evidence. *British Medical Journal, 309*, 1189-1202.

Poulton, E. C. (1982). Influential companions: Effects of one strategy on another in the within-subjects designs of cognitive psychology. *Psychological Bulletin, 91*, 673-690.

Prentice, D. A., & Miller, D. T. (1992). When small effects are impressive. *Psychological Bulletin, 112*, 160-164.

Price, G. R. (1955). Science and the supernatural. *Science, 122*, 359-367.

Raftery, A. E., & Zeh, J. E. (1993). Estimation of bowhead whale, *Balaena mysticetus*, population size. In C. Gatsonis, J. S. Hodges, R. E. Kass, & N. D. Singpurwalla (Eds.), *Case studies in Bayesian statistics* (pp. 163-240). New York: Springer-Verlag.

Rapola, J. M., et al. (1996). Effect of vitamin E and beta carotene on the incidence of angina pectoris. *Journal of the American Medical Association, 275*, 693-698.

Rapport, M. D., Jones, J. T., DuPaul, G. J., Kelly, K. L., Gardner, M. J., Tucker, S. B., & Shea, M. S. (1987). Attention deficit disorder and methylphenidate: Group and single-subject analyses of dose effects on attention in clinic and classroom settings. *Journal of Clinical Child Psychology, 16*, 329-338.

Rasmussen, J. L. (1989). Data transformation, Type I error rate and power. *British Journal of Mathematical and Statistical Psychology, 42*, 203-213.

Ratcliff, R. (1993). Methods for dealing with reaction time outliers. *Psychological Bulletin, 114*, 510-532.

Reichardt, C. S. (1979). The statistical analysis of data from nonequivalent group designs. In T. D. Cook & D. T. Campbell (Eds.), *Quasi-experimentation* (pp. 147-232). Chicago: Rand McNally.

Reichardt, C. S., & Gollob, H. F. (1997). When confidence intervals should be used instead of statistical tests, and vice versa. In L. L. Harlow, S. A. Mulaik, & J. H. Steiger, (Eds.), *What if there were no significance tests?* (pp. 259-284). Mahwah, NJ: Lawrence Erlbaum Associates.

Reinfurt, D. W., Campbell, B. J., Stewart, J. R., & Stutts, J. C. (1990). Evaluating the North Carolina safety belt wearing law. *Accident Analysis & Prevention, 22*, 197-210.

Rinck, M., Hähnel, A., Bower, G. H., & Glowalla, U. (1997). The metrics of spatial situation models. *Journal of Experimental Psychology: Learning, Memory, and Cognition, 23*, 622-637.

Rivers, P. C. (1994). *Alcohol and human behavior.* Englewood Cliffs, NJ: Prentice Hall.

Roberts, A. H. (1995). The powerful placebo revisited: Magnitude of nonspecific effects. *Mind/Body Medicine, 1*, 35-45.

Roberts, H. V. (1978). Bayesian inference. In W. H. Kruskal & J. M. Tanur (Eds.), *International encyclopedia of statistics* (pp. 9-16). New York: The Free Press.

Roberts, N. H. (1964). *Mathematical methods in reliability engineering.* New York: McGraw-Hill.

Roberts, S. (1987). Evidence for distinct serial processes in animals: The multiplicative-factors method. *Animal Learning & Behavior, 15*, 135-173.

Roberts, S., & Neuringer, A. (1998). Self-experimentation. In K. A. Lattal & M. Perone (Eds.), *Handbook of research methods in human operant behavior* (pp. 619-655). New York: Plenum.

Roberts, S., & Sternberg, S. (1993). The meaning of additive reaction-time effects: Tests of three alternatives. In D. E. Meyer & S. Kornblum (Eds.), *Attention and performance XIV: Synergies in experimental psychology, artificial intelligence, and cognitive neuroscience—A silver jubilee* (pp. 611-653). Cambridge, MA: MIT Press.

Rocke, D. M., Downs, G. W., & Rocke, A. J. (1982). Are robust estimators really necessary? *Technometrics, 24*, 95-101.

Rodin, J., & Langer, E. J. (1977). Long-term effects of a control-relevant intervention with the institutionalized aged. *Journal of Personality and Social Psychology, 35*, 897-902.

Rogosa, D. (1987). Causal models do not support scientific conclusions: A comment in support of Freedman. *Journal of Educational Statistics, 12*, 185-195.

Rokeach, M. (1964). *The three Christs of Ypsilanti*. New York: Knopf.

Rosenthal, R. (1968). Experimenter expectancy and the reassuring nature of the null hypothesis decision procedure. *Psychological Bulletin Monograph Supplement, 70*(6, Part 2), 30-47.

Rosenthal, R. (1987). *Judgment studies*. New York: Cambridge University Press.

Rosenthal, R., & Rosnow, R. L. (1969). *Artifact in behavioral research*. New York: Academic Press.

Rosenthal, R., & Rosnow, R. L. (1985). *Contrast analysis*. New York: Cambridge University Press.

Rosnow, R. L., & Arms, R. L. (1968). Adding versus averaging as a stimulus-combination rule in forming impressions of groups. *Journal of Personality and Social Psychology, 10*, 363-369.

Rosnow, R. L., & Rosenthal, R. (1991). If you're looking at the cell means, you're not looking at *only* the interaction (unless all main effects are zero). *Psychological Bulletin, 110*, 574-576.

Rothbart, M., Evans, M., & Fulero, S. (1979). Recall for confirming events: Memory processes and the maintenance of social stereotypes. *Journal of Experimental Social Psychology, 15*, 343-355.

Rulon, P. J. (1941). Problems of regression. *Harvard Educational Review, 11*, 213-223.

Sanford, R. L. (1994). The wonders of placebo. In C. R. Buncher & J-Y. Tsay (Eds.), *Statistics in the pharmaceutical industry* (pp. 247-266). New York: Marcel Dekker.

Sarbin, T. R. (1943). A contribution to the study of actuarial and individual methods of prediction. *American Journal of Sociology, 48*, 593-602.

Savage, L. J. (1962). *The foundations of statistical inference*. London: Methuen.

Sawilowsky, S. S., & Blair, R. C. (1992). A more realistic look at the robustness and type II error properties of the *t* test to departures from population normality. *Psychological Bulletin, 111*, 352-360.

Sawilowsky, S. S., Blair, R. C., & Higgins, J. J. (1989). An investigation of the Type I error and power properties of the rank transform procedure in factorial ANOVA. *Journal of Educational Statistics, 14*, 255-267.

Sawyer, J. (1966). Measurement *and* prediction: Clinical *and* statistical. *Psychological Bulletin, 66*, 178-200.

Scarr, S. (1985). Constructing psychology. *American Psychologist, 40*, 499-512.

Scarr, S. (1993a). A whistleblower's perspective on the Needleman case. *Pediatrics, 91*, 173-174.

Scarr, S. (1993b). Science, public policy, and a critic's dilemma. *The PSR Quarterly, 3*, 27-32.

Scarr, S. (1994). Psychological science in the public arena: Three cases of dubious influence. *Scandinavian Journal of Psychology, 36*, 164-188.

Scarr, S., & Ernhart, C. B. (1993). Of whistleblowers, investigators, and judges. *Ethics & Behavior, 3*, 199-206.

Schachter, S., & Singer, J. E. (1962). Cognitive, social, and physiological determinants of emotional state. *Psychological Review, 69*, 379-399.

Schachter, S., & Wheeler, L. (1962). Epinephrine, chlorpromazine, and amusement. *Journal of Abnormal and Social Psychology, 65*, 121-128.

Scheffé, H. (1959). *The analysis of variance*. New York: Wiley.

Schlottmann, A. (2000). Children's judgments of gambles: A disordinal violation of utility. *Journal of Behavioral Decision Making, 13*, 77-89.

Schlottmann, A. (in press). Children's probability intuitions: Understanding the expected value of complex gambles. *Child Development,*

Schlottmann, A., & Anderson, N. H. (1993). An information integration approach to phenomenal causality. *Memory & Cognition, 21*, 785-801.

Schmidt, C. F., & Levin, I. P. Test of an averaging model of person preference: Effect of context. *Journal of Personality and Social Psychology*, 1972, *23*, 277-282.

Schreibman, L., Kaneko, W. M., & Koegel, R. L. (1991). Positive affect of parents of autistic children: A comparison across two teaching techniques. *Behavior Therapy, 22*, 479-490.

Schroeder, L. D., Sjoquist, D. L., & Stephan, P. E. (1986). *Understanding regression analysis.* Newbury Park, CA: Sage.

Schwarz, C. J. (1993). The mixed-model ANOVA: The truth, the computer packages, the books. Part I: Balanced data. *The American Statistician, 47*, 48-59.

Searle, S. R. (1987). *Linear models for unbalanced data.* New York: Wiley.

Searle, S. R. (1993). Unbalanced data and cell means models. In L. K. Edwards (Ed.), *Applied analysis of variance in behavioral research* (pp. 375-420). New York: Marcel Dekker.

Sedlmeier, P., & Gigerenzer, G. (1989). Do studies of statistical power have an effect on the power of studies? *Psychological Bulletin, 105*, 309-316.

Seligman, M. E. P. (1995). The effectiveness of psychotherapy: The *Consumer Reports* study. *American Psychologist, 50*, 965-974.

Seligman, M. E. P. (1996). Science as an ally of practice. *American Psychologist, 51*, 1072-1079.

Shaffer, J. P. (1995). Multiple hypothesis testing. *Annual Review of Psychology, 46*, 561-584.

Shanteau, J. C. (1970). An additive model for sequential decision making. *Journal of Experimental Psychology, 85*, 181-191.

Shanteau, J. (1975). Averaging versus multiplying combination rules of inference judgment. *Acta Psychologica, 39*, 83-89.

Shanteau, J. (1991). Functional measurement analysis of response times in problem solving. In N. H. Anderson (Ed.), *Contributions to information integration theory. Vol. I: Cognition* (pp. 321-350). Hillsdale, NJ: Lawrence Erlbaum Associates.

Shanteau, J. C., & Anderson, N. H. (1969). Test of a conflict model for preference judgment. *Journal of Mathematical Psychology, 6*, 312-325.

Shanteau, J., & Anderson, N. H. (1972). Integration theory applied to judgments of the value of information. *Journal of Experimental Psychology, 92*, 266-275.

Shaughnessy, J. J., & Zechmeister, E. B. (1997). *Research methods in psychology* (4th ed.). New York: McGraw-Hill.

Sheldon, W. H., & Stevens, S. S. (1942). *The varieties of temperament: A psychology of constitutional differences.* New York: Harper & Row.

Shepard, R. N. (1962a). The analysis of proximities. Multidimensional scaling with an unknown distance function. I. *Psychometrika, 27*, 125-140.

Shepard, R. N. (1962b). The analysis of proximities. Multidimensional scaling with an unknown distance function. II. *Psychometrika, 27*, 219-246.

Shiu, L-P., & Pashler, H. (1992). Improvement in line orientation discrimination is retinally local but dependent on cognitive set. *Perception & Psychophysics, 52*, 582-588.

Shoben, E. J. (1982). Semantic and lexical decisions. In C. R. Puff (Ed.), *Handbook of research methods in human memory and cognition*, (pp. 287-314). San Diego: Academic Press.

Shryock, R. H. (1947). *The development of modern medicine.* New York: Knopf.

Siegel, S., & Castellan, N. J., Jr. (1988). *Nonparametric statistics for the behavioral sciences* (2nd ed.). New York: McGraw-Hill.

Siegler, R. S. (1976). Three aspects of cognitive development. *Cognitive Psychology, 8,* 481-520.

Siegler, R. S. (1981). Developmental sequences within and between concepts. *Monographs of the Society for Research in Child Development, 46*(2, Serial No. 189).

Sigall, H., & Aronson, E. (1969). Liking for an evaluator as a function of her physical attractiveness and the nature of the evaluator. *Journal of Experimental Social Psychology, 5*, 93-100.

Silverman, I. W., & Paskewitz, S. L. (1988). Developmental and individual differences in children's area judgment rules. *Journal of Experimental Child Psychology, 46,* 74-87.

Simon, H. A. (1976). Discussion: Cognition and social behavior. In J. S. Carroll & J. W. Payne (Eds.), *Cognition and social behavior* (pp. 253-267). Hillsdale, NJ: Lawrence Erlbaum Associates.

Singh, R. (1991). Two problems in cognitive algebra: Imputations and averaging versus multiplying. In N. H. Anderson (Ed.), *Contributions to information integration theory. Vol. II: Social* (pp. 143-180). Hillsdale, NJ: Lawrence Erlbaum Associates.

Smith, H. F. (1957). Interpretation of adjusted treatment means and regressions in analysis of covariance. *Biometrics, 13,* 282-308.

Snedecor, G. W., & Cochran, W. G. (1980). *Statistical methods* (7th ed.). Ames, IA: Iowa State University Press.

Snow, R. E. (1989) Aptitude–treatment interaction as a framework for research on individual differences in learning. In P. L. Ackerman, R. J. Sternberg, & R. Glaser (Eds.), *Learning and individual differences* (pp. 13-59). New York: Freeman.

Snyder, M., Tanke, E. D., & Berschied, E. (1977). Social perception and interpersonal behavior: On the sulf-fulfilling nature of social stereotypes. *Journal of Personality and Social Psychology, 35,* 656-666.

Soal, S. G., & Goldney, K. M. (1943). Experiments in precognitive telepathy. *Proceedings of the Society for Psychical Research, 47,* 21-150.

Sobell, M. B., & Sobell, L. C. (1973). Alcoholics treated by individualized behavior therapy: One year treatment outcome. *Behaviour Research and Therapy, 11,* 599-618.

Sobell, M. B., & Sobell, L. C. (1978). *Behavioral treatment of alcohol problems.* New York: Plenum.

Solso, R. L., Johnson, H. H., & Beal, M. K. (1998). *Experimental psychology: A case approach* (6th ed.). New York: Addison Wesley Longman.

Spiegelhalter, D. J., Freedman, L. S., & Parmar, M. K. B. (1996). Bayesian approaches to randomized trials. In D. A. Berry & D. K. Stangl (Eds.) *Bayesian biostatistics,* (pp. 67-108). New York: Marcel Dekker.

Stefurak, D. L. (1987). *Studies in chromatic induction.* Unpublished doctoral dissertation, University of California, San Diego.

Sternberg, R. J. (1993). *The psychologist's companion* (3rd ed.). New York: Cambridge University Press.

Sternberg, R. J., & Williams, W. M. (1997). Does the Graduate Record Examination predict meaningful success in the graduate training of psychologists? *American Psychologist, 52,* 630-641.

Sternberg, S. (1966). High-speed scanning in human memory. *Science, 153,* 652-654.

Sternberg, S. (1969). The discovery of processing stages: Extensions of Donders' method. *Acta Psychologica, 30,* 276-315.

Sternberg, S. (1998). Discovering mental processing stages: The method of additive factors. In D. Scarborough & S. Sternberg (Eds.), *An invitation to cognitive science, Volume 4: Methods, models, and conceptual issues* (pp. 703-863). Cambridge, MA: MIT Press.

Sternberg, S. (2000, 1 June). Separate modifiability, mental modules, and the use of pure and composite measures to reveal them. Third annual Norman Anderson Distinguished Lecture. Department of Psychology, University of California, San Diego.

Sternberg, S. (in press, 22 May, 2000). Separate modifiability, mental modules, and the use of pure and composite measures to reveal them. *Acta Psychologica.*

Stevens, S. S. (1951). Mathematics, measurement and psychophysics. In S. S. Stevens (Ed.), *Handbook of experimental psychology* (pp. 1-49). New York: Wiley,

Stevens, S. S. (1956). The direct estimation of sensory magnitudes—loudness. *American Journal of Psychology, 69,* 1-25.

Stevens, S. S. (1974). Perceptual magnitude and its measurement. In E. C. Carterette & M. P. Friedman (Eds.), *Handbook of perception*, Vol. 2, (pp. 361-389). New York: Academic Press.

Stoner, G., Carey, S. P., Ikeda, M. J., & Shinn, M. R. (1994). The utility of curriculum-based measurement for evaluating the effects of methylphenidate on academic performance. *Journal of Behavior Analysis, 27*, 101-113.

Strunk, W., Jr., & White, E. B. (1972). *The elements of style* (2nd ed.). New York: Macmillan.

Student. (1908). The probable error of a mean. *Biometrika, 6*, 1-25.

Student. (1931). The Lanarkshire milk experiment. *Biometrika, 23*, 399-406.

Surber, C. F. (1981). Effects of information reliability in predicting task performance using ability and effort. *Journal of Personality and Social Psychology, 40*, 977-989.

Surber, C. F. (1982). Separable effects of motives, consequences, and order of presentation on children's moral judgments. *Developmental Psychology, 18*, 257-266.

Surber, C. F. (1985). Measuring the importance of information in judgment: Individual differences in weighting ability and effort. *Organizational Behavior and Human Decision Processes, 35*, 156-178.

Swanberg, W. A. (1956). *Sickles, the incredible.* NY: Scribner.

Taylor, D. J., & Muller, K. E. (1995). Computing confidence bounds for power and sample size of the general linear univariate model. *The American Statistician, 49*, 43-47.

Tesman, J. R., & Hills, A. (1994). Developmental effects of lead exposure in children. *Social Policy Report, 8*(No. 3), 1-16. Ann Arbor, MI: Society for Research in Child Development.

Thompson, G. G., & Hunnicutt, C. W. (1944). The effect of repeated praise or blame on the work achievement of 'introverts' and 'extroverts.' *The Journal of Educational Psychology, 35*, 257-266.

Thompson, G. L. (1991). A note on the rank transform for interactions. *Biometrika, 78*, 697-701.

Toothaker, L. E. (1991). *Multiple comparisons for researchers.* Newbury Park, CA: Sage.

Townsend, J. T., & Ashby, F. G. (1984). Measurement scales and statistics: The misconception misconceived. *Psychological Bulletin, 96*, 394-401.

Trochim, W. M. K. (1984). *Research design for program evaluation: The regression-discontinuity approach.* Beverly Hills, CA: Sage.

Trochim, W. M. K. (1986). *Advances in quasi-experimental design and analysis.* San Francisco: Jossey-Bass.

Troutman, C. M., & Shanteau, J. (1977). Inferences based on nondiagnostic information. *Organizational Behavior and Human Performance, 19*, 43-55.

Tsujimoto, R. N. (1978). Memory bias toward normative and novel trait prototypes. *Journal of Personality and Social Psychology, 36*, 1391-1401.

Tukey, J. W. (1960). A survey of sampling from contaminated normal distributions. In I. Olkin, et al., (Eds.), *Contributions to probability and statistics* (pp. 448-485). Stanford, CA: Stanford University Press.

Tukey, J. W. (1969). Analyzing data: Sanctification or detective work? *American Psychologist, 24*, 83-102.

Tukey, J. W. (1977). *Exploratory data analysis.* Reading, MA: Addison-Wesley.

Tversky, A., & Kahneman, D. (1971). Belief in the law of small numbers. *Psychological Bulletin, 76*, 105-110.

Tversky, A., & Koehler, D. J. (1994). Support theory: A nonextensional representation of subjective probability. *Psychological Review, 101*, 547-567.

Ulrich, R., & Miller, J. (1994). Effects of truncation on reaction time analysis. *Journal of Experimental Psychology: General, 123*, 34-80.

Underwood, B. J. (1975). Individual differences as a crucible in theory construction. *American Psychologist, 30*, 128-134.

Underwood, B. J. (1983). *Attributes of memory*. Glenview, IL: Scott, Foresman.

Underwood, B. J., & Shaughnessy, J. J. (1983). *Experimentation in psychology* (reprint ed.). Malabar, FL: Robert E. Krieger. (Originally published 1975)

University of Pittsburgh Needleman Hearing Board. (1992). *Needleman hearing board final report*. Pittsburgh, PA: University of Pittsburgh.

United States Environmental Protection Agency. (1983). *Independent peer review of selected studies concerning neurobehavioral effects of lead exposures in nominally asymptomatic children: Official report of findings and recommendations of an interdisciplinary expert review committee* (EPA-600/8-83-028A). Research Triangle Park, NC: Author.

Velleman, P. F., & Wilkinson, L. (1993). Nominal, ordinal, interval, and ratio typologies are misleading. *The American Statistician, 47*, 65-72.

Von Winterfeldt, D., & Edwards, W. (1986). *Decision analysis and behavioral research*. New York: Cambridge University Press.

Voss, J. F., Perkins, D. N., & Segal, J. W. (1990). *Informal reasoning and education*. Mahwah, NJ: Lawrence Erlbaum Associates.

Wagner, C. H. (1982). Simpson's paradox in real life. *The American Statistician, 36*, 46-48.

Wagner, M. T. (1988). The story of surgery. *KPBS on Air*, September, 20-21, 52.

Wallis, W. A., & Roberts, H. V. (1956). *Statistics: A new approach*. New York: The Free Press.

Wang, M-S., & Yang, J. (1998). A multi-criterion experimental comparison of three multi-attribute weight measurement methods. *Journal of Multi-Criteria Decision Analysis, 7*, 340-350.

Ward, L. M. (1975). Heuristic use or information integration in the estimation of subjective likelihood? *Bulletin of the Psychonomic Society, 6,* 43-46.

Ware, M. E., & Brewer, C. L. (Eds.). (1988). *Handbook for teaching statistics and research methods*. Hillsdale, NJ: Lawrence Erlbaum Associates.

Washington, B. T. (1963). *Up from slavery*. New York: Bantam. (Originally published 1901)

Weiss, D. J. (1972). Averaging: An empirical validity criterion for magnitude estimation. *Perception & Psychophysics, 12*, 385-388.

Weiss, D. J., & Shanteau, J. C. (1982). Group-Individual POLYLIN. *Behavior Research Methods & Instrumentation, 14*, 430.

Welkowitz, J., Ewen, R. B., & Cohen, J. (2000). *Introductory statistics for the behavioral sciences* (5th ed., p. 260, problem 1). Fort Worth, TX: Harcourt Brace.

Wellman, B. L., Skeels, H. M., & Skodak, M. (1940). Review of McNemar's critical examination of Iowa studies. *Psychological Bulletin, 37*, 93-111.

Wesman, A. G. (1971). Writing the test item. In R. L. Thorndike (Ed.), *Educational measurement* (2nd ed., pp. 81-129). Washington, DC: American Council on Education.

Westfall, P. H., & Young, S. S. (1993). *Resampling-based multiple testing*. New York: Wiley.

Wickens, T. D. (1989). *Multiway contingency tables analysis for the social sciences*. Hillsdale, NJ: Lawrence Erlbaum Associates.

Wickens, T. D., & Keppel, G. (1983). On the choice of design and of test statistic in the analysis of experiments with sampled materials. *Journal of Verbal Learning and Verbal Behavior, 22*, 296-309.

Wilcox, R. R. (1994). Some results on the Tukey–McLaughlin and Yuen methods for trimmed means when distributions are skewed. *Biometrics Journal, 36*, 259-273.

Wilkening, F. (1982). Children's knowledge about time, distance, and velocity interrelations. In W. J. Friedman (Ed.), *The developmental psychology of time* (pp. 87-112). New York: Academic Press.

Wilkening, F., & Anderson, N. H. (1982). Comparison of two rule-assessment methodologies for studying cognitive development and knowledge structure. *Psychological Bulletin, 92,* 215-237.

Wilkening, F., & Anderson, N. H. (1991). Representation and diagnosis of knowledge structures in developmental psychology. In N. H. Anderson (Ed.), *Contributions to information integration theory. Vol. III: Developmental* (pp. 45-80). Hillsdale, NJ: Lawrence Erlbaum Associates.

Williams, J. M. (1997). *Style: Ten lessons in clarity and grace* (5th ed.). New York: Addison Wesley Longman.

Wilson, E. B., Jr. (1990). *An introduction to scientific research.* New York: Dover. (Originally published 1952)

Winer, B. J. (1971). *Statistical principles in experimental design* (2nd ed.). New York: McGraw-Hill.

Winer, B. J., Brown, D. R., & Michels, K. M. (1991). *Statistical principles in experimental design* (3rd ed.). New York: McGraw-Hill.

Winkler, R. L. (1967). The quantification of judgment: Some methodological suggestions. *Journal of the Americal Statistical Association, 62,* 1105-1120.

Wixted, J. T. (1990). Analyzing the empirical course of forgetting. *Journal of Experimental Psychology: Learning, Memory, and Cognition, 16,* 927-935.

Wolf, Y. (1995). Estimation of Euclidean quantity by 5- and 6-year-old children: Facilitating a multiplication rule. *Journal of Experimental Child Psychology, 59,* 49-75.

Wolf, Y. (2001). Modularity in everyday judgments of aggression and violent behavior. *Aggression and Violent Behavior, 6,* 1-34.

Wright, P. H. (1988). Interpreting research on gender differences in friendship: A case for moderation and a plea for caution. *Journal of Social and Personal Relationships, 5,* 367-373.

Wright, W. A. (1996). *The accuracy of cognitive self-report.* Unpublished doctoral dissertation. University of California, San Diego.

Wyer, R. S., Jr. (1975). Functional measurement methodology applied to a subjective probability model of cognitive functioning. *Journal of Personality and Social Psychology, 31,* 94-100.

Yeaton, W. H., & Sechrest, L. (1981). Meaningful measures of effect. *Journal of Consulting and Clinical Psychology, 49,* 766-767.

Zalinski, J., & Anderson, N. H. (1991). Parameter estimation for averaging theory. In N. H. Anderson (Ed.), *Contributions to information integration theory. Vol. I: Cognition* (pp. 353-394). Hillsdale, NJ: Lawrence Erlbaum Associates.

Zalinski, J., & Anderson, N. H. (1998). Testing goodness of fit for a nonlinear model with a replications method. Unpublished paper.

Zeiger, M. (1991). *Essentials of writing biomedical research papers.* New York: McGraw-Hill.

Zhu, S.-H. (1991). *Context effects in semantic interpretation: A study of probability words.* Unpublished doctoral dissertation, University of California, San Diego.

Zhu, S-H. (1999). A method to obtain a randomized control group where it seemed impossible. *Evaluation Review, 23,* 363-377.

Zhu, S.-H., & Anderson, N. H. (1991). Self-estimation of weight parameter in multiattribute analysis. *Organizational Behavior and Human Decision Processes, 48,* 36-54.

Zhu, S-H., Stretch, V., Balabanis, M., Rosbrook, B., Sadler, G., & Pierce, J. P. (1996). Telephone counseling for smoking cessation: Effects of single-session and multiple-session interventions. *Journal of Consulting and Clinical Psychology, 64,* 202-211.

Zimbardo, P. G. (1988). *Psychology and life* (12th ed.). Glenview, IL: Scott, Foresman.

AUTHOR INDEX

Subject Index